16625

D0161874

FIFTH EDITION

WILLS, TRUSTS, AND ESTATE ADMINISTRATION FOR THE PARALEGAL

The West Legal Studies Series

Your options keep growing with West Legal Studies
Each year our list continues to offer you more options for every area of the law to meet your course or on-the-job reference requirements. We now have over 140 titles from which to choose in the following areas:

Administrative Law	Family Law
Alternative Dispute Resolution	Federal Taxation
Bankruptcy	Intellectual Property
Business Organizations/Corporations	Introduction to Law
Civil Litigation and Procedure	Introduction to Paralegalism
CLA Exam Preparation	Law Office Management
Client Accounting	Law Office Procedures
Computer in the Law Office	Legal Research, Writing, and Analysis
Constitutional Law	Legal Terminology
Contract Law	Paralegal Employment
Criminal Law and Procedure	Real Estate Law
Document Preparation	Reference Materials
Environmental Law	Torts and Personal Injury Law
Ethics	Will, Trusts, and Estate Administration

You will find unparalleled, practical support
Each book is augmented by instructor and student supplements to ensure the best learning experience possible. We also offer custom publishing and other benefits such as West's Student Achievement Award. In addition, our sales representatives are ready to provide you with dependable service.

We want to hear from you
Our best contributions for improving the quality of our books and instructional materials is feedback from the people who use them. If you have a question, concern, or observation about any of our materials, or you have a product proposal or manuscript, we want to hear from you. Please contact your local representative or write us at the following address:

West Legal Studies, 3 Columbia Circle, P.O. Box 15015, Albany, NY 12212-5015

For additional information point your browser at
www.westlegalstudies.com

FIFTH EDITION

WILLS, TRUSTS, AND ESTATE ADMINISTRATION FOR THE PARALEGAL

DENNIS R. HOWER

University of Minnesota

WEST

THOMSON LEARNING

Australia Canada Mexico Singapore Spain United Kingdom United States

WEST LEGAL STUDIES

Wills, Trusts, and Estate Administration for the Paralegal 5E
Dennis R. Hower

Business Unit Director:
Susan L. Simpfenderfer

Executive Editor:
Marlene McHugh Pratt

Senior Acquisitions Editor:
Joan M. Gill

Development Editor:
Rhonda Dearborn

Editorial Assistant:
Lisa Flatley

Executive Production Manager:
Wendy A. Troeger

Production Manager:
Carolyn Miller

Production Editor:
Betty L. Dickson

Technology Project Manager:
James Considine

Executive Marketing Manager:
Donna J. Lewis

Channel Manager:
Nigar Hale

Cover Designer:
Dutton and Sherman Design

Cover Image:
Artville Stock Images

COPYRIGHT © 2002 by Delmar.
West Legal Studies is an imprint of Delmar,
a division of Thomson Learning, Inc. Thomson Learning™ is a
trademark used herein under license

Printed in the United States
3 4 5 05 04 03 02

For more information contact Delmar,
3 Columbia Circle, PO Box 15015,
Albany, NY 12212-5015.

Or find us on the World Wide Web at http://www.
westlegalstudies.com

ALL RIGHTS RESERVED. No part of this work covered by the
copyright hereon may be reproduced or used in any form or
by any means—graphic, electronic, or mechanical, including
photocopying, recording, taping, Web distribution or information storage and retrieval systems—without written permission of the publisher.

For permission to use material from this text or product,
contact us by   Tel   (800) 730-2214
                   Fax   (800) 730-2215
                   www.thomsonrights.com

Library of Congress Cataloging-in-Publication Data
Hower, Dennis R.
  Wills, trusts, and estate administration for the
    paralegal/Dennis R. Hower,—5th ed, p. cm.
  "West Legal Studies series,"
  Includes index,
  ISBN 0-7668-2051-3
  1. Wills—United States, 2. Trusts and trustees—United
States. 3. Probate law and practice—United States, 4. Legal
assistants—United States—Handbooks, manuals, etc. I.
  Title.
KF755 .H68 2001
346.7305'4—dc21

                                              2001025856

NOTICE TO THE READER

Publisher does not warrant or guarantee any of the products described herein or perform any independent analysis in connection with any of the product information contained herein. Publisher does not assume, and expressly dis-claims, any obligation to obtain and include information other than that provided to it by the manufacturer.

The reader is notified that this text is an educational tool, not a practice book. Since the law is in constant change, no rule or statement of law in this book should be relied upon for any service to any client. The reader should always refer to standard legal sources for the current rule or law. If legal advice or other expert assistance is required, the services of the appropriate professional should be sought.

The Publisher makes no representation or warranties of any kind, including but not limited to, the warranties of fit-ness for particular purpose or merchantability, nor are any such representations implied with respect to the material set forth herein, and the publisher takes no responsibility with respect to such material. The publisher shall not be li-able for any special, consequential, or exemplary damages resulting, in whole or part, from the readers' use of, or re-liance upon, this material.

For the Amazing Mrs. Z.

CONTENTS IN BRIEF

CONTENTS

PREFACE

Over the past thirty years, the performance of qualified and competent paralegals (legal assistants) has raised their status and established their work as a new and unique type of legal professional. The economic benefits paralegals bring both to their employers (supervising attorneys) and to the firm's clients have proven their need and value. Therefore, it was no surprise their vocation became one of the fastest growing professions during the past decade. Although the number of teaching institutions that offer paralegal training has diminished, the current national market for paralegals remains strong.

The goal of the fifth edition of *Wills, Trusts, and Estate Administration* is to continue to provide a textbook that explains the basic, practical, everyday duties of a paralegal in these fields of law and prepares paralegals, such as yourself, to confidently undertake and successfully accomplish these tasks. After using the text and obtaining work experience, you will attain the level of competence that will enable you to perform your work with confidence and continue the success and uphold the standards that your profession demands.

The text is written primarily for paralegals, but others such as trust officers and personal representatives appointed to administer the estate of a deceased person have found it useful. Law firms also include copies of the book in their office library. The text identifies the responsibilities and duties that a paralegal can perform under the supervision of an attorney when drafting a will or trust or assisting with the administration of a decedent's estate. The fifth edition provides a review of the terminology and general principles of law that are the basis for drafting wills and trusts, or planning and administering an estate, and identifies the participants and the duties they must perform in these legal areas. Next, a chronological treatment of the step-by-step procedures required to complete the will and trust drafts and the administration of a decedent's estate is presented, including sample drafts and the executed forms needed to administer the estate. Current federal and state tax information and the appropriate tax forms are also discussed. A new unit on long-term care and the need for insurance has been added. The final chapter addresses the ethical standards and guidelines that currently govern the conduct of legal assistants practicing in wills, trusts, and estate administration. A new and unique electronic Study Guide, discussed below, is a major supplement to this edition.

The author is indebted to the American Law Institute for granting permission to cite numerous sections of the Restatement (Second) or (Third) on Trusts, and to the National Conference of Commissioners on Uniform State Laws for permission to include the Uniform Probate Code in this text.

CHAPTER ORGANIZATION

To help students obtain confidence and proficiency, each chapter of the fifth edition contains the following features:

- *Objectives*. The objectives focus students on what they will learn upon completion of the chapter.
- *Scope of the chapter*. The scope identifies and lists, in order, the topics to be discussed within the chapter.
- *Terminology*. Key terms are printed in boldface type and are defined in the margin at their first appearance. Mini-glossary Boxes are used to group multiple definitions on a page. Key terms are also listed at the end of each chapter and defined in a comprehensive end-of-text glossary.
- *Examples, hypothetical situations, sample state statutes, legal forms, exhibits, checklists, drafted documents, and actual cases*. These are interspersed throughout the chapters to help students understand the concepts and procedures discussed.
- *Assignments*. Frequent assignments within the chapters require students to apply the chapter's legal concepts or to perform tasks required of a practicing paralegal.
- *Checklists*. Checklists that collect relevant client data and information are included in the text, and "*What You Do*" lists and "*You Must*" notations in the Estate Administration chapter emphasize and clarify the actual procedures and specific tasks the paralegal student must master to attain confidence and competency.
- *Ethical Issues*. These issues are found throughout the text to call attention to important ethical concerns that are relevant to the procedures discussed within the individual chapters.
- *Review Questions*. Review questions are included at the end of each chapter and revised to correspond to the changes in content within the chapters.
- *Case Problems*. These actual cases and hypothetical problems are included at the end of the chapters to enable the students to verify what they have learned and apply it to a specific problem or task discussed in the chapter.

CHANGES IN THE FIFTH EDITION

Major changes:

- *Online student resource*. An electronic Study Guide is available for free at *www.westlegalstudies.com*. This supplement to the textbook contains fact-based scenarios with relevant problems involving paralegals, and step-by-step instructions and examples which enable the student to learn how to abstract (brief) actual cases. Vocabulary questions, special projects, and chapter-specific online assignments involving the Internet are included.
- *Long-term care and the need for long-term care insurance*. An extensive discussion on the most important and challenging topics of the new millennium, long-term care and the need for insurance, has been added to Chapter 10.
- *Computer technology*. The text has been updated to provide the latest information on how computer technology is impacting the practice of wills, trusts,

and estates. The Study Guide and the computer technology additions include websites for current federal gift and estate tax laws and increased contributions to Roth and traditional IRAs.

Other changes:

- *Case references.* Numerous case references in the chapters and case problems have been supplemented with additional cases in the Study Guide to give students experience in reading and applying actual cases to the legal topics and concepts presented in the text.
- *Statutes.* State statutes have been added or updated that identify the variations in state laws and emphasize the need for paralegals to master the statutes of the state in which they live and practice.
- *State-by-state charts.* Revised charts show differences among all fifty states on topics such as State Courts and Spouse's Elective Share. A new chart covering Intestate Succession Statute Citations for all states has been added.
- *Letter of Instructions.* An expanded discussion and a new chart covering the subject matter of the Letter of Instructions are included.
- *Legal forms.* Legal forms have been updated within the chapters, and newly executed estate administration forms, including the essential tax forms, are included in Appendix A.
- *Checklists.* The checklists used for collecting data and information for drafting wills, trusts, or an estate plan have been expanded and revised where necessary.
- *Ethics.* The chapter on ethics has been updated. Additional information and assignments are included in the new Study Guide and in the Extensive Teaching Package discussed below.
- *Estate planning.* Estate planning coverage is expanded to include long-term care.
- *Right to die laws and advance medical directives.* The discussion on these topics has been revised and the documents updated.
- *Tax laws have been updated.*
- Premarital and postmarital agreements have been moved from Chapter 6 to Chapter 4.

EXTENSIVE TEACHING PACKAGE

- The **Instructor's Manual with Test Bank and Transparency Masters,** contains detailed lecture outlines, teaching suggestions, answers to the text questions and assignments, a test bank and transparency masters.
- The **Instructor's Manual with Test Bank and Transparency Masters** is also available online at *www.westlegalstudies. com.*
- **Online Student Resource** available for free at *www.westlegalstudies.com.* This electronic Study Guide contains fact-based scenarios with problems involving paralegals, edited cases with questions, vocabulary questions, special projects, and chapter-specific online assignments involving the Internet.
- **Computerized Test Bank** The Test Bank found in the Instructor's Manual is also available in a computerized format on CD-ROM. The platforms supported include Windows™ 3.1 and 95, Windows™ NT, and Macintosh. Features include:

- Multiple methods of question selection
- Multiple outputs—that is, print, ASCII, and RTF
- Graphic support (black and white)
- Random questioning output
- Special character support

- **State-Specific Supplements** are available for CA, FL, IL, NY, and TX. These supplements are keyed to each chapter in the text and point out state-specific information when it differs from the text's discussion. These supplements are available online at *www.westlegalstudies.com* as downloadable electronic supplements.

- **Web page** Come visit our website at *www.westlegalstudies.com,* where you will find valuable information specific to this book such as hot links and sample materials to download, as well as other West Legal Studies products.

- **WESTLAW**® West's online computerized legal research system offers students hands-on experience with a system commonly used in law offices. Qualified adopters can receive ten free hours of WESTLAW®. WESTLAW® can be accessed with Macintosh and IBM PC and compatibles. A modem is required.

- **Strategies and Tips for Paralegal Educators,** a pamphlet by Anita Tebbe of Johnson County Community College, provides teaching strategies specifically designed for paralegal educators. A copy of this pamphlet is available to each adopter. Quantities for distribution to adjunct instructors are available for purchase at a minimal price. A coupon in the pamphlet provides ordering information.

- **Survival Guide for Paralegal Students,** a pamphlet by Kathleen Mercer Reed and Bradene Moore covers practical and basic information to help students make the most of their paralegal courses. Topics covered include choosing courses of study and note-taking skills.

- **West's Paralegal Video Library,** West Legal Studies is pleased to offer the following videos at no charge to qualified adopters:
  - *The Drama of the Law II: Paralegal Issues Video*
    ISBN 0-314-07088-5
  - *I Never Said I Was a Lawyer Paralegal Ethics Video*
    ISBN 0-314-08049-X
  - *The Making of a Case Video*
    ISBN 0-314-07300-0
  - *Mock Trial Video—Anatomy of a Trial: A Contracts Case*
    ISBN 0-314-07343-4

- **Court TV Video** West Legal Studies is pleased to offer the following video from Court TV. Avaialable for a minimal fee:
  - *Garcia v. Garcia: Fighting Over Jerry's Money*
    ISBN 07668-0264-7

ACKNOWLEDGMENTS

The author would like to thank and acknowledge the work of Joan Gill, Senior Acquisitions Editor; Rhonda Dearborn, Developmental Editor; and Betty Dickson, Production Editor The author would like to especially thank Lisa Duncan, Central Carolina Community College, North Carolina for her excellent and practical technology contributions included in each chapter and for the unique electronic study guide that is a major addition to the fifth edition.

Special appreciation is extended to the following reviewers of the fifth edition:

Mark Ciccarelli
Kent State University, OH

Fernaundra Fergusson
University of West Florida

Thomas Higgins
Illinois Central College, IL

Cynthia Lauber
Community College of Aurora, CO

Jennifer Merton
Elms College, MA

Scott Myers
Marist College, NY

Carole Olson
El Centro College, TX

Clark Silliman
Edmonds Community College, WA

Carolyn Smoot
Southern Illinois University, IL

Christopher Whaley
Roane State Community College, TN

Please note the Internet resources are of a time-sensitive nature and URL addresses may often change or be deleted.

Contact us at westlegalstudies@delmar.com

THE PURPOSE AND NEED FOR A WILL

OBJECTIVES

After completing this chapter, you should be able to:

- ➤ Understand and explain the reasons why many Americans die without a will.
- ➤ Begin to identify and become familiar with the basic terminology of wills and trusts.
- ➤ Recognize and explain the function and purpose of wills.
- ➤ Begin to identify and contrast the procedures and outcomes when property is passed by testacy versus intestacy.
- ➤ Begin to recognize the terms used to identify the persons who make, manage, administer, or benefit from wills, trusts, and a deceased person's estate.
- ➤ Identify and understand the functions of fiduciaries including guardians, conservators, trustees, and personal representatives.
- ➤ Identify examples of instances where a person may not need a will.

SCOPE OF THE CHAPTER

This chapter begins with a brief explanation of the reasons people in this country die without wills. The terminology associated with the law of wills, trusts, and estate administration is introduced as you begin the process of mastering the terms and legal concepts essential to the practice of law in these areas. A discussion of the purpose and use of wills and the necessity of having a will, also called a **testament**, concludes this chapter.

Testament
Another name for a will.

AN INTRODUCTION TO WILLS

Will
The legally enforceable written declaration of a person's intended distribution of property after death.

Unfortunately, many people in the United States die without a valid **will**—the written declaration of a person's intended distribution of property after death. The result is they have no say in the way property they have accumulated over a lifetime will pass after they die.

Most young adults (over 18) have few possessions and dying is not their everyday concern. Correspondingly, in their view, neither is the need for a will. However, every adult owns some property, and most individuals want to determine to whom this property will be distributed after they die. Why then do so many people fail to make a will?

In the first place, almost everyone under 18 and adults who have a mental deficiency cannot make a will because legally they are either too young or they lack the mental health (sanity) required to create a valid will. Currently, financial planners nationwide recommend individuals make a will as soon as they reach the age of majority. Other reasons for failure to make a will include: some are reluctant to discuss their property and finances with "strangers"; others procrastinate, then die prematurely due to an accident or unexpected illness; some do not want to discuss or face their mortality; others cite cost as their reason (although attorneys generally charge minimal fees for preparing simple wills); and, finally, many people are aware each state has laws that determine the passage of their property to family and blood relatives if they die without a will, so they allow their state to "make a will" for them. It seems no matter how much effort is spent to encourage Americans to make a will, many are not convinced or motivated to act.

Statutory Requirements for a Will

As mentioned, one reason why the young and some adults die without wills is that not everyone can legally make a will. To begin with, state laws impose restrictions on the makers of wills and on the procedures for creating a valid will. Through its legislature, every state passes laws, called **statutes**, that determine the **legal capacity** (age) and **testamentary capacity** (sanity) requirements for a person to make a will. The maker or **testator/testatrix** must be old enough (usually 18) and be of **sound mind** (sane) at the time the will is made.

💻 HOW WILL THE INTERNET AFFECT ESTATE PLANNING?

Perhaps more Americans will consider the benefits of estate planning and preparing a will. Many estate planning services are prominently advertised on the Internet. Quizzes and self-tests can be taken on the Internet to ascertain if one needs a will. Many sites of-

MINI-GLOSSARY BOX

Statutes
Laws passed by state and federal legislatures.

Legal capacity
Age at which a person acquires capacity to make a valid will, usually 18.

Testamentary capacity
The sanity (sound mind) requirement for a person to make a valid will.

Testator/testatrix
A man or a woman who makes and/or dies with a valid will.

Sound mind
To have the mental ability to make a valid will. The normal condition of the human mind, not impaired by insanity or other mental disorders.

fer links to pages and/or sites that feature will writing, advantages of having a trust, minimizing estate taxes, and other related topics. Will this additional exposure to the topic of estate planning promote more Americans to write a will? Only time will tell.

In the case of *Matter of Yett's Estate*, 44 Or.App. 709, 606 P.2d 1174 (1980), a will was challenged on the basis the testator lacked testamentary capacity. The court held that to determine whether the maker of a will had testamentary capacity, great weight is accorded the testimony of attesting witnesses who were present at the execution of the will. It is the testatrix-decedent's capacity at that time, not her general condition over a span of time that determines testamentary capacity. In this case, the evidence indicated she had this capacity even though she suffered from a malignant brain tumor. The court also ruled the evidence failed to establish her illness, i.e., the tumor, had caused insane delusions which resulted in a decreased share of her estate passing to the contestant of the will. Consequently, the court ruled that the will was valid.

State statutes also establish formal requirements for the creation and **execution of a valid will**; e.g., most wills must be written, signed and dated by the maker, and attested and signed by two or three witnesses. To be properly executed, a will must conform to the laws of the state in which it is made. Each state enacts (passes) laws on the execution of wills, and these laws are not always the same. Laws differ, for example, on the method of writing that may be used (e.g., whether the will may be handwritten or **holographic**, typewritten, printed out on a computer printer, audiotaped, or videotaped) and on the placement of the testator's signature (e.g., whether it must be on every page, only at the end of the will, or simply anywhere on the will). Individuals who are unfamiliar with the laws of their state and try to create their own wills often make mistakes or omissions concerning their property, naming their **beneficiaries**, or attempting to satisfy the statutory requirements for a will. The result may be an unintended, incomplete, or invalid will. To become a well-trained and experienced paralegal, you need to learn and master the laws of your state, so you can explain the statutory requirements, terminology, and procedures associated with wills and help clients execute a valid and meaningful will that accurately fulfills their intent and desires.

Basic Terminology Related to Wills

Before proceeding further, it will be helpful to present some basic terminology related to wills and estates. Exhibit 1.1 explains the terms that are used to indicate whether a person died with or without a valid will.

Execution of a valid will
The acts of the testator who writes and signs the will and the two or more witnesses who attest and sign it to establish the will's validity.

Holographic will
A completely handwritten, signed, and usually dated will that often requires no witnesses.

Beneficiary (of a will)
A person who is entitled to receive property under a will or to whom the decedent's property is given or distributed.

Exhibit 1.1   Testacy versus Intestacy

Decedent

(the deceased or person who dies)

With a valid will

- Testacy. Death with a valid will.
- Testate. Any person who makes and/or dies with a valid will. The decedent's property is distributed to beneficiaries and devisees.
- Testator. A man who makes and/or dies with a valid will.
- Testatrix. A woman who makes and/or dies with a valid will.

Without a valid will

- Intestacy. Death without a valid will.
- Intestate. Any person who dies without a valid will. The decedent's property passes to heirs according to state laws called intestate succession statutes.

Note: Today, common practice often uses the term *testator* for both sexes. In most cases, this text will refer to any person (man or woman) who makes and dies with a valid will as a *testator*.

The following terms relate to the actual making of a will:

- *Execute*. To perform or complete, e.g., to write and sign a will.
- *Attest*. To bear witness; to affirm or verify as genuine, e.g., the witness who attests the testator's intent, capacity, and signature on a will.
- *Subscribe*. To sign one's name generally at the end of a will.
- *Witnesses*. Two or more persons who attest and subscribe (sign) the will.

Other important terms relate to the administration of the decedent's estate:

- *Estate*. Also called *gross estate*. The property accumulated during a person's lifetime and owned at the time of death.
- *Property*. Anything subject to ownership; classified as real property or personal property.
  - *Real Property*. Land, buildings, and things permanently attached to them.
  - *Personal Property*. Any property that is not real property.
- *Estate administration*. The process of appointing a personal representative (executor or administrator) to collect, preserve, manage, and inventory the decedent's estate; notifying creditors to present their claims; paying all the decedent's debts and death taxes due; and distributing the remaining estate property to beneficiaries named in the will or heirs according to state law if the decedent died intestate, i.e., without a will.
- *Probate*. Court procedure by which a will is proved to be valid or invalid. Probate has been expanded to include the legal process of the administration of a decedent's estate. The term is often used synonymously with estate administration. For example, the phrase "to avoid probate" means to avoid the process and procedures of estate administration. The probate process is required to legally establish the beneficiary's or heir's title to a decedent's property. The probate (estate administration) is performed by the personal representative, e.g., executor or administrator, of the estate under the supervision of the appropriate court, often called the probate court.

- *Probate court*. The general name for the court that has jurisdiction (authority) over the handling or administration of a decedent's estate and the distribution of the property; also called Chancery, Surrogate's or Orphans' Court.
- *Personal representative*. The person (man or woman) who is appointed by the probate court to manage the estate of the decedent and either distribute the estate assets according to a will or a state's intestate succession statute when there is no will. A personal representative includes:
  - *Executor/executrix*. The man or woman named in the will to carry out its provisions, i.e., administer the decedent's estate.
  - *Administrator/administratrix*. The man or woman appointed by the probate court to administer the decedent's estate when there is no will.

Other specialized types and titles of personal representatives are discussed in Chapters 3 and 11.

The following terms are used to refer to the recipients of the decedent's property:

Will Terms:

- *Beneficiary*. Traditionally, a beneficiary is a person who is entitled to receive property under a will or a person who has already received the property. Under common law, a beneficiary received the personal property of the decedent by will, but today, the term is used to describe a person entitled to any gift (real or personal property) under a will. Therefore, a beneficiary can include a devisee or legatee. This definition for beneficiary will be used throughout the text.
- *Devisee*. A person who receives a gift of real property under a will; or as defined by the **Uniform Probate Code (UPC)**, the person who receives a gift of either real or personal property. See complete text of the UPC in Appendix C.
- *Legatee*. A person who receives a gift of personal property under a will.

Intestate Terms:

- *Heir*. Under common law, an heir was a person entitled by statute to receive the real property of a decedent who died intestate. Today, an heir includes persons who are entitled by statute to receive or have already received any gift (real or personal property) of the intestate. In addition, although technically incorrect, the popular use of the word *heir* has also been expanded to include persons who receive any gift through a decedent's will. However, throughout the text, the term *heir* will include persons who receive any gifts by intestate succession statutes. See comparison chart on terminology, Exhibit 4.1.
- *Distributee*. A person who is entitled to share in the distribution of an estate of a decedent who dies intestate, or as defined by the UPC, any person who has received property of a decedent from the personal representative other than a creditor or purchaser.
- *Next of kin*. The nearest blood relatives of the decedent; or those who would inherit from a decedent who died intestate, whether or not they are blood relatives, e.g., a spouse.

Uniform Probate Code (UPC)
A uniform law available for adoption by the states to modernize and improve the efficiency of the administration of a decedent's estate.

THE PURPOSE OF WILLS

The primary function of a will is to allow individuals to distribute their property any way they choose. A will gives the testator the opportunity to accurately describe the

Probate court
The court that has jurisdiction (authority) over the probate of wills and the administration of the decedent's estate.

property owned at death and to designate to whom that property is to be distributed. Since **probate courts** closely scrutinize the language of the will to determine the testator's true intent, it is of paramount importance that no word or sentence within the will create a contradiction, ambiguity, or mistaken interpretation that could cause confusion that would change the testator's plan or, worse, invalidate the will.

> **Example:** In an early provision of her handwritten will, Thelma Parker leaves "all my antique furniture to my best friend, Maude Thompson." Later in the will, Thelma states that she wants the furniture to go to her only daughter, Betsy. In the final clause of the will, she selects five pieces of this furniture to be given to her housekeeper. Because of these and other contradictions, the court could declare the will invalid.

Since the context of the general language and particular words in a will is a major factor used to determine the testator's intent, it is essential the will be carefully constructed to ensure the testator's plan for the distribution of the estate property is clearly understood. The court in the case of *Richland Trust Co. v. Becvar*, 44 Ohio St.2d 219, 339 N.E.2d 830 (1975) stated: "The function of the court in a will construction case is to determine and apply the testatrix's intention, as expressed in the language of the whole will, read in the light of the circumstances surrounding its execution."

Without a will, the statutes of the decedent's **domicile** (home state) will determine to whom the decedent's property will be distributed with the exception that **real property,** i.e., land, buildings (house, cottage, apartment, or office building), and the like, will be distributed according to the laws of the state in which the property is located. One of your major tasks and responsibilities will be to prepare drafts of the will and review them carefully with the client *to ensure that the final draft contains complete, accurate, and clearly understandable language to enable readers, especially the probate court, to agree on the meaning of the will and the client's intent.*

ETHICAL ISSUE

Since all wills are **ambulatory**, i.e., subject to change or revocation anytime before death, a will takes effect only after the testator dies. While living, the testator can review and modify the will whenever he wishes by the addition, deletion, or modification of gifts, beneficiaries, clauses of the will, or fiduciaries (see further discussion below under Appointment of Fiduciaries). Also, the testator can sell or dispose of any property listed in the will before death. In the past, if the modification was a simple change, e.g., adding a new gift, a **codicil** or amendment to the will was sufficient. Today, codicils have become obsolete. With the change from typewriter to word-processing software which rapidly and easily produces legal documents, a "new will" is the preferred and more appropriate choice for *any* needed modification. Also, the use of a computer disk and printer to create

MINI-GLOSSARY BOX

Domicile
The location (state) of a person's true and legal home.

Real property
Land, buildings, and things permanently attached to them.

Ambulatory
Subject to change or revocation anytime before death, e.g., a will is ambulatory.

Codicil
A written amendment to the will that changes but does not invalidate it.

the "new will" eliminates the serious potential problem of locating two or more documents, i.e., a will and multiple codicils. For further discussion see Chapter 5.

In no particular order of importance, the next paragraphs discuss the testator's essential letter of instructions and some of the reasons for making a will.

Funeral and Burial Plans and the Letter of Instructions

The best and most appropriate method for individuals who preplan their funeral and burial arrangements is to include the plans in a **letter of instructions** and *not* in a will or codicil. One of the valuable uses of the letter of instructions is to provide a written document that identifies and explains a person's funeral and burial plans and is readily accessible for the testator's review and modification. After planning the funeral with a mortician (including costs and arrangements for a casket, church service, and reception) and purchasing a burial plot, a person can insert these plans into the letter of instructions and make them known to her family, physician, religious adviser, and future personal representative by giving them copies of the letter. Thus, the letter avoids a frequently unpleasant, and sometimes painful, problem the family faces when a loved one dies, often suddenly and unexpectedly, and the will or codicil cannot be found or obtained before the decedent-testator's burial.

> **Letter of instructions**
> A document that specifies the testator's instructions for organ donation and funeral and burial plans. It can also be an all-inclusive checklist of various personal and estate information to help the family and personal representative locate and identify property and documents necessary to administer the estate.

Preplanning and prepaying the costs of the funeral and burial takes a heavy burden off the grieving family, both economically and emotionally. Alternately, if the person prefers to be cremated and wants to ensure that her wishes will be followed without revealing the contents of the will, she can review the letter containing the cremation plans with family members; and, if there are any concerns or objections, they can be resolved prior to the person's death.

Unfortunately, if a testator places funeral and burial arrangements only in the will, all such preplanning may be an exercise in futility, either because the will is not found until after the testator has been buried, or because the family simply disregards or disobeys the instructions. Since statutes in most states allow the desires of a surviving spouse and next of kin to legally supersede the plans of the testator, often the family makes the final decisions concerning the disposal of the testator's body and the type of funeral or service. The following persons generally have priority in deciding on funeral and burial arrangements including cremation: the surviving spouse, an adult child, a parent, an adult sibling, the decedent's guardian, and any other authorized or obligated person, e.g., a personal representative or medical examiner. All too frequently, serious disagreements arise over such questions as whether there should be a burial or cremation, a denominational or nondenominational religious service, an open or closed casket, and the like.

> **Example:** Fred has told his family he wants to be cremated when he dies. After his death, Fred's family, for religious reasons, decides to have him buried in the family plot. Often the decedent's wishes are not followed, as in this example.

Sometimes the testator's family disregards the funeral plans outlined in the will because the arrangements are too elaborate, too expensive, or unreasonable.

> **Examples:** John wants to be cremated and have his ashes flown to Paris and spread from the top of the Eiffel Tower. Bill wants a horse-drawn carriage, a hundred-member band, and an all-night party. Honoring such requests may deplete the estate and create additional hardships for survivors.

The above problems can best be alleviated by preplanning and prepaying the funeral and burial arrangements, discussing them with family and the funeral director, and placing them in the letter of instructions. *Caveat*: Copies of the letter must be given to the family and the future personal representative.

Even though the funeral and burial arrangements are often made by someone other than the personal representative (such as a surviving spouse or other family member), the cost of all "reasonable" expenses is paid as a priority debt of the decedent's estate according to state law, as will be discussed in detail in later chapters. It will be your job to keep accurate records of the costs and *remind the personal representative so that these expenses remain "reasonable."* Personal representatives are liable to the estate if they allow these costs to become excessive due to their neglect.

ETHICAL ISSUE ┈┈┈►

If an individual intends to donate organs or remains for transplant or medical research, the donation instructions must also be included in the letter instead of a will which may not be discovered in time to make a "useful" organ donation. A donor card can be obtained from the National Kidney Foundation (see Exhibit 1.2). To be legal and enforceable, it must be signed by the donor and two witnesses.

Exhibit 1.2   Donor Card from the National Kidney Foundation

NATIONAL KIDNEY FOUNDATION
Please detach and give this portion of the card to your family.

This is to inform you that, should the occasion ever arise, I would like to be an organ and tissue donor. Please see that my wishes are carried out by informing the attending medical personnel that I have indicated my wishes to become a donor.
Thank you.

SIGNATURE _____   DATE _____

For further information write or call:
NATIONAL KIDNEY FOUNDATION
30 East 33rd Street, New York, NY 10016
(800) 622-9010

- -

UNIFORM DONOR CARD

Of _____
(print or type name of donor)

In the hope that I may help others, I hereby make this anatomical gift, if medically acceptable, to take effect upon my death. The words and marks below indicate my wishes.
I give: ☐ any needed organs or parts
            ☐ only the following organs or parts

_____
(specify the organ(s), tissue(s) or part(s))
for the purposes of transplantation, therapy, medical research or education;
            ☐ my body for anatomical study if needed.
Limitations or special wishes, if any: _____

THIS IS YOUR
UNIFORM DONOR CARD
from the
NATIONAL KIDNEY FOUNDATION

Here's all you have to do...
1. **Designate your wishes by filling out the card, and sign it in front of two witnesses**
2. **Discuss your wishes with your family and give them the top half of the card**
3. **Carry the bottom half of the card in your wallet**
4. **Tell someone else about the Organ Donor Program**

ORGAN DONATION... The GIFT of Life!

- -

Signed by the donor and the following two witnesses in the presence of each other:

_____   _____
Signature of Donor   *Date of Birth of Donor*

_____   _____
Date Signed   *City and State*

_____   _____
Witness   *Witness*

This is a legal document under the Anatomical Gift Act or similar laws.
☐ Yes, I have discussed my wishes with my family.
For further information consult your physician or

NKF **National Kidney Foundation**
30 East 33rd Street, New York, NY 10016

Source: The Uniform Donor Card is reprinted with permission from the National Kidney Foundation, Inc., copyright 1996, New York, NY.

Exhibit 1.3 Driver's License—Organ Donation

STATE OF CALIFORNIA
DEPARTMENT OF MOTOR VEHICLES
DMV
A Public Service Agency

Pursuant to the Uniform Anatomical Gift Act.
I hereby elect upon my death the following option(s):

A __ To donate any organ or parts

B __ To donate a pacemaker (date implanted _____)

C __ To donate parts or organs listed _____

_____

D __ To not donate any organs, parts or pacemaker.

_____   _____
SIGNATURE   DATE
DL 290   (REV 5/92)

NOTICE
If you are at least 18, you may designate on your driver license or I.D. card a donation of any needed organs, tissues or pacemaker for medical transplantation. Under the Uniform Anatomical Gift Act (Sec. 7150, Health & Safety Code) donation takes effect upon your death.
NEXT OF KIN (OPTIONAL)

NAME _____

ADDRESS _____

TELEPHONE NO. _____

DETACH HERE

IMPORTANT INSTRUCTION

To make a donation, fill out this card and put the "DONOR" dot on the front of your license or I.D. card as shown below. The card should be carried with your license or I.D. card. If you change your mind complete a new card and remove the dot. Whole Body donations require separate arrangement.

To refuse to donate, fill out this card and carry it with your license or I.D. card. Do not use the dot.

DMV CALIFORNIA
Driver License

DONOR | DONOR DOT

DETACH HERE

Additional information regarding the Donor program may be obtained by writing or calling The Gift of Life:

National Kidney Foundation of Southern California
- 5777 West Century Blvd.
  Suite 395
  Los Angeles, CA 90045-7404
  1/800 747-5527
  Southern California
- 17050 Bushard Street
  Suite 202
  Fountain Valley, CA 92708
  (714) 962-7675

- 2320 Fifth Avenue
  Suite 206
  San Diego, CA 92101-1633
  (619) 235-8280
  Northern California
- 553 Pilgrim Drive
  Suite C
  Foster City, CA 94404
  (415) 349-5111

Source: The Uniform Donor Card is reprinted with permission from The National Kidney Foundation, Inc., copyright 1996, New York, NY.

Some states provide a notation for an organ donation on the face or the back of the donor's driver's license (see Exhibit 1.3). A provision for organ donation can also be made in the health care directive of some states. For further discussion of funeral and burial arrangements and organ donation by the testator, see Chapter 7.

The letter of instructions is potentially a multipurpose document, but it is not legally enforceable. It is, therefore, not a substitute for a will. The letter's purpose can range from a document limited to funeral and burial plans, to an all-inclusive checklist that identifies the testator's personal and family history; assets and liabilities; various insurance policies; financial advisers; health and service providers; location of legal and personal documents; and many other matters. A checklist could be drafted from a list such as that shown in Exhibit 1.4. The subject matter list enables testators to select and create appropriate schedules for their personal letter of instructions.

Example: A sample schedule in the letter of instructions containing assets such as pension/retirement plans of the testator might appear as follows:

Pension/Retirement Plans	Location Home safe/ File cabinet	Designated Beneficiary	Present Value
Date _____			
Plan			
1. IRA—Traditional			
_____	_____	_____	_____
IRA—Roth			
_____	_____	_____	_____
2. 401(k) Plan			
_____	_____	_____	_____
3. Keogh Plan			
_____	_____	_____	_____
4. Profit-sharing Plan			
_____	_____	_____	_____
5. Pension Plan			
_____	_____	_____	_____
6. Other			
_____	_____	_____	_____

Example: Another common schedule identifies necessary service personnel:

Service Personnel			
Date _____			
Item	Name/Address/Phone	Item	Name/Address/Phone
1. Car	_____	6. Lawn Care	_____
2. Heating/Air Cond	_____	7. Computer/TV/VCR	_____
3. Appliances	_____	8. Veterinarian	_____
4. Electrician	_____	9. Snow Removal	_____
5. Plumber	_____	10. Other	_____

A third potential schedule could include a list of securities (stocks and bonds) within the letter of instructions to enable the investor to review and regularly update the entries so that necessary changes, e.g., number of shares, date acquired, purchase price, date sold, sales price, and stockbroker can be made. If the letter is on a computer disk, assets such as securities can be evaluated daily for future investment strategies.

By keeping the letter of instructions current and distributing copies to family members to inform them of its contents, especially funeral, burial, and organ donation plans, the letter becomes the ideal method for the documentation of this information in place of a will or codicil. Most importantly, it allows the testator's organ donation and funeral plans to be implemented when time is of the essence.

Exhibit 1.4   Letter of Instructions—Subject Matter

Personal Information
  Name/ (a/k/a)
  Address
  Prior Residences (Past 10 Years)
  Telephone Number (Home/Work)
  Date/Place of Birth (Certificate)
  Social Security Number
  Religion
  Date of Marriage (Certificate)
  Date of Divorce (Decree)
  Education
  Employment History
  Military Record
  Other

Organ Donation/Funeral Plan
  Organ Donation
    Donor Card
    Driver's License Provision
    Health Care Directive
  Body Donation
  Funeral Plan
    Prepaid Funeral/Burial Contract
    Funeral Service
    Burial/Cemetery Plot
  Other

Family Information
  Relationship (Spouse,
    Children, Grandchildren, etc.)
  Name
  Address
  Telephone Number (Home/Work)
  Date/Place of Birth
  Marital Status
  Date of Death
  Other

Fiduciaries
  Personal Representative
    Successor
  Guardian (Minor or
    Incapacitated Persons)
    Personal Guardian
    Property Guardian
    Conservator
    Successor
  Trustee
    Successor
  Other

Family Financial Advisers
  Accountant/Tax Adviser
  Appraiser
  Attorney
  Banker/Trust Officer
  Financial Planner
  Insurance Agent (Broker)
  Real Estate Agent (Broker)
  Stockbroker
  Other

Liabilities
  Automobile Loan
  Business Debts
  Charge Accounts
  Contract for Deed Payments
  Credit Card Charges
  Installment Purchases
  Loans on Insurance Policies
  Mortgages on Real Property
  Pledges to Charities,
    Religious Organizations, etc.
  Promissory Notes
  Taxes
  Other

Assets
  Automobile, Boat, etc.
  Bank Accounts
  Business (Family) Ownership
  Furniture/Household Goods
  Notes, Contracts for Deed, etc.
  Pension/Retirement Plans
  Real Property
  Royalties/Patents & Copyrights
  Securities
  Trusts
  Other

Additional Topics
  Credit Cards
  Insurance Policies
  Legal & Personal Documents
  Location of Documents
  Medical & Dental Providers
  Service Personnel
  Spiritual Advisers
  Safe Deposit Box
  Tax Returns
  Other

Apportionment for Death Taxes

By adding an appropriate **apportionment clause** to the will, the testator can determine the source from which death taxes (federal and state estate taxes and state inheritance taxes) will be paid. If the apportionment clause is explicit and included in the will, it determines the method of apportionment. On the other hand, if the will has no apportionment clause or is ambiguous, the statute of the testator's domicile determines the method of apportionment. The following is an example of an apportionment clause from West's McKinney's Forms, ESP, § 7:412:

> I direct that all estate, inheritance, succession and transfer taxes and other death duties, including any interest or penalties thereon, imposed or payable by reason of my death upon or in respect of any property passing under my will and required to be included in my gross estate for the purpose of such taxes, shall be paid out of my residuary estate as an administration expense and shall not be apportioned. (Reprinted with permission from West's McKinney's Forms, Copyright ©, by West Group.)

Many states place the burden of estate and inheritance taxes on the **residuary estate** of the will which is also the source of payment of creditors' claims. Other states apportion federal and state death taxes among the various persons (**legatees** or beneficiaries) on a **pro rata** basis (see N.Y. EPTL § 2–1.8).

The advantage of having the testator make the apportionment decision rather than leaving it to state law is that customarily the property included in the will's residue clause, often a substantial portion of the estate, is left to the surviving spouse and children. If this property is the primary or sole source of payment of creditors' claims and death taxes, *these family members may be unintentionally placed in a hardship situation by this major oversight.* It is your responsibility to recognize this mistake and bring it to your supervising attorney's attention. The attorney will explain its significance to the client and obtain permission for you to redraft appropriate provisions of the will for the attorney's approval.

The Uniform Estate Tax Apportionment Act of 1958 (Revised 1964 and 1982), which apportions federal and state death taxes among all beneficiaries on a pro rata basis, has been adopted in some states and is incorporated in the UPC § 3–916(a)(b). *Remember:* An apportionment clause in a will overrules any apportionment method established by state statute.

Property Distributions

With a will, the testator can avoid many ill-advised and awkward property distributions. Consider the following example:

Example: Jacob Weizman dies intestate. His only heirs are five unmarried daughters. Jacob's estate assets consist of three farms (each farm is located in Jacob's home state (domicile) and is worth $200,000) and a total of $100,000 in various banks. Jacob's state statute, like the law in most states, divides his assets equally among his five daughters. Dividing the money is easy—each daughter receives $20,000. The three farms, however, go to the five daughters in the form of co-ownership called **tenancy in common,** which creates for each co-owner (each daughter) an undivided, equal interest in each farm and the right to equal possession of the entire premises of each farm. As a **tenant in common,** each daughter, on her death, can pass her $20,000 and her equal interest (one-fifth) in each farm to the beneficiaries she names in her

---

Apportionment clause
A clause in a will that allocates the tax burden among the residuary estate and the beneficiaries of the will.

Residuary estate
The remaining assets (residue) of the decedent's estate after all debts have been paid and all other gifts in the will are distributed.

Legatee
A person who receives a gift of personal property under a will.

Pro rata
According to a certain rate or percentage.

ETHICAL ISSUE ▸

Tenancy in common
The ownership of an undivided interest in real or personal property by two or more persons without the right of survivorship, which allows each owner's interest to be passed to his or her beneficiaries or heirs upon death.

Tenant in common
One of two or more persons who own property in a tenancy in common.

will; if she dies intestate, the law of the state where the farms are located will determine who receives her one-fifth interest and her $20,000.

This example could become more complicated if, for example, two of the daughters want to live on one of the farms; the others want to sell them; or one or more of the daughters marry. The point is clear: Even if serious personality conflicts do not occur, the occupation and management problems of the property could create numerous and unfortunate consequences. Jacob could avoid this unpleasant situation if he discussed his assets with his daughters, so that, as a family, they could identify possible options which would enable him to make a decision and arrive at a compromise acceptable to all. In this way, Jacob's original plan to treat the daughters fairly could be accomplished harmoniously, and the solution could be included in his will.

🏛 ASSIGNMENT 1.1

Review the facts in the Jacob Weizman example above. Draw up three different plans that could be used as part of Jacob's will to transfer the three farms and the $100,000 to his five daughters in equal shares.

Provisions for Family Members

With a will, the testator can appropriately provide for a surviving spouse and the special needs of individual children. In most cases, the surviving spouse receives the majority of the testator's estate. If the testator's estate plan includes lifetime gifts and specific provisions in wills and trusts, death taxes, especially federal and state estate taxes, can be reduced, thereby maximizing the portion of the estate family members receive. These tax reductions could be lost if the decedent dies intestate. For a complete discussion of these problems and tax concerns, see Chapter 10.

When a spouse and minor children survive a decedent who failed to make a will, the **intestate succession statutes** of most states pass the estate property to the spouse individually, or for life, and to the children equally as tenants in common. Since the children are minors, a probate court would need to appoint a **guardian** (see Appointment of Fiduciaries below) to handle any property in which they have an interest. In such a case, the surviving spouse would be appointed guardian, but the appointment could cause additional expense and needless delay if the property had to be sold promptly, e.g., to provide funds for the family's necessary living expenses or if the family needed to relocate. For this reason, it is often best to leave the decedent's estate solely or as a life estate to the surviving spouse without minor children becoming the co-owners. This can be accomplished using a will and/or a trust.

The only person a testator cannot disinherit is a surviving spouse because the spouse has a statutory right to a share of the decedent spouse's estate. This is called the surviving **spouse's statutory, forced or elective share.** Every state has a statute with a provision for the benefit of the surviving spouse that makes it impossible for the deceased to leave the surviving spouse nothing. On the other hand, a decedent who dies testate can disinherit children. Of course, this happens at times, but more commonly, the testator wants the children to receive the estate equally. Due to special circumstances, the testator may grant unequal shares of the estate to meet the children's different needs (see the examples below).

Intestate succession statutes
Laws passed in each state establishing the manner in which a decedent's property will be distributed when death occurs without a valid will.

Guardian
The person or institution named by the maker of a will or appointed by the court when there is no will to care for the person and/or property of a minor or a handicapped or incompetent person.

Spouse's statutory, forced or elective share
The spouse's statutory right to choose a share of the decedent spouse's estate instead of inheriting under the provisions of the decedent's will.

Examples: In her will:
1. Kristin Neilsen leaves the entire estate to her three children equally.
2. Kristin Neilsen leaves the majority of the estate to her handicapped child and smaller shares to her other two children.
3. Kristin Neilsen intentionally and specifically states that one, two, or all three of her children (naming them) are not to receive any assets of the estate.

In the above examples, if the decedent, Kristin Neilsen, dies intestate, the children's special needs won't be met, but none of them will be disinherited. If the children are Kristin's only heirs, they will receive equal shares.

Numerous other problems concerning family members' inheritance rights are discussed in detail in Chapters 4 and 6.

Appointment of Fiduciaries: Guardians and Conservators

Ward
A minor or incompetent person placed by the probate court under the care and supervision of a guardian.

Incompetent person
A person under legal disability, e.g., a physically or mentally incapacitated person.

With a will, a testator can appoint guardians for a **ward** (minor or **incompetent persons**). Guardians appointed by the court are either **personal guardians** or **property guardians.** Both guardians are a type of **fiduciary**, a person in a position of trust who controls and manages property exclusively for the benefit of others and owes the highest duty of obedience, diligence, and good faith to those the person represents. Fiduciaries include guardians who act for minors or incompetent persons, trustees who act for beneficiaries of a trust, and personal representatives who act for beneficiaries of a will or for **heirs** when there is no will. The fiduciary is required to give absolute loyalty to the beneficiary or minor while performing **fiduciary duties**, i.e., all transactions that concern the property held in trust.

A personal guardian is an adult who has custody, control, and responsibility for the care and supervision of the minor child until the child reaches the age of majority, usually 18. If the decedent-testator is survived by the other natural or **adoptive parent**, that parent by law immediately becomes the personal guardian of the minor. An attempt by the testator to appoint some other person as the minor's guardian is not valid or binding, see Tex. Prob. Code Ann. § 676(b). This situation

---

MINI-GLOSSARY BOX

Personal guardian
An individual or trust institution appointed by a court to take custody of and care for a minor or an incompetent person.

Property guardian
An individual or trust institution appointed by a court to care for and manage the property of a minor or an incompetent person.

Fiduciary
A person, such as a personal representative, guardian, conservator, or trustee, who is appointed to serve in a position of trust and controls and manages property exclusively for the benefit of others. By law the fiduciary's conduct is held to the highest moral and ethical standard.

Heir
Traditionally, a person, including a spouse, who is entitled by statute to the real property of an intestate. Today, a person entitled to any gift (real or personal property) of the intestate or in the decedent's will.

Fiduciary duty
A duty or responsibility required of a fiduciary to act solely for another's benefit that arises out of a position of loyalty and trust.

Adoptive parent
A person who legally adopts another individual, usually a child.

frequently occurs when married couples divorce, and one of the former spouses is given custody of the minor children of the marriage. If the custodial spouse dies while the children are still minors, the attempt in a will to name a personal guardian who is not the other natural parent (the former spouse) would fail.

On the other hand, when there is no other surviving natural parent, the appointment of a personal guardian in the custodial parent's will is generally upheld by the court, and any further hearing on custody is unnecessary, see Mass. Gen. Laws Ann. ch. 201 § 3. The appointment of a personal guardian is discussed in detail with examples and cases in Chapters 7 and 12.

When parents die without a will or fail to appoint a guardian in a will, the probate court must select both a personal and a property guardian based on what is "in the best interests of the child." Usually, the court appoints a family member who may or may not have been the choice of the decedent. Without a will, the appointment of a guardian can lead to a time-consuming and expensive contest in probate court between relatives. Unfortunately, the dispute often has lasting harmful effects on the children.

> **Example:** Tal Anderson dies intestate. Tal had often talked to Cathy and Joe Merrill, Tal's close friends, about his desire to have them "take care of my children if I should die." Even though Cathy and Joe informed the probate court of Tal's wishes and their willingness to be the guardians, the probate court would most likely appoint blood relatives of Tal who agree to be the guardians.

> **Example:** The only blood relative of Rachel Weinstein, age 27, is her grandmother, age 70. Due to her grandmother's age and uncertain health, Rachel asked her close friend, Susan Johnson, if she would be the guardian of her 8-year-old daughter. Susan agrees, but Rachel dies intestate. The probate court would likely appoint as guardian, the grandmother, if she is willing to serve, even though she was not Rachel's choice.

Unlike the case of the personal guardian, the surviving natural or adoptive parent or the person appointed by the testator's will is not automatically appointed the property guardian for the decedent's minor or incompetent children. Such people may be appointed and often are, but the decision is made by the probate judge, who appoints the guardian.

The property guardian can be a natural person or a legal person such as a corporation, bank, or trust department which happens infrequently. The property guardian's responsibility is to take exclusive control of and manage the property inherited by a minor or incompetent person in order to preserve and increase its value. The guardian must perform the management and investment functions according to strict standards set by the court and state law. These standards cannot be changed, broadened, or made less rigid by the terms of a will even if that was the testator's intent.

A property guardian for an incompetent person whom the probate court has found to be incapable of managing property is, in a few states, called a **conservator**, another type of fiduciary. Typically, conservators are appointed for individuals who, due to advanced age or an illness such as Alzheimer's disease, are under a legal disability that makes them physically or mentally incapable of managing their property. States usually require that a conservator or guardian be appointed whenever an incompetent person owns property obtained through gifts or inheritance. Property guardians or conservators are discussed further in Chapters 7 and 12.

Conservator
A fiduciary; an individual or trust institution appointed by a court to care for and manage property of an incompetent person.

MINI-GLOSSARY BOX

Trust
A right of property, real or personal, held by one person (trustee) for the benefit of another (beneficiary).

Settlor
A person who creates a trust; also called donor, grantor, creator, or trustor.

Legal title (of a trust)
The form of ownership of trust property held by the trustee giving the trustee the right to control and manage the property for another's benefit, i.e., the holder of the equitable title.

Trustee
The person or institution named by the maker of a

will or a settlor of a trust to administer property for the benefit of another (the beneficiary) according to provisions in a testamentary trust or an *inter vivos* trust.

Beneficiary (of a trust)
The person or institution who holds equitable title and to whom the trustee

distributes the income earned from the trust property and, depending on the terms of the trust, even the trust property itself.

Equitable title (of a trust)
A right of the party who holds the equitable title or beneficial interest to the benefits of the trust.

Creation of Testamentary Trusts

Testamentary trust
A trust created in a will. It becomes operational only after death.

***Inter vivos* or living trust**
A trust created by a maker (settlor) during the maker's lifetime. It becomes operational immediately after the trust is created.

A testator can create either a **testamentary trust**, i.e., a trust within the will, which becomes operational only after the testator's death, or an ***inter vivos*** or **living trust,** which takes effect immediately after the trust is created. A **trust** is a legal agreement in which one person (the **settlor**) transfers **legal title** (ownership) to one or more persons (the **trustee** or co-trustees) who, as a fiduciary, holds and manages the property for one or more **beneficiaries** who receive the **equitable title** which gives them the right to the benefits of the trust. The settlor gives up possession, control, and ownership of the property to the trustee who is specifically instructed by the trust terms how the trust is to be managed and the trust property invested so that income produced (profits) can be distributed to the beneficiaries. All three positions (settlor, trustee, and beneficiary) can be held by the same person, but the fundamental characteristic of a trust is the trust splits title of the trust property into legal title (transferred to the trustee) and equitable title (given to the beneficiary), and requires that no one person can be the sole trustee and the sole beneficiary since that person would hold both titles, merging them and invalidating the attempt to create a trust. The solution to this problem is to have either co-trustees or co-beneficiaries so the "split title" requirement is satisfied.

Examples:

1. A trust is not created if the settlor, Mike Ford, names himself as both the sole trustee and the sole beneficiary.
2. A trust is created if the settlor, Mike Ford, names himself sole trustee and Carley Brown and himself as co-beneficiaries.
3. A trust is created if the settlor, Mike Ford, names Carley Brown and himself as co-trustees and himself as sole beneficiary.

All trusts whether testamentary or *inter vivos* (living) are either revocable or irrevocable. A revocable trust may be changed, amended, or canceled by the settlor while living, but, generally, they become irrevocable when the settlor dies. Irrevocable trusts are final from the moment of their creation. They cannot be changed or revoked. *Caveat:* Unless the trust document contains a clause that expressly reserves the right or power of the settlor to revoke the trust, the trust is irrevocable. The significance and consequences of revocable or irrevocable trusts

MINI-GLOSSARY BOX

Principal
In trust law, the capital or property of a trust, as opposed to the income, which is the product of the capital.

Federal estate tax
A tax imposed on the right to transfer property at death.

are discussed in Chapters 8 and 9. One of the most common uses of a testamentary trust is the **bypass trust** (also called Trust B of an A-B trust, credit shelter trust, exemption equivalent trust, family trust, and residuary trust) established for the benefit of a surviving spouse. By limiting the surviving spouse's right to a life estate in the **principal** of Trust B, the property is not included in the estate of the surviving spouse when he dies; thus, it avoids **federal estate tax**. By reducing federal taxes in this manner, more of the estate property is free to pass to future beneficiaries, usually the children (see the detailed discussion in Chapter 10). If a person dies without a will (intestate), this tax advantage would be lost.

Another common reason for creating testamentary or *inter vivos* (living) trusts is to counter and avoid the rigid control and considerable expense of a property guardian for minors or a conservator for incompetent persons. The following examples illustrate the advantages of trusts.

Bypass trust
An estate planning device whereby a deceased spouse's estate passes to a trust as a life estate for the surviving spouse rather than entirely to the surviving spouse, thereby reducing the likelihood that the surviving spouse's estate will be subject to federal estate tax.

Example: In a trust, trustee Edward Benson can be given discretion to choose among accumulating trust income, distributing income, or even distributing the principal of the trust for the benefit of one or more beneficiaries. The stricter regulations imposed on a property guardian or conservator would not grant this freedom.

Example: After reviewing the pros and cons of wills, trusts, and guardianships, Beverly and Howard Mayberry, who have two minor children, decide on the following: Since he has a terminal illness, Howard drafts and executes his will which leaves his entire estate to his surviving spouse, Beverly. He is confident that she will provide for their minor children and eventually transfer the balance of the property to them in her own will. Since no property is left to the minor children, guardianships (with their corresponding control and expense) are avoided. In the event that Beverly dies first, Howard adds a contingent testamentary trust, which leaves his estate to the trust for the benefit of his minor children.

Other reasons for the creation of trusts include the following:

- Trusts are used to provide professional management of the trust property for those beneficiaries (including a settlor-beneficiary) who do not have the time, inclination, or skill to manage the property themselves or, because of illness or incapacity, are no longer able to do so.
- Trusts known as **public (charitable) trusts** can be established for religious, scientific, charitable, literary, or educational purposes under IRC § 170(c)(4).
- Trusts can prevent spendthrift beneficiaries, including children, from recklessly depleting the trust fund and can also prevent their creditors from obtaining the trust principal on demand for the payment of debts.
- Trusts can save taxes and avoid probate expenses if properly established.

Public (charitable) trust
A trust established for the social benefit either of the public at large or the community.

MINI-GLOSSARY BOX

Personal representative
The person who administers and distributes a decedent's estate according to the will or the appropriate intestate succession statute. It includes executor and executrix when there is a will and administrator and administratrix when there is no will.

Executor/executrix
A man or woman named in the will by the maker to be the personal representative of the decedent's estate and to carry out the provisions of the will.

Administrator/ administratrix
The man or woman appointed by the probate court to administer the decedent's estate when there is no will.

A complete discussion of the formation, drafting, and types of trusts, including the popular living trust, is included in Chapters 8 and 9.

Selection of Personal Representative

The **personal representative** is a UPC term that identifies the man or woman who manages, administers, and distributes a decedent's estate according to the terms of a will or the appropriate state intestate succession statute if the decedent dies without a will; see UPC § 1–201(36). A personal representative includes an **executor** (man) or **executrix** (woman) who is selected by a testator to carry out the terms of a will or an **administrator** (man) or **administratrix** (woman) who is appointed by the court to administer the estate of a decedent who dies intestate. Throughout the remaining chapters of the text, the words *personal representative* will be used to identify any person who has the responsibility to administer the estate of a decedent who dies either testate or intestate. The various types of personal representatives and the important role they play in administering the decedent's estate are discussed in Chapters 3, 11, and 12.

Like trustees and guardians, the personal representative is a fiduciary who owes fiduciary duties (acts of trust, loyalty, and good faith) to the recipients of the decedent's estate, e.g., beneficiaries, heirs, and devisees. To acquire the authority and powers of the position, a personal representative must be appointed by the appropriate court, often called the probate court. Generally, in testacy cases, the court appoints the person nominated in the testator's will unless that person is not qualified under state law. Whether a person dies with or without a will, states usually have statutes that list the persons who are not qualified to be personal representatives (see Tex. Prob. Code Ann. § 78). The Texas list includes:

1. An incapacitated person, e.g., minors or incompetent persons.
2. A person convicted of a felony.
3. A nonresident (natural person or corporation) who has failed to appoint a resident agent to accept service of process.
4. A corporation that is not authorized to act as a fiduciary in the state.
5. A person whom the court finds "unsuitable."

Example: Carry Swanson's will names Jack Daniels to be the personal representative. Due to previous associations, Carry's family and heirs feel extremely hostile toward Jack. The hostility of beneficiaries toward a nominated personal representative does not ordinarily or automatically disqualify the person as "unsuitable." But see

Matter of Petty's Estate, 227 Kan. 697, 608 P. 2d 987 (1980), where the court refused to appoint the will's nominee to be personal representative, because the hostility between the beneficiaries and nominee could lead to unnecessary difficulties and expenses for the estate.

Caveat: If a testator selects a personal representative and also in the will names an attorney to assist the personal representative with the estate administration, the estate is not legally bound to this selection. Personal representatives have the right to select an attorney of their own choice to represent the estate. *It is a violation of the Code of Ethics for the attorney or paralegal to suggest that they be named in the will for such purpose.*

◀ **ETHICAL ISSUE**

Chapter 4 of this text discusses death with a will (testacy) and death without a will (intestacy) in more detail.

WILL SUBSTITUTES

In some cases it may not be necessary to have a will. However, the decision should be made only after consultation with an attorney knowledgeable about estate planning. It may be possible, especially with small estates, to employ "will substitutes" instead of a will to distribute a decedent's estate. Examples of will substitutes include (1) joint tenancy, (2) life insurance, (3) *inter vivos* trusts, (4) *inter vivos* gifts, and (5) the state of Washington's unique "community property agreement." The value and kinds of property owned by the client and the needs of the beneficiaries generally determine whether a will should be executed.

- Joint tenancy:

Example: Jean and her fiancé, Bill, own a house in **joint tenancy** valued at $90,000. They also have $1,200 in a checking account and $4,000 in a savings account, which are both joint tenancy accounts. They each own other separate property. Both Jean and Bill are salaried employees and contributed equal sums to purchase the home and to the checking and savings accounts. Jean dies without a will. As the sole surviving joint tenant, Bill will receive all the joint tenancy property, which was the couple's intent. Jean's individual or separate property has to go through probate. The tax consequences in such cases will be discussed in the tax chapter (see Chapter 14). A more complex problem could result, however, if the unmarried couple, Jean and Bill, were to die in a common accident and both die intestate.

- Life insurance:

Example: As another example of a will substitute, assume that Mary, a single parent, had only one major asset, a $100,000 life insurance policy through a group plan with premiums paid equally by Mary and her employer. Her son, Mike, is named as sole beneficiary. If Mary dies testate or intestate, Mike will receive the proceeds of the life insurance policy which do not go through the probate process. Under current tax law, the proceeds are not taxable income or a gift to Mike, so no income or gift taxes are owed (see Chapter 10).

- *Inter vivos* (living) trust:

Example: Serena owns an apartment building valued at $300,000. During her lifetime she places this property in an *inter vivos* (living) trust, naming her brother, Reginald, trustee, and two friends, Vaughn and Renee, beneficiaries. In the trust

Joint tenancy
Ownership of real or personal property by two or more persons with the right of survivorship.

instrument, Serena directs the trustee to pay the income from the trust property— the apartment building—to the beneficiaries, Vaughn and Renee, during their lifetimes and, at the death of the last of the two to survive, to convey the apartment building and land to the children of Renee (Christopher and Ann) as tenants in common. Even if Serena dies testate or intestate, the distribution of the trust income and the trust property will be determined by the trust instrument. Any remaining property in Serena's estate at her death will be distributed according to the provisions of her will or according to the state intestate succession statute. For a more complete discussion of the use of an *inter vivos* (living) trust as a substitute for a will, see Chapter 9.

- *Inter vivos* gift:

Example: Anyone may dispose of property while alive by gift. During his lifetime, Sherman gives to his relatives and friends $100,000 in cash, $50,000 in stocks and bonds, a pickup truck, and his collection of Chinese figurines. Once these gifts are delivered (executed) Sherman has no legal right to demand their return. Gift taxes may be due and payable on the *inter vivos* gifts if Sherman exceeds the $10,000 per donee annual exclusion. The exclusion is indexed annually for inflation. Annual gifts over a lifetime can reduce the size of the donor's estate and result in death tax savings. For a complete discussion of the gift tax laws, see Chapters 10 and 14.

- Community property agreement:

Example: The state of Washington has developed a unique document authorized under its community property law called the "community property agreement." The agreement acts as a will substitute and is often used by a married couple domiciled in Washington to transfer, at the death of the first spouse, all the community estate to the surviving spouse without the necessity of probate.

CHECKLIST TO DETERMINE THE NEED FOR A WILL

To determine whether a client needs a will, the following questions should be answered:

1. What property does the client own?

Domiciliary administration
The administration of an estate in the state where the decedent was domiciled at the time of death.

2. Where is the property located? Will a **domiciliary administration** be the only one required?

3. In what form of ownership, e.g., severalty (sole ownership), joint tenancy, or tenancy in common, is the property held?

4. Is the client aware of the intestate succession statute that determines who would take her property if the client died without a will? Would the client be content with these persons receiving the property, or does the client desire to leave the property to someone else, e.g., a close friend or institutions such as a church or a charity?

5. Are specific items of real or personal property to be given to certain beneficiaries or devisees?

6. Does the client want to donate organs or his body for medical or educational research?

7. Does the client wish to establish a testamentary trust for the purpose of maintaining an income for a surviving spouse, elderly parent, minor child, or spendthrift relative?

8. Is there a need for a guardian to be appointed over property or the person of minor children or incompetent persons?

9. Does the client want to select a personal representative (executor or executrix) to handle the administration of the estate?

10. Has the client considered the possible tax consequences to the estate, with or without a will, and to the beneficiaries, devisees, or heirs?

11. Does the client want any taxes owed, including state inheritance taxes, to be paid out of specific estate assets?

12. What powers and authority does the client wish to bestow on the personal representative (executor), guardian, conservator, or trustee?

13. If married, and the client and spouse were to die in a common accident, have the consequences to their respective estates been considered?

14. Does the client want to avoid the probate process and its corresponding expenses and delays?

15. Is the client aware that probate files are open to the public?

BASIC REQUIREMENTS FOR A LEGAL WILL— A REVIEW

The testator must have:

- Legal capacity—generally age 18 or older.
- Testamentary capacity—be of sound mind (sanity).

The will must:

- Be written, i.e., typewritten, printed on a computer printer (today's method), or handwritten (allowed in some states).
- Be signed by the testator usually in the presence of witnesses.
- Be dated (in most states).
- Be attested and signed by at least two witnesses.
- Select a personal representative (executor or executrix) to administer the decedent's estate.

See a detailed discussion of these requirements in Chapter 5.

THE NEED FOR A WILL—A CONCLUSION

In summary, there are numerous reasons why so many Americans die without a will. They include:

1. Some people, by statute, cannot make a valid will, e.g., minors and incompetent persons.

2. Everyone does not need a will. Some people have limited or no property, others have no heirs (and believe they have no need), and some are satisfied with the "will" their state makes for them, i.e., the intestate succession statute.

3. Some attempt to create a will, but it is declared invalid by the probate court due to improper execution.

4. Some people, concerned about the cost of a will or their reluctance to discuss their finances, procrastinate too long and die prematurely. Others simply do not bother.

5. Some use "will substitutes" instead of wills to distribute the decedent's estate.

As Chapter 2 explains, the need for a will is determined by the kind of property the individual possesses and the form of the possessor's ownership.

KEY TERMS

Testament	Ambulatory	Incompetent person	Equitable title (of a
Will	Codicil	Personal guardian	trust)
Statutes	Letter of instructions	Property guardian	Bypass trust
Legal capacity	Apportionment clause	Fiduciary	Principal
Testamentary capacity	Residuary estate	Heir	Federal estate tax
Testator/testatrix	Legatee	Fiduciary duty	Public (charitable)
Sound mind	Pro rata	Adoptive parent	trust
Execution of a valid	Tenancy in common	Conservator	Personal representative
will	Tenant in common	Testamentary trust	Executor/executrix
Holographic will	Intestate succession	*Inter vivos* or living	Administrator/
Beneficiary (of a will)	statutes	trust	administratrix
Uniform Probate Code	Guardian	Trust	Joint tenancy
(UPC)	Spouse's statutory,	Settlor	Domiciliary adminis-
Probate court	forced or elective	Legal title (of a trust)	tration
Domicile	share	Trustee	
Real property	Ward	Beneficiary (of a trust)	

REVIEW QUESTIONS

1. Explain the reasons why many Americans die without wills.
2. What does it mean to say the maker of a will has testamentary capacity? How does it differ from legal capacity?
3. List your state's statutory requirements for the execution of a will. How does your state's requirements for a valid will differ from those of other states?
4. Because the terminology included in this chapter is essential to your understanding of legal concepts and procedures presented in future chapters and your practice in the fields of wills, trusts, and estates, write out your own definition of each key term in this chapter. Are your definitions essentially the same as those in the text?
5. Can a will be changed or revoked? Explain.
6. List and explain the various reasons or purposes for making a will.
7. Identify five examples of "will substitutes" and discuss how each might possibly be used to eliminate the need for a will.

CASE PROBLEMS

Problem 1

Erik Larson handwrote a three-page will in pencil. At the end of the business day, he took the will to an attorney and asked that it be typed. Since Erik mentioned that he was leaving on a vacation and would be out-of-state for one week, the paralegal for the firm asked if he would like to sign the handwritten (holographic) will. Erik did sign the will, but he also stated that he would return after his trip to sign "his will," i.e., the typed will. While on vacation, Erik became ill and died. Answer the following:

A. Is a signed holographic will a valid will in your state?
B. Are witnesses required for a holographic will?
C. Should the executed holographic will operate as Erik's will pending the execution of the typewritten will? Explain. See and compare *In re Cosgrove's Estate*, 290 Mich. 258, 287 N.W. 456 (1939).

Problem 2

Otto Halverson died testate. He was survived by twenty-seven nieces and nephews. Otto had little formal education and had not learned how to write his signature; therefore, he signed his name with a mark, i.e., an "X." Otto's nieces and nephews challenged the validity of his will. They claimed the will had been improperly executed because he signed with an "X."

A. Is a testator's mark, i.e., an "X," sufficient to satisfy the signature requirement for a valid will in your state? Cite the statute or case law.

B. In your opinion, if there is no statute or case law on this issue in your state, how should your state court decide this issue? See and compare *In re Hobelsberger's Estate,* 85 S.D. 282, 181 N.W.2d 455 (1970).

CHAPTER 2

THE CONCEPT OF PROPERTY RELATED TO WILLS, TRUSTS, AND ESTATE ADMINISTRATION

OUTLINE

OBJECTIVES

After completing this chapter, you should be able to:

➤ Identify, explain, and classify the various kinds of property, such as real and personal property or probate and nonprobate property.

➤ Recognize and understand the terminology associated with property law.

➤ Distinguish the various forms of ownership of real and personal property and explain the requirements for their creation and function.

➤ Understand and explain why courts do not favor the creation of joint tenancies between parties other than spouses.

➤ Identify the community property states and differentiate between community and separate property.

➤ Explain the kinds, methods of creation, and characteristics of estates in real property.

SCOPE OF THE CHAPTER

Everyone owns some kind of property, e.g., a home, car, savings and checking accounts, appliances, clothes, jewelry, or stocks and bonds. While alive, the owner of certain property called probate property (discussed below) has the opportunity to transfer it by gift, sale, or the creation of an *inter vivos* (living) trust. After the owner dies, probate property can pass by will, testamentary trust, or **inheritance** according to state law. Without property, a will is unnecessary, and a trust cannot be created. Thus, property is the essential component that establishes the need for and purpose of wills and trusts. You must fully understand the law of property and its terminology before you can draft wills or trusts and assist with the administration of a decedent's estate. This chapter introduces the terminology of the law of property, explains its association with wills, trusts, and estate administration, and discusses related statutes and court decisions. Also introduced are ways or forms in which property can be owned; each form of ownership is identified, defined, and explained. Estates in real property (freeholds and leaseholds) are also covered.

Inheritance
Property that descends (passes) to an heir when an ancestor dies intestate.

PROPERTY: TERMINOLOGY AND CLASSIFICATION

Property is anything subject to ownership. It is classified as either real property or personal property.

Real Property

Real property (also called realty or real estate) is property that is immovable, fixed, or permanent. It includes:

- Land.
- Structures affixed to land such as houses, apartment buildings, condominiums, and office buildings.
- Objects attached to land and buildings called fixtures.
- Things grown on land except those for the purpose of sale (see below).

Owners of real property also have rights to airspace above their land and to the earth below it, including any minerals in the earth.

Fixtures

A **fixture** is real property that may once have been personal property but now is permanently attached to land or buildings. An example of a fixture that grows on land is a tree; however, growing crops which are annually cultivated for sale like corn, wheat, and vegetables are not fixtures. They are considered to be personal property. Carpeting nailed to the floor and a built-in dishwasher are examples of fixtures in buildings.

State courts apply three tests—annexation, adaptation, and intention—to determine if personal property has been converted into a fixture:

1. Annexation means that the personal property has been affixed or annexed to the real property.

Fixture
Something so attached to land as to be deemed a part of it, e.g., real property that may have once been personal property but now is permanently attached to land or buildings.

2. *Adaptation* means that the personal property has been adapted to the use or purpose of the real estate. The court asks whether the property is necessary or beneficial to the function or enjoyment of the real estate.

3. In most states, however, the *intention* of the person who annexed the personal property to the real property has been the controlling test that determines the existence of a fixture.

Courts throughout the country vary substantially on what constitutes a fixture, but generally, though not always, doors, fences, windows, stoves, refrigerators, electric lights, wall to wall carpeting, and the like are held to be fixtures. Compare the following cases:

- *Mortgage Bond Co. v. Stephens,* 181 Okl. 419, 74 P.2d 361 (1937), in which the court held that a refrigerator was a fixture.
- *Andrews v. First Realty Corp.,* 6 Cal.App.2d 407, 44 P.2d 628 (1935), in which the court held that a refrigerator was personal property.

Tenants often install fixtures on property they rent. A tenant farmer who raises chickens may build a shed to shelter them or install gasoline tanks to avoid long drives to town for fuel; a tenant who rents an apartment may add carpeting, bookshelves, and a door knocker for comfort and convenience. Previously, any such items a tenant attached to the real estate could not be removed when the tenant vacated. Today, however, tenants may remove property they have attached to real estate if the property falls under one of three exceptions, known as tenant's fixtures:

1. *Trade fixtures.* Property placed on the land or in a building to help the tenant carry on a trade or business.

Examples: Smokehouse, machinery, barber chairs, greenhouse, pipe organ.

2. *Agricultural fixtures.* Property annexed by the tenant for farming purposes.

Examples: Wooden silo, toolshed, henhouse, hay carrier, irrigation plant.

3. *Domestic fixtures.* Property attached by the tenant to make an apartment more comfortable or convenient.

Examples: Carpeting, dishwasher, clothes dryer, gas stove, bookshelves.

🏛 ASSIGNMENT 2.1

Henry recently sold his movie theater to Helma. Which of the following items are fixtures (real property) that now belong to Helma? Give reasons for your answers.

Seats in the auditorium	Popcorn machine	Furnace in the building
Computers in the office	Movie projector	Telephones in the building
Carpeting in the theater	Movie film	Mirrors in the restrooms

💻 USE TECHNOLOGY TO ASSESS REAL ESTATE RECORDS

Land record offices and for profit companies are making real property records, including deeds, mortgages, and tax information, accessible through the web. Information about a parcel of property may be accessed by owner's name, street address, or tax identification number.

....

Transfers of Real Property

When real property is transferred by gift or sale, the title or ownership is conveyed to the donee or buyer by a formal written document called a **deed.** Some of the more important terms associated with transfers of real property include the following:

evidences

Deed
A writing signed by the grantor whereby title to real property is transferred or conveyed to the grantee.

- *Transfer.* An act by which the title to property is conveyed from one party to another. A party may be a person, corporation, or the government.
- *Conveyance.* Any transfer by deed or will of legal or equitable title (see below) to real property from one person to another.
- *Disposition.* The parting with, transfer, or conveyance of property.
- *Grant.* A transfer of title to real or personal property by deed or other instrument.
- *Grantor.* The person who conveys (transfers) real or personal property to another. In the law of trusts, the creator of a trust, also called the settlor or trustor. *Gor*
- *Grantee.* The person to whom real or personal property is conveyed. *Gee*

Example: Abner conveys Blackacre, a farm, by deed to his friend, Charles. Abner is the grantor; Charles is the grantee. The act of conveyance of Blackacre to Charles is a disposition.

- *Deed.* A written, signed, and delivered legal document that transfers title or ownership of real property such as land or buildings from a grantor to a grantee.
- *Title.* In the law of property, the right to and evidence of ownership of real or personal property.
- *Legal title.* A title that is complete, perfect, and enforceable in a court of law, granting the holder the right of ownership and possession of property. In the law of trusts, the trustee receives legal title that provides the right of ownership and possession but no beneficial interest in the property which exists in another, i.e., the holder of the equitable title who is the beneficiary of the trust.
- *Equitable title.* In the law of trusts, a party who has equitable title has the right to have the legal title transferred to her. The person, i.e., beneficiary, who holds the equitable title has the beneficial interest, which includes the right to the benefits of the trust, and is regarded as the real owner although the legal title is placed in possession and control of the trustee.
- *Interest.* The terms "interest" and "title" are not synonymous. An interest entitles a person to some right in the property, but that right may be less than title or ownership.
- *Vest.* To deliver possession of land. At death, state law automatically vests title to the decedent's real property in beneficiaries of the will or in heirs if the decedent dies without a will "subject to" the right of the personal representative to devest or take away the property in order to pay claims of the decedent's creditors (see Cal. Prob. Code § 7000 and Tex. Prob. Code Ann. § 37).
- *Devest* or *divest.* To withdraw or take away title from the possessor.

The following example illustrates the use of these and earlier terms.

Example: Valerie agrees to buy Richard's cottage. At the closing, Richard *transfers title* to the cottage by the *conveyance* of a *deed* to Valerie. Since Richard is the person (seller) who transfers *real property* (the cottage) to another (Valerie, the buyer), Richard is also the *grantor*. Valerie is the *grantee*. Clearly, Valerie has an *interest* in the cottage, and in this case, her interest is the *ownership (title)* of the cottage. One year later Valerie dies in a car accident without having made a will. Title to real property (cottage) owned by the decedent (Valerie) *vests* in her heirs the moment she dies. If Valerie had substantial debts, her personal representative may have a right to *devest* (take away) the property from the heirs and sell it to pay creditors' claims. On the other hand, title to Valerie's *personal property* passes to her *personal representative* who uses the property, if necessary, to pay taxes due and creditors' claims or transfers it to *beneficiaries* of the will or to *heirs* if there is no will.

In another scenario, Valerie creates an *inter vivos* (living) trust and names her friend, Joe, *trustee*. The trust property is an apartment building which is conveyed by deed into the trust and splits title to the apartment so that Joe, the trustee, holds *legal title* and Valerie's daughter, Amy, the *beneficiary,* holds the *equitable title*. As trustee, Joe has *fiduciary duties* to manage and maintain the apartment for Amy's benefit until the trust terminates when he transfers the apartment building to Amy according to the terms of the trust.

Personal Property

Personal property is movable property. It is everything subject to ownership that is not real estate and includes such items as clothing, household furnishings, stocks, money, contract rights, and life insurance. A **chattel** is an item of personal property.

Chattel
Generally, any item of personal property.

At death, title to a decedent's real property vests directly in the decedent's beneficiaries or heirs. Title to the decedent's personal property passes to the personal representative (executor or administrator) appointed to handle the administration of the decedent's estate. If creditors must be paid, generally the decedent's personal property is used first to obtain the necessary funds and real property is the last asset used to pay estate debts.

Personal property can be subdivided into two categories:

1. *Tangible personal property.* Property that has a physical existence, i.e., it can be touched and is movable.

Examples:

Merchandise	Animals	Tools
Clothing	Household goods	Furniture
Appliances	Jewelry	Works of art
Books	China	Stamp/coin collections
Television sets	Cars	Boats
Airplane	RVs	Computers

2. *Intangible personal property.* Property that has no physical existence, i.e., it cannot be touched. Although such property has little or no value in itself, it establishes and represents the right to receive something of value. The ownership of intangible property is established by various documents, such as bank state-

ments, stock or bond certificates, and written contracts for life insurance and annuities.

Intangible personal property also includes a **chose in action,** a right to bring a civil lawsuit to recover possession of personal property or receive money damages, e.g., payment of a debt.

Chose in action
A right to bring a civil lawsuit to recover money damages or possession of personal property.

Examples: A ten dollar bill is just a piece of paper, but it represents the right to receive property worth ten dollars. A promissory note by itself has no value, but it represents the right to receive payment from a debtor. The ten dollar bill and the promissory note are intangible personal property. Other examples of intangible personal property include the following:

Cash	Savings and checking accounts
Profit-sharing plans	Shares of corporate stock
Annuities	Corporate and government bonds
Pension plans	Negotiable instruments (checks and promissory notes)
Life insurance proceeds	Government benefits such as Social Security
Patent rights	and veterans' benefits
Copyrights	Individual retirement accounts
Trademarks	Claims against another person for debts,
Royalties	property damage, personal injury, or wrongful death

⚜ ASSIGNMENT 2.2

Classify each of the following items by placing a mark (X) in the most appropriate column.

Item	Real Property	Tangible Personal Property	Intangible Personal Property
Car			
Cash in checking account			
Right to renew apartment lease			
House			
Life insurance proceeds			
Furniture			
Stocks and bonds			
Furnace			
Personal injury lawsuit			
Clothing			
Dishwasher (built-in)			
Dishwasher (portable)			
Mobile home on wheels			
Houseboat			
Tax refund check			
Television roof antenna			
Bookcase			
Trees on land			
Gun collection			
Corn growing on farm			

Your major role will be to help the personal representative find, collect, preserve, appraise, and liquidate or distribute the decedent's personal assets. These tasks will be discussed in more detail in future chapters. In addition, you will have to list all the decedent's assets and classify them as real property or tangible or intangible personal property. Since an accurate classification is essential to the administration of the estate, you must learn to distinguish the different types of property and *be sure to verify your classification with your supervising attorney.*

ETHICAL ISSUE

Probate Property or Probate Estate

All decedents own one or both of the two types of property (real and personal). Together, these assets are often called the decedent's estate. An **estate** (also called a gross estate) is all the property, real and personal, owned by any living person, or all the assets owned by a decedent at the time of death.

Estate
All property owned by a person while alive or at the time of death. Also called gross estate, probate estate, probate assets, or probate property.

> **Example:** Jana Bronowski is single. She owns her home, furniture, household goods, and clothes. She has money in savings and checking accounts, stocks and bonds, and valuable jewelry. She also owns a lake cottage with a boat and motor. All these property items, real and personal, constitute Jana's estate or gross estate.

Not all property owned by the decedent can be passed by will, however. The only type of property a decedent can distribute through a will or by intestate succession, if there is no will, is **probate property,** which is also referred to as probate assets, the probate estate, or simply the estate.

Probate property is all real or personal property that the decedent owned either individually as a single or sole owner, called ownership in **severalty,** or as a co-owner with another person or persons in the form of ownership called tenancy in common. Probate property is subject to estate administration by the personal representative (executor or administrator) according to the terms of the will or, if the decedent died intestate, according to the appropriate state intestate succession statute.

Probate property (estate)
Decedent's property that is subject to estate administration by the personal representative.

Severalty
Ownership of property held by one person only.

> **Example:** LaShanna Morgan owns her house, car, furniture, and savings account in severalty; i.e., she is the sole owner of each of these items of property. LaShanna also owns a boat and condominium equally with her best friend Sarah as tenants in common. If LaShanna dies and her debts and taxes due are paid, all of this property, including her one-half interest in the boat and condominium as a tenant in common, would be probate property and would pass to her named beneficiaries or devisees if she has a will or to her heirs if she died intestate.

Probate property includes the following:

Incidents of ownership
The right of the insured or her estate to the economic benefits of the life insurance policy.

- Real property owned in severalty (single ownership) or in a tenancy in common.
- Personal property owned in severalty or in a tenancy in common.
- Life insurance proceeds payable to the estate or a policy in which the decedent retained the **incidents of ownership** (see the discussion in Chapter 10).
- Debts owed the decedent for mortgages, promissory notes, contracts for deed, loans, rents, stock dividends, income tax refunds, interest, royalties, and copyrights.
- Gain from the sale of a business.

- Social Security, Railroad Retirement, and Veterans Administration benefits.
- Civil lawsuit for money damages.
- Testamentary trusts.

Probate property is subject to creditors' claims and federal and state death taxes (see below).

Nonprobate Property or Nonprobate Assets

Some of the real and personal property owned by the decedent at the time of death cannot be transferred by will or inheritance; therefore, it is not subject to probate. This is the decedent's nonprobate property, and it includes the following:

- Real and personal property owned and held in joint tenancy or tenancy by the entirety, both with the right of survivorship.
- Real and personal property transferred into an *inter vivos* (living) trust prior to the settlor's death.
- Money placed in a bank account as a **Totten trust,** also known as a pay-on-death (POD) account.
- Proceeds of a life insurance policy payable to a named beneficiary (recipient of the money) and not to the decedent's estate as long as the decedent relinquishes the incidents of ownership.
- Employment contract benefits that contain a named beneficiary (not the estate) such as profit-sharing plans, pension plans, group life insurance, 401(k) plans, employee stock ownership plans (ESOPs), and Keogh plans.
- Annuity contracts with a named beneficiary (not the estate).
- Individual retirement accounts (traditional and Roth IRAs) with a named beneficiary (not the estate).
- U.S. savings bonds payable on death to a named beneficiary (not the estate).
- Property owned in *tenancy in partnership* (see glossary).

> **Totten trust**
> A bank deposit of a person's money in her name as trustee for another person.

Each of these types of nonprobate property goes directly to the named beneficiary or to the surviving joint tenant(s) or partners by **operation of law.** If the decedent's entire estate consists of nonprobate property, there is no need for estate administration (probate).

Nonprobate property is real or personal property that is not part of the decedent's probate estate. For that reason, a decedent's nonprobate property is:

> **Operation of law**
> Rights pass automatically to a person by the application of the established rules of law, without the act, knowledge, or cooperation of the person.

- Not distributed according to the decedent's will.
- Not distributed according to intestate succession statutes if there is no will.
- Not subject to estate administration (probate) of the decedent's estate.
- Not subject to a spouse's claims.
- Not subject to claims of the decedent's creditors.

But nonprobate property is part of the decedent's *gross estate* for federal and state death tax purposes, i.e., it is subject to federal and state estate taxes and state inheritance tax, and, therefore, you must identify and keep accurate records of each property item for the preparation of required tax returns. See Exhibit 12.15 and Chapter 14.

STATUTES THAT GOVERN THE PASSAGE OF PROPERTY

The law of property is mostly statutory law. States have the power to enact statutes that govern the passage of property from one generation to another or from the deceased to someone in his own generation. The states derive such power from their right, under the U.S. Constitution, to levy and collect taxes and from their duty to protect the citizenry.

> **Example:** If Jane Doe dies with a will and owns property which includes her house and items of personal property such as household furniture, savings and checking accounts, and automobiles, what are the respective rights of her beneficiaries, heirs, and creditors? As an owner of an estate, Jane Doe may distribute her property as she wishes, as long as her plans do not conflict with the statutory rights of others, e.g., a spouse, children, or creditors. Generally, a spouse cannot be disinherited, and although children can be disinherited, minor children are entitled to support. Also, all creditors have the right to be compensated for their valid claims, and states establish statutory procedures whereby creditors may make claims against the decedent's estate whether or not the decedent has made a will.

Each state requires careful recording of all activity during the administration of a decedent's estate so it can fairly and accurately calculate the amount of tax that may be due from the estate of the decedent. Thus, the state becomes another "creditor" (see Chapter 14).

The state protects the decedent's rights by enacting statutes to ensure that each person will be allowed to make a will. If someone dies without a will, the state's statutes also provide for distribution of the property to those whom the decedent would probably have chosen if the decedent had made a will. These are the laws of **descent and distribution,** more commonly called *intestate succession statutes*. Exhibit 2.1 is the intestate succession statute of New York (for further discussion, see Chapter 4).

Descent and distribution
Refers to the distribution by intestate succession statutes.

🏛 ASSIGNMENT 2.3

1. Define the following new words contained in the New York statute (Exhibit 2.1) by using the Glossary at the end of this book (all these terms will be defined and discussed in later chapters): *dower, right of succession, distributee, issue, distributive share, per capita,* and *half blood.*
2. List seven types of property interests that are not part of the decedent's probate estate.

FORMS OF PROPERTY OWNERSHIP

Various forms of property ownership exist. They range from one person who owns or holds the entire interest in an item of real or personal property to situations where two or more persons share concurrent ownership rights as co-owners also called co-tenants. The most common forms of property ownership are *tenancy in severalty* (individual ownership) and *concurrent ownership* (joint ten-

Exhibit 2.1 New York State's Intestate Succession Statute

N.Y. Estates Powers and Trusts Law § 4-1.1
Descent and Distribution of a Decedent's Estate

The property of a decedent not disposed of by will shall be distributed as provided in this section. In computing said distribution, debts, administration expenses and reasonable funeral expenses shall be deducted but all estate taxes shall be disregarded, except that nothing contained herein relieves a *distributee* from contributing to all such taxes the amounts apportioned against him or her under 2–1.8. Distribution shall then be as follows:

(a) If a decedent is survived by:

(1) A spouse and *issue,* fifty thousand dollars and one-half of the residue to the spouse, and the balance thereof to the issue by representation.

(2) A spouse and no issue, the whole to the spouse.

(3) Issue and no spouse, the whole to the issue, by representation.

(4) One or both parents, and no spouse and no issue, the whole to the surviving parent or parents.

(5) Issue of parents, and no spouse, issue or parent, the whole to the issue of the parents, by representation.

(6) One or more grandparents or the issue of grandparents (as hereinafter defined), and no spouse, issue, parent or issue of parents, one-half to the surviving paternal grandparent or grandparents, or if neither of them survives the decedent, to their issue, by representation, and the other one-half to the surviving maternal grandparent or grandparents, or if neither of them survives the decedent, to their issue, by representation; provided that if the decedent was not survived by a grandparent or grandparents on one side or by the issue of such grandparents, the whole to the surviving grandparent or grandparents on the other side, or if neither of them survives the decedent, to their issue, by representation, in the same manner as the one-half. For the purposes of this subparagraph, issue of grandparents shall not include issue more remote than grandchildren of such grandparents.

(7) Great-grandchildren of grandparents, and no spouse, issue, parent, issue of parents, grandparent, children of grandparents or grandchildren of grandparents, one-half to the great-grandchildren of the paternal grandparents, per capita, and the other one-half to the great-grandchildren of the maternal grandparents, *per capita*, provided that if the decedent was not survived by great-grandchildren of grandparents on one side, the whole to the great-grandchildren of grandparents on the other side, in the same manner as the one-half.

(b) For all purposes of this section, decedent's relatives of the *half blood* shall be treated as if they were relatives of the whole blood.

(c) *Distributees* of the decedent, conceived before his or her death but born alive thereafter, take as if they were born in his or her lifetime.

(d) The right of an adopted child to take a *distributive share* and the *right of succession* to the estate of an adopted child continue as provided in the domestic relations law.

(e) A distributive share passing to a surviving spouse under this section is in lieu of any right of *dower* to which such spouse may be entitled.

ancy, tenancy in common, tenancy by the entirety, and community property). The term "tenant" or "tenancy," which is used to describe severalty and some of the types of concurrent ownership, is synonymous with "owner" or "ownership." Exhibit 2.2 summarizes the forms of property ownership.

Exhibit 2.2 Forms of Property Ownership

Real or personal property can be owned:

By one person (individual ownership)	or	By two or more persons (concurrent ownership)
▪ Tenancy in severalty		▪ Joint tenancy
		▪ Tenancy in common
		▪ Tenancy by the entirety
		▪ Community property

Tenancy in Severalty—Ownership by One Person

Disposition
The parting with, transfer of, or conveyance of property.

Tenancy in severalty (ownership in severalty, or individual ownership) means that one person is the sole owner of real property, such as land, or personal property, such as a car. As an individual, the owner in severalty has absolute ownership of the real or personal property with exclusive rights, privileges, and interests. The owner may voluntarily dispose of the property while living, either by gift or sale, or may dispose of it at death through a will. If no such **disposition** has taken place at the time of death, the property remains in the owner's estate and passes to certain specified takers under intestate succession statutes.

Example: John buys Joe's car. The title is transferred to John. John is the sole owner of the car. He owns it in severalty.

Example: Mary is given a ring by her aunt. Once delivered, the ring belongs to Mary, solely. She owns it in severalty.

Example: Uncle Henry died. In his will, he left his lake cottage to his niece, Kathy. Kathy owns the real property in severalty.

Example:

Blackacre—a farm

| Joel | Tenancy (ownership) in severalty |

No person, other than Joel, has any ownership right or interest in the property. He owns the property in a tenancy in severalty or simply referred to as *in severalty.*

Forms of Concurrent Ownership—Ownership by Two or More Persons

Concurrent ownership is a right of ownership in real or personal property shared by two or more persons. The most common forms of such multiple ownership are joint tenancy, tenancy in common, tenancy by the entirety, and community property.

Joint Tenancy

Joint tenants
Two or more persons who own or hold equal, undivided interests in property with the right of survivorship.

Right of survivorship
Passes the decedent joint tenant's interest in property automatically to the surviving joint tenant(s) by operation of law without the need for probate.

Joint tenancy is the ownership of real or personal property by two or more persons (called the **joint tenants**) who obtain an equal and undivided interest in the property by gift, purchase, will, or inheritance. The unique and distinguishing characteristic of a joint tenancy is the **right of survivorship.** On the death of one joint tenant, the right of survivorship passes the decedent's interest in the property automatically to the surviving joint tenants by operation of law, *without the need for probate* and with the last surviving joint tenant entitled to the whole property in severalty.

Example:

Blackacre—a farm	Blackacre	Sam and Ruth are joint tenants who concurrently own Blackacre. Ruth dies. Sam owns the undivided whole property in severalty (single ownership).
Sam Ruth →	Ruth dies → Sam	

The farm goes directly to Sam *without* passing through Ruth's estate. The farm is nonprobate property. Even if Ruth has a will, it does not affect property owned as joint tenants because she cannot pass joint tenancy property through a will.

In order for a joint tenancy to be created, common law requires "four unities": unity of time, unity of title, unity of interest, and unity of possession. According to common law, a simple conveyance of property that uses the words, "to two or more persons as joint tenants," does not necessarily create a joint tenancy unless the four unities also exist. The decision in *Cleaver v. Long,* 69 Ohio Law Abs. 488, 126 N.E.2d 479 (1955), supports the common law rules for the creation of a joint tenancy; in the case, the court said all joint tenants must:

- Have the same interest in land with respect to duration of the estate (unity of interest).
- Acquire their interest by the same title (unity of title).
- Receive their interest at the same time (unity of time).
- Take their right to possession of the estate at the same time (unity of possession).

Cleaver involved a quitclaim deed, to which husband and wife were both grantors and grantees; the deed created a joint tenancy for them with the right of survivorship. The court ruled that the deed was valid as long as the four unities under common law were present. The next paragraphs discuss the common law definitions of these "unities" in more detail.

Unity of Time. For unity of time to exist, joint tenant owners must receive or take their interests in the property together, i.e., at the same time.

Example: In most states, a single conveyance of property from Mary to Amy and Betty as joint tenants dated July 15, 2001, creates a joint tenancy. If, however, Mary conveys the property to Amy and Betty as joint tenants in a single transfer that takes effect on different dates, Amy receives an interest on July 15, 2001, and Betty receives an interest a day later, the conveyance fails in its attempt to create the interest desired, and a tenancy in common exists between Amy and Betty. Some states require an express statement to create a joint tenancy and avoid a tenancy in common (see the discussion below).

𝍔 ASSIGNMENT 2.4

Howard conveys a farm, Blackacre, by deed to "Brown and Jones as joint tenants and not as tenants in common." What form of ownership is presumed in your state by this conveyance?

Unity of Title.   For unity of title to exist, the tenancy must be created and the tenants must receive their title (ownership rights) from a single source, e.g., the same will or deed.

> **Example:** When Mary, in a single deed, transfers real property to Amy and Betty as joint tenants, unity of title exists and a joint tenancy is created. On the other hand, if Mary transfers property to Amy and Betty by will *and* deed, respectively, or by more than one deed, the use of multiple instruments of transfer fails to meet the unity of title requirement, and a joint tenancy is not created.

Some states do not allow the creation of a joint tenancy wherein the grantor names himself and another or others as joint tenants. For example, if Brown conveys a farm, Blackacre, which he inherited and now solely owns, to "Conrad and himself (Brown) as joint tenants with the right of survivorship," a joint tenancy, generally, does not result because of the lack of unities of time and title. The parties do not receive their interest in the property simultaneously since Brown already owned the farm, nor do they receive their title from one document since Brown received his title through inheritance.

To create a joint tenancy between an existing owner of the property (Brown) and one or more persons, Brown must first transfer a deed to the property to a third person, called the **straw man** (Jones); then, by a second deed, Jones, the straw man, immediately reconveys the property back to the original owner (Brown) and the new co-owner (Conrad) as joint tenants with the right of survivorship. The prevailing view in the majority of states today, however, is that, as in the *Cleaver* case, Brown can convey the farm from himself to "himself and Conrad" and create a valid joint tenancy.

Straw man
A person used to create a joint tenancy of real property between the existing owner of the property and one or more other persons.

𝍔 ASSIGNMENT 2.5

Determine whether your state statute would allow an existing owner to create a joint tenancy as Brown did in the last example by conveying the farm to "himself and Conrad as joint tenants."

Unity of Interest.   For unity of interest to exist, each tenant must have an interest in the property identical with that of the other tenants; the interests must be of the same quantity and duration.

> **Example:** If Mary conveys property to Amy, Betty, and Carol as joint tenants with the right of survivorship, a joint tenancy is created. If instead, Mary gives both Amy and Carol one-sixth shares of the ownership rights and Betty a two-thirds share, the unity of interest requirement is not met, and Amy, Betty, and Carol own the property as tenants in common, although the conveyance specifies they are joint tenants.

Unity of Possession. For unity of possession to exist, each joint tenant must own and hold the same undivided possession of the whole property held in joint tenancy. As part of the group that owns all the property, each joint tenant has an equal right to possess the entire property and share equally in the profits and losses derived from the property, e.g., the sale of crops or livestock.

Example:

Blackacre—a farm 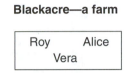	Alice, Roy, and Vera are joint tenants, and each has the right to possess the whole property concurrently with the other co-tenants. None has the right to exclude the others from possession of all or any part of the property, and each has the right to share in profits derived from the use of the farm.

Example: A conveyance of a farm, Blackacre, from Mary to "Amy and Betty as joint tenants with the right of survivorship," with no restrictions on the amount of their respective possession rights creates a joint tenancy. However, if Mary attempts to limit the possession rights of either Amy or Betty and states "to Amy and Betty as joint tenants, but only Betty has the right to possess Blackacre," the transfer fails to create a joint tenancy for lack of the unity of possession.

SUMMARY EXAMPLE: William conveys a farm to Jeff, Bob, and Greg as joint tenants on June 1, 2001 (unity of time), by a single deed (unity of title). Each co-owner receives a one-third undivided interest (unity of interest) of the whole property, and each has an equal right to possession of the whole (unity of possession). All four unities are present. Therefore, a valid joint tenancy is created if William complies with other state statutory requirements, e.g., uses language which indicates he desires to create a joint tenancy, such as "to Jeff, Bob, and Greg as joint tenants and not as tenants in common." If any of the four "unities" is not included in the conveyance of the property, the form of ownership created is *not* a joint tenancy but may be a tenancy in common (see the discussion below).

ASSIGNMENT 2.6

1. If Robert Green owned a farm in your state and died leaving by will the farm to "my three sons, Roger, John, and James as joint owners with equal shares," what form of ownership would the three sons have in your state?
2. If Robert Green in the problem above had devised the farm "to my three sons, Roger, John, and James as joint tenants and not tenants in common," would a joint tenancy be created according to the laws of your state?
3. Joyce, age 21, and Ellen, age 20, are sisters. When Aunt Mary dies, she leaves her country home "to Joyce immediately and to Ellen on her twenty-first birthday, as joint tenants with the right of survivorship." What form of ownership has Aunt Mary created?

The legal document in Exhibit 2.3, a deed, is executed to illustrate the creation of a joint tenancy with the required four unities. The type of ownership a person has in real property is determined by an examination of the deed to the property. Notice that the conveyance reads "to Roger L. Green, John M. Green, and James

Exhibit 2.3   Sample Deed Showing Creation of a Joint Tenancy

MD Form No. 5–M--WARRANTY DEED   Minnesota Uniform Conveyancing Blanks (6/1/97)   Miller-Davis Co., St. Paul, MN

Individual(s) to Joint Tenants

No delinquent taxes and transfer entered; Certificate
of Real Estate Value ( ) filed ( ) not required
Certificate of Real Estate Value No. _____

_____
(Date)

_____
County Auditor

by _____
Deputy

(reserved for recording data)

DEED TAX DUE: $ 282.70

Date: August 1, 2001

FOR VALUABLE CONSIDERATION, _____
   Henry J. Smith and Sara M. Smith,   husband and wife
                                                                                                      (marital status)

Grantor, hereby conveys and warrants to _____
   Roger L. Green, John M. Green, and James R. Green

Grantees, as joint tenants, real property in _____ Brownstad _____ County, Minnesota, described as follows:

   Lot 4, Block 12, Moser's Addition to Fairview Village

together with all hereditaments and appurtenances belonging thereto, subject to the following exceptions:

_____
_____
_____

Check box it applicable:
☐ The Seller certifies that the seller does not know of any wells on the described real property.
☐ A well disclosure certificate accompanies this document.
☐ I am familiar with the real property described in this instrument and I certify that the status and number of wells
   on the described real property have not changed since the last previously filed well disclosure certificate.

/S/ Henry J. Smith

Affix Deed Tax Stamp Here

/S/ Sara M. Smith

STATE OF MINNESOTA

COUNTY OF Brownstad   } ss.

This instrument was acknowledged before me on August 1, 2001
                                                                                    Date

by Henry J. Smith and Sara M. Smith, husband and wife

NOTARIAL STAMP OR SEAL (OR OTHER TITLE OR BANK)

/S/ Mary A. Williams

SIGNATURE OF NOTARY PUBLIC OR OTHER OFFICIAL

My commission expires on:
August 4, 2004

Check here if part or all of the land is Registered (Torrens) ☐

Tax Statements for the real property described in this instrument should
be sent to (include name and address of Grantee):

THIS INSTRUMENT WAS DRAFTED BY (NAME AND ADDRESS):

Dean T. Anderson
Plaza Bank Building
Minneapolis, MN 55455

Roger L. Green
1400 River Street
Minneapolis, MN 55455

Source: This form is property of Miller/Davis Company, St. Paul, MN, Telephone 651-642-1988. Reprinted with permission.

R. Green, grantees as joint tenants" and not as tenants in common. In some states, this language is necessary to create the joint tenancy. Since Roger, John, and James receive their co-ownership at the same time (August 1, 2001—the date on the deed); by the same legal document (the deed); with the same undivided interest in the whole (equal interest); and with the right to possess the entire property (equal possession), all four unity requirements are satisfied.

🏛 ASSIGNMENT 2.7

Assume you own the house in which you now live. Using your state form, draft a deed conveying the house to your two best friends as joint tenants. Draft a second deed conveying the house to your friends as tenants in common.

Besides the four unities, certain other characteristics distinguish joint tenancy from tenancy in common and other forms of co-ownership. They include the following:

- Right of survivorship.
- **Undivided interest.**
- **Severance.**

Right of Survivorship. When a joint tenant dies, the surviving joint tenants receive the interest of the deceased, i.e., the equal and undivided part, with nothing passing to the beneficiaries, heirs, or devisees of the decedent. The deceased joint tenant's ownership rights pass automatically to the other living joint tenants under the *right of survivorship.* Each joint tenant has this right of survivorship, which prevents a joint tenant from transferring property by a will. If all the joint tenants die except one, the surviving joint tenant owns the property *in severalty,* which means that the joint tenancy is destroyed and the lone survivor owns the property solely.

Undivided Interest. Joint tenants are entitled to the equal use, enjoyment, control, and possession of the property since they have an equal and undivided identical interest in the same property. Each joint tenant is considered to be the owner of the whole property and also of an undivided part. The undivided interest means that no joint tenant can say she owns a specific or individual part of the property. If a joint tenant did own a particular portion of the property, it would be owned as a single owner, *in severalty,* not as a co-owner, *joint tenant.* (See the example and further discussion under Tenancy in Common.)

Undivided interest
A right to an undivided portion of property that is owned by one of two or more joint tenants or tenants in common before the property is divided (partitioned).

Severance
The destruction of a joint tenancy by one of the joint tenants transferring while alive his interest in real property to another person by deed, thereby creating a tenancy in common with the new owner and the other remaining joint tenant(s).

🏛 ASSIGNMENT 2.8

1. Which of the following items of property can be owned in a joint tenancy?

Stocks	House
Bonds	Cottage
Art	Condominium
Jewelry	Boat
Car	Contents of a safe deposit box

2. Conchita and Emilio are not related by blood or marriage. All of the items in Question 1 are either given, sold, or willed to Conchita and Emilio as joint tenants with the right

of survivorship. Emilio dies and owes many debts. Do his creditors have any claim against the property? Can Emilio transfer by will any of the property to his spouse and family? When Emilio dies, who owns the property? What form of ownership is created by Emilio's death?

Severance.   While alive, each joint tenant has the right of severance, i.e., an act of severing, separating, or partitioning real property. Severance occurs when a joint tenant owner conveys her equal interest in the property during her lifetime, thereby destroying one of the four essential unities and terminating the joint tenancy. Such an "*inter vivos*" conveyance, i.e., a transfer of interest by gift or sale while the joint owner is alive, is the *only* way a joint tenancy can be severed. Severance of real property is accomplished when a deed is conveyed. After a joint tenancy is severed in this manner, the remaining joint tenants and the new tenant are tenants in common, and the new tenant has no right of survivorship. (See the examples below.)

Example: To illustrate joint tenancy ownership, suppose X dies and gives by will a farm to A and B as joint tenants. If during their lifetimes neither A nor B conveys (gives or sells) his interest in the farm by deed to another person and A dies, B becomes the sole owner (*in severalty*) of the farm through right of survivorship.

X	gives by will	A and B	A dies	B owns the
	→	⎵	→	property
decedent	property	joint tenants		in severalty

Assume that X dies and gives by will the farm to A, B, and C as joint tenants. C later conveys, by deed, his undivided one-third interest in the farm to D. This conveyance, as a severance, terminates the joint tenancy between (A and B) and (C) and creates a tenancy in common form of ownership between (A and B) and (D). Since they have done nothing to change (sever) their form of ownership, a joint tenancy still remains between A and B. Thereafter, if A dies and has made no conveyance of his interest, B would receive A's interest in the farm through right of survivorship. The result: B and D own the farm as tenants in common, i.e., B owns a two-thirds interest and D owns a one-third interest in the property. The unities of time, title, and interest have been destroyed and only the unity of possession remains.

Example:

A	gives by will	A, B, C	C	
→	→	→	→	to D
dies	property	joint tenants	conveys his ⅓ interest and severs the joint tenancy	

Result: A and B own a two-thirds interest in the farm, and they remain joint tenants (each owns a one-third undivided interest). A tenancy in common now exists between (A and B) and (D), who owns the other one-third.

Later:

A → dies	B receives A's $^1/_3$ interest → as surviving joint tenant	B and D are tenants in common $^2/_3$ interest for B _____ $^1/_3$ interest for D

As tenants in common, on the death of either B or D, the decedent's interest in the farm passes by will or inheritance to his beneficiaries, heirs, or devisees (see the discussion of tenancy in common below).

 ASSIGNMENT 2.9

Apply the previous illustration to the following cases and then answer the questions.

Case 1. Alice dies. In her will she leaves her farm, Blackacre, to her three nephews, Able, Baker, and Charlie, as joint tenants. Able is married and has eleven children; Baker is divorced and has two children; and Charlie is a bachelor. Able dies. His will leaves all his property to his wife, Agnes. Who owns Blackacre? What form or forms of ownership exist between the owners?

Case 2. Continue with the facts of Case 1 except Abel sold and deeded his interest in Blackacre to Dolan, and Charlie gave and deeded his interest to Elaine, his girlfriend. Who owns Blackacre? What form or forms of ownership exist between the owners? What happens to Baker's interest in the property when he dies? Does Able's wife, Agnes, have any interest in Blackacre?

Creation of a Joint Tenancy.   Today, state statutes determine whether a joint tenancy is legally created. Most states recognize joint tenancy, but they vary in the express language they require to create it. Proper use of the mandatory words and the intent of the creator of the joint tenancy determine whether a binding joint tenancy is established. For example, if Harold Wong wants to give his lake cottage to his two children, Sue and James, he may satisfy the statutes in most states by writing in the deed of conveyance "to my two children, Sue Wong and James Wong as joint tenants." Other states require more, such as ". . . as joint tenants with the right of survivorship" or, as some documents are written today, ". . . as joint tenants with the right of survivorship and not as tenants in common" (see the Illinois statute below). Some community property states (Arizona, Nevada, Texas, and Wisconsin) allow spouses to obtain joint tenancy benefits for their community property by including the words ". . . as community property with the right of survivorship" on deeds or in written contracts. Louisiana has no joint tenancy with survivorship rights. The remaining community property states create a joint tenancy by deed or contract and add a separate document, signed by the spouses, that states the property is held in joint tenancy for the purpose of avoiding probate, but the property preserves and maintains its community property character. This document allows California, Idaho, New Mexico, and Washington to create a joint tenancy with community property. See the forms of ownership by state in Exhibit 2.4.

Exhibit 2.4   Forms of Ownership by State

By One Person	By Two or More Persons			
Tenancy in severalty	Tenancy in Common	Joint Tenancy	Tenancy by the Entirety	Community Property
All states	All states	All states except as follows: Alaska—for personal property only Louisiana—not recognized Ohio—called survivorship tenancy Oregon—equivalent only if language reads "tenancy in common with the right of survivorship" Texas—for real property owners must sign a joint tenancy agreement	Alaska, Arkansas, Delaware, Florida, Hawaii, Maryland, Massachusetts, Mississippi, Missouri, New Jersey, Oklahoma, Pennsylvania, Rhode Island, Tennessee, Vermont, Virginia, Wyoming Illinois, Indiana, Kentucky, Michigan, New York, North Carolina, Oregon—for real property only Washington—no right of survivorship	Arizona*, California, Idaho, Louisiana, Nevada*, New Mexico, Texas*, Washington Wisconsin*—recognizes marital property equivalent of community property *These states allow spouses to hold community property with right of survivorship.

+Alaska Sort of [handwritten annotation]

Another variable among the states is their preference for certain forms of co-ownership of property. At one time, common law preferred the creation of a joint tenancy over a tenancy in common whenever a conveyance was unclear which of these two interests was intended by the grantor. Today, in most states, the reverse is generally true, and by statute, when the intention of the parties is not clear, tenancy in common is presumed and preferred over a joint tenancy since the legislatures believe the decedent's property should pass to beneficiaries, heirs, or devisees and not to surviving joint tenants. An example of one such statute is Minn. Stat. Ann. § 500.19(2), *Construction of grants and devises.* The decision in *Short v. Milby,* 31 Del.Ch. 49, 64 A.2d 36 (1949), illustrates the current preference. In this case, the court stated, "Joint tenancies are not favored and can only be created by clear and definite language not reasonably capable of any different construction." Notice the words required and preferred for the creation of concurrent ownership in the states of New York and Illinois:

N.Y. Estates Powers and Trusts Law § 6–2.2
The law provides that a grant of an estate (interest in property) to two or more persons ". . . creates in them a tenancy in common, unless expressly declared to be a joint tenancy."

Ill. Compiled Stat. Ann. Ch. 765 § 1005/1
The law states that the deed of conveyance must expressly provide that the property interest is granted ". . . not in tenancy in common but in joint tenancy . . ."

🏛 ASSIGNMENT 2.10

Using your state's codes, find and cite appropriate statutes, if any, that determine the form of ownership that would be created by the following conveyances by deed: (1) "to A and B jointly," (2) "to A and B as joint owners," (3) "to A and B equally," (4) "to A or to B," (5) "to A and to B." If your statutes or case law do not address this problem, find a statute from another state that does. Find and cite your state statute that determines the required words to create a joint tenancy or a tenancy in common.

Advantages and Disadvantages of Joint Tenancy. When working with clients, you will discover they frequently have created joint tenancies with spouses and others. When you discuss the following advantages and disadvantages with the client, *you must be careful not to attempt to respond to questions that seek legal advice or interpretations.* All such questions *must* be referred to your supervising attorney. Advantages of a joint tenancy:

ETHICAL ISSUE

- On the death of a joint tenant, title passes automatically to the surviving joint tenant(s) because of the right of survivorship.
- It avoids probate. No corresponding expenses and delays are necessary or required for the surviving joint tenant(s) to acquire title.
- Title passes to the surviving joint tenant(s) free of the claims of the decedent's creditors unless the joint tenancy was created to defraud creditors. The decedent's real estate is subject to certain unpaid debts such as mortgages, property taxes, and liens, e.g., a mechanic's lien for work or improvements to the property.
- If the joint tenants are husband and wife (but see tenancy by the entirety below), no federal gift tax is owed because of the unlimited marital gift tax deduction (this may also be true for state gift tax concerns). See discussion in Chapters 10 and 14.
- If real property located in other (foreign) states is in a joint tenancy, ancillary administration may be avoided (see discussion in Chapter 3).
- Joint tenancy of bank accounts, which include checking, savings, certificates of deposit, and Totten trusts (PODs), that are properly and legally created to establish the right of survivorship for the named co-owners or beneficiary, can avoid probate and provide immediate cash for family needs on the death of a spouse or parent. You must be careful to ensure the account is correctly created, e.g., all signature cards executed and state statutory requirements met.
- Creation of a joint tenancy is fast and inexpensive, whereas probate and the creation of a trust are expensive.

Disadvantages of a joint tenancy:

- The person who creates the joint tenancy no longer has complete control of the property.

Example: Shirley is a single parent who has a teenage son, Zachary. Shirley buys a house in joint tenancy with Zachary. A wonderful job opportunity becomes available in another state, and Shirley must immediately sell the house. Since Zachary is a minor and cannot convey real property, a court must appoint a guardian (Shirley) to represent and protect Zachary's interest in the house. However, this loss of control and subsequent delay may cause Shirley to lose the employment opportunity.

- Any joint tenant can terminate the joint tenancy without the agreement of the other joint tenant(s).

Example: The mother of Andre and Rachael dies and leaves the family farm to them as joint tenants. Rachael wants to live on the farm. Andre wants to sell his interest. If Rachael cannot afford to buy Andre's interest, the farm *may* have to be sold to a third party since it is Andre's right to terminate the joint tenancy.

- The surviving recipient of the property previously held in joint tenancy may not have been the intended beneficiary.

Example: In the preceding example, if Shirley died after creating the joint tenancy with Zachary, he would own the house. If Zachary was killed in a car accident a year later while still the owner of the house, the house will pass to his only heir, his father, if living, which may not be a result that Shirley would have intended.

- The stepped-up basis for full value of the proceeds is lost. See the discussion and example in Chapter 10.
- Other examples of problems created by joint tenancy follow.

Example: Robbie, age 19, wants to buy a car, but he is unable to obtain a loan to finance the purchase. His parents agree to cosign the promissory note required by the bank for the loan. The parents also list themselves as joint tenancy owners with Robbie on the title of the car. While driving the new car, Robbie is the sole cause of an accident in which the driver of the other car is seriously injured. The injured driver sues Robbie and his parents. If the injured driver wins the case and receives a judgment of $450,000 in damages, she can collect money damages from the personal assets of Robbie or his parents if they are not adequately insured.

Example: A married couple, Bert and Lil, want to avoid probate and see no reason to have individual wills, so they place all their real and personal property (including their home, cars, checking and savings accounts, stocks and bonds) in joint tenancy. When one of them dies, the title to all of the property will go to the surviving spouse because of the right of survivorship. However, if both spouses die in a common accident, for example, in a plane crash, the property will have to go through probate, and since they have no wills when the accident occurs, their property will be transferred to their heirs according to their state's intestate succession laws, which may be a distribution very different from what they wanted or intended.

Tenancy in Common

Tenancy in common is a form of concurrent ownership of real or personal property by two or more persons called tenants in common. Each tenant owns separate undivided interests in the property with the "unity" of possession. The tenants' interests may be equal or unequal. The "unity" of possession establishes each tenant's right to take and possess the whole property with the other co-tenants, and each is entitled to share proportionately in the profits derived from the property. A tenancy in common differs from a joint tenancy in several important ways, including the following:

- The undivided interest of the joint tenants *must* be equal; for tenants in common, it may be equal or unequal. Thus, when there are two tenants in common, each may own one-half of the property, i.e., an equal interest, or one may own three-fourths of the property and the other one-fourth, i.e., an unequal interest. Neither owns a specific portion of the property, because each has an undivided interest in the entire property.

Example: X may expressly create a tenancy in common in the following way:

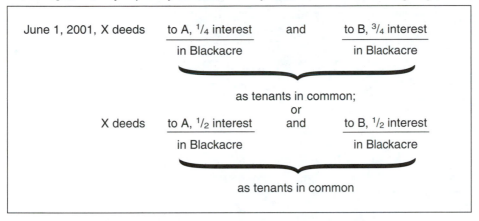

June 1, 2001, X deeds ⸻ to A, $^1/_4$ interest ⸻ and ⸻ to B, $^3/_4$ interest

in Blackacre ⸻⸻⸻⸻⸻⸻⸻⸻⸻ in Blackacre

as tenants in common;

or

X deeds ⸻ to A, $^1/_2$ interest ⸻ and ⸻ to B, $^1/_2$ interest

in Blackacre ⸻⸻⸻⸻⸻⸻⸻⸻⸻ in Blackacre

as tenants in common

- The creation of a joint tenancy must include the "four unities" (time, title, interest, and possession); a tenancy in common requires only "unity of possession."
- Property held in joint tenancy is nonprobate property; property held in a tenancy in common is probate property.
- The distinguishing characteristic of a joint tenancy is the right of survivorship; there is *no* right of survivorship in a tenancy in common. Therefore, unlike a joint tenancy, when a tenant in common dies, the decedent's interest goes to an heir or as directed in a will, and it is subject to estate administration (probate).

Example: Jeff Morrow dies with a will. In the will, he gives a one-half interest in his original Picasso painting to his only living relative, his nephew Charles Morrow. Jeff gives the other half of the ownership rights in the painting to his two close friends, Mike Flaherty and Dave Rossi, equally. Charles, Mike, and Dave are co-owners of the Picasso painting as tenants in common. If Mike Flaherty should die, his one-fourth interest in the painting would be transferred according to his will, if he has one, or to his heir (closest blood relative, if he is not married) according to state law.

Not only may tenants in common own different interests in terms of quantity and duration, but they may receive their interests from different parties through different instruments of conveyance at different times. Nevertheless, they retain an undivided interest in the property unless it is merged or severed.

Creation of a Tenancy in Common. A tenancy in common may be expressly created as in the deed in Exhibit 2.5, but as previously mentioned, a tenancy in common is also created when a grantor makes a conveyance and fails to use the terminology required to establish a joint tenancy. In addition, once a joint tenancy is validly established, if one of the joint tenants makes an *inter vivos* conveyance by deed to another person, the joint tenancy is severed, and a tenancy in common is created for the new owner (see the examples below).

Example: Most states today prefer the establishment of tenancy in common over a joint tenancy. Therefore, if William Kennedy dies and provides in his will that Blackacre is to go "to my sons, Joseph and Robert jointly in equal shares," the real property will pass to the two sons as tenants in common in states with such a preference. Note that the conveyance did not contain an explicit statement saying that a "joint tenancy" was to be created.

Exhibit 2.5 Sample Deed Showing Creation of Tenancy in Common

MD Form No. 1–M--WARRANTY DEED   Minnesota Uniform Conveyancing Blanks (6/1/97)   Miller-Davis Co., St. Paul, MN

Individual(s) to Individual(s)

No delinquent taxes and transfer entered; Certificate of Real Estate Value (   ) filed (   ) not required
Certificate of Real Estate Value No. _____

_____
(Date)

_____
County Auditor

by _____
Deputy

(reserved for recording data)

DEED TAX DUE: $ _282.70_____

Date: __September 12, 2001_____

FOR VALUABLE CONSIDERATION, _____
__David L. Smith and Sally J. Smith_____   __husband and wife__
(marital status)

Grantor, hereby conveys and warrants to_ Warren P. Jones and Mary S. Jones,_____
__husband and wife as tenants in common_____

Grantee, real property in __Lowry_____ County, Minnesota, described as follows:

     Lot Two(2), Block Five (5), Samuel's Addition to Lake Park

together with all hereditaments and appurtenances belonging thereto, subject to the following exceptions:

_____
_____

Check box it applicable:
☐ The Seller certifies that the seller does not know of any wells on the described real property.
☐ A well disclosure certificate accompanies this document.
☐ I am familiar with the real property described in this instrument and I certify that the status and number of wells on the described real property have not changed since the last previously filed well disclosure certificate.

/S/ David L. Smith

Affix Deed Tax Stamp Here

STATE OF MINNESOTA

/S/ Sally J. Smith

COUNTY OF _Lowry_____ } ss.

This instrument was acknowledged before me on _September 12, 2001_____
Date

by __David L. Smith and Sally J. Smith, husband and wife____

NOTARIAL STAMP OR SEAL (OR OTHER TITLE OR BANK)

My commission expires on:
June 4, 2003

/S/ Janice S. Brown

SIGNATURE OF NOTARY PUBLIC OR OTHER OFFICIAL

Check here if part of all or the land is Registered (Torrens) ☐

Tax Statements for the real property described in this instrument should be sent to (include name and address of Grantee):

THIS INSTRUMENT WAS DRAFTED BY (NAME AND ADDRESS):

Dean T. Anderson
Plaza Bank Building
Minneapolis, MN 55455

Mary S. Jones
1704 Northland Road
St. Paul, MN 55243

Source: This form is property of Miller/Davis Company, St. Paul, MN, Telephone 651-642-1988. Reprinted with permission.

Example: In another case, suppose William Kennedy creates a valid joint tenancy in his will which states Blackacre goes "to my sons, Joseph and Robert, as joint tenants with the right of survivorship and not as tenants in common." William dies. Joseph and Robert are joint tenants. Robert, by deed, sells his interest in Blackacre to Charles Brown. The result is the original joint tenancy is severed by Robert's *inter vivos* conveyance and a tenancy in common is created between Joseph and Charles.

🏛 ASSIGNMENT 2.11

1. If Michael conveys one-third of his farm, Blackacre, to Fred on August 15, 2001, and the remaining two-thirds to Bob on September 20, 2001, what form of ownership will Fred and Bob have according to the statutes or case law in your state?
2. If Peter and Mary are joint tenants, and Peter gives his interest in the property to Paul by a valid conveyance, what form of ownership exists according to your state law?

The state of New York, by statute, handles the transfer of property to two or more persons in the following way:

N.Y. Estates Powers and Trusts Law § 6-2.2
When Estate Is in Common, in Joint Tenancy or by the Entirety:

(a) A disposition of property to two or more persons creates in them a tenancy in common, unless expressly declared to be a joint tenancy.

(b) A disposition of real property to a husband and wife creates in them a tenancy by the entirety, unless expressly declared to be a joint tenancy or a tenancy in common.

(c) . . .

(d) . . .

(e) A disposition of property to two or more persons as executors, trustees or guardians creates in them a joint tenancy.

(f) Property passing in intestacy to two or more persons is taken by them as tenants in common.

Example: Phyllis, a resident of New York, dies without a will. Her husband, Martin, died a year earlier. She leaves a house, which is in her name only, and no debts. The law of descent and distribution of the state of New York entitles her children, Joan and Jack, to the house in tenancy in common.

🏛 ASSIGNMENT 2.12

1. Susan Sowles, a resident of New York, dies without a will. If she has a lakeshore cottage in New York and her heirs are her three children, what form of ownership of the cottage results for their benefit?
2. If Mary Main, also a resident of New York, dies with a will which transfers her homestead to her two nephews, who are the executors of her estate, what form of ownership exists between the nephews in New York and in your state?

Transfer of an Interest. Each tenant in common may transfer an interest by gift, will, or sale or may pledge it as security for a loan. When a tenant in common dies without having conveyed her share of the property, it passes to her beneficiaries, heirs, or devisees. The *right of survivorship* that accompanies a joint tenant interest does not exist with a tenancy in common.

Example: A, B, and C each own an undivided one-third interest in property as tenants in common. If A dies *intestate,* A's interest in the property will pass by descent to his heirs and not automatically go to B and C.

Concurrent Ownership of Blackacre			
A, B, and C are tenants in common			
A	B	C	A dies
1/3 interest	1/3 interest	1/3 interest	

Result: A heirs receive A's one-third interest (by descent). (A's heirs and B and C are tenants in common.)

If A died testate (with a will) in the above example, his will determines how and to whom his interest in Blackacre will be distributed. Such a testamentary transfer is not possible in a joint tenancy since the property held in joint tenancy is automatically transferred to the surviving joint tenant.

⚖ ASSIGNMENT 2.13

Abner, Boswell, and Clarence are owners of Blackacre as joint tenants. Clarence sells his interest and delivers a deed to Boswell. Abner gives his interest to Ruth by delivering a deed. What form of ownership exists? Name the owners and the amount of their interests. Explain what would happen to Boswell's interest if he died testate or intestate.

When a tenant in common disposes of an interest by gift, sale, or will, the new owner is also a tenant in common with the remaining co-tenants. Tenancy in common is destroyed by merger when the entire ownership rights pass to one person or by severance when the property is partitioned (see below).

Example: A and B are tenants in common. A purchases B's interest by deed. A now has merged the property and is the sole owner of the property *in severalty.*

Undivided Interest. As mentioned previously in the discussion of joint tenancy, an undivided interest is a right to an undivided portion of property that is owned by one of two or more *tenants in common* or joint tenants before the property is divided (partitioned). A farm, including the buildings (house, barn, etc.), the personal property (tractor, other machinery, and livestock), and the land itself, owned in joint tenancy or tenancy in common creates an *undivided interest* for each co-tenant. In a practical sense this means that each co-owner has a right or interest in the entire farm, but cannot claim a specific portion of the property, e.g., the house or the livestock, as the co-owner's own individual property. After partition, each person (co-owner) owns the apportioned part of the property in severalty, i.e., in single ownership. (See the example below and the subsequent discussion of partition).

Example:

Blackacre Roy Alice Vera Joint tenancy	Each of the three joint tenants has a one-third *undivided interest* in the whole property. Each has the equal right to use and possess the whole property and to share equally the profits from the crops, buildings, and livestock.
Blackacre Roy Alice Vera Tenancy in common	The dotted lines are used to show that the interests of tenants in common may be unequal. Roy and Alice each have a one-fourth *undivided interest* in the whole property; Vera has *a* one-half *undivided interest* in the whole property. Each has a right to use and possess the whole property.

Partition. One way to cause severance is for a joint tenant or tenant in common to ask the court to **partition** the property. Partition is the division of real property held by joint tenants or tenants in common into distinct and separate portions so that the individuals may hold the property in severalty. A partition can occur by a voluntary agreement of the co-owners, or it can be made by the court. If the co-owners cannot agree on a division, any one of the owners can petition the court for partition, which, in most cases, can force the sale of the property. The owners then split the proceeds. In some states, a court-ordered partition is not allowed for property in joint tenancy.

Once joint tenancy or tenancy in common property has been partitioned, severance results, and the former co-tenants each own a portion of the property in severalty. Joint tenancy property is partitioned into equal parts; tenancy in common property is partitioned into equal or unequal parts. (See the example below.)

Partition
The division of real property held by joint tenants or tenants in common into separate portions so that the individuals may hold the property in severalty, i.e., in single ownership.

Example: If a concurrently owned farm, Blackacre, is partitioned, it is divided into separate parts:

PARTITION—JOINT TENANCY	**PARTITION—TENANCY IN COMMON**
Blackacre	**Blackacre**
Before Partition After Partition	**Before Partition After Partition**
Roy Alice Vera │Roy││Alice││Vera│	Roy .... Roy ....
	.... Alice ....
Joint tenancy Each owns the	Alice .... Alice ....
Equal parts divided property as	.... Alice ....
(cannot be a single owner, i.e.,	
unequal) *in severalty.*	Vera Vera
	Tenancy Roy $1/5$
	in common Alice $3/5$
	Unequal parts Vera $1/5$
	(could be Each owns the
	equal) divided property
	in severalty.

Tenancy by the entirety
A form of joint tenancy available only to a husband and wife; it also has the right of survivorship.

Tenancy by the Entirety

Tenancy by the entirety is an estate available only to a husband and wife, which must be created in writing and is nonprobate property. It is essentially a special form of "joint tenancy" modified by the common law theory that husband and wife are one person. Therefore, in addition to the four unities of time, title, interest, and possession required for joint tenancy, tenancy by the entirety requires a fifth unity—the unity of person, i.e., a husband and wife are one.

Tenancy by the entirety has most of the same advantages and disadvantages of joint tenancy. However, unlike joint tenancy, neither husband nor wife in a tenancy by the entirety can mortgage, sell, or give the property to another or sever the tenancy while alive or by will or trust without the written and signed consent of the other spouse. Unless both husband and wife join in (i.e., sign) the conveyance, it is invalid. This characteristic distinguishes tenancy by the entirety from joint tenancy since joint tenants can transfer their interest (by deed) without obtaining the permission of the other joint tenants. Since it imposes such restrictions on the transfer of property, some states have abolished tenancy by the entirety as being against public policy. Consequently, tenancy by the entirety is not recognized in all states (see Exhibit 2.4).

The states that allow tenancy by the entirety differ in the wording they require in the deed or will that creates the tenancy. In some states, unless the deed or will provides differently, a conveyance to a husband and wife automatically creates a tenancy by the entirety. Other states require that the conveyance include explicit language, e.g., to husband and wife "as tenants by the entirety with the right of survivorship." Any conveyance without the exact words may result in the creation of another form of co-ownership, e.g., a tenancy in common, or simply fail to create the desired result.

> **Example:** A will states: "I hereby give and devise my farm, Blackacre, to Jim and Trudy Lozano, husband and wife, in tenancy by the entirety." But if the will had been worded "I hereby give and devise my farm, Blackacre, to Jim and Trudy Lozano, husband and wife, with the right of survivorship," the devise might have been interpreted to be a tenancy by the entirety in some states or a joint tenancy in other states. In the latter case, it could be severed and individually transferred by one of the joint tenants.

Most statutes concerning tenancy by the entirety are worded like the New York statute (N.Y. EPTL § 6–2.2):

> A disposition of real property to a husband and wife creates in them a tenancy by the entirety, unless expressly declared to be a joint tenancy or a tenancy in common.

But court interpretations of similar statutory language seem to vary among the states.

The predominant and distinguishing feature of both joint tenancy and tenancy by the entirety is the *right of survivorship,* which, on the death of one spouse, passes sole ownership of the property in severalty to the surviving spouse.

> **Example:** William and Margaret, husband and wife, own property as tenants by the entirety. William dies and wills all his property to his son by a previous marriage. The son does not receive any interest in the tenancy by the entirety property because of Margaret's right of survivorship. Margaret owns the property in severalty (single ownership).

A creditor of one spouse cannot foreclose on property held in tenancy by the entirety or enforce a judgment (court decision) against it, and a judgment against one spouse is not a claim (lien) against the property. On the other hand, a judgment against both spouses can become a lien against the property, and a creditor can foreclose.

In some states, e.g., New York and Massachusetts, the unity of person in a tenancy by the entirety is terminated by a divorce (dissolution). The divorced couple become tenants in common of the property with each former spouse owning a one-half interest in the property. Unlike a divorce, a legal separation does not terminate a tenancy by the entirety in most states.

Some commentators have argued that the common law tenancy by the entirety should be abolished for policy reasons. First, property owned in this form is not subject to the claims of creditors of a deceased tenant (spouse); second, the specific language that creates this form of ownership is not always clear; and finally, when marital problems and disagreements arise, the mutual consent required to transfer property held in tenancy by the entirety may be difficult to obtain.

▥ ASSIGNMENT 2.14

1. John and Mae are married and live in your state. The deed conveying their property states: "to John A. Kowalski and Mae F. Kowalski, husband and wife, as joint tenants and not as tenants in common." (a) Would this conveyance create a tenancy by the entirety in your state? (b) Cite your state statute, if any.
2. What five unities are necessary for the establishment of a tenancy by the entirety? Explain each one.
3. Which unity exists in tenancy by the entirety but not in joint tenancy?
4. Select a state that recognizes tenancy by the entirety (possibly your own state) and identify the type of tenancy created by the following conveyances according to the courts of that state. Each conveyance is to husband and wife with wording as indicated.

	Joint Tenancy	Tenancy by the Entirety	Tenancy in Common
▪ "as tenants by the entirety"			
▪ "as tenants by the entirety with the right of survivorship"			
▪ "with the right of survivorship"			
▪ "as joint tenants"			
▪ "as tenants in common"			
▪ no other words, just to "husband and wife"			

Community Property

Two classifications of marital property law systems exist in the United States: community property law and common law. Originally eight southern and western states (Arizona, California, Idaho, Louisiana, Nevada, New Mexico, Texas, and Washington) adopted by statute the form of ownership by spouses known as

Community property
All property, other than property received by gift, will, or inheritance, acquired by either spouse during marriage is considered to belong to both spouses equally in the nine community property states.

community property. Wisconsin, the only state to adopt the Uniform Marital Property Act, which is essentially the same as the community property system, joined the other eight states in 1986 (see Exhibit 2.4). The other forty-one states are classified as common law jurisdictions, and this marital property law system will be discussed under Dower and Curtesy below and in Chapter 4. The theory behind community property ownership is that a husband and wife should share equally in the property acquired by their joint efforts during marriage. Therefore, each spouse is considered to own an undivided half interest in all property acquired during their marriage even though one spouse may have earned considerably less than the other or even nothing at all. Also, both spouses have the right to convey by will their individual half of the community property to whomever they choose, but each spouse has no control over the other spouse's half of the property (see discussion below). Community property law is set entirely by state statutes which vary considerably among the nine states.

Community property states recognize two kinds of property: **separate property** and community property. Separate property includes:

Separate property
Property that the husband or wife owned prior to their marriage or acquired during marriage by gift, will, or inheritance.

- Property individually owned by the husband or wife prior to their marriage.
- Property acquired by an individual spouse during marriage by gift, will, or inheritance.
- Property which is currently separate property and is traded, replaced, or sold for other property and becomes "new" separate property.
- Social security, railroad retirement, and veterans' benefits.

Note: All of the above property will remain separate property if it is kept separate and not combined (commingled) with community property (see discussion below).

Caveat: Income earned during the marriage by the spouses' property is treated as follows:

- Income produced by community property of the spouses during their marriage is community property.
- Income produced by a spouse's separate property during the marriage is treated in a variety of ways:
  - In Idaho and Texas the income is community property.
  - In Arizona, California, Nevada, New Mexico, and Washington the income is separate property.

Although income earned by the individual spouses' employment during their marriage, as mentioned above, is classified as community property, it is possible for this income to be classified as separate property, e.g., if the spouses sign a written agreement in which they approve the separate property classification and place the employment income in their own separate bank accounts.

Separate property is entirely under the management and control of the spouse who owns it no matter how it is acquired, and it is free from all interests and claims of the other spouse. Without the consent of the other spouse, either spouse may dispose of separate property by gift, sale, or will as stated in the following statute:

Cal. Prob. Code § 6101 Property Which May Be Disposed Of By Will
A will may dispose of the following property:
(a) The testator's separate property.
(b) The one-half of the community property that belongs to the testator under Section 100.

(c) The one-half of the testator's quasi-community property that belongs to the testator under Section 101.

Community property includes:

- Property obtained during the marriage by gift, sale, or will which names both spouses as the recipients.
- Income earned or acquired during the marriage by either spouse's employment, except by gift, sale, will, or inheritance to just one spouse; but compare comment above on income produced by separate property during the marriage in the five states listed.
- Property obtained from community property income during the marriage.
- Property owned by the spouses in partnerships, stocks and bonds, and as tenants in common.
- Property that was originally separate but is now transformed into community property by a gift from one spouse made to both spouses during their marriage, e.g., one spouse transfers her individual bank account into an account in both spouses' names, or a spouse who owns real property signs a deed naming both spouses owners of the property as "community property."

If the spouses agree in writing, they can change separate property into community property. All other property acquired by either spouse during the marriage in any manner is *presumed* to be *community property* (see La. Civ. Code Ann. art. 2340). The presumption may be rebutted by valid evidence that proves the property is separate property.

To determine whether a married couple's property is separate or community property, the following factors should be considered:

- Whether the property was acquired by either spouse before or after their marriage.
- The language and date of the conveyance (deed or will).
- The intent of the grantor, if the conveyance was made by deed, or of the testator(trix) if made by will.
- Whether the property was given as a gift to one or both spouses.
- Whether the property was inherited by one or both spouses.
- Whether separate property of a spouse was sold or exchanged for other separate property, or whether the purpose of the sale was to use the proceeds for community purposes.
- The purpose and use of property acquired or obtained by the married couple.

Examples:

1. In a community property state, if a deed conveys real property to a husband and wife, it is community property.

2. On the other hand, a deed which expressly states the real property is separate property of either the husband or wife creates a conclusion that it is separate property.

3. A married woman's father dies and conveys community property in his will to her. The property is the woman's separate property.

4. If a married woman's father dies intestate and she is his only heir, she will inherit his community property as her separate property.

5. An employer gives $1,000 to a married man living in California. The man's wife claims the money is a salary bonus. The employer testifies in court that the $1,000 was a gift. The court disagrees. Therefore, it becomes part of the spouses'

community property. Conversely, if the court agrees the $1,000 was a gift, it becomes the husband's separate property.

Characteristics of Community Property. Formerly, a husband had sole control over community property and could convey or mortgage it without his wife's consent. Today, the community property states have enacted statutes requiring the signatures of both spouses on any transfer or mortgage of community property.

Since each spouse owns one-half of the community property, on the death of either (in the majority of the community property states), the surviving spouse is entitled to his or her one-half of the community property (see Cal. Prob. Code § 100). The decedent's will, if one exists, or the state's intestate succession statutes determine the disposition of the decedent's remaining half. Under no circumstances can either spouse dispose of more than one-half of the community property by will.

The statutes of the community property states differ on the division and distribution of property in cases involving intestacy, divorce, community property with right of survivorship, creditors' claims, commingling, and a new category of property created by these statutes called "quasi-community property." Each topic is discussed in more detail in the following paragraphs.

Intestacy. In some community property states, depending on the length of the marriage, when a spouse dies intestate, all of the decedent's community property passes to the surviving spouse but only a smaller share of the separate property. (see Cal. Prob Code § 6401 (a) & (c), but compare Tex. Prob. Code Ann. § 45 where a surviving spouse may not be entitled to all of the property and La. Civ. Code Ann. art 890). See also the case *In re Salvini's Estate,* 65 Wash. 2d 442, 397 P.2d 811 (1964), in which the court ruled a gift of store property to the deceased and her husband prior to her death was community property and, after her death, passed to her husband.

Divorce. In a divorce, the division of community property varies. If a married couple is divorced, the court generally divides the community property so that each party receives an equal share (see Cal. Fam. Code § 2550). Other states, such as Arizona, allow the court to use its discretion in deciding how to divide community property "equitably" (see Ariz. Rev. Stat. Ann. § 25–318). In most community property states, even without divorce, spouses may at any time enter into an agreement which dissolves the community relationship and divides the property. The share each spouse receives is his or her separate property.

Community Property With Right of Survivorship. A form of ownership of community property that allows a surviving spouse to automatically receive the property and avoid probate on the death of the other spouse. This form of community property is permitted in Arizona, Nevada, Texas, and Wisconsin.

Creditors' Claims. The classification of property as community or separate also affects claims of creditors. In some community property states, e.g., Arizona and Washington, a creditor of one spouse can attach only that spouse's separate property (see *Nationwide Resources Corp. v. Massabni,* 143 Ariz. 460, 694 P.2d 290 [App. 1984] and *Nichols Hills Bank v. McCool,* 104 Wash.2d 78, 701 P.2d 1114 [1985]).

In the *Massabni* case, the court acknowledged that in community property states, all property acquired by either spouse during marriage is presumed to be community property and a spouse's separate property can be transmuted (changed) into community property by agreement, gift, or commingling. In this complex case, however, the court held the property in question was the husband's separate property and, therefore, a judgment creditor of the husband could **garnish,** make a claim against, only his separate property to satisfy the debt, but could not make a claim against the spouses' community property for the husband's individual debt.

In the *Nichols* case, the court ruled "although one spouse's interest in community property can be reached (and used) to satisfy a tort judgment," a bank (the creditor) could not enforce a loan guaranty agreement signed only by the husband against his interest in the community property since the wife had neither signed nor ratified the agreement. The state of Washington statute requires consent of both spouses before a gift or transfer of community property can be legally enforced.

Other community property states allow creditors with community debts to satisfy their claims against the community property of the spouses and creditors with separate debts to satisfy their claims first against the individual spouse's separate property and then, if the debt is not paid in full, to collect the remainder of the debt from community property.

Commingling.   Another concern of spouses in community property states is the problem of commingled separate and community property. When extensive **commingling** occurs and it becomes impossible to identify the separate property, the presumption is that the commingled property is community property. To overcome this presumption, each spouse must keep complete and accurate records of how the property was obtained, as well as its purpose and use.

Quasi-community Property.   Property that is acquired in a common law state and then moved into a community property state or that is owned by spouses who have moved into a community property state is called **quasi-community property.** If the newcomer dies *domiciled* in the community property state, the presumption discussed earlier still stands; i.e., all of the decedent's property that is not separate property as defined by the current domicile state is community property. On the other hand, if the newcomer's domicile is considered to be the former, the common law state, the presumption can be rebutted and reversed. Conversely, when spouses move from a community property state to a common law state, the community property obtained while they lived in the community property state is not automatically converted into separate property solely by the change of domicile. However, all property acquired by either spouse after both spouses move to the common law state is considered separate property when purchased by a spouse with his or her own funds. When your clients are spouses seeking your assistance, *you must not forget to inquire about their state residences throughout their marriage.*

Community property states have abolished the form of co-ownership called a tenancy by the entirety, but, except for Louisiana, usually they continue to allow spouses to own property in a joint tenancy. Review Exhibit 2.4 and see Exhibit 2.6 for a summary and comparison of forms of concurrent ownership.

🏛 ASSIGNMENT 2.15

1. John and Mary Doe live in a community property state. They own the following property: a house in joint tenancy; two cars in both names; a camper given to John by his father; savings and checking accounts in both names; a boat purchased by Mary before their

---

Garnish
Make a claim against.

Garnishment
A three-party statutory proceeding in which a judgment creditor may demand that an employer who owes wages to an employee (the judgment debtor) pay these wages to the creditor to satisfy the creditor's claim against the employee (debtor).

Commingling
Combining community and separate property, e.g., into the same account or by using both to acquire a different item of property.

Quasi-community property
Property that is acquired in a common law state and then moved into a community property state or that is owned by spouses who have moved into a community property state.

ETHICAL ISSUE
◀ ⋯⋯⋯⋯⋯⋯⋯⋯⋯⋯⋯⋯

Exhibit 2.6 Summary and Comparison of Forms of Concurrent Ownership—Two or More Persons

Form of Ownership	Joint Tenancy	Tenancy in Common	Tenancy by the Entirety	Community Property
Formation: By deed—gift or sale or by will	Yes	Yes	Yes	No—by operation of law
Owners: Two or more named in conveyance	Yes	Yes	Two only—must be husband and wife	Two only—must be husband and wife by operation of law
Right of survivorship	Yes	No	Yes	No*
Unity of interest: Undivided and equal shares	Yes	Undivided but shares may be equal or unequal	Undivided but husband and wife as a unit own the property	Yes—of the community property
Unity of possession	Yes	Yes	Yes	Yes
Right of partition	Yes—but not in all states	Yes	No—except if spouses divorce	No—except if spouses divorce
Probate or nonprobate	Nonprobate	Probate	Nonprobate	Probate
Co-owner's right to sell or give by deed his or her interest in the property	Yes	Yes	No—spouses must agree to transfer in writing	No—of the community property
Creditors of individual co-owner may attach co-owner's interest	Yes	Yes	No—only creditors of both husband and wife	Yes—but only separate property in Arizona and Washington

*Spouses may create a right of survivorship in their community property (see Tex. Prob. Code Ann. § 451).

marriage; and furniture and household goods, a stereo, and television sets purchased during their marriage. John dies. Identify the property John can convey in his will.

2. If possible, obtain your family documents and determine the forms of ownership in which your family property is held, e.g., house, stocks, bonds, savings account.

Freehold estate
An estate in real property of uncertain duration. Examples include fee simple and life estates.

ESTATES IN REAL PROPERTY

The law divides estates in real property into two categories: **freehold estates** and nonfreehold or leasehold estates. The categories are distinguished by the extent and duration of the individual's interest. In other words, freeholds and leaseholds

Exhibit 2.7   Estates in Real Property

(1)
Freehold

Fee simple estate   Life estate

(2)
Leasehold

Tenancy for years

in real property are classified according to how long and how much an interest a person has in realty. Exhibit 2.7 illustrates the classification of estates that will be discussed.

Freehold Estates

Fee Simple Estate or Fee Simple Absolute

The vast majority of all real property, including houses, apartment and office buildings, and farms, is owned as a fee simple estate. A **fee simple estate,** also known as a fee simple absolute, an estate in fee, or simply as a fee, is the largest, best, and most extensive estate possible. An individual holding a fee estate has an absolute, unqualified, and unlimited interest in the real property. This means the fee estate is not subject to any restrictions, and the owner is entitled to all rights and privileges associated with the property, i.e., there is no limit on the estate's duration or on the owner's method of disposition. The owner has the unconditional power to dispose (sell or make a gift) of the property during his lifetime by deed and after death by will; if the owner dies intestate, the property descends (passes) to his heirs (see the statute and discussion below). Section 44–6–20 of the Georgia Code Annotated defines the estate as follows:

> An absolute or fee simple estate is one in which the owner is entitled to the entire property with unconditional power of disposition during his life and which descends to his heirs and legal representatives upon his death intestate.

In most states no special language is needed to establish a fee simple estate. Every conveyance is presumed to create a fee simple estate unless the conveyance expressly states an intent to create another type of estate such as a smaller estate or an estate of limited duration (see discussion below).

Characteristics of a Fee Simple Estate.   The following are characteristics of a fee simple estate in real property:

- *A fee simple estate is transferable during life by deed.*

Example: Jane Doe owns a farm, Blackacre, in fee simple. While alive, she can sell the farm or give it away by the transfer of the title to the real property as a fee simple estate to another person by conveying (delivering) a deed. Jane Doe sells Blackacre by deed to Tom Brown:

Fee simple estate
An estate in real property that is the largest, best, and most extensive estate possible. Also known as a fee simple absolute, an estate in fee, or simply a fee.

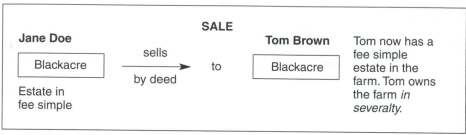

Jane Doe gives Blackacre to Tom Brown by delivering the deed to the farm to Tom:

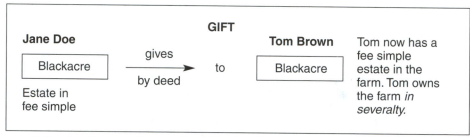

- *A fee simple estate is transferable after death by will.*

Example: Jane Doe owns Blackacre in fee simple. In her will she gives the farm, Blackacre, to her niece, Sheila Johnson. When Jane dies, Sheila will own Blackacre as a fee simple estate:

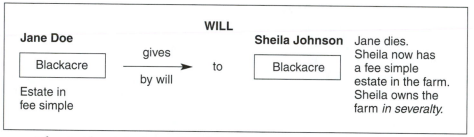

- *A fee simple estate descends to heirs if not transferred through a will.*

Example: Jane Doe owns Blackacre in fee simple and dies intestate. The state in which the farm is located will determine which of Jane's heirs are entitled to the farm in fee simple.

🏛 ASSIGNMENT 2.16

Assume Blackacre in the above example is located in your state. Jane Doe owns Blackacre, the family home, in her name only and dies intestate. She is survived by a husband, three children, her father, and two brothers. According to your state law, who owns Blackacre?

- *A fee simple estate is subject to the rights of the owner's surviving spouse.*

Example: Jane Doe owns Blackacre. She dies. Whether Jane dies testate or intestate, her surviving spouse, John, is entitled to an interest in Jane's property.

The current rights one spouse has in the decedent spouse's estate are discussed below.

- *A fee simple estate is subject to claims of creditors of the fee owner both before and after the owner's death.*

Example: Jane Doe owns Blackacre in fee simple. Jane owes Sam Bender $10,000, which is now due for payment. If Jane cannot pay this debt to Sam using her other assets, she may have to sell or mortgage Blackacre in order to satisfy the debt.

Creation and Transfer of a Fee Simple Estate. Under common law, a fee simple estate could be created in only one way. The fee owner was required to convey the title to real property by deed or will using the words "to A *and his heirs.*" (The letter A stands for the name of a person.) The words *and his heirs* create a fee simple absolute estate for A and were the only words allowed by common law to create this estate. Times have changed, however, and currently, the words "to A and his heirs" are infrequently used to create a fee simple estate. Today a fee simple estate can be created by any words that indicate an intent to convey absolute ownership, e.g., "to A in fee simple," "to A forever," or simply, "I give the land to A." Generally, whenever any real estate, e.g., a house, is purchased, the buyer becomes the fee owner.

Example: Steven Brown buys a business including the land and building in which the business operates. When the current fee owner, Janet Williams, transfers the deed to Steven, he becomes the sole owner of the property *in severalty* and holds the real property in a *fee simple estate.* The transfer of the deed accomplishes the following: (1) Steven now holds legal title to the property; (2) Steven, as sole owner, owns the property *in severalty*—single ownership; (3) Steven receives a *fee simple estate* in the realty since this is the estate Janet held and transferred to Steven by deed. All the rights associated with a fee owner are now Steven's.

Example: Susan and David Martin contract to buy a house from Stan Williams. When Stan delivers the deed to the real property (house) thereby transferring legal title to the Martins, the deed reads "to Susan Martin and David Martin, husband and wife as joint tenants in fee simple." Susan and David own the property as joint tenants with a fee simple estate. They are the fee owners.

Notice that the results would be the same even if the words "in fee simple" were not included in the deed because of the presumption that all conveyances create a fee simple estate unless expressly stated otherwise.

Keep in mind the characteristics of joint tenancy ownership and a fee simple estate while you review the following summary that explains the application and relationship of these different principles of property law, i.e., estates in real property versus forms of ownership.

- A fee simple estate allows the fee owner, while alive, the right to sell or give the property to another. But since the property is held in joint tenancy by a husband and wife, or in some states, tenancy by the entirety, both types of joint owners must join in the conveyance (sale or gift) to pass the title to the new owner(s). Thus, both Susan and David (in the previous example) must sign a deed which transfers their house to another as part of a sales contract or as a gift.

- Although another characteristic of a fee simple estate allows a fee owner to transfer the property through a will, neither Susan nor David can transfer by will her or his interest in the house to another because they are joint tenants or tenants by the entirety and have the right of survivorship; therefore, if Susan dies first, her interest automatically passes to David by operation of law. Thus, the survivor, David, would hold a fee simple estate as a single owner and could, subsequently, transfer the estate by will. While both Susan and David are alive, neither can pass the property by a testamentary disposition until after the death of the first joint tenant or tenant by the entirety.

𝍐 ASSIGNMENT 2.17

Zachary, a Montana farmer, deeds 20 acres of his land to his daughter, Catherine, in fee simple when she becomes engaged to Frank. Catherine marries Frank, and they have two children. Upon Catherine's death, Frank claims that he, and not the children, is the owner of the land as a joint tenant with the right of survivorship. Is Frank's claim correct? Explain.

Life Estate

A **life estate** in real property is another type of freehold estate in which an individual, called the **life tenant,** holds an interest in the property that lasts either for the lifetime of that individual or for the life of another person. If the life estate is created for the life of a person other than the life tenant, then it is known as an estate *pur autre vie.*

The next paragraphs discuss the characteristics of life estates and examine some property law concepts associated with them including future interests (reversion and remainder), dower and curtesy, a spouse's elective rights, and waste.

Characteristics of a Life Estate.   The characteristics of a life estate can be summarized as follows:

- *A life estate may last for the lifetime of the original owner (the person who conveys the estate).*

Example: Sam conveys Blackacre by a deed to "Shirley for the life of Sam." Shirley has a life estate based on Sam's lifetime. Shirley is the life tenant. Since real property is being conveyed, Sam is the grantor and Shirley is the grantee.

- *A life estate may last for the lifetime of the person enjoying the estate (the person to whom the estate is conveyed).*

Example: Sam conveys Blackacre by a deed to "Shirley for life." Shirley receives a life estate based on her own lifetime.

- *A life estate may last for the lifetime of a third person, called an estate pur autre vie.*

Life estate
A freehold estate in which a person, called the life tenant, holds an interest in land during his own or someone else's lifetime.

Life tenant
The person holding a life estate.

Pur autre vie
An estate lasting for the life of a person other than the life tenant.

Example: Sam conveys Blackacre by a deed to "Shirley for the life of Julie." Shirley has a life estate based on Julie's lifetime.

- *A life estate can be created by deed or will.*

Example: Sam sells Blackacre to "Shirley for life" and delivers a deed to her at the closing.

Example: Sam gives Blackacre to "Shirley for life" in his will.

- *Unlike a fee simple estate, a life estate cannot be transferred by will.*

Example: Shirley, a life tenant, could not transfer her life estate to another person through her will.

- *Life tenants while living may convey their interests in the property by sale or gift to a third person, however.*

Example: Shirley, a life tenant, sells her lifetime interest in Blackacre to Laverne. When Shirley gives a deed to Laverne, Laverne becomes the new life tenant and holds the property until Shirley dies. Shirley can sell only her interest in Blackacre, i.e., her life interest or life estate. Since a life tenant's death is inevitable but uncertain and it terminates the life estate, finding a buyer for a life estate is difficult and uncommon.

- *On the death of the life tenant, the life estate terminates, and no interest remains to be passed to heirs or by will; nor can it be probated or be subject to creditors' claims.* The property returns (reverts) to the grantor who created the life estate by conveying the property by deed.

Example: Sam conveys Blackacre by a deed to "Shirley for life." Shirley dies. The property is returned to Sam (see the discussion below).

Future Interests—Reversion and Remainder. Whenever a grantor, who owns a fee simple estate in real property, creates a life estate, one of two results occurs:

1. At the time of the creation of the life estate, the grantor retains a reversion or reversionary interest.
2. Alternatively, at the time of the creation of the life estate, a future remainder interest can also be created within the same conveyance. The person who receives the future remainder is called the remainderman.

Each of these possibilities is discussed in the next paragraphs.

Reversion. A **reversion** or **reversionary interest** is the interest or right a **grantor** alone has to the return of real property, at present in the possession of another (the **grantee**), on the termination of the grantee's preceding estate. A reversion exists only when the grantor holding a fee simple estate conveys an interest in property by deed or will that is less than the entire fee simple estate.

When a life estate is created and a reversion is retained, the following rules apply:

- The grantor is the only person entitled to a reversion.
- The grantor is entitled to the reversion (return) of the property, when the grantee's estate terminates, i.e., when the grantee dies.

MINI-GLOSSARY BOX

Reversion or reversionary interest
The interest in real property that a grantor retains when a conveyance of the property by deed or by will transfers an estate smaller than what the grantor

owns, e.g., when the grantor has a fee simple estate and conveys to the grantee a life estate. At some future time the real property reverts back to the grantor.

Grantor
The person who makes a conveyance (transfer) of real or personal property to another.

Grantee
The person to whom a conveyance of real or personal property is made.

- The grantor, while alive, can transfer the reversion by deed or will.
- If the grantor dies before the grantee, the reversion is not lost because the right to the reversion can be transferred by the grantor's will to beneficiaries; or if the grantor dies without a will, the right to the reversion can be inherited by the grantor's heirs.
- The real property that reverts (returns) does not go through the probate process of the life tenant's estate and is not subject to tax or creditors' claims.

The following example explains the grantor's right to a reversion or reversionary interest:

Example: Peter Nokamura owns a farm, Blackacre, in fee simple. Peter conveys (transfers) the farm by a deed to "Reiko Yoshida for life." Peter is the grantor who retains a reversion in the farm. Reiko receives a life estate and is both the grantee and life tenant. Reiko's life estate gives her the right to use and possess Blackacre or to convey her life estate to another for her own lifetime. When Reiko dies, the life estate ends, and the farm, because of the reversion, automatically reverts (returns) to the grantor, Peter, without going through probate. If Peter dies before Reiko, then his reversion in the property passes (reverts) to Peter's estate, and Peter's will, if he has one, or his state intestate succession statute, if he has no will, determine which of Peter's beneficiaries, heirs, or devisees will receive the property. Exhibit 2.8 diagrams a reversion of this example.

ASSIGNMENT 2.18

Jane Smallwood owns a lake cottage. In a deed she conveys the cottage "to my father, Brent Smallwood, for life, then to my sister, Sue Smallwood for life." Jane outlives her father but dies before her sister, Sue. Is Brent a life tenant? Who gets the property when he dies? What interest does Sue have at the time of Jane's conveyance? Explain what will happen to the property, and why, after the death of Sue.

Remainder
A future estate in real property that takes effect on the termination of a prior estate created by the same instrument at the same time.

Remainder. A **remainder** is a future estate in real property that will take effect on the termination of a prior estate created by the same instrument at the same time. A grantor who owns a fee simple estate in real property can create a life estate for one person and, in the same conveyance and at the same time, transfer the future fee simple estate to another person by deed. When the life tenant dies, the

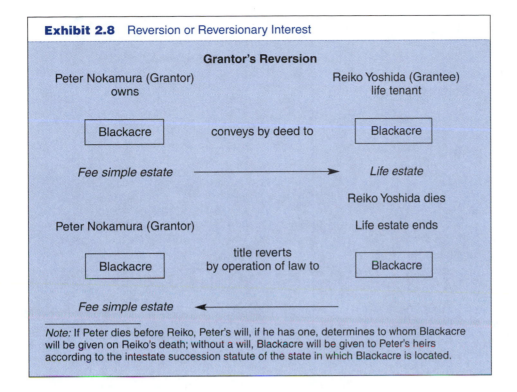

Exhibit 2.8   Reversion or Reversionary Interest

Grantor's Reversion

Peter Nokamura (Grantor)
owns

Reiko Yoshida (Grantee)
life tenant

Blackacre   conveys by deed to   Blackacre

Fee simple estate ⟶ *Life estate*

Reiko Yoshida dies

Peter Nokamura (Grantor)   Life estate ends

Blackacre   title reverts
by operation of law to   Blackacre

Fee simple estate ⟵

Note: If Peter dies before Reiko, Peter's will, if he has one, determines to whom Blackacre will be given on Reiko's death; without a will, Blackacre will be given to Peter's heirs according to the intestate succession statute of the state in which Blackacre is located.

property passes to the future fee owner who is called the **remainderman.** This term is used for any person (man or woman) who receives the future estate.

Example: Bill Maxwell conveys Blackacre by deed "to James Maxwell for life, then to Mary Wilson and her heirs" or "to James Maxwell for life, then to Mary Wilson." Result: By the same conveyance and at the same time, James receives a life estate and Mary receives a future fee simple estate. When James dies, the property does *not* revert to the grantor, Bill, but instead passes as a fee simple estate to Mary. Since he has a fee simple estate and conveys the property by deed, which gives a future fee simple estate to Mary, Bill terminates his grantor's right to a reversion in Blackacre. Once Mary becomes the fee owner, she is entitled to do with the property as she pleases, i.e., sell it, give it to another, or convey it after death through her will. The same result would have occurred if Bill had conveyed Blackacre "to James Maxwell for life, then to Mary Wilson forever," or "to Mary Wilson in fee simple." In such cases, where a person, other than the grantor, is entitled to the remainder of an estate in real property after another prior estate has expired, the person (Mary) is called the remainderman. Exhibit 2.9 presents a diagram of this example.

Remainderman
A person entitled to the future fee simple estate after a particular smaller estate, e.g., a life estate, has expired.

🏛 ASSIGNMENT 2.19

According to your state laws, what kind of an estate in real property would Mary Williams receive if her Uncle Charles deeded a farm to her in the following ways? (1) "to Mary"; (2) "to Mary and her heirs"; (3) "to Mary in fee"; (4) "to Mary forever"; (5) "to Mary for life"; (6) "to Mary for the life of Helen"; (7) "to Mary for as long as I live."

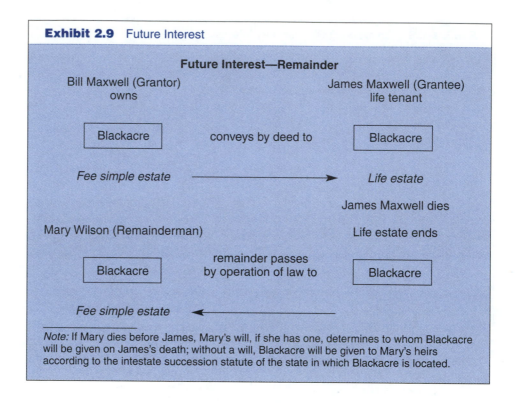

Exhibit 2.9 Future Interest

Future Interest—Remainder

Bill Maxwell (Grantor)
owns

James Maxwell (Grantee)
life tenant

Blackacre   conveys by deed to   Blackacre

Fee simple estate ⟶ *Life estate*

James Maxwell dies

Mary Wilson (Remainderman)   Life estate ends

Blackacre   remainder passes
by operation of law to   Blackacre

Fee simple estate ⟵

Note: If Mary dies before James, Mary's will, if she has one, determines to whom Blackacre will be given on James's death; without a will, Blackacre will be given to Mary's heirs according to the intestate succession statute of the state in which Blackacre is located.

Dower
At common law, the right of the surviving wife to a life estate in one-third of all real property her husband owned during the marriage.

Curtesy
The right of the surviving husband to a life estate in all of his wife's real property owned during the marriage, but only if the married couple had a child born alive.

Dower and Curtesy. Property law in America is derived from the English common law. The rights of spouses in each other's real, but not personal, property, called rights of **dower** and **curtesy,** developed through the common law system. Under common law, at the time of marriage, and to protect her from disinheritance, a wife was given dower rights to provide her with the means of support after her husband's death. Specifically, dower was the surviving wife's (widow's) right to a life estate in one-third of all the real property her husband owned during the marriage. Similarly, the husband was given curtesy rights to his wife's real property. Curtesy was the right of the surviving husband (widower) to a life estate in all of his wife's real property owned during the marriage, but only if the married couple had a child born alive. In the past under common law, the wife's dower right terminated if:

- She was divorced from her husband when he died; a legal separation did not terminate dower, however.
- Her husband held his real property in joint tenancy with another person; however, if the real property was held by the husband in a tenancy in common, his share was subject to his wife's dower right.

Dower and curtesy applied whether or not the decedent died testate. The surviving spouse had a right to a life estate in real property.

Both dower and curtesy have undergone numerous changes in every state. Most states (including UPC states) have abolished or materially altered dower and curtesy and replaced them with statutes establishing a surviving spouse's right to a share, often called an elective or forced share, of the entire estate (both real and personal property) in cases where the decedent spouse's will makes unreasonable or inadequate provisions or attempts to disinherit the surviving spouse. Nine states have replaced dower and curtesy with marital property rights established by community property statutes. Other states have retained their own versions of dower and curtesy rights, though with major modifications. A few states grant equivalent rights or shares to both spouses under the term "dower" (see Mass. Gen. Laws Ann. ch. 189 § 1). Even though this state uses the term "dower," it is not the same as common law dower; e.g., in Massachusetts "dower" is restricted to land owned by the decedent spouse at death. Other states have enacted "statutory" dower and curtesy where dower is not available if the decedent spouse dies intestate since the surviving spouse is an heir (see 20 Pa. Stat. Ann. § 2105). In these states, a conveyance of real property owned by one spouse requires written consent by the other spouse to release the statutory dower or curtesy interest in the property. Despite these variations, today, the few states that retain dower and curtesy agree on the following:

- Dower and curtesy occur only on the death of a spouse.
- Dower and curtesy provide the same rights to an interest in land to both spouses.
- Dower and curtesy apply even if the decedent died testate.
- Dower and curtesy are terminated by a divorce and the common law rules on real property owned in joint tenancy are retained.
- Dower and curtesy rights in property can be released by spouses only with their written consent.
- Dower and curtesy cannot and do not exist in community property states where the surviving spouse generally receives at least one-half of the community property.
- Dower and curtesy are exempt from the claims of the creditors of the decedent spouse or the decedent spouse's estate except for liens and encumbrances such as mortgages and judgments (see Mass. Gen. Laws Ann. ch. 189 § 1).

Policy reasons for replacing dower and curtesy include (1) the inadequate support they provide a surviving spouse under the common law rules; (2) the complications that occur in the transfer or clearance of title to real property for the benefit of prospective purchasers or for future beneficiaries, heirs, or devisees; (3) the fact they transfer only real property, and many estates contain only personal property, such as cash, stocks, and life insurance; and (4) the fact a surviving husband was treated more favorably than a surviving wife under common law rules.

Spouse's Right to Election or Elective Forced Share.   With the demise of dower and curtesy, most states, except community property states, give a surviving husband or wife the statutory right to avoid being disinherited by the will of the decedent spouse. The right is established by a statute that allows the surviving spouse to choose between the provisions made by the deceased spouse's will or the prescribed share set by state statute. This choice is called the spouse's right to an election. The statute granting the *right of election* to take "against the will" is the *elective* or *"forced share" statute*, and the property acquired by the selection is called the spouse's *forced share, elective share,* or *statutory share. Note:* The elective (forced) share statute is only applicable to cases in which the decedent spouse dies with a will. For a complete discussion on the elective (forced) share of the spouse, see Chapter 4.

Waste.   While in possession of real property, a life tenant has the absolute right to possess and use the property. However, because of the future reversion and remainder interests of grantors and remaindermen, the life tenant is under a duty to exercise reasonable and prudent care to protect and preserve the property and is required by law not to cause or commit "**waste.**" Waste is a legal term which refers to "any act or omission that does permanent damage to the real property or unreasonably changes its character or value." Therefore, waste occurs when a life tenant permits any unreasonable or unauthorized use or neglect of the real property that causes permanent physical damage, decreases the property's value, and detrimentally affects the persons entitled to the future interest, i.e., reversion and remainder interests. Specific examples of waste include:

Waste
Any act or omission that does permanent damage to real property or unreasonably changes its character or value.

- To fail to make necessary building repairs.
- To harvest and sell all trees on timberland.
- To strip-mine, remove, and sell excessive minerals from the land.
- To neglect to heat a house in winter causing major damage to the plumbing.

If guilty of waste, the life tenant may be subject to a lawsuit for damages, an injunction from an equity court, or—the extreme remedy—forfeiture (termination) of the tenant's life estate. Unless the facts are obvious, most courts are reluctant to find waste. In addition, state court decisions are inconsistent in determining what constitutes waste. A case involving waste that illustrates the limits placed on a life tenant concerning mineral rights is *Nutter v. Stockton,* 626 P.2d 861 (Okl. 1981).

Leasehold Estates

Leasehold estate
An estate in real property held under a lease.

Various types of **leasehold estates** exist including tenancy at will, tenancy at sufferance, and tenancy from month to month. This text will examine only one example, however, a tenancy or estate for years.

Tenancy for Years

A tenancy or estate for years creates an interest in real property that will last for a fixed period of time, e.g., a tenancy for 10 years. Such a tenancy is created and terminates according to its own terms. No notice to terminate is required.

> **Example:** John Kellar owns a farm, Blackacre, in fee simple. John conveys the farm by deed to "Maude Owens for 20 years." Maude holds Blackacre as a tenancy for 20 years. She has the right to use, possess, or even to sell her *interest* in the property. At the end of the 20-year period, however, Maude's interest ends, and the property reverts to John because of the grantor's reversionary interest. A tenancy for years may include a lease, but it must be clear that interest in real property is conveyed for the stated time period and not just rights to possession.

▥ ASSIGNMENT 2.20

On the basis of the above discussion, and after reviewing freehold estates, answer the following questions.

Amy conveys by deed her lake cottage to "Clare for life, then to Maxine for 20 years, then to Elizabeth and her heirs."

1. What kind of estate does Clare have?
2. Who receives the property when Clare dies?
3. If Maxine dies before Clare, who receives the property on Clare's death?
4. Does Amy have a reversionary interest in the property? Explain.
5. What interest does Elizabeth hold?
6. Two remaindermen are involved in the conveyance. Who are they and why are they so classified?
7. Do Elizabeth's heirs have any interest in the property by this conveyance?

Leaseholds, such as a tenancy for years, also include the standard landlord-tenant relationships. If Harold signs a lease, i.e., a contract to take possession of real property for a specified time period and agrees to pay rent while in possession, such a contract creates the estate called a tenancy for years. It is not the function of this text to review in depth this area of contract and property law, but it is important to understand the association of the landlord-tenant relationship with the terminology and legal concepts previously discussed. Confusion between such terms as landlord-tenant and joint tenancy, tenancy in common, tenancy by the entirety, and tenancy for years must be avoided.

KEY TERMS

Inheritance	Operation of law	Community property	*Pur autre vie*
Fixture	Descent and	Separate property	Reversion or
Deed	distribution	Garnish	reversionary interest
Chattel	Disposition	Garnishment	Grantor
Chose in action	Joint tenants	Commingling	Grantee
Estate	Right of survivorship	Quasi-community	Remainder
Probate property	Straw man	property	Remainderman
(estate)	Undivided interest	Freehold estate	Dower
Severalty	Severance	Fee simple estate	Curtesy
Incidents of ownership	Partition	Life estate	Waste
Totten trust	Tenancy by the entirety	Life tenant	Leasehold estate

REVIEW QUESTIONS

1. How does real property differ from personal property?
2. In whom and when does the real and personal property of the decedent vest (pass)?
3. What are the three tests state courts use to determine if property is a fixture?
4. What are trade fixtures? List three examples.
5. Write out your own definition of each key term in this chapter. Are your definitions essentially the same as those in the text?
6. How do tangible and intangible personal property differ?
7. What items of property are classified as probate property and what items are nonprobate property?
8. What is the significance of property being classified as probate or nonprobate property in terms of the need for probate, creditors' claims, and payment of federal estate and state estate and inheritance taxes?

9. What are the four common law "unities" required for the creation of a joint tenancy?
10. How does a joint tenancy differ from both a tenancy in common and a tenancy by the entirety?
11. How many states are community property states? List them.
12. In a community property state, what property is separate property and what is community property?
13. What is a fee simple estate and what are its characteristics?
14. Concerning future interests in real property, what are the differences between a reversion and a remainder?
15. How does dower differ from curtesy and why have most states replaced them with a spouse's right to elect "against a will"?
16. What responsibilities does a life tenant have concerning the problem of "waste"? Give an example of waste.

CASE PROBLEMS

Problem 1

A client of the law firm where you work as a paralegal, and with whom you have become acquainted, calls you at your home to discuss and ask your advice about the following matter. The client wants to change the form of ownership in a cottage she currently owns in severalty to either a joint tenancy or a tenancy in common with her two adult children and herself. She tells you her main concern is that she does not want her children's spouses to "ever have any interest in the cottage," and she wants your advice as to how she can obtain this result. Due to your experience, you feel you know the answer to the question. How should you respond to her request? Is this an ethical issue or concern for you as a paralegal? Explain.

Problem 2

When he died, Abner Huntington owned a magnificent and expensive home well known for its beautiful landscaping and flower gardens. In his will, he gave his children "all household furnishings, equipment, decorations, and appliances." The home was sold to a famous entertainer who claimed the children had improperly removed certain fixtures from the house and the premises. The property removed included garden statues, lighting fixtures, a pipe organ, metal decorative birds around the swimming pool, and inside the house, a large statue of Pegasus, the flying horse. Most of these property items could be easily removed.

A. In your opinion, are these items fixtures? Explain.

B. Read the case *Paul v. First National Bank of Cincinnati,* 52 Ohio Misc. 77, 369 N.E.2d 488 (1976). In that case, the court ruled that items similar to those in the example were fixtures. Do you agree?

THE PARTICIPANTS AND THE PROPER COURT

OBJECTIVES

After completing this chapter, you should be able to:

➤ Identify the participants who are essential for drafting wills and trusts and for administering the estate of a decedent and explain their basic functions.

➤ Identify the proper court that supervises the administration and distribution of a decedent's estate.

➤ Explain what is meant by probate and jurisdiction.

➤ Identify the various elements of jurisdiction required by a specific court, such as the probate court.

➤ Determine the proper place (county/state) to commence probate proceedings of a decedent's estate.

➤ Recognize the necessity for establishing a second or ancillary administration of a decedent's estate when property of the decedent is located in another state.

SCOPE OF THE CHAPTER

Many different participants are involved in the creation of wills and trusts and the administration of estates. This chapter reviews the basic functions of these participants and describes the role of the proper court in the administration of an estate. Important terms associated with the selection and function of the court, such as probate, jurisdiction, domicile, venue, and ancillary administration, are defined and explained in the second half of the chapter.

THE PARTICIPANTS

The following people are involved in the preparation of wills and trusts and the administration of a decedent's estate: the personal representative of the estate, an attorney, a paralegal, the probate court (judge), the registrar, and the clerk. We begin our discussion by examining the functions of each of these participants.

The Personal Representative

The personal representative is a person or corporate institution, such as a bank or trust department, appointed by a proper court, often called the probate court, to administer the estate of a decedent who died with or without a will. As a fiduciary, a person who serves in a position of trust and loyalty, a personal representative has obligations called "fiduciary duties" to act in good faith solely for the benefit of another person. Trustees, guardians, and conservators are three other types of fiduciaries commonly appointed by will. Personal representatives act for the beneficiaries or heirs of the estate; trustees act for beneficiaries of trusts; guardians act for minors; and conservators act for incompetent persons.

In most cases, before executing the final draft of the will, the testator asks the prospective personal representative if he is willing to serve. Even if the person agrees, he has a right to change his mind and reject the position before being appointed or resign the position after appointment by the probate court. *Note:* The personal representative can also be a beneficiary or heir of the decedent's estate.

Most personal representatives are family members or friends who accept their appointments. The knowledge that the court and professional assistance (an attorney and you, the paralegal) are available to help complete the necessary tasks can help reluctant personal representatives overcome their anxiety about dealing with matters that are unfamiliar to them.

Appropriate Terminology

If the personal representative named in the will is a man, he is also traditionally or commonly called the executor; if a woman, she is the executrix.

> **Example:** Howard dies with a will. He names his sister, Nanette, as his personal representative to administer his estate and distribute his property according to the terms of his will. Nanette is Howard's personal representative or executrix. If Howard had named the First National Bank's trust department as his personal representative to administer his estate, the bank would be his personal representative or executor.

If there is no will, the court appoints the personal representative, traditionally called an administrator (man) or administratrix (woman).

Example: Howard dies without a will. The probate court appoints his sister, Nanette, to oversee the distribution of his estate to his heirs as determined by state law. Nanette is Howard's personal representative or administratrix.

Generally, executors and administrators perform similar duties, face similar liabilities, and hold similar powers. Many states now use the term *personal representative* instead of executor or administrator, and this practice will be followed here. Throughout this book, any person (man or woman) who administers the estate of a decedent will be referred to as a personal representative, whether the decedent died with or without a will. The various types of personal representatives and the fiduciary duties they perform are discussed in detail in Chapter 11.

The Role of the Personal Representative

Although state statutes often grant numerous fiduciary powers to personal representatives, usually the powers are limited to those stated explicitly in the will or incorporated into the will by reference to a statute authorizing them. As an example, see Section 3–715 of the Uniform Probate Code, which lists twenty-seven transactions the personal representative can perform. You should review these functions carefully.

Generally, the role of the personal representative is:

- To probate the will or petition for estate administration when there is no will.
- To collect, protect, preserve, and manage the probate estate of the decedent.
- To publish notice to creditors to submit their claims by a specific date.
- To pay all federal and state taxes and approved creditor claims.
- To distribute the remaining assets to the beneficiaries named in the will or to the decedent's heirs if no will exists.
- To refrain from engaging in acts of self-dealing, often referred to as the duty of loyalty; e.g., *the personal representative cannot borrow, sell, or buy estate property. It may be appropriate for you to remind the personal representative of this duty.* **◄ ETHICAL ISSUE**
- To commence a civil lawsuit for claims on behalf of the estate or to defend the estate against claims brought by creditors or disgruntled family members.
- *To keep all collected estate assets separate from the personal representative's own assets*, i.e., to not commingle these assets. **◄ ETHICAL ISSUE**
- *To not delegate the management of the probate estate or these fiduciary duties to others.* Obviously, this does not prevent the personal representative from selecting and hiring professional advisers, e.g., an attorney and a paralegal, to help perform these duties. **◄ ETHICAL ISSUE**

Circumstances may arise that make the personal representative's task more difficult. Problems that may occur include the following:

- A beneficiary or heir cannot be found.
- A beneficiary or heir challenges the personal representative's appointment or authority to act and proposes an alternate candidate.
- Someone contests the will.
- Someone challenges the personal representative's payment to creditors or distributions to beneficiaries or heirs.

The court will ultimately resolve these problems, but they may cause lengthy delays in the estate administration and add considerable expense that depletes the assets of the estate.

The personal representative distributes only the probate property of the decedent's estate, i.e., the assets that are disposed of by will or that descend as intestate property. The personal representative does not have administrative power to distribute nonprobate property such as jointly owned property, the proceeds from an insurance policy payable to a named beneficiary other than the decedent's estate, and the like. Statutes generally require that the personal representative report all the property (probate and nonprobate) in the estate for tax purposes. These tax requirements will be discussed in Chapter 14.

Pre-Probate Duties of the Personal Representative

Neither this list of the personal representative's duties nor the lists in the following sections are intended to be all-inclusive. Not only do these duties vary from state to state, but many aspects of estate administration depend on the provisions of the will, if one exists, and the amount and nature of the assets the decedent owned. The personal representative will generally perform these tasks with the advice of an attorney and your assistance, which will be discussed in more detail in Chapters 11 and 12. The following are the main tasks of the personal representative prior to probate:

1. Upon request, assist with anatomical gifts and funeral arrangements. Obtain copies of the death certificate from the funeral director.

2. Although not mandatory, the personal representative will generally hire an attorney to *represent the estate* and to help with its administration.

3. Help find and review any existing will.

4. Contact all of the decedent's financial advisers to obtain information about business records, papers, a safe deposit box, and the like.

ETHICAL ISSUE

5. Convene a conference of family members and other interested persons to discuss the provisions of the will or intestate laws, election rights, immediate financial needs, maintenance, and similar matters. *Advise a surviving spouse of the right to obtain his or her own attorney and elect against the will.* Determine whether fiduciaries (guardians or conservators) are needed for minors and incompetent persons.

6. Locate and notify witnesses of the testator's death.

7. Discontinue the telephone and other utilities if advantageous and notify the post office to forward mail to the address of the personal representative. Stop newspaper and other deliveries.

8. Determine the appropriate probate proceedings—solemn (formal) or common (informal). See the discussion in Chapters 12 and 13.

Probate Duties prior to Appointment as Personal Representative

The personal representative is expected to file all required legal documents, petitions, and accounts, as discussed in detail in Chapters 11 and 12. Before being formally appointed, the personal representative should attend to the following:

1. Petition for probate of the will or for general administration if there is no will and, in either case, for appointment of the personal representative (out-of-state property may require ancillary administration, see later discussion in this chapter).

2. Give notice of the decedent's death and notice of the date for the hearing to probate the will and for appointment of the personal representative to beneficiaries, heirs, creditors, and other interested persons.

3. Notify the surviving spouse and minor children of their rights.

Estate Administration Duties from Appointment to Closing of the Estate

The personal representative will perform the following tasks in administering the estate:

1. Obtain from the court the **Letters Testamentary** or **Letters of Administration** that establish the authority of the personal representative and file an oath of office as personal representative. Letters are one-page certificates of appointment authorizing the personal representative to act on behalf of the decedent's estate in performing the tasks of estate administration.

2. Arrange for a **bond** with **surety** if necessary. Unless a state statute requires a bond, it may be waived in the will.

3. Apply for an Employer Identification Number (Form SS—4).

4. Open an estate checking account.

5. Open the decedent's safe deposit box.

6. Defend the estate against will contests.

7. Discuss the need for survivors to draft or rewrite their own wills and review their health and life insurance.

8. Protect, collect, and preserve assets:

   a. Find and review all documents, records, and papers (e.g., business records, checkbooks, tax returns, pension plans, insurance policies) concerning the decedent's financial affairs. Notify local banks of the decedent's death and request information on accounts or an unknown safe deposit box.

   b. Take possession of all personal property not set aside for the spouse and/or minor children and transfer all cash from such sources as savings and checking accounts, life insurance payable to the estate, and dividends from securities into the new estate checking account.

   c. Inspect the condition of all real estate and review all written documents, including promissory notes, leases, mortgages, and deeds. Arrange for security, management, and collection of rents and pay insurance premiums, rent, and other obligations.

MINI-GLOSSARY BOX

Letters Testamentary
The formal document of authority and appointment given to a personal representative (executor) by the proper court to carry out the administration of the decedent's estate according to the terms of a will.

Letters of Administration
The formal document of authority and appointment given to a personal representative (administrator) by the proper court to carry out the administration of the decedent's estate according to the proper state intestate succession statute.

Bond
A certificate whereby a surety company promises to pay money if the personal representative of a deceased fails to faithfully perform the duties of administering the decedent's estate. The bond is the contract that binds the surety.

Surety
An individual or insurance company that, at the request of a personal representative, agrees to pay money up to the amount of a bond in the event that the personal representative fails to faithfully perform his duties.

d. Determine the form of ownership of all real and personal property.

e. Protect both real and personal property with adequate and appropriate kinds of insurance coverage (obtain confirmation in writing) and keep all property in reasonable repair. Place valuable personal property in a new estate safe deposit box or vault.

f. Collect information on all nonprobate assets to be used later in preparing tax returns, e.g., property in joint tenancy or trusts and other assets designated for a named beneficiary (e.g., life insurance, IRA, and pension plans).

g. Collect all debts including family debts owed to the decedent and place the funds in the estate account. Contact the decedent's employer and collect any amounts owed to the decedent such as unpaid salary, bonus, and vacation pay. Make sure the decedent was not involved in any pending litigation. If the decedent or the estate is entitled to sue others, e.g., debtors and the like, then the personal representative must perform these tasks.

h. File claims for any Social Security, veterans' pension benefits, and the like to which the decedent's estate is entitled.

i. Determine whether the decedent made any gifts for which a gift tax return must be filed.

j. Determine whether ancillary administration of out-of-state assets is necessary and make appropriate arrangements for such administration when required (see the discussion under Ancillary Administration later in the chapter).

9. Ascertain whether the decedent owned any business (sole proprietorship or partnership) and determine whether the business should be liquidated, sold, or continued. Arrange proper management for the business as needed.

10. Review all securities (stocks and bonds) and collect all interest and dividends, make decisions on proper investments, and determine whether any of these assets will have to be liquidated to pay administration expenses, taxes, or creditors' claims.

11. Once the assets are determined and collected, inventory and make arrangements to have all assets appraised according to their value at the date of the decedent's death or the alternate valuation date.

12. Distribute family allowances, including support and maintenance to the surviving spouse and/or minor children, as determined by statute.

13. Examine all claims made against the estate; determine their reasonableness, timeliness, validity, and priority; defend the estate against any improper claims.

14. Defend the estate against any litigation filed against it.

15. Pay all allowed claims against the estate according to their statutory priority.

16. Prepare and file all necessary federal and state tax returns and pay all taxes due.

17. Terminate the ancillary administration, if one exists, and pay any debts or taxes due.

18. Obtain and keep detailed records of all receipts (income) and vouchers for all disbursements (expenses and debt payments) and prepare all necessary data for the final accounting, listing assets, receipts, disbursements, and sales (if any), noting any gains or losses, and providing a reconciliation of beginning and ending balances.

19. Obtain court approval of attorney's and personal representative's fees.

20. Distribute proper title to remaining assets of the estate to beneficiaries according to the will or to heirs according to the intestate statute.

21. After the final accounting, obtain approval of the settlement of the estate and a discharge of the personal representative by order of the court.

22. Cancel the personal representative's bond, if one was necessary, with the surety (bonding) company, claim any refund, and close the estate.

The Attorney

In many cases the personal representative appointed by the decedent will lack the knowledge, experience, or expertise to handle the complexities of estate administration. For this reason, the personal representative generally requests the assistance of an attorney. Once the attorney is hired, you also will begin your tasks.

Potential ethical problems, of which you, too, must be aware, arise for the supervising attorney who is hired to draft the will *whenever the following occur:*

ETHICAL ISSUE

1. The attorney or her family is named a beneficiary in the will. The case of *In re Peterson's Estate*, 283 Minn. 446, 168 N.W.2d 502 (1969) illustrates this problem.

> Grace Peterson, a 74-year-old spinster asked her attorney, Chester Gustafson, to draft her will. Over several years, the attorney prepared seven wills and a codicil for Peterson with the last will leaving her entire estate to Gustafson's children. Peterson died, and Gustafson sought to have the last will probated.

> - Issue: Is a will valid when the entire estate is left to the family of the attorney who drew the will?
> - Decision: No, said the Minnesota Supreme Court. The will was a product of the attorney's undue influence and cannot be probated.

Comment: Rule 1.8(c) of the Model Rules of Professional Conduct (see Chapter 15) specifically states:

> A lawyer shall not prepare an instrument giving the lawyer or a person related to the lawyer as parent, child, sibling, or spouse, any substantial gift from a client, including a testamentary gift, *except* where the client is related to the donee.

> **Example:** Attorney John Edwards drafts a will for Elizabeth Thompson, the mother of John's wife, Sarah Edwards. In the will, Elizabeth leaves her lake cottage in Maine to her daughter, Sarah Edwards. This gift would be ethically acceptable.

2. The attorney is named in the will to be the personal representative. *not suggested*

3. The attorney is named in the will as the testator's choice to assist the personal representative.

Both situations 2 and 3 both raise a serious ethical issue. In each case, the appointment would be financially rewarding to the attorney, especially when the compensation is a percentage of the estate. For this reason, *the attorney or paralegal must not solicit or suggest either appointment to the client*.

ETHICAL ISSUE

Comment: The Model Code of Professional Responsibility (EC 5–6) (the predecessor to the Model Rules discussed in Chapter 15) states:

> A lawyer should not consciously influence a client to name [the lawyer] as executor, trustee, or lawyer in an instrument. In those cases where the client wishes to name the lawyer as such, care should be taken by the lawyer to avoid even the appearance of impropriety.

A leading case on these issues is *State v. Gulbankian*, 54 Wis.2d 605, 196 N.W.2d 733 (1972), in which the Wisconsin Supreme Court stated:

> It is clear an attorney cannot solicit either directly or by any indirect means a request or direction of a testator that he or a member of his firm be named executor or be employed as an attorney to probate the estate. . . . An attorney, merely because he drafts a will, has no preferential claim to probate it.
>
> A lawyer must not only avoid solicitation but also the appearance of solicitation so as not to damage the confidence the public has in the legal profession.

The Wisconsin court added that a lawyer may draft a will that names him as executor *if* that is the *unprompted* intent of the client. The court also observed that testators rarely name the attorney who drafts the will to be their personal representative or to assist the personal representative.

Furthermore, even when the will recommends an attorney to assist in probating the estate, that attorney may not be the one to do so. The personal representative of the estate has the sole discretion to select the attorney and is under no obligation to choose one named in the will.

ETHICAL ISSUE →

Having been retained to help the personal representative settle an estate, the attorney has a duty to inform the beneficiaries or heirs of the estate that the attorney represents and works for the estate while advising the personal representative and not individually for them. In case of conflict, such as when named beneficiaries to the will want to sue the estate, they must hire their own attorney. *They cannot retain the attorney who is representing the estate because that would create a conflict of interest for the attorney.* The attorney, like the personal representative, has a fiduciary responsibility, a basic duty of loyalty to the client (the estate), and cannot become involved in a situation where a conflict may develop or where the attorney has a personal interest in the outcome of the proceedings.

THE PUBLIC IS USING THE INTERNET TO LOCATE AN ATTORNEY

The marketing of legal services on the Internet has exploded. Many attorneys and law firms have a web page advertising their services. The firm's address, telephone number and other vital information is often listed. Photographs and profiles of firm employees are a popular feature. A creative page will allow the prospective client to communicate with the firm, request information, or e-mail a question.

Some sites that assist clients in locating attorneys are *www.findlaw.com, www.lawoffice.com,* and *www.martindale.com.* FindLaw advertises its directory as the web's most useful. The directory at lawoffice.com lists more than one million lawyers and promotes the service as an easy to use system for locating legal counsel. The lawyer locator directory information published by Martindale Hubbell is extensive. Most on-line directories allow a user to search for an attorney by name, city, state, or area of practice.

ASSIGNMENT 3.1

Sharon, the personal representative of her father's estate, hires Tamara Colby, an attorney, to help administer the estate. The will names all of Sharon's brothers and sisters beneficiaries except Charles. Charles intends to contest the will. Answer the following questions yes or no and explain your position according to your state's statutory code for wills *and* the Model Rules of Professional Conduct (see Chapter 15).

1. Can Charles hire Tamara to represent him in the will contest?
2. If Tamara and Sharon's father were business partners, can Tamara accept the position offered by Sharon?
3. Can the attorney who drafted the will act as the attorney for the estate?
4. Charles owns his own business. On occasion, he has retained Tamara to handle various legal problems for the business. The business has no legal actions pending at this time. Can Tamara accept the position offered by Sharon?

The Paralegal or Legal Assistant

As the legal assistant, you must act under the direction and supervision of an attorney and cannot give legal advice. Many tasks must be performed when drafting wills and trusts and administering decedents' estates, but not all of them must be handled personally by an attorney. The specific duties you will perform when assisting the attorney and the personal representative in estate administration will be discussed in later chapters. The next paragraphs provide a brief overview of your tasks in wills, trusts, and estate administration.

Wills
Your tasks concerning wills include the following:

1. Collect all data and information necessary for making a client's will, including helping the client complete questionnaires and handling all communication (phone calls, letter writing, and interviews) to obtain the required information.
2. After reviewing the client's financial information, discuss with the attorney the contents of the will. You should be prepared to discuss such topics as the need to incorporate trusts; tax considerations, including methods of reducing taxes; the identification and clarification of all assets; and the beneficiaries to whom the property is to be distributed according to the client's wishes.
3. Prepare a preliminary draft of the will.
4. Review the draft with your attorney and the client and make any corrections, additions, deletions, or modifications necessary to avoid inconsistencies and ensure that the will reflects the wishes of the client.
5. Assist in the execution of the final draft of the will.

Trusts
The following are your main tasks in relation to trusts:

1. Obtain from the client data and information needed for the creation of a trust (e.g., the purpose of the trust, parties, property to be transferred, powers of the trustee, distributions of income and principal, and tax considerations).
2. Draft a preliminary trust.
3. Review the preliminary draft with your supervising attorney and the client and make corrections, additions, deletions, or modifications as necessary.
4. Assist in the final execution of the trust.

Estate Administration
Your *pre-probate tasks* in estate administration generally include the following:

1. If requested, help locate the will, if one exists.

2. Set up a family conference and notify all family members and beneficiaries or heirs.

3. Assist in reviewing the will or intestacy procedures with the family and beneficiaries of the will or the heirs of the intestate.

4. Explain the **"tickler" system** and probate procedures to the client.

5. Set up the "tickler" system with the personal representative and prepare for the maintenance and monitoring of the procedures (e.g., dates for filing, correspondence, and filing of documents).

Probate tasks include the following:

Tickler system
A chronological list of all the important steps and dates in the stages of the administration of the decedent's estate.

> **ETHICAL ISSUE**

1. Help locate, collect, preserve, and maintain assets and ensure that *estate assets are not commingled with other assets of the law firm.*

> **ETHICAL ISSUE**

2. Handle communication (phone calls, letter writing, and personal interviews) with parties holding assets (e.g., insurance companies, banks), creditors, beneficiaries, and heirs. *None of your communications may contain legal advice, and any information you receive must remain confidential.*

3. Assist in preparing preliminary drafts of legal documents (forms) associated with estate administration.

4. Maintain records of all collected assets (filing of documents, creditors' claims, and the like).

5. Prepare an inventory and appraisal of all probate assets and also list all nonprobate property and its value for federal and state death tax purposes.

6. Prepare preliminary drafts of final estate accounts and necessary tax returns.

7. Record the payment of debts and taxes due.

8. File legal documents (from the original petition to the final account).

9. File tax returns after review with the attorney.

Your handling of such tasks frees the attorney from the time-consuming but important details of estate administration, thus decreasing the cost of legal services. You are responsible for seeing that these matters move smoothly and chronologically. By doing so, you can handle queries that do not involve the dispensing of legal advice and can indirectly improve attorney-client rapport by allowing the attorney more time to advise the client. The ethical conduct required of paralegals when performing these tasks under the supervision of an attorney is discussed in Chapter 15 and throughout the text. Exhibit 3.1 summarizes the duties a paralegal can and cannot perform.

The Probate Court

Another participant with an essential role in the administration of a decedent's estate is the judge. The words *court* and *judge* are frequently used synonymously in statutes and in legal writings. As a courtesy, the judge who presides over a court is referred to as "the court." Throughout the remaining chapters of this text, the words will be used interchangeably. Chapters 11 and 12 discuss the role of the court in greater detail. In some states, the court that handles estate administration is called the probate court, but in other states, this court is called a Surrogate, Orphans', or Chancery Court. In many states, the court is part of the state's regular judicial system, e.g., a district, circuit, county, or superior court. The designation, probate court, will be used throughout this text. Exhibit 3.2 identifies the name of the appropriate court in each state.

Exhibit 3.1 Duties and Functions a Paralegal with Proper Supervision Can or Cannot Perform

Duties/Functions	Paralegal Can Perform	Paralegal Cannot Perform
Accept an employment (client) contract.		X
Establish legal fees with a client when working for a firm.		X
Interview a client to gather relevant data needed for drafting wills, trusts, and estate administration forms.	X	
Prepare questionnaires for estate planning and checklists for wills and trusts.	X	
Give legal advice on estate planning, e.g., gifts, taxes.		X
Perform legal research.	X	
Draft preliminary wills, trusts, and estate documents.	X	
Verify that the creation and execution of all documents and estate administration procedures comply with state statutes.	X	
Assist in the final execution of the will or trust.	X	
Set up and explain to appropriate parties the "tickler" system used in probate.	X	
Handle communication (phone calls, correspondence, interviews, etc.) with the decedent's family, beneficiaries, heirs, and creditors.	X	
Perform legal advocacy (represent a client before a court in a will contest).*		X
Identify and keep records of all probate and nonprobate property for preparing the estate inventory.	X	
File legal documents for probate and estate administration.	X	
Determine if federal and state death taxes are due and execute tax returns.	X	

*Exceptions currently allow paralegals or other nonlawyers to act on behalf of a client in a few situations, e.g., appeals at Social Security hearings.

In general, once the probate court has jurisdiction, its function is to ensure that the personal representative properly administers the estate so that (1) the homestead exemption, exempt property, family allowances, and maintenance are granted; (2) creditors who have valid claims are paid; (3) taxes owed are paid; (4) the remaining property is distributed to the rightful beneficiaries according to the testator's wishes as expressed in the provisions of the will if a will exists or, in the alternative, according to the controlling state intestate succession statute; and (5) disputes that may arise in the course of the administration of the estate are settled. By approving the will or identifying the decedent's rightful heirs according to statute, the probate court establishes clear title to the property distributed to the beneficiaries of the will or to the heirs. Terminology relating to the functions of the probate court will be covered in a later section of this chapter.

The Registrar

The **Registrar**, also known as **Surrogate** or Register of Wills, is an officer of the probate court who is in charge of keeping records and at times acts on behalf and in place of the court. The Registrar may be a judge but more often is a person designated by the judge to perform functions of the court in certain probate proceedings, e.g., common, independent, or informal proceedings in Uniform

Registrar (Surrogate)
A person designated by the judge to perform the functions of the court in informal proceedings.

Exhibit 3.2 State Courts Having Jurisdiction over Wills, Probate, and Distribution of Decedents' Estates

Probate court:	Alabama, Arkansas, Connecticut, Georgia, Maine, Michigan, New Hampshire, Rhode Island, South Carolina, Vermont
Probate and family court:	Massachusetts
Probate court or district court:	New Mexico
Surrogate's court:	New Jersey, New York
Orphans' court or circuit court in Hartford and Montgomery counties:	Maryland
Court of common pleas or orphans' court division of court of common pleas:	Pennsylvania
Probate division of court of common pleas:	Ohio
Court of chancery:	Delaware, Mississippi
Court of chancery, court of general sessions, or probate court in Davidson and Shelby counties:	Tennessee
District court:	Idaho, Iowa, Kansas, Kentucky, Louisiana, Montana, Nevada, Oklahoma, Utah, Wyoming
District court or Denver probate court:	Colorado
Probate division of district court:	Minnesota
Circuit court:	Florida, Hawaii, South Dakota, Virginia, Wisconsin
Probate division of circuit court:	Illinois, Missouri
Circuit court, superior court, or probate court in St. Joseph and Vigo counties:	Indiana
Superior court:	Alaska, Arizona, California, North Carolina, Washington
Circuit court or county court:	Oregon
County court:	Nebraska, North Dakota
County court or probate court:	Texas
County commission:	West Virginia

Probate Code states. Although Registrars cannot, by statute, give legal advice, they can answer questions about forms and procedures that are common concerns for paralegals working in estate administration.

The Clerk or Court Administrator

Clerk
An administrative assistant to the court who receives and files documents and keeps records of court proceedings.

The **clerk** (of the probate court) is an administrative assistant to the court (judge). The clerk administers oaths and authenticates and certifies copies of instruments, documents, and records of the court. Like the Registrar, the court clerk in the county of the decedent's domiciliary state cannot give legal advice, but both are essential and extremely helpful sources of information about probate procedures and the execution of the required forms. Since your county may follow "local customs" in administering decedents' estates, you should contact the Registrar or clerk and become familiar with their procedures. Frequently, these officers of the court have written a pamphlet or outline of "Guidelines for Probate Procedures" customarily followed in your county. The pamphlet usually identifies the rules, procedures, and required state forms you will use. Since you will file all forms and other documents with these officers of the court, you will find their help invaluable in assuring that your forms are complete and accurate.

𐫱 ASSIGNMENT 3.2

1. If Anna Brown was appointed executrix of her mother's estate, did her mother die intestate or testate?
2. Does either an executor(trix) or administrator(trix) have the duty to collect money from insurance policies naming a specific person as the beneficiary? Do they have this duty if the beneficiary predeceased the decedent?
3. To whom is a personal representative responsible?
4. Look up the sections in your state's statutes describing the appointment and duties of the personal representative. Cite the sections.

TERMINOLOGY RELATED TO PROBATE COURT PROCEEDINGS

Since probate court proceedings are an essential part of estate administration, you need to become familiar with the basic terminology related to probate. Jurisdiction, domicile, venue, and ancillary administration are all important aspects of probate proceedings.

Probate

Originally, the term **probate** referred to a proceeding in the appropriate court to prove that a certain document was a will. To prove a will means to acknowledge its existence and validity as the properly executed last will of a decedent. A will that is proved is said to be admitted to probate. Initially an adjective, *probate* today is commonly used as a noun meaning **probate proceedings**, which expands the definition and use of the term *probate* to include the process of distributing the estate assets of a person who died testate in accordance with the will or according to state intestate statutes if there is no will. The probate process passes title to the decedent's property to the beneficiaries or heirs. The term *probate* is also used to include all other matters over which probate courts have jurisdiction during the completion of the entire administration of the decedent's estate, including such matters as the settlement of a dispute concerning a will. Such suits, known as **will contests**—for example, a contest between two beneficiaries who claim that the same item of property was given to each of them—may arise after the will is admitted to probate. Further discussion concerning the actual procedures of probate versus estate administration is included in Chapter 12.

Probate (of a will)
The procedure by which a document is presented to the court to confirm it is a valid will.

Probate proceedings
The process of distributing the estate of a person who died testate or intestate; includes all other matters over which probate courts have jurisdiction.

Will contest
Litigation to overturn a decedent's will.

Jurisdiction

Jurisdiction is the authority by which a particular court is empowered by statute to hear and decide a certain kind of case and to have its decision enforced. As mentioned previously, the court that has authority (jurisdiction) over wills and the administration of decedents' estates is often called the probate court.

In general, the jurisdiction of a probate court extends to the administration and distribution of a decedent's estate, including the primary function of proving that

Jurisdiction
The authority by which a particular court is empowered by statute to decide a certain kind of case and to have its decision enforced.

a certain legal document is a will. The powers and duties of the probate court are set out in the statutes or constitution of each state. See the following Missouri statute:

Mo. Ann. Stat. § 472.020 Jurisdiction of Probate Division of Circuit Court

The probate division of the circuit court may hear and determine all matters pertaining to probate business, to granting letters testamentary and of administration, the appointment of guardians and conservators of minors and incapacitated and disabled persons, settling the accounts of personal representatives and conservators, and the sale or leasing of lands by personal representatives and conservators, including jurisdiction of the construction of wills as an incident to the administration of estates, of the determination of heirship, of the administration of testamentary and *inter vivos* trusts, of disability and incapacity proceedings as provided by law and of such other probate business as may be prescribed by law.

Note that in this statute the probate court operates as a division of the circuit court instead of a separate court. In other states, the probate court may be a division of another system of courts (e.g., of the court of common pleas, as in Ohio) or a special court (as in New York, where it is called the Surrogate's Court, or in Maryland, where it is called the Orphans' Court).

Note also that the Missouri statute enumerates the powers of the probate court. It may make orders or decrees (decisions) in respect to wills and estate administration. No other state court has jurisdiction over the construction of a decedent's will or to decide matters concerning the estate. Although the probate court's jurisdiction is limited to powers given it by statutory law, it has "superior" jurisdiction in the matters on which it rules; that is, its decisions can be overruled only by the highest state court, often called the state supreme court.

Domicile

Domiciliary state
The state in which the decedent's domicile (legal home) is located.

Domiciliary administration
The administration of an estate in the state where the decedent was domiciled at the time of death.

Domicile
The legal home where a person has a true, fixed, and permanent place of dwelling and to which the person intends to return when absent.

Residence
The dwelling in which one temporarily lives or resides.

Domicile (legal home) has been defined as the place a person has adopted as a permanent home, and to which the person intends to return when absent. A probate court has jurisdiction over decedents who were domiciles, i.e., legal residents within its authority (county). Determination of a person's **domiciliary state** is essential when the person dies and owns real and personal property located in more than one state. The domiciliary state has jurisdiction over the decedent and all of the decedent's property except real property located in the other state(s). The administration of the decedent's estate is referred to as the primary or **domiciliary administration.** Real property located in other states is probated through secondary court proceedings called ancillary administration (see further discussion in this chapter). The terms *domicile* and *residence* are often confused and frequently used interchangeably, but they are distinguishable. **Domicile** is the legal home, the fixed permanent place of dwelling, whereas **residence** is a temporary place of dwelling. Therefore, a temporary residence, such as a summer home, is not a domicile. A person may have more than one residence but only one domicile.

Example: Sam's permanent home is in Dayton, Ohio. He spends every winter at his condominium in Miami and two weeks each summer at a friend's cottage on Cape Cod. All three places are Sam's residences, but only the home in Dayton is his domicile.

Domicile, not residence, determines venue (see the next section). A permanent legal address is determined by where one lives, banks, goes to church, buys license plates, pays state taxes, and votes. If an uncertainty does arise, e.g., if a person abandons his domicile in one place and has not yet taken up another before dying, probate proceedings are usually conducted in the county where the assets of the decedent's estate are located. Some cases and examples will illustrate how a court determines a person's domicile.

In the case of *Application of Winkler*, 171 A.D.2d 474,567 N.Y.S.2d 53 (1991), the court held that a person's domicile is "determined by the conduct of the person and all the surrounding circumstances which may be proven by acts and declarations." Documentation, such as a person's voting records, passport, marriage certificate, and driver's license, as well as witnesses' testimony can also be used to verify a person's true intention as to domicile. In the case of *In re Estate of Elson*, 120 Ill.App.3d 649, 76 Ill. Dec. 237, 458 N.E.2d 637, (1983), the court was asked to decide whether Illinois or Pennsylvania was the true and intended domicile of the decedent. The court stated:

1. "Domicile" has been defined as the place where a person has her true, permanent home to which she intends to return whenever she is absent.

2. "Domicile" is a continuing thing, and from the moment a person is born she must, at all times, have a domicile.

3. A person can have only one "domicile," and once a domicile is established, it continues until a new one is actually acquired.

4. To effect a "change of domicile," there must be actual abandonment of the first domicile, coupled with intent not to return to it, and physical presence must be established in another place with intention of making the last-acquired residence a permanent home.

5. "Domicile" is largely a matter of intention and, hence, is primarily a question of fact.

6. Once a "domicile" is established, it is presumed to continue, and the burden of proof in such cases rests on the party who attempts to establish that change in domicile occurred.

7. Very slight circumstances often decide questions of "domicile," and the determination is made based on the preponderance of evidence in favor of some particular place as a domicile and depends upon facts and circumstances of the particular case.

In reaching a decision, the court considered various actions of the decedent: in particular, when the decedent left Illinois five or six days prior to her death, she took most of her personal possessions with her, closed her bank accounts in Illinois, and established new accounts in Delaware near her new home in Pennsylvania. In addition, in an unmailed letter she penned the day before her death, she wrote that she had "moved to Pennsylvania." The court found that this evidence was sufficient to support a finding that the decedent intended to abandon her Illinois domicile permanently and acquire a permanent domicile in Pennsylvania, despite other evidence that she intended to stay in Pennsylvania for only one year and planned to return to Illinois.

> **Example:** Whitney legally resides, i.e., is domiciled, in Kennebec County, Augusta, Maine. The probate court of Kennebec County in Maine would be the proper court to probate her will. Whitney moves her household goods from Augusta to Hartford, Connecticut, but dies before establishing legal residence there. If she still owned land in Augusta, the probate court of Kennebec County would remain the proper court to probate her will.

Example: Allisson owns real estate in more than one state, i.e., a house in Ohio, a farm in Kentucky, and a cottage in Minnesota, but only one residence is her domicile. Since the house in Ohio is Allisson's permanent address and Ohio is the state where she pays taxes, votes, and has a driver's license, Ohio would be Allisson's domiciliary state.

Venue

Venue
The particular place, city or county, where a court having jurisdiction may hear and decide a case.

Venue is the particular place (either city or county) where a court that has jurisdiction may hear and decide a case. Venue and jurisdiction are not interchangeable, although they are closely related. "Jurisdiction" is abstract, denoting the power or authority of a court to act; "venue" is concrete, denoting the physical place of a trial. "Venue" approximates the definition of territorial jurisdiction and will be used throughout this text to signify the location of the proper court, usually the county within a specific state.

In determining which probate court is the proper one to handle the decedent's estate, the question of the court's jurisdiction is primary. After that has been resolved, the question of venue arises. Usually, venue corresponds to the decedent's place of domicile (legal home) or to the decedent's residence at death. In other words, the proper venue (place) for the probate administration of the estate of a deceased state resident is usually the county in which the decedent was domiciled at his death. The venue for out-of-state residents is generally the county in which the nonresident left real property.

Example: Harold Wickes was living in Cook County, Chicago, Illinois, at the time of his death. The administration of his estate will be supervised by the probate (circuit) court of Cook County. Thus, the venue in this instance is Cook County. "Change of venue" means to transfer the location of the court proceedings; a change of venue may be granted if a devisee of the will shows a good reason for the transfer to another location. If Harold's will gave a farm located in Gogebic County, Michigan, to his cousin, and the cousin could prove that Harold's actual domicile was Gogebic County, the venue of the probate proceedings would be changed to that county in Michigan.

Example: Ralph Schollander wrote a will three years ago identifying himself as a resident "of the . . . County of Marion, State of Indiana." Last year he moved to St. Joseph County (Indiana) to live with his sister. Should Ralph die in St. Joseph County, venue for the probate of his will would be a question for the probate court of Marion County to decide. The court would have to consider, among other things, whether Ralph intended to give up permanent legal residence in Marion County and establish it in St. Joseph County (i.e., to remain there indefinitely).

The following are examples of statutory regulation of jurisdiction and venue:

Cal. Prob. Code § 7050 Jurisdiction over Estate Administration
The superior court has jurisdiction of proceedings under this code concerning the administration of the decedent's estate.

Cal. Prob. Code § 7051 Venue; County of Domicile
If the decedent was domiciled in this state at the time of death, the proper county for proceedings concerning administration of the decedent's estate is the county in which the decedent was domiciled, regardless of where the decedent died. [Compare Uniform Probate Code § 1–303.]

In addition to its value in determining the venue of a probate proceeding, the fact of the decedent's domicile aids the court in establishing ***in rem* jurisdiction** over the estate's probate assets. Similarly, when two or more states are involved in the probate of a single will, the state that can claim the testator as its citizen will collect the greater share of the state inheritance or estate taxes. The fact of domicile controls not only the state's power to levy taxes, but also its right to collect taxes on the decedent's property passed by will. Therefore, the tax liability of an estate may vary noticeably, depending on the inheritance tax demands, if any, of the state in which the estate assets are located.

In rem **jurisdiction**
The authority of the court over the decedent's property.

Ancillary Administration or Ancillary Probate Administration

As mentioned above, if at death the decedent-testator owns any real property (e.g., cottage, condominium, timeshare, or vacation home) in a state other than his domiciliary state and, in some cases, any tangible personal property in another state, his will must be admitted to probate in each state where the property is located. These separate or secondary court proceedings are known as ancillary probate administration or simply **ancillary administration.** Ancillary administration is necessary because the court in the county of the decedent's domicile has no jurisdiction over real property located in another state, often referred to as the **"foreign state."** Furthermore, by admitting the will to probate in each state and holding ancillary administration there, any local creditors of the decedent are protected. The court in the case of *First National Bank of Brush, Colo. v. Blessing*, 231 Mo. App. 288, 98 S.W.2d 149 (1936), provided a good explanation of ancillary administration.

> It seems to be well-settled law that the administration of the estate of a person who dies owning property in different states may be had in each of the states dealing with the property of the estate having a local situs [location] therein. Administration in the state where a person is domiciled at the time of his death is deemed the principal or primary administration and is ordinarily termed the "domiciliary administration"; and, in the state other than where he is domiciled where he has property, the administration is termed "ancillary" or "auxiliary." Administration either in the state of the decedent's domicile or the state other than the decedent's domicile in which he left property affects persons and things within that state only.

Ancillary administration
Additional administration used to dispose of and distribute that portion of the decedent's estate located in a state other than the decedent's domiciliary state.

Foreign state
Any state other than the decedent's domiciliary state.

Thus, when a person dies leaving real property in more than one state, not only are separate domiciliary and ancillary administrations required, but the property is administered under the laws of the state where it is located.

Usually, the testator or the court of the state of domicile appoints a person, called an **ancillary administrator(trix)**, to handle the administration in each state where the decedent's assets are located. Some states allow the personal representative of the domiciliary state to administer the ancillary proceedings. In such cases, the personal representative is also the ancillary administrator. However, state law often requires the ancillary administrator to be a resident of that state, thereby increasing the expense of ancillary administration. Exceptions are sometimes made to allow nonresident family members (e.g., the spouse of the testator) to serve as ancillary administrators, but at the same time, the court must take care to safeguard the rights of the creditors of the decedent who live

Ancillary administrator(trix)
The personal representative appointed by the court to distribute that part of a decedent's estate located in a state other than the decedent's domiciliary state.

in the foreign state. Section 3–203(g) of the Uniform Probate Code gives the domiciliary personal representative priority in being appointed the ancillary administrator. See Exhibit 3.3 for the various state requirements for personal representatives who want to be appointed the ancillary administrator in the foreign state. Consider the following examples.

Exhibit 3.3   State Eligibility Requirements for Personal Representatives

Age Requirements

21 or older: Arkansas, Colorado, Utah
19 or older: Alabama, Alaska, Nebraska
18 or older: All other states not listed

Unsuitability Disqualifications

Legal disqualifications:
- Felony or infamous crime conviction:
  Alabama, Arkansas, Delaware, Florida, Illinois, Indiana, Louisiana, Maryland, Mississippi, Missouri, Nevada, New York, North Carolina, Oklahoma, Oregon, South Dakota, Texas, Washington
- Disbarred from practice of law: Oregon
- Misdemeanor involving "moral turpitude": Washington
Capacity disqualifications:
- Mentally incapacitated: Delaware
- Adjudged disabled: Illinois
- Incapacitated: Indiana
- Mentally ill, retarded, an alcoholic, or a spendthrift: Iowa
- Bad moral character: Louisiana
- Mentally incompetent: Maryland
- Not having proper capacity: Massachusetts
- Mentally or physically unable to perform: Florida
- Unsound mind or not of sound mind:
  Arkansas, Illinois, Mississippi, Missouri, Washington, Wisconsin
- Incompetent, adjudged incompetent, or decreed incompetent:
  Alabama, Nevada, New York, North Carolina, Oklahoma, Oregon, South Dakota, Texas, Wyoming

Nonresident Requirements

- Nonresident must be approved by judge or consent to the jurisdiction of the state's court:
  Hawaii, Idaho, Minnesota, New Hampshire, Pennsylvania, Rhode Island
- Nonresident must appoint a specific person for service of process including probate judge, secretary of state, court surrogate, register, or clerk of court:
  Arkansas, Connecticut, Delaware, New Jersey, Tennessee, West Virginia
- Nonresident must appoint resident agent for service of process:
  Illinois, Indiana, Kansas, Louisiana, Maine, Maryland, Massachusetts, Michigan, Missouri, North Carolina, Oklahoma, South Carolina, South Dakota, Texas, Vermont, Washington, Wisconsin, Wyoming
- Nonresident must serve with co-administrator or resident fiduciary; or state prefers resident only:
  Iowa, New York, Tennessee, Virginia, Wyoming
- Nonresident may or can be executor if named in will or if a spouse, child, parent, or relative of the decedent:
  Alabama, Florida, Kentucky, Ohio, Tennessee, Virginia, West Virginia
- Nonresident cannot be administrator if decedent died intestate:
  Alabama, Kansas, Nevada, Ohio
- All other states not listed allow the appointment of nonresidents

Example: Toby resides in Virginia and owns a summer cottage in North Carolina. Several years ago she mortgaged the cottage to a bank in Raleigh. Should she die without having paid the mortgage, the bank would have no notice of her death even though it is an **"interested party"** by virtue of being her creditor. For this reason, an ancillary administration of her North Carolina property is necessary. In North Carolina the ancillary administrator must be 18 or older; must not be declared incompetent or convicted of a felony; and, if a nonresident, must designate a resident agent for service of process.

Example: North Dakota is Benjamin's domicile. Most of his assets are in North Dakota, but he has a winter home in Georgia. In his will Benjamin appoints his wife, Alesha, his personal representative. Under Georgia law, Alesha could also be appointed ancillary administratrix to administer the assets in Georgia including the winter home.

The ancillary administration in the foreign state generally includes the following procedures:

1. Acceptance by the foreign state court of the will admitted to probate in the decedent-testator's domiciliary state.

2. Issuance of letters of authority, e.g., Letters Ancillary Testamentary, to the ancillary administrator that permit the real property to be transferred to the designated devisee named in the will if all creditors of the testator in the foreign state have been paid.

3. If any inheritance or estate taxes are imposed by the foreign state, these taxes must be paid to that state and not to the testator's domiciliary state.

If the decedent died intestate, then the persons entitled to the decedent's real property in the foreign state will be determined by that state's intestate succession statute. However, generally, all of the decedent's personal property, wherever located, will pass to the persons entitled to it according to the decedent's domiciliary state's intestate succession statute. Specific tasks of paralegals concerning ancillary administration are discussed in Chapter 12.

> **Interested party (person)**
> A person including heirs, devisees, beneficiaries, personal representatives, creditors, and any others having a property right to or claim against the estate of a decedent.

KEY TERMS

Letters Testamentary	Clerk	Domiciliary	Ancillary administration
Letters of Administration	Probate (of a will)	administration	Foreign state
Bond	Probate proceedings	Domicile	Ancillary
Surety	Will contest	Residence	administrator(trix)
Tickler system	Jurisdiction	Venue	Interested party
Registrar (Surrogate)	Domiciliary state	*In rem* jurisdiction	(person)

REVIEW QUESTIONS

1. A personal representative is a fiduciary. What does that mean?
2. Who may act as a personal representative?
3. Why is a personal representative sometimes called an executor or an administrator?
4. What are Letters Testamentary and Letters of Administration and how do they differ?
5. Summarize the duties of a personal representative.

6. What are three ethical problems an attorney and paralegal face when drafting a client's will?
7. What are the general duties a paralegal may perform concerning wills, trusts, and estate administration?
8. What other titles besides probate court do states use to identify the court that supervises the administration of the decedent's estate?

9. How do the functions of a registrar and a court clerk differ?
10. Why are the terms *probate* and *probate proceedings* often confused? Explain.
11. Are domicile and venue the same thing? Explain.
12. When is an ancillary administration necessary and what is its purpose?
13. Who is authorized to act as an ancillary administrator in your state?

CASE PROBLEMS

Problem 1

Alberto Gomez owns real and personal property in three states, California, New Mexico, and New York. Alberto is 102 years old and has outlived his only spouse and their three children. When he dies intestate, Alberto has no surviving family, i.e., blood relatives. Answer the following:

A. What facts would be required for you to determine Alberto's domiciliary state?
B. What is the difference between Alberto's domicile and his residence?
C. Where would the proper venue be for Alberto's estate administration?
D. If a conflict arises over which of two or three states is the decedent's domicile, how does the Uniform Probate Code resolve the problem? See UPC § 3–202 and *Riley v. New York Trust Co.*, 315 U.S. 343, 62 S.Ct. 608, 86 L.Ed. 885 (1942).
E. Which state would determine how Alberto's property would be inherited? *Caveat:* Discuss both real and personal property. For personal property, see *Howard v. Reynolds*, 30 Ohio St.2d 214, 283 N.E.2d 629 (1972).

Problem 2

Maura Hanlon, legally a resident of Amarillo, Texas, dies while traveling in Waterford, Ireland. Maura owns a house in Amarillo and an apartment building in Tulsa, Oklahoma. Answer and explain each of the following:

A. In which state should Maura's will be probated?
B. Is an ancillary administration necessary in this case?
C. Whether Maura dies testate or intestate, is an ancillary administration still necessary?
D. What are the eligibility requirements for appointment of an ancillary administrator in the foreign state in this case?
E. Find and cite the section of the Uniform Probate Code or your state's statute, if any, that gives the domiciliary personal representative priority to be appointed the ancillary administrator.

THE LAW OF SUCCESSION: DEATH TESTATE OR INTESTATE

OBJECTIVES

After completing this chapter, you should be able to:

➤ Recognize, understand, and explain the basic terms, including the difference between orthodox (traditional) and UPC terminology, associated with testacy and intestacy.

➤ Read a will and identify the parties and gifts using both orthodox (traditional) and UPC terminology.

➤ Recognize and identify lineal and collateral relationships and determine who is entitled to receive a decedent's property under state intestate succession statutes.

➤ Understand the difference between the right of heirs of an intestate to take their share of the estate per capita or per stirpes.

➤ Explain the process of escheat.

➤ Explain the intestate succession statutory rights of family members versus the spouse's election rights when a decedent spouse dies with a will.

➤ Identify the advantages and disadvantages of a will.

SCOPE OF THE CHAPTER

Chapters 1 and 2 defined the basic terms associated with death with a will (testacy) and death without a will (intestacy) and identified the fiduciaries (personal representative, executor, administrator, trustee, and guardian) who are named in a will or appointed by the probate court. By now you are familiar with these and other terms such as decedent, intestate, and testator or testatrix. If your memory needs refreshing, review these terms in the opening chapters.

Before wills and trusts are drafted and the required forms for the administration of a decedent's estate are identified and executed, you need to add more terms to your basic vocabulary. This chapter defines the terms associated with the individuals and proceedings involved in the law of **succession.** The law explains how and to whom a decedent's property is distributed whether a person dies with or without a will. This acquired knowledge and the guidance of your supervising attorney will prepare you to perform your future tasks of drafting preliminary wills, trusts, and the numerous forms required for estate administration. Two sets of terminology, orthodox (traditional) and the Uniform Probate Code, used in the practice of law and by legal writers are identified, defined, and discussed. Both will be included throughout the remainder of the text.

First to be discussed are terms related to testacy—death with a will. A sample will is included with an illustrative review of the terminology. Next, terms that relate to death without a will—intestacy—are discussed, and the use of intestate terminology is also illustrated. The chapter concludes with a list of the advantages and disadvantages of wills.

Succession
The act of acquiring property of a decedent by will or by operation of law when the person dies intestate.

DEATH WITH A WILL—TESTACY

When death occurs, it is necessary to determine whether the decedent died testate or intestate. These terms refer to death with a valid will **(testacy)** or without a valid will **(intestacy).** The difference in the way and to whom property is distributed between testacy and intestacy is significant whenever the decedent's will is challenged, for example, in a will contest. If the challenge is successful and the will is declared invalid, the state intestate succession statute or a previous will determines who receives the decedent's property. These recipients may be entirely different from those individuals named in the contested will.

When a will exists, your training, experience, and investigatory skills should enable you to determine, with verification by your supervising attorney, if the will is valid, e.g., whether it was properly drafted and executed. If it is not valid, you must analyze and accurately apply your state's intestate succession statute to determine to whom the property will be distributed. Even when a will exists, its distribution provisions may not dispose of some probate property; for example, the will may not include a residuary clause. In such cases, the forgotten, overlooked, or excluded property not disposed of by the will passes by the state's intestate succession statute. To learn how to collect the requisite information and prepare the preliminary draft of a client's will, you must understand certain basic terms.

Testacy
Death with a valid will.

Intestacy
Death without a valid will.

Terminology Related to Wills

In general, two different types of terminology are used for wills:

- *Orthodox or traditional terminology.* Orthodox terminology refers to the traditional words related to wills and probate matters which were used universally before the adoption into law of the **Uniform Probate Code (UPC).**
- *UPC terminology.* The Code presents for adoption an alternative plan for probate procedures and new terminology for wills and estate administration. Many states have either adopted or modified the UPC or use the terminology it recommends. States that have adopted the UPC, or a modified version, include:

Alaska	Hawaii	Minnesota	North Dakota
Arizona	Idaho	Montana	South Carolina
Colorado	Maine	Nebraska	South Dakota
Florida	Michigan	New Mexico	Utah

Uniform Probate Code (UPC)
A uniform law available for adoption by the states to modernize and improve the efficiency of the administration of a decedent's estate.

Most states use a combination of UPC and orthodox terminology. Exhibit 4.1 lists both the traditional and UPC terms used in testacy and intestacy cases.

Wills are divided into four basic types and a separate document called a living will:

1. Holographic (also called an olographic) will. A holographic will is a will written in the maker's own handwriting. About half of the states and the UPC allow holographic wills, and, generally, such wills do not require witnesses or that the will be dated in order to be valid (see UPC § 2-502 and Exhibit 4.2). Compare Nev. Rev. Stat. § 133.090 and Okla. Stat. Ann. tit. 84, § 54, two states that require a date. In the case of *In re Mulkins' Estate,* 17 Ariz. App. 179, 496 P.2d 605 (1972),

---

Exhibit 4.1　Orthodox (Traditional) and UPC Terminology Compared

Testacy Terminology	Orthodox	UPC
Person appointed to administer an estate when there is a will	Executor (man) Executrix (woman)	Personal representative
Gift of money by will	Legacy	Devise
Gift of personal property by will (other than money)	Bequest	Devise
Gift of real property by will	Devise	Devise
Recipient of money by will	Legatee	Devisee
Recipient of personal property by will (other than money)	Beneficiary	Devisee
Recipient of real property by will	Devisee	Devisee

Intestacy Terminology	Orthodox	UPC
Person appointed to administer an estate when there is no will	Administrator (man) Administratrix (woman)	Personal representative
Person entitled by statute to real property of intestate	Heir or heir at law	Heir
Person entitled by statute to personal property of intestate	Distributee or next of kin	Heir
Passage of an intestate's property to the state when the decedent has no surviving blood relatives (kin)	Escheat	Escheat

Testacy or Intestacy Terminology	Orthodox	UPC
Person, other than creditors, entitled to the real or personal property of a decedent by will or through intestate succession	No all-inclusive word	Successor
Person, other than a creditor or purchaser, who has actually received real or personal property from the decedent's personal representative	No all-inclusive word	Distributee

the court held the handwritten words by the decedent on a publisher's will form was a valid holographic will. Many states require some or all of the following for a holographic will to be valid:

- The will must be "entirely" handwritten by the testator.
- The testator must have a clear intent to make a will.
- The testator's signature must be placed in a specific part of the will, e.g., at the "foot" or end of the will.
- The will must be dated.

Valid holographic wills have been written on envelopes, cabinet tops, and even petticoats. Audiotape or audio videotape recordings and typewritten wills are generally not recognized as valid holographic wills. See *Matter of Reed's Estate*, 672 P. 2d 829 (Wyo. 1983).

Nuncupative will
An oral will.

2. Nuncupative (oral) will.   A **nuncupative will** is an oral will spoken in the presence of witnesses; the will is valid only under exceptional circumstances, such as the imminent death of the person "speaking" the will. Nuncupative wills are prohibited in the majority of states (see Exhibit 4.2). However, when they are allowed, they must be probated within a statutory time period, and can generally pass only a limited amount of personal property of the speaker-testator (see Kan. Stat. Ann. § 59–608 and Tenn. Code Ann. § 32-1-106). Some states allow nuncupative (oral) wills such as soldiers' and sailors' wills made during military service in time of war, but a few states do not require formal hostilities; see Va. Code Ann. § 64.1-53, and N.Y. EPTL § 3-2.2(b). The Code does not allow oral wills (UPC § 2-502).

Statutory will
A fill-in-the-blank check-the-box will that is created and authorized by statute in a few states.

3. Statutory will.   A **statutory will** fulfills all the state's mandatory formal requirements for a will which are: the will must be written or typed; signed and dated by the testator; and attested and signed by at least two witnesses. A statutory will is a fill-in-the-blank check-the-box will and is an official legal document printed in the state statute for exclusive use in the testator's domiciliary state.

California, Louisiana, Maine, Michigan, and Wisconsin have developed their own unique statutory wills (see Exhibits 4.2, 4.3, and 6.7). Two other states, Massachusetts and New Mexico, have adopted the Uniform Statutory Will Act (see N.M. Stat. Ann. § 45-2A-17). Statutory wills are inexpensive and easy to execute. However, the options provided in a preprinted statutory form are often limited. Most of the decedent's property must go to spouses and children since the form has few, if any, options for close friends or charitable and religious organizations, and they cannot be amended to comply with alternative or additional estate plans. Therefore, spouses and children are the primary individuals for whom statutory wills are appropriate.

Exhibit 4.2   Types of Valid Wills by State

	Holographic	Nuncupative	State's Statutory Will Form	Uniform Statutory Will Act
Alabama	Prohibited (2)	Prohibited (6)		
Alaska	Valid	Prohibited		
Arizona	Valid	Prohibited		
Arkansas	Valid	Prohibited		

(continued)

Exhibit 4.2 Types of Valid Wills by State—*continued*

	Holographic	Nuncupative	State's Statutory Will Form	Uniform Statutory Will Act
California	Valid	Prohibited	X	
Colorado	Valid	Prohibited		
Connecticut	Prohibited (2) (6)	Prohibited		
Delaware	Prohibited (6)	Prohibited		
Florida	Prohibited (2)	Prohibited		
Georgia	Prohibited	Prohibited		
Hawaii	Valid	Prohibited		
Idaho	Valid	Prohibited		
Illinois	Prohibited	Prohibited		
Indiana	Prohibited (2) (6)	(4, 5)		
Iowa	Prohibited (6)	Prohibited		
Kansas	Prohibited (6)	(3, 5)		
Kentucky	Valid	Prohibited		
Louisiana	Valid	(7)	X	
Maine	Valid	Prohibited	X	
Maryland	Prohibited (1)	Prohibited		
Massachusetts	Prohibited (6)	(1)		X
Michigan	Valid	Prohibited	X	
Minnesota	Prohibited	Prohibited		
Mississippi	Valid	(3, 5)		
Missouri	Prohibited	(4, 5)		
Montana	Valid	Prohibited		
Nebraska	Valid	Prohibited		
Nevada	Valid	Prohibited		
New Hampshire	Prohibited	(3, 5)		
New Jersey	Valid	Prohibited		
New Mexico	Prohibited	Prohibited		X
New York	Prohibited (1)	(1)		
North Carolina	Valid	(3, 4, 5)		
North Dakota	Valid	Prohibited		
Ohio	Prohibited	(3, 5)		
Oklahoma	Valid	(1, 4, 5)		
Oregon	Prohibited	Prohibited		
Pennsylvania	Prohibited (2)	Prohibited		
Rhode Island	Prohibited	Prohibited		
South Carolina	Prohibited	Prohibited		
South Dakota	Valid	Prohibited		
Tennessee	Valid	(4, 5)		
Texas	Valid	(3, 5)		
Utah	Valid	Prohibited		
Vermont	Prohibited	(5)		
Virginia	Valid	(1)		
Washington	Prohibited (6)	(3, 5)		
West Virginia	Valid	(1)		
Wisconsin	Prohibited	Prohibited	X	
Wyoming	Valid	Prohibited		

(1) Prohibited except for mariners at sea or for military exceptions, e.g., armed forces members in actual service or during armed conflict.
(2) Prohibited unless it meets execution requirements, e.g., witnesses.
(3) Applies to anyone during their last illness.
(4) Applies to anyone in imminent peril of death and who dies from that peril.
(5) Prohibited unless declared in the presence of witnesses, reduced to writing, and/or probated within statutory time periods.
(6) Prohibited unless valid where executed.
(7) See La. Code of Civ. Proc. Art. 2884.

Exhibit 4.3 Wisconsin Basic Will

Signature of Testator ....

WISCONSIN BASIC WILL OF

....

(Insert Your Name)

Article 1. Declaration.

This is my will and I revoke any prior wills and codicils (additions to prior wills).

Article 2. Disposition of My Property

2.1 PERSONAL, RECREATIONAL AND HOUSEHOLD ITEMS. Except as provided in paragraph 2.2, I give all my furniture, furnishings, household items, recreational equipment, personal automobiles and personal effects to my spouse, if living; otherwise they shall be divided equally among my children who survive me.

2.2 GIFTS TO PERSONS OR CHARITIES. I make the following gifts to the persons or charities in the cash amount stated in words (. . . . . . Dollars) and figures ($ . . . . . .) or of the property described. I SIGN IN EACH BOX USED. I WRITE THE WORDS "NOT USED" IN THE REMAINING BOXES. If I fail to sign opposite any gift, then no gift is made. If the person mentioned does not survive me or if the charity does not accept the gift, then no gift is made.

FULL NAME OF PERSON OR CHARITY TO RECEIVE GIFT. (Name only one. Please print.)	AMOUNT OF CASH GIFT OR DESCRIPTION OF PROPERTY.	SIGNATURE OF TESTATOR.
		....
FULL NAME OF PERSON OR CHARITY TO RECEIVE GIFT. (Name only one. Please print.)	AMOUNT OF CASH GIFT OR DESCRIPTION OF PROPERTY.	SIGNATURE OF TESTATOR.
		....
FULL NAME OF PERSON OR CHARITY TO RECEIVE GIFT. (Name only one. Please print.)	AMOUNT OF CASH GIFT OR DESCRIPTION OF PROPERTY.	SIGNATURE OF TESTATOR.
		....
FULL NAME OF PERSON OR CHARITY TO RECEIVE GIFT. (Name only one. Please print.)	AMOUNT OF CASH GIFT OR DESCRIPTION OF PROPERTY.	SIGNATURE OF TESTATOR.
		....
FULL NAME OF PERSON OR CHARITY TO RECEIVE GIFT. (Name only one. Please print.)	AMOUNT OF CASH GIFT OR DESCRIPTION OF PROPERTY.	SIGNATURE OF TESTATOR.
		....

(continued)

Exhibit 4.3 Wisconsin Basic Will—*continued*

2.3   ALL OTHER ASSETS (MY "RESIDUARY ESTATE"). I adopt only one Property Disposition Clause in this paragraph by writing my signature on the line next to the title of the Property Disposition Clause I wish to adopt. I SIGN ON ONLY ONE LINE. I WRITE THE WORDS "NOT USED" ON THE REMAINING LINE. If I sign on more than one line or if I fail to sign on any line, the property will go under Property Disposition Clause (b) and I realize that means the property will be distributed as if I did not make a will in accordance with Chapter 852 of the Wisconsin Statutes.

PROPERTY DISPOSITION CLAUSES *(Select one.)*

(a)   TO MY SPOUSE IF LIVING; IF NOT LIVING, THEN TO MY CHILDREN AND THE DESCENDANTS OF ANY DECEASED CHILD BY RIGHT OF REPRESENTATION.   ....

(b)   TO BE DISTRIBUTED AS IF I DID NOT HAVE A WILL.   ....

Article 3. Nominations of Personal Represenative and Guardian

3.1   PERSONAL REPRESENTATIVE. *(Name at least one.)*
I nominate the person or institution named in the first box of this paragraph to serve as my personal representative. If that person or institution does not serve, then I nominate the others to serve in the order I list them in the other boxes. I confer upon my personal representative the authority to do and perform any act which he or she determines is in the best interest of the estate, with no limitations. This provision shall be given the broadest possible construction. This authority includes, but is not limited to, the power to borrow money, pledge assets, vote stocks and participate in reorganizations, to sell or exchange real or personal property, and to invest funds and retain securities without any limitation by law for investments by fiduciaries.

FIRST PERSONAL REPRESENTATIVE

SECOND PERSONAL REPRESENTATIVE

THIRD PERSONAL REPRESENTATIVE

3.2   GUARDIAN. *(If you have a child under 18 years of age, you should name at least one guardian of the child.)*
If my spouse dies before I do or if for any other reason a guardian is needed for any child of mine, then I nominate the person named in the first box of this paragraph to serve as guardian of the person and estate of that child. If the person does not serve, then I nominate the person named in the second box of this paragraph to serve as guardian of that child.

FIRST GUARDIAN

SECOND GUARDIAN

Signature of Testator ....

(continued)

Exhibit 4.3 Wisconsin Basic Will—*continued*

3.3 BOND.
My signature in this box means I request that a bond, as set by law, be required for each individual personal representative or guardian named in this will. I DO NOT SIGN IN THIS BOX, I REQUEST THAT A BOND NOT BE REQUIRED FOR ANY OF THOSE PERSONS.

I sign my name to this Wisconsin Basic will on . . . . (date), at . . . . (city). . . . . (state).

. . . .
Signature of Testator

STATEMENT OF WITNESSES *(You must use two adult witnesses.)*

EACH OF US DECLARES THAT THE TESTATOR SIGNED THIS WISCONSIN BASIC WILL IN OUR PRESENCE, ALL OR US BEING PRESENT AT THE SAME TIME, AND WE NOW, AT THE TESTATOR'S REQUEST, IN THE TESTATOR'S PRESENCE AND IN THE PRESENCE OF EACH OTHER, SIGN BELOW AS WITNESSES, DECLARING THAT THE TESTATOR APPEARS TO BE OF SOUND MIND AND UNDER NO UNDUE INFLUENCE.

Signature . . . .   Residence Address: . . . .
Print Name
Here: . . . .

Signature . . . .   Residence Address: . . . .
Print Name
Here: . . . .

. . . .
Signature of Testator

Source: Wisconsin Legal Blank Co., Inc. Reprinted with permission.

Joint will
A will for spouses that consists of a single document signed by them as their will.

Mutual (reciprocal) wills
Separate and identical wills made by spouses that contain reciprocal provisions and agree that neither spouse will change his or her will after the death of the first spouse.

Living will
A document, separate from a will, that expresses a person's wish to be allowed to die a natural death and not be kept alive by artificial means.

4. Joint and mutual (reciprocal) wills. When one document is made the will of two persons (usually spouses) and is signed by them, a **joint will** is created. The joint will is probated twice—on the death of each spouse. **Mutual (reciprocal) wills** are usually the separate and identical wills of spouses who make reciprocal provisions in each will and agree that neither spouse will change his or her will after the death of the first spouse. Many problems are created by these two types of wills, especially if the spouses divorce or one dies and the other spouse remarries and decides to make a different will or wishes to revoke the original joint or mutual will. An additional problem is created for spouses with mutual wills. After the death of the first spouse, the problem emerges if the surviving spouse decides to make substantial gifts of their combined estate assets to other than those beneficiaries named in the mutual wills. This may not change the terms of the mutual will, but it most assuredly changes the distribution of the estate. Most attorneys do not recommend or use joint or mutual wills.

Living will. A **living will** is a separate legal document from the standard will. When the maker of a living will is no longer able to make decisions regarding her medical treatment, the living will governs withholding or withdrawal of life-sustaining treatment in the event of an incurable or irreversible condition which will cause death within a short time. For further discussion and an example of a living will, see Chapter 7.

Types of Dispositions—Gifts Made in a Will

A will's dispositions are the various ways property is conveyed by the will. Dispositions include gifts that are called bequests, legacies, or devises.

Bequest, Legacy, or Devise) UPC

According to traditional terminology, a bequest or legacy is a gift of personal property, and a devise is a gift of real property. When gifts are made by a will, they are called a specific legacy or a specific devise. In cases in which a testator has mistakenly used the wrong term in connection with the transfer of real or personal estate property, e.g., "I *bequeath* my home to my daughter, Sarah," or "I *devise* my books and paintings to my son, Benjamin," the courts have consistently upheld such gifts because of the unmistakable intention of the testator. Therefore, the terms can be used interchangeably or applied to either real or personal property if the context of the will clearly indicates that such was the testator's intent. The states that have adopted the UPC use one term, *devise,* to include the transfer of all gifts of real or personal property by will. The next paragraphs define and explain the categories of dispositions of a will: specific legacy, specific devise, demonstrative legacy, general legacy, and residuary legacy or devise.

Specific Legacy. A specific legacy (also called a specific bequest or, in states that have adopted the UPC, a specific devise) is a gift of a particular item or class of personal property in a will.

> **Examples:** In his will, John Williams states:
> 1. "I give my 2000 Buick to my daughter, Marilyn Williams, if she survives me."
> 2. "I give my gun and stamp collections to my son, Henry Williams, if he survives me."
> 3. "I give my grand piano and all my sheet music to my niece, Linda Anderson, if she survives me."

4. "I give one half of all of the rest of my tangible personal property, that has not other-wise been specifically mentioned heretofore in this will, to my spouse, Elizabeth Williams, if she survives me. If my said spouse, Elizabeth Williams, does not survive me, I give the above-mentioned property to my children, Marilyn Williams and Henry Williams, in equal shares." (This is an example of a gift of a class of property.)

A specific legacy is the only type of testamentary gift subject to ademption (see discussion below).

Specific Devise.   A specific devise is a gift of real property in a will. In states that have adopted the UPC, a specific devise includes a gift of real or personal property in a will.

Example: In his will, John Williams states: "I give my homestead at 4645 Fair Hills Lane, City of Bloomingdale, County of Nobles, State of Indiana, and legally de-scribed as "Lot 7, Block 4, of Hillstrom's Addition to Stone Valley" to my spouse, Eliz-abeth Williams, if she survives me. If she fails to survive me, I give the hereinbefore described homestead to my son, Henry Williams, if he survives me."

Demonstrative Legacy.   A demonstrative legacy is a gift of a specific monetary amount to be paid from the proceeds of the sale of a particular item of property or from some identifiable fund.

Examples: In his will, John Williams states:
1. "I give $2,000 to be paid from the *sale* of my U.S. savings bonds to my nephew, Daniel Anderson, if he survives me."
2. "I give $5,000 to be paid out of my savings account on deposit in First State Bank, 1204 Main Street, City of Redwood Falls, County of Morgan, State of Oregon, to my niece, Linda Anderson, if she survives me."

A demonstrative legacy differs from a specific legacy as follows: If the fund from which the demonstrative legacy is to be paid has diminished or is nonexistent when the testator dies, the payment can come out of other estate funds the same as a general legacy. A demonstrative legacy differs from a general legacy as fol-lows: It does not *abate,* i.e., it is not subject to unpaid debts as is a general legacy, but instead, is used to pay debts like a specific legacy (see discussion of abate-ment below).

Since demonstrative legacies are similar to both specific and general legacies, the distinction between them can be difficult and lead to confusion. Therefore, drafters seldom include demonstrative legacies in wills. The court in the case of *In re Jeffcott's Estate,* 186 So.2d 80 (Fla.App. 1966), identifies and distinguishes general and demonstrative legacies.

General Legacy.   A general legacy (also called a pecuniary bequest) is a gift of a fixed amount of money from the general assets of the testator's estate or an amount of money derived from a source established in the estate by a calculated formula.

Examples: In his will, John Williams states:
1. "I give the sum of $20,000 to my niece, Linda Anderson, if she survives me."
2. "I give one-half of all the value of the stock I own at the time of my death to my daughter, Marilyn Williams, if she survives me." (Calculations are necessary to de-termine the actual amount Marilyn will receive.)

Residuary Legacy or Devise. A gift of all the testator's personal property not otherwise effectively disposed of by a will is a residuary legacy, and a gift of all the real property not disposed of is a residuary devise.

A residuary clause distributes the remaining assets (the residue) of the decedent-testator's estate after all other gifts in the will have been distributed. A residuary clause is the most important clause in a will because it generally passes the bulk of the decedent's estate after the payment of debts, taxes, and costs of administration and the distribution of specific, demonstrative, and general legacies. It is essential that every will include a residuary clause; otherwise all remaining assets, whether inadvertently overlooked, omitted, forgotten, or acquired after execution of the current will, pass through intestate succession statutes. Clearly, this would not reflect the intent of the will's maker since it defeats the will's purpose.

> **Example:** In his will, John Williams states: "I give all the rest, residue, and remainder of my estate, including all real and personal property wherever located that is not previously disposed of by this will, to my wife, Elizabeth Williams, if she survives me. If she does not survive me, I give this, my residuary estate, to my children, Marilyn Williams and Henry Williams, in equal shares."

If the decedent does not include any specific, demonstrative, or general legacies in the will, a gift by John Williams that states "I give all my real and personal property to my daughter, Marilyn Williams" acts as a residuary clause.

If any beneficiaries of the will, especially those named in the residuary clause, predecease the testator, the will should be reviewed and new or successor beneficiaries added to avoid passage of the property through intestate succession. These changes, even if minor, can best be accomplished by the creation of a new will using word-processing computer software.

Another important function of the residuary clause is that after any intestate property of the decedent, it serves as the next, and generally the major, source of payment of the decedent's debts, death taxes, and funeral, burial, and administration expenses. If property (funds) from the residue is insufficient to pay these debts and taxes, other gifts in the will are used to satisfy these obligations (see Abatement below).

Ademption, Lapses, and Abatement

The gifts (legacies or devises) distributed by will can be affected by ademption, lapses, and abatement.

Ademption. Whether a legacy, bequest, or devise, gifts of property made in a will may not be available for transfer to the named beneficiaries or devisees because the testator no longer owns the property at the time of death. After execution of the will, the testator, by an intentional act of **ademption,** has the right to:

- revoke or cancel any testamentary gift;
- deliver the gift to the beneficiary or someone else before the testator's death; or
- substitute a different gift for the original one.

As a result, the beneficiary or devisee does not receive the original gift through the will, and other property of the estate passes to the beneficiary or devisee as a substitute for the **adeemed** gift, *only if* the testator so indicated in the will or

Ademption
The intentional act of the testator, while alive, to revoke, recall, or cancel a gift made through the will or deliver the gift or a substitute to the beneficiary.

Adeem
To take away, extinguish, revoke, or satisfy a legacy or devise by delivery of the gift or a substitute to the beneficiary by the testator before death.

delivered the substitute gift before death. Of the three types of legacies, only the specific legacy is subject to ademption; however, in some states, a specific devise can be adeemed if the intention is expressed by the testator in writing as required by a state statute.

Ademption can occur by extinction or by satisfaction. Ademption by extinction occurs when the property is either nonexistent (destroyed by storm, fire, and the like) at the time of the testator's death or is given or sold by the testator to someone other than the person named in the will.

Examples:

1. In her will, Elizabeth leaves Arnold her champion thoroughbred racehorse, Secretary. Secretary dies before Elizabeth. The gift of the horse is "adeemed" by extinction.
2. In her will, Elizabeth leaves Arnold the horse, but she sells or gives the horse to another person before she dies. Again, the gift of the horse is "adeemed" by extinction.

See *Shriner's Hospital v. Stahl,* 610 S.W.2d 147 (Tex. 1980), in which the court ruled that a specific devise of property was "adeemed" when the testatrix sold the property before her death, and the proceeds of the sale passed under the residuary clause of her will.

Ademption by satisfaction occurs when the testator, while living, gives the gift in the will to the named beneficiary with the stated intent in writing that the gift will not be replaced with a substitute or additional gift.

Example: In her will, Elizabeth leaves Benedict her Renoir painting. Elizabeth decides to give Benedict the painting on his birthday. When she delivers the painting to him, Elizabeth adeems the specific legacy by satisfaction.

Lapse
Failure to distribute a gift in a will because the beneficiary or devisee dies before the testator.

Lapses.   A **lapse** is the failure to pass or distribute a gift in a will because the beneficiary or devisee dies before the testator. The beneficiary's death causes the gift in the will to lapse or fail and fall into the residue of the estate *unless* the will designates an alternate beneficiary or a statute provides for the gift's distribution. Such a state statute, called an **antilapse statute,** passes the gift to the decedent beneficiary's children or heirs who survive the testator. The antilapse statutes of Illinois, Mississippi, and Texas only pass the gift to the decedent beneficiary's heirs if the beneficiary is the child of the testator. Most states' antilapse statutes have expanded the eligible heirs who can receive the gift, but no state includes, as an heir, the spouse of the decedent beneficiary. If a testator wants to avoid the application of an antilapse statute, the words in the following clause accomplish that objective:

Antilapse statute
A statute that prevents a lapse (termination) of a clause in a will which would otherwise occur if the beneficiary who was to receive property under the clause dies before the testator.

"I give my Picasso painting to my daughter, Irene Benson, if she shall survive me."

If Irene dies before the testator, an antilapse statute would not apply for the benefit of Irene's children or heirs because of the above clause. Instead, the Picasso painting becomes part of the residue of the estate and is passed to the persons named as beneficiaries in the residuary clause of the will.

On the other hand, if the testator wants a successor to receive the gift if the beneficiary predeceases the testator, the clause would state:

". . . to Irene Benson, if she shall survive me, if she does not survive me, to my son, Howard Benson, if he shall survive me."

Abatement.   **Abatement** is the proportional reduction of the legacies and de-vises in a will because of inadequate available funds from the assets of the tes-tator's estate. Abatement determines the order in which gifts (legacies and de-vises) made by the testator in the will shall be applied to the payment of the decedent-testator's debts, taxes, and expenses. If required, such payments can and most assuredly will cause the gifts made in the will to be reduced or even eliminated. Abatement occurs whenever there are insufficient assets in the tes-tator's estate to pay all the death taxes, funeral, burial, and administration ex-penses, and other creditors' claims that must be paid before the remaining es-tate is distributed to beneficiaries and devisees. State statutes list the order in which the various assets and categories of gifts (legacies and devises) are used to pay these debts and taxes. Usually, the order is: first, any intestate property not disposed of by the will; second, residuary assets (legacies and devises); third, general legacies and devises; fourth, demonstrative legacies; and last, specific legacies and devises.

> **Example:** In the examples earlier in this chapter, John Williams made specific legacies (his car, gun and stamp collections, piano and sheet music, and all of the rest of his tangible personal property); a specific devise (his home); demonstra-tive legacies (sums of money from the sale of bonds or from an identifiable fund); general legacies (cash and money from a calculated source); and a final residuary gift. John dies. Before any of the property listed in the will can be distributed, John's debts, expenses, and taxes due must be paid. The gifts made in the will, with the exception of the homestead, are used according to the priority order of payment listed in the preceding paragraph.

This arrangement or ranking of testamentary gifts into a certain order to be used for the payment of debts is called **marshaling of assets** of the estate, and the assets used for payment are said to "abate." Generally, personal property is the source of the funds used to pay debts and taxes, but, if necessary, real property must be devested from devisees or heirs by the personal representa-tive and sold to pay the decedent's creditors. In a few states, the decedent's personal property in all categories must be used first before any real property is used to pay debts and taxes due (see Mass. Gen. Laws Ann. ch. 202 § 1). Other states only require that all personal property in each category be used for payments prior to the use of real property within the category (see Tex. Prob. Code Ann. § 322B). Today, the prevailing trend is to use gifts of real and personal property within the same category equally; see Cal. Prob. Code § 10000; N.Y. EPTL § 13-1.3(b); and UPC § 3-902. When property within each category "abates" to pay decedent's debts, the gifts are used for payment on a *prorated basis.*

> **Example:** Sydney makes the following testamentary gifts: $2,000 cash to Rita, a homestead valued at $45,000 to Ralph, and the residue (valued at $8,000) to Peter. Expenses, debts, and taxes amount to $12,000. The residue assets would first be applied to payment of expenses, debts, and taxes. Thus, Peter would lose all his $8,000. Second, the general gift, i.e., the sum of money left to Rita ($2,000) would be applied. Rita would lose all her $2,000. Third, Ralph would be required to pay the remaining deficiency of $2,000, or, depending on the state, the home-stead may have to be sold and $2,000 of the proceeds of the sale used to pay the deficiency. Ralph would get the remainder of the proceeds of the sale. If a spouse

Abatement
The process that determines the order in which gifts made by the testator in the will shall be applied to the payment of the decedent-testator's debts, taxes, and expenses.

Marshaling of assets
The arrangement or ranking of testamentary gifts into a certain order to be used for the payment of debts.

survives the decedent, however, the spouse will receive the statutory (elective) share of the decedent's estate before any of the other named devisees receive their gifts through the will.

Example: Oscar dies and leaves an estate valued at $175,000. It consists of a homestead owned in his name valued at $100,000, $30,000 in cash in a savings account, $30,000 in stocks and bonds, and $15,000 in household furnishings. Oscar leaves his home and $10,000 in cash to his spouse, Evelyn. He leaves $10,000 in cash to his nephew, Phil, and $10,000 to his niece, Trudy. His administration and funeral expenses, death taxes, and creditors' claims (debts) amount to $60,000. Since these obligations must be paid first (have priority), only $115,000 remains to be distributed among the named beneficiaries and devisees.

In the example above, because insufficient assets remain in the estate to distribute them as Oscar intended, the domiciliary state statute on abatement determines which beneficiaries or devisees lose their gifts. If Oscar's estate is probated in New Jersey, it would have to adhere to the New Jersey abatement statute. This statute is similar to other state laws that determine the order of payment when the decedent's assets are insufficient:

N.J. Stat. Ann. § 3B: 22-3 Abatement for Purpose of Paying Claims and Debts
Except as otherwise provided in a decedent's will, the property of a decedent's estate shall abate for the purposes of paying debts and claims, without any preference or priority as between real and personal property, in the following order:
a. Property passing by intestacy;
b. Residuary devises;
c. General devises; and
d. Specific devises.

USE OF TESTATE TERMINOLOGY

To better understand the meaning and usage of the terms discussed above, read the following facts and the will in Exhibit 4.4.

The Facts

Sheila M. Swanson has a will. In the will, she leaves a fur coat and her other clothing to a sister, Myrtle Jones. Sheila also gives $20,000 to each of her children living at her death. To a cousin, John Stewart, Sheila leaves her one acre of land in Northern County. The sum of $100,000 is left in trust for her surviving grandchildren, to be administered by Glen Howard of the Fullservice Bank. The rest of her estate is given to her husband, Frank, but if he does not survive her, then her surviving children receive the property in equal shares. In the event that Sheila and her husband die in a common accident before her children are adults, she nominates her sister, Myrtle, to be their guardian. Viola Larson is named personal representative to manage and distribute the estate according to the will, which is signed and witnessed by Charles Larson and Althea Gibbons.

| | **Exhibit 4.4** Last Will and Testament of Sheila M. Swanson |

I, Sheila M. Swanson, of the City of Winslow, in the County of Northern, and State of Maine, being of sound mind and memory, and not acting under duress, menace, fraud, or undue influence of any person whatsoever, do make, publish, and declare this instrument to be my Last Will and Testament. I do hereby cancel, revoke, and annul all former wills and testaments or codicils made by me.

First: I direct that all my valid debts, last illness, funeral, burial, and estate administration expenses be paid out of my estate as soon as possible after my death;

[Specific legacy]
Second: I give my fur coat and all other personal clothing to my sister, Myrtle Jones;

[Specific devise]
Third: I give my one acre of land with the following legal description, "Lot 1, Block 4, Brauer Addition," located in Northern County to my cousin, John Stewart, and his heirs;

[General legacy]
Fourth: I give $20,000 to each of my children living at my death;

[Demonstrative legacy]
Fifth: I give $100,000 from the sale of my Picasso painting entitled "Self Portrait" to Glen Howard of the Fullservice Bank to hold in trust for the benefit of my grandchildren. See attached testamentary trust.

[Residuary legacy or devise]
Sixth: All the rest, residue, and remainder of my estate, real, personal, or mixed of any kind, and wherever located, of which I die possessed or to which I am entitled at the time of my death, I give to my husband, Frank, if he survives me, and if he does not survive me, or we die in a common accident, I give this, my residuary estate, to my children that survive me in equal shares;

Seventh: In the event of a common accident in which both my husband and I die, I nominate and appoint my sister, Myrtle Jones, to be the personal and property guardian over any of my minor children living at the time of our deaths;

Eighth: Finally. I nominate and appoint Viola Larson to be the personal representative of this my last will and testament and direct that she not be required to give any bond or security for the proper discharge of her duties.

IN TESTIMONY WHEREOF I hereunto set my hand on this *10th* day of *March, 2001.*

[Signature] *Sheila M. Swanson*
[Address] *11712 Sundown Avenue*

The foregoing instrument, consisting of two pages, including this page, was, on the date hereof, signed, published, and declared by Sheila M. Swanson, the testatrix above named, at the City of Winslow, County of Northern, State of Maine as and for her last will and testament, in our presence, who, in her presence, at her request, and in the presence of each other hereunto set our names as witnesses.

Names	Addresses
Althea Gibbons	*4656 Gaywood Drive*
Witness	
Charles Larson	*401 Elm Street*
Witness	
	[*Signed by two witnesses*]

Review of Terminology

Since Sheila Swanson has a will, on her death, she will die *testate*. For her will to have validity, it must be *executed* carefully to comply with the requirements of state statutes which establish *testate succession*. The fact that Mr. Larson and Ms. Gibbons are required to *attest* and *subscribe* the will is an example of such statutory control.

Sheila Swanson, the *testatrix,* can change her mind and dispose of her estate prior to death in any manner she chooses. She also retains the option to cancel or destroy the will and either substitute a new will in its place or decide not to make a new will, in which event she would die *intestate.*

The *beneficiaries* in her will are Sheila's children and grandchildren living at her death, her sister Myrtle, cousin John, and husband Frank; these are the persons to whom she intends to leave her estate. Before any of the assets pass to these recipients, the will must be *probated,* i.e., declared by a *probate court* to be a valid testamentary disposition. This procedure for approval of a will and *estate administration* is discussed in detail in later chapters.

The following discussion illustrates the use of both orthodox and UPC terminology. The first term listed is the orthodox term; the corresponding UPC term, if different, is placed in parentheses (review Exhibit 4.1).

Distribution of Sheila's one acre of land is a *specific devise,* a gift of real property by will, and its taker, cousin John, is a *devisee* (or *successor*). Sheila devised the land to him. The $20,000 to be received by each of Sheila's surviving children, a gift of money, is a *general legacy (devise)*. Sheila's children are *legatees* (*devisees* or *successors*) of the money. Since she receives personal property under the will, Myrtle is a *beneficiary* (*devisee* or *successor*), but distribution of the fur coat and other clothing to her, since it is not money, is known as a *specific legacy* or *specific bequest (devise)*. Sheila bequeathed (devised) the clothing to her. Although it is important to keep the latter distinction in mind, in modern practice the terms *bequest* and *legacy* are used interchangeably. Generally, if orthodox terms such as "bequeath" or "bequest" are used in a will, they stand for a gift of any personal property, including money. In preparing wills today, however, most attorneys prefer to use the phrase "I give" in place of the words "I bequeath" or "I devise."

The $100,000 earmarked for the grandchildren is a *demonstrative legacy (devise)* which constitutes a *testamentary trust* (i.e., a trust created by will) and Glen Howard of the bank is its administrator, the *trustee*. Since Viola Larson has been named to manage the estate, she is its *executrix (personal representative)*. Had Viola's husband, Charles, been given the responsibility instead, he would be the *executor (personal representative)* of the estate. Sheila's sister, Myrtle, has a role beyond that of a *beneficiary (successor)*. As the person designated to care for the testatrix's minor children at her death, if Sheila's husband, Frank, is also deceased, Myrtle is a *guardian* for Sheila's children.

ASSIGNMENT 4.1

Read the following will, then answer the questions at the end.

LAST WILL AND TESTAMENT OF JOHN L. JONES

I, John L. Jones, of the City of Burnsville, in the County of Denton and State of Utah, being of sound and disposing mind and memory, and not acting under duress, menace, fraud, or undue influence of any person whatsoever, do make, publish, and declare this instrument to be my Last Will and Testament. I do hereby cancel, revoke, and annul all former wills and testaments or codicils made by me at any time.

First: I direct that all my just debts, last illness, funeral, burial, and estate administration expenses be paid out of my estate as soon as possible after my death.

Second: I give to my son, James, my diamond ring and all my other personal jewelry.

Third: I give to my son, James, the sum of five thousand dollars.

Fourth: All the rest, residue and remainder of my estate, real, personal, or mixed, of whatsoever character and wheresoever situated, of which I die seized or possessed or to which I am in any way entitled at the time of my death, I give to my wife, Mary, if she survives me, and if my said wife is not living at the time of my death or we both should die in a common accident, I give this my residuary estate to my son, James.

Fifth: I nominate and appoint Bill Brown to be the personal representative of this my last Will and Testament, and I direct that my said personal representative shall not be required to give any bond or security for the proper discharge of his duties.

IN TESTIMONY WHEREOF I hereunto set my hand on this *15th* day of *June, 2001*.

[*Signature*] _____ *John L. Jones* _____

[*Address*] _____ *798 Village Drive* _____

The foregoing instrument, consisting of two pages, including this page, was, on the date hereof, signed, published, and declared by JOHN L. JONES, the testator above named, at the City of Burnsville, County of Denton. State of Utah, as and for his Last Will and Testament, in our presence, who, in his presence, at his request, and in the presence of each other have hereunto set our names as witnesses.

Harry W. Potter	*1054 South Shore Drive*
Elizabeth B. Brown	*917 Hillcrest Street*

[*Signed by two witnesses*]

---

1. Who is the testator?
2. Is there a testatrix?
3. Did John Jones die testate or intestate?
4. Does the document name a guardian or trustee?
5. Is the document a will or a codicil?
6. What is the diamond ring given to James called according to the UPC?
7. Is a devisee named in the will?
8. Who are the beneficiaries named in the will?
9. Who is the personal representative?
10. Is there an executrix?

11. Does the document contain a testamentary trust?
12. Has the will been attested and subscribed?
13. Is this an example of a nuncupative or holographic will?
14. How many witnesses are required to sign this will according to your state statute?

DEATH WITHOUT A WILL—INTESTACY

A person who dies without a will dies intestate. He or she is called the intestate. In all states, the distribution of an intestate's estate is determined by state law called the intestate succession statute. Such statutes, in effect, write the will the decedent failed to make and determine the distribution of the intestate's property to the heirs. Each state has its own specific statutes and court decisions that cover and control intestacy. These laws and decisions vary substantially from state to state and identify the heirs, rights of family members, guardianship of minor children, procedures and rules for the administration of the estate, appointment of the personal representative or administrator, and the disposition of the estate property to the surviving spouse and blood relatives of the intestate. The controlling statutes are those of the state in which the intestate had her domicile *and* the states where any *real property* is located.

> **Example:** Sandra lives in Nebraska where she owns a house, is registered to vote, has her driver's license, and pays state income tax. Collectively, these factors determine that Nebraska is Sandra's true legal home—her domicile. She also owns real property in other states, i.e., a cottage in Wisconsin and a condominium in Florida. If Sandra dies intestate, Nebraska's statutes will determine how and by whom her house and personal property will be inherited; however, Wisconsin's statutes will decide who receives the cottage, and Florida's law, the condominium.

Through study, research, and experience, you must become knowledgeable of your state's intestate statute so that you can accurately explain and apply its provisions to the estate of the deceased.

Terminology Related to Intestacy

The following terms are associated with the persons and proceedings involved in the law of intestate succession:

- *Kindred.* Kindred refers to persons related to one another by blood. The persons are also referred to as kin or next of kin.
- *Consanguinity.* Consanguinity refers to persons who are related by blood through a common ancestor.

> **Example:** A child, grandchild, grandparent, aunt, uncle, and cousin are related to the decedent through a common ancestor and are kindred. Janice Rule is the granddaughter of Elliot Sanderson. She is related to her grandfather by consanguinity (blood) and is his kin.

- *Affinity.* Affinity refers to persons who are related by marriage. They include stepchildren, father- or mother-in-law, and brother- or sister-in-law. Since only blood relatives can inherit from the intestate's estate, none of the individuals related by affinity (except for a surviving spouse) can inherit from the intestate under the laws of intestate succession.

Exhibit 4.5 Examples of Lineal Ascendants and Descendants

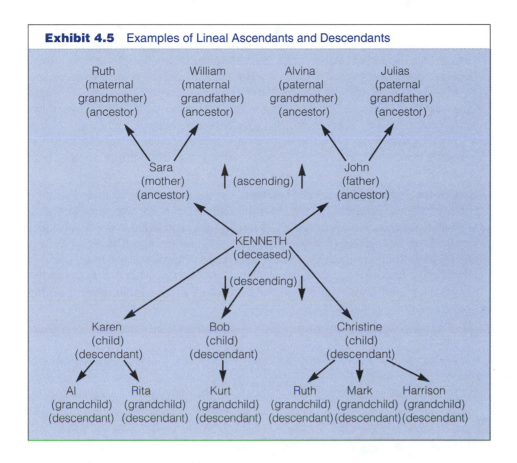

Example: In Exhibit 4.7, Nathan's wife, Ann, is related to Joe by affinity. She cannot inherit from Joe under intestate succession laws. The decedent and the person related to him by affinity have no common blood ancestor. This rule, of course, does not apply to the spouse of the decedent even though husband and wife are usually related solely by marriage (by affinity).

- *Ascendant or ancestor.* An ascendant or ancestor is a claimant to an intestate's share who is related to the decedent in an ascending lineal or collateral blood line.

Example: The parent of a decedent is a lineal ancestor. The sister of a decedent is a collateral relative.

- *Descendant.* A descendant is a claimant to an intestate's share who is related to the decedent in a descending lineal or collateral blood line.

Example: The child of a decedent is a lineal descendant. A niece is a collateral descendant.

- *Lineal.* As a noun, a lineal is an heir or relative related to an intestate decedent in a direct line either upward in an ascending bloodline (e.g., parents, grandparents, or great-grandparents) or downward in a descending bloodline (e.g., children, grandchildren, or great-grandchildren). See Exhibits 4.5, 4.7, and 4.9. Lineal consanguinity exists between persons when one is descended (or ascended) in a direct line from the other, e.g., a father to a son or daughter.

- *Collateral.* As a noun, in intestate terminology, a collateral is an heir or relative, not in a direct line of lineal ascent or descent, who traces a kinship relationship to an intestate decedent through a common ancestor (e.g., brothers, sisters, aunts, uncles, nieces, nephews, cousins, and other such relatives), forming a collateral line of relationship (see Exhibits 4.6, 4.7, and 4.9). Collateral consanguinity exists between persons who have the same ancestors, but who do not descend or ascend from each other, e.g., brother, uncle, or nephew.
- *Half blood.* Half blood is the degree of relationship that exists between persons who have the same mother or the same father in common, but not both parents.

Example: Paul and Mark are half brothers. They are related to each other through only one common ancestor, i.e., they have the same father but not the same mother. Most state statutes, including the UPC § 2–107, allow half blood and whole blood kindred to receive an equal share of the intestate's estate (see Cal. Prob. Code § 6406; Iowa Code Ann. § 633.219; Mass. Gen. Laws Ann. ch. 190 § 4; Mich. Comp. Laws Ann. § 700.2107; N.J. Stat. Ann. § 3B: 5–7; and N.Y. EPTL § 4–1.1[b]). Other states give the half blood kindred only half as much as a whole blood (see Fla. Stat. Ann. § 732.105 and Va. Code Ann. § 64.1–2).

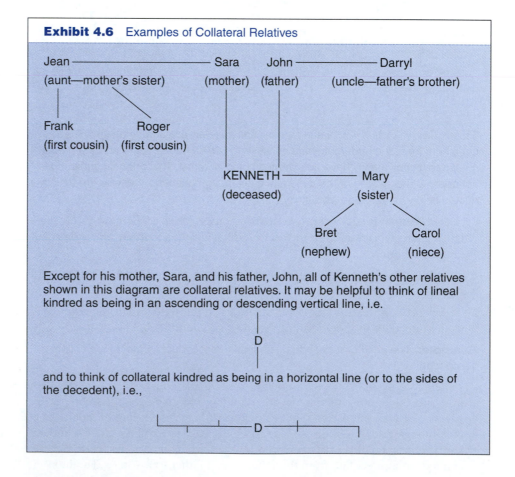

Exhibit 4.6 Examples of Collateral Relatives

Except for his mother, Sara, and his father, John, all of Kenneth's other relatives shown in this diagram are collateral relatives. It may be helpful to think of lineal kindred as being in an ascending or descending vertical line, i.e.

and to think of collateral kindred as being in a horizontal line (or to the sides of the decedent), i.e.,

Intestate Succession Laws

Each state has enacted its own intestate succession statute. These statutes vary considerably from state to state. They provide rules for descent and determine distribution of the probate property of the decedent. An important distinction exists, however, between real and personal property that involves the application of the intestate succession statute. Generally, the law of the intestate's domiciliary state determines the inheritance of personal property regardless of where the property is located. On the other hand, real estate passes according to the intestate succession statute of the state where the real property is located.

Example: Rosa Sanchez owns a house in South Dakota, her domiciliary state, and a cottage in Minnesota. She has furniture in both the home and the cottage and

Exhibit 4.7   Examples of Lineal and Collateral Relationships

Joe's three children are in his direct line—also called descending lineal bloodline.

Joe's lineal ancestors are his mother and father. Joe's sister, Brenda, and her children, Fran (niece) and Larry (nephew), are Joe's collateral kindred.

Nathan, Joe's uncle, is Joe's collateral kin. Nathan's wife, Ann, is not a direct lineal or collateral relative, i.e., she is not related to Joe *by blood*.

Nathan, Joe's uncle, has two children, Susan and Sally, who are Joe and Brenda's first cousins (see Exhibit 4.9) and are collateral kindred.

Sam is the son of Joe's great-grandparents and is Joe's great uncle who has two children, Mary and Sue. They are Joe's first cousins once removed (see Exhibit 4.9). Sam, Mary, and Sue are collateral kindred. Sam's wife, Shirley, is not a collateral relative. She is not related to Joe by blood.

savings accounts in banks in both states. If Rosa dies intestate, the intestate succession statute of South Dakota will determine the recipients of her house and all of her personal property, including her furniture and savings account in Minnesota. The real property in Minnesota—the cottage—however, will pass to the recipient according to Minnesota's intestate succession law.

Nonprobate property, such as property held in joint tenancy and tenancy by the entirety, is affected neither by a will nor by intestate succession statutes but instead passes automatically, due to the right of survivorship, to the surviving co-owners.

Some of the terms used in intestate statutes to identify heirs and methods of distributing the intestate's property include "issue," "per capita," "per stirpes," and distribution "by representation." The term "issue" refers to all of the lineal descendants from a common ancestor. The law of intestate succession rests on these basic principles:

1. The intestate's property passes first to the surviving spouse who is entitled to his or her intestate share; then, issue (children and other blood relatives) receive the remaining estate.

2. The intestate's property does not pass to all members of the class of persons defined as "issue" but only to persons closest in line to the intestate, e.g., generally children take before grandchildren and parents before grandparents.

3. The heirs can only be persons who survive the intestate; they must be living at the time of the intestate's death. A deceased person's "estate" cannot be an heir. Thus, if an intestate's child dies before the intestate, neither the child nor the child's estate is an heir. However, the deceased child's children living at the time of the intestate's death would be heirs. See the discussion and examples below.

An intestate's estate is distributed by one of two statutory methods: *per capita distribution* or *per stirpes distribution*.

Per Capita Distribution

Per capita distribution

The method of dividing an intestate estate and giving an equal share to a number of individuals without the right of representation.

"Per capita" means "equal to each person" or "by the heads." **Per capita distribution** is a method of dividing an intestate estate by giving an equal share to a number of persons all of whom are related to the decedent in the same degree of relationship (same-generation ascendants or descendants).

Example: Howard dies intestate. Since his wife predeceased him, his only heirs are his children, Betty, Sue, and Joe. The three children receive equal shares in Howard's estate per capita.

Per capita

Howard (decedent)

Betty — Sue — Joe

1/3   1/3   1/3

Example: Continuing with the above case, suppose not all of the heirs are of the same generation because one or more heirs in a class (generation) has predeceased Howard. Consequently, each living "head" of a descendant's line takes equally, per capita. For example, suppose Betty dies before Howard and has two surviving children, Bob and Sally, Howard's grandchildren. Per capita distribution in this case would be determined by counting the number of heirs that "head" each descendant's line (since Betty is dead, Bob and Sally "head" her line; Sue and Joe "head" their lines); therefore, there are four (4) heirs, and each would receive an equal one-fourth of Howard's estate per capita.

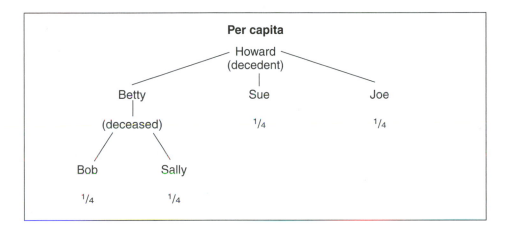

Right of Representation

When Betty died and was survived by her two children, Bob and Sally, the principle of **right of representation** gives Betty's children, Bob and Sally, the share in Howard's estate that Betty would have taken if she had survived Howard. All states allow distribution by right of representation, although some states limit it among collateral heirs, see and compare UPC § 2-103.

Per Stirpes Distribution

Per stirpes distribution means to take by class or by right of representation. Using the principle of right of representation, per stirpes distribution is the method of dividing an intestate estate wherein a class or group of heirs takes the share to which their deceased parent would have been entitled had he or she lived; thus, the heirs take by their right of representing their ancestor (parent) and not as so many individuals. A majority of the states employ this method. In per stirpes distribution, the heirs are related to the intestate in different degrees of relationship (intergenerational ascendants or descendants) with some heirs having predeceased the intestate. The descendants of such persons receive their shares through the predeceased heir by representation. Using the per stirpes method, the intestate's estate is divided into as many equal shares as the decedent has children (1) who are living or (2) who are already dead but have living descendants. The living children of any deceased parent take their parent's share per stirpes, by right of representation.

Example: Returning to the previous example, a per stirpes distribution would be as follows:

Right of representation
The right of a child to receive the share of an intestate's property the child's deceased parent would have received if the parent was still living.

Per stirpes distribution
A distribution of property that depends on the relationship to the intestate of those entitled to the estate. Distribution by representation.

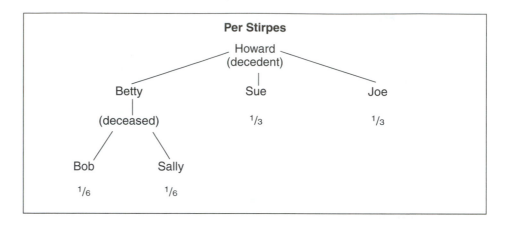

Per Stirpes

Method: Divide the estate into equal shares based on the living children and the children who have died but have living descendants. There are three (3) shares. Thus, Sue and Joe each receive one-third of the estate, and Bob and Sally receive their mother's (Betty's) one-third share equally by right of representation. Bob and Sally each receive a one-sixth share.

An example of a statute regulating per capita and per stirpes rights to an intestate's estate is Idaho Code § 15-2-103 on the share of heirs other than a surviving spouse:

The part of the intestate estate not passing to the surviving spouse under section 15-2-102 of this part, or the entire intestate estate if there is no surviving spouse, passes as follows:

(a) To the issue of the decedent; if they are all of the same degree of kinship to the decedent they take equally [per capita], but if of unequal degree, then those of more remote degree take by representation [per stirpes].

Example: Mary, a widow, has three children—Jim, Nora, and Kathryn. Jim is married and has two children—Matt and Colleen. Nora is single. Kathryn also was married and had three children—Charles, Darlene, and Elaine. Kathryn died two years ago. Now Mary dies. (Refer to Exhibit 4.8). If Mary dies intestate, leaving an estate valued at $225,000 after payment of debts, taxes, and all other expenses, and her only surviving relatives are two of her three adult children and her five grandchildren (three of whom are the children of her deceased daughter, Kathryn), her estate would be distributed according to the Idaho statute as follows:

- $75,000 to Jim (son) per capita—a one-third interest.
- $75,000 to Nora (daughter) per capita—a one-third interest.
- $25,000 to Charles (grandchild) per stirpes—a one-ninth interest.
- $25,000 to Darlene (grandchild) per stirpes—a one-ninth interest.
- $25,000 to Elaine (grandchild) per stirpes—a one-ninth interest.

If Kathryn had been alive at her mother's death, she would have taken a per capita share of $75,000 (one-third of the total estate). Since Kathryn died before her mother, Kathryn's children receive her share per stirpes (by right of representation), i.e., they "represent" their mother. This means Kathryn's share is divided equally among her children and each child receives a third of their mother's share. The other two grandchildren of the decedent receive nothing because their father, Jim, who was the son of the decedent, Mary, survived his mother. If Mary had died with

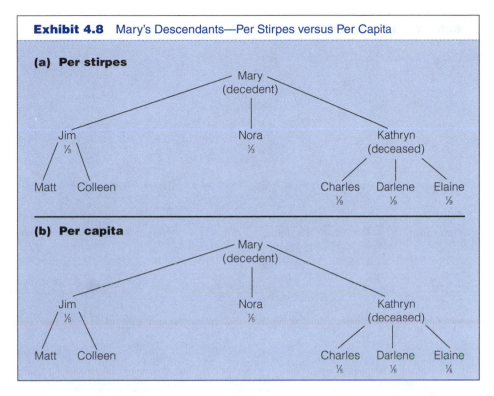

Exhibit 4.8   Mary's Descendants—Per Stirpes versus Per Capita

a will and left her estate to her then living children and to the issue of any deceased child of hers per capita, then Mary's estate would be distributed as follows: Jim, Nora, Charles, Darlene, and Elaine would each receive $45,000. See Exhibit 4.8.

Degree of Relationship

The **degree of relationship** is a method of determining which **collateral relatives** or heirs will inherit from an intestate with the use of a **degrees of kindred** genealogy chart (see Exhibit 4.9). When a person dies intestate, most state statutes and the UPC pass the decedent's estate in the following order:

1. First to a surviving spouse and lineal descendants (children), but if none, then to:

2. Other lineal descendants such as grandchildren or great-grandchildren, but if none, then to:

3. Lineal ascendants (ancestors) such as parents or grandparents, but if none, then to:

4. Collateral relatives who are lineal descendants of the decedent's parents such as brothers and sisters and their children who come before aunts, uncles, and cousins, and whose degree of relationship determines their inheritance rights.

5. Other next of kin, blood relatives of the decedent.

6. If there are none of the above, the decedent's property passes to the state by escheat, the right of the state to title of an intestate's property when no spouse or kindred survive the intestate. Reminder: Real property would pass by escheat to the state in which the real property is located.

To determine which collateral heirs receive the intestate's property to the exclusion of other collateral heirs, it is often necessary to ascertain the degree of

Degree of relationship
A method of determining which collateral relatives or heirs will inherit from an intestate.

Collateral heirs (relatives)
Heirs who do not ascend or descend from each other but descend from the same ancestor, e.g., sisters, aunts, nephews, cousins.

Degrees of kindred
The relationship between a decedent and his or her survivors which governs descent and distribution. A genealogy chart.

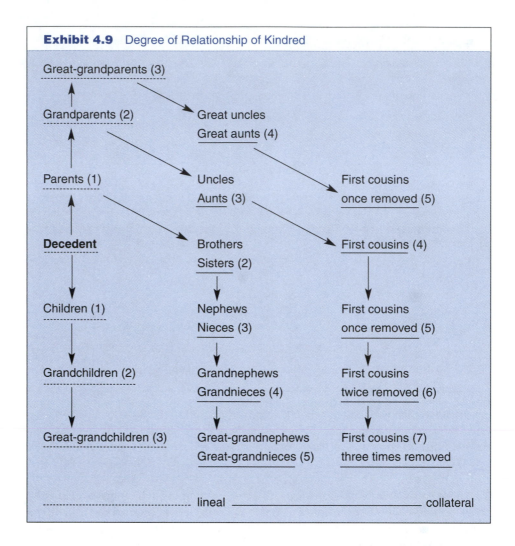

Exhibit 4.9   Degree of Relationship of Kindred

Great-grandparents (3)

Grandparents (2)   Great uncles
Great aunts (4)

Parents (1)   Uncles   First cousins
Aunts (3)   once removed (5)

Decedent   Brothers   First cousins (4)
Sisters (2)

Children (1)   Nephews   First cousins
Nieces (3)   once removed (5)

Grandchildren (2)   Grandnephews   First cousins
Grandnieces (4)   twice removed (6)

Great-grandchildren (3)   Great-grandnephews   First cousins (7)
Great-grandnieces (5)   three times removed

lineal   collateral

relationship between the decedent and the particular collateral heirs in question, i.e., which relative is most closely related to the decedent by blood. Most states and the UPC limit collateral heirs to the next of kin, i.e., to the collateral relatives of the decedent who are lineal descendants of the decedent's grandparents. These potential heirs are determined according to either the civil law or the common law as follows:

- *Civil law computation.* Obtain a genealogy (degrees of kindred) chart. See Exhibit 4.9. The chart illustrates the summary history of a family and assigns a degree of relationship number to each relative of the decedent to show how closely the persons listed are related to each other. Each degree (number) represents one generation, e.g., parents are related to the decedent in the first degree, grandparents in the second degree, etc. Under the civil law method, the degree of relationship of a relative is calculated by first counting up from the decedent-intestate to the *closest common ancestor* to both the decedent and the possible *heir,* and then counting down to the heir (see Exhibit 4.9). When counting, the decedent is excluded, and the possible heir is included. See Ga. Code Ann. § 53-2-1.

Example: Using Exhibit 4.9 to determine the degree of relationship of a grand-nephew, Jeffrey, to the decedent-intestate, Marilyn, count up to her parents (1), the closest common ancestor to both Marilyn and Jeffrey, and then down through brothers and sisters (2) and nephews and nieces (3), to Jeffrey, the grandnephew (4). Thus, the grandnephew, Jeffrey, is related to the decedent in the fourth degree.

Similarly, Marilyn's first cousin, Lisa, is also related in the fourth degree, i.e., parents (1), grandparents (2), uncles and aunts (3), to first cousins (4).

In states that follow the civil law computation, the collateral heir who is related to the decedent-intestate in the lowest degree (smallest number) receives the property to the exclusion of the other collateral heirs. If several collateral heirs are related in the same degree, they share equally; thus, in the example above, Jeffrey and Lisa would receive equal shares. However, some states specify that in case of a degree tie (same number) between collateral heirs, those related through the closest common ancestor take to the exclusion of the others; see Cal. Prob. Code § 6402(f); Mass. Gen. Laws Ann. ch. 190 § 3(6). Thus, in the example above, although Jeffrey and Lisa are both in the fourth degree, Jeffrey would receive Marilyn's property since he is related through her parents while Lisa is related through Marilyn's grandparents.

- *Common law computation*. This method computes the degree of relationship by first counting up from the decedent-intestate to the closest common ancestor to the decedent and the possible heir and, next, starting a new count down to the heir. The greater or higher this second number is in comparison with other possible collateral heirs determines who receives the inheritance.

Example: Using the Marilyn-Jeffrey-Lisa example above, the closest common ancestor between Marilyn and Jeffrey is Marilyn's parent. Counting from Marilyn to the parent is (1), and, starting the new count, from the parent to Jeffrey, the grand-nephew, is (3). Thus, (3) is the degree of relationship between Marilyn and Jeffrey. However, calculating the degree of relationship between Marilyn and Lisa using their common ancestor, the grandparent, leads to the degree of (2); i.e., counting from Marilyn to the grandparent is (2) and, starting the new count, from the grandparent to the first cousin is (2). Therefore, since Jeffrey has the higher number, he receives the inheritance.

No matter which system, the civil law or common law method, is used for determining degrees for collaterals, the decedent-intestate's property usually goes to the "nearest surviving kin" as established by state statutes. Most states give preference to descendants over ancestors, e.g., children over parents; brothers and sisters over grandparents; and nephews and nieces over first cousins. Since the variations in individual state laws are numerous, *you must carefully review your state's laws with the supervising attorney if they must be applied to determine a client's interest in an intestate's estate*.

ETHICAL ISSUE ◄··································

Escheat

Escheat is the passage of property to the state when an intestate leaves no surviving spouse or blood relatives (kindred) entitled to inherit the intestate's estate. Real property of an intestate escheats to the state in which it is located. For example, see Maryland's escheat statute (Md. Estates and Trusts Code Ann. § 3-105), which passes the intestate's property to the county board of education to be used in public schools of the county. Since heirs are generally found, escheat rarely occurs.

Escheat
The passage of an intestate's property to the state when there are no surviving blood relatives or a spouse.

Example: Bob dies intestate, leaving an estate valued at $100,000. There are no surviving relatives. The property "escheats" to the state; the state enjoys complete ownership and can use the property as it sees fit; it can sell or lease the property just as an individual owner could do.

Note: If a legitimate surviving heir is discovered after the intestate's property escheats to the state, the heir can usually claim the property or its value if the claim is made within the statute of limitations time period.

🏛 ASSIGNMENT 4.2

Armond died in Great Falls, Montana. Either by choice or through oversight, he had neither married nor drawn a will. At his death, Armond had the following blood relatives surviving him:

- A brother, Niles, living in Sacramento, California.
- A sister, Lorraine, living in London, England.
- A niece, Francine, living in Fridley, Minnesota, and a nephew, Frank, living in Albany, New York, both children of Armond's deceased brother, Harry.
- A mother, Lila, who lived with Armond.
- A grandfather, Alonzo, Lila's father, living in Cleveland, Ohio.
- An aunt, Rose, Lila's sister, living in Bangor, Maine.
- A first cousin, Judy, Rose's daughter, living in Lawrence, Kansas.

Answer the following questions:

1. Who of Armond's surviving blood relatives are lineal descendants?
2. Who of Armond's surviving blood relatives are lineal ascendants?
3. Who of Armond's surviving blood relatives are collaterals? What are their degrees of relationship?
4. What is the order of inheritance of Armond's surviving relatives in your state? Which heir receives property to the exclusion of others?
5. Do any of Armond's kindred receive his property per stirpes or per capita?
6. If Francine and Judy are Armond's only surviving relatives when he dies intestate, who receives his property according to your state statute? If Francine is dead but her son, Fred, and Judy are living when Armond dies, who receives the property?
7. Beginning with Alonzo, diagram a family tree for Armond's family.

General Rules of Distribution under State Intestate Succession Statutes

As we have emphasized throughout this discussion, intestate succession statutes vary from state to state. Nevertheless, many states do have similar rules on which surviving relatives will inherit an intestate's estate. The following scenarios illustrate some of these general rules of distribution. If the decedent-intestate is survived by:

- A surviving spouse and no blood relatives: The spouse receives the entire estate.
- A surviving spouse and children all born to the surviving spouse and the deceased: The spouse receives a lump sum of money (ranging from $7,500 to $150,000 depending on the state) and/or a portion (usually one-half) of the estate; the children receive the remainder of the estate equally.
- A surviving spouse and children, some or all of whom are not the children of the surviving spouse: The spouse receives a lump sum of money (ranging from

$7,500 to $150,000 depending on the state) and/or a portion (usually one-half) of the estate; the children receive the remainder of the estate equally.

- A surviving spouse, no children, but surviving parents: In most states, the surviving spouse gets everything; in other states, the spouse receives a lump sum ranging from $7,500 to $200,000 plus one-half of the remaining estate, and the parents receive the other half.
- A surviving spouse, no children and no parents, but brothers and sisters: In the majority of states, the surviving spouse receives everything; in a few states, the spouse receives one-half of the remaining estate, and the brothers and sisters receive the other half equally.
- No surviving spouse and no children: The parents receive the property followed by brothers and sisters, then their children and other collateral heirs.
- No spouse or kindred (blood relatives): The state receives the property by escheat.

ASSIGNMENT 4.3

Molly Brown dies intestate in your state. She had three children, Curly, Betty, and Moe. Curly and Betty each have two children. Curly's two daughters are Judy and Jody; Betty's two sons are Bobby and Billy. Moe died six months before Molly, and he had three children, Mark, Luke, and John. Answer the following according to your state statute:

1. Who receives Molly's property?
2. What portion does each recipient receive?
3. Is the inheritance per stirpes or per capita? Explain.
4. Does any of Molly's property escheat to the state?

RIGHTS OF FAMILY MEMBERS TO A DECEDENT'S ESTATE

On the death of the family "breadwinner", the surviving family members may face a financial crisis. This section examines the rights of a surviving spouse and children to the property of the decedent.

Caveat: You must not confuse the following two state statutes:

- The intestate succession statute which determines the inheritance of an intestate's surviving spouse and heirs; and
- The spouse's elective (forced) share statute which, as an option, is granted if the decedent spouse dies testate.

Rights of a Surviving Spouse

Surviving Spouse's Testate and Intestate Rights

When a married person dies testate, the rights of the surviving spouse to the decedent spouse's estate are usually determined by the will (but see section on elective share). When the decedent spouse dies without a will, the surviving spouse's rights to the intestate spouse's estate are determined by state statute and by which other family members, e.g., children, parents, brothers and sisters, and other kindred, survive the intestate. For an example of the rights of surviving spouses under state intestate succession statutes, see the New York statute in Exhibit 2.1. Exhibit 4.10 includes intestate succession statute citations for all states.

🖳 HOW TO LOCATE STATE LAWS, CODES, AND STATUTES

A very user friendly website is www.findlaw.com. State laws can be located on this cite. Click on the state needed and follow the prompts.

Exhibit 4.10	Intestate Succession Statute Citations for All States
Alabama	Ala. Code § 43-8-41; § 43-8-42
Alaska	Alaska Stat. § 13.12.102; § 13.12.103
Arizona	Ariz. Rev. Stat. Ann. § 14-2102; § 14-2103
Arkansas	Ark. Code Ann. § 28-9-204; § 28-9-205; § 28-9-206; § 28-9-214
California	Cal. Prob. Code § 6401; § 6402
Colorado	Colo. Rev. Stat. § 15-11-102; § 15-11-103
Connecticut	Conn. Gen. Stat. Ann. § 45a-437; § 45a-438; § 45a-439
Delaware	Del. Code Ann. Tit. 12 § 502; § 503
Florida	Fla. Stat. Ann. § 732.102; § 732.103
Georgia	Ga. Code Ann. § 53-2-1
Hawaii	Haw. Rev. Stat. § 560:2-102; § 560:2-103
Idaho	Idaho Code § 15-2-102; § 15-2-103
Illinois	Ill. Comp. Stat. Ann. Ch. 755 § 5/2-1
Indiana	Ind. Code Ann. § 29-1-2-1
Iowa	Iowa Code Ann. § 633.211; § 633.212; § 633.219
Kansas	Kan. Stat. Ann. §§ 59-504 to 59-508
Kentucky	Ky. Rev. Stat. Ann. § 391.010; § 391.030; § 392.020
Louisiana	La. Civ. Code Ann. Art. 889 to 902; Art. 1493
Maine	Me. Rev. Stat. Ann. Tit. 18-A § 2-102; § 2-103
Maryland	Md. Est. & Trst. Code Ann. §§ 3-102 to 3-105
Massachusetts	Mass. Gen. Laws Ann. Ch. 189 § 1; Ch. 190 §§ 1 to 3
Michigan	Mich. Comp. Laws Ann. § 700.2102; § 700.2103; § 700.2105
Minnesota	Minn. Stat. Ann. § 524.2-102; § 524.2-103
Mississippi	Miss. Code Ann. § 91-1-3; § 91-1-7; § 91-1-11
Missouri	Mo. Ann. Stat. § 474.010
Montana	Mont. Code Ann. § 72-2-112; § 72-2-113; § 72-2-115
Nebraska	Neb. Rev. Stat. § 30-2302; § 30-2303
Nevada	Nev. Rev. Stat. § 134.040; § 134.050
New Hampshire	N.H. Rev. Stat. Ann. S 561:1
New Jersey	N.J. Stat. Ann. § 3B:5-3; § 3B:5-4
New Mexico	N.M. Stat. Ann. § 45-2-102; § 45-2-103
New York	N.Y. EPTL § 4-1.1
North Carolina	N.C. Gen. Stat. § 29-14; § 29-15
North Dakota	N.D. Cent. Code § 30.1-04-02; § 30.1-04-03
Ohio	Ohio Rev. Code Ann. § 2103.02; § 2105.06
Oklahoma	Okla. Stat. Ann. Tit. 84 § 213
Oregon	Or. Rev. Stat. §§ 112.025 to 112.045
Pennsylvania	Pa. Stat. Ann. Tit. 20 § 2102; § 2103
Rhode Island	R.I. Gen. Laws § 33-1-5; § 33-1-6; § 33-1-10; § 33-25-1
South Carolina	S.C. Code § 62-2-102; § 62-2-103
South Dakota	S.D. Cod. Laws Ann. § 29A-2-102; § 29A-2-103; § 29A-2-105
Tennessee	Tenn. Code Ann. § 31-2-104
Texas	Tex. Prob. Code Ann. S 38
Utah	Utah Code Ann. § 75-2-102; § 75-2-103
Vermont	Vt. Stat. Ann. Tit. 14 § 551
Virginia	Va. Code Ann. § 64.1-1; § 64.1-11
Washington	Wash. Rev. Code Ann. § 11.04.015
West Virginia	W.Va. Code § 42-1-2; § 42-1-3
Wisconsin	Wis. Stat. Ann. § 852.01
Wyoming	Wyo. Stat. § 2-4-101

Surviving Spouse's Elective (Forced) Share

In a will, a testator is permitted to specifically disinherit anyone *except a surviving spouse*. As previously mentioned in Chapter 2, most states offer a surviving spouse the choice or **right of election** to either take the benefits in the will or to *elect* a **statutory forced share** of the deceased spouse's estate established by state statute. Generally, the surviving spouse chooses whichever share is greater. In a few states, the **elective share** of the surviving spouse is the same amount the spouse would receive if the decedent spouse died intestate.

The elective right has replaced common law provisions of dower and curtesy, which have been abolished or materially altered in most states (see UPC § 2-112). By statute, the spouse's election must be made within nine (9) months of death. If no election is made, the surviving spouse is required to take the share provided under the decedent spouse's will. The election is made when the spouse gives written notice to the personal representative and files the notice with the probate court. See Exhibit 4.11 for an example of a notice. The amount of the decedent's property that passes to the spouse as the elective share, excluding a life estate interest, qualifies for the estate tax marital deduction (see the discussion in Chapter 10).

If the choice is to elect "against the will," the spouse waives the will, renounces it, and takes what the state provides, thereby forfeiting any further claims to property under the will. States vary substantially in the amount a surviving spouse receives by statute. A few states determine the amount by their version of "dower or curtesy"; some set the amount by their intestate succession statute; others allow their method of "dower" and have an "elective right" statute; and the community property states grant each spouse one-half of the community property. Most states, however, grant one-third to one-half of the decedent's **augmented estate** to the surviving spouse.

The right of election does not apply if the surviving spouse has previously waived the right to the elective share by signing an agreement before marriage. Also, in some states like New York, a surviving spouse can be prohibited from the election if the spouse "abandoned" the deceased spouse prior to the latter's death or failed to provide required support for the deceased spouse for any period before death (see N.Y. EPTL §§ 5-1.1 and 5-1.2).

Sections 2–202 and 2–203 of the Uniform Probate Code set the spouse's elective share at the amount equal to the value of the elective-share percentage of the augmented estate, determined by the length of time the spouse and the decedent were married to each other, in accordance with the following schedule:

Right of election
The right of a surviving husband or wife to choose to take, under the decedent's state law, his or her statutory share in preference to the provision made in the deceased spouse's will.

Elective or forced share statute
The statute that grants the surviving spouse the election or choice. Also called statutory share.

Augmented estate
The value of all the decedent's property that consists of the sum of four components (see Glossary), reduced by funeral and administration expenses, homestead allowance, family allowances, exempt property, and enforceable creditors' claims.

If the decedent and the spouse were married to each other:	The elective-share percentage is:
Less than 1 year	Supplemental Amount Only.
1 year but less than 2 years	3% of the augmented estate.
2 years but less than 3 years	6% of the augmented estate.
3 years but less than 4 years	9% of the augmented estate.
4 years but less than 5 years	12% of the augmented estate.
5 years but less than 6 years	15% of the augmented estate.
6 years but less than 7 years	18% of the augmented estate.
7 years but less than 8 years	21% of the augmented estate.
8 years but less than 9 years	24% of the augmented estate.
9 years but less than 10 years	27% of the augmented estate.
10 years but less than 11 years	30% of the augmented estate.

11 years but less than 12 years . . . . .34% of the augmented estate.
12 years but less than 13 years . . . . .38% of the augmented estate.
13 years but less than 14 years . . . . .42% of the augmented estate.
14 years but less than 15 years . . . . .46% of the augmented estate.
15 years or more . . . . .50% of the augmented estate.

Note: In any situation, a $50,000 minimum elective-share is granted for the support of the surviving spouse, see UPC § 2–202(b). The augmented estate consists of the value of all property, whether real or personal, tangible or intangible, wherever situated, that constitutes the sum of four components (1) the decedent's net probate estate; (2) the decedent's nonprobate transfers to others; (3) the decedent's nonprobate transfers to the surviving spouse; (4) the surviving spouse's net assets and nonprobate transfers to others, reduced by funeral and administration expenses, homestead allowance, family allowances, exempt property, and enforceable creditors' claims, see UPC §§ 2–202 through 2–207. Exhibit 4.12 summarizes the spouse's elective share in all fifty states.

Exhibit 4.11   Notice of Election of Surviving Spouse

SURROGATE'S COURT: COUNTY OF _____

_____

   In the Matter of the Estate of

_____ ,

_____ Deceased.

NOTICE OF ELECTION

File No. _____

To: [*Insert name of fiduciary and clerk of court*]

   1. I,_____, am the surviving spouse of _____ , who died a domiciliary of the County of _____ , and the State of New York, on _____, 20____ .

   2. The said decedent left a certain Last Will and Testament dated the _____ day of _____ , 20___ , which was probated in the Surrogate's Court of the County of _____ , New York, on the _____ day of _____ , 20 _____ , and Letters Testamentary were issued to _____as Executor on _____ , 20_____.

   3. I, _____ , the surviving spouse of _____ , deceased, do hereby exercise the personal right of election given to me pursuant to the provisions of Section 5–1.1 of the New York Estates, Powers and Trusts Law, and I do hereby elect to take my elective share pursuant to the provisions of the New York Estates, Powers and Trusts Law.

   IN WITNESS WHEREOF, I have hereunto set my hand and seal this _____ day of _____, 20___.

[*Acknowledgement*]

_____   _____ L.S.

Source: Reprinted with permission from West's McKinney's Forms, ESP §7:499. Copyright ©, by West Group.

Exhibit 4.12 Summary of Spouse's Elective Share by State

Alabama	Lesser of (1) all of the decedent's estate reduced by the value of the surviving spouse's separate estate; or (2) one-third of decedent's estate (§ 43–8–70)
Alaska	One-third of decedent's estate (§ 13.12.202)
Arizona	One-half of community property (community property law) (§ 14-2301)
Arkansas	Dower or curtesy interest (§ 28-39-401)
California	One-half of community or quasi-community property (community property law) (§ 100)
Colorado	Up to one-half of the augmented estate determined by the length of time the spouse and the decedent were married to each other (§ 15-11-201)
Connecticut	One-third of decedent's estate for life (§ 45a-436)
Delaware	One-third of the elective estate (Tit. 12 S 901)
Florida	Thirty percent of the elective estate (§ 732.2065)
Georgia	One year's support from date of decedent's death (§ 53-3-1)
Hawaii	Up to one-half of the augmented estate determined by the length of time the spouse and the decedent were married to each other (§ 560:2-202)
Idaho	One-half of augmented quasi-community property; one-half of community property (community property law) (§ 15-2-203)
Illinois	One-third of estate if surviving descendants; one-half if no surviving descendants (Ch. 755 § 5/2-8)
Indiana	One-half of net estate if surviving spouse is first spouse of decedent; if not, separate rules apply and share is limited (§ 29-1-3-1)
Iowa	One-third of decedent's estate (§ 633.238)
Kansas	Up to one-half of the augmented estate determined by the length of time the spouse and the decedent were married to each other (§ 59-6a202)
Kentucky	Dower right (§ 392.080)
Louisiana	One-half of community property (community property law)
Maine	One-third of the augmented estate (Tit. 18-A § 2-201)
Maryland	One-third of net estate if surviving issue; one-half if no surviving issue (§ 3-203)
Massachusetts	One-third of estate if surviving issue; $25,000 plus life estate in one-half of remaining estate if surviving kindred but no issue; $25,000 plus one-half of remaining estate if no surviving kindred or issue (Ch. 191 § 15)
Michigan	One-half of intestate share, reduced by one-half of the value of all property received from decedent other than by testate or intestate succession; or dower right (§ 700.2202)
Minnesota	Up to one-half of the augmented estate determined by the length of time the spouse and the decedent were married to each other (§ 524.2-202)
Mississippi	Intestate share not to exceed one-half of the estate (§ 91-5-25)
Missouri	One-half of estate if no lineal descendants or one-third if lineal descendants, reduced by the value of all property derived by spouse from decedent (§ 474.160)
Montana	Up to one-half of the augmented estate determined by the length of time the spouse and the decedent were married to each other (§ 72-2-221)
Nebraska	One-half of the augmented estate (§ 30-2313)
Nevada	One-half of community property (community property law) (§ 123.250)

(continued)

Exhibit 4.12 Summary of Spouse's Elective Share by State—*continued*

New Hampshire	One-third of estate if surviving issue; $10,000 of personalty and realty each plus one-half of remaining estate if surviving parent or sibling but no issue; $10,000 plus $2,000 for each year of marriage to decedent plus one-half of remaining estate if no issue, parent, or sibling (§ 560:10)
New Jersey	One-third of the augmented estate (§ 3B:8-1)
New Mexico	One-half of community property (community property law) (§ 45-2-805)
New York	The greater of $50,000 or one-third of net estate (§ 5-1.1-A)
North Carolina	Intestate share (§ 30-3)
North Dakota	One-half of the augmented estate (§ 30.1-05-01)
Ohio	Intestate share not to exceed one-half of net estate; one-third if two or more surviving children or their lineal issue (§ 2106.01)
Oklahoma	One-half of all property acquired during marriage by the joint industry of the husband and wife (Tit. 84 S 44)
Oregon	One-fourth of net estate (§ 114.105)
Pennsylvania	One-third of decedent's estate (Tit. 20 § 2203)
Rhode Island	Life estate as provided by intestacy law (§ 33-25-2)
South Carolina	One-third of decedent's estate (§ 62-2-201)
South Dakota	Up to one-half of the augmented estate determined by the length of time the spouse and the decedent were married to each other (§ 29A-2-202)
Tennessee	Up to forty percent of the net estate determined by the length of time the spouse and the decedent were married to each other (§ 31-4-101)
Texas	One-half of community property (community property law)
Utah	One-third of the augmented estate multiplied by a fraction (§ 75-2-202)
Vermont	Dower or curtesy equal to one-third of real property; or intestate share (Tit. 14 § 402; § 461)
Virginia	One-third of the augmented estate if surviving children or their descendants; one-half if no surviving children or their descendants (§ 64.1-16)
Washington	One-half of community property (community property law)
West Virginia	Up to one-half of the augmented estate determined by the length of time the spouse and the decedent were married to each other (§ 42-3-1)
Wisconsin	One-half of the augmented deferred marital property estate (§ 861.02)
Wyoming	One-half of estate if no surviving issue or if spouse is also a parent of any surviving issue; one-fourth if spouse is not the parent of any surviving issue (§ 2-5-101)

Effect of Divorce and Marriage on a Spouse's Rights

Divorce

If the testator obtains a divorce (or annulment) *after* executing a will, the effect on the will is determined by state law. In most states, by statute or case law, a divorce revokes only the provisions that benefit the former spouse, not the will itself, and any gift to the divorced spouse passes to the residuary beneficiaries or devisees of the will (see Exhibit 4.13 and UPC §§ 2–802 and 2–804). The decision in *Matter of Seymour's Estate,* 93 N.M. 328, 600 P.2d 274 (1979) illustrates this position (for further discussion, see Chapter 5). A legal separation which does not terminate the spouse's marital status does not revoke a will's provisions for the benefit of a spouse; see Cal. Prob. Code § 6122(d).

Exhibit 4.13 Consequence of Divorce on Preexisting Will

Does not affect provisions of the will:
  Louisiana
  Mississippi
  Vermont
Revokes all the will provisions pertaining to the former spouse:
  All remaining states not listed above

Marriage

In some states, a testator's subsequent marriage after creating a will may revoke the entire will (see R.I. Gen. Laws § 33-5-9 and Exhibit 4.14). Since the majority of states allow a statutory forced share to a surviving spouse who elects against a decedent spouse's will, some of these states often have no "marriage revocation law" since the new spouse is covered by the election right. Community property states automatically pass one-half of the decedent's community property to the surviving spouse. Numerous states and the UPC give the new (omitted) spouse an amount equal to the intestate share of the decedent spouse's estate unless it can be shown the omission was intentional or the testator provided for the surviving spouse by transfer outside the will and intended the transfer be in lieu of a testamentary provision (see UPC §§ 2–301 and 2–508). See also the discussion in Chapter 5.

Other Spouses' Rights Before or After Marriage

Various methods allow widows, widowers, or divorcees, who are contemplating a second marriage, to transfer some of their currently owned assets to existing family members, e.g., children and grandchildren, by the elimination of these assets from the statutory elective share or intestate succession rights of their future spouse. Disclosure of the transfer of the property and its value to the future spouse is essential for approval by state courts. These methods can be created before or after the marriage.

Before marriage:

1. Creation of a joint tenancy.   As discussed in Chapter 2, on the death of one joint tenant, the title to property held in joint tenancy automatically passes to the surviving joint tenant.

Example: Ashley, a 62-year-old widow, and James, a 65-year-old widower, plan to marry. Ashley has two children from her first marriage; James has one child. Ashley owns a lake home, Tanglewood, that she and James plan to use as a vacation home during the summer months after they marry. Ashley wants Tanglewood to go to her children after she dies. Before the marriage, Ashley creates a joint tenancy with equal interests in Tanglewood for herself and each of her two children. Ashley tells James about the joint tenancy, and he acknowledges and states, "It's the right thing to do." They marry. If Ashley dies before James and her children, Tanglewood will belong to the children, and James will have no legal claim to the lake home.

Exhibit 4.14   Consequence of Marriage on Preexisting Will

Revokes the entire will:

Georgia	(marriage, birth, or adoption of a child by the testator)
Kansas	(marriage followed by birth or adoption of a child by the testator)
Maryland	(marriage followed by birth, adoption, or legitimation of a child by the testator, provided the child or the child's descendant survives the testator)
Massachusetts	
New Hampshire	(marriage followed by birth of a child by the testator)
Oregon	(if survived by a spouse)
Rhode Island	
Tennessee	(marriage followed by birth of a child by the testator)

Does not revoke the will:

Arkansas	Louisiana	Oklahoma
Illinois	Mississippi	Texas
Indiana	Missouri	Vermont
Iowa	North Carolina	Virginia
Kentucky	Ohio	Wyoming

Surviving spouse (omitted spouse) entitled to receive statutory intestate share unless otherwise provided for:
   All remaining states not listed above

---

2. Creation of a revocable living trust.   Prior to a second marriage, a revocable living trust can be established by a former spouse (widow, widower, or divorcee) for the benefit of his or her children for the purpose of transferring currently owned personal assets into the trust to avoid subjecting these assets to the statutory intestate succession or elective share claims of a future (new) spouse. Once the property is transferred, only the beneficiaries of the trust, i.e., the children, are entitled to it. Such a trust could be revoked during the lifetime of the spouse (settlor), but on that spouse's death, the trust becomes irrevocable. After the marriage, a claim by the new spouse that the living trust is an attempt to defraud said spouse from statutory rights would be declared invalid as long as disclosure of the trust's existence, value, and plan for property distribution was made to the new spouse prior to the marriage.

> **Example:** Rosa and Hector plan to marry. Rosa and her first husband, Juan, who died in 2000, owned and managed a successful restaurant for 32 years. Rosa's three adult children also work at the restaurant, and she wants them to have it after she dies. Rosa transfers title to the restaurant into a revocable living trust, naming herself trustee and her children beneficiaries of the trust. She informs Hector of the trust, its value, and her plan for the property distribution. Later, they marry. Under these circumstances, if Rosa dies before Hector, an attempt by him to claim the living trust is fraudulent would be denied.

Antenuptial (premarital) agreement
A contract made by a man and woman before their marriage or in contemplation of that marriage whereby the property rights of either or both the prospective husband or wife are determined.

3. Creation of an antenuptial agreement (contract) also called a prenuptial or premarital agreement.   Due to the increasing frequency of second marriages after a divorce or death of a spouse, the couple now contemplating marriage often wishes to pass their separate estates to the existing children of their earlier marriages free from claims of the new spouse. To accomplish these plans, mutual agreements called **antenuptial or premarital agreements** or contracts are created prior to the marriage. The provisions and validity of such agreements vary from state to state. See *In re Estate of Peterson,* 221 Neb. 792, 381 N.W.2d 109 (1986). Some states have adopted the Uniform Premarital Agreement Act that establishes the formalities for the execution and revocation of the agreement.

> **Example:** Julia and Robert have agreed to marry. Julia, a divorcee, has a son, Ryan; Robert has never married. Ryan has been raised and continues to live on Julia's ranch in Montana. Since she wants her son to own the ranch after her death, Julia tells Robert she will marry him only if they sign an antenuptial agreement legally transferring the ranch to Ryan on her death or if she and Robert divorce. Robert agrees. After Julia and Robert sign the agreement, they marry. Two years later, Julia is killed in an accident. Ryan is entitled to the ranch because of the antenuptial agreement.

After marriage:

4. Creation of a postnuptial agreement (contract). A **postnuptial agreement** is made after marriage between spouses while still married to determine the rights of each spouse in the other spouse's property in the event of death or divorce (see Ind. Code Ann. § 29-1-3-6 and UPC § 2–213). At death, postnuptial agreements allow a transfer of the decedent spouse's separate estate assets to children of a previous marriage and prevent the surviving spouse from making a successful claim for the property based on fraud.

> **Example:** Using the facts in the previous example, if Julia and Robert consented to create the identical antenuptial agreement for the benefit of Ryan after they were married, the executed contract would be a postnuptial agreement.

> **Postnuptial agreement**
> A contract made by spouses after marriage whereby the property rights of either or both spouses are determined.

The previously mentioned Uniform Premarital Agreement Act and another statute, the Uniform Marital Property Act, have proposed, for states that adopt these acts, the standards for their courts to resolve the antenuptial or postnuptial agreement problems concerning the claims of the spouse who waives statutory intestate succession or elective share rights by signing either of the two agreements. Both acts agree that the antenuptial or postnuptial agreements can be voided if: (1) the agreement (contract) is unconscionable, i.e., so one-sided as to be oppressive and unfair; and/or (2) there was inadequate disclosure concerning the property waived and its fair value. The Uniform Marital Property Act requires that both of the conditions above be met for antenuptial agreements, but, for postnuptial agreements, either one of the conditions is enough to make the agreements unenforceable.

Rights of Children (Issue)

Issue

All persons who have descended from a common ancestor are the **issue** of the ancestor. Issue is a broader term than children and, as it is normally used in wills, includes all blood descendants of the ancestor, not just lineal descendants, such as children, grandchildren, and great-grandchildren; see *In re Wolf's Estate,* 98 N.J. Super. 89, 236 A.2d 166 (1967). Formerly, the term included only legitimate issue, but in *Reed v. Campbell,* 476 U.S. 852, 106 S.Ct. 2234, 90 L.Ed.2d 858 (1986), the U.S. Supreme Court prohibited unjustified discrimination against children born out of wedlock. In some states, such as New York, a nonmarital child shares in the intestate estate of the child's father; see N.Y. EPTL§ 4–1.2. In trusts in Massachusetts,

> **Issue**
> All persons who have descended from a common ancestor.

the word "issue," which formerly meant legitimate children, today includes all biological descendants unless the settlor clearly expresses a different intent; see *Powers v. Wilkinson,* 399 Mass. 650, 506 N.E.2d 842 (1987). In addition, many states' intestacy statutes have established an adopted child is "issue" of the adoptive parents, which gives the child the same rights, including inheritance rights, as the adoptive parents' natural children. The next paragraphs discuss the rights of children in the following order: natural children, adopted children, nonmarital children, pretermitted (omitted) and posthumous children, and children who may be disinherited by statute.

Natural Children

A natural child is a child by birth of a mother and the biological father, as distinguished from a child by adoption. In addition, if a married woman gives birth to a child, her husband is presumed to be the father of the child. Although most testators leave all or most of their property to their surviving spouse, state intestate statutes differ sharply from those testamentary provisions. Under the statutes, whenever a spouse *and* child(ren) survive the intestate, the surviving spouse generally receives a lump sum amount of the estate plus half of the remainder, and the child(ren) receive the other half; alternatively, the spouse receives one-third to one-half of the estate with the remainder to the children. In either case, this distribution of a decedent's estate is substantially different from what the usual testator's will provides. Thereafter, except for specific bequests (gifts) to named children, most natural and, as we shall see, adopted children receive the estate of their parents when the second parent dies. Obviously, this is not the case in single-parent families, since the parent who dies testate generally leaves the entire estate to the children. When the single parent or the second parent-spouse dies intestate, the natural children are the first-in-line heirs and inherit the entire estate, except that a deceased child's share will pass per stirpes, by right of representation, to that child's issue.

In all states, parents are not required to leave anything to their children. Excluding children from sharing in an estate can be accomplished by inserting a clause in the will to the effect that the testator or testatrix has intentionally made no provision for a certain named child. However, despite a testator's intention to disinherit, if no specific exclusion is stated in the will, the child may ultimately receive a share as a result of an omitted child statute (see discussion below).

Divorce and remarriage often have a detrimental effect on the rights and opportunities of natural or adopted children to inherit by will or by law. In divorce decrees, the spouses may agree by stipulation that the spouse who is obligated to pay child support will make a will leaving a portion of the estate to the child(ren) or name the child(ren) as beneficiaries of a life insurance policy.

Adopted Children

Adoption is a legal process whereby state statutes terminate legal rights and duties between children and their natural parents and substitute similar rights and duties between the children and their adoptive parents. The state statutes are inconsistent in determining the inheritance rights of adopted children or adoptive parents. The modern trend is to treat the **adopted child** as a natural child of the adoptive parents and not as the child of the former natural parents for all legal

Adoption
The legal process by statute that establishes a relationship of parent and child between persons who are not so related by nature.

Adopted child
The person (child) adopted.

purposes including inheritance. The states that have adopted UPC § 2–114 have followed this trend. Consider the following examples:

Example: Karen Wilson's son, Ron, is adopted by Scott and Shirley Mikulski. The adopted child, Ron, has the right to inherit from either of the adoptive parents, Scott or Shirley, when they die intestate, and they have the right to inherit from Ron. However, Ron will no longer inherit from his natural mother, Karen, nor will she inherit from him.

Example: If, instead, Karen Wilson marries Fred Maxwell and Fred adopts Ron, Ron will continue to have the right to inherit from his natural mother, Karen, and also from his adoptive parent, Fred, and they, in turn, have a right to inherit from Ron.

Note: Not all states follow the procedures described in these examples. Several states allow adopted children to inherit from their biological kindred; see Ala. Code § 43–8–48; La. Civ. Code Ann. art. 214; and Wyo. Stat. § 2–4–107. Since a testator can leave an estate to anyone, with the exception that a surviving spouse cannot be disinherited, the adoption rules apply only to intestacy cases. When a testator has an adopted child whom he wants to treat equally as a natural child, a clause, such as the following, should be added to the will to avoid confusion:

Sample Clause
For the purpose of this will, the words "issue," "child," or "children" used within this will describing the relationship of a person or class of persons to another shall refer both to persons who are related by blood and also to any person whose relationship is acquired by adoption.

Adults can also be adopted. When this occurs, the purpose is generally to allow the adopted adult to inherit, or take by will, from the adopting person. The case *In re Adult Anonymous II,* 88 A.D.2d 30, 452 N.Y.S.2d 198 (1982), in which a gay lover was adopted, is an example of adoption for economic and inheritance purposes. Adult adoptions generally only affect the inheritance rights of the immediate parties.

Nonmarital Children

A **nonmarital child** is a child born to parents who are not married to each other. The child is said to be born out of lawful wedlock, i.e., illegitimate. A nonmarital child's inheritance rights are governed by state statute. Generally, they hold that the child has the right to inherit from and through the child's mother, but the statutes vary about the rights of the child to inherit from the father. However, since the U.S. Supreme Court's decision in *Trimble v. Gordon,* 430 U.S. 762, 97 S.Ct. 1459, 52 L.Ed.2d 31 (1977), established that a nonmarital child has a constitutional right to inherit from a father, most states have amended their statutes to avoid unjustified discrimination against nonmarital children. Some states continue to control the right of inheritance from the biological father by requiring either (1) an acknowledgment by the man that he is the father of the child or (2) convincing evidence in a civil paternity lawsuit that the man is the father of the child. Whenever either of these requirements is met, the nonmarital child has the right to inherit from the father; see Ark. Code Ann. § 28-9-209 and UPC § 2-114. Today, current DNA identification is an accurate method to establish paternity.

Reversing the roles, most states allow parents and their relatives to inherit from their nonmarital children who die intestate without issue (children). However, the

Nonmarital child
A child born to parents who are not married.

father must establish appropriate proof of paternity; see Ga. Code Ann. § 53-2-4 and Tex. Prob. Code Ann. § 42, and compare UPC § 2-114(c), in which the parent must have treated the child as his or hers and supported the child. Some states, like New York, have passed legislation preventing a parent from inheriting from a child whom the parent abandoned or failed to support during minority; see N.Y. EPTL § 4-1.4.

Pretermitted (Omitted) and Posthumous Children

Unlike a surviving spouse, children can be disinherited by their parents if the omission is intentional. A **pretermitted child** is a child omitted in a will by a parent. If a parent unintentionally does not mention a child or make a provision for a child in the will, and the child was either living at the date of the will's execution or was born thereafter, a statute may provide that the child, or the issue of a deceased child, shall receive a share in the estate as though the parent-testator had died intestate. The decision in *Crump's Estate v. Freeman,* 614 P.2d 1096 (Okl. 1980), illustrates this position. The court held that the omitted child (in the case) should receive the same share of the estate that the child would have taken if the testator had died intestate "unless the omission was intentional and not caused by accident or mistake." Most states have statutes that allow a child who is not named in the will to receive a share of the parent's estate. The UPC and other state statutes, however, include only children who were born after the will was executed; see UPC § 2-302 which limits the amount given to the omitted child to an equal amount that is given to other children. Other states cover children born before or after the testator's death; see Mass. Gen. Laws Ann. ch. 191 § 20. For an adopted child, the date of the adoption rather than the date of birth is controlling. An example of a state statute on the pretermitted child's right to inherit is Wis. Stat. Ann. § 853.25.

Under a pretermitted statute, a testator, while living, must either (1) make some settlement or give an equal share of property to the omitted child (or grandchild, if the child is dead and there is a grandchild) by way of advancement; (2) after death, name the child as a beneficiary in the will; *or* (3) make it clear in the will that the omission of the child was intentional. Thus, a parent can give a child little or nothing through a will but must do so expressly; if the child is not mentioned at all in the will, the assumption is that the omission was inadvertent and not intended. The testator should include a specific clause in the will to establish a clear intent and avoid potential problems concerning pretermitted or omitted children.

Sample Disinheritance Clause

I have intentionally not provided in this will for my daughter, Elizabeth May Johnson, and for my son, Robert Jay Johnson, and these omissions are not caused by accident or mistake.

Section 2-101(b) of the UPC officially recognizes the right of the testator to disinherit any heir, except a surviving spouse, by specifically excluding the named person or class of persons in the will.

A **posthumous child** is conceived before but born after the death of his or her father. Under most state statutes, the child is given an intestate share of the deceased father's estate.

Pretermitted (omitted) child
A child omitted in a parent's will.

Posthumous child
A child born after the death of his or her father.

Disinheritance of Heirs (Children and Others) by Statute

All states, by statutes or court decisions, abolish the right of a convicted murderer, including a spouse or child, to inherit by will or intestacy the property of the victim. These state statutes are often called slayer or homicide statutes (see Cal. Prob. Code § 250; Ill. Compiled Stat. Ann. Ch. 755 § 5/2–6; Tenn. Code Ann. § 31-1-106; and UPC § 2–803). Often the slayer statute considers the killer to have predeceased the murdered victim which may allow the inheritance to pass to the slayer's heirs, e.g., children. States have also passed legislation to abolish the inheritance rights of a beneficiary of a will who is convicted of killing other beneficiaries. *Note*: Mistreatment of a testator or an intestate by an heir has not been adequate evidence for disinheriting the heir.

Additional Rights or Protection for a Surviving Spouse and Children

In addition to the specific rights of a surviving spouse and children discussed above, these family members may receive benefits from a decedent spouse's estate that are not determined by the decedent's will or the state intestate succession statute. These benefits, established by other specific statutes, include the homestead exemption, homestead allowance, family or "widow's" support or allowance (sometimes called maintenance), and exempt property. They take priority not only over the decedent's will or the intestacy laws but also over creditor's claims against the decedent's estate.

Homestead Exemption

In some states, statutes protect a family that owns their house from eviction by creditors by allowing the **householder** or head of the family to designate a house and land as the homestead. The **homestead exemption** statute exempts the homestead from claims and execution by creditors regardless of the amount of the householder's debt.

The **homestead** is defined as the house and adjoining land occupied by the owner as a home. The amount of land comprising the homestead may be limited in acreage by statute. For example, in Kansas a rural homestead is limited to 160 acres and an urban homestead to one acre. The following Minnesota statutes define a homestead, identify its area limits, and explain its descent to surviving family members:

Minn. Stat. Ann. § 510.01 Homestead Defined; Exempt; Exception
The house owned and occupied by a debtor as the debtor's dwelling place, together with the land upon which it is situated to the amount of area and value hereinafter limited and defined, shall constitute the homestead of such debtor and the debtor's family, and be exempt from seizure or sale under legal process on account of any debt not lawfully charged thereon in writing, except such as are incurred for work or materials furnished in the construction, repair, or improvement of such homestead, or for services performed by laborers or servants and as is provided in section 550.175.

Minn. Stat. Ann. § 510.02 Area and Value; How Limited
The homestead may include any quantity of land not exceeding 160 acres, and not included in the laid out or platted portion of any city. If the homestead is within the laid

Householder
The head of the household or family who is entitled to the homestead exemption.

Homestead exemption
A statute that protects a family from eviction from their home by creditors.

Homestead
The house and adjoining land occupied by the owner as a home.

out or platted portion of a city, its area must not exceed one-half of an acre. The value of the homestead exemption, whether the exemption is claimed jointly or individually, may not exceed $200,000 or, if the homestead is used primarily for agricultural purposes, $500,000, exclusive of the limitations set forth in section 510.05.

Minn. Stat. Ann. § 524.2-402 Descent of Homestead

(a) If there is a surviving spouse, the homestead, including a manufactured home which is the family residence, descends free from any testamentary or other disposition of it to which the spouse has not consented in writing or as provided by law, as follows:

(1) if there is no surviving descendant of decedent, to the spouse; or

(2) if there are surviving descendants of decedent, then to the spouse for the term of the spouse's natural life and the remainder in equal shares to the decedent's descendants by representation.

(b) If there is no surviving spouse and the homestead has not been disposed of by will it descends as other real estate.

(c) If the homestead passes by descent or will to the spouse or decedent's descendants, it is exempt from all debts which were not valid charges on it at the time of decedent's death except that the homestead is subject to a claim filed pursuant to section 246.53 for state hospital care or 256B.15 for medical assistance benefits. If the homestead passes to a person other than a spouse or decedent's descendants, it is subject to the payment of expenses of administration, funeral expenses, expenses of last illness, taxes, and debts. The claimant may seek to enforce a lien or other charge against a homestead so exempted by an appropriate action in the district court.

(d) For purposes of this section, except as provided in section 524.2-301, the surviving spouse is deemed to consent to any testamentary or other disposition of the homestead to which the spouse has not previously consented in writing unless the spouse files in the manner provided in section 524.2-211, paragraph (f), a petition that asserts the homestead rights provided to the spouse by this section.

It is common practice for spouses to hold title to their home in joint tenancy or tenancy by the entirety. When one spouse dies, the homestead automatically passes to the surviving spouse as a result of the right of survivorship.

If both spouses are living, most states provide that the homestead cannot be sold without the consent and signature of each spouse.

To illustrate the passage of a homestead upon the intestate death of its owner, consider the following assignment.

🏛 ASSIGNMENT 4.4

Henry and Wilma have been married for the past 32 years. Henry owns their house, which he purchased before their marriage, in his name only. Henry dies without a will. He is survived by his widow, Wilma; two children, Abby and Beth; and six grandchildren: Cindy and Daniel, Abby's children; Elaine and Fred, Beth's children; and George and Ida, children of Henry's deceased child, Stanley. The house in which Henry and Wilma lived, has a lien against it for partial nonpayment of 2000 property taxes and a 30-year mortgage with 5 years remaining. According to your state laws, how, to whom, and in what shares will the house descend? Is the descent of the homestead free from creditors' claims against it?

Homestead Allowance

Instead of a homestead exemption, some states provide a cash award called a **homestead allowance** for the benefit of a surviving spouse or minor children. This allowance is also not subject to creditors' claims and is a priority payment made to the surviving spouse or minor children in addition to any property passing to them by the provisions of a will, by intestate succession, or by a surviving spouse's right to an elective share; see UPC § 2–402.

Exempt Property

Many states and the UPC also exempt some of the decedent's personal property up to a specific dollar amount, which is given to the surviving spouse and/or children free from claims of creditors. The property is often limited to a selection of household furniture, appliances, furnishings, automobiles, and personal effects, and the number of items in the various categories that constitute the **exempt property** can also be limited, e.g., one car; see Ala. Code § 43-8-111; R. I. Gen. Laws § 33-10-1; Va. Code Ann. § 64.1-151.2; and UPC § 2-403. Under the UPC, the selected exempt property either goes to the surviving spouse or to the children equally if there is no surviving spouse. Sections 271, 272, and 278 of the Texas Probate Code allow minor or adult children to receive exempt property. In cases in which the decedent did not own any qualifying exempt personal property, state laws may provide for a modest cash allowance in place of the property; see Tex. Prob. Code Ann. §§ 273–277. Exempt property is identified in the following statute:

Minn. Stat. Ann. § 524.2-403 Exempt Property

(a) If there is a surviving spouse, then, in addition to the homestead and family allowance, the surviving spouse is entitled from the estate to:

(1) property not exceeding $10,000 in value in excess of any security interests therein, in household furniture, furnishings, appliances, and personal effects, subject to an award of sentimental value property under section 525.152; and

(2) one automobile, if any, without regard to value.

(b) If there is no surviving spouse, the decedent's children are entitled jointly to the same property as provided in paragraph (a), except that where it appears from the decedent's will a child was omitted intentionally, the child is not entitled to the rights conferred by this section.

(c) If encumbered chattels are selected and the value in excess of security interests, plus that of other exempt property, is less than $10,000, or if there is not $10,000 worth of exempt property in the estate, the surviving spouse or children are entitled to other personal property of the estate, if any, to the extent necessary to make up the $10,000 value.

(d) Rights to exempt property and assets needed to make up a deficiency of exempt property have priority over all claims against the estate, but the right to any assets to make up a deficiency of exempt property abates as necessary to permit earlier payment of the family allowance.

(e) The rights granted by this section are in addition to any benefit or share passing to the surviving spouse or children by the decedent's will, unless otherwise provided by intestate succession or by way of elective share.

Family or "Widow's" Allowance

During the administration of the decedent spouse's estate, most states give the probate court the power to award the surviving spouse and/or minor children the

Homestead allowance
A statute that provides a modest cash award for the benefit of a surviving spouse or minor children; it is a priority payment to them and is not subject to creditors' claims.

Exempt property
The decedent's personal property up to a specific dollar amount that is given to the surviving spouse and/or minor children and is exempt from creditors' claims.

exempt property (see discussion on p.131)) *and* a monthly cash allowance for their maintenance and support; see Ariz. Rev. Stat. Ann. § 14-2404; Conn. Gen. Stat. Ann. § 45a-320; Or. Rev. Stat. § 114.015; and UPC § 2-404. The amount of the award varies and is determined by the probate court based on the assets and liabilities of the estate and the family needs. The award may be terminated by the death of the recipient(s) or remarriage of the surviving spouse, as illustrated by the case of *Hamrick v. Bonner,* 182 Ga.App. 76, 354 S.E.2d 687 (1987). The decedent's will cannot defeat this **"family" allowance** even if the decedent disinherited them, and it, too, is exempt from creditors' claims. In Tennessee, the award or allowance is called the "heirs' support."

The following statute provides an example of such an allowance:

Minn. Stat. Ann. § 524.2-404 Family Allowance

(a) In addition to the right to the homestead and exempt property, the decedent's surviving spouse and minor children whom the decedent was obligated to support, and children who were in fact being supported by the decedent, shall be allowed a reasonable family allowance in money out of the estate for their maintenance as follows:

(1) for one year if the estate is inadequate to discharge allowed claims; or

(2) for 18 months if the estate is adequate to discharge allowed claims.

(b) The amount of the family allowance may be determined by the personal representative in an amount not to exceed $1,500 per month.

(c) The family allowance is payable to the surviving spouse, if living; otherwise to the children, their guardian or conservator, or persons having their care and custody.

(d) The family allowance is exempt from and has priority over all claims.

(e) The family allowance is not chargeable against any benefit or share passing to the surviving spouse or children by the will of the decedent unless otherwise provided, by intestate succession or by way of elective share. The death of any person entitled to family allowance does not terminate the right of that person to the allowance.

(f) The personal representative or an interested person aggrieved by any determination, payment, proposed payment, or failure to act under this section may petition the court for appropriate relief, which may include a family allowance other than that which the personal representative determined or could have determined.

See also Chapter 12 on family allowances.

 ASSIGNMENT 4.5

Benjamin and Christy, husband and wife, have been married ten years. They have three minor children, Andrew, Shannon, and Lincoln. Benjamin is killed in an airplane mishap. He has no will, and his wife and children survive him. Christy has been advised that probate might be lengthy. Benjamin's estate encompasses (a) a $100,000 house; (b) household furnishings, clothing, and other like items valued at $20,000; (c) additional items of personal property amounting to $15,000; (d) a $10,000 family car. Christy estimates that upkeep for the family during probate of her husband's estate will cost $1,400 per month. At death, Benjamin's estate had $200,000 in assets and $5,000 in liabilities.

As an exercise in how to analyze a state statute, answer the following according to the family allowance and exempt property procedures under the Minnesota law, mentioned above.

Family allowance
A statute that allows the court to award to the surviving spouse and/or minor children a monthly cash allowance for their maintenance and support.

1. From what source and how much can Christy seek as the allowance and exempt property granted a surviving spouse?
2. Will Benjamin's children be entitled to receive the allowance, and if so, when?
3. Does the family allowance or exempt property in this case include the car?
4. Will the family receive a sum of money to maintain it for the balance of the time it takes to administer Benjamin's estate? If so, for how long? If not, why not?
5. Check to see if your state has a family allowance statute. If it does, answer the questions above according to your own state laws.

On the descent of other property, Minn. Stat. Ann. § 524.2-101 states that subject to the family allowances that are granted in cases of both testacy and intestacy, the items paid out of the estate are the expenses of probate administration, funeral expenses, expenses of the last illness, and taxes and debts under federal and state law (see UPC § 3–805). The balance of the estate, both real and personal property, descends and is distributed as follows:

Minn. Stat. Ann. § 524.2-102 Share of the Spouse
The intestate share of a decedent's surviving spouse is:
   (1) the entire intestate estate if:
   (i) no descendant of the decedent survives the decedent; or
   (ii) all of the decedent's surviving descendants are also descendants of the surviving spouse and there is no other descendant of the surviving spouse who survives the decedent;
   (2) the first $150,000 plus one-half of any balance of the intestate estate, if all of the decedent's surviving descendants are also descendants of the surviving spouse and the surviving spouse has one or more surviving descendants who are not descendants of the decedent, or if one or more of the decedent's surviving descendants are not descendants of the surviving spouse.

Minn. Stat. Ann. § 524.2-103 Share of Heirs Other Than Surviving Spouse
Any part of the intestate estate not passing to the decedent's surviving spouse under section 524.2-102, or the entire intestate estate if there is no surviving spouse, passes in the following order to the individuals designated below who survive the decedent:
   (1) to the decedent's descendants by representation;
   (2) if there is no surviving descendant, to the decedent's parents equally if both survive, or to the surviving parent;
   (3) if there is no surviving descendant or parent, to the descendants of the decedent's parents or either of them by representation;
   (4) if there is no surviving descendant, parent, or descendant of a parent, but the decedent is survived by one or more grandparents or descendants of grandparents, half of the estate passes to the decedent's paternal grandparents equally if both survive, or to the surviving paternal grandparent, or to the descendants of the decedent's paternal grandparents or either of them if both are deceased, the descendants taking by representation; and the other half passes to the decedent's maternal relatives in the same manner; but if there is no surviving grandparent or descendant of a grandparent on either the paternal or the maternal side, the entire estate passes to the decedent's relatives on the other side in the same manner as the half;
   (5) if there is no surviving descendant, parent, descendant of a parent, grandparent, or descendant of a grandparent, to the next of kin in equal degree, except that

when there are two or more collateral kindred in equal degree claiming through different ancestors, those who claim through the nearest ancestor shall take to the exclusion of those claiming through an ancestor more remote.

Finally, if neither a spouse nor any kindred survives the intestate, the estate passes to the state by the process of *escheat*. Personal property *escheats* to the state of the decedent's domicile at death as does real property located in that state. Real property situated outside the state of the decedent's domicile escheats to the state of its location.

USE OF INTESTATE TERMINOLOGY

The following situation illustrates the meaning and use of the terminology used in cases of intestacy.

The Facts

Toby Smith dies without a will. His survivors are Sally Smith, Toby's present wife; Wylie Smith and Margo Smith Tyler, children by his marriage to Sally; John Smith, an adopted son; Bob Smith, his brother; Sue Smith, his sister; Doris Smith, his mother; Kay and Mary Tyler, Margo's children; Bert and Thad Smith, Wylie's nonmarital children; Rosey Thorn, Sally's daughter by a previous marriage; Tom Johnson, a foster child who lives with the Smiths; Jane Carson, a woman Toby had lived with, but not married; and Carol Stuart, Toby's former wife. Frank Malcolm is appointed administrator by the probate court to manage and administer Toby's estate.

Review of Terminology

Toby Smith dies *intestate* because he left no will directing the distribution of his estate at his death. His death without a will is known as *intestacy,* and Toby, the decedent, is the *intestate*. What, how, and to whom the various items of property in his estate pass on his death are controlled by *intestate succession statutes,* state laws that govern the process by which intestate estates are distributed. In effect, the state writes the "will" when a decedent fails to write one.

In addition to the decedent's spouse, various family members, ranked in the order of closest blood relative to the intestate, are the *heirs, distributees,* or *successors* who share in the distribution of the *intestate's* estate. Under the UPC, an heir may receive either real or personal property, or both. Confusion exists in the terminology used to describe the manner in which property passes from an intestate. Under the orthodox terminology, an *heir* is one entitled to inherit the decedent's real property, and a *distributee* or *next of kin* is one entitled to inherit the decedent's personal property. However, these words are frequently used interchangeably.

All persons mentioned in the facts above who survived Toby, including his adopted son John, are potential *heirs, distributees,* or *successors,* except Rosey Thorn, Tom Johnson, Jane Carson, and Carol Stuart, who are not blood relatives and do not trace their relationship to Toby through *consanguinity*. His mother, Doris, is an *ascendant* who possesses an interest in the estate through a direct upward bloodline as an ascending *lineal ancestor*. Wylie, Margo, Bert, Thad, Kay, and Mary, Toby's children and grandchildren, who are in a direct bloodline downward as descending lineals, are his *descendants*. Bob and Sue, his brother and sister, are not direct blood *lineals,* but instead trace their relationship to him through their mother, Doris, as a common ancestor. They are *collaterals* in a collateral relationship line to Toby.

Toby's *adopted* son, John Smith, would be entitled to share in the estate. Statutes entitle *adopted children,* such as Toby's son, John Smith, to inherit from their *adoptive parents* (Toby) on the same basis natural children (Wylie and Margo) have for inheritance—lineal descent. In some states, adopted children are precluded from inheritance from their natural parents. However, in a few states, the adopted child (John) can inherit from both his natural parents in all circumstances and from his adoptive parents (Toby) but the natural parents do not inherit from or through the adopted child (John) (see R.I. Gen. Laws § 15–7–17 and Wyo. Stat. § 2–4–107).

The inheritance rights of a child whose natural parent dies and whose surviving parent remarries and the new spouse legally adopts the child are sometimes delineated by statute:

> *Conn. Gen. Stat. Ann. § 45a–731* Effects of Final Decree of Adoption—Surviving Rights
>
> A final decree of adoption, whether issued by a court of this state or a court of any other jurisdiction, shall have the following effect in this state: . . .
>
> (8) Notwithstanding the provisions of subdivisions (1) to (7), inclusive, of this section, when one of the biological parents of a minor child has died and the surviving parent has remarried subsequent to such parent's death, adoption of such child by the person with whom such remarriage is contracted shall not affect the rights of such child to inherit from or through the deceased parent and the deceased parent's relatives; . . . [see UPC § 2–114(b)].

Depending on the statutes of Toby's *domiciliary state,* Wylie's *nonmarital children,* Bert and Thad, may or may not inherit from Toby, since their inheritance through intestacy is possible only if Wylie dies before Toby. Most state statutes would allow Bert and Thad to inherit their mother's share of Toby's estate *by representation*. Tom Johnson, the foster child living with the Smiths, would not inherit from Toby.

🏛 ASSIGNMENT 4.6

After George's father died, his mother remarried; her second husband legally adopted George. Three weeks later, the brother of George's natural father died intestate, leaving no other surviving heirs. George wishes to claim his uncle's estate. Is he entitled? Cite statutory authority from the state of Connecticut. If this situation had occurred in your state, what statute(s) would control it?

In most states, all the heirs in the same *degree of relationship* to the intestate share equally through *per capita* distribution. For example, if Toby dies and only his children survive him, then Wylie, Margo, and John would each receive one-third of his estate per capita, a distribution equally divided among the heirs standing in the same degree of relationship to the intestate.

Example:

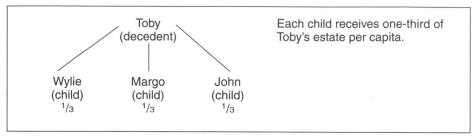

Each child receives one-third of Toby's estate per capita.

The same is true if only his grandchildren are living and Toby's domiciliary state statutes allow nonmarital children to inherit from their grandparent.

Example:

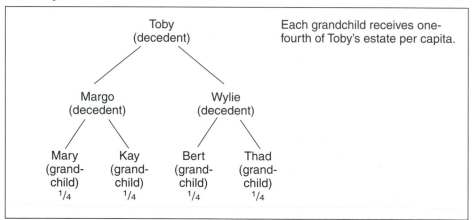

Each grandchild receives one-fourth of Toby's estate per capita.

The same is true if only his brother and sister survive his death.

Example:

Each sibling receives one-half of Toby's estate per capita.

A different result is reached when a successor (heir) predeceases the intestate. If Wylie dies before her father, and later Toby dies, his grandchildren, Bert and Thad, would receive Wylie's share of their grandfather's estate by right of representation (*per stirpes*) to be divided equally between them.

Example:

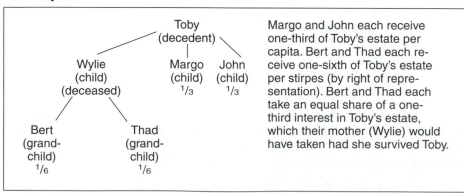

Margo and John each receive one-third of Toby's estate per capita. Bert and Thad each receive one-sixth of Toby's estate per stirpes (by right of representation). Bert and Thad each take an equal share of a one-third interest in Toby's estate, which their mother (Wylie) would have taken had she survived Toby.

If Toby dies without the aforementioned persons surviving him, or any other relatives entitled to inherit his estate, the property *escheats,* i.e., the state acquires title to the intestate's property.

Since Frank Malcolm is appointed to manage and distribute Toby's estate, he is the *administrator* or *personal representative* who acts under the supervision of the *probate court*. If, however, Frank's sister, Karen (or any other woman), is appointed by the probate court, she would be the *administratrix* of Toby's estate.

𝍌 ASSIGNMENT 4.7

Mary Worth dies without a will. The following relatives survive her: a husband, Atkinson; an adopted daughter, Lana; a foster son, Thomas; two sisters, Faith and Nadine; a brother, Thor; her mother, Theresa; father, Lorenzo; her mother-in-law, Islodean; Atkinson's sister, Cynthia; an aunt, Rose; an uncle, Oscar; two nephews, Donnie and Kevin, sons of her deceased brother, William; a niece, Diane, daughter of her deceased sister, Sharon; a grandson, David, son of her deceased daughter, Denise; a granddaughter, Luella, daughter of her deceased daughter, Nancy; and Manny, a husband by a prior marriage whom she divorced.

1. Who is the intestate?
2. Who is the administrator or administratrix?
3. Name the laws that govern the passage of the decedent's estate.
4. Find and cite the state statute that would determine the passage of Mary's estate in your state.
5. Name the decedent's lineal relatives who are ascendants and descendants.
6. Name the collaterals related to the decedent.
7. List all the potential successors (heirs) of the decedent.
8. Name the relationship that entitles the persons in question 7 to possibly share in the decedent's estate.
9. List persons who might be excluded from receiving any of the decedent's property.
10. How are the persons in question 9 related to the decedent?
11. Name relatives who might receive their share of the decedent's estate per capita.
12. Name relatives who might receive their share of the decedent's estate per stirpes.
13. What would happen if the decedent had no surviving spouse or relatives?
14. Diagram a family tree for Mary and her relatives.

ADVANTAGES AND DISADVANTAGES OF A WILL

Advantages of a Will

A will makes it possible for the testator to:

- Designate how much and to whom all property owned, real or personal, is to be distributed after death.
- Leave property to family members equally or in varying amounts based on need or the affection for or worthiness of the chosen recipients.
- Leave property to someone who would not take under intestate succession, e.g., close friends or special and faithful employees.

■ Make gifts to the testator's church, or to charitable, educational, scientific, and health institutions or organizations.

■ Subject to the approval of the probate court, nominate a personal guardian to care for any minor or incompetent person and a property guardian to manage the property inherited by the minor.

■ Appoint a trustee and create testamentary trusts which, through proper estate planning, can diminish death taxes, e.g., estate taxes.

■ Nominate a personal representative and grant the nominee special powers relating to the administration of the estate.

■ Avoid many legal problems that may accompany an intestate's estate administration, e.g., a will can waive the bond requirement for the appointed personal representative.

Disadvantages of a Will

Disadvantages include:

■ The probate of a will is often time-consuming and expensive and can cause inconvenience to the decedent's family.

■ In addition to the delays and costs, probating a will also causes bureaucracy (red tape) problems.

■ A will does not eliminate complicated procedures, e.g., the problems that accompany the transfer of ownership from the decedent to the beneficiary.

■ The loss of confidentiality concerning the decedent's property and named beneficiaries. All wills are filed in the county courthouse of the decedent's domiciliary state, and they are open to the public.

■ If the will is ill-fitting, poorly drafted, outdated, or inadequate, having no will might be more acceptable.

ASSIGNMENT 4.8

1. Review § 1–201 of the UPC in Appendix C on general definitions. Does your state's code have a separate section on such definitions? Note any differences from those presented in this text.

2. Does every eligible member of your family have a will? Why or why not? If a member of your family has no will, list reasons why that person should have one.

3. Secure a copy of someone's will (e.g., spouse, parent) or a sample will from a law library and identify as many of the terms defined in this chapter as possible.

KEY TERMS

Succession	Statutory will	Lapse	Per stirpes distribution
Testacy	Joint will	Antilapse statute	Degree of relationship
Intestacy	Mutual (reciprocal) wills	Abatement	Collateral heirs
Uniform Probate	Living will	Marshaling of assets	(relatives)
Code (UPC)	Ademption	Per capita distribution	Degrees of kindred
Nuncupative will	Adeem	Right of representation	Escheat

Right of election	Postnuptial agreement	Pretermitted (omitted)	Homestead
Elective or forced share	Issue	child	Homestead allowance
statute	Adoption	Posthumous child	Exempt property
Augmented estate	Adopted child	Householder	Family allowance
Antenuptial (premarital)	Nonmarital child	Homestead exemption	
agreement			

REVIEW QUESTIONS

1. What is a will contest? If the contestant of a will is successful and the will is declared invalid, what law determines how and to whom the intestate's in-state and out-of-state real and personal property is distributed?

2. Review the comparison of orthodox and UPC terminology in Exhibit 4.1. How do the meanings of the terms *heir* and *devisee* differ between the two sets of terminology?

3. What are four types of basic wills? Define and explain each one.

4. Explain the differences between (A) a bequest and a devise; (B) a specific legacy and a specific devise; (C) a demonstrative legacy and a general legacy; and (D) a residuary legacy and a residuary devise.

5. What does it mean when a gift in a will is adeemed or lapses?

6. When there are insufficient assets in the testator's estate to pay all debts, taxes, and expenses, what is the order of abatement of the decedent's assets including legacies and devises?

7. How does per capita distribution differ from per stirpes distribution in intestacy cases?

8. Which computation method, the civil law method or the common law method, do you prefer to determine the degree of relationship of collateral heirs? Explain.

9. What does the term *escheat* mean? When does escheat occur?

10. Why is it generally impossible for a testator to disinherit his or her surviving spouse? Explain.

11. What effect does a divorce or a marriage have on a preexisting will?

12. What are the inheritance rights of an adopted child; a stepchild; a nonmarital child; and a pretermitted child?

13. How does a homestead exemption differ from a homestead allowance? How do family allowances differ from exempt property?

14. What are the advantages and disadvantages of a will?

CASE PROBLEMS

Problem 1

Emmett Tomas, a bachelor, makes the following testamentary gifts: a house valued at $110,000 to his best friend, Roxanne Rudin; furniture and household appliances worth $8,000 to Roxanne; a television and stereo system worth $2,500 to his nephew, Roland Tomas; a 2000 Toyota Camry worth $15,000 to his only brother, William Tomas; a gift of $10,000 to his sister-in-law, Sally Tomas, to be paid out of his savings account in Metro State Bank in his hometown; a gift of $5,000 to his church; and a residue gift of his remaining property, which is all personal property worth $22,000, to the American Cancer Society.

A. Place each gift in the appropriate disposition category:
   Specific devise
   Specific legacy
   Residuary legacy
   General legacy
   Demonstrative legacy

B. After his death, Emmett's expenses, debts, and taxes amount to $50,000 and none of his assets pass outside his will as intestate property. Explain how Emmett's testamentary gifts are used to pay his obligations according to the abatement process.

C. If William dies before Emmett and no successor beneficiary is named to receive the Toyota before Emmett dies, what happens to this gift and how does it abate?

D. If the law in Emmett's domiciliary state "abates" a decedent's property within each disposition category and uses the property for payment of debts on a prorated basis, how much, if any, of the specific legacies does each beneficiary get to keep after the $50,000 obligation is paid? See *Matter of Estate of Wales,* 223 Mont. 515, 727 P.2d 536 (1986).

Problem 2

The following diagram shows the interest each descendant would receive in Howard's estate. All descendants are living except as noted.

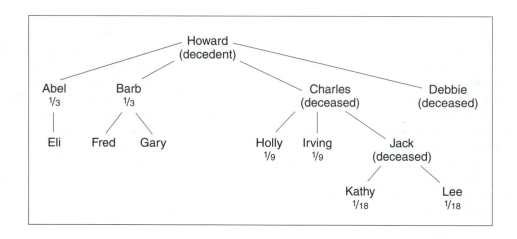

A. Is the distribution method per capita or per stirpes? See *Godwin v. Marvel,* 55 Del. 1, 99 A.2d 354 (1953), and *In re Morton's Estate,* 48 N.J. 42, 222 A.2d 185 (1966).

B. Explain how the shares of Abel and Barb are determined.

C. Eli, Fred, and Gary do not receive an interest. Why not? Explain.

D. Explain the calculation of the shares of Kathy and Lee.

E. If Debbie was married, would her surviving husband receive an interest? Explain.

CHAPTER 5

WILLS: VALIDITY REQUIREMENTS, MODIFICATION, REVOCATION, AND CONTESTS

OUTLINE

OBJECTIVES

After completing this chapter, you should be able to:

➤ Use the terminology associated with the validity, modification, and revocation of wills.

➤ Recognize the formal requirements for a valid will and verify that a client's will has satisfied all those requirements.

➤ Interpret statutes and statutory language so that you can apply the statutes to problems presented by a client's will.

➤ Understand the legal requirements for modifying an existing will and know how to avoid errors in making modifications.

➤ Identify and describe the various methods of revoking a will.

➤ Explain the legitimate grounds for contesting a will.

SCOPE OF THE CHAPTER

The execution, modification, and revocation of a will must be done according to specific statutory guidelines. This chapter discusses the terminology and basic requirements for creation of a valid will. Next the ways an existing will can be changed or modified are covered, as are the procedures which demonstrate the intention of a testator or testatrix to revoke a will. The chapter concludes with a discussion of will contests—the proper persons to contest the legality of a will and the grounds for commencement of a will contest.

REQUIREMENTS FOR THE CREATION OF A VALID WILL

Case law
Law made by judges' decisions.

A will is a legally enforceable, written declaration of a person's intended distribution of property after death. Because a will is "ambulatory," i.e., subject to change, the declaration is revocable during the testator's lifetime and is operative only upon death. Each state passes legislation that controls the right and power of a person to execute a valid will, and these statutes and subsequent **case law** (court decisions) establish the procedure that must be followed. The following state statutes are examples of the requirements for testamentary capacity and the proper execution of a will.

Ill. Compiled Stat. Ann. Ch. 755 § 5/4–1 Capacity of Testator
Every person who has attained the age of 18 years and is of sound mind and memory has power to bequeath by will the real and personal estate which he has at the time of his death.

Ohio Rev. Code Ann. § 2107.03 Method of Making Will
Except oral wills, every last will and testament shall be in writing, but may be handwritten or typewritten. Such will shall be signed at the end by the party making it, or by some other person in such party's presence and at his express direction, and be attested and subscribed in the presence of such party, by two or more competent witnesses, who saw the testator subscribe, or heard him acknowledge his signature.

⛉ ASSIGNMENT 5.1

Mike Hasper is 17 years old. He handwrites and signs a will leaving all his property to his brother, Matthew. There are no witnesses to the will. At age 23, Mike is killed while driving a car. Mike's only living relatives are Matthew and their mother, Mary. Answer the following questions according to your state law:
1. Is Mike's will valid? Explain.
2. Does Mike's holographic will need witnesses? Must it be dated?
3. What formal requirements for the proper execution of a will are lacking?
4. If both Mary and Matthew claim Mike's estate, who prevails? Explain.

The importance of learning your state's requirements for making a valid will cannot be overstated. At the same time, even though state statutes that regulate the preparation and execution of wills are not uniform, they do share some basic similarities. All wills must meet specific formalities to prevent fraud and uncertainty. Commonly, the requirements for a properly executed will are: (1) the maker must have testamentary intent and capacity; and (2) the will must comply with certain formal requirements, e.g., the will must be written, signed, and dated by the testator, and witnessed and signed by at least two persons.

Intent of the Testator

For a will to be declared a legal document that can transfer a decedent's estate after death, the maker must have **testamentary intent:** that is, the testator must establish that the written document currently operates as her last will. The document is a valid will only if the maker possesses the required *animus testandi, i.e.,* the intention to make a will with the express purpose of disposing of property upon death—but not before, as illustrated by the case of *Faith v. Singleton*, 286 Ark. 403, 692 S.W.2d 239 (1985). The testator's intent is revealed from the form, general language, and particular words used in the will itself. Many courts, however, also look at the surrounding circumstances in determining testamentary intent, e.g., the comments and activities of a person who is terminally ill, the collection and placement of important papers in a safe location, and comments made by a person about distribution plans after death. The absence of the ceremonial declaration "this is my last will" often creates doubt about whether a will is intended (see *Matter of Griffin's Will*, 81 A.D.2d 735, 439 N.Y.S.2d 492 [1981], in which the court ruled that because the testatrix, Griffin, did not declare or publish to the witnesses that she intended a document they signed to be her will, the document was not entitled to be probated). Courts have often ruled, however, a document need not be labeled a "will" to be a valid testamentary instrument. In the case of *Estate of Logan*, 489 Pa. 29, 413 A.2d 681 (1980), a paper stating, ". . . I give all my monies and estates to my sister Lillian . . . ," was declared a will and probated.

Caveat: With the exception of "statutory" wills, which have been adopted in a few states (see the detailed discussion in Chapter 6), writing one's own will or using preprinted will forms to avoid the expense of an attorney may be foolhardy. Even worse, it may end in the creation of a document that fails to satisfy the statutory requirements for a legal will regardless of the good intentions of the maker.

Capacity of the Testator

As explained in Chapter 1, **testamentary capacity** is necessary for the creation of a valid will. In all states, a testator must be of majority age (usually 18) and sane, i.e., have the required testamentary capacity to create a valid will (see UPC § 2–501). State statutes and court decisions have established, however, that a member of the armed forces or a married person can make a valid will even if under the age of majority (see Tex. Prob. Code Ann. § 57 and Iowa Code Ann. § 599.1). Sanity is the "soundness of mind" that enables a person to have sufficient mental capacity to create a valid will. In general, a testator must meet the following test for testamentary capacity (sound mind):

- The testator must remember and be aware of the persons who are the "**natural objects** of his or her bounty"—usually family members but also persons for whom the testator has affection.

Testamentary intent
Requirement for a valid will that the testator must intend the instrument to operate as his/her last will.

Testamentary capacity
The sanity (sound mind) requirement for a person to make a valid will.

Natural objects of the testator's bounty
Family members and other persons (friends) and institutions (charitable or religious organizations) for whom the testator has affection.

- The testator must know and be aware of the kind, extent, and nature of the property to be distributed.
- The testator must formulate a plan, e.g., a will, for distribution of the property to the intended beneficiaries, i.e., family and friends, and understand the effect of the dispositions of the plan.

The case *In re Lacy's Estate,* 431 P.2d 366 (Okl. 1967), illustrates the application of this test. The court stated, "A person has 'testamentary capacity' when his mind and memory are such that he knows, in a general way, the character and extent of his property, understands his relationship to the objects of his bounty and those who ought to be in his mind on the occasion of making a will, and comprehends the nature and effect of the testamentary act."

This test for "sound mind," which was formed in case law instead of statutes, relates to the testator's ability, not to his actual knowledge of details. Still a testator must be able to hold these facts in mind long enough to make a rational judgment. Such capacity is needed only at the time of making and executing the will. Even though a person has a low level of intelligence or suffers from a mental illness or senility, it does not mean the person necessarily lacks testamentary capacity. The individual case and circumstances must be investigated and judged on the basis of the test, as established in cases such as *Estate of Wrigley,* 104 Ill.App.3rd. 1008, 60 Ill.Dec. 757, 433 N.E.2d 995 (1982). Case law has consistently held that neither eccentricities or peculiarities of the will nor uncleanliness, slovenliness, neglect of person and clothing, and offensive and disgusting habits of a testator constitute an "unsound mind."

A common question when determining testamentary capacity is whether a person suffering "delusions" lacks such capacity. Some courts have held that a testator suffering delusions is not mentally competent. Most have decided that the presence of **insane delusions** is not inconsistent with testamentary capacity, if the delusions are of such a nature that they cannot reasonably have affected the dispositions made by a will. The testimony of witnesses to the will is often critical in court decisions on "delusions" as noted in *Yett's* case in Chapter 1. See also *Matter of Coleman's Estate,* 1 Haw. App. 136, 615 P.2d 760 (1980), in which the court held that during a **"lucid interval,"** a mentally ill person can execute a valid will.

In will contest cases, Section 3–407 of the Uniform Probate Code places the burden of proof of the lack of the testator's capacity on the contestant—the person contesting the will (this was the decision in *Lacy's Estate,* cited above). Some states, however, place the burden of proof of the testator's "sound mind" on the proponent—the person who submits or delivers the will to the court—as in the case of *Croucher v. Croucher,* 660 S.W.2d 55 (Tex. 1983). The procedures generally followed to satisfy the burden of proof and establish testamentary capacity (i.e., sound mind) include:

- The filing of the will.
- The witnesses give testimony or affidavits are filed that acknowledge the proper completion of formal procedures required for a valid will and the testator's rational behavior and comments *at the time of the execution of the will.*
- The order of the probate court admitting the probate of the will.

Next, during the contest of the will, others, in addition to the witnesses, may testify concerning the testator's "sound mind." Family members, the testator's

Insane delusions
A person with a disordered mind imagines facts to exist for which there is no evidence.

Lucid interval
A temporary restoration to sanity during which an incompetent person has sufficient intelligence and judgment to make a valid will.

personal physician, and other medical care providers may testify, for example. Since the determination of testamentary capacity is a "fact issue," the decision of capacity or lack thereof is generally left to a jury or the court. As a paralegal, if you are asked to witness a will, you must make your judgment of the testator's capacity at the time of the execution of the will with the understanding that *if the testator obviously lacks capacity you should not sign the will*.

ETHICAL ISSUE

🏛 ASSIGNMENT 5.2

1. Billy Budd, age 18, inherited an estate valued at $150,000 from his father. Billy wants his property to go to his dog, Snoopy. Therefore, Billy executes a formal written will that passes all his property to his best friend, Fred, to be used solely for the benefit of the dog and provides that when the dog dies, the remaining property is to be given to the Animal Humane Society. At age 20, while walking on the railroad tracks, Billy is killed by a train. Billy's only living relative, his mother, claims his estate. Was Billy's will valid in your state when he died? Who would receive Billy's estate according to the law in your state?
2. Bradford, age 85, is not married and has no heirs besides his sisters, Katherine and Clara, who live with him and are completely dependent on him for support. He dies and, in his will, gives his entire estate of $100,000 to the American Lung Association. Would Katherine and Clara have grounds on which to challenge the will by alleging that Bradford lacked the capacity to make a valid will? Answer the question according to your state's law.

Formal Requirements of a Will

In addition to testamentary intent and capacity to create a valid will, a testator must execute it with certain formal requirements.

A Written Will

By either statute or case law, a majority of the states require a will to be in writing to be valid (see UPC § 2–502). Generally, a will must be either typed, printed, or handwritten to fulfill the requirement. *Note:* Today, the most common method to create a written will is to use a computer disk and word-processing software, and print out the will on a computer printer. A completely handwritten or holographic will is valid in many states, but it must meet the other formal requirements unless otherwise provided by statute. Section 133.090(1) of the Nevada Revised Statute provides:

> A holographic will is a will in which the signature, date, and material provisions are written by the hand of the testator, whether or not it is witnessed or notarized. It is subject to no other form, and may be made in or out of this state.

Currently, over half of the states allow holographic wills, but the requirements for their validity differ from state to state. In the case *Matter of Estate of Cunningham,* 198 N.J.Super. 484, 487 A.2d 777 (1984), the court did not require a holographic will to be completely handwritten. Instead, the court held that all that is required to admit the writing to probate as a holographic will is that the signature and material provisions in the will be in the handwriting of the testator. Some states require the will to be signed and dated in the testator's handwriting, but compare UPC § 2–502, which does not require a holographic will to be dated (see Exhibit 4.2 in Chapter 4). The courts have held that neither an audiotape nor an audio videotape recording of an oral statement can be probated as a will.

🏛 ASSIGNMENT 5.3

Jim Brown executed an instrument in his own handwriting, in which he wrote: "To whom it may concern. When I die, I sign everything I own over to my best friend, Sarah Williams." Signed and dated: Jim Brown, August 13, 2000. Mr. Brown was a bachelor. Two witnesses also signed the instrument. Would this document be considered a valid will? Were the witnesses necessary for this will? Answer these questions according to your state statutes or case law.

As mentioned earlier, a few states allow oral wills under specific conditions. An oral will is called a nuncupative will. It is usually made during a terminal illness in the presence of witnesses or during military service in time of war. When allowed by statute, oral wills generally can pass only personal property (see North Carolina and Texas statutes below). If a nuncupative will is reduced to a writing by the still living testator or by disinterested witnesses (usually two are required) who can attest to the decedent's oral declaration within a statutory time period (e.g., ten to thirty days) after it was spoken, it may be probated. The following are examples of statutes that recognize nuncupative wills.

N.C. Gen. Stat. §31–3.2 Kinds of Wills

* * *

(b) Personal property may also be bequeathed by a nuncupative will which complies with the requirements of G.S. 31–3.5.

N.C. Gen. Stat. §31–3.5 Nuncupative Will
A nuncupative will is a will
(1) Made orally by a person who is in his last sickness or in imminent peril of death and who does not survive such sickness or imminent peril, and
(2) Declared to be his will before two competent witnesses simultaneously present at the making thereof and specially requested by him to bear witness thereto.

Tex. Prob. Code Ann. § 64 Capacity to Make a Nuncupative Will
Any person who is competent to make a last will and testament may dispose of his personal property by a nuncupative will made under the conditions and limitations prescribed in this Code.

Tex. Prob. Code Ann. § 65 Requisites of a Nuncupative Will
No nuncupative will shall be established unless it be made in the time of the last sickness of the deceased, at his home or where he has resided for ten days or more next preceding the date of such will, except when the deceased is taken sick away from home and dies before he returns to such home; nor when the value exceeds Thirty Dollars, unless it be proved by three credible witnesses that the testator called on a person to take notice or bear testimony that such is his will, or words of like import.

Nuncupative wills play a minimal role in actual probate proceedings. The Uniform Probate Code and the majority of the states do not allow oral wills.

🏛 ASSIGNMENT 5.4

Helen Anderson is dying of cancer at the county hospital. In the presence of her doctor and two nurses, Helen, who has no written will, announces that it is her intent to leave her entire estate to her favorite niece, Alice Marble. She asks those present to act as witnesses of her intention and oral declaration. Helen's only other living relative is another niece, Carla Bergen, whom Helen states she wishes to disinherit. Later that day, Helen dies. According to your state statutes, would Alice be entitled to Helen's estate? Are nuncupative wills on the "deathbed" of the speaker-decedent valid in the majority of the states?

Signature of the Testator

A will must ordinarily be signed by its maker. However, because of illness or illiteracy, the mere making of a mark, e.g., an "X" or an initial, can suffice in some situations. See *Estate of Mangeri,* 55 Cal.App.3d 76, 127 Cal.Rptr. 438 (1976), where the court ruled that a signature by mark was permitted (but other statutory requirements were not met), and *Mitchell v. Mitchell,* 245 Ga. 291, 264 S.E.2d 222 (1980), where an "X" was allowed when it was directed and intended to be a signature, thereby authenticating the will. Also, a New York statute, N.Y. EPTL § 3–2.1, requires that a will bear the testator's signature or some mark that can be regarded as the testator's signature. In addition, in all states a person other than the testator may sign the maker's name to the will in her presence, but such signing must occur at the express direction of the maker, given in a clear manner. The express direction must precede the signing.

> **Example:** If Sam's wife, Mary, signs his name on his will for Sam, her signing alone does not validate the will. Sam must direct or request that she sign for him. The case of *Matter of Kelly's Estate,* 99 N.M. 482, 660 P.2d 124 (App. 1983), illustrates this requirement. The court ruled that another person who signs the testator's name on the will must be directed by the testator and that two witnesses must attest to the request and the substitute's signature; since those requirements were not met in this case, the will was not admitted to probate.

Courts have also consistently held that subsequent ratification of a prior will signed by a substitute person is not sufficient to reinstate the prior will. On the other hand, at his request, the hand of the testator may be guided by another to aid in the signing. All wills should also be dated in the testator's handwriting, but it is somewhat perplexing that this is not a common requirement except in the holographic wills that are recognized in some states (see Mich. Comp. Laws Ann. §700.2502).In the case of *Randall v. Salvation Army,* 100 Nev. 466, 686 P.2d 241 (1984), the court ruled that "the fact that the instrument bears more than one date does not necessarily make its date uncertain or otherwise prevent it from being probated as a holographic will."

The placement of the testator's signature has created a lot of controversy. In most cases, the maker's signature need not be at the end of the will if it can be shown that the intention to authenticate the will was present. See *In re Estate of Carroll,* 192 Ill. App.3d 202, 139 Ill. Dec. 265, 548 N.E.2d 650 (1989), in which the

Exhibit 5.1   Formal Requirements for a Valid Basic Will by State

	Age	Testamentary Capacity	Testator's Signature Required	Witnesses
Alabama	18	(2)	Yes	Two
Alaska	18	(2)	Yes	Two
Arizona	18	(2)	Yes	Two
Arkansas	18	(2)	Yes (4)	Two
California	18 (1)	(2)	Yes	Two
Colorado	18	(2)	Yes	Two
Connecticut	18	(2)	Yes	Two
Delaware	18	(2)	Yes	Two
Florida	18	(2)	Yes (4)	Two
Georgia	14	(2)	Yes	Two
Hawaii	18	(2)	Yes	Two
Idaho	18 (1)	(2)	Yes	Two
Illinois	18	(2)	Yes	Two
Indiana	18 (1)	(2)	Yes	Two
Iowa	18 (1)	(2)	Yes	Two
Kansas	18	(2)	Yes (4)	Two
Kentucky	18	(2)	Yes	Two
Louisiana	16	(2)	Yes (5)	Two (6)
Maine	18	(2)	Yes	Two
Maryland	18	(2)	Yes	Two
Massachusetts	18	(2)	Yes	Two
Michigan	18	(2)	Yes	Two
Minnesota	18	(2)	Yes	Two
Mississippi	18	(2)	Yes	Two
Missouri	18	(2)	Yes	Two
Montana	18	(2)	Yes	Two
Nebraska	18	(2)	Yes	Two
Nevada	18	(2)	Yes	Two
New Hampshire	18 (1)	(2)	Yes	Two
New Jersey	18	(2)	Yes	Two
New Mexico	18	(2)	Yes	Two
New York	18	(2)	Yes (4)	Two
North Carolina	18	(2)	Yes	Two
North Dakota	18	(2)	Yes	Two
Ohio	18	(2, 3)	Yes (4)	Two
Oklahoma	18	(2)	Yes (4)	Two
Oregon	18 (1)	(2)	Yes	Two
Pennsylvania	18	(2)	Yes (4)	Two
Rhode Island	18	(2)	Yes	Two
South Carolina	18 (1)	(2)	Yes	Two
South Dakota	18	(2)	Yes	Two
Tennessee	18	(2)	Yes	Two
Texas	18 (1)	(2)	Yes	Two
Utah	18	(2)	Yes	Two
Vermont	18	(2)	Yes	Three
Virginia	18	(2)	Yes	Two
Washington	18	(2)	Yes	Two
West Virginia	18	(2)	Yes	Two
Wisconsin	18	(2)	Yes	Two
Wyoming	18	(2)	Yes	Two

(1) Younger if: emancipated minor; member of Armed Forces; or married.
(2) Sound mind; mentally competent; or legally competent.
(3) Not under restraint.
(4) Signature at end of will.
(5) Signature at end of each separate page of will.
(6) Notary required.

Illinois court ruled it is immaterial where the signature is written in the will so long as there was intent to authenticate. However, some states insist that the testator's signature appear at the end of the will. Under New York law, the testator's signature marks "the end of the will"; see N.Y. EPTL § 3–2.1. Accordingly, the New York court in the case of *In re Winters' Will,* 302 N.Y. 666, 98 N.E.2d 477 (1951), held the testator must sign at the end of the will. Therefore, testators domiciled in the state of New York should not sign the bottom of each page of their will. The Kansas Supreme Court took a similar position in the case of the *Matter of Reed's Estate,* 229 Kan. 431, 625 P.2d 447 (1981), where the court held that a will must be signed at the end by the testator in order for it to be probated. But compare the comment to UPC § 2–502, which states that if the testator "writes his name in the body of the will, and intends it to be his signature, this would satisfy the statute" and the will can be probated. Because the proper place for a signature varies from state to state, the statutes of the state that has jurisdiction over the decedent's estate must be checked.

A lengthy will of several pages must be carefully drafted and should be typed using computer technology to prevent unscrupulous persons from inserting additional words, names, or even pages into the will. To ensure that there is no opportunity to alter the will, each page should be numbered; no spaces on any page should be large enough for additions or modifications; and the total number of pages should be specifically identified in an attestation clause that states: "The foregoing last will and testament consisting of eight pages, including this page, etc. . . ." In some states when a will consists of multiple pages, it might be wise for the maker to sign or initial each page; however, all states have routinely validated wills that are signed only on the last page (see Exhibit 5.1).

ASSIGNMENT 5.5

1. Michael Shain was 85 years old and suffered from arthritis. He asked that a will be drawn for him. The will was delivered to Michael's hospital room, and in the presence of three witnesses, he said, "This is my last will. I want my property to be distributed according to its provisions." Michael did not sign the will or direct anyone to sign for him. Does this document fulfill the requirements for a valid will in your state based on statute or case law? Compare your answer with Ky. Rev. Stat. Ann. § 394.040.

2. Viola Carter drew a will satisfying all other statutory requirements of her state, but she signed the eight-page document on the first page only. Would her will be valid in your state? Cite the controlling law and see UPC § 2–502, Tex. Prob. Code Ann. § 59, and Ga. Code Ann. § 53–4–20, and compare 20 Pa. Stat. Ann. § 2502.

3. If Viola had asked Jane to sign Viola's name for her on all eight pages, would her will be valid in your state? Cite the controlling law.

4. If Viola had a twenty-page will and page five was missing when she signed the will, would the will or any part of the will be valid in your state? Cite the controlling law and review *Matter of Griffin's Will,* discussed previously, and compare it to *In re Beale's Estate,* 15 Wis.2d 546, 113 N.W.2d 380 (1962).

5. If Viola misspelled her name or used a nickname when she signed her will, would her will be valid in your state? Cite the controlling law. Compare your answer with 72 ALR 2d 1267 and 98 ALR 2d 841.

6. Viola writes, "I, Viola Carter, leave my property to Phyllis Meyer," but does not sign after the statement. Does the fact that Viola wrote out her name in the statement

constitute a "signature"? See *Matter of Estate of Cunningham,* previously cited, and *In re McNair's Estate;* 72 S.D. 604, 38 N.W.2d 449 (1949).

Signatures of Witnesses

The purpose of witnesses is to validate the document declared to be a will was freely and intentionally signed by a competent testator. As the court explained in *Ferguson v. Ferguson,* 187 Va. 581, 47 S.E.2d 346 (1948), the function of the witnesses' subscription "is to establish the genuineness of the testator's signature." The witnesses are not required to read the will or even to be told its contents, but they must be made aware that what they are signing is the testator's will. Witnesses are required to perform two duties: **attest** and **subscribe** the will.

Statutes provide that to be valid a will must be signed in the maker's presence by two or three competent witnesses (but compare UPC § 2–502, which also allows the testator to acknowledge to the witnesses that she signed the will). A written will is not valid without witnesses unless it is a holographic will. State statutes establish the required number of witnesses; currently, all states require two witnesses, except Vermont, which requires three (see Exhibit 5.1). In addition, the witnesses must be competent, i.e., capable of testifying as to the facts of execution of the will and the mental capacity of the testator. Various factors help determine the **competency of a witness,** although age does not appear to be one of them. The minimum age to be a witness is below the age of majority in some states. The following questions must be answered in order to assess competency. The list also helps identify who is and who is not an appropriate witness.

- *Is the witness capable of testifying as to the facts of the execution of the will?* (See the next example.)
- *Is the witness able, by legal standards, to testify as to the mental capacity of the testator?*

Example: Sam Jones attests (witnesses) and subscribes (signs) Greg Hartman's will. Sam is acquainted with Greg, knows the document is Greg's last will, remembers and can relate the facts of the execution of the will, i.e., declared and signed by Greg, and can testify to Greg's mental capacity. Thus, Sam is a competent (capable) witness.

- *When is the competency of the witness required?* The witness must be competent at the time of the execution of the will. If the witness is incompetent at the execution of the will but later becomes competent to testify, the will is invalid.

Example: Stephen Hart is intoxicated. He is asked to witness Kevin Hanson's will. Stephen signs his name unaware of what he is signing. Later, when sober, Stephen is told he witnessed and subscribed Kevin's will. The witness's competence must exist at the time of the execution of the will. The will is not valid.

Conversely, if the witness is competent at the time a will is attested, subsequent incompetency does not invalidate the will. See Mass. Gen. Laws Ann. ch. 191 § 3.

Example: Stanley Novak attests and subscribes Allan Sheppard's will. Five years later Stanley becomes mentally ill and is hospitalized. Stanley's subsequent insanity

---

Attest (a will)
To bear witness; to affirm or verify a will as genuine.

Subscribe (a will)
To sign one's name at the end of a will.

Competent witness
A person who is legally capable and suitable to act as a witness to a will.

would not affect the validity of Allan's will. The purpose of the statutory requirement that a will be witnessed by a competent person is that such a person might later be required to testify that the deceased testator was of sound and disposing mind and memory at the time of the will's execution.

■ *Can the personal representative (executor) or trustee named in the will also act as a competent witness?* The prevailing view is that a person named as personal representative (executor) or trustee in a will, if *not* a beneficiary or devisee of the will, is not disqualified from acting as a proper witness to a will. The basis for the rule is the opinion that an executor does not have a direct interest in the will by virtue of the duty to see that the testator's wishes are carried out, even though the executor claims a personal representative's fee from the estate. The fact that an executor's interest is not "pecuniary, legal and immediate," as is a beneficiary's, qualifies the executor to be a witness. However, it is preferable that a personal representative not be a witness.

Example: Fred Johnson names Robert Olson executor of his will. Robert also attests and subscribes the will. Most states consider Robert a competent witness. (Check your state to see if it follows the majority view.)

■ *Is a person disqualified as a competent witness because the testator owes her a debt?* Generally, a creditor is competent to act as a witness as long as no bequest or devise other than the debt owed is mentioned in the will.

Example: In her will, Janet Martin provides that all her approved debts, funeral expenses, and taxes should be paid out of assets of her estate. Marian Cooper is a creditor of Janet's. No other provisions in the will mention Marian. Marian is a competent witness.

■ *Is an "interested witness," i.e., a person who is both a witness and a beneficiary, or devisee named in a will, a competent witness?*

Example: In his will, Daniel Kane gives a valuable ring to his sister, Margaret Wilson. Margaret can testify to Daniel's mental capacity and is one of the witnesses and subscribers to the execution of his will. She is a competent witness. However, Margaret's act of attesting a will in which she is named a devisee may cost her the ring because she is an **interested witness**—a witness who is also a beneficiary of the will. If there are two other witnesses, the gift to Margaret is valid. If she is one of only two witnesses, however, the gift to Margaret is void, in some states, even though she remains a competent witness. Finally, under some state statutes such as the Tennessee statute below, Margaret may be able to retain the gift even if she is one of only two witnesses, because as an heir, she would receive her intestate's share within the limits of the value of the gift she was to receive through the will. See UPC § 2–505, which provides that a will is valid even if it is attested by an interested witness and allows the witness-beneficiary to receive the gift.

> **Interested witness**
> A person who is a beneficiary and a witness of the same will.

The following is a state statute that addresses itself to this problem:

Tenn. Code Ann. § 32–1–103 Witnesses—Who May Act

(a) Any person competent to be a witness generally in this state may act as attesting witness to a will.

(b) No will is invalidated because attested by an interested witness, but any interested witness shall, unless the will is also attested by two (2) disinterested witnesses, forfeit so much of the provisions therein made for him as in the aggregate exceeds in value, as of the date of the testator's death, what he would have received had the testator died intestate. . . .

This statute is typical in states that have not enacted the Uniform Probate Code.

Good legal practice dictates that a beneficiary or devisee, although competent to act as a witness, should never be a witness to a will from which the beneficiary or devisee benefits, since the bequest or devise (gift of real or personal property) may be voided or may possibly invalidate the entire will. It is also unwise for the attorney who drafts a client's will to act as a witness. Although no statute forbids an attorney from being a witness, this is seldom done since any challenge to the will could require the attorney to cease to represent the estate if the attorney is likely to be called as a witness in a will contest. *A paralegal who acts as a witness could run into the same ethical problem.* However, compare Rule 3.7 of the Model Rules of Professional Conduct which appears to allow an attorney who is also a witness to turn the will contest over to another member of the law firm and resume acting as attorney for the estate after the will is proved (accepted).

In summary, a witness should be acquainted with the testator to establish competency but should not be a beneficiary of the will.

ETHICAL ISSUE

ASSIGNMENT 5.6

Answer the following according to your state laws:
1. Can an heir of an intestate, who becomes a beneficiary or devisee when the intestate makes a will, be a competent witness?
2. In such a case, can the heir-devisee or heir-beneficiary receive any property from the decedent testator?
3. Linda is Sara's daughter and only heir. Sara dies testate. In her will, she leaves Linda the following property: a diamond ring valued at $2,500; silverware worth $750; an $1,800 fur coat; and a lake cottage appraised at $25,000. The rest of Sara's estate is given to charity. The total value of the estate after deducting expenses, debts, and taxes is $100,000. Linda and Sara's best friend, Sylvia, witness and sign the will. In Tennessee, is Linda a competent witness? In your state is Linda competent? In your state would Linda be entitled to receive any of her mother's estate? If so, how much? In your state, what effect does Linda's signature as a witness have on the validity of the will?
4. Determine whether the following persons can act as competent witnesses in your state: (a) a minor, (b) the attorney drafting the will, (c) the spouse of the testator, (d) the personal representative (executor) not named a devisee, (e) a parent of the testator, (f) a creditor of the testator, (g) the probate judge, (h) a spouse of a beneficiary or devisee named in the will.
5. If you are drafting your own will, should the age of an adult witness (person over 18) have any bearing on whether you choose a witness younger or older than yourself? Explain.

In most states the witnesses to the will must sign in the conscious presence of the testator (see Conn. Gen. Stat. Ann. § 45a–251, but compare UPC § 2–502 where presence is not required). In a few states, the witnesses do not necessarily have to sign in one another's presence so long as they both were present when the testator signed the will. In common practice, however, subscribing (signing) by witnesses is accomplished in the presence of both the maker of the will and each other. The signatures of the witnesses attest to the act of signing by the testator, his age and sound mind, and that they themselves signed in his presence. In addition, some states require the addresses of the witnesses be given. Although witnesses need not know the contents of a will, they usually must be aware that what they have subscribed is a will. To help resolve doubts that the testator and the witnesses were present together when all signatures were made, they all should sign with the same pen. For an example of a standard attestation clause used in drafting a will, see Exhibit 5.2.

In summary, the individual state's statutory requirements concerning the maker of the will (testator), witnesses, and signatures vary substantially and may or may not require any or all of the following:

- The will must be written.
- Usually two and sometimes three witnesses are required (see Exhibit 5.1).
- The testator must declare (publish) to the witnesses that the document is her will (this is called publication) and request they sign it (see N.Y. EPTL § 3–2.1[a] [3], [4]). **Publication,** as the term is used in the law of wills, is the declaration or act of the testator at the time of execution of a will that manifests intent that the document is a will; any communication made to witnesses by word, sign, motion, or conduct is sufficient to constitute a publication. This was the definition of publication upheld by the court in the *Matter of Kelly's Estate* case cited previously. But see and compare *Matter of Estate of Polda,* 349 N.W.2d 11 (N.D. 1984). Publication is becoming an unnecessary formality in many states, and it is not required under the Uniform Probate Code.
- The testator must sign the will in the presence of the witnesses.

Publication
In the law of wills, the formal declaration made by a testator at the time of signing a will that it is her last will and testament.

Exhibit 5.2 Sample Signature and Attestation Clauses

Signature Clause
I, Jane C. Doe, have signed this my last will and testament consisting of ten (10) typewritten pages including this page, on June 15, 2000.

_____
Jane C. Doe, Testatrix

Attestation Clause
We certify that in our presence on the date appearing above the testatrix, [name], signed the foregoing instrument and acknowledged and declared it to be her will, that at her request and in her presence and in the presence of each other, we have signed our names below as witnesses, and that we believe her to be eighteen (18) years of age or more, of sound mind, and under no constraint or undue influence.

_____	residing at	_____
(Witness)		(Address)
_____	residing at	_____
(Witness)		(Address)
_____		

Note: Although an attestation clause is not required, all states recommend its use.

- The testator's signature must be at the end of the will.
- The witnesses must see the testator sign the will, or the testator must acknowledge in their presence that the signature on the will is his (see Cal. Prob. Code § 6110[c] or N.Y. EPTL § 3–2.1[a] [2]).
- The witnesses must sign (subscribe) in the presence of the testator and/or at the testator's request (see *Matter of Graham's Estate,* 295 N.W.2d 414 [Iowa 1980]).
- The witnesses must sign in each other's presence (see Ky. Rev. Stat. Ann. § 394.040 or Fla. Stat. Ann. § 732.502). But the placement of the witnesses' signatures may vary according to individual state laws, as noted in the cases cited previously.

Note: The modern way to satisfy these requirements is to include signature and attestation clauses, which state that all the formalities listed above have been properly performed (see Exhibit 5.2). The most common method to resolve these requirements is the use of a self-proving affidavit of witnesses that creates a self-proved will (see Chapter 7). In some states, e.g., Indiana, a videotape may be used to verify that these formalities have been met to establish the validity of the document (see Ind. Code Ann. § 29–1–5–3[c]).

For the most part, statutes have not established many qualifications for attesting witnesses; e.g., in many states, there are no age requirements for witnesses, but they must be competent as previously discussed. When choosing attesting witnesses, good practice would be to choose adult, mature, literate witnesses who are younger than the testator, especially if the testator is elderly, and acquainted with her. If not acquainted, such witnesses should engage in conversation with the testator prior to the execution of the will to establish some rapport and most importantly to reassure the attesting witnesses that the testator exhibits both testamentary intent and capacity should they later be asked to verify these requirements in court.

🏛 ASSIGNMENT 5.7

David Erickson executes a will and declares to three competent witnesses, "This is my last will and testament." In the will, Erickson leaves part of his estate to Allan Potter, who is also a witness to the will. Answer the following questions according to your state's law:

1. Must the witnesses know the contents of Erickson's will before they attest and subscribe their names to the document in order for it to be valid?
2. Can Potter receive his benefit from the will?
3. Is the will valid?

MODIFICATION OF A WILL—CODICIL V. NEW WILL

Because people are living longer, many years may pass between the date a will is executed and the death of the maker of the will. During that time, the testator's wishes concerning the beneficiaries or devisees of the estate assets may dramatically change, as may the potential beneficiaries themselves. For example, the testator's decisions may be influenced by the birth, death, adoption, marriage, divorce, legal separation, change of a minor's guardian, change of state of residency, or change in financial standing. The testator's property may no longer be the same due to additions, sales, gifts, losses, destruction, or a change in value. *Caveat:* As a result of such events or changes, it becomes absolutely essential to update and revise the testator's original will and estate plan.

The most appropriate way to accomplish these major and necessary changes in the will is to execute a "new" updated will that specifically states all earlier wills are revoked. *Therefore, when you are asked to prepare a codicil for a client, you should always discuss the reasons for drafting a "new" will as the preferred document.*

In the past, the most common method to change or modify provisions in a will was a codicil (see Exhibit 5.3). Today, codicils are almost obsolete. In this age of computers, modern practitioners agree the use of codicils to modify or change existing wills is not sound judgment. Because today's will is on a computer disk, it is faster, easier, and less expensive to create a "new" will whenever any changes,

---

Exhibit 5.3 Sample Codicil

[The facts: Henry Hamilton executed a will on June 1, 1998. One provision of the will gives his gun collection to his son, John; another gives his faithful employee, Joe Spencer, $10,000. In 1999, John lost an arm in a hunting accident. That same year, Joe Spencer died. Henry therefore executes the following first codicil to his will.]

CODICIL

I, Henry Hamilton, of River City, Cornwald County, State of A, do make, publish, and declare this to be the first codicil to my last will and testament, executed June 1, 2001.

First: Whereas in Article IV in my said last will and testament, I gave my gun collection to my son, John; and whereas my said son is no longer able to use said gun collection, I hereby give said gun collection to my son, Edwin Hamilton, if he survives me.

Second: Whereas in Article V, I gave $10,000 to my employee, Joseph Spencer; and whereas my said employee has died, I give said $10,000 to his wife, Renee Spencer, if she survives me.

Third: Except as modified by this codicil, in all other respects, I ratify, confirm, and republish all of the provisions of my said last will and testament dated June 1, 1998.

IN WITNESS WHEREOF, I have hereunto set my hand to this, the first Codicil to my Last Will and Testament, dated this 26th day of February, 2000.

Henry Hamilton
_____
2114 Oak Street
_____

THIS INSTRUMENT, bearing the signature of the above-named Testator, was by him on the date thereof willingly signed, published, and declared by him to be a Codicil to his Last Will and Testament, in our presence, who, at his request and in his presence, and in the presence of each other, we believing him to be of sound mind and under no constraint or undue influence, have hereunto subscribed our names as attesting witnesses.

Mary Ann Garsity   residing at   *9341 Silverman Avenue*

Lawrence Escrach   residing at   *87 Coronada Circle*

whether minor or substantial, are necessary. Equally important, the computer technology eliminates the need and expense to create, revise, and eventually find and probate multiple documents, i.e., the will and one or more codicils, after the testator's death. Any will that has been substantially rewritten by one or more codicils is bound to be awkward and confusing.

Interlineation
The act of writing between the lines of an instrument.

To cross out terms or a clause of a will and write in new words or a provision (called **interlineation**) does not create a new will because the act does not meet the statutory requirements for a valid will. In other words, the will, prior to interlineation, was executed validly with respect to attestation, signature, and the like, but that validity does not apply to the will in its interlineated state. The will must meet the formal requirements of the maker's state statutes (see N.Y. EPTL § 3–4.1[a]). Example clauses of wills are discussed in Chapter 7.

🏛 ASSIGNMENT 5.8

On July 15, 2000, Colleen Shannon executes a will. In one of its provisions, she leaves a $50,000 diamond brooch to Susan Slade, a lifelong friend. Sometime afterward, Susan and Colleen have a falling out. No longer wanting Susan to receive the brooch, Colleen crosses out Susan's name from the will and writes in Diane Pylkas as the new beneficiary. A short time later, after having won $100,000 on a television quiz show, Colleen adds a page to her will giving the prize money to Patty Barron. According to your state's law, are the changes Colleen made to her will valid? Explain.

REVOCATION AND REJECTION OF A WILL

A will is operative only after the testator or testatrix dies. Until then, it is ambulatory, i.e., revocable and subject to change. A will can be changed or revoked at any time before death by methods authorized by statute or case law. Whenever the maker of the will changes the way estate property is to be distributed upon death, revocation results, and it terminates the existence of a will. Revocation may be accomplished in three ways:

1. Revocation by physical act.
2. Revocation by operation of law.
3. Revocation by subsequent writing.

Revocation by Physical Act

The following are examples of revocation by a physical act:

- Keri Wilson burns her will.
- Steven Wong tears his will in half.
- Kendra Espinoza writes the word "canceled" across each page of her will.
- Jack Miles uses a pen to cross out all clauses of his will.
- Sally Smallwood, who suffers from frostbite on both hands, asks Julie Adams to burn Sally's will. Julie, in the presence of her husband, Sam Adams, and under specific directions by Sally, burns the will.

All these deliberate physical acts, i.e., burning, tearing, canceling, obliterating, or otherwise destroying a will, or directing and consenting to have another person do the same, allow the maker to revoke the will. Once revoked, if the testator later changes her mind, she cannot revive or reinstate the original will unless she writes a new will. The case of *In re Bonner's Will,* 17 N.Y.2d 9, 266 N.Y.S.2d 971, 214 N.E.2d 154 (1966), illustrates a revocation of a will by deliberate act:

> A will of Merritt Bonner that had been cut-in-two was found after his death. The executors named in the severed will offered it for probate, and the decedent's father opposed the petition to admit the will on the grounds that the will had been revoked. The court ruled that cutting a will in two was an act of revocation that canceled the will.

When destruction is by another person, the direction and consent of the testator and the fact of such destruction must comply with the state statute which regulates the revocation of a will by destruction by a person other than the testator. Some states require such destruction to be witnessed by two persons, neither of whom is the destroyer; others require only that the destruction be at the direction and with the consent of the testator. The following Pennsylvania statute is typical of state statutes that outline procedures for the revocation of wills:

> *20 Pa. Stat. Ann. § 2505* Revocation of a Will
> No will or codicil in writing, or any part thereof, can be revoked or altered otherwise than:
> (1) *Will or codicil* By some other will or codicil in writing;
> (2) *Other writing* By some other writing declaring the same, executed and proved in the manner required of wills; or
> (3) *Act to the document* By being burnt, torn, canceled, obliterated, or destroyed, with the intent and for the purpose of revocation, by the testator himself or by another person in his presence and by his express direction. If such act is done by any person other than the testator, the direction of the testator must be proved by the oaths or affirmations of two competent witnesses [Compare UPC § 2-507].

When the testator's intent is not destruction but to delete or cross out specific words or clauses in the will, the deletions are allowed without the required witnesses' signatures if the testator's intent can be proven. That is the problem. Since the testator often dies before the deletions are discovered, the subsequent confusion often leads to an expensive will contest.

Lost Wills

Sometimes a will cannot be found even though individuals acknowledge it existed. A lost will that cannot be found is not necessarily considered to be a revoked will by a physical act. Many states have statutes or allow case law to decide whether a "lost will" can be probated. With or without a statute, courts require "clear and convincing proof" of a lost will, as in the case of *In re Thompson's Estate,* 214 Neb. 899, 336 N.W.2d 590 (1983), where a second will revoked the original but the second will could not be found. Thus, the required standard of "clear and convincing proof" was not met, and the original will was probated. State laws vary on the question of whether a "lost will" is revoked or can be probated. The decision is generally based on the following:

- Proof the will was properly executed.
- Proof while the will was under the control of the decedent-testator, she did not expressly revoke it.
- Proof of the contents of the will.

One method of satisfying the "proof of execution" requirement is to have the two or three witnesses to the lost will, if available, testify that the "lost" will was acknowledged and signed by the testator. Depending on the circumstances, a true and complete copy of the lost will may or may not be admitted to probate. Consider the following examples:

Example: Martina Martinez's will is properly executed and left in her attorney's office. Martina dies and her will cannot be found. The state statute requires two witnesses to testify concerning the "lost will," but only one witness is discovered. The result could be the same as in the famous lost will case, *Howard Hughes Medical Institute v. Gavin,* 96 Nev. 905, 621 P.2d 489 (1980). There the court denied probate because the statute governing lost wills required evidence from two witnesses and only one witness was found.

Example: Peter Wheaton properly executes a will in 1995. During the last five years, Peter has frequently mentioned to his attorney, beneficiaries, and heirs that he is happy with his estate plans and keeps his will at home. He has shown his family the contents of his will. When Peter dies, the will cannot be found. Any statutory presumption that this will is revoked by physical act can be opposed and refuted by the facts, e.g., the will was under the control of the decedent-testator. See *Matter of Travers' Estate,* 121 Ariz. 282, 589 P.2d 1314 (App. 1978), in which the court ruled that the evidence supported the trial court's finding in a will contest that the will had been destroyed by the testator with intent to revoke. If the other issues, such as proper execution of the will and no expressed revocations by the testator while the will was under his control, are resolved, then a lost will can be probated if its contents are satisfactorily proved.

Example: Boris Decker properly executed his will. When he died, his will could not be found. The attorney who drafted the will retained a photocopy of the original will. This copy could be used as evidence to prove the contents of the will (see *Matter of Wheadon's Estate,* 579 P.2d 930 [Utah 1978], but compare the case of *In re Sage's Will,* 76 Misc.2d 676, 351 N.Y.S. 2d 930 [1974], in which the court disapproved the use of a photocopy in place of the original will).

Case law has generally held that in will contests involving lost or misplaced wills, the burden of proof is on the proponent of the lost will to prove that the testator did not intentionally revoke the lost, misplaced, or destroyed will during his lifetime. This was the position of the Supreme Court of Nevada in the case of *Estate of Irvine v. Doyle,* 101 Nev. 698, 710 P.2d 1366 (1985). In *Barksdale v. Pendergrass,* 294 Ala. 526, 319 So.2d 267 (1975), another case in which the original will could not be found, the court stated that the burden was on the proponent alleging a lost will to establish (1) the existence of a will; (2) the loss or destruction of the will; (3) the nonrevocation of the will by the testatrix; and (4) the contents of the will. The court affirmed the jury's decision that the original will was either lost, misplaced, or destroyed but not with the testatrix's intent.

Finally, a lost will may be found after the administration of a decedent's estate is completed. In that case, if the will is offered for probate and a request to reopen the administration is made, the following factors apply:

- The request may be barred by a statute of limitations. Some states like Texas have a four-year limit after death (see Tex. Prob. Code Ann. § 73[a]); others like California have no time limit (see Cal. Prob. Code § 8000, and compare UPC § 3–108).

- Generally, creditors, banks, trustees or guardians of property, and "good faith" purchasers of estate property are exonerated and protected by the previous estate administration; see Tex. Prob. Code Ann. § 73(b).
- In some states, however, beneficiaries, devisees, or heirs are subject to the distribution provisions of the lost will; see UPC § 3–108.

Revocation by Operation of Law

A will can be revoked wholly or partially by the following:

- By marriage.
- By divorce.

A will can be revoked by other than a deliberate physical act on the part of the maker or another person. A state statute may automatically revoke or amend a will without the testator's knowledge of or agreement to the revocation. For example, by **operation of law,** a will is often affected by the marriage or divorce of the testator or testatrix. If the testator marries after executing a will, it is revoked in some states by operation of law, and the testator's property passes by intestacy. Under UPC § 2–508 and a majority of the states, a subsequent marriage does not revoke a will. The surviving spouse receives an intestate share of the decedent spouse's estate, and the rest of the estate passes under the will (see UPC § 2–301). On the other hand, if a maker is divorced after executing a will, all provisions in favor of the maker's former spouse are revoked by operation of law in most states leaving the rest of the will intact. This is especially appropriate because the divorce decree usually contains a property settlement between the spouses. For the effects of divorce and marriage on an existing will in all states, review Exhibits 4.13 and 4.14. An example of a state statute explaining the effect of marriage on an existing will follows:

> *Or. Rev. Stat. § 112.305* Revocation by Marriage
> A will is revoked by the subsequent marriage of the testator if the testator is survived by a spouse, unless:
> (1) The will evidences an intent that it not be revoked by the subsequent marriage or was drafted under circumstances establishing that it was in contemplation of the marriage; or
> (2) The testator and spouse entered into a written contract before the marriage that either makes provision for the spouse or provides that the spouse is to have no rights in the estate of the testator. [Compare UPC § 2–301.]

Operation of law
Rights pass to a person by the application of the established rules of law, without the act, knowledge, or cooperation of the person.

🏛 ASSIGNMENT 5.9

Harold and Maude are close friends. Maude has drawn her will leaving half her estate to Harold and the other half to charity. If, subsequently, Harold and Maude marry, would Maude's will be revoked by operation of law in Oregon? What would your answer be according to the laws of your state? Would the charity receive half of Maude's estate in your state?

The following Pennsylvania statute addresses itself to the effect of a divorce on an existing will:

20 Pa. Stat. Ann. § 2507 Modification by Circumstances
Wills shall be modified upon the occurrence of any of the following circumstances, among others:

(2) Divorce. If the testator is divorced from the bonds of matrimony after making a will, any provision in the will in favor of or relating to his spouse so divorced shall thereby become ineffective for all purposes unless it appears from the will that the provision was intended to survive the divorce. . . . [Compare UPC § 2–802.]

🏛 ASSIGNMENT 5.10

Frank and Eleanor are single and both have their own wills. Frank and Eleanor marry. Both execute new wills. Subsequently, the couple obtains a divorce. Answer the following according to the statutes of your state:
1. What effect did the marriage have on the wills Frank and Eleanor made before marrying?
2. What effect does their divorce have on the former spouses' wills?

Revocation by Subsequent Writing

Both of the following are examples of a revocation of a will by subsequent writing:

- Samantha Nguyen writes a new will.
- Lee Shapiro adds a codicil to her will.

A current will can be expressly revoked only by a written document executed with the same formalities required for a valid will. The law is well settled that the last will and codicil executed with these formalities is the valid will of the decedent. This is the decision of the courts whenever more than one will or codicil is discovered after the death of a testator. Today, in our computer world, codicils are rarely used and have been replaced by "new" wills.

A revoked will is usually destroyed, but it may be advisable to retain the former will when the testator's testamentary capacity is questioned or there is a possibility of a will contest. The reason for saving the will is that the revocation of the earlier will may turn out to be dependent on the validity of the later will. Possibly, too, the testator may change her mind and decide she prefers the terms of the earlier will. If the later will is held invalid, it may be possible and appropriate to probate the earlier will. An example of a statute concerned with the retention and validity of an earlier will is 20 Pa. Stat. Ann. § 2506:

If, after the making of any will, the testator shall execute a later will which expressly or by necessary implication revokes the earlier will, the revocation of the later will shall not revive the earlier will, unless the revocation is in writing and declares the intention of the testator to revive the earlier will, or unless, after such revocation, the earlier will shall be reexecuted. Oral republication of itself shall be ineffective to revive a will. [Compare UPC § 2–509.]

Example: In 1997, Richard makes a will and leaves $4,000 to his niece, Myrrha. In 2000, he revokes but does not destroy the first will and writes a second will, which gives $2,000 to Myrrha and $2,000 to her sister, Melisande. Later, Richard destroys the second will because he does not approve of the person Melisande marries. Although he intends to revive the first will, he dies before this task is accomplished. In the eyes of the law, Richard died intestate. Myrrha would not be entitled to the $4,000 because the first will was rendered ineffective by Richard's deliberate revocation of it. The second will was revoked when Richard destroyed it, but this revocation does not revive the first will.

ASSIGNMENT 5.11

1. In the above example, would Myrrha be entitled to the $4,000 in your state?
2. How could Richard, while living, revive the first will after he destroyed the second will?

WILL CONTESTS

A will contest is a lawsuit commenced in probate court that challenges the validity of an existing will. Very few wills are contested and most contests are unsuccessful. State statutes govern will contests, but they vary regarding when a hearing on a will contest must occur. In the *Tobin* case discussed below, the Illinois court allowed a niece, who was not given notice, to contest the will 18 years after the will was admitted to probate. As a rule, the hearing is prior to or shortly after a will is admitted to probate by the court. Before the hearing, the contesting party files an affidavit of objection to the petition for probate and lists the grounds for the objection.

Who Can Contest a Will

A lawsuit must be commenced by a person who has "standing" and, consequently, may make an objection to the probate court and request that a will offered for probate be rejected. A person with **standing** is someone who stands to lose a pecuniary interest, i.e., a share of the decedent's estate, if a will is allowed, such as a spouse, beneficiary, or heir of an earlier will. The person who contests the will has the burden of proving his objection by "clear and convincing evidence," a standard that is more than a mere preponderance of the evidence (the civil law standard) but less than beyond a reasonable doubt (the criminal law standard). Generally, creditors are *not* proper contestants since they can pursue their claims in a separate lawsuit in civil court, but they must be given notice of the probate proceeding so they can pursue their claims. If probate is denied, i.e., the will is successfully contested and declared invalid by the probate court, then the decedent's estate passes according to intestate succession laws, and all belongings are distributed as if the decedent had left no will. This law is the reason an heir, who would inherit if the decedent is declared intestate, has standing, i.e., the right to contest the will, but creditors do not have standing.

Most states have a statute of limitations, i.e., a limited time period during which the contestant must file the appropriate documents to contest the will. If the time

Standing
The requirement that a person stands to lose a pecuniary interest in a decedent's estate if a will is allowed.

limit is not strictly followed, the opportunity to contest the will is lost regardless of the validity of the contestant's challenge (but read and compare the *Tobin* case below).

 ASSIGNMENT 5.12

Harry is not mentioned in the will of his father, George. In their domiciliary state, Harry receives a share of his father's estate if George dies intestate. George's will provides that half his estate goes to his wife, Helen, and the remaining half goes to charity. As an heir, Harry contests the will and establishes his right to inherit the property in the case of intestacy. According to your state's laws, is Harry entitled to contest the will? Would this will contest succeed? If Harry wins the case, how much of his father's estate does he receive in your state?

ASSIGNMENT 5.13

Joan is named beneficiary in her Aunt Grace's will, dated April 10, 1995. In 2000, Grace executes a new will, which states that it revokes all prior wills and codicils. Joan is not mentioned in the new will. Joan establishes that the will dated April 1995 had been properly executed while the will written in 2000 was witnessed by two persons also named as beneficiaries. According to your state's laws, is Joan a proper will contestant? Would Joan's contest succeed? Explain.

WILL MORE WILL CONTESTS BE FILED IN THE FUTURE?

With more do-it-yourself will kits on the market and proper will execution methods doubtful, it is possible that the filings of lawsuits involving a will contest may rise. It is much easier for a client to attempt to prepare his own will on the family computer. Problems with these homemade wills may prompt surviving family members and other interested parties to question the validity of the document.

Grounds for Contesting a Will

The probate court may refuse to accept a will that has been presented to it for approval for several reasons. In some of the cases, the court finds legitimate grounds for a successful will contest. The following are grounds for contesting a will:

- *The will is not properly executed.*

Examples: (1) John writes but does not sign his will. (2) John writes and signs the will, but it is not witnessed. (3) John writes and signs the will, but the witnesses are not competent (review the discussion on competency in this chapter).

- *No notice of the probate of a will is given to heirs or creditors.*

Example: John's estate is administered and distributed without notice of the proceedings being given to one of John's sons or to a creditor. The requirement of notice is illustrated by *In re Estate of Tobin,* 152 Ill.App.3d 965, 105 Ill.Dec. 891, 505 N.E.2d 17 (1987). In that case, the court ruled that a niece, who was an heir of the decedent but did not receive notice, was entitled to contest the will even though 18 years had passed.

▪ *The will or the testator's signature is forged.*

Examples: (1) John's signature is copied and written by another. (2) John's written (holographic) will is a forgery. Handwriting experts could be retained to determine authenticity.

▪ *The testator lacks testamentary capacity.*

Examples: (1) John lacks legal capacity. He is a minor. (2) John lacks testamentary capacity. He is of "unsound mind." He is mentally ill or mentally retarded and lacks knowledge and understanding of the nature and extent of his property and of the persons who are the natural objects of his bounty at the time of the execution of the will. In the case *In re Stitt's Estate,* 93 Ariz. 302, 380 P.2d 601 (1963), which involved a will contest, the court stated that "in determining testamentary capacity, the law is concerned only with the testator's state of mind at the time of the execution of the will." As previously discussed, the Uniform Probate Code places the burden of proof on the contestant to establish the testator's lack of mental or testamentary capacity, i.e., a sound mind; see UPC § 3-407.

▪ *The will has been revoked.*

Examples: (1) John has written a new will. (2) John has destroyed or canceled his existing will. (3) John has married or been divorced since writing his will.

▪ *The testator is induced by fraud to write or change the will.*

Examples: (1) John is tricked into leaving his estate to his nephew who causes John to believe erroneously that his only other heir is dead. (2) John disinherits his daughter after he was lied to by his son that the daughter hates John.

In order for a probate court to disallow a will on the grounds the testator was deceived into making it, the contestant must prove (1) a beneficiary of the will actually led the testator into an erroneous belief concerning the disposition of the property (as in the first example above, where John's nephew caused him to believe his only other heir was dead) and (2) the testator, who believed the false statement to be true, relied on it and wrote a will accordingly. (If John did not believe his nephew, but nevertheless wrote a will favoring the nephew over the other heir, the court would allow the will to be probated and disregard the claim of fraud. The testator's reliance on the beneficiary's willful misrepresentation is essential.)

▪ *The will contains material contradictions, ambiguities, or mistakes.*

Examples: (1) John's will leaves the same items of property to different persons. (2) John's will is written so ambiguously it is impossible to determine his intent. (3) John did not know he was signing a will.

A material mistake is one that alters the substance or matter of the provision in which it appears. If John had given his automobile to Eugene and to Eloise in the same will, both gifts to take effect at the same time, John's mistake would be material; it would alter the bequest itself. Without further evidence to show which beneficiary John intended to have the automobile, the probate court would hold the gift invalid. Although a probate court does not have the power to rewrite the will in its entirety, the court may strike down individual provisions on the grounds the testator's wishes concerning the bequests or devises therein cannot be determined; the remaining portions of the will would then be admitted. Sometimes a mistake may invalidate a will. If the mistake is material, e.g., a mistake as to the document signed, the entire will is invalid.

> **Example:** John signs a document which he believes to be his will, when in fact it is his wife's will. This document is not valid.

On the other hand, if the mistake is a simple drafting error, e.g., the will lists the address of the testator as 4711 Fair Hills Avenue instead of 4771, this will is valid.

- *The testator is forced by duress or persuaded by undue influence to sign the will.* The contestant in this situation alleges the testator did not execute the will independently or voluntarily.

> **Examples:** (1) John is forced by physical threats to himself or his family to sign the will. (2) John is influenced by another with whom John has a close personal (confidential) relationship to include that person in his will while excluding his rightful beneficiaries or heirs, e.g., his spouse and children. (3) John makes a will leaving a substantial amount of his estate to his housekeeper, Mary, who also signs the will as one of the two required witnesses. As previously discussed, some states presume there was undue influence in this case, while other states declare the will invalid because Mary is an "interested witness" or at least deny her the benefits she would receive through John's will but do not invalidate the rest of the will.

In the above examples, John, at first glance, may have written and executed a proper will and satisfied the required formalities of the law of wills in his state, yet the probate court could hold the will invalid because John's free will to dispose of the property according to his own wishes has been denied. To create a valid will, the requisite testamentary intent must be present. A will is invalid if obtained through physical threats or mental influence that destroys the freedom of choice and intent of its maker. To threaten the maker or members of his immediate family with violence to force the execution of a will constitutes duress and physical coercion—factors that invalidate the will. To substitute by force someone else's wishes in place of the maker's is another example of the use of coercion in drafting a will. Although not physical in nature as with duress, nor apparent from the appearance of the will as with mistake, undue or extraordinary influence on the mind of the maker can also render the will invalid.

A will might be disallowed because of both fraud and undue influence, as illustrated by the case of *Cook v. Loftus,* 414 N.E.2d 581 (Ind.App. 1981), in which a beneficiary of a new will falsely told the testator the beneficiaries under his prior will planned to put him in a nursing home. The court upheld the prior will.

The presence of undue influence is especially difficult to determine for there are as many kinds of undue influence as there are personalities. The probate court must consider the testator, the person who allegedly exerted the undue influence, and the circumstances. The court may infer undue influence if the testator ignores blood relatives and names, as beneficiary, a nonrelative who is in constant close contact with the testator and thus in a position to unduly influence her. Nevertheless, undue influence must still be proven.

Example: An in-law or friend caring for the deceased at the time of death is named beneficiary to the exclusion of all family members. See *In re Estate of Price,* 223 Neb. 12, 388 N.W.2d 72 (1986), in which the court found that in this instance there had been no undue influence. See also the case of *Succession of Bacot,* 502 So.2d 1118 (La.App. 1987), in which the court upheld a devise of the decedent's estate to a gay lover instead of to the family.

In some states, a presumption of undue influence is raised if a contestant (opponent) of the will shows (1) a confidential relationship (doctor, attorney, legal assistant, caregiver, priest or minister, fiduciary) allowed the alleged influencer an opportunity to control the testamentary act; (2) the testator's weakened physical and mental condition easily permitted a subversion of free will; (3) the influencer actively participated in preparing the will; or (4) the influencer unduly profited as a beneficiary or heir under the provisions of the will. *Note:* In most states, not to mention the canons of professional ethics, *a lawyer or paralegal who is intended to be a beneficiary or heir under a will must refrain from drafting and designing the will.* See Rule 1.8(c) of the Model Rules of Professional Conduct.

◄ ETHICAL ISSUE

But see *In re Conduct of Tonkon,* 292 Or. 660, 642 P.2d 660 (1982), where the attorney (Tonkon) represented his client (testator) for many years and the client's final will left Tonkon a gift of $75,000. Even though Tonkon did not advise the client to consult another attorney, the Oregon Supreme Court held he did not violate the Code of Professional Responsibility. As an attorney or paralegal in a situation like Tonkon's, the following are other procedures you could and should use to avoid this ethical problem:

1. Refuse to draft the will.
2. Insist another attorney of the client's choice draft the will but not an associate or partner from your law firm. See Model Rule 1.10(a).
3. Fully disclose the Code of Conduct to your client.
4. Make sure you do not in any way suggest or encourage the gift and that the client originated the bequest.
5. Make sure the gift is not the major asset of the estate.

⚏ ASSIGNMENT 5.14

Review the resolutions of the ethical problem above; then answer the following:

1. You are asked to draft a client's will that includes a gift to you as in the *Tonkon* case. What should you do if the client is so near death there is no time to obtain another attorney?
2. Could you argue the gift is appropriate because you are a "close personal friend" of the client and, therefore, "a natural object of the testator's bounty"?

The burden of proving undue influence, fraud, duress, mistake, or revocation is generally on the contestant and, as mentioned earlier, the proof must be "clear and convincing" (see UPC § 3–407). Once the contestant has established sufficient evidence of the truth of her contention, she has established a **prima facie** case. Now the burden of establishing evidence to the contrary that establishes the will's validity shifts to the proponent of the will. Exhibit 5.4 illustrates the method and legal form used to contest a will in the state of New York.

Prima facie
At first sight; on the face of it. A fact presumed to be true unless disproved by evidence to the contrary.

In Terrorem or "No Contest" Clause—A Forfeiture Clause

People who have wills are concerned about will contests even though very few contests are successful. If the maker of a will fulfills all requirements for a valid will and executes it correctly, the probate court will uphold it. Nevertheless, any will is open to a will contest whether by legitimate persons or unscrupulous ones. Unfortunately, even though the will contest has no merit, the cost of the potential litigation may be so high that a settlement is reached, and gives the contestants part of the estate even though this was not the intent of the testator.

In anticipation that an omitted family member or disgruntled heir may contest the will, the testator may attempt to prevent a will contest by such person by including in the will a "no contest" or **"in terrorem" clause.** Such clauses state that if a beneficiary or heir named in the will disputes the validity of the will, objects to the probate of the will, or challenges the dispositions, i.e., the kind and amount of the gifts that pass to the named persons listed in the will, that contestant forfeits all benefits of the will. Some states, e.g., Indiana, declare such in terrorem

In terrorem clause
A clause in a will that if a beneficiary of the will objects to probate or challenges the will's distributions, that contestant forfeits all benefits of the will.

Exhibit 5.4   Objection to Probating a Will

Surrogate's Court: County of _____

    In the Matter of the Objections to Probate against   Objections to Probate
the Last Will and Testament of _____,   File No. _____
Deceased.

_____, a distributee objects to the probate of the instrument propounded herein as the last will and testament of _____, late of the County of _____, deceased, upon the following grounds:
    First: That the alleged will was not duly executed by the said _____, deceased, that she did not publish the same as her will in presence of the witnesses whose names are subscribed thereto, that she did not request the said two witnesses to be witnesses thereto, and that the said alleged witnesses did not sign as witnesses in her presence or in the presence of each other.
    Second: That on the _____ day of _____, 20 ____, the said decedent, _____, was not of sound mind or memory and was not mentally capable of making a will.
    Third: That the said paper writing was not freely or voluntarily made or executed by the said _____, as her last will and testament, but that the said paper writing purporting to be her will was obtained and the subscription and publication thereof if it was in fact subscribed or published by her, were procured by fraud and undue influence practiced upon the decedent by _____ and _____, the principal legatees and devisees named in said paper, or by some other person or persons acting in concert or privity with them, whose name or names are at the present time unknown to this contestant.
    Fourth: A trial by jury of the issues raised by this answer is hereby demanded.
    Wherefore, the above named contestant prays that this proceeding may be dismissed, with costs.

                                                   _____
                                                   Attorney for Objecting Distributee
                                                   P.O. Address
                                                   Tel. No.

[*Verification*]

This form is used in New York when an interested party (beneficiary, distributee, or heir at law) objects to the acceptance and probate of a will.
_____

Source: Reprinted with permission from West's McKinney's Forms, ESP, § 7:523. Copyright ©, by West Group.

clauses unenforceable; some, e.g., New York and Wyoming, strictly enforce the clause; others disregard the clause if the contestant had "probable cause" to commence the will contest. See N.Y. EPTL § 3–3.5 and *Dainton v. Watson,* 658 P.2d 79 (Wyo. 1983), in which the court ruled that "a no contest or in terrorem clause in the will, which required forfeiture of the bequest to the [beneficiary] as a result of the beneficiary's unsuccessful will contest, was valid and did not violate public policy." The following is an example of an in terrorem clause:

> If a beneficiary or devisee under this will contests or challenges the probate of this will or any of its clauses in any manner, in such event the bequest or devise of my estate given to such beneficiary or devisee under this will is hereby revoked and forfeited, and said bequest or devise shall be distributed as part of my residuary estate.

KEY TERMS

Case law	Insane delusions	Interested witness	Prima facie
Testamentary intent	Lucid interval	Publication	In terrorem clause
Testamentary capacity	Attest (a will)	Interlineation	
Natural objects of the testator's bounty	Subscribe (a will)	Operation of law	
	Competent witness	Standing	

REVIEW QUESTIONS

1. Who may make a valid will?
2. Can an attorney or a paralegal prepare and draft a will for a client who is of unsound mind? Explain.
3. What are the statutory or formal requirements for executing a will?
4. What are the signature requirements, e.g., types of signatures or placement of signatures, for testators and witnesses?
5. How is a witness determined to be competent?
6. Can an attorney or a paralegal be a competent witness to a will? Should they be witnesses?
7. Is an attestation clause required in every will? Explain.
8. In what three ways can a will be revoked? Explain.
9. Under what circumstances can a "lost will" be probated?
10. Only a person with "standing" can contest a will. What does this mean?
11. What are the appropriate reasons or grounds for contesting a will? Explain.
12. Are in terrorem clauses in a will enforced in your state? Cite the appropriate statute or case law.

CASE PROBLEMS

Problem 1

Bill Jorgenson is terminally ill. Suppose Bill's son, Harold, convinces his father that Cheryl Jorgenson, Bill's wife and Harold's mother, is initiating institutional commitment proceedings against Bill. In fact, that is not true. Nevertheless, Bill changes his will because of this allegation and leaves everything to Harold. According to your state's law, what are the grounds for contesting a will? Which grounds can Cheryl use to contest Bill's will? What other rights does Cheryl have if the will is declared valid? See the *Cook* case previously cited.

Problem 2

A will was drafted for Melinda Wadsworth. Melinda's attorney, Malcolm Edwards, was present when she signed the will. Malcolm then signed as one of the attesting witnesses. It was Malcolm's intent to have Jaclene Morgan, a paralegal working for his law firm, be the second required witness. However, Jaclene was out of the office when Melinda and Malcolm signed the will. When Jaclene returned, Melinda had left the office. Malcolm showed the will to Jaclene, informed her that it was Melinda's will and signature, and asked Jaclene to witness and sign the will. Instead of immediately signing the will, Jaclene first called Melinda and verified that it was Melinda's will and signature. Then, Jaclene signed as a witness to the will.

A. Is the above procedure for executing a will proper? Explain.

B. Would this will be valid in your state? Cite the statute or case law. See *Matter of Jefferson's Will,* 349 So.2d 1032 (Miss. 1977).

CHAPTER 6

PREPARATION TO DRAFT A WILL: CHECKLISTS AND THE CONFERENCE WITH THE CLIENT

OBJECTIVES

After completing this chapter, you should be able to:

➤ Collect and assimilate the relevant facts in preparation for the preliminary draft of a will.

➤ Identify, explain, and interpret the sources of law, e.g., common (case) law and statutes which determine the validity of a will.

➤ Develop and use checklists to elicit the information necessary for the preliminary draft of a will.

➤ Ensure all necessary pertinent information obtained from appropriate checklists is accurate and complete.

➤ Recognize when additional information is needed.

➤ Identify and follow guidelines used to prepare wills.

SCOPE OF THE CHAPTER

This chapter is concerned with the procedures prior to making a will. A will must be prepared with meticulous care and follow the standards prescribed by case law and state statutes. If not careful, a drafter can fail to execute a valid and appropriate will if essential information is not elicited from the client and certain rules of practice are not followed.

The chapter begins with the initial meeting with the client. It identifies the checklists that are created and used to gather facts to determine to whom the client's assets will be transferred, and how tax burdens and miscellaneous problems can be minimized or resolved. Definitions and examples of terms used in the checklists precede the individual lists. Sample checklists used to prepare a draft of the will are illustrated. You must learn to develop checklists and questionnaires appropriate for your client's needs. Next comes a discussion of some pitfalls in the preparation of the rough draft of a will. Guidelines to make the document a purposeful, legally enforceable, and unimpeachable testamentary disposition are presented.

THE CONFERENCE WITH THE CLIENT: INITIAL INTERVIEW, CHECKLISTS, AND OTHER MATTERS

When you and the attorney meet with a client to discuss preliminary matters prior to drafting a will, you must collect information about the client's finances and family. Checklists will be used or created to obtain the necessary data.

In order to assist the attorney to formulate an appropriate will for a client, you will need to develop interviewing, data-collecting, drafting, and counseling skills to help clients overcome the normal reluctance most people have when they discuss family relationships and financial matters. By being positive, cooperative, reassuring, informative, and professional in appearance and demeanor, you can help the client overcome this reluctance and understand that his or her best interests will be served by an open and frank discussion of complete financial data

ETHICAL ISSUE ➤ and information. *You should also assure the client that strict confidentiality of all matters which concern family and finances will be maintained.* Once a client who seeks a will or an estate plan hires your supervising attorney, your work as a legal assistant will commence.

TECHNOLOGY ADVANCES MAY MEAN CLIENT HAS CREATED HIS OWN WILL

Will preparation kits are sold in office supply stores, book stores, and in major retail outlets. These products can also be ordered from catalog companies and from e-commerce retailers. Some will forms are available for free on the Internet. The easy access to these forms may result in some attempts by clients to draft their own wills. It is questionable how adequate and valid these documents are. Rarely will clients fully understand the terminology used. It is doubtful that the will execution was properly performed. If a client has attempted to prepare his own will and is now seeking assistance from a law office, he should be commended for realizing that professional counsel is needed. Use the client's draft to assist with the interview.

Initial Interview

The development of a will begins with an initial and lengthy interview of the client by the attorney. Assuming a "comfort" level has been reached and the client is willing to be open and frank about financial data in front of others, you will be asked to attend the interview. Your first task will be to help the client identify all facts, data, and information needed to create a draft of the will. You must develop checklists and questionnaires or expand, amend, or modify existing copies of these documents and thoroughly review them with the client to ensure they elicit the information necessary for the draft. Exhibits 6.1 through 6.6 are examples of the checklists that will enable you to obtain the requisite information.

You will need to collect information concerning the client's financial affairs and family members names, addresses, domicile, and marital status. A chart showing the family tree should be drawn. It should identify adopted and nonmarital children and include the general health of all family members. Assets and liabilities should be listed. Beneficiaries, including charities, should be named, and the assets to be transferred to them should be identified and valued. All fiduciaries, e.g., personal representatives, trustees, guardians, or conservators, should be named. All known creditors and the amounts of the debts owed to them should be listed. Finally, the specific wishes of the client for disposition of the estate should be determined and carefully considered in order to anticipate, counter, or prevent potential will contests by disgruntled family members who may receive nominal gifts of the estate or be completely disinherited.

Once the checklists have been executed and the questionnaires answered, you will review them with the client to ensure they are complete and accurate. Then you can discuss how best to achieve the specific objectives of the client. In addition, one of the more important tasks the attorney undertakes is to help the client reduce death taxes. The attorney should familiarize the client with the taxes imposed on a decedent's estate and give legal advice, *something you must not do*, on how to minimize them. This can be accomplished by reducing the decedent's gross estate through lifetime gifts and increasing the potential deductions from the gross estate such as the marital and charitable deductions. Finally, the client should be informed of the necessity of making decisions about how best to achieve an effective, valid distribution of her estate, at death, in a manner of her own choosing.

ETHICAL ISSUE

If it is obviously apparent that a person lacks mental capacity—a sound mind—the attorney and paralegal cannot accept employment. On the other hand, the lawyer and paralegal should not be judgmental about the client's plans for the will, even if they are eccentric. The paralegal should be helpful and encourage the client to carefully examine, analyze, and determine her true feelings toward beneficiaries and the distributions planned for them. The attorney and paralegal can help the client focus on whether the will should distribute the testator's estate (1) on the basis of a property distribution plan in which the closest family members receive the greater share and other relatives and friends a lesser amount, (2) on the basis of family need, or (3) a combination of these two. Some clients may adopt an unduly submissive or subordinate attitude toward their attorney or the paralegal and may even suggest or request the attorney or you advise them as to what they should do with their estate property. *This request must be adamantly denied to avoid unethical consequences.*

ETHICAL ISSUE

ETHICAL ISSUE

After the interview, you should prepare optional drafts of the will distribution plans for consideration and review by the client. The plans should include comparisons of their tax consequences and other expenses including attorney's fees. The drafts should be summarized and explained in plain language to the client so that any modifications can be noted and incorporated into the appropriate selected draft. Once the client is satisfied with the changes, the final will is prepared and properly executed. *While you must avoid improper solicitation*, you should recommend periodic reviews of the will whenever the client's marital status (divorce or marriage), domicile, or the law changes, or when additional children are born or adopted.

ETHICAL ISSUE ▸

Use of Checklists to Obtain Basic Data

The following discussion illustrates the development and use of checklists, which help to assemble the data necessary to draft a will appropriate for the individual needs of the client. Definitions and examples of terms used within the checklists precede the individual lists. In addition to being used during the formation of the will, the information is helpful to determine the proper venue for probating the estate and the location of beneficiaries, devisees, and assets of the deceased. The client should be given a copy of each checklist before the conference so he can gather the information requested. The client should not attempt to complete the checklists alone, however, but should obtain the assistance of family members and financial advisers. You will also help obtain the information. *If an earlier will exists, obtain a copy from the client for review.*

ETHICAL ISSUE ▸

The purpose of checklists is to ensure accurate, complete, and requisite information is obtained. As you review each checklist, you need to analyze and interpret the collected data and recognize when supplementary information is needed.

The sample checklists in this chapter are (1) Family Data, (2) Family Advisers, (3) Assets, (4) Liabilities, (5) Life Insurance Policies, and (6) Locations of Important Documents. In Chapter 7 you will be asked to draft your own will from these sample checklists or from those you develop for yourself. The same or similar checklists will be used to establish an estate plan in Chapter 10. In specific instances, additional or supplementary checklists may be needed, and you will be asked to produce them.

Terminology Associated with Family Data Checklists

The following are terms you are likely to encounter when you prepare a family data checklist:

Advancement

Money or property given by a parent while living to a child in anticipation of the share the child will inherit from the parent's estate and in advance of the proper time for receipt of such property.

- *Advancement.* An **advancement** is money or property given by a parent to a child in anticipation of the share the child will inherit from the parent's estate. Prior to the parent's death, it is given to the child and is intended to be deducted from the share of the parent's estate the child eventually receives after the parent's death.

Example: Shirley Wilson has 100 shares of valuable stock. Under intestate succession laws, Shirley's only daughter is entitled to the 100 shares. While alive, Shirley gives her daughter 50 shares. The 50 shares would be considered an advancement unless Shirley dies testate or other evidence is presented that rebuts the advancement presumption. The laws of most states require a written confirmation of an advancement must exist on the date of the donor's death. The rule of advancement generally applies when there is no will.

- *Disinheritance*. Disinheritance by will is the act by which the testator of an estate specifically deprives another, who would otherwise be the testator's legal heir, from receiving the estate.

Example: Susan York specifically states in her will "I, intentionally and with full knowledge, leave nothing to my son, Leonard, from the assets of my estate." *Note:* Compare this to the "no contest" (in terrorem) clause in Chapter 5.

- *Life estate*. A life estate is an interest in real property, e.g., land and buildings, for a lifetime, either the lifetime of the person holding the estate or of some other person. A person who holds a life estate, called the life tenant, possesses and is entitled to use the real property only during the lifetime of the person named in the will or deed which granted the life estate.

Example: Barry receives a life estate in a lake cottage through his uncle's will. Barry may use and possess the cottage until he dies.

- *Spendthrift*. A spendthrift is one who spends money unwisely and wastefully.

Example: George wastes the estate left him by his father by drinking, gambling, idleness, and the like.

Checklist for Family Data

As a paralegal, part of your investigatory duties is to collect complete information concerning your client, the client's family, and the beneficiaries or devisees to be named in the will. You should obtain the following:

- Full names, addresses, and phone numbers of the participants: maker of the will; beneficiaries or devisees; executor (or executrix); witnesses; guardians; and trustee, if any.
- Age and marital status of the maker, beneficiaries, and devisees.
- Relationship of appropriate participants to the client.
- Mental and physical health of the client, spouse, and other beneficiaries.
- Financial status (worth) of the client, spouse, and family, and the nature of any business in which the client has an interest.
- Family affairs, including tensions, possible mistreatment of the client and the source of such mistreatment, debts owed the maker by family members, advancements (property previously transferred) given to some members, spendthrifts, persons incapable of handling their own financial affairs who may need a trustee, and other pertinent matters.

Using a checklist like the one in Exhibit 6.1, you can collect and organize the family data.

The Need for Supplementary Data.   In some instances, information provided by the checklists will not be adequate to inform the attorney of all the client's needs or plans to dispose of estate property. As an observant practitioner, you should note situations likely to lead to problems with specific devises (gifts) and should further pursue these matters with the client after first bringing them to the attention of the supervising attorney. *You should not discuss any circumstances or suggest resolutions to problems which may involve giving legal advice.*

ETHICAL ISSUE

Exhibit 6.1 Family Data

CHECKLIST: FAMILY DATA

Client
Name and address: _____City, State _____
Alias or a.k.a _____
Telephone number: Home _____Other _____
Social Security number: _____
Date of birth: _____City, State _____
Marital status: _____Maiden name _____
Date of marriage: _____City, State _____
Date of divorce: _____City, State _____
Date of death: _____City, State _____
Present health: _____
Occupation/business: _____
Name of employer: _____Telephone _____
Employer address: _____

Family Members (use additional sheets as necessary) (Spouse, children, grand-children, parents, other dependents, relatives, and beneficiaries)
Name: _____
Relationships: _____
Telephone number: Home _____Other _____
Address: _____
Date of birth: _____City, State _____
Marital status: _____Maiden name _____
Date of death: _____City, State _____
Present health: _____

Domicile of Client	Address	City	County	State
Home:				
Other residences (homes, cottages, etc.):	_____			
	_____			
	_____			
Prior residences over past 10 years, especially if in a community property state:	_____			
	_____			

Business
Name of business: _____
Business address: _____
Telephone number: _____
Type of business (purpose): _____
Form of ownership (interest):
    Sole proprietor: _____
    Partner: _____
    Limited partner: _____
    Corporation: _____
    Other: _____

Family Concerns
Antenuptial or postnuptial agreements: _____

(*continued*)

Exhibit 6.1   Family Data—*continued*

Previous marriages:	_____
Children of previous marriages:	_____
Divorce or legal separation:	_____
Settlement information (child support, maintenance, etc.):	_____
Special dependency cases:	
Handicapped child, parent, relative:	_____
Mental disability:	_____
Emotional problems:	_____
Other health problems:	_____

Trusts

Spendthrift child:	_____
Life estate to be transferred:	_____
Potential inheritance:	_____

Persons to be disinherited (specific reasons listed below):

_____

_____

Advancements (property previously transferred before client's death):

_____

_____

Names and Addresses of Potential Fiduciaries and Successors

Personal representative (Executor/trix):	_____
Successor:	_____
Guardian for minor children:	_____
Successor:	_____
Trustees:	_____
Successor:	_____

Example: Suppose George Samson, the client, indicated he had been previously married and had two children by that marriage. The paralegal would have to determine (1) whether the former spouse and children are still living; (2) whether a satisfactory property settlement and child support agreement were reached by all interested parties in the prior marriage, and the terms of those agreements; and (3) whether the client intends to leave any part of his estate to his former wife and children of the marriage.

ETHICAL ISSUE

Example: Suppose the client, George, has an invalid mother who is 75 years old. He has supported his mother for the past 15 years and wants to continue this support for her lifetime. The original checklist only includes information that the client's mother is alive and currently an invalid. Questions you put to the client could obtain additional information about his mother and the method by which George wishes to maintain support for her in case he should die first, *but legal advice must come from the attorney.*

Example: Suppose George does not want any of his estate to go to his brother, Henry. The reasons for this decision and the manner in which George's intent can be manifested in his will must be discussed with the client under the supervision of the attorney.

Example: Suppose, while he completes the checklist, George comes to the question of advancements and remembers he gave his youngest son $500 to buy a used motorbike last year. Like most people, George is not sure what an advancement is. This concept must be reviewed and explained. You could explain this term and probable results or outcomes; *however, any counseling or legal advice must come from the attorney* during the conference with the client.

ETHICAL ISSUE

The checklists help you to draw out general information and to clarify the client's intentions. If additional data about specific matters and details to be incorporated into the future will must be obtained, you perform that task.

Checklist for Family Advisers

A list of the names of the client's advisers is helpful to obtain information about the names of creditors or debtors and the location of the client's assets, personal records and documents, beneficiaries, successors, or previous will (see Exhibit 6.2).

Terminology Associated with Assets and Liabilities Checklists

The following terms may appear in your assets and liabilities checklist:

- *Dividend.* The share of profits or property to which the owners of a business are entitled; e.g., stockholders are entitled to dividends authorized by a corporation in proportion to the number of shares of the corporation's stock owned by each stockholder.
- *Fair market value.* The fair market value is the monetary amount an item of property, e.g., a house, would bring if sold on the open market. Usually, it is the price agreed to by a willing seller and a willing buyer, neither party being compelled to offer a price above or below the average price for such an item.

Example: Fred Morley offers $120,000 to buy Sam Hacker's house. Houses of this type usually command a price of at least $120,000. Sam accepts Fred's offer. The fair market value of the house is $120,000.

- *Homestead.* A homestead is the family home and the adjoining land (within statutory limits) where the head of the family lives; it is the family's fixed place of residence. Most states allow the head of the family to exempt the homestead from claims and executions by creditors.

Terms associated with miscellaneous property include the following:

- *Copyright.* A government grant to an author of an exclusive right to publish, reprint, and sell a manuscript for a period of the life of the author plus fifty years after the author's death for works written after January 1, 1976.

Exhibit 6.2 Family Advisers

CHECKLIST: FAMILY ADVISERS

	Name	Address	Telephone Number
Accountant:			
Tax preparer:			
Appraiser:			
Attorney:			
Banker:			
Physician:			
Insurance agent:			
Financial planner:			
Trust officer:			
Stockbroker:			
Religious adviser:			
Others:			

- *Patent.* A government grant to an inventor of an exclusive right to make, use, and sell an invention for a nonrenewable period of seventeen years.
- *Royalty.* A payment made to an author, composer, or inventor by a company that has been licensed to publish or manufacture the manuscript or invention of that author, composer, or inventor.
- *Receivables.* Receivables are debts (such as promissory notes) established in the course of business that are currently due from others or due within a certain time period.

The following terms describe liabilities you are likely to encounter:

- *Contract for deed.* An agreement or contract to sell real property on an installment basis. On payment of the last installment, the title to the property is transferred by delivery of the deed to the purchaser.
- *Installment purchase.* The purchase of goods on credit whereby the purchaser pays for them over a period of time. The purchaser (in the case of a small-loan purchase) immediately obtains the title, or ownership, of the purchase; the seller retains a security interest until the purchaser has paid the full price.
- *Mortgage.* A mortgage is a contract by which a person pledges property to another as security in order to obtain a loan.

Example: Debbie Johnson obtains a $70,000 mortgage from her bank as a loan in order to finance the purchase of a house costing $90,000.

- *Mortgagor.* The person who mortgages property; the borrower or debtor.
- *Mortgagee.* The person to whom property is mortgaged; the lender, e.g., bank.

Example: Debbie Johnson in the example above would be the mortgagor (borrower), and the bank would be the mortgagee (lender).

- *Promissory note.* A promissory note is a promise in writing to pay a certain sum of money at a future time to a specific person.

Checklists for Assets and Liabilities

Lists of all assets and liabilities of the client are made, and the form of ownership of each asset is noted, e.g., whether the asset is solely owned or concurrently owned, such as a homestead in joint tenancy between a husband and wife. The lists should include the following information:

- *Real property*, including the legal description and estimated fair market value of the homestead, all other land, and business buildings. Determine whether the property is owned individually in severalty or concurrently in joint tenancy, tenancy by the entirety, tenancy in common, or as community property (see Chapter 2). Check the location of the property. If it is outside the client's domiciliary state, ancillary administration might be necessary.
- *Tangible personal property*, including personal effects and clothing of considerable value, furniture and household goods, automobiles, boats, jewelry, antiques, art and stamp collections, and other miscellaneous items.
- Other items of personal property such as savings and checking accounts, safe deposit box, stocks and bonds, cash on hand, promissory notes receivable, mortgages, patents, and copyrights.
- Insurance policies, including life, disability, health and accident, hospitalization, and annuities, must be scrutinized to determine how and to whom payments are to be made on the client's death.
- Employee benefits like Social Security, veterans' benefits, pension plans, profit-sharing plans, death benefits, stock options, and all other claims to which the client's estate or successors may be entitled.
- Business interests in a corporation, partnership, or sole proprietorship, with complete details about the client's interest, rights, and responsibilities therein.
- All debts owed by the client, including outstanding mortgages, promissory notes payable, business debts, payments owed on contracts for deed, and accounts with a stockbroker.
- Interest and duties in trust assets (property transferred, beneficiary, trustee, trust agreement) or estates of others, including powers of appointment (a power to dispose of property not owned by the holder of the power), which the decedent may hold by virtue of being given this power by another's will or trust. A general power of appointment held by the decedent is taxable to the decedent's estate (see Chapter 10).

Using checklists like those in Exhibits 6.3 and 6.4, you can collect and organize the data on the client's assets and liabilities.

☷ ASSIGNMENT 6.1

Your law firm's client is heavily invested in the bond and stock markets. As a paralegal for the firm, you have been asked to collect the necessary data concerning the extent and value of the client's holdings. Due to the client's extensive holdings, you will need a more detailed checklist than the one shown in Exhibit 6.3. You have been asked to include the number of shares, ownership, date of purchase and cost basis, and current

Exhibit 6.3 Assets

CHECKLIST: ASSETS

List the item (by name), the estimated fair market value of the property owned, the location, the form of ownership, e.g., single ownership by husband (H) or wife (W), joint tenancy (J), tenancy by the entirety (E), tenancy in common (T), or community property (C) for each item, and the beneficiary or beneficiaries (Bene.).

			Form of Ownership	
Item	**Value**	**Location**	**(H/W/J/E/T/C)**	**Bene.**

Cash
Cash and checking
   accounts: _____
Savings accounts: _____
Money market accounts: _____
Certificates of deposit: _____

Stock and Bonds
Stocks (Name and no. of
   shares): _____
Stock options: _____
Brokerage accounts: _____
U.S. government bonds: _____
Municipal bonds: _____
Mutual funds: _____
Other: _____

Real Property
Residential (homestead): _____
Business building: _____
Recreational (summer
   cottage): _____
Rental property: _____
Timeshare: _____
Foreign real estate: _____
Other: _____

Personal Property
Furniture and household
   goods: _____
Furs and jewelry: _____
Automobiles (model and
   year):
   (1) _____
   (2) _____
Collections (art, guns,
   coins, stamps,
   antiques, etc.): _____
Other vehicles (boats,
   trailers, campers,
   snowmobiles,
   motorbikes, etc.): _____
Wearing apparel and
   personal effects: _____
Other: _____

(*continued*)

179

Exhibit 6.3 Assets—*continued*

Business Interests
Sole proprietorship: _____
Partnership: _____
Limited partnership: _____
Corporation: _____
Buy-sell agreements: _____
Other: _____

Receivables
Accounts receivable: _____
Promissory notes
  (payable to client): _____
Contract for deed (client
  is seller): _____
Other: _____

**Employee, Corporate,
  and Other Benefits**
Pension plan: _____
Stock bonus: _____
Profit-sharing plan: _____
401(k) plan: _____
Keogh plan: _____
Individual retirement
  account (IRA)
  Traditional: _____
  Roth: _____
Health insurance
  Accident and health: _____
  Medical and surgical: _____
  Hospitalization: _____
Social Security: _____
Union benefits: _____
Railroad retirement
  benefits: _____
Veterans' benefits: _____
Fraternal organization
  benefits: _____
Other: _____

**Interests in Trusts
Power of Appointment
(General or Special)** _____
**Insurance and Annuities
  (See Exhibit 6.5)**
Straight life, universal
  life, or term: _____
Endowment or annuity: _____
Group life insurance: _____

Miscellaneous Property
Patents: _____
Copyrights: _____
Royalties: _____
Other: _____

TOTAL ASSETS (value): _____

Exhibit 6.4 Liabilities

CHECKLIST: LIABILITIES

List the item, its location, the estimated value of each debt, the parties indebted, i.e., husband (H), wife (W), or both (B), and the creditor.

Type of Liability	Item	Value	Location	Form of Liability (H/W/B)	Creditor
Promissory notes (to banks, loan companies, individuals, etc.):					
Mortgages—on real property:					
Payment on contracts for deed:					
Charge accounts and installment purchases:					
Automobile loans:					
Credit card charges:					
Loans on insurance policies:					
Business debts:					
Enforceable pledges to charitable and religious organizations:					
Taxes owed:					
TOTAL LIABILITES (value):					

---

market value for all stocks, bonds, and mutual funds owned by the client. Draft an appropriate checklist.

··

   If the client has substantial stock holdings, separate lists of the holdings should be attached to the assets checklist. The value of assets such as patents, art and coin collections, hobby equipment, or business interests may be difficult to estimate accurately; therefore, you should ask the client to recommend appraisers and collectors or suggest potential buyers interested in these items. A separate list should be made of this information.

Terminology Associated with a Life Insurance Policies Checklist

The life insurance policies checklist may include the following terms:

- *Life insurance.* Life insurance is a contract, a legally binding agreement, by which one party (the insurance company) promises to pay another (the policyholder or designated beneficiary) a certain sum of money if the policyholder sustains a specific loss (e.g., death or total disability). For this protection the policyholder makes a payment called a premium on a regular basis, usually annually, to the insurance company. Life insurance includes term, ordinary (whole or straight) life, and universal life insurance (see Chapter 10).

- *Annuity.* An annuity is a fixed sum to be paid at regular intervals, such as annually, for either a certain or indefinite period, as for a stated number of years or for life.
- *Primary beneficiary.* A primary beneficiary is the person who has a superior claim over all others to the benefits of a life insurance contract. The policyholder selects the primary beneficiary.
- *Secondary (contingent) beneficiary.* A secondary beneficiary is the person selected by the policyholder as a successor to the benefits of a life insurance policy whenever the proceeds of the policy are not paid to the primary beneficiary.
- *Cash surrender value.* In ordinary (straight) life insurance, the cash surrender value is the cash reserve that increases (builds) each year the policy remains in force as a minimum savings feature. After the policy has been in force for a period specified by the insurer (company), the policyholder may borrow an amount not to exceed the cash value.
- *Premium.* The sum paid or agreed to be paid annually by the insured person (policyholder) to the insurance company (insurer) as the consideration for the insurance contract.
- *Settlement option.* A settlement option is one of a number of alternatives that parties to an insurance contract agree to follow to discharge their agreement.

Checklist for Life Insurance Policies

Exhibit 6.3 (Assets) includes basic information about the existence and types of life insurance owned by the client. If necessary, more detailed information about such policies must be compiled. This is an example of an instance in which you must develop a checklist within a checklist. Exhibit 6.5 is a checklist of information on the client's life insurance policies. Information on the insurance policies of the client's spouse and children should also be obtained.

> **Example:** Charles Rivera is the named primary beneficiary of his deceased parent's life insurance policy. The policy gives Charles the option of receiving payment in a lump sum or in monthly payments over a period of years. The option selected by Charles acts as a present or eventual discharge of the contract.

🏛 ASSIGNMENT 6.2

John Smith owns a straight life insurance policy with the Life Assurance Company of Kingstown with $50,000 as its face value. John names his wife, Mary Smith, as his primary beneficiary and his son, William Smith, as the secondary beneficiary. The cash value of the policy at the time of John's death is $8,700. The year before John's death, he obtained a $2,500 loan on his insurance from the insurance company at 5 percent interest. When John died, a $1,200 balance, including interest, was unpaid on the loan. To whom will the life insurance be paid? How much will the beneficiary receive?

Checklist for Important Documents

You collect all documents involving the client's property and business interests for review with the attorney. These documents may include stock certificates and op-

Exhibit 6.5   Life Insurance Policies

CHECKLIST: LIFE INSURANCE DATA

Policyholder (owner): _____

Insured: _____

Insurance agent: _____Phone: _____

	Company 1	Company 2	Company 3	Company 4	Totals
Name/Policy no.					
Location of policy					
Type of insurance					
Face or death value					
Dividends					
Annual premium					
Cash (surrender) value					
Loan on cash value					
Primary beneficiaries					
Secondary beneficiaries					
Settlement option installment					
Annuity					
Others					

tions, contracts, deeds, receivables, insurance policies, gift tax returns, income tax returns for the past three years (the Internal Revenue Service can challenge the accuracy of a taxpayer's income tax return for the three previous taxable years, although if fraud is involved, the statute of limitations does not apply; see IRC §§ 6501 and 6531), divorce decrees and alimony or child support payments or other property settlements from a previous marriage, antenuptial agreements, mortgages, *inter vivos* (living) trust agreements in which the client is either the donor or beneficiary, and any existing will the client may have. Exhibit 6.6 is a sample checklist to collect information about the existence and location of these important documents.

Exhibit 6.6 Locations of Important Documents

CHECKLIST: RECORDS OR DOCUMENTS (COPIES)

List the applicable documents' location or comment on missing items. Use additional sheets as necessary. If any documents are kept in a safe deposit box, list its location.

Checklists   Location
   Checklists: _____

Personal Data (Client and Family Members)
   Birth certificate: _____
   Social Security card: _____
   Medicare card: _____
   Marriage certificate: _____
   Separation agreement: _____
   Divorce decree: _____
   Antenuptial agreement: _____
   Postnuptial agreement: _____
   Adoption papers: _____
   Naturalization papers: _____
   Passports: _____
   Military records: _____
   Death certificate: _____
   Cemetery deed: _____
   Other: _____ _____

Real Property
   Abstracts of title: _____
   Deeds: _____
   Contracts for deed: _____
   Leases: _____
   Appraisals: _____
   Property tax valuation notices: _____
   Other: _____ _____

Personal Property
   Titles/registrations for
     Automobiles: _____
     Recreational vehicles: _____
     Trailers: _____
     Boats: _____
     Airplanes: _____
   Other: _____ _____

Cash, Stocks, and Bonds
   Bank account statements: _____
   Investment account statements: _____
   Certificates of deposit: _____
   Bonds and other debentures: _____
   Stock certificates: _____
   Other: _____ _____

Miscellaneous Property
   Patent agreements: _____
   Copyright agreements: _____
   Royalty agreements: _____
   Promissory notes: _____
   Other: _____ _____

(continued)

Exhibit 6.6   Locations of Important Documents—*continued*

Business Interests
Partnership agreements: _____
Limited partnership agreements: _____
Franchise agreements: _____
Buy-sell agreements: _____
Corporation documents
   Charter: _____
   Bylaws: _____
   Stock certificates: _____
   Stock options: _____
Other:_____ _____

Retirement Plans
Pension plan: _____
Profit-sharing plan: _____
401(k) plan: _____
Keogh plan: _____
Individual retirement
   account (IRA)
   Traditional: _____
   Roth: _____
Social security: _____
Veterans' benefits: _____
Other:_____ _____

Interests in Trusts
Trust agreements: _____
Declaration of trust: _____
Powers of appointment: _____
Other:_____ _____

Insurance Policies
Life insurance: _____
Annuity contracts: _____
Accidental insurance: _____
Health insurance: _____
Disability insurance: _____
Title insurance: _____
Homeowners' insurance: _____
Mortgage insurance: _____
Automobile insurance: _____
Boat insurance: _____
Other:_____ _____

Liabilities
Promissory notes: _____
Mortgages on real property: _____
Contracts for deed: _____
Loans on insurance policies: _____
Installment purchases
   Automobile loans: _____
   Credit card charges: _____
Business debts: _____
Other:_____ _____

(continued)

Exhibit 6.6   Locations of Important Documents—*continued*

Miscellaneous (specify)
   Credit cards:
   ATM cards: _____
   Other:_____   _____

Tax Returns
   Federal income tax (3 years):
   State income tax (3 years):   _____
   Federal gift tax (all years):   _____

Current Will or Trust
   Original (client):
   Original (spouse):   _____
   Codicil: _____
   Trust documents: _____
   Letter of instructions: _____
   Memorandum of personal
      property: _____

Advance Directives
   Living will: _____
   Durable power of attorney
      for health care: _____
   Health care proxy or
      appointment of a health
      care agent: _____

Safe Deposit Box Location: _____

ASSIGNMENT 6.3

Using the checklists in this chapter as a guide, develop and fill in the checklists necessary to prepare a preliminary draft of your will or the will of some member of your family, e.g., a spouse, parent, brother, or sister.

PRELIMINARY TAX ADVICE AND OTHER MATTERS

At the conference with the client, in addition to eliciting information by means of the checklists, the attorney or the supervised paralegal should explain the tax consequences of death in terms understandable to the client. The resolution of tax problems under the supervision of an attorney is an important function of a paralegal. Chapter 14 of this text identifies and defines the various types of federal and state taxes, explains how the basic tax regulations are applied to analytical problems, and demonstrates the necessary tax calculations. Therefore, the chapter must be reviewed before you can perform the duties outlined below during the conference.

At the conference the following matters should be explained and discussed. The tax items are discussed in more detail in later chapters.

- For smaller estates, joint tenancy ownership can avoid additional administration expenses. You must guard against overemphasizing the advantages of this form of property ownership. Since the transfer of property into joint tenancy divides the ownership and control of the property, it becomes impossible to sell the entire property without the consent of both joint tenants.
- You must determine if the federal estate tax can be reduced by using the marital and charitable deductions to which a client's estate is entitled (see Chapter 10).
- The use of certain *inter vivos* gifts or trusts to lower administration expenses and death taxes by reducing the client's gross estate.
- Whether the client wants taxes on the estate paid from estate funds or whether the individual beneficiaries or devisees are to pay taxes on their shares.

During the conference you should clarify other pertinent matters for the client and determine the client's desires in a number of situations. Particularly important are the spouse's right of election and the children's right to inherit.

Spouse's Right of Election—A Review

The client should be reminded that a married testator cannot determine conclusively the disposition of the entire estate by will because a surviving spouse cannot be completely disinherited. Most states offer a surviving spouse the right to renounce the will and elect a statutory share of a certain minimum portion of the deceased spouse's estate, thus invalidating an exclusion from the will. Therefore, your state's right of election should be explained to the client. A typical state statute which addresses this matter is N.C. Gen. Stat. § 30–3, which allows a surviving spouse to take an elective share equal to the intestate share (but compare UPC §§ 2–202 and 2–203).

For a review of this topic, see Chapter 4.

Examples: John Evans dies testate and leaves his surviving spouse, Bette (1) *all* his property; (2) *some* of his property; (3) *nothing*—he disinherits Bette. In Case 1, Bette would receive through John's will all his property as his sole successor. In Case 2, Bette would have the election (statutory) right to take either through John's will or by statute. Usually, she would choose whichever was the greater. She cannot take both. In Case 3, John would fail in his attempt to disinherit his wife since in most states she is entitled to the statutory elective share, which she would naturally choose.

ASSIGNMENT 6.4

If John Evans is domiciled in your state and attempts through his will to leave all, some, or none of his property to his surviving spouse, how would your state handle each conveyance? Cite and explain your statute.

🏛 ASSIGNMENT 6.5

1. Jerry and Audrey Maxwell are husband and wife. They have no children. If on Audrey's death Jerry were to choose to take the surviving spouse's elective share according to your state's statute, how much of Audrey's property would Jerry receive?

2. In another example, Jerry and Audrey have five children—Marty, Mike, Marc, Mary, and Michelle. Marc died in a childhood accident; all the other children are married and have two children. On Jerry's death, what would Audrey's share be if she elected against the will based on your state's statute?

3. In a third case, Jerry and Audrey have one child, Marty, who is married and has three children. Marty dies in an industrial accident. Then Jerry dies one year later. Audrey elects against the will. What will her statutory elective share be according to your state statute?

Children's Right to Inherit—A Review

It should be made clear to the client that parents are not required to leave anything to their children. Nevertheless, if children are to be excluded from a share of a parent's estate, it is best accomplished by the insertion of a clause in the will that states the parent has intentionally made no provision for a clearly identified child named in the will. When a child is not specifically excluded in the will, the child may ultimately receive a share as a result of a state's Pretermitted (Omitted) Child Statute, despite the parent's intent to disinherit. Most parents, however, have no intention of disinheriting their children, but they may wish to pass their estates to their children in unequal proportions because of the children's different financial or health status.

🏛 ASSIGNMENT 6.6

In the completion of the family data checklist illustrated earlier in this chapter, William Richardson, age 68, the testator, indicates that of his four adult children, Duane, James, Amy, and Beth, and one minor child, Susan, age 17, only Amy has consistently shown an interest in her father's health and welfare. Therefore, William intends to leave his entire estate to Amy. Answer the following according to your state laws:

1. Can William disinherit his three adult children other than Amy? If so, how could this be done?

2. Can William disinherit his minor child, Susan? Explain.

3. If Duane, one of William's adult children, is physically handicapped or mentally retarded, can William disinherit him? Explain.

4. William stated in a clause in his will, "Because of their mistreatment of me, I intentionally disinherit all my other children, Duane, James, and Beth, and leave my entire estate to Amy." Susan is not mentioned, yet the words *all my other children* are included in the will. After William dies, Susan and the other adult children, Duane, James, and Beth, contest their father's will. Who prevails according to your state laws?

GUIDELINES FOR PREPARATION OF A WILL

In addition to the collection of pertinent facts from the client for the creation of a first draft of a will, you should follow general guidelines to ensure the will's effectiveness and validity and to decrease the likelihood that persons who claim an interest in the decedent's estate might challenge it in a will contest. The following are guidelines for the creation of a valid testamentary document. They provide a convenient checklist of good construction habits to develop in preparation for the execution of a will. Actual drafts will be included in Chapter 7.

Guideline 1: Avoid the Use of Preprinted Will Forms

Preprinted will forms should seldom be used. They may not fill the special needs of the testator and can cause problems. For instance, if part of the form is printed, part is typed, and part is handwritten, a will contest based on forgery could result. An alteration of any kind in a will usually casts doubt on whether the altered section is the work of the testator or of some other person. *Note:* The state "statutory will" forms available in California, Louisiana, Maine, Michigan, and Wisconsin are a major exception to the caveat on using printed or computerized forms. These are preprinted fill-in-the-blank forms with written instructions to the maker of the will, and they require choices which must be made on the form; see Cal. Prob. Code §§ 6220–6226 and Mich. Comp. Laws Ann. § 700.2519 and compare the California and Wisconsin statutory wills in Exhibits 6.7 and 4.3.

Another problem is that words on preprinted forms are often crossed out or deleted by ink or type. Sometimes corrections or changes called interlineation are written on the forms. In such cases, the question arises as to who made these changes and the reason for them. Thus, the validity of the will is in jeopardy.

A third problem is that preprinted forms are written in generalities and therefore do not address the specific problems or objectives of the testator. Property may be inadvertently omitted, intended beneficiaries or devisees may be excluded, and tax advantages may be overlooked.

> **Example:** Louise Pendleton, using a preprinted will form, forgot to include a residuary clause to pass the residue or remainder of her estate to a named person. Louise had made a number of specific gifts to relatives and friends, but the bulk of her estate was in the residue. Since Louise used a preprinted form and no residuary clause was included, the residue of her estate would pass by intestate succession statutes.

ASSIGNMENT 6.7

In the example above, if Louise had only two relatives, Peter, a nephew, and Clara, a grandparent, how and to whom would Louise's residuary estate be transferred according to your state laws?

Exhibit 6.7   California Statutory Will

CALIFORNIA STATUTORY WILL OF

Print Your Full Name

1. **Will.** This is my Will. I revoke all prior Wills and codicils.

2. **Specific Gift of Personal Residence.** (Optional - use only if you want to give your personal residence to a different person or persons than you give the balance of your assets to under paragraph 5 below). I give my interest in my principal personal residence at the time of my death (subject to mortgages and liens) as follows: (Select one choice only and sign in the box after your choice.)

a. <u>Choice One</u>: All to my spouse, if my spouse survives me; otherwise to my descendants (my children and the descendants of my children) who survive me.

b. <u>Choice Two</u>: Nothing to my spouse; all to my descendants (my children and the descendants of my children) who survive me.

c. <u>Choice Three</u>: All to the following person if he or she survives me: (Insert the name of the person):

_____

d. <u>Choice Four</u>: Equally among the following persons who survive me: (Insert the names of two or more persons):

_____
_____
_____

3. **Specific Gift of Automobiles, Household and Personal Effects.** (Optional - use only if you want to give automobiles and household and personal effects to a different person or persons than you give the balance of your assets to under paragraph 5 below). I give all of my automobiles (subject to loans), furniture, furnishings, household items, clothing, jewelry, and other tangible articles of a personal nature at the time of my death as follows: (Select one choice only and sign in the box after your choice.)

a. <u>Choice One</u>: All to my spouse, if my spouse survives me; otherwise to my descendants (my children and the descendants of my children) who survive me.

b. <u>Choice Two</u>: Nothing to my spouse; all to my descendants (my children and the descendants of my children) who survive me.

c. <u>Choice Three</u>: All to the following person if he or she survives me: (Insert the name of the person):

_____

d. <u>Choice Four</u>: Equally among the following persons who survive me: (Insert the names of two or more persons):

_____
_____
_____

4. **Specific Gifts of Cash.** (Optional) I make the following cash gifts to the persons named below who survive me, or to the named charity, and I sign my name in the box after each gift. If I don't sign in the box, I do not make a gift. (Sign in the box after each gift you make.)

Name of Person or Charity to receive gift (Name one only - please print)	Amount of Cash Gift
	Sign your name in this box to make this gift.

(continued)

Exhibit 6.7   California Statutory Will—*continued*

| Name of Person or Charity to receive gift (Name one only - please print) | Amount of Cash Gift |
| | Sign your name in this box to make this gift. |

| Name of Person or Charity to receive gift (Name one only - please print) | Amount of Cash Gift |
| | Sign your name in this box to make this gift. |

| Name of Person or Charity to receive gift (Name one only - please print) | Amount of Cash Gift |
| | Sign your name in this box to make this gift. |

| Name of Person or Charity to receive gift (Name one only - please print) | Amount of Cash Gift |
| | Sign your name in this box to make this gift. |

5. **Balance of My Assets.** Except for the specific gifts made in paragraphs 2, 3 and 4 above, I give the balance of my assets as follows: (Select <u>one</u> choice only and sign in the box after your choice. If I sign in more than one box or if I don't sign in any box, the court will distribute my assets as if I did not make a Will).

a. <u>Choice One</u>: All to my spouse, if my spouse survives me; otherwise to my descendants (my children and the descendants of my children) who survive me.

b. <u>Choice Two</u>: Nothing to my spouse; all to my descendants (my children and the descendants of my children) who survive me.

c. <u>Choice Three</u>: All to the following person if he or she survives me: (Insert the name of the person):

_____

d. <u>Choice Four</u>: Equally among the following persons who survive me: (Insert the names of two or more persons):

_____
_____
_____

6. **Guardian of the Child's Person.** If I have a child under age 18 and the child does not have a living parent at my death, I nominate the individual named below as First Choice as guardian of the person of such child (to raise the child). If the First Choice does not serve, then I nominate the Second Choice, and then the Third Choice, to serve. Only an individual (not a bank or trust company) may serve.

| Name of First Choice for Guardian of the Person | Name of Second Choice for Guardian of the Person |

| Name of Third Choice for Guardian of the Person |

7. **Special Provision of Property of Persons Under Age 25.** (Optional - Unless you use this paragraph, assets that go to a child or other person who is <u>under</u> age 18 may be given to the parent of the person, or to the guardian named in paragraph 6 above as guardian of the person until age 18, and the court will require a bond; and assets that go to a child or other person who is age 18 or older will be given outright to the person. By using this

(continued)

Exhibit 6.7 California Statutory Will—*continued*

paragraph you may provide that a custodian will hold the assets for the person until the person reaches any age between 18 and 25 which you choose). If a beneficiary of this Will is between age 18 and 25, I nominate the individual or bank or trust company named below as First Choice as custodian of the property. If the First Choice does not serve, then I nominate the Second Choice, and then the Third Choice, to serve.

Name of First Choice for Custodian of Assets	Name of Second Choice for Custodian of Assets

Name of Third Choice for Custodian of Assets

Insert any age between 18 and 25 as the age for the person to receive the property: (If you do not choose an age, age 18 will apply.)........

8. I nominate the individual or bank or trust company named below as First Choice as executor. If the First Choice does not serve, then I nominate the Second Choice, and then the Third Choice, to serve.

Name of First Choice for Executor	Name of Second Choice for Executor

Name of Third Choice for Executor

9. **Bond.** My signature in this box means a bond is <u>not</u> required for any person named as executor. A bond may be required if I do not sign in this box:
No bond shall be required.

(Notice: You must sign this Will in the presence of two (2) adult witnesses. The witnesses must sign their names in your presence and in each other's presence. You must first read to them the following two sentences.)
This is my Will. I ask the persons who sign below to be my witnesses.
Signed on _____ at
(date)

_____, California.
(city)

Signature of Maker of Will

(Notice to Witnesses: Two (2) adults must sign as witnesses. Each witness must read the following clause before signing. The witnesses should not receive assets under this Will.)
Each of us declares under penalty of perjury under the laws of the State of California that the following is true and correct:
a. On the date written below the maker of this Will declared to us that this instrument was the maker's Will and requested us to act as witnesses to it;
b. We understand this is the maker's Will;
c. The maker signed this Will in our presence, all of us being present at the same time;

d. We now, at the maker's request, and in the maker's and in each other's presence, sign below as witnesses;
e. We believe the maker is of sound mind and memory;
f. We believe that this Will was not procured by duress, menace, fraud or undue influence;
g. The maker is age 18 or older; and
h. Each of us is now age 18 or older, is a competent witness, and resides at the address set forth after his or her name.

Dated: _____, _____

Signature of Witness

Signature of Witness

Print name here:

Print name here:

Residence Address:

Residence Address:

Source: Wolcotts Forms. Reprinted with permission.

Guideline 2: Use the Same Word-Processing Software and Computer Printer Typeface

Among the good habits to develop in the creation of wills is to use the same word-processing software and typeface for the entire testament. The use of different typefaces makes it appear someone other than the testator's drafter has inserted provisions. In addition, the typist should not leave blank spaces in the will, which might make possible the addition of words or names or even an entire page. Such procedures help ensure that the decedent's heirs will be protected from persons who could change the will to benefit themselves.

Example: Michael intends to leave the bulk and residue of his considerable estate to five friends—Mary Brown, Adam Korkowski, Elmer Bartholomew, Jean Olson, and Stanley Weskoskowitz. Because of the length of Stanley's last name, the typist of the will left some space at the end of a line of the will and started Stanley's name on the next line. Michael's residuary clause reads:

"I give and bequeath all the rest, residue and remainder of my property to Mary Brown, Adam Korkowski, Elmer Bartholomew, Jean Olson,
and Stanley Weskoskowitz share and share alike."

Joe Blitz typed his name in the empty space left on the line after Jean Olson's name. Unless the addition is detected and deleted before Michael's death, Joe may become a residuary beneficiary or devisee of Michael's will.

Example: Paul has typed a six-page will. Before it is witnessed and signed, his brother, Robert, adds an extra page to the will in which most of Paul's estate passes to Robert. Even if Paul does not notice the additional page, he could have protected himself by signing each of the original pages and stating in the attestation clause that the will contained only six pages.

Another advantage of typing the entire will is that uncertainties so often found in holographic (handwritten) wills due to the illegible handwriting of the testator can be avoided. Computer typed wills are easier to read and errors are more readily identified and corrected than in handwritten wills. However, typed wills prove disadvantageous if the will is contested because of forgery or undue influence, or if a question arises concerning the testator's knowledge of the contents of the will; if the testator had written a holographic will, it could avoid these contentions.

Example: Joan is elderly and suffers from severe arthritis. She is concerned her signature on the will may be contested as a forgery. What procedures might be followed to avoid a foreseeable will contest? (1) Joan could identify her affliction within the will's provisions so all interested parties have notice of her infirmity. A will contest on the grounds of forgery requires that many persons testify to the genuineness of the writing; the testatrix's own declaration as to the reason for her unusual signature would eliminate the need for calling a great number of witnesses and provide direct evidence in the matter. (2) A better procedure is to have Joan write in her own hand the testimonium clause so that, if necessary, a handwriting expert could compare and identify the validity of Joan's signature. (3) The best procedure would be to have her personal physician witness the will so that, if called to testify, the physician could explain the reason for the shaky signature.

Guideline 3: Use Words That Avoid Ambiguity

The will must be written so that the testator's intent is clear. Chapter 7 discusses the creation of a will and includes sample clauses or provisions to illustrate its step-by-step formation. Our immediate concerns are the uncertainties, ambiguities, and alterations the testator must avoid. The will should be clear and understandable.

> **Example:** Marcia's will provides: (1) I give my diamond ring to my best friend, Florence Williams. (2) I give $5,000 to my faithful employee, Steven Newell. (3) *All my personal property* I leave to my beloved son and only heir, Kevin. A conflict such as this in which the testator apparently leaves the same gifts to different persons may result in a will contest.

Guideline 4: Use Simple Language

As noted in Chapter 4, the UPC attempts to resolve confusion surrounding terminology used to identify gifts transferred through a will and the recipients of such gifts. Because the traditional terms "bequest," "legacy," and "devise" are used interchangeably, misunderstanding and confusion result. The proper way to solve this problem is to use the phrase "I *give* my diamond ring to my daughter, Marilyn," rather than "I *bequeath* my ring, etc." The use of simple and more recognizable terms is the better practice in will construction.

Guideline 5: Place Small Estates in Joint Tenancy

In appropriate cases, small estates can be placed in joint tenancy, one of the most common ways to avoid probate, to diminish administrative procedures and expenses.

Guideline 6: Sign the Will According to State Statutes, but Do Not Sign Copies

The original will must be signed and should be dated. If the will consists of multiple pages, all pages of the original should be signed or initialed except in states such as New York which require the signature to be only at the end of the will. If copies are made, they should not be signed. To have many original executed wills in existence is a potential problem because it increases the possibility of will contests. All copies that are executed (signed and witnessed) must be presented in court, or the law presumes the will was revoked. Therefore, you should make copies of the original will before it is signed. Give one to the personal representative and another to the spouse, if he or she is not the personal representative, and explain where the original will is located.

ASSIGNMENT 6.8

Joyce's original will cannot be found. A photocopy with Joyce's signature has been located, however. According to the laws of your state, would the copy be a valid testament? See *Matter of Wheadon's Estate,* 579 P. 2d 930 (Utah 1978).

Guideline 7: Include a Residuary Clause

The testator's entire estate must be transferred. This requires the use of a residuary (or residue) clause such as the following:

> I give all the rest, residue, and remainder of my estate, consisting of all property, real, personal, or mixed, of whatever kind and wherever located, that I can dispose of by will and not effectively disposed of by the preceding articles of this will, as follows:

Guideline 8: Choose Witnesses Carefully

To improve the probability the witnesses will be available when the will is probated, it is good practice to have the will witnessed by individuals who live in the same county, know, and are younger than the testator. Also, the witnesses should not be beneficiaries or devisees of the will. If the testator's mental capacity might be questioned, the testator's physician should be one of the witnesses (see the previous discussion and examples of who may be a competent witness in Chapter 5). Some states now provide for attestation clauses that result in "self-proved" wills (see Chapter 7).

Guideline 9: Tell Witnesses What Might Be Expected of Them

The witnesses should be informed they are witnessing the testator's signature on a will and that they may be called on to testify to this fact in court. They need not read the will, however, nor be informed of its contents before they sign as witnesses.

Guideline 10: Do Not Make Additions after Execution

Generally, if words are added to the will after execution, they do not revoke or affect the will's validity. However, additions to the will are not legally enforceable unless the testator and two witnesses sign the will a second time. If the testator wants to make valid major or minor additions to the existing will, the proper and best way to accomplish this result is by the creation of a new will.

▥ ASSIGNMENT 6.9

After executing and signing her will, Laura writes the following beneath her signature: "All of the provisions of my will previously mentioned shall take effect after my death unless my son, Randall, predeceases me." What effect, if any, would such an alteration have on Laura's will in your state?

Guideline 11: Use Computer Technology for All Changes

With the use of computer technology, a new will should be drafted for all will modifications including minor changes. This is faster and more efficient than the use of an obsolete codicil.

Guideline 12: Avoid Erasures and Corrections

Great care should be taken to avoid all erasures and corrections in the final draft of a will. When a page is found to contain an error, the entire page should be retyped. Where, because of time and unusual circumstances, it is necessary to use an altered page, the testator should approve it by dating, signing, or initialing the alteration in the margin of the page. The witnesses should also sign in the margin to indicate that the alteration was made prior to execution of the will. It is also a good idea to identify the corrections made in the attestation clause.

Guideline 13: Word Conditions to Avoid Ambiguity

If a condition is added to a devise, it can change the effect of the gift and possibly negate the testator's wishes. The drafter must recognize the importance of using correct words. A conditional devise is one which takes effect, or continues in effect, with the occurrence of some future event. A **condition precedent** is one in which a specified event must occur before the estate or interest vests in (passes to) the named devisee. A **condition subsequent** is one in which an estate that is already vested in a named devisee will not continue to be vested unless a specified event occurs. If it does not occur, the devisee will be divested of the estate and will not continue to receive the interest.

Condition precedent
A condition or specific event that must occur before an agreement or obligation becomes binding.

Condition subsequent
A condition that will continue or terminate an existing agreement or duty if the condition does or does not occur.

Condition Precedent

When a decedent devises property with a condition precedent attached, title (ownership) in the property does not vest until the stated event (condition) occurs. The devisee must perform some act *before* (precedent to) ownership of the devise will vest in the devisee.

> **Example:** Andrew devises Blackacre "to Ralph when he marries Florence." Ownership of Blackacre will vest in Ralph only if and when Ralph marries Florence. If the marriage never occurs, the ownership of property will not pass to Ralph but will pass to another person named in the will or, if no one is named, will revert to the testator or his heirs by operation of law.

> **Example:** Andrew makes a gift of $20,000 "to Renee when she receives her college degree."

> **Example:** Andrew devises Blackacre "to Saul at such time as he comes back to Texas to live and takes possession of Blackacre." (Saul is living in California at the time the will is drafted.)

The will may provide that the condition precedent be an act performed by the testator or by another person.

> **Example:** Andrew gives "the automobile owned by me at the time of my death to my son, Chris." Andrew might buy and sell many cars prior to his death. However, only the car owned by Andrew at his death will go to Chris. If Andrew does not own a car at his death, Chris is out of luck; he will get no car.

> **Example:** Andrew makes a gift of $30,000 "to the person who is taking care of me at death." The person taking care of Andrew at his death may be different from the one taking care of him at the time he drafts the will. The fact that Andrew may not now know the identity of his devisee does not invalidate the devise. The identity of

the "person who is taking care of me at death" is ascertainable. Whoever that person is would be entitled to the $30,000 gift.

Caution must be taken to prevent vague conditions from being inserted into a will. The last example illustrates a potential problem. At his death, Andrew may have several people caring for him, e.g., his niece, with whom he lives; a nephew who helps dress and feed Andrew; his doctor, who visits him routinely; and a physical therapist who daily helps Andrew exercise.

When a decedent-testator places a condition precedent on a gift, the condition may fail because it is regarded as socially unacceptable.

> **Example:** Andrew makes a gift of $1,000,000 "to my daughter Rachael, if she divorces the man to whom she is now married."

Condition Subsequent

A condition subsequent is one in which the nonhappening of the event or a violation (breach) of a condition will terminate an estate that has already vested. If an estate vests in (passes to) the devisee when the will becomes operative but is subject to being divested on the future happening or nonhappening of an event or on a breach, the condition is subsequent. If the event occurs or fails to occur, or if a specified condition is breached, the devisee will be divested of ownership of the devise (property) by "operation of law." This is also called *defeasance*.

> **Example:** Ralph devises Blackacre "to my wife, Tina, to hold while she remains a widow." The estate vests in Tina on the death of her husband, Ralph, and will be divested on Tina's remarriage.

> **Example:** Sara devises her summer home "to my daughter, Rose, but if Rose fails to return to the family home within five years, then to my son, Waldo." The devise vests in Rose on her mother's death. If Rose does not return to the family home within five years from the date of Sara's death, Rose will then be divested of the estate, and it will vest in Waldo. Waldo's potential future estate is not subject to divestment (i.e., not subject to any condition) but is a *fee simple absolute*.

In theory, the defeasance occurs by operation of law; in practice it occurs after a court action has been brought. If the devisee who has been divested of ownership in the property is in actual physical possession of the property, it will nearly always be necessary for the grantor, the grantor's heirs, or another person named by the grantor to retake or recover ownership of the property after the defeasance to (1) exercise a right of reentry (this must be a positive physical act of reentering the land) and (2) bring an action in **ejectment** in court to regain possession of the property.

Ejectment
An action (a lawsuit brought in a court) for the recovery of the possession of land.

Generally, the determination of whether a condition is precedent or subsequent will depend on the intention of the testator as interpreted from the language of the will in light of the circumstances. The particular expression used is not conclusive. Because the law prefers a vested estate, the presumption of courts favors a condition subsequent rather than a condition precedent. Therefore, the courts will construe ambiguous testamentary language as a condition subsequent rather than a condition precedent. The reason for this is that a vested estate is more marketable, i.e., it can be sold or conveyed more easily.

Guideline 14: Include Full Data on Beneficiaries and Devisees

The full names, addresses, and relationship to the testator of the beneficiaries and devisees in the will must be accurately written. This avoids uncertainty as to whom the assets are to be transferred. When the beneficiary or devisee is a charitable corporation, the corporate name and address should be given.

Guideline 15: Give the Client a Rough Draft

Check and verify that all client information transferred from checklists and attorney or client notes has been accurately incorporated into the will. A rough draft of the will should be presented to the client to be scrutinized so the client can make corrections, deletions, or additions. Also, clearly mark the document as a rough draft so the client does not sign it.

KEY TERMS

Advancement   Condition precedent   Condition subsequent   Ejectment

REVIEW QUESTIONS

1. What procedures would you recommend to put a new client at ease and overcome his or her reluctance when you need to elicit confidential family and financial information for the preparation of legal documents such as wills?
2. Are there additional checklists you recommend to obtain the necessary information for drafting wills?
3. What would you add to the checklists in the text to make them more comprehensive and useful?
4. Diagram your family tree beginning with your grandparents and including all their descendants.

5. What are some of the tax issues and rights of the surviving spouse and children that the attorney and paralegal must discuss at the family conference?
6. Which states have statutory wills? What are statutory wills?
7. What is the distinction between a condition precedent and a condition subsequent?
8. What are the guidelines recommended for the preparation of wills?
9. Are there any other guidelines for preparing wills you would add to those in the text?
10. What are the advantages of a typewritten will versus a holographic will?

CASE PROBLEMS

Problem 1

Liza Mills owns a considerable amount of personal property. She is an only child, and her parents and other blood relatives are all deceased. Liza's domestic partner is Alecia Browning. Liza is dying of AIDS.

A. If Liza dies intestate, to whom will her property pass?
B. List three suggestions you could make to Liza that would enable her to ensure that her property will go to Alecia.

C. If Liza had a brother who survived her, would your suggestions successfully prohibit or disallow any claim he might make to obtain her property?

Problem 2

Based on the guidelines for drafting a will, point out as many errors in the following sample will as you can.

LAST WILL AND TESTAMENT OF
Ben Brady

1. I, <u>Ben Brady</u>, declare this my last will and testament.
2. I direct that my debts be paid out of my estate.
3. I give my son, George, my ~~two~~ *three* rings, ~~10~~ *8* guns, clothing, and all my other personal property.

4. I give my beloved wife, Sarah, my interest in our home that we own jointly; all the money (cash) I have in savings and checking at our local bank; and, if she does not remarry, my interest in the summer cottage I own with my brother.
5. I request that no bond be required of my executor.
6. If my wife does not survive me, I request that ~~Robert Brown~~ *Jerry Clark* be executor of this will, and he be appointed guardian of any minor children of mine.

IN WITNESS WHEREOF, I set my hand to this my last will and testament.

Date: _____   __*Ben Brady*_____

_____

unisex
page break at each article

16. do not direct just debts be paid in a will

17 funeral info

18 avoid per capita per stirpes — simple terms

19 do not use precatory language

20 specific names of assets (car model)

21 no derogatory comments

22 don't disinherit by leaving $

CHAPTER 7

FINAL DRAFT AND EXECUTION OF A VALID WILL

OUTLINE

OBJECTIVES

After completing this chapter, you should be able to:

➤ Analyze the collected data and make sure the information conforms to the client's objectives when preparing a draft of the will.

➤ Identify and include the appropriate clauses for the client's will.

➤ Verify the will's construction and execution have followed the relevant state statutes.

➤ Draft a preliminary will, for the supervising attorney's review, that is free from errors of construction that might invalidate the will or lead to a will contest.

➤ Explain the purpose and function of a self-proving affidavit, living will, health care proxy, and durable power of attorney.

SCOPE OF THE CHAPTER

This chapter covers the procedures involved in drafting a client's will under an attorney's supervision, an important task of the paralegal. Exhibit 7.1 outlines these procedures. The contents of a standard will are discussed, and a formal will is provided. Sample clauses used in drafting a will and statutes that pertain to such clauses are examined, as are other documents that are not part of a standard will but are related to it. These include a self-proving affidavit, letter of instructions, right-to-die advance directives such as a living will, health care proxy, and a durable power of attorney.

CONTENTS OF A STANDARD WILL.

A standard will has the following clauses or provisions:

1. Introductory or exordium and publication clause.
2. General revocation clause.
3. Provision for payment of debts and funeral expenses.
4. Instructions for funeral and burial.
5. Specific testamentary gifts.
6. Provision for residue of estate.
7. Appointment of personal representative.
8. Appointment of personal and/or property guardian.
9. Simultaneous death clause.
10. Testamentary trust clause.
11. Testimonium clause.
12. Testator's signature.
13. Attestation clause of witnesses.
14. Witnesses' signatures and addresses.

The next sections discuss each of these clauses and provisions in detail, along with relevant statutes and sample clauses.

In addition, the following documents, which are not part of a standard will but are related to it, are identified and discussed:

1. Self-proving affidavit clause.
2. Letter of instructions.
3. Power of attorney.
4. Living will.
5. Medical power of attorney.

SOFTWARE AND COMPUTER ADVANCES MAKE PREPARING A WILL EASIER

Many computer products are available that will make preparation of a will easier. A law firm may have a word processor enter drafts of wills, standard clauses, and other related estate planning documents into the computer system thereby making the draft of a will from scratch a rarity.

Legal forms, including wills, are available on CDs. However, careful, personalized drafting is still required. The appropriate form can be downloaded from a

CD into a word-processing system for easy will preparation. West's Legal Forms, for example, a traditional multi-volume legal formbook series, is available on CD. A new CD is sent from the publisher when updates are made. The easy computer and word-processing access to CDs and the minimum storage requirements of CDs make the purchase of these products attractive.

1. Introductory or Exordium and Publication Clause

Exordium clause
The beginning or introductory clause of a will.

The **exordium clause** identifies the maker of the will and states or declares the maker's intention that the provisions in this written document be followed after death. To be valid and enforceable, the document must appear to be a will or testamentary in nature. The introductory clause should also include the address, city, county, and state of its maker which help to determine domicile for probate proceedings; any alias or other name by which the maker is known (often written "a/k/a"—also known as) so all property owned by the maker can be identified, located, and properly transferred or eventually distributed; and a statement of the maker's capacity and freedom from undue influence.

Sample Exordium Clause:

I, Rowley D. Morse, also known as R. David Morse, of 4607 Elmors Drive, City of Middleton, County of Heather, and State of Iowa, being of sound mind and not acting under undue influence of any person whomsoever, do make, publish, and declare this document to be my last will and testament. I do hereby cancel, revoke, and annul all former wills and testaments or codicils made by me.

The purpose of the exordium clause is to declare to the public the following: (1) the identity of the testator, (2) the testator has the intent and capacity to create a will, (3) the document is the testator's last will, and (4) the location of the testator's principal residence (city, county, and state) or domicile, which enables

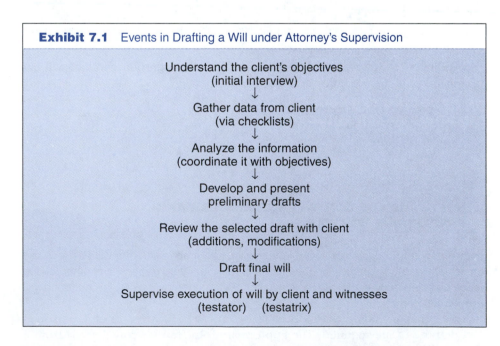

Exhibit 7.1 Events in Drafting a Will under Attorney's Supervision

Understand the client's objectives
(initial interview)
↓
Gather data from client
(via checklists)
↓
Analyze the information
(coordinate it with objectives)
↓
Develop and present
preliminary drafts
↓
Review the selected draft with client
(additions, modifications)
↓
Draft final will
↓
Supervise execution of will by client and witnesses
(testator)   (testatrix)

the personal representative to determine which state has the proper authority to tax the testator's property and which court has jurisdiction over the administration of the decedent-testator's estate.

🏛 ASSIGNMENT 7.1

1. Examine the following exordium clause: "Being of sound mind and body, I, D. E. Pearson, of 2914 Columba Street, Bloomington, dispose of the following property by will:. . . ."

   a. Is this adequate for the purposes of an exordium clause? Why or why not?

   b. Could any word or phrase be misinterpreted so as to prevent the document's admission to probate?

   c. Redraft the parts of the clause likely to cause difficulty. If necessary, include information not found in the original clause and explain the reasons for including it.

2. Tom Hardy lives in Zuma, Arizona. He owns a cottage in Wisconsin and has a savings and checking account in Zuma. The deed to the cottage is written to "Thomas William Hardy," and both bank accounts are in the name, Tom W. Hardy. Draft an appropriate exordium clause for Tom and explain your reasons for the draft.

2. General Revocation Clause

A decedent's new will generally revokes an earlier will. State statutes vary on the requirements necessary for a new will to revoke a prior will. Some require a specific statement saying the new will revokes the prior will; in most states, however, a prior will is automatically revoked when the maker writes, dates, and signs a new will. The testamentary document last in time also supersedes existing codicils attached to previous wills. The safest way to ensure revocation by a new will is to include a **revocation clause** as part of the exordium clause. For example: "I hereby revoke all prior wills and codicils made by me, and declare this to be my last will and testament." Review Chapter 5 on the revocation of wills.

Revocation clause
A clause or statement in a will that revokes all prior wills and codicils.

3. Provision for Payment of Debts and Funeral Expenses

The maker of a will often directs the named personal representative or executor to pay all debts, administration expenses, and expenses of the last illness, funeral, and burial out of estate funds before the decedent's property is distributed. These duties are automatic responsibilities of the personal representative of the estate, however, and need not be embodied in a formal clause. The phrasing of the debt payment clause can also present a problem. For example, if the clause reads "I direct my personal representative or executor to pay all of my valid debts and administration expenses out of the residue of my estate," and the decedent-testator was personally liable for a debt such as a mortgage on the decedent's home, the specific devisee of the home in the will, who would normally be responsible for the mortgage payment, could require that the mortgage be paid out of the residue (according to the rules of abatement). Many states avoid this problem by statute, unless the decedent's will specifically states otherwise; see Cal. Prob. Code

§ 21131; Mass. Gen. Laws Ann. ch. 191 § 23; N.Y. EPTL § 3-3.6; and UPC § 2-607. A more appropriate clause is the following.

> *Sample Debt Payment Clause:*
> I direct my personal representative hereinafter named, to pay all my just debts, estate administration expenses, and expenses of my last illness, funeral, and burial out of my estate as soon as possible after my death.

The inclusion of a clause in the testator's will that requires payment of debts and administration expense from the estate can lead to a deduction from federal estate or income taxes for those payments (see IRC §§ 2053 and 212).

The cost of funeral and burial expenses continues to escalate. When the burden of making the necessary arrangements falls on the bereaved family, emotions often play a part in their financial decisions concerning, for example, the casket, flowers, headstone, reception, and religious service. To alleviate this unpleasant burden, many people prearrange and pay for their funeral and burial prior to death. You should discuss this sensitive but responsible option with the client and suggest possible methods to accomplish it; e.g., the client could open a bank savings account covering the estimated cost of a client-selected casket, headstone, reception, and so on, or execute a simple trust agreement with a funeral home in which the money for these expenses would be held in trust by the funeral director until the client's death. However, this prepayment plan could result in the loss of the tax deduction for funeral expenses for death tax purposes. Some state statutes establish monetary limits for the funeral and burial expenses. If the decedent has many creditors and the personal representative overspends the reasonable limit, the personal representative is liable for this breach of fiduciary duty, and the court can order the personal representative to pay damages to the estate.

𐐒 ASSIGNMENT 7.2

1. Check your state statutes and determine the priority of payment of decedent's debts in your state (compare UPC §§ 3-805 and 3-807).
2. In writing his will, Quincy Rudd included a clause directing his executor to pay the debts owed by him at the time of his death from the residue of the estate. Draft a clause for Quincy's will to this effect. Explain the hardship that your draft may cause if the residuary clause is the sole provision in a testator's will that provides for the surviving spouse and children.
3. Draft a clause for Quincy Rudd's will that identifies how any taxes owed by his estate will be paid.

4. Instructions for Funeral and Burial

As previously mentioned, a letter of instructions rather than a will is the more appropriate and preferred written document used to contain the plans for a testator's funeral and burial arrangements. Since copies of the letter are given to the family and personal representative, a primary advantage of the letter is it ensures the funeral plans are known at the time of the testator's death, whereas a will may not be found in time. Having stated the above preference, it is a fact many testators continue to place, or already have, funeral instructions in their wills or codicils. Therefore, the discussion that follows has been retained in the text.

A simple clause such as the following may be included in a will to inform the decedent's family of the previous plans or instructions the deceased has made for her funeral:

Sample Clause:

I direct that my funeral is to be conducted according to my letter of instructions, a copy of which is on file at the Benson Funeral Home, 1404 Second Avenue, City of Cedar Falls, County of Polk, State of Iowa. The said written instructions are hereby incorporated into and made part of this will.

Including funeral and burial instructions in a will may be futile, because the will may not be found in time or, in many states, the desires of the decedent's surviving spouse or next of kin legally supersede any such instructions by the decedent. A conflict between the wishes of the family and the testator may also arise when the testator desires to be cremated. Concerning cremation, a testator can simply add a clause in the will that states:

Sample Clause:

At my death, I direct that my body be taken to the Nielson Chapel and Crematory, my remains cremated, and my ashes buried in our family plot.

Another challenge to burial instructions may occur when the testator desires to donate his body for educational or medical purposes (e.g., to an organ transplant bank), but the nearest relatives object. To resolve questions associated with anatomical gifts, the Uniform Anatomical Gift Act, which has been adopted in all fifty states, provides the maker may legally determine in a will the disposition of all or any part of the body for organ transplant, medical research, or educational purposes. Although the words have been modified in some states, the act substantively regulates who may be a donor and a donee, the manner of executing, delivering, and amending the gift, and the rights and duties of the parties. A sample clause follows:

Sample Clause:

I hereby direct my personal representative on my death to see that my body be delivered to the State University Medical School to be used for educational purposes.

In addition to a provision in a will, under the act, any person, 18 or older, may donate organs by a donor card or other document that becomes legally enforceable once the signatures of the donor and two attesting and subscribing witnesses are obtained. The act permits medical schools, universities, physicians, hospitals, and organ banks to receive the body or organ donations. See and review Exhibit 1.2 for a card and comments. Whenever the testator intends to donate his body or organs for transplants or medical research, he should carry a written expression of those wishes, such as a donor card, on his person at all times. Otherwise, by the time the will is located and read, his body may have been cremated or buried, or the organs to be donated may not be useful for transplants.

If a potential organ donor has taken no action during her lifetime to make a gift of body organs, only specific relatives have the ability to make a gift of the decedent's organs (absent any evidence of a contrary decision by the decedent). The following are excerpts of typical state statutes concerning anatomical gifts and the relatives of the decedent who are allowed to make the gifts:

Fla. Stat. Ann. § 732.912 Persons Who May Make an Anatomical Gift
(1) Any person who may make a will may give all or part of his or her body for any purpose specified in § 732.910, the gift to take effect upon death. . .
(2) . . .
(3) . . . a member of one of the classes of persons listed below, in the order of priority stated and in the absence of actual notice of contrary indications by the decedent or actual notice of opposition by a member of the same or a prior class, may give all or any part of the decedent's body for any purpose specified in § 732.910:
    (a) The spouse of the decedent;
    (b) An adult son or daughter of the decedent;
    (c) Either parent of the decedent;
    (d) An adult brother or sister of the decedent;
    (e) A grandparent of the decedent;
    (f) A guardian of the person of the decedent at the time of his or her death; or
    (g) A representative ad litem . . . .
(4) If the donee has actual notice of contrary indications by the decedent or, in the case of a spouse making the gift, an objection of an adult son or daughter or actual notice that a gift by a member of a class is opposed by a member of the same or a prior class, the donee shall not accept the gift.
(5) The person authorized by subsection (3) may make the gift after the decedent's death or immediately before the decedent's death.
(6) A gift of all or part of a body authorizes any examination necessary to assure medical acceptability of the gift for the purposes intended.
(7) Once the gift has been made, the rights of the donee are paramount to the rights of others except as provided by § 732.917.

Fla. Stat. Ann. § 732.913 Persons and Entities That May Become Donees; Purposes for Which Anatomical Gifts May Be Made
The following persons or entities may become donees of gifts of bodies or parts of them for the purposes stated:
    (1) Any hospital, surgeon, or physician for medical or dental education or research, advancement of medical or dental science, therapy, or transplantation.
    (2) Any accredited medical or dental school, college, or university for education, research, advancement of medical or dental science, or therapy.
    (3) Any bank or storage facility for medical or dental education, research, advancement of medical or dental science, therapy, or transplantation.
    (4) Any individual specified by name for therapy or transplantation needed by him.

ASSIGNMENT 7.3

1. Margaret is dying. She is unconscious and in a coma from which her doctors do not expect her to recover. Margaret's family is aware another patient is seeking a kidney transplant, and the doctors have informed the family Margaret could be a successful donor. Margaret's husband and children are in favor of donating Margaret's kidneys after her death; Margaret's parents are opposed. How would this conflict be resolved in Florida? In your state?

2. Claudia's will does not contain an anatomical gift clause. She thinks it would be a good idea to leave her eyes to the State Society for the Prevention of Blindness eye bank. Draft such a provision for the revised will she is writing.

3. Claudia realizes her family may hold the funeral and burial before reading her will and the provision mentioned above. What should she do to prevent this potential problem?

5. Specific Testamentary Gifts

It is important to remember that under the orthodox system of terminology "legacies" are gifts of money, "bequests" are gifts of personal property, and "devises" are gifts of real property. Nevertheless, these terms are often used interchangeably. Under UPC terminology, the disposition of both real and personal property under a will is called a devise. Both sets of terminology are used in this section of the text.

One of the most important functions of a will is the determination of "what goes to whom." To prevent family arguments over specific items of a decedent's estate, the will should provide for the disposition of property as its maker chooses. The maker may have many reasons for leaving specific property to certain individuals. These gifts must be made before the maker transfers the remaining assets in a residuary clause. Marital deduction provisions (discussed in Chapters 10 and 14) must also be stated before the residue is transferred. For example, John Harrington has three sons. His will provides:

Sample Clause:

I give the sum of Two Thousand Dollars ($2,000) to my son, James L. Harrington; my diamond ring to my son, Thomas J. Harrington; and my collection of guns and rifles to my son, Harold L. Harrington. If any of my three sons predeceases me, the gift designated for that son shall pass into the residue of my estate. All my sons' addresses are currently the same as my own.

I give the land that I own in the County of Adams, State of Iowa, legally described as follows: Lot 17, Block 8, consisting of twenty acres, known as Stonybroke, according to the plat filed with the Registrar of Titles in and for the County of Adams, State of Iowa, to my wife, Jeanine Harrington, as fee owner in severalty, if she survives me. If not, I give the aforementioned land, legally described above, known as Stonybroke, to my three sons equally as tenants in common. Also, I give my automobiles and other items of personal property to my wife, Jeanine Harrington, to do with as she sees fit, if she survives me. If not, I give the aforementioned property to my three sons equally.

An important point to recall is that a will is ambulatory (not yet operative), so regardless of a clause like the above, its maker is free before death to destroy the will, give away, or sell any property constituting a specific gift in the will. Any intentional act of the testator can cancel a gift in the will, such as the destruction, sale, or gift of the property to another person. In such cases, the testamentary gift is adeemed, and the beneficiary or devisee is not entitled to receive the property unless a substitute for the gift is mentioned in the will.

Example: In the clause above, if the diamond ring and gun collection are not in John Harrington's estate at his death, the two sons do not receive their specific bequests or devises.

⛪ ASSIGNMENT 7.4

1. Roger's will provides, in part: "To my daughter, Nadine, I give 100 shares of common stock in the Hopewell Corporation, if she survives me." What kind of gift is this? If Roger owns 75 shares of common stock in the Hopewell Corporation at the time of his death, would Nadine be entitled to them plus the fair market value of 25 shares? Why or why not?
2. Lillian wishes to leave her antique rosewood furniture to her daughters, Kimberly and Ellen. Draft a provision in Lillian's will for this gift (bequest or devise).
3. At Lillian's death Kimberly and Ellen are living in separate houses. They cannot agree on the division of the furniture. Could Lillian's will have been written to avoid the dispute? If necessary, redraft your provision to illustrate.
4. "To my son, Gerald, I leave 30 acres of land in Marsh County." What kind of devise is this? Is it defeasible (see the Glossary)? Why or why not?

Memorandum
A written list of the testator's personal property and the name of the beneficiary who receives each item. It is signed by the testator but is not a legally enforceable document.

In most states, statutes have established procedures for the disposition of the tangible personal property, other than money, that remains after the testator has made specific testamentary gifts (see UPC § 2-513). The testator is allowed to write a separate **memorandum** (list of property) in the handwriting of the testator and signed by the testator. The memorandum describes the property, item by item, and the beneficiary or devisee who is to receive it with "reasonable certainty." The following sample will clause identifies the separate memorandum that lists the decedent's tangible personal property and names the beneficiary who is to receive each item listed.

Sample Clause:

I give my tangible personal property to the beneficiaries and devisees named herein, in accordance with any written list or memorandum which is signed and dated by me and is incorporated by reference in this will, and which is prepared in accordance with the provisions of [add appropriate state statute]. The most recent memorandum shall control if there are inconsistent dispositions. I give all tangible personal property not disposed of by the provisions of any such memorandum to my wife, if she survives me, or if she does not survive me, I give such property in equal shares to my children who survive me.

Such statutes allow the testator who owns numerous items of tangible personal property, such as cars, boats, antiques, jewelry, art objects, stamp or coin collections, and the like, to identify and list the property and the beneficiaries and devisees to whom it is to be given on a separate memorandum from the will. The testator can easily add to or modify this memorandum without having to revoke the will and draft a new one.

Family complications make it necessary to draft the will carefully to satisfy the purposes and intentions of the client. These complications may occur when the testator has been married more than once and two or more sets of children are potential beneficiaries or devisees. The rule that the testator may favor or exclude family and others in the will still applies, but so does the rule that a spouse cannot be disinherited. Children, however, can be disinherited according to the wishes of the testator. The following illustrates a typical family problem that could affect the validity of a will.

Example: A man divorces his first wife, with whom he had two children, remarries, and has a child by his second wife. His will, written during the first marriage, leaves half his estate to the wife and children of the first marriage and, obviously, says nothing of the second wife or their child. Should he die without revising his will, his estate may be distributed as if he had died intestate, since the will may be revoked by "operation of law" by some state statutes. For example, in states that have adopted the Uniform Probate Code, his divorce revokes the provisions of the will that benefit his first wife (UPC §§ 2-802 and 2-804); in others, remarriage or remarriage and the birth of issue may revoke a will. The result of such revocation is the same as if the testator died without a will, i.e., intestate. In such a case, the second wife and all his children will take under the state intestate succession statute; the first wife will be entitled to nothing.

During will construction, problems may arise concerning the client's children, e.g., natural, adopted, nonmarital, and stepchildren, when the client attempts to identify the persons to be included or excluded in the will. Words such as "issue," "heirs," "descendants," and, of course, "child" or "children," are often ambiguous or misleading. In the statutes of most states, the terms just mentioned include natural and adopted children of the testator, exclude stepchildren, and may vary concerning nonmarital children. To resolve these problems, the following clause should be used if it matches the client's wishes:

Sample Clause:
As used in this will, words such as "issue," "child," and "children," describing a person or class of persons by relationship to another, shall refer to persons who are related by blood and also to persons who are related by adoption.

If the testator wishes to make a provision for stepchildren, that intention must be expressly stated in the will. Understanding the law of wills and careful drafting are necessary to resolve such problems.

🏛 ASSIGNMENT 7.5

Harold Wilson is currently married to his second wife, Cheryl. They have two teenage children, James and Barbara. Previously, Harold was married to and later divorced from Margaret Wilson. Harold and Margaret were married for ten years and also had two children, Wilbur and Maude. The following is an excerpt from a will written by Harold when he was married to Margaret.

Article IV
I give all my personal effects, including books, art objects, jewelry, furnishings, and other tangible items, to my wife, Margaret, and children, Wilbur and Maude, to be divided equally, as determined by my executrix.

Article V
I give the sum of two thousand dollars ($2,000) to my secretary, Jerome Davis, if he is employed by me at the time of my death.

Article VI
I give the sum of ten thousand dollars ($10,000) to be divided equally to my children, if they survive me, or if they do not survive me, then to my issue who survive me, per stirpes.

Article VII
I give the sum of five thousand dollars ($5,000) and all stocks, bonds, and debentures which I shall hold at the time of my death to my wife, if she survives me, or if she does not survive me, to my children who survive me in equal shares.

Answer the following questions and draft appropriate clauses to change or modify Harold's will as requested:

1. If Harold and his first wife, Margaret, as part of their divorce agreement, had a fair and complete property settlement between themselves and for the benefit of their two children, Wilbur and Maude, could Harold exclude these three members of his first family from the benefits of his current will according to your state laws? Draft the necessary provisions in Harold's will that would exclude all three members of his first family.

2. Suppose in the example above that Maude is now married and has a son, Thomas, who is Harold's grandson. Thomas is physically handicapped. According to your state's laws, could Harold exclude Thomas from his will? Could Harold include Thomas, but exclude Maude? Draft sample will provisions that accomplish these purposes if allowed by your state statutes.

3. Suppose, while married, Harold and Margaret had adopted a daughter, Marjory. At the time of the divorce, Marjory had requested that she be allowed to live with her father, Harold. The request was granted. In your state, what are the rights of an adopted child to inherit from either of the adoptive parents? Due to his affection for Marjory, Harold wants half of his entire estate to go to her with the remaining half to be split equally by his current wife, Cheryl, and his two minor children, James and Barbara. Would such a provision be legal in your state? If so, draft the appropriate provision(s).

4. While married to his first wife, Margaret, Harold fathered a nonmarital son, Charles. Although their relationship is known by all, Harold has never acknowledged in writing that he is Charles's father.

   a. According to your state's laws, what rights would a nonmarital child (Charles) have in his father's (Harold's) estate?

   b. Must a provision be included in Harold's will in order to exclude Charles?

   c. If Harold had acknowledged Charles as his son in writing or in any requisite statutory manner, could Charles claim a share in Harold's estate even though he (Charles) was not mentioned in the will?

   d. Can any children, natural, adopted, or nonmarital, demand or claim a share of their parent's estate when they are not mentioned in their parent's will? What are the rights of stepchildren?

   e. Can property from an estate be willed to some of the testator's children while other children are disinherited? If so, draft such a provision in Harold's will including James, Barbara, and Marjory but excluding Wilbur and Maude.

5. A different complication would result if the facts in the Harold Wilson case were changed as follows: Instead of Harold and his second wife, Cheryl, having two children, they are childless. If Harold were to die testate and leave his entire estate to Cheryl, on Cheryl's subsequent death her relatives may receive the entire estate to the exclusion of Harold's children by his first wife. Harold wants to leave his estate to Cheryl if she survives him, but he also wants to provide for his two children, Wilbur and Maude. How could this be accomplished? Draft at least two clauses, one of which includes a life estate that would allow Harold to ensure that all or part of his estate would be received by his children on the death of either Harold or Cheryl.

6. Suppose that Harold Wilson was injured in an automobile accident, crippling him for life. He decided to leave his entire estate to his faithful nurse, Agnes, who had cared for him continuously since the year of the accident. According to your state laws, can Harold leave his estate to his nurse, excluding his wife and children?

6. Provision for Residue of Estate

The **residuary clause** allows the maker to transfer the remaining property of an estate that has not been specifically given to beneficiaries or devisees. This includes any additional property that may come into the estate after the will has been executed or after the maker's death. Generally, the bulk of an estate falls within the residue, which is usually the source for paying all federal and state death taxes, debts, and expenses of the decedent. *Remember:* Always name an alternate or successor residuary beneficiary. The following is an example of a residuary clause:

> *Sample Clause:*
> I give all the rest, residue, and remainder of my estate, of whatever kind, real, personal, or mixed, and wherever located, not effectively disposed of by the preceding articles of this will, to my surviving spouse, [add name], if she survives me, but if she does not survive me, to my children in equal shares.

When the residue is insufficient to meet priority obligations of the estate, e.g., debts, taxes, and expenses, payment must come from legacies or devises made in the will. *Remember:* The *abatement* process will determine the order in which property in the estate will be applied to the payment of such obligations causing some gifts to be diminished or totally abolished. Consequently, state statutes that control the abatement process must be checked (see UPC § 3-902).

Some residuary clauses are simple, leaving everything to one person. Others are complex, with lengthy provisions concerning the establishment of testamentary trusts and the powers and duties of the named trustee. In either case, the will's maker must remember that if the named residuary beneficiaries or devisees should predecease the maker, there would be no one to receive the residue, so all or part of it will be distributed according to appropriate state intestate succession statutes. Thus, the residuary clause must be carefully drafted to cover potential problems caused by the sequence of deaths of named devisees and must list alternative or successor beneficiaries or devisees.

Finally, it is important to keep in mind that without a residuary clause or in any circumstances in which some or all of the decedent's estate passes by intestacy, there are no specific or general legacies or devises. Therefore, the estate's net assets or income are divided among the heirs on a pro rata basis. An example of a case in which the decedent died testate but the will contained an invalid residuary clause, thereby causing the property not disposed of to pass by the state's intestate succession statute, is *Estate of Cancik,* 121 Ill.App.3d 113, 76 Ill.Dec. 659, 459 N.E.2d 296 (1984).

Residuary clause
A clause in a will that disposes of the remaining assets (residue) of the decedent's estate after all debts and gifts in the will are satisfied.

ASSIGNMENT 7.6

1. Suppose in the John Harrington example above in which James received $2,000, Thomas the diamond ring, and Harold the gun collection, the testator, John Harrington, added the following provision, "all the rest, residue, and remainder of my estate I leave to my wife, Jeanine Harrington." The residue is valued at $10,000. If John died and left debts and expenses amounting to $11,000, how would his testamentary gifts abate according to your state's laws?
2. In the Harrington case, if Jeanine, the residual beneficiary, predeceases John, the testator, and he has not named a successor residual beneficiary, all the assets included

in the residue will pass according to the intestate succession statute. Check to see how this problem is handled in your state.

3. Draft a residuary clause for John Harrington containing a successor residual beneficiary.

7. Appointment of Personal Representative

To acquire the powers and authority of a personal representative, a person must be appointed by a court (e.g., the probate judge or, for informal proceedings, a registrar). Generally, unless the person is unqualified, the court approves and appoints the personal representative named in the will. Since personal representatives are *fiduciaries* who are entrusted with the assets and property of others (the decedent), they must be intelligent, organized, honest, and loyal to the beneficiaries or devisees of the estate while performing all estate administration tasks. They must also be capable of engaging in business transactions or making contracts such as selling assets. Therefore, they should not be minors, incompetent persons, felons, or persons who have or *may have a conflict of interest, e.g., an attorney or paralegal who drafts a will and who influences a client to name him as the personal representative* (see UPC § 3-203 and Tex. Prob. Code Ann. § 78).

ETHICAL ISSUE ▶

State statutes often enumerate the powers granted a personal representative or trustee. The testator, however, may want to list certain specific powers and duties to help the personal representative facilitate the administration of the estate. Giving the personal representative the power to sell one's property, for instance, saves time and perhaps money; otherwise, the personal representative would have to obtain permission from the probate court for such a sale. Such permission is called a *license to sell.* When the estate requires detailed handling, it is best the testator direct the personal representative's course of action. For example, promissory notes payable to the testator should be collected by the personal representative. Unless the testator mentions collection on such notes in the letter of instructions, the personal representative might overlook this detail, with the result that the probate court might hold the personal representative liable. In addition, just as a contingent devisee should always be named in the event the original devisee predeceases the maker, a contingent or alternate personal representative should be selected in case the original one is unable or unwilling to serve in that capacity (for an example of a statute on executor's and administrator's powers and duties, see Wash. Rev. Code Ann. § 11.48.010 and compare UPC §§ 3-701 and 3-703).

Sample Clause:

I nominate and appoint my son, Marvin Jameson, as personal representative of this my last will and my estate and authorize him to (among other powers) sell at public or private sale any real or personal property of my estate. If Marvin Jameson predeceases me, fails to qualify, or ceases to act as my personal representative for any reason, I nominate and appoint my daughter, Myrtle B. Jameson, as successor personal representative with all powers hereinbefore mentioned, and I request that my personal representative be permitted to serve without bond or surety thereon. [See detailed discussion of bond and surety in Chapter 11].

A typical statute on the time for commencing the personal representative's duties is the following North Dakota law.

N.D. Cent. Code § 30.1-18-01 Time of Accrual of Duties and Powers
The duties and powers of a personal representative commence upon appointment. The powers of a personal representative relate back in time to give acts by the person appointed which are beneficial to the estate occurring prior to appointment the same effect as those occurring thereafter. Prior to appointment a person named executor in a will may carry out written instructions of the decedent relating to the decedent's body, funeral, and burial arrangements. A personal representative may ratify and accept acts on behalf of the estate done by others where the acts would have been proper for a personal representative.

The personal representative appointed is responsible for collecting and preserving the estate assets, paying all allowed debts of the decedent, as well as estate expenses and taxes, and distributing the balance to devisees named in the will (see UPC § 3-703). The procedures for appointing the personal representative are discussed in Chapters 11 and 12.

It is important that you be able to interpret statutory language correctly. A phrase in the North Dakota statute above, "The powers of a personal representative relate back in time," refers to the fact that although personal representatives do not have authority to handle the administration of the estate until appointed, they do possess limited authority (e.g., to preserve the assets of the estate before the personal representatives can be duly appointed), a universal though unwritten rule that several states, including UPC states, have incorporated into their probate codes. Formal qualification of the personal representative requires a hearing before a probate judge, registrar, or clerk of the court, an order signed by the judge, and issuance of documents called Letters Testamentary or Letters of Administration (see Chapter 11), which officially authorize the named personal representative to commence the administration.

The cost of selecting and utilizing fiduciaries such as personal representatives, trustees, or attorneys handling an estate is governed by state law. In some states, such as New York, California, and Iowa, personal representatives are paid commissions (fees) according to a sliding scale based on the monetary value of the estate or trust. Typically, the statutory fee percentage of the estate's value decreases as the value of the estate increases. The statutory fees paid personal representatives in the above states are as follows:

- California: Up to 4 percent of first $15,000; 3 percent on next $85,000; 2 percent on next $900,000; 1 percent on next $9,000,000; 0.5 percent on next $15,000,000; and a "reasonable rate" for anything over $25,000,000 (see Cal. Prob. Code § 10800).
- Iowa: Up to 6 percent of first $1,000; 4 percent on next $4,000; and 2 percent on anything over $5,000 (see Iowa Code Ann. § 633.197).
- New York: 5 percent of first $100,000; 4 percent on next $200,000; 3 percent on next $700,000; 2.5 percent of next $4,000,000; and 2 percent on anything over $5,000,000 (see N.Y. SCPA § 2307).

New York also uses such scales to compensate trustees, while California uses them for personal representatives and attorneys but not for trustees. Formerly, state bar associations established minimum attorney fee schedules based on the size of the estate. But the U.S. Supreme Court in *Goldfarb v. Virginia State Bar,* 421 U.S. 773, 95 S.Ct. 2004, 44 L.Ed.2d 572 (1975), ruled that such minimum fee schedules were prohibited by antitrust laws as a method of price fixing. Currently, the trend is to use "reasonable compensation" commensurate with the value of personal representative and attorney services rather than the value of the estate to determine fees. Today, many states and the UPC use the "reasonable compensation" method; see UPC § 3-719. Custom and local practice play a major part in determining what constitutes "reasonable compensation," but the court makes the final decision and must also approve the payment of fees to the personal representative and estate attorney.

8. Appointment of Personal and/or Property Guardian

A parent has a statutory obligation to support children until they reach majority. The law establishes two types of guardianships: a personal guardian and a property guardian. Whenever the testator has minor or physically or mentally handicapped children and the other parent is deceased or unable to care for them, a personal guardian should be named in the will to ensure proper care of the children after the testator's death. Otherwise, if there is no will, the court is required to determine who shall have custody and/or *guardianship of the person,* i.e., the child or the incompetent).

> **Example:** Bryan dies testate. He had sole custody of his minor daughter, Kate. Bryan's wife had died several years earlier. Bryan's brother, Gerald, with whom Bryan and Kate had lived for a number of years, and Kate's maternal grandmother both claim to be the better choice for guardian of the child. The probate court must choose between the two if Bryan's will fails to name a guardian.

The testator should also appoint a *guardian of the property* or *conservator* to manage property left to minor or incompetent children. If such an appointment is not made, the probate court must do so. The testator should empower the property guardian or conservator to hold, accumulate, and manage the funds and property for incapacitated or minor devisees or beneficiaries under a trust for the duration of their minority or incapacity (compare UPC§ § 5-209, 5–309, and 5–401). The personal guardian and the property guardian may or may not be the same person. The following is an example of a clause which appoints a personal and property guardian:

> *Sample Clause:*
>
> I nominate and appoint Francine E. Richter as personal and property guardian of my minor child, Debra G. Thorsby, and empower her with the right to have care, custody, and control of said minor child, and to collect, invest, and manage, without court approval, any property passing to said minor child by this will. The guardian may use the income from the property for the support, education, and well-being of said child and distribute the principal balance to her on her 25th birthday or her marriage, whichever occurs first. In the event Francine E. Richter fails to qualify or is unable, or unwilling, or ceases to act as guardian, I nominate and appoint William B. Kruger to serve in her place as successor personal and property guardian with all the hereinbefore mentioned powers. I direct that the appointed guardian in this will shall not be required to give any bond or other surety in connection with qualifying or acting in this capacity.

A statute that grants testamentary appointment of a guardian is *Tex. Prob. Code Ann. § 676(d),* Guardians of Minors:

The surviving parent of a minor may by will or written declaration appoint any eligible person to be guardian of the person of the parent's minor children after the death of the parent. Unless the court finds that the person designated in the will or declaration to serve as guardian of the person of the parent's minor children is disqualified, is dead, refuses to serve, or would not serve the best interests of the minor children, the court shall appoint the person as guardian in preference to those otherwise entitled to serve as guardian under this chapter. On compliance with this code, an eligible person is also entitled to be appointed guardian of the children's estates after the death of the parent.

A statute that treats the order of preference for the appointment of a guardian is *Ind. Code Ann. § 29-3-5-5,* Consideration for Appointment of Guardian; Order of Consideration; Priorities:

> Sec. 5 (a) The following are entitled to consideration for appointment as a guardian under section 4 of this chapter in the order listed:
> (1) A person designated in a durable power of attorney.
> (2) The spouse of an incapacitated person.
> (3) An adult child of an incapacitated person.
> (4) A parent of an incapacitated person, or a person nominated by will of a deceased parent of an incapacitated person or by any writing signed by a parent of an incapacitated person and attested to by at least two (2) witnesses.
> (5) Any person related to an incapacitated person by blood or marriage with whom the incapacitated person has resided for more than six (6) months before the filing of the petition.
> (6) A person nominated by the incapacitated person who is caring for or paying for the care of the incapacitated person.
> (b) With respect to persons having equal priority, the court shall select the person it considers best qualified to serve as guardian. The court, acting in the best interest of the incapacitated person or minor, may pass over a person having priority and appoint a person having a lower priority or no priority under this section.

A controversial and often stressful situation arises whenever a single parent attempts to appoint a guardian for a child in a will and specifically excludes from the appointment the other natural parent. The surviving natural parent, without regard to marital status, has the right to custody of the child and to be the guardian unless the parent is found to be unfit. The custodial parent cannot change the rights of the surviving parent (see Minn. Stat. Ann. § 525.6155).

> **Example:** In her will, Sandra, the custodial parent, selects her sister, Ruth, to be the personal guardian of Sandra's minor son, William. Sandra also states she does not want her former husband, Roy, who is the father of William, to obtain custody of William. Upon Sandra's death, the court would appoint Roy the personal guardian unless he was unwilling or unfit.

⚊ ASSIGNMENT 7.7

Rhoda's husband, Steven Clark, has a will, leaving his estate equally to Rhoda and their three-year-old adopted daughter, Karen, who has muscular dystrophy.
1. Draft a provision to be added to Steven's will that adequately protects Karen's interest in her father's estate.

2. If Rhoda remarries and dies intestate five years after Steven's death, would her new husband or Karen's maternal grandparents have a statutory preference to the appointment of guardian for Karen in the state of Indiana? In your state?

9. Simultaneous Death Clause

Most states have enacted statutes that govern the distribution of a decedent-testator's property when there is insufficient evidence to determine if a beneficiary survived the testator. Due to the frequent occurrence of these inheritance and distribution problems whenever two people, such as a married couple or a parent and adult child, die at the same time in a common accident, nearly all states have adopted the Uniform Simultaneous Death Act. The act provides where the inheritance of property depends on the priority of death of the decedents, and there is no sufficient evidence that the decedents have died other than simultaneously, the property of each decedent involved shall be distributed as if he or she had survived the other (see UPC § 2–702). This provision can be added to the decedent's will. A typical state statute is *Conn. Gen. Stat. Ann. § 45a–440,* Simultaneous Death; Disposition of Property:

> (a) When no sufficient evidence of survivorship. When the title to property or the devolution thereof depends upon priority of death and there is no sufficient evidence that the persons have died otherwise than simultaneously, the property of each person shall be disposed of as if he had survived, except as provided otherwise in this section.

Example: Margaret and her daughter, Mary, are at home asleep. Gas leaks into the house causing an explosion that destroys the house and kills Margaret and Mary. Margaret's will named Mary as her sole beneficiary, but in the event of Mary's death before Margaret, the property was to pass to Margaret's brother, Adam. The will contained a **simultaneous death clause** that allowed the property to go to Adam instead of possibly passing into Mary's estate.

Simultaneous death clause
A clause in a will that determines the distribution of property in the event there is no evidence as to the priority of time of death of the testator and another, usually the testator's spouse.

The Uniform Simultaneous Death Act has also resolved the following problem. If two individuals owning property in joint tenancy die simultaneously under circumstances in which it cannot be determined who died first, the property is divided equally and distributed to the beneficiaries named in the residuary clause of their respective wills. In the previous example, if Margaret and Mary owned a house in joint tenancy and they died simultaneously in a plane crash, half of the value of the house would pass to Margaret's brother, and the other half would pass to Mary's beneficiaries or heirs depending on whether she died testate or intestate.

Unfortunately, the act can result in a significant financial loss to surviving beneficiaries and devisees, because the act implies that if there is adequate proof of the sequence of deaths, the surviving beneficiary, no matter how long the person survives, will be entitled to the property passed by will from the first decedent's estate. For example, suppose a wife, who died a few days after her husband in a common accident, was the sole beneficiary of her husband's will; after his estate is taxed and debts are paid, the residue would be added to the wife's estate, where it would be taxed again. Most states, including those that have adopted the UPC, have eliminated this problem by adding a "delay clause" to the simultaneous death provision which requires that a person must survive the first decedent in the common accident by at least 120 hours to qualify as a surviving beneficiary. If the beneficiary does not survive the decedent-testator by 120 hours, the beneficiary does not receive the property through the will. *Caution*: A delay clause that exceeds 180 days will disqualify a bequest to the spouse for the marital deduction (see U.S.C.A. § 2056[b] [3]; Federal Tax Regulations, § 20. 2056). The following is a sample clause, taken from West's McKinney's Forms, ESP, § 7:255, that can be used to resolve the "delay" problem:

> *Sample Clause:*
> In the event that my said wife shall die within a period of [six] months (180 days) after the date of my death, my said wife shall be deemed to have predeceased me, and all provisions contained herein for her benefit shall be cancelled and my estate shall be administered and the assets of my estate distributed as though I had died immediately after the death of my said wife. (Reprinted with permission from West's McKinney's Forms, Copyright ©, by West Group).

In cases involving intestacy and simultaneous deaths, Section 47 of the Texas Probate Code establishes a "delay" period of 120 hours (5 days) that must pass in order for an heir to "survive" and inherit from the intestate. If the heir does not survive the intestate by the 5 days, the beneficiary is considered to have predeceased the intestate, and none of the intestate's property will be passed to the beneficiary. The UPC § 2–104 has the same provision.

Although the Uniform Simultaneous Death Act is the most common provision for directing how a testator's property will be distributed, i.e., that the beneficiary in the will predeceased the testator, a different presumption of death can be established in the will by an appropriate provision. For example, when estate planning for spouses is an important consideration, it is common to provide that the spouse with the smaller estate is determined to survive in the event of simultaneous death.

⚖ ASSIGNMENT 7.8

Ruth and Edmund Barnet, husband and wife, live in Connecticut. Edmund's will gives his country house to Ruth, if she should survive him, but if she does not, to his sister, Estelle. Ruth's will gives her collection of antiques to Edmund, if he should survive her, but if he does not, to her brother, Keith. Ruth and Edmund die simultaneously in an automobile collision. Answer these questions according to your state laws:

1. Who inherits which property?
2. Would your answer differ if Ruth had died one day later than Edmund? Is there "sufficient evidence" to prevent the Connecticut statute above from operating?
3. If Ruth receives injuries in the accident and dies 90 days afterward, would she be entitled to receive Edmund's gift? Would Estelle?

10. Testamentary Trust Clause

Often, a person wishes to transfer ownership of property to another without giving the recipient full power over the designated property. In a will, a method frequently used for the benefit of minor children is a *testamentary trust*. The will, and therefore the trust, takes effect when the testator dies and the probate court assumes the management and administration of the trust.

> *Sample Clause:*
>
> In the event any of my children are under the age of 18 at the time of my death, I give the remainder of my estate to the trustee, hereinafter named, in trust for the benefit of said child or children until they reach the age of 21. I direct said trustee to pay or apply the net income of this trust for the support, maintenance, and education of said children. When all my surviving children reach the age of 21, I direct the trustee to give the remainder of the trust to said children equally.

The probate court requires annual accounting by the trustee throughout the life of the trust.

11. Testimonium Clause

Testimonium clause
A clause in a will in which the maker states that she has freely signed and dated the will and requests the proper number of witnesses to do the same.

The **testimonium clause** contains a statement by the maker of the will that it has been freely signed and a request has been made of the proper number of witnesses to do the same.

Since the testimonium clause does not contain any new information and in most instances only repeats what the testator has stated in the opening paragraphs, it would appear to be expendable. Although each state demands the will conform to standards that require wills be written, signed by the testator, and witnessed, state statutes do not prescribe a form for the testimonium clause. Likewise, the use of a seal to indicate the identity of the testator or the substitution of L.S. (Lieu of Seal; set in place of a seal) is disregarded today by most will-drafters, although there are adherents to the practice. The following is an example of a testimonium clause:

> *Sample Clause:*
>
> In Witness Whereof, I, the undersigned testator (trix), do hereby declare that I willingly sign and execute this instrument as my last will consisting of _____ pages, including this page, on this _____ day of _____, 20 _____, at City of _____, County of _____, State of _____, in the presence of the witnesses whose names appear hereafter.
>
>
>
>   Testator(trix)

A typical statute on this matter is *N.J. Stat. Ann. § 3A:3-2,* Formal Requisites of a Will:

> Except as provided in Section 3A:3-5 of this title, a will to be valid shall be in writing and signed by the testator, which signature shall be made by the testator, or the making thereof acknowledged by him, and such writing declared to be his last will, in the presence of 2 witnesses present at the same time, who shall subscribe their names thereto, as witnesses, in the presence of the testator.

⚖ ASSIGNMENT 7.9

After reading a copy of a will prepared for him by an attorney, Owen decides that he does not like the antiquated language of the testimonium clause. He crosses it out and writes the following clause in its place.

At the time this will was executed, the testator knew of and fully complied with the statutes of this state relating to the execution of wills.

/S/ _____
(*Testator*)

Witnessed this same day, April 13, 2000.

/S/ _____
(*Witness*)

/S/ _____
(*Witness*)

1. Would this clause serve in lieu of the traditionally worded testimonium clause? Why or why not?
2. Point out potential difficulties caused by this testimonium clause when the will's executor offers the document for probate. Are there any words or omissions likely to be challenged in a will contest? Why?
3. If necessary, add to or modify the clause to make it conform both to the requirements of the law and to Owen's desire to modernize its language.

12. Testator's Signature

For a will to be valid, its maker must sign, make a mark, or direct another to sign. In most states, the signature must be witnessed by two or more persons acting as attesting witnesses. The date, either in the beginning, within, or at the end of the will, is essential. Without it, it may be impossible to prove the will is the last (in time) made by the testator.

A typical statute on the execution of a will is *Ill. Compiled Stat. Ann. Ch. 755 § 5/4-3*, Signing and Attestation:

(a) Every will shall be in writing, signed by the testator or some person in his presence and by his direction and attested in the presence of the testator by 2 or more credible witnesses. [Compare UPC § 2-502.]

Example: Walter typewrites his will. He puts his signature at the beginning of it, but types his name at the end. In some states, e.g., New York, the will may not be valid for lack of a proper signature in the proper place.

Example: Luke writes a second will but neglects to date it. Previously, he made a will but decided to discard it. He did not destroy the former will. Both documents are found after his death. The latter will may not supersede the former or prevail over it for lack of evidence that it was written at a later time.

🏛 ASSIGNMENT 7.10

Edith wishes to make a will, but she is partially paralyzed and cannot write her name. Her nephew, Arthur, agrees to draw up the will and to witness the X she will make in place of her name. The clause preceding the signature follows.

I, the testatrix, Edith B. Pendergast, on this 19th day of March, 1998, subscribe my mark to this will.

I, Arthur G. Pendergast, have witnessed this mark made by Edith B. Pendergast who affixed it in lieu of her signature.

_____

_____

1. Do these clauses fulfill your state's statutory requirements for a signature by the testator? Why or why not?
2. If necessary, add to or modify the clauses to make them conform to your answer in question 1 (compare UPC § 2-502). Is Arthur's signature sufficient to validate the will?

13. Attestation Clause of Witnesses

Attestation clause
Witnesses to a will state that they have attested the maker's signature and that they have subscribed (signed) a clause in the will to this effect.

The **attestation clause** identifies the individuals who are witnesses to the will. Witnesses must state they have attested the maker's signature on the will and sign the clause. As in the case of the testimonium clause, each state has legislation requiring subscription by witnesses, although none prescribes the words or form to be used to accomplish this. The traditional form of the attestation clause, like the familiarly worded testimonium clause, is illustrated below.

Sample Clause:
The above and foregoing instrument, consisting of three (3) typewritten pages including this page, was on the date hereof, signed by _____, the testator herein named and published and declared by him to be his last will and testament, in our presence, and we at his request and in his presence and in the presence of each other, have hereunto signed our names as witnesses and believe the testator to be 18 years of age or older, of sound mind, and under no constraint or undue influence.

_____ address _____
(Witness)

_____ address _____
(Witness)

Note: Some states have enacted statutes that substitute a self-proving affidavit clause for the traditional attestation clause (see discussion below).

🏛 ASSIGNMENT 7.11

"We, the undersigned, declare that Lyman Jarrett validly signed and executed this will. We sign at his request, all of us signing in each other's presence."
1. Does such a clause comply with statutory requirements? Why or why not?
2. If necessary, add to or modify the clause to make it conform to the statutory requirements.

14. Witnesses' Signatures and Addresses

Only the original copy of the will is signed. Copies should be made before the original is signed. All states require at least two witnesses sign the will, except

Vermont, which requires three witnesses' signatures. Witnesses should sign using the same pen as the testator.

Example:

	Address
Pamela C. Hunter	*111 Wheelock Drive*
Fredrick G. Burns	*2307 Ayleshire Avenue*
Marshall Jayner	*417 Kenyan Place*

ASSIGNMENT 7.12

You are a paralegal and also a notary public. At the execution of a will, while you are discussing the procedures with the attorney, the testator inadvertently signs the will, and now wants you to notarize it. What would you have the testator do to resolve this problem?

SAMPLE PRELIMINARY WILL

Exhibit 7.2 is a worksheet used to prepare a draft of a client's will. The will drawn from the information on the worksheet follows.

In a hypothetical situation, Leona Bayn Farrell wishes to make a will. She is married and has a husband, Oren, and four children, Randolph, Jonathan, Daria, and Thomas. Her estate consists of both real and personal property, all of which she acquired prior to the marriage or as gifts to her individually as separate property during the marriage. Leona lives in Arizona, a community property state, which allows her to convey by will her separate property and half of the community property acquired by Leona and her husband while they are married.

ASSIGNMENT 7.13

Peter Rice Cochran wishes to make a will. He is currently unmarried. He divorced Viola Leigh after a five-year marriage during which two children, Nancy and Jean, were born. His estate consists of both real and personal property, namely, a townhouse; household goods; automobile; checking account of $587; certificate of deposit of $7,000; insurance policy on his life, payable to his brother, Desmond Cochran, $10,000; 100 shares of Xerox Corporation stock; and a savings account of $10,525.

1. Make a preliminary outline of a will for Peter Cochran using the form suggested by the Leona Farrell example. Make up facts in the testator's life (e.g., devisees who are not named above, testamentary trusts to be created) if you wish.
2. Using the will of Leona Farrell that follows as a guide, write a will for Peter Cochran. (Assume the testator lives in your state. Be sure to consult the probate laws of your state before drafting the will.)

Exhibit 7.2 Sample Worksheet for Drafting a Will

Client's Name: <u>Leona Bayn Farrell (also known as Leona Alice Bayn)</u>
Address: <u>913 Garth Avenue</u>, City <u>Santa Maria</u>, County <u>Harkness</u>, State <u>Arizona</u>
(if more than one) <u>17 Mesa Grande, Dorado, New Mexico.</u>

Permanent Residence (Domicile): <u>913 Garth Avenue, Harkness County, Santa</u>
<u>Maria.</u>

Funeral and Burial Directions: <u>I direct that my kidneys be delivered, immediately</u>
<u>upon my death, without autopsy having been performed, to the Dorado State</u>
<u>School of Medicine, 403 Alamoreal Street, Dorado, New Mexico, to be used for</u>
<u>educational purposes.</u>

Method (source of payments of debts and all taxes): I direct that my executor pay
all my expenses, debts, and taxes from the residue of my estate.
Specific Gifts
Personal Property (community property)

Beneficiary: <u>Oren Johnstone Farrell</u>   Contingent beneficiary: <u>Children</u>
Relationship: Husband   Relationship: Sons and daughters
Item: Share of community property consisting of household furnishing, clothing,
jewelry, books, and other personal effects.
Method: Legacy
Personal property

Beneficiary: <u>Randolph Bayn Farrell</u>   Contingent beneficiary: <u>Ella Gamble</u>
                                                 <u>Dean</u>
Relationship: Son   Relationship: Niece
Item: The Buick automobile that I own, serial number 70–5015–9229
Present location: <u>At my permanent residence, 913 Garth Avenue</u>
Method: Legacy
Personal Property

Beneficiary: <u>Oren Johnstone Farrell</u>   Contingent beneficiary: <u>Jonathan</u>
                                                 <u>Bayn Farrell</u>
Relationship: Husband   Relationship: Son
Item: All the farm equipment located at Siete Rios
Method: Legacy
Personal Property

Beneficiary: <u>Jonathan Bayn Farrell</u>   Contingent beneficiary: <u>Angela</u>
                                                 <u>Bayn Rodgers</u>
Relationship: Son   Relationship: Niece
Item: All the horses and riding equipment located at Vallejo Grande
Method: Legacy
Real Property: Ranch—"Vallejo Grande"

Beneficiary: <u>Jonathan Bayn Farrell</u>   Contingent beneficiary: <u>Angela</u>
                                                 <u>Bayn Rodgers</u>
Relationship: Son   Relationship: Niece
Legal description of "Vallejo Grande": <u>"The West half of Section 12, being 320 acres</u>
<u>more or less, Township 4 North, Range 28 West of the 4th Principal Meridian, ac-</u>
<u>cording to the United States Government survey."</u>

(*continued*)

Exhibit 7.2 Sample Worksheet for Drafting a Will—*continued*

Location: County: Almedo   State: New Mexico

Amount of interest: Fee simple

Method: Fee simple devise

Real Property: Farm—"Siete Rios"

Beneficiary: Oren Johnstone Farrell   Contingent beneficiary: Daria Eileen Farrell

Relationship: Husband   Relationship: Daughter

Location: County: Dorado   State: New Mexico

Legal description of "Siete Rios": "The Southwest Quarter of Section 13, being 160 acres more or less, Township 4 North, Range 28 West of the 4th Principal Meridian, according to the United States Government survey."

Amount of Interest: Fee simple

Method: Fee simple devise

Residue

Beneficiary: Daria Eileen Farrell   Contingent beneficiary: Randolph Bayn Farrell

Relationship: Daughter   Relationship: Son

Interest given: Legacy or devise; if any residue remains after payment of debts, expenses, and taxes

Name and Address of Executor: Randolph Bayn Farrell
                              119 Golden Valley Road
                              Santa Maria, Arizona

Contingent (Successor) Executor: Farmers National Bank, Santa Maria, Arizona

Powers of Executor: To sell publicly or privately all or part of my residual property to carry on the operations of "Vallejo Grande" and "Siete Rios" until the dispositions thereof are complete

Trusts

Trustee: Carl A. Woodward, Farmers National Bank, Santa Maria, Arizona

Property: $75,000 (cash)

Location: Farmers National Bank, Account #922160

Duration of trust (life, years, etc.): For the life of my son, Thomas Earl Farrell

Remainder: First United Methodist Church of Waco, Texas

Trustee's powers

Investment: To invest and reinvest the corpus

Management: To distribute the earned income for the benefit of Thomas Earl Farrell

Payment of income: Quarterly if possible; at least semiannually

Payment of principal: At the trustee's discretion or at the request of Thomas Earl Farrell's natural or legal personal guardian

Power of sale: N/A

Special Provisions: Both principal and interest may be used for education, training, and maintenance of Thomas Earl Farrell. If guardian and trustee disagree, guardian's opinion is to prevail.

Guardians

Guardian of person: Oren Johnstone Farrell, my husband

Name and address: 913 Garth Avenue, County of Harkness, City of Santa Maria, Arizona

(*continued*)

Exhibit 7.2　Sample Worksheet for Drafting a Will—*continued*

Ward: Thomas Earl Farrell

Successor Guardian: Randolph Bayn Farrell

Bond: None required

Guardian of property: Randolph Bayn Farrell, my son

Name and address: 119 Golden Valley Road, County of Harkness, City of Santa Maria, Arizona

Ward: Thomas Earl Farrell

Successor Guardian: Oren Johnstone Farrell

Bond: None required

Common Disaster Provision: If my husband and I should die under circumstances which make it impossible to determine the order of deaths, he shall be deemed to have predeceased me.

Witnesses

Name and Addresses: Raymond Meador, Route 34, White Plains, Arizona
Mildred Wagoner, Route 7, Adolphus, Arizona

General Notes

Location—safe deposit box: Leona and Oren Farrell, joint tenants, Farmers National Bank

Location where will shall be placed: In the custody of Frank R. Goad, Attorney-at-law

Will prepared by: Joyce Bell, paralegal assistant under supervision of attorney Judith K. Larson

Date: July 6, 2000

Affidavit
A printed declaration made voluntarily under oath or affirmed before a notary public.

Notary Public
A person authorized by the state whose function is to administer oaths, certify documents and deeds, and attest to the authenticity of signatures.

Self-proving affidavit (clause)
A clause at the end of a will which contains an acknowledgment or affidavit of the testator and affidavits of witnesses signed by them in the presence of a notary public who also signs and seals it. This clause is used to replace the traditional attestation clause.

ADDITIONAL NONTESTAMENTARY DOCUMENTS

Several other documents are not part of the formal will itself, but are related to it. Depending on the circumstances, the client may require some or all of the documents discussed in the next paragraphs.

1. Self-Proving Affidavit Clause That Creates a Self-Proved Will

As noted above, some states have adopted a statute that provides an option for "self-proving" a will without the witnesses' testimony in court. The statute requires an acknowledgment or **affidavit** of the testator and the affidavits of the witnesses which are made before an officer authorized to administer oaths by the state, e.g., a **notary public.** In a few states, the testator and the two witnesses sign the same **self-proving affidavit** as shown in Exhibit 7.3. The acknowledgment or affidavits can be signed either at the time of the execution of the will, which is generally the case and thereby replaces the attestation clause, or at any subsequent date during the lifetime of the testator and witnesses. The document recites the testator is of sound mind and the testator and the subscribing witnesses followed the

---

Exhibit 7.3 Kentucky Self-Proving Affidavit Clause

I, _____, the testator, sign my name to this instrument this _____ day of _____, 20___, and being first duly sworn, do hereby declare to the undersigned authority that I sign and execute this instrument as my last will and that I sign it willingly (or willingly direct another to sign for me), that I execute it as my free and voluntary act for the purposes therein expressed, and that I am eighteen (18) years of age or older, of sound mind, and under no constraint or undue influence.

_____
TESTATOR

We, _____ and _____, the witnesses, sign our names to this instrument, being first duly sworn, and do hereby declare to the undersigned authority that the testator signs and executes this instrument as his last will and that he signs it willingly (or willingly directs another to sign for him), and that each of us, in the presence and hearing of the testator, and in the presence of the other subscribing witness, hereby sign this will as witness to the testator's signing, and that to the best of our knowledge the testator is eighteen (18) years of age or older, of sound mind, and under no constraint or undue influence.

WITNESSES   ADDRESSES

_____   _____
_____   _____

THE STATE OF _____)
COUNTY OF _____)
Subscribed, sworn and acknowledged before me by _____, the testator, and subscribed and sworn before me by _____ and _____, witnesses, this _____ day of _____, 20__.

_____
OFFICIAL CAPACITY OF OFFICER

_____
_____

My Commission Expires:
This form is used when it is executed at the same time the will is executed.
Source: Ky. Rev. Stat. Ann. § 394.225(1).

---

required formalities for the proper and legal execution of the will. The testator and the witnesses sign the document in the presence of a notary public who also signs and seals it, thereby creating a **self-proved will.**

A form for the acknowledgment and affidavit of self-proved wills is provided in § 2-504 of the UPC.

The self-proving provision or affidavit signed and sealed by a notary public at the end of the will is *not* required to validate the will. The execution of the affidavit supplies the requisite evidence to admit the will to probate, but the affidavit does not waive the formal requirements for a valid will, nor does it prevent a will contest on legitimate grounds such as duress, fraud, undue influence, revocation, or lack of testamentary capacity of the testator. *Remember.* To be a valid *self-proved will*, the self-proving affidavit must strictly follow the statutory language required by the state where the testator lives.

Self-proved will
A will that replaces the traditional attestation clause with another state statute clause which contains a self-proving affidavit signed by the testator and witnesses in the presence of a notary public who also signs and seals it, thereby creating the self-proved will.

LAST WILL AND TESTAMENT
OF
LEONA BAYN FARRELL

Exordium clause →

I, Leona Bayn Farrell, a/k/a (also known as) Leona Alice Bayn, residing at 913 Garth Avenue, City of Santa Maria, County of Harkness, State of Arizona, being of sound and disposing mind and memory, and not acting under undue influence of any person whomsoever, make, publish, and declare this document to be my last will and testament, and

Revocation clause →

expressly revoke any prior wills and codicils, made by me.

Article I

Payment of debts, expenses, and taxes →

I direct my personal representative hereinafter named, to pay all my just debts, and expenses of my last illness, funeral, burial, and estate administration out of the residue of my estate. I further direct my personal representative to pay out of my residuary estate all estate, income, and inheritance taxes assessed against my taxable estate or the recipients thereof, whether passing by this will or by other means, without contribution or reimbursement from any person.

Article II

Organ donation →

I direct my personal representative to notify the Dorado State School of Medicine, 403 Alamoreal Street, Dorado, New Mexico, of my death, so that it may receive the gift of my kidneys to use for medical or educational purposes. I further request that no autopsy or embalming be performed upon my body unless ordered by the aforesaid school.

Article III

Burial →

I direct my personal representative, after having completed the gift in Article II, to deliver my body to be interred in my family lot in the Paz de Christo cemetery, 528 Memorial Park, Santa Maria, Arizona.

Article IV

I give the portion of our community property which I own, consisting of household furnishings, clothing, jewelry, books, and personal effects of every kind used about my home or person to my husband, Oren Johnstone Farrell, to do with as he sees fit, if he survives me; if he does not survive me, to my children that survive me in shares of substantially equal value, per stirpes.

Article V

Specific legacies →

I give the Buick automobile which I own, serial number 70–5015–63–9229, to my son, Randolph Bayn Farrell, if he survives me. If he does not survive me, I give said Buick automobile to my niece, Ella Gamble Dean.

Article VI

I give all the farming equipment located at my farm, "Siete Rios," hereinafter legally described, to my husband, Oren Johnstone Farrell, if he survives me. If he does not survive me, I give said farming equipment to my son, Jonathan Bayn Farrell.

Article VII

I give all the horses and riding equipment located at my ranch, "Vallejo Grande," to my son, Jonathan Bayn Farrell, if he survives me. If he does not survive me, I give said horses and said equipment to my niece, Angela Bayn Rodgers.

Article VIII

I give my ranch, "Vallejo Grande," in Almedo County, New Mexico, legally described: "The West half of Section 12, being 320 acres more or less, Township 4 North, Range 28 West of the 4th Principal Meridian, according to the United States Government survey," to my son, Jonathan Bayn Farrell, in fee simple if he survives me. If he does not survive me, I give said ranch in fee simple to my niece, Angela Bayn Rodgers.

Article IX

Specific devises →

I give my farm, "Siete Rios," in Dorado County, New Mexico, legally described: "The Southwest Quarter of Section 13, being 160 acres more or less, Township 4 North, Range 28 West of the 4th Principal Meridian, according to the United States Government survey," to my husband, Oren Johnstone Farrell, in fee simple if he survives me. If he does not survive me, I give said farm in fee simple to my daughter, Daria Eileen Farrell.

(continued)

Article X

I give to Carl A. Woodward of Farmers National Bank, Santa Maria, Arizona, the sum of $75,000 to hold in trust for the life of my son, Thomas Earl Farrell. The trustee shall invest and reinvest the corpus of said trust and distribute the income earned thereby for the benefit of Thomas Earl Farrell at least semiannually, or, if possible, quarterly. Payment of the principal shall be made at the discretion of the trustee or at the request of Thomas Earl Farrell's natural or legal personal guardian, but if the trustee and the personal guardian cannot agree on the dispensing of the principal, the personal guardian's word shall be conclusive in the situation. On the death of my son, Thomas Earl Farrell, the remainder of the trust property, if any, is to be given to the First United Methodist Church of Waco, Texas. ← **Testamentary trust**

Article XI

I nominate and appoint as personal guardian of my minor son, Thomas Earl Farrell, Oren Johnstone Farrell, my husband.

I nominate and appoint as property guardian of my minor son, Thomas Earl Farrell, Randolph Bayn Farrell, my oldest son.

If either guardian becomes disabled or declines to serve, I nominate the other to serve in the former's capacity as well as the capacity in which he is presently serving. ← **Appointment of personal and property guardians and successors**

I direct that bond be required of neither of said guardians for the performance of the duties of their respective offices. ← **No bond required**

Article XII

I give all the rest, residue, and remainder of my estate, real, personal, or mixed, of whatever kind and wherever located, after the payment of debts, expenses, and taxes, as mentioned in Article I, and after transfer of my community property mentioned in Article IV, subject to the laws of this state regarding community property, to my daughter, Daria Eileen Farrell, if she survives me. If she does not survive me, I give said residue to my son, Randolph Bayn Farrell. ← **Residuary clause**

Article XIII

In the event that my husband, Oren Johnstone Farrell, and I die under such circumstances that it is difficult or impossible to determine who died first, it shall be presumed that my husband predeceased me. ← **Simultaneous death clause**

Article XIV

I nominate and appoint my son, Randolph Bayn Farrell of 119 Golden Valley Road, Santa Maria, Arizona, to be personal representative of this will, and to serve without bond. ← **Nomination of personal representative; no bond required**

If Randolph Bayn Farrell does not survive me or does not qualify as personal representative, I nominate Farmers National Bank, a national banking institution located in Santa Maria, Arizona, to be successor personal representative of this will. ← **Nomination of successor personal representative**

My personal representative shall have the power to sell publicly or privately all or part of the residue of my property in the event that such sale will become necessary for the payment of debts, taxes, or expenses; to carry on the operations of "Vallejo Grande" and "Siete Rios" until the testamentary dispositions thereof are complete; and to settle all valid claims against my estate. ← **Powers of personal representative**

I freely and willingly subscribe my name to this will consisting of three pages on this 18th day of July, 2000, at Santa Maria, County of Harkness, State of Arizona, in the presence of these witnesses; Raymond Meador and Mildred Wagoner, each of whom I have requested to subscribe their names in my presence and in the presence of all the others. ← **Testimonium clause**

/S/ Leona Bayn Farrell ← **Signature of testatrix**

On the last date shown above, Leona Bayn Farrell, known to us to be the person whose signature appears at the end of this will, declared to us, the undersigned, that the foregoing instrument was her will. She then signed the will in our presence; at her request, we now sign our names in her presence and the presence of each other. ← **Attestation clause**

Names	Addresses
/S/ Raymond Meador	Route 34, White Plains, Arizona
(Witness)	
/S/ Mildred Wagoner	Route 7, Adolphus, Arizona
(Witness)	

← **Signatures of witnesses**

2. Letter of Instructions

The letter of instructions is not part of the will and has no legal effect. It may be incorporated by reference into the will. It is a letter to the personal representative and family that explains where the will and important assets and records are located including all bank accounts, safe deposit boxes, and other legal documents; lists current market values of assets or recommends appraisers; and makes management suggestions and investment recommendations to the personal representative. The letter should be updated each year.

3. Power of Attorney

A **power of attorney** is a written document that grants to another person, called the **agent** or **attorney in fact,** the power and right to act legally on behalf of the person, called the **principal,** who authorizes and grants the power. Notwithstanding the title of the document, the agent authorized to act does not have to be an attorney. Spouses usually name their husband or wife to be their agent. The power of attorney is often granted for a specific time period, e.g., while the principal is out of the country or hospitalized; for a specific purpose, e.g., to run a business or purchase a home; or for a specific circumstance, e.g., to manage property because of the principal's illness. A power of attorney granted during the principal's life terminates at the moment of the principal's death.

4. Right to Die Laws and Related Advance Medical Directive Documents

Over the past twenty-five years, state statutes and case law have established and recognized the right of a dying person to refuse extraordinary medical treatment to prolong life or the right of a person's guardian or proxy to make such a request. The development of **right to die laws** began with the landmark case of *Matter of Quinlan,* 70 N.J. 10, 355 A.2d 647 (1976), which involved a young woman, Karen Ann Quinlan, who had lapsed into a coma. When it became clear their daughter would not recover, her parents went to court to request that the respirator supporting Karen's breathing be removed. After a long court battle, the New Jersey Supreme Court ordered the respirator removed. The case caused the legal and medical professions to resolve their differences concerning the legal and medical positions on a person's right to die and to acknowledge and eventually to agree to grant that all persons have the right to determine their quality of life, including the right to die.

In a later case, *Cruzan v. Director, Missouri Dept. of Health,* 497 U.S. 261, 110 S.Ct. 2841, 111 L.Ed.2d 224 (1990), the U.S. Supreme Court confirmed the constitutional **right to die.** In this case the patient, Nancy Cruzan, was critically injured in a car accident leaving her in a coma with no hope of recovery. Her family knew she would not want to live in this condition and asked the hospital to stop her tube feeding. Since Nancy had not made her wishes known in a writing such as a living will, the Missouri Supreme Court rejected the family's request. The family appealed to the U.S. Supreme Court. The Court ruled that the tube could not be removed (thereby allowing the tube feeding to continue), but the Court said it assumed the right to die existed and a competent person could refuse medical treatment as long as the wishes of the person are known and "clear and convincing evidence" of those wishes is established. The Court acknowledged that competent and incompetent persons have the same rights, but that a surrogate or agent must be named to exercise the rights for the incapacitated person, e.g., a patient such as Nancy Cruzan.

To alleviate an individual's concern and anxiety about becoming incompetent due to aging, illness, or accident, several forms of right to die **advance medical directives** have been established by state legislatures. These directives allow a competent person to determine, in advance and in writing, the kind of future medical care and treatment he wishes to have in case he becomes incapacitated or terminally ill, or to appoint a surrogate, agent, or proxy to exercise his wishes to continue or discontinue future medical treatment. The two forms of advance directives used to make medical decisions for disabled or terminally ill persons are (1) a living will and (2) a medical power of attorney. Each state has various forms of one or both of these documents. See definitions in Exhibit 7.4.

The Patient Self-Determination Act enacted by Congress in 1991 was created to bring the existence of the directives to the attention of the public and promote their use. The law requires health care providers who work with the Medicaid and Medicare programs to provide each patient or the patient's authorized surrogate, usually a family member, with written information about the patient's right to (1) make health care and medical treatment decisions including the use of life support systems, (2) be informed on admission by the health care facility, e.g., the hospital, hospice, or nursing home in which the patient resides or is being treated, of its policies concerning patient's rights, and (3) sign any of the above-mentioned advance directives for health and medical care decisions. Information on advance directives and state-specific forms is available on the internet at *http://www.partnershipforcaring.org*.

Living Will: Death with Dignity

Although it has been a long and hard-fought battle, it is apparent that constitutional and common law assure any adult person the right to refuse medical treatment, including life-sustaining treatment; however, an incompetent person, e.g., a terminally ill patient, may be unable to communicate her wishes to exercise that right. The controversial decision to withhold or withdraw medical care and treatment must be made on the patient's behalf by someone else, e.g., a family member, doctor, or other medical care provider. Legislation has been passed and the U.S. Supreme Court has issued decisions that have established guidelines for the execution and implementation of a terminally ill patient's advance written health care directives including what is commonly known as a **living will.** Such a will

---

MINI-GLOSSARY BOX

Right to die laws
Cases and statutes that recognize the right to die and the right of a dying person's guardian to ask the court to substitute its judgment for that of the dying person who no longer has the mental capacity to make such a judgment.

Right to die
The right of a dying person to refuse extraordinary medical treatment to prolong life.

Advance medical directives
Various legal documents individuals execute and use to ensure their wishes for medical care and treatment are followed after they become terminally ill and can no longer make their own decisions.

Exhibit 7.4   Legal Terminology of Titles and Sources of Authority

Titles:

Principal
A person who permits or directs an agent to act for the principal's benefit subject to the principal's direction and control; such acts of the agent become binding on the principal.

Agent
A person authorized to act for the principal. Also called surrogate or proxy.

Attorney in fact
An agent, not necessarily an attorney, who is given authority by the principal in a written document called a power of attorney to perform certain specific acts on behalf of the principal.

Sources of Authority:

Power of attorney
A written document in which a principal appoints and authorizes an agent or attorney in fact to perform specific acts or kinds of acts on behalf of the principal and grants either a general (full) power of attorney or special (limited) power of attorney.

Durable power of attorney
A written document whereby a principal grants a power of attorney which continues to be or becomes effective in the event the principal later becomes disabled, e.g., mentally incapacitated. If the power does not take effect until the principal becomes disabled (incapacitated), the power is called a springing durable power of attorney. All states have statutes which establish the exact words required for this document (see UPC § 5-501).

Advance Medical Directives—Sources of Authority:

Living will
A written document that expresses a terminally ill person's wish to be allowed to die a natural death and not be kept alive by life-sustaining treatment.

Medical power of attorney
A written document that enables the principal patient to appoint an agent, proxy, or surrogate to make decisions for medical care when the principal becomes incapacitated and is unable to make such decisions. It may be called a durable power of attorney for health care, health care proxy, or appointment of a health care agent.

> **Durable power of attorney for health care**
> A written document signed by the principal that gives an agent the power and authority to make all medical and health care decisions which become or remain effective when the principal is disabled and unable to make the decisions.

> **Health care proxy**
> A written document in which a patient designates and authorizes a proxy, surrogate, or agent to make future medical and health care decisions if the patient becomes incapacitated. The proxy receives full information of the patient's medical condition before a decision is made.

---

states that in the event a person becomes incompetent due to a physical or mental disability with no reasonable expectation or hope for recovery, and because of the disability is unable to take part in decisions, the person can request he not be kept alive by artificial means, e.g., life-support treatment. Examples of famous public persons who have elected to make this request in their living wills are former First Lady Jacqueline Kennedy Onassis and former President Richard Nixon. The purpose of the request is to relieve family members from the responsibility of making the decision, to alleviate guilt feelings on their part, and to protect the physician and health care institution from personal liability if they refrain, as requested, from using certain medical treatment. The patient can revoke the living will at any time by spoken or written directions in the presence of witnesses. Due to their preference for the appointment of a health care agent *only,* three states, Massachusetts, Michigan, and New York, do not authorize living wills. Instead, they incorporate the language of a living will into their *medical power of attorney* in the form of a health care proxy or agent. On the other hand, Alaska authorizes *only* living wills.

The living will is not part of the will a testator makes to transfer property after death. It is a separate and distinct document. To be valid in most states, the living will must either be signed by the testator and two witnesses in the presence of one another or signed by the testator and notarized. Generally, neither of the witnesses may be: related to the testator; beneficiaries or heirs of the testator's estate; the attending physician; or employees of the physician, hospital, or care facility. Copies of the living will should be placed in the testator's medical record file and given to family members and the testator's personal representative. A copy should be placed with the testator's will and a notation of the will's location should be made in the letter of instructions. See Georgia's living will in Exhibit 7.5.

Medical Power of Attorney

The **medical power of attorney** is a second type of right to die advance directive which is used in place of a living will. It may be called a **durable power of attorney for health care, health care proxy,** or appointment of a health care agent. It is a written document that gives another person (agent), as a substitute for the patient (principal), the power and authority to make all decisions relating to the performance of medical and health care treatment by health care providers such as doctors, surgeons, and nurses. Some states use the term *durable power of attorney for health care* for their medical power of attorney. A person granted a **durable power of attorney** does more than simply act as an agent for another. Instead, the durable power of attorney for health care allows the authorized designated agent not only to make health care and medical decisions in place of the patient (principal) when the patient is disabled and unable to make such decisions, but also to direct the withholding or withdrawal of such care and life-sustaining treatment. These decisions are based on current medically known facts and the wishes of the patient, even though he is incompetent. The durable power of attorney for health care document also gives the designated agent the right to (1) employ and discharge health care personnel (doctors, nurses, etc.); (2) obtain and disclose the principal's medical records; and (3) select the health care facility, e.g., elder care, nursing home, or hospital, as the appropriate residence for the principal based on his level of need for medical care and assistance. Unlike the living will, which is limited to situations where the principal (patient) has a terminal condition due to illness or injury and death is imminent, the durable power of attorney for health care has no such limitation, has a broader grant of authority, and gives the patient a wider range to exercise self-determination.

All states, except Alaska, have statutes that authorize an agent, also called a proxy or surrogate. Alaska does have a durable power of attorney, but it does not cover end-of-life: therefore, a living will is required. Ohio's durable power of attorney for health care appears in Exhibit 7.6.

Exhibit 7.5   Georgia Living Will

Georgia Living Will

INSTRUCTIONS

PRINT THE DATE

PRINT YOUR
NAME

CHECK THE
OPTIONS THAT
APPLY

CHECK THE
OPTIONS THAT
REFLECT YOUR
WISHES ABOUT
ARTIFICIAL
FEEDING

ADD PERSONAL
INSTRUCTIONS
(IF ANY)

© 2000
PARTNERSHIP
FOR CARING, INC.

Living will made this _____ day of _____ .
                   (date)   *(month, year)*

I, _____ ,
                                         (name)

being of sound mind, willfully and voluntarily make known my desire that my life shall not be prolonged under the circumstances set forth below and do declare:

1. If at any time I should (*check each option desired*):
   ( ) have a terminal condition,
   ( ) become in a coma with no reasonable expectation of regaining consciousness, or
   ( ) become in a persistent vegetative state with no reasonable expectation of regaining significant cognitive function,

as defined in and established in accordance with the procedures set forth in paragraphs (2), (9), and (13) of Code Section 31-32-2 of the Official Code of Georgia Annotated, I direct that the application of life-sustaining procedures to my body be withheld or withdrawn and that I be permitted to die.

With regard to artificially supplied nutrition and hydration, I direct that (*check the option desired*):
   ( ) artificial nutrition be provided.
   ( ) artificial nutrition be withheld or withdrawn.
(*check the option desired*):
   ( ) artificial hydration be provided.
   ( ) artificial hydration be withheld or withdrawn.

Other directions:

(*continued*)

Exhibit 7.5 Georgia Living Will—*continued*

2. In the absence of my ability to give directions regarding the use of such life-sustaining procedures, it is my intention that this living will shall be honored by my family and physician(s) as the final expression of my legal right to refuse medical or surgical treatment and accept the consequences from such refusal;

3. I understand that I may revoke this living will at any time;

4. I understand the full import of this living will, and I am at least 18 years of age and am emotionally and mentally competent to make this living will; and

5. If I am a female and I have been diagnosed as pregnant, I want this living will to be carried out despite my pregnancy.

_____ (*initial*)

Signed _____

City _____

County _____

State of Residence _____

I hereby witness this living will and attest that:
    (1) The declarant is personally known to me and I believe the declarant to be at least 18 years of age and of sound mind;
    (2) I am at least 18 years of age;
    (3) To the best of my knowledge, at the time of the execution of this living will, I:
        (A) Am not related to the declarant by blood or marriage;
        (B) Would not be entitled to any portion of the declarant's estate by any will or by operation of law under the rules of descent and distribution of this state;
        (C) Am not the attending physician of declarant or an employee of the attending physician or an employee of the hospital or skilled nursing facility in which declarant is a patient;
        (D) Am not directly financially responsible for the declarant's medical care; and
        (E) Have no present claim against any portion of the estate of the declarant;

INITIAL THIS STATEMENT IF IT REFLECTS YOUR WISHES

SIGN THE DOCUMENT AND PRINT YOUR CITY, COUNTY AND STATE OF RESIDENCE

WITNESSING PROCEDURE

WITNESSES MUST SIGN AND PRINT THEIR ADDRESSES ON THE FOLLOWING PAGE

© 2000
PARTNERSHIP FOR CARING, INC.

(continued)

Exhibit 7.5 Georgia Living Will—*continued*

GEORGIA LIVING WILL — PAGE 3 OF 3

(4) Declarant has signed this document in my presence as above instructed, on the date above first shown.

WITNESS #1

Witness _____

Address _____

_____

WITNESS #2

Witness _____

Address _____

_____

RESIDENTS OF A HOSPITAL OR NURSING HOME MUST HAVE ONE ADDITIONAL WITNESS

Additional witness required when living will is signed by a patient in a hospital or skilled nursing facility.

I hereby witness this living will and attest that I believe the declarant to be of sound mind and to have made this living will willingly and voluntarily.

Witness _____

(Medical director of skilled nursing facility or staff physician not participating in care of the patient, or chief of the hospital medical staff or staff physician or hospital designee not participating in care of the patient.)

© 2000
PARTNERSHIP FOR CARING, INC.

Courtesy of **Partnership for Caring, Inc.** 6/96
1035 30th Street, NW Washington, DC 20007   800-989-9455

Source: Reprinted by permission of Partnership for Caring, 1035 30th Street, NW, Washington, DC 20007, 800-989-9455.

Exhibit 7.6 Ohio Durable Power of Attorney for Health Care

INSTRUCTIONS

PRINT YOUR NAME AND ADDRESS

PRINT THE NAME, ADDRESS AND TELEPHONE NUMBERS OF YOUR AGENT

© 2000

Ohio Durable Power of Attorney for Health Care

1. DESIGNATION OF attorney in fact.

I, _____ , presently residing at
                  (name)

_____ , Ohio,
               (address)

intending to create a Durable Power of Attorney for Health Care under Chapter 1337 of the Ohio Revised Code, do hereby designate and appoint:

_____ presently residing at
(name of agent)

_____
(address)

_____
(home telephone number)   *(work telephone number)*

as my attorney in fact who shall act as my agent to make health care decisions for me as authorized in this document.

2. GENERAL STATEMENT OF AUTHORITY GRANTED. I hereby grant to my agent full power and authority to make all health care decisions for me to the same extent that I could make such decisions for myself if I had the capacity to do so, at any time during which I do not have the capacity to make or communicate informed health care decisions for myself. My agent shall have the authority to give, to withdraw or to refuse to give informed consent to any medical or nursing procedure, treatment, intervention or other measure used to maintain, diagnose or treat my physical or mental condition. In exercising this authority, my agent shall make health care decisions that are consistent with my desires as stated in this document or otherwise made known to my agent by me or, if I have not made my desires known, that are, in the judgment of my agent, in my best interests.

(continued)

Exhibit 7.6 Ohio Durable Power of Attorney for Health Care—*continued*

3. ADDITIONAL AUTHORITIES OF AGENT. Where necessary or desirable to implement the health care decisions that my agent is authorized to make pursuant to this document, my agent has the power and authority to do any and all of the following:

(a) If I am in a terminal condition, to give, to withdraw or to refuse to give informed consent to life-sustaining treatment, including the provision of artificially or technologically supplied nutrition or hydration;

(b) If I am in a permanently unconscious state, to give informed consent to life-sustaining treatment or to withdraw or to refuse to give informed consent to life-sustaining treatment; *provided, however, my agent is not authorized to refuse or direct the withdrawal of artificially or technologically supplied nutrition or hydration unless I have specifically authorized such refusal or withdrawal in Paragraph 4;*

(c) To request, review, and receive any information, verbal or written, regarding my physical or mental health, including, but not limited to, all of my medical and health care facility records;

(d) To execute on my behalf any releases or other documents that may be required in order to obtain this information;

(e) To consent to the further disclosure of this information if necessary;

(f) To select, employ, and discharge health care personnel, such as physicians, nurses, therapists and other medical professionals, including individuals and services providing home health care, as my agent shall determine to be appropriate;

(g) To select and contract with any medical or health care facility on my behalf, including, but not limited to, hospitals, nursing homes, assisted residence facilities, and the like; and

(h) To execute on my behalf any or all of the following:

(1) Documents that are written consents to medical treatment or written requests that I be transferred to another facility;

(2) Documents that are Do Not Resuscitate Orders, Discharge Orders or other similar orders; and

(3) Any other document necessary or desirable to implement health care decisions that my agent is authorized to make pursuant to this document.

© 2000
PARTNERSHIP FOR CARING, INC.

(continued)

Exhibit 7.6 Ohio Durable Power of Attorney for Health Care—*continued*

Check box and initial space if you want to refuse tube feeding if you become permanently unconscious

4. <u>WITHDRAWAL OF NUTRITION AND HYDRATION WHEN IN A PERMA-NENTLY UNCONSCIOUS STATE.</u>

☐ _____ IF I HAVE MARKED THE FOREGOING BOX AND HAVE PLACED MY INITIALS ON THE LINE ADJACENT TO IT, MY AGENT MAY REFUSE, OR IN THE EVENT TREATMENT HAS ALREADY COMMENCED, WITHDRAW INFORMED CONSENT TO THE PROVISION OF ARTIFICIALLY OR TECHNOLOGICALLY SUPPLIED NUTRITION AND HYDRATION IF I AM IN A PERMANENTLY UNCONSCIOUS STATE AND IF MY ATTENDING PHYSICIAN AND AT LEAST ONE OTHER PHYSICIAN WHO HAS EXAMINED ME DETERMINES, TO A REASONABLE DEGREE OF MEDICAL CERTAINTY AND IN ACCORDANCE WITH REASONABLE MEDICAL STANDARDS, THAT SUCH NUTRITION OR HYDRATION WILL NOT OR NO LONGER WILL SERVE TO PROVIDE COMFORT TO ME OR ALLEVIATE MY PAIN.

5. DESIGNATION OF ALTERNATE AGENT. Because I wish that an agent shall be available to exercise the authorities granted hereunder at all times, I further designate each of the following individuals to succeed to such authorities and to serve under this instrument, in the order named, if at any time the agent first named (or any alternate designee) is not readily available or is unwilling or unable to serve or to continue to serve:

Alternate Agents

PRINT THE NAMES, ADDRESSES, PHONE NUMBERS OF AND RELATIONSHIP TO YOUR ALTERNATE AGENTS

First Alternate Agent: _____ ,
                                    (*name*)   (*relationship*)

presently residing at _____
                                          (*address*)

_____
(*home telephone number*)   (*work telephone number*)

Second Alternate Agent: _____
                                       (*name*)   (*relationship*)

presently residing at _____
                                          (*address*)

_____
(*home telephone number*)   (*work telephone number*)

Each alternate shall have and exercise all of the authority conferred above.

© 2000
PARTNERSHIP FOR CARING, INC.

(continued)

Exhibit 7.6 Ohio Durable Power of Attorney for Health Care—*continued*

OHIO DURABLE POWER OF ATTORNEY FOR HEALTH CARE—PAGE 9 OF 10

SIGN AND DATE YOUR DOCUMENT AND PRINT YOUR CITY OF RESIDENCE

6. NO EXPIRATION DATE. This Durable Power of Attorney for Health Care shall not be affected by my disability or by lapse of time. This Durable Power of Attorney for Health Care shall have no expiration date.

7. SEVERABILITY. Any invalid or unenforceable power, authority or provision of this instrument shall not affect any other power, authority or provision or the appointment of my agent to make health care decisions.

8. PRIOR DESIGNATIONS REVOKED. I hereby revoke any prior Durable Powers of Attorney for Health Care executed by me under Chapter 1337 of the Ohio Revised Code.

I understand the purpose and effect of this document and sign my name to this Durable Power of Attorney for Health Care after careful deliberation on

_____ at _____ , Ohio,
     (date)   *(city)*

_____
                       (principal)

WITNESSING PROCEDURE

WITNESSES MUST SIGN AND DATE YOUR DOCUMENT AND PRINT THEIR NAMES AND ADDRESSES BELOW

WITNESS #1

© 2000
PARTNERSHIP FOR CARING, INC.

THIS DURABLE POWER OF ATTORNEY FOR HEALTH CARE WILL NOT BE VALID UNLESS IT IS EITHER (1) SIGNED BY TWO ELIGIBLE WITNESSES AS DEFINED BELOW WHO ARE PRESENT WHEN YOU SIGN OR ACKNOWLEDGE YOUR SIGNATURE OR (2) ACKNOWLEDGED BEFORE A NOTARY PUBLIC.

I attest that the principal signed or acknowledged this Durable Power of Attorney for Health Care in my presence, that the principal appears to be of sound mind and not under or subject to duress, fraud or undue influence. I further attest that I am not the agent designated in this document, I am not the attending physician of the principal, I am not the administrator of a nursing home in which the principal is receiving care, and that I am an adult not related to the principal by blood, marriage or adoption.

Signature: _____

Print Name: _____

Residence Address: _____

Date: _____

(continued)

Exhibit 7.6 Ohio Durable Power of Attorney for Health Care—*continued*

OHIO DURABLE POWER OF ATTORNEY FOR HEALTH CARE—PAGE 10 OF 10

WITNESS #2

Signature: _____

Print Name: _____

Residence Address: _____

Date: _____

OR

OR

ACKNOWLEDGEMENT

A NOTARY PUBLIC MUST COMPLETE THIS SECTION OF YOUR DOCUMENT

State of Ohio

County of _____ , s.s.:

On this the _____ day of _____ , 20 _____ ,

before me, the undersigned Notary Public, personally appeared _____
_____ , known to me
or satisfactorily proven to be the person whose name is subscribed to the above Durable Power of Attorney for Health Care as the principal, and acknowledged that (s)he executed the same for the purposes expressed therein. I attest that the principal appears to be of sound mind and not under or subject to duress, fraud or undue influence.

My Commission Expires:

_____
notary public

© 2000
PARTNERSHIP FOR CARING, INC.

Courtesy of **Partnership for Caring, Inc.** 6/96
1035 30th Street, NW Washington, DC 20007   800-989-9455

Source: Reprinted by permission for Caring, 1035 30th Street, NW, Washington, DC 20007, 800–989–9455.

WHERE TO KEEP THE WILL

The will should be kept in a safe and accessible location. It is good practice to include the location of the will in the letter of instructions. The will itself is often kept in one of four places: (1) in the lawyer's office vault which was the traditional practice but not commonly done today; (2) with the client, the most frequent location today because it is readily available for review (good choices would be a fireproof metal box or family safe at the client's home or office); (3) in a personal safe deposit box in a bank; or (4) filed with the clerk of the appropriate probate court which is allowed in a few states. If the choice for safekeeping a will is the latter, anyone holding the receipt issued for the filed will and signed by the testator may obtain the original will while the testator is living. After the testator's death, the probate court retains the original will and gives copies to the personal representative (see UPC § 2-515).

A will kept in a personal safe deposit box is less desirable because it makes the will less accessible. This is also the case if the will is filed. If the will is in a safe deposit box, probate proceedings may be delayed. Ordinarily, a person must have permission from the state tax commission representative or a county treasurer to open the safe deposit box belonging to another. Generally, when the safe deposit box is rented in the decedent's name only, bank representatives will seal the box when they are notified of the person's death after first removing the will if it is known that the box contains the will. However, once the box is sealed, a court order is often required to open the box to remove the will (see the Petition and Order to Open Safe Deposit Box in Exhibit 7.7). After the will is removed, the box is resealed. Depending on the state in which the testator resides, one of the following procedures is advisable:

1. If the testator lives in a state in which the county treasurer or the state tax representative does not have to be present when the safe deposit box is opened, the box should be rented in the names of the testator and the testator's spouse or another person as joint tenants. Whenever either spouse dies, the other may open the box. Widows, widowers, or single parents may want to name themselves and an adult child as the joint tenants for the same reason.

2. If the testator lives in a state in which the county treasurer or the state tax representative must be present, the testator should put the will in a safe deposit box rented in the name of the testator's spouse. Upon the testator's death, the testator's will is readily accessible.

If the safe deposit box is placed in joint tenancy between spouses or others, the joint owners must remember to state in detail on the bank account cards whether or not the joint tenants also share ownership of all the contents in the box and not just access to it. For further discussion on opening a safe deposit box, see Item 19 in Chapter 12.

Leaving the will with the testator's lawyer with whom the testator is familiar and has had a long time working relationship based on confidence and trust makes for easy access and convenient periodic review of the will whenever the testator wishes. A request for the review should be initiated by the testator and *not be solicited by the attorney or paralegal.*

ETHICAL ISSUE

Exhibit 7.7 Petition and Order to Open Safe Deposit Box

Approved, SCAO

OSM CODE: DBP, DBO

STATE OF MICHIGAN PROBATE COURT COUNTY OF	PETITION AND ORDER TO OPEN SAFE DEPOSIT BOX TO LOCATE WILL OR BURIAL DEED	FILE NO.

Estate of _____

PETITION

1. I am an interested person as _____ of decedent, who died _____.

                                     Heir, devisee, etc.   Date

2. _____ , as lessor, leased to decedent, alone or jointly, safe

   Name of bank, trust company, or safe deposit company

   deposit box number _____ , located at _____ in _____ in this

                                               Branch   City or township

   county, and the safe deposit box may contain decedent's will or a deed to a burial plot in which the decedent is to be interred.

3. I REQUEST that this court issue an order directing the lessor to permit _____

                                                                        Name

   to examine the contents of the safe deposit box in the presence of an officer or other authorized employee of lessor for the purpose of locating and removing a will and deed to a burial plot only.

I declare under the penalties of perjury that this petition has been examined by me and that its contents are true to the best of my information, knowledge, and belief.

_____

Date

_____   _____

Attorney signature   Petitioner signature

_____   _____

Name (type or print)   Bar no.   Name (type or print)

_____   _____

Address   Address

_____   _____

City, state, zip   Telephone no.   City, state, zip   Telephone no.

ORDER

IT IS ORDERED:

4. The above petition is granted and the lessor is ordered to permit _____

to examine the above described safe deposit box in the presence of an officer or other authorized employee of the lessor. Only a will of the decedent and a deed to a burial plot shall be removed from the box and shall be delivered by the above named person to the probate register or deputy register of this court.

5. At the time of the opening of the safe deposit box, all persons in attendance shall execute a written statement certifying whether a will or deed to a burial plot was found and that no other items were removed from the safe deposit box. The person named above shall file that written statement with the probate register or deputy register of this court within 7 days of opening the box.

_____   _____

Date   Judge   Bar no.

Do not write below this line - For court use only

MCL 700.2517; MSA 27.12517

⚖ ASSIGNMENT 7.14

1. Explain your position on a living will, health care proxy, and a durable power of attorney for health care. Are you in favor of any of them or not? Has your state passed any of these directives?
2. In your state, must a doctor or hospital follow the patient's requests that are written in a living will? If they are required to honor the requests, are there any exceptions? Discuss these questions with your family physician.
3. Are patients who execute a living will in your state allowed to designate a proxy? Who would you select as your proxy? Why?
4. Must a patient hire a lawyer to make a valid living will, a health care proxy, or a durable power of attorney? If not, why might the patient choose to have a lawyer draft these directives?
5. If you execute a valid living will in your home state and then move your domicile (home) to another state that has no living will statute, will your wishes in the living will be honored in your new domicile? Explain.
6. Draft a living will. Obtain your state's living will form and compare it to your draft. How do they differ? How are they similar? Also draft and execute forms for a health care proxy and a durable power of attorney for health care and compare them to your state's forms, if any.

KEY TERMS

Exordium clause	Affidavit	Principal	Durable power of
Revocation clause	Notary public	Right to die laws	attorney for health
Memorandum	Self-proving affidavit	Right to die	care
Residuary clause	(clause)	Advance medical	Health care proxy
Simultaneous death	Self-proved will	directives	Durable power
clause	Power of attorney	Living will	of attorney
Testimonium clause	Agent	Medical power	
Attestation clause	Attorney in fact	of attorney	

REVIEW QUESTIONS

1. What is the purpose of the following clauses of a will? Exordium, Revocation, Residuary, Simultaneous death, Testimonium, and Attestation.
2. If a testator uses more than one name or alias when signing written statements or documents, is it necessary to include all such names in the will? Explain.
3. How does any person who wishes to donate body organs accomplish that purpose both within a will and using other nontestamentary documents?

4. According to your state statute, if any, who may make an anatomical gift in addition to the testator-decedent?
5. When a testator has numerous items of tangible personal property that she wishes to leave to an equal number of beneficiaries, how can she list these items and ensure that they are distributed to the desired recipients without writing them directly into the will?
6. Confusion exists in the law of wills concerning the use of the words *issue, child, heirs, descendants,* and *adopted, natural, nonmar-*

ital, and *stepchildren.* How would you avoid this confusion when drafting a client's will?

7. If there is no residuary clause in a will and not all the testator's estate is distributed to named beneficiaries, how and to whom would such property be distributed?

8. How are personal representatives appointed (authorized to act)? In general, what are the powers granted to them?

9. What is the difference between a property guardian and a conservator?

10. Does your state have any requirements for the placement of the testator's signature on the will? Are initials, a nickname, or simply an "X" valid signatures in your state?

11. Which of the statutory requirements of a will is eliminated by the self-proving affidavit or the self-proved will?

12. What are the purposes of the two kinds of advance medical directives, i.e., the living will and the medical power of attorney? How do these directives differ?

13. Where is the best place to keep your will?

CASE PROBLEMS

Problem 1

Hans Heidelberger died testate. He owned a considerable amount of property and made many specific legacies and devises to numerous relatives and friends. However, his will had no residue clause. In the will, Hans specifically disinherited by name his only two children. A number of very valuable stock certificates and bonds that Hans owned were not included as gifts in the will. Answer and explain the following:

A. Through what process and to whom will the valuable stocks and bonds be distributed?

B. Since Hans specifically stated that his two children were not to receive any of his estate, does that provision of the will bar them from receiving an interest in the stocks and bonds? See *Ferguson v. Croom,* 73 N.C.App. 316, 326 S.E.2d 373 (1985).

Problem 2

While on a weekend trip, Stewart and Patricia Kincaid and their two minor children die simultaneously in a plane crash. Two adult children, Frank and Ruth, living at home, are the surviving family members. The major asset Stewart owned was a life insurance policy worth over $500,000 payable to Patricia as the primary beneficiary and to all four children as the secondary beneficiaries. The Kincaids live in a state that has adopted the Uniform Simultaneous Death Act. Under the Act, when the insured policyholder (Stewart) and the beneficiary (Patricia) die simultaneously, the life insurance proceeds are distributed as if the insured has survived the beneficiary.

A. To whom would the life insurance proceeds be paid? How is this decision determined?

B. If all six members of the Kincaid family had died in the crash, to whom would the life insurance proceeds be paid? Explain. See *Keegan v. Keegan's Estate,* 157 N.J.Super.279, 384 A.2d 913 (1978).

C. If Stewart and Patricia had owned property in joint tenancy, how does the Uniform Simultaneous Death Act resolve the problem of dividing the jointly owned property?

CHAPTER 8

INTRODUCTION TO TRUSTS

OUTLINE

OBJECTIVES

After completing this chapter, you should be able to:

➤ Understand the basic terminology of trusts.

➤ Identify and define the essential elements of trusts.

➤ Identify the participants in the creation and operation of a trust and be able to explain their functions and roles.

➤ Explain the ways in which a trust terminates.

SCOPE OF THE CHAPTER

To practice successfully in the field of trusts, you must learn the terminology of trust law. Once you acquire a basic vocabulary, you will be able to identify the various kinds of trusts, understand their functions, and draft trust agreements that meet your client's objectives. After you gain work experience under the supervision of a trust attorney, you will be able to handle these matters with confidence. The purpose of this and the following chapter on trusts is to help you obtain that confidence.

Although all states have adopted or enacted some form of probate code by statute, very few states have trust codes. A major authority on trusts, often cited by legal scholars, is the Restatement of Trusts published by the American Law Institute. For the most part, the law of trusts is found in a combination of state statutes, judicial decisions, and the Restatement.

🖥 RESTATEMENT INFORMATION ONLINE

Learn more about the Restatement of Trusts and the American Law Institute at *www.ali.org*. The Institute, which was created in 1923, has published restatements in many areas of the law.

This chapter begins with the terminology associated with trusts and presents an example of how a trust works. You will be asked to identify the terms in an actual trust instrument. The remaining units of the chapter discuss the purposes and elements of a trust, including the participants, their interests, selection, duties, and liabilities; the trust property; and the ways in which a trust terminates.

TERMINOLOGY RELATED TO TRUSTS

Before you can prepare a preliminary draft of a trust agreement, you must master the terminology of trusts. The major terms are defined as follows:

- *Trust.* A trust is a property arrangement in which real or personal property is transferred from the settlor to one or more trustees who hold the legal title to the property for the benefit of one or more beneficiaries who hold the equitable title.

Example: Barry gives Charles $30,000 to hold and invest in trust for the benefit of William.

- *Settlor.* The person who creates a trust is the settlor, also called the creator, donor, grantor, or trustor. In the above example, Barry is the settlor.
- *Trustee.* The trustee (or co-trustees) is the person who holds the legal title to property in trust for the benefit of one or more beneficiaries. A trustee is a fiduciary and, as such, is required to perform all trustee duties according to the terms of the trust instrument with loyalty, honesty, and in good faith for the sole benefit of the beneficiary. In the above example, Charles is the trustee; he holds legal title to the property and must invest it for the benefit of William, the beneficiary.

- *Legal title.* Legal title is a title, enforceable in a court of law, that is the complete and absolute right of ownership and possession. However, in the law of trusts, the trustee, who manages and administers the trust, holds the legal title but without the benefits of the trust, i.e., without the right to receive financial profit from it. The benefits of the trust go to the beneficiary who holds this beneficial interest, called the equitable title.

Example: By deed, John transfers a farm to Mary to hold in trust for the benefit of Shirley. Mary is the trustee and has legal title. Shirley is the beneficiary and holds the equitable title.

- *Beneficiary or "cestui que trust."* The beneficiary (also called the cestui que trust) is the person (or persons) who has the enjoyment and benefit of the property. The beneficiary is said to hold equitable title; i.e., the beneficiary has the right to the benefits (profits) of the trust.
- *Equitable title.* In the law of trusts, equitable title, or beneficial title, refers to the right of the beneficiary to receive the benefits of the trust. Another way to view equitable title is that the beneficiary of the trust is regarded as the real "owner"; i.e., the beneficiary is entitled to the beneficial interest (the right to profit or benefit from the trust property), although the legal title to the property is held by another, the trustee (see Exhibit 8.1).
- *Trust property.* The trust property is the real or personal property that the trustee holds subject to the rights of one or more beneficiaries. The trust property in the example above is the farm transferred by John. Other names for trust property are the trust corpus, trust res, trust fund, trust estate, or subject matter of the trust.
- *Trust instrument.* A written instrument that creates a trust, i.e., a will, trust agreement, or declaration of trust. These terms are defined as follows:
  - *Will.* A trust included in a will is called a testamentary trust.
  - *Trust agreement.* A written agreement (contract) between the settlor and trustee(s) that creates the trust and is signed by them (see Exhibit 8.2). In a trust agreement, the settlor transfers the legal title to the trustee and either retains the equitable title or transfers it to another person but not to the trustee.
  - *Declaration of trust.* A document that creates a trust in which the settlor is also the trustee. The document declares the creation of a trust in which the settlor names herself as trustee and retains the legal title but transfers the equitable title to the trust property to another person, the beneficiary. When the property being transferred to a trust is real estate, the method

---

Exhibit 8.1 Creation of a Trust

of transfer is often a *deed of trust* or a *trust transfer deed*. (For further discussion, see Chapter 9 and Exhibits 9.3 and 9.5).

- *Revocable living trust.* A revocable living trust is a trust that the settlor has a right or power to revoke or change at any time prior to death. Such a power must be expressly stated or reserved by the settlor in the trust instrument; otherwise trusts are generally irrevocable. Property placed in revocable living trusts becomes a nonprobate asset and is not subject to probate or creditors' claims. It is included in the decedent's gross estate and, therefore, is subject to federal estate tax.
- *Irrevocable living trust.* Once created, an irrevocable living trust cannot be revoked or changed by the settlor. Property placed in the trust is not subject to probate or federal estate tax.
- *Principal.* The principal is the capital or property of a trust as opposed to the income, which is the product or profits generated by the capital.

Example: The farm John transferred to Mary would be the principal, and the profits generated by the farm would be the income.

- *Income.* Income is the financial gain measured in money that is generated from the principal.
- *Income beneficiary.* The income beneficiary is the person or charity that is entitled to receive the income produced from trust property (principal).
- *Restatement of Trusts.* In 1935, recognizing the need to simplify and clarify the American law of trusts, a group of trust experts working for the American Law Institute set forth the existing rules of law affecting trust creation and administration and included illustrations and comments. The completed work was called the Restatement of the American Law of Trusts which is considered to be the authority on trust law in most states. In 1959, the original Restatement was revised, and the revisions were incorporated into the Restatement (Second) of Trusts. In 1992, another partial revision was completed. Throughout the trust chapters of this book, relevant sections of the Restatement (Second) or (Third) of Trusts will be cited.[1]
- *Parol evidence.* Parol evidence is oral or written evidence.
- *Statute of Frauds.* State laws which provide that no lawsuit or civil action shall be maintained on certain classes of oral contracts unless the agreement is put in writing in a note or memorandum and signed by the party to be charged, i.e., the person being sued, or an authorized agent of the person. The statute's objective was to avoid numerous frauds and perjuries. In the law of trusts, the majority of states requires trust agreements that transfer title of real property to the trust to be written and signed by the parties to the contract. The Statute of Frauds makes oral trusts of real property invalid.

Use of Trust Terminology

To better understand the meaning and use of trust terms, consider the following situation.

The Facts

Jack Alston Carter gives 600 shares of Successful Corp. stock to his financial adviser and best friend, Timothy Connor McEvoy, to hold in trust and to invest for

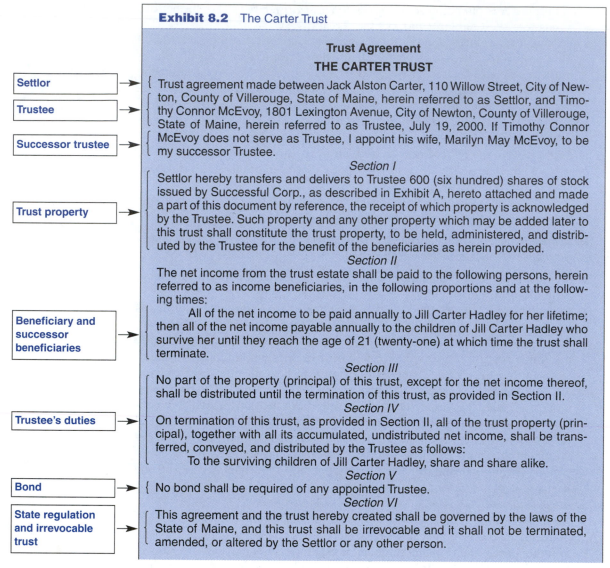

Exhibit 8.2 The Carter Trust

Settlor

Trustee

Successor trustee

Trust property

Beneficiary and successor beneficiaries

Trustee's duties

Bond

State regulation and irrevocable trust

Trust Agreement

THE CARTER TRUST

Trust agreement made between Jack Alston Carter, 110 Willow Street, City of Newton, County of Villerouge, State of Maine, herein referred to as Settlor, and Timothy Connor McEvoy, 1801 Lexington Avenue, City of Newton, County of Villerouge, State of Maine, herein referred to as Trustee, July 19, 2000. If Timothy Connor McEvoy does not serve as Trustee, I appoint his wife, Marilyn May McEvoy, to be my successor Trustee.

Section I

Settlor hereby transfers and delivers to Trustee 600 (six hundred) shares of stock issued by Successful Corp., as described in Exhibit A, hereto attached and made a part of this document by reference, the receipt of which property is acknowledged by the Trustee. Such property and any other property which may be added later to this trust shall constitute the trust property, to be held, administered, and distributed by the Trustee for the benefit of the beneficiaries as herein provided.

Section II

The net income from the trust estate shall be paid to the following persons, herein referred to as income beneficiaries, in the following proportions and at the following times:

All of the net income to be paid annually to Jill Carter Hadley for her lifetime; then all of the net income payable annually to the children of Jill Carter Hadley who survive her until they reach the age of 21 (twenty-one) at which time the trust shall terminate.

Section III

No part of the property (principal) of this trust, except for the net income thereof, shall be distributed until the termination of this trust, as provided in Section II.

Section IV

On termination of this trust, as provided in Section II, all of the trust property (principal), together with all its accumulated, undistributed net income, shall be transferred, conveyed, and distributed by the Trustee as follows:

To the surviving children of Jill Carter Hadley, share and share alike.

Section V

No bond shall be required of any appointed Trustee.

Section VI

This agreement and the trust hereby created shall be governed by the laws of the State of Maine, and this trust shall be irrevocable and it shall not be terminated, amended, or altered by the Settlor or any other person.

(continued)

the benefit of Jack's only child, Jill, and Jill's children, Mary and Joe. Named as successor trustee is Timothy's wife, Marilyn May McEvoy, who is also an accountant. This instrument (written agreement) provides that Timothy will pay Jill the income from the stock annually for the rest of her life, and after Jill's death, the stock will be given to Jill's children (Jack Carter's grandchildren). Exhibit 8.2 presents the trust agreement establishing the Carter Trust.

Review of Terminology

Jack Carter, the person who creates the trust, is the *settlor,* a word that comes from traditional legal language of "settling the property in trust." He may also be called the *trustor, donor, grantor,* or *creator.* The *trustee,* the person to whom the property is transferred in trust for the benefit of another and who manages and

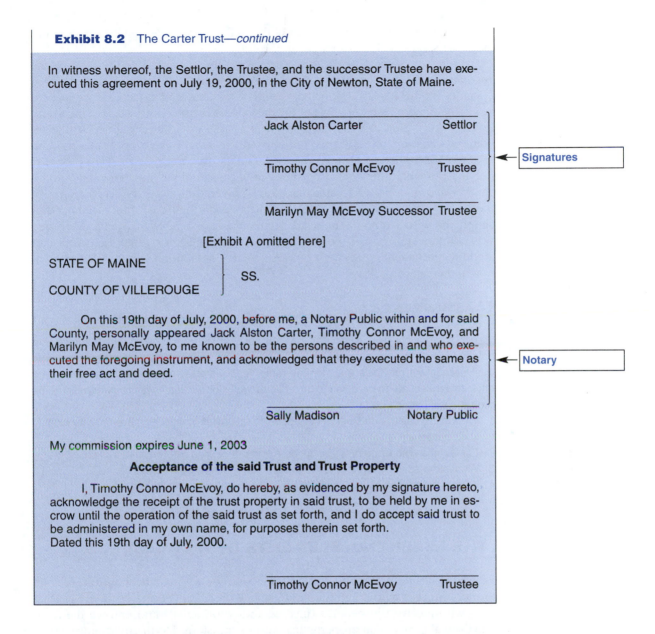

Exhibit 8.2 The Carter Trust—*continued*

In witness whereof, the Settlor, the Trustee, and the successor Trustee have executed this agreement on July 19, 2000, in the City of Newton, State of Maine.

> Jack Alston Carter   Settlor
>
> Timothy Connor McEvoy   Trustee   ← **Signatures**
>
> Marilyn May McEvoy   Successor   Trustee

[Exhibit A omitted here]

STATE OF MAINE }

       SS.

COUNTY OF VILLEROUGE }

    On this 19th day of July, 2000, before me, a Notary Public within and for said County, personally appeared Jack Alston Carter, Timothy Connor McEvoy, and Marilyn May McEvoy, to me known to be the persons described in and who executed the foregoing instrument, and acknowledged that they executed the same as their free act and deed.   ← **Notary**

> Sally Madison   Notary Public

My commission expires June 1, 2003

Acceptance of the said Trust and Trust Property

    I, Timothy Connor McEvoy, do hereby, as evidenced by my signature hereto, acknowledge the receipt of the trust property in said trust, to be held by me in escrow until the operation of the said trust as set forth, and I do accept said trust to be administered in my own name, for purposes therein set forth.
Dated this 19th day of July, 2000.

> Timothy Connor McEvoy   Trustee

administers the trust, is Timothy McEvoy. The *legal title* to the property is held by Timothy, the trustee, while the right to the use and benefit of the income from the property, i.e., the *equitable title,* is enjoyed (held) by the beneficiaries, Jill and Jill's children. Another name for the *beneficiary* is "*cestui que trust,*" which means "he for whom certain property in trust is held." Property held in trust (in this case the 600 shares of stock) is called the *trust property, trust fund, trust corpus, trust estate, trust res,* or the *subject matter of the trust.* The *trust instrument* that created this contract or agreement between the settlor, Jack, and the trustee, Timothy, is the Carter Trust. The objectives of the Carter Trust are to vest in (transfer to) the trustee and the beneficiaries the property interests it describes and to establish the parties' respective rights and duties. If the trustee fails to perform the terms of the trust or to act within the laws of the state (Maine), the beneficiaries are entitled to seek remedies from a *court of equity.*

A distinction is made between the *principal,* the property held in trust, and the *income,* which is earned by the principal and distributed by the trustee to the beneficiaries. In this case, the principal would be the shares of stock, and the income would be the profits in the form of dividends paid by the corporation to the shareholders. According to the trust instrument's provisions, Jill is entitled to the income (dividends) from the trust property (stock) for the duration of her life. Jill's children are entitled to a future interest called the *remainder* in the trust property, i.e., the principal (the stock) remaining after their mother dies. The children are called *remaindermen.* A trustee may also be given the power to distribute part of the *trust property* (the stock) to the beneficiaries on the basis of financial need or simply the wishes of the beneficiary. In this *trust agreement,* however, the trustee was not given this power. *Powers* are granted by the settlor when the trust is created (see Restatement [Second] of Trusts § 3 for definitions and § 37 for reservation and creation of powers).

🏛 ASSIGNMENT 8.1

Mary Schrader gives a four-unit apartment building to her nephew, John Simmons, to hold in trust for the benefit of his children (Mary's grandnieces and grandnephews). The trust agreement provides the monthly rents, less maintenance, insurance, taxes, and other expenses, are to be given to the children until John's death, when ownership of the property will pass to them.

1. Who is the cestui que trust in the above case? What other terms are used to identify such persons?
2. Explain the difference between income and principal in reference to this case.
3. Who is the settlor? What other terms are used to identify the settlor?
4. Who is the trustee? What is the trustee's function?

THE ESSENTIAL ELEMENTS OF A TRUST

Each trust has the following elements: (1) a settlor who creates the trust; (2) one or more trustees who administer and manage the trust; (3) one or more beneficiaries who receive the benefits (income and/or principal) and enforce the trust; and (4) real or personal property that must be transferred to the trust. Since a trust differs from other legal property transactions, such as a sale or gift of property, it is essential that all participants' interest in a trust be understood. After a sale or gift of property, the entire legal title passes from seller to buyer (sale) or from donor to donee (gift). But after the creation of a trust, title to property placed in the trust passes to at least two persons. The title is "split" into legal title and equitable title. The trustee receives the legal title, and the beneficiary receives the equitable title. For this reason, the trustee and the beneficiary are indispensable to the existence of a trust. In fact, a trust does not begin until legal and equitable interests (title) in specific property are vested in different individuals or sets of individuals, i.e., co-trustees or co-beneficiaries. The trust relationship commences when the separation of legal and equitable title takes place; see *In re Coutts' Will,*

260 N.Y.128, 183 N.E.200 (1932). Once a trust is created, the settlor's involvement often ends (see discussion below).

Another feature that distinguishes a trust from a sale is that consideration, i.e., payment to the settlor based on the trust property's reasonable value, is not a requirement for the creation of a trust. In other words, when property is placed in trust for the beneficiary, the settlor does not require the beneficiary to pay for the transfer. A trust is a gratuitous transfer of property; consideration is not necessary (Restatement [Second] of Trusts §§ 28, 29).

The Settlor: The Creator of the Trust

When a trust is created by the settlor, it is common practice to execute a written document called a **trust agreement** or **declaration of trust.** Provided the settlor manifests a clear intent to establish a trust, i.e., the settlor expressly imposes a duty on the trustee with respect to specific property, no particular words are necessary to create the trust so long as the trust purpose, property, and beneficiaries are designated (Restatement [Second] of Trusts §§ 23, 24). A common trust provision is "to X, as trustee, to have and hold under the trust's provisions hereinafter set forth," but the settlor could also establish a valid trust by giving property "to X for the benefit of Y." Use of the word "trust" or "trustee" is helpful but not mandatory, as illustrated by the case of *Mahoney v. Leddy,* 126 Vt. 98, 223 A.2d 456 (1966), in which Teresa Egan signed a paper stating that "in the event of my death" certain stock held in her name "belongs to Miss Peck." This was held to be a trust. Also, as noted above, the settlor's creation of the trust is not invalidated by its gratuitous nature; i.e., the beneficiary is not required to give the settlor money, service, or any other consideration in return for the settlor's act of establishing the trust.

Trust agreement
A written agreement (contract) between the settlor and trustee(s) that creates the trust and is signed by them.

Declaration of trust
A document that creates a trust in which the settlor is also the trustee.

⚖ ASSIGNMENT 8.2

Shirley gives Joanna $30,000 cash to hold and invest for the benefit of Carl. A trust is created even though the words "trust" and "trustee" are not used in its creation. The trust property is transferred as a gift. Neither Joanna nor Carl has purchased the property, so neither of them pays for receiving it.

1. Name the settlor, beneficiary, trustee, and trust corpus.
2. How does this trust differ from a sale or a gift?

Who may be a settlor? What qualifications or limitations exist that allow courts to enforce the trust the settlor creates? To be a settlor, a person must own a transferable interest in property, have the right or power of disposing of a property interest, and have the ability to make a valid contract. Only those who have contractual capacity, i.e., who are not insane, intoxicated, or minors, can make an outright transfer of property into a trust (Restatement [Second] of Trusts §§ 18–22). Thus, the limitations placed on persons to make contracts, wills, and other legal transactions are also limitations on settlors of trusts. Unless a person meets the qualifications, he cannot create a trust, and any attempt to do so is voidable. In addition, even though a person is qualified to make a trust, if the property transfer is accomplished through duress, fraud, or undue influence, the settlor may avoid or cancel the trust.

Once the settlor intentionally creates a trust, assuming he does not appoint himself trustee or beneficiary, the settlor's functions terminate, i.e., he has no further rights, duties, or liabilities with respect to the trust administration.

Example: Harding owns a farm, Blackacre, which he conveys by deed to Barrett in trust for the benefit of Stewart. Harding is the settlor and retains no interest. He has no further powers, duties, rights, or liabilities concerning the trust administration. Barrett is the trustee and has legal title. Stewart is the beneficiary and has equitable title. Blackacre is the trust property.

At the termination of the trust, the settlor may have the right to the return of the trust property, i.e., the settlor's (grantor's) reversionary interest (see Chapter 2).

While alive, the settlor may expressly retain the power to revoke or cancel the trust and recover the trust property. When the settlor has such a power, the trust is called a **revocable trust** (Restatement [Second] of Trusts § 330). When the settlor does not expressly reserve this power, the trust is **irrevocable.**

At first, the settlor may want the trust to be revocable in order to have the opportunity to see how well it works and what changes, if any, are necessary before the trust is made irrevocable. Eventually, the settlor may wish to make the trust irrevocable, since the retention of control over the trust arrangement, including the power to revoke, exposes the settlor to tax liability for the trust income. Generally, the settlor must make the trust irrevocable and retain only limited powers over the trust before death; if these requirements are not met, the trust income and principal will be included in the settlor's gross estate and will be subject to estate and inheritance taxes.

The Settlor as Trustee or Beneficiary

Although three parties usually participate in the creation of a trust, the law demands the involvement of at least two. The same person cannot be the settlor, trustee, and beneficiary, but the same person could be the settlor and trustee, or the settlor and beneficiary. Thus, a settlor may appoint herself sole trustee and legally transfer the trust property from herself personally to herself as trustee using a declaration of trust document.

Example: Harding owns 1,000 shares of IBC, Inc. stock and declares himself trustee of the stock for the benefit of Stewart. Harding is the settlor and trustee who retains legal title. Stewart is the beneficiary and has equitable title. The IBC, Inc. stock is the trust property.

A settlor may also convey property in trust to another for her own benefit, i.e., the settlor is the beneficiary.

Example: Harding owns a farm which he conveys by deed to Barrett in trust for the benefit of himself (Harding). Harding is the settlor and beneficiary with an equitable interest in the farm. Barrett is the trustee and has legal title. The farm is the trust property.

Notice, however, the same person cannot be both the sole trustee and the sole beneficiary. A trust exists when the trustee has a fiduciary obligation to administer the trust property for the benefit of another, i.e., the beneficiary, who can enforce the obligation. Therefore, a sole trustee cannot also be a sole beneficiary because there would be no one to enforce the trust. If the trustee, who holds legal title to the trust property, acquires the equitable title of the beneficiary, the legal

Revocable trust
A trust that the settlor has a right or power to cancel or revoke.

Irrevocable trust
A trust that may not be revoked by the settlor after its creation.

and equitable titles merge, and the trust ends. On the other hand, when the sole trustee is also one of several beneficiaries, or the sole beneficiary is also one of several trustees, the legal and equitable titles do not merge, and the trust is valid (Restatement [Second] of Trusts § 99). Thus, the settlor can name himself sole trustee and co-beneficiary or co-trustee and sole beneficiary, but not sole trustee and sole beneficiary (see Exhibit 8.3).

> **Example:** A settlor, Ray Norton, signs a declaration of trust naming himself trustee of stock certificates for the benefit of himself and his wife, Vera. Because he holds complete legal title but only partial equitable title to the trust property, Ray is allowed to fill all three of these roles (settlor, trustee, and co-beneficiary) while Vera is alive. When Vera dies, however, Ray holds the entire equitable as well as legal title. This merger of title in one person ends the trust.

The Trustee: The Fiduciary and Administrator of the Trust

The trustee is the participant in a trust who holds legal title to the trust property for the benefit of the beneficiary. The trustee is a fiduciary and, as such, owes fiduciary duties to act honestly and loyally for the sole benefit of the beneficiary. This fiduciary relationship between the trustee and the beneficiary is identified and defined in the case of *Scotti's Drive In Restaurants, Inc. v. Mile High-Dart In Corp.,* 526 P.2d 1193 (Wyo. 1974). Normally, the settlor has the right or power to select the trustee, but this right may be given to the beneficiary or to another; *failure of the settlor to name a trustee is not fatal to the trust,* however, because in such cases the court will appoint a trustee.

Natural or Legal Person as Trustee

Generally, the trustee selected is a person, either natural (e.g., settlor, family member, attorney, or financial adviser) or legal (e.g., a private corporation authorized to act as a trustee by its charter and state statute, such as a trust company or bank). If a trust is created to last a considerable length of time, it may be best to select a corporate trustee (bank) to assure continued reliable management. As a matter of practicality, settlors often choose a bank as the trustee or co-trustee because of the experience and expertise of bank trust officers. The cost of using such trustees is always an important consideration. Corporate trustees make their published fee schedules available to attract prospective clients. Close family members may not charge any fee, but their management advice may not be as productive.

Any natural person who has the legal capacity to hold, own, and administer property may receive trust property as a trustee. However, even though minors, intoxicated individuals, and mentally incompetent persons can take and own property, they lack the capacity to make a valid contract; therefore, they cannot properly administer a trust since their contracts are voidable (revocable). In other words, if such persons make contracts as part of their duties while administering a trust, they can avoid, disaffirm, or cancel their contracts because their contracts are voidable. Therefore, such trustees will ordinarily be removed and a new trustee appointed by the equity court on request of the beneficiary.

In most cases the settlor selects the trustee on the basis of the person's proven integrity, ability, experience, and, of course, capacity. If there is a question about the selected person's fitness or capacity, the equity court either ratifies (confirms) or denies the selection. Therefore, in some instances, the settlor is considered to have only nominated a trustee; selection is within the court's prerogative (see Cal. Prob. Code § 17200). But the *most important rule* of trust law concerning the selection of a trustee is that the court will not allow a trust to fail for lack of a trustee. Thus, the court has the power and authority to appoint or replace a trustee if any of the following events occurs:

1. No one is nominated as trustee.
2. The trustee dies.
3. The trustee is incompetent.
4. The named trustee declines the position.
5. No successor is named as a replacement in the provisions of the trust.

Example: The trust department of the Lincoln National Bank, a private corporation, has experienced financial advisers who offer their services to the public as professional trustees. Since the bank's charter enables it to act as a trustee, it does so through these employees. Betty White transfers her Microsoft stock to the bank to hold and manage for the benefit of her son, Willard. The bank's trust advisers perform this service for an agreed-on fee.

Example: Ella Cunningham, age 80, transfers part of the assets of her estate in trust to her favorite niece, Paula, age 17. Ella is the beneficiary. Paula signs a contract as trustee, but, as a minor, she decides not to honor her obligation. Because minors make voidable contracts, they may choose to avoid or cancel them. Since Paula avoided the trust agreement, Ella may appoint a successor trustee.

Example: Darnella Swanson, a single parent, appoints Newton Marshall, a close friend, trustee of a trust for the benefit of her son, Roy. Newton sells some of his property to the trust, buys other trust property for his family, and adds the money to his account instead of the trust account. Because of these serious breaches of his fiduciary duties, Darnella can have Newton replaced as trustee.

Exhibit 8.3   Creation of Valid or Invalid Trusts

Valid Trust Combinations

Settlor	Trustee or Co-Trustees	Beneficiary or Co-Beneficiaries
Tom	Mary	Joe
Tom	Tom and Mary	Joe
Tom	Mary	Tom and Joe
Tom	Tom and Mary	Tom and Joe
Tom	Tom	Joe
Tom	Mary	Tom
Tom	Tom and Mary	Tom
Tom	Tom	Tom and Joe

Invalid Trust Combinations

Settlor	Trustee or Co-Trustees	Beneficiary or Co-Beneficiaries
Tom	Tom	Tom
Tom	Mary	Mary

These last two examples do not create a valid trust because the same individual cannot be the sole trustee and the sole beneficiary; that would cause the legal and equitable titles to be merged and would automatically terminate the trust.

Co-Trustees

The following rules generally apply when co-trustees have been appointed and decisions concerning the administration of the trust must be made:

- If there are two trustees, both must agree on any action concerning trust property.
- If there are more than two trustees, the general rule is that all must agree, but the trust document determines whether action can be taken only by unanimous vote, majority vote, or even by one trustee (usually the settlor-trustee) acting alone (Restatement [Second] of Trusts § 194). Some states allow a majority vote when more than two people are co-trustees.

Acceptance or Disclaimer of Trusteeship

Normally, the settlor will name a trustee, but if the settlor does not, a trustee will be appointed by a court (Restatement [Second] of Trusts § 108). Since the trust imposes fiduciary duties on the trustee, the trustee has the right to renounce or reject (disclaim) the trust. The person named as trustee is free to choose whether to accept or reject the appointment by words or conduct.

In the absence of a definite rejection or **disclaimer,** acceptance will be presumed, and any positive act such as taking possession of the trust property will confirm the trustee's acceptance. Likewise, the failure of a trustee to do or say anything to indicate acceptance within a reasonable length of time will be considered a disclaimer.

> **Disclaimer**
> The right a person has to refuse or reject appointment as trustee of a trust.

> **Example:** Lydia Metaxis creates a testamentary trust for her grandchildren and names her friend, Isabel Leclerc, trustee. Isabel is unable to carry out the tasks of administration. Therefore, she executes a disclaimer of responsibility as trustee and files it with the probate court that has jurisdiction over Lydia's will. The court will appoint a different trustee. Isabel's disclaimer is shown in Exhibit 8.4.

Once disclaimed, a trusteeship cannot thereafter be accepted. The disclaimer does not affect the validity of the trust, however, because a court will appoint a successor trustee if the settlor did not provide for one. The best way to eliminate any doubt of the trustee's acceptance or rejection is for the trustee to deliver to the proper person, e.g., the settlor, a signed document of the decision to accept or disclaim.

Removal or Resignation of Trustee

Trusteeship is a solemn undertaking. After accepting the duties outlined in a trust, a trustee can be relieved of the duties and office by the settlor, by death, by

---

Exhibit 8.4   Sample Disclaimer

I, Isabel Andrewes Leclerc, named as trustee under the will of Lydia Metaxis, deceased, respectfully decline to act as said trustee.
In witness whereof, I have executed this instrument at the City of Puentavilla, Tarpon County, Florida.

_____
Isabel Andrewes Leclerc

January 16, 2001

removal by the equity or probate court, or by resignation (Restatement [Second] of Trusts §§ 103, 104, 105, 106). Resignation is an exercise of the trustee's discretion and must be accepted by the proper court (a court of equity or probate court). Removal of the trustee is an exercise of the court's discretion when it believes the continuation of acts by the trustee would be detrimental to the beneficiary's interests (Restatement [Second] of Trusts § 107). Grounds for the removal of a trustee include:

- Lack of capacity.
- Commission of a serious breach of trust.
- Refusal to give bond when bond is required.
- Refusal to account for expenditures, investments, and the like.
- Commission of a crime, particularly one involving dishonesty.
- Long or permanent absence from the state.
- Showing of favoritism to one or more beneficiaries.
- Unreasonable failure to cooperate with the co-trustee if one exists (Restatement [Second] of Trusts § 107).

If the trustee selected is a corporation, the beneficiaries are given the right to remove the trustee and name a successor corporate trustee. However, mere friction between the trustee and the beneficiary is not sufficient grounds for removal. Remember, if a trustee resigns or is appropriately removed, the court will appoint a new (successor) trustee as a replacement unless the trust document provides for a successor.

Unless required by a state statute, by terms of the trust, or by an order of a court of equity, a trustee is not required to take an oath that he will faithfully discharge the duties or to secure a certificate of authority from a court. Whether or not an oath is required, the trustee still has a fiduciary duty to the beneficiary. In some jurisdictions, becoming a trustee depends on performance of one or more of these acts, and failure to perform the act prevents the person from assuming the office. In other jurisdictions, failure of the trustee to perform a required qualifying act does not prevent assumption of the office, but is considered a breach of trust that will allow the court to remove the trustee at the request of a beneficiary and to appoint another trustee (Restatement [Second] of Trusts § 107).

Powers of the Trustee

The powers of the trustee are determined by the following:

- The express authority granted by the terms of the trust instrument.
- The statutes in the state in which the trust is established; for an example of the powers granted by a typical state statute, see N.Y. EPTL § 11–1.1.

The powers granted to the trustee by the trust document are often purposely broad to give the trustee the flexibility, like that of the owner-settlor, to manage and administer the trust property. It is common, in modern trusts, to give the trustee wide discretionary powers to determine and resolve problems that the settlor could not have foreseen.

Example: By the terms of the trust, Hannah, the trustee, is given discretionary power to "use and disburse principal as well as income if, in the opinion of the trustee, it is necessary for the education or medical care of the beneficiary."

A trustee in the trust instrument is granted the power to:

1. Sell assets, including real estate, and reinvest the proceeds.
2. Lease or rent trust property.
3. Carry on a business.
4. Vote stock and give proxies.
5. Lend or borrow money, including pledging or mortgaging trust property.
6. Hire attorneys, stockbrokers, accountants, and insurance agents.
7. Compromise, settle, contest, or arbitrate claims and disputes.
8. Subdivide, exchange, develop, or improve real property.
9. Do anything necessary to carry out any of the above.
10. Do whatever a legal owner of property can do subject to the required performance of the trustee to act as a fiduciary.

Duties of the Trustee

In general, a trust does not exist unless specific actions and enforceable duties are performed by the trustee, such as a duty to manage the property in some manner or to exercise discretion or judgment (Restatement [Second] of Trusts § 25). The settlor's mere order to the trustee to hold the property in trust without any direction as to its use or distribution does not suffice to create a valid trust; it creates, instead, a passive trust which the law declares void (see Chapter 9).

> **Example:** In his will, George, the decedent, gives $100,000 to Howard and expresses the hope that Howard will use the money "for religious and family purposes." Such phraseology does not clearly indicate George is "settling" or creating a trust. He has not identified the duties Howard must perform as the trustee of an active trust. George might well have intended the $100,000 as a gift to Howard with "advice" on its use.

When a trust is created, it establishes a fiduciary relationship of trust and confidence between the trustee and beneficiary, in which the trustee, as the fiduciary, must faithfully follow the directions of the trust and be loyal to the beneficiary throughout its duration. Acting as a fiduciary, the trustee has the following duties:

1. *Duty of performance and due care (Restatement [Second] of Trusts § 169).*
   - The trustee's main duty is to carry out the terms and purpose of the trust. The trustee is personally liable, i.e., must pay out of personal funds, for any loss sustained by failure to perform the duties of the trust unless the failure can be justified. There is no personal liability for loss sustained if the trustee has exercised the degree of care a reasonable person would exercise under the circumstances.
   - The trustee cannot delegate the performance of personal duties (Restatement [Third] of Trusts § 171). The case of *U.A. of Joliet v. First National Bank of Joliet,* 93 Ill.App.3d 890, 49 Ill.Dec. 250, 417 N.E.2d 1077 (1981), illustrates a trustee's inability to delegate duties.
   - The trustee has a fiduciary duty to use ordinary, reasonable skill, prudence, and diligence in the administration of the trust and in the performance of trust duties (Restatement [Second] of Trusts § 174). In other words, the trustee must use the care a reasonable, prudent person would exercise under the circumstances. In the case of *Costello v. Costello,* 209 N.Y. 252, 103 N.E. 148

(1913), the court defined a trustee's responsibility as follows: "...trustees are bound in the management of all matters of the trust to act in good faith and employ such vigilance, diligence, and prudence as in general, prudent men of discretion and intelligence in like matters employ in their affairs." The law does not hold a trustee who acts in accord with such a rule responsible for errors in judgment.

Example: Nathan Maxwell transfers 100 shares of stock to William Mann in trust to hold and invest for the benefit of Nathan's invalid mother, Marilyn.

Whether a trustee, such as William Mann in the example above, receives compensation for his services or not, he must use at least ordinary care, skill, prudence, and diligence in the execution (performance) of the trust. The degree of ability required may be increased if William actually has greater than normal abilities or if he, as trustee, represented to the settlor that he possessed unusual capabilities before the trust was created. Therefore, professional fiduciaries, such as banks and trust companies with specialists in various areas of trust work, may be held to a higher standard since they give a sense of security to a trust, because of their claims of special expertise and because of the rule that more is expected of a trustee who has a special skill or knowledge of the subject. At the very least, professional fiduciaries must measure up to the standard of skill and prudence of the average, ordinary professional corporate trustee located in the community where the trust is created.

The law would not hold William, as trustee, responsible for every error in judgment he might make, but he is obliged to use the care and skill of an ordinary capable person who is charged with conserving a trust. If William disregards this obligation, he cannot defend himself against liability on the grounds he acted in good faith or did not intentionally misuse the trust property. In addition, William, as trustee, cannot disclaim any personal liability on the grounds he was simply following the practices the settlor had previously followed when ordinary skill and prudence would dictate another course.

⚎ ASSIGNMENT 8.3

In performing the following acts, is William Mann violating his duty of reasonable care of the trust property? Why or why not?

1. William receives a dividend on one of the shares of stock in the amount of $90. He uses it to buy a birthday present for Marilyn.
2. One of the stocks William holds is performing poorly. On the advice of another executive in the corporation where William works, he sells the stock and invests in Goldbrick, Inc., which subsequently falls in value below the level of the stock formerly owned.

2. *Duty of loyalty (Restatement [Third] of Trusts § 170).*
   - The trustee is not permitted to profit personally from her position as trustee, other than to receive the compensation allowed by contract or by law. The loyalty duty applies to all persons in a fiduciary capacity.

Example: The will of Colin Wilcox appoints Judith Ames trustee of a business, the Wilcox Bakery, for the benefit of Colin's minor sons, Reynold and Richard.

Loyalty to the beneficiaries of the trust is one of the most important duties of a trustee. The duty of loyalty means that the trustee is obliged to act solely in the best interests of the beneficiary. A disloyal act would include any transaction by Judith as trustee that creates a **conflict of interest** between herself and the beneficiaries of the trust, or between the beneficiaries and third persons. A conflict of interest is the creation of circumstances by the fiduciary (trustee) in the administration of the trust that benefits someone other than the beneficiary, thereby establishing the conflict. The other party benefited is most often the trustee, but it could be any person. In the case above, a disloyal act by Judith is not automatically void. The beneficiaries may elect to disaffirm and avoid such transactions or to treat them as legal and binding. As trustee, Judith must avoid placing herself in a position where her personal interest or that of a third person might conflict with the interest of the beneficiaries.

> **Conflict of interest**
> Divided loyalties (it would be a conflict of interest for an attorney to represent both sides in a dispute).

The trustee must act in the sole and exclusive interests of the beneficiaries. In the above example, *if Judith buys or leases trust property for herself, or profits from the sale of her own property to the trust, she commits acts of disloyalty*. It does not matter that Judith acted in good faith or with honest intentions, or that the beneficiaries suffered no loss because of her disloyal acts. It is also immaterial that the trustee has made no profit for herself from her disloyal transaction, even though in most cases she does benefit in some manner. When responsible for such disloyal acts, the trustee (Judith), may be held liable for the amount of gain to herself or a third person, and the court may even remove her from the trusteeship. These strict standards are designed not only to prevent actual unfair dealing but also to help trustees avoid a conflict of interest.

> **ETHICAL ISSUE**

⚖ ASSIGNMENT 8.4

Judith Ames performs the following acts in the course of trusteeship. Are they disloyal? Are they voidable? What additional facts, if any, would you need in order to answer these questions?

1. In the example above, Judith buys a display case from the bakery. She pays fair market value for it. Reynold is fully aware of the purchase.
2. Colin Wilcox dies and his executor prepares to sell some real estate as instructed by the will. Judith withholds one piece of property from the sale so a friend may buy it. Her friend pays the amount of the property's appraised value.
3. As trustee, Judith persuades the bakery manager to sign a contract to buy flour from the Hanrahan Co. for the next year. Hanrahan does not offer the lowest contract price for flour, nor is there any evidence that its product is better than that of other companies; however, the Ameses and the Hanrahans have been friends for many years.

   3. Duty to take possession of and preserve trust property (Restatement [Second] of Trusts § 176).

- The trustee has a duty to take possession of and preserve the trust property from possible loss or damage, and if the property includes outstanding debts, the trustee has the duty to collect them, *but the trustee must not add the money collected to her own bank account.*

> **ETHICAL ISSUE**

Example: John Yeats creates a living trust that consists of an apartment building, stocks, bonds, and promissory notes for the benefit of his son, Roderick. He names as trustee his sister, Marcela, who is an attorney.

In accordance with the terms of the trust instrument, Marcela has the duty to take possession of the property. If the trust property consists of money or goods and chattels, she should take immediate possession of the chattels and open a separate fiduciary bank account for the cash. Such an account should be identified as a trust account, i.e., "Marcela Yeats, Trustee for Roderick Yeats." Since Marcela handles funds for the benefit of Roderick, she has a duty to keep the trust property separate from her own individual property and from property held for other trusts. Since the trust property includes promissory notes, bonds, shares of stock, and a deed to the apartment, Marcela should take possession of the documents representing title (ownership) to such property and place them in a safe deposit box registered in the name of the trust. If you are a paralegal who works for Marcela, you should remind her that *all trust property should be clearly distinguished from Marcela's own property*. If it is not, Marcela will have the burden of proving which commingled property belongs to whom and might even lose her own property in the process if a court rules that the mixture of trust and personal property belongs to the trust. Possession is usually obtained from the settlor, or, if the trust was created in a will (a testamentary trust), from the named executor or personal representative. The failure to act promptly and reasonably to secure possession of the trust property makes the trustee personally liable for any loss caused by such negligence.

> **ETHICAL ISSUE**

In brief, Marcela has the duty to perform whatever acts a reasonably prudent businesswoman would deem necessary in order to preserve and protect the trust property. Such acts would include placing cash in a trust account; filing legal documents such as deeds and mortgages; depositing important legal papers, documents, and valuable personal property in an appropriate place such as a safe deposit box; paying taxes on realty and maintaining the property in reasonable condition to avoid deterioration; transferring shares of stock to the appropriate person's name; maintaining adequate insurance coverage on all appropriate trust property; and the like.

🏛 ASSIGNMENT 8.5

Are the following acts examples of a violation of the trustee's duty to preserve and protect the trust property? What additional facts would you want to know to assist you in answering the questions?

1. Marcela withdraws a substantial part of the trust fund from its bank account and gives it to a friend to invest. Her friend is not a professional investor, and the advice proves shortsighted financially. All the investments depreciate.
2. Same facts as in question 1 above except the friend's advice is very lucky. The earnings on the investments suggested by Marcela's friend triple the trust account.
3. The apartment which Marcela holds in trust for Roderick has a defective staircase. While on a visit to the apartment, Flora Atkinson falls down the stairs and is injured. Was Marcela's failure to repair the staircase a breach of her fiduciary duty?

4. *Duty to invest the trust property (Restatement [Third] of Trusts §§ 181, 207, and 227).*

- The trustee is required to invest the money or property in enterprises or transactions that will yield an income to the trust.

Example: Carmine diGrazia, a widower living in Maryland, created a testamentary trust of $100,000 and his interest in a building construction business for the benefit of his two sons, Paola and Carlo. He appoints as trustee his cousin, Katarina, who is his accountant. Carmine dies and Katarina assumes trusteeship.

Katarina must make the trust property productive by investing it in income-producing investments as soon as possible. Delay could constitute negligence and make her liable for any loss. Generally, Katarina's investment policies are controlled by the authority granted her by Carmine, by the court, and by statute. Today some states establish by statute a list of specific types of investments that may or must be made by the trustee. The law of the state of Maryland lists examples of the statutory investments fiduciaries may make.

Md. Estates and Trusts Code Ann. § 15–106 Lawful Investments

(a) *List of lawful investments*—The following investments shall be lawful investments for any person:

(1) Debentures issued by federal intermediate credit banks or by banks for cooperatives;

(2) Bonds issued by federal land banks or by the Federal Home Loan Bank Board;

(3) Mortgages, bonds, or notes secured by a mortgage or deed of trust, or debentures issued by the Federal Housing Administration;

(4) Obligations of national mortgage associations;

(5) Shares, free-share accounts, certificates of deposit, or investment certificates of any insured financial institution, as defined in § 13–301(g) of this article;

(6) Bonds or other obligations issued by a housing authority pursuant to the provisions of Article 44A of the Code, or issued by any public housing authority or agency in the United States, when such bonds or other obligations are secured by a pledge of annual contributions to be paid by the United States or any agency of the United States;

(7) Obligations issued or guaranteed by the International Bank for Reconstruction and Development.

* * *

(e) *Liability for lack of reasonable care*—This section shall not be construed as relieving any person from the duty of exercising reasonable care in selecting securities.

* * *

(g) *Other investments*—This section shall not be construed to make unlawful any investment not listed in this section.

Katarina must periodically review her investment methods and policies. If she fails to examine or review at regular intervals the investments which she has made, she can be liable for the loss or decrease in the value of the trust property.

The case of *Witmer v. Blair,* 588 S.W.2d 222 (Mo.App. 1979), involved this duty. Because the trustee of the testamentary trust had kept no records and had not invested the money of the trust, the court ruled the trustee had violated the fiduciary duty to "make the trust property productive" by properly investing the trust funds.

Unless the trust property consists solely of real estate or a family business, corporate trustees, because of their experience and expertise, are sometimes selected over family members when trust property is to be invested. A comparison of average annual rates of return of the management and investment performance of professional corporate trustees over a number of years can be evaluated and ranked. This comparison is useful for two reasons. It allows the settlor to:

1. Choose a comfort level on the degree of risk he or she is willing to take in the investment, e.g., *safe* versus *high risk.*
2. Select a leading corporate trustee who has a history of successful, dependable, and acceptable investment strategies.

ASSIGNMENT 8.6

Katarina makes the following investments. Do they violate her duty to make the trust property productive? What additional facts must you know to assist you in answering the following?

1. Carmine had recently complained that his building construction business was unprofitable. At the time of his death, he was preparing to sell it to a business associate. Katarina, who was also named executrix of Carmine's estate, executes the sale in the name of the estate and adds the money to the trust fund.
2. Katarina buys bonds issued by the Vittore Emanuele Lodge, to which Carmine had belonged. The bonds pay 8 percent annual interest. Several of Katarina's neighbors and friends hold similar bonds. Other kinds of debentures that cost the same price yield higher rates of interest.
3. After Carmine's death, Katarina is preoccupied with details of his funeral and putting his affairs in order. She neglects to deposit part of the cash portion of the trust, i.e., $8,000, in a bank until it is too late to earn interest on the money for the quarter. Carmine kept the $8,000 in a small safe at home.

5. *Duty to make payments of income and principal to the named beneficiaries (Restatement [Second] of Trusts § 182).*

- Most trusts establish two kinds of beneficiaries: income beneficiaries, who receive the net income from the trust property for a determined number of years or for the beneficiaries' lives, and remainder beneficiaries, who receive the principal of the trust after the rights of the income beneficiaries in the trust are terminated. A person who receives the property after an income beneficiary is called the remainderman.

Example: Celia Brosniak, the oldest child in her family, is named trustee of a large sum of money in the will of her aunt. The trust is for the benefit of Celia's brothers and sisters, who are to receive investment income from the money until the youngest attains majority. At that time, according to the will, Celia is to receive the balance (principal) of the trust fund. Celia's brothers and sisters are the income beneficiaries, and Celia is the remainder beneficiary and remainderman.

If the settlor provides for separate disposition of the trust income and trust principal, and if the trust property is cash, it is advisable that the trustee open two accounts, one for the principal and one for the interest. In the example above, this would be necessary. The aunt not only designated income-receiving beneficiaries but also chose Celia to receive the principal as a lump sum. Celia should open a separate principal account so that she may readily take her gift when the time comes. Also, when there are two or more beneficiaries, as in this case, the trustee, Celia, must deal with them impartially, i.e., treat them equally.

It may happen that during the course of the trust administration, Celia will obtain money or property other than what she was given in the trust. In such cases she must decide whether to credit the receipt of such property to the income or principal account of the trust. If a trust agreement does not specify how to allocate the trust funds, a statute, the Uniform (or Revised Uniform) Principal and Income Act adopted in most states, provides for the method of allocation. These acts define in detail the duties of the trustee in regard to the receipt of property and its disbursement into the income or principal account. Trustees are personally liable for any loss if they fail to comply with the trust agreement or the statute.

The general rule for disbursement is that money paid for the use of the trust property and any benefit received from the employment of that property are to be treated as trust income, while substitutes for the original trust property, such as the proceeds from the sale of the property, are to be considered trust principal. When allocating receipts or expenses between the income beneficiaries and remaindermen, the general rule is that ordinary or current receipts and expenses are allocated or assigned to the income beneficiary, whereas extraordinary receipts and expenses are allocated to the remaindermen (see Exhibit 8.5).

Example: Howard wills his property to a trust. The trustees are to pay the income from the property to his wife, Mary, during her life and to distribute the property to their children when Mary dies. Howard can direct the trustees to allocate receipts and charge expenses between the income beneficiary (Mary) and the remaindermen (children).

Exhibit 8.5 Allocation of Ordinary and Extraordinary Receipts and Expenses between Beneficiaries and Remaindermen

Ordinary—Income Beneficiary	Extraordinary—Remaindermen
Receipts	Receipts
Rents	Proceeds from sale or exchange of trust principal
Royalties	**Stock Dividends**
Cash dividends	**Stock Splits***
Interest	Settlement of claims for injury to principal
Expenses	Expenses
Insurance	Extraordinary repairs
Ordinary taxes	Principal amortization
Ordinary repairs	Costs incurred in the sale or purchase of principal
Depreciation	Long-term improvements
Interest payments	

*A stock split is the issuance by a corporation of a number of new shares in exchange for each old share held by a stockholder; the result is a proportional change in the number of shares owned by each stockholder. A common purpose of a stock split is to reduce the per share market price to encourage wider trading and ownership and eventually a higher per share value (i.e., price).

Stock dividend
A dividend of shares of stock distributed to stockholders.

Stock split
One share of stock is split into a larger number of shares resulting in a proportional change in the number of shares owned by each stockholder.

🏛 ASSIGNMENT 8.7

If the trust agreement in the Celia example authorized her to distribute income "at best, quarterly, and at least, annually," would she be acting within her fiduciary obligations if she withheld certain amounts from the quarterly distributions for possible emergency expenses and thereby created a separate fund?

6. *Duty to account (Restatement [Second] of Trusts § 172).*
   - The trustee must keep accurate records so that it can be determined whether the trust has been properly administered.

Example: Nicholas Walheimer creates a living trust for the benefit of his mentally handicapped son, David. He names Felix Basch trustee of the fund, which consists of $65,000 worth of stock. Felix is given the power to sell and invest the stock. Nicholas dies. Frederika Wolfram is appointed David's personal and property guardian.

Felix has the duty to render an account (complete and accurate information) of his administrative activities at reasonable intervals to those who are "interested" in the trust, namely, the settlor, Nicholas, while alive, and the beneficiary, David, acting through his personal and property guardian, Frederika. The trustee, Felix, alone has the right to manage and control the trust property. He must retain trust documents and records, secure and file vouchers for all expenditures and disbursements, and keep an accurate and complete set of books. He is obliged to show these to Nicholas and Frederika on request. Felix has a fiduciary duty to account voluntarily (e.g., quarterly) for changes in the trust property. If the trustee fails to perform these duties, the trustee may be removed by the court, denied compensation, or even charged with the cost to the beneficiary of an accounting proceeding.

🏛 ASSIGNMENT 8.8

Felix has been a trustee for two years. He tries to make periodic reports on the trust, but this is not always feasible because he frequently travels while conducting business. In performing the following acts, did Felix violate his duty to account? (These are opinion questions, but you must give reasons for your answers).

1. Felix sells some stock from the trust and buys land in the Santo Affonso Valley. Frederika asks him to account for this, so he sends her copies of the contract of sale and the deed of title.

2. At the end of the calendar year, Felix sends a balance sheet indicating the financial status of the trust property but neglects to include a dividend paid one week before the issue date of the balance sheet. Later he discovers his error. He sends Frederika a receipt for payment of the dividend, informing her that he will rectify the error on the next annual statement.

3. Felix has the second annual statement prepared by an accountant. Having read it, Frederika complains that it is too technical for her to understand. Felix replies that the statement is correct to the best of his knowledge and that he has fulfilled the duty to account required of a trustee.

⚎ ASSIGNMENT 8.9

1. John Williams, a customer's representative in a stock brokerage firm, is appointed sole trustee of the Carter Trust. If John uses the firm to buy and sell stock for the trust, is this a violation of John's fiduciary duty? If so, which duty?
2. Continuing with the John Williams case in question 1, if John temporarily put the money obtained from the sale of trust property, e.g., shares of stock owned by the trust, into his own bank account, would this violate his fiduciary duty? If so, which duty?
3. Sally Feldman is an attorney and sole trustee of a trust. An unhappy beneficiary of the trust demands that Sally transfer the trust property to an investment company, which will manage and invest the property. Must Sally make the transfer? Would this violate her fiduciary duty? If so, which duty?

Liability of Trustee to Beneficiary

A breach of trust by the trustee may occur in a variety of ways, which in turn determine the remedies available and the party who is entitled to bring suit. To restore the damage committed by a trustee, the beneficiary has the right to judicial remedies at law or a suit in equity. An action at law is a civil lawsuit commenced by the person, called the plaintiff, who seeks the remedy at law called damages, i.e., to be compensated monetarily.

- The beneficiary can maintain a civil lawsuit to compel the trustee to reimburse the trust for any loss or depreciation in value of the trust property caused by the trustee's breach of the trust instrument (Restatement [Second] of Trusts §§ 199, 205).

Example: Sharon has agreed to act as trustee for Joan's benefit. The trust property is a lake cottage. Sharon has obtained the deed but has not insured the property. Lightning strikes the cottage, and it is destroyed. Sharon would be personally responsible and liable for this loss.

- The beneficiary can obtain an injunction, i.e., a court order, to compel the trustee to do, or refrain from doing, an act that would constitute a breach of trust.

Example: Stephen Adams holds shares of stock in trust for Evelyn Sandberg. According to the terms of the trust agreement, he is not authorized to sell the stock. The value of the stock has recently increased substantially. Stephen intends to sell the stock. Evelyn, on learning of the pending sale, could obtain an injunction from the equity court forbidding the sale by Stephen.

- The beneficiary can trace and recover the trust property that the trustee has wrongfully taken, unless the property has been acquired by a purchaser who, believing the trustee has a right to sell, pays an adequate price and purchases the property without having been informed of the breach of trust (Restatement [Second] of Trusts §§ 202, 284).

Example: In the preceding example, Stephen sells the stock to Jane Brown, who pays full market value for the stock unaware that Stephen has no right to sell the stock or that the stock is trust property. Jane becomes the owner of the stock. Evelyn would not have a right to sue Jane, a good-faith purchaser, but she would have a right to sue Stephen for damages because of his fraud.

- The beneficiary can request the court of equity to remove the trustee for misconduct and to appoint a successor trustee (Restatement [Second] of Trusts §§ 107, 108, 109). The *Witmer v. Blair* case previously discussed illustrates the removal of a trustee for misconduct, i.e., failure to invest the trust property.

Example: Ronald Caster is the trustee, and Vincent Prima is the beneficiary of a trust. The trust agreement gives Ronald the discretion of determining the amount of income from the trust property that Vincent shall receive each year. The amount actually given to Vincent by Ronald causes a great deal of friction between them. Vincent can petition the court to remove Ronald as trustee, but the court will not do so unless Vincent can prove that the hostility causes Ronald to mismanage his trusteeship. By itself, hostility between the trustee and beneficiary is not enough reason for the court to remove the trustee.

- The beneficiary can sue for specific performance to compel the trustee to perform the duties created by the terms of a private trust (Restatement [Second] of Trusts §§ 198, 199).

Example: According to the trust agreement, the trustee, Monica Murphy, is to give the trust property to the beneficiary, Julie Anderson, when she reaches age 21. Six months have passed since Julie's twenty-first birthday, and Monica has not transferred the property. Julie sues Monica in the court of equity for specific performance of the agreement. If Julie proves Monica has violated her duty, Monica must complete the transfer.

- The beneficiary can sue for breach of the trustee's loyalty (Restatement [Second] of Trusts § 206). Breach of loyalty by the trustee includes many things. In general, breach of loyalty is any action by the trustee that upsets the trustee-beneficiary relationship. It results from the trustee's failure to administer the trust solely in the interest of the beneficiary.

Example: By will, Hollis Stately leaves his ranch, Bluelake, to Lavinia Turner in trust for his son, Francis, directing her to sell or exchange Bluelake for investment securities. Lavinia sells Bluelake for $200,000 and uses the money to buy bonds that she owns. Lavinia has breached the duty of loyalty by "self-dealing" with trust money (the proceeds of the sale).

Cost of a Trustee

Trustees perform work for the trust when they buy, sell, invest, and receive income, on behalf of the beneficiary, and they must be paid, although trustees who are family members may decline compensation. The settlor may provide a reasonable fee for the trustee in the trust instrument; if the settlor does not, state statutes fix the amount, or in the absence of such statutes, the courts will fix a reasonable annual compensation. There is an opinion (originating in common law) that the trustee should not make an unreasonable profit from the trust; therefore the actual amount of compensation is usually a small percentage of the trust's annual income and principal set by statute (see N.J. Stat. Ann. § 3B: 18–24, 18–25). In a testamentary trust, the probate court may set the annual fee for a corporate trustee, such as a bank, at an appropriate percentage of the fair market value of the trust estate. In determining whether the fee charged is reasonable, the court considers the size of the estate, the services performed, the time spent, and the results achieved. In a living trust, fees are generally negotiated. State statutes may also set fees in some cases.

The Beneficiary: The Recipient of the Trust Property or Benefits

Every trust must have a beneficiary. In a private trust, the beneficiaries must either be identified by name, description, designation of the class to which the beneficiaries belong, or if no beneficiary is in existence at the time the trust is created (such as a trust for the benefit of unborn children), the trustee must be able to ascertain the identity of the beneficiary within the period of the Rule Against Perpetuities (Restatement [Second] of Trusts § 112). In a charitable trust, however, it is sufficient that the beneficiaries be members of the public at large or a general class of the public (Restatement [Second] of Trusts §§ 122, 123, 364, 375).

To create a private trust, the settlor must name or sufficiently describe a beneficiary or co-beneficiaries, of whom the settlor may herself be one, to receive the equitable interest in the trust property. If the trust instrument describes the beneficiary too vaguely, a court of equity cannot validate the trust. There must be someone to enforce the trust and to ensure that the trustee will faithfully perform the previously mentioned duties. That was the position in the case of *Scotti's Drive In Restaurants, Inc. v. Mile High—Dart In Corp.,* cited earlier, where the court stated: "A trust is an obligation imposed, either expressly or by implication of law, whereby the obligor [trustee] is bound to deal with property over which he has control for the benefit of certain persons [beneficiaries], of whom he may himself be one, and any one of whom may enforce the obligation." Consequently, the beneficiaries of a trust must be specifically identified.

> **Example:** Howard establishes a trust and directs Mary, the trustee, to pay the trust income to "whomever Mary selects" without adequately describing the persons or class of persons from which the selection is to be made. Such a trust is too vague and is invalid.

Any person who is capable of owning property, including infants, insane persons in some states, and public or private corporations, may be a beneficiary in a trust, but incompetents and minors generally require guardians to act as "beneficiaries" for them. Trusts in which aliens, the United States, a state, a municipality, and a foreign country are beneficiaries have been upheld. In sum, the beneficiary may be any entity capable of taking title to property in the manner as a person, whether natural or created by law, e.g., a corporation, state, or nation. It is important to note that the beneficiary of the trust, however, need not have capacity to hold property or to make a contract, since the trustee has legal title to and control of the trust property. Many trusts are created specifically because the beneficiary lacks legal or actual capacity to manage property without assistance.

> **Example:** Martha Kirk places $20,000 in trust for the benefit of the Red Cross. The Red Cross is a "corporate person." It is a definite beneficiary. This trust is as valid as if Martha had created it for the benefit of a natural person.

> **Example:** Giovanna Bonetto belongs to a card club. The members meet once a month to play cards and perform works of charity. She dies and leaves a trust fund to enable the members of the club to continue to carry on their activities. This trust will fail because the card club, as such, is not a "person." The individual members are. Had Giovanna's trust named them individually as beneficiaries, the trust would have been valid.

Although it is required that the beneficiaries be definite, they need not be, and frequently are not, described by name but rather by class designation. Examples of such designation are "my grandchildren" or "my issue," in which cases the identification of the beneficiaries is ascertainable, i.e., capable of being determined (Restatement [Second] of Trusts § 120). Words such as "friends," "family," and "relatives," used to designate beneficiaries, have sometimes caused trusts to fail for lack of definite beneficiaries because such terms have broad and varied application. A trust to benefit "relatives," however, occasionally proves an exception to the rule. A court, construing "relatives" to mean those who would inherit the settlor's property according to the statutes of descent and distribution rather than those who are related to the settlor either closely or remotely by either blood or marriage, would in all likelihood uphold the trust (Restatement [Second] of Trusts § 121). Similarly, interpretation of the word "family" to mean "the settlor's spouse and issue" leads to the same result (Restatement [Second] of Trusts § 120b). Note that this requirement of definiteness of beneficiary for a private trust directly opposes the requirement of indefiniteness of beneficiary for a public (charitable) trust.

Beneficiaries need not always be persons or institutions. As the case *In re Searight's Estate*, 87 Ohio App. 417, 95 N.E.2d 779 (1950), illustrates, placing property "in trust for" the care and benefit of pets, such as dogs or cats, or for the maintenance of pet cemeteries has been declared valid and enforceable because of the social interests that are involved. But compare *In re Estate of Russell*, 69 Cal.2d 200, 70 Cal.Rptr. 561, 444 P.2d 353 (1968).

🏛 ASSIGNMENT 8.10

1. Harding Mulholland lived at the home of his niece, Cecelia, and her husband, Edwin. He provided in his will that a trust be set up for the benefit of his nieces and nephews, Cecelia being the only one of that class at the time. Subsequently, another niece, Teresa, was born, and Cecelia died in the same year. When Harding died, Edwin petitioned the court to set aside the trust, claiming that Harding neither knew nor could have known of the current beneficiary, Teresa. Should the trust fail for lack of a definite beneficiary?

2. Willis Rokeby lives in Bangor, Maine. For five months each year, he visits his daughter in Texarkana. He hires Jacques Santin, a citizen of Canada, to take care of his house in Maine. He pays Jacques a small salary and creates a testamentary trust of the house and surrounding land for Jacques's benefit. After Willis's death, his sister, named trustee in the trust instrument, claims that Jacques cannot be the beneficiary because he is not subject to the laws of either Maine or the United States. Is she correct?

Nature of the Beneficiary's Interest (Restatement [Second] of Trusts § 130)

The length of time the beneficiary holds the equitable interest in the trust property may be limited to a period of years, to the life of the beneficiary or that of someone else, to a condition precedent, to a condition subsequent, or to the nonoccurrence of a specified event.

Example: Patrice Avery sets aside stocks and bonds for living trusts for each of her three children: The first is created for her son, Vinton, on the condition that he return to the family home in West Virginia. This trust is based on a condition precedent.

The second is for her daughter, Susanna, on the condition that she continue to support Patrice as she had been doing. This trust is created on a condition subsequent. The third is for her daughter, Alberta, as long as she continues to study medicine at State University. This trust is created on the nonhappening of a specific event, e.g., Alberta's switching to another course of study or another school.

Note that both Susanna's and Alberta's trusts begin immediately but the possibility of the premature termination of the trusts exists, whereas Vinton's does not begin until he has complied with the condition precedent.

The beneficiary's equitable interest in realty (real property) usually passes on his or her death to the beneficiary's heirs or devisees; personal property passes to the beneficiary's personal representative, e.g., the administrator or executor. Another possible result is that the trust instrument itself may provide that the beneficiary's interest terminates on death, as in the case in which the beneficiary receives a life estate.

A single trust may have more than one beneficiary. Multiple beneficiaries usually hold the property as tenants in common unless the settlor expressly makes the beneficiaries joint tenants or tenants by the entireties. The doctrine of survivorship applies if the co-beneficiaries are joint tenants or tenants by the entireties (Restatement [Second] of Trusts § 113). For example, if Charles and Dennis are co-beneficiaries as joint tenants, and Charles dies, Dennis will then be the sole beneficiary and will own the entire equitable interest in the trust property, just as any joint owner with the right of survivorship succeeds to full ownership upon the death of the other joint owner.

The beneficiary of a trust is free to transfer the interest in trust property by mortgage or devise, in the absence of any restriction imposed by statute or by the terms of the trust, to the same extent that a person who holds both equitable and legal titles is free to do so (Restatement [Second] of Trusts § 132). In some states, all transfers of beneficial interests must be in writing and signed by the beneficiary; in other states, this requirement applies only to the transfer of real property (Restatement [Second] of Trusts § 139).

Unless prohibited by statute or the trust agreement, beneficiaries may ordinarily transfer their interest in a trust by an assignment. This legal transaction allows the beneficiary to transfer to another the benefits of the trust. This may be done to make a gift of the trust benefits or to pay the beneficiary's debts.

Example: Greg receives an income as a beneficiary of a trust. He assigns his interest (transfers his right to receive income) to June. Thereafter, June receives the income from the trust.

Creditors may attach the beneficiary's equitable interest in trust property unless statutes or trust provisions exempt the interest from creditors' claims (Restatement [Second] of Trusts § 147). If statutes exempt a legal interest from creditors' claims, a corresponding equitable interest of a beneficiary in trust property is also exempt, e.g., homestead exemptions (which apply to both legal and equitable interests). The method by which a creditor reaches an equitable interest varies from state to state. The only remedy in some states is a creditor's bill in chancery (equity) in which the creditor commences the lawsuit in an equity court. In other states, the equitable interest is subject to execution, attachment, and garnishment by the beneficiary's creditors just as if it were a legal interest. An exception occurs when the settlor has restricted the trust so that the beneficiary cannot assign nor creditors reach the equitable interest of the beneficiary; such a trust is commonly called a spendthrift trust (see the discussion in Chapter 9).

Trust Property

The trust property is the property interest that is transferred to the trustee to hold for the benefit of another. It is sometimes called the *res, corpus, principal,* or *subject matter* of the trust. Any transferable interest in an object of ownership may become trust property. This includes ownership of real or personal property. Thus, a fee simple estate in land, a co-owner's interest (joint tenants, tenants in common, and the like), a mortgage, a life estate in land, a right to remove coal, a business interest, promissory notes, bonds or shares of stock (securities), a trade secret, copyright, patent, or cash could serve as trust property. Examples of nontransferable property are government pensions, existing spendthrift trusts, or tort claims for wrongful injury, i.e., the victim's right to sue a negligent party for personal injury. Nontransferable property interests may not be the subject matter of a trust.

A trust involving the transfer of personal property only may be created orally, but a settlor transferring title to real property to a trust must comply with the state statute, i.e., the Statute of Frauds, requiring a written agreement establishing the details of the trust. The latter requirement is designed to prevent fraud and perjury (see further discussion below). The court in *State ex rel. Wirt v. Superior Court for Spokane County,* 10 Wash.2d 362, 116 P.2d 752 (1941), expressed this principle when it ruled: "It has become the settled law of this state, in harmony with the general accepted rule in this country, that an express trust in real property cannot rest in parol [oral evidence], but must be evidenced in writing." See also the *Mahoney* case, cited earlier, where the court stated that a "trust involving only personal property may be instituted [commenced] without being reduced to writing." The terms of the written trust agreement as designated by the settlor must include the purpose of the trust, the length of time the trust will last, and a description and conveyance of the trust property. It must also include the names of the trustee and beneficiary, and the powers, duties, and rights of such parties, including how much the beneficiaries are to receive, and when they will receive it. It is not necessary to use a particular form or particular language to frame the trust as long as the settlor makes these elements clear.

Statute of Frauds
State laws which provide that no lawsuit or civil action shall be maintained on certain classes of oral contracts unless the agreement is put in writing in a note or memorandum and signed by the party to be charged, i.e., the person being sued, or an authorized agent of the person.

 ASSIGNMENT 8.11

Read the Carter trust (see Exhibit 8.2) and determine whether the requirements in the preceding two paragraphs have been met.

The English **Statute of Frauds** was enacted in 1677 to prevent fraud and perjury between sellers and buyers by requiring certain kinds of contracts to be written. Its American counterparts, drawn chiefly from sections 4 and 17 of the original statute, demand that a written contract, signed by the parties, be used in certain transactions. If the trust property transferred into an *inter vivos* (living) trust is an interest in land, the Statute of Frauds requires that, if it is to be enforced, it must be written, signed, and include the essential elements of a trust (Restatement [Second] of Trusts, § 40). Many states have enacted statutes that require certain trusts to be written to be valid. North Dakota is an example.

> *N.D. Cent. Code § 59–03–03* Requisites of Trust Relating to Real Property
> No trust in relation to real property is valid unless created or declared:
>   1. By a written instrument, subscribed by the trustee or by the trustee's agent thereto authorized in writing;
>   2. By the instrument under which the trustee claims the estate affected; or
>   3. By operation of law.

In addition to requiring a written agreement whenever land is transferred in trust, the method of transfer is also strictly regulated. Land must be transferred by specific legal documents, e.g., either a deed or a will. Personal property, on the other hand, may be simply delivered to the trustee.

> **Example:** Sharon signed a trust agreement transferring title to Greenvale, a country home, to Susan in trust for the benefit of Thomas. Sharon executed and delivered the deed to Greenvale to Susan. Sharon and Susan are parties to a trust agreement. Sharon is the grantor. Susan is the trustee and holds the legal title that she received from Sharon. Thomas is the beneficiary (*cestui que trust*) of the agreement and holds equitable title.

The agreement satisfies the state Statute of Frauds because it is written. It also complies with requirements for trusts of this nature, i.e., trusts to which real property is transferred, and is therefore enforceable.

🏛 ASSIGNMENT 8.12

Simon Rothstein executes a trust instrument with the Third National Bank, placing his lakeshore property in trust for the benefit of his nephew, Norman. However, Norman is unaware of the trust. Simon dies one year later. His widow, Evelyn, contends that the trust is not valid because it was not signed by Norman. Norman contends that it is valid. Who is right?

As noted above, the trust instrument must either specifically describe the trust property or clearly define the manner to be followed in identifying it. The validity of a trust depends on its enforceability. If a court is to enforce a trust, the trust property must be *in existence* (i.e., definite and certain on the *date* the trust is created, or definitely ascertainable) and *owned* by the settlor.

> **Example:** Mary Holland is an investor and collector of art. If Mary attempts to create a trust by declaring herself trustee of the next work of art she buys, no trust is created, because the trust property is neither specifically identifiable nor owned and in existence at the time of the trust creation.

On the other hand, a testamentary trust created in the "residue of the decedent's estate" *is* valid, even though the exact amount of the residue cannot be determined until the decedent's assets and liabilities are known. In this case, the facts needed to specifically identify the amount of the residue do exist on the date the trust is created, i.e., the date of the testator's death.

Example: In a living trust instrument, Alicia Schell states, "I give to Joan Warfield, to hold and to manage, the amount of my savings and checking accounts for the benefit of Roberta Polenek." This instrument creates a valid trust. The trust corpus is not stated, but it is ascertainable. It is the amount of money in Alicia's checking and savings accounts on the date of the trust instrument's execution.

The fact that trust property may change from time to time during the trust period does not make the trust void.

Example: Alex Knight, trustee of real estate for the benefit of Letita Kruse, has the power of sale and reinvestment. He sells part of the land for cash and deposits this cash in the Citizens Bank. He buys bonds for the trust and pays for them by drawing a check on the Citizens Bank. He has effected three changes in the trust property—real estate into cash, cash into a claim on the bank (i.e., a right to withdraw the amount deposited), and the claim on the bank into bonds. The trust property has changed, but the trust is still valid.

TERMINATION OF TRUSTS

A trust may be terminated in the following ways:

- In accordance with the trust's terms (Restatement [Second] of Trusts §§ 330, 334).

Example: Sarah gives Roberta $100,000 to hold and invest in trust for Katherine and to pay the income produced to Katherine annually for ten years. At the end of the ten years, the trust terminates.

- By the completion of the trust's valid purpose (Restatement [Second] of Trusts § 337).

Example: Sarah gives Roberta $100,000 to hold and invest and to pay the income produced to Sarah's mother annually for her lifetime and then return the trust property to Sarah. When Sarah's mother dies and the property is returned, the trust purpose is accomplished.

- By revocation by the settlor when allowed by the terms of the trust (Restatement [Second] of Trusts § 330).

Example: Sarah creates a trust which includes a provision that states, "This trust is revocable and the settlor reserves the right to amend or revoke the trust in whole or in part at any time." The trust will terminate if Sarah chooses to revoke it.

- By merger of all interests (legal and equitable) in the same person (Restatement [Second] of Trusts §§ 337, 341).

Example: Sarah creates a trust in which she names herself trustee and names Roberta and herself the beneficiaries. Roberta dies, and Sarah now holds both the legal and equitable titles to the trust property by herself. Since the titles have merged in one person, the trust terminates.

- On the request of all the beneficiaries when there is no express purpose that requires continuation of the trust (Restatement [Second] of Trusts § 337).

The majority of U.S. courts holds that if one or more of the settlor's purposes for creating the trust can still be achieved by the continuance of the trust, the court will not allow termination unless all beneficiaries join in the request for termination with the settlor. When a trust does terminate, the trustee must also account for all assets and obtain a receipt and release from the recipients. But, remember, a trust does not terminate for want of a trustee.

KEY TERMS

Trust agreement	Irrevocable trust	Conflict of interest	Stock split
Declaration of trust	Disclaimer	Stock dividend	Statute of Frauds
Revocable trust			

REVIEW QUESTIONS

1. What is meant by the following statement: "The most unique feature of a trust is that a trust splits title to property." Explain.
2. In trust law, what is the difference between legal and equitable title?
3. In what ways can a trust be created?
4. What are the essential elements of a valid trust?
5. What are the qualifications required for a person to become a settlor, the creator of a trust?
6. Why would a settlor create a revocable trust, and what are the advantages of making the trust irrevocable?
7. What are the standard powers and duties of a trustee who, like a personal representative, is a fiduciary?
8. What are the beneficiary's rights for breach of trust by a trustee? Explain.
9. Must a person have contractual capacity to be a beneficiary of a trust? Explain.
10. May a settlor be the sole trustee and sole beneficiary of a trust? Explain.
11. Does a trust always have to be in writing? Explain.
12. Are there any limits on the kind of property that can be placed in trust? Explain.
13. How are trusts terminated?

CASE PROBLEMS

Problem 1

Suki Nakajima, a widow in failing health, intends to leave her estate equally to her adult children, a daughter, Tomoko, and a son, Hito. Suki has two concerns. With good reason, she lacks confidence that Hito can manage property because of his irresponsible spending habits, and she does not want any property she gives to Tomoko to pass to Tomoko's husband. Suki writes, but does not sign, a letter to her best friend, Tomura, requesting that he manage money for the benefit of her two children, and asking him, if he agrees, to sign and return the letter. After receiving the letter back from Tomura with his signature and acceptance, Suki mails a cashier's check for $200,000 to Tomura. Answer and explain the following:

A. Is Suki's letter a valid holographic will?
B. Is the use of the words "trust" or "trustee" in a formal written document necessary to create a valid trust?

C. Does Suki's letter create an *inter vivos* (living) trust? See *In re Barker's Estate,* 82 Misc.2d 974, 370 N.Y.S.2d 404 (1975).
D. *If* a trust exists, must it be written and signed to be valid?

Problem 2

In a testamentary trust, Alanzo Lopez names his friend, Ricardo LaPalma, trustee of substantial property placed in trust for the benefit of Alanzo's wife, Maria, and his sister, Yolanda. Hostility existed between Ricardo and Maria long before the trust was created, and it became worse soon after Alanzo's death when the trust became active. Alanzo gave Ricardo broad discretion in distributing trust income, and when Ricardo distributed a much greater percentage of the trust's annual income to Yolanda than to Maria, Maria became outraged. She demanded that Ricardo be removed as an unsuitable trustee because of his act of disloyalty by favoring one beneficiary over another.

   A. Is hostility between a trustee and beneficiary a valid reason for the removal of a trustee?

   B. If there were five beneficiaries in the trust and three were pleased with the trustee's actions and two were incensed and wanted the trustee removed, should the "majority rule" apply to this decision?

   C. Read and compare the following cases: *Matter of Brecklein's Estate,* 6 Kan.App.2d 1001, 637 P.2d 444 (1981) and *Edinburg v. Cavers,* 22 Mass. App. Ct. 212, 492 N.E.2d 1171 (1986). What are the circumstances a court should consider before deciding a request for removal of a trustee based on hostility between the trustee and a beneficiary?

Note

1. *For the Restatements:* © 1959 and 1992 by The American Law Institute. Reprinted with permission.

CLASSIFICATION OF TRUSTS, THE LIVING TRUST, AND OTHER SPECIAL TRUSTS

OUTLINE

OBJECTIVES

After completing this chapter, you should be able to:

➤ Identify and define the classes of trusts.

➤ Explain the uses and functions of the various kinds of trusts.

➤ Explain the formation, use, advantages, and disadvantages of revocable and irrevocable living trusts.

➤ Identify and explain the function of Totten, spendthrift, and sprinkling trusts and a pour-over will.

➤ Prepare preliminary drafts of private express trusts including living trusts.

➤ Avoid common errors in the initial drafts of living trusts.

SCOPE OF THE CHAPTER

This chapter identifies and discusses the various kinds of trusts which include the increasingly popular living *(inter vivos)* trust. The chapter begins with the classification of trusts, followed by an examination of a private express trust including various examples that eventually lead to a detailed discussion of the living trust. The chapter outlines the steps necessary for drafting trusts including the accumulation of data through appropriate checklists. Actual drafts of these trusts and a pour-over will are also contained in the chapter.

CLASSIFICATION OF TRUSTS

Express trust
A trust created or declared in explicit terms for specific purposes by a written document (deed or will) or an oral declaration.

All trusts may be divided into two major categories, express and implied. An **express trust** is created or declared in explicit terms for specific purposes and is represented by a written document (deed or will) or an oral declaration. A simple statement that a settlor intends to hold property in trust for another creates a trust by declaration. No special words, such as *trust* or *trustee,* are required to create an express trust, provided the intent of the settlor to establish the trust is clear. In most jurisdictions, as previously mentioned, an express trust of real property *must be in writing* to meet the requirements of the Statute of Frauds.

Depending on the purpose for which they are created, express trusts fall into the following subcategories: (1) private or public (charitable) trusts; (2) active or passive trusts; or (3) *inter vivos* (living) or testamentary trusts. The most common types of express trusts are the testamentary and living trusts. The living trust is one of the major topics of this chapter.

Implied trust
A trust created by operation of law or the equity court based on the implied or presumed intent of the person who holds legal title and, generally, to prevent fraud.

Implied trusts are created not by the settlor's expressed terms but by the implied or presumed intent of the person holding legal title or by a decree (order) of the equity court generally to prevent fraud. Implied trusts are either resulting trusts or constructive trusts (see Exhibit 9.1).

Express Trusts—Private versus Public (Charitable)

Private Trust
A *private trust* is created expressly (orally or in writing) between a person who has the power to be a settlor and one or more trustees who hold legal title to trust property for the financial benefit of a certain named beneficiary or beneficiaries. The essential elements of an express private trust are as follows:

- The settlor must intend to create a private trust.
- A trustee must be named to administer the trust.
- A beneficiary must be named to enforce the trust.
- The settlor must transfer sufficiently identified property to the trust.

The court in *City Bank Farmers' Trust Co. v. Charity Organization Society,* 238 App.Div. 720, 265 N.Y.S. 267 (1933), upheld these elements as being essential for a private trust.

Exhibit 9.1 Classification of Trusts

Example: Loraine Katz owns a one-third interest in a boutique. In her will she gives the interest to her nephew, David, to hold and manage in trust for the benefit of her niece, Tracy. Loraine, the owner of the interest, is the settlor. David, to whom she conveys the legal title to the one-third interest, is the trustee. Tracy, who is to receive the benefit of the interest (i.e., one-third of the profits of the boutique), is the beneficiary. This is a private (for benefit of a person), express (written), and testamentary (established by will) trust.

🏛 ASSIGNMENT 9.1

Sidney Benchman transfers (assigns) the royalties to his book, to which he holds the copyright, to his business adviser, Martin Lorenz, to hold and invest for the benefit of Martitia Hughes.
1. Does the settlor intend to create a trust?
2. Is there a trustee to administer the trust?
3. Is trust property included in the instrument?
4. Is there a beneficiary or *cestui que trust*?

Public Trust

A *public* or *charitable trust* is an express trust established for the purpose of accomplishing social benefit for the public or the community (Restatement [Second] of Trusts §§ 348, 349). Although charitable trusts are public trusts, the beneficiary of the trust does not have to be the *general* public. The trust fund, however, must be designated either for the benefit of the general public, e.g., a charitable trust that benefits a hospital, *or* a reasonably large, **indefinite class** of persons within the public who may be personally unknown to the settlor, e.g., a charitable trust that benefits the deaf in a certain city (Restatement [Second] of Trusts §§ 362, 364, 368–374). If the terms of the trust limit the distribution of its fund to named individuals rather than to an indefinite class of persons, the trust will not be classified as public. Instead, it would be a private trust. In the majority of states, the true test for creation of a valid public trust is not the indefiniteness of the persons aided

Indefinite class
A group of persons within the public whose number is not specified and are unknown to the settlor of the trust.

by the trust but rather the amount of social benefit given to the public (Restatement [Second] of Trusts § 375). Also, the purpose of the charitable trust must not include profit-making by the settlor, trustee, or other persons (Restatement [Second] of Trusts § 376). Therefore, the essential elements of an express public (charitable) trust are as follows:

- The settlor must intend to create a public trust.
- A trustee must be named to administer the trust.
- Property must be transferred to the trust.
- A charitable purpose must be expressly designated.
- The general public must be benefited, or
- An indefinite class of persons must be named beneficiaries.

Examples of charitable trusts that advance the public welfare are trusts created to maintain or propagate religion, religious education, and missionary work (see *In re Dobbins' Will,* 206 Misc. 64, 132 N.Y.S.2d 236 [1953]); further health and relieve poverty and human suffering by the establishment of health care clinics and other institutions, fund scientific research into the causes of numerous diseases, and provide direct aid of food, clothing, shelter, and medical care to the needy; found or maintain educational institutions, art galleries, museums, or libraries (see *In re Tiffany's Estate,* 157 Misc. 873, 285 N.Y.S. 971 [1935]); aid students or teachers; care for and maintain public cemeteries; erect monuments to public figures or national heroes; construct and maintain public buildings or improvements, such as an irrigation system or a playground; further patriotism; conserve natural resources and scenery; and prevent cruelty to animals.

> **Example:** Agnes Swanson died testate, providing in her will, "I give State University $100,000 to provide scholarships for single mothers who major in the field of nurse's training." In the absence of other evidence, an express, testamentary, charitable trust is created.

Agnes is the settlor, State University is the trustee, and "single mothers who major in nurse's training" are the beneficiaries. The $100,000 is the trust property. Agnes intended to create a public or charitable trust, which she expressed in her will. The class of persons to be benefited is smaller than "the general public" but sufficiently large and indefinite enough to enable the trust to be classified as public. For example, Sheila Johnson, a single mother, decides to major in nurse's training a year after Agnes dies; therefore, Agnes could not have named Sheila a beneficiary. Sheila was not a member of the class to be benefited when Agnes made her will, but now she qualifies. She and others in the same situation are indefinite beneficiaries.

The mere fact the purpose of a trust is to give money to others does not make it a charitable trust. The settlor of a charitable trust must describe a purpose that is of substantial public benefit.

ASSIGNMENT 9.2

Mark Nelson gives $100,000 to Luke Mellows to be distributed as Luke feels is appropriate for the support of orphans living in South Dakota.
1. Did the settlor intend to create a trust?
2. Is there a trustee to administer the trust?

3. Is trust res (property) included?
4. Is a charitable purpose expressly designated?
5. Will the general public be benefited?
6. Are there indefinite beneficiaries within a definite class who are the persons who actually receive the benefit?

Public Trust—*Cy-pres* Doctrine

Where it is clear the donor intended a private trust to be performed exactly as indicated or not at all, the trust fails (terminates) when it is not possible to follow such direction. However, in the absence of this clear intent by the donor in the trust agreement, the law will *not* permit a *public charitable* trust to end (fail) even though the beneficiary no longer exists or the original purpose has been accomplished or can no longer be achieved. Instead, the courts will apply the doctrine of **cy-pres** (an abbreviation of the French words *cy pres comme possible* or "as near as possible") (Restatement [Second] of Trusts § 399), which is applicable only to public (charitable) trusts. In practice, the **cy-pres doctrine** means that where a settlor makes a gift to charity or for a charitable purpose and it subsequently becomes impossible or impractical to apply the gift to that particular charity, the equity court may order the gift applied to another charity "as near as possible" to the one designated by the settlor.

> **Example:** Etta Barranger establishes a trust fund to provide relief to victims who suffer from a particular kidney disease. Later, an inventor creates a kidney machine that alleviates the problem. In order to continue the trust, it is necessary for the court to apply the *cy-pres* doctrine by the substitution of another charity whose purpose corresponds "as near as possible" to Etta's original motives for the trust. For example, the court might apply the trust principal to a charity that aids the victims of a liver ailment.

The rationale behind the application of *cy-pres* is that the law desires to continue the operation of charitable trusts in order to avoid the termination of public benefits. If a charitable trust fails for lack of foresight on the part of its settlor or simply due to modern-day advances in medical science and technology, a court will review the settlor's intended use of the trust and, if possible, transfer the trust fund to a charity with a more viable use which approximates the intent. The courts are anxious for the public to receive the benefits. For the doctrine to be applied to a charitable trust, however, the settlor's intent must be broad and general and not restricted to one specific objective or to one particular method of accomplishing the purpose of the trust.

> **Example:** Through his will, Elmer Wilson gives the National Polio Foundation $500,000. Dr. Salk discovers a vaccine that prevents polio. Elmer's heirs ask the court to distribute the money to them now that the disease is preventable. Instead, the court of equity would apply the *cy-pres* doctrine and transfer the balance of the funds to a charity as near as possible to the testator's (Elmer's) wishes, e.g., the court may give the money to the National Crippled Children's Foundation.

The case of *In re Bletsch's Estate,* 25 Wis.2d 40, 130 N.W.2d 275 (1964), illustrates the use of the *cy-pres* doctrine. The testator, Jack Bletsch, left his entire estate to his wife and daughter if they survived him, but if they did not, he left his estate to the Masonic Home for Crippled Children in Illinois. Both his wife and

Cy-pres
As near as possible

Cy-pres doctrine
The equity court may order a gift intended for a charity, or for a charitable purpose, that is now nonexistent be given or applied to another charity whose purpose is as near as possible to the one originally chosen by the settlor.

daughter predeceased Jack, but there was no Masonic Home for Crippled Children in Illinois. However, there was a Shriner's Hospital for Crippled Children in Illinois. The Wisconsin court ruled the hospital was "... an identifiable beneficiary whose charitable or public program and goals are reasonably close to those expressed by the testator." The estate passed to the Shriner's Hospital, because the *cy-pres* doctrine was applied and upheld by the court.

Express Trusts—Active versus Passive

Active trust
A trust in which a trustee performs active duties of management for the benefit of the beneficiary.

Passive trust
A trust in which the trustee has no active duties to perform.

The features that distinguish *active trusts* from *passive trusts* are the obligations of management and administration that active trusts impose on the trustee. An **active trust** is an express trust which can be either private or public (charitable). A settlor who desires to create an express private active trust must give oral or written affirmative powers and duties to a trustee to perform discretionary acts of management or administration for the benefit of named beneficiaries.

In contrast, in a **passive trust,** the trustee does not have responsibilities or discretionary duties to perform; in fact, a passive trust often involves no administrative duties at all. The trustee of a passive trust merely holds the trust property for the beneficiary with no obligations or administrative powers. Implied trusts, such as resulting and constructive trusts, are passive trusts. Modern-day passive trusts stem from the failure of the settlor to create an active trust, either accidentally, e.g., through a poor choice of words in the trust instrument, or deliberately, e.g., an attempt to evade the law for the settlor's own fraudulent purposes. To avoid accidentally creating a passive trust, the drafter must properly designate the active functions or duties of the trustee. The following example illustrates a trust declared passive by the equity court.

> **Example:** Silvia appoints Arnold trustee of securities for the benefit of Harriet but neglects to give him duties to perform. Silvia dies. Legal title to the securities would normally pass to Arnold, but instead, under these circumstances, it passes directly to Harriet who holds equitable title as well. Since the legal and equitable titles are held by one person, no trust is created.

Additional examples involving resulting and constructive trusts are discussed below.

▥ ASSIGNMENT 9.3

Neal Sanderson owns a farm, Springlake, which he conveys by deed to Rudolf Meyerling for the benefit of Barbara Jacoby. Neal directs Rudolf to rent the land to tenants and to use part of the income produced thereby to pay taxes and to apply the remainder for Barbara's benefit at his own discretion. Answer the following and compare your answers with the statements in the next paragraph:
1. Is the trust express or implied?
2. Is the trust private or public?
3. Are there administrative duties that the trustee must perform?
4. Is the trust active or passive?

This trust is a private express trust. Neal Sanderson, the settlor, conveyed his farm, the trust property, to Rudolf Meyerling, the trustee. Barbara Jacoby is the beneficiary. The trust is active because Rudolf has the duties of renting the farm, collecting income (rent), paying taxes, and paying the remainder of the income to Barbara.

Express Trusts—*Inter Vivos (Living)* versus Testamentary

The most common types of express trusts are living trusts and testamentary trusts. Both *inter vivos (living) trusts* (Restatement [Second] of Trusts §§ 17, 31) and *testamentary trusts* (Restatement [Second] of Trusts §§ 33, 54) refer to express trusts either private or public in nature. As the generic names of these trusts imply, they are created at different times in the settlor's life: *inter vivos* (pertaining to a gift in trust made "between living persons" and hereafter called living trusts) and testamentary (pertaining to a gift in trust made after death as a testament, i.e., as part of a last will). In the event of a question of whether a trust is living or testamentary, the criterion will be the time at which the trust became effective. If a settlor wishes to see how well the trust operates while she is alive, a living trust should be established. Otherwise the living trust differs little from the testamentary trust. Both types of trusts are widely employed as a means of conserving property for the benefit of a surviving spouse and children or for the child or children of a single parent. *Note:* The testamentary trust is probated; the living trust is not.

🏛 ASSIGNMENT 9.4

Herb gives Janet $40,000 to be distributed as she sees fit for the benefit of poor Amish children in Kentucky between the ages of 6 and 12. Determine whether the essential elements of an express, active, living, public trust are present:
1. Does the settlor intend to create a trust?
2. Is there a trustee to administer the trust?
3. Is trust res included?
4. Is a charitable purpose expressly designated?
5. Is the general public benefited?
6. Are there indefinite beneficiaries within a definite class who are the persons who actually receive the benefit?

The **Rule Against Perpetuities,** a common law rule that originated in England, affects the validity and duration of *all private noncharitable trusts.* The rule places a term (time limitation) on how long a private noncharitable trust may exist. The rule regulates the creation of future interests in trusts and holds that to be valid, an interest in property must vest (take effect); that is, some future beneficiary must get full and unrestricted possession and control over the property, no later than 21 years, plus the period of gestation, after some life or lives in being (a living person or persons) at the time of the creation of the interest. The word vest referred to above creates an immediate interest, not an immediate possession. A future interest may vest in interest long before it vests in possession.

The Rule Against Perpetuities has an important bearing on testamentary trusts that prevents testator-settlors from controlling property long after they are dead. Since public policy, as enunciated in the rule, opposes the accumulation and monopolization of property and income over many generations, the maker of a will may not create a trust that lasts longer than 21 years together with the period of gestation after the life of a named living person. The life of such a person is referred to as a "life in being" when the trust is created. To illustrate: A settlor of property currently without children cannot create a testamentary trust for grandchildren (children's children, neither of which class is yet born), since there is no "life in being" at the time of the creation of the trust. The trust is void

Rule Against Perpetuities
The principle that no interest in property is good (valid) unless it must vest (take effect), if at all, not later than 21 years, plus the period of gestation, after some life or lives in being at the time of the creation of the interest. The rule fixes the time within which a future interest must vest. The period of gestation is included to cover cases of posthumous birth.

because of the rule. On the other hand, if the settlor were to create a trust leaving property at death in trust to a daughter now living—the "life in being"—and on her death to the daughter's children, the trust would be legal since the duration of the trust would be measured by the life of the daughter. The trust terminates no later than 21 years after her death, at which time her child or children would receive the trust property. If the daughter were to die childless, the trust property would revert (return) immediately to the settlor or the settlor's beneficiaries or heirs.

> **Example:** In her will, Lashandra creates a trust to pay the income to her husband, Rashad, for life, and then to pay the income to her two children, Kendra and Kirby, for their lives, and on the death of the last child, to pay the principal to her grandchildren. Lashandra dies survived by her husband and children. This trust does not violate the rule and is valid.

Most states have enacted the rule into statutory law, but some states have modified it to inquire whether the gift did in fact vest within the time period. If it did vest, the gift is upheld (valid).

The following Iowa law exemplifies state statutes on the Rule Against Perpetuities:

> *Iowa Code Ann. § 558.68* Perpetuities
> 1. A nonvested interest in property is not valid unless it must vest, if at all, within twenty-one years after one or more lives in being at the creation of the interest and any relevant period of gestation.

A sample clause in a will which contains the rule is the following:

> All the remainder of my estate, I give to the Fourth Western Bank to hold in trust, invest, reinvest, and distribute the net income accruing from the date of my death, for the benefit of my son, Jeremy, for life, and the remainder to such child or children of him who reach the age of 18 years.

To avoid a violation of the Rule Against Perpetuities when a will is drafted is difficult, as evidenced by the great number of lawsuits brought by persons who allege certain trust provisions violate the rule. For this reason, you must go over the perpetuities statute of the state where the trust is to take effect in detail to ensure the trust harmonizes with it.

The above-quoted Iowa statute, for example, holds the effective term of a trust to be the remaining length of the lives of persons named in the instrument, plus 21 years, plus nine months (the "usual period of gestation"—this provision provides for persons not yet born at the time of the trust execution). The trust set up in the sample clause could last for the rest of the life of Jeremy (the life in being) and continue for 21 years and nine months. The clause falls within the limits set by the Rule Against Perpetuities.

Note: Since the rule does not affect charitable trusts, such trusts have an unlimited duration.

⚖ ASSIGNMENT 9.5

What is the Rule Against Perpetuities and does it affect both private and public trusts?

Implied Trusts—Resulting and Constructive

The second major category in the classification of trusts is the *implied trust,* subdivided into *resulting trusts* and *constructive trusts.* Both types of implied trusts are also passive trusts. Implied trusts are trusts imposed on property by the equity courts when trust intent is lacking. Such trusts, also known as involuntary trusts, are said to be created by "operation of law." Unlike express trusts, implied trusts have no named settlor. The settlor who creates an express trust does so with intent, even though the details (i.e., the language of the trust instrument or identities of the trustee or beneficiaries) might be vague enough to require court interpretation. It is impossible, however, for any person in the capacity of settlor to create an implied trust since they, by definition, are involuntary trusts imposed by the equity court.

Resulting Trusts

A **resulting trust** is created by operation of law under circumstances in which one person becomes the possessor or holder of property with the legal title but is obligated by the equity court to hold "in trust" the title and property for another person's benefit even though there is no stated declaration to create a trust and fraud is not involved. The argument for the creation or use of the resulting trust is that property is always held for the *true owner.* Frequently, the courts use a resulting trust to settle legal disputes. There are three common situations in which implied, resulting trusts are created.

Situation One. *The purchase-money resulting trust.* When one person pays for land or personal property, but the legal title of the property is conveyed to another person, the law presumes that a resulting trust, called a **purchase-money resulting trust,** has been created for the benefit of the person who paid the money. That person receives equitable title to the property. The person to whom the property was conveyed, i.e., the holder of legal title to the property, is considered the trustee (Restatement [Second] of Trusts § 440).

Since a purchase-money resulting trust is created by implication and operation of law, it need not be in writing. However, if there is a conflict later, it may be difficult to prove whether the conveyor intended to make a gift to the alleged trustee instead of allowing a resulting trust to be created by implication.

Generally, courts require clear and convincing proof to establish a resulting trust. The evidence must be strong and unmistakable, and the burden of proof rests on the party who seeks to establish the trust. To establish proof, the court allows **parol evidence,** i.e., oral testimony or written evidence, to be used in these cases. Although a person who makes a gratuitous conveyance most likely intends to make a gift, the grounds for the court's presumption that a purchase-money resulting trust is created are that a person who furnishes consideration, pays for a conveyance to another, probably does so for reasons other than a gift. The person may intend to facilitate resale of the property, repay a debt, obtain services of management from the transferee, or seek to avoid creditors. Due to these difficulties and uncertainties, several states have abolished or modified purchase-money resulting trusts by statute.

> **Example:** Aron Samuels, age 75, buys 500 shares of Honeywell, Inc., stock with money that he needs to live. He instructs the corporation's agent to issue the certificates in the name of Miriam Slater. Miriam is not related by blood or marriage to Aron.

Resulting trust
A trust created by operation of law from circumstances implied from the intentions of the parties that the person who holds legal title is obligated to hold it "in trust" for another person's benefit, even though there is no stated intention to create a trust and no fraud is involved. Resulting trusts often occur when an attempt to create a valid express trust fails for lack of one or more of the essential elements.

Purchase-money resulting trust
A resulting trust in which property is purchased and paid for by one person, and at his direction, the seller transfers possession and title to another person.

Parol evidence
Oral testimony or written evidence.

In the absence of further evidence, Miriam holds the shares as trustee in a *resulting trust* for Aron.

Situation Two.   *The failed trust.* When a settlor creates a private express trust gratuitously (without requiring payment of the beneficiary) and the trust fails or is declared void for any reason except that it has an illegal objective, a resulting trust arises for the benefit of the settlor or the settlor's successors (Restatement [Second] of Trusts § 411). In other words, the trust arrangement no longer exists, but the trust property does, and so does the problem of disposing of it. Should the settlor be allowed to recover the property? In general, the law considers such recovery to be the only fair solution. However, if the court rules the private express trust was created for an illegal purpose, it generally does not decree (order) a resulting trust for the benefit of the settlor but instead declares the trust void. In such cases, the settlor of an illegal trust is generally not allowed to recover the trust property from the trustee since equity discourages such transactions and will not be a party to their enforcement.

Example: Perrin Williams conveys his farm, Oakburne, by deed to Lee Hunter in trust for Stephen Grant. Unknown to Perrin, Stephen is dead at the time of the conveyance. The trust property now reverts to Perrin, but until Perrin takes possession of it, Lee holds Oakburne in a resulting trust for Perrin.

A resulting trust also arises when a charitable trust fails in an instance where the court cannot apply the *cy-pres* doctrine. The trust property is held by the trustee for the benefit of the original settlor or the settlor's successors.

🏛 ASSIGNMENT 9.6

Allen Greenfield gratuitously transfers by deed his lakeshore cottage to Patricia Williams in trust for the benefit of Allen's son. Unknown to Patricia, Allen makes the transfer to avoid claims of his creditors. The creditors seek to have the trust set aside so they can attach the property in payment of their claims. Patricia agrees the trust should be declared void because of its illegal purpose, but she claims, as an innocent party, she should be entitled to keep the property since equity should not return it to the fraudulent settlor. Who wins? Answer the question according to the laws of your state.

Situation Three.   *The excessive endowment trust.* When the property of a private express trust exceeds what is needed for the purpose intended by the settlor, or some part of the trust property remains after the trust has ended, the court may establish a resulting trust for the benefit of the settlor or the settlor's successors (Restatement [Second] of Trusts § 430).

Example: Regina Andrews provides in her will "I give my shares of Highly Successful, Inc., stock to Harriet Backer in trust to pay the income to Timothy Collins for life." The will does not mention who will receive the remainder. After Timothy dies, there is a resulting trust for Regina's successors of the remaining principal in the trust fund.

🏛 ASSIGNMENT 9.7

In 2000, Eustacia gives by deed all the land she owns in Pike County to the Westside State Bank for the benefit of her children and grandchildren. Her children, Daniel and Dorothy, die in 2001 without children or wills. Two months later, Eustacia dies.

1. What kind of trust, if any, did Eustacia create in 2000?
2. What kind of trust, if any, is formed in 2001?
3. Dorothy's cousin, Laverne, claims the land because she is Dorothy's next of kin. Is she entitled to it?
4. Who receives the equitable and the legal titles, respectively?

Constructive Trusts

A **constructive trust** is *not* created by written agreement or the stated intent of the settlor. That is an express trust. Nor is a constructive trust created by the implied or presumed intent of a property holder of legal title whose acts cause the equity court to enforce a trust established by operation of law. That is a resulting trust. The point of similarity between a constructive trust and a resulting trust is that both are implied, passive trusts. Resulting trusts arise by implication of law or by an equity court decree that declares the property holder to be a trustee either as a result of implied intent or because of presumed intent of the parties based on the consequences of their acts. Constructive trusts are not based on express or even implied or presumed intent. A constructive trust is exclusively a creation of the equity court and is established for the purpose of rectifying a serious wrong such as fraud, duress, unconscionable conduct, or preventing unjust enrichment of the wrongdoer.

Constructive trust
An involuntary trust created by operation of law to recover property from a person who has improperly obtained possession of or legal rights to property by fraud, duress, abuse of confidence, or other unconscionable conduct.

Case One. In the case of *Beatty v. Guggenheim Exploration Co.,* 225 N.Y. 380, 122 N.E. 378 (1919), Supreme Court Justice Cardozo identified a constructive trust as "the formula through which the conscience of equity finds expression. When property has been acquired in such circumstances that the holder of the legal title may not in good conscience retain the beneficial interest, equity converts him into a trustee" [of a constructive trust].

When a person has acquired title to property by unlawful or unfair means or by breach of duty as trustee, the court will construct a trust for the benefit of the person rightfully entitled to that property. In such cases, the court declares that the person who has acquired or retained property wrongfully holds the property as "constructive trustee" for the person who has been unjustly deprived of the property. Therefore, a constructive trust is imposed to remedy a wrong and to prevent unjust enrichment by the person who acquired title at the expense of another. The constructive trustee has no administrative duty other than the obligation to transfer the title and possession of the property to the proper person.

Case Two. The case of *Sharp v. Kosmalski,* 40 N.Y.2d 119, 386 N.Y.S.2d 72, 351 N.E.2d 721 (1976), illustrates the creation of a constructive trust. Rodney Sharp was a 56-year-old farmer whose education did not go beyond the eighth grade. On the death of his wife of 32 years, he developed a very close relationship with Jean Kosmalski, 16 years his junior. Sharp proposed marriage to her, but she refused. He continued to make substantial gifts to her which included the execution of a deed that named her a joint owner of the farm. Later, Sharp transferred his remaining joint interest in the farm to Kosmalski. She ordered Sharp to move out of the house and vacate the farm. Sharp brought this action to impose a constructive trust on the property transferred to Kosmalski. The court ruled that a person may be determined to be unjustly enriched if that person has received a benefit, the retention of which would be unjust, as in this case; therefore, the court decided in favor of Sharp.

The court may also construct a trust for the benefit of the rightful owner when a person obtains property by fraud or willfully converts another's personal property for her own use.

Example: Clare Allison works for the Benedict Corporation. She embezzles $10,000 from the corporation and uses the money to buy a speedboat. Under these circumstances, the equity court could decree Clare to be a constructive trustee for the corporation with the duty to transfer possession and title of the speedboat to the company.

See Exhibit 9.2 for a summary of the types of trusts.

Exhibit 9.2   An Outline Summary of the Main Types of Trusts

A. Two main types of trusts
  1. **Express trust** A trust intentionally created or declared in express terms either by oral declaration or by a written instrument. Express trusts may be—
      a. Private or public (charitable) trusts.
      b. Active or passive trusts.
      c. *Inter vivos* (living) trusts or testamentary trusts.
  2. **Implied trust** A trust imposed on property by the court when trust intent is lacking but the acts of the parties make the imposition necessary. Implied trusts may be—
      a. Resulting trusts.
      b. Constructive trusts.
B. **Express trusts**
  1. Private or public (charitable) trusts
      a. **Private trust** An oral or written trust created for the financial benefit of a certain named individual or individuals.
      b. **Public trust** An express trust created for the social benefit of the public, or specific groups within the public; often called a charitable trust.
  2. Active or passive trusts
      a. **Active trust** A trust that gives the trustee the power and duty to perform discretionary acts of management or administration.
      b. **Passive trust** A trust in which the trustee is a mere holder of the legal title and has no duties of administration or only minor duties that are of a mechanical or formal nature. All implied trusts are passive trusts.
  3. *Inter vivos* or testamentary trusts
      a. ***Inter vivos* (living) trust** An express active trust, either private or public, created during the settlor's lifetime.
      b. **Testamentary trust** An express active trust, either public or private, created in a decedent's will.
C. **Implied trusts**
  1. **Resulting trust** An implied trust created by the equity court to carry out the true intent of a property holder of legal title or settlor in cases where the intent of such person is inadequately expressed.
  2. **Constructive trust** An implied trust imposed by courts of equity as a means of accomplishing justice and preventing unjust enrichment. Such trusts are not based on either actual or presumed intent of the parties.

⛬ ASSIGNMENT 9.8

1. Russell Haberman owned a tract of land he believed was practically worthless. His brother-in-law, Francis Holgate, offered to buy the land for one dollar an acre. Francis knew it contained valuable mineral deposits of which Russell was unaware. Russell sold the land and, subsequently, discovered its true value. Has Francis been unjustly enriched by the transaction? What should Russell do?

2. In a will dated June 6, 1997, Michelle Walker named her nephew, Clarence Wilson, beneficiary of a substantial portion of her estate. In 2001, Michelle wrote a new will in which Clarence was left nothing; later that year Michelle died. Clarence discovered the second (2001) will but concealed its existence until the probate of the first (1997) will was completed. A beneficiary of the second will uncovered the truth. Some states hold that a constructive trust may be created in this case. How would your state decide this matter?

Miscellaneous Trusts

A number of special trust forms need to be discussed. These include the spend-thrift, Totten, and sprinkling trusts. Charitable remainder trusts and other tax-saving trusts are discussed in Chapter 10.

Spendthrift Trusts

Spendthrift trusts are commonly created by parents for children they feel are financially irresponsible. A spendthrift is a person who spends money improvidently, compulsively, and foolishly and thereby wastes the funds. As defined in the *Matter of Sowers' Estate,* 1 Kan.App.2d 675, 574 P.2d 224 (1977), *spendthrift trusts* are trusts created to provide a fund for the maintenance of a beneficiary while safeguarding the fund against the beneficiary's own extravagance or inexperience in spending money. In such trusts, only a certain portion of the total amount of the funds is given to the spendthrift beneficiary at any one time. The trustee is given discretion to decide the amount of income given to the beneficiary. The settlor provides that the beneficiary cannot assign (transfer) to anyone the right to receive future payments of income or principal from the trust (which the settlor believes the beneficiary would do in times of financial difficulty). At the same time, the settlor declares that creditors of the spendthrift beneficiary cannot reach the trust benefits by obtaining a court order that awards the trust benefits to the creditors. In this way, settlors seek to protect the beneficiary who cannot or will not handle money wisely. This protection ends once the beneficiary actually receives the distribution of the trust income from the trustee.

Spendthrift trusts do not place limitations on income once it is received by the beneficiary, who may spend it, give it away at will, or use it to satisfy creditors' claims, but the beneficiary cannot pledge future trust income as security for a loan. The trust only guarantees the beneficiary will not lose the income before receiving it. Principal or income is subject to creditors' claims only after it is received by the beneficiary; see N.H. Rev. Stat. Ann. § 498:8 and 9. A majority of states allows settlors to create a spendthrift trust and prohibits creditors from attaching the trust in order to obtain a beneficiary's interest. However, if there is no spendthrift provision, the creditors can enforce their claims. State statutes and case law do allow creditors to reach the beneficiary's trust income despite a spendthrift clause if they have supplied **"necessaries"** to the beneficiary. See Ky. Rev. Stat. Ann. § 381.180(6)(b), and *Matter of Dodge's Estate,* 281 N.W.2d 447 (Iowa 1979). Necessaries include necessary services a creditor performs for a beneficiary or necessary supplies a creditor delivers to the beneficiary. See *In re Mayer's Will,* 59 N.Y.S.2d 561 (1945).

Necessaries
Necessary items that supply the personal needs of an individual or family, such as food, clothing, or shelter.

> **Example:** Leo Demarest, a resident of Nevada, wishes to leave a considerable amount of property to his son, Robert, although he knows Robert is irresponsible and wastes his money. He fears that Robert may go into debt and pledge the income received from the trust to pay his creditors. Leo could enable Robert to keep the right to the trust income by inserting the following "spendthrift trust" clause in his will: "It is the purpose of this trust to protect Robert Demarest from want or his own mismanagement and improvidence and to provide him with a reasonable means of support free from claims or interest of any other person. The beneficiary, Robert Demarest, of this trust shall not have the power to transfer, pledge, or assign his interest in the principal or the income of this trust in any manner, nor shall such interest be subject to the claims of his creditors, attachment, garnishment, execution, or other process of law. All payments from the trust shall be paid directly to Robert Demarest and to no other person or entity."

ASSIGNMENT 9.9

Theodore Phelps wishes to make a gift of his utility company stocks to his daughter, Jana, who is about to be married. He knows Jana, who is inexperienced in handling securities, might sell them at a loss, and being headstrong, she would not listen to sound advice. Would a gift of the property be wise? Is it advisable for Theodore to establish a spendthrift trust for her? Explain.

Totten Trusts

A *Totten trust,* also called a POD (payable or pay on death) account, is a savings account in a bank in which money is deposited in the depositor's name as trustee for another person named as beneficiary. The name derives from the first case in which such trusts were upheld—*In re Totten,* 179 N.Y. 112, 71 N.E. 748 (1904). Commonly, the trust is created by A, the depositor, in the name of "A, in trust (or as trustee) for B," or in the name of "A, payable on death to B." Such deposits permit the depositor-trustee to withdraw money while alive and allow any remaining balance of the funds to be transferred to the beneficiary after the depositor's death. If the named beneficiary dies before the depositor, the trust terminates, and the money passes into the depositor's probate estate on his death. In addition, some courts hold the depositor may revoke the "trust" by withdrawing the entire fund or changing the form of the account. The requirements for the creation and distribution of funds in such trusts vary from state to state. Therefore, the individual state statutes must be checked to determine how Totten trusts will be administered. Sections 6–212 and 6–223 of the UPC states that a bank account, such as a Totten trust, belongs to the beneficiary when the trustee dies. In the case of *Hall's Estate v. Father Flanagan's Boys' Home,* 30 Colo.App. 296, 491 P.2d 614

(1971), the court ruled that a Totten trust was created, and the beneficiary, "Boys Town, Nebraska," actually known as Father Flanagan's Boys' Home, was entitled to the trust funds. The money in a Totten trust is a nonprobate asset and is, therefore, not part of the depositor's estate, i.e., not subject to probate or to creditors' claims of the depositor.

> **Example:** Esther Brown changes a savings account in her name to "Esther Brown, in trust for Jean Brown." Esther has converted her account into a Totten trust, which is allowed in her state. She has the option of withdrawing any or all of the money as she wishes during her lifetime because the Totten trust is revocable until the settlor's death. On Esther's death, Jean, the beneficiary, will own the remaining funds in the savings account. If Jean dies before Esther, however, the Totten trust ends, and the money in the savings account belongs to Esther. If no change is made in this savings account and Esther dies after Jean, the money will be transferred to Esther's estate and will be subject to probate.

Sprinkling Trusts

A **sprinkling trust** gives the trustee the authority and power to accumulate or distribute the income of the trust, the principal, or both among the trust beneficiaries in varying amounts. The financial needs of family members named as beneficiaries constantly change, and a trustee with sprinkling powers has the opportunity to change distributions from the trust to meet the needs of the beneficiaries.

> **Example:** Barbara is a single parent with three adult children. Barbara dies with a testamentary trust in her will that gives the trustee discretionary power to "sprinkle" income to the beneficiaries (the three children) in greatest need. Barbara's youngest child, Sara, is permanently injured in an accident and is obviously in greater financial need than Barbara's other two children, Susan and Elizabeth, both of whom are married and financially secure. The trustee accomplishes what Barbara herself would have wanted by giving the trust's income to Sara.

> **Example:** Barbara's testamentary trust in the above example would also allow her trustee to save income tax dollars since any distribution to the daughters, Susan and Elizabeth, would be taxed at a higher rate because of their family income.

A sprinkling trust also offers two other advantages: the trust funds are more difficult for creditors of the beneficiaries to reach since the trustee alone decides how much to give each beneficiary; and such trusts may help to reduce estate taxes.

> **Example:** Wanda sets up a sprinkling trust for her husband, Harold, for life, then to their children. Harold spends his own estate funds, and the trustee allows Wanda's trust funds to accumulate. The trust funds pass to the children on Harold's death free of estate tax.

A disadvantage of a sprinkling trust is that if the trust is intended to qualify for the marital deduction on the decedent's estate tax return, the surviving spouse must receive all the income during the spouse's lifetime.

Since the trustee is given the authority to make important family financial decisions, the person selected must be someone the settlor knows is reliable, experienced, and reasonable. The following is an example of a sprinkling trust provision from West's McKinney's Forms, ESP, § 10:593:

Sprinkling trust
The trustee has the authority and discretion to accumulate or distribute trust income, principal, or both among the trust beneficiaries in varying amounts.

It is desired that, while the underlying principle of equality shall be followed in making distributions of net income or principal to or for the benefit of any beneficiary, the Trustee is to be entirely free to pay out either more or less to or for the benefit of any particular beneficiary as it deems advisable because of variations in health, character, education, or other requirements, and the Trustee may use both net income and principal in disproportionate amounts to provide security and opportunities for higher education for each beneficiary during the term of the trust. . . . The judgment of the Trustee shall be final and conclusive upon all persons. (Reprinted with permission from West's McKinney's Forms, Copyright ©, by West Group.)

THE PURPOSES OF TRUSTS

A trust can be created for any lawful purpose, but it must not contravene common or statutory law (Restatement [Second] of Trusts § 59). Most trusts are created to distribute the income from the trust property to family members, friends, or a charity and/or to preserve the trust property for later distribution to such persons on termination of the trust. This can be accomplished during the settlor's lifetime by a living trust or at death by a testamentary trust.

A trust is a practical way to manage and transfer property in the best interests of a beneficiary. On the creation of a trust, the trustee assumes the duty to administer the trust, and relieves, if desired, both the settlor (grantor) and the beneficiary from the responsibility of managing and conserving the property. Numerous advantages of trusts become obvious. A living trust is created in each of the following examples. By means of such a device, the settlor can provide:

- Funds for the support of dependent family members, e.g., parents, spouse, children.

Example: Clinton McBride supports his elderly mother, Martha. Due to her age and frail health, Martha will most likely predecease Clinton. The transfer of income-producing property by outright gift in order to have the income taxed in Martha's lower tax bracket would be illogical, since gift taxes would be owed and on her death the property would return to Clinton, reduced by his mother's estate and administration expenses. If Clinton places the property in a living trust for his mother for life, with the remainder to his only child, Jennifer, the income would be taxed to Martha without her receiving legal title to the property. When Martha dies, the property will pass to Jennifer, if she survives Martha.

- Funds for the college education of children.

Example: Kathleen Shannon, a widow, has been a homemaker and mother all her adult life. Her husband died two years ago, and left her a substantial life insurance benefit. She wants to establish a fund for the college education of her two children. Since she lacks business experience and the children are minors, the creation of a living trust and the selection of an experienced trustee to invest the trust property would be good decisions.

- Professional financial management for those inexperienced in handling large sums of money, which relieves a spouse or children from this responsibility and spares a settlor the burden of property management.

Example: Kevin Perry, a single parent, age 55, has recovered from a series of mild heart attacks. He owns property that he wants to transfer by will to his children, Abby and James. Since Kevin is concerned about the way the property may be used or spent by his children, he would prefer to transfer it now, while he is alive, in order to determine how well the property is managed. A living trust with a spendthrift clause under experienced and expert corporate management could relieve the children of this administration responsibility, benefit them immediately, and continue after Kevin's death.

- A method to avoid probate.

Example: Marc Livingston wants to avoid the expense of probate, ancillary proceedings, and the publicity of probate. He may, therefore, choose to create, as a will substitute, a revocable living trust to continue after his death. A will is probated; a living trust is not.

- A public, charitable trust for an educational, health, scientific, or religious institution.

Example: Anna wants to give a substantial amount of money to St. Mary's Hospital, but she wants to control the way the money will be used. She could establish a living trust and name herself as trustee with such powers.

ASSIGNMENT 9.10

Charlotte dies testate. She gives her farm, Longacre, "to Wallace in trust for my husband, Gerard, for his lifetime, and at his death, in equal shares as tenants in common, to our two children, Wilma and Richard." At the time of Charlotte's death, all other parties mentioned are living. Does this provision of the will create a trust? Classify it. Wilma and Richard are remaindermen. What does the term mean?

ASSIGNMENT 9.11

Jean-Luc Bernadois, a naturalized citizen, wishes to set up a trust for the benefit of his sister, Claire, who has recently arrived from Martinique and has little knowledge of financial matters. He has government bonds valued at $25,000.

1. Assuming that Jean-Luc does set up a trust, identify the settlor, the beneficiary, and the trust property.
2. Whom might the settlor appoint trustee? Why?
3. Would it be advisable to make a gift of the bonds rather than a transfer of them in trust? Why or why not?

Legal Restrictions

Generally, a trust can be created for any purpose that is legal, but the law has imposed some restrictions on what constitutes a legal purpose (Restatement [Second] of Trusts §§ 59, 60). Restrictions on purposes of trusts fall into several categories. There are restrictions on purposes contrary to public policy, such as imposing total restraint on marriage or attempting to encourage divorce (Restatement [Second] of Trusts § 62).

Example: Otto Lindberg tells his son, Scott, he will transfer his ski resort, Arrowhead, to Daniel Maulkin in a living trust for Scott's benefit if Scott will divorce his wife, Elizabeth. Such a condition is against public policy and would invalidate the trust. In this case, Otto would retain the trust property.

Some restrictions are imposed by statute. Statutes restricting trusts are usually framed in general language, e.g., N.Y. EPTL § 7–1.4 states: "An express trust may be created for any lawful purpose." The definition of what is "lawful" is then subject to interpretation by the New York courts. Some statutes contain further restrictions, usually in the area of real property trusts.

Example: Hermann Pfalz lives in South Dakota. As a gift to his daughter, Freida, he transfers to her in a living trust a part of his wheat acreage. Hermann's gift must be in writing to be valid, according to S.D. Cod. Laws Ann. § 55–1–1.

Some restrictions are imposed on private noncharitable trusts by the Rule Against Perpetuities, which prohibits indefinite accumulations of wealth or property. The perpetuation of a trust that effectively prohibits any but members of a certain class from possessing the trust property beyond an extended statutory period contravenes public policy and the Rule Against Perpetuities.

Example: In his will, Howard Engel gives $100,000 in trust to Investors, Inc., to hold and invest, to accumulate the income of the trust property for the next 100 years, and then to transfer the trust estate to the heirs of Howard equally. The testamentary trust is invalid because the rule against perpetual interests in trust property requires that the period be no greater than the continuance of lives in being at the time the trust instrument takes effect and 21 years thereafter plus the period of gestation.

Another restriction is a valid trust cannot be formed if it is based on an illegal contract or agreement. Where a trust is created and income is to be paid to the beneficiary on condition the beneficiary aids in the commision of criminal acts, the purpose is illegal and the trust is invalid. Any illegal purpose, such as inducing the beneficiary to live in adultery with the settlor or defrauding the settlor's creditors, will invalidate the trust. Any trust designed to induce criminal acts is invalid, e.g., a trust set up to reward a beneficiary for committing perjury or to pay legal costs and fines for a beneficiary who commits a crime (Restatement [Second] of Trusts §§ 62b, d, and 63).

🏛 ASSIGNMENT 9.12

Sherman Aldrich, retired president of a paper products firm, creates the Northwest Environmental Trust to preserve valuable forest land in the Pacific Northwest. He endows the trust with $500,000 and, in the trust instrument, directs the trustees to invest and reinvest the money for the cultivation and reforestation of certain tracts of land and to encourage legislation favorable to the continuation of these aims.
1. Is this trust legal or illegal? Why? (See Restatement [Second] of Trusts § 65.)
2. Under what circumstances, if any, might this trust be declared invalid?
3. In the event that one of the purposes of the trust becomes or is declared to be illegal, could the remainder of the trust be enforced?

Just as a trust may not violate statutory law, it may not violate public policy. A provision in a trust imposing total restraint on a beneficiary to marry is generally invalid (but see *Young v. Kraeling,* 134 N.Y.S.2d 109 [1954], in which the court held a remarriage caused the widower to lose his trust fund). For instance, if the trust provides that a beneficiary will be divested of an interest if the beneficiary should *ever* marry anyone, the provision is invalid since it is against public policy to prevent a person from marrying, having children, and a normal family life (Restatement [Second] of Trusts § 62h). A trust that provides income payments to a person whose spouse has died until the person remarries, does not oppose public policy however, since it restrains not marriage but remarriage. Courts have generally upheld trusts that provide that the beneficiary will lose her interest if she:

- marries a particular person
- marries before reaching majority
- marries before reaching majority without the consent of the trustee (or someone else)
- marries a person of a particular religious faith
- marries a person of a faith different from that of the beneficiary

These restrictions are considered to not "unduly" restrain marriage and are referred to as "reasonable restraints." In determining the validity or invalidity of a partially illegal trust, the court will likely declare the trust valid if it determines the settlor's intent was not to restrain marriage but merely to provide support to the beneficiary as long as the beneficiary remains single. The facts, in particular the settlor's intent, are crucial to the court's decision.

If a testamentary trust provides that a beneficiary will be divested for marrying without the consent of executors and trustees, and, if under provisions of the will those persons will profit by refusing to consent to the beneficiary's marriage, the provision is invalid. Provisions that are designed to prevent hasty or imprudent marriages and that subject a minor to the restraint of parents or friends during minority are allowed. The reasoning is that the law should uphold such a provision because it protects the minor from unscrupulous persons who could dissipate the proceeds established for the minor's benefit.

Likewise, a provision in a trust that divests beneficiaries of their interests if they communicate or have social relations with certain other family members is invalid as being against public policy and disruptive of family relations (Restatement [Second] of Trusts § 62g).

Another invalid provision is one that constitutes an inducement to change the religious faith of the beneficiary (Restatement [Second] of Trusts § 62i). For example, if a trust provides that Maureen Shannon is to receive her interest only if she changes her religious faith or that her interest ceases if she does not change her religious faith, the courts hold as a general rule that enforcement of such provisions restrains the religious freedom of the beneficiary by improperly inducing her to change or not to change her faith.

INFORMAL AND INCOMPLETE CREATION OF A TRUST

When competent legal advice is not sought, a private express living or testamentary trust might be drafted improperly, and litigation could result. The following are some of the major mistakes made in an improperly drafted trust:

Precatory words
Words such as *hope, desire, request, ask, beseech, wish,* or *recommend* which are ineffective to dispose of property.

- A testator-settlor, in a hand-drawn will, indicates that he wants certain testamentary trust objectives accomplished but expresses this using **precatory words** such as *hope, desire, request,* or *wish* rather than expressing it as a mandate.
- The trust document does not sufficiently identify the beneficiary or fails to name a beneficiary.
- The trust instrument fails to name a trustee or fails to name a successor when the named trustee does not want to serve.
- The document names the trustee and describes the beneficiaries but does not specify the duties of the trustee.
- Although the trust instrument purports to be transferring legal title, the trust terms are not specified, or they have only been implied in an informal oral agreement.

Failure to Make Intentions Clear

It is possible to create a trust without actually using the words "trustee" or "in trust." On the other hand, in a hand-drawn instrument the use of these words is not conclusive evidence of the intent to create a trust. In order to create an express trust, the court must be satisfied the settlor manifested an intention to impose enforceable duties on the trustee to manage the property for the benefit of others. When a testator uses precatory words such as "hope," "wish," "desire," or "recommend" to devise the property of his estate, the court must determine whether he intended an absolute gift or a trust (Restatement [Second] of Trusts § 25). It will consider all relevant factors before reaching a conclusion.

> **Example:** Desmond Cormac's will provides, in part: "I give to my wife in the event of my death all my interest in the farm we own as tenants in common and all the stock, farm implements, etc., after my debts are paid. To have and to hold the same in fee simple and to dispose of the same among the children as she may think best." An argument could be made that the will establishes a testamentary trust in the property for the benefit of the children, but another view is the devisee (the wife) is given an estate in fee simple.

> **Example:** John Vanderhaavn's will gives property to his wife "to be her absolute estate forever." He added the words, "It is my request that on her death, my said wife shall give, devise, and bequeath the real property given her to persons named in the fourth clause of this will." An ambiguity is created because the testator cannot create a fee simple estate for his wife and then request the same property be transferred to others on her death. That right belongs to the fee owner, i.e., the testator's wife. The court held the wife took the property in fee simple and not in trust.

These examples illustrate the effects unclear terms may have on an intended trust. In some cases, inclusion of these precatory words results in the undoing of the would-be settlor's intentions.

Precatory trust
A trust created by precatory words, e.g., "wish and request," or "have fullest confidence," which the courts have held sufficient to constitute a trust.

The early English view held the use of such words as "request," "desire," "hope," and "wish" were a courteous means of creating duties enforceable by the courts. Some courts hold the use of such *precatory words* does *not* create a trust. The intent to create a trust containing such words must be proven by other sections of the trust instrument or by extrinsic circumstances (Restatement [Second] of Trusts § 25). Other courts hold the words create a **precatory trust** and allow the trust to be performed.

Example: Suppose a testator, Marvin Rothman, wills all his property to his wife, and adds, "I recommend to her the care and protection of my mother and sister, and request her to make such provision for them as in her judgment will be best." Both mother and sister are invalids and in need, and the testator had supported them for some time before his death. A court could hold his wife takes the property in trust with the obligation to make a reasonable provision for the continual care of the testator's mother and sister. Such a testamentary trust is poorly drafted because it creates an ambiguity, i.e., a conveyance of the estate property to the testator's spouse but with a request the spouse "care and protect" the testator's invalid mother and sister. A court's decision to call this will provision a testamentary trust could be based on the circumstances, i.e., the fact the mother and sister are invalids, and the testator had previously cared for them. But consider and compare the case of *In re Lubenow's Estate,* 146 N.W.2d 166 (N.D. 1966), in which the testator left his estate to his nephew with directions, "to see to it that my brothers are provided for." The court held "these [precatory] words do no more than express a wish or desire on the part of the testator." Therefore no testamentary trust was created. The nephew received the entire estate.

When drafting wills and trusts, it is best to avoid these precatory words altogether.

Failure to Name or Identify the Beneficiary

When the trust instrument fails to name a beneficiary, a few cases give the trustee absolute ownership, but the general rule is a "resulting trust" arises in favor of the decedent's estate if the trust instrument was testamentary (Restatement [Second] of Trusts §§ 44e and 45e). If a living trust is created and it fails to name a beneficiary, the attempt to create a trust fails.

Example: If Mel Bowles sets aside money for a living trust, executes the instrument, and directs the trustee to distribute the income to persons the trustee considers deserving, the trust fails because Mel did not clearly identify the beneficiaries. Had he augmented the description, e.g., "to be distributed to my nieces and nephews" or "to the descendants of my sister, Judith," the beneficiaries would at least be identifiable.

Failure to Name a Trustee or a Successor Trustee

A valid trust will not fail for want of a trustee or successor trustee. Lack of a trustee to administer the trust may come about in any of the following ways:

- If the settlor does not name a trustee in the trust instrument or fails to name a successor trustee to resolve the problem of the original trustee's death, resignation, or nonacceptance, i.e., the trustee's unwillingness or inability to serve.
- If the named trustee does not qualify, e.g., refuses to accept the duty, dies before the effective date of the trust, or is refused confirmation of the office by the court because of incompetence.
- If the named trustee does not have legal capacity to hold property in trust, e.g., in some states an unincorporated association.
- If the named trustee is removed or resigns after the effective date of the trust.

Courts will preserve trusts. Normally, the court will not allow a trust to fail for any of the above reasons and will appoint a new trustee as long as the trust is otherwise valid. Where a trustee is needed to execute and manage a trust, state statutes authorize the court to appoint the following: (1) an original trustee where the trust document or will creating the trust has not nominated a trustee or the nominee is unable or unwilling to serve; and (2) a successor trustee, when the original trustee has ceased to act and a replacement is required to finish the administration of the trust. The trust will fail only if it can be shown the settlor intended only the named person and no one else could be the trustee.

Although the laws of a few states prohibit the creation of joint tenancy, this prohibition does not apply to property held in trust. Co-trustees generally hold title to trust property as joint tenants with the right of survivorship, so if one dies, disclaims, resigns, or is removed by a court, legal title passes to the remaining co-trustee(s) by operation of law (Restatement [Second] of Trusts § 103).

> **Example:** Curt Baird places 500 shares of Behl, Inc., in trust for the benefit of his son, Kyle, and names Curt's three brothers trustees as joint tenants. Later, one brother resigns due to ill health. The court decides two trustees will suffice because the settlor did not specify there must be three at all times. Therefore, the court does not appoint a new trustee. At the annual stockholders' meeting of Behl, the two trustees vote in the name of the trust. Another major stockholder contends the Baird trust votes were invalid because they were cast by two, not three, trustees. The votes are valid. The two trustees hold the entire legal title to the trust by right of survivorship.

LIVING (*INTER VIVOS*) TRUSTS

A living trust is one of the two ways property can be placed in a trust; the other is a testamentary trust. A living trust is created by a settlor and operates during the settlor's lifetime. The trust property is a nonprobate asset; therefore, it is not part of the decedent's probate estate and is not under the jurisdiction or supervision of the probate court.

A living trust can be created by either of the following:

1. A *declaration of trust* in which the settlor retains the legal title to the trust property and is, therefore, also the trustee and, thereafter, names another person or persons to be the beneficiaries. The declaration of trust must be signed by the settlor and at least two witnesses or notarized (see Exhibit 9.3 for a sample declaration of trust).

2. A *trust agreement* in which the settlor transfers legal title to another party, the trustee, who manages or administers the property in trust for the beneficiary who holds the equitable title and receives the benefits of the trust (see the Carter Trust in Exhibit 8.2).

A settlor's *declaration of trust* or a conveyance of trust that uses a *trust agreement* are simple methods of establishing a living trust. In the former, the owner of property, i.e., the settlor, simply declares herself trustee of the property for the benefit of another person. The conveyance of trust method requires the settlor to sign a *trust agreement* with a trustee and a successor trustee and transfer property to create the trust. As mentioned previously, the settlor and the trustee or the settlor and the beneficiary may be the same person depending on the type

---

Exhibit 9.3   Sample Declaration of Trust

Declaration of Trust

This declaration of trust is made on _____ [date], by _____, of _____ [address], _____ [city], _____ [county], _____ [state], referred to as trustor.

Section One

Declaration of Trust

I _____ as trustor, have assigned myself as trustee and declare that I hold in trust the securities described in the attached Schedule A, which is incorporated by reference. I declare that I and my successor trustee will hold the described securities, and all substitutions and additions, as the trust estate for the use and benefit of _____, of _____ [address], _____ [city], _____ [county], _____ [state], referred to as beneficiary, for the following purposes and on the following terms and conditions: [see 17 Am. Jur. Legal Forms 2d § 251:21 for complete text.]

* * *

_____

Source: Reprinted with permission from American Jurisprudence Legal Forms 2d. Copyright ©, by West Group.

---

of trust selected. No trust is created, however, until the declaration or the transfer of the trust property takes place. If the conveyance is a transfer of personal property to a living trust, no formalities are required for the declaration of trust except that the settlor-trustee must manifest an intention to hold or place the property in trust. If the trust property is realty, the settlor must put the declaration of trust or trust agreement in writing to satisfy the requirements of the Statute of Frauds (Restatement [Second] of Trusts § 40). Likewise, delivery requirements are simple. For example, if the conveyance is a gift of land, the settlor must deliver the deed to the trustee; if the gift is personal property, usually delivery of the gift itself is necessary.

> **Example:** Carol Flexner, a widow with four children, received her father's resort, Edgewater, from his estate. If Carol wishes to create a living trust using this property, she will have to put the trust agreement in writing. She will also have to deliver the deed to Edgewater to the trustee.

Revocable Living Trusts

A living trust is either revocable or irrevocable. In a revocable trust, the settlor reserves the right to amend, revoke, or cancel the trust at any time while living. On the death of the settlor, the living trust becomes *irrevocable* and the trust property is disposed of or distributed according to the terms of the trust. Since revocable trusts avoid the need for and cost of probate or estate administration, they are commonly used in estate planning (see Chapter 10). A revocable living trust is not a device for saving estate taxes, however; only an irrevocable trust offers that additional tax benefit (see the discussion below). Many people today are using a revocable living trust as a substitute for a will. The trust allows the settlor to transfer the entire estate to the trust, manage and retain full control over the assets of the trust, receive the income from the trust during his or her lifetime, distribute the trust property after death to the named beneficiaries (usually children), and avoid the often substantial costs and delays of probate. The trust becomes the legal owner of the property both before and after the settlor's death and is responsible for the payments of all outstanding debts and taxes.

When a revocable living trust is created a trustee must be named to manage and control the trust. Frequently, the settlor will name himself trustee, or, if married, the settlor and the settlor's spouse will act as co-trustees or joint-trustees, which grants either spouse the legal authority to act as trustee. If one spouse becomes disabled or dies, the other spouse automatically has control of the trust without the delays and expense of the probate process or the intervention of the probate court. Even though a settlor no longer owns the trust property, the revocable living trust enables the settlor-trustee to retain complete control of the property and to avoid paying any management fees. As trustee, the settlor can invest, buy, and sell the trust property, distribute the income from the trust to himself or to whomever the settlor chooses, change the trust beneficiaries, or, because it is revocable, cancel the trust at any time. The former owner (settlor) of the trust property who is now the trustee is obligated to preserve, maintain, and insure the property and file the annual income tax returns. If the settlor appoints someone else trustee, the trust agreement usually provides the trustee is to manage and invest the trust property for the benefit of the settlor-beneficiary for life, and pay to the settlor-beneficiary all the income and as much of the principal of the trust as the trustee determines to be required for the settlor-beneficiary's care. Problems that arise due to the disability, incompetence, or death of the settlor are discussed below.

In the past, the revocable living trust was most commonly used for the primary benefit of an elderly settlor who owned a substantial amount of income-producing property (assets) and desired to be relieved of the responsibility of managing the property. Today, many people of all income brackets are substituting revocable living trusts for wills.

Transfer of Trust Property to a Living Trust

If a revocable living trust is to act as a will substitute, all assets (real and personal property) owned by the settlor or in which the settlor has or acquires an interest must be transferred to the living trust. When property is transferred into a revocable living trust, a gift is not made by the settlor. Therefore, no federal or state gift taxes are due. No matter in which state it is located and whether or not it is income producing, *all real estate* including rental units such as apartment buildings, duplexes, rooming houses, and commercial buildings plus residential property including the settlor's house, vacation home, cottage, or condominium *must be* transferred to the trustee(s) of the trust. When asked to assist the settlor with these transfers, you will most likely use a quit-claim deed (Exhibit 9.4) or a deed of trust [trust transfer deed] (Exhibit 9.5) as the document to correct or change title (ownership) of real property either from an individual or from spouses holding title as joint tenants to the trustee(s) of the living trust. This is just a change of title, not a transfer of title. The executed deed must be delivered to the trustee(s) but does not nec-

Exhibit 9.4   Sample Quitclaim Deed

RECORDING REQUESTED BY

AND WHEN RECORDED MAIL THIS DEED AND, UNLESS OTHERWISE SHOWN BELOW, MAIL TAX STATEMENT TO:

NAME

STREET ADDRESS

CITY, STATE & ZIP CODE

TITLE ORDER NO. _____   ESCROW NO. _____

SPACE ABOVE THIS LINE FOR RECORDER'S USE

QUITCLAIM DEED

DOCUMENTARY TRANSFER TAX $ _____
☐ computed on full value of property conveyed, or
☐ computed on full value less liens and encumbrances remaining at time of sale.

Signature of Declarant or Agent Determining Tax   Firm Name

_____,
(NAME OF GRANTOR(S))

the undersigned grantor(s), for a valuable consideration, receipt of which is hereby acknowledged, do__ hereby remise, release and

forever quitclaim to _____
(NAME OF GRANTEE(S))

the following described real property in the City of _____, County of _____, State of _____:

Assessor's parcel No. _____

Executed on _____, _____, at _____
(CITY AND STATE)

_____

STATE OF _____   _____

COUNTY OF _____   _____

On _____ before me, _____
(NAME/TITLE, i.e. "JANE DOE, NOTARY PUBLIC")

personally appeared _____ personally known to me (or proved to me on the basis of satisfactory evidence) to be the person(s) whose name(s) is/are subscribed to the within instrument and acknowledged to me that he/she/they executed the same in his/her/their authorized capacity(ies), and that by his/her/their signature(s) on the instrument the person(s) or the entity upon behalf of which the person(s) acted, executed the instrument.

WITNESS my hand and official seal.

RIGHT THUMBPRINT (Optional)

TOP OF THUMB HERE

_____
(SIGNATURE OF NOTARY)   (SEAL)

CAPACITY CLAIMED BY SIGNER(S)
☐ INDIVIDUAL(S)
☐ CORPORATE _____
    OFFICER(S) _____
                        (TITLES)
☐ PARTNER(S)   ☐ LIMITED
                      ☐ GENERAL
☐ ATTORNEY IN FACT
☐ TRUSTEE(S)
☐ GUARDIAN/CONSERVATOR
☐ OTHER: _____

MAIL TAX STATEMENTS TO: _____

Before you use this form, fill in all blanks, and make whatever changes are appropriate and necessary to your particular transaction. Consult a lawyer if you doubt the form's fitness for your purpose and use. Wolcotts makes no representation or warranty, express or implied, with respect to the merchantability or fitness of this form for an intended use or purpose.

WOLCOTTS FORM 790   ©1994 WOLCOTTS FORMS, INC.
QUITCLAIM DEED   Rev. 3-94b (price class 3A)

SIGNER IS REPRESENTING:
(Name of Person(s) of Entity(ies))
_____
_____

7 67775 39790 1

Source: Wolcotts Forms. Reprinted with permission.

Exhibit 9.5 Sample Deed of Trust

WOLCOTTS FORM 822   — DETACH STUB BEFORE RECORDING —

RECORDING REQUESTED BY

AND WHEN RECORDED MAIL THIS DEED AND, UNLESS
OTHERWISE SHOWN BELOW, MAIL TAX STATEMENT TO:

NAME

STREET
ADDRESS

CITY, STATE &
ZIP CODE

TITLE ORDER NO._____ ESCROW NO._____

SPACE ABOVE THIS LINE FOR RECORDER'S USE

SHORT FORM DEED OF TRUST AND ASSIGNMENT OF RENTS (With Future Borrowing Clause)
incorporating by reference certain provisions of a fictitious deed of trust of record

This Deed of Trust, Made this   day of   ,between

                                                                    herein called TRUSTOR,

whose address is

(Number and Street)   (City)   (State)   (Zip)

herein called TRUSTEE, and

herein called BENEFICIARY.

WITNESSETH: That Trustor IRREVOCABLY GRANTS, TRANSFERS AND ASSIGNS TO TRUSTEE IN TRUST, WITH POWER OF SALE, that

property in   County, California, described as:

TOGETHER WITH the rents, issues and profits thereof, SUBJECT, HOWEVER, to the right, power and authority given to and conferred upon Beneficiary by paragraph (10) of the provisions incorporated herein by reference to collect and apply such rents, issues and profits.
For the Purpose of Securing: 1. Performance of each agreement of Trustor incorporated by reference or contained herein. **2.** Payment of the indebtedness evidenced by one promissory note of even date herewith, and any extension or renewal thereof, in the principal sum of $_____ executed by Trustor in favor of Beneficiary or order. **3.** Payment of such further sums as the then record owner of said property hereafter may borrow from Beneficiary, when evidenced by another note (or notes) reciting it is so secured.
To protect the Security of This Deed of Trust, Trustor Agrees: By the execution and delivery of this Deed of Trust and the note secured hereby, that provisions (1) to (14), inclusive, of the fictitious deed of trust recorded June 1, 1953, in the book and at the page of Official Records in the office of the county recorder of the county where said property is located, noted below opposite the name of such county, viz.:

COUNTY	BOOK	PAGE	COUNTY	BOOK	PAGE	COUNTY	BOOK	PAGE	COUNTY	BOOK	PAGE
Alameda	7043	119	Kings	558	124	Placer	629	311	Sierra	6	1
Alpine	G	65	Lake	235	108	Plumas	64	277	Siskiyou	315	114
Amador	52	393	Lassen	90	305	Riverside	1477	255	Solano	670	214
Butte	675	4	Los Angeles	41866	80	Sacramento	2420	317	Sonoma	1210	616
Calaveras	81	369	Madera	582	315	San Benito	196	295	Stanislaus	1154	443
Colusa	198	142	Marin	808	420	San Bernardino	3179	87	Sutter	397	248
Contra Costa	2133	208	Mariposa	43	242	San Diego	4874	512	Tehama	244	379
Del Norte	37	241	Mendocino	345	92	San Francisco	6165	282	Trinity	52	167
El Dorado	325	506	Merced	1110	55	San Joaquin	1528	314	Tulare	1679	106
Fresno	3313	673	Modoc	109	221	San Luis Obispo	712	43	Tuolumne	62	47
Glenn	295	536	Mono	30	343	San Mateo	2425	243	Ventura	1137	136
Humboldt	252	449	Monterey	1458	561	Santa Barbara	1156	1	Yolo	395	302
Imperial	862	639	Napa	415	331	Santa Clara	2627	445	Yuba	179	259
Inyo	103	83	Nevada	186	337	Santa Cruz	916	153			
Kern	2070	417	Orange	2512	500	Shasta	402	1			

(which provisions, identical in all counties, are printed on pages 3 & 4 hereof) hereby are adopted and incorporated herein and made a part hereof as fully as though set forth herein at length; that he will observe and perform said provisions; and that the references to property, obligations, and parties in said provisions shall be construed to refer to the property, obligations, and parties set forth in this Deed of Trust.

The undersigned Trustor requests that a copy of any Notice of Default and of any Notice of Sale hereunder be mailed to him at his address hereinbefore set forth.

_____
Signature of Trustor

MAIL TAX
STATEMENTS   _____   _____
TO: _____   _____

WOLCOTTS FORM 822 - rev. 4-94b (price class 2C)
SHORT FORM DEED OF TRUST   ©1994 WOLCOTTS FORMS, INC.
Before you use this form, fill in all blanks, and make whatever changes are appropriate and necessary to your particular transaction. Consult a lawyer if you doubt the form's fitness for your purpose and use. Wolcotts makes no representation or warranty, express or implied, with respect to the merchantability or fitness of this form for an intended use or purpose.

RECORD PAGES 1 & 2 ONLY, Page 1 of 4

(continued)

Exhibit 9.5   Sample Deed of Trust—*continued*

State of _____

County of _____

RIGHT THUMBPRINT (Optional)

TOP OF THUMB HERE

RIGHT THUMBPRINT (Optional)

TOP OF THUMB HERE

On _____ before me, _____
              (DATE)   (NAME/TITLE OF OFFICER-I.E."JANE DOE, NOTARY PUBLIC")
personally appeared _____
                              (NAME(S) OF SIGNER(S))

_____

_____

☐ personally known to me -**OR**- ☐   proved to me on the basis of satisfactory evidence to be the person(s) whose name(s) is/are subscribed to the within instrument and acknowledged to me that he/she/ they executed the same in his/her/their authorized capacity(ies), and that by his/her/their signature(s) on the instrument the person(s), or the entity upon behalf of which the person(s) acted, executed the instrument.

Witness my hand and official seal.

_____
         (SIGNATURE OF NOTARY)

CAPACITY CLAIMED BY SIGNER(S)

☐ INDIVIDUAL(S)
☐ CORPORATE _____
    OFFICERS _____
                (TITLES)
☐ PARTNER(S) ☐ LIMITED
            ☐ GENERAL
☐ ATTORNEY IN FACT
☐ TRUSTEE(S)
☐ GUARDIAN/CONSERVATOR
☐ OTHER_____

_____

_____

_____

SIGNER IS REPRESENTING:
(NAME OF PERSON(S) OR ENTITY(IES)):

_____

_____

_____

RECORD PAGES 1 & 2 ONLY, Page 2 of 4

Source: Wolcotts Forms. Reprinted with permission.

essarily need to be recorded. However, if the deed is recorded, the legal forms required by the local county tax assessors in the county the real property is located must be executed to establish that the property is now trust property. In addition, some states have statutes or rules of procedure that ensure the transfer of the settlor's domiciliary residence (homestead) into the trust does not cause the loss of the **homestead exemption** for property tax purposes. *Caveat:* Permission must be obtained from the bank which holds the mortgage on real property the settlor intends to transfer to the trust, because the transfer may trigger a clause (provision) in the mortgage loan agreement which requires immediate repayment of the loan. This approval must be obtained *before* recording any transfer of the property.

> **Example:** To change the title to his real property, Adam T. Jones, a single person, would sign the trust transfer deed from "Adam T. Jones, single" to "Adam T. Jones, as Trustee of the Adam T. Jones Revocable Living Trust, under trust dated August 1, 2001."

> **Example:** If Alex R. Brown and his wife, Janet M. Brown, own real property as joint tenants, they could change the title by both signing the deed from "Alex R. Brown and Janet M. Brown, husband and wife as joint tenants" to "Alex R. Brown and Janet M. Brown, as Trustees of the [name of trust], under trust dated August 1, 2001."

You must also change (reregister) title to personal property such as checking and savings accounts, stocks, bonds, certificates of deposit, money market and mutual funds, partnerships, cars, boats, and any other titled property to the name of the trustee(s) using the designated language as shown in the Adam T. Jones example above. Untitled personal property such as clothing, furs, jewelry, art objects, antiques, stamp and coin collections, and household furnishings can easily be transferred into the trust by a written assignment from the settlor to the trustee(s) that states the property is to be added to the trust. You must also have the assignment document in which the property is listed, signed and notarized. Some states have an assignment form that transfers all untitled personal property to the trustee(s) of the living trust (see N.Y. EPTL § 7–1.18). A copy of the assignment should be attached to the trust document. Any future untitled personal property should also be assigned to the trustee(s). In addition, all property that allows the settlor to name a beneficiary (such as life insurance policies, annuities, IRAs [traditional or Roth], 401(k), pension, profit-sharing, and Keogh plans) could be changed so that the primary beneficiary is the spouse or children and the secondary or successor beneficiary is the trustee(s) of the revocable living trust. Although the above property items that name a beneficiary already avoid probate, it is helpful to change the secondary or successor beneficiary to the trustee(s) of the revocable living trust to consolidate these assets, resulting in a more efficient and better coordinated administration, *and* to avoid the possible dilemma which may occur if the current owner and primary beneficiary die in a common accident. *Caveat:* Title or ownership of all retirement benefits, e.g., annuities, IRAs, and all the other retirement plans listed above **MUST NOT BE CHANGED** or **TRANSFERRED** to the living trust but should remain in the settlor's name. The change of ownership to the trustee would constitute a withdrawal and become a taxable event. Ownership of these benefits should and must *not* be transferred to the trust. Also, if the settlor is the insured person and the owner of a life insurance policy, the only change required is to name the trustee(s) the beneficiary. The settlor retains all ownership rights and should *not* transfer ownership or title to the name of the trustee(s).

Homestead exemption
Property tax reductions or exemptions available in some states for homestead property. A formal declaration is recorded annually to establish the homestead or whenever the property changes owners.

Advantages of a Revocable Living Trust as a Substitute for a Will

The following are some of the advantages of a revocable living trust:

- It avoids probate since trust property is a nonprobate asset, and it avoids probate expense—the costs of probating the estate of a decedent who dies with a will or intestate may include filing fees, court costs, publication and advertising expenses, appraisal and auction fees, bond expense, costs of will contests, expenses of challenges to creditors' claims, expenses of establishing guardianships for minor children, and, most expensive of all, the fees for attorneys and personal representatives. It is estimated the average total probate expense ranges from 5 to 15 percent of an estate's gross value. Also, the smaller the gross estate, the higher the percentage cost. In comparison, the cost of establishing a living trust generally averages $1,200 to $2,000 depending on the complexity of the settlor's estate. Both wills and trusts need to be updated which adds another expense.
- It avoids the lengthy delays often associated with estate administration—even if a testamentary trust is included in a decedent's will, it takes time to have a trustee appointed whenever beneficiaries of the will are minors, disabled, or incompetent persons.

Other routine problems that delay probate include locating assets, finding beneficiaries, and simply waiting for a court calendar date. It is not unusual for the final distribution of the estate property to beneficiaries and the closing of the probate process to take a year or more.

- It can also diminish the cost and delays caused by will contests or invalid creditors' claims. *Note:* A living trust can be contested but not as easily as a will. Time is also a factor when a will is contested by disgruntled family members who are not included as named beneficiaries of the decedent or who are disappointed in the amount of property left to them. Since the settlor creates and often administers the trust while living, it is in operation while the settlor can personally alter it; thus, the trust establishes persuasive evidence of the settlor's competence and clearly reflects the settlor's true wishes. Consequently, the probate court would be reluctant to change it. On the other hand, where a will exists, all persons who would inherit from the decedent if the decedent died intestate must be notified of the petition to probate the will. This allows, even invites, the disinherited or dissatisfied family members to challenge the will's validity. Even if this will contest is unfounded, delays and expense are the result. Creditors may also make unsubstantiated claims against the decedent's estate, which the personal representative must challenge in a court hearing. All of these concerns take time and cost money. If a living trust is already in operation, the delays and added costs described above are usually avoided.
- It avoids publicity—the will, its contents, and the probate file and documents are public records (i.e., they are open to the public). This means anyone can examine these records to determine what property the decedent owned at the time of death and who the beneficiaries are. Vulnerable family members, especially elderly surviving spouses, may possibly be exploited by individuals who obtain information from these public records and offer to sell investments, or worthless and unsolicited merchandise, unnecessary or expensive

insurance, or management services. Business competitors may attempt to take advantage of an owner-manager's death by offering to buy the business at unfavorable prices or other terms. The use of a revocable living trust can assure the settlor-decedent of complete privacy in the distribution of the trust property and enable surviving family members to avoid the potential problem of dishonest opportunists.

- It is not under the control or supervision of the probate court. Instead, it enables the settlor, while living, or the settlor's trustee, to continue to control and manage the property; and after the settlor's death, the family members can retain control of the trust property. Whereas with a will, the family may find they must obtain court approval before any assets of the deceased can be distributed to named beneficiaries or sold. As noted above, this process is time-consuming and expensive.

- It also affords the settlor, while living, an opportunity to view the operation of the trust, verify its performance, and make necessary and appropriate changes, such as granting more or less power to trustees, changing beneficiaries, or selling and giving away trust property. Settlors can even cancel the revocable trust whenever they wish.

- It provides lifetime or longer management of trust assets by experienced professional corporate trustees for the benefit of the settlor, the settlor's spouse and family, or other named beneficiaries. A will, on the other hand, obviously takes effect only after death.

- It allows the settlor who owns real estate in other states to avoid the time and expense of an ancillary administration normally required to pass the title to such real estate to beneficiaries of the trust. An ancillary administration is required because only the state in which the real estate is located has jurisdiction to convey (transfer) title to the property. A will would necessitate the ancillary procedures, a living trust would avoid them.

- It avoids the need, expense, and delay of appointing a guardian or conservator required under state law should the settlor become disabled or be declared incompetent. A living trust provides a convenient, reviewable, and private administration of the settlor's affairs by a trustee who can control all of the settlor's property, wherever located, with much more flexible powers of investment and property management than a court-appointed guardian or conservator who must report to the probate court and whose functions and duties can be restricted by both the court and state statutes. In addition, the trustee may continue to administer trust assets after the settlor's death, whereas a guardian or conservator's authority to act terminates at death.

- It also eliminates the need, expense, and delay for court-appointed guardians for minors or conservators for dependents with special needs due to physical or mental incapacity. A living trust can provide for these individuals specifically and also reassure the settlor, while living, that they are properly cared for and will continue to be cared for after the settlor's death. A will cannot verify such matters for a testator who must die before the will takes effect.

- It may allow the settlor to save on death taxes, e.g., the federal estate tax, the state inheritance tax, and the state estate tax, but only if it is an irrevocable living trust. However, wills containing testamentary trusts may also limit these taxes. Either a testamentary or a living trust make it possible to pass the decedent's estate tax-free to a surviving spouse; however, the testamentary trust must go through probate.

Disadvantages of a Revocable Living Trust

The following are some of the disadvantages of a revocable living trust:

- It may be more costly to create the trust than to draft a will depending on the amount of assets the settlor-testator owns or the complexity of the estate, and the trustee's management and administration fees are a continual expense throughout the life of the trust. However, wills are frequently changed and redrawn, often many times, and the total cost of many wills plus the probate costs will most likely exceed the cost of a living trust.
- It requires all of the settlor's assets, except for life insurance and retirement benefits previously discussed, to be transferred into the living trust by changing titles to real property, reregistering titled personal property, assigning untitled personal property, and placing all newly acquired property in the name of the trustee(s) of the trust. This makes the trust and not the settlor the owner of the assets. If this is not done because the settlor forgets or procrastinates, the property whose title is unchanged must go through the probate process.

Pour-Over Wills

If a revocable living trust is substituted for a will as the legal document of choice to avoid the probate process and to transfer and distribute the settlor's property after death, a **pour-over will** should also be executed. The pour-over will allows the testator to direct or pass the residue of the estate into an existing living trust. The will ensures that property acquired by the settlor after the revocable living trust was established or property the settlor forgot to transfer into the trust will be distributed according to the terms of the trust rather than pass by intestate succession.

Pour-over will
A will provision in which the testator directs (passes) the residue of the estate into an existing living trust.

As a companion to the revocable living trust, the pour-over will can perform the following important functions:

1. It can dispose of property the testator neglected to add to the trust before death.
2. It can dispose of property acquired through gifts, inheritance, or good fortune shortly before death.
3. It can allow the testator to specifically disinherit family members, e.g., children and other heirs which can only be done by a clear and expressed statement in the will.
4. It can allow the testator to name a personal and/or property guardian (conservator) for minor children.
5. It can allow the testator to name the same person as trustee of the living trust and personal representative of the will.

See the examples of a revocable living trust and a pour-over will in Exhibits 9.6 and 9.7.

Exhibit 9.6 Sample Revocable Living Trust

William T. Brown Trust Agreement

This trust agreement is made on _____, 20 _____, between William T. Brown of _____ County, State of _____, hereinafter called the "settlor," and William T. Brown of _____ County, State of _____, Charles T. Brown of _____ County, State of _____, and Sarah J. Brown of _____ County, State of _____, hereinafter collectively called the "trustees."

Recitals

I have transferred certain property to the trustees contemporaneously with signing this trust agreement, the receipt of which they acknowledge and which is described on Exhibit "A" attached hereto; and the parties to this agreement acknowledge that all property transferred or devised to the trust now or in the future is to be administered and distributed according to the terms of this trust agreement.

Article I
Reservation of Rights

During my life I reserve the following rights, to be exercised without the consent or participation of any other person:

1. To amend, in whole or in part, or to revoke this agreement by a written declaration.

2. To add any other real or personal property to the trust by transferring such property to the trustees, and to add any other property by my will. The trustees shall administer and distribute such property as though it had been a part of the original trust property.

3. To make payable to the trustees death benefits from insurance on my life, annuities, retirement plans, or other sources. If I do so, I reserve all incidents of ownership, and I shall have the duties of safekeeping all documents, of giving any necessary notices, of obtaining proper beneficiary designations, of paying premiums, contributions, assessments or other charges, and of maintaining any litigation.

4. To receive annual written accounts from all trustees (or the personal representative of any deceased trustee). My approval of these accounts by writings delivered to another trustee shall cover all transactions disclosed in these accounts and shall be binding and conclusive as to all persons.

5. To direct the trustees as to the retention, acquisition, or disposition of any trust assets by a writing delivered to the trustees. Any assets retained or acquired pursuant to such directions shall be retained as a part of the trust assets unless I otherwise direct in writing. The trustees shall not be liable to anyone for any loss resulting from any action taken in accordance with any such direction of mine.

6. To examine at all reasonable times the books and records of the trustees insofar as they relate to the trust.

Article II
Disposition of Trust Assets

Unless I am disabled, the trustees, after paying the proper charges and expenses of the trust, shall pay to me during my lifetime the entire net income from the trust property in monthly installments, and the trustees shall also pay to me and any other person who is a financial dependent of mine, in accordance with my written instructions, such portions of the principal of the trust property as I direct. If I become disabled by reason of illness, accident, or other emergency, or I am adjudicated incompetent, the trustees, other than myself, are authorized and directed to pay to me or for my benefit such portions of the trust income or principal as the trustees deem necessary to provide for my care, comfort, support, and maintenance.

On my death, the trustees, if requested by the personal representative of my estate shall, or in their own discretion may, directly or through the personal representative of my estate, pay the expenses of my last illness and funeral, my valid debts, the expenses of administering my estate, including nonprobate assets; and pay all estate, inheritance, generation-skipping, or other death taxes that become due because of my death, including any interest and penalties.

Also, on my death, I give all my tangible personal property to Charles T. Brown, my son, if he survives me, or if he does not survive me, to Sarah J. Brown, my daughter. (I request the recipient of any such tangible personal property to distribute the same as I may have indicated informally by memorandum or otherwise.) The trustees shall distribute all the trust property not effectively disposed of by the preceding provisions of this agreement in equal shares to the persons named below. If any person named below does not survive me, such person's share shall be distributed per stirpes to such person's descendants who survive me.

Charles T. Brown, my son
Sarah J. Brown, my daughter

(continued)

Exhibit 9.6   Sample Revocable Living Trust—*continued*

Article III
Selection of Trustees

Trustees shall be appointed, removed, and replaced as follows: unless I am disabled, I reserve the right and power to remove any trustee and to appoint successor or additional trustees. If I become disabled, I shall cease to be a trustee. On my death or disability, my son, Charles T. Brown, may at any time appoint an individual or corporate trustee and may remove any individual or corporate trustee so appointed.

Article IV
Trustee Powers and Provisions

The powers granted to my trustees may be exercised during the term of this trust and after the termination of the trust as is reasonably necessary to distribute the trust assets. All of the powers are to be discharged without the authorization or approval of any court. I hereby give to my trustees the following powers: (specific administrative powers are listed).

Among the administrative provisions of this trust, I request no bond or other indemnity shall be required of any trustee nominated or appointed in this trust. I expressly waive any requirement that this trust be submitted to the jurisdiction of any court, or that the trustees be appointed or confirmed, that their actions be authorized, or that their accounts be allowed, by any court. This waiver shall not prevent any trustee or beneficiary from requesting any of these procedures.

(General governing provisions may also be added).

The settlor and the trustees have signed this agreement in duplicate on or as of the date appearing at the beginning of this agreement and the trustees accept their appointments as trustees by signing this agreement.

Note: Signatures and notary have been omitted.

Irrevocable Living Trusts

An irrevocable living trust may not be amended, revoked, or canceled after its creation. Living trusts are generally irrevocable unless the trust instrument contains a provision stating it is revocable. To avoid any confusion concerning a settlor's intent, the trust should include a provision such as, "The settlor hereby declares this trust agreement and all its provisions shall be irrevocable and not subject to any amendment or modification by the settlor or any other person." An irrevocable living trust not only has the advantages of avoiding probate and its expense, but also can be used as a tax saving device:

- Although a living trust cannot save on income taxes, it can save on federal estate tax, in appropriate trusts, by excluding the trust property from the decedent-settlor's gross estate, thereby reducing or avoiding the federal estate tax. This is commonly accomplished using an irrevocable life insurance trust.

Example: Pauline Hayes is a single parent with two teenage children. The total value of her gross estate including the face amount (proceeds) of her life insurance for the year 2001 is over $675,000. If Pauline wishes to avoid probate, but completely control her property, she could create two trusts: a revocable trust, into which she would place all of her property except her life insurance, and an irrevocable life insurance trust, into which she would place her life insurance polices worth $300,000 and the ownership of them. By funding the irrevocable trust with an amount of money sufficient to pay the annual life insurance premiums, when Pauline dies, the amount of the life insurance will be paid to the trust, but it will not be added to Pauline's gross

Exhibit 9.7 Sample Pour-Over Will

WILL
OF
WILLIAM T. BROWN

I, William T. Brown, of _____ County, _____ State, revoke any prior wills and codicils and make this my last will.

Article I
Payment of Taxes and Expenses

I direct my personal representative to pay from my estate or to direct the trustee of the William T. Brown Trust under Agreement dated _____, 20___, (referred to hereafter as the "William T. Brown Trust") to pay, or both, as determined in the sole discretion of my personal representative all expenses of my last illness and funeral, my valid debts, the expenses of administering my estate, including nonprobate assets; and to pay all estate, inheritance, generation-skipping, or other death taxes that become due because of my death, including any interest and penalties.

Article II
Special Gifts

I give all my tangible personal property to Charles T. Brown, my son, if he survives me, or if he does not survive me, to Sarah J. Brown, my daughter. (I request the recipient of any such tangible personal property to distribute the same as I may have indicated informally by memorandum or otherwise.)

Article III
Residue

I give the rest, residue, and remainder of my estate consisting of all the real, personal, or mixed property whatsoever and wheresoever located, that I can dispose of by will and not effectively disposed of by preceding articles of this will to the trustee or trustees of the William T. Brown Trust, executed by me on _____, 20___, at [city], [state], as amended and existing at my death, to be added to the remaining assets of that trust and disposed of according to the terms and provisions of that trust.

Article IV
Personal Representative

I nominate and appoint Charles T. brown, my son, as my personal representative. If Charles T. Brown fails or ceases to act or is unable or unwilling to serve as personal representative; I nominate and appoint Sarah J. Brown, my daughter, as successor personal representative.

Article V
Personal Representative and Trustee Provisions

My personal representative, in addition to all other powers conferred by law that are not inconsistent with those contained in this will, shall have the power, exercisable without authorization of any court, to sell at private or public sale, to retain, to lease, and to mortgage or pledge any or all of the real or personal property of my estate; and to settle, contest, compromise, submit to arbitration or litigate claims in favor of or against my estate. I request that my estate be administrated as an Informal Administration and that no bond or other indemnity shall be required of my personal representative. I expressly waive any requirement that the William T. Brown Trust be submitted to the jurisdiction of any court, or that the trustees be appointed or confirmed, or that their actions be authorized, or that their accounts be allowed, by any court. This waiver shall not prevent any trustee or beneficiary from requesting any of these procedures.

(Other Articles may be added.)

I have signed this Will consisting of _____ pages, including this page on _____, 20___.

_____

William T. Brown—Testator

Note: Attestation clause, signatures of witnesses, and self-proving affidavit have been omitted.

estate. This will keep the estate value under $675,000 and thereby avoid the U.S. (federal) estate tax (see the discussion and details in Chapter 10).

Example: In 2001, spouses such as Harold and Marilyn Sheppard, who have three children, can also take advantage of a revocable trust and an irrevocable life insurance trust to preserve an estate worth $1,850,000. Assume, for example, that their life insurance is worth $500,000. Using a revocable trust, they can control their property during their lifetime and avoid probate at death. Using one or more irrevocable life insurance trusts as appropriate, they can eliminate the value of their life insurance from their gross estate(s) and thereby pass to their children the maximum amount of their estate by avoiding the federal estate tax (see the discussion of estate planning in Chapter 10).

AUTOMATED DOCUMENTS

Research Institute of America is just one of many companies that markets an automated estate planning system. Automated products allow users to customize various estate planning forms and checklists, including trusts. Go to *www.riahome.com* to learn more about these types of products.

DRAFTING AN IRREVOCABLE LIVING TRUST

An irrevocable living trust is a convenient device to transfer assets out of a settlor's estate. Its greatest advantage is its flexibility, its adaptability to many purposes. It is important to delegate the drafting of a trust instrument only to counsel knowledgeable in this area. Often you will be asked to prepare a preliminary draft. The instrument must conform not only to the requirements of the Internal Revenue Code but to state law as well. Therefore, before preparing the preliminary draft of an irrevocable living trust under the attorney's supervision, you must have a clear understanding of the settlor's purposes and desires for creation of the trust as well as the applicable federal and state tax consequences.

The hypothetical case below describes the settlor's purposes for establishing a trust and provides a sample checklist of information you need to prepare a preliminary draft. On the basis of the checklist data, a sample agreement is drawn, creating a private express irrevocable living trust.

The Facts

Helen A. Flynn, age 60, lives at 1520 Holly Drive, Flowertown, Apple County, State A. Helen is a widow with two adult children, Jerry Flynn, residing at 1402 Oak Drive, Flowertown, and Janet Flynn, living at home with her mother. Helen has been a very successful businesswoman. She has also been a wise investor. Helen wants to transfer 10,000 shares of common stock of Golden Harvest. Inc., to an irrevocable living trust for her son's benefit (to be designated Trust I). The annual income produced by the stock varies. Jerry has had serious business reverses, and his mother wants to help him overcome these problems. Helen wants the income produced from the stock paid to Jerry annually for the next five years.

At the end of the time period, Helen instructs the trustee to transfer the trust property into two separate, equal trusts, Trust II and Trust III, for the benefit of her two children, as successor beneficiaries, for their respective lifetimes. On the death of Janet and Jerry, Helen wants the trusts to terminate and the principal of the trust (stock) to pass into their respective estates. Therefore, Janet and Jerry will have the opportunity to determine through their individual wills to whom the stock will eventually be transferred.

Helen names her close friend and financial adviser, Betty R. White, trustee. Betty lives at 1040 Merry Lane, in Flowertown. Helen names Betty's husband, Bob, successor trustee. He would take over Betty's duties, e.g., pay trust income to the beneficiaries, should Betty become legally unable to perform. Betty and Bob agree to serve without compensation. The powers and duties granted by Helen to her trustee include the trustee's right to vote the stock, to sell and reinvest in other stocks or bonds when in the best interests of the beneficiaries, and to distribute the income and principal as outlined in the trust agreement. Also, Helen wants to retain the right to remove any trustee she selects or to allow the beneficiaries to remove the trustee.

Using a Checklist

A checklist similar to the one in Exhibit 9.8 should be used to gather the information necessary for drafting the Flynn trust. This checklist is for illustrative purposes only. It reflects details to be included in the prospective trust instrument based on the fact situation previously outlined. Drafters of trust instruments would not and should not use this checklist in every situation. For example, the settlor might not want to name a successor beneficiary who would receive the benefit of the trust should the first-named beneficiary die.

 ASSIGNMENT 9.13

From the completed checklist in Exhibit 9.8, draft a private express irrevocable living trust with the appropriate provisions based on the facts in the Flynn case. Compare your draft with the annotated sample trust in Exhibit 9.9 and point out the similarities and differences in the two drafts.

 ASSIGNMENT 9.14

George Conover decides to create a living trust for his children, Melissa and Gary, with his wife, Grace, as trustee and trust property consisting of real estate in your state that he operates as a summer residence for tourists. Using this information, and supplying more, as necessary to indicate the settlor's intention, compile a checklist similar to the one in Exhibit 9.8 and draft an irrevocable living trust for the Conover Trust.

 ASSIGNMENT 9.15

In Assignment 9.14, George Conover created an irrevocable living trust. Draft a self-proved pour-over will to accompany the Conover Trust.

Exhibit 9.8 Sample Checklist for Drafting a Private Express Irrevocable Living Trust

Names and Addresses of Necessary Parties

Settlor:	Helen A. Flynn	1520 Holly Drive, Flowertown Apple County, State A
Trustee:	Betty R. White	1040 Merry Lane Flowertown Apple County, State A
Successor trustee:	Robert C. White	1040 Merry Lane Flowertown Apple County, State A
Relationship of trustee(s) to settlor:	Financial adviser and friend	

Beneficiaries:

Income beneficiary:	Jerry Flynn, son	1402 Oak Drive, Flowertown Apple County, State A
Successor beneficiary:	Jerry Flynn and	Same as above
	Janet Flynn, daughter	Same as Helen (mother)
Remainderman:	Respective estates of Jerry and Janet Flynn	
Relationship of beneficiaries to settlor:	Beneficiaries (Janet and Jerry) are the children of settlor (Helen)	

Trust Property

Stocks:	10,000 shares of common stock, Golden Harvest, Inc.
Location:	Stock shares—transferred to trustee on acceptance

Revocability of Trust

Trust is irrevocable

Trustee's Powers and Duties

Payment of income (Trust I):	Annually to Jerry for five years
Payment to successor beneficiaries (Trusts II & III):	After five years, income to be paid equally to Janet and Jerry for life
Payment (transfer) of principal:	Principal transferred in equal shares to the respective estates of Janet and Jerry on their deaths
Investment powers:	Invest and reinvest the securities and other general powers

Term of Trustee

Removal:	Removal may be by either settlor or both beneficiaries acting jointly
Successor in office:	Robert White, husband of proposed trustee

(continued)

Exhibit 9.8 Sample Checklist for Drafting a Private Express Irrevocable
Living Trust—*continued*

Trustee's Rights

Acceptance or rejection (determine trustee's intention):	Trustees agree to serve
Compensation:	Trustees agree to serve without charge

Termination of Trust

Duration of trust:	Settlor intends to transfer income to son for five years (Trust I); then in equal shares (Trusts II and III) to both children for life. Remainder to the children's estates
Distribution of principal of Trust I on termination of trust:	Transferred in equal shares to Trusts II and III
Distribution of principal and income of Trusts II and III on termination of said trusts:	Transferred in equal shares to respective estates of Janet and Jerry on their deaths

Exhibit 9.9 Annotated Sample Irrevocable Living Trust

HELEN A. FLYNN
TRUST AGREEMENT

This trust agreement is made June 1, 2000, between Helen A. Flynn of 1520 Holly Drive, City of Flowertown, County of Apple, State of A, hereinafter referred to as Settlor, Betty R. White of 1040 Merry Lane, City of Flowertown, County of Apple, State of A, hereinafter referred to as Trustee, and Robert C. White of 1040 Merry Lane, City of Flowertown, County of Apple, State of A, hereinafter referred to as Successor Trustee.

COMMENT: The major purpose of the introductory clause in a trust is to identify the parties involved. Always include addresses to assist in proper identification.

Settlor and trustees agree to the following:

Article I

Settlor hereby transfers to trustee 10,000 shares of common corporate stock of Golden Harvest, Inc., described in Schedule A, annexed hereto and made a part hereof by this reference, the receipt of which property is hereby acknowledged by trustee, to be held in trust based on the terms herein set forth.

COMMENT: This article identifies the property of the trust. It also establishes the willingness of the person nominated to act as trustee and to accept the responsibilities outlined in later articles. Incorporation by reference, i.e., use of the words, "Schedule A, annexed hereto," enables the drafter to define the trust estate without making the trust instrument unduly long.

Article II

Trustee is authorized to receive property added to the trust estate from any person, provided such property is acceptable to the trustee.

COMMENT: If the trustee is to care for property added to the trust throughout its duration, such as stock resulting from a split, this must be stipulated. Generally, property can be added to the trust throughout its existence.

(*continued*)

Exhibit 9.9   Annotated Sample Irrevocable Living Trust—*continued*

Article III

Trustee shall hold, invest, and reinvest the trust property; collect the dividends, interest, and other income thereof; and, after deducting all necessary administration expenses, dispose and distribute the net income and principal as follows:

First: The net income from the trust estate shall be placed in a trust, Trust I, and shall be paid annually to Jerry Flynn, son of the settlor, of 1402 Oak Drive, Flowertown, Apple County, State A, for five (5) years commencing from the date of this agreement.

Second: At the end of the five-year period, the trustee shall divide the trust principal and income into equal amounts and place them into two separate trusts, Trust II and Trust III. Trust II shall be established for the benefit of Jerry Flynn and Trust III for Janet Flynn, daughter of settlor, currently residing at settlor's address. The net incomes of Trust II and Trust III shall be paid annually to the respective beneficiaries, Jerry and Janet, until their deaths. The death of each beneficiary named herein shall terminate the respective trust created for his or her benefit, and the principal and remaining income of the trust shall become part of the decedent beneficiary's estate and shall be distributed to the beneficiary's personal representative.

COMMENT: This article describes in detail the way income and principal of the trust estate shall be distributed. The settlor's directions for payment should be clear, specific, and complete. Ambiguities should be avoided. For example, the instrument should not recite: "The settlor wishes the trustee to manage and invest the trust estate and pay the income to Jerry Flynn for five years, and thereafter to Jerry Flynn and Janet Flynn in equal shares." Perhaps the settlor knows exactly what she intends the trust to accomplish, but the trust instrument does not convey this. The lack of definiteness leads to questions concerning the implementation of the trust. Is the trustee obliged to reinvest the trust funds? May she deduct administrative expenses? Could the trust continue indefinitely? Spelling out the powers and duties of the trustee will lessen the risk of injured feelings and litigation.

Article IV

The trustee shall have the following powers and discretions in addition to those conferred by law:
(a) To retain the property described in "Schedule A," and any other property added to the trust estate;
(b) To invest and reinvest, to sell or exchange the principal of this trust in such stocks or bonds as trustee shall in her discretion deem to be reasonable, expedient or proper regardless of whether such stocks, bonds, or other property shall be legal investments for trusts under the laws of State A;
(c) To vote in person or by proxy all stocks or other securities held by trustee;
(d) To exchange the securities of any corporation or company for other securities issued by the same, or by any other corporation or company at such times and upon such terms, as trustee shall deem proper; and
(e) To exercise with respect to all stock, bonds, and other investments held by trustee, all rights, powers, and privileges as are lawfully exercised by any person owning similar property in his/her own right.

COMMENT: All powers that a settlor wishes to grant to the trustee should be included in the trust instrument and clearly defined. Limitations, if desired, should also be specifically enumerated. The settlor of this trust has definite ideas about what she wants the trustee to do. Section *b* above, for example, states that the trustee shall decide what investments shall be made on behalf of the trust, despite the statutes of State A, which declare and enumerate permissible trust investments. It is possible, and perfectly legal, for settlors to include such provisions in trust agreements. It is only when the settlor fails to mention the type of investments the trustee may make that such statutes go into effect. The intent of these statutes is benevolent rather than restrictive. They are designed to help inexperienced investors to invest prudently.

Article V

The settlor hereby declares that this agreement and the trusts hereby created shall be irrevocable and not subject to modification by the settlor or any other person and the settlor further declares that no trustee shall be required to furnish bond or other security to any court.

COMMENT: Placing property in trust saves estate tax only if the trust is irrevocable and not included in the settlor's estate. The settlor is taxed on the income and capital gains of the trust property if:
1. The settlor retains the right to revoke the trust (IRC § 676).
2. The settlor or the settlor's spouse currently or at any time in the future receive or "may receive" the trust income (IRC § 677 [a]).
3. The settlor retains certain dispositions or administrative powers (IRC §§ 674 and 675).
It is common today that trustees can serve without bond.

(continued)

Exhibit 9.9 Annotated Sample Irrevocable Living Trust—*continued*

Article VI

Both trustee and successor trustee have agreed to waive compensation for their services.

COMMENT: The trust instrument should expressly provide for the trustee's compensation or its waiver. In the absence of such a provision, statutes in many states fix or limit the rates of the commission. Unless the settlor indicates whether the trustee shall receive or forgo compensation as agreed, the court may order the statutory amount paid from the trust income.

Article VII

The settlor hereby appoints as successor trustee, Robert C. White of 1040 Merry Lane, Flowertown, Apple County, State A. In the event that trustee or successor trustee shall die, resign, become incapacitated, or for any reason fail or refuse to act as trustee, settlor shall have the power to appoint a successor. Any successor trustee shall have all the powers and obligations of the trustee named herein.

COMMENT: It is important for the settlor to name a successor in case the original trustee is unable or unwilling to serve. Because of their fiduciary responsibilities, all trustees should be selected with care, keeping in mind the specific purposes for which the trust is created.

Article VIII

The validity of this trust and the construction of its provisions shall be governed solely by the laws of the State of A as they now exist or may exist in the future.

COMMENT: Each state may have certain restrictions on trusts that may affect the purpose of the trust. Such restrictions must be determined before a workable instrument can be drafted. A clause similar to this may prove more valuable than it would appear. For example, Helen Flynn, the settlor, lives in State A, as does Betty White, the trustee. At the inception of the trust, at least, it will be governed by the laws of A because that is the place where it is to be administered (carried out by the trustee), according to Article VIII. However, this situation can change. Suppose Betty moves to the State of N and transacts business there. The laws of N regarding trusts might be quite different from the laws of A, with the result that new limitations are placed on Betty and the trust does not achieve what Helen had intended. Or suppose that a year from now state A enacts a special tax on living trusts. Does the Flynn Trust have to pay the tax since such a law was not in existence at the time of the trusts's creation? A court could resolve such problems, but the process would be both time-and money-consuming (e.g., the question involving the laws of two states, A and N, might require a federal action). It is advisable to include a clause that prevents such questions from arising.

IN WITNESS WHEREOF, settlor and trustees have executed this agreement at Flowertown, the day and year written above.

IN PRESENCE OF:

_____   _____
(Witness)   (Settlor)

_____   _____
(Witness)   (Trustee)

                                              _____
                                                  (Successor Trustee)

STATE OF <u>A</u>   ⎫
                        ⎬ ss.
County of <u>Apple</u>   ⎭

   The foregoing instrument was acknowledged before me this <u>1st</u> day of <u>June</u>, 2000, by <u>Helen A. Flynn</u> as settlor and <u>Betty R. White</u> and <u>Robert C. White</u>, as trustees.

[*Notarial Seal*]

                                              _____
                                                  Notary Public

KEY TERMS

Express trust
Implied trust
Indefinite class
Cy-pres
Cy-pres doctrine

Active trust
Passive trust
Rule Against
   Perpetuities
Resulting trust

Purchase-money
   resulting trust
Parol evidence
Constructive trust
Necessaries

Sprinkling trust
Precatory words
Precatory trust
Homestead exemption
Pour-over will

REVIEW QUESTIONS

1. What are the differences between the following kinds or classes of trusts: express versus implied: private versus public; active versus passive; *inter vivos* (living) versus testamentary; and resulting versus constructive?
2. What elements are necessary to create an express private trust? How do they differ from the elements needed to create an express public trust?
3. Does the *cy-pres* doctrine apply to all trusts? Explain.
4. What is meant by the phrase "the law allows resulting trusts to be proved by parol evidence"?
5. What are spendthrift and sprinkling trusts, and why would a settlor create them?
6. What is the proper way of creating a Totten trust, and can it be used to disinherit a surviving spouse? Explain.
7. What are some of the most common reasons or purposes for creating trusts?
8. Give three examples of trust restrictions that are "reasonable restraints" and do not violate public policy.
9. When is a precatory trust declared valid?
10. What is the court's position on a trust that has all its required elements but lacks a trustee? Explain.
11. Why are living trusts today often considered to be more desirable than wills? Which do you prefer? Why?
12. What are the major disadvantages of revocable living trusts?
13. How are real and personal property transferred into a living trust?
14. What is the purpose of a pour-over will? Do assets included in such a will have to be probated? Explain.
15. What are some of the uses of an irrevocable living trust?

CASE PROBLEMS

Problem 1

Duncan Bennett, a single parent, wants to leave his entire estate to his only child, Bonnie. He knows Bonnie is extravagant and often spends her money foolishly; therefore, he establishes a trust with a spendthrift provision, "to protect Bonnie from her own mismanagement and wasteful habits in spending money." The trust also provides that Bonnie cannot transfer, pledge, or assign her interest in the trust income or principal in any manner and that such interest is not to be subject to any of Bonnie's creditors' claims by attachment, garnishment, execution, or other process of law. Answer the following:

A. Are spendthrift trusts valid in all states?
B. Would this trust be valid in your state? If so, cite the statute.
C. If one of Bonnie's creditors supplies her with property items that are obviously "necessaries," can that creditor reach (obtain) Bonnie's trust income despite the spendthrift clause? See *Erickson v. Bank of California,* 97 Wash.2d 246, 643 P.2d 670 (1982).

Problem 2

Amy purchased twenty acres of land from Ben. Because Amy was immediately leaving the country to serve in the Peace Corps for two years and was unable to attend the closing, she asked Ben to deed the property to her close friend, Sally. Ben conveyed the property by deed to Sally in her name. When Amy returns, Sally refuses to turn over the property and claims the property was a gift to her from Amy. Amy denies the property was a gift and demands that Sally return the property. Answer and explain the following:

A.   Since real property (land) is involved in this case, does the Statute of Frauds apply?

B.   In this case, can parol evidence be used to determine whether or not a resulting trust is established?

C.   If Amy and Sally go to court, what methods might a court use to decide whether Sally's claim is correct?

D.   If it goes to court, in your opinion, which party would win this case? See *Rainey v. Rainey,* 795 S.W.2d 139 (Tenn.App. 1990).

E.   If Amy died while in the Peace Corps, would the property belong to Sally?

ESTATE PLANNING AND LONG-TERM CARE

OUTLINE

OBJECTIVES

After completing this chapter, you should be able to:

➤ Explain the need for and purpose of an estate plan and the procedures and documents used to create a plan.

➤ Understand the adverse factors that diminish an estate's value and how to minimize them.

➤ Utilize the knowledge acquired from earlier chapters to draft appropriate wills and trusts necessary for an estate plan.

➤ Identify and incorporate into an estate plan the tax-saving devices that increase the deductions from the gross estate or reduce the gross estate, thereby reducing or possibly eliminating federal and/or state death taxes.

➤ Identify the users and their need for long-term care. Explain how the cost of such care is financed by individual assets, state and federal sources, and long-term care insurance.

SCOPE OF THE CHAPTER

This chapter discusses the need for an estate plan and the process for its creation. The legal documents, e.g., wills and trusts, required for an estate plan are discussed in detail as are devices that save estate tax either by reducing the decedent's gross estate or by increasing the deductions from the estate. In addition, due to the enormous increase in our nation's aging population in the first half of the new millennium, the estate plan must include financial planning for future disability and long-term care needs. This chapter concludes with a discussion of long-term care.

THE ESTATE PLAN

Estate planning is the determination and utilization of a method to accumulate, manage, and dispose of real and personal property by the owner of the property during life and after death and to minimize the income, gift, inheritance, and estate taxes due. The purpose of estate planning is to identify, preserve, and increase the assets owned and provide for distribution of these assets, with the least possible tax expense, to family members and institutions the owner wishes to benefit. If estate planning is properly performed, the intent and desires of the owner will be accomplished, and the beneficiary-recipients (primarily family) will receive the maximum benefit and enjoyment of the property.

Unfortunately, most people are so involved in their daily activities, they give little thought to the consequences of their deaths. Many realize the importance of purchasing life insurance to protect their dependents, and as people grow older, they give thought to their mortality. But people often die prematurely and fail to provide through a valid will or an appropriate trust for those for whom they care. The consequences of these acts of procrastination can be financially devastating.

Earlier chapters in this book explained in detail how you can assist in the creation and use of trusts and wills to resolve and avoid these unfortunate consequences. It is also important that you are prepared to assist those who have the responsibility for estate planning and administration, i.e., your supervising attorney and the personal representative of the decedent's estate.

In addition to the attorney, numerous other individuals are qualified to give estate planning advice. They include trust officers from banks and trust companies, accountants, investment advisers, financial planners, and life insurance agents. Acting as a team, many of these advisers will take an active role in the development of an appropriate estate plan for each client. The attorney you assist will give advice on legal matters; the accountant will handle tax concerns; the financial planner will advise on investments; and the life insurance agent may play a key role in the formation of an insurance policy to ensure financial security for the client's family. While you assist these estate planners, your tasks will be to gather information, maintain records, and communicate by phone or letters to update and keep the client and planners informed of the plan's progress. *Such tasks require you to neither divulge confidential information nor submit or propose unauthorized legal advice even in response to a specific request.*

ETHICAL ISSUE ➤

🖳 ESTATE PLANNING ADVICE IS EVERYWHERE!

Advertisements for estate planning tips and asset protection tools flourish on the Internet. Television commercials are common for mutual funds and related products. More and more insurance agents and stockbrokers are presenting investment/estate planning seminars. Seniors are not the only target market. Presentations are made in the workplace, to civic groups, at business expos—really just about everywhere. In our wealthy country, there are many companies that wish to influence how Americans spend and invest their money. Some nonlawyers may have given legal advice to clients, and therefore, clients may need to be reminded that legal advice comes from attorneys. Other investment and retirement planning advice needs to come from the appropriate professionals.

Everyone who lives a normal life span accumulates assets he wants to transfer after death. Real estate, cash, art, jewelry, securities, business ownership, boats, planes, antiques, profit-sharing plans, pension plans, life insurance, IRAs, 401(k) plans, Social Security, and other employment and government benefit plans are a few examples of the wide variety of assets frequently acquired during one's life. The total value of the property items that form an individual's estate can be considerable and may be much larger than initially anticipated; e.g., the value of an appreciated home and other unencumbered real estate, sizable pension plans, and often the proceeds of life insurance policies alone may add substantially to the estate.

These assets and their value create a need to formulate a sound and appropriate financial plan—called an **estate plan.** The estate plan is an arrangement of a person's estate that takes into account the laws of wills, property, trusts, insurance, and taxes in order to gain maximum financial benefit of all these laws for the **disposition** (distribution) of the property during life and after death. If the plan is properly formed and executed, it should produce the best possible economic security for the individual and her family. The estate plan encompasses the creation of the estate, its maximum growth and conservation, and, ultimately, its distribution. It necessitates active planning strategies during the individual's life and important postmortem decisions after death. If designed appropriately, the estate plan should meet all the individual's objectives and provide her with (1) a comfortable retirement income; (2) financial protection for her family; (3) proper custodial care should incompetency or any serious physical or other mental health problem occur; (4) a minimum of taxes and expenses throughout the implementation of the plan; and (5) expedient, efficient, and harmonious distribution of the estate according to her wishes after death.

The development of an estate plan for the client commences once the client reaches a "comfort level" with the supervising attorney and paralegal which allows the paralegal to accumulate the personal and financial data. To help the client create an appropriate estate plan, you will use all of the same techniques (interviewing, negotiating, drafting, and counseling skills) and professional conduct which were described earlier in the discussion of drafts of wills and trusts.

Estate plan
An arrangement of a person's estate using the laws of various disciplines, e.g., wills, trusts, taxes, insurance, and property, to gain maximum financial benefit of all the laws for the disposition of a person's assets during life and after death.

Disposition
The distribution, transfer, or conveyance of property.

🏛 ASSIGNMENT 10.1

1. A new client has come to your office to discuss a will. You have not met the client, but your supervising attorney has told you the client is shy, reserved, and reluctant

to discuss private family and financial matters with "strangers." Explain some of the things you might do or say to establish a "comfort level" between the client and yourself so you can obtain the requisite information to draft the will.

2. Review the checklists in Chapter 6 (Exhibits 6.1 through 6.6), and determine if they are adequate to elicit the necessary information to develop and draft an estate plan. What is missing? What could you add?

Before the utilization of the data and information accumulated through the interview, checklists, worksheets, and questionnaires is discussed, it will be helpful to summarize the potential adverse factors which will diminish any estate. It is necessary to identify and understand these factors so measures can be included in the estate plan to diminish their effect. Five factors in particular require attention: federal and state death and gift taxes; administration expenses; losses resulting from the forced liquidation (sale) of assets to raise funds to pay debts of the deceased; and financial losses due to the termination of the decedent's employment.

1. *Federal gift and estate tax.* This tax is imposed on the privilege of transferring property while living by gift and at death whether to beneficiaries of a will or to heirs by the intestate succession statutes (IRC § 2001 et seq.). Federal law exempts from federal gift and estate tax transfers from the decedent of up to $675,000 in value for 2001 (see Exhibit 14.3). Thus, anyone can give while living and transfer after death assets worth $675,000 to donees, beneficiaries, or heirs without paying any federal gift and estate tax. Although the number of individuals dying with estates valued over $675,000 is increasing, the percentage of the population dying with such estates is still small. Since the federal gift and estate tax rates range from a low of 37 percent for estates over $675,000 to 55 percent on estates over $3,000,000, any procedure that can diminish the tax must be included in the estate plan. With proper planning in 2001, a married couple can use planning devices, such as trusts, to transfer $1,350,000 free of estate tax after the deaths of both spouses. *Caveat: The Economic Growth and Tax Relief Reconciliation Act of 2001 increases the exemption amount and decreases teh tax rates beginning in 2002 (see Chapter 14).*

2. *State death taxes.* The taxes imposed by the states vary considerably. State taxes may include estate taxes (which only two states impose); a "credit estate tax" (which all states impose) that "picks up" or absorbs the amount of the federal estate tax credit allowed for taxes paid to the state and is commonly referred to as the state estate tax; or an inheritance tax (a tax on the beneficiaries of property received from a decedent's estate). The inheritance tax is determined by the value of property received and the relationship of the beneficiaries to the decedent. *Caveat:* If the *only state tax* is the equivalent of the federal estate tax credit, this state estate tax does not present a tax planning problem for two reasons: (1) if no federal estate tax is due, no state estate tax is levied either, and (2) if federal estate tax is levied, the state tax offsets the federal tax so that the total tax remains the same. *Note: See credit for state death taxes on U.S. Treasury Form 706 (Form 88, Appendix A).* Also, see Exhibit 14.1 in Chapter 14, which lists the taxes of each state.

3. *Administration expenses.* The commission (fee) of the personal representative, attorney's fee, court costs and filings, and costs of administering the estate including the decedent's funeral and burial expenses are all incurred during an

estate administration. All of these expenses must be paid from the assets of the decedent's estate and may substantially lessen its value. If the decedent owned property in more than one state, ancillary administration expense will add to these costs. Obviously, any method that reduces the decedent's gross estate, e.g., by making lifetime gifts, also reduces the probate fees and administration expenses, which are commonly computed as a percentage of the probate estate. The personal representative may elect to take the administration expenses as a deduction on the decedent's federal estate tax return (IRC § 2053) or as a deduction on the estate's fiduciary income tax return (IRC § 642[g]).

4. *Forced liquidation.* The personal representative may be forced to sell (at a sacrifice) assets of the estate in order to obtain the cash needed to pay legitimate and approved creditors, claims, federal and state taxes, and administration expenses. After reviewing the potential property to be sold with the beneficiaries, the personal representative will select and sell, according to statutory guidelines, the assets that cause the least shrinkage from their fair market value and consequently from the estate.

5. *Termination of employment.* A substantial loss of income to the estate may result for many reasons including the direct consequence of the employee's untimely and unexpected death.

The adverse effects of some or all of these factors cannot be entirely eliminated, but a well-designed estate plan can help to minimize them.

After information has been obtained from interviews and questionnaires and reviewed with the client, an estate plan is created using the following documents and devices which save estate tax either by an increase in the deductions from the gross estate or by reducing the gross estate itself:

- Documents:
  - Wills and trusts.
- Estate tax-saving devices that increase the deductions from the gross estate:
  - The marital deduction.
  - The charitable deduction.
- Estate tax-saving devices that reduce the gross estate:
  - Gifts.
  - Powers of appointment.
  - Trusts.
  - Life insurance.

The next sections discuss the role these elements play in the development of an estate plan. Earlier chapters described in detail the plans, drafts, and uses of wills and trusts, therefore, this chapter will emphasize the tax-saving devices.

Periodic Review

No matter how well an estate plan is designed to meet the objectives of a client, changes in tax laws, domicile, family relationships (including marital status, birth or death of a child or other beneficiaries and heirs), and accumulated assets necessitate periodic review of the plan. *Another ethical issue could result if the attorney or paralegal openly solicited clients to conduct this review.* Therefore, it must be made clear to the client that she is responsible for initiating a review when changes known only to her occur which mandate the modification of the estate plan.

ETHICAL ISSUE

DOCUMENTS USED TO CREATE THE ESTATE PLAN

Wills

A will is one of the most common and important estate planning documents. As part of an estate plan, a will allows the testator to:

- Leave the entire estate to a surviving spouse *or* limit the spouse's interest to the share required by state statute since the surviving spouse cannot be disinherited (see the discussions of elective or forced share of a surviving spouse and the method used in community property states in Chapters 2 and 4).
- Leave the estate to children, e.g., natural, adopted, or nonmarital, *or* disinherit one or more or all of them.
- Leave the estate to anyone, such as friends or faithful employees, whether or not they are family members.
- Leave the entire estate to charity or other public institutions, except for the surviving spouse's elective share.
- Identify the estate assets and the beneficiaries who are to receive them, thereby minimizing confusion and the possibility of costly will contests.
- Appoint both personal and property guardians for minor children. One person may serve as both types of guardian, or a financial institution, e.g., a bank, may be the property guardian, while a relative or friend is the personal guardian.
- Establish testamentary trusts within the will to reduce or even avoid estate taxes and select the trustee who will administer the trusts.
- Appoint an executor or executrix or, using the UPC term, a personal representative to carry out the terms of the will and administer the estate.

A will can be changed throughout the testator's lifetime since the will takes effect only on death. It should be reviewed periodically and, when necessary, updated.

Trusts

Trusts are the other key planning documents. As previously discussed, a trust can be created *inter vivos,* the living trust, or placed in a will, the testamentary trust. A living trust can be revocable or irrevocable. If it is irrevocable, the income produced by the trust property is taxable to the trust as a legal entity, or to the beneficiaries, if they receive the income, but in either case, the trust property is no longer part of the settlor's assets. Estate planners can use trusts to benefit family members in numerous other ways:

- Provide lifetime income for a surviving spouse and then pass the property to children and grandchildren.
- Protect a spendthrift child.
- Preserve privacy, because, unlike a will, a trust is not a public document.
- Obtain professional management of the trust property to maximize its income potential.
- Spread or sprinkle trust income or principal to family members years after the testator's death when their needs are better known.

- Enable the trust property to be controlled by the settlor-trustee while living and, after the settlor's death, by the successor trustee for the benefit of the beneficiary.
- Avoid the lengthy delays and expense of probate including ancillary administration expense.
- Diminish problems such as will contests.
- Eliminate the need for the probate court to appoint a guardian or conservator for minors or for oneself due to declining health.
- Reduce federal and state death taxes by using trusts to increase the marital and charitable deductions and allow a married couple to make maximum use of their estate tax exclusions after their deaths (see the discussion of estate tax-saving devices in the next sections).

ESTATE TAX-SAVING DEVICES THAT INCREASE DEDUCTIONS FROM THE GROSS ESTATE

Two types of deductions are frequently used to produce a lower net estate subject to the federal estate tax. They are (1) the marital deduction and (2) the charitable deduction.

The Marital Deduction

The **marital deduction** is an unlimited federal tax deduction allowed on the transfer of property from one spouse to another. The unlimited deduction is allowed under the federal gift tax for *inter vivos* (lifetime) transfers between spouses (IRC § 2523) and also under the federal estate tax for property passing from a decedent to a surviving spouse by will or inheritance (IRC § 2056). The unlimited marital deduction is an essential consideration in estate tax planning for a married couple since spouses frequently leave their estates to the surviving spouse. *Note:* Without an appropriate estate tax plan, however, considerable federal estate tax that could have been avoided may be owed on the death of the second spouse.

> **Example:** William and Melva are married. William owns assets worth $350,000; Melva's assets are worth $1,000,000. If William dies first in 2001 and leaves everything to Melva, his estate would pay no tax because of the unlimited marital deduction. *Note:* Although William's estate pays no estate tax on his death, he has lost the opportunity to take advantage of every person's right to the $675,000 estate tax exemption (exclusion). When Melva dies in 2001 (assuming she does not remarry), her $1,350,000 estate will pay approximately $270,750 in taxes (calculated as $491,300 tentative tax on the $1,350,000 estate minus $220,550 unified credit (applicable credit amount) = $270,750; for more on the calculation of federal estate tax, see Chapter 14). To avoid this estate tax and enable more of their combined estates to pass to their children, Melva, while living, could transfer by gift $325,000 of her estate to William so that each would have assets of $675,000. (This suggestion assumes Melva and William are not contemplating a legal separation or divorce and they want to maximize the estate they pass to their children.)

This process of rearranging property ownership of total estate assets so each spouse's estate has approximately the same value, which enables each spouse to take the maximum advantage of the unified credit amount, is called **estate**

Marital deduction
An unlimited amount of the decedent's gross estate, which may be given to the surviving spouse without being subject to federal estate tax levied against the decedent's estate.

Estate equalization
Rearranging property ownership of total estate assets owned by the spouses so that each spouse's individual estate has approximately the same value.

▶ **ETHICAL ISSUE**
.........................➤

Bypass trust
This trust, also called Trust B of an A-B trust, credit shelter trust, exemption equivalent trust, residuary trust, or family trust, is an estate planning device whereby a portion of a deceased spouse's estate passes to a trust rather than directly to the surviving spouse, thereby reducing the likelihood that the surviving spouse's subsequent estate will exceed the federal estate tax threshold. Typically, the surviving spouse is given a life estate in the trust.

Charitable deduction
Under tax law IRC § 170(c), a charitable deduction is any contribution by a person to a qualified charity or other tax-exempt institution for which the taxpayer can claim a deduction on her income tax return.

equalization. *The attorney and paralegal must be especially careful when acting for and advising both spouses about interspousal gifts because serious ethical problems can result when the attorney advises one spouse to make substantial gifts to the other spouse.* The ethical concern of the attorney is that the marriage might subsequently be dissolved. The solution for the attorney and paralegal is to explain the dilemma and make sure both spouses understand the situation, acknowledge their awareness of the potential problem, and indicate their consent to this estate plan, in writing. If William dies first, he can create what is called a **bypass trust** in which a deceased spouse's estate passes to a trust (bypass trust) rather than to the surviving spouse. The bypass trust is established with William's $675,000 estate. The trust will pay the income to Melva for life but then pass the remainder to their children without being taxed when she dies. Melva can then pass her $675,000 estate, free of estate tax, to their children because she still has her individual $675,000 estate tax exemption (exclusion) available. See Exhibit 10.1 illustrating this tax planning example.

The bypass trust is funded with all of the first deceased spouse's (William's) $675,000 unused estate tax exemption (exclusion) without incurring any estate tax. Since the interests of the surviving spouse (Melva) as beneficiary of the bypass trust are sufficiently limited (to only a life estate), when she dies, the trust assets are not included in her gross estate for estate tax purposes. Thus, the trust "bypasses" Melva's taxable estate, and the assets pass tax-free to their children. Melva's own $675,000 estate tax exemption (exclusion) will apply to her separate property, which is valued at exactly $675,000.

Melva is giving up a lot. She has transferred $325,000 to William by gift, and in return, she receives only a life estate in his now combined $675,000 estate. If she is willing to make this arrangement, however, after both spouses die, $1,350,000 of their property will pass to their children free of estate tax, saving $270,750. Although Melva must forgo ownership of the assets used to fund the bypass trust, she still receives substantial benefits from the trust. She receives all trust income during her lifetime, and principal may be distributed to her at the discretion of the trustee: *she* may even act as trustee or co-trustee, but in such cases, the discretion to distribute principal to herself is limited to an "ascertainable standard," such as her need for health, education, support, or maintenance (IRC § 2041[b][1]). Melva may also have the right to appoint principal of the trust during her lifetime or at death, provided she does not appoint the property to herself, her estate, her creditors, or creditors of her estate. *Note,* however, she does not have a general power of appointment (see the discussion below) over the trust assets, which would cause them to be taxable to her estate when she died.

Section 2056 of the IRC establishes that a "qualifying" marital deduction is not limited to gifts through a will or to transfers made at the time of the decedent's death. The following transfers all qualify as part of the marital deduction from the gross estate of the decedent spouse for property that passes to the surviving spouse: bequests and inheritances; joint tenancy property; *inter vivos* gifts; trust transfers; pension plan benefits; life insurance proceeds; and transfers made through the exercise of powers of appointment.

The Charitable Deduction

To be a **charitable deduction,** a gift must be made for religious, scientific, charitable, literary, or educational purposes (IRC § 170[c]). A charitable deduction is

---

Exhibit 10.1   Tax Planning Illustration

Case One		Case Two

First estate:
   William dies in 2001
   leaving $350,000
   to Melva.

First estate qualifies
for marital deduction;
no federal estate tax.

Compare after Melva gives
William $325,000, which
is not taxed because of
the unlimited marital gift
tax deduction.

The success of this
financial plan to pass the
maximum estate to the
couple's children depends
solely on Melva's willingness to gift $325,000 of
her property to her
husband. Marital problems
between them might make
this impractical and dis-
advantageous to Melva
with ethical consequences
for any attorney or
paralegal acting for both
spouses.

First estate:
   William dies in 2001,
   leaving $675,000 in a
   life estate for Melva in
    a bypass trust.

First estate qualifies for
$675,000 individual
estate tax exemption
(exclusion); **no** federal
 estate tax.

Bypass trust:
   Since Melva receives
   a life estate, she has no
   interest in this property
   when she dies, and it is
   not taxed to her estate;
   no federal estate tax.

Second estate:
   Melva dies in 2001,
   leaving $1,350,000
   to children.

Second estate
qualifies for only
$675,000 individual
estate tax exemption
(exclusion).

Second estate:
   Melva dies in 2001,
   leaving separate
   $675,000 to children.

Second estate qualifies
for her $675,000
individual estate tax
exemption (exclusion).

Result: $270,750
   federal estate tax

Result: **No** federal
   estate tax

---

also applicable to trusts (IRC § 512[b][11]). If a trust is to qualify and be approved as a charitable trust, it must be established for one of these purposes. A charity cannot be an individual.

Gifts made to qualified charities during the donor's lifetime can be used to reduce both estate and income taxes. The value of real or personal property given by a will or trust to certain kinds of qualified charities is deductible from the donor's gross estate for federal estate tax purposes (IRC § 2055). A lifetime donor or a testator often makes a direct, outright charitable gift of cash; alternatively, the donor may give highly appreciated securities and real estate because doing so can reduce both estate taxes and **capital gains taxes.** In addition, a settlor-donor can establish a trust with a gift called a **charitable remainder** (see discussion below).

Charitable Remainder Trusts

A charitable remainder trust allows a settlor or the named beneficiary to retain the income from the trust, generally for life; after death, the trust property is given to a "qualified" charity. Charitable remainder trusts can provide the following benefits:

- Reduce income tax by allowing the settlor-donor an income tax deduction for the gift in the year the contribution is made to the trust.
- Increase current income by providing a life income for the settlor or other named beneficiaries by using property that currently does not provide income (real estate such as the settlor's home or other residential property).
- Avoid capital gains tax on gifts of long-term appreciated property (securities or real estate).
- Reduce federal estate tax liability. Gifts to charities, in general, are exempt from federal estate tax as long as the recipient of the gift qualifies as a charity (IRC § 2055). If real estate is given to the charity, the value would not be included in the gross estate of the settlor-decedent, thereby decreasing the federal estate tax on the decedent's estate.
- Provide funds from lower taxes and increased income to the settlor that can be used to purchase life insurance through an irrevocable life insurance trust to replace the value of the donation (e.g., real estate) and pass the insurance proceeds through the trust to the heirs (children, etc.).
- Allow the settlor-donors to make substantial gifts to charities of their choice.

Two types of irrevocable charitable remainder trusts are the Charitable Remainder Unitrust and the Charitable Remainder Annuity Trust.

Charitable Remainder Unitrust.   In a **Charitable Remainder Unitrust,** the settlor places cash or property in the trust, which pays an annual distribution of a fixed percentage of not less than 5 percent of the fair market value of the trust property (determined annually) to a noncharitable beneficiary for life (IRC § 664[d][2] & [3]). The noncharitable income beneficiary may be the settlor-donor or other named beneficiaries. When the life beneficiary dies, the trust property passes to the qualified charity. The settlor-donor and the charitable organization negotiate the specific percentage to be paid (at least 5 percent) at the time the trust is established. Additional assets can be contributed to the trust at any time. Once the fixed percentage is agreed on by the settlor and charity, it cannot be changed. However, payments to the beneficiary will vary annually depending on the increase in the value of the trust property. If the property's value increases, so does the beneficiary's income. The unitrust provides for this potential income growth and thereby counteracts the effects of inflation.

Charitable Remainder Annuity Trust.   In a **Charitable Remainder Annuity Trust,** the settlor places property in the trust, which must pay a fixed amount (sum certain) of income at least annually to a noncharitable beneficiary for life. When the beneficiary dies, the trust property passes to the qualified charity. Un-

---

Capital gains tax
An income tax on profits from the sale or exchange of a capital asset at a lower rate than the rates applied to ordinary income. Capital assets are all property held by a taxpayer, e.g., house, car, and stocks, except for assets listed in IRC § 1221.

Charitable remainder
A gift to a qualified charity after an intervening estate which qualifies as a tax deduction under certain circumstances.

Charitable Remainder Unitrust
A trust that specifies the noncharitable income beneficiary or beneficiaries are to receive annual payments for life based on a fixed percentage (at least 5 percent) of the net fair market value of the trust's assets as determined each year.

Charitable Remainder Annuity Trust
A trust that must pay the noncharitable income beneficiary or beneficiaries a sum certain annually for life, or more frequently if desired, which is not less than 5 percent of the initial net fair market value of all property placed in the trust as determined for federal tax purposes.

der Section 664(d)(1) of the IRC, the fixed annual income given to the noncharitable life beneficiary must be at least 5 percent of the initial net fair market value of all property placed in the trust. This annual income amount can never change. The court in the case of *In re Danforth's Will,* 81 Misc.2d 452, 366 N.Y.S.2d 329 (1975) upheld this definition of a Charitable Remainder Annuity Trust. If the trust property's income diminishes for some reason such as a slump in the economy, the annual fixed payment must come from the principal of the trust. On the other hand, if the economy flourishes, the excess income, after the fixed payment is paid, remains in the trust. Therefore, this trust is primarily for individuals who want a guaranteed fixed income. Unlike the unitrust, the annuity trust does not allow additional contributions to be made to the trust property.

If a client does not have enough property to set up one of these charitable remainder trusts by herself, she can contribute her property to a public "pooled income" fund such as the American Cancer Society or the March of Dimes. All individual gifts are placed in the larger "pooled" fund, and each donor receives annual income based on her contribution compared to the value of the entire fund. When the client dies, her property passes to the charity.

ESTATE TAX-SAVING DEVICES THAT REDUCE THE GROSS ESTATE

When preparing an estate plan, one of the most important goals is to identify and incorporate into the plan various ways to reduce or eliminate federal and state estate taxes. Among the most common methods used to reduce these death taxes are:

- Gifts made during the donor's lifetime.
- Powers of appointment.
- Trusts that qualify for the martial deduction or avoid multiple taxation.
- Life insurance.

Gifts Made During the Donor's Lifetime— The Gift Tax Annual Exclusion

According to tax law (IRC § 2503[b]), any **donor** can make a gift of up to $10,000 to *any number* of recipients (**donees**) *each year* during the donor's life without being required to pay gift tax. Beginning in 1999, the $10,000 amount has been indexed annually for inflation (cost of living) rounded to the closest thousand dollars; e.g., the total increase must exceed $1,000 before the annual exclusion is increased to $11,000. The gift tax annual exclusion remains unchanged at $10,000 for the year 2001. In addition, spouses may join in the annual gift to the donees and combine their individual $10,000 gifts so as to give $20,000 to each donee free of gift tax. This practice is called **gift splitting,** and it is only available between spouses (IRC § 2513). In such cases a gift tax return must be filed with the Internal Revenue Service. In appropriate family situations, lifetime gifts are important tax-saving devices that are essential to a well-designed estate plan. Whenever donors are looking for a method to reduce their estates in order to diminish their potential federal estate tax liability, as well as to reduce the cost of probate administration of their estate, gift giving is an obvious solution.

Donor
A person who makes a gift.

Donee
A person who receives a gift.

Gift splitting
For gift tax purposes, an election by spouses to make a gift by one of them to a third party as being made one-half by each spouse.

Example: Bob and Mary have five children. To reduce their estate and the corresponding federal estate tax, they can give each of their five children $20,000 (adjusted for inflation) each year for a total of $100,000 or more. If they make these same gifts for ten years, Bob and Mary will reduce their estate by $1,000,000 or more.

Assuming that a donor has not made any previous gifts that year to the donees, he can give them each $10,000 (indexed annually for inflation) on his deathbed to diminish his federal estate tax. Such gifts would qualify for the annual exclusion.

The annual gift tax exclusion is available only for **present interests,** i.e., unrestricted rights to the immediate possession, use, or enjoyment of property (or the income of property). A gift of a present interest results whenever the donor makes a direct transfer of property to a donee. Donors may be individuals during life or may act through wills, trusts, estates, or guardianships. An unrestricted right to receive trust income, a **legal life estate,** and a gift to a **custodian** under the Uniform Transfers (Gifts) to Minors Act are all examples of a present interest. This act allows any kind of real or personal property to be transferred to a custodian for the benefit of a minor. The **custodianship,** however, must end and all property must be transferred to the minor at age 18, 21, or, in a few states, 25 (see the discussion of this act in Chapter 14).

Gifts of **future interests,** such as gifts of remainder interests and gifts in trust subject to a preceding life estate, do *not* qualify for the annual gift tax exclusion. Sometimes clients must be cautioned not to become too eager to part with their property to reduce federal tax liability since the gifts, once executed, transfer title to the property and its control. Once clients have gifted away their property, unforeseen and disastrous financial circumstances could cause them to become dependent on others for support.

In addition to the annual exclusion, no gift tax is owed for gifts made directly to a college or university to pay for a student's tuition and gifts made directly to a hospital or doctor for another person's medical care regardless of the relationship of the donor to the donee (IRC § 2503[e]). *Remember:* Other examples of gifts that are excluded from federal gift and estate tax are property to a tax-exempt charity (IRC §§ 2522 and 2055) and gifts to spouses (IRC §§ 2523 and 2056).

All lifetime gifts made to a donee in a given year that exceed the annual exclusion must be reported on Form 709 or Form 709A, if the gift is split between spouses. Such lifetime gifts are taxed by the federal government as part of the estate tax law. However, no tax is owed or paid for gifts over the $10,000 annual exclusion (indexed annually for inflation) until the unified credit (applicable

---

MINI-GLOSSARY BOX

Present interest
An immediate and unrestricted interest in real or personal property including the privilege of possession or enjoyment of the property.

Legal life estate
A life estate created by operation of law and not directly by the parties themselves.

Custodian
A person who has charge or custody of property for the benefit of another, usually for a minor.

Custodianship
An alternative to a trust or guardianship that allows a person (called a custodian) to be appointed by the court to manage property for the benefit of a minor.

Future interest
Any fixed estate or interest, except a reversion, in which the privilege of possession or enjoyment is future and not present.

credit amount) based on the gross estate of the current year (applicable exclusion amount) is exceeded, e.g., $675,000 for 2001 (see Exhibit 14.3). Any gift tax owed is assessed against the donor who is primarily obligated to pay it.

A donor who plans to make gifts to children should leave them highly appreciated property, such as real estate (e.g., a house, cottage, condominium, apartment building, or securities) in a will or trust and give them other property during his lifetime. The problem with making a gift of highly appreciated property while living is that the advantage of the **"stepped-up basis"** of the property is lost. Property "basis" is the value that is used to determine loss or gain for income tax purposes. The difference (loss or gain) between what the donor paid for the property and the amount received when the property is sold is taxable. If the donor, while alive, gives the property to his children, the property retains the donor's basis. However, if the donor passes the property to his children through a will or trust when he dies, the property takes a new "stepped-up basis," which is the current value of the property on the date of the donor-testator's death or **alternate valuation date.**

> **Example:** Debbie, the donor, purchased a lakeshore cottage in Minnesota in 1960 for $10,000. In her will, Debbie leaves the cottage to her two children. When Debbie dies in 2001, the property is worth $200,000. The children receive the property with the stepped-up basis of $200,000. If they sell the property for $200,000 in 2001, they will owe no federal income tax on the sale because there was no income gain. (*Note:* The stepped-up basis of $200,000 would be included in Debbie's gross estate for estate tax purposes and could result in an estate tax liability if her gross estate exceeds $675,000.) On the other hand, if the property had been given to the children while Debbie was alive, the basis for the property when it was sold would be Debbie's basis of $10,000. There is *no* stepped-up basis when property is passed by gift while the donor is alive. Therefore, if the basis is $10,000 and the children sell the cottage for $200,000 in 2001, the gain of $190,000 would be subject to income tax.

Powers of Appointment

A power of appointment is created by will or in a trust when one person (a testator or settlor, now also called the **donor**) confers a power or authority upon another (called the **donee**) to appoint (i.e., to select and nominate) the person who is to receive and enjoy an estate, or an income therefrom, or receive a trust fund after the donee's death. The purpose of a power of appointment is to enable the persons (called the **appointees**) who will receive the estate or trust fund to be named later when their needs are better known.

Section 2041 of the IRC identifies two types of powers:

1. A **general power of appointment,** which the Code defines as follows:

The term general power of appointment means a power which is exercisable in favor of the decedent, his estate, his creditors, or the creditors of his estate. . . .

> **Example:** In her will, Margaret Brower, creates a testamentary trust naming her daughter, Elizabeth Brower, beneficiary of the trust and provides that all income of the trust will be distributed to Elizabeth during her lifetime. On Elizabeth's death, she will be given the power to "appoint" the principal of the trust to anyone she selects.

Stepped-up basis
An increase in the income tax basis of appreciated (increase in value) property. The property is valued on the date of death or the alternate valuation date.

Alternate valuation date
A date six months from the date of death or the date the property is disposed by the estate, whichever comes first.

Donor (of a power of appointment)
The testator or settlor who creates and confers a power or authority upon another (called the donee) to appoint, that is, to select the person(s) (called the appointee) to receive an estate or an income therefrom after the testator's or donee's death.

Donee (of a power of appointment)
The person to whom a power of appointment is given, also called the holder, who selects the appointee to receive an estate or an income therefrom.

Appointee
The person who is to receive the benefit of the power of appointment.

General power of appointment
The right to pass on an interest in property to whomever a donee chooses, including herself, her estate, her creditors, or creditors of her estate.

- Margaret Brower is the testatrix and donor who creates the power of appointment.
- Elizabeth is the beneficiary of the testamentary trust and donee who holds the power of appointment. She has the right to exercise the power during her life or after death in her own will by naming anyone, including herself or her estate, her creditors, or the creditors of her estate, as the beneficiaries of the trust principal.
- The person appointed by Elizabeth is the appointee.
- Elizabeth has a general power of appointment.

Note: Only a general power of appointment causes the value of the property appointed to be included in the gross estate of the person who possesses the power of appointment for federal estate tax purposes. For further discussion of general power of appointment trusts, see below.

Special power of appointment
A power of appointment that cannot be exercised in favor of the donee or his estate, but only in favor of identifiable person(s) other than the donee.

2. **A special or limited power of appointment** in which the donor limits the donee's right of appointment to an identified person or persons, other than the donee, to whom the property can be distributed.

> **Example:** In the above example, Margaret, in the testamentary trust, gives Elizabeth the power to "appoint" the principal only to Elizabeth's brother, Henry, or only to any siblings that survive Elizabeth.

- Margaret is still the testatrix and donor.
- Elizabeth is still the beneficiary and donee who holds the power of appointment.
- Henry, or Elizabeth's siblings, are the appointee(s).
- Elizabeth has a special power of appointment.

A common use of a special power of appointment occurs between spouses whenever one spouse, e.g., the husband in a trust or will, names his wife as his beneficiary and gives her a power to appoint the principal only to their children. This special power of appointment does *not* cause the value of the property appointed to be included in the gross estate of the wife, who is the beneficiary (donee).

Trusts That Qualify for the Marital Deduction or Avoid Multiple Taxation

Transfers of property that qualify for the gift or estate tax marital deduction include the following: (1) outright transfers between spouses by gift or trust; (2) life estate with general power of appointment trusts; (3) qualified terminable interest property (QTIP) trusts; and (4) bypass trusts, which are also known as Trust B of A-B trusts, credit shelter trusts, exemption equivalent trusts, residuary trusts, or family trusts.

Outright Transfers Between Spouses by Gift or Trust

Direct transfer of ownership from one spouse to the other spouse by a gift, will, or operation of law is the simplest and most common form of a marital deduction transfer. Due to the unlimited marital deduction for these direct transfers between spouses, no federal gift or estate tax is owed. A transfer in trust may be more appropriate, however, if the recipient spouse is unable to manage the trust property properly or if the settlor-donor wants to determine and select the ultimate beneficiaries of the property at the spouse's death instead of allowing the surviving spouse to make that decision. Consider the following trust examples.

Example: Maria establishes a trust that states "on Maria's death, the trustee shall distribute all principal and income directly to Maria's surviving spouse, Howard." This is an outright transfer by trust of property that qualifies for the marital deduction from Maria's gross estate.

The major tax problem created by an outright transfer to a spouse is that the entire trust property is now part of the surviving spouse's estate and may be liable for estate taxes upon that spouse's death if the value of his estate is greater than $675,000 in 2001 increasing to $1,000,000 in 2002.

Life Estate with General Power of Appointment Trusts

A common alternative to an outright transfer that also qualifies trust property for the marital deduction is the general power of appointment trust. This living or testamentary trust alternative established by the settlor spouse requires the trustee to distribute trust income to the surviving spouse *for life* and gives the spouse an unqualified general power to appoint the trust property to "anyone," including herself, her estate, her creditors, or the creditors of her estate, that she names in her will. Since no limitations exist on the spouse's exercise of the power of appointment, this is a general power of appointment. When the general power is given to the surviving spouse, it causes the trust property to be included in the gross estate of the "person who possesses the power," i.e., the surviving spouse (IRC § 2041[a][2]).

Example: In his will, Sherman creates a trust transferring property to his spouse, Roxanne, for life and giving Roxanne on her death the power to appoint the balance of the trust principal to "such beneficiaries as she may designate in her will." Since there are no limitations on the power of appointment, and Roxanne can appoint the remaining principal at her death to "herself, her estate, her creditors, or the creditors of her estate," this is a general power of appointment, and the trust property will be added to Roxanne's estate and is subject to federal estate tax when she dies.

A general power of appointment also occurs, for example, when a decedent spouse in a testamentary trust gives property for life to the surviving spouse and gives that spouse an unrestricted right to withdraw all or any part of the principal at any time. This would give the surviving spouse the power to appoint the principal to herself at any time and thus becomes a general power of appointment.

As mentioned previously, to avoid the unfavorable estate tax consequences of the general power of appointment trust, a special power of appointment trust can be created instead, if appropriate. Such trusts limit the surviving spouse to appointing only an identifiable person or class of persons designated in the trust document creating the power. The appointee(s) cannot be the spouse or the spouse's estate or creditors. When special powers of appointment are created, the trust property is not included in the surviving spouse's estate on death.

Under a general power of appointment trust, the surviving spouse must receive all the trust income at least annually for life; *only* the surviving spouse may have the power to appoint the trust property or any part of the property to herself, her estate, her creditors, or the creditors of her estate; and no other person has the power to appoint property to anyone but the surviving spouse (IRC § 2056[b][5]). If the spouse fails to exercise the power of appointment in her own will, the trust assets pass as directed in the trust document. An advantage of this trust is that it may permit the surviving spouse to make gifts of trust property to children that may qualify for the gift tax annual exclusion, which, in turn, reduces estate taxes at the surviving spouse's death. However, the general power of appointment trust fails to protect the estate of the settlor-spouse, who creates the trust, from the surviving spouse's power to change who will ultimately receive the trust property. The QTIP trust, discussed below, eliminates this problem.

QTIP Trusts

QTIP trust (qualified terminable interest property)
A type of trust that will qualify for the marital deduction in which the surviving spouse receives all the income for life but is not given a general power of appointment.

Since its creation in 1982, the **qualified terminable interest property (QTIP) trust** has been very popular. This type of trust, which can be a testamentary or living trust, allows a settlor-spouse to transfer the income from trust property to a surviving spouse for life, and then pass the remainder (principal) to someone else, usually children.

Generally, the marital deduction (for federal gift and estate tax purposes) is not available if the property transferred by one spouse (transferor) will terminate on the death of the surviving spouse (transferee) and pass to someone else. For example, if a husband places property in trust for his wife for life, and passes the remainder to their children when his wife dies, this is a **terminable interest** that does *not qualify* as a marital deduction for the husband or the husband's estate because it does not give the wife sufficient control over the trust property and is not considered a transfer to her. A QTIP trust resolves this problem because "qualified terminable interest property" (QTIP) is excluded from the terminable interest rule, and, therefore, the QTIP qualifies for the unlimited marital deduction.

Terminable interest
An interest in property which terminates on the death of the holder or on the occurrence of some other specified event. The transfer of a terminable interest from one spouse to the other spouse does not qualify for the marital deduction.

To qualify as QTIP and thereby make possible the QTIP election, as explained below, the settlor-spouse of a QTIP trust must:

- Give the surviving spouse the right to all the income from the trust property for life, payable at least annually (IRC § 2056 [b][7][B][ii][I]). *Note:* This also gives the surviving spouse the right to use the trust property, e.g., to live in the family home or vacation home for life; and
- Not allow any person, including the surviving spouse, to have a power to appoint any part of the property to any person other than the surviving spouse for the spouse's lifetime (IRC § 2056[b][7][B][ii][II]).

In a QTIP trust, the trustee may be allowed to use some of the trust principal, but usually only when necessary for the surviving spouse's "health, education, support, or maintenance" (IRC § 2041[b][1][A]). *Note:* Although the surviving spouse in a QTIP trust receives all the income for life, the settlor-spouse can designate and pass the principal (remainder) of the trust to someone other than the surviving spouse, e.g., children. Therefore, the surviving spouse is *not* given a *general power of appointment,* and the settlor-spouse, even though the first to die, determines the trust property distribution after the death of the surviving spouse through the trust.

Caveat: For property to qualify as QTIP for the marital deduction, an election (called the QTIP election) must be made on Schedule M of Form 706, the U.S. Estate (and Generation-Skipping Transfer) Tax Return (see text Form 88* and IRC § 2056[b][7][B][v]). The election is irrevocable. If the property is transferred as a gift

---

*See Appendix A

through a living trust, the settlor-spouse (donor) is the person who makes the QTIP election which results in the property qualifying for the gift tax marital deduction. If the trust property is transferred after the settlor-spouse's (testator's) death through a testamentary trust, the personal representative (executor) of the estate makes the election on Form 706 (IRC § 2056[b][7][B][i][III]). The executor (or the settlor-donor in the case of the living trust) may elect to qualify all or any portion of the QTIP trust assets for the marital deduction based on the most advantageous tax strategy and benefits to the recipients. Once the QTIP election is made, the property transferred into the trust is treated as qualified terminable interest property which causes the terminable interest restriction to be waived with the result that the marital deduction is allowed. *Note:* In exchange for this earlier marital deduction for the settlor-spouse, the surviving spouse's gross estate must include the value of the QTIP election assets (remaining principal) of the trust property at the surviving spouse's death for federal estate tax purposes even though the surviving spouse has no control over the ultimate disposition of these assets (IRC § 2044).

Thus, the QTIP trust offers two unique advantages. First, the settlor-spouse (testator) of a testamentary trust or the settlor-spouse (donor) of an irrevocable living QTIP trust is allowed to direct the disposition (distribution) of the trust principal at the death of the surviving spouse. This assures that the testator's or settlor's children or other intended family members will be the ultimate beneficiaries of the trust. The second advantage is the trust's flexibility for purposes of the gift or estate tax marital deduction. The testator of a testamentary trust can direct the personal representative (executor) or the settlor-donor can direct the trustee (who may be the settlor) in the irrevocable living trust to elect on the estate or gift tax return to qualify all or any part of the trust principal for the marital deduction. The portion of the trust for which the election is made must be included in the surviving spouse's gross estate for federal estate tax purposes. The result is that the federal estate tax is not avoided, but it is postponed, which is another reason for the use of the QTIP trust since the postponement of paying federal estate tax when the settlor-spouse dies makes more property assets available to the surviving spouse and ultimate heirs. Another advantage is that QTIP assets are not probated after the surviving spouse's death. QTIP trusts are primarily used by spouses whose estates exceed their combined personal federal estate tax exemptions (exclusions). The QTIP trust is particularly useful when creating estates for spouses who have children from earlier marriages.

Example: Betty and Bob are married. Betty has two children by a previous marriage, and Bob has three children by a previous marriage. If Betty dies leaving all her property to Bob in her will, no federal estate tax will be owed on her death because of the marital deduction. When Bob dies, however, he may pass all the property he inherited from Betty to only his children. Using a QTIP trust, Betty can create a testamentary trust that pays all the trust income annually to Bob for life; on his death, the trust principal passes to *her* children. In addition, Betty can direct her personal representative to elect on her federal estate tax return, Form 706, that all or part of the trust property be treated as QTIP property and therefore qualify for the marital deduction. *Note:* The decision to make the QTIP election by the personal representative (executor) is after the first spouse (Betty) dies which makes possible important postmortem estate planning. On Bob's death, the value of the QTIP election assets, which qualified for the marital deduction on Betty's death and now pass to her children, must be included in Bob's gross estate and may be subject to federal estate tax. If Bob remarries after Betty's death, the QTIP trust prevents him from transferring trust property to his new spouse.

The major disadvantage of the QTIP trust is that the surviving spouse is not permitted to make gifts to children from the trust principal.

Bypass Trusts

As discussed, a bypass trust (also called Trust B of an A-B trust, credit shelter trust, exemption equivalent trust, residuary trust, or family trust) is an estate planning device whereby a deceased spouse's estate passes to a trust rather than directly to the surviving spouse, thereby reducing the likelihood that the surviving spouse's subsequent estate will exceed the federal estate tax threshold and be taxed. In the trust, the surviving spouse is given a life estate which ends at the spouse's death and passes the remainder of the estate to named beneficiaries, usually children. This trust allows spouses with substantial estates to transfer their property, after both have died, to their children and avoid paying any federal estate tax by appropriately planning and using the marital deduction and their individual $675,000 estate tax exemptions (exclusions). As long as a husband and wife each hold $675,000 in separately owned assets, and they do not use the marital deduction exclusively for those assets, the couple can use a marital deduction trust (Trust A) and a bypass trust (Trust B) to retain combined total assets worth up to $1,350,000 that will avoid federal tax liability. The individual exemption (exclusion) increases to $1,000,000 and $2,000,000 for a married couple in 2002. See an example bypass trust within a testamentary trust in Appendix B.

As explained earlier, the process of rearranging the spouses' assets so that each spouse's estate takes maximum advantage of its unified credit is known as estate equalization. Harmony between the spouses is essential to this strategy. Marital friction and discord may make this sound estate planning device impossible.

Life Insurance

When designing an estate plan, one of the important planning devices available to conserve the value of the estate is *life insurance*. Life insurance is a contract between the *policyholder,* in most cases, the owner of the policy and the person whose life is insured, and an insurance company whereby the company agrees, in return for annual *premium* payments, to pay a specific sum of money, i.e., the *face value,* to the designated *beneficiary* upon the death of the policyholder. The insurance company is called the *insurer* or *carrier;* the policyholder is the owner and can also be the *insured.*

> **Example:** Sarahana contracts with Metro Life Insurance Company to buy a $200,000 term life insurance policy. Sarahana pays an annual *premium* of $600 to the company. She has named her son, Joshua, as her primary *beneficiary.* When Sarahana dies, the insurance company must pay Joshua $200,000. Sarahana is the *policyholder* or *insured.* Metro Life Insurance Company is the *insurer* or *carrier.* Joshua is the *beneficiary.* The *premium* is $50 per month or $600 per year, and the *face value* or *amount* of the policy or contract is $200,000.

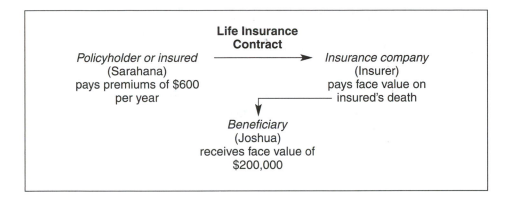

Types of Life Insurance

The three major types of life insurance are ordinary, straight, or whole life insurance; term life insurance; and universal life insurance.

1. *Ordinary, straight, or whole life insurance.* Whole or straight life insurance combines lifetime protection with a minimum savings feature called *cash surrender value* or, more commonly, *cash value.* Premium payments remain the same during the contract and are required throughout the policyholder's lifetime. After the first few years, the cash value slowly increases throughout the duration of the contract. The policyholder may *surrender* (cash in) the policy at any time and take out the cash value (money) for his own use or retain the policy until death for the benefit of the named beneficiary.

Example: Phyllis buys a $50,000 policy of straight life insurance, naming her daughter, Barbara, *beneficiary.* Each year Phyllis pays the *premium* for the policy. If Phyllis desires, she may at any point withdraw for her own use the *cash value* (savings) accumulated, but she must *surrender* (terminate) the policy to obtain the cash value. If Phyllis dies before the policy is terminated, Barbara will receive the proceeds ($50,000).

2. *Term life insurance.* Term insurance is life insurance which is pure protection without savings (*cash surrender* or *loan value*). It is by far the least expensive insurance. It requires the insurance company to pay the face value (amount) of insurance, i.e., the proceeds, to the beneficiary if the policyholder dies within a given time period (term). It is generally renewable from term to term without an additional medical examination. The cost to renew term insurance increases with the age of the insured.

Example: If, in the above example, Phyllis had bought a ten-year policy of term insurance in the amount of $50,000 and died within that period, Barbara would receive the proceeds.

3. *Universal life insurance.* Universal life insurance is life insurance that covers a specific period of time and builds *cash value* for the policyholder over that time. This coverage emphasizes the separation of the portion of the premium that is used to cover the insurance protection from the portion of the premium allocated to an investment that is used to build the policy's cash value. Investments are usually flexible and selected with a view to maximize the rate of return.

Tax Consequences of Life Insurance

Regardless of the type of life insurance, the entire proceeds, i.e., the face amount of the policy, are included in the decedent-policyholder's estate if (1) the proceeds are payable to the decedent's estate or (2) the proceeds are payable to other beneficiaries and the decedent retained any "incidents of ownership" in the life insurance policy prior to death. An **incident of ownership** is an element or right of ownership or degree of control over a life insurance contract. The following are examples of incidents or rights of ownership:

Incident of ownership
An element or right of ownership or degree of control over a life insurance contract.

- The right to change the named beneficiary of the policy.
- The right to cancel or surrender (cash in) the policy.
- The right to transfer or assign ownership of the policy to another person or to a trust.
- The right to pledge the policy as collateral for a loan.
- The right to obtain a loan against the cash value of the policy from the insurer (insurance company).

Caveat: The retention by the policyholder of any *incident of ownership* in a life insurance policy will cause the policy proceeds (face amount) to be included in the policyholder's gross estate on death and be subject to federal estate tax; see IRC § 2042(2). In the case of *In re Lumpkin's Estate,* 474 F.2d 1092 (1973), the U.S. Court of Appeals ruled the decedent taxpayer (Lumpkin), under the provisions of a group term life insurance policy, had the right to alter the time and manner of the benefits of the policy and thereby possessed an incident of ownership with respect to the policy. Therefore, the court decided the value of the insurance proceeds must be included in Lumpkin's gross estate and be subject to federal estate tax. *Note:* The policyholder and owner can avoid this detrimental tax consequence to his estate in one of three ways:

1. Transfer the ownership of an existing policy to a trust or to another person (but not to a spouse since there is no tax advantage because of the unlimited marital deduction).

2. In a written statement given to the insurance company, formally relinquish (give up) all incidents of ownership in an existing policy.

In both cases above, however, the Internal Revenue Code also requires the policyholder to *live three more years* after the date of the transfer or the date of the formal relinquishment in order for the proceeds of the policy to *not* be included in the decedent's gross estate and thus *not* be subject to federal estate tax.

3. When the insurance policy is purchased, another person (not the insured) pays the premiums and, thereby, is the owner of the policy and possessor of the incidents of ownership instead of the insured. When the insured dies, the beneficiary receives the face value (amount) of the policy, but the proceeds are *not* included in the insured's gross estate, and, therefore, are *not* subject to federal estate tax.

Another important tax outcome associated with life insurance is the payment of the proceeds to the named beneficiary. Generally, when the proceeds are paid to the beneficiary on the death of the policyholder, they are exempt from federal and state income tax (IRC § 101[a]).

Life insurance proceeds are distributed by various methods. If the policyholder's *estate is the beneficiary,* the proceeds are normally distributed as a lump sum since it provides immediate cash for the family and a source of funds to pay creditors, claims and administration expenses. As noted above, however, the proceeds are subject to federal estate tax; since they enlarge the gross estate, they also increase the probate costs. When the *beneficiary is an individual,* several settlement options are available under most policies, including the following:

- The company holds the proceeds and interest accumulates.
- The company pays the beneficiaries the proceeds and interest in installments over a specific time period.
- The company uses the proceeds to purchase an annuity for lifetime payments to the beneficiary.
- The company pays the beneficiary a lump sum to be invested or used as the beneficiary wishes.

Life insurance proceeds can be used for many purposes besides the payment of the decedent's debts, taxes, and administration expenses. The proceeds can supply a source of funds to replace the lost income of the decedent wage earner, maintain a family's lifestyle, pay for the college education of children, help to cover the ongoing expenses of an elderly parent or handicapped child, and provide for the financial security of future generations of family members.

Life Insurance Trusts

One method often used by families to conserve wealth is the **irrevocable life insurance trust,** a common device used in estate planning to pass proceeds of a life insurance policy to heirs tax-free. A settlor establishes an irrevocable life insurance trust by assigning the ownership of an existing policy to the trust or the trustee can purchase a new policy on the settlor's life. Each year while alive, the settlor gives the trust a certain amount of money with which the trustee pays the existing or new policy premiums. The life insurance policy is owned by the trust. When the settlor dies, the proceeds of the policy are paid to the trust, which is the named beneficiary of the policy. This process enables the settlor to direct the trustee to pass the proceeds to the trust's named beneficiaries (usually children) and keeps the proceeds from being included in the settlor's taxable estate for federal estate tax purposes. *Note:* If the settlor transfers an existing policy to the trust, thereby relinquishing the incidents of ownership, the settlor must live for three years from the date of the establishment of the irrevocable life insurance trust for the proceeds to avoid federal estate tax. In addition, depending on the replacement value of the existing policy, i.e., the amount of money it would cost to buy the policy at the present time, gift tax may be due, unless the cost was under the annual $10,000 gift tax exclusion (indexed annually for inflation).

If the life insurance trust is designed properly, it can take advantage of an important decision on tax law that establishes the opportunity for the annual gift tax exclusion to be allowed for transfers into trusts. The decision came in the case of *Crummey v. Commissioner,* 397 F.2d 82 (9th Cir. 1968). The money the settlor contributes each year to pay the insurance premiums is not given to the beneficiaries (the children) directly, but goes instead to the trustee of the trust. The trustee must give each beneficiary (child) a written notice, called a Crummey letter, indicating the gift from the settlor has been delivered and each beneficiary may elect

Irrevocable life insurance trust
A living trust that cannot be revoked or amended which is established by a settlor who assigns the ownership of a new or existing life insurance policy on her life to the trust and contributes money annually to the trust to pay the premiums. The policy proceeds are payable to the trust on the death of the settlor.

(demand) to receive the gift at this time. If the demand is not made, the trustee will invest the money by paying the premiums due on the policy. Since the settlor's annual gift to the trust can be acquired by the beneficiaries each year, it constitutes a *present interest* and, therefore, qualifies for the annual $10,000 gift tax exclusion (indexed annually for inflation). See Exhibit 10.2 for an illustration of an irrevocable life insurance trust.

🏛 ASSIGNMENT 10.2

In the chart below, fill in the missing Yes or No for each estate planning device (document).

	Documents		
This Document Can (be)	Will (without a testamentary trust)	Recovable Living Trust	Irrevocable Living Trust (if funded)
1. Private.	No	_____	Yes
2. Avoid probate.	_____	Yes	Yes
3. Avoid court appointment of fiduciaries.	_____	Yes	Yes
4. Use professional management.	Yes	_____	Yes
5. Protect a spendthrift child.	No	_____	Yes
6. Avoid ancillary administration.	No	_____	Yes
7. Allow maker to control assets while alive.	Yes	Yes	_____
8. Delay inheritance.	_____	Yes	Yes
9. Avoid federal estate tax.	No	No	_____
10. Diminish contests of the document.	No	Yes	_____
11. Revoked.	Yes	Yes	_____
12. Provide for the maker's disability.	_____	Yes	Yes

Exhibit 10.2   Irrevocable Life Insurance Trust Illustration

Settlor
Annually gives money to trustee in trust. The trust is the owner and beneficiary of the life insurance policy.

→**Trustee**
Annually gives written notice of the gift and right to elect by the beneficiaries of the trust.

→**Beneficiaries**
Refuse the gift.

→**Trustee**
Uses gift to pay annual life insurance premium.

→When settlor dies, the face amount of the policy is paid to the trust.

→**Trustee**
Distributes life insurance proceeds to beneficiaries as directed by settlor.

POSTMORTEM ESTATE PLANNING

Important estate planning opportunities are available even after the testator's death. This estate planning is called **postmortem** planning, and it is often used for tax-saving purposes. Disclaiming an inheritance is an example of such planning.

> **Example:** At age 82, Barney dies, leaving half of his estate to his wife, Wilma, who is 86 and the other half to their only child, Doreen. Either Wilma or Doreen could reject the testamentary gifts from Barney by a disclaimer.

A **disclaimer** is a refusal to accept a bequest, inheritance, or gift acquired through a will, trust, or the law of intestate succession or to accept proceeds from life insurance or other gratuitous transfers. Named beneficiaries disclaim gifts primarily because of their age, health, and financial security and because disclaimers offer the opportunity to make sound tax-saving decisions. The following are some examples of how disclaimers and other strategies can be used to save on taxes after the testator's death:

- *Gift and estate tax savings.* When a beneficiary or donee disclaims a gift of an estate that results in a transfer of the property from the disclaimant to another person, the question arises whether the transfer is subject to gift or estate tax. The case of *Brown v. Routzahn,* 63 F.2d 914 (6th Cir. 1933), has settled the issue that a "valid" transfer or qualified disclaimer is not subject to either tax. In the *Brown* case, the court ruled that a donee's rejection of a testamentary gift before the distribution of the estate was not a taxable transfer and therefore was not subject to tax. The types of disclaimers that qualify to avoid gift and estate tax are found in state statutes and in Section 2518 of the Internal Revenue Code, which provides:
  1. The disclaimant must make an irrevocable and unqualified refusal to accept an interest in property.
  2. The refusal must be in writing.
  3. The written instrument of disclaimer must be received by the personal representative (or trustee in a trust) no later than nine (9) months after the decedent's death. If the potential disclaimant is a minor, the time for the disclaimer may be the date the minor reaches age 21. See Exhibit 10.3 for a sample written disclaimer.
  4. The disclaimant must not accept an interest or any of its benefits.
  5. The refusal must be legally effective to pass the specific gift to another person without direction from the disclaimant.

As a result of the disclaimer, the interest does not pass to the disclaimant and therefore is not subject to gift or estate tax.

> **Example:** Tom's will leaves a majority of his estate to Jolene, his wife. Jolene is financially secure, so she executes a written disclaimer and gives it to the personal representative and files a copy with the probate court. The disclaimer keeps the property out of Jolene's estate and is not subject to gift or estate tax. It also allows the property to pass directly to their children, which, although not specified by Jolene, is actually what she wishes.

Postmortem
After death; pertaining to matters occurring after death.

Disclaimer
The right of a beneficiary or heir to refuse a gift by will, trust, or inheritance without any adverse tax consequences.

Exhibit 10.3 Sample Disclaimer

STATE OF NEW YORK
SURROGATE'S COURT: COUNTY OF _____

In the Matter of the Administration
of the Estate of _____,
                         Deceased.

RENUNCIATION OF INTEREST IN ESTATE
PURSUANT TO EPTL 2-1.11
File No. _____

TO THE SURROGATE'S COURT OF THE COUNTY OF _____:
  I, the undersigned, _____, domiciled at _____, New York, pursuant to Section 2-1.11 of the New York Estates, Powers and Trusts Law, irrevocably renounce wholly all of the right, title, and interest in and to any portion of the estate of _____, deceased, to which I may be or become entitled under the laws of the State of New York.

                                             _____ [L.S]

[Notary]
_____

Source: Reprinted with permission from West's McKinney's Forms, ESP, § 7:418. Copyright ©, by West Group.

A disclaimer is accomplished by delivering the written disclaimer to the personal representative and filing a copy with the probate court. In the case of a trust, the disclaimer would be given to the trustee. Estate tax reduction after death can also be achieved by purposely allowing the personal representative to transfer the amount of the property disclaimed to a charity or spouse. This strategy can substantially increase the charitable and marital deductions and thereby lower the gross estate of the decedent and correspondingly the estate tax. A surviving spouse's elective rights against a will can also be used to increase the marital deduction if the elective share is greater than the amount the spouse receives through the will.

- *State inheritance tax savings.* Inheritance taxes levied by some states are based on the amount of the property given to the recipient and the relationship of the person to the testator. Assuming a bequest to a child in the testator's will would be taxed at a lower rate than a bequest to a surviving spouse, the testator—decedent's spouse, by a disclaimer, may cause the property to pass to the child and be taxed at a lower rate for inheritance tax purposes. See *Matter of Wisely's Estate,* 402 N.E.2d 14 (Ind.App. 1980), in which the court held the beneficiary's renunciation of her interest in the decedent's estate under the will related back to the time of the decedent's death. Consequently, none of the estate had been transferred to her under the will, and therefore there was no basis for assessment of inheritance tax to her.
- *Federal and state income tax savings.* The decedent's estate as a taxable entity and the beneficiaries' income taxes may be affected by controlling the

timing and amount of property distributed to the beneficiaries or prolonging the time period of the estate administration into a second taxable year if this procedure is economically sound.

- *Deduction for administration expenses.* As a final postmortem tax-saving method, the personal representative can also elect to use estate administration expenses as a deduction for either estate tax or income tax purposes.

LONG-TERM CARE

History and Development of Long-Term Care

During the past twenty-five years health and medical advances have increased the lifespan of our nation's population, thereby creating a new field of law. It is called **Elder Law,** i.e., specialized legal services for our aging population. All Elder Law attorneys and legal assistants recognize that wills and/or trusts are an essential part of a client's *estate plan*. Today, such a plan should also include financial planning for future disability and long-term care needs. While assisting your supervising attorney and the client, you will need to familiarize yourself with the new or revised federal and state programs' eligibility rules, benefits, forms, and procedures for the practice of Elder Law according to federal and your state statutes. This constant updating is especially needed if you work with attorneys in state-administered public legal aid clinics (offices) for low income individuals. Coordination and utilization of legal documents (wills, trusts, and advance directives), federal and your state programs, local legal services, and public housing and benefit programs are essential to competently alleviate the aging client's long-term care concerns.

For its predominant impact on how people lived, the last half of the twentieth century has been considered the "Age of the Computer." Subsequently, the first half of the twenty-first century is destined to be the "Era of the Seniors." As we move into the new millennium, the *baby boomers* will reach their senior years and cause a dramatic increase in the number of elderly persons who will require special housing and long-term medical care. It is estimated by the U.S. Census Bureau that the percentage of the U. S. population older than 65 will rise from 11.3 percent in 1990 for ages 65 to 84 to 15.4 percent for the same ages in 2050, and people over 85 will increase from 1.2 percent (1990) to 4.6 percent (2050). Although most of the aging *baby boomers* will initially stay in their homes, by the year 2030 (when they begin to reach the age of 85) other housing, especially nursing homes, will likely be their option.

Definition and Goal

Long-term care is the support people need when they can no longer care for themselves because of disability, frailty, or a lingering illness. This support can range from assistance with daily activities at home, such as bathing or dressing, to highly skilled care in a nursing home. Unlike traditional medical care performed by doctors, nurses, and other medical staff to cure the sick and heal the injured, long-term care provides a wide variety of services for elderly people with a chronic illness, disability, or **cognitive disorder,** e.g., Alzheimer's disease. These medical problems limit the person's ability to function independently and perform the six "**activities of daily living**" which include bathing, dressing,

Elder Law
Specialized legal services for our aging population.

Long-term care
The support that disabled, frail, or chronically ill people need when they can no longer care for themselves.

eating, **toileting, continence,** and **transferring** (see discussion below). The *goal* of long-term care is to help the elderly maintain their level of functioning as opposed to curing or correcting specific medical problems.

Users and Costs of Long-Term Care

In most cases, the elderly receive long-term care services in their home, but they are also cared for in nursing homes, **adult day care centers,** or in **assisted living facilities** such as a **continuing care retirement community.** In the United States, more than 1.6 million elderly people live in nursing homes.

Although the numbers vary among the states, approximately 43 of 100 individuals who live to age 65 will enter a nursing home during their remaining years.[1] About 24 of the 43 will remain in the nursing home for at least one year, and 9 will stay for five years or longer. The average length of stay in a nursing home is two and one-half years.[2] As each year passes for the elderly, the need for **nursing home care** increases, e.g., while slightly over 1 percent of seniors age 65 to 74 live in nursing homes, nearly 25 percent of individuals over 85 live in a nursing home, and women outnumber men by more than three to one.[3]

The annual cost of nursing home care is averaging over $56,000,[4] with much higher expenses reported in some states. A government study by the House of Representatives Select Committee on Aging found 66 percent of all single elderly patients who enter nursing homes depleted their entire savings to pay for just one year of care. Most long-term care is provided at home by family and friends with the part-time assistance of **home health care** and **respite** caregivers, but even those costs can run between $40 and $135 per day and there is an associated emotional expense. Caring at home for an aging family member with a chronic illness or disability can be physically and emotionally exhausting, especially for the inexperienced caregiver. It has been projected by the American Council of Life Insurance that the annual cost of nursing home care will be $190,000 by the year 2030.

Need for Long-Term Care

The need for and financing of long-term care has become one of the most serious concerns of our nation's aging population. The questions each person must answer are:

- How soon must I plan for long-term care before the actual need arises?
- How much inheritance, if any, do I want to leave my family?

MINI-GLOSSARY BOX

Cognitive disorder (impairment)
A mental incapacity that causes disorientation, loss of memory, and lack of safety awareness, e.g., Alzheimer's disease.

Activities of daily living (ADLs)
Six everyday functions and activities people do without help including bathing, eating, dressing, toileting, continence, and transferring.

Toileting
Getting to and from, on and off the toilet, and performing personal hygiene.

Continence
The ability to control bowel and bladder function.

Transferring
Moving in or out of bed, a chair, or wheelchair.

- How will I pay for housing, health, and medical expenses during the last years of my life?

For some people these expenses will be enormous. Without proper financial planning, the costs of housing and medical care may eliminate all potential inheritance to family and friends, deplete the individual's assets, impoverish the person, and make him or her a ward of the state. The sad fact is the majority of Americans over 65 have made no plans for long-term care.

Financing Long-Term Care

Many people continue to believe that when they need long-term care our government will pay their expenses. This belief, of course, is a fantasy and not true. The reality is that the resources (income and assets) of each person combined with federal and state government sources (e.g., Social Security, Supplemental Security Income, Medicare, and Medicaid) will determine the person's ability to pay for necessary long-term care and also will identify the need and appropriateness of adding another resource: *long-term care insurance*. Choices for financing long-term care will vary according to each person's level of income and assets. There are three levels: (1) low; (2) moderate; or (3) high. The need for long-term care and methods of paying for it by a person in each of the three levels of income will be discussed next.

Resources Available to Help Pay Long-Term Care Expenses

Obviously, personal resources available to pay the cost of long-term care include an individual's income and assets from employment, home ownership, investments (stocks and bonds), and retirement plans including pension and profit-sharing plans, IRAs, 401(k) plans, and Keogh plans (retirement plans for self-employed taxpayers). Federal programs such as Social Security, Medicare, and Medicaid also are sources that provide income, hospital and medical insurance, and medical assistance for people who are aged or whose income falls below a certain minimum

---

MINI-GLOSSARY BOX

Adult day care center
Senior service centers that are community-based group programs which give care during the day for adults with functional or cognitive impairments and provide assistance to caregivers.

Assisted living facility
A community residential living arrangement that provides individual per-

sonal care and health services for a person who requires help with activities of daily living (ADLs).

Nursing home care
A residential institution that provides care and services for the elderly or infirmed.

Continuing care retirement community
A campus-style community that provides a combina-

tion of housing, services, and nursing care, at one location, to meet the various needs of residents as they grow older. The community generally charges a standard fee to enter and a flexible fee for a package of contract-specified services that vary as the resident's needs change.

Home health care
Medical and nonmedical (including household) services provided by doctors, nurses, therapists, home health aides, and homemakers for sick, disabled, or infirmed persons in their homes.

Respite care
Care offered to relieve family caregivers for a few hours or up to several days.

standard. *Note:* Since the programs discussed below annually change their statistical information, e.g., percentages, monetary amounts, and income limits, you must use the Research Boxes to update facts and procedures.

RESEARCH BOX

To obtain information about Social Security programs, call this toll-free number **1-800-772-1213** and order the following publications any time any day:

Social Security—Basic Facts (Publication 05–10080)
Social Security—Understanding Benefits (Publication 05–10024)
Social Security—Retirement Benefits (Publication 05–10035)
Social Security—Survivor Benefits (Publication 05–10084)
Social Security—Disability Benefits (Publication 05–10029)
Social Security—SSI (Publication 05-11000)
Medicare & You (Publication HCFA-10050)

Access information and the publications on the internet at: **http://www.ssa.gov**

Social Security

The official name for Social Security is the Federal Old Age, Survivor's, and Disability Insurance (OASDI) Benefits Program which clearly identifies its purpose. For many Americans, Social Security is the main and, in some cases, the sole resource for their retirement.

Social Security is funded through taxes paid by workers, employers, and self-employed people. The law that authorizes taxes for Social Security and Medicare is the Federal Insurance Contributions Act (FICA). In 2001, the worker and employer each pay 7.65 percent (6.2 percent for Social Security and 1.45 percent for Medicare) of the worker's gross salary up to $80,400. If the worker earns more than $80,400 in 2001, the worker and employer both continue to pay the 1.45 percent Medicare tax on the rest of the worker's earnings. Self-employed persons pay 15.30 percent on net earnings from self-employment up to $80,400 for 2001 and continue to pay the Medicare tax of 2.9 percent on the rest of their earnings.

Social Security benefits paid to eligible workers are based on the worker's earnings while employed at a job covered by this federal program. Most self-employed persons also receive benefits based on their earnings. In addition, an eligible worker is allowed to take early retirement with reduced benefits at age 62 or wait and take full benefits at 65. In the year 2003, the full benefit retirement age will slowly begin to rise from 65 and will continue rising until the end of 2027 when the retirement age with full benefits will be 67. Age 62 will remain the age for early retirement with reduced benefits. *Note:* Social Security is not a program that pays benefits based on financial need. All eligible workers and self-employed persons regardless of their personal wealth receive benefits.

Social Security benefits, subject to certain age and other conditions, are paid to the following:

- Retired workers, age 65, and their dependents.
- Disabled workers (any age) who have qualified for disability and their dependents.
- Surviving dependents of deceased workers.
- Surviving dependents of deceased disabled workers.

- Former spouses, if married for at least ten years. *Note:* If a former spouse receives benefits on the worker's account, it does not affect the amount of any benefits payable to other survivors of the worker who are also on the worker's account.

Finally:

- Every qualified worker is also entitled to a special one-time death benefit payment of $255.
- Some higher income taxpayers may have to pay income tax on a portion of their Social Security benefits.

Supplemental Security Income (SSI)

Both Social Security and SSI are administered by the Social Security Administration. However, SSI is financed from the general revenue funds of the U.S. Treasury and not from Social Security taxes. The program makes monthly payments based on need to low income people who have few assets. To receive the SSI basic monthly benefit you must be a U.S. citizen, live in the United States, and be:

- 65 or older; or   Basic monthly check (year 2001)
- Blind; or   Individual $530
- Disabled.   Couple $796

Children can also receive SSI benefits due to blindness or disability. Most individuals receiving SSI benefits are eligible for food stamps and Medicaid (see discussion below).

SSI sets the income and asset limits for benefit eligibility. Some states add funds to the basic federal SSI monthly benefit, so you must check the local Social Security office in your state for the income limits and amount of the benefit. The asset limits, unlike the income limits, do not vary from state to state. If eligible, people may receive both Social Security and SSI benefits.

▥ ASSIGNMENT 10.3

Assume you are a legal assistant working in a legal aid clinic for low income individuals. Determine whether your state adds funds to the federal SSI monthly benefit. What are your state's income limits for eligibility, and what is the maximum amount of the benefit your state allows?

> **RESEARCH BOX**
> To obtain annual updated statistical information, call this Medicare hotline toll-free number **1-800-633-4227** or visit internet sites:
>
> **http://www.medicare.gov**
> **http://www.HCFA.gov**

Medicare

Medicare is a federal program that provides hospital and medical insurance for people age 65 and older, certain disabled persons under 65 who qualify under

Social Security, and people with permanent kidney failure treated with dialysis or a transplant. The Health Care Financing Administration is the federal agency within the U.S. Department of Health and Human Services that administers the Medicare and Medicaid programs. These two programs benefit approximately 75 million Americans. Medicare has two parts: A and B.

Part A is a hospital insurance program that pays for the following four kinds of medically necessary care:

- Inpatient hospital care.
- Home health care.
- **Hospice care.**
- Inpatient care in a skilled nursing facility following a required three-day hospital stay.

⚱ ASSIGNMENT 10.4

After obtaining a current Medicare booklet which is updated each year, list the services covered and *not* covered under Part A for inpatient hospital care.

To be eligible for coverage under Part A for inpatient care in a **skilled nursing facility,** the patient, based on a physician's orders, must require daily skilled nursing or skilled rehabilitation services performed by, or under the supervision of, licensed nursing personnel. In the United States, many nursing homes provide custodial or personal care only and are *not* skilled nursing facilities.

Custodial (personal) care consists of helping the patient with daily living and personal needs provided by people lacking professional skills or training. It includes assistance in walking, bathing, dressing, eating, and taking medicines. Much of the care for the elderly that allows them to stay in their own homes is also custodial care. When workers and their spouses who are eligible for Social Security benefits reach the age of 65, they are automatically covered under Part A even if the worker has not retired. In addition, workers, regardless of age, who qualify for disability under Social Security and receive benefits for two years are also eligible for Medicare.

Part B is a medical insurance program that helps pay for the following:

- Doctor's services.
- Outpatient hospital care.
- Diagnostic tests.
- Durable medical equipment.
- Necessary ambulance services.
- Home health visits needed after an injury, illness, or surgery.

⚱ ASSIGNMENT 10.5

Using your Medicare booklet, list the doctor and outpatient hospital services covered and *not* covered by Medicare Part B.

Medicare has consistently expanded its services so that relevant diagnostic tests and treatments are now covered, including yearly mammograms (breast cancer);

Hospice care
A public agency or private organization that provides supportive care at home or in an institution (e.g., hospital) for the terminally ill, i.e., persons certified by their doctor to have a life expectancy of six months or less.

Skilled nursing facility
A Medicare qualified facility that specializes in skilled nursing or rehabilitation services under the supervision of licensed nursing personnel and based on a doctor's orders.

Custodial (personal) care
Care that consists of helping the patient with daily living and personal needs provided by people lacking professional skills or training.

pap smears (cervical and vaginal cancer); colorectal cancer screening; diabetes monitoring and self-management; bone mass measurements; flu, pneumonia, and Hepatitis B shots; and prostate cancer screening, which includes a prostate-specific antigen (PSA) test. In summary, Medicare pays for approximately 90 percent of the hospital and doctor bills for eligible recipients. To pay for the remainder and some other expenses Medicare does not cover, many participants buy Medicare Supplement Insurance, also known as Medigap policies. *Note:* Part A and Part B of the Medicare program do not pay for long-term care expenses in a nursing home, or at home, and neither does any Medicare Supplement Insurance policy. In most states Medicare pays for less than 5 percent of all nursing home care. To recap: Medicare only pays for a limited amount of nursing home and at-home care called skilled nursing care which is not the same as custodial or personal care. The latter is the kind of long-term care most elderly people need, but it is not paid for by Medicare.

Medicaid

Medicaid is a form of public assistance, sponsored and funded jointly by the federal and state governments, which provides medical aid for people whose income and assets fall below a certain level. The federal government sets the guidelines for the Medicaid program which the individual states administer, but some states have substantially modified the rules within the limits of the federal statutes and regulations. For example, two-thirds of the states automatically grant Medicaid assistance to all individuals who are eligible for SSI, i.e., over 65, blind, or disabled. The remaining states have different and more restrictive eligibility requirements concerning income and resources than allowed under SSI. In most states the list of medical care covered by Medicaid includes:

- Physician services.
- Most prescription drugs.
- Dental care.
- Medical tests.
- Home health care.
- Physical therapy.
- Eyeglasses.
- Hearing aids.
- Hospital and long-term nursing home care.

Requirements for Medicaid Eligibility

The amount of money and assets a person eligible for Medicaid is allowed to keep differs among the states.

ASSIGNMENT 10.6

List the eligibility requirements for nursing home residents in your state. *Note:* Each state has a toll-free 800 number for state residents to obtain this information.

Medicaid pays the medical treatment and housing expenses for nursing home or in-home care not only for those individuals who have little or no resources (income and assets) but also for some middle-income individuals who may become unable to continue to pay unexpected, catastrophic long-term nursing home expenses. Once they have spent most of their financial resources, they, too, become eligible for Medicaid. The result is that nearly half of all nursing home care expenses in the United States is paid by Medicaid. Furthermore, nursing homes cannot discriminate between Medicaid patients and other patients; i.e., the Medicaid patients must be given services and care that are equal to the care received by patients who pay their own expenses.

Other middle-income spouses (parents) who wish to leave their children an inheritance, but realize one of them (husband or wife) faces a debilitating illness that will wipe out their resources, will attempt to use a method, often referred to as the **spend-down** procedure, to qualify for Medicaid but pass the inheritance without impoverishing the healthy spouse. The parents' procedure is to pass by gift (spend down) enough of their assets to their children to qualify the parents for Medicaid. However, Medicaid has a restriction that prohibits spouses (parents) and others in such cases from becoming eligible for medical assistance if any transfer of assets is done for less than fair market value during a thirty-six-month period immediately preceding an application for Medicaid.

Spend-down
A procedure that requires an individual to spend enough income and resources to qualify for Medicaid eligibility.

> **Example:** Gladys and Henry are both 70 years old, own an estate worth $700,000 including a home, and have five married children and seven grandchildren. They wish to leave a substantial amount of their estate to their family. Henry, who has smoked cigarettes for over fifty years, has emphysema which will eventually require him to use oxygen for treatment and almost assuredly necessitate his move to a nursing home. Theoretically, if Henry and Gladys transfer by gift enough assets from their estate to their seventeen family members, i.e., five children, five spouses, and seven grandchildren, in one year they can remove $340,000+ from their estate. *Note:* Spouses who join in making a gift can transfer $20,000+ (indexed annually for inflation) to each recipient every year free from gift tax. Under the example, this would allow Gladys and Henry to pass a substantial amount of their estate to their family, Gladys could remain in their home, and Henry would eventually qualify for Medicaid when, three or more years later, he enters a nursing home. Assumption: Long-term care insurance is not an option for Henry because of his uninsurable pre-existing medical condition.

As the previous example illustrates, you must familiarize yourself with the statutes and administrative rules of your state concerning Medicaid's procedures since they may become an increasingly important and essential part of your client's estate plan. Common financial advice for clients facing Medicaid's eligibility rules and restrictions is to convert liquid assets into exempt assets, such as a home. When spouses, like Gladys and Henry, own a home, it is good tax and estate planning advice for them to pay off any existing mortgage so Gladys (referred to as the "community spouse" using Medicaid terminology) can continue to live there without mortgage payments. Another possible tax advantage is for spouses to buy a home, such as a condominium, so if one spouse (referred to as the "institutional spouse") moves into a nursing home covered by Medicaid, the "community spouse" will have an exempt home. A carefully created trust for a disabled child covered by Medicaid is a third potential financial consideration.

> **RESEARCH BOX**
> A Children's Health Insurance Program is available in your state. For more information call **1-877-543-7669**.

Children's Health Insurance Program

The Children's Health Insurance Program is administered by the Health Care Financing Administration and the Health Resources and Services Administration. This program began in October 1997 and provides $24 billion in federal matching funds spread over five years (1997–2002) to help states expand health care coverage to some of the approximately 10 million uninsured children in the United States.

The federal agencies have set broad guidelines for the program, allowing the individual states to establish eligibility and coverage requirements. The method of providing services is also determined by the states. Eligible recipients in all states must: (1) have low income; (2) be ineligible for Medicaid; and (3) be uninsured. Not all states have established benefits for the program, and existing state programs are not all the same. However, all states must cover at least the following services:

- Inpatient and outpatient hospital services.
- Doctor's surgical and medical services.
- Laboratory and x-ray services.
- Well baby/child care, including immunizations.

Additional benefits are available in many states. Applications for this children's benefit program are available at state or county social service agencies, human resource (services) agencies, and public health agencies.

Need for Long-Term Care Insurance

Now that the sources of income and the federal and state public assistance programs available to the elderly and disabled have been identified, the methods of paying for long-term care expenses for individuals included in each of the three levels of income and assets can be discussed.

Low Income and Assets

Low income individuals often receive nominal Social Security benefits, generally qualify for SSI, and, therefore, are eligible for Medicaid in most states. Consequently, they *cannot* afford and have no need for long-term care insurance.

High Income and Assets

High income individuals, including married couples, with comfortable assets and income, have sufficient resources to pay for any possible long-term care expenses. Consequently, they *can* afford but have no need for long-term care insurance.

Caveat: Dr. Benjamin Spock, author of the 1946 classic, *Baby and Child Care,* sold over 50 million copies of the book, was very wealthy, and never considered purchasing insurance to cover the cost of long-term nursing care. However, before his death in 1998 at the age of 94, his family needed financial assistance to help pay for his in-home nursing care expenses. Dr. Spock's legacy: Sometimes, even with the best of intentions and thoughtful planning, a savings plan for retirement may not be sufficient if you unexpectedly need long-term round-the-clock care in a nursing home or even at home as in the Doctor's case.

Moderate Income and Assets

Moderate income individuals are generally considered to have assets over $75,000, not including a home or car, and annual income of up to $40,000 for an individual and up to $70,000 for a married couple. It is this group of individuals who can afford to buy long-term care insurance and thereby protect their estate assets.

Caveat: Unfortunately, even those who purchase long-term care insurance, because of spiralling inflation costs and the underestimated magnitude of long-term care expenses, especially those in nursing homes, may be forced to participate, as mentioned earlier, in the Medicaid spend-down program. In all states, the majority of nursing home residents are on Medicaid, and over half a million people in America become eligible for Medicaid each year. Many members of the *baby boomer* generation recognize the cost of their parents' long-term nursing home care may ultimately become their responsibility. To cover the considerable expense of long-term care for their parents, some have purchased the insurance for them. At the present time, however, statistics show the *boomers* need to be more concerned about their own long-term care needs. A survey by the American Health Care Association found 68 percent of them are not financially prepared for long-term health care. In addition, 50 percent admitted they had not given any thought as to how they will finance the costs of long-term care.

Long-Term Care Insurance

Definition

Long-term care insurance
Insurance that pays a fixed monetary benefit, usually per day, for a designated benefit period during which the insured generally receives care at home or in a nursing home.

Long-term care insurance pays a fixed monetary amount (benefit) usually per day or per month for a designated period of time (benefit period) during which the insured can receive long-term care services in an assisted living facility, a nursing home, or at home. Long-term care insurance is not a typical health and medical insurance program. Instead, its purpose is to provide the insured with funds to maintain estate assets. These funds (benefits) are paid by the insurance company in one of two ways: (1) either it pays the insured or the provider for services up to the policy limits, or (2) it pays the insured only the amount stated in the policy regardless of the services received.

Goals of Long-Term Care Insurance

The goals of long-term care insurance are to enable the insured to:

- Identify the need and qualifications for long-term care insurance while factoring into the decision to buy the insurance the concern that future health restrictions or accident injuries may disqualify the applicant.
- Pay the expenses of long-term care.
- Maintain and protect estate assets.
- Leave an inheritance to family (the most common incentive and justification for the purchase of this insurance).

- Select the location (facility) where long-term care is received (assisted living facility, adult day care center, continuing care retirement community, nursing home, or at home—where this care is given most often).
- Select caregivers (doctors, nurses, home care providers, etc.) and care facilities (hospital, clinic, etc.).
- Receive federal income tax benefits, including allowing policy premiums to be deductible as medical expenses (subject to qualification and limits) and permitting all or most of the policy benefits to be tax-free (see Tax Advantages discussion below).
- Most importantly, maintain independence and dignity without having to rely on the generosity of others.

Tax Advantages Associated with Long-Term Care Insurance

Since the passage of the Health Insurance Portability and Accountability Act of 1996, two important tax benefits are available to policyholders with tax-qualified long-term care insurance:

- Benefit payments from long-term care insurance policies are treated as tax-free income and are not subject to federal taxation.
- Premium payments for a **tax-qualified long-term care insurance policy** are deductible as personal medical expenses if the policyholders itemize their deductions and their total medical expenses (including the long-term care insurance premiums) exceed 7.5 percent of their adjusted gross income. Deductions are available for individuals, their spouses, and tax dependents, e.g., parents. The deductible amount is subject to dollar limits based on the individual taxpayer's attained age before the close of the tax year. These limits are indexed annually for inflation (see following chart).

Tax-qualified long-term care insurance policy
A policy that conforms to specific standards under federal law and offers certain federal tax advantages.

Maximum Federal Income Tax Deductible Amounts—2001

Age	Individual	Couple
Under 40	$ 230	$ 460
40–49	$ 430	$ 860
50–59	$ 860	$1720
60–69	$2290	$4580
Over 70	$2860	$5720

Long-Term Care Insurance Policy Options

Before purchasing a long-term care insurance policy, the available and affordable contract options from competing companies must be carefully compared.

These options include the following items.

1. *Amount of the maximum benefit*. Most companies will clearly list the maximum benefit they will pay over the time period set in the policy. Other companies limit the maximum benefit to a total dollar amount. Benefits are usually paid on a daily, monthly, or annual basis. The amounts offered range from $50 to $250 per day or $1,500 to $7,500 per month for care in nursing homes. Coverage approved for in-home care services is usually $40 to $125 per day.

2. *Duration of the coverage*. Choosing the length of time for coverage is a difficult decision. Since the average stay in a nursing home, as noted earlier, is two

and one-half years, and the vast majority of patients stay less than four years, four years may be the maximum time period needed versus unnecessary and more expensive lifetime coverage which, according to statistics, the majority of Americans will never need.

3. *Types of coverage.* Types of coverage include coverage only in a nursing home, only at home, or a combination covering both. Since insurers estimate that seven of ten people who live past age 65 will use home care,[5] buying coverage for home care only is a viable option. It is the place where most people want to stay, and it is also less expensive than nursing home coverage. However, the down side of home coverage only is that anybody frail enough to need this care may also need nursing home care in the near future. On the other hand, buying only nursing home care could be a regrettable mistake since the buyer may never need it. The best choice may be the combined home and nursing home policy, but it is more expensive. You must prepare and consistently update a comparison of the available insurance policies in your state to enable your client to make the best and most appropriate personal selection. Some policies pay benefits that include care and services in any or all facilities.

4. *Cost of the policy.* In the year 2000, the average annual premium including inflation protection and nonforfeiture benefits for a person age 65 is $2,305 and $7,022 for a person age 79.[6] Obviously, the younger a buyer is when the policy is purchased, the cheaper the cost. If buyers wait until they are older, they run the risk that their health will deteriorate, and they will not be able to qualify at any price. The premium cost of a long-term care insurance policy is determined by the policyholder's choice of the amount of the benefit and the length of time of the policy. The quality and coverage of nursing home care and the costs vary among the states, but the average cost, according to the Health Insurance Association of America, is approximately $110 per day. To determine how much coverage prospective buyers need, they should research and compare the average daily cost of care in their state in local nursing homes and at home, if that location is a viable option. Subsequently, they should obtain quotes from at least three insurance companies comparing the same levels of coverage and benefits. The final choice should at least cover the average cost of the daily benefit plus the cost of inflation protection (see discussion below). Each of the following can add to the cost of the premium of a long-term care insurance policy: (1) the age of the person when the policy is purchased; (2) the amount of the maximum benefit and length of the benefit period; (3) the addition of home health care coverage to a nursing home policy or the reverse; (4) the addition of nonforfeiture benefits; (5) the shortening of the waiting (elimination) period; and (6) the addition of inflation protection that, by itself, can increase the premium by 25 to 40 percent.

5. *Housing facilities and services provided.* It is essential the person seeking long-term care insurance be aware of which housing facilities are covered by the selected policy. If the insured is placed in a facility that is not covered by the policy, generally, the insurance company is not obligated to pay for the services provided. For example, some policies may require the insured to reside in a state-licensed facility (such as a licensed nursing home); therefore, such policies would not cover an unlicensed rest home or homes for the aged. Long-term care insurance policies may cover the following:

- Nursing home care.
- Home health care.

- Personal care in your home.
- Services in assisted living facilities.
- Services in adult day care centers.
- Services in other community facilities.

Today, almost all policies cover Alzheimer's disease but sometimes only if the policy is purchased before the disease is diagnosed.

Check the policies that cover home health care very thoroughly. Some policies pay for home care only by licensed home health agencies. Others pay for care from licensed health care providers such as practical nurses; speech, physical, or occupational therapists; and/or home health care aides who may help with custodial (personal) care needs. *Note:* Family members who take care of a loved one at home are not paid benefits by most insurance companies.

🏛 ASSIGNMENT 10.7

Which of the following services are not covered by long-term care insurance policies?
- Alcohol or drug addiction;
- Illness or injury caused by an act of war;
- Attempted suicide;
- Intentional self-inflicted injuries.

6. ***Waiting (elimination) period.*** The waiting period is the amount of time the insureds must wait from the date they are certified as chronically ill until the date benefit payments for covered services begin. In other words, the insured patients will not receive benefits the first day they arrive and receive care at the nursing home nor when they begin receiving services at home. Most companies have a waiting or elimination period during which time benefits do not begin until a set number of days (30, 60, 100, or 180 days) have passed after the start and use of qualifying long-term care services. Premiums can be reduced by choosing a longer elimination period.

The insured becomes **chronically ill** when he or she is incapable of performing, without substantial assistance from another person, two or more of the activities of daily living (ADLs) for a period of at least ninety consecutive days or the person requires consistent supervision because of his or her severe cognitive impairment that threatens the person's health and safety. To recap: The six activities of daily living include bathing, eating, dressing, continence, toileting, and transferring. Before the insured can receive benefit payments under a long-term care insurance policy, most companies require that the insured must be unable to perform any two of these activities.

7. ***Inflation protection.*** Due to inflation, the insured must recognize the need for increasing insurance protection. If the inflation rate is 5 percent per year, nursing home care that currently costs $110 per day will cost $292 per day in twenty years. Although the cost for inflation protection increases the premium each year, it is recommended the insured purchase at least 5 percent inflation protection compounded annually. A policy a person age 55 buys today, may not pay benefits until the person enters a nursing home at age 75. Unless the policy benefit is compounded annually to help keep up with inflation, the amount of the benefit will fall far short of the actual costs. Some states require that inflation

protection be compounded, but this also increases the cost of the policy premium. *Caveat:* Long-term care insurance should not be purchased if the buyer cannot realistically expect to be able to afford the substantial increases in premiums in future years due to inflation. A buyer could waste thousands of dollars on a policy that lapses before it is needed.

8. ***Pre-existing condition limitation.*** If a buyer of long-term care insurance had a medical problem (pre-existing condition) that was diagnosed and treated prior to an application for the insurance, the policy, if acquired, may not cover the expense for the condition or may delay coverage for a stated period of time before payments begin. For example, almost all long-term care insurance policies cover Alzheimer's disease if the disease occurs after the policy is in effect. However, as a pre-existing condition, many companies do not offer insurance to patients who already have Alzheimer's disease when they apply. *Note:* Long-term care insurance policies that contain an exclusion for Alzheimer's disease are prohibited in many states.

9. ***Nonforfeiture benefit.*** A provision in a long-term care insurance policy that refunds at least part of the premium if the insured cancels the policy or lets it lapse for nonpayment.

10. ***Waiver of premium payment.*** A provision in a long-term care insurance policy that allows insureds to stop paying the premium once they enter a nursing home, and the company begins to pay benefits. The waiver of premium payments may not apply to insureds receiving home health care.

11. *Third-party notification.* The third-party notification option allows the insured to name a third person who is to be notified if the policy is about to lapse for nonpayment of the premium.

12. *Premium refund on death.* After paying premiums for a set number of years or if death occurs before a specific age, an insured may be entitled to a refund payable on death to the estate.

Methods of Purchasing Long-Term Care Insurance

Long-term care insurance policies are sold by over 120 private insurance companies. Policies may be purchased in many ways through:

MINI-GLOSSARY BOX

Waiting (elimination) period
The amount of time in calendar or benefit days after the initial use of qualifying long-term care services in a nursing home or at home before benefits are paid.

Chronically ill
A continuing or recurring illness that prevents the person from performing activities of daily living or requires supervision because of a cognitive impairment.

Inflation protection
A policy option that provides for increases in benefit amounts to help pay for expected increases in the costs of long-term care services due to inflation.

Pre-existing condition limitation
An illness or disability for which the insured was diagnosed or treated during a period of time before applying for a long-term care insurance policy.

Nonforfeiture benefit
A policy feature that returns a portion of the premiums if the insured cancels the insurance policy or allows it to lapse.

Waiver of premium payment
A provision in a long-term care insurance policy that allows the insured to stop paying premiums once benefits are received.

- Agents.
- By mail or by phone without an agent.
- Senior citizen organizations and fraternal associations.
- Employers who may offer a group insurance policy.
- Continuing care retirement communities that offer or require residents to pass a physical and enroll in group policies.
- A combination of life insurance and long-term care insurance using an "accelerated benefit," a benefit of life insurance the insured uses while living.
- Long-term care "partnerships" that exist between four states, i.e., California, Connecticut, Indiana, and New York, and their Medicaid agencies that allow resident purchasers of a long-term care insurance policy to go on Medicaid when the policy benefits are exhausted without first having to deplete (spend down) their own assets to become eligible.

Insurance Selection—Rating Services

Since a long-term care insurance policy may last for many years, the insured, before buying the policy, should select a company that has an established history of prompt payments and excellent service. Several private companies, called rating services, investigate and analyze the financial strength of long-term care insurance companies and rate them. Ratings from the services are available free at most public libraries. Some of these rating services include:

- A.M. Best Company 1–908–439–2200 or on the internet at *http://www.ambest.com.*
- Standard & Poor's Insurance Rating Services 1–212–438–2400 or on the internet at *http://www.standardpoor.com.*

Recommendation: If a person has decided to buy long-term care insurance, the following is suggested:

- Buy a policy that covers both in-home and nursing home care and lasts for at least four years.
- Buy at least $100,000 in lifetime benefits.
- Buy a policy with at least $125 per day for nursing home care and $65 per day for home care with a minimum of five visits per week.
- Buy 5 percent inflation protection compounded annually.
- Keep your existing policy and change it only for a good reason.

Alternatives to Long-Term Care Insurance

Instead of buying insurance, a person might pay for long-term care by the following:

- Borrow from the cash value of a whole-life insurance policy.
- Accelerate death benefits from life insurance while the insured is still living.
- Use a reverse mortgage on the home owned by the person to help pay for long-term care.

When deciding whether to purchase long-term care insurance, consider this fact: No matter what a person's current age, the cost of the total premiums for long-term care insurance over the required years of payments will be less than the amount the person would pay for one year living in a nursing home. At the start of the new millennium only 10 percent of Americans over 65 purchase long-term care insurance.

Current Trends

The general dissatisfaction with the nursing home option for long-term care housing needs of the elderly and infirmed has established almost a universal mindset in our nation: No one wants to live in a nursing home. However, many have no alternative.

During the 1990s, a transition began which changed the housing system from a domination of highly state-regulated nursing homes to one of broader consumer choices in housing and health services which can be delivered in homes, apartments, and specialized nursing homes. With the help of family, home health aides, and other available assistance, the first choice of the elderly is usually to stay in their own homes if it is physically, mentally, and financially possible. For those who cannot or choose not to stay in their homes, the second housing option is independent assisted living which is rapidly increasing in demand for those who can afford it.

The change occurring within the long-term care housing system is due to the combination of market forces, i.e., the *baby boomers* who want options other than nursing homes, and the general agreement of the need for new options among care providers, advocates for the elderly who use the services, and state and federal regulators who oversee their long-term care housing needs.

Although the *baby boomers* will be wealthier and better educated than their counterparts of today, careful financial planning will be necessary for them to attain the goals for their long-term care housing needs. Remaining in their homes with family and other help, in assisted living apartments, and in specialized nursing homes will surely be options. However, the ever-increasing cost of long-term care housing will continue to dictate and severely limit the housing options of low and moderate income people.

As an added incentive for the purchase of long-term care insurance, look for legislation in the coming years that offers new or increased tax deductions for insurance premiums.

KEY TERMS

Estate plan
Disposition
Marital deduction
Estate equalization
Bypass trust
Charitable deduction
Capital gains tax
Charitable remainder
Charitable Remainder
  Unitrust
Charitable Remainder
  Annuity Trust
Donor
Donee

Gift splitting
Present interest
Legal life estate
Custodian
Custodianship
Future interest
Stepped-up basis
Alternate valuation
  date
Donor (of a power of
  appointment)
Donee (of a power of
  appointment)
Appointee

General power of
  appointment
Special power of
  appointment
QTIP trust (qualified
  terminable interest
  property)
Terminable interest
Incident of ownership
Irrevocable life
  insurance trust
Postmortem
Disclaimer
Elder Law

Long-term care
Cognitive disorder
  (impairment)
Activities of daily
  living (ADLs)
Toileting
Continence
Transferring
Adult day care center
Assisted living facility
Continuing care
  retirement
  community
Nursing home care

Home health care	Spend-down	Waiting (elimination) period	Nonforfeiture benefit
Respite care	Long-term care insurance	Chronically ill	Waiver of premium payment
Hospice care		Inflation protection	
Skilled nursing facility	Tax-qualified long-term care insurance policy	Pre-existing condition limitation	
Custodial (personal) care			

REVIEW QUESTIONS

1. Who are the individuals you would choose to help you prepare an estate plan for a client?
2. What is the purpose of an estate plan? Methods for reducing or avoiding taxes are part of every estate plan. Such tax avoidance methods may be legal, but are they ethical?
3. How do potential adverse factors diminish the value of an estate? List at least three such factors.
4. What are the two key documents used to prepare an estate plan? How does each document benefit a decedent's surviving family members?
5. How is the marital deduction used to lower the net estate that is subject to federal estate tax?
6. Under what circumstances does estate equalization between spouses become important?
7. How does the charitable deduction reduce both federal estate and income taxes?
8. How does a charitable remainder unitrust differ from a charitable remainder annuity trust? What function does each charitable trust serve?
9. What are the most common methods used to reduce federal and state death taxes? List four methods and explain how each reduces these taxes.
10. According to current federal tax law, what are the gift tax annual exclusion, the marital deduction, and the unified transfer tax credit for gifts and estates? Explain how each is used to reduce federal taxes.
11. What is the distinction between a general and a special power of appointment? Why is a power of appointment used in a will or a trust?
12. What are four methods of transferring property that qualify for the gift or estate tax marital deduction? Explain each one.
13. What is a QTIP trust? Explain its function and advantages.
14. Why is life insurance such an important planning device for an estate plan? What is the function of an irrevocable life insurance trust?
15. What are the incidents of ownership of a life insurance policy? What effect do they have on a decedent-policyholder's potential federal estate tax?
16. Using your Medicare booklet, list the services covered and *not* covered under Medicare Part A for each of the following: services provided by a skilled nursing facility; home health care; and a hospice.

CASE PROBLEMS

Problem 1

Marsha Thompson, age 34, is a single parent who divorced her husband, Ben Thompson, three years ago. Marsha has custody of their two children, Andrea, age 12, and Jonas, age 8. Marsha is a marketing manager for a local retail store. She earns $35,000 per year. The company provides Marsha and her dependents with a health insurance plan; a group term life insurance policy worth $20,000; and a 401(k) employee benefit plan to which the company annually contributes 3 percent of her salary. Marsha makes contributions of $200 per month to the 401(k) plan, and she has named her two children the beneficiaries of the plan and her life insurance. Marsha has a checking account of $1,200; owns a 1999 Ford; and after the divorce, has title to a house worth $85,000 with equity of $15,000. She has no other savings or investments.

Marsha's former husband, Ben, is a salesman who has difficulty keeping a job because of his dependency on alcohol. Currently, he sells new and used cars. He has visitation rights with the children, but he frequently fails to show up. Ben has been ordered to pay monthly child support of $300, which he has paid sporadically depending on whether he has a job. He is now $4,500 behind in support payments, and Marsha has little hope of enforcing payment. According to your state statutes, answer and explain the following:

A. As part of an estate plan for Marsha, would you recommend a will, a will with a testamentary trust, or a revocable living trust?
B. Name the fiduciaries who would need to be appointed as part of Marsha's estate plan.
C. If Marsha were to die first, can she exclude her former husband, Ben, from becoming the guardian of the person of her minor children? What about the guardian of the property?
D. Are the children old enough to voice their preference for a guardian?
E. What other kinds of insurance, if any, would you recommend Marsha buy, e.g., homeowners, car, life, disability, health, or long-term care?
F. What kinds of investments, if any, would you recommend, e.g., stocks, bonds, certificates of deposit, and IRAs?

Problem 2

Jake Costello, a confirmed bachelor, has been a workaholic his entire life. Financially, he has been immensely successful. Jake's net worth is over $10 million. Now 86 years of age and in failing health, Jake has outlived his immediate family members and has no surviving relatives. Realizing "you can't take it with you," Jake decides the one beneficiary he does not want to receive any death benefits, i.e., federal taxes, from his estate is the government. What options could you suggest to Jake to accomplish his wish or is it a fantasy?

Problem 3

Mary Olson, a widow, is age 62. Her husband, George, died last year of lung cancer. Due to George's poor health for the past twenty years, Mary had been the sole breadwinner of the family. She has two adult children and one grandchild who live in a neighboring state. Mary's mother, Alice, who is 88, lives in a nearby nursing home. All of Alice's assets were used to pay for her health care and living expenses. She is now supported by Social Security and Medicaid. Mary's only sibling, a sister, died two years ago at age 52 of breast cancer. Mary plans to leave her estate to her children and grandchild. Mary's assets consist of the following:

- Home (no mortgage), current value $285,000.
- 401(k) plan, current value $315,000.
- Savings, investments, IRA, and miscellaneous personal property, current value $165,000.

Should Mary purchase long-term care insurance? Explain.

Notes

1. *Journal of Financial Planning* (3/99).
2. *Boston Globe* (5/12/97).
3. *New England Journal of Medicine* (2/28/91).
4. *The Washington Post* (7/2/00).
5. *Business Week* (7/20/98).
6. *The Washington Post* (7/2/00).

CHAPTER 11

PERSONAL REPRESENTATIVES: TYPES, PRE-PROBATE DUTIES, AND APPOINTMENT

OUTLINE

OBJECTIVES

After completing this chapter, you should be able to:

➤ Identify and define the various types of personal representatives involved in the administration of decedents' estates.

➤ From the dialogue, identify and appreciate your role in the practice of the law of wills and probate.

➤ Understand the procedures for appointment of the personal representative in formal probate proceedings.

➤ Explain the basic functions and duties performed by the personal representative in the preparation of probate and estate administration.

➤ Recognize your role as an assistant to the personal representative in the performance of the required duties of estate administration.

SCOPE OF THE CHAPTER

This chapter provides a more in-depth review of the law governing personal representatives. It identifies and defines them and reviews their duties in preparation for the administration of a decedent's estate. The chapter discusses only those functions that must be performed soon after the decedent's death, i.e., duties the personal representative should be ready to perform even before the probate court confirms his appointment. Since you will often be asked to assist the personal representative, knowledge of these duties is essential.

The chapter begins by defining additional types of personal representatives not previously discussed, describing their powers and functions, and citing sample statutes that establish their authority. Next, the basic powers and duties of the personal representative in preparation for formal proceedings are explained, along with your role in assisting with these duties. For an overview of the duties of the personal representative, see Chapter 3.

TYPES OF PERSONAL REPRESENTATIVES

The UPC term *personal representative* refers to anyone empowered or authorized to administer the estate of the deceased, whether the deceased died testate or intestate. Minors, incompetent persons, convicted felons, and judges of a court are prohibited from being personal representatives. Personal representatives must be U.S. citizens.

The role of the personal representative may be performed by a private individual (usually a family member), an attorney, or a trust officer of a corporate business such as a bank or trust company. In intestacy cases, the personal representative is selected according to the order of preference for appointment set by statute. An example of a state statute illustrating the order of preference is 20 Pa. Stat. Ann. § 3155 Persons Entitled:

> (a) *Letters testamentary*—Letters testamentary shall be granted by the register to the executor designated in the will, whether or not he has declined a trust under the will.
>
> (b) *Letters of administration*—Letters of administration shall be granted by the register, in such form as the case shall require, to one or more of those hereinafter mentioned and, except for good cause, in the following order:
>
> (1) Those entitled to the residuary estate under the will.
>
> (2) The surviving spouse.
>
> (3) Those entitled under the intestate law as the register, in his discretion, shall judge who will best administer the estate, giving preference, however, according to the sizes of the shares of those in this class.
>
> (4) The principal creditors of the decedent at the time of his death.
>
> (5) Other fit persons.
>
> (6) If anyone of the foregoing shall renounce his right to letters of administration, the register, in his discretion, may appoint a nominee of the person so renouncing in preference to the persons set forth in any succeeding paragraph.
>
> (c) *Time limitation*—Except with the consent of those enumerated in clauses (1), (2), and (3), no letters shall be issued to those enumerated in clauses (4) and (5) of

subsection (b) until seven days after the decedent's death. [For comparison see UPC § 3–203 in Appendix C.]

💻 INFORMATION FOR THE PERSONAL REPRESENTATIVE

Estate law firms need to provide information to the personal representative about the duties of the job. Creative brochures or handouts containing the information can be created on the office computer. A good brochure will include a summary of the required duties and the law office's contact information. Web articles exist that discuss the personal representative's duties. The court's probate office may also provide such information.

In some states, if no one appears who is entitled to act as administrator, the court or registrar may appoint an official, called the public administrator, to administer the estate of an intestate decedent. This and other terms relating to personal representatives not previously discussed are defined below:

- *Special administrator or administratrix.* The special administrator or administratrix is the personal representative, either man or woman, appointed temporarily by a probate court to handle certain immediate needs of an estate, such as managing a business in place of the decedent, until a general administrator or executor can be appointed. This representative usually handles Summary Administration proceedings when the amount of the decedent's property qualifies as a "small estate" (see Chapter 12).
- *Administrator or administratrix* cum testamento annexo. The administrator or administratrix *cum testamento annexo,* also called administrator C.T.A. (means administrator with the will annexed), is the personal representative appointed by the court in two situations: (1) where the maker of the will does not name an executor or executrix or (2) where the maker of the will does name an executor or executrix but the latter cannot serve because of a deficiency in qualifications or competency. The following state statutes identify the position of administrator C.T.A.

20 Pa. Stat. Ann. § 3325 Administrator C.T.A.
An administrator with the will annexed shall have all the powers given by the will to the executor, unless otherwise provided by the will. When he has been required to give bond, no proceeds of real estate shall be paid to him until the court has made an order excusing him from entering additional security or requiring additional security, and in the latter event, only after he has entered the additional security.

Cal. Prob. Code § 8441 Priority for Appointment
(a) Except as provided in subdivision (b), persons and their nominees are entitled to appointment as administrator with the will annexed in the same order of priority as for appointment of an administrator.

Cal. Prob. Code § 8442 Authority over Estate
(a) Subject to subdivision (b), an administrator with the will annexed has the same authority over the decedent's estate as an executor named in the will would have. (c) If the will confers a discretionary power or authority on an executor that is not conferred by law and the will does not extend the power or authority to other

personal representatives, the power or authority shall not be deemed to be conferred on an administrator with the will annexed, but the court in its discretion may authorize the exercise of the power or authority.

Example: Geraldine writes and executes a will, but she neglects to name an executor. On her death, the probate court will decide if the document is admissible to probate and, if so, will appoint an administrator C.T.A. for Geraldine's estate.

■ *Administrator or administratrix* de bonis non. The administrator or administratrix *de bonis non,* also called administrator D.B.N. (means administrator of goods not administered), is a court-appointed personal representative who replaces a previous personal representative who has begun but failed to complete the administration of a decedent's estate for any reason, including death. The following is a sample statute that creates the administrator D.B.N. position.

20 Pa. Stat. Ann. § 3326 Administrator D.B.N. and D.B.N.C.T.A.
An administrator de bonis non, with or without a will annexed, shall have the power to recover the assets of the estate from his predecessor in administration or from the personal representative of such predecessor and, except as the will shall provide otherwise, shall stand in his predecessor's stead for all purposes, except that he shall not be personally liable for the acts of his predecessor. When he has been required to give bond, no proceeds of real estate shall be paid to him until the court has made an order excusing him from entering additional security or requiring additional security, and in the latter event, only after he has entered the additional security.

Example: Frazier is named executor in Eleanor's will. While in the process of settling her estate, he dies. The probate court will appoint a replacement who will have the title of administrator D.B.N.C.T.A.

■ *Public administrator.* The public administrator is a public official appointed by the court to administer the property of an intestate who has left no kindred (blood relative) entitled to apply for appointment and Letters of Administration.

Example: Arnold dies intestate. He never married and has no blood relatives (kindred). Some states would appoint a public administrator to handle Arnold's estate. Exhibit 11.1 summarizes the different types of personal representatives.

Exhibit 11.1   Types of Personal Representatives: Summary Chart

■ The personal representative of a testate decedent is called executor (if a man) or executrix (if a woman).
■ The personal representative of an intestate decedent is called general administrator or simply the administrator (if a man) or administratrix (if a woman).
■ A special administrator (-trix) is appointed by the probate court to handle problems and immediate needs of the estate administration that arise before the court appoints a personal representative.
■ A public administrator is appointed by the probate court to administer the property of an intestate who has left no person entitled to appointment.
■ In special cases the personal representative for either a testate decedent or an intestate decedent may be called:
1. An administrator (-trix) C.T.A. is the person appointed by the court when the maker of the will either does not name an executor or does name one, but that person cannot serve.
2. An administrator (-trix) D.B.N. is the person appointed by the court to replace a previous personal representative who has failed to complete the administration of a decedent's estate.
3. An ancillary administrator (-trix) is the person appointed by the court to oversee the administration of a decedent's estate located in a foreign state.

⚎ ASSIGNMENT 11.1

Joshua Foley's will named his son, William, to be executor, but William refused to serve after Joshua's death and no contingent (successor) executor was named in the will.

1. If Joshua's wife, Ethel, was appointed as personal representative by the probate court, what title would she have?
2. If instead William had commenced probate proceedings but was unable to complete them due to illness, and Ethel was then appointed by the court as his replacement, what would her title be?
3. If Ethel was appointed by a probate court to handle the administration of the estate of her brother, George Clark, who lived and died in another state, what would her title be?
4. If Joshua had forgotten to name an executor, what would the court most likely do?
5. If Joshua had been in the process of completing a transfer of the majority interest in a corporation when he died and the court named a person to continue the transfer before a regular probate proceeding could be held, what would be the title of the person?

INTRODUCTION TO ESTATE ADMINISTRATION: A DIALOGUE

The following discussion describes the probate procedures involved in a typical case. The participants include the decedent's named personal representative (the executor), the attorney for the estate, and the paralegal. It is essential the participants maintain continuous communication between and among themselves so the administration of the decedent's estate will be timely and efficient. The participants and facts of the case are as follows:

Participants

- Decedent—John T. Smith
- Executor—William R. Smith
- Attorney—Ms. Brown
- Paralegal—Ms. Jones

Facts.   John T. Smith, the decedent, died August 15, 2000, owning property in two states, State A and State B. He was domiciled at 1024 Pleasure Lane, Heavenly City, in Cotton County, State A, owning a house there. In addition to the homestead held in joint tenancy with his wife, John owned the following property: a car, licensed in State A and owned in his name only; stocks and bonds owned jointly with his wife; a savings account jointly owned; a checking account in his name only; a life insurance policy with his wife named beneficiary; some valuable paintings given to him by his grandfather; and a summer cottage in his name only, located in State B. John had only a few debts at the time of his death, and no one owed him any money. He was survived by his wife, Mary, and only child, William, age 22.

An attorney, Ms. Brown, had previously been retained to draft John Smith's will. Ms. Jones, the paralegal, had collected all the pertinent information from John Smith and had written a preliminary draft of the will, which had been finalized in a meeting between John Smith, Ms. Brown, and Ms. Jones on January 10, 1998 (see Exhibit 11.2). The final draft of the executed will had been placed in a vault in Ms. Brown's office at Mr. Smith's request.

The provisions of John's will left his wife all property not already transferred to her by joint ownership, gift, or other means. William R. Smith, son of the decedent, had been named executor of the will. He had made all the necessary funeral arrangements for his father's burial according to the directions in his father's letter of instructions, and, knowing he had been named executor, went to the office of Ms. Brown to discuss the procedures for the administration of his father's estate.

In the presence of the paralegal (Ms. Jones), the attorney (Ms. Brown), and the executor (William Smith), the following dialogue takes place.

Attorney: Come in and sit down, William. Here is your father's will. As you know, you have been asked to be his executor.

Executor: (Reads the will) Before his death, my father and I discussed his will and estate. I knew he had named me executor, and I agreed to serve. We also decided, and my mother agreed, to ask you, Ms. Brown, to act as the estate's attorney and help me carry out the duties of the executor since I have no experience in these matters and feel I should learn and understand my responsibilities.

Attorney: I will be happy to serve as the attorney for the estate. It has been the practice of this law firm when advising clients named as executors to work with our paralegal in the field of estate administration. As you know, William, Ms. Jones helped collect the necessary data and prepare the preliminary draft of your father's will. Now, under my supervision, she will handle many of the details necessary to help settle your father's estate. She will participate in our conferences on administration, and will keep you informed of all meetings, hearings, correspondence, and the current status of the administration of your father's estate. She will be available to answer some of the questions you might have about your executor's duties. Others she will discuss with me, and then we shall communicate the information to you. Please feel free to ask any questions or contact us any time you have matters you want to discuss.

Executor: Yes, I have met Ms. Jones. My father told me how pleased he was with the help she had given him in drafting his will. I am very happy Ms. Jones will be working with us.

Paralegal: Thank you. Before we begin our discussion about your father's will and the administration of his estate, let me review for you the things that have been done to this point. As you know, our firm assisted your father in planning for the distribution of his estate after his death. Ms. Brown discussed with him the purpose of and need for a will. I compiled checklists of all the property your father owned or in which he had any interest. After discussing the estate plan with Ms. Brown, I drew up a preliminary draft of the will. Ms. Brown, utilizing methods that took advantage of all possible tax considerations, prepared the final draft of your father's will in its present form. The will ensures the estate will be distributed according to your father's wishes.

Estate administration procedures

Attorney: Let's get started. What we try to accomplish, William, when we assist executors, is to explain the basic procedure that must be followed in administering an estate from beginning to end.

Exhibit 11.2 John T. Smith's Will

LAST WILL AND TESTAMENT
OF
JOHN T. SMITH

I, John T. Smith, residing at 1024 Pleasure Lane, Heavenly City, Cotton County, State A, declare this instrument to be my Last Will and Testament, hereby revoking all former Wills and Codicils by me made.

Article I

I direct that all my just debts, expenses of my last illness, funeral expenses, and expenses of the administration of my estate be paid as soon as possible after my death.

Article II

I give all of my property, now owned or hereafter acquired by me, to my wife, Mary K. Smith, if she survives me.

Article III

In the event my said wife, Mary K. Smith, shall predecease me, or if we should die in a common accident, then I give all of my said property, now owned or hereafter acquired by me, to my son, William R. Smith, now residing at 1024 Pleasure Lane.

Article IV

I hereby nominate and appoint my son, William R. Smith, Executor of this, my Last Will and Testament. In the event he should predecease me or should be unwilling or unable to serve in that capacity, then I hereby nominate and appoint my brother, Joseph B. Smith, Executor of this, my Last Will and Testament. I hereby give and grant unto my said Executor full power to sell and convey, lease or mortgage any and all real estate that I may own at the time of my death or which may be acquired by my estate, without license or leave of court.

Article V

No bond shall be required of any individual named above as Executor of this Will.

IN WITNESS WHEREOF, I have hereunto signed this my last Will and Testament this 10th day of January, 1998.

John T. Smith
_____
John T. Smith—Testator

THIS INSTRUMENT, consisting of one (1) typewritten page, bearing the signature of the above named Testator, was on the date hereof signed, published and declared by him to be his Last Will and Testament in our presence, who, at his request and in his presence, and in the presence of each other, we believing him to be over 18 years of age, of sound mind and disposing memory, and under no constraint or undue influence hereunder do sign our names as attesting witnesses.

Francis A. Miller	residing at	*1712 State Street*
Witness		
Janet F. Strom	residing at	*34 S. Seventh Street*
Witness		

Executor: A few years ago my uncle died without a will. I recall my aunt talking about it. Are the same procedures followed whether a person dies with or without a will?

Attorney: I intend to discuss with you procedures that occur whether a decedent dies *testate,* meaning with a will, as in your father's case, or *intestate,* which means without a will, as in your uncle's case. In either case, a *personal representative* must be appointed to administer the decedent's estate. In the situation such as your father's, where someone has died leaving a will, the personal representative named in the will is generally called an *executor,* if a man, or an *executrix,* if a woman. When a person has died without a will, the personal representative is referred to as an *administrator,* if a man, or an *administratrix,* if a woman. An executor is named in the will and confirmed by the court to handle the estate. An administrator, however, must be appointed by the court when there is no will. You, William, will perform the duties of an executor.

Executor: Well, how do we begin? What must I do?

Attorney: Any personal representative must perform three basic duties:

> **Personal representative's duties**

1. All your father's assets must be collected.
2. His debts, claims against the estate, and taxes due must be paid.
3. The remainder of his estate or property must be distributed according to his will within guidelines set by the *statutes* or laws of this state.

> **Domicile and venue identified**

When a person dies, the state which is the decedent's *domicile* (legal home) and the county which is the proper *venue,* become the location for the *domiciliary administration* of the decedent's estate. In this state, as in many states, the court that handles the decedent's estate is called the *probate court.* Each county has its own probate court. The right, power, and authority a probate court has to hear and decide these matters is referred to as the court's *jurisdiction.* Jurisdiction of the probate court over the administration of a decedent's estate continues until the proceeding is finished. Since your father also owned *real property,* your summer cottage in State B, a second or *ancillary administration* must be commenced in that state. The county in which the property is located is the proper venue for the ancillary proceeding. Ms. Jones will give you additional information and assistance in handling such matters.

> **Probate court's jurisdiction**

Executor: So far I believe I understand the basic functions that must be performed and how the probate court fits into the picture. Since my father named me executor, do I give the money and property to the people mentioned in his will?

Attorney: Not right away. Although you have been named executor, you have no authority to act as personal representative until you file a petition and are appointed by the probate court. This will be done once your father's will has been admitted, which means the will is validated and accepted by the probate court. Now that we are ready to discuss procedural steps and the checklists of information necessary to accomplish them, I am turning you over to Ms. Jones to have her go through the steps with you. As we previously mentioned, if you have any questions about your responsibilities, please call. We shall see that any problems are resolved.

Executor: Thank you for the information, Ms. Brown. If I have any problems, I'll be sure to ask you. Good-bye, and thanks again.

> **Petition to probate will**

Paralegal: As Ms. Brown mentioned, in order for you to become authorized as executor, you must petition the court to admit and accept your father's will. This is done by filling out one of the numerous forms required for estate administration. We have in our law office all the necessary forms you must complete as part of this administration. In addition, we will set up what is called a "tickler" system, which lists chronologically all the important steps and dates in the stages of the administration of the estate.

Tickler system

Here is an example of a "tickler" form (see Exhibit 11.3). Using both this system and a list of procedural steps will help reduce the possibility some important detail or significant date might be forgotten, with resulting damage to the beneficiary's *(successor's)* interest and with potential liability to you, the executor.

Executor: In that case, let's set up this "tickler" system right away. If we each have a copy, we can remind one another of the essential steps and important dates. Right?

Paralegal: Yes. This is exactly what we will do. But remember, you must first get your position as executor authorized as well as establish the necessary ancillary administration in State B where the summer cottage is located. You recall that administration in your father's county of residence is called the "domiciliary" administration. Administration necessary in any other state is "ancillary." Although your father left a will naming you as executor of his estate, a person must also be appointed in State B to handle the ancillary administration. Even though there is a will, that person, who is usually a resident of State B, is called the *ancillary administrator.*

Executor: Now I understand the term. But how is the ancillary administrator authorized, and what does he or she do?

Paralegal: You and your mother are given the opportunity to select the person from State B to act in this *fiduciary* capacity. As a representative of the estate, the ancillary administrator must submit a copy of your father's will, a certified copy of his death certificate, and a petition for appointment to the probate court of the county in which the *real property,* the cottage, is located, using a form similar to the one you will use for authorization in our state. Once authorized by the local county probate court in State B, the ancillary administrator will:

1. Collect the local assets.
2. Pay the local creditors and taxes, if any.
3. Transfer the balance of the estate to you, the domiciliary representative.

Some states allow the domiciliary representative to apply for appointment as ancillary administrator if there is no law to the contrary. We shall check this out because, if it is allowed, your acting as ancillary as well as domiciliary representative might be desirable. If there are creditors of your father in State B, you will be faced with the choice of paying their claims out of ancillary assets or the domiciliary estate funds. If you want to protect the summer cottage against being sold to satisfy such debts, you must discuss this with Ms. Brown.

Executor: By all means, I will consult with Ms. Brown. We would not want to sell the summer cottage unless necessary, since both my mother and I enjoy it so much.

Paralegal: Once you petition the court for probating the will, and the court has proved and accepted it, you will be the authorized personal representative—the executor. The probate court signs an order admitting the will as valid and issuing to you *Letters Testamentary*. This particular legal form is the authorization given to executors to handle the administration of a decedent's estate. If your father had died intestate, without a will like your uncle, either your mother or you as *next of kin* would petition the probate court for general administration of your father's estate,

Letters testamentary

Exhibit 11.3 Sample "Tickler" Form

ESTATE OF JOHN T. SMITH
"Tickler"

ESTATE OF _____ deceased, _____, 20_____

Date of Death _____ Date of Birth _____ Domicile _____

Probate Court _____ County, File No. _____

Name, Mailing Address, and Telephone of Personal Representative and Date of Appointment: _____

_____

Ancillary Administration Necessary _____

Date of Last Will _____ Tax Identification No. _____

Proceeding	Person Who Performed	Due or Dated	Filed or Paid
Original will filed with probate court			
Petition for probate, administration, etc.	_____	_____	_____
Mailing of notice of hearing	_____	_____	_____
Hearing on petition for probate or appointment with registrar	_____	_____	_____
Affidavit of mailing (family allowances, etc.)	_____	_____	_____
Bond	_____	_____	_____
Letters issued	_____	_____	_____
Notice to creditors and affidavit of mailing	_____	_____	_____
Inventory and appraisement	_____		
Personal property tax		Feb.	_____
Real estate taxes: (First half		May 15	_____
Second half) if necessary		Oct. 15	_____
Last date for spouse's election	_____	_____	_____
Property set apart for surviving spouse and/or minor children	_____	_____	_____
Maintenance ordered	_____	_____	_____
State and other inheritance tax waivers obtained	_____	_____	_____
Last date for filing claims	_____	_____	_____
Claims hearing	_____	_____	_____
Decedent's final income and gift tax returns due			
Federal	_____	_____	_____
State	_____	_____	_____
Fiduciary's final income tax returns due			
Federal	_____	_____	_____
State	_____	_____	_____
Last date for filing claims with leave of court	_____	_____	_____
Optional alternative valuation date	_____	_____	_____
Federal estate tax return due	_____	_____	_____
State inheritance and/or estate tax due	_____	_____	_____
Closing letter (federal estate tax)	_____	_____	_____
Date maintenance ends	_____	_____	_____
Final account	_____	_____	_____
Closing statement	_____	_____	_____
Hearing on final account	_____	_____	_____
Decree or order of distribution issued	_____	_____	_____
Discharge of personal representative	_____	_____	_____
Bond refund	_____	_____	_____

and request the probate court appoint one or both of you as administrators. The form used to authorize an administrator is called *Letters of Administration*.

Executor: Letters Testamentary authorize an executor named in a will to handle the decedent's estate, and Letters of Administration authorize a general administrator to do the work when the decedent dies leaving no will. Are the duties of the executor and administrator the same?

Paralegal: Basically, yes. Administrators do much the same thing as executors, but they must rely on the state laws to guide their actions, whereas executors follow the provisions of the will within statutory limitations, of course.

Executor: I've heard in some cases an estate can be probated in a simpler manner—informally, I believe it is called. Is this possible?

Paralegal: That is a good question. Many states, including our own, have adopted the *Uniform Probate Code*'s recommendations for administration of decedents' estates. Two forms of probate procedures are included in the Code: *formal* or *solemn* and *informal* or *common*. Some states use only the formal procedures; some follow the Uniform Probate Code and use both formal and informal procedures; other use a variation of these forms.

Basically, formal probate refers to proceedings or a hearing conducted before a *judge* with the requirement that *notice* be given to all *interested persons,* such as beneficiaries, devisees, or heirs, so they might be present to contest the will or, in *intestacy* cases, to contest the appointment of a general administrator. Informal probate, on the other hand, is also known as unsupervised probate since it is necessary only to present a will or petition for administration to an appropriate court representative, who may be a judge but more likely will be a *registrar* or *clerk.* After the will has been admitted or the administrator appointed, no notice to interested parties is necessary. The administration of the decedent's estate can therefore be completed faster. Another advantage of informal probate is that it may reduce the expenses of administration, including the elimination of the need for an attorney to assist in the procedures. Every personal representative should consider informal administration.

After hearing of the person's death, interested parties such as beneficiaries, heirs, or devisees of the decedent who want to contest the validity of the will or the appointment of the administrator must request a formal hearing. An original informal proceeding then becomes a formal one, with all associated procedures. Due to the size of your father's estate and the real property involved, you will have to discuss with Ms. Brown the type of proceeding to be followed.

Executor: So what are the advantages of formal as opposed to informal probate for an estate like my father's?

Paralegal: Basically, the choice of formal or informal probate depends on a number of variables, such as the nature of estate assets and the preferences of the personal representative. The probate court must supervise formal probate, whereas it does not have to supervise informal probate unless someone who has an interest in the estate requests it. The personal representative might feel that it would be better for the court rather than the registrar to oversee administration of the estate because of problems presented by certain assets. Since your father's estate hasn't been inventoried or valued yet, I can't give you facts or figures. However, Ms. Brown will advise you of the method that would better suit your case. One word of caution—informal probate sounds effortless, but I assure you it

Letters of administration

Estate administration

isn't. It allows the personal representative to administer the estate with the help of the registrar. The court will step in only when requested, but knowing when to request the court's help isn't all that easy.

Executor: I can see the procedures can be complicated. What information is needed to commence the formal probate?

Paralegal: First, we need a *petition to prove the will* (see Form 1*). It requests the following information:

- The name, age, and usually the Social Security number of the decedent.
- His domicile.
- The place and date of his death.
- The name and address of the executor (personal representative) named in the will.
- The date and original copy of the will being probated.
- The estimated value of the decedent's estate, including both real and personal property.
- The names, ages, relationships, and addresses of the decedent's known beneficiaries, heirs, and devisees.
- The will be admitted to probate, and the petitioner be appointed executor and Letters Testamentary issued.

The petition, like many of the forms we use, may be verified, that is, signed and sealed by a notary public. A certified copy of the decedent's death certificate usually accompanies the petition.

Executor: What happens after the petition is completed?

Paralegal: We file the petition with the probate court, which establishes the court's jurisdiction over the estate, and the probate judge sets a date and time for the hearing on the petition. This order also limits the time for any of your father's creditors to file their claims and sets the date for hearing any disputed claim. Notice of the hearing is given to all interested parties either by direct mail to each beneficiary, heir, or devisee, or by publication once a week for three weeks in a legal newspaper within the county for the benefit of creditors. Copies of this notice are also given to the state's tax department.

Executor: What happens at the hearing?

Paralegal: Before the actual hearing, we will correspond with the witnesses to your father's will and make arrangements to have them meet you and Ms. Brown at the judge's chambers on the hearing day. Ms. Brown will have with her at that time the necessary forms for presentation to the court. You and I shall prepare these forms with Ms. Brown's supervision and review. The forms include:

- A *proof of publication* of notice of the hearing (Form 5*).
- An *affidavit* stating when and where publication was made, obtained from the newspaper publishing the notice (Form 6*).
- An *order admitting the will to probate* (Form 11*), which states that this is the last will of the decedent, grants *Letters Testamentary* (Form 16*), and specifies the amount of *bond* (Form 68*), if required.
- The personal representative's *oath of office* (Form 13*).

*See Appendix A

We shall also prepare Letters Testamentary for the signature of the probate judge. These authorize you to act as the executor of your father's estate. Remember, had your father died intestate like your uncle, we would prepare Letters of Administration instead.

Executor: Yes, now I understand.

Paralegal: The final forms we prepare and present to the court are:
- The *order appointing the appraisers,* which names the persons who will appraise or value the estate (Form 21*).
- The *notice to the surviving spouse,* your mother, of her *right to renounce* or waive what your father left to her in the will and take, instead, a percentage of his total probate estate, as she is allowed by statute (Form 8*). Widows or widowers who receive little under their spouse's will find this *statutory election,* also known as the "forced or elective share," advantageous, but since your father left your mother everything, she will obviously not pursue this right.

Executor: All right. We have the forms and the witnesses to my father's will at the courtroom. Are we ready for the hearing?

Paralegal: Yes. As petitioner, you will take the stand and be sworn in. Ms. Brown will elicit from you the information contained in the petition. Under oath, you will verify that it is correct and request appointment as executor of your father's estate. Then Ms. Brown will ask the witnesses who *attested* and *subscribed* your father's will to take the stand and under oath testify that your father *acknowledged* the document as his last will and signed it in their presence and that they each signed in each other's presence as attesting witnesses. They will also testify that your father was of sound mind at the time he signed the will. Ms. Brown then asks the court to admit the will to probate and that you be authorized as executor.

> **Hearing on petition to probate will**

Executor: What happens if my father's brother, Uncle Joe, objects to the will?

Paralegal: Good question. That's called a contest of the will. The probate court would have to set up a separate hearing date for the will contest. Do you expect this to happen?

Executor: No, I was just wondering about the procedure.

Paralegal: In that case, I assume the probate judge will agree to the requests made by Ms. Brown. The execution of the will is thereby proved, and probate of the estate can begin.

Executor: What happens at the hearing?

Paralegal: The probate judge asks you to take the required oath and sign the executor's *bond* if the judge deems it necessary. Since your father's will specifically requested that his representative be exempted from this, the judge will try to comply with the request, unless our statute requires the personal representative to be bonded in estates like your father's. A bond guarantees to the court and to those parties with an interest in the decedent's estate (beneficiaries, devisees, creditors, and the like) that you, the executor, will act in a fiduciary manner and perform your duties faithfully. The amount of the bond is determined by the court, and if it is needed, we will seek the lowest amount possible to lessen the bond premium expense.

> **Bond**

*See Appendix A

After you have signed the bond and it is approved by the court, Ms. Brown asks the court to appoint two persons, previously agreed on, as appraisers for your father's estate. Not all states require appraisers, but ours does. Before the hearing, we will contact and receive the consent of these persons to act as appraisers. They are paid for their work out of the assets of the estate by you, the executor.

Letters testamentary issued

Finally, Ms. Brown requests the clerk to issue *Letters Testamentary* to you. These become your official authorization from the court to act as executor of your father's will and estate. You will use the Letters to obtain the assets of your father's estate that are currently in the possession of others such as banks and corporations. A few of the forms I have mentioned are provided by the court, but it will be necessary for us to prepare and execute most of the forms we previously discussed.

Executor: The procedures are just as complex as I imagined. What next?

Paralegal: Well, remember we discussed ancillary administration?

Executor: Yes, in connection with the summer cottage.

Paralegal: That's right. We petition the county probate court in State B, where the cottage is located, asking that you be appointed ancillary administrator. I shall check to make sure you qualify. If I remember correctly, State B does not require the personal representative to be a resident of that state. I will check on this and on all similar matters under instructions from Ms. Brown before we act. If you are appointed, you will follow procedures similar to those we have discussed. You should notify creditors, if any, collect other assets, and pay taxes and debts. Doing these things will prevent creditors from attaching the cottage to satisfy debts, so you will be able to transfer it to your mother according to your father's wishes.

Executor: I am sure my father had no debts in State B where the cottage is located.

Paralegal: We must still go through these procedures, but the ancillary administration should create no problems.

Inventory and appraisal

Executor: Good. Let's get back to our state procedures.

Paralegal: The next step is to prepare a complete inventory of your father's property with an estimate of the value of each asset. I prepare an *inventory and appraisal form* (Form 22*), which Ms. Brown reviews. The two appointed appraisers will value the inventory according to one of the methods allowed by Section 2032 of the Internal Revenue Code—assigning to each asset either the value it had at the time your father died or the value it had six months after his death. We will discuss the tax advantages of both methods and choose the one we think best once we have completed the inventory. The inventory and appraisal serve as a basis for the federal and state tax returns that must be filed and provide information to all interested parties concerning the value of the estate. You will also find them helpful when filing your *final account* (Form 32*) after completing all required procedures.

Executor: I was wondering about the taxes. What taxes must be paid and when are they due?

Paralegal: This area, resolving tax problems, is probably one of the most important functions Ms. Brown and I will help you perform in administering the estate. Death tax laws, both state and federal, are very complex. Ms. Brown determines whether any of the following tax returns must be filed and paid: *federal estate tax* (Form 88*), *State A and B inheritance tax* (Form 93*) *and/or estate tax*

---

*See Appendix A

(Form 92*), *federal and state individual income tax* (Forms 74* and 78*), *federal and state fiduciary income tax* (Forms 83* and 85*), *federal and state gift tax* (Forms 86* and 87*).

	Federal and state tax forms

Now you see why the "tickler" system and the checklists we previously discussed are so valuable. They help us avoid forgetting any important step or date in the administration of the estate. They are especially useful and timely when dealing with potential tax problems.

I prepare all the necessary tax returns, and we review them thoroughly with Ms. Brown. She files them, along with your check as executor for any tax payments due, with the appropriate federal or state tax department as well as the probate court.

Executor: I am glad we have the opportunity to review the tax consequences together because I know very little about this area, but I have been interested in it.

Paralegal: Now, let's discuss the major items of property included in your father's estate. As you know, your duties as executor are basically to collect the estate assets, to pay your father's creditors and necessary taxes, and to distribute the remaining assets according to the provisions of his will.

Some of your father's property was owned by him and your mother in *joint tenancy* and will automatically pass to her by *operation of law*. This results from the *right of survivorship,* which means that the surviving joint tenant (your mother) gets the property without having to wait for a court order. The home, the stocks and bonds, and the savings account automatically belong to your mother because she is a joint tenant owner. These property items, along with the benefits from your father's life insurance policy, are called *nonprobate assets* since they do not have to be disposed of by will nor do they *descend* to an heir as intestate property. Other items, which he owned, were in his name alone, such as the car, the checking account, the paintings, and the summer cottage. These are *probate assets,* and, I might add, anything he may have owned as a tenant in common with someone else would be a probate asset also. Tenancy in common is a form of ownership between two or more persons. It differs from joint tenancy in that each co-owner can transfer his property interest not only while alive as in joint tenancy but also, unlike joint tenancy, after death, for example, through a will.

	Probate and nonprobate assets

As executor, you must collect and preserve only *probate assets* such as the car, paintings, and checking account. All probate and generally all nonprobate assets are included, however, in the decedent's estate for computing death taxes. There are additional procedural steps we will follow to clear the passage of the nonprobate property to your mother.

Executor: What do we need to do now?

Paralegal: At this time, you must open a checking account at your father's bank in your name as executor of his estate. In order to do this, we must file for an employer identification number using Form SS-4 from the Internal Revenue Service and a Notice Concerning Fiduciary Relationship (see Forms 81 and 82 in Appendix A). These forms must be executed and the employer identification number obtained before we can open the account. Here is an example of what the check imprint on your father's account should look like (see Exhibit 11.4). You can then submit to the bank Letters Testamentary authorizing you to withdraw your father's checking account and have it transferred to the estate account. All

---

*See Appendix A

Exhibit 11.4   Sample Check Imprint for Deceased's Estate

No. _____

Heavenly City, State A _____ 20 _____

PAY TO THE
ORDER OF _____ $ _____

_____ DOLLARS

FIRST NATIONAL BANK
Heavenly City, State A

Estate account of John T. Smith, deceased, by *William R. Smith* _____
                                                    Executor*

*Or other titles for the personal representative may be used.

---

the estate funds you collect must be deposited into this account, and receipts for such funds and any disbursements you make must be retained. You will need the canceled checks and other receipts or vouchers you receive during the administration of the estate when you present your *final account* to the probate court. It is essential that you keep complete and accurate records of all transactions affecting the estate because the court will hold you personally responsible for any discrepancies or negligence.

Executor: What about some of the other property that I can't deposit—the probate assets I believe you called them—like the car, the paintings, and Dad's life insurance?

Paralegal: Let's back up one moment and discuss again which are probate assets and which are nonprobate assets. Probate assets are those that can be passed by will or by intestate succession statutes. They include property owned solely in the decedent's name or, as previously mentioned, owned as a tenant in common. No other person takes them automatically when the owner dies. The car and the paintings that belonged to your father are probate assets because he alone owned them. The life insurance benefits are different. When the owner dies, the named beneficiary more-or-less automatically becomes the owner of the benefits—because life insurance benefits are derived from a contract between an insured person and an insurer (the insurance company) to pay a certain sum of money to a third person, the beneficiary, after the insured die. When your father died, your mother, whom he named beneficiary, became entitled to the insurance benefits directly, without having to wait for the probate court's approval.

Executor: I see. The insurance benefits are nonprobate assets like the property my parents owned as joint tenants?

Life insurance and incidents of ownership

Paralegal: That's right. You must notify the insurance agent of your father's death and verify the agent receives the policy so your mother can be given its proceeds without their passing through probate. Remember, however, we still must report this insurance as part of your father's *gross (total) estate* for federal estate tax purposes, unless he had relinquished the *"incidents of ownership"* on the policy. If your father contacted his insurance agent three years before his death and gave up the incidents of ownership, which are certain contractual rights under the policy, such as the right to cancel the policy or change the beneficiary and the right to borrow on or assign the policy, then the amount of the policy will not be part of his gross estate for federal estate tax purposes. We must check this out.

Executor: It's getting complicated.

Paralegal: Right now I'm sure it seems complicated. Let me assure you that if we work on this together in a systematic manner, everything will go smoothly.

Let's see. We were discussing the car and the paintings. The title to the car must be transferred to your mother. This cannot be accomplished until you receive Letters Testamentary. The following, however, will be necessary:

- The *title registration card* (Exhibit 11.5) or certificate of title must be executed (filled in with any required information and signed by you as executor).
- A transfer fee must accompany the executed registration card or certificate and be mailed within a prescribed time, e.g., 14 days of the date of transfer, to the state motor vehicle office to avoid penalties.
- A certified copy of Letters Testamentary—your authorization from the court to act as executor.
- A certified copy of the *Order Setting Apart Personal Property* (Form 25*). (We will discuss this in greater detail later.)

The paintings, like the car, are part of the inventory, and title will be transferred to your mother after creditors' claims and taxes due are paid. Determination of your father's debts and payment of those claims are other topics we must discuss.

Creditors' claims

Executor: Suppose my mother wanted to obtain and use some of the probate property now. Could she?

Paralegal: Yes. Some states, including ours, allow a surviving spouse and/or minor child to petition the probate court for a *family maintenance allowance* and the receipt of certain *exempt personal property* reserved for them by law. Your mother can petition for these things as the surviving spouse. Since your father was solvent and left his entire estate to your mother, I do not believe this will be necessary. If some unknown creditors of your father with considerable claims appear, we will then review the situation.

Executor: If the creditors do appear and there isn't enough property in my father's estate to pay all of them, would my mother still receive these things?

Paralegal: Yes. This is true in our state. Such claims of the spouse are given priority even over funeral expenses as well as various other debts within statutory limitations. Now, concerning creditors' claims, do you remember what was said during our earlier discussion about creditors and the hearing on the petition to approve the will?

Executor: Yes. You mentioned that time limits are set for filling creditors' claims against my father's estate.

Paralegal: Right. When that time expires, we shall check to determine whether any filed claims should be contested. If you reasonably believe a particular claim is not legitimate, you will file an *Objections to Claim* form with the probate court and serve a copy on the alleged creditor. Contested claims are not heard on the

---

*See Appendix A

Exhibit 11.5   Registration Card or Certificate of Title

STATE OF MINNESOTA
CERTIFICATE OF TITLE
TO A MOTOR VEHICLE
THIS TITLE IS PRIMA FACIE PROOF OF OWNERSHIP
KEEP IN A SAFE PLACE – ANY ALTERATION OR ERASURE VOIDS THIS TITLE

VEHICLE IDENTIFICATION NUMBER

MAKE   YEAR   TYPE

TITLE NUMBER   DATE ISSUED   NEW OR USED   IF NEW, DATE OF FIRST SALE   FOR CENTRAL OFFICE USE ONLY

FIRST SECURED PARTY'S INTEREST RELEASED BY: SECOND SECURED PARTY'S INTEREST RELEASED BY:

AUTHORIZED SIGNATURE   X   AUTHORIZED SIGNATURE

ASSIGNMENT BY RECORDED OWNER(S): I (WE), CERTIFY THIS VEHICLE IS FREE FROM ALL SECURITY INTERESTS , WARRANT TITLE, AND ASSIGN THE VEHICLE TO:

PRINT BUYER'S NAME(S)   OWNER'S SIGNATURE(S) ALL OWNERS MUST SIGN   DATE OF SALE

X

APPLICATION FOR TITLE BY BUYER(S)   **COMPLETE FRONT AND BACK**   **PLEASE PRINT (DARK INK)**

PRINT BUYER'S NAME(S) LAST, FIRST, AND MIDDLE   DATE OF BIRTH

STREET ADDRESS   CITY   COUNTY   STATE   ZIP CODE

IS THIS VEHICLE SUBJECT TO SECURITY AGREEMENT(S)?   YES ☐   NO ☐   **IF YES, COMPLETE SECTION BELOW**

FIRST SECURED PARTY (PRINT NAME)   DATE OF SECURITY AGREEMENT

STREET ADDRESS   CITY   STATE   ZIP CODE

SECOND SECURED PARTY (PRINT NAME)   DATE OF SECURITY AGREEMENT

STREET ADDRESS   CITY   STATE   ZIP CODE

IF THERE IS AN ADDITIONAL SECURITY AGREEMENT(S) COMPLETE AND ATTACH DPS2017.   NAME OF INSURANCE COMPANY   POLICY NUMBER

BUYER SUBSCRIBED AND SWORN TO BEFORE ME:

X

NOTARY SIGNATURE   DATE

I (we), certify I (we) am (are) of legal age, have bought this vehicle subject to liens shown and no others, this vehicle is and will continue to be insured while operating upon the public streets and highways, and all of my (our) declarations are true and correct.

X

COUNTY   DATE MY COMMISSION EXPIRES   BUYER'S SIGNATURE(S) ALL BUYERS SIGN.

DETACH THIS PORTION   **DO NOT SEPARATE UNTIL SOLD**

MINNESOTA MOTOR VEHICLE REGISTRATION CARD   **RECORDED OWNER(S) RECORD OF SALE**

PLATE NUMBER   TITLE NUMBER   PLATE NUMBER

PLATES EXPIRE   TAX   TAX BASE   TITLE NUMBER

MAKE   MODEL YEAR   TYPE   V.I.N.

V.I.N.   STICKER NUMBER

RECORDED OWNER(S)   BUYER'S SIGNATURE(S)   SALE DATE

STREET ADDRESS

CITY   STATE   ZIP CODE

same date as uncontested claims. A separate hearing date is set, at which time the court will decide which contested claims are to be allowed. Since it appears that your father had only a few debts and you have already acknowledged their validity, a hearing for contested claims may not be necessary. If one is necessary, however, you must pay the claims the court allows.

Executor: How do I pay the claims?

Paralegal: By writing checks on the estate account. Remember to ask for receipts from each creditor so the receipts and the canceled checks can be filed with the court as evidence of payment. Be cautioned that overpayment to a creditor, or payment of an invalid claim, makes you, the executor, personally liable. This means you must be very careful not to pay any doubtful claim until the hearing is over.

Executor: What if debts occur during our handling of the estate?

Paralegal: These expenses, including the fee our law firm will charge for its assistance in handling the estate, are priority debts according to statute and are paid just before you make the final distribution of the assets of the estate. As executor, you also are entitled to reasonable compensation as the personal representative of the estate, which is another priority debt.

Executor: My father mentioned that to me, but I do not intend to charge a fee.

Paralegal: That, of course, is entirely up to you. After claims are paid and receipts filed, the *final account* can be prepared. Each state generally sets a time limit for settlement of an estate, which the court may extend for proper reasons. This state allows the personal representative, you as executor, one year from the date of the appointment to settle the estate. Again, a hearing is held for final settlement, and forms must be prepared.

Final account

Executor: What forms are required, and what is the procedure?

Paralegal: To close the estate after having distributed its assets—

- You must submit a *final account* which contains a list of all the assets you have collected, such as personal property and monies from sales, rents, and other sources.
- You must list the liabilities you claim as credits against the estate, including payments for expenses of administration, creditors' claims allowed by the court, funeral expenses, taxes due, and other necessary and proper expenses. Your account must show in detail these receipts and disbursements.
- You must sign and file a *petition for settlement and distribution* (Form 33*).
- You must prove you have distributed the *remaining assets* of the estate, and this figure must correspond to the actual inventory.

The court will then issue an *order* (Form 34*) setting a hearing on the final account so parties interested in the estate can have the opportunity to be present and make any objections to the accounting.

As with the hearing to prove the will, *notice* (Form 6*) must be published within a prescribed time, e.g., once a week for three consecutive weeks, in a local newspaper for the probate court. Copies of the notice must be sent to all beneficiaries, heirs, or devisees as well as the state Department of Taxation within a specified statutory time period before the hearing. In our state, it is 14 days. *Proof* of this publication and mailing must be filed with the court (Forms 6* and 35*).

---

*See Appendix A

Executor: Then is the hearing held?

Paralegal: Yes. At the hearing, if satisfied the final account is correct and all taxes due have been paid, the probate judge will sign an order allowing the final account. Proof of payment of necessary taxes is provided by a certificate of release of tax lien. All the tax returns I have previously mentioned must be filed and any tax due must be paid before the court will determine the persons entitled to the remaining assets of the estate. The court will then issue the *Decree of Distribution* (Form 37*) assigning these assets. The Decree of Distribution states that: notice of the final account and settlement was given; the decedent died testate; the final account was approved and allowed; all allowed claims were paid; all other expenses, such as funeral and administration expenses have been paid; and all beneficiaries or heirs are named and the share of the decedent's property to which each is entitled is listed.

Decree of distribution

Executor: Is that it? Are my duties finished?

Paralegal: No. You must record a certified copy of the Decree of Distribution with the county recorder's office, specifically the register of deeds, for the real estate your father willed to your mother. Other documents might also have to be recorded in State B, depending on its laws.

   Finally, you can distribute the estate in compliance with the Decree of Distribution. Each distributee or recipient must sign a receipt for the property passed to him or her, and you must file the receipts with the court. The last act is *petitioning* the court for your discharge as personal representative (Form 39*). In this case, the court will sign an *order* discharging you, as executor (Form 40*). If there was a bond, a certified copy of the order should be sent to the surety company, and you should request any refund. With that, you have completed your responsibilities.

Executor: And there are quite a few! I very much appreciate your taking the time to explain the probate procedures to me. It gives me a much clearer picture of what happens in an administration and what duties I have to perform.

Paralegal: Well, I enjoy being able to assist you in these matters. I am sure we will work well together. I have some questionnaires and checklists for you to complete, and I will give you some written materials on the duties of a personal representative and procedures for probating a will that our office has prepared. I would like you to take these home and read them. Also, our local county probate court in the county courthouse offers a pamphlet on probate and estate administration that I will obtain for you. It explains the tasks you will perform and may clear up any confusion you may have about the things we have discussed today. We may need to cover some matters more fully, such as what happens if you decide to sell any of your father's real property, but we can wait to discuss those matters with Ms. Brown when they arise. Now let's set up our "tickler" system.

PREPARATION FOR PROBATE AND ESTATE ADMINISTRATION—GENERAL OVERVIEW

The personal representative has a fiduciary obligation with respect to the assets of the estate, that is, a duty to utilize the highest degree of care and integrity in

---

*See Appendix A

handling the decedent's property for the benefit of the estate beneficiaries and devisees. Once appointed by the court, the personal representative has the following general responsibilities:

1. To discover, collect, and preserve all probate assets of any value and manage the probate estate of the decedent if it includes real estate, securities, or an ongoing business until the estate is settled.

2. To notify the deceased's creditors of the death, give them the opportunity to present their claims, settle all just claims against the estate, and verify the creditors are paid (money for this will come out of the estate assets).

3. To file all required federal and state income, gift, estate, or inheritance tax returns and pay all taxes due.

4. To distribute the remainder of the estate as required by the terms of the will or by law (the intestate succession statutes when there is no valid will).

The mechanics of administering an estate are complex and varied. The authority of the personal representative to administer the decedent's property is governed by the will or state statute. Statutes vary from state to state. Therefore, the list of duties presented here is intended only to provide a basis for understanding the major duties in any given administration; it is not meant to be all-inclusive or exhaustive.

Pre-Probate Duties of the Personal Representative and Paralegal

Both you and the personal representative will have numerous duties to perform in the days immediately after the decedent's death. If the decedent left a letter of instructions concerning her funeral and burial or had entered into a prepaid contract with a funeral director, the personal representative will help the family make the necessary arrangements according to the decedent's wishes or will defer to those of the surviving spouse and family members. Generally, your supervising attorney will be hired by the personal representative at this time, and your work as the paralegal in this case will begin.

Preparations for probate should begin immediately after the death of the testator. The needs of the family take priority on the death of one of its members, especially when the decedent was the family breadwinner. As the paralegal acting for the law firm selected by the personal representative to assist in administering the estate, you must see that the family's needs are satisfied. The duties you may be asked to perform include the following: (1) search for and obtain the will and other personal and business records; (2) notify appropriate parties of the decedent's death; (3) obtain certified copies of the death certificate from the funeral director; and (4) after contacting the appropriate persons, set a date for the family conference.

Search for and Obtain the Will and Other Personal and Business Records

One of your first responsibilities while assisting the client, i.e., the personal representative, in testate proceedings is to obtain, review, and make copies of the will. As you perform this investigative function, you should check the letter of instructions for the will's location or your law firm's files. If your firm did not draft the will, you should contact the office of the decedent's attorney who drafted the will. At this point, if you have not discovered the will, check other locations such as the decedent's safe deposit box and places in the decedent's home considered secure. You should also determine if the will was filed with the court.

Example: Maxine has a will. Her husband, Malcolm, has seen the will and knows he has been named executor. Maxine dies and her will cannot be found. Malcolm believes the will is located in Maxine's safe deposit box. Although a bank must seal the safe deposit box on learning of the owner's death, generally an officer of the bank will be allowed to determine whether the owner's (decedent's) will is in the box. If it is, before sealing the safe deposit box, the bank may forward the will directly to the probate court, thereby avoiding unnecessary delays in locating the will and enabling the decedent's estate administration to begin.

You must interview family, friends, business advisers, and associates (such as partners, accountants, brokers, agents, and the employer of the decedent), or contact them by phone or mail and request information about the will's existence and location and about other personal or business records that may help you locate all assets belonging to the decedent. If the search is successful and the will is found, copies of the will are prepared for the beneficiaries, devisees, and the court, and a summary of the contents of the will is made. The original will must be given to the probate court in the county of the state that is the decedent's legal home (domicile) within a specific time period, usually thirty days after death. Any person in possession of a will who neglects or refuses to deliver the will to the court may, by law, be civilly liable for damages caused by such neglect or possibly criminally prosecuted. Some states have established a "procedure to compel production of a will" when there is reason to believe that a will or codicil exists but the written document cannot be located. The petition requests the judge issue an order that requires the person who allegedly has knowledge of the location or existence of the document to appear and be examined in court. A case that illustrates the use of this procedure to compel production to determine the existence of a will is *In re Vieillard's Will,* 17 Misc.2d 703, 182 N.Y.S.2d 558 (1959).

ASSIGNMENT 11.2

To test your investigatory abilities, make a list of as many places as possible where a will might be kept. Select members of your family, e.g., spouse, parents, brothers, or sisters, who have made wills and determine if your list would help you find their wills. If your list does not locate their wills, what additional steps would you follow to discover whether a will exists and its location?

Notify Appropriate Parties of the Decedent's Death

After finding the will, you may be asked to summarize it and send copies to persons named in the will. You also must locate and notify by phone or mail the witnesses and other appropriate parties, such as banks or depositories, e.g., savings and loan associations or credit unions, of the decedent's death so these financial institutions may meet certain legal obligations including the following:

- Prevent persons (holders of accounts with the decedent) from withdrawing money from the decedent's accounts in an attempt to avoid death taxes levied on the transfer of assets at the time of death.
- Provide for the safekeeping of any safe deposit box contents.
- Close all demand accounts (checking accounts) of the decedent.
- Cancel all credit cards.

Obtain Certified Copies of the Death Certificate

Your attorney will seldom be contacted to assist in sorting out a decedent's estate before the funeral arrangements are complete. The funeral director obtains the necessary burial permits and the death certificate, which is the document executed by a physician listing the name of the decedent and the place, time, date, and cause of death. Once your attorney is employed, you will obtain certified copies of the death certificate from the funeral director. If additional copies are needed, you may obtain them from the State Health Department, the Bureau of Vital Statistics, the clerk of district court, or a state Registrar. A certified copy of the death certificate is usually filed with the Petition for Probate. Also, you must include a certified copy when you apply to file claims, obtain life insurance or accidental death benefits, open a decedent's safe deposit box, collect money from POD accounts, end a joint tenancy, transfer stocks, collect benefits from Social Security or the Veterans Administration, and file deeds transferring title to real estate with the county recorder's office or the Registrar of Deeds office (see the sample death certificate in Exhibit 11.6).

Set a Date for the Family Conference

Shortly after the decedent's death, you will schedule a family conference. All persons named in the will should be asked to attend this conference. In addition, whether the decedent died testate or intestate, you must give notice of the death to all heirs (blood relatives of the decedent) and request that they—and, of course, the surviving spouse—attend the family conference. In some states, a convenient time for this meeting may be on the day of the opening of the safe deposit box, if the decedent had one.

The Family Conference

At the family conference, you must obtain information pertinent to future administrative duties. While assisting the personal representative, you or your supervising attorney should openly discuss the following points with the family:

1. *Explain the provisions of the will* if it is available. If no will exists, you must explain in detail how the intestate-decedent's property will be inherited, by whom, and which state statute will apply to specific property of the deceased. Only a paralegal who has mastered the intestate succession statutes and is experienced in responding accurately to any questions should perform this function, *but remember legal advice about family concerns must come from the attorney*. If **ETHICAL ISSUE** property such as real property is located in another state, you must explain the need for an ancillary administrator. The attorney and you should also explain the general nature of probate administration, including the appointment of the personal representative, the preparation of the inventory and appraisal, the various tax returns, and the final account and decree of distribution. You should point out the dates by which these steps must be taken and explain how a "tickler" system can prevent important deadlines from being overlooked (see No. 16 below). If possible, provide an estimate of how long the administration will take.

2. *Discuss with the family the need for appointing fiduciaries,* e.g., guardians for minors or conservators for incompetent persons, if the decedent died intestate. If there is a will, and the persons selected to act in these capacities, including a trustee named in a testamentary trust, are present at the conference, find out whether they are willing to serve.

Exhibit 11.6 Death Certificate

Type/Print
in Permanent
Black Ink

MINNESOTA DEPARTMENT OF HEALTH.
Section of Vital Statistics
CERTIFICATE OF DEATH

Local File Number   State File Number

Signature of Sub-Registrar / Date

1a Name of Deceased - First	Middle	Last	Suffix

1b Alias	2 Social Security No.	3 Sex	4 Date of Death

5 Date of Birth	6a Age (in years)	Under 1 Yr. 6b months / 6c days	Under 1 Day 6d hours / 6e minutes	7 Place of Birth (city and state/foreign country)

8a Father's Name (first, middle)	8b Father's Last Name	9 Mother's Name (first, middle, maiden surname)

10 Race	11a Hispanic Origin ___No ___Yes →	11b If Yes, Specify Cuban, Mexican, etc...	12 Decedent's Education 12a Primary/Secondary (0-12) 12b College (1-4, 5+)

13a Marital Status ___Mar. ___Div. ___Wid. ___Never Mar.	13b Name of Spouse (If wife, specify maiden name)	14 Decedent's Usual Occupation

15 Kind of Business or Industry	16 U.S. Veteran ___No ___Yes	17a State of Residence	17b County of Residence

17c City or Township of Residence	17d Address of Decedent (number, street, zip)

17e Residence in City or Township ___City Limits ___Township Limits	18a City or Township of Death	18b County of Death

19a Place of Death (specify one) ___Hosp. ___N.H. ___Res. ___Other →	Specify	19b If Hospital (specify one) ___Inpatient ___ER ___DOA ___Other

19c Name of Facility Where Death Occurred (if not institution, specify address)

COPY

20a Name of Informant	20b Informant is _____ of the deceased (spouse, child, parent, sibling, etc.)

21 Method of Disposition (check all that apply) ___Burial ___Cremation ___Donation ___Entombment ___Other →	Specify	22 Date of Disposition

23 Name of Cemetery	City	State

24 If Cremation, Specify Name of Crematory	25 If Cremation, Specify Name of M.E. / Coroner Authorizing Cremation

26a Name of Funeral Establishment	26b License No.	27a Signature of Funeral Service Licensee	27b License No.	28 Date Signed

29a Name of Person Certifying Cause of Death (please type)	29b Title (check one) ___M.D. ___Coroner / M.E. ___D.O.	29c License No. of Certifier #

29d Address of Certifier (street & number)	29e City	29f State	29g Zip Code

30 Signature of M.D. / M.E. / Coroner / D.O.	31 Date Signed	32 Signature of Registrar	33 Date Filed

PLEASE TYPE

34 PART I
IMMEDIATE cause of death (final disease or condition resulting in death)

Enter the diseases, injuries, or complications that caused death. Do not enter the mode of dying, such as cardiac or respiratory shock or heart failure. List only one cause per line.

Interval between onset and death.

a. _____

Sequentially list conditions, if any, leading to immediate cause. Enter UNDERLYING cause last, (disease or injury that initiated events resulting in death).

b. _____

c. _____

35 I attended the deceased from _____ to _____ and last saw him/her on _____. I viewed the body after death ___Yes ___No

36 PART II Other significant conditions contributing to death but not resulting in the underlying cause given in Part I.

38 Time of Death

37 Was Female Pregnant: At Death? ___Yes ___No ___Unknown In Last 12 Months? ___Yes ___No ___Unknown

39 MANNER OF DEATH ___Natural	40 M.E./Coroner Notified ___Yes ___No	41 Autopsy ___Yes ___No	42 Were autopsy results available when filling in cause of death ___Yes ___No	43 Diagnosis Deferred ___Yes

MUST BE REFERRED TO M.E. or CORONER {
___Accident
___Homicide
___Suicide
___Pending Inves.
___Cannot be Det.
___Not Classifiable

44a Place of Injury (street & number, city / township, state)

44b Describe How Injury Occurred

44c Type of Place Where Injury Occurred	44d Date of Injury	44e Time of Injury	44f Injury at Work? ___Yes ___No

3. *Obtain information from the family about the general size and nature of the decedent's estate* using checklists similar to those in Chapter 6. You will need to explain that only probate assets will be subject to probate and that nonprobate property passes directly to the beneficiary or joint owners. The total value of probate and nonprobate assets is included in the decedent's estate for federal and state death tax purposes but only probate assets are subject to creditors' claims. Nonprobate assets include property in joint tenancy, property in living trusts, and assets where a named beneficiary is to receive the property, as in life insurance policies, annuities, pension or profit-sharing, Keogh, and 401(k) plans, or IRAs (traditional and Roth). Based on the information obtained in the checklists, determine the type of probate proceeding to be used, or for UPC states, determine whether formal or informal probate proceedings should be followed or whether it is possible to settle the estate by a method other than probate proceedings. (See the discussion on administering "small estates" by affidavit or by Summary Administration in Chapter 12.)

4. *Verify that the personal representative protects and sufficiently insures* all real and personal property and any premiums due are paid. Written verification of coverage must be obtained from insurance agents. You should also advise the personal representative to safeguard expensive personal property such as jewelry, coin collections, and other valuables by placing them in a newly opened safe deposit box.

5. *Identify and obtain a list of personal debts and those relating to any business interest* of the decedent known to family members so you can give these creditors actual notice of the death and the need to file their claims. Other creditors will be given notice by publication, which is discussed in detail in Chapter 12.

6. *Obtain the facts necessary to prepare the Petition to Prove the Will,* if the decedent died testate, or Petition for General Administration, if the decedent died intestate. Be sure you use the appropriate state or county forms for these and subsequent petitions.

7. *If the deceased owed any members of the family a debt,* explain to that creditor the need to file a claim. The time limits for procedures to approve such claims will be discussed in the following chapters.

8. *To alleviate the family's anxiety and concern about immediate financial matters,* you must discuss the various forms of protection given a surviving spouse and children by some state statutes, such as the homestead exemption or allowance; exempt property; family allowances or maintenance; dower, curtesy, or election rights of a surviving spouse; and children's rights, including rights of pretermitted children, adopted children, and nonmarital children. You should determine the wishes of these family members and prepare the necessary documents and forms to implement their requests.

9. *Explain what a disclaimer is,* its procedures, and effects. Some states allow a beneficiary or devisee to disclaim in whole or in part any interest received from the will by filing a disclaimer in probate court (see Exhibit 10.3). If a beneficiary or devisee determines a disclaimer is in the best interests of both the family and himself, you may be asked to obtain and execute the disclaimer form and file it with the probate court. Disclaimers can also be executed and filed by an executor or administrator on behalf of the estate of a deceased devisee or beneficiary or by a guardian on behalf of a minor. The interest disclaimed will be distributed according to the directives of the will or by intestate succession, and it will be

disposed of just as if the disclaimant had died immediately before the decedent (compare UPC § 2-801).

10. *Determine whether assets will need to be sold during probate administration* to pay debts, taxes, and expenses of the decedent's estate. If assets must be sold, ask the family whether they wish to retain any particular items. Otherwise, if the personal representative has been given the power of sale by the will, he might sell an item of property, e.g., a painting, that the family would prefer to keep for sentimental reasons. If property must be sold to pay debts, you will have to explain the abatement process to the family and heirs.

11. *If authorized by state statute or the decedent's will,* you must discuss the arrangements that will be necessary for the continuation or sale of the decedent's business, e.g., a sole proprietorship, partnership, or limited partnership.

ETHICAL ISSUE ⤍

12. *Check the estate plans of the surviving spouse* and, if requested, make arrangements to amend his will. *Be careful about improper solicitation for this will.* If there is no surviving spouse and the decedent was the last occupant in a home, you may be asked to notify the post office to forward mail to the personal representative of the estate and stop newspapers and all other deliveries.

13. *In all cases, you must determine if the decedent made any advancements* to any of the beneficiaries or heirs.

14. *Discuss or inquire about any other documents that may have a direct or indirect bearing on the status or transfer of the decedent's estate,* such as marital agreements, a legal separation or divorce, or transactions such as living trust agreements.

15. *Obtain names and addresses of the decedent's financial advisers,* including tax advisers, accountant, banker, trust officer, insurance agent or broker, and stockbroker.

16. *In preparation for the probate procedure,* you must create a checklist of probate procedures and prepare a calendar checklist (tickler) of important tax dates and deadlines (Exhibit 11.3). After you obtain the necessary information, explain the probate process, and answer the questions of the family members, the conference is concluded. Your duties and the duties of the personal representative, however, are just beginning.

Appointment Procedure—The Beginning

To begin the probate process and obtain appointment, the personal representative must complete the following steps. You will assist the personal representative in performing some of these tasks.

- File the original will and codicil if there is one.
- File a petition either for (1) probate of the will and appointment of the personal representative (executor) or for (2) administration and appointment of the personal representative (administrator). These petitions are usually two separate forms that request, basically, the same information.
- Contact the witnesses to the will who, if needed, must be present to testify at the hearing for probate of the will and appointment of the personal representative (executor). Witnesses are not needed if the will is self-proved.
- File a death certificate, if required.
- Pay filing fees, which you will verify.
- Arrange for bond, if necessary (see the discussions of bond and surety in the next sections).

In some states, e.g., Minnesota, the mechanics for beginning the probate procedures when a decedent dies testate or intestate require the use of one of two legal forms. When the decedent dies with a will, the form that commences probate is called the Petition for Probate of Will and for Appointment of Personal Representative (Executor). If the decedent dies without a will, the form is called the Petition for Appointment of Administrator. Both petitions contain facts which establish that a specific probate court has jurisdiction. *Note:* Whether the decedent died testate or intestate, these petitions must list all heirs, i.e., persons who would have inherited under the laws of intestate succession. For their protection, these heirs must be given notice of the court hearing on the petition and also the opportunity to be present to contest the will or challenge the personal representative's appointment. In most states, the petitions include the name and domicile (address) of the decedent; the date and place of death; the names, ages, relationship to the decedent, and addresses of heirs; the value and the nature of the decedent's real and personal property; the decedent's debts; and the name and address of the petitioner. As you would expect, the forms used for this petition vary from state to state. Other states, e.g., Michigan, use the same form for commencing probate for all decedents, whether they die with or without a will, by simply having the petitioner check the appropriate box on the form. The following state forms reflect this diversity:

- Exhibit 11.7 Michigan Petition for Probate and/or Appointment of Personal Representative (Testate/Intestate)
- Exhibit 11.8 Delaware Petition for Authority to Act as Personal Representative

In both testate and intestate cases, the probate court sets a time and place for a hearing on the petition. At the hearing, after the witnesses testify, if the probate court allows the will or grants administration, the court appoints the personal representative (executor or administrator), who must file an oath of office and in some cases post a bond, which constitutes an expense of the estate and may be deducted on the death tax forms. These procedural matters will be discussed in greater detail in subsequent chapters.

Bond

A bond or surety bond is a certificate in which a "surety," an individual or insurance company, promises to pay up to the amount of the bond to the probate court if the personal representative fails to faithfully perform the duties of administering the decedent's estate (see Form 68*). A "surety or bonding" company is licensed to offer bonds to fiduciaries, such as personal representatives. The purpose of the bond is to protect beneficiaries, heirs, creditors, and government tax collectors from losses due to the personal representative's improper, negligent, or fraudulent administration of the decedent's estate. If required, a bond must be filed at the time of the personal representative's appointment or shortly thereafter. Often an employee of a bonding company will be present at court on hearing days with the appropriate bond forms, and arrangements can be made to complete and file the bond with the court immediately after the hearing.

---

*See Appendix A

Exhibit 11.7   Michigan Petition for Probate

Approved, SCAO

OSM CODE: PFA

STATE OF MICHIGAN PROBATE COURT COUNTY OF	PETITION FOR PROBATE AND/OR APPOINTMENT OF PERSONAL REPRESENTATIVE (TESTATE/INTESTATE)	FILE NO.

Estate of _____

1. I,_____ , am interested in the estate and make this petition as

    Name of petitioner

   _____ as defined by MCL 700.1105(c).

    Relationship to decedent, i.e., heir, devisee, child, spouse, creditor, beneficiary, etc.

2. Decedent information: _____ _____ m. _____ _____

                                         Date of death   Time (if known)   Age   Social Security Number

   Domicile (at date of death): _____ _____ _____

                                              City/Township/Village   County   State

   Estimated value of estate assets: Real estate: $_____   Personal estate: $_____

3. So far as I know or could ascertain with reasonable diligence, the names and addresses of the heirs and/or devisees of the decedent, the relationship to the decedent, and the ages of any who are minors are as follows:

NAME	ADDRESS	RELATIONSHIP	AGE (if minor)

Of the above interested persons, the following are under legal disability or otherwise represented and presently have or will require representation:

NAME	LEGAL DISABILITY	REPRESENTED BY Name, address, and capacity

4. ☐ a. Venue is proper in this county because the decedent was domiciled in this county on the date of death.

   ☐ b. The decedent was not domiciled in Michigan, but venue is proper in this county because property of the decedent was located in this county at the date of death.

5. ☐ An application was previously filed and a personal representative was appointed informally.

PLEASE SEE OTHER SIDE

Do not write below this line - For court use only

PC 559   (3/00)   **PETITION FOR PROBATE AND/OR APPOINTMENT OF PERSONAL REPRESENTATIVE (TESTATE/ INTESTATE)**   MCL 700.3402; MSA 27.13402, MCL 700.3502; MSA 27.13502, MCR 5.302(A), MCR 5.308, MCR 5.310(B)

(continued)

Exhibit 11.7   Michigan Petition for Probate—*continued*

6. ☐ A personal representative has been previously appointed in _____ County, _____
and the appointment has not been terminated. The personal representative's name and address are: State

_____   _____
Name   Address

_____
City, state, zip

7. ☐ The decedent's will, dated _____ , with codicil(s) dated _____
is offered for probate and is   ☐ attached to this petition.   ☐ already in the court's possession.
☐ An authenticated copy of the will and codicil(s), if any, probated in _____County, _____
is offered for probate, and documents establishing its probate accompany this petition.   State
☐ Neither the original will nor an authenticated copy of a will probated in another jurisdiction accompanies the petition. The
will is lost, destroyed, or otherwise unavailable, but its contents are: (attach additional sheets as necessary)

_____

8. ☐ The decedent's will was ☐ formally ☐ informally   probated on _____ in _____County.
9. To the best of my knowledge, I believe that the instrument(s) subject to this petition, if any, was validly executed and is the
decedent's last will.   After exercising reasonable diligence, I am unaware of an instrument revoking the will or codicil(s).
10. ☐ After exercising reasonable diligence, I am unaware of any unrevoked testamentary instrument relating to property located
in this state as defined under MCL 700.1301.

11. ☐ I nominate _____ , as personal representative, who is qualified and has priority
Name

as: _____ . His/her address is: _____
Address

_____
City, state, zip

Other persons having prior or equal right to appointment are:

_____   _____
Name   Name

_____   _____
Name   Name

12. ☐ The will expressly requests the personal representative serve with bond.
13. ☐ a. The decedent left a will that directs supervised administration.
☐ b. The decedent left a will that directs unsupervised administration, but supervised administration is necessary for the
protection of persons interested in the estate because: (complete on line below)
☐ c. The decedent died intestate or left a will that does not direct supervised administration, but supervised administration is
necessary because: (complete on line below)

_____

14. ☐ A special personal representative is necessary because _____ .

I REQUEST:
15. ☐ An order determining heirs and that the decedent died   ☐ testate.   ☐ intestate.
16. ☐ Formal appointment of the nominated personal representative   ☐ with   ☐ without   bond.
17. ☐ Supervised administration.
18. ☐ Appointment of a special personal representative pending the appointment of the nominated personal representative.

I declare under the penalties of perjury that this petition has been examined by me and that its contents are true to the best of my
information, knowledge, and belief.

_____
Date

_____   _____
Attorney signature   Petitioner signature

_____   _____
Attorney name (type or print)   Bar no.   Petitioner name (type or print)

_____   _____
Address   Address

_____   _____
City, state, zip   Telephone no.   City, state, zip   Telephone no.

Exhibit 11.8   Delaware Petition for Authority to Act as Personal Representative

FORM NO. 1 - PETITION FOR AUTHORITY TO ACT AS PERSONAL REPRESENTATIVE

TO: The Register of Wills for the County of New Castle in the State of Delaware

In the matter of the estate of:

. . . . } **PETITION**

                                                                                            Decedent

I. . . . . , the "Petitioner(s):

    represent(s) that:

    (1) The decedent died on . . . . a resident of . . . .

    . . . .

    (2) The decedent had a/had no will dated . . . .

    (3) Since the execution of the will (if referred to above), the decedent has/has not married, and . . . . child(ren) were born
        to the decedent.

    (4) Petitioner(s) basis for qualification to act or other explanation:. . . . .

    . . . .

    . . . .

II. Petitioner(s) request(s) the grant of: (check one)

     . . . . . . Letters Testamentary.   . . . . . . Letters of Ancillary Administration with Will Annexed.
     . . . . . . Letters of Administration.   . . . . . . Letters for Appointment of a Successor Administrator/rix.
     . . . . . . Letters of Administration with Will Annexed.   . . . . . . Letters for Appointment of a Successor Administrator/rix
     . . . . . . Letters of Ancillary Administration.   Will Annexed.

III. The decedent was survived by the following persons:

NAME	RELATIONSHIP	ADDRESS
SPOUSE:		
NEXT OF KIN: (BLOOD RELATIVE)		

IV. The decedent owned personal property valued at $ . . . . and/or real estate to the value of $ . . . .

     located in. . . . . County, State of Delaware, as follows: (describe real estate). . . . .

     . . . .

     . . . .

V. A bond is/is not required.

    STATE OF DELAWARE } SS.
    NEW CASTLE COUNTY }

    . . . . named in this application, being duly

    sworn according to law say(s) that the matters alleged in this petition are true and correct to the best of . . . . knowledge
    and belief.

    Attorney of Record. . . . .

    Address. . . . .

    . . . .

    SWORN TO AND SUBSCRIBED before me, at Wilmington, Delaware this. . . . . .day of. ;

    A.D. . . . .

                                              . . . . REGISTER OF WILLS

The requirement that a personal representative file a bond is generally set by state statute. Typical statutes are Sections 8480(a) and 8481(a)(1) of the California Probate Code:

Cal. Prob. Code § 8480
(a) Except as otherwise provided by statute, every person appointed as personal representative shall, before letters are issued, give a bond approved by the court. If two or more persons are appointed, the court may require either a separate bond from each or a joint and several bond.

Cal. Prob. Code § 8481
(a) A bond is not required in either of the following cases:
    (1) The will waives the requirement of a bond.

Another example of a statute requiring a bond is:

20 Pa. Stat. Ann. § 3175 Requiring or Changing Amount of Bond
The court, upon cause shown and after such notice, if any, as it shall direct, may require a surety bond, or increase or decrease the amount of an existing bond, or require more or less security therefor. (See also UPC §§ 3–603 and 3–604 for examples of when a bond is required and the amount of the bond.)

The requirements for a bond and surety vary from state to state:

- In some states, a bond may be required of all personal representatives.
- A bond is generally required if the testator requests it in the will, but the court can decide it is "unnecessary."
- In most states, a bond is not required if the testator states in the will that the personal representative may serve without bond. A sample clause reads:

I direct that no bond or other indemnity shall be required of any personal representative including successor personal representatives nominated or appointed pursuant to this will. The term personal representative shall include any person appointed to administer this will.

- Even if the will waives the bond, a probate court may agree to require one at the request (sometimes a demand) and for the protection of interested parties, e.g., beneficiaries and creditors (see Md. Estates and Trusts Code Ann. § 6–102[b]); Ohio Rev. Code Ann. § 2109.04; and Cal. Prob. Code § 8481(b). But compare the comment in UPC § 3–603 rejecting the idea that a bond always be required, or required unless the will waives the bond.)
- If a will does not mention the bond, and the personal representative is a family member or close friend and a resident of the state in which the estate is administered, the court can agree to exclude a bond if all the beneficiaries agree and waive the filing of a bond.
- *No bond* is required if a corporation, e.g., a bank or trust company, is appointed personal representative.
- If there is no will, generally the personal representative must post a bond, especially if one or more minor children survive the intestate.

Today the majority of financial planners believe a bond is unnecessary. When a bond is required, the amount of the bond is based on the value of the estate, the type of assets, the relationship of the personal representative to the decedent, and other relevant facts including the demands of beneficiaries and creditors. The amount varies from state to state and ranges from the same as the estimated value of the decedent's personal property to twice that amount. Generally, the value of real property, unless sold at the direction of the testator's will to pay for estate debts, is not included in determining the value of the bond.

If a bond is required, you must remind the personal representative to purchase the bond and file it promptly. Since the bond premium is payable annually and is automatically renewed, you must cancel the bond as soon as the estate is closed, deliver a copy of the Order Discharging the Personal Representative to the surety company, and request a refund of the unearned premium (see Form 40*). Since the testator can waive the requirement of a bond in the will, this expense can be avoided. In any event, the cost of the personal representative's bond is charged to the estate and paid with estate funds.

Surety

The surety is an insurance company or individual who guarantees payment of a specified sum of money to the court if the personal representative fails to properly perform his/her fiduciary duties.

🏛 ASSIGNMENT 11.3

Determine whether your state has bond requirements. If so, state briefly what they are. Cite all relevant statutes.

Probating (Proving) the Will or Granting Administration

Depending on the state, a will is proved in a variety of ways. The court may require the subscribing witnesses to testify to the following in court:

- That the testatrix, her attorney, and the two witnesses were present in the lawyer's office.
- That the testatrix declared to the witnesses the document she held in her hand was her will and requested them to act as witnesses to the execution of her will. *Note:* The witnesses are not asked to read the will.
- That the witnesses watched the testatrix sign the will and also sign her initials in the margin on each page of the will.
- That the testatrix handed the will to one witness who, at the request of the testatrix, read aloud the attestation clause that precedes the place for the witnesses' signatures.
- That both witnesses knew the testatrix and that she was over the age of majority (18), of sound mind, and not acting under any constraint or undue influence.
- That each witness then signed the will and added his address while the testatrix and the other witness watched.

---

*See Appendix A

Note: If a notary public is present at the execution of the will, hears the oaths and observes the acknowledgments and signatures, and officially notarizes the will, the will is "self-proved," and the witnesses' testimony in court is not necessary.

Another method used to prove a will is to have an affidavit signed by one or more of the witnesses who attest to the facts and the proper execution of the will (see Exhibit 11.9).

Once the probate court has approved the will or, in intestate cases, has granted administration, the court issues **Letters of Authority.** These are certificates of appointment that are often called Letters Testamentary or Letters of Administration.

Letters Testamentary and Letters of Administration

When the probate court grants Letters Testamentary, an executor or executrix is appointed; when it grants Letters of Administration, an administrator or administratrix is appointed (see Forms 16* and 69*). Both Letters Testamentary and Letters of Administration are conclusive proof and evidence that the person named therein is the duly appointed, qualified, and acting personal representative of the decedent's estate with the powers, rights, duties, and obligations conferred by law. Certified copies of the letters issued to the personal representative by the probate court or registrar will be required for specific estate administration procedures including the following:

- Open the decedent's safe deposit box, remove contents, and cancel the box.
- Open an estate safe deposit box to safeguard certain valuable assets, such as expensive jewelry, coins, and other valuables, and documents, such as deeds, birth and marriage certificates, divorce decrees, passports, insurance policies, stock certificates, record of military service, automobile and boat titles and registrations, mortgages, savings certificates, promissory notes, bills of sale, and other contracts.

Letters of Authority
Certificates of appointment called either Letters Testamentary, when there is a will, or Letters of Administration, when there is no will.

Exhibit 11.9   Affidavit of Attesting Witnesses

The undersigned, being severally duly sworn on their respective oaths, depose and say that on the _____ day of _____, 20___. _____, the Testator of the attached Will, in their presence, subscribed said Will at the end thereof and at the time of making such subscription declared the instrument so subscribed by him [her] to be his [her] Last Will and Testament; that they, at the request of said Testator and in his [her] presence and in the presence of each other, thereupon witnessed the execution of said Will by said Testator by subscribing their names as witnesses thereto; that in their opinion said Testator at the time of the execution of said Will was in all respects competent to make a Will and not under any restraint; and that they make this affidavit at the request of said Testator.

Witness

_____

Witness

_____

[Notary]

_____

Source: Reprinted with permission from West's McKinney's Forms, ESP, § 7:85. Copyright ©, by West Group.

---

*See Appendix A

- Withdraw money from existing savings and checking accounts of the decedent.
- Open a bank account for the estate to hold all cash from the decedent's accounts and from all property sold by the personal representative, debts collected, dividends from securities, salary checks, and other funds or benefits owed to the decdent.
- Transfer all assets (e.g., sale of real estate, sale or gift of stock, life insurance proceeds when the estate is the beneficiary, and so on).
- Forward the decedent's mail to the personal representative.

The person who applies for either Letters Testamentary or Letters of Administration must be competent, i.e., suitable in the opinion of the court, to discharge the personal representative's obligations. A person who has a felony record, is not a resident of the domicile state, or has a history of mental illness may be rejected as "unsuitable." The decision on competency is an exercise in discretion by the court. An executor is named by the will, so the court cannot arbitrarily appoint someone else to fill the position. This does not mean, however, that the court is compelled to appoint the named executor or that the appointee must be the most suitable and competent of all possibilities. For example, the court will not name a minor as executor even though he was selected by the testator. The minor lacks competency since a minor cannot make binding contracts for the estate. If the minor, however, had attained majority age at the time of the testator's death or subsequently at the time for admission or proof of the will, he can be competent to act as personal representative and may be appointed by the court.

The appointment of an administrator calls for greater discretion on the part of the court. Where the decedent has not designated a person to distribute the estate, the court will decide which applicant is appropriate. In many states the order of preference is set by statute. Again, the court cannot overrule a preference with or without cause unless the state statutes grant the court this power, but the court may use its discretion to appoint someone who occupies a lower position in the statutory order.

> **Example:** Ridgely names his wife, Yvonne, personal representative in his will. Following his death, she will be appointed executrix unless the court finds her incompetent or otherwise subject to disqualification. Ridgely's sister, Loretta, is an accountant and more experienced in business than Yvonne, but the court will not replace Yvonne with Loretta or anyone else unless it finds Yvonne unqualified. Similarly, if Ridgely had died intestate, Yvonne, his wife, would be the first choice in most states to be appointed personal representative.

If, in intestacy, an administrator has been appointed, but later a will is discovered and admitted to probate, the court will terminate the powers of the administrator and appoint the named executor, who will continue the probate of the estate. The following statute illustrates the basis for the termination of an intestate or testate appointment.

20 Pa. Stat. Ann. § 3181 Revocation of Letters

(a) When no will—the register may revoke letters of administration granted by him whenever it appears that the person to whom the letters were granted is not entitled thereto.

(b) When a will—The register may amend or revoke letters testamentary or of administration granted by him not in conformity with the provisions of a will admitted to probate. [Compare UPC § 3–612.]

Example: Roxanne Bridges dies intestate. After her husband, Neil, is appointed administrator and Letters of Administration are issued, he discovers a will drawn by Roxanne in an old shoebox in the family home. Roxanne named her father, Harold Jensen, executor of the will. On the basis of this discovery, if the court decides it is appropriate, Neil's administration terminates, and Harold will be appointed personal representative in order to continue the probate administration.

The specific procedures of administration and the personal representative's duties after appointment are discussed in succeeding chapters.

ASSIGNMENT 11.4

Juliana was in her last illness when she made a will naming her brother, Roland, executor. Unknown to her, Roland had been declared legally insane the previous year. A month after Juliana's death, Roland is declared sane and applies for Letters Testamentary. Juliana's sister, Clarissa, contests Roland's application, and states that his insanity disqualifies him from acting as executor. In your state, is she correct?

KEY TERM

Letters of Authority

REVIEW QUESTIONS

1. Who is prohibited from being a personal representative?
2. What is the difference between the following: an executor v. an executrix; a general administrator v. a special administrator; an administratrix *cum testamento annexo* v. an administratrix *de bonis non;* and a public administrator v. an ancillary administrator?
3. The personal representative is one type of a fiduciary. What does that mean? List other fiduciaries.
4. What are the primary or general duties of a personal representative when administering a decedent's estate?
5. How is a "tickler" system used for an estate administration?
6. Is there a time limit for commencing probate in your state? How long does your state allow for the completion of an estate administration? Cite your state statute for each time period.
7. In general, what are a paralegal's duties in organizing, preparing, and conducting a family conference after a testator's death?
8. When does the probate court require a personal representative to post a bond? What is a surety bond? Draft a bond using your state's form.
9. How do Letters Testamentary and Letters of Administration differ?
10. Using the attesting and subscribing witnesses, what procedures are required to prove a will's validity?

CASE PROBLEMS

Problem 1
Assume some married member of your family has died. Perform the following tasks. (To preserve confidentiality, you should change the names of all parties concerned.)
A. Determine whether the decedent left a will.
B. If a will exists, locate it.
C. Using the sample from this text, prepare a "tickler" system.
D. Using the text's checklists or your own, determine the assets and liabilities of the "decedent's" estate. Fill in the checklists.

E. Obtain the facts necessary for the Petition to Prove the Will or, if no will exists, the Petition for General Administration. Then fill out the appropriate form.

F. Assume the decedent owed you a $5,000 debt based on a promissory note and you are willing to cancel the debt. How might this be done?

G. Determine whether your state grants an election right to a surviving spouse. Cite the statute and determine whether the decedent's spouse would receive a greater share under the will or under the statute.

H. Assume you are named as a beneficiary or devisee in the will. Fill out the disclaimer form. Can you assign your interest to your best friend?

I. Cite your state statute, if any, on maintenance, family allowance, and exempt property. Fill out the forms that pass these property items to family members.

J. Check to see if the "decedent's" spouse has a will. Ethically, could your supervising attorney be hired by the spouse to prepare the will? Explain.

Problem 2

Carmella Lamas is a wealthy widow. She has prepared a preliminary draft of her will but has not decided who she will name as her personal representative. Answer and explain the following questions according to your state's statutes:

A. Carmella's favorite relative is her nephew, Ferdinand, age 19. If she names him to be her personal representative, is he qualified to serve in your state? See and compare UPC § 3-203(f).

B. Would Ferdinand be eligible to serve if he had been convicted of the felony of possessing and using drugs? See *Smith v. Christley,* 684 S.W.2d 158 (Tex.App. 1984).

Unless the person is unsuitable, courts routinely appoint the personal representative the testator names in her will.

A. If Carmella appoints her brother, Carlos, personal representative, can Carlos be removed after his appointment because he is insolvent? See *In re Quinlan's Estate,* 441 Pa. 266, 273 A.2d 340 (1971).

B. Once appointed, can Carlos be removed for any of the following acts of misconduct?
    1. Carlos fails to file a final account.
    2. Carlos omits items from the inventory he files with the court. See *Matter of Aaberg's Estates,* 25 Wash.App. 336, 607 P.2d 1227 (1980).
    3. Carlos makes payments to himself for work he performs while administering Carmella's estate.

Since all states provide for the choice of a personal representative for an intestate's estate, answer the following if Carmella dies intestate:

A. Since Carmella is a widow and never remarried, who has priority in your state to be appointed her personal representative?

B. Some states do not allow persons who live in another state to become personal representatives. If Carlos lived in a different state than Carmella's domicile (your state), could he be appointed her personal representative?

PROBATE AND ESTATE ADMINISTRATION

OUTLINE

OBJECTIVES

After completing this chapter, you should be able to:

➤ Explain the distinction between probate proceedings and estate administration.

➤ Identify and explain state alternative procedures to probate and estate administration when administering "small estates."

➤ Recognize and define the traditional forms of probate and estate administration and compare the Uniform Probate Code alternative.

➤ List the circumstances under which solemn or formal probate proceedings are appropriate.

➤ Identify and explain the use of formal probate procedures and forms for administering a decedent's estate whether death occurred testate or intestate.

➤ Explain the potential liability of the personal representative.

➤ Apply the procedures and prepare the legal forms used in formal probate and estate administration for a set of facts involving a decedent's estate.

SCOPE OF THE CHAPTER

The probate and estate administration procedures involved in administering a testator's or an intestate's estate are the concerns of this and the next chapter. The distinction between probate and estate administration is explained, and alternative methods for administering "small estates" are listed and discussed. The two traditional methods of probate and estate administration, solemn and common, are explained, and the Uniform Probate Code alternatives, formal and informal probate, are introduced. The chapter then discusses the procedures and forms used in administering a typical estate using the formal probate method. The chapter ends with illustrated case problems, one with accompanying executed forms (found in Appendix A), and one with an assignment asking you to complete a similar case problem.

PROBATE OR ESTATE ADMINISTRATION

In previous chapters of the text, you have learned the identity, role, and duties of the participants (e.g., personal representative, attorney, paralegal, probate judge, registrar, clerk) in preparation for the administration of a decedent's estate. You have traveled through the procedures that begin soon after death, whether the decedent died testate or intestate. For example, you possibly helped to arrange for the funeral and burial; find the will, if one exists; hold the family conference; locate witnesses, if necessary; and obtain the information to begin the probate process.

The remaining steps of the probate procedures involved in the administration of an intestate's or testator's estate are the concerns of this and the following chapter. The word *estate,* also called the gross estate, includes the interest in every type of property, real and personal, owned by the decedent at the time of death. When death occurs, everything the decedent owns becomes part of the estate. The decedent's personal representative holds and manages only the probate assets of the estate until those who are entitled to them (beneficiaries and devisees, if the decedent left a will; heirs, if the decedent died without a will) can assume ownership. In either instance, the personal representative's work is termed estate administration or the probating of the estate of the deceased. The decedent's estate, or gross estate, includes probate as well as nonprobate property, and is subject to federal and state taxes when the owner dies. Only the probate property, however, is subject to the payment of creditors' claims. These assets are the ones handled by the probate court whether or not a will exists. A decedent's will gives the court specific instructions as to what is to be done with the decedent's probate property, i.e., the solely owned property and any property owned in tenancy in common. It has no effect on nonprobate assets. Estate administration is not an issue and is not needed if the decedent's entire estate consists of nonprobate property. If there is no will, the court follows the probate procedures under the laws of intestate succession.

This chapter deals with the required probate procedures for the administration of an estate when the decedent dies either testate or intestate. Included in the discussion are samples of the various forms that must be completed. It is the personal representative's duty to see that these procedures and forms are properly and timely executed. With your assistance, the attorney will help the personal representative perform this duty. The "tickler system" (Exhibit 11.3) will play an important role in keeping the estate administration on schedule.

The term *probate* initially meant "the act or process of proving the validity of a will." Over the years, the term has evolved so that, in many states, probate generally refers to all matters over which the court, often called the probate court, has jurisdiction. Thus the probate court has the power and authority to:

- Establish the validity of a will and appoint the personal representative (executor) or appoint the personal representative (administrator) of an estate when there is no will.
- Determine and verify the statutory rights of a spouse and children.
- Supervise the guardianship of minors or incompetent persons.
- Supervise and approve the personal representative's payment of creditors' claims, administration expenses, taxes due, and distribution of the decedent's estate.
- Supervise all other matters pertaining to these subjects.

Sometimes the terms *probate administration* (or probate proceedings) and *estate administration* are used synonymously to refer to the actual administration of the decedent's estate from appointment of the personal representative to the final distribution of the property and the personal representative's discharge. Therefore, to avoid confusion, this chapter and Chapter 13 will use the term *probate* to refer to the process and procedures that establish the validity of a will and the appointment of the personal representative in testate or intestate cases. The term *estate administration* will be used for the remaining procedures and duties of the personal representative, which include the collection and inventory of assets, the payment of approved claims against the estate, the payment of all state or federal taxes due, and the final distribution of the remaining assets to the beneficiaries, devisees, or heirs entitled to them.

Before we discuss the various methods and procedures individual states use to administer a decedent's estate, it is important to identify those cases in which estate administration may not be needed. In some states, such cases may avoid estate administration if the decedent:

1. Has no property in registered form, e.g., recorded deeds for real property and certificates for securities (stocks and bonds).

2. Has no individually owned property in the possession of third parties, e.g., savings and checking accounts, employee benefit plans, and the like, which cannot be transferred to a personal representative without the authorization of Letters Testamentary or Letters of Administration.

3. Has no outstanding creditors' claims, e.g., the decedent has no debts or all creditors have been paid.

4. Has an estate that is classified as a "small estate" where all assets consist entirely of exempt property with a limited monetary value such as family allowances or a homestead and no other real property (see Tex. Prob. Code Ann. §§ 137 and 138; Cal. Prob. Code § 13100; and compare UPC §§ 3–1203 and 3–1204).

As an alternative to probate and estate administration, some states allow the heirs and devisees to collect, divide, and distribute the decedent's assets in "small estates" subject to their personal liability for paying all valid creditors' claims and all taxes (see Cal. Prob. Code §§ 13650–13655; and compare UPC §§ 3–312 to

3–322). In addition, as previously discussed, there is no need for estate administration if all of the decedent's assets consist of nonprobate property.

Small Estate Settlement and Administration

All states allow decedents with "small estates" to avoid the more common, but also more expensive, methods of probate or estate administration. Most states set a certain monetary limit for the total value of an estate's assets that can qualify as a **small estate.** The amount varies from state to state. If the value of a decedent's estate is below the statutory amount, the estate can be administered as a "small estate." Lengthier, more expensive probate procedures are unnecessary. Small estate procedures are simple: for example, collection of assets is quick and easy; court fees are greatly reduced; debts are generally minimal and promptly paid; death taxes are usually not owed; and assets can be distributed almost immediately, typically to a spouse and children. State statutes also commonly identify **"qualified small estates"** as those in which estate assets are within a certain limited monetary amount and/or consist entirely of exempt property, homestead allowance or exemption, family allowances, and where the estate debts are limited to funeral and burial expenses, and hospital and medical costs of the decedent's last illness (see UPC § 3-1203).

The procedures adopted by state legislatures for expediting the distribution of small estates vary widely. You must review your state statutes and these procedures and familiarize yourself with the required forms, some of which will be available from your local county probate court. *Note:* The county clerks or registrars will give you the forms they can distribute. In addition, they often have developed an outline, pamphlet, or booklet for personal representatives that lists the required forms and procedures for handling small estates. Other necessary forms will generally be available from local or state publishers of legal documents.

Although specific procedures for small estate administration vary from state to state, in general four traditional methods are used: Collection by Affidavit, Summary Administration, Universal Succession, and Family Settlement Agreements.

Collection by Affidavit

Many states allow an affidavit procedure to collect and transfer personal property to a beneficiary, devisee, or heir; to collect debts owed the decedent; or to take possession of the decedent's property held by third parties, e.g., banks and credit unions (see UPC § 3-1201 and Exhibit 12.1). Title and possession of personal property is transferred without involvement of others, e.g., this collection method eliminates the need for the appointment of a personal representative, for supervision by the probate court, or for notice to creditors. To collect the property, the beneficiary, devisee, or heir must present a certified copy of the decedent's death certificate to the debtor or possessor of the property with an affidavit stating:

- That the value of the entire estate, less liens and encumbrances, does not exceed the state's maximum limit (up to $200,000 depending on the state).
- That a minimum number of days, usually thirty (30) to forty-five (45), have elapsed since the death of the decedent to allow creditors to present their claims.

Small estate
A decedent's estate with few assets and a limited monetary value.

Qualified small estate
A decedent's estate that consists entirely of statutory exempt property or allowances and funeral and administration expenses, and is within a certain limited monetary value.

Exhibit 12.1 Affidavit for Collection of Personal Property

MD Form No. P-680   Minn. Stat. 524.3-1201   Miller/Davis Co., St. Paul, MN (800) 752-4221
Minnesota Continuing Legal Education © 1994 MCLE

STATE OF MINNESOTA)
)
COUNTY OF _____)

Estate of

_____

_____   **AFFIDAVIT FOR COLLECTION
OF PERSONAL PROPERTY**
     Decedent
_____

I, _____ ,
Affiant, state:

1. My address is:

2. Decedent died on _____ . A certified copy of Decedent's death certificate is attached to this Affidavit.

3. I am the successor of the Decedent because:

~~VOID~~

4. The value of the probate estate, wherever located, involving any contents of a safe deposit box, less liens and encumbrances, does not exceed $20,000.

5. Thirty days have elapsed since the death of the Decedent or, in the event the property to be delivered is the contents of a safe deposit box, 30 days have elapsed since the filing of an inventory of the contents of said box.

6. No application or petition for the appointment of a personal representative is pending or has been granted in any jurisdiction.

7. I, as claiming successor, am entitled to payment or delivery of the following described property:

_____

_____

_____

_____

NOTARIAL STAMP OR SEAL (OR OTHER TITLE OR RANK)	
	Affiant Date
	Signed and sworn to (or affirmed) before me on
	_____ by
	_____
	Affiant.

               SIGNATURE OF NOTARY PUBLIC OR OTHER OFFICIAL

NOTE: Submit this Affidavit in duplicate or as required by statute.

MD   MCLE P-680   Affidavit for Collection of Personal Property

Source: This form is property of Miller/Davis Company, St. Paul, MN. Telephone 651-642-1988. Reprinted with permission.

- That no application or petition for the appointment of a personal representative (executor) is pending or has been granted in any state court.
- That the claiming beneficiary or heir is legally entitled to inherit the decedent's estate including the right to the payment or delivery of the property.

The affidavit procedure can be used to transfer insurance proceeds, accounts in banks or credit unions, promissory notes, and the property kept in a safe deposit box so long as their combined value does not exceed the maximum limit set by statute. Generally, real property cannot be transferred by affidavit. If the decedent died with a will, some possessors, e.g., banks, may require a copy of the will plus an affidavit and death certificate before they will transfer the property. In Illinois, the affidavit method allows the holder of the property, e.g., a debtor who pays the beneficiary or heir, to be discharged of the debt (see Ill. Compiled Stat. Ann. Ch. 755 § 5/25–1). After the property is transferred, the affiant-recipient is personally liable for the decedent's debts if, subsequently, they become known. For example, if the **affiant** was not legally entitled to the collected property, the affiant is responsible to the person who had the legal right to possession of the property, and the former possessor (such as the debtor above) who acted in good faith on the affidavit is released from any further liability based on the transfer.

Affiant
The person who makes, subscribes, and files an affidavit.

> **Example:** Tom's will left his entire estate to his daughter, Carol, his only heir. When he died, Tom had $1,500 in a savings account; a fishing boat in joint tenancy with his best friend, Fred; a $75,000 life insurance policy naming Carol the beneficiary; and an unpaid debt of $15,000 owed to Tom by Mark for a car Tom sold to Mark. The boat and the proceeds of the life insurance are nonprobate assets and do not apply toward the state maximum for collection by affidavit, which is $50,000 in Illinois, Tom's domiciliary state. After thirty days, Carol can execute an affidavit stating she is Tom's only heir and entitled to his estate under his will and the total value of Tom's probate assets (i.e., $16,500) is below the state's limit. With an affidavit and death certificate, Carol would be entitled to collect the $16,500 (the savings account plus the debt) from the bank and from Mark. Carol may also have to present a copy of Tom's will with the affidavit.

Other individual state restrictions on the use of an affidavit for collection include the following: allowing only spouses and children to collect by affidavit; allowing only certain personal property (e.g., bank accounts) to be collected by affidavit; and requiring some minimal court involvement such as filing the affidavit with the probate court.

Summary Administration

After appointment, a personal representative may apply for a special form of administration called Summary Administration for certain small estates. This form of administration, which is shorter and simpler than the regular estate administration, can be utilized when the sum of the decedent's probate assets does not exceed the maximum limit set by state statute. Many states have both a Collection by Affidavit and a Summary Administration procedure for administering small estates. Exhibit 12.2 lists the maximum amounts allowed for settling small estates by Affidavit or Summary Administration in each state which has these procedures. Summary Administration is generally limited to small estates that have survivors which include a spouse and minor children and insufficient assets to pay all creditors. In other words, if the value of the entire estate, less liens and encumbrances, does not surpass the amount payable for exempt property, family allowances, administration expenses, reasonable funeral and burial costs, the homestead exemption or allowance, and reasonable and necessary hospital and medical expenses of the last illness of the decedent, then Summary Administration may be permitted (see UPC § 3–1203). When this method is allowed, the personal representative immediately distributes the estate assets according to the will or in the order of priority set by an intestate statute and files a sworn closing statement with the probate court (see UPC § 3–1204 and Exhibit 12.3). Accordingly, the intermediate procedures required under the solemn or formal probate process may be eliminated including notice to creditors, presentation of their claims, the formal inventory and appraisal, and the court's decree of distribution.

Example: Richard dies intestate and is survived by his spouse, Mary, and a minor child. Mary is appointed his personal representative. A preliminary inventory of the estate's probate property shows that the estate assets are not sufficient to pay Richard's unsecured creditors' claims. Richard's estate qualifies for Summary Administration as a "small estate." Mary immediately distributes Richard's assets according to the order of priority set by his state's statute and files a sworn closing statement with the court. Copies are sent to all distributees (recipients) of the estate and known creditors (see UPC § 3-1204).

Exhibit 12.2   Monetary Limits That Allow the Transfer of Small Estates by Affidavit or Summary Administration by State

State	Amount	State	Amount
Alabama	$ 3,000	Montana	7,500
Alaska	15,000	Nebraska	25,000
Arizona	50,000	Nevada	200,000
Arkansas	50,000	New Hampshire	10,000
California	100,000	New Jersey	5,000/10,000
Colorado	27,000	New Mexico	30,000
Connecticut	20,000	New York	20,000
Delaware	20,000	North Carolina	10,000/20,000
Florida	60,000/25,000	North Dakota	15,000
Georgia	No ceiling	Ohio	35,000/85,000
Hawaii	60,000	Oklahoma	60,000
Idaho	25,000	Oregon	50,000/90,000
Illinois	50,000	Pennsylvania	25,000
Indiana	25,000	Rhode Island	15,000
Iowa	50,000	South Carolina	10,000
Kansas	10,000/25,000	South Dakota	25,000
Kentucky	(1)	Tennessee	25,000
Louisiana	50,000	Texas	50,000
Maine	10,000	Utah	25,000
Maryland	30,000	Vermont	10,000
Massachusetts	15,000	Virginia	10,000
Michigan	15,000	Washington	60,000
Minnesota	20,000	West Virginia	50,000
Mississippi	20,000	Wisconsin	20,000/50,000
Missouri	40,000	Wyoming	70,000

(1) Available where the exemption of the surviving spouse alone, or together with preferred claims, equals or exceeds the amount of probatable assets.

MD Form No. P-688   Minn. Stat. 524.3-1204   Miller/Davis Co., St. Paul, MN (800) 752-4221
Minnesota Continuing Legal Education © 1994 MCLE

STATE OF MINNESOTA   **DISTRICT COURT**
                                                             PROBATE DIVISION
COUNTY OF _____ **JUDICIAL DISTRICT**

                                                             Court File No. _____

Estate of

_____   **SMALL ESTATE:**
_____   **CLOSING BY SWORN STATEMENT OF**
                    Decedent   **PERSONAL REPRESENTATIVE**

    I, _____ , state:

1. My address is:

VOID

2. I am the Personal Representative of this Estate.

3. The Estate has been administered under the summary procedure of Minn. Stat. 524.3-1203. The
    Estate is not subject to supervised administration, nor does any order of the court prohibit summary
    closing of this Estate.

4. To the best of my knowledge, the entire Estate, less liens and encumbrances, did not exceed:

    (i)   an exempt homestead as provided for in Section 524.2-402,

    (ii) the allowances provided for in Section 524.2-403 and524.2-404, and

    (iii) costs and expenses of administration, reasonable funeral expenses, and reasonable and
          necessary medical and hospital expenses of the last illness of the Decedent.

5. I have fully administered the Estate by distributing it to the persons entitled to the Estate.

6. I have sent a copy of this Closing Statement to all distributees of the Estate and to all creditors or other
    claimants of whom I was aware whose claims are neither paid nor barred and have furnished a full
    account in writing of my administration to the distributees whose interests are affected.

    Under penalties for perjury, I declare or affirm that I have read this document and I know or believe its
representations are true and complete.

                                                             _____
Attorney For Personal Representative

    ┌─────────────────────────────────────┐
    │ THIS INSTRUMENT WAS DRAFTED BY (NAME AND ADDRESS): │   Personal Representative   Date
    │   │
    │   │
    │   │
    │   │
    │   │
    │   │
    └─────────────────────────────────────┘

MD   MCLE P-688   Small Estate: Closing By Sworn
                                              Statement of Personal Representative

Source: This form is property of Miller/Davis Company, St. Paul, MN. Telephone 651-642-1988. Reprinted with
permission.

In the states of New Hampshire and New York, the person who performs duties similar to those involved in Summary Administration is called a "voluntary administrator." In Florida, the administration of small estates up to $60,000 is called Family Administration (see Fla. Stat. Ann. § 735.101).

Universal Succession

The Uniform Probate Code has established another method of transfer of a decedent's estate which requires an application to a registrar and no further court involvement. It is called Universal Succession and is included in UPC §§ 3-312 through 3-322. The recipients of the estate are designated the universal successors, and there is no limit on the value of an estate that can be distributed to them. Universal succession allows heirs of an intestate or beneficiaries and devisees under a will, except minors and incapacitated, protected, or unascertained persons, to take possession, control, and title to a decedent's property. The universal successors assume personal liability to pay taxes, debts, claims against the decedent, and distributions to others legally entitled to share in the decedent's estate. At least 120 hours must elapse after the decedent's death before an application can be made. If it is granted, the registrar issues a written statement which identifies and describes the assets of the estate and states the applicants are the universal successors who have title to the assets and assume liability for the obligations of the decedent.

Family Settlement Agreements

A Family Settlement Agreement is a private written agreement among heirs of an intestate or beneficiaries of a will by which these parties unanimously agree on the distribution of the decedent's estate without supervision by the court having jurisdiction over the estate. In either testate or intestate cases, the settlement must be agreed to by all interested parties, and once it is executed, the settlement agreement supersedes and replaces the intestate succession statute or the will (see UPC § 3–912). The Uniform Probate Code requires the settlement agreement to be in writing. Although the Family Settlement Agreement speeds the distribution of estate assets, a court order is still required to protect the estate from creditors and to clear title to the assets involved (see UPC §§ 3-1101 and 3-1102).

FORMS OF PROBATE OR ESTATE ADMINISTRATION

Before the creation and subsequent adoption of the Uniform Probate Code, traditionally two forms of probate or estate administration, *solemn* and *common* probate, were used. Many states continue to use these two methods today. With **solemn probate,** also called probate in solemn form, formal court supervision is required throughout the administration of the estate, and notice must be given to all *interested parties,* e.g., beneficiaries, heirs, and creditors of the decedent, so they may be present at an initial hearing to contest the validity of the will or the appointment of a personal representative. Solemn probate procedures are followed in intestate as well as testate estates. Solemn probate is established by an order of the court that recognizes the existence and validity of a will and may be used to set aside an earlier common probate proceeding or prevent a pending petition for common probate.

Solemn probate
Formal probate proceedings that require court supervision throughout the administration of the decedent's estate.

Common probate
Informal probate proceedings that involve limited court supervision, if any, and are primarily used for smaller estates.

Common probate, which is primarily used for smaller estates and is usually uncontested, is less formal, and involves less supervision or none. It is a simpler procedure that does not require notice to all interested parties. In company with the witnesses to the will, the nominated personal representative delivers the will to an officer of the court, usually a Registrar or Surrogate. This officer has the power and authority to do what the probate judge would normally do, i.e., appoint the personal representative, either the executor or administrator, and make findings of fact in relation to the will or the intestate succession statutes when there is no will. Under oath, the witnesses attest that: the testator asked them to sign the will; they saw the testator sign it; and their signatures are also on the will. Once this is done, the will is considered proven (admitted to probate). If others contest the will, they must petition the clerk, Registrar, or Surrogate to hold a formal hearing to determine the will's validity. The burden of proof is on the contestant. As mentioned above, common probate may be superseded and set aside by a request of an interested party for implementation of solemn probate. Common probate provides a faster and less expensive statutory method of administering an estate than solemn probate (see and compare Cal. Prob. Code §§ 10500 and 10501; Tex. Prob. Code Ann. §§ 145 et seq.; and Wash. Rev. Code Ann. § 11.68.011).

The Uniform Probate Code has added another method for administering an estate. The options are similar to the traditional forms of probate except they are called *formal* and *informal* probate rather than *solemn* and *common* probate. Under the Code, formal probate (proceedings) is conducted under the supervision of the judge with notice to interested persons; informal probate (proceedings) is conducted, without notice to interested persons, by an officer of the court acting as a Registrar for probate of a will or appointment of a personal representative; see UPC §§ 1-201(18) and (23). "Interested persons" are heirs, devisees, children, spouses, creditors, beneficiaries, and any others having a property right or claim against . . . the estate of a decedent; see UPC § 1-201(24). Formal probate can be either supervised or unsupervised. With formal (supervised) probate, the probate court has supervision over the entire duration of the estate administration. With formal (unsupervised) probate, the estate administration commences formally, but it becomes less supervised by the court after the appointment of the personal representative unless an interested party requests that formal (supervised) probate continue.

The purpose of the Uniform Probate Code is primarily to:

- Simplify and clarify the law, terms, and procedures in estate administration.
- Lessen the expense and time for the administration.
- Provide an alternative system, which, if adopted by the states, establishes uniform law.

The states are not required to adopt the Code, although they are free to adopt it individually through their legislatures. As noted earlier, many estates have continued to use the more traditional methods of estate administration, sometimes in revised form. Exhibit 12.4 identifies the states that use the traditional forms of estate administration and those that have adopted the Uniform Probate Code. As the exhibit shows, sixteen states have adopted the Uniform Probate Code, and ten have followed the solemn-common form. The remainder either follow a hybrid mixture that possibly combines some features of the Code with

---

Exhibit 12.4   Method of Estate Administration by State

States that have followed the English system of common and solemn form probate:

Delaware	Mississippi
Georgia	New Hampshire
Indiana	Tennessee
Kentucky	Virginia
Louisiana	West Virginia

States that have adopted the Uniform Probate Code with some modifications:

Alaska	Idaho	Nebraska
Arizona	Maine	New Mexico
Colorado	Michigan	North Dakota
Florida	Minnesota	South Carolina
Hawaii	Montana	South Dakota
		Utah

States that require some form of notice prior to the admission of a will to probate and afford an opportunity to interested persons to object to the probate of the will:

Alabama	Missouri	Pennsylvania
Arkansas	Nevada	Rhode Island
California	New Jersey	Texas
Connecticut	New York	Vermont
Illinois	North Carolina	Washington
Iowa	Ohio	Wisconsin
Kansas	Oklahoma	Wyoming
Maryland	Oregon	
Massachusetts		

---

their own statutes or have adopted an independent method. *Note:* A few states have established a type of estate administration called *independent administration* that is essentially free of court supervision or intervention. The person appointed to administer the estate is sometimes called the *independent administrator* (see Ill. Compiled Stat. Ann. Ch. 755 § 5/28-1, Mo. Ann. Stat. § 473.780, Tex. Prob. Code Ann. § 145, and Wash. Rev. Code Ann. § 11.68.011). Whatever the method, all states require some form of notice prior to the admission of a will to probate and afford an opportunity to interested parties to object to the probate of the will or to the appointment of the personal representative or executor.

In the majority of cases, formal or solemn probate is used for the administration of decedents' estates. Formal probate is unnecessary, however, when the value of the estate is minimal (see the earlier discussion of small estates), when the estate is not complex, or when the estate assets consist solely of nonprobate property. In such cases, the services of an attorney are generally not required. Formal probate would normally be the choice in any of the following situations: some beneficiaries are minors whose rights must be protected; real estate problems exist; a beneficiary or creditor intends to challenge the proceedings; the estate presents tax law difficulties; in an intestate case, the number of the decedent's heirs is uncertain; in a testate case, the beneficiaries cannot be located; or family members disagree about their respective inheritances or the continuation or sale of a family business.

COMMENCING PROBATE AND ESTATE ADMINISTRATION PROCEEDINGS

Assuming all the preliminary work and correspondence have been completed by the personal representative with the attorney's assistance and your help, probate and estate administration can begin.

You will assist the personal representative with the following procedures and prepare the necessary probate forms:

ELECTRONIC FORMS

In many states the process of estate administration involves filing many documents with the proper court official. Some jurisdictions will allow those forms to be sent electronically. Trips to the courthouse to obtain the proper forms are being eliminated. The necessary forms can be assessed through the Internet from either the local court system or from the appropriate state agency that creates and supplies the documents.

The data that needs to be entered on these forms can be done on the computer, eliminating the necessity of preparing the form on a typewriter. Typo's and other typing mistakes often made preparation of these forms on a typewriter a frustrating experience!

1. Petition for probate of will or petition to prove a will.
2. Petition for administration when no will exists.
3. Obtain an Order for Hearing the Petition to Prove a Will or for Administration.
4. Arrange for publication of the Notice of Order for Hearing and Affidavit of Publication.
5. Mail the Notice of Order for Hearing and Affidavit of Mailing Notice to all interested persons including creditors.
6. Mail notice of rights to the spouse and minor children and prepare an Affidavit of Mailing.
7. Pay funeral bills and obtain a receipt for the records.
8. Identify and review objections and arrange for the appearance of witnesses.
9. Miscellaneous duties before the hearing.

Probate forms and procedures vary from state to state. You must become familiar with your state forms and the time limits for filing them.

The following discussion includes a series of "**What You Do**" lists or "**You Must**" notations which identify tasks you may be asked to perform. Although not mentioned in each "What You Do" list, you should always be in contact with the clerk or registrar of the probate court to verify that you have completed the required forms and procedures accurately and to obtain helpful advice and guidance. However, the clerk or registrar is forbidden by law to give you legal advice.

1. *Petition for probate of will or petition to prove a will.* The form used to commence probate proceedings with a will is the Petition for Probate of Will or Petition to Prove a Will (Form 1* and Exhibit 12.5). The petitioner may be any person who has an interest in the estate, such as a spouse, adult child, beneficiary, heir, devisee, successor, the named executor, or creditor of the decedent, and may

---

*See Appendix A

Exhibit 12.5   Petition for Probate of Will

DE-111

ATTORNEY OR PARTY WITHOUT ATTORNEY *(Name, state bar number, and address)*:	TELEPHONE AND FAX NOS.:	*FOR COURT USE ONLY*

ATTORNEY FOR *(Name)*:

SUPERIOR COURT OF CALIFORNIA, COUNTY OF

STREET ADDRESS:

MAILING ADDRESS:

CITY AND ZIP CODE:

BRANCH NAME:

ESTATE OF *(Name)*:

DECEDENT

PETITION FOR
- ☐ **Probate of Will and for Letters Testamentary**
- ☐ **Probate of Will and for Letters of Administration with Will Annexed**
- ☐ **Letters of Administration**
- ☐ **Letters of Special Administration**
- ☐ **Authorization to Administer Under the Independent Administration of Estates Act** ☐ **with limited authority**

CASE NUMBER:

HEARING DATE:

DEPT.:   TIME:

1. Publication will be in *(specify name of newspaper)*:
   a. ☐ Publication requested.   b. ☐ Publication to be arranged.
2. **Petitioner** *(name of each)*: **requests**
   a. ☐ decedent's will and codicils, if any, be admitted to probate.
   b. ☐ *(name)* :
      be appointed (1) ☐ executor   (3) ☐ administrator
                    (2) ☐ administrator with will annexed   (4) ☐ special administrator
      and Letters issue upon qualification.
   c. ☐ that ☐ full ☐ limited   authority be granted to administer under the Independent Administration of Estates Act.
   d. (1) ☐ bond not be required for the reasons stated in item 3d.
      (2) ☐ $ bond be fixed. It will be furnished by an admitted surety insurer or as otherwise provided by law.
            (Specify reasons in Attachment 2 if the amount is different from the maximum required by Probate Code section 8482.)
      (3) ☐ $ in deposits in a blocked account be allowed. Receipts will be filed. *(Specify institution and location)*:

3. a. Decedent died on *(date)*:   at *(place)*:
      (1) ☐ a resident of the county named above.
      (2) ☐ a nonresident of California and left an estate in the county named above located at *(specify location permitting publication in the newspaper named in item 1)*:
   b. Street address, city, and county of decedent's residence at time of death *(specify)*:

   c. Character and estimated value of the property of the estate:
      (1) Personal property: $
      (2) Annual gross income from
          (a) real property: $
          (b) personal property: $
                      Total: $
      (3) Real property: $ *(If full authority under the Independent Administration of Estates Act is requested, state the fair market value of the real property less encumbrances.)*
   d. (1) ☐ Will waives bond.   ☐ Special administrator is the named executor and the will waives bond.
      (2) ☐ All beneficiaries are adults and have waived bond, and the will does not require a bond. *(Affix waiver as Attachment 3d(2).)*
      (3) ☐ All heirs at law are adults and have waived bond. *(Affix waiver as Attachment 3d(3).)*
      (4) ☐ Sole personal representative is a corporate fiduciary or an exempt government agency.
   e. (1) ☐ Decedent died intestate.
      (2) ☐ Copy of decedent's will dated: ☐ codicils dated: are affixed as Attachment 3e(2).
          ☐ The will and all codicils are self-proving (Prob. Code, § 8220).
                        (Continued on reverse)

Form Approved by the Judicial Council of California DE-111 [Rev. January 1, 1998] Mandatory Form [1/1/2000]	**PETITION FOR PROBATE**	**WEST GROUP** Official Publisher	Probate Code, §§ 8002, 10450

(continued)

Exhibit 12.5 Petition for Probate of Will—*continued*

ESTATE OF *(Name):*	CASE NUMBER:
DECENT	

3. f. **Appointment of personal representative** *(check all applicable boxes):*

> Include in Attachment 3e(2) a typed copy of a handwritten will and a translation of a foreign language will.

(1) Appointment of executor or administrator with will annexed:

(a) ☐ Proposed executor is named as executor in the will and consents to act.

(b) ☐ No executor is named in the will.

(c) ☐ Proposed personal representative is a nominee of a person entitled to Letters. *(Affix nomination as Attachment 3f(1)(c).)*

(d) ☐ Other named executors will not act because of ☐ death ☐ declination ☐ other reasons *(specify in Attachment 3f(1)(d).*

(2) Appointment of administrator:

(a) ☐ Petitioner is a person entitled to Letters. *(If necessary, explain priority in Attachment 3f(2)(a).)*

(b) ☐ Petitioner is a nominee of a person entitled to Letters. *(Affix nomination as Attachment 3f(2)(b).)*

(c) ☐ Petitioner is related to the decedent as *(specify):*

(3) ☐ Appointment of special administrator requested. *(Specify grounds and requested powers in Attachment 3f(3).)*

g. Proposed personal representative is a ☐ resident of California ☐ nonresident of California *(affix statement of permanent address as Attachment 3g)* ☐ resident of the United States ☐ nonresident of the United States.

4. ☐ Decedent's will does not preclude administration of this estate under the Independent Administration of Estates Act.

5. a. The decedent is survived by *(check at least one box in each of items (1)-(3))*

(1) ☐ spouse ☐ no spouse as follows: ☐ divorced or never married ☐ spouse deceased

(2) ☐ child as follows: ☐ natural or adopted ☐ natural adopted by a third party ☐ no child

(3) ☐ issue of a predeceased child ☐ no issue of a predeceased child

b. Decedent ☐ is ☐ is not survived by a stepchild or foster child or children who would have been adopted by decedent but for a legal barrier. *(See Prob. Code, § 6454.)*

6. *(Complete if decedent was survived by (1) a spouse but no issue (only a or b apply), or (2) no spouse or issue. Check the **first** box that applies):*

a. ☐ Decedent is survived by a parent or parents who are listed in item 8.

b. ☐ Decedent is survived by issue of deceased parents, all of whom are listed in item 8.

c. ☐ Decedent is survived by a grandparent or grandparents who are listed in item 8.

d. ☐ Decedent is survived by issue of grandparents, all of whom are listed in item 8.

e. ☐ Decedent is survived by issue of a predeceased spouse, all of whom are listed in item 8.

f. ☐ Decedent is survived by next of kin, all of whom are listed in item 8.

g. ☐ Decedent is survived by parents of a predeceased spouse or issue of those parents, if both are predeceased, all of whom are listed in item 8.

h. ☐ Decedent is survived by no known next of kin.

7. *(Complete only if no spouse or issue survived decedent)* Decedent ☐ had no predeceased spouse ☐ had a predeceased spouse who (1) ☐ died not more than 15 years before decedent owning an interest in **real property** that passed to decedent, (2) ☐ died not more than five years before decedent owning **personal property** valued at $10,000 or more that passed to decedent, (3) ☐ neither (1) nor (2) apply. *(If you checked (1) or (2), check only the **first** box that applies):*

a. ☐ Decedent is survived by issue of a predeceased spouse, all of whom are listed in item 8.

b. ☐ Decedent is survived by a parent or parents of the predeceased spouse who are listed in item 8.

c. ☐ Decedent is survived by issue of a parent of the predeceased spouse, all of whom are listed in item 8.

d. ☐ Decedent is survived by next of kin of the decedent, all of whom are listed in item 8.

e. ☐ Decedent is survived by next of kin of the predeceased spouse, all of whom are listed in item 8.

8. **Listed in Attachment 8** are the names, relationships, ages, and addresses, so far as known to or reasonably ascertainable by petitioner, of (1) all persons named in decedent's will and codicils, whether living or deceased, (2) all persons named or checked in items 2, 5, 6, and 7, and (3) all beneficiaries of a devisee trust in which the trustee and personal representative are the same person.

9. Number of pages attached: _____

Date:

▶ _____

* *(Signature of all petitioners also required (Prob. Code, § 1020).)*   (SIGNATURE OF ATTORNEY *)

I declare under penalty of perjury under the laws of the State of California that the foregoing is true and correct.

Date:

▶ _____

· · · · · · · · · · · · · · · · · · · ·
(TYPE OR PRINT NAME)   (SIGNATURE OF PETITIONER)

▶ _____

· · · · · · · · · · · · · · · · · · · ·
(TYPE OR PRINT NAME)   (SIGNATURE OF PETITIONER)

DE-111 [Rev. January 1, 1998]   **PETITION FOR PROBATE**   WEST GROUP Official Publisher   Page two

Source: Reprinted with permission from California Forms: Legal and Business. Copyright ©, by West Group.

file the will and a petition with the court to have the will proved (admitted to probate). Most states have a statute of limitations that limits the time allowed to file the petition, e.g., Arizona, Kansas, and Montana (see *Matter of Estate of Taylor,* 207 Mont. 400, 675 P.2d 944 [1984], which allowed a limit of three years after the decedent's death, and compare UPC § 3–108). Other states have no limits on the time for allowing probate, e.g., Oklahoma.

A petition is a written document addressed to a court or judicial official that requests the court order certain legal actions. The petition and subsequent order establishes the court's jurisdiction over the decedent's estate. The original will is filed with the petition. To establish jurisdiction, the petition to prove a will generally must include the following:

- The name and aliases, date of death, age, place of death of the decedent, and, if required, the Social Security number.
- The domicile of the decedent.
- The existence and date of the will and, in some cases, the names of its witnesses. Unless it has previously been forwarded to the court, the original will usually accompanies and is filed with the petition.
- The name and address of the petitioner named in the will who seeks appointment as personal representative (executor or executrix) and requests Letters Testamentary. Verification that the petitioner is legally qualified for the appointment is often required.
- Names, addresses, ages, relationship to the decedent, and identity of those persons under legal disability (e.g., incompetents), of all devisees, and also of those heirs who would be entitled to distribution of the decedent's estate in the absence of the will. *Caveat:* For all estates, whether testate or intestate, the heirs must be listed in the court petition for probate of a will or for administration of an intestate's estate.
- The estimates value of the real and personal property that are probate assets.
- The amount and general character of the decedent's debts, if known.
- In some states, if the decedent was survived by children and a spouse, a statement that "the children of the decedent are/are not also children or issue of the decedent's surviving spouse." *Note:* This statement and the affidavit of Medical Assistance which follows are also included in the petition for administration when no will exists.
- In some states, if the decedent was over sixty-five years of age, an affidavit of Medical Assistance must be filed and sent to the Department of Welfare with a copy of the Petition for Probate of Will if the decedent received any health benefits from the state's Medical Assistance program.

What You Do:
- Contact the county clerk or registrar and obtain the forms and information they provide for commencing probate. Obtain all other required forms from local (state) legal form publishers. Your law office will have most of these forms utilizing computer software to produce and prepare them.
- Collect all necessary information needed to complete and execute the Petition for Probate of Will.

- Make sure you or the personal representative files the will, petition, and death certificate, if required.
- Obtain and file an affidavit of Medical Assistance, if needed.
- Whenever any document is filed, see that the personal representative pays the filing fee. *Note:* Filing fees will be required on many occasions, so this statement will not be repeated on the ensuing pages.

2. *Petition for administration when no will exists.* When there is no will, a form called the Petition for Administration (Form 2*) sets forth facts similar to the Petition for Probate of Will. It should contain the following:

- The name and aliases, date of death, age, place of death of the decedent, and, if required, the Social Security number.
- The domicile of the decedent.
- The name and address of the petitioner requesting appointment as personal representative (administrator or administratrix) and Letters of Administration.
- The name and address of the surviving spouse of the decedent, if any.
- The names, ages, relationship to the decedent, and addresses of all heirs or heirs at law of the decedent so far as they are known to the petitioner.
- The estimated value of the real and personal property that are probate assets.
- The amount and general character of the decedent's debts, if known.

As a general rule, the surviving spouse has first priority to be appointed as general administrator, then the next of kin, or both, at the discretion of the court. If the surviving spouse or next of kin so choose, they may nominate another person to serve as administrator. If all of the possible administrators are incompetent, unsuitable, or unwilling to serve, or if no petition has been filed within a statutory number of days, e.g., forty-five days after the decedent's death, administration may be granted to one or more creditors of the decedent or to the creditors' nominee. In that case, the petition must be accompanied by an itemized and verified statement of the creditor's claim. Generally, minors, mentally incompetent persons (as determined by a court), and often nonresidents of the state cannot act as personal representatives. Additional probate proceedings, called ancillary administrations, are necessary whenever a decedent-intestate owns real property or, in some cases, tangible personal property in more than one state.

What You Do:
- Obtain the information needed to execute the required forms and obtain the forms from the county clerk or local publishers of legal forms if your firm does not have them.
- Check your state statutes on priority of appointment of a personal representative (administrator) and ask the person who has first priority, i.e., the surviving spouse, whether he or she is willing to serve (see UPC § 3-203[a]).
- Make sure you or the personal representative files the petition and death certificate, if required.

3. *Obtain an Order for Hearing the Petition to Prove a Will or for Administration.* As soon as possible after the filing of the petition either to have the will admitted

---

*See Appendix A

to probate or for administration of the intestate estate, the court will make and enter its order (also called a **citation**) fixing a date, time, and place for hearing the petition. In some states the date of the order generally signals the beginning of the statutory period for creditors of the estate to file their claims against the estate (see the discussion of claims below). A court officer, such as the clerk, may prepare the order, but you should check to make sure this is done (Forms 3* and 4*).

4. *Arrange for publication of the Notice of Order for Hearing and Affidavit of Publication.* The next task you must perform for the attorney and client is to contact a legal newspaper (one that specializes in printing legal notices), or at least a newspaper that is generally circulated in the county in which the proceedings are pending, and arrange for publication of the Notice of the Order for Hearing (Form 5*).

What You Do:

- Call the county clerk for information about procedures for publication. The clerk may tell you which newspapers are available for this purpose. Then contact a local "legal notice" newspaper publisher and arrange for publication of the executed Notice of the Order for Hearing. Make sure the order is published within the statutory time required *before* the hearing is held.
- File the Affidavit (Proof) of Publication. This affidavit will include an attached cut-out copy of the notice as it appeared in the newspaper. For an example of such a publication, see Form 6*.

Publication requirements vary from state to state. In some states, the order must be published once a week for two or three consecutive weeks. The first newspaper publication must occur within a statutory time period, e.g., two weeks after the date of the court order fixing the time and place for the hearing. In addition, the Affidavit (Proof) of Publication must be filed with the probate court within a statutory number of days (usually fifteen days) prior to the hearing. Sometimes the county clerk of the probate court makes the arrangements for publication, but **You Must** check to be sure it is done within the time allotted by court rules. In some counties, the newspaper publisher sends the Affidavit of Publication directly to the court; in others the publisher fills out the affidavit, which is filed with the probate court by the personal representative, the attorney, or you. Discuss the procedure with the publisher.

5. *Mail the Notice of Order for Hearing and Affidavit of Mailing Notice to all interested persons including creditors.* The Order for Hearing requires the petitioner to serve the order personally or, after the order is published in a local legal newspaper, to mail the publication attached to the Notice of Order for Hearing the Petition to all interested persons named in the petition and to creditors whose names and addresses are known, informing them that the petition has been filed and the order given listing the date, time, and place for the hearing (Form 7*). In states like New York that use the *citation,* the form contains notice and the affidavit of service which all interested persons must receive.

"Interested persons" who must receive formal legal notice include all those who have a property right or claim against the decedent's estate; they include creditors as well as all heirs, devisees, beneficiaries, spouses, and children (see UPC § 1-201[24]). Therefore, **You Must** identify all known individuals or businesses to whom the decedent owed money (e.g., family, friends, business associates, credit card

---

*See Appendix A

Citation
The legal form, used in some states, that is the court's order fixing a date, time, and place for hearing the petition to prove a will or for administration; the petitioner is required to give notice of the hearing to all interested persons.

companies, loans from banks, utilities, hospitals, doctors, financial advisers) and see that they receive actual notice, i.e., you will deliver notice to them personally or mail a copy of the notice to their homes and place of business. Other unknown creditors will be given notice by publication, as mentioned above, in a local newspaper as required by state statutes. Notice is required to set the starting date for the statutory time period, usually two to six months from the date of the order *or* the appointment of the personal representative and issuance of the Letters of Authority, that creditors have to file their claims with the court stating the amount and basis of their claim. Once a creditor files a claim, the creditor is known as the **claimant.** Notice also serves the purpose of allowing the interested person to file an objection to the appointment of the personal representative and propose another candidate or to contest the will. In addition, notice allows the surviving spouse to choose the elective share rather than the will's provisions and enables the family to claim the statutory family allowance available in many states (see Item 6).

Notice is necessary to establish the court's jurisdiction over the decedent's estate, and the proceedings will be invalid if it is not delivered and/or mailed. If there are no heirs, beneficiaries, or devisees, the property will escheat (pass) to the state, and notice should be sent to the state attorney general. If an heir does not receive notice, the heir may later contest the will (see the *Tobin* case in Chapter 5). If the decedent was born in a foreign country, notice must also be mailed to the consul or other representative of that country if a consul resides in the state and has filed a copy of her appointment with the state's secretary of state. The personal representative must submit the affidavit, attesting to the mailing of the notices, to be filed with the court.

What You Do:

- Mail a copy of the Notice of Order for Hearing to all interested persons listed in the petition, e.g., heirs, beneficiaries, devisees, and all known creditors. Actual notice to known creditors informs them of the deadline they have to file a claim against the decedent's estate.
- Make sure personal (actual) service or service through the local paper is accomplished. Prepare the Affidavit of Mailing notice and verify the personal representative sends the Affidavit of Mailing of these notices, and that it is filed with the court.

Any person (called the **demandant**) having financial property interests in the decedent's estate may file with the court a demand for notice of any order of filing pertaining to the estate. The **demand** must state the person's name, address, and the nature of her interest in the estate (Form 10*). The clerk mails a copy of the demand to the personal representative who must, in turn, mail the Notice of the Order for Hearing the Petition to the demandant (see also Chapter 13).

6. *Mail notice of rights to the spouse and minor children and prepare an Affidavit of Mailing.* In most states, if a decedent has left a spouse or minor children, a notice of right to the *homestead exemption* (unless it is in joint tenancy between spouses), *exempt property,* and *family allowances* must be mailed to each such person within a period of time set by statute, e.g., fourteen days prior to the date set for hearing on the petition (Form 8*). Also, if the spouse has not already

Claimant
A creditor who files a claim against the decedent's estate.

Demandant
Any person who has a financial or property interest in a decedent's estate and who files with the court a demand for notice of any order or filing pertaining to the estate.

Demand
To assert and file a claim for payment based on a legal right.

---

*See Appendix A

contested the will, notice of rights dealing with renunciation and *election* must be mailed to the spouse. **You Must** prepare these notices and the affidavit the personal representative must file with the court showing the mailing of the notices. *Note:* An explanatory letter accompanying these notices can help avoid confusion. A child of the testator does not have the right to elect against the will. Only the surviving spouse has the *right of election*.

7. *Pay funeral bills and obtain a receipt for the records.* The funeral bill is a debt for which a claim can be filed by the funeral director. The personal representative cannot pay the bill until appointed and need not pay it until the claim period expires; however, it may be possible to obtain a discount by paying the bill promptly. Sometimes, by statute, there is a limit on the amount that can be spent for funerals. In addition, the *funeral bill* is generally a *preferred claim* (see the discussion of priority of debts later in the chapter). Timely payment is important when an estate has few assets since failure to pay this bill and other priority debts before distributing the assets can lead to individual liability for the personal representative.

What You Do:

- You must contact the decedent's spouse and family or the funeral director to determine how payment is to be made. Sometimes the decedent prepaid the expenses by arrangement with the funeral director. In other cases, the spouse and family make separate arrangements for the funeral, burial, and reception with the funeral director and pay the bill themselves with the understanding the decedent's estate will reimburse them. You must remind the personal representative that funeral expenses must be "reasonable" considering the amount of assets and liabilities of the estate and these expenses must be discussed with the family. You must also obtain copies of the receipts for all funeral and related expenses from family members or the funeral director.

8. *Identify and review objections and arrange for the appearance of witnesses.* If anyone with an interest in the estate raises objections to the will, he must file them with the court before the hearing and the witnesses to the will must be contacted. Objections are most commonly filed by the following:

- A spouse dissatisfied with the amount received in the will.
- A child who has been omitted or disinherited.
- A devisee who claims the will is a forgery or was signed under fraud or undue influence.
- A devisee who claims the testator was incompetent.

What You Do:

- If there are any objections to the will, you must arrange for the witnesses to the will to appear in court to testify the testator knew and declared the document to be a will and freely signed it in accordance with state statutes. If a witness lives more than a hundred miles away from the place of the hearing, a written statement the witness affirms to be true (a **deposition**) may serve in lieu of testimony in open court (Exhibit 12.6 and Form 9*). Usually, the testimony of one witness is sufficient to establish the will's validity. If neither

Deposition
A written statement signed under oath by a witness that may serve to validate a will in place of testimony given in open court.

---

*See Appendix A

Exhibit 12.6 Deposition of Witness

MD Form No. P-272   Minn. Stat. 524.3-405   Miller/Davis Co., St. Paul, MN (800) 752-4221
Minnesota Continuing Legal Education © 1994

STATE OF MINNESOTA   **DISTRICT COURT**
                                                         PROBATE DIVISION
COUNTY OF _____ **JUDICIAL DISTRICT**

                                              Court File No. _____
Estate of

_____
                                              COMMISSION TO TAKE DEPOSITION
_____   **OF WITNESS TO WILL**
            Decedent

You are appointed commissioner to take the deposition of _____
_____ , a subscribing witness to the last will of Decedent, which is
transmitted with this Commission. You have the authority to require the witness to appear before you at a
time and place designated by you and to examine the witness, under oath or affirmation, respecting the
execution of the will. Immediately after the examination you shall return the deposition signed by the
witness and certified by you, together with this Commission and the will, by registered mail in a sealed
envelope addressed to the District Court, Probate Division, _____
_____

Minnesota _____ .

VOID
                                              _____
                                              Judge   Date
                              DEPOSITION

("Deponent"), residing at _____,
_____

being duly sworn deposes and says that:

1. I am one of the subscribing witnesses to the instrument dated _____ ,
   which purports to be the last will of _____ ,
   who resided at _____
   _____
   County of _____ , State of _____ , which is now being shown to me.

2. I am of legal age and was so at the time I witnessed the signing of Decedent's will.

3. I knew the Decedent or met the Decedent at the signing of the Decedent's will. At that time the
   Decedent declared the instrument to be Decedent's will and in my presence signed the will.

4. In the presence of and at the request of Decedent, I signed the instrument declared to be Decedent's
   will.

5. To the best of my knowledge, at the time of the witnessing of Decedent's will, the Decedent was of
   sound mind and memory, of lawful age, and under no restraint.

                                              _____
                                              Deponent   Date

MD   MCLE P-272   Commission to Take Deposition of Witness to Will

(continued)

Exhibit 12.6 Deposition of Witness—*continued*

Court File No._____

COMMISSIONER'S CERTIFICATE

STATE OF MINNESOTA   } ss

COUNTY OF _____

I, _____ ,
a notary public licensed under the laws of _____ in
_____ County, took the attached deposition pursuant to the above
commission. Under said commission I administered an oath to the witness and took the witness' testimony.
The witness swore to give truthful testimony relative to the cause specified in the commission. The witness,
after giving testimony, read the testimony given and signed the deposition as the Deponent's free act.

_____

(COURT SEAL)   Commissioner   Date

VOID

MD   MCLE P-272/PPage 2   Commission to Take Deposition of Witness to Will

Source: This form is property of Miller/Davis Company, St. Paul, MN, telephone 651-642-1988. Reprinted with permission.

witness can be found, then others familiar with the testator's signature, such as a banker or business associate, may acknowledge the validity of the signature. Many states provide for the self-proved will, which makes the testimony of subscribing witnesses in court unnecessary (see UPC § 2-504). Also, holographic wills do not have to be witnessed, but they are not legal in all states.

9. *Miscellaneous duties before the hearing.* Before the hearing, you may be asked to perform various other tasks under the supervision of an attorney.

What You Do:

- Send copies of the will and a preliminary estimate of the estate to the appropriate beneficiaries, devisees, and/or heirs.
- Collect all available pertinent information for final income tax returns and prepare a "tickler" form (Exhibit 11.3), a list of the probate and estate administration procedures with all deadline dates and the person who performs the tasks.
- Assemble data on nonprobate property (see the discussion later in the chapter).
- If the decedent owned real property in joint tenancy with another, contact the state department of taxation and determine whether an affidavit of survivorship will be necessary to resolve tax concerns (Exhibit 12.7). Since the title to the property will now be in the name of the survivor, check the state public records division to verify the documents required to transfer the title are accurate. Frequently, the survivorship affidavit must be cleared with the proper county tax official and filed with the county real estate recorder along with a certified copy of the decedent's death certificate, if required. Your state procedure must be followed.
- Inquire into all substantial gifts made by the decedent and all transfers made in trust. Such items have special tax considerations and are discussed further in Chapter 14.

PROBATE COURT PROCEDURE

The next steps in probate and estate administration include the following:

10. Hearing on petition to prove the will or petition for administration.
11. Selection of the personal representative.
12. Order admitting the will or granting administration.
13. Issuance of Letters Testamentary or Letters of Administration.
14. File for a federal employer identification number.
15. Open a checking account for the estate.
16. Notice to creditors.
17. Appointment of trustees and guardians.
18. Order admitting a foreign will to probate.

10. *Hearing on petition to prove the will or petition for administration. Note:* This discussion covers both testacy and intestacy cases. On the date set for the hearing to prove the will or, if there is no will, for general administration, the petitioner seeking appointment as personal representative and at least one subscribing witness, if a testate case, should accompany the attorney to court. **You Must** make arrangements to see that the witness(es) are notified and appear in court

Exhibit 12.7 Affidavit of Survivorship

Form No. 119-M   Minnesota Uniform Conveyancing Blanks (1981)   Miller-Davis Co., St. Paul, MN

AFFIDAVIT OF IDENTITY AND SURVIVORSHIP

Transfer entered

_____ , _____
(Year)

_____
County Auditor

By _____
Deputy

(reserved for recording data)

STATE OF MINNESOTA _____ } ss.   **NAME OF DECEDENT**

COUNTY OF _____

_____

I, _____

Name of Affiant   and   Address of Affiant

being first duly sworn, on oath state from personal knowledge:

That the above named **decedent** is the person named in the certified copy of Certificate of Death attached hereto and made a part hereof.

That the name(s) of the survivor(s) is/are _____

That said decedent on date of death was an owner as a joint tenant/life tenant of the land legally described as follows:

VOID

(If more space is needed, continue on back)

as shown by instrument recorded in Book _____ of _____

Page_____ , or as Document No._____ in the office of the County

Recorder of _____ County, Minnesota, or as shown on Certificate of Title

No. _____ , Files of the Registrar of Titles of _____ County, Minnesota.

SIGNATURE OF AFFIANT

THIS INSTRUMENT WAS DRAFTED BY (NAME AND ADDRESS):

Subscribed and sworn to before me

this _____ day of_____ , _____ .
(Year)

_____
SIGNATURE OF NOTARY PUBLIC OR OTHER OFFICIAL

NOTARIAL STAMP OR SEAL (OR OTHER TITLE OR RANK):

Tax Statements for the real property described in this instrument should be sent to:

Source: This form is property of Miller/Davis Company, St. Paul, MN, telephone 651-642-1988. Reprinted with permission.

on time on the appropriate day. No testimony from a subscribing witness is necessary if the will is self-proved. Any person who has an interest in the estate and who wishes to contest the validity of the will or the appointment of the petitioner as administrator must file the objection with the court and should appear at the hearing. *Remember:* Creditors can challenge the appointment of the personal representative, but they cannot contest the will. For a will contest, the court will set a different hearing date and time. If no interested person raises an objection, the petitioner, i.e., either the person who petitions to have the will admitted to probate or the person seeking appointment as administrator, testifies to the facts of the will or intestacy. Usually, this testimony will suffice to prove the will or to appoint the administrator (but compare UPC § 3–405). If the petitioner is unable to testify to the facts, another person who can give such evidence must be present at the hearing. This person testifies under oath and answers questions that elicit such information as the date of the decedent's birth, death, and will, the domicile of the decedent, the probable value of the decedent's estate and debts, and the names of devisees, heirs, and other interested parties (any person entitled to receive a share of the decedent's assets). If necessary when the hearing is to prove a will, one or both of the subscribing witnesses are also sworn and testify as to the execution of the will and the capacity (age and sanity) of the testator. In addition, they verify the testimony of the first witness, the petitioner, insofar as possible. Exhibit 12.8 is an example of a typical transcript at a hearing to prove a will. Note that the questions are asked by the attorney from the information requested on the petition itself in a manner that requires a simple yes or no answer (Form 1*). Proof of publication and mailing of notice of the hearing to all interested parties should also be offered in evidence at this hearing. Finally, after the hearing, the testimony of the subscribing witness(es) should be signed and delivered to the judge unless the signature(s) may be waived.

If the will is contested and a date is set for the contest hearing, all witnesses to the will's execution should be present to testify at the hearing. A witness living more than a hundred miles away or an ill or disabled witness may testify by deposition, as mentioned above. If the party contesting the will is successful, the probate court may set aside part or all of the will and declare it invalid. The decedent's estate will then pass by the state's intestate succession statute.

11. *Selection of the personal representative.* As discussed in Chapter 11, the kind of personal representative the court appoints at the hearing depends on the action, or lack of action, taken by the decedent. If the decedent names a personal representative in the will, the court usually confirms and appoints that individual executor (or executrix) to carry out the directions and requests of the testator. If the decedent dies intestate, the courts appoints an administrator to handle the estate. Review the priority of appointment of the administrator in Chapter 11 and compare UPC § 3-203(a).

12. *Order admitting the will or granting administration.* At testate proceedings, after the witness(es) testify and the will has been proved, the court makes its order admitting the will to probate (Form 11* and Exhibit 12.9). In intestate proceedings, the court issues an order granting administration of the estate (Form 12*). In both cases, the court appoints a personal representative (i.e., executor or administrator) and fixes the amount of the personal representative's bond, if one is needed, based on the value of the estate, the type of assets, the relationship of the personal representative to the decedent, and other relevant facts.

---

*See Appendix A

Exhibit 12.8 Transcript of Hearing to Prove a Will

1. Are you the petitioner _____ as named in the petition for the probate of the estate of _____, the deceased?
2. And you reside at _____?
3. And have an interest in the proceeding as _____?
4. And to your knowledge decedent was born _____ at _____?
5. And that the decedent died on _____ at _____?
6. And the decedent at the time of his death resided at _____ in the city of _____, county of _____, state of _____?
7. And that the names and addresses of decedent's spouse, children, heirs, and devisees and other persons interested in this proceeding and the ages of any who are minors so far known or ascertainable with reasonable diligence by you are _____? Is that correct?
8. And that no personal representative of the decedent has been appointed in this state or elsewhere whose appointment has not been terminated?
9. And that the original of decedent's last will duly executed on _____, _____, is in the possession of the court, and there is no codicil or codicils to the will?
10. And that to the best of your knowledge, you believe the will has been validly executed. Is that correct?
11. And that you are unaware of any instrument revoking the will?
12. And that you are entitled to priority and appointment as personal representative because you are nominated in the last will of the decedent as personal representative with no bond required. Correct?

Finally, that you request the court enter a judicial order formally:
1. Finding that the testator is dead
2. Finding that venue is proper
3. Finding that the proceeding was commenced within the time limitations prescribed by the laws of this state
4. Determining decedent's domicile at death
5. Determining decedent's heirs
6. Determining decedent's state of testacy
7. Probating the valid and unrevoked last will or decedent including any valid and unrevoked codicil thereto
8. Determining that petitioner is entitled to appointment as personal representative under the laws of this state
9. Appointing petitioner as the executor of the estate of decedent with no bond in a(n) (formal) (informal) administration
10. Authorizing issuance of letters testamentary to petitioner upon qualification and acceptance
11. Granting such other and further relief as may be proper

Before a bond is purchased from a surety (bonding) company, **You Must** shop around for the best price and make arrangements with the bonding agent. Although the bond may be prepared by a surety (bonding) company or others, the personal representative or the attorney is responsible for it. Therefore, it may become your task to prepare the form(s) of both bond and oath (Forms 68* and 13*). To facilitate this process, an employee of a bonding company may be present in court on hearing days with appropriate bond forms. In that case, the bond and oath can be completed and you can file them with the court immediately after the hearing. The order will require the filing of an acceptance of the position of

---

*See Appendix A

Exhibit 12.9 Order for Probate

DE-140

ATTORNEY OR PARTY WITHOUT ATTORNEY *(Name, state bar number, and address)*:	TELEPHONE AND FAX NOS.:	*FOR COURT USE ONLY*

ATTORNEY FOR *(Name)*:

SUPERIOR COURT OF CALIFORNIA, COUNTY OF
STREET ADDRESS:
MAILING ADDRESS:
CITY AND ZIP CODE:
BRANCH NAME:

ESTATE OF *(Name)*:

DECEDENT

ORDER FOR PROBATE	CASE NUMBER:

ORDER APPOINTING
- [ ] Executor
- [ ] Administrator with Will Annexed
- [ ] Administrator [ ] Special Administrator
- [ ] Order Authorizing Independent Administration of Estate
  - [ ] with full authority [ ] with limited authority

WARNING: THIS APPOINTMENT IS NOT EFFECTIVE UNTIL LETTERS HAVE ISSUED.

1. Date of hearing: Time: Dept./Room: Judge:

THE COURT FINDS

2. a. All notices required by law have been given.
   b. Decedent died on *(date)*:
      (1) [ ] a resident of the California county named above.
      (2) [ ] a nonresident of California and left an estate in the county named above.
   c. Decedent died
      (1) [ ] intestate
      (2) [ ] testate
      and decedent's will dated: and each codicil dated:
      was admitted to probate by Minute Order on *(date)*:

THE COURT ORDERS

3. *(Name)*:
   is appointed **personal representative**:
   a. [ ] executor of the decedent's will
   b. [ ] administrator with will annexed
   c. [ ] administrator
   d. [ ] special administrator
      (1) [ ] with general powers
      (2) [ ] with special powers as specified in Attachment 3d(2)
      (3) [ ] without notice of hearing
      (4) [ ] letters will expire on *(date)*:
   and letters shall issue on qualification.

4. a. [ ] **Full authority** is granted to administer the estate under the Independent Administration of Estates Act.
   b. [ ] **Limited authority** is granted to administer the estate under the Independent Administration of Estates Act (there is no authority, without court supervision, to (1) sell or exchange real property or (2) grant an option to purchase real property or (3) borrow money with the loan secured by an encumbrance upon real property).

5. a. [ ] Bond is not required.
   b. [ ] Bond is fixed at: $ to be furnished by an authorized surety company or as otherwise provided by law.
   c. [ ] Deposits of: $ are ordered to be placed in a blocked account at *(specify institution and location)*:
      and receipts shall be filed. No withdrawals shall be made without a court order. [ ] Additional orders in Attachment 5c.
   d. [ ] The personal representative is not authorized to take possession of money or any other property without a specific court order.

6. [ ] *(Name)*: is appointed probate referee.

Date:

_____
JUDGE OF THE SUPERIOR COURT

7. Number of pages attached: _____   [ ] SIGNATURE FOLLOWS LAST ATTACHMENT

Form Approved by the
Judicial Council of California
DE-140 [Rev. January 1, 1998]
Mandatory Form [1/1/2000]

ORDER FOR PROBATE

WEST GROUP
Official Publisher

Probate Code, §§ 8006, 8400

Source: Reprinted with permission from California Forms: Legal and Business. Copyright © by West Group.

personal representative of the estate (Form 13*). No bond is required in the case of a corporate representative, and bond may not be required of a personal representative. The court will consider, and usually grants, a request for a minimum bond or no bond when the request is made in a decedent's will or is signed by all persons interested in the estate and submitted at or before the time of the hearing (Form 14*). The personal representative will normally make this request for the benefit of interested parties.

13. *Issuance of Letters Testamentary or Letters of Administration.* After the court has signed an order appointing the personal representative and approved the bond, if one is required, the personal representative will file an oath of office, and the court issues the appropriate documents conferring authority on the personal representative. In most states, these documents, for an executor or executrix, are called Letters Testamentary; for an administrator or administratrix, they are called Letters of Administration.

The authority conferred by these letters is the same. The letters are certified (accompanied by a certificate from the clerk of the probate court stating they are in full force). The personal representative is then authorized and qualified to act for the decedent's estate (Forms 16*, 69*, Exhibit 12.10, and Exhibit 12.11).

14. *File for a federal employer identification number.* After the appointment, one of the first duties of the personal representative is to file Form SS–4 to obtain a federal employer identification number, which is required on fiduciary income tax returns and is needed before a Notice Concerning Fiduciary Relationship can be filed as required by the IRC § 6903 (Forms 81* and 82*). Because the decedent's estate is an entity in itself and will be taxed as such on income produced by the estate after the decedent's death, **You Must** prepare and file these forms to establish that a fiduciary relationship exists. The employer number identifies the fiduciary responsible for preparing the fiduciary income tax return and for paying any tax due. This filing enables the Internal Revenue Service to mail the notices and tax forms to the new fiduciary (personal representative) who is now responsible for the tax liability of the decedent's estate.

15. *Open a checking account for the estate.* To help the personal representative keep complete and accurate records of all financial transactions throughout the administration of the decedent's estate, a bank checking account for the estate must be opened. Once the federal employer identification number is obtained, the account is opened in the name of the estate of the decedent with the personal representative authorized to make deposits or withdrawals. The estate checking account allows the personal representative to consolidate and deposit into this one account all current and future liquid probate assets, e.g., all existing cash and funds obtained from the sale of estate assets; payments of debts owed to the decedent; dividends from stock; checking and savings deposits located in other banks, credit unions, or savings and loan associations; proceeds from life insurance, pension or profit-sharing plans, and other retirement plans *if* the estate was named the beneficiary; and all other funds that belong to the decedent's estate as they mature during the estate administration.

---

*See Appendix A

Exhibit 12.10 Letters of Authority

DE-150

ATTORNEY OR PARTY WITHOUT ATTORNEY *(Name, state bar number, and address):*	TELEPHONE AND FAX NOS.:	*FOR COURT USE ONLY*

ATTORNEY FOR *(Name):*

SUPERIOR COURT OF CALIFORNIA, COUNTY OF

STREET ADDRESS:

MAILING ADDRESS:

CITY AND ZIP CODE:

BRANCH NAME:

ESTATE OF *(Name):*

DECEDENT

LETTERS

□	**TESTAMENTARY**	□	**OF ADMINISTRATION**	CASE NUMBER:
□	**OF ADMINISTRATION WITH WILL ANNEXED**	□	**SPECIAL ADMINISTRATION**	

LETTERS

1. □ The last will of the decedent named above having been proved, the court appoints *(name):*

   a. □ executor.
   b. □ administrator with will annexed.

2. □ The court appoints *(name):*

   a. □ administrator of the decedent's estate.
   b. □ special administrator of decedent's estate
      (1) □ with the special powers specified in the *Order for Probate.*
      (2) □ with the powers of a general administrator.
      (3) □ letters will expire on *(date):*

3. □ The personal representative is authorized to administer the estate under the Independent Administration of Estates Act □ **with full authority**
   □ **with limited authority** (no authority, without court supervision, to (1) sell or exchange real property or (2) grant an option to purchase real property or (3) borrow money with the loan secured by an encumbrance upon real property).

4. □ The personal representative is not authorized to take possession of money or any other property without a specific court order.

WITNESS, clerk of the court, with seal of the court affixed.

(SEAL)	Date:
	Clerk, by
	_____
	(DEPUTY)

AFFIRMATION

1. □ PUBLIC ADMINISTRATOR: No affirmation required (Prob. Code, § 7621(c)).

2. □ INDIVIDUAL: **I solemnly affirm** that I will perform the duties of personal representative according to law.

3. □ INSTITUTIONAL FIDUCIARY *(name):*

   I solemnly affirm that the institution will perform the duties of personal representative according to law. I make this affirmation for myself as an individual and on behalf of the institution as an officer.
   (Name and title):

4. Executed on *(date):*
   at *(place):*   , California.

   ▶ _____
   (SIGNATURE)

CERTIFICATION

I certify that this document is a correct copy of the original on file in my office and the letters issued by the personal representative appointed above have not been revoked, annulled, or set aside, and are still in full force and effect.

(SEAL)	Date:
	Clerk, by
	_____
	(DEPUTY)

Form Approved by the
Judicial Council of California
DE-150 [Rev. January 1, 1998]
Mandatory Form [1/1/2000]

LETTERS
(Probate)

WEST GROUP
Official Publisher

Probate Code, §§ 1001, 8403,
8405, 8544, 8545;
Code of Civil Procedure, § 2015.6

Source: Reprinted with permission from California Forms: Legal and Business. Copyright © by West Group.

Exhibit 12.11 Domicillary Letters

STATE OF WISCONSIN, CIRCUIT COURT, _____ COUNTY   -PROBATE-

IN THE MATTER OF THE ESTATE OF

_____   **DOMICILIARY**
_____   **LETTERS**

File No. _____

To: _____
                              Name(s)

The above named person died, domiciled in _____ County, Wisconsin, on
_____.
                Date
You are appointed personal representative and have fully qualified.

THEREFORE, these Letters are issued to you, and you are ordered to administer this estate according to law.

BY THE COURT:

Seal

_____
                                    Circuit Judge

_____
                                    Date

PR-1403, 6/85 - (16A) DOMICILIARY LETTERS   Wisconsin Legal Blank Co., Inc.
  s.856.21, Wisconsin Statutes   Milwaukee, WI

Source: Wisconsin Legal Blank Co., Inc. Reprinted with permission.

All cash transactions of the estate will be handled through the estate checking account. Therefore, using the estate checks, the personal representative pays the decedent's debts, taxes due, and all of the expenses throughout the estate administration including funeral expenses, court costs and filing fees, costs of insuring and maintaining estate property, and fees of the personal representative and attorney. The remaining property is distributed to the estate beneficiaries or heirs.

The estate checking account allows the personal representative and you to keep an accurate and complete accounting of all receipts and disbursements. The final account that is filed with the probate court to settle and close the estate and the death tax returns that must be prepared are absolutely dependent upon the accuracy and completeness of the checkbook records. The checks accomplish three essential record-keeping functions:

- They establish a record of all payments and disbursements.
- Once the check is endorsed, they act as creditors' admissions of the payment of their debts.
- When canceled, they serve as evidence and verification of payment of taxes and the personal representative's final account.

The personal representative should select a competitive interest-bearing checking account that is insured by the FDIC (Federal Deposit Insurance Corporation). See Exhibit 11.4 for a sample check imprint for a deceased's estate.

What You Do:

- If the personal representative asks you to open a checking account for the estate and cannot come with you to the bank, you should bring to the bank a signature card signed by the personal representative, a check for the initial deposit, a certified copy of the Letters Testamentary or Letters of Administration, and the death certificate, if required.

16. *Notice to creditors*. Many states give notice to creditors either by formal (actual) notice or by publication *after* the Notice of Order for Hearing or the "Letters" have been issued. The procedure covered previously in Item 5 would be performed at this time. The United States Supreme Court has held that actual notice, i.e., delivery of notice directly to a creditor or by mail, must be given to all known or readily identified creditors of the deadline to file a claim against a decedent's estate.

17. *Appointment of trustees and guardians*. Other fiduciaries besides the personal representative can be selected and appointed by the testator. While alive, the testator can establish testamentary trusts in the will to take effect upon death. This allows the testator to appoint a trustee who will administer the trust created in the will. Since the will and therefore the trust become effective only on the death of the testator, technically, the trustee is appointed at that time. The trustee's powers must conform to statutory guidelines whether or not the testator incorporated them into the testamentary trust. A better choice and another possibility would be for the parent to create a living trust for the benefit and care of the child(ren) since it would be in operation while the parent was alive and could be modified to meet the child's needs as determined by the parent.

Other fiduciaries appointed by the probate court include guardians for minor children of the deceased. The guardian *of the person* of a minor is responsible for the custody and care, specifically, the education, health, and welfare of the minor. The guardian or conservator *of the property* is responsible for managing and safeguarding the minor's property, prudently investing the assets when appropriate, and making disbursements in accordance with the will or living trust and the laws of the state until the minor reaches adulthood. Both guardians should be named in the will and may be the same person, but like the personal representative, they must be approved and appointed by the probate court. Once appointed, the guardians are accountable to the court (Form 17*). The guardian's duties and powers are set by statute or the will's provisions. When acting in the name of the minor, the guardian should always sign legal documents listing the minor's name followed by the words "by _____, guardian."

If the decedent-testator has included a clause that names and appoints a surviving spouse as guardian of the person and property of minor children, the court generally appoints the spouse. If the decedent fails to name either type of guardian or dies intestate, the court will appoint a suitable guardian(s) for the benefit of the minor children. Guardians or conservators may also be appointed for

---

*See Appendix A

persons who may or may not be minors but are physically or mentally handicapped. In choosing a person to administer a will or trust or a guardian of a minor's property, the testator or settlor should select a person who is responsible, competent, experienced in the management of property and investments, and capable of maintaining well-organized checkbooks and records.

What You Do:

- Contact the local county clerk and identify and/or obtain the proper forms used by the county for the appointment of fiduciaries and review procedures with the clerk.
- If the deceased died intestate, your work will be more complex and time-consuming since substantial legal research may be necessary to convince the probate judge your client's nominee for guardian is "in the best interests of the minor (or incapacitated) children," the criterion used by the court when considering the application for guardianship. For example, your research would discover that in cases involving a minor child age 14 or older, some states allow the child to request a person other than the natural parent be appointed guardian (see UPC § 5–203).

Parents are considered, by law, to be the natural guardians of their children, but are not necessarily considered natural guardians over the children's property. Usually, a parent will act as guardian of both the child's person and the child's property, but in all states, the court has the final word in the appointment of guardians. State laws that allow a parent to act as guardian of the child's property or to act as guardian of both the child's person and property are permissive rather than mandatory. The following example illustrates a typical problem of guardianship.

Example: In his will, John Casey leaves his estate to his wife, Sharon, and their two minor children, Kimberly, age 16, and James, age 13, equally as tenants in common. John dies. Sharon is appointed guardian of the children. If Sharon wants or needs to use inherited family funds, sell family property, or move to another state, she must get permission from the court. This is both time-consuming and expensive. Using similar facts, except John dies intestate, the state intestate succession statute also passes John's estate to Sharon and the two children. Sharon is again appointed guardian, and once again, she will need court approval for decisions involving the property. John could have avoided these problems if he had left all his estate to Sharon and relied on her to care properly for their children or if he had established a living or testamentary trust, naming Sharon the trustee or co-trustee with another responsible and suitable person. Unlike a testamentary trust, the assets in the living trust are nonprobate property, and the court has no control over them.

18. *Order admitting a foreign will to probate.* The decedent may die leaving real property or, in some cases, tangible personal property in another state (foreign state) as well as in the state of domicile. All of the decedent's property, wherever located, must be distributed to interested parties, e.g., beneficiaries, devisees, heirs, or creditors. As previously discussed, the disposition of property in the state of residence is the domiciliary administration, and the disposition of property located in a different state, the foreign state, requires a separate procedure called ancillary administration. If a will has been admitted to probate by a proper court in the state where the decedent was domiciled, this will may thereafter be admitted to probate as a foreign will in the other state. In many states, the personal

representative appointed to administer this property in the other (foreign) state is called the ancillary administrator, and the form used is the Petition for Probate of Foreign Will discussed below.

If the decedent was born in or has left heirs in another country and no petition has been filed within a statutory number of days, e.g., thirty days after the decedent's death, administration may be granted to the consul or other representative of that country or his nominee, but only if the person appointed ancillary administrator resides in the state and files a copy of the appointment with the state's secretary of state. Finally, administration may be granted to any suitable and competent person, whether the person has an interest in the estate or not, provided the court considers the appointment to be in the best interest of the estate and heirs.

According to provisions in the will or the statutes, the ancillary administrator collects assets and pays debts and taxes due in the state where the property is located and remits the residue and final documents to the personal representative of the principal (domiciliary) state for final settlement. The estate cannot be closed until the ancillary administration is completed since the determination of estate tax cannot be settled until the property, debts, and claims in all states are known.

The ancillary procedures in the foreign state generally include the following:

- The Petition for Probate of a Foreign Will must be filed (Form 18*). Along with the petition, the personal representative may be asked to send the following documents: an authenticated copy of the will; a certified copy of the death certificate, if required; a certificate from the clerk of the court in the domiciliary state affirming the will's correctness; a certificate from the probate judge reinforcing the clerk's certificate; a certificate affirming the court's authority to admit the will; and a copy of the order admitting the will to probate in the domiciliary state. Note, however, the requirements vary from state to state.
- The Order for Hearing on the Petition must be published, and notice of the Order for Hearing must be sent to all interested persons including creditors (Form 19*).
- After the hearing on the petition, the court will execute an order accepting and admitting the will admitted to probate in the testator's domiciliary state and appointing the ancillary administrator (Form 20*). In a few states, a person appointed ancillary administrator must meet the same qualifications as a domiciliary administrator. Most states, however, do have specific qualifications for a person to be appointed an ancillary administrator (see Exhibit 3.3).
- The court will issue Letters of Authority, e.g., Letters Ancillary Testamentary, to the ancillary administrator. The Letters permit the real property located in the foreign state to be transferred to the designated devisee named in the will if all creditors of the testator in the foreign state have been paid.
- If the foreign state imposes any inheritance or estate tax, these taxes must be paid to that state before the property can be transferred back to the domiciliary state.

What You Do:
- Identify the property that must be administered and its location (county) in the foreign state.

---

*See Appendix A

- Check the foreign state's statutes to determine the qualifications and residency requirements for the ancillary administrator, and see if your client, the domiciliary personal representative, qualifies. If so, you will continue to do the remaining tasks.
- Contact the county court personnel in the foreign state and obtain the forms and written procedures they make available for ancillary administration and solicit their advice and guidance regarding any local requirements.
- Execute all required forms and documents (see the listed examples above) and file them with the foreign state's court.
- Verify that all foreign state creditors and death taxes, if any, are paid and retain receipts.
- Verify that legal title to property in the foreign state has been cleared and is submitted to the domiciliary state court for distribution to the beneficiaries or devisees of the decedent's will or to the heirs of the decedent according to the foreign state's intestate succession statute for appropriate assets, e.g., real property located in the foreign state.

What You Do (if the ancillary administrator is a resident of the foreign state rather than the domiciliary personal representative)

- Obtain the name and address of the person selected by the testator's will or by the personal representative to be the ancillary administrator in the other state.
- Obtain all required documents listed above, or others required by the local county court, execute them with appropriate signatures, and mail them to the ancillary administrator for filing.
- Keep in contact to help with any other data or documents the ancillary administrator may need.
- Once the foreign state's court accepts the approved will from the domiciliary state, the court issues the Letters Ancillary Testamentary to the ancillary administrator to authorize that person to administer the property of the decedent located in the foreign state. If there is no will, Letters of Ancillary Administration are issued.
- After the court in the foreign state completes its responsibilities, obtain the final documents and personal property from the foreign state and add it to the inventory. If the property consists of real estate, the personal representative generally does not include it in the inventory, but may elect to include it in a memorandum at the end of the inventory.

Exhibit 12.12 is a summary comparison of the procedures to follow in formal probate administration for testate and intestate cases. Note there are some differences between the two procedures (testate and intestate) up to the point of appointment and acceptance. Thereafter, for all practical purposes, the testate and intestate procedures are similar until it is time to distribute the assets of the estate. Then, either the will directs the personal representative, or the intestate succession statute does.

PROCEDURES BEFORE ESTATE DISTRIBUTION

We have covered probate procedures up to and including the order appointing the personal representative and the establishment of the personal representative's authority by issuance of Letters. In both testacy and intestacy, before the estate is distributed, the personal representative must be concerned with the following:

Exhibit 12.12   Comparison of Formal Testate and Intestate Procedures

Testate Procedures	Intestate Procedures
1. File will (and codicils if any) and petition to prove (admit) will and for appointment of the personal representative (executor) and, if required, file death certificate.	1. File petition for administration and appointment of the personal representative (administrator) and, if required, file death certificate.
2. Order for hearing on petition.	2. Order for hearing on petition.
3. See to publication of order for hearing (in some counties the clerk does this).	3. See to publication of order for hearing (in some counties the clerk does this).
4. File affidavit of publication (in some counties the publisher does this).*	4. File affidavit of publication (in some counties the publisher does this).*
5. Mail notices to interested parties entitled to them.	5. Mail notices to interested parties entitled to them.
6. Mail notice of rights of spouse and minor children, if required.	6. Mail notice of rights of spouse and minor children, if required.
7. File affidavit of mailing notices.	7. File affidavit of mailing notices.
8. Ensure appearance of petitioner and witness(es) to will at hearing.	8. Ensure appearance of petitioner at hearing.
9. File request for reduced bond, if appropriate. Will can waive bond.	9. File request for reduced bond, if appropriate.
10. Hearing to prove will.	10. Hearing for administration.
11. Order admitting will to probate and appointing personal representative (in some counties this is prepared by the clerk).	11. Order granting administration and appointing administrator (in some counties this is prepared by the clerk).
12. Prepare and file bond and oath (if personal representative is an individual).	12. Prepare and file bond and oath (if personal representative is an individual).
13. Prepare and file acceptance (if personal representative is a corporation).	13. Prepare and file acceptance (if personal representative is a corporation).
14. Issuance of Letters Testamentary.	14. Issuance of Letters of Administration.
15. Apply for federal employer identification number.	15. Apply for federal employer identification number.
16. Send notice of fiduciary relationship to IRS.	16. Send notice of fiduciary relationship to IRS.
17. Establish checking account for estate.	17. Establish checking account for estate.
18. Notice to creditors.	18. Notice to creditors.
19. Appointment of guardians or trustees, if any.	19. Appointment of guardians or trustees, if any.
20. Review ancillary administration matters, file petition for probate of foreign will, and obtain order admitting foreign will.	20. Review ancillary administration matters.

*Some publishers send the affidavit directly to the probate court; others fill out the affidavit form, but the personal representative must file it with the court.

---

19. Open the safe deposit box.
20. Collect and preserve the decedent's assets.
21. Prepare the inventory.
22. Prepare an appraisal (can be same form as for inventory).
23. Prepare a schedule of nonprobate assets.
24. File the inventory and appraisal.

It is essential the personal representative, with the attorney's and your assistance, accomplishes these tasks accurately and expeditiously since complete information as to the value of the decedent's gross estate, including the probate and nonprobate assets, is necessary for the determination of death taxes. Thus the personal representative must not only take possession of all property when required to do so, but must also inventory (list) all probate assets accurately and report all non-probate assets, making certain these assets are properly valued in preparation for executing and filing the necessary federal and state tax returns.

19. *Open the safe deposit box.* Most states require that once a bank learns of a decedent's death, it must freeze all savings and checking accounts and seal any safe deposit box leased by the decedent (whenever the decedent held the box solely) until the contents of the box have been examined by the county treasurer's office or a representative thereof. Bank requirements to open a safe deposit box frequently vary, but most banks require, at minimum, a certified copy of the decedent's death certificate (see Exhibit 11.6). In some states the statutory requirements for opening the box may cause serious problems because of the delay in obtaining the will. In many states, if the decedent's will is in the safe deposit box, the bank usually is allowed to take it out and forward it to the probate court before sealing the box. It is the responsibility of the bank to prevent anyone from removing any other contents of the box. The box should be unsealed only when the personal representative, the county treasurer or deputy, a representative of the bank, and you or the estate's attorney are present. After the box is unsealed, the bank's representative is permitted to distribute the contents to the personal representative. **You Must** make a complete inventory of the contents of the box.

Proper disposition of the contents may present problems. In some states, if the box had been owned jointly, the surviving owner could be entitled to its contents. If the contents were not also jointly owned, however, the survivor is not entitled to them and may have to relinquish possession if the will or intestacy statute gives them to others.

Often life insurance policies are kept in safe deposit boxes. When the named beneficiary is someone other than the estate of the decedent, the policies may be handed over to the appropriate beneficiary, but, **You Must** make and retain photocopies so they can be used in the calculation of possible state and/or federal death taxes. If a federal estate tax return must be filed, U.S. Treasury Form 712 must be completed for each policy and filed with the return (Form 89*). This form lists the names of the beneficiary, decedent, insurance company, face amount of the policy, premium cost, and the like.

20. *Collect and preserve the decedent's assets.* One of your vital duties and major responsibilities is to help the personal representative find, collect, preserve, value, and either liquidate or distribute all of the decedent's probate personal property. The personal representative does not take title to the decedent's real property unless it must be used to satisfy creditor claims. Your job concerning the real property is to locate it and keep records for future tax concerns or distribution. Apart from personal property set aside as family allowances or exempt property for the surviving spouse and minor children, all personal property owned solely by the decedent comes under the care of the personal representative. The court holds the personal representative personally responsible for collecting and preserving existing probate assets. On request, you will help the personal representative perform the following duties:

a. To locate the decedent's real and personal property. It will be necessary for the personal representative and you, by phone, by letter, or in person, to contact many people: relatives, friends, business associates, tax adviser, banking officials, stockbrokers, accountant, attorneys, trust officers, insurance agent

---

*See Appendix A

or broker, employers, and persons handling the decedent's claims within the Social Security Administration and the Veterans Administration. With the help of the family or these advisers, examine financial records to find all bank accounts, stock and bond holdings, insurance policies (including credit life insurance on any credit cards, loans, or savings accounts), outstanding loans or other debts owed to the decedent, and any stock options or deferred compensation.

b. To take possession of all the decedent's probate personal property. Nonprobate assets, including jointly owned property, life insurance benefits, and the like, are not subject to the marshaling (collection) authority of the personal representative. You will prepare a separate list of nonprobate assets that must be maintained (see the later discussion). Title to the decedent's personal property passes to (vests in) the personal representative when appointed by the probate court. This passage of title is retroactive to the decedent's death. In other words, title vests in the personal representative as if the personal representative had assumed title as soon as the decedent died.

What You Do:

At the direction and with the consent of the personal representative:

- You must identify all nonprobate assets and list them for future required documents, e.g., a schedule of nonprobate assets required for filing death tax returns.
- You will contact in person or by phone all persons listed above and prepare all correspondence, e.g., letters to banks (for checking and savings accounts), insurance companies (for policies and named beneficiaries), stockbrokers (for all investments), and business associates, for the personal representative's signature to identify, locate, and collect, when appropriate, all personal property of the decedent to which the personal representative is entitled and required to possess. With the use of Letters of Authority and certified copies of the death certificate, if needed, you will obtain the assets mentioned below. You will verify all checking and savings accounts wherever located are closed and the cash and money obtained from the sale of all personal property is transferred into the estate account. You will also verify proceeds collected from life insurance and retirement plans naming the estate the beneficiary are deposited in the account. If the will specifically states that securities (stocks and bonds), certificates of deposits, and mutual funds are to be given to named persons, these will pass through the will; otherwise the personal representative may have to sell them. The money from this sale must also be transferred to the estate account. The collected assets, wherever located, are to be used to pay all valid creditors' claims and death taxes due. After payment of all debts and taxes, the personal representative will distribute the remaining personal property to those who are entitled to it.

Title to the decedent's real property, however, vests immediately, upon the decedent's death, in the beneficiaries or devisees of a testate estate or the heirs of an intestate estate, but it is subject to divestiture (to be taken away) to pay creditors of the estate. In appropriate instances, therefore, the personal representative may obtain possession of real property (by entering onto the land with a court order) and convey (sell) it in order to satisfy creditors' claims. A typical state statute on this matter is Pennsylvania's:

20 Pa. Stat. Ann. § 3311 Possession of Real and Personal Estate; Exception

A personal representative shall have the right to and shall take possession of, maintain and administer all the real and personal estate of the decedent, except real estate occupied at the time of death by an heir or devisee with the consent of the decedent. He shall collect the rents and income from each asset in his possession until it is sold or distributed, and, during the administration of the estate, shall have the right to maintain any action with respect to it and shall make all reasonable expenditures necessary to preserve it. The court may direct the personal representative to take possession of, administer and maintain real estate so occupied by an heir or a devisee if this is necessary to protect the rights of claimants or other parties. Nothing in this section shall affect the personal representative's power to sell real estate occupied by an heir or devisee. [Compare UPC § 3–709.]

c. To keep all real property (e.g., houses and other buildings) protected and in reasonably good repair.

What You Do:

■ You must contact an insurance company and obtain information so the personal representative can maintain reasonable coverage for all real property. This must include both property and liability insurance usually in the form of a "homeowner's policy." If such a policy already exists, you will determine the expiration date. If necessary, a policy must be purchased until the home is sold or transferred to the devisee. If the property needs repair, you must inform the personal representative so the property is properly maintained until it is distributed or sold. You must also make sure no property taxes or mortgage payments become delinquent. The transfer or distribution of real estate is discussed in detail later in this chapter. You must immediately notify all tenants in possession of any real property owned by the decedent that rent is to be paid to the personal representative and give them her name and address. You must verify all such rent payments are included in the estate account.

d. To search for important documents, records, and papers that might contain information on the location of unknown assets.

What You Do:

■ You may be asked to help in finding checkbooks, saving account statements, insurance policies, charge account cards, credit cards, canceled or uncashed checks, income tax returns for the last three years and any gift tax returns, deeds, contracts for deed, trust documents, bills of sale for personal property, title cards or certificates for automobile, boat, and mobile home ownership transfer, and cards for membership in various agencies and fraternal organizations. You must review records filed with various county and city departments for additional clues to unknown or missing property.

e. To protect certain items of value in the estate, once they are collected, including stocks, bonds, insurance policies, promissory notes, mortgages, jewelry, and stamp or coin collections. **You Must** contact a bank and, with the personal representative, rent a safe deposit box for their safekeeping.

f. To check other insurance policies (life, hospitalization, disability, and automobile liability) for coverage and expiration dates. Although the personal representative decides these matters, **You Must** prepare all the correspondence to terminate, continue, or transfer the benefits under the policies to the appropriate parties or to transfer ownership to the "Estate of John Doe" account. You also verify these transfers.

g. Miscellaneous. Inheritance due the decedent from others (predeceased family and friends not yet collected). **You Must** discover, collect, and add this property to the assets of the estate.

Procedures for Collecting Specific Estate Assets

Collecting estate assets can be complex work, depending on the number and diversity of the assets. The personal representative of a typical estate will be dealing with such assets as bank accounts, securities, debts owed the decedent, causes of action, jointly owned property, insurance benefits, sale of a business, death benefits, and automobiles. Complete, accurate, and detailed records of each asset must be kept, including a record of all cash receipts and expenditures on a check register (see the previous discussion of opening a checking account.)

- *Bank accounts.* Accounts solely in the name of the decedent will be released only to the personal representative of the estate. After determining the location of the decedent's bank accounts (savings, checking, and credit union), the personal representative must withdraw the funds using the decedent's bank statement and certified copies of the Letters Testamentary or Letters of Administration and the death certificate. The personal representative may wait to withdraw these funds until after the interest earning period, e.g., monthly or quarterly. The withdrawn funds are to be placed in the "Estate of John Doe" account.

What You Do:

If asked by the personal representative:

- You must prepare a letter for the signature of the personal representative with an order directing that the account be closed and a check for the balance including interest payable to the estate of the decedent be sent to the personal representative's address. Other required documents, e.g., Letters Testamentary or Letters of Administration and the death certificate, must accompany your letter.

Joint accounts must also be located, although these accounts go to the surviving joint tenant, e.g., a spouse. The date on which the joint account was established, the source from which the account was created, and the amounts must be obtained and reported on the death tax forms. For further discussion on tax consequences of joint ownership, see Chapter 14.

"Totten trusts" or POD (payable on death) accounts (savings account trusts in the decedent's name for the benefit of another) are payable directly to the named beneficiary in many but not all states. For tax purposes, you must obtain information on Totten trusts and the date the account was opened.

- *Securities.* Securities are often found either among the decedent's possessions or in a safe deposit box.

What You Do:

- You must search for all the decedent's securities (stocks, bonds) including accounts with brokers or stocks held in the broker's name. Generally, securities remain registered in the decedent's name and are transferred to the proper beneficiaries or devisees named in the will or to heirs through intestate succession after administration of the estate is completed. Determination must be made as to whether the decedent, before death, effectively transferred ownership of the stock to another. Transfer of securities is discussed in detail later in the chapter. In other situations, the personal representative must decide whether to liquidate (sell) the securities immediately or wait until a later time when their value may increase. When the securities are sold, you must verify the proceeds are placed in the estate checking account.

- *Debts owed the decedent.* Inquiries should be made into all outstanding debts owed to the decedent.

What You Do:

- You must review county and city records and files to determine whether the decedent held any mortgages, contracts for deed, promissory notes, or similar evidences of indebtedness to the decedent.
- You must interview family to determine if such debtors may include friends, relatives, devisees, or heirs. Since they must repay the estate, their debts might cancel out the benefits they receive from it unless their debts are forgiven in the will.
- You must arrange by letter, phone, or personally for the continued collection of loans, rents from tenants, interest from financial institutions, alimony (maintenance) from a divorced spouse, dividends, royalties from publishers, unemployment compensation, worker's compensation, and federal or state income tax refunds and attempt to collect delinquent obligations. These monies must be transferred into the estate account. At the request of the personal representative, you may have to contact and hire a collection agency to collect delinquent debts. The probate court will approve a reasonable compromise settlement of a disputed debt owed to the decedent so long as it appears to be in the best interest of the estate. *Since legal advice may be involved in the settlement, this must be done by the attorney and personal representative.*

- *Causes of action.* A legal wrong for which a civil lawsuit for **damages** can be brought creates for the wronged or injured party a **cause of action,** i.e., a right to sue. If the person suing dies while in the process of litigation, the claim or "cause of action" may also die (end). When by statute, the personal representative is allowed to pursue the "cause of action" for the benefit of the decedent's estate or heirs, any recovery in damages becomes an asset of the estate. State statutes on the subject of "causes of action" as assets of the estate allow or bar such lawsuits depending on the circumstances surrounding death, the nature of the action, and many other factors.

What You Do:

- You must carefully read the state statutes and commentaries on them and perform any necessary legal research to determine if a particular decedent's

ETHICAL ISSUE

Damages
The monetary remedy from a court of law that can be recovered by the person who has suffered loss or injury to her person, property, or rights by the unlawful act, omission, or negligence of another.

Cause of action
The right of a person to commence a lawsuit.

ETHICAL ISSUE

"cause of action" survives the decedent's death and should be continued. *The findings must be discussed with the supervising attorney for final resolution.*

Example: Betty Simmons negligently backs her car into her neighbor's yard striking a supporting beam of the neighbor's porch, which causes the porch roof to collapse. Considerable property damage results. Susan Swanson, the neighbor, sues Betty in civil court, but after commencing the lawsuit, Susan dies. The personal representative of Susan's estate must continue the suit if no settlement is reached. Any recovery becomes an asset of Susan's estate and is paid into the estate's checking account.

Example: Tom Jensen is struck by a car driven negligently by Michael Howard. Although Tom is seriously injured, causing him to be hospitalized, his doctors assure him he will completely recover in time. While convalescing two months after the accident and after commencing a lawsuit against Michael, Tom has a heart attack and dies. Medical experts establish the heart attack is totally unrelated to the previous accident. Under these circumstances in some states, Tom's "cause of action" dies with him. The personal representative of Tom's estate would not be allowed to continue Tom's lawsuit except to recover "special damages," i.e., the medical and hospital expenses and loss of wages incurred by Tom because of the automobile accident. "Pain and suffering" damages are not recoverable.

- *Jointly owned property.* Property of any kind, real or personal, held in the form of ownership known as joint tenancy does not become a probate asset of the decedent's estate. If the decedent held such property with another person as joint tenants, the property would automatically become the surviving joint tenant's upon the decedent's death.

What You Do:

To clear title to real property held in joint tenancy by the decedent, you must help the personal representative to take the following steps:

- Execute in duplicate an Affidavit of Survivorship if the property is the homestead and the surviving joint tenant is the decedent's spouse (see Exhibit 12.7). *Remember:* Due to the *homestead exemption,* in some states, a surviving spouse and family are protected from eviction from their home by creditors whether the homestead was owned in joint tenancy or in severalty.
- File a certified copy of the death certificate of the decedent and one copy of the Affidavit of Survivorship with the proper section of the county land office, i.e., the county recorder or registrar (see Exhibit 11.6).
- Send one copy of the Affidavit of Survivorship to the office of the commissioner of taxation or the appropriate state tax officer.
- If the real property is Torrens (registered) property, the surviving joint tenant must also file an Affidavit of Purchaser of Registered Land and the owner's duplicate Certificate of Title.
- A Decree of Distribution will also be recorded (see Item 35 below).

In some states, when the value of the homestead does not exceed a statutory amount and the homestead goes to the surviving joint tenant, i.e., the spouse, the above procedures may cancel the state inheritance tax lien (claim) on the homestead that would otherwise exist. To cancel an inheritance tax lien on all other jointly held real property, the surviving joint tenant must file the following with the county land office:

- An Affidavit of Survivorship on which the appropriate state tax official, e.g., commissioner of taxation, has certified that no inheritance tax is due or that the tax has been paid.
- A certified copy of the decedent's death certificate.

- *Insurance benefits.* A life insurance policy is a written contract between the buyer (our decedent) and an insurance company in which the buyer pays annually a specified amount of money called a premium to the company and it, in turn, agrees to pay a designated beneficiary named by the buyer an agreed-on amount of money, usually at the time of the buyer's death. If the decedent held life insurance policies payable to named beneficiaries (e.g., a spouse or children) and did not retain any incidents of ownership (see below), then the proceeds of the policy are paid directly to the beneficiaries, are not part of the estate and, therefore, are not subject to federal estate tax. They are also exempt from federal income tax. For each policy to be listed on the federal estate tax return, the personal representative should obtain U.S. Treasury Form 712 Life Insurance Statement (Form 89*). These forms must be filed with the return and contain information needed in order to prepare the death tax returns (see Chapter 14).

If the decedent retained any of the incidents of ownership (e.g., the right to change the beneficiary, to assign ownership of the policy to another person, or to cancel it altogether), the Internal Revenue Service considers the decedent held enough control over the policy for it to be considered an asset of the estate. As such, it is subject to both state and federal death taxes. Death benefits will go directly to the named beneficiary without being subject to tax, *only if* the insurance company was informed in writing that the insured person was giving up these rights (incidents of ownership) at least three years before death (see IRC § 2042 and Chapter 14). *Caveat:* No death taxes are due on an insurance policy if the policy is taken out on the decedent's life *by another person* (owner) who pays the premiums, unless the beneficiary is the decedent's estate.

What You Do:
- At the request of the personal representative, obtain and partially complete Form 712 for every insurance policy on the life of the decedent. Mail the forms to each insurance company for final completion and signature.
- When the decedent's estate is the beneficiary of the policy, help the personal representative execute the proper forms for filing the claim to receive the proceeds from the policy. Notice of the date of the decedent's death should be given to the insurance company, and all other documents required by the company should be prepared. These generally include a certified copy of the death certificate, the return of the original life insurance policy, and, if required, a certified copy of the Letters Testamentary or Letters of Administration. Make sure you keep a copy of the life insurance policy.

---

*See Appendix A

- Hospitalization, medical (doctor), and disability insurance companies must be notified, especially where the decedent was hospitalized for any length of time due to a last illness before death. Payments from these policies may be made directly to those who provided care during the last illness; otherwise, they are paid directly into the decedent's estate. Receipts must be obtained for these payments. Any uncollected claims owed and unpaid by an insurance company due to incidents prior to the decedent's death must be paid into the estate checking account. Cancellation of life, disability, auto, home, and other types of insurance premiums, when appropriate, must be made, and refunds received should be paid into the estate checking account. As needed, you will perform the above tasks.

- *Sale of or continuation of a business—sole proprietorship, partnership, or limited partnership.* If the decedent was the sole owner and manager of a business, the personal representative may have to run the business until it can be liquidated. A personal representative has no authority to continue a decedent's business, and most states hold that the business must be liquidated. However, if the testator-decedent named a devisee to inherit the business and/or manage it, or a state statute authorizes it, the personal representative may select a long-time employee willing to continue to manage the business until the devisee or heir takes over or the business is liquidated. Complete and accurate records of all business activities must be kept and reviewed by the personal representative during this transition.

If the decedent was a partner in a partnership or limited partnership, the personal representative must obtain a copy of the partnership or limited partnership agreement to determine the procedures and partner's rights when a partner dies. If the agreement contains a clause that allows a buyout of the decedent partner's interest, the personal representative must see that a fair price is obtained for the estate.

> *Sample Clause [Will]: (West's McKinney's Forms ESP, § 7:393)*
> I authorize my Personal Representative(s) for the time being to carry on the whole or any part of the [name of business] now operated and managed by me at [address] until such time as they shall deem it expedient to sell the same or to wind up the said business, as the case may be. (Reprinted with permission from West's McKinney's Forms, Copyright ©, by West Group.)

- *Death benefits.* Other death benefits, payable to the decedent's estate, must be collected.

What You Do:
- You must contact federal and state government benefit plans, such as Medicare, Medicaid, Social Security, and, if appropriate, farm subsidy benefits, Railroad Retirement Fund benefits, and the Veterans Administration for benefits.
- You must contact the decedent's employer to determine if the decedent was entitled to accrued earned pay, accrued vacation pay, commissions, sick leave, terminal pay, pension or profit-sharing plans, 401(k) plans, deferred compensation plans, employee stock-ownership plans, group insurance plans, stock options, year-end bonus, or back pay uncollected, and labor union benefit plans. Such compensation should go into the estate checking account.

If the benefits are a form of employee compensation such as pension or profiting-sharing plans, the personal representative must identify them and determine to whom these benefits are to be paid.

If the decedent was a veteran of any war, including WWII, Korean, Vietnam, and Persian Gulf Wars, the decedent's beneficiaries or heirs may be entitled to benefits such as insurance, pensions, and burial expenses, according to the rules of the Veterans Administration or state law. Death benefits under Social Security and veterans benefits are generally either paid directly to the surviving spouse or applied to the payment of funeral and burial expenses. The Social Security death benefit is a maximum of $255.

A union or fraternal lodge to which the decedent may have belonged should be checked to see if any benefits are due the decedent or the successors. In addition, the surviving spouse and minor children of a decedent covered under Social Security benefits may have the right to a claim for monthly income benefits given to survivors of the decedent. The local Social Security office must be contacted.

- *Automobiles*. As owner of the decedent's automobile(s), the estate or the personal representative could become legally liable for injuries or damage caused by improper and negligent use. Therefore, the automobile(s) should be transferred to the persons entitled to them as soon as possible after the death of the decedent or, if a state statute demands, within a certain number of days. The ways of transferring title to the decedent's car to the appropriate person vary from state to state. State statutes or regulations control the transfer of title to the car. The appropriate person to whom title is transferred could be a surviving spouse who elects to take the car (see Minn. Stat. Ann. § 524.2–403 for a typical state statute), a surviving joint tenant owner, a devisee in the decedent's will, or a purchaser who pays the market value to the personal representative. The statutory requirements or regulations for title transfer must be checked.

21. *Prepare the inventory*. An **inventory** is a complete physical check of all the probate assets owned by the decedent and a detailed listing of these assets and their estimated fair market value at the time of the decedent's death on the forms provided for the inventory (Form 22*, Exhibit 12.13, and Exhibit 12.14). The inventory should be made jointly by the personal representative and either the attorney or you. In practice, this becomes one of your more important paralegal tasks. Nonprobate assets are not included in the inventory but are listed separately for death tax purposes. The organization of the inventory and the degree of particularity with which items should be listed are matters of judgment, but the inventory should include serial numbers of certificates for stocks, automobiles, or deposits; account numbers for savings or checking; and legal descriptions of real property. Real property must be included in the inventory and the final account of the personal representative. The inventory should be well organized, complete, and accurate. The appraisers hired by the personal representative and appointed by the court (if required by state law or on demand by an interested party) can then expeditiously appraise and value the assets. **You Must** complete and file this inventory so all data will be available as necessary for the preparation of the

Inventory
A detailed list of property and other assets containing a description or designation of each specific item and its value at the time of the decedent's death.

---

*See Appendix A

Exhibit 12.13 Inventory and Appraisal

DE-160, GC-040

ATTORNEY OR PARTY WITHOUT ATTORNEY *(Name, state bar number, and address):* TELEPHONE AND FAX NOS.:	FOR COURT USE ONLY
ATTORNEY FOR *(Name):*	

SUPERIOR COURT OF CALIFORNIA, COUNTY OF

STREET ADDRESS:

MAILING ADDRESS:

CITY AND ZIP CODE:

BRANCH NAME:

ESTATE OF *(Name):*

☐ DECEDENT   ☐ CONSERVATEE   ☐ MINOR

INVENTORY AND APPRAISAL

☐ **Partial No.:**   ☐ **Corrected**

☐ **Final**   ☐ **Reappraisal for Sale**

☐ **Supplemental**   ☐ **Property Tax Certificate**

CASE NUMBER:

Date of Death of Decedent or of Appointment of Guardian or Conservator:

APPRAISALS

1. Total appraisal by representative, guardian, or conservator (Attachment 1): $
2. Total appraisal by referee (Attachment 2): $

                     TOTAL: $

DECLARATION OF REPRESENTATIVE, GUARDIAN, CONSERVATOR, OR SMALL ESTATE CLAIMANT

3. Attachments 1 and 2 together with all prior inventories filed contain a true statement of
   ☐ all   ☐ a portion   of the estate that has come to my knowledge or possession, including particularly all money and all just claims the estate has against me. I have truly, honestly, and impartially appraised to the best of my ability each item set forth in Attachment 1.

4. ☐ No probate referee is required   ☐ by order of the court dated *(specify):*

5. **Property tax certificate.** I certify that the requirements of Revenue and Taxation Code section 480
   a. ☐ are not applicable because the decedent owned no real property in California at the time of death.
   b. ☐ have been satisfied by the filing of a change of ownership statement with the county recorder or assessor of each county in California in which the decedent owned property at the time of death.

I declare under penalty of perjury under the laws of the State of California that the foregoing is true and correct.

Date:

▶

_ _
(TYPE OR PRINT NAME; INCLUDE TITLE IF CORPORATE OFFICER)   (SIGNATURE)

STATEMENT ABOUT THE BOND
(Complete if required by local court rule)

6. ☐ Bond is waived, or the sole fiduciary is a corporate fiduciary or an exempt government agency.
7. ☐ Bond filed in the amount of: $ ☐ Sufficient   ☐ Insufficient
8. ☐ Receipts for: $ have been filed with the court for deposits in a blocked account at *(specify institution and location):*

Date:

▶

_ _
(TYPE OR PRINT NAME)   (SIGNATURE OF ATTORNEY OR PARTY WITHOUT ATTORNEY)

(Continued on reverse)

Form Approved by the
Judicial Council of California
DE-160, GC-040 [Rev. January 1, 1998]
Mandatory Form [1/1/2000]

INVENTORY AND APPRAISAL

WEST GROUP
Official Publisher

Probate Code, §§ 2610-2616,
8800-8980

(continued)

Exhibit 12.13 Inventory and Appraisal—*continued*

ESTATE OF (*Name*):	CASE NUMBER:

☐ DECEDENT ☐ CONSERVATEE ☐ MINOR

DECLARATION OF PROBATE REFEREE

9. I have truly, honestly, and impartially appraised to the best of my ability each item set forth in Attachment 2.

10. A true account of my commission and expenses actually and necessarily incurred pursuant to my appointment is

Statutory commission: $

Expenses (*specify*): $

TOTAL: $

I declare under penalty of perjury under the laws of the State of California that the foregoing is true and correct.

Date:

▶

. . . .
(TYPE OR PRINT NAME)

_____
(SIGNATURE OF REFEREE)

INSTRUCTIONS

(See Probate Code sections 2610-2616, 8801, 8804, 8852, 8905, 8960, 8961, and 8963 for additional instructions.)

1. See Probate Code section 8850 for items to be included in the inventory.

2. If the minor or conservatee is or has been during the guardianship or conservatorship confined in a state hospital under the jurisdiction of the State Department of Mental Health or the State Department of Developmental Services, mail a copy to the director of the appropriate department in Sacramento (Prob. Code, § 2611).

3. The representative, guardian, conservator, or small estate claimant shall list on Attachment 1 and appraise as of the date of death of the decedent or date of appointment of the guardian or conservator at fair market value moneys, currency, cash items, bank accounts and amounts on deposit with each financial institution (as defined in Probate Code section 40), and the proceeds of life and accident insurance policies and retirement plans payable upon death in lump sum amounts to the estate, except items whose fair market value is, in the opinion of the representative, an amount different from the ostensible value or specified amount.

4. The representative, guardian, conservator, or small estate claimant shall list in Attachment 2 all other assets of the estate which shall be appraised by the referee.

5. If joint tenancy and other assets are listed for appraisal purposes only and not as part of the probate estate, they must be separately listed on additional attachments and their value excluded from the total valuation of Attachments 1 and 2.

6. Each attachment should conform to the format approved by the Judicial Council (see *Inventory and Appraisal Attachment* (form DE-161, GC-041) and Cal. Rules of Court, rule 201).

DE-160, GC-040 [Rev. January 1, 1998]   **INVENTORY AND APPRAISAL**   WEST GROUP
Official Publisher   Page two

Source: Reprinted with permission from California Forms: Legal and Business. Copyright © by West Group.

Exhibit 12.14 Inventory

STATE OF WISCONSIN, CIRCUIT COURT, _____ **COUNTY** **-PROBATE-**

IN THE MATTER OF THE ESTATE OF

_____

_____ } **INVENTORY**

File No. _____

I, the undersigned personal representative, certify that to the best of my knowledge this Inventory (with attached schedules) includes all property, encumbrances, liens or charges of the decedent required to be shown and identifies marital property, if any.

Subscribed and sworn to before me

on _____

_____   _____
Notary Public, Wisconsin   Signature

My commission expires: _____   _____
                                                                                                          Signature

SUMMARY OF PROPERTY (Value of Decedent's Interest at Date of Death)	Date of Death	TOTAL VALUES
1. PROPERTY SUBJECT TO ADMINISTRATION		
(a) Net Value of Property Other Than Marital Property (Individual and Predetermination Date Property)	$_____ *	
(b) Net Value of Decedent's Interest in Marital Property	$_____ *	
NET VALUE OF PROPERTY SUBJECT TO ADMINISTRATION		$_____
2. PROPERTY NOT SUBJECT TO ADMINISTRATION		
(a) Net Value of Decedent's Interest in Joint Property	$_____ *	
(b) Net Value of Decedent's Interest in Survivorship Marital Property	$_____ *	
(c) Other (s. 814.66, Wis. Stats.)	$_____ *	
NET VALUE OF PROPERTY NOT SUBJECT TO ADMINISTRATION		$_____
TOTAL VALUE OF PROPERTY		$_____

*ATTACH SCHEDULES SHOWING DETAILS.

PR-1422, 3/86-(19A) INVENTORY
s. 858.01 and 858.07, Wisconsin Statutes

Wisconsin Legal Blank Co., Inc.
Milwaukee, WI

Source: Wisconsin Legal Blank Co., Inc. Reprinted with permission.

federal estate tax return, and you must mail or deliver copies of the inventory to the surviving spouse, beneficiaries, devisees, heirs, creditors, and all interested parties who requested a copy. Some states do not require an inventory to be filed and use their state death tax return instead. Often both of these documents are filed at the same time for those states that use an inventory. The time limit for filing the inventory is determined by state statute, but is usually between sixty and ninety days. As previously mentioned, the value of securities for purposes of the inventory is generally computed as of the date of the decedent's death or the alternate valuation date, as are all the other assets, and must include the following often forgotten items: (1) interest and rent accrued at the date of death and (2) any dividends declared before death. A preliminary or partial inventory can be made if it is necessary to sell assets before the inventory and appraisal can be completed; if additional property is found, an amended inventory may be required.

Appraisal (appraisement)
A true and just valuation of the decedent's real or personal property by a recognized expert (appraiser).

22. *Prepare an appraisal.* An **appraisal** or **appraisement** is a true and just valuation of the decedent's real or personal property by a recognized expert called an appraiser. The inventory and appraisal are often combined on the same form and, therefore, are filed together. All estate property must be appraised, but if the value of the property can be easily estimated, the personal representative is allowed to do it. When the estate property is real estate or expensive personal property such as art, jewelry, antiques, collections of coins or stamps, furs, boats, or aircraft, **You Must** employ professional appraisers, or the court will appoint them (usually two are selected). Once the inventory is completed and the personal representative has signed an oath stating that all known property of the decedent has been inventoried, ask the clerk which type of appraisers you will need and, if court-appointed appraisers are necessary, how to contact them. Generally, if real property is involved, the appraisers are real estate agents or brokers selected from the local real estate association. An appraiser must not have any interest in the estate or property.

In states that require appointment of appraisers, the probate judge generally appoints qualified persons to determine the value of the particular type of property of the estate (Form 21*). Often the appointment is made at the original hearing without the necessity of filing a petition. Even in those states in which appointment of appraisers is not required, the personal representative, the court, or any interested party may request a professional appraisal.

Before the appraisers begin their work, they should sign the oath of appraisers (Form 23*). Then, accompanied by the attorney or more often by you, they should complete their work. Appraisers are often used to resolve disagreements between heirs or devisees about the value of the decedent's property. They are also used when the beneficiaries are uncertain about the property's true market value.

After a written appraisal is obtained, you will assign the appraised fair market value to each property item as of the date of the decedent's death or the alternate valuation date and ensure the personal representative files this inventory and appraisal with the probate court and pays the appraisers' fees. The normal fee for each appraiser is generally set by statute (either a percentage of the estate or whatever the court determines to be fair and reasonable). Some states set minimum and/or maximum appraisal fees depending on the size of the estate. Other states no longer permit percentage fees. Fees charged by the appraisers can be deducted as a proper administration expense on both federal and state estate tax returns.

*See Appendix A

23. *Prepare a schedule of nonprobate assets.* Previously, we have discussed probate and nonprobate assets (property). In summary, property that passes by will is probate property and is the only property subject to estate administration. After the decedent's assets have been collected and the inventory and appraisal have been completed, assets that are not part of the probate estate but are included in the decedent's gross estate for estate tax purposes must be identified. All such assets are exempt from creditors' claims since only probate assets are subject to the debts of the decedent. Exhibit 12.15 contains examples of nonprobate and probate assets.

24. *File the inventory and appraisal.* When completed, the original Inventory and Appraisal form with attached appraisal reports from any independent or court-appointed appraisers, is filed with the probate court. **You Must** also mail copies to the surviving spouse and interested persons, i.e., heirs, beneficiaries, devisees, and creditors who have requested it.

DISTRIBUTION OF THE ESTATE AND PAYMENT OF CLAIMS

The following procedures are essential for the distribution of a decedent's estate:

25. Distribute family allowances (including maintenance) and/or exempt property to surviving spouse and/or minor children.

26. Attend hearing on creditors' claims and pay allowed or approved claims.

27. Transfer of assets—real estate and securities (corporate stock). See 27A and 27B.

Exhibit 12.15 Nonprobate and Probate Assets

Nonprobate Assets Not Subject to Creditors' Claims but are Subject to Federal Estate Tax	Probate Assets Subject to Creditors' Claims and Federal Estate Tax
1. Real property owned in joint tenancy or tenancy by the entirety.	1. Real property owned in severalty (single) ownership or tenancy in common.
2. Personal property owned in joint tenancy or tenancy by the entirety (automobile, stocks and bonds, jewelry, art, savings and checking accounts, etc.)	2. Personal property owned in severalty or as tenants in common (jewelry, art, automobile, boat, coin collection, stocks and bonds, bank accounts, etc.).
3. Life insurance proceeds with a named beneficiary and not payable to the estate so long as the policyholder retains incidents of ownership.	3. Life insurance proceeds payable to the estate.
4. Annuity contracts with named beneficiary (not the estate).	4. Debts owed the decedent (mortgage, promissory notes, contracts for deed, loans, rents, dividends, income tax refunds, interest, royalties, copyrights, etc.).
5. Employment contract benefits that contain named beneficiary (pension, profit-sharing, 401[k], group life insurance, etc.) and not payable to the estate.	5. Sale of business.
6. Individual retirement accounts (IRAs) with named beneficiary (not the estate).	6. Social Security, Railroad Retirement, and Veterans Administration benefits.
7. Trusts (Totten trust and living trust).	7. Civil lawsuit for money damages.
8. U.S. savings bonds payable on death to a named beneficiary (not the estate).	8. Testamentary trusts.

25. *Distribute family allowances (including maintenance) and/or exempt property to surviving spouse and/or minor children.* After the property is appraised, and the Inventory and Appraisal form is filed, the surviving spouse or minor children, or the guardian of minor children, may submit a petition to set apart the exempt personal property of the decedent allowed by statute whether the decedent died testate or intestate (Form 24*). **You Must** prepare the petition. Most states grant the family allowance and/or exempt property to a surviving spouse and/or minor children, and some states also grant a homestead allowance or exemption prior to the payment of any creditor claims, but care must be taken to avoid premature or improper distributions. Some states, e.g., Pennsylvania, include the family allowance or exemption in their priority of payment of debts (see the later discussion). After approving the petition, the court will issue an order "setting apart" said property (Form 25*). In some states, separate petitions and orders are used, one for the homestead, another for the personal property.

We have already discussed the types and value of the property that can be set aside according to one state's law (see Chapter 4). If the homestead passes directly by state statute to the surviving spouse and/or the minor children, you also determine if the state exempts the homestead from inheritance taxation. If a fee simple ownership in the homestead passes directly to a surviving spouse, federal tax law will allow the homestead to qualify as part of the marital deduction for federal estate tax purposes. It would not qualify for the marital deduction if the spouse receives only a life estate in the homestead (IRC § 2056). *Note:* State statutes should be consulted to determine if any family allowance or exemption is allowed for inheritance tax purposes. No federal estate tax deduction is granted for such property (see IRC §§ 2056 and, generally, 2053–2057, 2106).

Until final settlement of the estate, the surviving spouse and/or minor children may receive reasonable maintenance from the assets of the estate. The amount is determined by the value of the estate and the socioeconomic status of the decedent, but compare Tex. Prob. Code Ann. § 288, where no family allowance is granted if the surviving spouse has adequate separate property. State statutes determine the length of time the family may receive maintenance (e.g., usually twelve to eighteen months). The court, at its discretion, may lengthen this period. In most states, the statutory family allowances including maintenance are exempt from the claims of all creditors, including claims for administration of the estate and funeral expenses, but compare 20 Pa. Stat. Ann. § 3392, where a family allowance (exemption) is granted after administration expenses. The Petition for an Order Allowing Maintenance and the order from the court granting it to the decedent's family are found on Forms 26* and 27*.

26. *Attend hearing on creditors' claims and pay allowed or approved claims.* After the family allowances (including maintenance) and exempt property have been set apart (granted), the decedent's valid and approved debts must be paid before any of the decedent's assets can be distributed to the beneficiaries, devisees, or heirs of the estate. Those to whom the decedent owed money are given actual notice or notice through publication (see Items 5 and 16) that their debtor has died and they must file their claims with the probate court or with the decedent's personal representative within the time period set by each state.

---

*See Appendix A

What You Do:

- You collect and keep complete records of all claims sent to the personal representative and those filed with the probate court.
- You determine and verify all claims have been filed within the required time period.
- You refer the personal representative to the attorney for legal advice to contest any claim. If appropriate, the clerk of court should be contacted to help explain the procedures to deny claims.

Statutes have established a definite time and procedure to file and hear creditors' claims. In most states, the time limits for creditors to file their claims are established by either (1) the court's order setting the date for the hearing of the Petition to Prove the Will or the Petition for Administration or (2) the official appointment of the personal representative and the issuance of Letters. For this purpose, creditors should use the Proof of Claim form containing the claimant's address and signature and the affirmation of a notary public (Form 59*, Exhibit 12.16, and Exhibit 12.17). Section 3–804 of the Uniform Probate Code allows a claimant to file the claim with the probate court or "deliver or mail to the personal representative a written statement of claim." If the claim is based on any written instrument, such as a contract, promissory note, or bank draft, the claimant must attach a copy of the instrument to the Proof of Claim. Records must be kept of all claims.

In many states, creditors have from two to six months from the date of the first publication of notice to creditors to file their claims; alternatively, the time period commences after the "Letters" are issued by the court and the personal representative is officially appointed. An estate cannot be closed before this time period has expired. If the claimant does not act within the time allowed, the right to present the claim, even if valid, is lost. **You Must** remind the personal representative that payment of late claims will create personal liability. If, however, the claimant can demonstrate a good reason for requesting an extension, the court may extend the period by giving notice to the personal representative.

During and after the time period for filing claims, **You Must** check with the personal representative to determine whether any of the claims should be contested. If the decision is made to contest a claim, the personal representative must, before or on the date of the hearing, file all objections to the claim or file a claim against the claimant (a counterclaim) asserting that the decedent was actually entitled to the property. The document you prepare to file an objection or counterclaim is called the Objection to Claim and is served on the claimant and filed with the probate court. Contested claims are not heard on the date set for hearing allowed claims, but on another hearing date, for which arrangements must be made. Notice of this second date for contested claims must be given to the creditors.

The personal representative of the estate can admit, in writing, the claims that are valid and proper debts of the decedent. All contested claims must be proven legitimate at this second hearing in order to be allowed (approved) by the court. Also, claims of the personal representative or claims in which the personal representative has an interest are allowed only if proven by evidence satisfactory to the court. Once the claims are allowed, it is the duty of the personal representative to pay them and to file receipts or vouchers (canceled checks). **You Must** keep records of all

---

*See Appendix A

Exhibit 12.16 Creditor's Claim

DE-17

ATTORNEY OR PARTY WITHOUT ATTORNEY *(Name, state bar number, and address):*	TELEPHONE AND FAX NOS.:	*FOR COURT USE ONLY*

ATTORNEY FOR *(Name):*

SUPERIOR COURT OF CALIFORNIA, COUNTY OF

STREET ADDRESS:

MAILING ADDRESS:

CITY AND ZIP CODE:

BRANCH NAME:

ESTATE OF *(Name):*

DECEDENT

CREDITOR'S CLAIM	CASE NUMBER:

You must file this claim with the court clerk at the court address above before the LATER of (a) four months after the date letters (authority to act for the estate) were first issued to the personal representative, or (b) sixty days after the date the *Notice of Administration* was given to the creditor, if notice was given as provided in Probate Code section 9051. You must also mail or deliver a copy of this claim to the personal representative and his or her attorney. A proof of service is on the reverse.

WARNING: Your claim will in most instances be invalid if you do not properly complete this form, file it on time with the court, and mail or deliver a copy to the personal representative and his or her attorney.

1. Total amount of the claim: $
2. Claimant *(name):*
   a. ☐ an individual
   b. ☐ an individual or entity doing business under the fictitious name of *(specify):*

   c. ☐ a partnership. The person signing has authority to sign on behalf of the partnership.
   d. ☐ a corporation. The person signing has authority to sign on behalf of the corporation.
   e. ☐ other *(specify):*
3. Address of claimant *(specify):*

4. Claimant is ☐ the creditor ☐ a person acting on behalf of creditor *(state reason):*

5. ☐ Claimant is ☐ the personal representative ☐ the attorney for the personal representative
6. I am authorized to make this claim which is just and due or may become due. All payments on or offsets to the claim have been credited. Facts supporting the claim are ☐ on reverse ☐ attached.

I declare under penalty of perjury under the laws of the State of California that the foregoing is true and correct.

Date:

▶

. . . .
(TYPE OR PRINT NAME AND TITLE)   (SIGNATURE OF CLAIMANT)

INSTRUCTIONS TO CLAIMANT

A. On the reverse, itemize the claim and show the date the service was rendered or the debt incurred. Describe the item or service in detail, and indicate the amount claimed for each item. Do not include debts incurred after the date of death, except funeral claims.

B. If the claim is not due or contingent, or the amount is not yet ascertainable, state the facts supporting the claim.

C. If the claim is secured by a note or other written instrument, the original or a copy must be attached *(state why original is unavailable.* If secured by mortgage, deed of trust, or other lien on property that is of record, it is sufficient to describe the security and refer to the date or volume and page, and county where recorded. *(See Prob. Code, § 9152.)*

D. Mail or take this original claim to the court clerk's office for filing. If mailed, use certified mail, with return receipt requested.

E. Mail or deliver a copy to the personal representative and his or her attorney. Complete the *Proof of Mailing or Personal Delivery* on the reverse.

F. The personal representative or his or her attorney will notify you when your claim is allowed or rejected.

G. Claims against the estate by the personal representative and the attorney for the personal representative must be filed within the claim period allowed in Probate Code section 9100. See the notice box above.

(Continued on reverse)

Form Approved by the Judicial Council of California DE-172 [Rev. January 1, 1998]	**CREDITOR'S CLAIM** (Probate)	**WEST GROUP** Official Publisher	Probate Code, §§ 9000 et seq., 915

(continued)

Exhibit 12.16 Creditor's Claim—*continued*

ESTATE OF *(Name):*		CASE NUMBER:
	DECEDENT	

Date of item	**FACTS SUPPORTING THE CREDITOR'S CLAIM** ☐ **See attachment** *(if space is insufficient)* Item and supporting facts	Amount claimed
	TOTAL:	$

PROOF OF ☐ **MAILING** ☐ **PERSONAL DELIVERY** **TO PERSONAL REPRESENTATIVE**
(Be sure to mail or take the original to the court clerk's office for filing)

1. I am the creditor or a person acting on behalf of the creditor. At the time of mailing or delivery I was at least 18 years of age.
2. My residence or business address is *(specify):*

3. I mailed or personally delivered a copy of this *Creditor's Claim* to the personal representative as follows *(check either a or b below):*
    a. ☐ **Mail.** I am a resident of or employed in the county where the mailing occurred.
        (1) I enclosed a copy in an envelope AND
            (a) ☐ **deposited** the sealed envelope with the United States Postal Service with the postage fully prepaid.
            (b) ☐ **placed** the envelope for collection and mailing on the date and at the place shown in items below following our ordinary business practices. I am readily familiar with this business' practice for collecting and processing correspondence for mailing. On the same day that correspondence is placed for collection and mailing, it is deposited in the ordinary course of business with the United States Postal Service in a sealed envelope with postage fully prepaid.
        (2) The envelope was addressed and mailed first-class as follows:
            (a) Name of personal representative served:
            (b) Address on envelope:

            (c) Date of mailing:
            (d) Place of mailing *(city and state):*
    b. ☐ **Personal delivery.** I personally delivered a copy of the claim to the personal representative as follows:
        (1) Name of personal representative served:
        (2) Address where delivered:

        (3) Date delivered:
        (4) Time delivered:

I declare under penalty of perjury under the laws of the State of California that the foregoing is true and correct.
Date:

▶

· ·
_____
(TYPE OR PRINT NAME OF CLAIMANT)

_____
(SIGNATURE OF CLAIMANT)

DE-172 [Rev. January 1,1998]

CREDITOR'S CLAIM
(Probate)

WEST GROUP
Official Publisher

Page two

Source: Reprinted with permission from California Forms: Legal and Business. Copyright © by West Group.

Exhibit 12.17   Claim Against Estate

STATE OF WISCONSIN, CIRCUIT COURT, _____ **COUNTY**   **-PROBATE-**

IN THE MATTER OF THE ESTATE OF

_____

_____   } **CLAIM AGAINST ESTATE**

File No. _____

Name of claimant: _____

STATEMENT OF CLAIM: (*If a claim is founded on a written instrument, a copy with all endorsements must be attached.*)

If the decedent was survived by a spouse, the classification of the obligation is as follows:

☐ Support obligation owed spouse or child [s. 766.55(2)(a), Wis. Stats.].
☐ Obligation incurred in the interest of the marriage [s. 766.55(2)(b), Wis. Stats.].
☐ Obligation incurred prior to marriage or prior to January 1, 1986 [s. 766.55(2)(c), Wis. Stats.].
☐ Tort [s. 766.55(2)(cm), Wis. Stats.].
☐ Other [s. 766.55(2)(d), Wis. Stats.].

I swear that this statement is correct and there is due to claimant from this estate

$ _____

No payments have been made which are not credited, and there are no offsets except as stated above.

Subscribed and sworn to before me

on _____   _____
                                                          Signature of Claimant

_____   _____
        Notary Public, Wisconsin   Address

My commission expires: _____   _____

_____
        Attorney for Claimant

_____
        Address

_____

NOTE: A statutory filing fee of $3.00 shall accompany each claim.

PR-1421, 3/86-(25A) CLAIM AGAINST ESTATE   s. 859.13, Wisconsin Statutes   Wisconsin Legal Blank Co., Inc.
                                                                                         Milwaukee, WI

Source: Wisconsin Legal Blank Co., Inc. Reprinted with permission.

payments for the Final Account (Form 32* and Exhibit 12.18) when it is presented to the probate court. Payments to creditors should be made from the estate checking account. *Note:* Creditors' debts are generally payable only from probate assets, but taxes due are payable from *both* probate and nonprobate assets.

The laws that regulate probate procedures have given certain kinds of debts priority. In the event assets of the decedent's estate are insufficient to pay all valid creditors' claims in full, all states have statutes that set the priority of payment of debts. In most states, any or all of the following may be paid before the debts: maintenance and family allowances, homestead allowance or exemption, and the exempt property. The priority of debts in the following Pennsylvania statute is typical:

> *20 Pa. Stat. Ann. § 3392* Classification and Order of Payment
> If the applicable assets of the estate are insufficient to pay all proper charges and claims in full, the personal representative, subject to any preference given by law to claims due the United States, shall pay them in the following order, without priority as between claims of the same class:
> (1) The costs of administration.
> (2) The family exemption.
> (3) The costs of the decedent's funeral and burial, and the costs of medicines furnished to him within six months of his death, of medical or nursing services performed for him within that time, of hospital services including maintenance provided him within that time, and of services performed for him by any of his employees within that time.
> (4) The cost of a gravemarker.
> (5) Rents for the occupancy of the decedent's residence for six months immediately prior to his death.
> (6) All other claims, including claims by the Commonwealth [compare UPC § 3–805].

Notice that, unlike many states, the Pennsylvania statute lists the costs of administration before the amount of the family exemption granted in Pennsylvania.

Example: In Pennsylvania, Rashanna's estate has assets worth $40,500. The approved claims against her estate are as follows:
a. $2,500 in administration expense.
b. $6,000 for family exemption.
c. $4,000 for funeral and burial.
d. $50,000 for medical, hospital, and nursing expenses.
e. $2,000 in credit card expenses.

The $2,500 in administration expenses is paid first; then the $6,000 family exemption is granted; next, since the funeral/burial expenses ($4,000) and the expenses for medical, hospital, and nursing services ($50,000) are on the same priority level (3) and their sum exceeds the remaining assets of the estate, each creditor on that level gets a prorated share of the remaining assets calculated as follows:

Total estate assets	$40,500
Less administration expenses and family exemption	8,500
Remaining estate assets	$32,000
Combined level 3 claims	$54,000
Percentage of remaining assets to level 3 claims	59.259%

*See Appendix A

Exhibit 12.18 Final Account and Petition

STATE OF WISCONSIN, CIRCUIT COURT, _____ COUNTY   -PROBATE-

IN THE MATTER OF THE ESTATE OF

_____

_____ } **FINAL ACCOUNT AND PETITION**

File No. _____

I, the personal representative of this estate, certify that this Final Account is true and correct, and this estate is ready for final settlement.

The following is my account of the administration of this estate from

_____ to _____

ATTACH SCHEDULES SHOWING DETAILS AND A LIST OF INTERESTED PERSONS (Include Addresses).

RECEIPTS		ITEMS	DISBURSEMENTS		ITEMS
Inventoried Assets		$	Funeral Expenses	(Schedule F)	$
Added Property	(Schedule A)		Debts	(G)	
Dividends	(B)		Claims by Judgment	(H)	
Interest	(C)		Taxes Paid	(I)	
Capital Gains (Losses)	(D)		Interest Paid	(J)	
Other Receipts	(E)		Administration Expenses		
			Other Than Fees	(K)	
			Other Payments	(L)	
			Distributions Paid to Date	(M)	
			TOTAL DISBURSEMENTS		$
			Assets on Hand	(N)	$
BALANCING TOTALS		$			$

Assets on Hand (Schedule N) $ _____

Less Requested Fees:

   Attorney $ _____

   Personal Representative   _____

   Guardian Ad Litem   _____ - $ _____

BALANCE AVAILABLE FOR DISTRIBUTION $ _____

Schedule O, showing the proposed distribution of the balance is attached.

The personal representative requests that the Court schedule a hearing to approve this account, the classification of assets, and the allocation of expenses; to certify that the decedent's interest in life estates and joint tenancies has terminated and that survivorship marital property has vested in the surviving spouse; and to assign the assets of the estate.

Subscribed and sworn to before me

                                                   _____

                                                      Signature of Personal Representative

on _____

                                                      _____

                                                      Name (Typed)

_____

                       Notary Public, Wisconsin   Address

My commission expires: _____

PR-1423, 3/86-(27A) FINAL ACCOUNT AND PETITION   s. 862.07, Wisconsin Statutes

Source: Wisconsin Legal Blank Co., Inc. Reprinted with permission.

There are ten creditors in priority level 3 with claims of varying amounts for a total of $54,000. Each creditor will receive 59.259 percent of his total claim using up the remaining $32,000 of estate assets. The credit card company would receive nothing for its $2,000 claim.

For the priority of creditors' claims as set out in Section 3–805 of the Uniform Probate Code, see Exhibit 12.19.

One of the personal representative's primary functions is to pay all approved creditors' claims from the estate assets according to the domiciliary state's statutory list of priorities. **You Must** identify, locate, and give notice to all creditors and then review their claims. Your next tasks will be to classify the approved claims

ETHICAL ISSUE

and categorize them by priority. *The accuracy of your classification must, of course, be confirmed by your supervising attorney.* All creditors must be paid according to their priority rights before the personal representative can distribute the balance of the estate assets according to the decedent's will or by intestacy when the decedent died without a will.

Remember: Only probate assets of the decedent's estate are subject to creditors' claims. Nonprobate assets and statutory allowances or exemptions are not.

Since creditors have a prior claim to the assets of the decedent's estate, the named devisees of the testator or the heirs may receive nothing from the estate through the will or the intestate statute. It is quite possible that no assets will be left after all the creditors have been paid. An estate that has more debts than assets is called an insolvent estate. Unless they are co-signers with the decedent on any of the debts, the spouse and family have no personal liability to pay all or any part of the debts. The decedent's probate estate is solely responsible.

▥ ASSIGNMENT 12.1

Erma Gledig dies and leaves the bills listed below. According to your state law, in what order are the following to be paid, if at all, by her executor, Sherwin Gledig, her husband?

1. Salary payable to Erma's nurse-companion for a week prior to Erma's death.
2. State inheritance tax due on a devise to Erma from her brother, who predeceased her.
3. Attorney's fee payable to a lawyer who advised Erma during a real estate transaction.
4. Claim for services rendered by the Cahill Funeral Home.
5. Claim from the U.S. Commissioner of Internal Revenue for income tax unpaid in the previous year.
6. Sherwin's executor's bond.
7. Unpaid installment on an automobile owned jointly by Erma and Sherwin.

27A. *Transfer of assets—real estate.* If the decedent's personal property is sufficient to pay the allowances, expenses, taxes, and the rest of the debts, all real estate will pass free and clear to the named devisees in the will or to heirs by intestate succession. Since title to real property vests in the devisees or heirs on the death of the owner, the personal representative is usually not authorized or obliged to take possession of the real estate but, if required, must manage it or verify that monthly mortgage payments, insurance premiums, real property taxes, utility bills, and maintenance expenses are paid until it is distributed to the devisees or heirs or sold. In addition, if the decedent's personal property assets are insufficient to pay the debts, the personal representative is obligated to divest possession of the real estate (excluding the homestead, if exempt) from the

1. **Costs and expenses of administration.** Expenses of the estate administration such as mailing and filing fees; court costs; publication and advertising expenses; renting an estate safe deposit box; opening an estate checking account; bond fees; costs for protecting, preserving, and selling estate property; appraisers' and auctioneers' costs; and attorney and personal representative fees are examples of debts within this priority.

2. **Reasonable funeral expenses.** As determined by the probate court, reasonable expenses include transporting the body to the funeral home; the funeral director's fees; burial or cremation costs; and payment for religious services, reception expenses, and other necessary funeral costs.

3. **Debts and taxes with preference under federal law.** Any financial obligations the decedent owed the federal government while alive, including debts and taxes, are the next priority. The federal estate tax is not included in this priority category, however, because it is a death tax, i.e., payable after death. The following are examples of federal debts and federal taxes included in this priority category:

Federal Debts

- Student loans
- Tax court judgments
- Fines for criminal convictions
- Overpayments for:
  - Medicare
  - Welfare benefits
  - Social Security benefits or disability
  - Veterans' benefits

Federal Taxes

- Individual income tax
- Gift tax
- Tax lien levied against the decedent for prior years

4. **Expenses of the last illness.** This category includes unpaid debts that were incurred during the decedent's last illness such as the following:
   - Reasonable and necessary medical (doctor), nurse, and hospital services
   - Hospice care
   - Outpatient and home health care by professional personnel
   - All prescription drugs
   - Physical, occupational, and speech therapy
   - Necessary medical equipment, e.g., walker, wheelchair, hospital beds, and the like
   - Drug and alcohol treatment
   - Personal live-in attendant, e.g., nurse or companion who cared for the decedent in the last months before death and may qualify for this category

5. **Debts and taxes with preference under state law.** Included are debts due the individual state government and state agencies and those due local, county, and city government agencies, which may be a state specific priority, e.g., a creditor priority for only the domiciliary state, not for other states where the decedent had debts or taxes that were due. State taxes are also part of this priority; however, state death taxes such as the inheritance tax, estate tax, and credit estate tax are excluded. The following are examples of items in this category:

State Debts

- Waste disposal
- Water and sewer charges
- Overpayments for:
  - Medicaid
  - Unemployment compensation
  - Worker's compensation

State Taxes

- Individual income tax
- Property tax
- Sales tax
- Gift tax
- Tax lien

Some states combine federal and state debts and taxes into one priority category.

6. **All other claims.** The remaining creditors of the decedent constitute the last category of priority creditors. Although a contract for personal services, e.g., a singer to perform a concert, a tailor to make a suit of clothes, a surgeon to perform an organ transplant, or a professional athlete to play a game, may obviously be terminated by injury or death, most other creditor claims are binding and can be collected from the decedent's estate.

Example: If Karl negligently causes bodily harm to Leonard or damages Leonard's property, or if Leonard sells a car to Karl or lends Karl money, and Karl dies before paying Leonard in each of these cases, Leonard is the creditor, and Karl's estate is responsible for these creditor's claims.

person with vested title and sell it to satisfy these obligations. Also, the court may decide the sale of the real estate is in the best interest of the persons with an interest in the realty and order such a sale. The homestead, however, may not be sold without written consent of the surviving spouse, which must be filed with the court.

The assistance of a real estate broker is usually obtained when real estate is to be sold. The sale can be accomplished in two ways: (1) if the decedent's will gives the personal representative the power to sell the estate's real estate, the personal representative needs no court order to proceed; (2) if the decedent had no will or failed to include in the will a power of sale, the personal representative may not proceed without a court order, which may authorize either a private or public sale of the real property. In either instance, the personal representative must execute numerous legal forms. **You Must** prepare all the necessary documents for execution by the personal representative and the purchasers including a certified copy of the will, a certified copy of the Order Admitting Will to Probate, a certified copy of the Letters Testamentary, and a Probate Deed (Form 31*). *Caution:* The personal representative may *not* sell, encumber, lease, or distribute real estate for thirty days from the date the Letters are issued.

If the decedent's will does not contain a power of sale or if the decedent dies intestate and the personal representative determines it is necessary to sell the real estate owned by the decedent, the probate court may authorize a *private sale* as requested. Note: The procedures that follow present the sale of real estate in the estate administration process in its most formal format. Most judges conduct these procedures less formally. **You Must** learn your local customs. The county clerk and staff will be an immense help and valuable advisers. They cannot give legal advice, such as how to fill out forms, but they will identify the required documents and review your executed forms to determine if they are complete and accurate.

What You Do:

- You must assist the personal representative to prepare and file a Petition to Sell-Mortgage-Lease Real Estate to be presented to the court after the Inventory and Appraisal has been filed.
- The probate judge signs the Order for Hearing Petition to Sell-Mortgage-Lease Real Estate requested by the personal representative. The order sets the date, place, and time for the hearing and must be published and printed in the same manner as the hearing to prove the will. You send notice of this hearing in the form of the publication or a copy of the Order for Hearing to the devisees or heirs in order to comply with the general probate notice requirements.
- At the Hearing on the Petition to Sell-Mortgage-Lease, the personal representative presents certified copies of the will, the Order Admitting Will to Probate, the Letters Testamentary, and a Probate Deed, along with the probate judge's order and testifies to the facts set forth in the petition. If satisfied the need to sell the real estate exists, the judge signs the Order for Sale-Mortgage-Lease of Real Estate at Private Sale.

---

*See Appendix A

- When a considerable period of time has elapsed since the earlier order was issued, the court may require the real estate to be reappraised because of the possible substantial increase or decrease in the property's value. The form used is the Warrant to Appraisers at Private Sale. Therefore, you contact the appraisers who are usually the same persons who made the original appraisal. Once the market value of the realty has been determined, the property cannot be sold at private sale for less than that price. The appraisers sign the Oath of Appraisers and Appraisal of Lands Under Order for Sale.
- At its discretion, the court may require the personal representative to post an additional bond (Form 68*).
- Once the private sale is completed, you prepare and you or the personal representative files the Report of Sale of Land at Private Sale Under Order for Sale with the court.
- After the personal representative files the report and complies with the Order for Sale, the court approves the sale and enters its Order Confirming Private Sale of Real Estate (Form 30*). Next, the court authorizes the personal representative to execute and deliver the Probate Deed (Form 31*).
- To complete the sale and to ensure the buyer will have clear and marketable title to the land, you must verify the personal representative has filed the following in the county real estate recorder's office: certified copies of the Letters of Administration or Letters Testamentary, the Order for Sale of Real Estate at Private Sale, the Order Confirming Private Sale of Real Estate, and the Probate Deed issued by the personal representative, often called either the administrator's deed or the executor's deed.

Public sale of real estate may also be authorized by the court. The personal representative executes the same documents as those used in a private sale, including the Petition and Order for Hearing to Sell Real Estate; the Order for Sale of Real Estate at Public Auction; the Report of Sale of Land at Public Auction; and the Order Confirming Sale of Real Estate at Public Auction. **You Must** obtain these documents, file an additional bond, if necessary, and prepare and file certified copies of the same instruments used in the private sale previously mentioned. The only additional requirement for the public auction is if such a sale is authorized by the court, published notice of the time and place of the sale are often required for a specific statutory notice period. Proof of such publication must be filed with the court before the court will formally confirm the sale. You perform these tasks (see the procedures previously discussed).

27B. *Transfer of assets—securities (corporate stock).* As a general rule, stocks need not be transferred to the name of the personal representative of the estate. They may be left in the name of the decedent and sold or transferred to the persons entitled to them at the conclusion of the administration of the estate. *If the securities are sold, the proceeds must be placed in the estate checking account and not, even temporarily, in the personal representative's account.* Whenever stock is transferred from one person to another, whether by sale, gift, devise, or inheritance, the transfer is handled by a transfer agent or corporation. A transfer agent (often a bank) is the party designated by the corporation as the one to be contacted whenever a stock transfer, e.g., a sale or gift of stock, is performed. When

◄ ETHICAL ISSUE

---

*See Appendix A

the decedent's stock is to be transferred to a devisee under the will or an heir under intestacy proceedings, **You Must** give the transfer agent the following:

- The stock certificate which represents the number of shares to be transferred, endorsed (signed) by the personal representative, whose signature is guaranteed by a bank or a member firm of the New York Stock Exchange.
- A certified copy of the Letters Testamentary or Letters of Administration.
- A certified copy of the Decree of Distribution (Form 37*).
- The name, address, and Social Security number of the devisee or heir receiving the stock.

If the securities are registered in the name of the decedent and another person as joint tenants, a transfer from joint tenancy to sole ownership requires, in addition to the documents and data mentioned above, that you send to the transfer agent a certified copy of the decedent's death certificate, an Affidavit of Survivorship (see Exhibit 12.7), and a state inheritance tax waiver for those states that require a stock transfer tax to be paid. After these required documents are received, the transfer agent changes the registry on the corporate books by writing in the new owner's name and address and issues new stock certificates to the new owner. Questions about transferring corporate stock can best be answered by contacting the appropriate stock transfer agent.

If the decedent lived in a rural area, you should make inquiries concerning the decedent's ownership of stock in a grain elevator, creamery, or other farmer cooperatives. It is possible the decedent kept no records of such stock ownership in obvious locations such as the safe deposit box or at home; consequently, a thorough check of outside sources (e.g., the associations themselves) is necessary.

If the decedent owned any U.S. savings bonds that were not redeemed before death, they should be presented immediately for payment if they have matured and no longer bear interest. Most banks are able to assist the personal representative to reissue bonds in the name of the distributee, if that is the person's preference. The personal representative will be required to endorse the existing bonds in the presence of the appropriate bank official.

THE FINAL ACCOUNT AND CLOSING THE ESTATE

Before the probate court can discharge the personal representative, the following final procedures must be completed:

28. File the Final Account and Petition for Settlement and Distribution.
29. Request Order for Hearing on Final Account and Petition for Distribution.
30. Give notice of the hearing to interested parties.
31. Prepare and file copies of federal and state estate and income tax returns with the Final Account.
32. Explain and defend the Final Account and Petition for Distribution.
33. Request Order Allowing Final Account.
34. Compute and file state inheritance tax return or waiver.
35. Receive Order for Settlement and Decree of Distribution.
36. Collect receipts for assets by distributee.

---

*See Appendix A

37. File Petition for Discharge of Personal Representative.
38. Request Order Discharging Personal Representative.
39. Cancel personal representative's bond.

28. *File the Final Account and Petition for Settlement and Distribution.* Once all just claims have been paid and receipts for such payments collected, **You Must** prepare and the personal representative must file a verified (notarized) final account (Form 32* and Exhibit 12.18) and petition the court for settlement of the estate (Form 33*). Beginning with the original inventory, the personal representative's final account must show all changes in the assets of the estate, including debits and credits of cash and any interest that may have accrued during administration of the estate. This final account should fully disclose the balance of property available for distribution to named devisees under the will or to heirs by inheritance after the payment of creditors.

You Must identify property remaining on hand for distribution in such a way that the personal representative may readily determine the persons entitled to receive such property. The personal representative should keep vouchers in the form of canceled checks or receipts to substantiate the payments for any and all disbursements or for assets distributed during administration of the estate including the personal representative's own fees and claims against the estate, and you must keep records of all these matters.

You Must verify the final account is filed within the time allotted by statute for settlement of the estate, which in some states is one year from the date of the personal representative's appointment. For good cause, the probate court may grant an extended time for settlement.

The form for the final account lists the steps and information that must be included for the court's review. Incidental expenses (for miscellaneous items such as copies of the final decree and filing fees) necessarily occur after the final decree has been granted and can only be estimated.

29. *Request Order for Hearing on Final Account and Petition for Distribution.* The probate court issues an order for a hearing on the final account, setting the time and place for the hearing (Form 34*). Notice of the hearing must be published in conformity with the state's statutory requirements, e.g., publication of the notice once a week for two or three weeks in a legal newspaper in the county of the court's jurisdiction. As before, **You Must** handle this notice requirement. Either the newspaper is required to file an affidavit with the probate court to prove the notice was published and to send a copy of this proof to the personal representative or you must file the affidavit (Form 6*).

30. *Give notice of the hearing to interested parties.* On request of the personal representative, **You Must** give notice of the hearing to interested parties by mailing a copy of the court's order for a hearing to each devisee or heir within a statutory time period, e.g., at least fourteen days before the hearing. You also prepare an affidavit, which the personal representative submits to the court, verifying that notice has been mailed to these persons and also the state's tax official, e.g., the state officer of taxation (Form 35*).

31. *Prepare and file copies of federal and state estate and income tax returns with the Final Account.* Before the final account is allowed and the Decree of

---

*See Appendix A

Distribution is issued, **You Must** complete all federal and state death and income tax returns and file them with the final account (see Chapter 14).

32. *Explain and defend the Final Account and Petition for Distribution*. The hearing on the Final Account and Petition for Distribution gives all parties with an interest in the estate of the decedent the opportunity to appear and examine the personal representative's accounting. Explanations and corrections of the account and the intended distribution are discussed and resolved at this time. Then the personal representative requests the court accept the final account.

33. *Request Order Allowing Final Account*. After all taxes have been paid and the final account has been accepted, the court signs an Order Allowing Final Account (Form 36*).

34. *Compute and file state inheritance tax return or waiver*. In states that have an inheritance tax, **You Must** file a copy of the Order Allowing the Final Account with the state's official tax collector. You also prepare a tax return if an inheritance tax is due and is an obligation of the estate, in which case, the personal representative pays the tax after the final account has been allowed. If no tax is due, the personal representative prepares the tax waiver. Within a specified time after filing the tax return, objections to the amount of tax may be made. After this time period expires, the state inheritance tax return becomes final.

35. *Receive Order for Settlement and Decree of Distribution*. After the final account has been allowed, the court enters an Order of Complete Settlement of the Estate and Decree of Distribution (Form 37*). In its decree, the court determines the persons entitled to the estate, names the heirs, beneficiaries, or devisees, states their relationship to the decedent, describes the property, and determines the property to which each person is entitled. This decree also states: (1) that notice for the final hearing was duly given; (2) that the deceased died testate or intestate, including the date of death and the residency of the decedent; (3) that the estate has been fully administered, including the payment of all allowed claims, and administration, funeral, and last illness expenses; (4) that the final account has been approved and settled; and (5) that all inheritance, gift, estate, and income taxes have been paid.

Once the final decree is entered, the assets of the decedent's estate can be transferred. The personal representative distributes and passes legal title to personal property to the appropriate heirs, beneficiaries, or devisees. In some states, real property passes differently. Excluding the homestead, the right to possess the decedent's real property passes to the heirs or devisees after the Decree of Distribution is executed, but legal title may remain with the personal representative until a certified copy of the decree has been filed with the county real estate recorder or other official in the county where the land is located. The statutes of the individual state must be checked to determine the exact procedure.

Remember: To transfer legal title to real property held in joint tenancy by the decedent to the surviving joint tenant or tenants, the following must be filed with the county recorder: an Affidavit of Survivorship that has been certified by the state department of taxation, a certified copy of the death certificate, and a certified copy of the Decree of Distribution.

36. *Collect receipts for assets by distributee*. After all distributions have been made, the personal representative must collect receipts for all property distrib-

---

*See Appendix A

uted, real or personal, from each person to whom property has been distributed. **You Must** add these receipts to your records. The personal representative must file these receipts in order to account for all the assets transferred (Form 38*).

37. *File Petition for Discharge of Personal Representative.* When the distributions have been made and the receipts obtained from the heirs, beneficiaries, or devisees, the personal representative (executor or administrator) files a form **You Must** prepare called the Petition for Discharge of Personal Representative (Form 39*).

38. *Request Order Discharging Personal Representative.* After presenting the Petition for Discharge, the personal representative will request an Order for Discharge from the probate court. This order or, in some states, the form called the Order for Final Distribution terminates the potential personal liability of the personal representative. Local custom determines whether the attorney for the estate or the probate court prepares this order allowing the personal representative to close the estate (Form 40*). You may have to prepare this form.

39. *Cancel personal representative's bond.* **You Must** send a copy of the Order Discharging Personal Representative to the bonding company (surety) to cancel the personal representative's bond and request the return of any unused premium for the bond. This act terminates the administration of a decedent's estate.

SPECIAL PROBATE PROCEEDINGS

In certain circumstances, special probate proceedings may be required. They include special administration, administration of omitted property, and decree of descent.

Special Administration

In some states, special administration is a procedure used by the probate court to administer the estate of a decedent under specific circumstances. It has limited purposes and is commenced only when a good reason for it exists. Reasons for appointing a special administrator include the following: (1) to preserve the decedent's estate until an executor or administrator is appointed, e.g., in cases where a will or the appointment of an executor or administrator is being contested; and (2) to give immediate attention, when necessary, to the management of a business left by the decedent.

Special administration is accomplished in the following manner:

1. A person having an interest in the estate files a Petition for Appointment of a Special Administrator (Form 41*). The petition includes an itemized listing of the estate's real and personal property and a valid reason why it is necessary and expedient to have a special administrator appointed.

2. The judge signs the Order Granting Special Administration and appoints the special administrator (Form 42*).

3. The special administrator files the *bond* (Form 68*). The amount of the bond is fixed by the court. You must check individual state statutes to see if a bond is required.

---

*See Appendix A

4. The court issues Letters of Special Administration conferring appropriate powers on the special administrator (Form 43*).

5. The special administrator files an Inventory and Appraisal of the personal property of the decedent (Form 22*). As a rule, if another person is to act as general administrator, the special administrator does not take possession or control of real property. If there is to be a summary distribution without general administration, then the special administrator must include real estate in the inventory and may take possession of it.

6. The powers of the special administrator officially cease when the personal representative is appointed and the Letters Testamentary or Letters of Administration are issued. Before being discharged, the special administrator must file a Final Account and Report of the Special Administrator, including vouchers and receipts for all disbursements (Form 44*). This final account will also provide for all remaining assets of the estate to be delivered into the hands of the new personal representative.

7. The probate judge signs the Order Approving the Final Account and Report of the Special Administrator (Form 45*). The order allows the final account and discharges the special administrator and the sureties. When the special administrator and the personal representative are the same person, only one inventory and one final account need be filed.

Administration of Omitted Property

After the estate has been closed and the personal representative discharged, someone may discover additional property belonging to the decedent that has not been administered (e.g., rare books, to which the will referred but which could not be located during administration). Proper disposition of the assets will necessitate reopening the estate. A petition may be filed by any person claiming an interest in the omitted property (Form 46*). The court that has jurisdiction of the recently discovered assets will, on petition by the interested person, appoint a personal representative, the same person as previously appointed, if possible (see UPC § 3–1008). Reopening the estate and subsequent administration are both court-supervised proceedings. At the hearing on the petition, the court will determine to whom the omitted property will be distributed. The court can then, without notice, summarily decree the distribution of the property once all tax liability has been paid (Form 47*).

Decree of Descent

When more than three years have passed since the date of the decedent's death and no probate proceedings have been commenced, an interested party may petition the court to determine the descent of the decedent's property. The petition requires that a formal proceeding be held with notice and a hearing (Form 48*).

---

*See Appendix A

LIMITATIONS ON AND LIABILITY OF THE PERSONAL REPRESENTATIVE

Throughout the collection and management of the assets of an estate, the personal representative cannot personally profit because profit taking would violate the fiduciary duty to the estate. Therefore, the personal representative is not allowed to purchase property or encumbrances against the estate or to sell property to the estate while retaining a personal interest in the estate (compare UPC § 3–713).

> **Example:** Paulina Neven, the administratrix of Charlotte Neven's estate, obtained an order from the probate court allowing her to rent out land belonging to Charlotte while the estate was being settled. Paulina rents it to herself. If one of Charlotte's heirs objects to this apparent self-dealing, Paulina would have to prove that she had paid as much or more rent than anyone else would have been charged.

The personal representative who acts reasonably and in good faith faces no personal liability for decreases in the value of estate assets during administration. If decreases occur because of a breach of fiduciary duties due to negligence or delay, however, the court will impose damages on the personal representative to compensate the estate for the loss. The compensation, often called a **"surcharge,"** is paid by the personal representative out of her personal funds (compare UPC § 3–808).

Surcharge
An overcharge beyond what is just and right, e.g., an amount the fiduciary is required by court order to make good because of negligence or other failure of duty.

> **Example:** If in the above example the court had found Paulina guilty of self-dealing with the estate's assets, it would require her to compensate the estate, e.g., by paying, from her own funds, the amount of loss she had caused the estate.

When total assets of an estate are not sufficient to pay all approved debts and other charges against it, the law provides an order of priority for payments, as described earlier. The personal representative is individually liable for placing a less preferred creditor in a more favorable position than is appropriate and thus causing improper payment.

> **Example:** Charlotte died with unpaid bills for her last illness, federal taxes payable for the previous year, and a bill from a local grocery. Paulina pays the grocer's bill before the federal tax lien. Because the grocer is a "less preferred creditor," Paulina must pay the amount due the federal government from her own funds if the estate cannot pay it.

If the decedent's estate owes any federal taxes, the personal representative is held personally liable for any taxes that are not paid; see IRC § 2002.

KEY TERMS

Small estate	Common probate	Demand	Inventory
Qualified small estate	Citation	Deposition	Appraisal
Affiant	Claimant	Damages	(appraisement)
Solemn probate	Demandant	Cause of action	Surcharge

REVIEW QUESTIONS

1. What are the steps in the probate or estate administration of a decedent's estate? List each step and explain your function in the performance of each procedure.

2. What is the distinction, if any, in your state between the words *probate* and *estate administration?*

3. How are "small estates" administered in your state? What is the monetary limit in your state that allows an estate to be classified as a "small estate"?

4. How do the following differ: solemn v. common probate; formal v. informal probate; and solemn v. formal probate (under the UPC)?

5. When would you choose to follow formal (solemn) probate instead of informal (common) probate when administering a decedent's estate?

6. In what ways can a county clerk or registrar assist you in your estate administration tasks? What are some things they cannot do?

7. What information must you obtain to complete the form used to petition to probate a will? Are this information and the form the same when a person dies intestate?

8. In your state, what are the statutory requirements for giving notice to creditors? When and how is the notice given in your state, and what is the time limit creditors have to file their claims?

9. How is a personal representative appointed? What document authorizes a personal representative to manage a decedent's estate? How is a fiduciary employer identification number obtained, and for what purposes does a personal representative use it?

10. What are the various assets you will help the personal representative collect and preserve in an estate administration, and what procedures do you use for the collection? List ten assets.

11. What are the inventory and appraisal, and how are they prepared?

12. How does a creditor present a claim against the decedent's estate, and how does the personal representative contest a claim?

13. What is your state's priority for payment of creditors' claims? Cite the statute and give examples of items within each category.

14. How is the final account prepared, and what does it contain?

15. At what point can the personal representative transfer the decedent's assets (both real and personal property) to the appropriate parties? When does legal title pass to them?

16. Can a decedent have more than one domicile? How would you resolve this problem so that ancillary proceedings can be finalized?

17. What happens to property of the decedent that is discovered after the estate administration has been completed?

18. Who is responsible for paying a surcharge, and under what circumstances would this occur?

19. Should all states adopt the Uniform Probate Code? Explain.

CASE PROBLEMS

Problem 1

Jane M. Doe of 1005 Elm Street, St. Paul, Minnesota, died testate (with a will) on September 20, 2000. She was married to John C. Doe, age 83, and had one child, Sandy R. Doe, age 55. Mrs. Doe was born on November 6, 1912, in the state of Michigan. Her parents moved to Minnesota that year. On September 4, 1936, she married John C. Doe in St. Paul, Minnesota. Mrs. Doe was a retired real estate broker, and her legal residence (domicile) at the time of her death was St. Paul, Minnesota. Mrs. Doe died in the Porta Veta Hospital in St. Paul after suffering from cancer for approximately nine months. Her attending physician was Dr. Norma J. Dennison, 2067 Doctor's Exchange Building, St. Paul, Minnesota. Her attorneys were

Cranwall and Schuster, First Trust Company Building, St. Paul, Minnesota.

Beneficiaries under Mrs. Doe's will are her husband, John C. Doe, who is also the personal representative of the estate; daughter Sandy R. Doe; the American Cancer Society; Girls' Clubs of America; and the Newark Institute of Higher Learning. Beneficiaries under insurance contracts are her brother, Jay A. Daw; husband, John C. Doe; and the estate.

Exhibit 12.20 shows the assets that Mrs. Doe individually owned or in which she owned an interest as specified at her death. Exhibit 12.21 shows liabilities and debts owed by Mrs. Doe at her death. Exhibit 12.22 shows costs incurred after Mrs. Doe's death. Exhibit 12.23 shows the

Exhibit 12.20 Assets of Jane M. Doe

Cash*

Traveler's checks (not cashed)	$ 1,000
Checking account—First National City Bank of St. Paul no. 55–5555	50,000
Savings deposit—American National Bank of St. Paul no. 44–4444	15,000

Stocks and Bonds

Tenneco, Inc., 100 shares (6 months after Mrs. Doe's death decreased in value to $4,800)	$ 5,000
Minnesota Co-op, 1,000 shares	4,500
American National Slide Rule, 1,000 shares (joint tenancy with husband)	75,000
Minnesota Company, 100 shares (joint tenancy with daughter)	5,000

U.S. Government Bonds

Bond No. R4502363E	$ 574
Bond No. R4502364E	574

Personal Property

Clothing—personal effects	$ 4,500
Furs—mink coat	11,500
Automobile—1998 Mazda	12,000
Furniture and household goods	22,000

Real Property

Residential (homestead)	$350,000
1005 Elm Street	
St. Paul, MN	

Legal description: Lot 615, Block 42, Reiser's Addition to St. Paul
Mortgage $130,000 at St. Paul Bank and Trust Company

Rental Property

Duplex	$ 22,750
776 Cliff Road	
St. Paul, MN	

Legal description: Lots 16 & 17, Block 20, Lovey's Addition to St. Paul
  $91,000: ¼ interest = $22,750
Mortgage $10,000 at St. Paul Bank and Trust Company
  $40,000: ¼ interest = $10,000

Receivables

Johnson Furriers—Promissory Note (accrued interest = $350)	$ 10,350
Judgment against Forrest R. Redding	20,000

Interests in Trusts and Other Estates

St. Paul Trust Co.—Annual income to Mrs. Doe until her death, then to her daughter, Sandy R. Doe until her death. Established by Mrs. Doe's uncle.	$ 6,000 annual
Power of Appointment (general; unexercised)—To distribute income or corpus (500 shares Green Giant). Established by Mrs. Doe's father.	50,000

Insurance and Annuities

Prudential Life Insurance Company—No dividends. Beneficiary: Jay A. Daw (brother).	$ 50,000
Minnesota Life Insurance Company—Dividends. Beneficiary: Estate	120,000
Accumulated dividends.	100
Ecko Life Insurance Company (premiums of $50 per month paid by Order of the Doves). $100 per month to Mrs. Doe for life; then $100 per month to her husband for his life.	100 per month
Life expectancy of 4 years.	4,800 ($100 per month times 48 months)

---

*Note: Five months prior to her death, Mrs. Doe transferred funds from her checking account to her husband ($30,000) and to her daughter ($20,000). Mrs. Doe obtained this cash by selling Airco Corporation stock that she owned, and she then placed the cash in her checking account.

Exhibit 12.21 Liabilities and Debts of Jane M. Doe

Liabilities

Mortgage on homestead, 1005 Elm Street, St. Paul Bank and Trust Company	$130,000
Mortgage on duplex, 776 Cliff Rd., St. Paul Bank and Trust Company ($40,000; $1/4$ interest = $10,000).	10,000
Total	$140,000

Debts

Approved claims against the estate

Ace's Plumbing Co. (company claims *$480* is owed; Mrs. Doe's personal representative claims *$230* is owed) (contested claim)	$ 480
St. Paul Telephone Company	50
St. Paul Electric Company	100
Harvey's Garbage Pickup	50
Dr. Norma J. Dennison	600
St. Paul Rents (rental of wheelchair)	50
Total	$ 1,330

Exhibit 12.22 Costs Incurred after Jane Doe's Death

Funeral Expenses

Newark and Newark Funeral Home	$ 9,500
Morningside Florists	100
Riverside Cemetery	1,000
Brown Monument Company—gravestone	500
Rev. B. Stone	25
Total	$11,125

Administration Expenses

Philip Masterson Co., Inc., appraisals	$ 500
Smith & Smith, Inc., preparation of tax returns	250
Attorney's fees	15,000
Compensation of personal representative	10,000
Publication of orders	50
Certified copies	5
Bond premiums (none)	0
Miscellaneous expenses	450
Expenses of last illness unpaid at death (Porta Veta Hospital)	850
Total	$27,105

---

beneficiaries of Mrs. Doe's estate and the maintenance of the family during administration.

Forms must be completed (executed) for the formal probate of the Jane M. Doe estate. From the information given in the above exhibits, the following sample forms (found in Appendix A) have been executed.

1. Petition for Formal Probate of Will and for Formal Appointment of Personal Representative (Form 1*).

2. Notice and Order of Hearing on Petition for Probate of Will and Appointment of Personal Representative and Notice to Creditors (Form 3*).

Exhibit 12.23   Those Who Receive Benefits from the Estate of Jane M. Doe

Individuals
John C. Doe (husband)
  Under will—Any interest in real property, and residue after
    specific gifts (bequests) $502,378
    Joint tenancy—Stock   75,000
    Gift—Cash   30,000
Sandy R. Doe (daughter)
    Joint tenancy—Stock $ 5,000
    Gift—Cash   20,000
Jay A. Daw (brother)
    Life insurance policy $ 50,000
Charitable Devises
American Cancer Society
    Under will $ 10,000
Girls' Clubs of America
    Under will $ 5,000
Newark Institute of Higher Learning
    Under will $ 1,000
Estate
Life insurance policy (part of residue, see above) $120,100
Family Maintenance during Administration
$400 per month for 12 months $ 4,800

---

3. Proof of Placing Order for Publication (Form 5*).

4. Affidavit of Publication (Form 6*).

5. Affidavit of Mailing Order or Notice of Hearing (Form 7*).

6. Notice to Spouse and Children and Affidavit of Mailing (Form 8*).

7. Testimony of Witness to Will (Form 9*).

8. Order of Formal Probate of Will and Formal Appointment of Personal Representative (Form 11*).

9. Acceptance of Appointment as Personal Representative and Oath by Individual (Form 13*).

10. Bond, if required, or Request for Waiver of Bond (Form 15*).

11. Letters Testamentary (Form 16*).

12. Application for Employer Identification Number (Form 81*).

13. Notice Concerning Fiduciary Relationship (Form 82*).

14. Inventory (Form 22*).

15. Petition to Allow Selection of Personal Property (Form 24*).

16. Order Allowing Selection of Personal Property (Form 25*).

17. Petition for Family Maintenance (Form 26*).

18. Order for Family Maintenance (Form 27*).

19. Final Account (Form 32*).

20. Petition to Allow Final Account, Settle and Distribute Estate (Form 33*).

---

*See Appendix A

21. Notice and Order for Hearing on Petition for Formal Settlement of Estate (Form 34*).

22. Affidavit of Mailing Order or Notice of Hearing on Final Account (Form 35*).

23. Federal and state death and income tax returns (see Chapter 14).

24. Order Allowing Final Account (Form 36*).

25. Order of Complete Settlement of the Estate and Decree of Distribution (Form 37*).

26. Receipt for Assets by Distributee (Form 38*).

27. Petition for Discharge of Personal Representative (Form 39*).

28. Order Discharging Personal Representative (Form 40*).

A. Review the checklists shown in Exhibits 12.20 through 12.23 and the executed forms in Appendix A in the Jane M. Doe case. Develop checklists and add to your checklists the data necessary to fill in the required forms for formal (solemn) probate of a testator's estate in your state. Use and follow the probate procedures in your state to execute (complete) the necessary forms.

B. Using the facts and information you have added to complete the forms in the Jane M. Doe case above, identify and complete the forms for formal probate if Jane M. Doe had died intestate in your state.

---

*See Appendix A

INFORMAL PROBATE ADMINISTRATION

OBJECTIVES

After completing this chapter, you should be able to:

➤ Identify and explain the informal probate method of administering decedents' estates under the Uniform Probate Code.

➤ Recognize the circumstances under which informal probate procedures are appropriate.

➤ Explain the steps in informal probate administration of a decedent's estate.

➤ Apply the procedures and prepare the legal forms used in informal probate administration for a set of facts involving a decedent's estate.

SCOPE OF THE CHAPTER

This chapter outlines the method of selection and the proceedings involved in informal probate according to the Uniform Probate Code (UPC). The procedures are listed, the relevant UPC sections are cited, and sample forms that are available in Appendix A are identified. Next, a case study of an estate that would appropriately be administered by informal probate procedures is presented. You are taken step by step through the informal proceedings so you can become familiar with the procedures. Case problems involving both testate and intestate situations illustrate estate administrations that use informal probate procedures. Executed forms required for informal probate administration are available in Appendix A for your review.

THE CHOICE OF FORMAL OR INFORMAL PROBATE

The administration of a decedent's estate may be initiated by any of several procedures under the Uniform Probate Code.

- Formal appointment of the personal representative and formal proceedings thereafter, in testacy and intestacy (UPC §§ 3–401 through 3–414) (see the discussion in Chapter 12).
- Informal appointment of the personal representative and informal proceedings thereafter, in testacy and intestacy (UPC §§ 3–301 through 3–311).
- Collection of the decedent's personal property by Affidavit and Summary Administration proceedings thereafter for small or moderate-sized estates (UPC §§ 3–1201 through 3–1204) (see the discussion in Chapter 12).

Some states require the personal representative to follow a formal, also called solemn or probate in solemn form, procedure in the course of administration. Others combine the UPC procedures, noted above, with local practices such as elimination or lowering of the requirement for a personal representative's bond. The states that have adopted all or part of the UPC are able to offer the above-mentioned procedures. Note-worthy contributions of the UPC include the introduction of (1) procedures that are unsupervised or only partially supervised by the court and are called informal, common, or probate in common form, and (2) simplified affidavit or summary administration procedures that reduce the expenses of administration and make the transfer of small estates to the heirs or devisees easier. In view of the great diversity among state practices, even among those that have enacted the UPC, your wisest course is to become familiar with the laws and estate administration procedures of the state in which you live and work.

When one applies for the position of personal representative of an estate that exceeds the limits for summary administration proceedings (see Exhibit 12.2), the applicant may select a formal or informal method of settling the estate. The UPC defines formal proceedings as "those conducted before a judge with notice to interested persons" (UPC § 1–201[18]) and informal proceedings as "those conducted without notice to interested persons by an officer of the court acting as a registrar for probate of a will or appointment of a personal representative" (UPC § 1–201[23]). In informal probate, a court-appointed officer (registrar, surrogate, or Register of Wills) skilled in overseeing decedents' estates takes the place of the judge. That officer has the power to do whatever the judge normally would do (e.g., appoint the personal representative and make findings of fact in relation to the will).

The UPC allows a unique *in and out* method of settling estates—partly "in" the probate court (formally) even though most of the administration takes place "out" of it (informally). In informal proceedings, the personal representative or any person interested in the estate, as defined by UPC § 1–201(24), may petition the court to adjudicate a disputed issue (e.g., the amount of a creditor's claim). After settlement of the dispute, the personal representative may resume informal procedures. This flexible *in and out* use of formal proceedings within informal probate proves advantageous to the personal representative who prefers the freedom of informal probate but who may encounter a complexity the court is better suited or may be required to handle.

> **Example:** Reginald Canby died testate leaving all his property to his son, Damon. Reginald's wife predeceased him. Vanessa, Reginald's daughter, contends that Damon unduly influenced their father during his last illness to persuade him to write the will. Although the executor of Reginald's estate had elected to follow informal probate procedures, Vanessa may petition the probate court to settle this question using formal probate procedures. After the court has made its decision, it may allow the estate to resume informal probate or order it to continue formal, supervised probate (UPC §§ 3–501, 3–502).

Informal probate generally reduces the time required to complete the administration of a decedent's estate. It involves fewer steps and less complicated procedures (e.g., the filing of fewer papers) than formal probate. The estate can be more easily distributed since the personal representative does not have to give notice of hearings, or obtain court approval for every item distributed, and may not be required to obtain a bond or submit an account at the end, depending on the circumstances.

The personal representative may request formal court supervision at any time; however, informal probate does not demand the court supervise even the personal representative's closing of the estate after administering it. Since the purpose of informal probate is in part to help relieve congestion in the probate court, the greater part of informal probate transactions are carried out without the court's direct involvement. Not infrequently a hearing to prove the will and to appoint a personal representative is the only in-court proceeding. Of course, this is not always the case since any person interested in the estate (e.g., a creditor, heir, or devisee) may petition the court to determine a matter using formal proceedings.

> **Example:** Fred McManus dies intestate, survived by a son, Bruce, and a brother, Paul. The registrar, who is empowered to conduct informal probate proceedings, appoints Paul personal representative of Fred's estate. Bruce successfully challenges the informal appointment of his uncle, Paul. Therefore, the court will appoint a personal representative in a formal proceeding, according to the order of priority (see the next section).

Although informal probate eliminates the required appraisal of estate assets unless demanded by the personal representative, another interested party, or the court, the value of real estate and closely held businesses should be appraised by an independent expert. The personal representative is entitled to hire and pay the appraiser(s) out of estate assets (UPC § 3–707).

Example: According to her will, Tillie's estate is to be divided equally among her two sisters, Sherie and Noreen, and one brother, Waldo. Included in her estate are valuable paintings. Waldo, who is informally appointed to administer the estate, sets the value of the paintings at $50,000. The remaining property in the estate is sold at public auction for $100,000 cash. Waldo decides to keep the paintings for himself and give Sherie and Noreen each $50,000 in cash. The two sisters, who believe the art collection is worth much more, can demand that it be appraised by an art expert.

The availability of informal proceedings to probate a will and settle the estate is one of the chief advantages of the Uniform Probate Code.

PRIORITY OF PERSONS SEEKING APPOINTMENT AS PERSONAL REPRESENTATIVES

In both formal and informal proceedings, persons who qualify as personal representative of the estate are considered in the following order of priority:

1. The person named as personal representative in the will, if there is one.
2. The surviving spouse of the decedent who is a devisee of the decedent.
3. Other devisees of the decedent.
4. The surviving spouse of the decedent.
5. Other heirs of the decedent.
6. Any creditor of the decedent, provided no one with a higher priority standing has applied for appointment within forty-five days of the death of the decedent (UPC § 3–203[a]). Compare a non-Uniform Probate Code state statute, Mass. Gen. Laws Ann. ch. 193 § 1.

The person who has the highest standing in this order and who is willing to serve does not always become the personal representative. The court or the registrar must appoint the personal representative but will not appoint a person who is under the age of eighteen, a felon, or otherwise unsuitable for the position. This decision must be made by the court on the petition of an interested person.

In some instances, persons having priority fail to apply or are in some way disqualified. If that happens, the court, in a formal proceeding, will consider the nominees or persons having priority and try to arrive at a solution beneficial to the estate and satisfactory to those interested in it (UPC § 3–203[b]). Any objection to the appointment of a personal representative must be made in a formal proceeding.

APPLICATION FOR INFORMAL PROBATE AND APPOINTMENT OF PERSONAL REPRESENTATIVE

Informal probate commences when an applicant who seeks to be appointed personal representative submits a completed application for informal probate and informal appointment to the registrar for screening and acceptance. If your firm has been hired to assist the personal representative, you will be asked to perform the following tasks to help with these procedures:

- Gather the information necessary to complete the forms.
- Prepare the forms and file them or verify the filing.
- Communicate with the personal representative and registrar to ensure all procedures and forms are properly executed.

The applicant must verify (i.e., swear under oath) that the application is accurate and complete to the best of the applicant's knowledge. It is filed with the registrar or clerk of the probate court (UPC § 3–301 and Form 49*).

1. The following general information is required on all applications for informal probate of a will or for informal appointment:

- The interest of the applicant in the decedent's estate (e.g., named personal representative—executor).
- Name, age, date of death of decedent, county and state of decedent's domicile at time of death; names and addresses of spouse, children, heirs, devisees, and ages of those who are minors.
- A statement indicating the county or city where the proceedings are to take place, if decedent was not domiciled at the date of death in the state where the application for informal probate has been filed.
- The name and address of any personal representative of the decedent who has been appointed in this state or elsewhere whose appointment has not been terminated.
- A statement that the applicant has not received nor is aware of any "demand for notice of any probate or appointment proceeding concerning the decedent that may have been filed in this state or elsewhere."
- A statement that the time limit for informal probate or appointment has not expired either because three years or less have passed since the decedent's death or, if more than three years from death have passed, circumstances as described by UPC § 3–108 authorizing late probate or appointment have occurred.

2. If the application is for informal probate of a will, it must, in addition to the information and statements listed under 1 above, affirm:

- That the court has possession of the original last will, or that the original will or an authenticated copy probated in another jurisdiction is included with the application.
- That the applicant believes the will to have been validly executed.
- That the applicant is unaware of any instrument that revokes the will and believes the submitted instrument is the decedent's last will.

3. An application for informal appointment of a personal representative to administer an estate under a will sets forth the following in addition to the general information referred to in 1 above:

- A description of the will by date of execution.
- The time and place of probate or the pending application or petition for probate.
- An adaptation of the statements in the application or petition for probate and the name, address, and standing of the applicant among those who are entitled to be personal representative under UPC § 3–203.

4. In addition to the statements listed in 1 above, an application for informal appointment of an administrator when the decedent died intestate states the following:

- That the applicant is not aware of any unrevoked testamentary instrument relating to property located in the state, or if the applicant is aware of any such instrument, the reason for its not being probated (UPC § 3–301[4]).

---

*See Appendix A

- The priority of the applicant, and the names of any other persons who have a prior or equal right to the appointment under UPC § 3–203 (Form 62*).

Example: Martha Engle's father died testate and named Martha executrix of his will. Martha desires to be appointed informally and to have the will probated informally. She must complete the data listed in 1, 2, and 3 above.

Example: Corey Davis desires to be named personal representative of the estate of his father who died intestate. Corey's mother predeceased his father. Corey must complete the data listed in 1 and 4 above.

In the example of Martha Engle, after her father died, no will could be found, and Maria Engle, Martha's sister, was informally appointed personal representative in intestacy. Subsequently, the will was discovered and Martha sought the appointment. Martha would have to complete, in addition to the data listed in 1, 2, and 3, a "change of testacy status" form, requesting that she replace Maria (UPC § 3–301[5]).

In the example of Corey Davis, after his father died, Corey's brother, Alton, produced an instrument that resembled a will in which Alton was named executor, and, therefore, he was appointed personal representative by the court. Subsequently, the instrument was proved not valid, and Corey sought appointment as personal representative. Corey would also have to complete a "change of testacy status" form because the decedent, formerly considered testate, is now intestate.

By definition, informal probate of a will and informal appointment are proceedings conducted "without notice to interested persons" (UPC § 1–201[23]). A person applying for informal appointment and/or informal probate of a will does not have to notify persons interested in the estate unless those persons have filed a written demand to be notified in accordance with UPC § 3–204 (see also UPC § 3–306). The applicant must, however, notify anyone who has a superior right to be personal representative, e.g., a person who has been previously appointed personal representative or a person who stands higher in the order of priority for appointment.

Example: Ernest Falcott wants to be informally appointed personal representative to his father's estate and have the will informally probated. No personal representative has been previously appointed. His cousin, Julia, files a demand to be notified. Ernest must, therefore, notify Julia of his applications for informal probate of a will and informal appointment. He must also notify his mother, Letitia, who has a superior right to be personal representative.

Persons applying for informal proceedings must verify under oath the statements on their applications (e.g., Form 50*). The registrar is required to make "proofs and findings" for informal probate and informal appointment applications to check the truth and accuracy of statements therein and has the power to disqualify or decline applications if not satisfied (UPC §§ 3–303, 3–305, 3–308, 3–309). Unintentional mistakes made by the applicant are correctable, but deliberate falsification that injures someone interested in the estate will give the injured person a cause of action against the applicant (UPC §§ 1–106 and 3–301[b]).

---

*See Appendix A

ACCEPTANCE BY THE REGISTRAR

After the forms necessary for informal proceedings are executed, the applicant submits them to the registrar, who scrutinizes them for errors or omissions which might invalidate the application. The registrar must be satisfied with the following:

- That the applicant has carried out the requirements of the Uniform Probate Code.
- That the applicant has solemnly affirmed the statements made in the application to be true to the best of the applicant's knowledge.
- That the applicant is an interested person as defined by UPC § 1–201(24).
- That the applicant has chosen the proper venue (county) for the will to be probated or for the appointment of the personal representative.
- That persons who have demanded notice of proceedings (UPC § 3–204) have been notified.
- That 120 hours have elapsed since the decedent's death—UPC § 2–104 requires that a person must survive the decedent for 120 hours to be an heir.

In addition, the registrar will check each application for particular requirements. For example, for informal probate, the registrar must possess the original of a properly executed will that has not been revoked, the statutory time limit for probate must not have expired, and the will must be the kind that may be probated informally. Informal probate of certain wills, may not be advisable. The registrar has a duty to decline informal probate of alleged copies of lost or destroyed wills, wills consisting of a series of testamentary instruments (rather than a single one), and other irregular instruments. For informal appointment, the priority of the person who is entitled to appointment is determined by statute (UPC § 3–203).

The registrar may not be satisfied with the contents of the application for any of several reasons. Some examples are illustrated below.

Example: The registrar denies Joceyln Galbreth's application for informal probate of her brother's will because another sister, Elin Galbreth, had applied for probate earlier.

Example: The registrar denies Gilbert Havlicek's application for informal probate of his mother's will because the will is written on two apparently unconnected papers and it is not clear if one revokes the other.

Example: The registrar denies Conrad Marquart's application for informal appointment as personal representative of his sister's estate because another person with a higher priority had been appointed and has not died or resigned.

Example: The registrar denies Marina Yladak's application for informal appointment as personal representative of her father's estate because she indicated on her application that her father might have had another will that is still in existence (UPC §§ 3–305, 3–309).

Informal probate is available only for uncomplicated wills or estates. The registrar's denial of an application usually results in the commencement of formal probate proceedings. When the registrar accepts an application, it does not constitute a recommendation of informal over formal probate for a particular estate. The responsibility for that choice belongs to the applicant. The acceptance of an application by the registrar means only that the application meets the statutory requirements for filing.

If satisfied with the information contained in the application for informal proceedings, and if 120 hours have elapsed since the decedent's death, the registrar signifies acceptance of the application by issuing a written Statement of Informal Probate (Form 51*) and/or appoints the applicant the personal representative of the estate by issuing Letters Testamentary or Letters of Administration (Forms 57* and 69*). The Letters empower the applicant to assume the powers and duties of the office of personal representative but do not take effect until the applicant has filed a statement of acceptance of these powers and duties and has paid the necessary fees (Form 56*). At this time, the personal representative's bond, if required, must be filed with the court (Form 68*). Any person who has an interest in the estate worth more than $1,000, including creditors with claims greater than $1,000, may demand the personal representative be required to post a bond, or the court may require it (UPC §§ 3–603 and 3–605).

ASSIGNMENT 13.1

Laurel Shepard, the granddaughter of Maryanna Means, who died intestate, intends to apply to be informally appointed personal representative (administratrix) of her grandmother's estate. Before she submits the application, she brings it to be checked by you, the legal assistant of the attorney who represents the estate. Comment on the following concerns you must bring to the attention of the attorney:

1. Laurel is not sure she qualifies as an "interested person" because she had seen her grandmother only two or three times before her death.
2. Laurel believes her priority may be inferior to that of Florence Kingsley, Maryanna's nurse for seventeen years, who had lived with and cared for Maryanna.
3. Laurel has not given notice to Georgina Means, Maryanna's daughter, because she does not know Georgina's address and has not been in contact with her for a long time.
4. Maryanna resided and died in Lawrence County, Idaho, but left a farm and a bank account in Orange County, California. Laurel does not know if Lawrence County, where she intends to submit her application, is the proper place for administration.
5. Laurel thinks her uncle, Jason Means, who lives in Orange County, may have been appointed personal representative. If so, this might present a challenge to her own application.
6. Laurel does not believe she can affirm the truth of her statements in the application because of the uncertainties stated above.

NOTICE REQUIREMENTS

Informal probate is not supervised by the probate court and does not require notice be given to interested parties. However, persons who have an interest in the estate may file a demand to be notified (Demand for Notice, Form 10*) of the petitioner's application for informal probate or informal appointment (UPC § 3–204). (See the discussion of notice requirements and methods below.) An interested person might be one who has a financial interest in the estate, a previously

---

*See Appendix A

appointed personal representative who is still acting in that capacity, or someone who occupies a place in the order of priority for appointment (UPC §§ 1–201[24] and 3–203).

Once a demand has been filed, the registrar will notify the personal representative to keep the demandant informed of proceedings related to the estate. If the demandant believes that the applicant is not qualified to be the personal representative, is using a revoked will, or otherwise objects to informal proceedings, the demand for notice ensures an opportunity to request formal or supervised administration when necessary. If the demandant is not given notice of a subsequent order or proceeding, it remains effective. However, the personal representative will be liable for any damages the demandant suffers as a result of the absence of notice (UPC § 3-204).

Notice of Application for Informal Probate

After the registrar accepts the application and grants informal probate and appointment of the personal representative, the petitioner who seeks informal probate must give notice as required by UPC § 1-401 of the application for informal probate to any person who demands it pursuant to UPC § 3-204 and Form 52*. No other notice of informal probate is required.

Notice of Application for Informal Appointment

The petitioner seeking informal appointment as personal representative must give notice as required by UPC § 1-401 of the intention to seek an informal appointment to any person who has a financial or property interest and who demands notice pursuant to UPC § 3-204 and to any person who has a prior or equal right to appointment not waived in writing and filed with the court (UPC § 3-310 and Form 52*). No other notice of an informal appointment proceeding is required.

Demand for Notice of Order or Filing

At any time after the death of the decedent any person who has a financial or property interest in a decedent's estate may file a demand with the court for notice of any order or filing relating to the estate (see UPC §§ 3-204, 3-306). The demand for notice must state the name of the decedent, the nature of the demandant's interest in the estate, and the person's address or that of the attorney who represents the person (Form 10*). The clerk will mail a copy of such demand to the personal representative, if any. After such a demand is filed, no order or filing to which the demand relates can be made or accepted without notice to the demandant or her attorney, as required in UPC § 1-401. If such notice is not given, the order or filing is still valid, but the person who receives the order or makes the filing may be liable for any damage caused by the absence of notice.

The notice requirement arising from a demand may be waived in writing by the demandant and will cease when the demandant's interest in the estate terminates. Interested persons are protected by their right to demand prior notice of informal

---

*See Appendix A

proceedings (see UPC § 3-204) or to contest a requested appointment by use of a formal testacy proceeding, or by use of a formal proceeding seeking the appointment of another person. Interested persons also have available to them the remedies provided in UPC § 3-605 (demand for bond by interested persons) and § 3-607 (order restraining personal representative).

Although not obligated to do so unless a demand has been filed, since publication under UPC § 3-801 is sufficient, the personal representative should give personal notice to creditors. The Uniform Probate Code allows creditors four months from the date of the first publication of notice to file claims (see UPC §§ 3-801, 3-802, and 3-803). If the estate is still open, the court has the discretion to allow late claims, but can refuse them unless good cause is shown. Once the account of the personal representative is settled, the court cannot allow the claim (Forms 28*, 29*, 52*, and 59*).

Method and Time for Giving Notice

If notice of a hearing on any petition, application, order, or filing is required (except for specific notice requirements as otherwise provided in the UPC), the petitioner or applicant must give notice of the time and place of hearing of any petition, application, order, or filing to any interested person or to her attorney (UPC § 1-401). Again, if requested, the petitioner must give notice in one of three ways:

- By mailing a copy of the notice at least fourteen days *before the time set* for the hearing by certified, registered, or ordinary first class mail addressed to the person being notified at the post office address given in the demand for notice, or at the person's office or place of residence.
- By delivering a copy of the notice to the person being notified personally at least fourteen days before the time set for the hearing.
- If the address, or identity of any person is not known and cannot be ascertained with reasonable diligence, by publishing at least once a week for three consecutive weeks a copy of the notice in a newspaper having general circulation in the county where the hearing is to be held, the last publication of which is to be at least ten days before the time set for the hearing.

For good cause, the court may provide a different method or time of giving notice for any hearing. Prior to or at the hearing, proof of giving the notice and the Affidavit of Mailing Notice must be made and filed (see UPC § 1-401 and Forms 53* and 54*). Any person, including a *guardian ad litem,* conservator, or other fiduciary (see Glossary), may waive notice by a writing signed by the person or her attorney and filed in the proceeding in court (see UPC § 1-402).

Notice must be given to every interested person or to one who can bind an interested person, as described in UPC § 1-403, which also describes pleading and notice requirements when parties are bound by others.

---

*See Appendix A

DUTIES AND POWERS OF THE PERSONAL REPRESENTATIVE IN INFORMAL PROBATE

The primary responsibility of the personal representative is the proper distribution of the decedent's estate. In a testate administration, the personal representative distributes the estate assets according to the will and within the bounds of the law (e.g., the personal representative pays priority family allowances and debts first). In an intestate administration, the personal representative distributes the estate assets according to state statutes of descent and distribution (intestate succession statutes).

The duties and powers of the personal representative in informal probate are outlined generally in UPC §§ 3-701 to 3-721.

As a fiduciary, the personal representative must observe the standards of care applicable to fiduciaries. Since it is necessary for the personal representative to hold temporary title to personal property assets that belong and are distributed to others (devisees or heirs), the personal representative is liable to successors for damage resulting from improper use of power or mishandling estate assets, e.g., selling an asset when there was no need to do so (UPC §§ 3–703, 3–712).

An informally appointed personal representative who possesses Letters Testamentary or Letters of Administration needs no further approval before beginning distribution (Forms 57* and 69*). Only when the personal representative or another interested person requests court supervision of heretofore unsupervised proceedings (the "in and out" feature) does the personal representative have to obtain the court's order to proceed (UPC § 3–704).

Notification to Devisees or Heirs and Creditors

No later than thirty days following appointment, the personal representative must notify the decedent's devisees or heirs of the appointment (UPC § 3–705). The notice is sent by ordinary mail and must include the name and address of the personal representative, indicate that it is sent to all persons who have or may have some interest in the estate, indicate whether bond has been filed, and describe the court where all estate documents are on file. This notice is part of the fiduciary obligation, but the personal representative's neglect to give notice will not invalidate the appointment or powers of the office. If it causes loss or damage to a devisee or heir, however, that person has a cause of action for damages against the personal representative for breach of the fiduciary duty (UPC §§ 3–204 and 3–712).

> **Example:** Eula Gribben died intestate in Colorado leaving a small estate. All of her heirs live in Colorado except her son, Lewis, who lives in Delaware. Her brother, Lloyd Adcock, was informally appointed personal representative (administrator) and gave notice to all of the heirs except Lewis. Should Lloyd omit Lewis in the distribution of the estate, Lewis would have a cause of action against Lloyd for the omitted share and possibly for damages (e.g., needless expense of court fees).

The personal representative must also notify creditors of the estate of the appointment by publishing in a general-circulation county newspaper the announcement of the personal representative's appointment. The notice must appear once a week for three successive weeks. Creditors have four months after the date of the first publication to present their claims; otherwise the claims are barred (UPC § 3–801 and Form 59*).

---

*See Appendix A

Payment of Creditors' Claims

After the four-month period, the personal representative must pay creditors' claims that are determined to be valid (i.e., are approved or allowed). The order in which valid claims are to be paid is found in UPC §§ 3–805 to 3–807. The personal representative has the power to disallow or disqualify claims creditors have made fraudulently or otherwise unjustly against the estate (UPC § 3–803). The creditors can appeal the personal representative's decision in court.

> **Example:** Bertrand Dorn had a credit account with the National Oil Company. Before his death, the company sent him a bill for $148.79. Bertrand disputed it and claimed that he owed only $48.79 according to service station receipts. His personal representative may refuse to pay the additional $100 claim by following UPC procedures for "allowance of claims" (UPC § 3–806).

Inventory Property

Within the time set by state statute, e.g., three to six months after appointment or nine months after the date of the decedent's death, the personal representative must prepare an inventory of all real or personal property owned by the decedent at the time of death and mail it to the surviving spouse and all other interested persons who request it. The personal representative may also file the original copy of the inventory with the court (UPC § 3–706). The inventory must list the assets of the estate with sufficient description for accurate identification, value the assets at fair market value, and include the kind of mortgage or other encumbrance on each item and the amount of the encumbrance (Form 58*).

Two typical inventory problems may arise: the nature and kind of estate assets may be so unique the personal representative is unable to adequately estimate their fair market value; or the court may order an independent person who has no interest in the estate to appraise these difficult-to-value estate assets. In either case, the personal representative usually has permission to hire independent appraisers to assist in valuation, and if they do perform appraisals, the personal representative must list on the inventory their names, addresses, and the items they valued (UPC § 3–707).

Hold and Manage the Estate

Until discharged or released from the appointment, the personal representative has the same power over the title to the decedent's personal property as the decedent (UPC § 3–711). Both a trustee and the personal representative hold title in a similar manner and are given powers and duties that require the exercise of prudence and restraint expected of a fiduciary for the benefit of others: the trustee for beneficiaries; the personal representative for devisees, heirs, or creditors. The personal representative is liable for loss or damage caused to such persons by improper exercise of these powers (UPC § 3–712).

> **Example:** Merle Hendricks, the informally appointed personal representative for his father's estate, was given the power of sale by the will. He sells an antique lamp

---

*See Appendix A

from the estate to his wife at a lower price than he would have asked of a stranger. Merle has violated his fiduciary duty by self-dealing with estate assets (UPC § 3–713).

The various transactions authorized and performed by a personal representative, e.g., acquire or dispose of assets; sell, mortgage, or lease real or personal property; and vote shares of stock are listed in UPC § 3–715.

Final Account and Closing the Estate

After the minimum time period for closing an estate has passed and all approved creditor claims have been paid, the personal representative must prepare and file the final account. It consists of a list of the decedent's probate assets; any increases or decreases in the assets; the payment of creditors' claims; administration expenses; funeral and last illness expenses; taxes; and the balance of assets on hand for distribution. Only after a copy of the final account has been given to every distributee of the estate can the personal representative distribute the remaining assets to the persons entitled to receive them and seek a discharge (termination) from office.

An informally appointed personal representative may choose to close the estate informally and be discharged by signing a sworn **closing statement** (affidavit) to the effect that he believes the estate's assets have been distributed correctly and its business transacted (Form 61*). The personal representative may use this method if the administration has not been continuously supervised by the court. In the case of continuous supervision, the UPC demands a final account and formal closing, as described in detail in Chapter 12, by either of the methods described in UPC §§ 3–1001, 3–1003, and 3–505 or 3–1002 (Forms 32* and 40*).

The personal representative's sworn closing statement informally closing the estate must verify the following:

Closing statement
An affidavit signed by the personal representative at the end of informal probate proceedings to close the estate and to be discharged.

- That a notice to creditors was published more than six months before the date of the present statement.
- That the personal representative has fully administered the estate, paid all federal and state taxes and valid claims (including creditors' and successors' claims), and that the assets of the estate have been distributed to the persons entitled. If the personal representative has not completed distribution, the reasons for partial distribution must be explained in the closing statement.
- That the personal representative has mailed a copy of this closing statement to all of the claimants (creditors) who have made themselves known and to all distributees of the estate (see UPC § 3–1003). Once copies have been mailed, the original "Statement to Close" is filed with the probate court.

The time periods creditors have to assert and present claims include the following:

- Under UPC § 3–803, all claims against a decedent's estate that arose before the decedent's death are barred against the estate, the personal representative, and the heirs and devisees of the decedent unless presented within four

---

*See Appendix A

months after the date of the first publication of notice to creditors if notice is given in compliance with UPC § 3–801, or within one year after the decedent's death, if notice to creditors has not been published.

- Under UPC § 3–1005, the rights of all creditors whose claims have not been previously barred against the personal representative for breach of fiduciary duty (see UPC § 3–803 above) are barred unless a proceeding to assert the claim is commenced within six months after the filing of the personal representative's *closing statement*. Creditors do, however, have the right to recover from a personal representative for fraud or inadequate disclosure related to the settlement of the decedent's estate.

If a personal representative has distributed the assets of the estate to other claimants, e.g., devisees, heirs, or other creditors, a creditor with a valid but undischarged claim must press the claim in a judicial proceeding against one or more of those who received the assets (UPC § 3–1004).

> **Example:** Annelise Frechette closes her mother's estate informally by filing a sworn statement with the probate court. Two months afterward, the owner of a gift shop who had not been given notice presents a bill for some items that Annelise's mother had bought on credit. Annelise is personally liable to the creditor for not having given him notice as she had given the other creditors. The creditor can obtain payment of the bill by initiating a judicial proceeding against Annelise or any distributee, but the creditor cannot collect from both. If the creditor obtains a judgment and payment from Corinee Mays, one of the five distributees, then Corinee may demand of the other four distributees, who were given notice of the creditor's claim and pending litigation, four fifths of the amount she had to pay so all will bear the burden equally.

If no proceedings involving the personal representative are pending in the court one year after the closing statement is filed, the personal representative's appointment is terminated (UPC § 3–1003). Termination does not automatically accompany closing. The authority of the personal representative remains active for one year. Once the authority is terminated, the personal representative has no power to conduct affairs in the name of the estate. The UPC provides the one-year grace period between closing and termination for the resolution of unforeseen business, such as in the preceding example.

It is important the personal representative obtain receipts or evidence of payment for everything distributed from the estate whether or not he has decided to close the estate under one of the methods described in UPC § 3–1001 through § 3–1003. *(Note:* It is legitimate but impractical not to close the estate at all but simply to rely on the receipts collected to show the estate has been fully distributed. Relying on receipts affords no protection to the personal representative should complications arise.) Collecting and retaining receipts enables the personal representative to support the closing statement and the request that the court formally close the estate. Alternatively, the personal representative may obtain an affidavit from each distributee which states he or she received the correct amount.

After the estate has been closed and the personal representative discharged, someone may discover additional omitted property that belonged to the decedent and obviously has not been administered, e.g., rare books referred to in the will but not located during administration. Proper disposition of the assets will necessitate reopening the estate (UPC § 3–1008).

STEP-BY-STEP PROCEDURES IN INFORMAL PROBATE

The following case study describes an estate that could conveniently be administered through the use of the UPC informal probate procedures by an informally appointed personal representative. Follow the personal representative step by step through the informal procedures. As a further review of informal probate procedures, three Case Problems, with appropriate forms and/or questions, are included.

Case Study

Elvira Krueger died testate on February 4, 2000, in a state that has adopted the Uniform Probate Code. Elvira left a son, Ralph, and two daughters, Sara and Christa, none of whom are minors. Elvira's husband predeceased her. Elvira owned property valued at $16,500 at the time of her death: household furniture and goods valued at $12,500, antique furniture valued at $2,000, an automobile valued at $1,400, and a tent trailer for camping valued at $600. In her will, Elvira appointed her daughter, Sara, personal representative (executrix) of her estate and directed the estate assets be distributed as follows: "the automobile and tent trailer to my son, Ralph; the antique furniture to my daughter, Sara; and the household furniture and goods to be sold and the proceeds to be distributed to my three children, Ralph, Sara, and Christa so each of them will receive an equal amount of my property." Sara later sells the household furniture and goods for $12,500.

Under the terms of the will, Sara must distribute the antique furniture (valued at $2,000) and $3,500 cash to herself (total—$5,500), $5,500 cash to Christa, and the automobile (valued at $1,400), the tent trailer (valued at $600), and $3,500 cash to Ralph. These devises, however, will be reduced by expenses and debts that must be paid first out of the estate assets.

Informal Procedures

Sara files an application with the registrar which requests both informal probate of her mother's will and her informal appointment as personal representative (executrix). She verifies the application is accurate and complete to the best of her knowledge and belief. The application must include Sara's interest in the estate and identify the required information about the decedent, e.g., name, age, domicile, date of death, and the names and addresses of her children (UPC § 3–301). Since Elvira resided in the state in which Sara is applying for informal appointment, Sara must wait 120 hours (five days) after Elvira's death before the registrar will finalize her appointment (UPC § 2–104).

Sara must give notice of the application for informal probate and appointment by one of the methods specified by UPC § 1–401 to (1) any interested person who has filed a written demand with the clerk pursuant to UPC § 3–204; (2) any personal representative of the decedent whose appointment has not been terminated; and (3) any interested person who has a prior or equal right to appointment that has not been waived in writing and filed with the court (UPC §§ 3–306 and 3–310).

File Application

Notice

Both Ralph and Christa have filed demands for notice with the court. Therefore, Sara gives notice of the application to her sister and brother. The validity of an order that is issued or a filing that is accepted without notice to Ralph or Christa will not be affected by the lack of notice, but Sara may be liable for any damage caused to either of them by the absence of notice (UPC § 3–204).

> **Example:** In her demand, Christa stated her interest as a devisee in Elvira's estate and signed her name and address. Sara discovered it was necessary to use all the money from the sale of Elvira's household goods to pay creditors and obtained a court order permitting her to do this. Christa's share in the proceeds of the sale is therefore reduced, but in anticipation of the share of cash she was to receive originally, she had negotiated a bank loan. If Sara fails to notify her of the order that permitted payment to creditors and Christa is subsequently unable to repay the loan, Christa may have a cause of action against Sara.

Application for appointment

After a review of Sara's application, the registrar makes the findings required by UPC § 3–303 and issues a written Statement of Informal Probate. The informal probate is conclusive on all persons unless the probate court, upon petition of an interested party, issues a superseding order that changes the estate administration to a formal testacy proceeding. Defects in Sara's application or in procedures followed in informally probating her mother's will do not by themselves render the probate void (UPC § 3–302).

Appointment of personal representative

When the registrar approves Sara's application for informal probate and appointment as personal representative, she must qualify and file her acceptance pursuant to UPC §§ 3–307, 3–601 and 3–602. Once the registrar issues the Letters of Authority (Letters Testamentary or Letters of Administration) (UPC § 1–305), Sara will have all the powers and be entitled to perform all the duties pertaining to her office pursuant to UPC Article III, Part 7.

Bond

As an informally appointed personal representative, Sara will not have to file a bond. She would be required to post a bond if it is demanded by any interested party, e.g., a creditor or devisee, who has an interest in the estate exceeding $1,000, or if the will had required her to file a bond, or if she had been appointed special administratrix (see Chapter 11) (UPC §§ 3–603, 3–605). The person who demands a bond must file a written request with the court (UPC §§ 3–603, through 3–606). For example, if Ralph files a written demand for a bond with the court, the registrar will mail a copy of the demand for a bond to Sara. Sara must then obtain a bond and file it with the court unless the court determines in formal proceedings that a bond is unnecessary or that Sara had deposited cash or collateral with an agency of the state to secure performance of her duties (UPC §§ 3–603, 3–605).

If the registrar is satisfied that Elvira had complied with the requirements for executing a will pursuant to UPC § 2–502, e.g., that the will contains the required signatures of two witnesses and attestation clause, the registrar will allow the proceedings to continue without further proof. The registrar may assume execution if the will appears to have been properly executed or may accept an affidavit (sworn statement) of any person who has knowledge of the circumstances of execution, whether or not that person actually witnessed the will (UPC § 3–303[c]).

Acceptance of application

Elvira's will contained signatures of two competent witnesses (her brother and aunt) and a proper attestation clause. The registrar approved Sara's application for informal probate and appointment. If for any reason the registrar had decided the will should not be admitted to probate or the informal appointment should be denied, the application would have been denied. In that case, if the estate is to be administered, Sara would be required to initiate formal probate proceedings (UPC §§ 3–305 and 3–309).

Sara is now officially Elvira's personal representative. She possesses the powers (e.g., to distribute the assets according to the will) and duties (e.g., to pay creditors before devisees) of a personal representative (UPC § 3–307[b]). Her appointment can be terminated, either voluntarily or by court order, at any time during administration of the estate. Sara's death, disability (such as being declared legally insane), or resignation would terminate her office. She might be removed by court order after a hearing initiated by a person interested in the estate (UPC §§ 3–608 through 3–612).

> **Example:** Marston Keefe, a creditor of Elvira, believes Sara should be removed from office for failing to pay his claim against the estate. Pursuant to UPC § 3–611, he files a petition with the court for a hearing seeking her removal. The court arranges a hearing at which Sara must appear to defend her action. If the court decides she has abused the power of a personal representative, it may direct that Sara be removed and someone else appointed to the position. Also, the court may regulate the disposition of assets remaining in the estate until a successor is appointed.

Sara must inform the heirs and devisees, Ralph and Christa, of her appointment by personal delivery or ordinary mail not later than thirty days after the appointment. Her failure to do this constitutes a breach of her fiduciary duty but does not render invalid her acts as personal representative (UPC § 3–705).

Within three months after her appointment, Sara must prepare and file with the court, either by mail or in person, an inventory of all property owned by Elvira at the time of her death. The inventory must list all assets with reasonable detail and indicate, for each listed item, its fair market value at the date of her mother's death and the type and amount of all encumbrances against any item (UPC § 3–706). Sara is allowed to appoint appraisers without the approval of the court, but the appointment may be challenged by an interested party as provided by UPC § 3–607. Sara must send a copy of the inventory to interested persons who have requested it (UPC § 3–706). She may also file the original with the court.

Inventory

A personal representative owes a fiduciary duty to the devisees comparable to that of a trustee and is not permitted to engage in "self-dealing," i.e., dealing for one's own benefit (UPC § 3–713).

> **Example:** Sara appraises the fair market value of a grand piano at $1,500 and decides she will purchase it from the estate. Ralph and Christa object, and assert the fair market value of the piano is at least $5,000. Ralph petitions the probate court to issue an order to restrain Sara from purchasing the piano and orders an independent appraisal, pursuant to UPC § 3–607. The court issues an order which temporarily prohibits Sara from proceeding with the purchase and notifies both of them of a hearing on the matter to take place within ten days. At the hearing, the court decides Sara's course of action is improper and issues an order permanently restraining Sara's action.

Sara would be liable to Ralph and Christa for any damage or loss resulting from any breach of her fiduciary duty to the same extent as a trustee of an express trust.

If Sara had bought the piano from the estate for $1,500 instead of its fair market value, i.e., $5,000, the estate would suffer because less money would be available to pay Elvira's creditors or to be distributed to her devisees. According to law, creditors are the first to be paid from nonspecific or general devises, e.g., in this example, the sale proceeds (money). If Elvira left many debts and expenses, these obligations might consume much of the general devise and diminish the distribution to Ralph or Christa (UPC § 3–712).

> **Example:** Suppose the sale of household goods brings $7,500 to the estate. If Elvira's bills total $7,600, all of which must be paid from the estate's assets, the $7,500 will have to be apportioned among the creditors. They will receive a percentage of what Elvira had owed them. Any of the creditors would have a cause of action against Sara, who undervalued the piano.

Elvira specified in her will that Sara would not receive any compensation for her services as personal representative, but nothing was mentioned about payment of creditors' claims, funeral expenses, and the like. Elvira had hospitalization and medical insurance that paid all the expenses of her last illness except for $300 to her doctor and $735 to the hospital. She also owed $90 to a local department store for clothing she had purchased. There was no provision in the will for payment of these obligations or for payment of funeral expenses ($1,800) or expenses of administration, such as filing fees ($75). Since the funeral and administration expenses have priority, Sara must pay these bills before the other debts (UPC § 3–805).

Since none of Elvira's three children are minors or dependent children, UPC § 2–402 (homestead allowance) and UPC § 2–404 (family allowance) are not applicable to her estate. The three children, however, are entitled to share the $10,000 exempt property allowance (UPC § 2–403). Together they are entitled to a sum not exceeding $10,000 in the form of household furniture, automobiles, furnishings, appliances, and personal effects, except for the portion of these chattels owned by creditors with security interests, e.g., an unpaid car dealer who sold the decedent a car on an installment payment plan.

> **Example:** Two months prior to her death, Elvira had bought a $900 stove from an appliance dealer. She agreed to make a down payment and pay $25 per month plus interest. The dealer was to retain title to the stove as a security interest until Elvira had finished paying for it. At the time of her death, she had paid $150 toward the purchase price. Under the terms of the contract, the dealer could repossess the stove if Elvira died before completing the payments. Therefore, the stove is not available as part of the exempt property. The children's rights to the exempt property have priority over all claims against the estate. Homestead and family allowances, however, are not applicable in this case because there is no surviving spouse or minor children. Elvira's estate has sufficient assets, after distributing the exempt property ($10,000) to Sara, Ralph, and Christa, to pay debts, expenses of a last illness, and expenses of administration. Therefore, Sara will distribute the assets of her mother's estate as follows:

Exempt property (to be shared by Sara, Ralph, and Christa)	$10,000
Funeral expenses	1,800
Administration expenses	75
Doctor	300

Hospital	735
Department store	90
Total prior obligations	$13,000
Value of all estate assets	16,500
Less prior obligations	13,000
	$3,500

After prior obligations are accounted for, $3,500 in estate assets remain. Sara will add that amount to the $10,000 exempt property to determine the shares of the three children.

$$\begin{array}{r} \$10,000 \\ +3,500 \\ \hline \$13,500 \div 3 = \$4,500 \end{array}$$

Each child is entitled to estate assets valued at $4,500. The children will receive less than Sara had determined prior to consideration of debts and expenses. Originally, each child would have received estate assets and/or cash valued at $5,500. After payment of debts and expenses, each child is entitled to receive estate assets and/or cash valued at $4,500.

Therefore, Sara may distribute the assets of Elvira's estate to Ralph, Christa, and herself as follows:

Sara		Ralph		Christa	
Antique furniture	$2,000	Automobile	$1,400	Cash	$4,500
Cash	2,500	Tent trailer	600		
Total	$4,500	Cash	2,500	*Total*	$4,500
		Total	$4,500		

Asset distribution

Sara must make the distribution expeditiously and may do so without order by the court (UPC § 3–704). Ralph, Christa, Sara (the distributees of the estate), and Elvira's creditors take the property subject to the proviso they return it to the personal representative should some unexpected event occur (UPC § 3–909). This section of the UPC protects the personal representative from unjustified litigation by distributees. The personal representative is liable, however, for improper distribution or payment of claims (UPC §§ 3–703, 3–712, and 3–808).

> **Example:** If Sara had overlooked the hospital bill ($735) and therefore paid $245 more to each devisee, each devisee (including herself) would be responsible for returning his or her share of the money improperly paid plus one-third of the interest that would have accrued on $735 from the date of distribution to the present date. The reason for the payment of interest is the creditor does not have the use of the money until later, so interest is added.

Persons who purchase from the distributees are also protected (UPC § 3–910). Sara will execute instruments or deeds of distribution which transfer or release the antique furniture, automobile, and the tent trailer to Ralph and herself as evidence of their respective titles to these assets (UPC § 3–907).

Once she completes the distribution of estate assets, Sara's last duty is to close the estate (wind up its affairs) in one of two ways:

Closing the estate

- Formally, by petitioning the court to declare that the estate has been settled fully in regard to all persons interested in it. This method protects the estate against potential danger from details overlooked by the personal representative, e.g., the payment of inheritance taxes, because it avails the estate of the court's experience (UPC § 3–1001).

- Informally, by filing a sworn closing statement with the court in which Sara verifies she has completed every detail of the administration.

If Sara chooses to close her administration by filing a closing statement with the court, she need not file a formal accounting with the court. She must, however, furnish Ralph and Christa and other interested parties with a full account in writing, together with a copy of the verified closing statement filed with the court (UPC §§ 3–1001, 3–1002, and 3–1003).

Sara elects to close the estate by filing a sworn closing statement with the court pursuant to UPC § 3–1003. No earlier than six months after the date of her original appointment, she files a verified statement which asserts she has (1) published notice to creditors and the first publication occurred more than six months prior to the date of the present statement; (2) fully administered her mother's estate by making payment, settlement, or other disposition of all claims presented, paying expenses of administration and estate, inheritance, and other death taxes, except as specified in the statement, and distributing the assets of the estate to the persons entitled; and (3) sent a copy of the closing statement to all the distributees of the estate and to all creditors or other claimants of whom she is aware whose claims are neither paid nor barred, and has furnished a full account in writing of her administration to the distributees (UPC § 3-1003).

> **Closing statement sent to creditors and distributees**

If no proceedings which involve Sara are pending in court one year after the closing statement is filed, her authority (appointment) terminates. An order closing an estate under UPC § 3-1001 or 3-1002 would terminate Sara's appointment. Her closing statement under UPC § 3-1003 would not terminate the appointment, however, because the statement is an affirmation by Sara that she believes the affairs of the estate are completed. Any creditor not paid whose claim has not been barred by the time limit can assert the claim against the distributees, i.e., Sara, Ralph, and Christa (UPC § 3-1004).

Example: When Sara was appointed, she published a notice to creditors in accordance with UPC § 3-801. Several creditors presented claims within the period allowed for presentation, and Sara paid all except the $90 clothing bill from a local store. The store may obtain payment, even though Sara has filed a closing statement, by demanding $90 from one of the three distributees. The distributee is then entitled to demand $30 from each of the other distributees so they will have contributed an equal amount. Sara can also be sued pursuant to UPC § 3-608 for actions she performed before the termination of her appointment. Under UPC § 3-610(a), her authority ends one year after she has filed the closing statement. Even after termination, Sara remains subject to a lawsuit unless the applicable statute of limitations has run or her administration has been terminated by an adjudication which settles her accounts (UPC § 3-1005).

Example: Before giving the automobile to Ralph as Elvira had directed in her will, Sara used it for her personal convenience. She was involved in a collision resulting in $1,000 damage to the automobile. Because this occurred while Sara was the personal representative of the estate, Ralph may sue her for having failed to exercise due care with respect to one of the estate's assets during or within six months after the termination of her administration.

Suits against Sara by successors of the will and creditors for breach of her fiduciary duty are barred unless begun within six months after Sara filed the closing statement. Rights of successors and creditors to recover for fraud, misrepresentation, or inadequate disclosure are not barred by the six-month limitation (UPC §§ 3-1005, 3-807, and 3-808).

Using a closing statement offers Sara more protection than if she had relied merely on the receipts collected to show the estate has been fully distributed.

Sections 3-1001, 3-1002, and 3-1003 of the Uniform Probate Code provide for judicial proceedings for closing by which Sara could gain protection from all interested persons or from Ralph and Christa, the other devisees (successors), only. Section 3-703 of the UPC provides very limited protection for a personal representative who relies only on receipts. These sections afford protection to the personal representative for acts or distributions which were authorized when performed but became doubtful because of a later change in testacy status. There is no protection against later claims of breach of fiduciary obligation except for those arising from consent or waiver of individual distributees who may have bound themselves by receipts given to the personal representative. In addition, the closing statement method provides notice to third persons that Sara's authority has terminated, whereas reliance on receipts alone does not. The closing statement method provides a useful means of closing small, uncomplicated estates where the distributees are all members of the family and disputes are unlikely.

> **Termination of administration**

🏛 ASSIGNMENT 13.2

1. Make a list of and obtain all the forms Sara would use to administer her mother's estate according to the Uniform Probate Code. Fill in the forms after reviewing Case Problem 2 below.
2. Suppose six months before Sara filed the closing statement, Christa found a will which devised all Elvira's property to Christa. The will was executed by Elvira at a date later than the probated will. What should Christa do?
3. Would distribution of the assets of Elvira's estate have been different if Christa had been a minor at the time of her mother's death? If so, how? Suppose Elvira in her will had appointed neither a personal guardian nor a property guardian for Christa. How would the guardianship be determined?
4. Ralph claims he, not Sara, should be appointed personal representative because he is the oldest of the children and thus has a higher priority. Should he petition the court to remove Sara and appoint himself on these grounds?
5. In her inventory, Sara omits a living-room chair valued at $50. If she discovers the error but neglects to file an amended inventory, what is the consequence?
6. Before her death, Elvira began negotiations for the sale of her automobile to Moira Byrne, but they had not agreed on a purchase price. Sara completes the sale at a price of $1,350. She intends to give the money, instead of the automobile, to Ralph. Has Sara breached her fiduciary duty?
7. Sara discovers a policy of insurance on Elvira's life which Elvira had taken out twenty-five years ago and was not mentioned in the will. The beneficiary of the policy is Elvira's estate. Should Sara record the value of this policy in her inventory of estate assets? May she use the proceeds to pay Elvira's creditors?

8. Elvira had opened a charge account at a local department store. Prior to her death she had charged but had not yet paid for $50 worth of merchandise. The credit manager of the store wants to be sure Sara will not overlook or disallow the claim. Could he demand Sara be bonded to ensure against loss to the store?

9. The registrar declines to issue an order of informal probate because the registrar doubts Elvira's signature on the will is genuine. One of the witnesses to the will is deceased, and the other cannot be located. How could Sara have the will admitted to probate? Could she still follow informal procedures as planned?

KEY TERM

Closing statement

REVIEW QUESTIONS

1. According to your state statute, who has top priority to be appointed the personal representative of a testator's estate? Of an intestate's estate?

2. What function does a registrar or surrogate perform in an informal or common probate administration?

3. How do informal probate procedures differ in testate versus intestate cases?

4. Under what circumstances can a registrar reject an application for informal probate proceedings? If the registrar denies an application, what results?

5. Since informal probate procedures are not supervised by the court and do not require notice be given, what rights and procedural steps are available to creditors?

6. Explain what is meant by the Uniform Probate Code's *in and out* feature available for those using informal probate proceedings.

7. Must an inventory be prepared in informal probate? If required, to whom must the inventory be given?

8. Using informal probate, how is an estate administration closed?

9. In informal probate, what time limits are placed on creditors for claims against the decedent's estate and the personal representative for breach of fiduciary duty?

10. In informal probate, when does the personal representative's authority officially terminate?

CASE PROBLEMS

Problem 1

Carl Bergmeister dies intestate on September 19, 2000, leaving outstanding assets valued at $322,800:

Homestead	$88,000
Furniture and household items	16,000
Shares of stock in Alcoa Aluminum	62,000
One-half interest in an apartment building held in tenancy in common (building valued at $250,000)	125,000
Two Miro paintings	28,000
1996 automobile	3,800
Total	$322,800

Several relatives survive Carl: Jenneille Bergmeister, wife; Naomi Bergmeister, daughter; Scott Bergmeister, son, who is a minor; David Bergmeister, son from a previous marriage; Carolyn Bergmeister, mother; Gustaf Bergmeister, father; Nora Stark, sister; Robin Stark, niece (daughter of Nora); Jarod Harrison, brother-in-law (wife's brother); and Verlayne Sather, first cousin.

Naomi Bergmeister, Carl's daughter, makes an application for informal appointment of herself in intestacy pursuant to UPC § 3-301.

A. Who has priority for such an appointment?

B. If someone else who has priority over Naomi is an invalid and does not feel capable of assuming the duties of administering Carl's estate, could the person decline the appointment? How can the priority be waived?

C. What steps must Naomi take to assure her informal appointment? What forms would she use?

Assume that Naomi is appointed personal representative.

A. Describe the steps she will take to administer, distribute, and close her father's estate. Use the informal methods you think most appropriate.

B. Make a list of and fill in all forms Naomi will use. Assume prior to his death on September 19, 2000, Carl earned $30,000 from his employment, $8,000 from dividends on his stock, and accrued but unpaid dividends amounted to $1,000. Assume, also, a $10,000 mortgage exists on the homestead; funeral expenses were $3,500; expenses for Carl's last illness were $270 to his doctor and $420 to the hospital; and Carl owed $4,200 to a contractor for repairs on the homestead.

C. It must also be determined whether federal or state estate and/or inheritance taxes must be paid. Read Chapter 14 and obtain and complete the necessary tax forms for the Bergmeister estate, including the decedent's final income tax return and the fiduciary income tax return for income earned by the estate

With regard to the administration of the real property owned by Carl at his death, Naomi should consider UPC § 3-715, especially subparagraphs 3, 6, 7, 8, 9, 10, 11, 15, 18, and 23, which discuss the transactions authorized for a personal representative that relate to land transactions. She must also consult the probate court of the county where Carl's land is located (if different from the county of his domicile) to see if there are local laws pertaining to real estate transactions (e.g., the personal representative must obtain the court's permission to sell, mortgage, or lease real estate, and wait a certain number of days before finalizing such transactions).

How will Naomi convey real property to heirs entitled to it—by deed or otherwise?

Assume that David Bergmeister, Carl's son by a previous marriage, files a petition with the probate court for *formal* appointment of a personal representative because he is dissatisfied with Naomi's appointment. What is the result? Could Naomi still exercise her powers while the formal proceeding is pending (see UPC § 3-401)?

What documents, if any, should Naomi file in order to convey a clear marketable title to the successors?

Problem 2

Cheryl Ann Kennedy died testate on August 1, 2000, at 1010 Willow Street in Hennepin County, Minneapolis, Minnesota 55409. She was born January 13, 1960, in Minneapolis, Minnesota.

Cheryl's successors include her husband, Charles; two twin daughters, Cherry and Cindy; three sons, Carl, Corey, and Christopher; her mother, Catherine Kelly; and one sister, Karen Kelly. The ages of the family members are Charles, 40, Cherry and Cindy, the twins, age 3, Carl is 5, Corey is 9, Christopher is 10, Catherine Kelly is 60, and Karen Kelly is 38. All members of the family live at 1010 Willow Street.

Cheryl's estate included the following assets:

- A home, the family residence, owned by Cheryl before her marriage and still recorded in her name only, valued at $95,000.
- A summer cottage in joint tenancy with Charles, given to Cheryl and Charles by Cheryl's father, valued at $35,000.
- A savings and a checking account in joint tenancy with Charles with a total value of $10,000.
- One thousand shares of Execo stock in joint tenancy with Charles worth $12,000.
- Fifty shares of Users, Inc., stock left to Cheryl by her father, worth $2,000 in her name only.
- A car (1998 Ford) worth $5,500 in her name.
- A life insurance burial policy payable to Charles with a face value of $5,000.
- A diamond ring worth $1,500.
- A mink coat worth $4,000.
- Household goods worth $5,000.
- Other personal property worth $300.
- Clothing worth $200.

The only debt Cheryl owed was $110 for two wigs purchased from Beauty Products, Inc.

Except for the diamond ring, which was left to her sister, Karen, Cheryl's will stated all of her estate should go to her husband, Charles, if he survived her, and if not, to her children in equal shares. The will names Charles personal representative (executor) and was executed on November 21, 1998. Charles hires an attorney, Susan Brown, 1400 Main Street, Minneapolis, Minnesota 55455, to help with the estate administration.

For the informal, unsupervised probate administration of Cheryl's will, the following forms must be executed. Review them in Appendix A.

1. Application for Informal Probate of Will and for Informal Appointment of Personal Representative (Form 49*).
2. Testimony of Witness to Will (not executed; see Form 9*).
3. Statement of Informal Probate of Will and Order of Informal Appointment of Personal Representative (Form 51*).
4. Notice of Informal Probate of Will and Appointment of Personal Representative and Notice to Creditors (Form 52*).
5. Proof of Placing Order for Publication (Form 53*).
6. Affidavit of Publication, often provided to registrar by publisher (not executed; see Form 6*).
7. Affidavit of Mailing Notice of Informal Probate of Will (Form 54*).
8. Notice to Spouse and Children and Affidavit of Mailing (Form 55*).
9. Acceptance of Appointment as Personal Representative and Oath by Individual (Form 56*).
10. Bond, if required (not executed; see Form 68*).
11. Letters Testamentary (Form 57*).
12. Inventory (Form 58*).
13. Written Statement of Claim (Form 59*).
14. Final Account (not executed; see Form 32*).
15. Receipt for Assets by Distributee (Form 60*).
16. Unsupervised Personal Representative's Statement to Close Estate (Form 61*).

Problem 3

All the facts in the Cheryl Kennedy case, including the assets and liabilities listed, are the same, except in this instance Cheryl died intestate. The forms that must be executed for the informal probate administration of Cheryl's estate in Minnesota are the following:

1. Application for Informal Appointment of Personal Representative (Intestate) (Form 62*).
2. Notice of Informal Appointment of Personal Representative and Notice to Creditors (Intestate) (Form 63*).
3. Proof of Placing Order for Publication (Form 64*).
4. Affidavit of Publication, often provided to registrar by publisher (not executed, see Form 6*).
5. Affidavit of Mailing Notice of Informal Appointment (Form 65*).
6. Notice to Spouse and Children and Affidavit of Mailing (Form 66*).
7. Acceptance of Appointment as Personal Representative and Oath by Individual (Form 67*).
8. Bond, if required (Form 68*).
9. Letters of General Administration (Form 69*).
10. Inventory (Form 58*).
11. Written Statement of Claim (Form 59*).
12. Final Account (not executed; see Form 32*).
13. Deed of Distribution by Personal Representative (Form 70*).
14. Receipt for Assets by Distributee (Form 71*).
15. Unsupervised Personal Representative's Statement to Close Estate (Form 61*).
16. Application for Certificate from Registrar—Application for Release of Bond (Form 72*).
17. Certificate of Registrar—Release of Bond (Form 73*).
    A. Review the forms that must be executed in Case Problem 3, the Cheryl Ann Kennedy intestate case. Identify and complete the forms required for the probate administration of her estate if Cheryl had died intestate in your state. Compare your executed forms with those in Appendix A.

*See Appendix A

CHAPTER 14

TAX CONSIDERATIONS IN THE ADMINISTRATION OF ESTATES

OUTLINE

OBJECTIVES

After completing this chapter, you should be able to:

➤ Distinguish and identify the income, gift, and death taxes that must be paid.

➤ Understand and explain various ways to transfer assets while alive in order to lessen the amount of taxes owed to the state and federal governments by a decedent's estate.

➤ Understand the current tax consequences for gifts and estates created by changes in the tax laws.

➤ Prepare the tax returns of a decedent's estate.

SCOPE OF THE CHAPTER

Although the personal representative and the attorney have the ultimate responsibility for probating an estate properly and promptly, as the paralegal assisting the attorney, you must also be knowledgeable about legal and procedural matters applicable to estate administration, including the tax consequences to the estate of the decedent. If you intend to specialize in estate administration, you will need to acquire an extensive knowledge of tax laws and procedures. Federal and state statutes must be checked to see if they have been repealed or amended, or if new statutes have been enacted. A good source for updated federal tax laws is the Commerce Clearing House (CCH) loose-leaf tax service as well as Internal Revenue Service (IRS) (*www.irs.ustreas.gov*) and state publications. *You will need*

ETHICAL ISSUE

to consult with other professionals, i.e., the attorney and an accountant, who are familiar with current tax laws and the preparation of tax returns.

This chapter provides a foundation for understanding tax considerations in the administration of estates. For purposes of illustration, it incorporates the basic materials used in the preparation of federal tax returns and some state death tax returns. State tax forms vary substantially. You must familiarize yourself with your state's forms and tax law. The forms mentioned appear in Appendix A.

The first part of this chapter provides an introduction to tax concerns and a discussion of such tax considerations as: the unified credit (applicable credit amount) and exemption equivalent (applicable exclusion amount); the unified transfer gift and estate tax rates; the marital deduction; trusts; lifetime gifts; and generation-skipping transfers. Next, the tax returns themselves are discussed, including the decedent's final income tax returns, federal and state; the fiduciary's income tax returns, federal and state; the gift tax returns, federal and state; the estate tax returns, federal and state; and the state inheritance tax return.

INTRODUCTION TO TAX CONCERNS

Income Tax

The federal government and many state governments levy and collect taxes on income. The income subject to such tax includes personal income, corporate income, and trust income, which is a form of personal income. It is the duty of the personal representative of the decedent's estate to file the decedent's personal income tax returns for the decedent's year of death and to see that any income tax owed the federal and state governments is paid out of estate assets. In addition, the personal representative must file federal and state income tax returns for any income that accrues or is earned after the decedent's death until the close of the taxable year or until the date of final distribution of the estate. These tax returns are called U.S. or state fiduciary income tax returns.

Death Tax

Death taxes are measured by the amount of property transferred at death. There are two kinds of death taxes: federal and state *estate taxes* and state *inheritance taxes.*

The estate tax is a tax levied on the privilege of transferring property at death. This tax is levied on the estate itself, not on the **successors.** The rate and amount of the estate tax are determined by the size of the estate; like the income tax, the estate tax is progressive, i.e., the larger the estate, the higher the tax rate. At the present time, the *federal gift and estate tax rate* ranges from 18 percent to 55 percent (see Exhibit 14.2). Under the Economic Growth and Tax Relief Reconciliation Act of 2001, the top rate is scheduled to decrease to 50 percent in 2002 and 45 percent in 2007 (see Exhibit 14.4). Generally, state estate taxes are imposed in an amount equal to the credit allowable under the federal estate tax law. Currently, two states have both a credit estate tax and an estate tax (see Exhibit 14.1).

A state inheritance or succession tax is levied on the privilege of receiving property from a decedent at death. The rate or amount of this tax is determined by state law and depends on the amount of the share of the decedent's estate received by a particular successor and on the relationship of the successor to the decedent. It is also a progressive tax. Eleven states impose an inheritance tax on successors (see Exhibit 14.1). Individual state statutes must be checked.

> **Successor**
> An all-inclusive UPC term meaning any person, other than a creditor, who is entitled to real or personal property of a decedent either under the will or through intestate succession.

Gift Tax

A gift tax is a tax levied on the privilege of transferring property during life. This is a tax on the donor, not on the donee. The federal gift tax rate is the same schedule used for the federal estate tax. The state gift taxes generally follow the rates and exemptions prescribed under the state death tax statutes.

The federal government imposes an estate tax and gift tax but no inheritance tax. States usually have either an estate tax, an inheritance tax, a gift tax, or some combination of the three. The federal and state estate, gift, and inheritance tax statutes require the personal representative to file the appropriate tax returns by a prescribed time, unless he or she has filed an Application for Extension of Time to File with the appropriate agencies. These statutes also require the personal representative to pay the tax due within the prescribed time. Generally, extensions of time to file do not extend the time to pay taxes, which are due by the regular due date. Extensions may be allowed in certain cases where reasonable cause can be shown. *A personal representative who fails to make timely payment is personally liable for any interest charged or penalties resulting from this neglect. You must remind him of such deadlines.*

> **ETHICAL ISSUE**

The personal representative is responsible for paying all taxes out of the estate assets. These include income, fiduciary, gift, estate, and inheritance taxes, unless the will specifies that the devisees pay the inheritance tax out of their legacies or devises. If prior to distribution of the estate the personal representative proves the estate does not have enough cash (or assets to be sold) to pay the taxes and this shortfall is not due to any fault on her part, she is free from individual liability to pay the taxes. If the personal representative distributes the estate, however, and does not have enough assets left to pay the taxes, she must pay the taxes out of her own pocket (IRC § 2002). Therefore, it is imperative the personal representative makes sure sufficient assets remain for the payment of all taxes and debts before distributing any of the estate assets. Certain preferred claims have priority for payment before taxes are paid, e.g., administrative expenses, funeral expenses, and expenses of the last illness (see Chapter 12 for an example of a priority of debts statute, but compare UPC § 3–805).

Exhibit 14.1 Income, Gift, Estate, Inheritance, and Generation-Skipping Transfer Taxes Imposed by States

State	Income Tax	Gift Tax	Estate Tax	Credit Estate Tax	Inheritance Tax	Generation-Skipping Transfer Tax
Alabama	×			(2)		(3)
Alaska				(2)		
Arizona	×			(2)		(3)
Arkansas	×			(2)		
California	×			(2)		(3)
Colorado	×			(2)		(3)
Connecticut	×	× (§ 12–640)		(2)	× (§ 12–344)	(3)
Delaware	×			(2)		
Florida				(2)		(3)
Georgia	×			(2)		
Hawaii	×			(2)		(3)
Idaho	×			(2)		(3)
Illinois	×			(2)		(3)
Indiana	×			(2)	× (§ 6–4.1–5–1)	(3)
Iowa	×			(2)	× (§ 450.10)	(3)
Kansas	×			(2)		(3)
Kentucky	×			(2)	× (§ 140.070)	
Louisiana	×	× (§ 47:1201)		(2)	× (§ 47:2403)	
Maine	×			(2)		
Maryland	×			(2)	× (§§ 7–203,4)	(3)
Massachusetts	×			(2)		(3)
Michigan	×			(2)		(3)
Minnesota	×			(2)		
Mississippi	×			(2)		
Missouri	×			(2)		(3)
Montana	×			(2)		(3)
Nebraska	×			(2)	× (§§ 77–2004,5,6)	(3)
Nevada				(2)		(3)
New Hampshire	(1)			(2)	× (§ 86:6)	
New Jersey	×			(2)	× (§ 54:34–2)	
New Mexico	×			(2)		
New York	×			(2)		(3)
North Carolina	×	× (§ 105–188)		(2)		(3)
North Dakota	×			(2)		
Ohio	×		× (§ 5731.02)	(2)		(3)
Oklahoma	×		× (T 68 § 803)	(2)		
Oregon	×			(2)		
Pennsylvania	×			(2)	× (T 72 § 9116)	
Rhode Island	×			(2)		(3)
South Carolina	×			(2)		(3)
South Dakota				(2)		
Tennessee	(1)	× (§ 67–8–101)		(2)	× (§ 67–8–314)	(3)
Texas				(2)		(3)
Utah	×			(2)		

(continued)

Exhibit 14.1   Income, Gift, Estate, Inheritance, and Generation-Skipping Transfer Taxes
Imposed by States—*continued*

State	Income Tax	Gift Tax	Estate Tax	Credit Estate Tax	Inheritance Tax	Generation-Skipping Transfer Tax
Vermont	×			(2)		(3)
Virginia	×			(2)		(3)
Washington				(2)		(3)
West Virginia	×			(2)		
Wisconsin	×			(2)		
Wyoming				(2)		

(1) Interest and dividend income only.
(2) An estate tax is imposed to absorb the credit against the federal estate tax for state death taxes paid.
(3) A generation-skipping transfer tax is imposed to absorb the federal transfer tax credit.

GENERAL TAX CONSIDERATIONS

Beginning in 1976, Congress has extensively overhauled the federal estate and gift tax laws, the most recent being the Economic Growth and Tax Relief Reconciliation Act of 2001. The changes have had a tremendous impact on estate planning and administration as well as on income tax considerations for grantors, testators, and beneficiaries. Many of the provisions are complex and require numerous qualifying regulations and rulings. Attorneys, paralegals, and others who specialize in estate planning and administration must be well versed on these comprehensive changes and their effects. Under these laws, death tax payments are assessed only against the wealthy and the moderately wealthy. Smaller estates have benefited from the changes; the vast majority of estates that were previously required to file federal estate tax returns and pay estate taxes are now required to do neither.

Before turning to the various tax returns that usually must be completed as part of the administration of a decedent's estate, certain general tax considerations need to be mentioned. One should remember that after the decedent's death, the estate is a new legal being; the legal existence of the decedent has terminated. The estate has rights and obligations, and it is a taxpayer.

Everybody wants to reduce the death taxes owed the government or to avoid them entirely whenever legally possible. There are numerous ways to accomplish tax savings on a decedent's estate. The most frequently used methods include: (1) making use of the unified credit (applicable credit amount) and exemption equivalent (applicable exclusion amount), and the Unified Transfer Tax Rate Schedule for federal estate and gift taxes; (2) making use of the marital deduction; (3) creating trusts; and (4) making gifts during the decedent's lifetime.

Unified Credit (Applicable Credit Amount) and Unified Transfer Gift and Estate Tax Rates

The 1976 Tax Reform Act (TRA) not only created a unified transfer tax credit for gifts and estates, but also unified federal gift and estate tax rates into a single schedule.

Unified Credit (applicable credit amount) A credit against the federal unified transfer tax on gifts (prior to death) and estates (after death).

The unified rate is applied to all transfers of assets subject to tax, whether the transfers occur during life by *inter vivos* gift or after death by will or intestate succession.

Exhibit 14.2   Unified Transfer Tax Rate Schedule for Gift and Estate Taxes: For Gifts Made and for Deaths after 1983 and before 2002

If the Amount with Respect to Which the Tentative Tax to Be Computed Is:	The Tentative Tax Is:
Not over $10,000	18 percent of such amount.
Over $10,000 but not over $20,000	$1,800 plus 20 percent of the excess of such amount over $10,000.
Over $20,000 but not over $40,000	$3,800 plus 22 percent of the excess of such amount over $20,000.
Over $40,000 but not over $60,000	$8,200 plus 24 percent of the excess of such amount over $40,000.
Over $60,000 but not over $80,000	$13,000 plus 26 percent of the excess of such amount over $60,000.
Over $80,000 but not over $100,000	$18,200 plus 28 percent of the excess of such amount over $80,000.
Over $100,000 but not over $150,000	$23,800 plus 30 percent of the excess of such amount over $100,000.
Over $150,000 but not over $250,000	$38,800 plus 32 percent of the excess of such amount over $150,000.
Over $250,000 but not over $500,000	$70,800 plus 34 percent of the excess of such amount over $250,000.
Over $500,000 but not over $750,000	$155,800 plus 37 percent of the excess of such amount over $500,000.
Over $750,000 but not over $1,000,000	$248,300 plus 39 percent of the excess of such amount over $750,000.
Over $1,000,000 but not over $1,250,000	$345,800 plus 41 percent of the excess of such amount over $1,000,000.
Over $1,250,000 but not over $1,500,000	$448,300 plus 43 percent of the excess of such amount over $1,250,000.
Over $1,500,000 but not over $2,000,000	$555,800 plus 45 percent of the excess of such amount over $1,500,000.
Over $2,000,000 but not over $2,500,000	$780,800 plus 49 percent of the excess of such amount over $2,000,000.
Over $2,500,000 but not over $3,000,000	$1,025,800 plus 53 percent of the excess of such amount over $2,500,000.
Over $3,000,000*	$1,290,800 plus 55 percent of the excess of such amount over $3,000,000.

*For large taxable transfers (generally in excess of $10 million) there is a phase-out of the benefits of the graduated rates and the unified tax credit.

tops out at 48% for over 2.5

Unified Credit (Applicable Credit Amount)

The 1997 Taxpayer Relief Act, which took effect on January 1, 1998, replaced the **unified credit** with an **applicable credit amount,** which is subtracted from the tax due (see Exhibit 14.3).

Unified Transfer Gift and Estate Tax Rates

In the 1976 TRA, the tax rates for estate and gift taxes were unified into a single schedule. The rates are progressive and are based on cumulative lifetime and deathtime transfers (see Exhibit 14.2).

    With the Economic Growth and Tax Relief Reconciliation Act of 2001, the top applicable rate will be 45 percent by 2007 and the **exemption equivalent (applicable exclusion amount)** will be $3,500,000 by 2009. The estate tax and generation-skipping transfer tax are scheduled to be repealed by 2010. The gift tax exemption will be $1,000,000 effective in 2002 and thereafter. The gift tax will be retained in 2010 at the top income tax rate for the applicable year which is scheduled to be 35 percent under the act. *Caveat:* The economic climate during the next ten years will dictate whether these changes become effective (see Exhibit 14.4).

Exemption equivalent (applicable exclusion amount)
The maximum value of property that can be transferred to others without incurring any federal gift or estate tax because of the application of the unified credit (applicable credit amount).

Exhibit 14.3   Unified Credit (Applicable Credit Amount) and Exemption Equivalent (Applicable Exclusion Amount)

Year	Unified Credit (Applicable Credit Amount)	Exemption Equivalent (Applicable Exclusion Amount)
1987–1997	$192,800	$600,000
1998	202,050	625,000
1999	211,300	650,000
2000 and 2001	220,550	675,000

Exhibit 14.4   Economic Growth and Tax Relief Reconciliation Act of 2001

Year	Estate Tax Exemption Equivalent (Applicable Exclusion Amount)	Generation-Skipping Transfer Tax Exemption	Gift Tax Exemption	Top Tax Rate
2002	$1,000,000	$1,000,000	$1,000,000	50%
2003	1,000,000	1,000,000	1,000,000	49
2004	1,500,000	1,500,000	1,000,000	48
2005	1,500,000	1,500,000	1,000,000	47
2006	2,000,000	2,000,000	1,000,000	46
2007	2,000,000	2,000,000	1,000,000	45
2008	2,000,000	2,000,000	1,000,000	45
2009	3,500,000	3,500,000	1,000,000	45
2010	Repealed	Repealed	1,000,000	35*

*The gift tax is retained at the top income rate for the applicable year.

Example: Jody Carter died in November 2000, leaving a taxable estate of $675,000. The formula for computing the federal estate tax was $155,800 plus 37 percent of the excess of such amount over $500,000, equaling a tentative tax of $220,550. In 2000, the unified credit (applicable credit amount) of $220,550 was allowed, which canceled out the $220,550 tentative tax. Therefore Jody Carter's estate owed no federal estate tax.

Any taxpayer who dies leaving a taxable estate of the value of the applicable exclusion amount (i.e., $675,000 for 2000 and 2001; $3,500,000 by 2009) or less would not be liable for any federal estate tax.

Under the law, gift taxes are computed by applying the Unified Transfer Tax Rate Schedule to cumulative lifetime taxable transfers and subtracting the taxes paid for prior taxable periods. Federal estate taxes are computed by applying the Unified Transfer Tax Rate Schedule to cumulative lifetime and deathtime transfers, then subtracting the gift taxes paid. Thus, if you give away $200,000 of property during your lifetime, over and above the $10,000 per donee per year exclusion (indexed annually for inflation), you have only $475,000 (2000 and 2001) of property available to pass tax-free at death. In some circumstances, adjustments must be made for taxes in lifetime transfers in the decedent's estate (see the discussion under Lifetime Gifts below). (*Note:* In general, any portion of the unified credit (applicable credit amount) that is used against gift taxes will reduce the credit available to be used against the federal estate tax.) The amount of the unified credit allowed cannot be greater than the amount of the computed transfer tax.

Calculating the Federal Estate Tax

The amount of the federal estate tax is computed by applying the unified rates to the decedent's cumulative lifetime transfers and transfers made at death, then subtracting the taxes paid on the lifetime transfers (the gift tax, as computed by applying the unified rate, would have been paid previously at the time assets were transferred during the decedent's life). The computation of the federal estate tax is outlined in Exhibit 14.5. Review the outline carefully for future computation examples. See also the discussion and examples under The Marital Deduction below.

The tax credits listed in Exhibit 14.5 include the previously discussed unified credit; the credit for state death taxes, i.e., the decedent's estate is allowed a federal credit for the state death taxes actually paid up to specific limits; the credit for foreign death taxes, i.e., credit allowed for death taxes actually paid to a foreign country by the decedent's estate; and for estate taxes paid by the estates of other decedents for assets included in the current decedent's estate. This is called the "credit for tax on prior transfers" and is allowed only if the two deaths occur within a short time of each other, e.g., within ten years before or two years after the current decedent's death. The purpose of this credit is to prevent the same property from being taxed too often. The credit is limited to the smaller of the following amounts:

1. The amount of the federal estate tax attributable to the transferred property in the transferor's estate, or
2. The amount of the federal estate tax attributable to the transferred property in the current decedent's estate.

Exhibit 14.5 Method for Computing Federal Estate Tax

Gross Estate (all property owned at decedent's death)		$_____
Less:		
Qualified conservation easement exclusion		_____
Equals:		
Total Gross Estate less Exclusion		_____
Less:		
Funeral and administration expenses	_____	
Debts including taxes accrued prior to death	_____	
Mortgages and liens	_____	
Losses during administration	_____	
Total	======	_____
Equals:		
Adjusted Gross Estate		_____
Less:		
Marital deduction	_____	
Charitable deduction	_____	
Qualified family-owned business interest deduction	_____	
Total	======	
Equals:		
Taxable Estate (Gross estate less deductions)		_____
Plus:		
Adjusted taxable gifts (post-1976 lifetime taxable transfers not included in gross estate)		_____
Equals:		
Tentative Tax Base (Taxable Amount)		======
Compute:		
Tentative tax	_____	
Less:		
Gift taxes paid or payable on post-1976 taxable gifts	_____	
Equals:		
Gross Estate Tax before Credits		_____
Less:		
Unified credit (applicable credit amount)	_____	
Credit for state death taxes	_____	
Credit for foreign death taxes	_____	
Credit for estate taxes on prior transfers	_____	
Total Tax Credits	======	_____
Equals:		
Federal Estate Tax Due		_____
Plus:		
Generation-skipping transfer taxes		_____
Equals:		
Total Transfer Taxes Due		$_____

Note: When a decedent leaves everything to his or her surviving spouse, there would be no estate tax because of the unlimited marital deduction.

Exhibit 14.6   The Credit for Tax on Prior Transfers

Period of Time Exceeding	Not Exceeding	Percent Allowable
. . . .	2 years	100
2 years	4 years	80
4 years	6 years	60
6 years	8 years	40
8 years	10 years	20
10 years	. . . .	none

Note: See Instructions for Form 706, Schedule Q.

The credit is allowed in a declining percentage of the smaller of these amounts (see Exhibit 14.6).

Example: Mary Perkins dies, leaving her daughter, Molly, property worth $400,000. Mary's estate paid $80,000 in federal estate taxes on the property transferred to Molly. Now Molly dies. Assuming the $80,000 of federal estate tax is the same or the smaller under the two limitations above, the amount of the credit available to Molly's estate would be as follows:

Year of Molly's Death after Mary's Death	Credit to Molly's Estate
1 or 2 years	$80,000 (100%)
3 or 4 years	$64,000 (80%)
5 or 6 years	$48,000 (60%)
7 or 8 years	$32,000 (40%)
9 or 10 years	$16,000 (20%)
Over 10 years	No credit

The Marital Deduction

The marital deduction can be a substantial tax-saving device for an estate (see the discussion under Determining the Taxable Estate below). The 1981 Economic Recovery Tax Act (ERTA) provided for an unlimited federal estate tax marital deduction for transfers between spouses. A testator's estate is entitled to the marital deduction if there is a surviving spouse and if the decedent leaves all or a portion of his or her estate to the surviving spouse. If the decedent spouse dies intestate, the surviving spouse is entitled to a statutory share of the decedent's estate. The amount of the surviving spouse's statutory share is the amount of the marital deduction in such cases.

The 1981 ERTA also added language to IRC § 2056, pertaining to the estate tax marital deduction, and to IRC § 2523, pertaining to the gift tax marital deduction (see Gifts and the Marital Deduction below). The 1981 law contains a "terminable interest rule," which allows certain property to qualify for the estate and gift tax marital deduction that previously did not qualify. The eligible property is called "qualified terminable interest property" (QTIP), i.e., property that passes from the decedent spouse in which the surviving spouse has a qualified income interest for life. Examples of QTIP property that qualify for marital deduction treatment are (1) trusts with a life interest to the surviving spouse, the remainder to the children; and (2) a legal life estate to the surviving spouse and the remainder to others, e.g., their children.

As Chapter 10 observed, the qualifying of QTIP property for the marital deduction can be an important estate-planning tool that also permits the testator to direct the disposition of the trust principal at the death of the surviving spouse (e.g., providing for children of a previous marriage and the like).

In order for property to qualify as QTIP property for marital deduction treatment, the following are necessary:

- The surviving spouse life tenant must have a "qualifying income interest for life" in the property. The surviving spouse has a qualified income interest for life if (1) the surviving spouse is entitled to all the income for life from the property, payable at least annually or at more frequent intervals, and (2) no person during the surviving spouse's lifetime has the power to appoint any part of the property to any person other than the surviving spouse.
- The personal representative or executor of the decedent spouse's estate must *elect* to treat the property as QTIP property on the decedent's federal estate tax return (Form 706 and Form 88 in Appendix A). If the executor makes the election, the property will qualify for the marital deduction. In the case of a lifetime transfer, however, the donor-spouse makes the QTIP election (see definition in the Glossary).

The use of a testamentary trust with a life interest to a surviving spouse is one method of substantially reducing the tax consequences to a decedent's estate. An example of such a trust is included in Appendix B.

Gifts and the Marital Deduction

The marital deduction can also be used when there is a transfer by gift of any property between spouses. The annual gift tax exclusion is $10,000 per donee per year (indexed annually for inflation), and the marital deduction on gift taxes for lifetime transfers (gifts) of any property between spouses is unlimited. Therefore, whether John gives his spouse, Mary, $10,000, $100,000, or $1,000,000, none of the property or cash is subject to gift tax. There is no upper limit on how much John can give his spouse. Regardless of the amount of the gift transferred between spouses that is offset by the unlimited marital deduction, such gifts do not require the filing of the gift tax return Form 709 (see Form 86*). Computation of the federal gift tax is outlined in Exhibit 14.7.

Creation of Trusts

Another method used to diminish death taxes is the creation of trusts (see Chapters 8 and 9). It is possible to leave property in a testamentary trust for beneficiaries named by the testator-settlor so that additional estate taxes are not due at the death of the beneficiary. If properly planned and executed, one such trust, combined with the marital deduction, can result in substantial savings to the

---

*See Appendix A

estate of a decedent over the course of two generations (see the discussion under Determining the Taxable Estate). Taxes can also be diminished using *inter vivos* or lifetime trusts.

Lifetime Gifts

A person who makes a gift is called a *donor,* and a person who receives a gift is called a *donee.* A federal gift tax is levied on the right to transfer property from a donor to a donee for less than full or adequate consideration. The donor is respon-

---

Exhibit 14.7   Method for Computing Federal Gift Tax

Total Gifts made during current calendar year (IRC §§ 2511–2519)		$_____
Less:		
Political organization exclusion (IRC § 2501[a][5])	_____	
Educational exclusion (IRC § 2503[e])	_____	
Medical exclusion (IRC § 2503[e])	_____	
Annual exclusion (IRC § 2503[b]) ($10,000 per donee indexed for inflation)	_____	
Unlimited marital deduction (IRC § 2523)	_____	
Charitable deduction (IRC § 2522)	_____	
Total Exclusions and Deductions	=====	_____
Equals:		
Taxable Gifts for calendar year (IRC § 2503[a])		_____
Plus:		
Taxable Gifts for prior years (IRC § 2504)		_____
Equals:		
Total Taxable Gifts (current and prior years)		=====
Compute:		
Tentative tax		
Less:		
Tentative tax on prior taxable gifts		_____
Equals:		
Gift Tax before unified credit		_____
Less:		
Allowable unified credit (IRC § 2505)		_____
Equals:		
Federal Gift Tax Due (for current period)		_____
Plus:		
Generation-skipping transfer taxes (for current period)		_____
Equals:		
Total Transfer Taxes Due		$_____

sible for the payment of the tax. Gifts made during the lifetime *(inter vivos)* of the decedent can in some cases result in tax advantages. Tax laws have unified the gift and estate tax rates into a single rate schedule with progressive rates that are computed on the basis of cumulative transfers made both during lifetime and at death. All taxable gifts made after December 31, 1976 (called adjusted taxable gifts) are included in the decedent's gross estate and are subject to the federal estate tax. A credit against the tax for gift taxes previously paid is then deducted.

But some incentives for *inter vivos* gift giving remain under the laws. The annual exclusion was increased to $10,000 per donee to allow larger gifts to be exempt from the federal gift tax. Beginning in 1999 an annual inflation adjustment was added. The increase reflects the economy's inflationary trend and encourages compliance with the tax law by taxpayers. Any appreciation in value of a lifetime gift that may accrue between the date the gift is made and the date of the donor's death is not subject to a transfer tax. *Note:* When the donee sells the property, any appreciation will be subject to income tax. Income taxes may be reduced when the gift property produces income and the property is transferred during life to a donee who is in a lower income tax bracket than the donor. Finally, lifetime gifts can reduce the value of the decedent's estate and thereby also reduce the federal estate tax, especially in the estate of the surviving spouse.

The laws governing gifts and taxes on such gifts provide as follows:

- A gift must be intended and delivered by the donor.
- Any person can give a gift of up to $10,000 per year (indexed annually for inflation) tax-free to each donee, and, if the donor's spouse joins in the gift, the exclusions of both spouses may be used, resulting in an exclusion of $20,000 or more when adjusted for inflation. This is called *gift splitting*. These joint gifts are tax-free to both the donor and the donee.
- Some gifts made within three years of the donor's death are automatically included in the donor-decedent's gross estate and are subject to federal estate tax (IRC § 2035).
- The federal unified gift and estate tax rate is a progressive and cumulative tax.
- When the gift is to the donor's spouse, there is an unlimited gift tax marital deduction (IRC § 2523).
- When a gift is made to a charitable organization, some limits are placed on the amount of the charitable deduction from the gift tax, depending on the type of gift and the charity to which it is given (IRC § 2522).
- Transfers to a political organization (IRC § 2501[a][5]) or amounts paid on behalf of a donee to an educational organization as tuition or a care provider for medical care (IRC § 2503[e]) are not subject to the gift tax.

Before becoming too enthusiastic about transferring property by gift, it is well to remember that, once transferred, the property can no longer be controlled by the donor. The property passes to the new owner, the donee, and that person alone has title to it. Also, one must guard against giving gifts with strings attached. In most cases, when the donor retains control over the gift, income from the gift property will be taxed to the donor, and the property will be included in the donor's gross estate for federal estate tax purposes upon the donor's death (IRC §§ 2036–2038).

Example: In 2001, Janet Brown made a gift to her niece, Sue, of property valued at $173,625. Janet had made no previous taxable gifts. The unified credit for 2001 is $220,550. Janet computes her gift tax for 2001 as follows:

Total gifts for 2001	$173,625	Tentative gift tax on total taxable gifts[1]	$43,160
Annual exclusion (adjust for inflation)	− 10,000	Tentative gift tax on prior taxable gifts	− 0
Taxable gifts for 2001	$163,625	Gift tax before unified credit	$43,160
Taxable gifts from prior years	+ 0	Allowable unified credit	− 220,550
Total Taxable Gifts	$163,625	Federal Gift Tax Due	$ 0

In order to avoid any gift tax for 2001, Janet would use only $43,160 of the $220,550 credit for that year and would thereby have no gift tax liability. *Note:* If Janet died in 2001 and had made no other taxable gifts that year, her estate would have, from the unified gift and estate tax schedule, $177,390 ($220,550 − $43,160) remaining as her unified credit that could be subtracted from any estate tax liability she might have at the time of her death.

Gift making, gift splitting between spouses, and the unified credit are all means of reducing tax liability. But remember the unified credit is allowed against lifetime gift taxes, or estate taxes, or both. Unlike the $10,000 per donee annual exclusion (indexed for inflation) which is available to the donor each year, once the unified credit is used, it is terminated. It can be used to diminish or eliminate the tax on lifetime gifts or to diminish or eliminate the estate tax.

The Gift-Splitting Provision

Gift splitting by spouses has been retained under the current law. When married, the donor, with the other spouse's consent, may split the lifetime gift to the donee. The gift will then be treated as though half was given by the donor and the other half by the spouse even though the entire gift comes from only one spouse's assets. Thus, the spouses may give $20,000 or more annually, when adjusted for inflation, to each donee tax-free if each spouse consents to having the gift treated as being given half by each spouse. As a result, a married donor can put more property into a trust while paying less gift tax than a single person would pay (IRC § 2513).

Example: Using the $10,000 annual exclusion, a gift may be given free of gift tax as in the following examples:

If You Are	Married	Single
and giving to one person	two $10,000 annual exclusions = $20,000	one $10,000 annual exclusion = $10,000
and giving to two persons	four $10,000 annual exclusions = $40,000	two $10,000 annual exclusions = $20,000
and giving to three persons	six $10,000 annual exclusions = $60,000	three $10,000 annual exclusions = $30,000

---

[1]This figure is obtained from the Unified Tax Rate Schedule using the over $150,000 but not over $250,000 line. The tentative tax is $38,800 plus 32 percent of the excess over $150,000. This becomes $38,800 plus $4,360, which equals $43,160.

⛩ ASSIGNMENT 14.1

Michele and Bruce, husband and wife, decided to give $700,000 to their niece, Trudy, in December 2000. Assuming the couple has not used either of their $10,000 exclusions for Trudy for 2000 nor the $220,550 unified credit, compute the aggregate gift tax the couple would have to pay on the gift (before the unified credit is subtracted), using the Unified Tax Rate Schedule. Now, assume the couple chooses to reduce the gift tax as much as possible. (Remember that a *credit* is deducted *after* the tax has been computed and the spouses each file separate returns.) How much gift tax would the couple pay?

Do the same computations, except the amount of the gift is $1,000,000.

Uniform Transfers to Minors Act

Today, all states, except South Carolina and Vermont, have adopted the Uniform Transfers to Minors Act (UTMA) which revised and replaced the Uniform Gifts to Minors Act (IRC § 2503[c]). The UTMA allows *any kind* of real or personal property, wherever located, to be transferred to a custodianship as a gift to a minor. Money and securities are common gifts to minors, but others include annuities, life insurance policies, and real estate. In addition to lifetime gifts, transfers from trusts and wills can be added to the custodianship. A person or financial institution, called the custodian, is selected by the donor of the gift to manage and invest the property for the support, education, and welfare of the minor who, as the donee, has legal title to the property (assets). The custodian can be a parent or other family member; a guardian; a bank; or a trust company. However, a parent-donor should not be named custodian because, if the parent-donor dies before the minor-donee receives the final distribution of the assets (gifts) at age 18, 21, or 25 (depending on the state), the assets will be taxed as part of the parent-donor's estate.

A custodianship is a less expensive alternative to the appointment of a guardian in a will because a will must be probated and the probate court has strict rules on how funds can be invested. Court approval or supervision of a custodian's investment decisions is not required.

Although a will or living trust can be used to establish a custodianship, a faster and easier method is to use a written instrument which transfers the property to the name of the custodian followed by the words "as custodian for the donee, [name of the minor], under the State of [name of state] Uniform Transfers to Minors Act" for the appropriate state, which can be the residence of the custodian, donor, minor, or the location of the property. This procedure incorporates by reference all provisions of the state's act and requires that each gift must be made to just one minor with only one person acting as the custodian. For their services, custodians are paid "reasonable compensation" from the transferred property.

Any gift transferred under the act is irrevocable. It belongs to the minor, and both the property and its income must be used solely for the benefit of the minor. Accurate records must be kept for all investments, and annual tax returns must be filed by the custodian for the minor since income earned on the property is taxable to the minor. When the minor reaches age 18, 21, or 25 (depending on the state), the custodianship terminates, and the custodian must transfer all assets and any undisposed income to the minor (see chart below). If the minor dies before age 18, 21, or 25, the property passes to the minor's estate or to whomever the minor may appoint under a general power of appointment.

For the donor, the creation of a custodianship under the Uniform Transfers to Minors Act is a gift of a present interest, and as such it qualifies for the $10,000 annual gift tax exclusion which is indexed annually for inflation.

Age at Which a UTMA Custodianship Must Terminate by State

Age	State
18	Kentucky, Louisiana, Michigan, Oklahoma, Rhode Island, South Dakota
18 (up to 21)	Maine, Virginia
18 (up to 25)	Alaska, California, Nevada
21 (down to 18)	Arkansas, New Jersey, North Carolina
21	All the remaining states (except South Carolina and Vermont)

Generation-Skipping Transfers and Their Tax Consequences

Generation-skipping transfer
A transfer of assets to a person two or more generations below the transferor, e.g., from a grandparent to a grandchild.

Generation-skipping transfer trust
A trust that partially avoids federal gift and estate taxes on transfers of large sums of money or other valuable assets established to transfer these assets to a benificiary two or more generations below the transferor.

Generation-skipping transfer tax
A federal tax on the transfer of property when its value exceeds $1,000,000 (indexed for inflation) to a person two or more generations below the generation of the transferor (donor or decedent), e.g., a grandparent who transfers property to a grandchild thereby skipping a child.

Transferor
The decedent or donor who creates a generation-skipping transfer trust.

Transferee
The beneficiary who receives the benefits of a generation-skipping transfer trust.

The stated purpose of the federal estate and gift taxes is not only to raise revenue but also to tax death transfers consistently generation by generation. Congress realized a tax loophole existed by which family members could create a **generation-skipping transfer** using a **generation-skipping transfer trust** to partially avoid federal gift and estate taxes on large transfers of money or other valuable assets between generations of family members. Therefore, Congress closed the tax loophole by creating the **generation-skipping transfer tax** so that every generation-skipping transfer is subject to the generation-skipping transfer tax (IRC § 2601). *Caveat:* The definitions and rules concerning generation-skipping transfers and their tax computations are complicated. You must review the Code provisions carefully and work closely with your supervising attorney when preparing the appropriate tax returns.

The generation-skipping transfer tax is levied on transfers of property that exceed $1,000,000 (indexed for inflation) under trusts which have beneficiaries who are two or more generations below that of the **transferor,** and by direct transfers to persons who are two or more generations below that of the transferor. The generation-skipping transfer tax applies to lifetime transfers by gift or transfers by will or trust.

The generation-skipping transfer tax is imposed on the following generation-skipping transfers whenever any one of these three taxable events occurs:

- **A direct skip.** A generation-skipping transfer of assets made to a **skip person** that is also subject to federal gift or estate tax. A skip person is the person who receives the property in a generation-skipping transfer and who is two or more generations younger than the transferor (IRC § 2612[c][1]). The transferor is subject to federal gift or estate tax, and the **transferee** is a skip person. The phrase "subject to federal gift or estate tax" means that the asset transfer must be a gift or included in the transferor's gross estate, but it does not require that actual gift or estate tax liability must occur. Direct skips are of two types: (1) an outright transfer to persons two or more generations lower than the transferor's generation or (2) a transfer in trust for the exclusive benefit of persons two or more generations lower than the transferor's generation. When a direct skip is made, the taxable amount is based on the value of the property received by the transferee. If a lifetime direct skip is made to an individual, the tax return is filed and the generation-skipping transfer tax is paid by the transferor while living or by the transferor's personal representative for direct skips occurring at death (IRC § 2603[a][3]). However, when the direct skip is made from a trust, the tax is paid by the trustee.

Example: The most common example of a direct skip is a gift made by a grandparent to a grandchild whose parent is living. Henry Howard makes a gift of $1,500,000 to his granddaughter, Debbie, while Henry's son, Richard Howard (Debbie's father), is alive. Henry is the transferor, Debbie is the transferee and skip person, Richard is a non-skip person, the taxable amount is the $1,500,000, which is subject to federal gift tax, and the generation-skipping transfer tax is paid by the transferor (Henry). *Note:* If Richard Howard is not living at the time of Henry's transfer (gift), the transfer of the gift to the grandchild is not a direct skip (IRC § 2612[c][2]). In this case, Debbie has "moved up" to her father's generation and has become a non-skip person; therefore, this is not a generation-skipping transfer.

Example: Henry makes the same $1,500,000 gift as above, but this time he transfers the money to a trust in which the trustee is to pay the income and eventually the principal exclusively for the benefit of Henry's granddaughter, Debbie. In this case, the trust itself is the skip person because no non-skip person (e.g., Henry's child, Richard) has any "interest" in the property. The taxable amount is still $1,500,000, which is subject to federal gift tax, but the generation-skipping transfer tax is now paid by the trustee.

The current generation-skipping transfer tax is a flat rate (the maximum rate allowed under the unified gift and estate tax schedule) and is reported on either U.S. Treasury Form 706 or Form 709.

- **A taxable termination.** An interest in property held in trust terminates and trust property is held for or distributed to a skip person (IRC § 2652[c]). The trustee of the trust is responsible for filing the generation-skipping transfer tax return and for payment of the generation-skipping transfer tax (IRC § 2603[a][2]). The trustee must obtain a taxpayer identification number once a trust is created.
- **A taxable distribution.** Any distribution from a trust (income or principal) that is not a taxable termination or direct skip (IRC § 2612[b]). The transferee of a taxable distribution is responsible for the filing of the return and the payment of the generation-skipping transfer tax (IRC § 2603[a][1]). Transfers that are not subject to gift tax because of the $10,000 annual exclusion (indexed annually for inflation) and the unlimited exclusion for direct payment of medical and tuition expenses are not subject to generation-skipping transfer tax (IRC § 2642[c][1]).

$1,000,000 Exemption

Every transferor, including, after death, the transferor's personal representative, is allowed a $1,000,000 lifetime exemption from the generation-skipping transfer tax, which can be applied to any generation-skipping transfer (IRC § 2631). The $1,000,000 exemption is indexed for inflation beginning in 1999 and has increased each year. For 2001 the exemption is $1,060,000. Effective in 2002 to

2009 the exemption will be an amount equal to the exemption equivalent (applicable exclusion amount) (see Exhibit 14.4). If spouses elect to split their gifts, the total amount of the exemption becomes $2,120,000 for 2001 (IRC § 2652[a][2]). The exemption can be applied to whichever transfers the transferor or personal representative chooses. The tax is calculated by multiplying the taxable amount of the generation-skipping transfer by the applicable rate (IRC § 2602). Because of these exemptions, the generation-skipping transfer tax can be reduced or eliminated. This exemption applies at the time of transfer as selected by the transferor, and any appreciation of the asset or property transferred is not subject to the generation-skipping transfer tax.

💻 CONTACTING THE IRS IS EASY

Some estates will require the filing of tax forms with the IRS. Access the IRS at *www.irs.ustreas.gov.* On line you can request forms to be sent through the mail or forms can be downloaded. Information about estate taxes, gift taxes, returns, and electronic filing is included at this site.

TAX RETURNS

It is the responsibility of the personal representative (the fiduciary) of the decedent's estate to file tax returns for the estate and to pay any taxes owed out of the estate assets. Depending on the situation, the personal representative may have to file some or all of the following returns:

- Federal Individual Income Tax Return
- State Individual Income Tax Return
- Federal Fiduciary Income Tax Return
- State Fiduciary Income Tax Return
- Federal Gift (and Generation-Skipping Transfer) Tax Return
- State Gift Tax Return
- Federal Estate (and Generation-Skipping Transfer) Tax Return
- State Estate Tax Return
- State Inheritance Tax Return

MINI-GLOSSARY BOX

Direct skip
A generation-skipping transfer of an interest in property to a skip person; a direct skip is subject to the federal generation-skipping transfer tax and also the federal gift or estate tax.

Skip person
An individual (such as a grandchild) who receives the property in a generation-skipping transfer and is two or more generations below the generation of the transferor.

Taxable termination
Any termination of an interest in property held in trust.

Taxable distribution
Any distribution of income or principal from a trust to a skip persona that is not a taxable termination or direct skip.

Decedent's Final Income Tax Returns, Federal and State

The personal representative, also called the fiduciary, of the decedent's estate has the obligation to file the required federal and state income tax returns for the decedent (IRC § 6012[b], and Minn. Stat. Ann. § 289A.08). The filing and payment of the income tax due must be completed within the time period determined by law, e.g., on or before the fifteenth day of the fourth month following the close of the taxable year in which the decedent died. Failure to do this may make the personal representative personally liable for any interest and penalties assessed.

The Internal Revenue Code § 6109 requires an identification number on tax returns and other documents. On the decedent's final federal income tax return, this number is the decedent's Social Security number.

Federal Individual Income Tax Return

A final Form 1040, U.S. Individual Income Tax Return (see Form 74*) must be filed for persons having a specified minimum of gross income (IRC § 6012).

Examples of income that must be reported include income from wages, salaries, tips, self-employment, rents, pensions, annuities, royalties, alimony, dividends, profits from partnerships, income from trusts or estates, bartering income, and interest on deposits, bonds, or notes. Examples of income that need not be reported are gifts and inheritances, compensation for injuries or sickness, child support, life insurance proceeds received due to a person's death, interest on most state or local bonds, and the $250,000 (single) or $500,000 (joint return) exclusion of gain from the sale of a home.

If a refund is due for income withheld for taxes during the year of the decedent's death, the personal representative can file a Statement of Person Claiming Refund Due a Deceased Taxpayer along with the federal income tax return (see Form 75*). Alternatively, the personal representative can attach to the return a copy of the court certificate showing her appointment as personal representative.

When preparing the decedent's final federal income tax return, there are a number of special tax considerations. First, if the decedent is survived by a spouse, a joint return can be filed if the surviving spouse agrees and if the surviving spouse has not remarried before the close of the taxable year (IRC § 6013). A joint federal return includes the income of the decedent to the date of death and the income of the surviving spouse for the entire year. For the client's benefit, both federal and state tax returns should be computed separately and jointly to determine which method results in the lesser tax and whether prompt filing or requesting an extension would be more advantageous. If the decedent's final federal income tax return is filed as a separate return, it may be advantageous to file the return as soon as possible and to request early audits by the Internal Revenue Service. This prevents the discovery of a large unplanned tax deficiency at some later date. With a joint federal return, the proportion of the total tax due to be paid by each spouse is determined by the percentage of the total income each earned during the year.

Second, IRC § 213(c) permits the personal representative to treat the decedent's medical expenses (including prescription drug expenses) that are paid from the estate within one year after death, as deductions on the income tax return for the year. If the personal representative makes this election, a Medical Expenses Deduction

---

*See Appendix A

Waiver must be filed, waiving the right to claim the medical expenses as an estate tax deduction (IRC § 2053) (see Form 1040, Schedule A, Itemized Deductions, in Appendix A as Form 76). The personal representative has the option of using the medical expenses either as a deduction for the final income tax return or as an expense of the decedent's last illness on the estate tax return. Generally, the choice should be made on the basis of which offers the greater tax saving, e.g., if the decedent's income was small for that year but he dies leaving a large estate, it would be more advantageous to use medical costs as an expense for estate tax purposes, if an estate tax is due after the unified credit (applicable credit amount) and marital deduction, because this deduction will reduce the taxable estate. This election may not be available on a state return. *Note:* Only medical and dental expenses that exceed 7.5 percent of the taxpayer's adjusted gross income may be deducted.

Third, on the decedent's final federal income tax return, a personal exemption is allowed for each taxpayer. An additional exemption is allowed for a spouse and for each dependent who qualifies under the tax law.

Finally, income "in respect of the decedent" is the gross income the decedent had a right to receive or could have received had he continued to live. This income should properly be included in the decedent's final return. The interest on stocks, bonds, income from sales of assets on an installment basis, and the like are examples of continuing income that should be included in the decedent's final return. For various reasons, certain income may be omitted from the decedent's final return, e.g., where the decedent's final return is filed before such income is received by the executor. Income "in respect of the decedent" that has been omitted from the decedent's final income tax return would then be included in the fiduciary's income tax return for the year in which the income is received. For example, if the decedent died in December 2000, interest on bonds received in May 2001 (which would have been omitted from the decedent's final income tax return filed by April 15, 2001) would be included in the fiduciary's income tax return. Tax may be saved on certain bonds, e.g., U.S. savings bonds, by electing not to pay the tax on the interest earned until they are cashed (IRC § 454).

State Individual Income Tax Return

On the state level, a final individual income tax return is also required. The following states do *not* have a state income tax: Alaska, Florida, Nevada, South Dakota, Texas, Washington, and Wyoming. As an example, in Minnesota, the personal representative of the estate of a decedent who was a resident, a non-resident, or a person who moved into or out of Minnesota during the year must file a return if the decedent earned enough income in Minnesota to require a filing (Minn. Stat. Ann. § 289A.08). A form called the Minnesota Individual Income Tax Return (Form M–1) is used for this purpose (see Form 78*). The personal representative may also file a claim for a state refund on behalf of the decedent's estate if a refund is due (see Form 79*).

Both the federal Form 1040 and Minnesota's M–1 form are due on or before the fifteenth day of April or the fourth month following the close of the decedent's tax year, unless that day falls on a weekend.[2] These returns must include all the decedent's income from the first day of the taxable year until the date of death. The opportunity to request an extension of time to file these final returns is allowed at both the federal and state levels.

---

[2]The U.S. Individual Income Tax Return must be filed with the Internal Revenue Service Center for the district in which the decedent was domiciled at the date of death.

Extensions for Federal and State Returns

An Application for Automatic Extension of Time to File U.S. Individual Income Tax Return (U.S. Treasury Form 4868; see Form 77*) may be filed, *except* in cases where the Internal Revenue Service is requested to compute the tax, there is a court order to file the return by the original due date, or a six-month extension while traveling abroad has been given previously. This application must be filed on or before April 15 or the normal due date of the return.

The extension of time for filing usually does *not* extend the time for payment of the tax due. With a payment equal to the estimated tax, the form is completed in duplicate, signed by the personal representative, and sent to the District Director of Internal Revenue. If the tax is not paid at this time, interest accrues from the regular due date of the return until the tax is paid. In addition, for each month the return is late, the law provides a 5 percent penalty of the tax due, not to exceed a maximum of 25 percent. If the taxpayer intends to request an extension to file both federal and state income tax returns, a copy of the federal automatic extension form must accompany the state return when that return is filed.

States may or may not require that the taxpayer file a form requesting an extension to file, but as with the federal extension, all tax must be paid on or before the original due date, i.e., April 15, even if the return is not filed. For example, Minnesota residents file Form M–13, Extension Payment of Income Tax (see Form 80*). Like the federal form, it must be submitted on or before the due date for filing the return. The form is sent to the Department of Revenue with payment. Interest and penalties apply to any unpaid tax.

🏛 ASSIGNMENT 14.2

Find out how a taxpayer in your state obtains an extension of time to file the state income tax return. Is there a form? If so, what is it called and what is its number? Check your state statutory code and/or your state tax regulations on this. If an extension is permitted in your state, for how long and under what conditions can it be obtained? Is there an interest assessment? Any penalty?

Fiduciary's Income Tax Returns, Federal and State

Federal Fiduciary Income Tax Return

In addition to filing the decedent's final federal individual income tax return, the personal representative of the estate must also file the federal fiduciary income tax return (IRC § 6012). This return includes accrued income and income earned after the decedent's death that is not included on the decedent's final individual income tax return. The personal representative is obligated to prepare and file such an income tax return for the estate for the period from the date of the decedent's death to the date of final distribution. Any tax due the federal government for that time period must be paid by the personal representative out of estate assets.

---

*See Appendix A

Within a statutory number of days of appointment (e.g., thirty days), the personal representative must file a Notice Concerning Fiduciary Relationship with the Internal Revenue Service (see IRC § 6903 and Form 82*). Accompanying the form must be satisfactory evidence that the personal representative has the authority to act as a fiduciary, such as a certified copy of the Letters appointing the personal representative.

The identification number used on the fiduciary income tax return is not the decedent's Social Security number. Instead, the personal representative or trustee uses the Employer Identification Number obtained from the Internal Revenue Service Center for the district where the decedent lived (see Form 81*).

Form 1041, U.S. Income Tax Return for Estates and Trusts (see Form 83*), must be filed for all domestic decedent estates with gross income for the taxable year of $600 or more; for estates that have a beneficiary who is a nonresident alien; and for some domestic trusts (IRC § 6012). The return must be filed on or before the fifteenth day of the fourth month following the close of the taxable year of the estate or trust. When filing the first return, a personal representative may choose the same accounting period as the decedent, e.g., a calendar year or any fiscal year. If the decedent's accounting year (most likely a calendar year) is chosen, the first return will cover that part of the year from the decedent's date of death to the end of the tax year. For consistency in filing returns, the personal representative should choose a taxable year that coincides with the state estate filing requirements. The return is sent to the Internal Revenue Service Center for the state where the fiduciary resides.

If an extension of time is needed, the personal representative can file an Application for Extension of Time to File Fiduciary and Certain Other Returns (see Form 84*). Once the tax payment is due, interest and penalties will accrue on the tax due from the due date until total payment is made. Prior to distribution of the estate assets, the fiduciary pays the tax on income earned; after distribution, the successors (heirs or devisees) pay tax on income earned from assets that were distributed to them.

> **Example:** Jean Carlton died on February 3, 2000. Stocks that Jean owned earned dividends of $5,000 between the date of Jean's death and October 19, 2000, the date of distribution of estate assets to heirs and devisees. The $5,000 will be included in the federal fiduciary income tax return. All dividends earned by the stock after October 19, 2000, will be income of the heirs or devisees to whom the stocks were distributed. For instance, if the stock was distributed to Karen Woods and earned $2,000 in dividends from October 19, 2000, through December 31, 2000, Karen would report the $2,000 on her own individual income tax return for the year 2000, which she will file on or before April 15, 2001.

When the federal fiduciary return is filed, a copy of the will, if any, must be filed with it only if the IRS requests it. When a copy of the will is required, the personal representative must attach to the copy a written declaration that it is a true and complete copy; the personal representative should also include a statement that the will, in her opinion, determines the extent to which the income of the estate is taxable to the estate and the beneficiaries, respectively (Reg. § 1.6012–3[a][2]).

---

*See Appendix A

State Fiduciary Income Tax Return

On the state level, using Minnesota as an example, the personal representative of every estate must obtain a Minnesota identification number and file a Form M–2, Minnesota Fiduciary Income Tax Return (see Form 85*) if the income of the decedent's estate for the year is more than $600. The first fiduciary return covers the period from the date of the decedent's death to the close of the taxable year, and subsequent returns cover a full twelve-month period.

Important considerations for fiduciary income taxes are the determination of the state's share of distributable net income, distribution deductions, the character of distributed income, simple or complex trusts, and the like. Ancillary administration in another state could entail the filing of more than one state's fiduciary return.

Like the federal form, the state fiduciary income tax return is due on or before the fifteenth day of the fourth month following the close of the taxable year of the estate or trust. The return is submitted to the state fiduciary income tax division at the state Revenue Department. States may require that a copy of the federal fiduciary income tax return be attached to the state return as well as a copy of the will and a statement similar to that required by the federal government.

 ASSIGNMENT 14.3

1. Whose obligation is it to complete and file income tax returns for a decedent's estate in your state?
2. How much interest, if any, is charged in your state for filing a late income tax return? Are there any penalties? Who is liable for interest and penalties in your state?
3. What constitutes sufficient income to require filing of a decedent's final income tax and fiduciary income tax returns—state and federal?
4. What are the conditions under which a joint tax return can be filed by the surviving spouse?
5. Describe the content and purposes of the federal fiduciary income tax return. Where is this explained in the Internal Revenue Code?

ASSIGNMENT 14.4

John Jones died in June. Following his death, his personal representative received checks from the A & M Mining Co. ($350), Bester Power & Light ($50), and Pronot Can Co. ($500). Will the personal representative have to file a federal fiduciary income tax return? Assume that the estate earned no other income after John's death.

*See Appendix A

Decedent's Gift Tax Returns, Federal and State

Federal Gift (and Generation-Skipping Transfer) Tax Return

U.S. Treasury Form 709, the U.S. Gift (and Generation-Skipping Transfer) Tax Return (see Form 86*), must be executed and filed whenever a donor makes an *inter vivos* gift in excess of $10,000 (indexed annually for inflation) in any calendar year to any person (donee). The method of calculating the gift tax was discussed previously under Lifetime Gifts. The return is due on or before the fifteenth day of April following the close of the calendar year the donor made the gifts. If the donor dies, the personal representative must file the return no later than the earlier of the due date for the donor's estate tax return or April 15. The identification number used on this return is the donor's Social Security number. Payment of the tax is due when the tax return is filed. U.S. Treasury Form 709 is also used to report generation-skipping tax due the federal government on *inter vivos* direct skips. An extension of time for filing the return can be accomplished by letter or by extending the time to file the federal income tax return which will also extend the time to file the gift tax return. A separate request must be made for an extension of time to *pay* the gift or generation-skipping transfer taxes. Penalties apply for late filing of returns, late payment of tax, and valuation understatements that cause an underpayment of tax. A married couple may not file a joint gift tax return. If, however, the couple agrees to split the gifts (see discussion in Chapter 10), both individual tax returns should be filed together. If a donor elects gift-splitting for his or her gifts and no tax is due, a Form 709-A, U.S. Short Form Gift Tax, can be filed by the donor spouse and the consenting spouse signifies consent to the gift-splitting on that form. The instructions that accompany Form 709 (the U.S. Gift Tax Return) should be reviewed carefully.

State Gift Tax Return

In addition to the federal gift tax, the following states impose a state gift tax: Connecticut, Louisiana, North Carolina, and Tennessee. When applicable, refer to the individual state's forms and instructions for filing. Form 87 in Appendix A is an example of the Tennessee Gift Tax Return.

Decedent's Estate Tax Returns, Federal and State

Federal Estate (and Generation-Skipping Transfer) Tax Return

U.S. Treasury Form 706, U.S. Estate (and Generation-Skipping Transfer) Tax Return (see Form 88*), must be filed within nine months of the decedent's death for the estate of every citizen or resident of the United States whose gross estate on the date of the person's death is greater than $675,000 for 2000 and 2001; $1,000,000 for 2002 and 2003; $1,500,000 for 2004 and 2005; $2,000,000 for 2006, 2007, and 2008; and $3,500,000 for 2009. The same Form 706 is also used to report any generation-skipping transfer tax owed the federal government on direct skips occurring at death. The identification number used on this return is the decedent's Social Security number. An extension of time to file Form 706 and to pay the tax may be obtained by completing the application on Form 4768, Application for Extension of Time to File a Return and/or Pay U.S. Estate (and Generation-Skipping Transfer) Taxes (see

---

*See Appendix A

Form 91*). Like the gift tax, penalties apply for late filing and late payment as well as underpayment of tax due to valuation understatements.

The federal government imposes a tax on the total value of a decedent's estate, i.e., the value of all property, real or personal, tangible or intangible, wherever situated, to the extent of the decedent's interest therein at the time of death (IRC §§ 2031, 2033). However, any personalty (household furnishings, stocks and bonds, an automobile, and the like) that a surviving spouse claims belongs to said spouse is not included in the deceased person's total estate for estate tax purposes if such a claim can be reasonably supported. The value of the decedent's property transferred under circumstances subject to the tax is called the gross estate (IRC § 2033).

Determining the Gross Estate

The gross estate includes all assets owned by the decedent at death and the value of any interest the decedent held in any property, e.g., the entire interest in a home less the mortgage balance. The gross estate will also include lifetime gifts of property in which the decedent retained "incidents of ownership."

For estate tax purposes, the property owned by a decedent that is included in the gross estate is valued in one of two ways. The assets may be valued on the basis of their fair market value on the date of the decedent's death. This date-of-death rule is established by statute (IRC § 2031). Or the personal representative of the decedent's estate may elect an *alternate valuation date* for determining the fair market value of the decedent's property (IRC § 2032). (But note, if the election is to be allowed, the alternate valuation date must decrease both the value of the gross estate and the federal estate tax liability.) The purpose of the alternate valuation date is to prevent an unreasonable tax liability on the decedent's estate whenever the value of this property takes a drastic plunge shortly after the decedent's death. For example, if the decedent owned a large number of shares of stock and the stock's value on the market decreased substantially shortly after her death, the estate could have an enormous tax burden if the property was valued at the date of death for estate tax purposes. Therefore, the IRC provides that property included in the gross estate that has not been distributed, disposed of, sold, or exchanged as of the alternate valuation date, a date six months after the decedent's death, may be valued as of that date if the personal representative so elects instead of assigning the value that prevailed at the date of death (IRC § 2032). The personal representative must elect the alternate valuation date on the decedent's estate tax return during the statutory time period allotted for filing such a return, e.g., nine months after the date of the decedent's death unless an extension of time has been properly requested and granted; otherwise the right to the election is lost. Once the alternate date is elected, it cannot be changed and all property included in the gross estate is valued at the alternate valuation date. Property that is sold, exchanged, distributed, or otherwise disposed of during the six-month period is valued on the date of disposition rather than the alternate valuation date.

> **Example:** Ben died on July 2, 2000. On that date, 1000 shares of stock that he owned in Benville Mining Company were valued at $100,000. Six months later, the value of the stock had dropped to $75,000 (a $25,000 loss). In determining the value of Ben's gross estate, the personal representative has the option of assigning the value to the stock (and all other estate assets) that prevailed on July 2, 2000, i.e., the

---

*See Appendix A

stock would be valued at $100,000, or assigning the value to the stock (and all other estate assets) that prevailed on January 2, 2001, six months after Ben's death, i.e., the stock would be valued at $75,000.

In the example above, assuming the value of other estate assets had not increased sufficiently to offset the $25,000 loss on the stock, it would be advantageous to the estate to choose the alternate valuation date. Since the gross estate would therefore be reduced by $25,000, no estate tax would be paid on that amount.

The problem of taxing the proceeds from life insurance policies is also resolved by the IRC. Obviously, if the decedent's estate or personal representative (executor) is the named beneficiary of the life insurance policy, the proceeds of the policy are part of the decedent's gross estate for tax purposes. Under IRC § 2042, the gross estate will also include the proceeds of all life insurance policies payable to all other beneficiaries in which the decedent at her death possessed any of the "incidents of ownership," or, within three years of her death, had assigned all the "incidents of ownership," as defined by the IRC. "Incidents of ownership" refer to the right of the insured (decedent) or the estate to the economic benefits of the policy. Therefore, they include the right to change the beneficiary or to cancel the policy.

The assets comprising the decedent's gross estate must be listed in separate sections, called schedules, and identified as Schedules A through I in the U.S. Estate Tax Return. Exhibit 14.8 describes some of the basic data to be included on each schedule. For more complete information on the individual schedules, see the updated instructions for Form 706, U.S. Estate Tax Return, published by the Internal Revenue Service.

Exhibit 14.9 shows a gross estate as an example of some of the kinds of property found in Schedules A through I.

Determining the Taxable Estate

After all the decedent's property subject to the federal estate tax, i.e., the gross estate, has been determined, the qualified conservation easement exclusion (see Exhibit 14.10, Schedule U), if any, is applied, and the various exemptions, deductions, and claims allowed by statute are subtracted from the gross estate to determine the *taxable estate,* which is the estate on which the tax is imposed (IRC § 2051).

In determining the taxable estate and computing the tax, the deductions, claims, and credits allowed by statute include the following:

- Specific deductible items (expenses, liens, encumbrances, debts, and taxes).
- Losses during the handling of the estate.
- Marital deduction.
- Charitable deductions.
- Qualified family-owned business interest deduction.
- Unified credit (applicable credit amount) and other allowable credits, e.g., state death taxes.

Deductions, credits, and special taxes are reported on Schedules J through U of the U.S. Estate Tax Return. Exhibit 14.10 shows the basic data to be included in Schedules J through U.

Deductible Items.   IRC § 2053 identifies deductible expenses and liabilities. The expenses that are deductible from the gross estate include funeral and es-

Exhibit 14.8   Basic Data for Schedules A–I of the U.S. Estate Tax Return

Schedule A—Real Estate

Regardless of the property's location, all interests in real property (except joint tenancy and tenancy by the entirety) owned by the decedent in severalty and the decedent's share of property owned with others as tenants in common at the time of death must be listed in Schedule A at their fair market value. This includes all land, buildings, fixtures attached to the real estate, growing crops, and mineral rights. The value of the real property includes all mortgages for which the decedent is personally liable. The mortgage will be listed as a debt of the decedent on Schedule K. Property owned in joint tenancy and tenancy by the entirety is not included in Schedule A, but is listed in Schedule E.

Schedule A-1—Section 2032A Valuation

The personal representative may elect to value certain real property in the decedent's estate that is devoted to farming or used in a closely held business on the basis of the property's actual use for these purposes, as opposed to its fair market value based on its potential or best use. Property passing in trust and property owned indirectly through a corporation or partnership qualify for this valuation. *This is a complex schedule that will require the expertise of other professionals (i.e., an attorney and tax accountant) to prepare.*

Schedule B—Stocks and Bonds

All stocks and bonds owned by the decedent are listed in Schedule B at their fair market value. The exact name of the corporation, the number of shares, the class of shares (common or preferred), the price per share, the CUSIP (Committee on Uniform Securities Identification Procedure) number, and the par value, if any, are some of the data listed for stocks. The principal stock exchange on which the stock is listed and traded should be given. For unlisted stock, the state and date of incorporation and the location of the principal place of business must be given.

The data on bonds must include the number held, the principal amount, the name of the obligor, the date of maturity, the rate of interest, the dates on which interest is payable, the series number if there is more than one issue, and the principal exchange on which the bonds are listed. Also, interest accrued on bonds to the date of the decedent's death must be shown. For unlisted bonds, the business office of the obligor must be given.

Schedule C—Mortgages, Notes, and Cash

Information on Schedule C should include the following:

- Mortgages owned by the decedent (original face value and unpaid balance of principal, date of mortgage, date of maturity, name of maker, property mortgaged, interest dates, and rate of interest).
- Promissory notes owned by the decedent (principal amount and unpaid principal and interest, date given, date of maturity, name of maker, interest dates, and rate of interest).
- Contracts to sell land (description of interest owned by the decedent, name of buyer, date of contract, description of property, sale price, initial payment, amounts of installment payments, unpaid balance of principal and accrued interest, interest rate, last date to which interest has been paid, and termination date of the contract).
- Cash and its location, whether in possession of the decedent, other person, or safe deposit box.
- All bank accounts except accounts in joint tenancy (name and address of bank, amount on deposit, account or serial number, whether checking, savings, or time deposit account, rate of interest, and amount of interest accrued and payable as of date of death).

Schedule D—Insurance on the Decedent's Life

Included in Schedule D are proceeds of insurance on the decedent's life received or receivable by or for the benefit of the decedent's estate or personal representative; insurance on the decedent's life receivable by any other beneficiary if the decedent at death possessed any incidents of ownership in the policy or

(continued)

Exhibit 14.8   Basic Data for Schedules A–I of the U.S. Estate Tax Return—*continued*

within three years of death had assigned all the incidents of ownership; benefits received from fraternal benefit societies operating under a lodge system, group insurance, accidental death benefits, double indemnity, and accumulated dividends on life insurance, but not annuities (annuities are included in Schedule I).

Schedule E—Jointly Owned Property

Schedule E includes the value of any interest in property held by the decedent and any other person in joint tenancy or tenancy by the entirety. The full value of jointly owned property must be included in the decedent's gross estate, except where a surviving joint tenant can prove he provided all or a portion of the consideration for the property or that the property or a fractional share therein was acquired by gift, bequest, devise, or inheritance. However, if the property is owned in a joint tenancy by a husband and wife, regardless of who paid for the property, only one-half of the value of the property is included in the estate of the first spouse to die.

Schedule F—Other Miscellaneous Property Not Reportable Under Any Other Schedule

Schedule F is a catchall schedule for probate assets owned by the decedent but not reportable in other schedules. It includes debts due the decedent; interest in business (sole proprietorship or partnership); patents, copyrights, and royalties; leaseholds; judgments; insurance on the life of another; household goods, clothing, and personal effects; automobiles; farm machinery; livestock; farm products and growing crops that have been severed from the land; reversionary or remainder interests; interests in other trusts and estates; uncashed checks payable to the decedent; and numerous other items.

Schedule G—Transfers During Decedent's Life

Transfers made by the decedent during life where the decedent retained the benefits of the property (except life insurance included in Schedule D) or transferred the benefits within three years of death, by trust or otherwise, except for bona fide sales for an adequate and full consideration in money or money's worth, are subject to tax and are included in Schedule G.

Schedule H—Powers of Appointment

Included in the gross estate under Schedule H is the value of certain property with respect to which the decedent possessed a general power of appointment at the time of death or once possessed a general power of appointment and exercised or released that power prior to death, unless the decedent released the power completely and held no interest in or control over the property.

Schedule I—Annuities

Annuities (periodic payments for a specified period of time) are included in Schedule I. These include annuities or other payments receivable by any beneficiary by reason of surviving the decedent under any form of contract or agreement (other than life insurance) entered into after March 3, 1931. The amount to be included is only that portion of the value of the annuity receivable by the surviving beneficiary that the decedent's contribution to the purchase price of the annuity or agreement bears to the total purchase price. Such benefits as pension, retirement, and profit-sharing plans and IRAs are included in this schedule.

tate administration expenses, e.g., the fees for the personal representative and the attorney (if used) for the estate. As such, these fees are deductible either for federal estate tax purposes (IRC § 2053) or for purposes of figuring the federal fiduciary income tax of the estate (IRC § 642). If administration expenses are taken as a deduction on the federal estate tax return, they cannot be used again as a deduction on the federal fiduciary income tax return. The same is true of medical expenses for the last illness, which cannot be used again on the decedent's final individual income tax return. Proper administration expenses besides the personal representative's compensation and attorney's fees include such miscellaneous items as court costs, surrogate's (judge's) fees, accountant's fees, appraiser's fees, storing costs, and other expenses necessary for preserving and distributing the assets of the estate. The rule regarding funeral expenses is that "a reasonable amount may be spent." What is reasonable must be considered in

Exhibit 14.9 Sample Gross Estate

1. Home	$140,000
Household furniture	20,000
IT&T Stocks	50,000
2. Joint tenancy with spouse in an apartment building, which, when established, was not subject to a gift tax. One-half of the value is included in decedent's gross estate.	$150,000
3. 100 shares of Nelson Manufacturing Co. stock, Decedent devised the income (dividends) from the stock to his son for life, the stock itself to be transferred to the decedent's daughter upon his son's death.	$25,000
4. *Office building* Decedent had placed the building in a trust for his niece—the income to be paid to himself for 10 years, then the building to be transferred to the niece. The decedent, however, had retained the right to change the beneficiary of the trust and to revoke it.	$100,000
5. *Annuity* Decedent made deductible payments of $1,500 each for five years to an individual Retirement Account. In addition, nondeductible payments of $1,000 each were made for five years. The surviving spouse is eligible to receive the benefits of this account as an annuity having a value of $18,000. The amount of the annuity to be included is arrived at as follows:	$7,200

$$\frac{\text{Nondeductible payments}}{\text{Total payments}} \quad \frac{1,000 \times 5}{2,500 \times 5} = \frac{5,000}{12,500} = 40\% \text{ of } 18,000 = 7,200$$

6. The decedent's uncle established a trust in which he placed $100,000 worth of various stocks. The trust named the decedent the trustee and gave the decedent a general power of appointment over the trust income and the trust property.	$100,000
7. Accumulated, undistributed income from trust.	$10,000
8. Life insurance policy naming the executor as beneficiary.	$10,000
9. Life insurance policy naming the estate as beneficiary.	$5,000
TOTAL ASSETS (gross estate)	$617,200

Exhibit 14.10 Basic Data for Schedules J–U of the U.S. Estate Tax Return

Schedule J—Funeral Expenses and Expenses Incurred in Administering Property Subject to Claims

All deductible funeral expenses, including burial, headstone, mausoleum, cost of transporting the body to the funeral home, and payment of clergy, are included in Schedule J. Funeral expenses must be reasonable, as judged by the size of the decedent's estate. Other deductible expenses are the administration expenses, including the personal representative's commission, attorney's fees, court filing fees, accountant's fees, expenses of selling assets if the sale is necessary to pay decedent's debts, and so on.

Schedule K—Debts of the Decedent, and Mortgages and Liens

Only valid debts owed by the decedent at the time of death can be included on Schedule K. Any debt that is disputed or the subject of litigation cannot be deducted unless the estate concedes it is a valid claim. Property tax deductions are limited to taxes that accrued prior to the date of the decedent's death. Federal taxes on income during the decedent's lifetime are deductible, but taxes on income received after death are not deductible. Notes unsecured by a mortgage or another lien are also included in this schedule. "Mortgages and liens" are those obligations secured on property that are included in the gross estate at the full values and are deductible only to the extent that the liability was contracted for an adequate and full consideration in money or money's worth.

(continued)

Schedule L—Net Losses During Administration and Expenses Incurred in Administering Property Not Subject to Claims

Included in Schedule L are losses limited strictly to those that occur during the settlement of the estate from fire, storm, shipwreck, or other casualty, or from theft to the extent that such losses are not compensated for by insurance or otherwise. Expenses incurred in administering property not subject to claims are usually expenses resulting from the administration of trusts established by the decedent before death or the collection of other assets or the clearance of title to other property included in the decedent's gross estate for estate tax purposes but not included in the decedent's probate estate.

Schedule M—Bequests, etc., to Surviving Spouse (Marital Deduction)

Schedule M lists any property that passes to the surviving spouse. The marital deduction is authorized for certain property interests passing from the decedent to the surviving spouse. It includes property interests that are part of the decedent's gross estate. The QTIP marital deduction election is made on this schedule.

Schedule O—Charitable, Public, and Similar Gifts and Bequests

Included in Schedule O are charitable gifts or transfers made during life or by will or other written instruments. A gift is charitable if it is for a public purpose, such as the furtherance of religion, science, literature, education, art, or to foster national or international amateur sports competition, and the prevention of cruelty to children and animals.

Schedule P—Credit for Foreign Death Taxes

Schedule P includes credit for foreign death taxes, which is allowable only when the decedent was a citizen or resident of the United States. In some cases, noncitizens who are residents may claim credit if the president has issued a proclamation granting the credit to citizens of a foreign country of which the resident was a citizen and if that country allows a similar credit to decedents who were citizens of the United States residing in that country.

Schedule Q—Credit for Tax on Prior Transfers

Included in Schedule Q is property received by the transferee (the decedent) from a transferor who died within 10 years before or 2 years after the decedent (see the earlier discussion). Credit is allowable for all or a part of the federal estate tax paid by the transferor's estate with respect to the transfer as long as the specified period of time has not elapsed. Where the transferee was the transferor's surviving spouse, no credit is given to the extent that a marital deduction was allowed the transferor's estate. Also, no credit is authorized for federal gift taxes paid in connection with the transfer of the property to the transferee.

Schedules R and R-1—Generation-Skipping Transfer Tax

Included in Schedules R and R-1 are the reporting and computation of the generation-skipping transfer tax imposed only on "direct skips occurring at death."

Schedule T—Qualified Family-Owned Business Interest Deduction

Schedule T is for certain estates that elect to deduct up to $675,000 of a qualified family-owned business included in the gross estate. The deduction is scheduled to be repealed in 2004.

Schedule U—Qualified Conservation Easement Exclusion

Schedule U is for the election and exclusion of a portion of the value of land included in the gross estate that is subject to a qualified conservation easement.

light of the size of the estate and the amount of indebtedness. Objections usually come from other successors, not from the Internal Revenue Service. If one successor spends too much out of the residuary estate for funeral or other expenses, other successors can object. If the court determines that such expenditure was unreasonable, it may order the spender to reimburse the estate. When the estate is small after obligations are paid, the court is concerned that enough will be left to support the family and will not allow excessive funeral expenses.

The lifetime debts of the decedent are proper deductions. Debts incurred after death as part of the administration of the estate are not deductible as debts of the decedent, but they may be deductible as administration expenses. All allowed debts, including unpaid mortgages, are proper deductions.

The deduction for taxes is limited to taxes that accrued against the decedent while alive. It does not extend to taxes accruing after death. Thus, the final federal income tax paid by the personal representative for the decedent's own income is deductible, but the income tax on the estate's income is not. Federal estate and state inheritance taxes paid for the privilege of transferring the estate are not deductible. Certain credits, however, are allowed for state and foreign death taxes that must be paid (see below).

Note: Although double deductions (Form 706 and 1041) are disallowed, deductions for taxes, interest, and business expenses accrued at the date of the decedent's death are allowed both as (1) claims against the estate (Schedule K, Form 706), see IRC § 2053(a); and (2) deductions in respect of the decedent (Form 1041), see IRC § 691(b).

Losses. The next deduction subtracted from the gross estate is for losses sustained during the administration of the decedent's estate (IRC § 2054). Such losses do not include the lessening of the value of assets of the estate, e.g., a drop in the value of stock or the loss in the sale of some property. Losses that are deductible are theft and casualty losses that occur during the administration of the estate. Casualty losses include losses due to fires, storms, shipwrecks, and the like. When such losses are recovered from insurance policies or from a suit for damages, they are not deductible. In addition, if the casualty or theft loss has already been deducted from the decedent's or the estate's income tax, such losses cannot be deducted from the gross estate for tax purposes.

When the above expenses, losses, and debts have been subtracted from the gross estate, what remains is called the adjusted gross estate. After the adjusted gross estate has been computed, the marital deduction, charitable deduction, and qualified family-owned business interest deduction are subtracted to arrive at the taxable estate.

Marital Deduction. The next and potentially most valuable deduction, the marital deduction, is then calculated (IRC § 2056). The current statute gives each spouse the right to leave to the surviving spouse an unlimited amount of the decedent spouse's estate free from estate tax.

For example, suppose a decedent's gross estate is $1,000,000. The total amount of deductions allowed for expenses, liens, debts, taxes, and losses is $300,000. The decedent has left $100,000 to various charitable organizations, with the balance of the estate going to the decedent's surviving spouse. The *adjusted gross estate* is the gross estate minus the deductions for expenses, encumbrances, indebtedness, taxes, and losses previously mentioned. Therefore, the adjusted gross estate in our example is $1,000,000 less the $300,000—or $700,000. Note that the charitable deduction is not involved in determining the adjusted gross estate. It is a proper deduction in determining the *taxable estate,* but it is deducted only after the amount of the marital deduction has been determined and deducted.

The marital deduction allowed in this illustration would then be $600,000 since the decedent has left the entire estate (less the $100,000 to various charities) to her spouse. If a decedent had left the surviving spouse less than $600,000, e.g., had given the spouse $400,000, the amount of the marital deduction would be limited to the amount passing to the spouse outright, the $400,000.

Note that in every state a surviving spouse is entitled to common law dower or curtesy rights, or statutory rights in lieu thereof. If a decedent devises less to the surviving spouse than the amount to which he or she is entitled under applicable state law, the spouse may elect to receive the amount to which he or she is entitled under the above rights. The amount received by the spouse pursuant to such election then becomes the amount of the marital deduction up to the statutory maximum.

The marital deduction applies to either the husband's estate or the wife's estate when one dies and the other spouse survives. Due to its tax-saving advantages, the marital deduction is an important tax consideration in estate planning. However, indiscriminate use of the marital deduction without regard for other methods of disposition, such as successive estates to avoid a second tax upon the death of the surviving spouse, may actually increase rather than decrease the tax liability of the two estates. Such overuse of the marital deduction may needlessly subject too much property to taxation when the surviving spouse dies.

> **Example:** Suppose a husband has an adjusted gross estate valued at $2,200,000. Assuming he dies in 2000 without having made any taxable lifetime gifts, he could leave his entire estate to his wife outright, and with the unlimited marital deduction, no tax would be due from his estate on his death. However, his wife now has the entire estate, and assuming her adjusted gross estate totals the same $2,200,000 at her death in 2001, her estate is taxed on the entire $2,200,000. The tax is $878,800 less her $220,550 unified credit (applicable credit amount), or $658,250 (see Exhibit 14.2).

From a tax-saving viewpoint, it is more economical for the husband to leave $1,100,000 of his estate to his wife outright or in a so-called "marital deduction trust." This trust could provide for investment advice or management protection, but it makes the property available to the spouse (wife) on her request. The other $1,100,000 is placed in a "bypass trust," with all income from the trust payable to the spouse (wife) for her lifetime; the remainder goes to their children at the death of the wife. Using this method, the tax on the husband's estate at his death in 2000 is calculated as follows:

Adjusted gross estate	$2,200,000	
Marital deduction	−1,100,000	(Marital deduction trust)
Taxable estate	$1,100,000	(Bypass trust)
Tentative tax	$ 386,800	(Exhibit 14.2)
Unified credit	− 220,550	(Exhibit 14.3)
Net estate tax	$ 166,250	

On the wife's death in 2001, the bypass trust in which she had only a life estate is not taxable to her estate. It passes free of tax to the remaindermen (the children). The tax on the wife's estate is calculated as follows:

Adjusted gross estate	$1,100,000	(Marital deduction trust)
Marital deduction	− 0	
Taxable estate	$1,100,000	
Tentative tax	$ 386,800	(Exhibit 14.2)
Unified credit	− 220,550	(Exhibit 14.3)
Net estate tax	$ 166,250	

The estate tax for both estates is $332,500 ($166,250 plus $166,250) for a tax saving of $325,750 ($658,250 less $332,500) using the second method rather than the first.

Therefore, a principal means of reducing the tax impact when there is a surviving spouse is the creation of two testamentary trusts. It is very important in this case to follow the requirements laid out in the Internal Revenue Code. For example, assuming the *wife* is the decedent, her estate may be divided into two testamentary trusts. One trust is called the "marital deduction trust" (Trust A), representing an amount equal to half the adjusted gross estate, which the husband receives tax-free, as previously discussed. The husband has the right to use the income from this trust (and as much of the principal as he desires, if this provision is included in the trust instrument), and he can dispose of Trust A property at his death according to his own wishes. Only the property the husband disposes of at his death is taxable against his estate, i.e., the value of his adjusted gross estate. The husband's estate will be entitled to subtract his available unified credit (applicable credit amount) from the tax payable. None of the property in Trust A is taxable against his deceased wife's estate.

The second half of the decedent wife's estate is put into a second trust, the bypass trust, (Trust B). Trustees will pay to the surviving spouse, the husband in this case, the income from this trust for his life and as much of the principal as they in their discretion deem necessary. On the death of the widower, the balance of the property remaining in Trust B goes to the children or other named beneficiaries. Therefore, the property in Trust B is not subject to estate tax when the widower dies (IRC § 2033). However, Trust B property may be subject to the estate tax on the death of the decedent wife. The wife's estate is entitled to subtract her available unified credit (applicable credit amount) for the year of her death from the tax payable.

To avoid subjecting Trust A property to estate tax on the death of the decedent wife, the surviving husband, in addition to being entitled to all the income from the trust, must be given a general power of appointment over the assets of this trust, including the right to direct how and to whom the property in Trust A is to be distributed during his lifetime and after his death through his will. The income from Trust A is distributed at least annually to the widower. Trust B is responsible for all debts, taxes, and expenses of the decedent wife's estate. All the income and as much of the principal of the bypass trust (Trust B) as the trustees deem necessary go to the widower during his life, the remainder to their children on his death.

In this way, only the portion of the decedent wife's estate that is placed in Trust B (i.e., one-half) is subject to tax at her death, and only the amount still remaining of the portion of her estate that is placed in Trust A is taxed at the subsequent death of the widower, her husband. A substantial tax saving is therefore possible. Other factors, such as the value of the surviving husband's property prior to the wife's death, may limit the tax advantages of the "marital deduction trust."

Many spouses were reluctant to take advantage of the marital deduction because they did not want to give their spouses the general power of appointment that allowed the surviving spouse to determine to whom the trust property would be given on that spouse's death. They wanted to be sure, for example, that the assets acquired during a first marriage eventually went to the children of that marriage. Granting a general power of appointment made property eligible for the marital deduction tax advantages, but it also created the problem of the children's inheritance if, for example, the surviving spouse remarried or chose to leave the property to someone other than the children. This problem was resolved with the creation of the "qualified terminable interest property" (QTIP) and its QTIP trust. This trust allows property to qualify for the marital deduction *and* ensures the right of the children to receive the assets when the second spouse dies. The requirements for property with its "qualifying income interest" to be used in a QTIP trust were discussed previously and must be reviewed. The essential difference between the standard marital deduction trust with the general power of appointment and the QTIP trust is the executor's election on the decedent spouse's estate tax return to specifically elect QTIP status for that trust. In other words, in our example above, the QTIP trust, like Trust B, would give income to the husband for life, then the remainder to the children, but the husband has no power to dispose of the principal at his death. The executor would elect to have this trust become a QTIP trust, and the property would then be transferred to the children when the husband dies. The one disadvantage is that the executor's election causes the QTIP trust property to be taxed in the second spouse's (the husband's in our case) estate when he dies even though he does not get the property or have the right to determine to whom it will go. The IRC provides that any additional taxes generated by the QTIP trust will be paid from assets of the QTIP trust unless the surviving spouse (the husband in our example) directs otherwise. In other words, those who inherit the QTIP property must pay these additional taxes.

Charitable deduction
Under tax law, a contribution to a qualified charity or other tax exempt institution for which a taxpayer may claim a deduction on her income tax return (IRC § 170[c]). Also applicable to trusts (IRC § 512[b][11]).

Charitable Deductions.　Another federal estate tax deduction allowed by statute is the **charitable deduction** (IRC § 2055). The charitable deduction includes any transfer of estate assets for public, charitable, educational, and religious purposes. The amount of the charitable deduction allowed under IRC § 2055 is the value of property in the decedent's gross estate which was transferred by the decedent during life or by will to a charitable institution. The deduction is limited to the amount actually available for charitable uses. Therefore, if under the terms of a will the federal estate tax, the federal generation-skipping transfer tax, or any other state estate or inheritance tax is payable in whole or in part out of any bequest, legacy or devise that would otherwise be allowed as a charitable deduction, the amount that can be deducted is the amount of the bequest, legacy, or devise reduced by the total amount of these taxes. The kinds of transfers that qualify for the charitable deduction are described in IRC § 2055 and include the following:

(a) *In general*—For purposes of the tax imposed by section 2001, the value of the taxable estate shall be determined by deducting from the value of the gross estate the amount of all bequests, legacies, devises, or transfers.—

(1) to or for the use of the United States, any State, any political subdivision thereof, or the District of Columbia, for exclusively public purposes;

(2) to or for the use of any corporation organized and operated exclusively for religious, charitable, scientific, literary, or educational purposes, including the encour-

agement of art, or to foster national or international amateur sports competition (but only if no part of its activities involve the provision of athletic facilities or equipment), and the prevention of cruelty to children or animals, no part of the net earnings of which inures to the benefit of any private stockholder or individual, which is not disqualified for tax exemption under section 501(c)(3) by reason of attempting to influence legislation, and which does not participate in, or intervene in (including the publishing or distributing of statements), any political campaign on behalf of any candidate for public office;

(3) to a trustee or trustees, or a fraternal society, order, or association operating under the lodge system, but only if such contributions or gifts are to be used by such trustee or trustees, or by such fraternal society, order, or association, exclusively for religious, charitable, scientific, literary, or educational purposes, or for the prevention of cruelty to children or animals, such trust, fraternal society, order, or association would not be disqualified for tax exemption under section 501(c)(3) by reason of attempting to influence legislation, and such trustee or trustees, or such fraternal society, order, or association, does not participate in, or intervene in (including the publishing or distributing of statements), any political campaign on behalf of any candidate for public office;

(4) to or for the use of any veterans' organization incorporated by Act of Congress, or of its departments or local chapters or posts, no part of the net earnings of which inures to the benefit of any private shareholder or individual; or

(5) to an employee stock ownership plan if such transfer qualifies as a qualified gratuitous transfer of qualified employer securities within the meaning of section 664(g).

For the purposes of this subsection, the complete termination before the date prescribed for the filing of the estate tax return of a power to consume, invade, or appropriate property for the benefit of an individual before such power has been exercised by reason of the death of such individual or for any other reason shall be considered and deemed to be a qualified disclaimer with the same full force and effect as though he had filed such qualified disclaimer.

Since charities may have similar names, it is important that the charity be designated in the will or trust by its full and correct name. It is also possible that another charity may have the same name. It is wise to consider this possibility and make sure the charity is properly identified to prevent later conflicts. The testator may limit the use of the gift if he wishes. Gifts made to individuals are not deductible under the charitable deduction provision. Two tax advantages may be obtained by making charitable gifts: (1) by decreasing the value of the donor's estate and (2) by claiming an income tax deduction for the amount of the gift on the donor's federal income tax return.

Qualified Family-Owned Business Interest Deduction. Certain qualifying estates meeting ownership and participation requirements can elect to deduct up to $675,000 of a qualified family-owned business interest from the decedent's gross estate. The qualified family-owned business interest deduction in coordination with the applicable exclusion amount (exemption equivalent) in effect at the time of the decedent's death cannot exceed a maximum of $1,300,000 of the value of the qualifying family-owned business interest. The deduction will be repealed in 2004.

Gross Estate Tax. After the taxable estate (total gross estate less allowable deductions) is determined, the *adjusted taxable gifts* made by the decedent after 1976 (lifetime taxable gifts from all the decedent's gift tax returns, Form 709, not included in the gross estate [see Schedule G]) are added to the taxable estate. A tentative estate tax is calculated on this sum using the Unified Tax Rate Schedule (see Exhibit 14.2). The *gift* tax payable on the post-1976 adjusted taxable gifts is then subtracted from the tentative tax to arrive at the gross estate tax, which is subject to the allowable credits.

Credits. The following credits against the gross estate tax are included under IRC §§ 2010–2015:

- The unified credit (applicable credit amount) (IRC § 2010).
- The credit for state death taxes that have actually been paid to the decedent's state (IRC § 2011). The credit allowed is limited to the lesser of the amount of tax actually paid or the amount provided for in Exhibit 14.11. The adjusted taxable estate is the federal taxable estate less $60,000. If the adjusted taxable estate is $40,000 or less, no credit for state death taxes is allowed.
- The credit for federal gift taxes on certain transfers the decedent made before January 1, 1977, that are included in the gross estate (IRC § 2012). Obtain Form 4808, Computation of Credit for Gift Tax, to calculate this credit.
- The credit for foreign death taxes (to help alleviate the burden of double taxation on the decedent's estate from two or more nations) (IRC § 2014).
- The credit for tax on prior transfers, e.g., a credit for estate taxes paid on the estate of the spouse of the decedent when the spouse died ten years or less prior to or two years after the decedent (IRC § 2013).

Net Estate Tax. Once the allowable credits are determined and subtracted from the gross estate tax, the remaining figure, called the net estate tax, is the tax due the federal government.

Additional Taxes. The following additional tax is added to the net estate tax to arrive at the total transfer taxes to be paid when the federal estate tax return is filed:

- The generation-skipping transfer tax imposed on direct skips.

Federal estate, state estate, and state inheritance taxes must be paid either out of the estate assets or by the persons to whom the estate assets are distributed. The will may contain a provision that requires such persons to pay estate and/or inheritance taxes due on a devise; otherwise, these taxes are generally paid out of the residue of the estate. Sometime after the personal representative files the estate tax return, the IRS sends an "estate tax closing letter" or notifies the personal representative that the return is not acceptable. If it is not acceptable, the IRS will determine the proper tax and request prompt payment. Since an estate tax return is routinely audited, the personal representative should file Form 2848, Power of Attorney and Declaration of Representative (see Form 90 in Appendix A), with the federal estate tax return, authorizing the attorney for the personal representative to represent the estate.

ASSIGNMENT 14.5

1. Review the section in the Internal Revenue Code dealing with special use valuation. What is its purpose?
2. Define "incidents of ownership." On what tax form does this phrase appear?
3. List examples of property subject to federal estate tax. Give imaginary figures for your examples (e.g., $10,000 to Mary Doe as provided in paragraph 3 of decedent's will). Using the examples, create a fact situation from which a sample federal estate tax return can be completed.
4. Explain the marital deduction and its use. Review the section of the Internal Revenue Code where it is discussed.
5. List the expenses, claims (debts), deductions, and credits allowed by the federal government when computing the federal estate tax.
6. Describe the marital deduction trust and its tax-saving function.
7. List examples of charitable deductions.

State Estate Tax Return

State estate taxes are imposed on the decedent's privilege of transferring property and are measured by the value of the property transferred. Only the state of the decedent's domicile has power to impose an estate tax on the decedent's estate. The exception to this general rule is that property located in a state other than the decedent's domicile is taxable in that state.

Most states levy an estate tax equal to the credit for state death taxes allowed on the federal estate tax return (see Exhibit 14.11). Form 92 in Appendix A is an example of the Minnesota Estate Tax Return. Individual state statutes must be checked for any estate taxes imposed in addition to the credit estate tax and for applicable deductions, exemptions, and credits.

The due date for the state estate tax return is usually the same as for the federal return, and any extension of time granted for the federal return automatically extends the filing deadline for the state return. State statutes vary, however, and should be reviewed.

State Inheritance Tax Return

A number of states impose an inheritance tax on the recipients of both real and personal property transferred to them from the estate of a decedent resident of the state. It is a tax on inherited property, i.e., a tax on the beneficiaries' right to receive the decedent's property, and the rate of tax (usually graduated) varies with the relationship of the heir or devisee to the decedent and the value of the property received (see Exhibit 14.12 for the inheritance tax rates of individual states). As with the estate tax, state statutes must be checked for deductions, exemptions, and credits that apply to the inheritance tax as well as due dates and extensions of time to file and pay the tax. Form 93 in Appendix A is an example of the Tennessee Inheritance Tax Return.

Exhibit 14.11   Computation of Maximum Credit for State Death Taxes

(A) Adjusted Taxable Estate* Equal to or More Than:	(B) Adjusted Taxable Estate* Less Than:	(C) Credit on Amount in Column (A)	(D) Rates of Credit on Excess over Amount in Column (A)
$ 0	$ 40,000	$ 0	None
40,000	90,000	0	0.8%
90,000	140,000	400	1.6
140,000	240,000	1,200	2.4
240,000	440,000	3,600	3.2
440,000	640,000	10,000	4.0
640,000	840,000	18,000	4.8
840,000	1,040,000	27,600	5.6
1,040,000	1,540,000	38,800	6.4
1,540,000	2,040,000	70,800	7.2
2,040,000	2,540,000	106,800	8.0
2,540,000	3,040,000	146,800	8.8
3,040,000	3,540,000	190,800	9.6
3,540,000	4,040,000	238,800	10.4
4,040,000	5,040,000	290,800	11.2
5,040,000	6,040,000	402,800	12.0
6,040,000	7,040,000	522,800	12.8
7,040,000	8,040,000	650,800	13.6
8,040,000	9,040,000	786,800	14.4
9,040,000	10,040,000	930,800	15.2
10,040,000		1,082,800	16.0

*Adjusted Taxable Estate = Taxable Estate − $60,000.

The state death tax credit is scheduled to be reduced over four years: 2002 − 25%; 2003 − 50%; 2004 − 75%; and 2005 − 100%. In 2005, the state death tax credit is changed to a deduction.x

KEY TERMS

Successor
Unified credit
  (applicable credit
  amount)
Exemption equivalent

(applicable exclusion
  amount)
Generation-skipping
  transfer
Generation-skipping

transfer trust
Generation-skipping
  transfer tax
Transferor
Direct skip

Skip person
Transferee
Taxable termination
Taxable distribution
Charitable deduction

Exhibit 14.12   Inheritance Tax Rates for Individual States

State	Surviving Spouse	Other Beneficiaries
Connecticut (phased out by 2005)	0	3–14%
Indiana	0	1–20%
Iowa	0	5–15%
Kentucky	0	2–16%
Louisiana	0	2–10%
Maryland	0.9%	0.9 & 5%
Nebraska	0	1 & 6–18%
New Hampshire	0	0 & 18%
New Jersey	0	0 & 11–16%
Pennsylvania	0	6 & 15%
Tennessee	0	5.5–9.5%

Rates are generally graduated for different classes of beneficiaries grouped according to relationship to the decedent; lower rates apply to closer relationships. Check individual states for classification of beneficiaries, exemptions, and applicable rates of tax.

REVIEW QUESTIONS

1. What is the difference between estate and inheritance taxes? Are they levied by both the state and federal governments?
2. What types of taxes, e.g., income, gift, or death taxes, are imposed or levied by your state?
3. Who is responsible for paying taxes of the estate, and what funds are used to pay them?
4. What is the alternate valuation election? Under what circumstances is it used?
5. Explain the unified credit (applicable credit amount) and the unified transfer gift and estate tax rates. Under current law, what increases are scheduled for the unified credit? What is meant by the "exemption equivalent (applicable exclusion amount)"?
6. How does the use of the marital deduction save estate taxes?
7. What is QTIP property and how does it qualify for the marital deduction?
8. How are gifts made between spouses taxed before and after death? Also explain gift splitting.
9. Briefly explain the Uniform Transfers to Minors Act.
10. Who is responsible for filing the decedent's tax returns? What liability exists? How is a tax refund obtained?
11. Which states have no income tax? Which states have a gift tax?
12. When preparing the federal estate tax return, how are the decedent's gross estate and taxable estate determined?
13. Briefly explain the generation-skipping transfer tax.
14. Does your state have an inheritance tax? How is this tax determined? Who pays the tax?

CASE PROBLEMS

Problem 1

Return to the Jane Doe case in Chapter 12. After reading the case, review the executed federal estate tax form found in Appendix A (Form 88). Assume you have been appointed personal representative of your estate (even though that would be impossible), and now you must file estate tax returns for the federal government and, if required, for your state government.

A. Develop appropriate checklists for your set of circumstances, e.g., assets, liabilities, forms of ownership, and beneficiaries.

B. Execute the required federal and state estate tax returns using the forms in the Jane Doe case as a guide.

Problem 2

A. Describe the types of property that are included on an inheritance tax return, if any, in your state. Give imaginary monetary figures for each item of property. Describe and list the deductions, exemptions, and credits allowed by your state's inheritance tax return. Cite the authority and give figures for each item on your list.

B. Using this information, create your own fact situation and complete the following forms according to the laws of your state: Inventory and Appraisal, Schedule of Nonprobate Assets, and Inheritance Tax Return.

CHAPTER 15

ETHICAL PRINCIPLES RELEVANT TO PRACTICING LEGAL ASSISTANTS

OBJECTIVES

After completing this chapter, you should be able to:

➤ Identify, understand, and explain the ethical employment responsibilities of practicing legal assistants in the field of wills, trusts, and estate administration.

➤ Understand the types of legal tasks that a paralegal may perform and be able to identify and therefore avoid those that would constitute the "unauthorized practice of law."

➤ Identify the codes and rules, specifically the 1969 Model Code of Professional Responsibility and the 1983 Model Rules of Professional Conduct written by the American Bar Association, that establish the ethical guidelines for the practice of law and provide the basis for disciplining attorneys and paralegals.

➤ Identify the specific rules and opinions adopted and enforced by the bar association of the specific state in which you live and intend to practice law.

SCOPE OF THE CHAPTER

This chapter discusses the standards of legal ethics that apply to individuals who practice law, e.g., lawyers and nonlawyers (including paralegals). To understand your employment responsibilities as a practicing paralegal, the legal and ethical principles that affect your work must be examined. The chapter identifies the various ethical standards and guidelines that apply to typical legal assistant employment tasks. These ethical standards, which are established by the American Bar Association (ABA), the National Association of Legal Assistants (NALA), and the National Federation of Paralegal Associations (NFPA), set the guidelines that help to identify and direct the ethical conduct required for practicing paralegals.

PARALEGALS AND CANONS OF ETHICS

Ethical standards and guidelines that apply to the legal profession are written by the **American Bar Association (ABA)** and published in codes and rules that, although not binding on individual state bar associations, have by and large been enacted by these organizations. The 1969 **Model Code of Professional Responsibility**[1], the 1983 **Model Rules of Professional Conduct**[2], and their amendments are the regulatory cornerstones of the legal profession. Both were enacted to establish ethical guidelines for the practice of law as well as to provide a basis for disciplining attorneys whose professional conduct violates the guidelines. A violation of either the Model Code or the Model Rules can result in a disciplinary action that could cost the offending attorney his license to practice law. Courses on legal ethics are usually required in law school, and state bar examinations include ethics questions. Both the ABA and state bar associations issue **opinions** that interpret and apply these standards to everyday legal practices and issues.

    It is important for you as a practicing paralegal to know the ethical standards and guidelines that direct attorneys in their legal practice so you can avoid violating the directives. Additionally, *ABA guidelines require attorneys to educate the legal assistants they employ on the various ethical issues that affect the practice of law.*

ETHICAL ISSUE ➤

MINI-GLOSSARY BOX

American Bar Association (ABA)
A national association of attorneys in the United States that sets the ethical standards and guidelines that apply to the legal profession.

Model Code of Professional Responsibility
Rules of conduct that govern the legal profession written by the ABA and adopted by some states.

Model Rules of Professional Conduct
Standards of conduct written by the ABA to establish ethical guidelines for the practice of law and adopted by most states.

Opinions
Statements issued by the ABA and state bar associations that interpret and apply their codes and rules that establish ethical guidelines for the practice of law.

MINI-GLOSSARY BOX

Canons of Ethics
General rules or principles that establish behavior and professional responsibilities which apply to attorneys in their practice of law.

Disciplinary Rules (DR)
Statements of minimum professional conduct that, if violated, lead to sanctions against the offending attorney.

Ethical Considerations (EC)
Ideals of professional conduct that attorneys should strive to achieve.

The Model Code, forerunner of the Model Rules, is made up of **Canons of Ethics** (general rules or statements that establish behavior and professional responsibilities which apply to lawyers in their practice of law), **Disciplinary Rules (DR)** (statements of minimum professional conduct that if violated lead to sanctions against the offending lawyer), and **Ethical Considerations (EC)** (ideals of professional conduct that attorneys should strive to achieve). The Canons consist of the following:

- Lawyers should help preserve the competence and integrity of the legal profession.
- Lawyers should facilitate the broad availability of legal counsel.
- Lawyers should seek to prevent the unauthorized practice of law.
- Lawyers should preserve client confidences and secrets.
- Lawyers should provide clients with independent professional judgment.
- Lawyers should represent clients zealously without violating the law.
- Lawyers should represent clients competently.
- Lawyers should promote progress and improvement of the legal system.
- Lawyers should refrain from engaging in conduct that creates the appearance of professional impropriety.

The Model Rules consolidate the Canons, Disciplinary Rules, and Ethical Considerations of the Code into a *single* set of rules that govern the following areas of the legal profession: attorney-client relationship; lawyer as counselor; lawyer as advocate; lawyers dealings with nonclients; law firms and associations; community service; legal services information; and the preservation and the promotion of the integrity of the legal profession.

Since legal assistants are excluded from full bar association membership, neither the Model Code nor the Model Rules directly apply to their employment activities. *Paralegals are therefore not subject to disciplinary action (reprimand, private and public censure, suspension, or disbarment) as are attorneys for violations of these ethical guidelines. Instead, attorneys are disciplined for the unethical conduct of legal assistants under their control and supervision.* This fact is reflected in the following excerpt from the Model Code:

Obviously the Canons, Ethical Considerations, and Disciplinary Rules cannot apply to nonlawyers; however, they do define the type of ethical conduct that the public has a right to expect not only of lawyers but also of their nonprofessional employees and associates in all matters pertaining to professional employment. A lawyer should ultimately be responsible for the conduct of employees and associates in the course of the professional representation of the client.

The Model Rules also address this issue in the Comment that follows Rule 5.3:

> A lawyer should give [legal] assistants appropriate instruction and supervision concerning the ethical aspects of their employment . . . and should be responsible for their work product. The measures employed in supervising nonlawyers should take account of the fact that they do not have legal training and are not subject to professional discipline.

Thus, the attorney-paralegal relationship is governed by the Model Code and the Model Rules. It is the supervisory function of attorneys who work with legal assistants that forms the basis of authority that allows law office use of legal assistants. In this capacity, attorneys are directly responsible to assure paralegals do not engage in the unauthorized practice of law. Likewise, paralegals must not engage in obviously unethical practices that are requested or directed by the supervising attorney, and paralegals must insist that any unethical activities they become aware of are brought to the attorney's attention and immediately discontinued. It is therefore essential for you as a paralegal to know the ethical guidelines that govern the practice of law, especially the Model Code and the Model Rules provisions that are relevant to the attorney-paralegal business relationship.

Model Code Provisions Relevant to the Attorney-Paralegal Relationship

Although legal assistants, under the supervision of an attorney, may perform a considerable amount of the work normally undertaken by a lawyer, care must be taken not to delegate improper responsibilities to the paralegal since Canon 3 of the Code prohibits nonlawyers from performing tasks reserved exclusively for attorneys. For example, legal assistants may not "act in matters involving professional judgment. Where this professional judgment is not involved, nonlawyers . . . may engage in occupations that require a special knowledge of law in certain areas" (EC 3-5). "A lawyer often delegates tasks to . . . lay persons. Such delegation is proper if the lawyer maintains a direct relationship with a client, supervises the delegated work, and has complete professional responsibility for the work product" (EC 3-6).

Issues and problems relating to confidential and privileged communications are covered under Canon 4. "It is a matter of common knowledge that the normal operation of a law office exposes confidential professional information to nonlawyer employees. . . . [T]his obligates a lawyer to exercise care in selecting and training employees so that the sanctity of all confidences and secrets of clients may be preserved" (EC 4-2). "A lawyer should endeavor to act in a manner which preserves this evidentiary privilege. . . . [A lawyer] should avoid professional discussions in the presence of persons to whom the privilege does not extend" (EC 4-4). The disciplinary rule that accompanies Canon 4 warns lawyers to use care in preventing employees from revealing or using confidential information (DR 4-101D). This duty applies to legal assistants as well.

Issues that involve conflicts of interest are covered by Canon 5. Situations in which lawyers are cautioned against accepting clients or cases because of potential conflicts of interest may also apply to legal assistants. When such problems arise, you must inform your supervising attorney.

Model Rules Provisions Relevant to the Attorney-Paralegal Relationship

Practicing attorneys employ extensive support staff, e.g., clerks, interns, secretaries, and investigators, to help maintain daily law office operations. Over the past three decades, the emergence and growth of paralegals as a distinct profession have led to the creation of a specific provision in the Model Rules that covers law office employment of nonlawyer assistants. Rule 5.3, Responsibilities Regarding Nonlawyer Assistants, states:

With respect to a nonlawyer employed or retained by or associated with a lawyer:

(a) A partner in a law firm shall make reasonable efforts to ensure that the firm has in effect measures giving reasonable assurance that the person's conduct is compatible with the professional obligations of the lawyer;

(b) A lawyer having direct supervisory authority over the nonlawyer shall make reasonable efforts to ensure that the person's conduct is compatible with the professional obligations of the lawyer; and

(c) A lawyer shall be responsible for conduct of such a person that would be a violation of the Rules of Professional Conduct if engaged in by a lawyer if:

(1) the lawyer orders or, with the knowledge of the specific conduct, ratifies the conduct involved; or

(2) the lawyer is a partner in the law firm in which the person is employed, or has direct supervisory authority over the person, and knows of the conduct at a time when its consequences can be avoided or mitigated but fails to take reasonable remedial action. [Also, see Model Rule 8.4.]

The Model Rules also contains guidelines that direct the manner in which lawyers may delegate work to nonlawyer office personnel. Under Rule 5.5(b), attorneys are cautioned not to assist a person who is a non-member of the bar in the performance of activity that constitutes the unauthorized practice of law. The Comment following this Rule goes on to say that the Rule "does not prohibit a lawyer from employing the services of paraprofessionals and delegating functions to them, so long as the lawyer supervises the delegated work and retains responsibility for their work."

American Bar Association Committees Dealing with Legal Assistants

The ABA Standing Committee on Legal Assistants has taken a leading role in the identification of the rights and duties of paralegals as practicing professionals. The following is the current American Bar Association definition of paralegal:

A legal assistant or paralegal is a person, qualified by education, training or work experience who is employed or retained by a lawyer, law office, corporation, governmental agency or other entity and who performs specifically delegated substantive legal work for which a lawyer is responsible. (Reprinted by permission of the American Bar Association.)

Other activities of this committee include accrediting legal assistant education programs, issuing reports on various issues related to the profession (an example is whether legal assistants should be certified to practice), and publishing articles on how paralegals can be effectively used in law offices. In 1991 this committee prepared and the American Bar Association published the ABA Model Guidelines for the Utilization of Legal Assistant Services (see Exhibit 15.1). Current information about the ABA with the text of the Model Guidelines is available on the internet at *http://www.abanet.org*.

The ABA Committee on Ethics and Professional Responsibility has produced several advisory opinions on the proper role of legal assistants in law offices. Committee action approved the use of paralegals' names on law office letterheads and business cards so long as the paralegals are conspicuously identified as "Legal Assistants." Bar associations in some states do not allow paralegals' names to appear on the letterhead of a law firm. However, such states generally do allow paralegals to author and sign correspondence on the firm's letterhead so long as the paralegal's status is disclosed and no legal advice or opinions are given in the correspondence.

Ethical Guidelines and State Action

Various state bar associations have issued guidelines that identify the proper role of legal assistants in law offices. An example is the New York State Bar Association guidelines, which address the requirement that lawyers preserve "direct relationships" with clients if they delegate work to paralegals. New York guidelines determine that "direct relationships" does not mean attorneys must contact clients with a "specified degree of regularity or frequency." Instead, the guidelines instruct attorneys to be available "at all reasonable times" for client consultation and to promote the interest of the client when they supervise a paralegal's work. However, today's legal assistants are faced with an ongoing dilemma concerning their professional conduct. At this time, although the states have discussed and proposed various kinds of regulation including certification and licensing legislation, they have not established a uniform position on the statutory regulation of the work performed by practicing legal assistants. Since no single national regulatory agency has been authorized to govern legal assistant conduct, two existing legal assistant associations have sought to address the dilemma (see the discussion below).

Professional Standards and Paralegal Associations

The **National Federation of Paralegal Associations (NFPA)** in Kansas City, Missouri, and the **National Association of Legal Assistants (NALA)** in Tulsa, Oklahoma, have both issued ethical guidelines regarding the attorney-paralegal relationship. The following information is taken from the preamble of the NFPA Model Code and Model Rules. In 1993, NFPA, which consists of paralegal associations and individual paralegals throughout the United States and Canada, adopted its Model Code of Ethics and Professional Responsibility ("Model Code") to delineate the principles for ethics and conduct to which every paralegal should aspire. In 1997, NFPA adopted the Model Disciplinary Rules ("Model Rules") to make possible the enforcement of the Canons and Ethical Considerations contained in the NFPA Model Code. A concurrent determination was made that the Model Code, formerly aspirational in nature, should be recognized as setting forth the enforceable obligations of all paralegals. The Model Code and Model Rules offer a framework for professional discipline, either voluntarily or through formal regulatory programs.

This document is presented in a condensed version as Exhibit 15.2. Current information about NFPA, its programs, and the full text of its Model Code and Model Rules are available on the internet at *http://www.paralegals.org.*

NALA, an organization of individual paralegals and state and local affiliates, has published its Code of Ethics and Professional Responsibility (Exhibit 15.3) as well as its Model Standards and Guidelines for Utilization of Legal Assistants (Exhibit 15.4). Current information about NALA, its programs, and the full text of its Code of Ethics and the annotated version of its Model Standards and Guidelines are available on the internet at *http://www.nalanet.org.*

The Model Standards and Guidelines published by NALA present minimum qualifications for paralegals and list employment responsibilities appropriate for them. Establishing minimum competency standards for paralegals, gained either through formal educational programs or on-the-job training, is a concept strongly endorsed by NALA. This organization also supports the certification of paralegal professional competence, and it administers a national certification program through an examination it developed and gives to applicants on a voluntary basis. Applicants must pass a two-day exam on topics that include communications, ethics, human relations and interviewing techniques, judgment and analytical ability, legal research, legal terminology, and four topics selected from administrative law, bankruptcy, business organizations/corporations, contracts, criminal law and procedure, family law, litigation, probate and estate planning, and real estate. Those who pass the test and complete continuing-education requirements are entitled to use the designation CLA (the abbreviation for Certified Legal Assistant) after their names, on their offices, and on their communications and advertisements. A CLA who passes a second exam on one of several specialty topics can use the designation CLAS (the abbreviation for Certified Legal Assistant Specialists) as well.

In the fall of 1994, the National Federation of Paralegal Associations changed its position on the use of standardized tests for experienced paralegals and joined NALA to advocate the use of a competency exam for paralegals. NFPA's proficiency exam, called the Paralegal Advanced Competency Exam (PACE), differs in several ways from the CLA exam. The PACE was developed by a professional testing company supported by an independent committee of lawyers, paralegals, educators, and members of the general public, and is administered by an independent agency. Before a paralegal is eligible to take the two-tiered exam, specific educational and experience requirements must be satisfied. The first tier of the test, which includes general questions, ethics, and state specific

MINI-GLOSSARY BOX

National Federation of Paralegal Associations (NFPA)
One of the two national professional associations of paralegals that issues recommended ethical guidelines regarding the attorney-paralegal relationship. The other is the NALA.

National Association of Legal Assistants (NALA)
One of the two national professional associations of paralegals that issues recommended ethical guidelines regarding the attorney-paralegal relationship. The other is the NFPA.

Exhibit 15.1 ABA Model Guidelines for the Utilization of Legal Assistant Services

Preamble

State courts, bar associations, or bar committees in at least seventeen states have prepared recommendations for the utilization of legal assistant services. While their content varies, their purpose appears uniform: to provide lawyers with a reliable basis for delegating responsibility for performing a portion of the lawyer's tasks to legal assistants. The purpose of preparing model guidelines is not to contradict the guidelines already adopted or to suggest that other guidelines may be more appropriate in a particular jurisdiction. It is the view of the Standing Committee on Legal Assistants of the American Bar Association, however, that a model set of guidelines for the utilization of legal assistant services may assist many states in adopting or revising such guidelines. The Standing Committee is of the view that guidelines will encourage lawyers to utilize legal assistant services effectively and promote the growth of the legal assistant profession. In undertaking this project, the Standing Committee has attempted to state guidelines that conform with the American Bar Association's Model Rules of Professional Conduct, decided authority, and contemporary practice. Lawyers, of course, are to be first directed by Rule 5.3 of the Model Rules in the utilization of legal assistant services, and nothing contained in these guidelines is intended to be inconsistent with that rule. Specific ethical considerations in particular states, however, may require modification of these guidelines before their adoption. In the commentary after each guideline, we have attempted to identify the basis for the guideline and any issues of which we are aware that the guideline may present; those drafting such guidelines may wish to take them into account.

Guideline 1: A lawyer is responsible for all of the professional actions of a legal assistant performing legal assistant services at the lawyer's direction and should take reasonable measures to ensure that the legal assistant's conduct is consistent with the lawyer's obligations under the ABA Model Rules of Professional Conduct.

Guideline 2: Provided the lawyer maintains responsibility for the work product, a lawyer may delegate to a legal assistant any task normally performed by the lawyer except those tasks proscribed to one not licensed as a lawyer by statute, court rule, administrative rule or regulation, controlling authority, the ABA Model Rules of Professional Conduct, or these Guidelines.

Guideline 3: A lawyer may not delegate to a legal assistant:

(a) Responsibility for establishing an attorney-client relationship.
(b) Responsibility for establishing the amount of a fee to be charged for a legal service.
(c) Responsibility for a legal opinion rendered to a client.

Guideline 4: It is the lawyer's responsibility to take reasonable measures to ensure that clients, courts, and other lawyers are aware that a legal assistant, whose services are utilized by the lawyer in performing legal services, is not licensed to practice law.

Guideline 5: A lawyer may identify legal assistants by name and title on the lawyer's letterhead and on business cards identifying the lawyer's firm.

Guideline 6: It is the responsibility of a lawyer to take reasonable measures to ensure that all client confidences are preserved by a legal assistant.

Guideline 7: A lawyer should take reasonable measures to prevent conflicts of interest resulting from a legal assistant's other employment or interests insofar as such other employment or interests would present a conflict of interest if it were that of the lawyer.

Guideline 8: A lawyer may include a charge for the work performed by a legal assistant in setting a charge for legal services.

Guideline 9: A lawyer may not split legal fees with a legal assistant nor pay a legal assistant for the referral of legal business. A lawyer may compensate a legal assistant based on the quantity and quality of the legal assistant's work and the value of that work to a law practice, but the legal assistant's compensation may not be contingent, by advance agreement, upon the profitability of the lawyer's practice.

Guideline 10: A lawyer who employs a legal assistant should facilitate the legal assistant's participation in appropriate continuing education and pro bono publico activities.

THE STANDING COMMITTEE ON
LEGAL ASSISTANTS OF THE
AMERICAN BAR ASSOCIATION
May 1991

Source: "ABA Model Guidelines for the Utilization of Legal Assistant Services," © 1991 American Bar Association. Reprinted by permission.

Exhibit 15.2 NFPA Model Code of Ethics and Professional Responsibility and Guidelines for Enforcement (Condensed Version)

§1. NFPA MODEL DISCIPLINARY RULES AND ETHICAL CONSIDERATIONS

1.1 A PARALEGAL SHALL ACHIEVE AND MAINTAIN A HIGH LEVEL OF COMPETENCE.

1.2 A PARALEGAL SHALL MAINTAIN A HIGH LEVEL OF PERSONAL AND PROFESSIONAL INTEGRITY.

1.3 A PARALEGAL SHALL MAINTAIN A HIGH STANDARD OF PROFESSIONAL CONDUCT.

1.4 A PARALEGAL SHALL SERVE THE PUBLIC INTEREST BY CONTRIBUTING TO THE IMPROVEMENT OF THE LEGAL SYSTEM AND DELIVERY OF QUALITY LEGAL SERVICES, INCLUDING PRO BONO PUBLICO SERVICES.

1.5 A PARALEGAL SHALL PRESERVE ALL CONFIDENTIAL INFORMATION PROVIDED BY THE CLIENT OR ACQUIRED FROM OTHER SOURCES BEFORE, DURING, AND AFTER THE COURSE OF THE PROFESSIONAL RELATIONSHIP.

1.6 A PARALEGAL SHALL AVOID CONFLICTS OF INTEREST AND SHALL DISCLOSE ANY POSSIBLE CONFLICT TO THE EMPLOYER OR CLIENT, AS WELL AS TO THE PROSPECTIVE EMPLOYERS OR CLIENTS.

1.7 A PARALEGAL'S TITLE SHALL BE FULLY DISCLOSED.

1.8 A PARALEGAL SHALL NOT ENGAGE IN THE UNAUTHORIZED PRACTICE OF LAW.

§2. NFPA GUIDELINES FOR THE ENFORCEMENT OF THE MODEL CODE OF ETHICS AND PROFESSIONAL RESPONSIBILITY

2.1 BASIS FOR DISCIPLINE

2.2 STRUCTURE OF DISCIPLINARY COMMITTEE

2.3 OPERATION OF COMMITTEE

2.4 PROCEDURE FOR THE REPORTING OF ALLEGED VIOLATIONS OF THE MODEL CODE/DISCIPLINARY RULES

2.5 PROCEDURE FOR THE INVESTIGATION OF A CHARGE OF MISCONDUCT

2.6 PROCEDURE FOR A MISCONDUCT HEARING BEFORE A TRIBUNAL

2.7 SANCTIONS

2.8 APPELLATE PROCEDURES

Source: National Federation of Paralegal Associations, Inc., Model Code of Ethics and Professional Responsibility and Guidelines for Enforcement (1997). Reprinted with permission.

---

sections, requires the paralegal to finish the necessary educational background plus two years of work experience. Paralegals who take the second tier exam must have four years of work experience. The PACE is voluntary unless a state adopts the test and its legislature makes it mandatory. Applicants who pass PACE and complete continuing-education requirements are entitled to use the designation PACE-Registered Paralegal or RP.

The **American Association for Paralegal Education (AAfPE)** was established in 1981 "to promote high standards for paralegal education." Its document, A Guide to Quality Paralegal Education, is the result of a joint effort by AAfPE and NFPA "to identify and publicize a common set of national recognized standards as to the various elements that should be included in paralegal educational programs." Current information about AAfPE, its programs, and the full text of the Guide and the Statement on Academic Quality are available on the internet at *http://www.aafpe.org.*

American Association for Paralegal Education (AAfPE)
An organization established to promote high standards for paralegal education.

Preamble. A legal assistant must adhere strictly to the accepted standards of legal ethics and to the general principles of proper conduct. The performance of the duties of the legal assistant shall be governed by specific canons as defined herein so that justice will be served and goals of the profession attained. (See Model Standards and Guidelines for Utilization of Legal Assistants, Section II.)

The canons of ethics set forth hereafter are adopted by the National Association of Legal Assistants, Inc. as a general guide intended to aid legal assistants and attorneys. The enumeration of these rules does not mean there are not others of equal importance although not specifically mentioned. Court rules, agency rules and statutes must be taken into consideration when interpreting the canons.

Definition. Legal assistants, also known as paralegals, are a distinguishable group of persons who assist attorneys in the delivery of legal services. Through formal education, training and experience, legal assistants have knowledge and expertise regarding the legal system and substantive and procedural law which qualify them to do work of a legal nature under the supervision of an attorney.

Canon 1. A legal assistant must not perform any of the duties that attorneys only may perform nor take any actions that attorneys may not take:

Canon 2. A legal assistant may perform any task which is properly delegated and supervised by an attorney, as long as the attorney is ultimately responsible to the client, maintains a direct relationship with the client, and assumes professional responsibility for the work product. (See NALA Model Standards and Guidelines, Section IV, Guideline 5.)

Canon 3. A legal assistant must not: (See NALA Model Standards and Guidelines, Section IV, Guideline 2.)

    (a) engage in, encourage, or contribute to any act which could constitute the unauthorized practice of law; and

    (b) establish attorney-client relationships, set fees, give legal opinions or advice, or represent a client before a court or agency unless so authorized by that court or agency; and

    (c) engage in conduct or take any action which would assist or involve the attorney in a violation of professional ethics or give the appearance of professional impropriety.

Canon 4. A legal assistant must use discretion and professional judgment commensurate with knowledge and experience but must not render independent legal judgment in place of an attorney. The services of an attorney are essential in the public interest whenever such legal judgment is required. (See NALA Model Standards and Guidelines, Section IV, Guideline 3.)

Canon 5. A legal assistant must disclose his or her status as a legal assistant at the outset of any professional relationship with a client, attorney, a court or administrative agency or personnel thereof, or a member of the general public. A legal assistant must act prudently in determining the extent to which a client may be assisted without the presence of an attorney. (See NALA Model Standards and Guidelines, Section IV, Guideline 1.)

Canon 6. A legal assistant must strive to maintain integrity and a high degree of competency through education and training with respect to professional responsibility, local rules and practice, and through continuing education in substantive areas of law to better assist the legal profession in fulfilling its duty to provide legal service.

Canon 7. A legal assistant must protect the confidences of a client and must not violate any rule or statute now in effect or hereafter enacted controlling the doctrine of privileged communications between a client and an attorney. (See NALA Model Standards and Guidelines, Section IV, Guideline 1.)

Canon 8. A legal assistant must do all other things incidental, necessary, or expedient for the attainment of the ethics and responsibilities as defined by statute or rule of court.

Canon 9. A legal assistant's conduct is guided by bar associations' codes of professional responsibility and rules of professional conduct.

Source: Copyright 1975, revised 1979, 1988, 1995. National Association of Legal Assistants, 1516 S. Boston, Ste. 200, Tulsa, OK 74119. Reprinted with permission.

I. PREAMBLE

Proper utilization of the services of legal assistants contributes to the delivery of cost-effective, high-quality legal services. Legal assistants and the legal profession should be assured that measures exist for identifying legal assistants and their role in assisting attorneys in the delivery of legal services. Therefore, the National Association of Legal Assistants, Inc., hereby adopts these Standards and Guidelines as an educational document for the benefit of legal assistants and the legal profession.

II. DEFINITION

The National Association of Legal Assistants adopted the following definition in 1984:

Legal assistants, also known as paralegals, are a distinguishable group of persons who assist attorneys in the delivery of legal services. Through formal education, training, and experience, legal assistants have knowledge and expertise regarding the legal system and substantive and procedural law which qualify them to do work of a legal nature under the supervision of an attorney.

III. STANDARDS

A legal assistant should meet certain minimum qualifications. The following standards may be used to determine an individual's qualifications as a legal assistant:

1. Successful completion of the Certified Legal Assistant ("CLA") certifying examination of the National Association of Legal Assistants, Inc.;
2. Graduation from an ABA approved program of study for legal assistants;
3. Graduation from a course of study for legal assistants which is institutionally accredited but not ABA approved, and which requires not less than the equivalent of 60 semester hours of classroom study;
4. Graduation from a course of study for legal assistants, other than those set forth in (2) and (3) above, plus not less than six months of in-house training as a legal assistant;
5. A baccalaureate degree in any field, plus not less than six months in-house training as a legal assistant;
6. A minimum of three years of law-related experience under the supervision of an attorney, including at least six months of in-house training as a legal assistant; or
7. Two years of in-house training as a legal assistant.

For purposes of these Standards, "in-house training as a legal assistant" means attorney education of the employee concerning legal assistant duties and these Guidelines. In addition to review and analysis of assignments, the legal assistant should receive a reasonable amount of instruction directly related to the duties and obligations of the legal assistant.

IV. GUIDELINES

These Guidelines relating to standards of performance and professional responsibility are intended to aid legal assistants and attorneys. The ultimate responsibility rests with an attorney who employs legal assistants to educate them with respect to the duties they are assigned and to supervise the manner in which such duties are accomplished.

Guideline 1

Legal assistants should:

1. Disclose their status as legal assistants at the outset of any professional relationship with a client, other attorneys, a court or administrative agency or personnel thereof, or members of the general public;
2. Preserve the confidences and secrets of all clients; and
3. Understand the attorney's Rules of Professional Responsibility and these Guidelines in order to avoid any action which would involve the attorney in a violation of the Rules, or give the appearance of professional impropriety.

Guideline 2

Legal assistants should not:
1. Establish attorney-client relationships; set legal fees; give legal opinions or advice; or represent a client before a court, unless authorized to do so by said court; nor
2. Engage in, encourage, or contribute to any act which could constitute the unauthorized practice of law.

(*continued*)

Exhibit 15.4   NALA Model Standards and Guidelines for Utilization of Legal Assistants—*continued*

Guideline 3

Legal assistants may perform services for an attorney in the representation of a client, provided:

1. The services performed by the legal assistant do not require the exercise of independent professional legal judgment;
2. The attorney maintains a direct relationship with the client and maintains control of all client matters;
3. The attorney supervises the legal assistant;
4. The attorney remains professionally responsible for all work on behalf of the client, including any actions taken or not taken by the legal assistant in connection therewith; and
5. The services performed supplement, merge with and become the attorney's work product.

Guideline 4

In the supervision of a legal assistant, consideration should be given to:

1. Designating work assignments that correspond to the legal assistant's abilities, knowledge, training and experience;
2. Educating and training the legal assistant with respect to professional responsibility, local rules and practices, and firm policies;
3. Monitoring the work and professional conduct of the legal assistant to ensure that the work is substantively correct and timely performed;
4. Providing continuing education for the legal assistant in substantive matters through courses, institutes, workshops, seminars and in-house training; and
5. Encouraging and supporting membership and active participation in professional organizations.

Guideline 5

Except as otherwise provided by statute, court rule or decision, administrative rule or regulation, or the attorney's rules of professional responsibility, and within the preceding parameters and proscriptions, a legal assistant may perform any function delegated by an attorney, including, but not limited to the following:

1. Conduct client interviews and maintain general contact with the client after the establishment of the attorney-client relationship, so long as the client is aware of the status and function of the legal assistant, and the client contact is under the supervision of the attorney.
2. Locate and interview witnesses, so long as the witnesses are aware of the status and function of the legal assistant.
3. Conduct investigations and statistical and documentary research for review by the attorney.
4. Conduct legal research for review by the attorney.
5. Draft legal documents for review by the attorney.
6. Draft correspondence and pleadings for review by and signature of the attorney.
7. Summarize depositions, interrogatories and testimony for review by the attorney.
8. Attend executions of wills, real estate closings, depositions, court or administrative hearings and trials with the attorney.
9. Author and sign letters providing the legal assistant's status is clearly indicated and the correspondence does not contain independent legal opinions or legal advice.

Source: Copyright 1984, revised 1991, 1997. National Association of Legal Assistants, 1516 S. Boston, Ste. 200, Tulsa, OK 74119. Reprinted with permission.

ATTORNEY-CLIENT-PARALEGAL ISSUES

Two major areas of concern that involve the attorney-paralegal professional relationship are the issues of the unauthorized practice of law and privileged/confidential communications. What is the proper procedure for legal assistants to resolve these issues? What problems might arise? How should they be resolved? These topics occupy the balance of this discussion.

Unauthorized Practice of Law

As previously discussed, regulations that govern the practice of law allow attorneys to delegate various responsibilities to legal assistants and other nonlawyer staff. Typical tasks assigned to legal assistants include interviewing clients and witnesses, drafting documents, conducting case investigations, and performing legal research. Usually, such work does not breach the prohibition against the **unauthorized practice of law** so long as a lawyer oversees the legal assistant's work and maintains an active, direct relationship with the client for whom the tasks are performed. Generally, paralegals are prohibited from the performance of any work that involves exercising professional judgment usually reserved for an attorney. Accordingly, legal assistants may not offer legal advice or counsel to a client, nor may they make a court appearance in a formal judicial proceeding. Various states, however, permit nonlawyers (including legal assistants) to make appearances at certain administrative proceedings, e.g., a nonlawyer may act on behalf of clients at Social Security disability hearings. The regulations dealing with nonattorney appearances at administrative proceedings vary from state to state. Your state laws must be reviewed carefully before any such activity is undertaken.

Usually, so long as legal assistants work under an attorney's supervision, no controversies involving the unauthorized practice of law arise. Such problems may occur when legal assistants offer unsupervised professional advice and counsel to persons who encounter routine legal transactions. Various state associations have prosecuted nonlawyers for services they performed that helped people obtain default divorces, assisted them to draft wills and contracts, or guided them through bankruptcy proceedings. Courts have ruled that nonlawyers may sell sample forms and informational publications, but, generally, they are not allowed to advise clients about legal remedies, inform clients on the use of the proper forms, help clients fill out forms, or prepare pleadings for clients. Certain exceptions to these limitations are recognized in some states. For example, real estate brokers or agents are allowed to use standard legal forms in real estate transactions without risking unauthorized practice of law charges.

It has been proposed that paralegals who work in the area of public law could provide standardized, routine legal advice if the following conditions are met:

- The legal assistants advise the client of their nonlawyer status.
- The legal assistants work under the close supervision of an attorney.
- The supervising attorney maintains ready access to the client to check the competence of the paralegal's work and to make changes necessary to correct mistakes.
- The client is cautioned not to rely on nor take any action based on the paralegal's advice without first consulting with the supervising attorney.

In conclusion, to effectively avoid any unauthorized practice of law problems when you work with clients, *you should always inform the client of your nonlawyer status at the first conference with the client*. This can prevent any misunderstanding regarding your role or responsibilities. Additionally, *before you meet and talk with a client, you should obtain approval from your supervising lawyer.*

Unauthorized practice of law
To engage in any legal work that involves exercising professional judgment or advice usually reserved for an attorney.

ETHICAL ISSUE

ETHICAL ISSUE

Rules Protecting Client Confidences

Under present-day rules of civil and criminal procedure, the court can order the disclosure of evidence to an opponent that is pertinent to pending litigation or other legal proceedings. During the investigation and pretrial discovery stages, or at a trial, civil and criminal courts allow few exceptions to the duties of witnesses to offer testimony, or of parties and their counsel to produce material documents or other relevant evidence vital to a case. Exceptions that are recognized to this general policy favoring parties sharing evidence are called "privileges," which allow witnesses to refuse to give testimony and allow attorneys to refuse to turn over documents or otherwise cooperate in providing requested evidence. Such evidentiary privileges in a criminal prosecution include protection against self-incrimination and the privilege that prevents married persons from testifying against one another. Most relevant to the work of paralegals, whether engaged in civil or criminal legal matters, are the **attorney-client privilege** and the attorney's **work product privilege.** Therefore, understanding the meaning of these privileges and their application to the legal assistant profession is crucial.

The attorney-client privilege protects confidential statements, e.g., secrets of the client exchanged between attorney and client, from being disclosed in an open court hearing or other judicial proceeding. The purpose of this doctrine is to encourage open, unrestrained communication between an attorney and client based on the total confidence that these communications will not be conveyed to others. This enables the attorney to obtain the fullest range of information from a client necessary to prepare the strongest case on the client's behalf. The scope, meaning, and application of the privilege are complicated and are not consistent among the states. In general terms, the doctrine prevents compulsory disclosure of spoken or written statements from a client to an attorney that are intended to be confidential. Similarly, statements from an attorney to a client are protected against disclosure although in some cases, usually involving no intended client confidentiality, courts lift the protection of the privilege to compel disclosure of relevant, material information. The protection under this privilege is also lifted when statements between attorney and client are made with other persons present or are later disclosed to another person. The complex elements of the attorney-client privilege, seen in the context of the attorney-client-legal assistant relationship, pose such difficult legal issues that a detailed examination is beyond the scope of this discussion.

Another exception to the policy favoring mandatory disclosure of information relates to the work of an attorney associated with pending litigation, called "work product." Referred to as the "work product" privilege, this disclosure shield

---

MINI-GLOSSARY BOX

Attorney-client privilege A rule that confidential communications in the course of professional employment between attorney and client may not be divulged by the attorney without the client's consent.

Work product privilege Work of an attorney for a client that includes private memoranda prepared in anticipation of litigation or for trials that does not have to be disclosed (given to the opposing party).

applies to "documents . . . prepared in anticipation of litigation or for trials" from being disclosed to aid adversaries (Fed.R.Civ.P. 26[b][3]). The purpose of the doctrine is to facilitate the lawyer's preparation and presentation of a client's case without fear of outside interference that might threaten confidentiality or disrupt the smooth, orderly flow of office operations. The work product rule is not, however, an absolute privilege. Its protection is lifted and disclosure is required upon a showing that the party seeking discovery has substantial need of the materials in the preparation of the case and that the party is unable to obtain the substantial equivalent of the materials by other means without undue hardship. Work consisting of "mental impressions, conclusions, opinions or legal theories of an attorney or other representatives of a party concerning the litigation," however, is usually given complete protection in most cases by the majority of courts.

As mentioned, ABA ethical standards require confidentiality. The Model Code of Professional Responsibility states that "[a] lawyer should preserve the confidences and secrets of a client" (Canon 4). This Canon is enforced through DR 4-101, which requires lawyers to preserve client confidences regarding information subject to the attorney-client privilege as well as information "gained in the professional relationship that the client has requested to be held inviolate or the disclosure of which would be embarrassing or would be likely to be detrimental to the client." Further elaboration of the lawyer's duty of confidentiality under EC 4-4 requires attorneys to meet this responsibility "without regard to the nature or source of the information or the fact that others share the knowledge." Under the Model Rules of Professional Conduct, the lawyer's duty of confidentiality is defined as follows, subject to certain exceptions: "[a] lawyer shall not reveal information relating to representation of a client unless the client consents after consultation" (Model Rule 1.6[a]). Comments accompanying this rule state that it should be interpreted broadly to include information obtained prior or subsequent to the existence of an attorney-client relationship. This policy is intended to eliminate the potentially disruptive and burdensome tasks of clients having to specify which statements are intended to be confidential and attorneys having to decide which statements contain potentially embarrassing or confidential information.

The Model Code and the Model Rules both require that lawyers act to prevent disclosing information falling within the attorney-client privilege and the work product doctrine as well as information arising out of and related to representing a client. Only when a client consents to disclosure, or disclosure is otherwise required by law, may an attorney disclose information. Lawyers who violate these rules are subject to significant disciplinary action.

It is important for legal assistants to be familiar with the doctrines relating to client confidences and the attorney-client privilege. You need to be aware of the risks of disclosing otherwise protected information that could result in weakening a client's case and possibly exposing the supervising attorney to malpractice liability. You will face this problem in many different aspects of your employment responsibilities, especially in document discovery settings. Although the supervising attorney has the final word regarding what information may, may not, or must be disclosed, you can perform the crucial task of recognizing potential confidential information, especially while examining and preparing documents for delivery to an opposing party. Caution must be exercised since turning over just one privileged document could trigger wholesale waiver of the protection granted under the privilege, in turn possibly undermining the strength of a client's case.

Paralegals should recognize that a considerable amount of their work falls within the scope of the work product disclosure restrictions. Although a few states limit the work product doctrine to lawyers only, most states apply the protection under this doctrine not only to direct work undertaken by attorneys, but to "other representative[s] of a party concerning litigation" as well.

For attorneys to represent their client effectively, they must be able to carry out their professional responsibilities efficiently. Efficiency is enhanced by careful delegation of duties to responsible, competent staff. To help lawyers accomplish these goals, courts have acknowledged the need to extend the protection of the work product doctrine to various classes of employees who usually assist attorneys in handling cases. Such subordinates as messengers, accountants, law clerks, secretaries, and special agents, working under the direct supervision of an attorney, have been accorded the protection of the work product doctrine in various court rulings. As a general proposition, paralegals employed directly under an attorney's supervision should have their work protected by the work product doctrine under circumstances where their efforts as subordinates to the attorney are reasonably related to professional services carried out on their client's behalf.

Ethical standards governing the practice of law contain provisions for protecting client confidences against disclosure by nonlawyers. DR 4-101(D) implementing Canon 4 states: "A lawyer shall exercise reasonable care to prevent employees, associates, and others whose services are utilized by him from disclosing or using confidences or secrets of a client, except that a lawyer may reveal the information allowed [to be disclosed] through an employee."

Regarding a lawyer's duty of confidentiality, the Model Rules state that "a lawyer having direct supervisory authority over [a] nonlawyer shall make reasonable efforts to ensure that the person's conduct is compatible with the professional obligations of the lawyer" (Model Rule 5.3[b]). The comment accompanying the Rule states "a lawyer should give assistants appropriate instruction and supervision concerning the ethical aspects of their employment, particularly regarding the obligation not to disclose information relating to representation of the client."

It is clear that paralegals are covered by both the protections and duties of these disclosure rules. You need to be aware of these doctrines and exercise sound judgment to safeguard client confidences. You must refrain from sharing information or experiences with others, including family, friends, and colleagues, to ensure that client confidences are not compromised. Merely revealing that a client has retained an attorney can be potentially embarrassing for a client and might possibly jeopardize the client's position. Additionally, you should avoid any relations with the news media and leave that task for the attorney or client to handle.

THE USE OF TECHNOLOGY TO HELP THE PROFESSIONAL PARALEGAL

In addition to the national paralegal organizations mentioned in this chapter, there are many state and local paralegal organizations. These groups sponsor continuing legal education seminars, publish informative magazines, provide networking support, maintain websites with chat groups, and offer other valuable professional assistance. Contact with such a group may provide the help you may need when faced with an ethical question.

Educational seminars have existed for some time to educate legal professionals about issues and legal changes. Now online classes exist, making these seminars easy to attend and learning available 24 hours a day, 7 days a week. A great paralegal resource center can be accessed at *www.WestLegalStudies.com.*

KEY TERMS

American Bar Association (ABA)
Model Code of Professional Responsibility
Model Rules of Professional Conduct
Opinions

Canons of Ethics
Disciplinary Rules (DR)
Ethical Considerations (EC)
National Federation of Paralegal Associations (NFPA)

National Association of Legal Assistants (NALA)
American Association for Paralegal Education (AAfPE)

Unauthorized practice of law
Attorney-client privilege
Work product privilege

REVIEW QUESTIONS

1. Identify, explain, and distinguish the two major ethical standards (codes) established by the American Bar Association that have been adopted in the majority of states.
2. Explain the functions of the Ethical Considerations (EC) and Disciplinary Rules (DR) within the Model Code.
3. Determine if one of the national paralegal (legal assistant) organizations is located in your county or state. If you joined the organization, what kind of resources would be available to you, e.g., job searches, job listings, job placement, and so on?
4. What are the ethical responsibilities of a supervising attorney toward nonlawyer assistants (including paralegals)?
5. In your opinion, should a nationally authorized regulatory agency or association be established to certify and govern the conduct of all paralegals? Explain.

6. Review the Codes of Ethics from the ABA, the NFPA, and the NALA and prepare a single consolidated list of their rules of ethical conduct, i.e., a "do and do not do" list, for paralegals. What, if anything, would you add to this list?
7. What is meant by the "unauthorized practice of law"? List some examples.
8. Are standardized tests given to experienced paralegals the best way to determine competency? Should such tests be mandatory?
9. Explain the differences between the NALA's CLA exam and the NFPA's PACE. What qualifications are required of paralegals before they can take each exam?
10. Explain the attorney's "work product privilege" and list some examples.

CASE PROBLEMS

Problem 1

Jerome Thompson hires an attorney, Sahandra Adams, to advise him about the need for and, if necessary, the filing of a petition for bankruptcy. After the initial interview, Sahandra asks her certi-

fied legal assistant (CLA), Kathryn Clark, to obtain the necessary data to complete the required forms for filing. Jerome gave Kathryn information about his assets and liabilities for purposes of preparing the bankruptcy petition and other forms, e.g., bankruptcy schedules. Some of Jerome's assets were omitted from the bankruptcy schedules. After Jerome stated in his deposition that "all information regarding assets had been given to and discussed with the CLA," a motion was made to the U.S. Bankruptcy Court to compel discovery in the form of a deposition of the CLA, Kathryn, with regard to Jerome's communications concerning those assets. At the deposition, Sahandra, the attorney, instructed Kathryn not to answer questions relating to the initial "data-gathering" interview, and Kathryn, therefore, refused to answer several questions on the topic she considered protected by the attorney-client privilege. The issue before the court is whether Kathryn should be compelled to provide those answers. Answer the following:

A. Explain what is meant by the attorney-client privilege.
B. Could Kathryn disobey her attorney's instructions not to answer the deposition questions? Ethically, should she?
C. The information sought by the questions was factual data about a debtor's assets to prepare the forms for bankruptcy. In your opinion, should that information be privileged? Explain. (See *In re French,* 162 B.R. 541 [Bkrtcy. D.S.D. 1994]).

Problem 2

Margerita Clark, a paralegal, discovered that her supervising attorney, Edgar Carmella, billed their client for the billable hours Margerita had worked on the client's case at his hourly rate rather than her lower hourly rate. In addition, no notice was given to the client that much of the work done on the case was done by a nonlawyer (Margerita). She brought this information to Edgar's attention, but nothing was done. Later, her supervisors directed Margerita at times to bill her work directly as attorney's time instead of at her hourly rate despite her protests that the practice was improper. When she continued to protest, the firm responded by imposing new work rules and hours, and subsequently, she was terminated. Margerita brought a lawsuit for wrongful discharge from her employment. Her former employers moved to dismiss the case. Answer the following:

A. After Margerita told her attorney about the improper billing and the firm directed her to bill her time as attorney's time, what would you recommend that she do?
B. If Margerita had informed the clients and authorities of the firm's fraudulent billing practices, what would be her purpose in "blowing the whistle" on the firm? What would you expect the court's decision to be?
C. Should the court allow the case to go to court? Explain your answer. (See *Brown v. Hammond,* 810 F.Supp. 644 [E.D. Pa. 1993]).

Notes

1. Model Code of Professional Responsibility, copyright © 1980 by the American Bar Association. Reprinted by permission.
2. Model Rules of Professional Conduct, copyright © 1998 by the American Bar Association. Reprinted by permission.
   Copies of ABA Ethics Opinions are available from Service Center, American Bar Association, 750 North Lake Shore Drive, Chicago, IL 60611–4497.

   Copies of the ABA *Model Rules of Professional Conduct* and the ABA *Model Code of Professional Responsibility* are available from Member Services, American Bar Association, 750 North Lake Shore Drive, Chicago, IL 60611–4497, (312) 988–5522.

APPENDIX A

SAMPLE FORMS

Form*

1. Petition for Formal Probate of Will and for Formal Appointment of Personal Representative
2. Petition for Formal Adjudication of Intestacy, Determination of Heirs, and Appointment of Personal Representative
3. Notice and Order of Hearing on Petition for Probate of Will and Appointment of Personal Representative and Notice to Creditors
4. Notice and Order of Hearing on Petition for Formal Adjudication of Intestacy and Determination of Heirship
5. Proof of Placing Order for Publication
6. Affidavit (Proof) of Publication
7. Affidavit of Mailing Order or Notice of Hearing for Formal Probate of Will
8. Notice to Spouse and Children and Affidavit of Mailing
9. Testimony of Witness to Will
10. Demand for Notice
11. Order of Formal Probate of Will and Formal Appointment of Personal Representative
12. Order of Formal Adjudication of Intestacy, Determination of Heirs, and Appointment of Personal Representative
13. Acceptance of Appointment as Personal Representative and Oath by Individual
14. Petition to [] Excuse Bond [] Increase Bond [] Reduce Bond
15. Request for Waiver of Bond
16. Letters Testamentary
17. Order Appointing Guardian
18. Petition for Formal Probate of Will and for Formal Appointment of Personal Representative (Ancillary Proceeding)
19. Notice and Order of Hearing on Petition for Probate of Will and Appointment of Personal Representative and Notice to Creditors (Ancillary Proceeding)
20. Order for Formal Probate of Will and Formal Appointment of Personal Representative (Ancillary Proceeding)
21. Order Appointing Appraisers
22. Inventory
23. Appraisal
24. Petition to Allow Selection of Personal Property
25. Order Allowing Selection of (Setting Apart) Personal Property
26. Petition for Family Maintenance
27. Order for Family Maintenance
28. Personal Representative's Petition for Late Disallowance of Claim
29. Order Authorizing Late Disallowance of Claim
30. Order Confirming Private Sale, Made Pursuant to License
31. Personal Representative's Deed
32. Final Account
33. Petition to Allow Final Account, Settle and Distribute Estate
34. Notice and Order for Hearing on Petition for Formal Settlement of Estate
35. Affidavit of Mailing Order or Notice of Hearing on Final Account and Petition for Formal Settlement of Estate
36. Order Allowing Final Account
37. Order Allowing Final Account and Settling Estate and Decree of Distribution
38. Receipt for Assets by Distributee
39. Petition for Discharge of Personal Representative
40. Order Discharging Personal Representative
41. Petition for Formal Appointment of Special Administrator
42. Order of Formal Appointment of Special Administrator
43. Letters of Special Administration
44. Final Account in Special Administration
45. Order Allowing Account and Discharging Special Administrator
46. Petition for Determination of Descent of Omitted Property
47. Decree of Descent of Omitted Property
48. Decree of Descent

---

*These forms are for purposes of illustration only. They represent the types of documents that might be used in particular situations and jurisdictions

49. Application for Informal Probate of Will and for Informal Appointment of Personal Representative
50. Verification under Oath
51. Statement of Informal Probate of Will and Order of Informal Appointment of Personal Representative
52. Notice of Informal Probate of Will and Appointment of Personal Representative and Notice to Creditors
53. Proof of Placing Order for Publication
54. Affidavit of Mailing Notice of Informal Probate of Will
55. Notice to Spouse and Children and Affidavit of Mailing
56. Acceptance of Appointment as Personal Representative and Oath by Individual
57. Letters Testamentary
58. Inventory
59. Written Statement of Claim
60. Receipt for Assets by Distributee
61. Unsupervised Personal Representative's Statement to Close Estate
62. Application for Informal Appointment of Personal Representative (Intestate)
63. Notice of Informal Appointment of Personal Representative and Notice to Creditors (Intestate)
64. Proof of Placing Order for Publication
65. Affidavit of Mailing Notice of Informal Appointment of Personal Representative
66. Notice to Spouse and Children and Affidavit of Mailing
67. Acceptance of Appointment as Personal Representative and Oath by Individual
68. Bond
69. Letters of General Administration
70. Deed of Distribution by Personal Representative
71. Receipt for Assets by Distributee

72. Application for Certificate from Registrar—Release of Bond
73. Certificate of Registrar—Release of Bond
74. U.S. Individual Income Tax Return (Form 1040)
75. Statement of Person Claiming Refund Due a Deceased Taxpayer (Form 1310)
76. Schedule A—Itemized Deductions (Form 1040)
77. Application for Automatic Extension of Time to File U.S. Individual Income Tax Return (Form 4868)
78. State (Minnesota as Example) Individual Income Tax Return
79. Claim for a Refund Due a Deceased Taxpayer (Minnesota)
80. Extension Payment of Income Tax (Minnesota)
81. Application for Employer Identification Number (Form SS-4)
82. Notice Concerning Fiduciary Relationship (Form 56)
83. U.S. (Fiduciary) Income Tax Return for Estates and Trusts (Form 1041)
84. Application for Extension of Time to File Fiduciary and Certain Other Returns (Form 2758)
85. State (Minnesota as Example) Fiduciary Income Tax Return
86. United States Gift (and Generation-Skipping Transfer) Tax Return (Form 709)
87. State (Tennessee as Example) Gift Tax Return
88. United States Estate (and Generation-Skipping Transfer) Tax Return (Form 706)
89. Life Insurance Statement (Form 712)
90. Power of Attorney and Declaration of Representative (Form 2848)
91. Application for Extension of Time to File a Return and/or Pay U.S. Estate Taxes (Form 4768)
92. State (Minnesota as Example) Estate Tax Return
93. State (Tennessee as Example) Inheritance Tax Return

Form 1 Petition for Formal Probate of Will and for Formal Appointment of Personal Representative

MD Form No. P-200   Minn. Stat. 524.3-401; 524.3-502; Minn. Gen. R. Prac. 409(a)   Miller/Davis Co., St. Paul, MN (800) 752-4221
Minnesota Continuing Legal Education © 1994 MCLE

STATE OF MINNESOTA

COUNTY OF   Ramsey

Second

DISTRICT COURT
PROBATE DIVISION
JUDICIAL DISTRICT

Court File No.   999999

Estate of

Jane M. Doe

Decedent

**PETITION FOR FORMAL PROBATE OF
WILL AND FOR FORMAL APPOINTMENT
OF PERSONAL REPRESENTATIVE**

I,   John C. Doe   , state:

1. My address is:

   1005 Elm Street
   St. Paul, MN 55102

2. I am an interested person as defined by Minnesota law because I am:

   spouse, heir, devisee, and nominated personal
   representative in the will.

3. Decedent was born on Nov. 6, 1912 , at (city, state)   Detroit, MI   .

4. Decedent died on Sept. 20, 2000 , at (city, state)   St. Paul, MN   .

5. Decedent at the time of death resided in   Ramsey   County, at (address):

   1005 Elm Street
   St. Paul, MN 55102

6. Decedent's Social Security number is   321-54-9876   .

7. The names and addresses of Decedent's spouse, children, heirs, devisees and other persons interested in
   this proceeding so far as known or ascertainable with reasonable diligence by the Petitioner are:

Name and Mailing Address	Relationship and Interest (list all)	Birthdate of Minors
John C. Doe 1005 Elm Street, St. Paul, MN 55102	Spouse/heir/devisee/ nominated personal rep.	
Sandy R. Doe 1005 Elm Street, St. Paul, MN 55102	Daughter/heir/devisee	
American Cancer Society 222 Glen Acre Drive, St. Paul, MN 55102	Devisee	
Girls' Clubs of America 111 Aspen Lane, St. Paul, MN 55102	Devisee	
Newark Institute of Higher Learning 444 Wirth Drive, St. Paul, MN 55102	Devisee	

(Attach separate schedule, if necessary)

MD   MCLE P-200

Petition for Formal Probate of Will and for
Formal Appointment of Personal Representative

(continued)

Form 1   Petition for Formal Probate of Will and for Formal Appointment of Personal Representative
continued

Court File No. ____999999____

8. Negative Allegation Statement (see Minn. Gen. R. Prac. 409(a)):

    Decedent left surviving no spouse, children, or parents, other than herein named, and no issue of deceased children.

9. All persons identified as heirs have survived the Decedent by at least 120 hours.

10. (Check appropriate boxes)
    ☐ Decedent left no surviving spouse.
    ☐ Decedent left no surviving issue.
    ☒ All issue of Decedent are issue of Decedent's surviving spouse except for: none

    ☐ There are issue of the surviving spouse who are not issue of the Decedent.

11. Venue for this proceeding is in this County of the State of Minnesota because:
    ☒ The Decedent was domiciled in this County at the time of death and was the owner of property located in the State of Minnesota.
or
    ☐ Though not domiciled in the State of Minnesota, the Decedent was the owner of property located in this County at the time of death.

12. I estimate the Decedent's assets and indebtedness are as follows:

Probate Assets		Non-Probate Assets	
Homestead	$ 220,000. (net)	Joint Tenancy $	80,000.
Other Real Estate	$ 12,750. (net)	Insurance $	50,000.
Cash	$ 76,350.	Other $	0
Securities	$ 10,648.		
Other	$ 240,100.		

Approximate Indebtedness $ ____2,180.____

13. There is no personal representative of the Decedent appointed in Minnesota or elsewhere whose appointment has not been terminated.

14. ☒ I have not received a demand for notice and am not aware of any demand for notice of any probate or appointment proceeding concerning the Decedent that may have been filed in Minnesota or elsewhere.
or ☐ Proper notice has been given to those persons who have filed a demand for notice.

15. Decedent's Will is comprised of the following:
    ☒ Last will dated ____June 2, 1985____ .
    ☐ Codicil(__) dated _____ .
    ☐ Separate writing(__) under Minn. Stat. 524.2-513 dated _____ .

    ☐ (check if applicable) The Will refers to a separate writing but none has been found.

16. To the best of my knowledge and belief, the Will has been validly executed.

17. Having conducted a reasonably diligent search, I am unaware of any instrument revoking the Will or of any other unrevoked testamentary instrument.

Petition for Formal Probate of Will and for
Formal Appointment of Personal Representative

(continued)

Form 1 Petition for Formal Probate of Will and for Formal Appointment of Personal Representative
continued

Court File No. _____999999_____

18. The documents comprising the Will:
   - [x] accompany this Petition.
   - [ ] are in the Court's possession.
   - [ ] have been probated elsewhere and an authenticated copy of the Will and statements or order probating the same accompany this Petition.
   - [ ] are unavailable, but a Statement of Contents of Lost, Destroyed or Otherwise Unavailable Will accompany this Petition.

19. The Will nominates _____John C. Doe_____
    as personal representative.
   - [x] The nominated personal representative is willing to serve and is not disqualified.

    or
   - [ ] The nominated personal representative is unable or has declined to serve.

    _____

    has priority to serve as personal representative because:

    and is willing to serve and is not disqualified.

20. The Will specifies:

    Bond:
    - [x] No Bond
    - [ ] Minimum Bond
    - [ ] $_____ bond
    - [ ] Unspecified

    Administration:
    - [x] Undesignated
    - [ ] Unsupervised
    - [ ] Supervised

21. Not more than 3 years (except as permitted by Minn. Stat. 524.3-108), have elapsed since Decedent's death.

WHEREFORE, I request the Court fix a time and place for a hearing on this Petition and enter an order formally:

1. Finding the Decedent is dead;
2. Finding venue is proper;
3. Finding the proceeding was commenced within the time limitation prescribed by Minnesota law;
4. Determining Decedent's domicile at death;
5. Determining Decedent's heirs;
6. Determining Decedent's testacy status;
7. Determining the Will is valid and unrevoked should be probated;
8. Determining _____John C. Doe_____ is entitled to appointment as personal representative and should be appointed;
9. Appointing _____John C. Doe_____ as Personal Representative with ____no____ bond, in [ ] an unsupervised [x] a supervised administration;
10. Authorizing issuance of letters testamentary upon qualification and acceptance; and
11. Granting such other relief as may be proper.

   Under penalties for perjury, I declare or affirm that I have read this document and I know or believe its representations are true and complete.

Attorney For Petitioner

_____/S/ John C. Doe_____

THIS INSTRUMENT WAS DRAFTED BY (NAME AND ADDRESS):
John W. Cranwall First Trust Co. Bldg. St. Paul, MN 55101 Telephone: (651) 555-5555 Attorney License No. 1234567

Petitioner   September 26, 2000   Date

Petition for Formal Probate of Will and for
Formal Appointment of Personal Representative

Source: This form is property of Miller/Davis Company, St. Paul, MN, Telephone 651–642–1988. Reprinted with permission.

Form 2   Petition for Formal Adjudication of Intestacy, Determination of Heirs and Appointment
of Personal Representative

M/D Form No. P-205   Minn. Stat. 524.3-401; 524.3-502; Minn. Gen. R. Prac. 409(a)   Miller/Davis Co., St. Paul, MN (800) 752-4221
Minnesota Continuing Legal Education © 1994 MCLE

STATE OF MINNESOTA

COUNTY OF _____   _____

Estate of   Court File No. _____

_____   **PETITION FOR FORMAL ADJUDICATION**
_____   **OF INTESTACY, DETERMINATION OF**
_____   **HEIRS AND APPOINTMENT OF**
                        Decedent   **PERSONAL REPRESENTATIVE**
_____

I, _____ , state:

1. My address is:

2. I am an interested person as defined by Minnesota law because I am:

VOID

3. Decedent was born on _____ , at (city, state) _____ .

4. Decedent died on _____ , at (city, state) _____ .

5. Decedent at the time of death resided in _____ County, at (address):

6. Decedent's Social Security number is _____ .

7. The names and addresses of Decedent's spouse, children, heirs, devisees and other persons interested in
this proceeding so far as known or ascertainable with reasonable diligence by the Petitioner are:

Name and Mailing Address	Relationship and Interest (list all)	Birthdate of Minors

(Attach separate schedule, if necessary)

M/D   MCLE P-205   Petitition for Formal Adjudication of Intestacy, Determination
                                              of Heirs and Appointment of Personal Representative

(continued)

Form 2 Petition for Formal Adjudication of Intestacy, Determination of Heirs and Appointment of Personal Representative   *continued*

Court File No. _____

8. Negative Allegation Statement (see Minn. Gen. R. Prac. 409(a)):

9. All persons identified as heirs have survived the Decedent by at least 120 hours.
10. (Check appropriate boxes)
    ☐ Decedent left no surviving spouse.
    ☐ Decedent left no surviving issue.
    ☐ All issue of Decedent are issue of Decedent's surviving spouse except for:

    ☐ There are issue of the surviving spouse who are not issue of the Decedent.

11. Venue for this proceeding is in this County of the State of Minnesota because:
    ☐ The Decedent was domiciled in this County at the time of death and was the owner of property located in the State of Minnesota.
    or
    ☐ Though not domiciled in the State of Minnesota, the Decedent was the owner of property located in this County at the time of death.

12. I estimate the Decedent's assets and indebtedness are as follows:

Probate Assets		Non-Probate Assets	
Homestead	$_____	Joint Tenancy	$_____
Other Real Estate	$_____	Insurance	$_____
Cash	$_____	Other	$_____
Securities	$_____		
Other	$_____		

VOID

Approximate Indebtedness $_____

13. There is no personal representative of the Decedent appointed in Minnesota or elsewhere whose appointment has not been terminated.

14. ☐ I have not received a demand for notice and am not aware of any demand for notice of any probate or appointment proceeding concerning the Decedent that may have been filed in Minnesota or elsewhere.
    or ☐ Proper notice has been given to those persons who have filed a demand for notice.

15. Having conducted a reasonably diligent search, I am unaware of any unrevoked testamentary instrument relating to property having a situs in Minnesota and believe that the Decedent died leaving no will.

16. _____

    is entitled to priority and appointment as personal representative because:

    and is willing to serve and is not disqualified. There is no other persons having a prior or equal right to the appointment under Minnesota law except:

    who have either renounced their right for appointment or have joined in nominating _____
    _____

Petition for Formal Adjudication of Intestacy, Determination of Heirs and Appointment of Personal Representative

(continued)

Form 2   Petition for Formal Adjudication of Intestacy, Determination of Heirs and Appointment
of Personal Representative   *continued*

Court File No. _____

17. Not more than 3 years (except as permitted by Minn. Stat. 524.3-108), have elapsed since Decedent's death.

WHEREFORE, I request the Court fix a time and place for a hearing on the Petition and enter an order formally:

1. Finding the Decedent is dead;
2. Finding venue is proper;
3. Finding the proceeding was commenced within the time limitation prescribed by Minnesota law;
4. Determining Decedent's domicile at death;
5. Finding Decedent left no will and therefore died intestate;
6. Determining Decedent's heirs;
7. Appointing _____ as
   Personal Representative of the Estate with _____ bond, in ☐ an unsupervised ☐ a supervised administration;
8. Authorizing issuance of letters of general administration upon qualification and acceptance; and
9. Granting such other relief as may be proper.

Under penalties for perjury, I declare or affirm that I have read this document and I know or believe its representations are true and complete.

VOID

_____

Petitioner   Date

Attorney For

THIS INSTRUMENT WAS DRAFTED BY (NAME AND ADDRESS):

Petitition for Formal Adjudication of Intestacy, Determination
of Heirs and Appointment of Personal Representative

Source: This form is property of Miller/Davis Company, St. Paul, MN, Telephone 651–642–1988. Reprinted with permission.

Form 3 Notice and Order of Hearing on Petition for Probate of Will and Appointment of Personal Representative and Notice to Creditors

MD Form No. P-220   Minn. Stat. 524.3-403; 524.3-502; 524.3-801   Miller/Davis Co., St. Paul, MN (800) 752-4221
Minnesota Continuing Legal Education © 1994

STATE OF MINNESOTA   DISTRICT COURT
                                                         PROBATE DIVISION
COUNTY OF   Ramsey   Second   JUDICIAL DISTRICT

                                            Court File No.   999999
Estate of   **NOTICE AND ORDER OF HEARING
                                            ON PETITION FOR PROBATE OF WILL
_____ Jane M. Doe _____   AND APPOINTMENT OF PERSONAL
                                            REPRESENTATIVE AND
Decedent   NOTICE TO CREDITORS**

It is Ordered and Notice is given that on ____October 31, 2000____ ,at __10:00__ (a.m.) (p̶.m̶.),
a hearing will be held in this Court at _____ St. Paul
_____, Minnesota, for the formal probate of an instrument
purporting to be the will of Decedent, dated ____June 2, 1985____ , and codicil (__) to the
will dated _____, and separate writing ( ) under Minn. Stat. 524.2-513 ("Will"), and
for the appointment of _____ John C. Doe

whose address is   1005 Elm Street
                                St. Paul, MN 55102

as personal representative of the Estate of the Decedent in ☐ an UNSUPERVISED ☒ a SUPERVISED administration. Any objections to the petition must be filed with the Court prior to or raised at the hearing. If proper and if no objections are filed or raised, the personal representative will be appointed with full power to administer the Estate, including the power to collect all assets, pay all legal debts, claims, taxes and expenses, to sell real and personal property, and do all necessary acts for the Estate.

Notice is also given that (subject to Minn. Stat. 524.3-801) all creditors having claims against the Estate are required to present the claims to the personal representative or to the Court Administrator within four months after the date of this Notice or the claims will be barred.

                                        /S/ Richard B. Evans

(COURT SEAL)

                                        Judge   September 30, 2000   Date

                                        /S/ Thomas Malone

                                        Court Administrator   September 30, 2000   Date

Attorney For Personal Representative

THIS INSTRUMENT WAS DRAFTED BY (NAME AND ADDRESS):

John W. Cranwall
First Trust Co. Bldg.
St. Paul, MN 55101
Telephone: (651) 555-5555
Attorney License No. 1234567

NOTE: If notice to creditors has been previously given, delete the notice to creditors.
NOTE TO PUBLISHER: Do not publish text that is unchecked and text of Notes.

MD   MCLE P-220

NOTICE AND ORDER OF HEARING ON PETITION FOR
PROBATE OF WILL AND APPOINTMENT OF
PERSONAL REPRESENTATIVE AND NOTICE TO CREDITORS

Source: This form is property of Miller/Davis Company, St. Paul, MN, Telephone 651–642–1988. Reprinted with permission.

Form 4   Notice and Order of Hearing on Petition for Formal Adjudication of Intestacy and Determination of Heirship

MD **Form No. P-226**   Minn. Stat. 524.3-403; 524.3-502; 524.3-801   Miller/Davis Co., St. Paul, MN (800) 752-4221
Minnesota Continuing Legal Education © 1994

STATE OF MINNESOTA   **DISTRICT COURT**
                                                         PROBATE DIVISION
COUNTY OF _____   _____ **JUDICIAL DISTRICT**

                                                         Court File No. _____

Estate of   **NOTICE AND ORDER OF HEARING ON**
                                                         PETITION FOR FORMAL ADJUDICATION
_____   **OF INTESTACY AND DETERMINATION**
_____   **OF HEIRSHIP**
                    Decedent

   It is Ordered and Notice is given that on _____ ,at _____ (a.m.) (p.m.),
a hearing will be held in this Court at _____
_____ , Minnesota, for the
adjudication of intestacy and determination of heirship of the Decedent. Any objection to the petition must
be filed with the Court prior to or raised at the hearing.

VOID

      (COURT SEAL)   _____

                                            Judge   Date

                                            _____

                                            Court Administrator   Date

Attorney For Petitioner

┌───┐
│ THIS INSTRUMENT WAS DRAFTED BY (NAME AND ADDRESS): │
│   │
│   │
│   │
│   │
│   │
└───┘

                                            Notice and Order of Hearing on Petition for
                                            Formal Adjudication of Inestacy and
                                            Determination of Heirship

MD   MCLE P-226

Source: This form is property of Miller/Davis Company, St. Paul, MN, Telephone 651–642–1988. Reprinted with permission.

Form 5 Proof of Placing Order for Publication

STATE OF MINNESOTA PROBATE COURT

COUNTY OF RAMSEY COURT FILE NO. <u>999999</u>

In Re: Estate of PROOF OF PLACING ORDER
FOR PUBLICATION

<u>Jane M. Doe</u>
Deceased

TO THE CLERK OF PROBATE COURT:

That is to verify that <u>John C. Doe, whose address is 1005 Elm St., St. Paul,</u>
<u>MN 55102</u>, applicant(s)

has ~~have~~ made arrangements for the publication of:

☐ NOTICE OF INFORMAL APPOINTMENT OF PERSONAL
REPRESENTATIVE(S) AND NOTICE TO CREDITORS

☒ NOTICE OF FORMAL PROBATE OF WILL AND APPOINTMENT OF
PERSONAL REPRESENTATIVE(S) AND NOTICE TO CREDITORS

☐

once a week for two consecutive weeks in the <u>FINANCE AND COMMERCE</u>
Daily Newspaper

and this is to confirm that the same will be published accordingly commencing in the next available issue, and that
arrangements for payment of the cost of said publication have been made.
Dated: <u>September 30, 2000</u>

<u>FINANCE AND COMMERCE Daily Newspaper</u>
Publisher

By: <u>/S/ Dorothy L. Wolf</u>

Form 6　Affidavit (Proof) of Publication

AFFIDAVIT OF PUBLICATION

State of Minnesota,

County of **Ramsey** ⎫ *ss*

COURT FILE NO. 999999

ORDER AND NOTICE OF
HEARING ON PETITION FOR
PROBATE OF WILL
, AND
APPOINTMENT OF
PERSONAL REPRESENTATIVES
IN SUPERVISED
ADMINISTRATION AND NOTICE
TO CREDITORS

STATE OF MINNESOTA
COUNTY OF Ramsey
PROBATE COURT

In Re: Estate of
　　Jane M. Doe,
　　Deceased.

TO ALL INTERESTED PERSONS
AND CREDITORS:

It is ordered and notice is herby given that on Monday, the 31st day of October, 2000, at ten o'clock A.M., a hearing will be held in the above named Court at C-4 Ramsey County Court House, St. Paul, Minnesota, for the probate of an instrument purporting to be the Will of the above decedent and for the appointment of John C. Doe, whose address is 1005 Elm St., St. Paul, Minnesota 55102.

, as personal representative of the estate of the above named decedent in supervised administration. That, if proper, and no objections are filed, said personal representative will be appointed to administer the estate, to collect all assets, pay all legal debts, claims, taxes, and expenses, and sell real and personal property, and do all necessary acts for the estate. upon completion of the administration, the representatives shall file a final account for allowance and shall distribute the estate to the persons thereunto entitled as ordered by the Court, and close the estate.

Notice is further given that ALL CREDITORS having claims against said estate are required to present the same to said personal representatives or to the Clerk of Probae Court within four months after the date of this notice or said claims will be barred.

Dated: September 30th, 2000,
　　　HON, Richard B. Evans,
　　　Judge of Probate Court.
　　　Thomas Malone,
　　　Clerk of Probate Court.

(COURT SEAL)

By: John Cranwall,
　　Attorney,
　　First Trust Bldg.
　　St. Paul, MN 55101

Warren E. Maul , *being duly sworn, on aoth says: that ...he now is, and during all the times herein stated has been the editor and publisher of the newspaper known as* **Finance and Commerce** , *and has full knolwedge of the facts herinafter stated.*

(1) *That said newspaper is printed in the English language in newspaper format and in column and sheet form equivalent in printed space to at least 1200 square inches;*

(2) *That said newspaper, if a weekly, be distributed at least once each week for 50 weeks each year, or if a daily, at least five days each week; but in any week in which a legal holiday is included, not more than four issues of a daily paper are necessary;*

(3) *That said newspaper has 25 percent, if published more often than weekly, or 50 percent, if a weekly, of its news columns devoted to news of local interest to the community which it purports to serve, and it may contain general news, comment, and miscellany, but not wholly duplicate any other publication, or be made up entirely of patents, plate matter, and advertisements;*

(4) *That said newspaper is circulated in and near the municipality which it purports to serve, has at least 500 copies regularly delivered to paying subscribers, has an average of at least 75% of its total circulation currently paid or no more than three months in arrears, and has entry as second-class matter in its local postoffice;*

(5) *That said newspaper has its known office of issue in the County of* **Ramsey** *in which lies, in whole or in part, the municipality which the newspaper purports to serve;*

(6) *That said newspaper files a copy of each issue immediately with the State Historical Society;*

(6a) *Be made available at single or subscription prices to any person, corporation, partnership or other unincorporated association requesting the newspaper and making the applicable payment.*

(7) *That said newspaper has complied with all the foregoing conditions of this subdivision for at least one year last past.*

(8) *That said newspaper has filed with the Secretary of State of Minnesota prior to January 1, of each year, an affidavit in the form prescribed by the Secretary of State and signed by the publisher or managing officer and sworn to before a Notary Public stating that the newspaper is a legal newspaper.*

That the printed Probate Notice hereto attached as a part herof was cut from the columns of said newspaper; was published therein in the English Language once each week for **2** *successive weeks; that it was first so published on the ...* **30th** *... day of* **September** *, 2000 and thereafter on* **Wednesday** *of each week to and including the* **11th** *day of* **October** *, 2000; and that the following is a copy of the lower case alphabet which is acknowledged as the size and kind of type used in the printed publication of said notice.*

abcdefghijklmnopqrstuvwxyz

/s/　Warren E. Maul

Subscribed and sworn to before me this **30th** *day of* **September** *, 2000,*

/s/　Dorothy L. Wolf

Notary Public **Ramsey** *County, Minnesota*

My Commission Expires **September 23** *, 2005*

Form 7 Affidavit of Mailing Order or Notice of Hearing for Formal Probate of Will

MD Form No. P-015   Minn. Stat. 524.1-401; 525.83   Miller/Davis Co., St. Paul, MN (800) 752-4221
Minnesota Continuing Legal Education © 1994 MCLE

STATE OF MINNESOTA

COUNTY OF ___Ramsey___   Probate Court

                                         Court File No. ___999999___

Estate of

_____Jane M. Doe_____   **AFFIDAVIT OF MAILING**
_____   **ORDER OR NOTICE**
          Decedent

STATE OF ___Minnesota___ }ss.

COUNTY OF ___Ramsey___

I, _____J. M. Golden_____,
being first duly sworn, on oath state that on _____October 5, 2000_____, at
_____St. Paul, MN_____ (city, state), I mailed a copy of the
attached Order or Notice to each person or entity named below by mailing a copy in a sealed envelope,
postage prepaid, with the U.S. Postal Service as follows:

Name and Mailing Address	Relationship and Interest (list all)	Birthdate of Minors
John C. Doe 1005 Elm Street, St. Paul, MN 55102	Spouse/heir/devisee/ nominated personal rep.	
Sandy R. Doe 1005 Elm Street, St. Paul, MN 55102	Daughter/heir/devisee	
American Cancer Society 222 Glen Acre Drive, St. Paul, MN 55102	Devisee	
Girls' Clubs of America 111 Aspen Lane, St. Paul, MN 55102	Devisee	
Newark Institute of Higher Learning 444 Wirth Drive, St. Paul, MN 55102	Devisee	

(Attach separate schedule, if necessary)

___/S/ J. M. Golden___

Affiant   October 5, 2000   Date

NOTARIAL STAMP OR SEAL (OR OTHER TITLE OR RANK)

Signed and sworn to (or affirmed) before me on
___October 5, 2000___ by
___J. M. Golden___.
Affiant.

___/S/ Judith Harris___
SIGNATURE OF NOTARY PUBLIC OR OTHER OFFICIAL

INSTRUCTIONS: (1) A copy of the Order or Notice must be mailed to each heir, devisee, personal representative, the foreign consul pursuant to Minn. Stat. 524.3-306 and 524.3-403, lawyers representing interested parties pursuant to Minn. Stat. 524.1-401(a), and the Minnesota Attorney General, if a devisee is a charitable organization or if the decedent left no devisee or heirs. In determining the persons or entities entitled to receive this order or notice, see Minn. Stats. 501B.41(5), 524.1-201(19), 524.1-403 and 524.1-404 and Minn. Gen. Rules of Practice 404(b) and 408(d). If the Decedent is survived by a spouse or minor child, also use Notice to Spouse and Children. (2) Attach to this affidavit another copy of the Order or Notice which was sent. (3) It may be necessary to give notice to creditors. See Minn. Stat. 524.3-801(3) and Supplementary Notice to Known and Identified Creditors form.

MD   MCLE P-015   Affidavit of Mailing Order or Notice

Source: This form is property of Miller/Davis Company, St. Paul, MN, Telephone 651–642–1988. Reprinted with permission

Form 8   Notice to Spouse and Children and Affidavit of Mailing

MD Form No. P-016   Minn. Stat. 524.1-401   Miller/Davis Co., St. Paul, MN (800) 752-4221
                                                                   Minnesota Continuing Legal Education © 1994 MCLE

STATE OF MINNESOTA   DISTRICT COURT
                                                          PROBATE DIVISION
COUNTY OF _____Ramsey_____   ___Second____   JUDICIAL DISTRICT

                                            Court File No. ___999999_____
Estate of

_____Jane M. Doe_____   **NOTICE TO SPOUSE AND CHILDREN**
_____   **AND AFFIDAVIT OF MAILING**

                Decedent

TO: Surviving spouse and children of the Decedent.

This notice is to advise you of your rights regarding the Estate of _____Jane M. Doe_____.
Under Minnesota law you, as surviving spouse or children or the Decedent, may have some or all of the
rights summarized below.

Surviving Spouse:

1.   The right to elect a percentage of the "augmented estate" which is provided under Minnesota
     Statutes §§ 524.2-201 through 524.2-214. This right to elect is personal to the surviving spouse
     and must be made within 9 months after the date of the Decedent's death; except that for property
     subject to probate the election may be made within 6 months after the probate of the Decedent's
     will, even if the 9 month period has already expired.

2.   If the Decedent's will was made prior to your marriage to the Decedent, the right to choose the
     intestate share of the Estate under Minnesota Statutes § 524.2-301. This right has some limitations
     and exceptions.

3.   The right, under Minnesota Statutes § 524.2-402 to the entire homestead if the Decedent did not
     leave any surviving descendants or the right to a life estate if the Decedent left surviving
     descendants.

4.   The right to allowances under Minnesota Statutes § 524.2-403, which permits the surviving spouse
     the right to select:

     a.   Household furniture, furnishings, appliances, and personal effects not exceeding $10,000, net
          of security interests, but subject to an award of sentimental value property under Minnesota
          Statutes § 525.152; provided, however, if the encumbered property and the value in excess
          of security interests, plus that of other exempt property, is less than $10,000, or if there is
          not $10,000 worth of exempt property in the Estate, the surviving spouse is entitled to other
          personal property of the Estate, if any, to the extent necessary to make up the $10,000 value;
          and

     b.   One automobile, if any, without regard to value.

5.   The right to a family allowance from the Estate under Minnesota Statutes § 524.2-404 of up to
     $1,500 per month (or more if authorized by the court) for one year if the estate is insolvent or for
     18 months if the Estate is solvent.

Minor Children of Decedent:

6.   If the Decedent had an obligation to support you, the right to family allowance from the Estate
     under Minnesota Statutes § 524.2-404 of up to $1,500 per month (or more if authorized by the
     court) for one year if the Estate is insolvent or for 18 months if the Estate is solvent.

MD   MCLE P-016   Notice to Spouse and Children and Affidavit of Mailing

(*continued*)

Form 8   Notice to Spouse and Children and Affidavit of Mailing   *continued*

Court File No. ___999999___

Adult Children of Decedents

7.   If you were being supported by Decedent, the right to family allowance from the Estate under Minnesota Statutes § 524.2-404 of up to $1,500 (or more if authorized by the court) per month for one year if the Estate is insolvent or for 18 months if the Estate is solvent.

Minor and Adult Children of Decedent:

8.   If there is no surviving spouse, the right to allowances under Minnesota Statutes § 524.2-403:

   a.   Household furniture, furnishings, appliances, and personal effects not exceeding $10,000, net of security interests, but subject to an award of sentimental value property under Minnesota Statutes § 525.152; provided, however, if the encumbered property and the value in excess of security interests, plus that of other exempt property, is less than $10,000, or if there is not $10,000 worth of exempt property in the Estate, the children are entitled to other personal property of the Estate, if any, to the extent necessary to make up the $10,000 value; and

   a.   One automobile, if any, without regard to value.

   If you have any questions regarding interpretation of these statutes or the effect of these or other rights, please consult with an attorney of your own choice or the attorney for the Personal Representative. Copies of the statutes can be obtained at the local county law library or from the Personal Representative.

___/S/ John C. Doe___

October 5, 2000
Personal Representative   Date

Attorney For Personal Representative

> THIS INSTRUMENT WAS DRAFTED BY (NAME AND ADDRESS):
>
> John W. Cranwall
> First Trust Co. Bldg.
> St. Paul, MN 55101
> Telephone: (651) 555-5555
> Attorney License No. 1234567

(continued)

Form 8   Notice to Spouse and Children and Affidavit of Mailing   *continued*

Court File No. _____999999_____

STATE OF **MINNESOTA** _____ } ss.

COUNTY OF __Ramsey_____ }

I, _____J. M. Golden_____ ,

being first duly sworn, on oath state that on _____October 5, 2000_____ , at

_____St. Paul, MN_____ (city, state), I mailed a copy of the attached Notice to each person or entity named below by mailing a copy in a sealed envelope, postage prepaid, with the U.S. Postal Service as follows:

Name and Mailing Address	Relationship and Interest (list all)	Birthdate of Minors
John C. Doe 1005 Elm Street, St. Paul, MN 55102	Spouse	

(Attach separate schedule, if necessary)

_____/S/ J. M. Golden_____

Affiant   October 5, 2000   Date

Signed and sworn to (or affirmed) before me on
__October 5, 2000_____ by
__J. M. Golden_____ .
Affiant.

NOTARIAL STAMP OR SEAL (OR OTHER TITLE OR RANK)

_____/S/ Judith Harris_____
SIGNATURE OF NOTARY PUBLIC OR OTHER OFFICIAL

Source: This form is property of Miller/Davis Company, St. Paul, MN, Telephone 651–642–1988. Reprinted with permission.

Form 9   Testimony of Witness to Will

MD Form No. P-062   Minn. Stat. 524.2-502; 524.3-303; 524.3-405   Miller/Davis Co., St. Paul, MN (800) 752-4221
Minnesota Continuing Legal Education © 1994 MCLE

STATE OF MINNESOTA   **DISTRICT COURT**
                                                             PROBATE DIVISION
COUNTY OF   Ramsey   Second   **JUDICIAL DISTRICT**

                                           Court File No.   999999

Estate of

_____ Jane M. Doe _____   **TESTIMONY OF WITNESS**
                                           TO [X] WILL [ ] CODICIL

Decedent

STATE OF MINNESOTA
                                           } ss
COUNTY OF   Ramsey

    I,   Harvey R. Horwell   , state:

1. My address is:
            999 Okinawa St.
            St. Paul, MN 55101

2. I am one of the subscribing witnesses to the Instrument purporting to be:

    [X] Decedent's Last Will and Testament dated   June 2, 1985   .
    or
    [ ] the _____ Codicil dated _____ to Decedent's will.

3. On that date the Decedent signed the Instrument in my presence or the Decedent acknowledged the signature as Decedent's signature or as having been made in Decedent's presence and at Decedent's direction.

4. Then, at Decedent's request, I signed my name as a witness in the presence of Decedent.

5. To the best of my knowledge and belief, Decedent at the time of the execution of the Instrument was 18 or more years of age, of sound mind, memory and understanding, of lawful age and under no constraint or undue influence.

                                           /S/ Harvey R. Horwell

NOTARIAL STAMP OR SEAL (OR OTHER TITLE OR RANK)

                                           Witness   October 7, 2000   Date

                                           Signed and sworn to (or affirmed) before me on
                                           October 7, 2000   by
                                           Harvey R. Horwell   .

Attorney For Witness   Witness

THIS INSTRUMENT WAS DRAFTED BY (NAME AND ADDRESS):   /S/ Judith Harris
                                                       SIGNATURE OF NOTARY PUBLIC OR OTHER OFFICIAL
    John W. Cranwall
    First Trust Co. Bldg.
    St. Paul, MN 55101
    Telephone: (651) 555-5555
    Attorney License No. 1234567

MD   MCLE P-062   Testimony of Witness to[ ] Will [ ] Codicil

Source: This form is property of Miller/Davis Company, St. Paul, MN, Telephone 651–642–1988. Reprinted with permission.

Form 10 Demand for Notice

MD Form No. P-020   Minn. Stat. 524.3-204   Miller/Davis Co., St. Paul, MN (800) 752-4221
Minnesota Continuing Legal Education © 1994 MCLE

STATE OF MINNESOTA   **DISTRICT COURT**
PROBATE DIVISION
COUNTY OF _____   _____ **JUDICIAL DISTRICT**

                                                         Court File No. _____
Estate of

                                                         Date of Death _____
                                                         Social Security No. _____

_____
_____   **DEMAND FOR NOTICE**
              Decedent
_____

    I, _____ , state:

1. My address is:

2. My telephone number is:

3. I have a financial or property interest in the Estate of the Decedent, for the following reasons:

VOID

    WHEREFORE, I demand notice of all orders and filings pertaining to the Estate. Notice shall be served upon me at the address stated above, or my attorney, named below.

    Under penalties for perjury, I declare or affirm that I have read this document and I know or believe its representations are true and complete.

                                             _____

                                             Demandant   Date

Attorney For Demandant

THIS INSTRUMENT WAS DRAFTED BY (NAME AND ADDRESS):

MD   MCLE P-020   Demand for Notice

Source: This form is property of Miller/Davis Company, St. Paul, MN, Telephone 651–642–1988. Reprinted with permission.

Form 11 Order of Formal Probate of Will and Formal Appointment of Personal Representative

MD Form No. P-230   Minn. Stat. 524.3-409; 524.3-414; 524.3-502;   Miller/Davis Co., St. Paul, MN (800) 752-4221
Minnesota Continuing Legal Education © 1994

STATE OF MINNESOTA

COUNTY OF ___Ramsey_____   ___Probate Court___

Court File No. ___999999_____

Estate of

_____Jane M. Doe_____   **ORDER OF FORMAL PROBATE OF WILL**
_____   **AND FORMAL APPOINTMENT**
Decedent   **OF PERSONAL REPRESENTATIVE**

The Petition for the Formal Probate of Will and Formal Appointment of Personal Representative, signed
by _____John C. Doe_____ , came before this Court on
___September 26, 2000_____ . The Court, having heard and considered the Petition, determines
the following:

1. This Court has jurisdiction and venue in this County is proper.

2. The Petition is complete.

3. The Petitioner has declared or affirmed that the representations contained in the Petition are true and complete to the best of the petitioner's knowledge or belief.

4. The Petitioner is an interested person as defined by Minnesota law.

5. Any notice required by Minnesota law has been given.

6. The Decedent died on ___September 20, 2000_____ .

7. Decedent's Will is comprised of the following:

   [x] Last will dated _____June 2, 1985_____ .
   [ ] Codicil(__) dated _____ .
   [ ] Separate writing(__) under Minn. Stat. 524.2-513 dated _____ .

   [ ] (check if applicable) The Will refers to a separate writing but none has been found.

8. The documents comprising the Will:

   [x] are in the Court's possession.

   [ ] have been probated elsewhere and an authenticated copy of the Will and statement or order probating the same accompanied the Petition.

   [ ] are unavailable, but a Statement of Contents of Lost, Destroyed or Otherwise Unavailable Will is in the Court's possession.

9. It appears from the Petition that the proceeding was commenced within the time limitation prescribed by Minn. Stat. 524.3-108.

10. The Petition indicates that there is no personal representative appointed in this or another county of Minnesota whose appointment has not been terminated.

MD   MCLE P-230   **ORDER OF FORMAL PROBATE OF WILL
AND FORMAL APPOINTMENT OF PERSONAL REPRESENTATIVE**

(continued)

Form 11   Order of Formal Probate of Will and Formal Appointment of Personal Representative
continued

Court File No. _____999999_____

11. The Petition does not indicate the existence of a possible unrevoked testamentary instrument which may relate to property subject to Minnesota law, and which is not filed for probate in this Court.

12. The person appointed below has priority and is entitled to be appointed personal representative and is not disqualified to serve as personal representative.

13. The Will provides for:

Bond: [x] No bond   Administration: [x] Undesignated
      [ ] Minimum bond   [ ] Unsupervised
      [ ] $_____ bond   [ ] Supervised
      [ ] Unspecified

14. Decedent's heirs under Minnesota law are as identified in the Petition commencing this proceeding.

15. All persons identified as heirs have survived the Decedent by at least 120 hours.

16. (Check appropriate boxes)

[ ] Decedent left no surviving spouse.

[ ] Decedent left no surviving issue.

[x] All issue of Decedent are issue of Decedent's surviving spouse except for: none

[ ] There are issue of the surviving spouse who are not issue of the Decedent.

17. No objections to the Petition have been asserted.

IT IS ORDERED:

1. The Petition is granted.

2. The Will is formally probated.

3. _____John C. Doe_____
   is formally appointed the Personal Representative of Decedent's Estate with _____no_____ bond, in [ ] an unsupervised [x] a supervised administration.

4. Upon filing of any required bond and statement of acceptance and oath, letters testamentary will be issued.

_____/S/ Richard B. Evans_____

(COURT SEAL)   Judge   October 31, 2000   Date

**ORDER OF FORMAL PROBATE OF WILL
AND FORMAL APPOINTMENT OF PERSONAL REPRESENTATIVE**

Source: This form is property of Miller/Davis Company, St. Paul, MN, Telephone 651–642–1988. Reprinted with permission.

Form 12 Order of Formal Adjudication of Intestacy, Determination of Heirs, and Appointment of Personal Representative

M/D **Form No. P-235** Minn. Stat. 524.3-409 Miller/Davis Co., St. Paul, MN (800) 752-4221
Minnesota Continuing Legal Education © 1994

STATE OF MINNESOTA

COUNTY OF _____

Estate of

_____
Decedent

DISTRICT COURT
PROBATE DIVISION
_____ **JUDICIAL DISTRICT**

Court File No. _____

ORDER OF FORMAL ADJUDICATION OF INTESTACY, DETERMINATION OF HEIRS, AND APPOINTMENT OF PERSONAL REPRESENTATIVE

The Petition for the Formal Adjudication of Intestacy and Determination of Heirs, and Appointment of Personal Representative, signed by _____, came before this Court on _____. The Court, having heard and considered the Petition, determines the following:

1. This Court has jurisdiction and venue in this County is proper.

2. The Petition is complete.

3. The Petitioner has declared or affirmed that the representations contained in the Petition are true and complete to the best of the Petitioner's knowledge or belief.

4. The Petitioner is an interested person as defined by Minnesota law.

5. Any notice required by Minnesota law has been given.

6. The Decedent died on _____ .

7. The Petition states that after conducting a reasonably diligent search, Petitioner is unaware of any testamentary instrument relating to property having a situs in this state under Minnesota law.

8. Decedent left no will, and any codicil (___) to the will, and, therefore, died intestate.

9. Decedent's heirs are ☐ as identified in the Petition or ☐ as follows:

Name and Mailing Address	Relationship and Interest (list all)	Birthdate of Minors

10. All persons identified as heirs have survived the Decedent by at least 120 hours.

Order of Formal Adjudication of Intestacy, Determination of Heirs, and Appointment of Personal Representative

M/D MCLE P-235

(*continued*)

Form 12   Order of Formal Adjudication of Intestacy, Determination of Heirs, and Appointment of
Personal Representative   *continued*

Court File No._____

11. (Check appropriate boxes)

☐   Decedent left no surviving spouse.

☐   Decedent left no surviving issue.

☐   All issue of Decedent are issue of Decedent's surviving spouse except for:

☐   There are issue of the surviving spouse who are not issue of the Decedent.

12. It appears from the Petition that the time limit for original testacy and appointment proceedings have not expired.

13. The Petition indicates that there is no personal representative appointed in this or another county of Minnesota whose appointment has not been terminated.

14. The person appointed below has priority and is entitled to be appointed personal representative and is not disqualified to serve as personal representative.

15. No objections to the Petition have been asserted.

IT IS ORDERED:

1.   The Petition is granted.

2.   Decedent left no will and, therefore, died intestate.

3.   The heirs of the Decedent are as identified above.

4.   _____
     is formally appointed the Personal Representative of Decedent's Estate with_____ bond,
     in ☐ an unsupervised ☐ a supervised administration.

5.   Upon filing of any required bond and statement of acceptance and oath, letters of general administration shall be issued.

_____

(COURT SEAL)   Judge   Date

Order of Formal Adjudication of Intestacy,
Determination of Heirs, and Appointment of
Personal Representative

MD   MCLE P-235/Page 2

Source: This form is property of Miller/Davis Company, St. Paul, MN, Telephone 651–642–1988. Reprinted with permission.

Form 13 Acceptance of Appointment as Personal Representative and Oath by Individual

MID Form No. P-001   Minn. Stat. 524.3-601   Miller/Davis Co., St. Paul, MN (800) 752-4221
Minnesota Continuing Legal Education © 1994 MCLE

STATE OF MINNESOTA

COUNTY OF   Ramsey   Probate Court

Court File No.   999999

Estate of

    Jane M. Doe

Decedent

**ACCEPTANCE OF APPOINTMENT
AS PERSONAL REPRESENTATIVE
AND OATH BY INDIVIDUAL**

STATE OF   Minnesota

COUNTY OF   Ramsey   } ss

I,   John C. Doe   ,
residing at ,   1005 Elm Street
St. Paul, MN 55102

as a condition to receiving letters as Personal Representative in this Estate, (1) accept the duties of the office, (2) agree to be bound by the provisions of the statutes relating to the office, (3) submit to the jurisdiction of the Court in any proceeding relating to this Estate, and (4) swear that I will faithfully perform all duties of the office that I now assume to the best of my ability.

/S/ John C. Doe

Signature   October 31, 2000   **Date**

Signed and sworn to (or affirmed) before me on
   October 31, 2000   by
   John C. Doe   .
   Personal Representative

/S/ Judith Harris
SIGNATURE OF NOTARY PUBLIC OR OTHER OFFICIAL

NOTARIAL STAMP OR SEAL (OR OTHER TITLE OR RANK)

Attorney For Personal Representative

THIS INSTRUMENT WAS DRAFTED BY (NAME AND ADDRESS):

John W. Cranwall
First Trust Co. Bldg.
St. Paul, MN 55101
Telephone: (651) 555-5555
Attorney License No. 1234567

MID   MCLE P-001

Acceptance of Appointment as
Personal Representative and Oath by Individual

Source: This form is property of Miller/Davis Company, St. Paul, MN, Telephone 651–642–1988. Reprinted with permission.

Form 14   Petition to [ ] Excuse Bond [ ] Increase Bond [ ] Reduce Bond

MD Form No. P-075   Minn. Stat. 524.3-604   Miller/Davis Co., St. Paul, MN (800) 752-4221
Minnesota Continuing Legal Education © 1994 MCLE

STATE OF MINNESOTA   **DISTRICT COURT**
                                                                         PROBATE DIVISION
COUNTY OF _____   _____   **JUDICIAL DISTRICT**

                                                                Court File No. _____
Estate of

_____   **PETITION TO**
                                                             [ ] **EXCUSE BOND**
_____   [ ] **INCREASE BOND**
                                                             [ ] **REDUCE BOND**
                    Decedent

I, _____ , state:

1. My address is:

2. I am an interested person as defined by Minnesota law because I am:

3. I request that the bond on the personal representative be

    [ ]   excused
    [ ]   increased from $_____ to $_____
    [ ]   reduced from $_____ to $_____

    for the following reasons:

WHEREFORE, I request the Court:

1. Fix a time and place for a hearing on this Petition;

2. Enter an Order [ ] excusing [ ] increasing [ ] reducing the bond; and

3. Grant such other relief as may be proper.

    Under penalties for perjury, I declare or affirm that I have read this document and I know or believe its representations are true and complete.

Attorney For Petitioner

THIS INSTRUMENT WAS DRAFTED BY (NAME AND ADDRESS):

_____
Petitioner   Date

MD   MCLE P-075   Petition to [ ] Excuse [ ] Increase [ ] Reduce Bond

Source: This form is property of Miller/Davis Company, St. Paul, MN, Telephone 651–642–1988. Reprinted with permission.

Form 15   Request for Waiver of Bond

MD Form No. P-074   Minn. Stat. 524.3-603   Miller/Davis Co., St. Paul, MN (800) 752-4221
Minnesota Continuing Legal Education © 1994 MCLE

STATE OF MINNESOTA   **DISTRICT COURT**
                                                         PROBATE DIVISION
COUNTY OF   Ramsey   Second   **JUDICIAL DISTRICT**

                                            Court File No.   999999

Estate of

                Jane M. Doe   **REQUEST FOR WAIVER OF BOND**

                Decedent

NOTICE: The purpose of the bond is to protect the beneficiaries of the Estate. A bond protects the beneficiaries of the Estate against the personal representative's wrongful action.

Each of the undersigned is an interested person in this Estate with an apparent interest in excess of $1,000.00, other than as a creditor. I am aware that any bond filed in this Estate is to cover damages in the event of mismanagement or misappropriation of funds by the personal representative. I request that no bond be required of _____ John C. Doe _____ , the nominated or appointed personal representative in this Estate.

_____ /S/ John C. Doe _____

Signature   October 31, 2000   Date

_____

Signature   Date

_____

Signature   Date

_____

Signature   Date

MD   MCLE P-074   Request for Waiver of Bond

Source: This form is property of Miller/Davis Company, St. Paul, MN, Telephone 651–642–1980. Reprinted with permission.

Form 16   Letters Testamentary

MD Form No. P-010   Minn. Stat. 524.3-601   Miller/Davis Co., St. Paul, MN (800) 752-4221
Minnesota Continuing Legal Education © 1994 MCLE

STATE OF MINNESOTA   **DISTRICT COURT**
                                                                         PROBATE DIVISION
COUNTY OF   Ramsey   Second   **JUDICIAL DISTRICT**

                                                     Court File No.   999999
Estate of

_____   **LETTERS**
          Jane M. Doe   ☒ **TESTAMENTARY**
_____   ☐ **OF GENERAL ADMINISTRATION**

          Decedent

1. The Decedent died on   Sept. 20, 2000 .

2. _____John C. Doe_____ has
   been appointed Personal Representative of Decedent's Estate in

   ☐ an unsupervised
   ☒ a supervised administration

   and is now qualified to act as Personal Representative of the Estate and has authority to administer the
   Estate according to law.

                                          ___/S/ Richard B. Evans_____

                                          Judge/Registrar   October 31, 2000   Date

          (COURT SEAL)

MD   MCLE P-010   **Letters**
                                                          ☐ Testamentary ☐ of General Administration

Source: This form is property of Miller/Davis Company, St. Paul, MN, Telephone 651–642–1988. Reprinted with permission.

Form 17   Order Appointing Guardian

MD Form No GC-14 (Revised 10/98)   Minn. Stat. 525.551, #1   Miller/Davis Co., St. Paul, MN (800) 752-4221

STATE OF MINNESOTA

COUNTY OF _____

In Re: Guardianship of

_____
_____
                           Ward

DISTRICT COURT
PROBATE DIVISION
_____ **JUDICIAL DISTRICT**

Court File No. _____

ORDER APPOINTING
GENERAL GUARDIAN OF THE
PERSON AND ESTATE

This matter came duly on for hearing on _____ , _____ , on the petition of
                                                                    Year
_____ seeking appointment
of a guardian for _____ .
Petitioner appeared personally and by and through his / her attorney _____
_____ , Esq. The above named ward appeared personally and by and through
His/Her   attorney, _____ , Esq.
The Court having considered the evidence and being fully advised in the premises now makes the following:

_____
_____
_____
_____
_____
_____
_____
_____
_____
_____
_____

VOID

FINDINGS OF FACT

1. (In a meeting with a Court appointed visitor the ward waived His/Her right to be present personally and to be represented by an attorney.) (The ward was unable to attend the hearing by reason of medical condition as evidenced by a written statement from a licensed physician.)

2. The ward lacks sufficient understanding or capacity to make or communicate responsible decisions concerning His/Her person.

3. The ward has demonstrated behavioral deficits evidencing inability to meet His/Her needs for medical care, nutrition, clothing, shelter, or safety.

4. The ward lacks sufficient understanding or capacity to make or communicate responsible decisions concerning His/Her estate or financial decisions.

5. The ward has demonstrated behavioral deficits evidencing inability to manage His/Her estate.

6. The ward has property which will be dissipated without proper management. (Funds are needed for the care, support, and welfare of the ward and / or those entitled to the support of the ward.)

7. No appropriate alternative to guardianship exists which is less restrictive of civil rights and liberties, including any protective arrangement under M.S. 525.54 Subd. 7.

8. The ward is incapable of exercising the following rights and powers:

    a. To establish His/Her place of abode.

    b. To determine His/Her food, clothing, shelter, health care, social and recreational requirements, and training, educational and rehabilitation requirements.

    c. To dispose of His/Her clothing, personal effects, vehicles, furniture or other property.

MD   GC-14   Order Appointing General Guardian of the Person and Estate

Source: This form is property of Miller/Davis Company, St. Paul, MN, Telephone 651–642–1988. Reprinted with permission.

Form 18   Petition for Formal Probate of Will and for Formal Appointment of Personal Representative (Ancillary Proceeding)

MD Form No. P-930   Minn. Stat. 524.3-401; 524.3-502   Miller/Davis Co., St. Paul, MN (800) 752-4221
Minnesota Continuing Legal Education © 1994 MCLE

STATE OF MINNESOTA   **DISTRICT COURT**
                                                         PROBATE DIVISION
COUNTY OF _____   _____ **JUDICIAL DISTRICT**

                                                         Court File No. _____
Estate of

_____   **PETITION FOR FORMAL PROBATE OF WILL**
_____   **AND FOR FORMAL APPOINTMENT**
                                        OF PERSONAL REPRESENTATIVE
                Decedent   **(ANCILLARY PROCEEDING)**

I, _____ , state:

1. My address is:

2. I am an interested person as defined by Minnesota law because:

    ☐ I have been appointed Personal Representative of Decedent's Estate by a court or registrar in the Decedent's domicile.
    or
    ☐ Other:

3. Decedent was born on _____ , at (city, state) _____ .

4. Decedent died on _____ , at (city, state) _____ .

5. Decedent at the time of death resided in _____ County, at (address):

6. Decedent's Social Security number is _____ .

7. The names and addresses of Decedent's spouse, children, heirs, devisees and other persons interested in this proceeding so far as known or ascertainable with reasonable diligence by the Applicant are:

Name and Mailing Address	Relationship and Interest (list all)	Birthdate of Minors

(Attach separate schedule, if necessary)

MD   MCLE P-930   Petition for Formal Probate of Will and for Formal Appointment
                                           of Personal Representative (Ancillary Proceeding)

Source: This form is property of Miller/Davis Company, St. Paul, MN, Telephone 651–642–1988. Reprinted with permission.

Form 19 Notice and Order of Hearing on Petition for Probate of Will and Appointment of Personal Representative and Notice to Creditors (Ancillary Proceeding)

MD Form No. P-932   Minn. Stat. 524.3-403; 524.3-502; 524.3-801; 524.4-207   Miller/Davis Co., St. Paul, MN (800) 752-4221
Minnesota Continuing Legal Education © 1994 MCLE

STATE OF MINNESOTA

COUNTY OF _____

Estate of

_____

_____

Decedent

DISTRICT COURT
PROBATE DIVISION
_____ **JUDICIAL DISTRICT**

Court File No. _____

NOTICE AND ORDER OF HEARING
ON PETITION FOR PROBATE OF WILL
AND APPOINTMENT OF PERSONAL
REPRESENTATIVE AND NOTICE
TO CREDITORS (ANCILLARY PROCEEDING)

It is Ordered and Notice is given that on _____ , at _____ (a.m.) (p.m.) a hearing will be held in this Court at _____ , Minnesota, for the formal probate of an instrument purporting to be the will of Decedent, dated _____ , and codicil(___) to the will dated _____ , and separate writing(___) under Minn. Stat. 524.2-513 ("Will") and for the appointment of _____ , whose address is

as ancillary Personal Representative of the Estate of the Decedent in ☐ an UNSUPERVISED ☐ a SUPERVISED administration. Any objections to the petition must be filed with the Court prior to or raised at the hearing. If proper and if no objections are filed or raised, the Personal Representative will be appointed with power to administer the assets of the Estate in Minnesota including the power to collect all assets, pay all legal debts, claims, taxes and expenses, and sell real and personal property, and do all necessary acts for the Estate.

Notice is also given that (subject to Minn. 524.3-801) all creditors having claims against the Estate are required to present the claims to the personal representative or to the Court Administrator within four months after the date of this Notice or the claims will be barred.

VOID

_____
Judge   Date

_____
Court Administrator   Date

Attorney For Personal Representative

THIS INSTRUMENT WAS DRAFTED BY (NAME AND ADDRESS):

NOTE: If notice to creditors has been previously given, delete the notice to creditors.
NOTE TO PUBLISHER: Do not publish text of notes.

MD   MCLE P-932

Notice and Order of Hearing on Petition for Probate of Will
and Appointment of Personal Representative
and Notice to Creditors (Ancillary Proceeding)

Source: This form is property of Miller/Davis Company, St. Paul, MN, Telephone 651–642–1908. Reprinted with permission.

Form 20 Order for Formal Probate of Will and Formal Appointment of Personal Representative (Ancillary Proceeding)

M/D Form No. P-934   Minn. Stat. 524.3-409; 524.3-414; 524.3-502   Miller/Davis Co., St. Paul, MN (800) 752-4221
Minnesota Continuing Legal Education © 1994 MCLE

STATE OF MINNESOTA

COUNTY OF _____

Estate of

_____
_____
                    Decedent

DISTRICT COURT
PROBATE DIVISION
_____ **JUDICIAL DISTRICT**

Court File No. _____

ORDER FOR FORMAL PROBATE OF WILL
AND FORMAL APPOINTMENT
OF PERSONAL REPRESENTATIVE
(ANCILLARY PROCEEDING)

The Petition for the Formal Probate of Will and Formal Appointment of Personal Representative (Ancillary Proceeding), signed by _____
_____
came before this Court on _____ . The Court, having heard and considered the petition, determines the following:

1. This Court has jurisdiction and venue in this County is proper.

2. The Petition if complete.

3. The Petitioner has declared or affirmed that the representations contained in the Petition are true and complete to the best of Petitioner's knowledge or belief.

4. The Petitioner is an interested person as defined by Minnesota law.

5. Any notice required by Minnesota law has been given.

6. Decedent died on _____ .

7. Decedent's Will relating to property in Minnesota is comprised of the following:

    ☐ Last will dated _____ .
    ☐ Codicil(___) dated _____ .
    ☐ Separate writing(___) under Minn. Stat. 524.2-513 dated _____ .

    ☐ (check if applicable) The Will refers to a separate writing but none has been found.

8. The Decedent's Will was probated by the _____ Court of
    _____ County, _____ , by an
    Order or Statement dated _____ , in File No. _____ .

9. _____
    was appointed Personal Representative of Decedent's Estate in the proceeding described in Paragraph 8.
     The Petition does not indicate that any personal representative has been appointed in this or any other county of Minnesota whose appointment has not been terminated.

10. Authenticated copies of the Will and Order or Statement probating the Will and appointing the personal representative are in the Court's possession.

VOID

M/D   MCLE P-934

Order for Formal Probate of Will and Formal Appointment
of Personal Representative (Ancillary Proceeding)

Source: This form is property of Miller/Davis Company, St. Paul, MN, Telephone 651–642–1988. Reprinted with permission.

Form 21   Order Appointing Appraisers

MD Form No. P-086 | Minn. Stat. 525.312 | Miller/Davis Co., St. Paul, MN (800) 752-4221
Minnesota Continuing Legal Education © 1994 MCLE

STATE OF MINNESOTA

COUNTY OF _____

DISTRICT COURT
PROBATE DIVISION
JUDICIAL DISTRICT

_____

Court File No. _____

Estate of

_____

_____

Decedent

ORDER APPOINTING APPRAISERS

The Petition for Order Appointing Appraisers, signed by _____

_____

came before the Court on _____ . The Court having heard
and considered the Petition, determines the following:

1. The Petition is complete.

2. The Petitioner has declared or affirmed that the representations contained in the Petition are true and complete to the best of Petitioner's knowledge or belief.

3. Any notice required by Minnesota law has been given.

4. The Petitioner is an interested person as defined by Minnesota law.

5. Appraisers should be appointed in the Estate because:

6. The following persons are qualified to be appraisers:

IT IS ORDERED:

1. The petition is granted.

2. The persons named in Paragraph 6, above, are appointed appraisers.

_____

Judge   Date

MD   MCLE P-086   Order Appointing Appraisers

Source: This form is property of Miller/Davis Company, St. Paul, MN, Telephone 651–642–1988. Reprinted with permission.

Form 22 Inventory

MD Form No. P-600   Minn. Stat. 524.3-706   Miller/Davis Co., St. Paul, MN (800) 752-4221
                                                              Minnesota Continuing Legal Education © 1994 MCLE

STATE OF MINNESOTA

COUNTY OF ___Ramsey___   Probate Court

                                              Court File No. ___999999___
Estate of

                                              INVENTORY
                                              [X] **ORIGINAL**
                                              [ ] **AMENDED**
                                              [ ] **SUPPLEMENTAL**

___Jane M. Doe___

Decedent   Date of Death ___September 20, 2000___
                                      Social Security Number ___321-54-9876___

___John C. Doe___,
the Personal Representative of the Estate, states:

1. The following is a true and correct inventory at date of death values of all the property of the Estate, both real and personal, which has come into my possession as Personal Representative. If an appraisal of any asset has been made, the name and address of each appraiser used is included. After diligent search and inquiry concerning the assets of the Estate, the following is a list of the Estate assets by category:

SCHEDULE	VALUE
Schedule A: Real Estate	372,750.
Schedule B: Stocks, Bonds, and Other Securities	10,648.
Schedule C: Bank Accounts, Mortgages, Contracts for Deed, Notes and Cash	76,350.
Schedule D: Other Personal Property	240,100.
SUBTOTAL	699,848.
Less Schedule E: Mortgages and Liens	(140,000.)
TOTAL	559,848.

2. A copy of this Inventory, including all schedules, has been mailed to the surviving spouse, if any, and to all residuary distributees of the Decedent and to interested persons and creditors who have requested a copy of the Inventory.

   Under penalties for perjury, I declare or affirm that I have read the Inventory and I know or believe its representations are true and complete.

Attorney For Personal Representative

THIS INSTRUMENT WAS DRAFTED BY (NAME AND ADDRESS):   /S/ John C. Doe

John W. Cranwall
First Trust Co. Bldg.
St. Paul, MN 55101
Telephone: (651) 555-5555   Personal Representative December 21, 2000 Date
Attorney License No. 1234567

MD   MCLE P-600   Inventory

(continued)

Form 22 Inventory *continued*

Court File No. ___999999___

SCHEDULE A: REAL ESTATE

INSTRUCTIONS for Schedule A:

1. Include both the legal description and the street address. If rural property also include acreage.
2. For Contracts for Deed: If Decedent owned a Vendor/Seller's interest describe the land on Schedule A, valuing it at zero and show the remaining contract balance on Schedule C. If Decedent owned a Vendee/Buyer's interest, describe the property on Schedule A valuing it at its fair market value.
3. County Assessor's market value can be obtained from the County Assessor or department of taxation.
4. List only Minnesota real estate. DO NOT list real estate located in other states.

Item Number	Description of Property	County Assessor's Market Value	Fair Market Value

1	Homestead in the County of ___Ramsey___
	1005 Elm Street, St. Paul, MN
	Legally described as follows, to wit:
	  Lot 615, Block 42, Reiser's
	  Addition to St. Paul (Plat
	  #22760 Parcel #7600)
		$ 337,500.	$ 350,000.

		Sub Total	350,000.
	Other Real Estate in the County of ___Ramsey___	$	$

2	An undivided 1/4 interest in duplex located at 776 Cliff Road, St. Paul, MN
	Legally described as follows, to wit:
	  Lots 16 & 17, Block 20, Lovey's
	  Addition to St. Paul (Plat
	  #32689 Parcel #5562)
		68,250.(Total)
		17,063.(1/4)
			91,000.(Total)
			22,750.(1/4)

		Sub Total	22,750.
	Schedule A: Real Estate	TOTAL	372,750.

(continued)

Form 22 Inventory *continued*

Court File No. ___999999___

SCHEDULE B: STOCKS, BONDS AND OTHER SECURITIES

INSTRUCTIONS for Schedule B:

1. Specify face value of bonds, number of shares of stock, stock certificate number and CUSIP number, if available.
2. List each bond issue, stock, or certificate separately.

Item Number	Description of Property	Unit Value	Fair Market Value
		$	$
1	Stocks: 100 Shares Tenneco, Inc., Common Stock, CUSIP 674322189, Cert. C068297 dated 12/31/72, N.Y.S.E.	50.	5,000.
2	1000 Shares Minnesota Co-op, Common Stock, Cert. D2289663 dated 12/31/74	4.50	4,500.
3	United States Savings Bonds: $500 U.S. Savings Bond, Series E, Bond R4502363E, 04/90		574.
4	$500 U.S. Savings Bond, Series E, Bond R4502364E, 04/90		574.

	Sub Total	10,648.
Schedule B: Stocks, Bonds and Other Securities	TOTAL	10,648.

(continued)

Form 22 Inventory *continued*

Court File No. _____999999_____

SCHEDULE C: BANK ACCOUNTS, MORTGAGES, CONTRACTS FOR DEED, NOTES AND CASH

INSTRUCTIONS for Schedule C:

1. List Vendor/Seller's interest in Contract for Deed on this Schedule. Also include the date of the contract, name of Vendee/Buyer, interest rate and unpaid balance at date of death, and accrued interest, if any. List Mortgages owned by Decedent as assets, NOT mortgages for which Decedent is liable or mortgages
2. secured by property in the Estate.

Item Number	Description of Property	Fair Market Value
		$
1	American Express Traveler's Checks #10008–10017, $100/ea.	1,000.
2	First National City Bank of St. Paul – Checking Account No. 55-5555.	50,000.
3	American National Bank of St. Paul – Savings Certificate No. 44-4444, at 5.5% per annum.	15,000.
4	Johnson Furriers, Promissory Note dated 03/20/94, payable 03/20/01 with interest at 7% per annum.	10,000.
5	Accrued interest on Item 4 from 03/20/00 to 09/20/00.	350.

		Sub Total	76,350.
	Schedule C: Bank Accounts, Mortgages, Contracts for Deed, Notes and Cash	TOTAL	76,350.

(continued)

Form 22 Inventory *continued*

Court File No. ___999999___

SCHEDULE D: OTHER PERSONAL PROPERTY

INSTRUCTIONS for Schedule D:

1. List on this schedule, any personal property owned by Decedent and not reported on other schedules. Examples of property to be listed on this schedule include: refunds, wearing apparel, household goods, automobiles, furniture, business interests, and insurance payable to the Estate.
2. Where appropriate, specify the location of the property.
3. Use actual value or specify if asset has no pecuniary value.
4. DO NOT list non-probate property.

Item Number	Description of Personal Property	Fair Market Value
		$
1	Furniture and household goods.	22,000.
2	Furs – Mink Coat.	11,500.
3	Clothing and personal effects.	4,500.
4	1998 Mazda, Vehicle Identification No. 6778899926, Title No. 03618957.	12,000.
5	Judgment dated February 19, 1997 for personal injuries in auto accident against Forrest R. Redding collected in full on December 20, 2000.	20,000.
6	Minnesota Life Insurance Company Policy J666221, face amount $120,000, accumulated dividends $100. Beneficiary: Estate of Jane M. Doe.	120,100.
7	Power of Appointment. Trust created under agreement dated 12/02/65 by father of decedent for decedent's benefit under which decedent had a general power of appointment (to distribute income and/or principal) which power had not been exercised during decedent's lifetime, but which decedent exercised under her will. The assets remaining in this trust and subject to this power are 500 shares of Green Giant common stock and undistributed earnings (dividends) thereon. Unit value $100 per share.	50,000.
	Sub Total	240,100.
	Schedule D: Other Property TOTAL	240,100.

(continued)

Form 22 Inventory *continued*

Court File No. ___999999___

SCHEDULE E: MORTGAGES AND LIENS

INSTRUCTIONS for Schedule E:

1. Show any mortgages and liens secured by property in the Estate. Detail the date of the installment, names of the parties, interest rate, payment terms, and any other relevant data. Indicate the Schedule and Item Number of the secured property from prior schedule. The remaining balance of Contracts for Deed in which Decedent was the Vendee/Buyer or was the mortgage debtor should be listed on this Schedule. Also include interest and taxes due at date of death.

Item Number	Description of Mortgage or Lien	Asset Secured (Schedule and Item Number)	Balance as of Date of Death
1	Mortgage on homestead. St. Paul Bank and Trust Company, Note dated 02/15/96 at 7.25% due 03/01/2010.	Sch. A, Item 1	$ 130,000.
2	Mortgage on duplex. St. Paul Bank and Trust Company, Note dated 03/01/91 at 9.00% due 03/01/2006. Balance – $40,000. 1/4 interest – $10,000.	Sch. A, Item 2	10,000.
		TOTAL	140,000.
	Schedule E: Mortgages and Liens	TOTAL	140,000.

MCLE P-600/Page 6

Inventory

Source: This form is property of Miller/Davis Company, St. Paul, MN, Telephone 651–642–1988. Reprinted with permission

Form 23 Appraisal

MD Form No. P-601   Minn. Stat. 524.3-707   Miller/Davis Co., St. Paul, MN (800) 752-4221
                                                                        Minnesota Continuing Legal Education © 1994 MCLE

STATE OF MINNESOTA

COUNTY OF _____   _____

Estate of   **Court File No.** _____

_____   **APPRAISAL**

_____   **Date of Death** _____
                    Decedent

_____

STATE OF MINNESOTA

COUNTY OF _____ } ss.

   I, _____ ,
residing at: _____ ,
as a condition to being appointed appraiser for the Estate, agree to perform the duties of an appraiser to
the best of my abilities and submit to the jurisdiction of the Court appointing me.

VOID

_____

Appraiser   Date

NOTARIAL STAMP OR SEAL (OR OTHER TITLE OR RANK)	Signed and sworn to (or affirmed) before me on
	_____ by
	_____
	_____ ,
	Appraiser
	_____
	SIGNATURE OF NOTARY PUBLIC OR OTHER OFFICIAL

MD   MCLE P-601   Appraisal

(continued)

Form 23   Appraisal   *continued*

Court File No. _____

APPRAISAL

Item Number	Legal Description of Real Property (Include street address of city realty; acreage of rural land; and liens, if any)	County Assessor's Market Value	Fair Market Value
	Homestead in the County of _____	$	$
		Sub Total	
	Other Real Estate in the County of _____	$	$
		Sub Total	
		TOTAL	

I certify that I have appraised the property described above as of the date of death of Decedent and I believe the Fair Market Value stated above accurately reflects the fair market value of the assets shown above.

_____

Appraiser   Date

MCLE P-601/Page 2   Appraisal

(continued)

Form 23 Appraisal *continued*

Court File No. _____

PERSONAL PROPERTY

Item Number	Description of Personal Property	Appraised Value
		$

VOID

		Sub Total	
	Personal Property	TOTAL	

I certify that I have appraised the property described above as of the date of death of Decedent and I believe the Fair Market Value stated above accurately reflects the fair market value of the assets shown above.

_____

Appraiser

MD   MCLE P-601/Page 3   Appraisal

Source: This form is property of Miller/Davis Company, St. Paul, MN, Telephone 651–642–1988. Reprinted with permission.

Form 24 Petition to Allow Selection of Personal Property

MD Form No. P-556   Minn. Stat. 525.151   Miller/Davis Co., St. Paul, MN (800) 752-4221
Minnesota Continuing Legal Education © 1994 MCLE

STATE OF MINNESOTA   **DISTRICT COURT**
                                                 PROBATE DIVISION
COUNTY OF ___Ramsey___   ___Second___   **JUDICIAL DISTRICT**

                                                 Court File No. ___999999___

Estate of

_____Jane M. Doe_____   **PETITION TO ALLOW SELECTION**
_____ **OF PERSONAL PROPERTY**

                Decedent

I, _____John C. Doe_____, state:

1. My address is:
        1005 Elm Street
        St. Paul, MN 55102

2. I am an interested person as defined by Minnesota law because I am:
        spouse, heir, devisee, personal representative

3. The Decedent was survived by a spouse, ___John C. Doe_____,
    and the following minor children whose names and ages are:
        none

4. I now select the following items of personal property listed and described in the inventory of Decedent's Estate (attach schedule, if necessary):

Description of Property   **Value**

1998 Mazda, Vehicle Identification No. 6778899926,   12,000.
Title No. 03618957

                                        TOTAL VALUE $12,000.

WHEREFORE, I request the Court:

1. Fix a time and place for a hearing on this Petition;
2. Enter an Order allowing the selection of property shown above; and
3. Grant such other relief as may be proper.

Under penalties for perjury, I declare or affirm that I have read this document and I know or believe its representations are true and complete.

Attorney For Petitioner   ___/S/ John C. Doe_____

THIS INSTRUMENT WAS DRAFTED BY (NAME AND ADDRESS):

    John W. Cranwall   Petitioner   December 21, 2000   Date
    First Trust Co. Bldg.
    St. Paul, MN 55101
    Telephone: (651) 555-5555
    Attorney License No. 1234567

MD   MCLE P-556   Petition to Allow Selection of Personal Property

Source: This form is property of Miller/Davis Company, St. Paul, MN, Telephone 651–642–1988. Reprinted with permission.

Form 25   Order Allowing Selection of (Setting Apart) Personal Property

MD Form No. P-557 | Minn. Stat. 525.151 | Miller/Davis Co., St. Paul, MN (800) 752-4221
Minnesota Continuing Legal Education © 1994 MCLE

STATE OF MINNESOTA

COUNTY OF ___Ramsey___

Estate of

_____ Jane M. Doe _____

Decedent

DISTRICT COURT
PROBATE DIVISION
___Second___ **JUDICIAL DISTRICT**

Court File No. ___999999___

ORDER ALLOWING SELECTION OF PERSONAL PROPERTY

The Petition for Allowance of Selection of Personal Property, signed by _____
_____ John C. Doe _____
came before this Court on _____ December 21, 2000 _____ . The Court, having heard
and considered the Petition, determines the following:

1. The Petition is complete.

2. Any notice required by Minnesota law has been given.

3. The Petitioner has declared or affirmed that the representations contained in the Petition are true and complete to the best of the Petitioner's knowledge or belief.

4. The Petitioner is an interested person as defined by Minnesota law.

5. The Decedent was survived by a spouse, _____ John C. Doe _____,
    and the following minor children whose names and ages are:

6. The Petitioner has selected certain items of personal property listed and described in the Inventory of Decedent's Estate.

MD   MCLE P-557

Order Allowing Selection of Personal Property

(continued)

Form 25 Order Allowing Selection of (Setting Apart) Personal Property *continued*

Court File No. _____999999_____

IT IS ORDERED:

1. The Petition is granted.

2. The Petitioner's selection of the following personal property is allowed:

Description of Property	Value
1998 Mazda, Vehicle Identification No. 6778899926, Title No. 03618957	12,000.

TOTAL VALUE $12,000.

3. The Personal Representative of the Estate will immediately transfer said personal property to the Petitioner.

_____/S/ Richard B. Evans_____

(COURT SEAL)   Judge   January 20, 2001   Date

MCLE P-557/Page 2   Order Allowing Selection of Personal Property

Source: This form is property of Miller/Davis Company, St. Paul, MN, Telephone 651–642–1988. Reprinted with permission.

Form 26   Petition for Family Maintenance

MD Form No. P-560   Minn. Stat. 525.151   Miller/Davis Co., St. Paul, MN (800) 752-4221
Minnesota Continuing Legal Education © 1994 MCLE

STATE OF MINNESOTA   **DISTRICT COURT**
                                                                               PROBATE DIVISION
COUNTY OF ___Ramsey___   Second   **JUDICIAL DISTRICT**

                                                    Court File No. ___999999___
Estate of

_____ Jane M. Doe _____   **PETITION FOR**
_____   **FAMILY MAINTENANCE**
              Decedent

I, _____ John C. Doe _____ , state:

1. My address is:
            1005 Elm Street
            St. Paul, MN 55102

2. I am an interested person as defined by Minnesota law because I am:
            spouse, heir, devisee, personal representative

3. The Decedent was survived by a spouse, ___John C. Doe_____ ,
   and the following minor or dependent children whose names and ages are:
                        none

4. Decedent's Estate is [x] solvent [ ] insolvent.

5. A reasonable and necessary family maintenance of ___$4,800.___ should be paid to and
   for the use and benefit of Decedent's surviving spouse and minor or dependent children constituting the
   family of Decedent.

   WHEREFORE, I request the Court:

1. Fix a time and place for a hearing on this Petition;
2. Enter an Order directing the payment of a family maintenance in the amount of ___$400.___
   per month commencing on ___January 21, 2001___ ; and
3. Grant such other relief as may be proper.

   Under penalties for perjury, I declare or affirm that I have read this document and I know or believe its
representations are true and complete.

                                              ___/S/ John C. Doe_____

Attorney For Petitioner

THIS INSTRUMENT WAS DRAFTED BY (NAME AND ADDRESS):
John W. Cranwall First Trust Co. Bldg. St. Paul, MN 55101 Telephone: (651) 555-5555 Attorney License No. 1234567

                                              Petitioner   December 21, 2000   **Date**

MD   MCLE P-560   Petition for Family Maintenance

Source: This form is property of Miller/Davis Company, St. Paul, MN, Telephone 651–642–1988. Reprinted with permission.

Form 27   Order for Family Maintenance

MD Form No. P-562   Minn. Stat. 525.151   Miller/Davis Co., St. Paul, MN (800) 752-4221
Minnesota Continuing Legal Education © 1994 MCLE

STATE OF MINNESOTA

COUNTY OF   Ramsey   Second

DISTRICT COURT
PROBATE DIVISION
JUDICIAL DISTRICT

Court File No.   999999

Estate of

Jane M. Doe

ORDER FOR
FAMILY MAINTENANCE

Decedent

The Petition for Family Maintenance, signed by _____
_____ John C. Doe _____
came before this Court on _____ December 21, 2000 _____ . The Court, having heard
and considered the Petition, determines the following:

1. The Petition is complete.

2. Any notice required by Minnesota law has been given.

3. The Petitioner has declared or affirmed that the representations contained in the Petition are true and complete to the best of Petitioner's knowledge or belief.

4. The Petitioner is an interested person as defined by Minnesota law.

5. The Decedent was survived by a spouse, _____ John C. Doe _____ ,
and the following minor or dependent children whose names and ages are:
none

6. Decedent's Estate is [x] solvent [ ] insolvent.

7. A family maintenance of _____ $4,800. _____ is reasonable and necessary for the use and benefit of Decedent's surviving spouse and minor or dependent children constituting the family of Decedent.

IT IS ORDERED:

1. The Petition is granted.

2. The personal representative is directed to pay to _____ John C. Doe _____ ,
the sum of _____ $400. _____ per month commencing on _____ January 21, 2001 _____
for the use and benefit of the surviving spouse and minor or dependent children constituting the family of Decedent.

_____ /S/ Richard B. Evans _____

(COURT SEAL)

Judge   January 20, 2001   Date

MD   MCLE P-562   Order for Family Maintenance

Source: This form is property of Miller/Davis Company, St. Paul, MN, Telephone 651–642–1988. Reprinted with permission.

Form 28 Personal Representative's Petition for Late Disallowance of Claim

MD Form No. P-534   Minn. Stat. 524.3-803; 524.3-806   Miller/Davis Co., St. Paul, MN (800) 752-4221
Minnesota Continuing Legal Education © 1994 MCLE

STATE OF MINNESOTA   **DISTRICT COURT**
                                                                PROBATE DIVISION
COUNTY OF _____   _____ **JUDICIAL DISTRICT**

                                                                Court File No. _____

Estate of

_____   **PERSONAL REPRESENTATIVE'S PETITION**
_____   **FOR LATE DISALLOWANCE OF CLAIM**
                   Decedent
_____

I, _____,
Personal Representative of the Estate, state:

1. _____,
   Claimant, presented a written statement of claim on _____ in the amount of
   $_____ ("Claim"). The Claim has been filed with the Court or a copy of the Claim
   accompanies this Petition.

2. The Claim should be disallowed because:

3. No notice of disallowance was mailed to claimant within two months after the time for original
   presentment of the Claim had expired.

4. Payment of the Claim has not been made.

   VOID

   WHEREFORE, I request the Court:

1. Fix a time and place for a hearing on this Petition;

2. Enter an Order formally disallowing the Claim; and

3. Grant such other relief as may be proper.

   Under penalties for perjury, I declare or affirm that I have read this Petition and I know or believe its
representations are true and complete.

                                          _____

Attorney For Personal Representative

| THIS INSTRUMENT WAS DRAFTED BY (NAME AND ADDRESS): | Personal Representative   Date |

MD   MCLE P-534   Personal Representative's Petition
                                                          for Late Disallowance of Claim

Source: This form is property of Miller/Davis Company, St. Paul, MN, Telephone 651–642–1988. Reprinted with permission.

Form 29   Order Authorizing Late Disallowance of Claim

MD Form No. P-536   Minn. Stat. 524.3-803; 524.3-806(a)   Miller/Davis Co., St. Paul, MN (800) 752-4221
Minnesota Continuing Legal Education © 1994 MCLE

STATE OF MINNESOTA

COUNTY OF _____

DISTRICT COURT
PROBATE DIVISION
_____ **JUDICIAL DISTRICT**

Court File No. _____

Estate of

_____
_____
Decedent

ORDER AUTHORIZING LATE
DISALLOWANCE OF CLAIM

The Petition to Present and Allow Late Claim, signed by _____
_____

came before this Court on _____ . The Court, having heard and considered
the petition, determines the following:

1.   The Petition is complete.

2.   Any notice required by Minnesota law has been given.

3.   The Petitioner has declared or affirmed that the representations contained in the Petition are true and
complete to the best of the Petitioner's knowledge or belief.

4.   The Petitioner is an interested person as defined by Minnesota Law.

5.   _____ ,
Claimant, presented a claim on _____ in the amount of
$_____ ("Claim").

6.   No notice of disallowance was mailed to Claimant within two months after the time for original
presentment of the Claim had expired.

7.   Payment of the Claim has not been made.

8.   The Personal Representative should be permitted to disallow the Claim because:

IT IS ORDERED:

VOID

1.   The Petition is granted.

2.   The Claim is formally disallowed.

(COURT SEAL)   _____

Judge   Date

MD   MCLE P-536   Order Authorizing Late Disallowance of Claim

Source: This form is property of Miller/Davis Company, St. Paul, MN, Telephone 651–642–1988. Reprinted with permission.

Form 30   Order Confirming Private Sale, Made Pursuant to License

MID Form No. 93-M --Order Confirming Private Sale,   Minnesota Uniform Conveyancing Blanks   Miller/Davis Co., St. Paul, MN
Made Pursuant to Licence.

STATE OF _____ ⎫   **IN COUNTY COURT,**
                                    ⎬ ss.   Probate Division
COUNTY OF _____ ⎭

In the Matter of the Estate of   File No. _____

_____ ⎫   **Order Confirming Private Sale,**
_____ ⎭   **Made Pursuant to License.**

The above entitled matter came on to be heard on the _____ day of _____ , _____ upon the
report of _____
as _____
                                    (Representative or Guardian)
in the above entitled matter of the sale by_____ of certain lands pursuant to the order or license of this court
to _____ granted therefor, and _____ petition for the confirmation of said sale; and the court having considered the
said report, and examined _____
relative to the same, and having examined the files and records in said matter, finds herein the following facts, to-wit:

FIRST-That pursuant to a petition duly made and filed in this court, and the citation of this court duly issued for hearing
on said petition, and notice of said hearing duly given as provided by law, and a hearing duly had by this court on said petition
an order of license in said above entitled matter was duly made and filed in this court whereby the said _____
_____
of said estate was authorized and directed to sell at private sale the real estate hereinafter described.

SECOND-That pursuant to said order of license, the said_____
_____
took, subscribed and filed in this court the oath required by law and the said order of license, before making the sale of real
estate specified in said report and hereinafter referred to; and also before making said sale, executed and filed in this court the
bond required by law and said order of license, which bond was duly approved by this court.

THIRD-That the said _____
before making said sale, did cause the real estate hereinafter and in said order of license described to be reappraised by the
persons appointed for that purpose in said order of license, and their re-appraisal thereof to be filed in this court _____
_____

FOURTH-That on the _____ day of _____ , _____ the said
_____
pursuant to said order of license, did sell, at private sale, to _____
for the sum of _____ DOLLARS,
the tract _____of land, described in said order of license lying and being in the County of _____
State of Minnesota, described as follows, to-wit:

Source: This form is property of Miller/Davis Company, St. Paul, MN, Telephone 651–642–1988. Reprinted with permission.

Form 31 Personal Representative's Deed

MD Form No. 109-M Personal Representative's Deed Minnesota Uniform Conveyancing Blanks (8/24/95) Miller-Davis Co., St. Paul, MN

Individual Personal Representative(s) to Individual(s)

No delinquent taxes and transfer entered; Certificate of Real Estate Value (   ) filed (   ) not required Certificate of Real Estate Value No. _____

_____ , _____
(Year)

_____
County Auditor

by _____
Deputy

DEED TAX DUE: $_____

Date: _____

(reserved for recording data)

FOR VALUABLE CONSIDERATION, _____ ,

as Personal Representative(s) of the Estate of _____
Decedent, single ☐   married ☐   at the time of death (if "married" is checked, attach a Consent of Spouse [Form No. 106-M]), Grantor, conveys to _____
_____ , Grantee,
real property in _____ County, Minnesota, described as follows:

VOID

together with all hereditaments and appurtenances belonging thereto.

☐ The Seller certifies that the seller does not know of any wells on the described property.

☐ A well disclosure certificate accompanies this document.

☐ I am familiar with the property described in this instrument and I certify that the status and number of wells on the described real property have not changed since the last previously filed well disclosure certificate.

Affix Deed Tax Stamp Here

PERSONAL REPRESENTATIVE(S)

STATE OF MINNESOTA _____

COUNTY OF _____ } ss.

This instrument was acknowledged before me on _____
(Date)

by _____

_____ , as Personal Representative(s)
of the Estate of _____ , Decedent.

NOTARIAL STAMP OR SEAL (OR OTHER TITLE OR RANK):

SIGNATURE OF NOTARY PUBLIC OR OTHER OFFICIAL

Check here if part or all of the land is Registered (Torrens) ☐

Tax Statements for the real property described in this instrument should be sent to (include name and address of Grantee):

THIS INSTRUMENT WAS DRAFTED BY (NAME AND ADDRESS):

Source: This form is property of Miller/Davis Company, St. Paul, MN, Telephone 651–642–1988. Reprinted with permission.

Form 32   Final Account

Probate 605
Minn. Stat. 524.3-1001; 524.3-1002; 524.3-1003

Miller/Davis Co., St. Paul, MN 800-752-4221

STATE OF MINNESOTA

COUNTY OF   Ramsey

DISTRICT COURT
PROBATE DIVISION
Second   **JUDICIAL DISTRICT**

Court File No.   999999

ESTATE OF

Jane M. Doe

FINAL ACCOUNT
[x] **ORIGINAL**
[ ] **AMENDED**
[ ] **SUPPLEMENTAL**

DECEDENT

READ INSTRUCTIONS AT END OF FORM

	DEBITS	CREDITS
DEBITS		
Estate described in Inventory		
Schedule A: Real Estate $ 372,750.		
Schedule B: Securities $ 10,648.		
Schedule C: Bank Accounts/Cash $ 76,350.		
Schedule D: Other Personal Property $ 240,100.		
SUBTOTAL $ 699,848.		
Less Schedule E: Mortgages/Liens ($ 140,000.)		
TOTAL	$ 559,848.	
Increases:		
Assets Omitted from Inventory $		
Advances to Estate $		
Interest $ 23,230.		
Dividends $ 2,460.		
Dividend Reinvestment $		
Refunds $		
Gain on sale of property $		
Other $		
Rents $ 1,100.		
$		
$		
$		
$		
$		
$		
$		
TOTAL	$ 26,790.	
ASSET ADJUSTMENTS (see Instruction A and attach schedule)	$	$
CREDITS-DISBURSEMENTS		
Decrease in Estate:		
Loss on sale of property $		
Other $		
$		
$		
$		
$		
TOTAL Decrease		$

Final Account

(continued)

Form 32 Final Account *continued*

	Court File No. 999999	DEBITS	CREDITS
MAINTENANCE AND SELECTION			
Family maintenance	$ 4,800.		
Statutory selection	$ 10,000.		
	$		
	$		
	$		
	$		
TOTAL Maintenance and Selection			$ 14,800.
EXPENSES OF ADMINISTRATION			
Probate Court Filing Fees	$ 2.		
Publication Fees	$ 50.		
Bond Premiums	$		
Copy Fees	$ 5.		
Appraiser Fees	$ 500.		
Compensation of Representative	$ 10,000.		
Expenses of Representative (attach Schedule)	$		
Attorneys' Fees to Date	$ 15,000.		
Estimated Future Fees to be Charged	$		
Repayment of Advances to Estate	$		
Accounting Fees/Tax Returns	$ 250.		
Miscellaneous	$ 448.		
	$		
	$		
	$		
	$		
	$		
	$		
	$		
	$		
TOTAL Expenses of Administration			$ 26,255.
FUNERAL EXPENSES			
Mortician	$ 9,500.		
Marker	$ 500.		
Flowers	$ 100.		
Cemetery	$ 1,000.		
Rev. B. Stone	$ 25.		
	$		
	$		
	$		
	$		
	$		
TOTAL Funeral Expenses			$ 11,125.
EXPENSES OF LAST ILLNESS			
Hospital	$ 850.		
	$		
	$		
	$		
	$		
	$		
	$		
	$		
	$		
	$		
TOTAL Expenses of Last Illness			$ 850.

Final Account

(continued)

Form 32 Final Account *continued*

Court File No. _____999999_____

	DEBITS	CREDITS
TAXES		
Real Estate Taxes:		
Homestead . . . . $____3,650.____		
Other Real Estate . . . . $____250.____ $____3,900.____		
Income Taxes of Decedent:		
Minnesota . . . . $_____		
Federal . . . . $_____ $_____		
Fiduciary Income Taxes:		
Minnesota . . . . $_____		
Federal . . . . $_____ $_____		
Estate Taxes:		
Minnesota . . . . $_____		
Federal . . . . $_____ $_____		
	$_____	
	$_____	
	$_____	
	$_____	
	$_____	
	$_____	
TOTAL Taxes		$____3,900.____
PAYMENTS MADE ON MORTGAGE, CONTRACT FOR DEED, AND OTHER LIENS		
Principal	$____3,600.____	$____3,600.____
Interest . . . . $____10,250.____		
Other . . . . $_____		
TOTAL Interest/Other Payments Made		$____10,250.____
OTHER CLAIMS ALLOWED AND PAID		
Ace's Plumbing Co. $____230.____		
St. Paul Telephone Co. $____50.____		
St. Paul Electric Co. $____100.____		
Harvey's Garbage Pickup $____50.____		
Dr. Norma J. Dennison $____600.____		
St. Paul Rents $____50.____		
_____ $_____		
_____ $_____		
_____ $_____		
_____ $_____		
_____ $_____		
_____ $_____		
_____ $_____		
_____ $_____		
_____ $_____		
_____ $_____		
_____ $_____		
_____ $_____		
_____ $_____		
_____ $_____		
_____ $_____		
_____ $_____		
_____ $_____		
_____ $_____		
TOTAL Claims Paid		$____1,080.____

Final Account

(*continued*)

Form 32 Final Account *continued*

	Court File No. 999999	
	DEBITS	**CREDITS**

CLAIMS ALLOWED AND NOT PAID
(See Instruction E)

$		
$		
$		
$		
$		
$		
$		
$		
$		
$		
$		
$		
$		
$		
$		
$		
$		
$		
$		
$		
$		
TOTAL Claims Allowed Not Paid		$

INTERIM DISTRIBUTIONS TO DEVISEES AND HEIRS
(See Instruction F)

$		
$		
$		
$		
$		
$		
$		
$		
$		
$		
$		
$		
$		
$		
$		
$		
$		
$		
$		
TOTAL Devisees Paid and Distributed		$
SUBTOTAL DEBITS AND CREDITS	$ 590,238.	$ 71,860.
PLUS: TOTAL PROPERTY ON HAND FOR DISTRIBUTION (From page 5)		$ 518,378.
TOTAL (debits should equal credits)	$ 590,238.	$ 590,238.

Final Account

(continued)

Form 32   Final Account   *continued*

Court File No. ___999999___

PERSONAL PROPERTY ON HAND FOR DISTRIBUTION

Stocks, Bonds, and Other Securities _____ $_____
  100 Shares Tenneco, Inc., Common Stock, Certificate C068297   5,000.
  1000 Shares Minnesota Co-op, Common Stock, Certificate D2289663   4,500.
  $500 U.S. Savings Bond R4502363E   574.
  $500 U.S. Savings Bond R4502364E   574.

Mortgages, Contracts for Deed, Notes, Etc. _____
  Johnson Furriers, Promissory Note dated 03/20/94 due 09/20/01   10,350.
  (Due date extended)

Cash on Hand _____ 161,030.

All Other Personal Property (Describe) _____
  Furniture and household goods   22,000.
  Furs – Mink coat   11,500.
  Clothing and personal effects   4,500.
  1998 Mazda   12,000.
  Power of Appointment Trust   50,000.

Less: Amounts reserved for future payments _____ (_____)
Less: Liens on Personal Property (See Instruction H) _____ (_____)
Other: _____ (_____)
    TOTAL Personal Property $ 282,028.

REAL ESTATE ON HAND FOR DISTRIBUTION
    (Include Legal Descriptions. Attach schedule, if necessary. Use Inventory values.)

Homestead: $ 350,000.
  Homestead being in the County of Ramsey, State of Minnesota:
  Legally described as follows, to wit:
  Lot 615, Block 42, Reiser's Addition to St. Paul
  (Plat #22760 Parcel #7600)

Other Real Estate:
  An undivided 1/4 interest in duplex located in Ramsey County:
  Legally described as follows, to wit:
  Lots 16 & 17, Block 20, Lovey's Addition to St. Paul
  (Plat #32689 Parcel #5562) $ 22,750.
Less: Mortgages, Contracts for Deed & Liens Unpaid   (136,400.)
  (See Instruction H)
    TOTAL Real Estate $ 236,350.

TOTAL PROPERTY ON HAND FOR DISTRIBUTION $ 518,378.

Under penalties for perjury, I declare or affirm that I have read this Final Account and I know or believe its representations are true and complete.

Attorney For Personal Representative

    /S/ John C. Doe

THIS INSTRUMENT WAS DRAFTED BY (NAME AND ADDRESS):

  John W. Cranwall
  First Trust Co. Bldg.
  St. Paul, MN 55101
  Telephone: (651) 555-5555
  Attorney License No. 1234567

Personal Representative   August 3, 2001   Date

Final Account

Source: This form is property of Miller/Davis Company, St. Paul, MN, Telephone 651–642–1988. Reprinted with permission.

Form 33   Petition to Allow Final Account, Settle and Distribute Estate

MD Form No. P-610   Minn. Stat. 524.3-1001   Miller/Davis Co., St. Paul, MN (800) 752-4221
Minnesota Continuing Legal Education © 1994 MCLE

STATE OF MINNESOTA   **DISTRICT COURT**
                                           PROBATE DIVISION

COUNTY OF   Ramsey   Second   **JUDICIAL DISTRICT**

                                         Court File No.   999999

Estate of

       Jane M. Doe   **PETITION TO ALLOW FINAL ACCOUNT,**
                                          SETTLE AND DISTRIBUTE ESTATE

             Decedent

I,   John C. Doe   , state:

1. My address is:

         1005 Elm Street
         St. Paul, MN 55102

2. I am an interested person as defined by Minnesota law because I am:

         spouse, heir, devisee, personal representative

3. Decedent was born on Nov. 6, 1912 , at (city, state) Detroit, MI .

4. Decedent died on Sept. 20, 2000 , at (city, state) St. Paul, MN .

5. Decedent at the time of death resided in Ramsey County, at (address):

         1005 Elm Street
         St. Paul, MN 55102

6. Decedent's Social Security number is 321-54-9876 .

7. The names and addresses of Decedent's spouse, children, heirs, devisees and other persons interested in this proceeding so far as known or ascertainable with reasonable diligence by the Petitioner are:

Name and Mailing Address	Relationship and Interest (list all)	Birthdate of Minors
John C. Doe 1005 Elm Street, St. Paul, MN 55102	Spouse/heir/devisee/ personal representative	
Sandy R. Doe 1005 Elm Street, St. Paul, MN 55102	Daughter/heir/devisee	
American Cancer Society 222 Glen Acre Drive, St. Paul, MN 55102	Devisee	
Girls' Clubs of America 111 Aspen Lane, St. Paul, MN 55102	Devisee	
Newark Institute of Higher Learning 444 Wirth Drive, St. Paul, MN 55102	Devisee	

(Attach separate schedule, if necessary)

MD   MCLE P-610   Petition to Allow Final Account,
Settle and Distribute Estate

(continued)

Form 33   Petition to Allow Final Account, Settle and Distribute Estate   *continued*

Court File No. _____999999_____

8. Negative Allegation Statement (see Minn. Gen. R. Prac. 409(a)):
    Decedent left surviving no spouse, children, or parents, other than
    herein named, and no issue of deceased children.

9. All persons identified as heirs have survived the Decedent by at least 120 hours.

10. (Check appropriate boxes)
    ☐ Decedent left no surviving spouse.
    ☐ Decedent left no surviving issue.
    ☒ All issue of Decedent are issue of Decedent's surviving spouse except for:
       No exceptions.

    ☐ These are issue of the surviving spouse who are not issue of the Decedent.

11. Venue for this proceeding is in this County of the State of Minnesota because:
    ☒ The Decedent was domiciled in this County at the time of death and was the owner of property
       located in the State of Minnesota.
    or
    ☐ Though not domiciled in the State of Minnesota, the Decedent was the owner of property located in
       this County at the time of death.

12. This Court's order dated ____October 31, 2000____ determined that: (check appropriate boxes)

    ☒ Decedent died testate.
       Decedent's Will is comprised of the following:
       ☒ Will signed and dated ____June 2, 1985_____ .
       ☐ Codicil(___) signed and dated _____ .
       ☐ Separate writing(___) under Minn. Stat. 524.2-513 dated _____ .
       was probated by the Order of this Court dated _____ .
    or
    ☐ Decedent died intestate.

13. No Personal Representative of the Decedent has been appointed in Minnesota or elsewhere whose
    appointment has not been terminated.

14. The Estate has been fully administered and all expenses, debts, valid charges and claims allowed have
    been fully paid, except (if none, so state):
    none

15. A final account is filed and presented for consideration and approval.

16. The time for presenting claims which arose prior to the death of the Decedent has expired.

Petition to Allow Final Account,
Settle and Distribute Estate

(continued)

Form 33 Petition to Allow Final Account, Settle and Distribute Estate *continued*

Court File No. _____999999_____

17. The property on hand for distribution is as reflected in the final account and should be distributed to the following named persons in the following named proportions or parts:

American Cancer Society	Charitable Devisee	$ 10,000.
Girls' Clubs of America	Charitable Devisee	5,000.
Newark Institute of Higher Learning	Charitable Devisee	1,000.
John C. Doe, Husband, all the rest, residue, and remainder of the real and personal property of the decedent's estate.		502,378.

WHEREFORE, I request the Court fix a time and place for hearing this Petition, and enter an order:

1. Finding the venue is proper;
2. Determining testacy as it affects any previously omitted or unnotified persons and other interested parties, if any, and confirming any previous order of testacy as it affects all interested persons;
3. Determining Decedent's heirs;
4. Construing Decedent's Will, if any;
5. Confirming the acts of the Personal Representative as shown by the Final Account and this Petition.
6. Allowing the Final Account;
7. Determining the persons entitled to distribution of the Estate and their respective interests;
8. Approving settlement of the Estate and
   [x] Issuing a decree of distribution assigning the Estate to the persons entitled to the Estate.
   or
   [ ] Directing or approving the distribution of the Estate by the Personal Representative to the persons entitled to the Estate; and
9. Granting such other relief as may be proper.

Under penalties for perjury, I declare or affirm that I have read this document and I know or believe its representations are true and complete.

/S/ John C. Doe _____

Petitioner   August 3, 2001   Date

Attorney For Petitioner

THIS INSTRUMENT WAS DRAFTED BY (NAME AND ADDRESS):

John W. Cranwall
First Trust Co. Bldg.
St. Paul, MN 55101
Telephone: (651) 555-5555
Attorney License No. 1234567

Petition to Allow Final Account,
Settle and Distribute Estate

Source: This form is property of Miller/Davis Company, St. Paul, MN, Telephone 651–642–1988. Reprinted with permission.

Form 34   Notice and Order for Hearing on Petition for Formal Settlement of Estate

M/D Form No. P-611 | Minn. Stat. 524.3-1001; | Miller/Davis Co., St. Paul, MN (800) 752-4221
Minn.Gen.R.Prac.404(b) | Minnesota Continuing Legal Education © 1994 MCLE

STATE OF MINNESOTA

COUNTY OF ___Ramsey___   ___Second___

Estate of

___Jane M. Doe___

Decedent

DISTRICT COURT
PROBATE DIVISION
JUDICIAL DISTRICT

Court File No. ___999999___

**NOTICE AND ORDER FOR HEARING
ON PETITION FOR FORMAL
SETTLEMENT OF ESTATE**

The Personal Representative of the Estate has filed a Final Account and a petition which requests formal allowance of the final account, an order of complete settlement of the Estate and an order or decree of distribution to the persons entitled to the Estate.

IT IS ORDERED and notice is given that the Petition will be heard on ___September 18, 2001___, at ___10:00___ (a.m.)(p̶.̶m̶.̶), by this Court at ___St. Paul___, Minnesota.

Any objections to the Petition must be filed with the Court prior to or at the hearing.

(1) Notice shall be given to all interested persons (Minn. Stat. 524.1-401) and persons who have filed a demand for notice pursuant to Minn. Stat. 524.3-204.

(2) Notice shall be given by:

[x] Mailing a copy of this Notice and Order by U.S. Postal Service at least 14 days prior to the hearing date.

[ ] Delivering a copy of this Notice and Order to _____ at least 14 days prior to the hearing date.

[ ] Publishing this Notice and Order in accordance with law by: _____

(COURT SEAL)

___/S/ Richard B. Evans___

Judge   August 10, 2001   **Date**

___/S/ Thomas Malone___

Court Administrator   August 10, 2001   **Date**

Attorney For Petitioner

THIS INSTRUMENT WAS DRAFTED BY (NAME AND ADDRESS):

John W. Cranwall
First Trust Co. Bldg.
St. Paul, MN 55101
Telephone: (651) 555-5555
Attorney License No. 1234567

M/D   MCLE P-611

Notice and Order for Hearing on Petition
for Formal Settlement of Estate

Source: This form is property of Miller/Davis Company, St. Paul, MN, Telephone 651–642–1988. Reprinted with permission.

Form 35   Affidavit of Mailing Order or Notice of Hearing on Final Account and Petition for Formal Settlement of Estate

MD Form No. P-015   Minn. Stat. 524.1-401; 525.83   Miller/Davis Co., St. Paul, MN (800) 752-4221
Minnesota Continuing Legal Education © 1994 MCLE

STATE OF MINNESOTA

COUNTY OF   Ramsey   Probate Court

Court File No.   999999

Estate of

_____ Jane M. Doe _____   **AFFIDAVIT OF MAILING**
ORDER OR NOTICE

Decedent

STATE OF   Minnesota   } ss.

COUNTY OF   Ramsey

I,   J. M. Golden   ,
being first duly sworn, on oath state that on   August 11, 2001   , at
St. Paul, MN   (city, state), I mailed a copy of the
attached Order or Notice to each person or entity named below by mailing a copy in a sealed envelope,
postage prepaid, with the U.S. Postal Service as follows:

Name and Mailing Address	Relationship and Interest (list all)	Birthdate of Minors
John C. Doe 1005 Elm Street, St. Paul, MN 55102	Spouse/heir/devisee/ personal representative	
Sandy R. Doe 1005 Elm Street, St. Paul, MN 55102	Daughter/heir/devisee	
American Cancer Society 222 Glen Acre Drive, St. Paul, MN 55102	Devisee	
Girls' Clubs of America 111 Aspen Lane, St. Paul, MN 55102	Devisee	
Newark Institute of Higher Learning 444 Wirth Drive, St. Paul, MN 55102	Devisee	

(Attach separate schedule, if necessary)

/S/ J. M. Golden

Affiant   August 11, 2001   Date

NOTARIAL STAMP OR SEAL (OR OTHER TITLE OR RANK)

Signed and sworn to (or affirmed) before me on
August 11, 2001   by
J. M. Golden   .
Affiant.

/S/ Judith Harris

SIGNATURE OF NOTARY PUBLIC OR OTHER OFFICIAL

INSTRUCTIONS: (1) A copy of the Order or Notice must be mailed to each heir, devisee, personal representative, the foreign consul pursuant to Minn. Stat. 524.3-306 and 524.3-403, lawyers representing interested parties pursuant to Minn. Stat. 524.1-401(a), and the Minnesota Attorney General, if a devisee is a charitable organization or if the decedent left no devisee or heirs. In determining the persons or entities entitled to receive this order or notice, see Minn. Stats. 501B.41(5), 524.1-201(19), 524.1-403 and 524.1-404 and Minn. Gen. Rules of Practice 404(b) and 408(d). If the Decedent is survived by a spouse or minor child, also use Notice to Spouse and Children. (2) Attach to this affidavit another copy of the Order or Notice which was sent. (3) It may be necessary to give notice to creditors. See Minn. Stat. 524.3-801(3) and Supplementary Notice to Known and Identified Creditors form.

MD   MCLE P-015   Affidavit of Mailing Order or Notice

Source: This form is property of Miller/Davis Company, St. Paul, MN, Telephone 651–642–1988. Reprinted with permission.

Form 36   Order Allowing Final Account

MD Form No. P-612   Minn. Stat. 524.3-1001; 524.3-1002; 525.51   Miller/Davis Co., St. Paul, MN (800) 752-4221
Minnesota Continuing Legal Education © 1994 MCLE

STATE OF MINNESOTA   **DISTRICT COURT**
                                                          PROBATE DIVISION
COUNTY OF ___Ramsey_____   ___Second___ **JUDICIAL DISTRICT**

                                        Court File No. ___999999_____

Estate of

                                        ORDER ALLOWING ACCOUNT
_____Jane M. Doe_____   [x] **FINAL**
                                        [ ] **SUPPLEMENTAL**
_____   [ ] **INTERIM**
              Decedent   [ ] **AMENDED**

The Personal Representative's [x] Final [ ] Supplemental [ ] Interim [ ] Amended account dated
___August 3, 2001_____ has been filed with this Court.

IT IS ORDERED, that the Account is settled and allowed as:

[x]   Filed.

[ ]   Corrected (explain correction below):

(COURT SEAL)   ____/S/ Richard B. Evans_____

                                Judge   September 18, 2001   Date

MD   MCLE P-612   Order Allowing Account

Source: This form is property of Miller/Davis Company, St. Paul, MN, Telephone 651–642–1988. Reprinted with permission.

Form 37 Order Allowing Final Account and Settling Estate and Decree of Distribution

M/D Form No. P-613   Minn. Stat. 524.3-1001; 524.3-1002   Miller/Davis Co., St. Paul, MN (800) 752-4221
Minnesota Continuing Legal Education © 1994 MCLE

STATE OF MINNESOTA

COUNTY OF _____Ramsey_____

Estate of

_____Jane M. Doe_____

Decedent

DISTRICT COURT
PROBATE DIVISION
Second **JUDICIAL DISTRICT**

Court File No. _____999999_____

**ORDER ALLOWING FINAL ACCOUNT
AND SETTLING ESTATE AND
DECREE OF DISTRIBUTION**

The Petition for an Order Allowing Final Account and Settling Estate and Decree of Distribution, signed by
_____John C. Doe_____ came before this Court on
_____August 3, 2001_____ . The Court, having heard and considered the Petition, determines the following:

1. The Court has jurisdiction and venue in this County is proper.

2. The Petition is complete.

3. [x] Any notice required by Minnesota law has been given.
   or
   [ ] Consents to the Final Account and to issuance of a Final Decree, and waivers of further notice or hearing have been signed by all interested persons and filed with the Court.

4. The Petitioner has declared or affirmed that the representations contained in the Petition are true and complete to the best of Petitioner's knowledge or belief.

5. The Petitioner is an interested person as defined by Minnesota law.

6. The Decedent died on _____Sept. 20, 2000_____ , at (city, state) _____St. Paul, MN_____ .

7. This Estate has been in all respects fully administered, and all expenses, debts, valid charges and all claims allowed against this Estate have been paid. (If any exceptions, so state.)

M/D   MCLE P-613

Order Allowing Final Account and
Settling Estate and Decree of Distribution

(*continued*)

Form 37 Order Allowing Final Account and Settling Estate and Decree of Distribution *continued*

Court File No. ___999999___

8. The Personal Representative has filed a Final Account for consideration and approval which accounts for every part of the Estate.

9. (Check appropriate boxes)
    [x] Testate.
    Decedent's Will is comprised of the following:
    [x] Will dated ____June 2, 1985____ .
    [ ] Codicil(__) dated _____ .
    [ ] Separate writing(__) under Minn. Stat. 524.2-513 dated _____ .

    [x] The Will was formally probated by the Order of this Court dated ___October 31, 2000___ .
    or
    [ ] The Will is formally probated by this Order.

    The Court construes the Will as follows:

    The estate of decedent is devised as follows:

American Cancer Society	Charitable Devisee	$ 10,000.
Girls' Clubs of America	Charitable Devisee	5,000.
Newark Institute of Higher Learning	Charitable Devisee	1,000.

    John C. Doe, Husband, all the rest, residue, and remainder of
      the real and personal property of the decedent's estate.   502,378.

    [ ] Intestate.
        [ ] A previous Order of this Court dated _____ , determined Decedent died intestate.
        or
        [ ] This Court determines by this Order that the Decedent died intestate.

MCLE P-613/Page 2

Order Allowing Final Account and
Settling Estate and Decree of Distribution

(continued)

Form 37 Order Allowing Final Account and Settling Estate and Decree of Distribution *continued*

M D Form No. P-613   Minn. Stat. 524.3-1001; 524.3-1002   Miller/Davis Co., St. Paul, MN (800) 752-4221
Minnesota Continuing Legal Education © 1994 MCLE

Court File No.   999999

The following named persons are all the heirs of the Decedent and their relationship to Decedent is as follows:

Name and Mailing Address	Relationship and Interest (list all)	Birthdate of Minors
John C. Doe 1005 Elm Street, St. Paul, MN 55102	Spouse/heir/devisee/ personal representative	
Sandy R. Doe 1005 Elm Street, St. Paul, MN 55102	Daughter/heir/devisee	

(Attach separate schedule, if necessary)

Order Allowing Final Account and
Settling Estate and Decree of Distribution

(continued)

Form 37   Order Allowing Final Account and Settling Estate and Decree of Distribution   *continued*

MD Form No. P-613   Minn. Stat. 524.3-1001; 524.3-1002   Miller/Davis Co., St. Paul, MN (800) 752-4221
Minnesota Continuing Legal Education © 1994 MCLE

Court File No.   999999

10. The property of the Decedent on hand for distribution consists of the following:

(A) Personal property of the value of ___ $282,028. ___ described as follows:

Item Number	Description of Personal Property	Fair Market Value
	Stocks and Bonds	$
1	100 Shares Tenneco, Inc., Common Stock, Certificate C068297	5,000.
2	1000 Shares Minnesota Co-op, Common Stock, Certificate D2289663	4,500.
3	$500 U.S. Savings Bond R4502363E	574.
4	$500 U.S. Savings Bond R4502364E	574.
	Note	
5	Johnson Furriers, Promissory Note dated 3/20/94 due 9/20/01	10,350.
6	Cash on hand	161,030.
	All other personal property	
7	Furniture and household goods	22,000.
8	Furs – Mink coat	11,500.
9	Clothing and personal effects	4,500.
10	1998 Mazda	12,000.
11	Power of Appointment Trust	50,000.
	Sub Total	282,028.
(A) Personal Property	TOTAL	282,028.

(continued)

Form 37 Order Allowing Final Account and Settling Estate and Decree of Distribution *continued*

MD Form No. P-613   Minn. Stat. 524.3-1001; 524.3-1002   Miller/Davis Co., St. Paul, MN (800) 752-4221
Minnesota Continuing Legal Education © 1994 MCLE

Court File No. ___999999___

(B) Real Property described as follows (Legal description) Identify if homestead):

Item Number	Description of Property	County Assessor's Market Value	Fair Market Value
	Homestead in the County of __Ramsey__	$	$
1	Lot 615, Block 42, Reiser's Addition to St. Paul (Plat #22760 Parcel #7600)	337,500.	350,000.
	Lien: Mortgage balance at St. Paul Bank and Trust Co.		127,000.
	Net		223,000.
	Sub Total		223,000.
	Other Real Estate in the County of __Ramsey__	$	$
2	Lots 16 & 17, Block 20, Lovey's Addition to St. Paul (Plat #32689 Parcel #5562)	17,063.	22,750.
	Lien: Mortgage balance at St. Paul Bank and Trust Co.		9,400.
	Net		13,350.
	Sub Total		13,350.
(B) Real Estate		TOTAL	236,350.

MD   MCLE P-613/Page 5

Order Allowing Final Account and
Settling Estate and Decree of Distribution

(continued)

Form 37   Order Allowing Final Account and Settling Estate and Decree of Distribution   *continued*

Court File No. _____999999_____

IT IS ORDERED AND DECREED:

1. The Petition is granted.

2. (Testate)
    [x] If not previously probated, Decedent's Will is formally probated. Decedent's Will is construed as stated above.

    (Intestate)
    [ ] The heirs of the Decedent are determined to be as stated above.

3. Any previous order determining testacy is confirmed by this Order as it affects any previously omitted or unnotified persons and other interested persons.

4. The acts of the Personal Representative as shown by the Final Account and the Petition are confirmed.

5. The property of the Decedent on hand for distribution is as stated above.

6. The Final Account of the Personal Representative is allowed.

7. By this Decree, title to the personal and real property described above, subject to any prior disposition, is assigned to and vested in the following named persons in the following proportions or parts:

    The whole thereof to decedent's husband, John C. Doe.

_____/S/ Richard B. Evans_____

(COURT SEAL)   Judge   September 18, 2001   Date

Order Allowing Final Account and
Settling Estate and Decree of Distribution

Source: This form is property of Miller/Davis Company, St. Paul, MN, Telephone 651–642–1988. Reprinted with permission.

Form 38 Receipt for Assets by Distributee

MD Form No. P-615	Minn. Stat. 524.3-1001(4); 524.3-1003(2)	Miller/Davis Co., St. Paul, MN (800) 752-4221 Minnesota Continuing Legal Education © 1994 MCLE

STATE OF MINNESOTA

COUNTY OF ___Ramsey___

	DISTRICT COURT
__Second__	**PROBATE DIVISION**
	JUDICIAL DISTRICT

Court File No. ___999999___

Estate of

_____Jane M. Doe_____

_____
Decedent

RECEIPT FOR ASSETS BY DISTRIBUTEE

I, ___Phyllis L. Taylor for the American Cancer Society___
the undersigned distributee, acknowledge receipt from the Personal Representative of this Estate, of the following assets in [x] full [ ] partial satisfaction of my distributive share:

Charitable Devise $ 10,000.

AMERICAN CANCER SOCIETY

BY: /S/ Phyllis L. Taylor

Distributee   September 20, 2001   Date

MD   MCLE P-615   Receipt for Assets by Distributee

Source: This form is property of Miller/Davis Company, St. Paul, MN, Telephone 651–642–1988. Reprinted with permission.

Form 39   Petition for Discharge of Personal Representative

MD Form No. P-640   Minn. Stat. 524.3-1001; 524.3-1002 Miller/Davis Co., St. Paul, MN (800) 752-4221
Minnesota Continuing Legal Education © 1994 MCLE

STATE OF MINNESOTA

COUNTY OF _____Ramsey_____   _____Second_____

DISTRICT COURT
PROBATE DIVISION
JUDICIAL DISTRICT

Court File No. ____999999____

Estate of

_____Jane M. Doe_____

Decedent

PETITION FOR DISCHARGE OF
PERSONAL REPRESENTATIVE

I, _____John C. Doe_____ , state:

1. My address is:

   1005 Elm Street
   St. Paul, MN 55102

2. I am an interested person as defined by Minnesota law because I am:

   spouse, heir, devisee, personal representative

3. The Personal Representative has fully administered the Estate of the Decedent, and has paid all expenses, debts and charges chargeable upon the Estate.

4. The final account has been presented to and allowed by the Court, and the decree or order of distribution made, and all taxes required to be paid by the Personal Representative have been paid and proper receipts have been filed.

5. The balance of the Estate remaining in my possession for distribution pursuant to the Order Allowing Final Account, has been paid out and distributed in accordance with the Decree or Order of Distribution as follows:

LEGACIES (AND)(OR) DISTRIBUTIVE SHARES	SHARE VALUE
1. American Cancer Society, 222 Glen Acre Dr., St. Paul, MN	$ 10,000.
2. Girls' Clubs of America, 111 Aspen Lane, St. Paul, MN	5,000.
3. Newark Institute of Higher Learning, 444 Wirth Dr., St. Paul, MN	1,000.
4. John C. Doe, Surviving Spouse, 1005 Elm St., St. Paul, MN	502,378.
5.	
6.	
7.	
8.	
9.	
10.	
11.	
12.	

6. I have filed in this Court proper receipts from all parties for their respective legacies (and)(or) distributive shares.

MD   MCLE P-640   Petition for Discharge of Personal Representative

(continued)

Form 39   Petition for Discharge of Personal Representative   *continued*

WHEREFORE, I request the Court: **Court File No.** ___999999___

1. Fix a time and place for a hearing on this Petition;

2. Enter an order formally discharging the Personal Representative and releasing and discharging any sureties upon the Personal Representative's bond; and

3. Grant such other and further relief as may be proper.

Under penalties for perjury, I declare or affirm that I have read this document and I know or believe its representations are true and complete.

___/S/ John C. Doe_____

Petitioner   September 29, 2001   Date

Attorney For Petitioner

THIS INSTRUMENT WAS DRAFTED BY (NAME AND ADDRESS):

John W. Cranwall
First Trust Co. Bldg.
St. Paul, MN 55101
Telephone: (651) 555-5555
Attorney License No. 1234567

MD   MCLE P-640/Page 2   Petition for Discharge of Personal Representative

Source: This form is property of Miller/Davis Company, St. Paul, MN, Telephone 651-642-1988. Reprinted with permission,

Form 40 Order Discharging Personal Representative

MD Form No. P-642   Minn. Stat. 524.3-1001; 524.3-1002;   Miller/Davis Co., St. Paul, MN (800) 752-4221
                                525.51   Minnesota Continuing Legal Education © 1994 MCLE

STATE OF MINNESOTA

COUNTY OF ____Ramsey_____   Probate Court

                                              Court File No. ____999999_____
Estate of

_____Jane M. Doe_____   **ORDER DISCHARGING**
_____   **PERSONAL REPRESENTATIVE**
              Decedent

The Petition for an Order Discharging Personal Representative, signed by _____
_____John C. Doe_____

came before this Court on ___September 29, 2001_____ . The Court, having considered the petition,
determines the following:

1. The Petition is complete.

2. Any notice required by Minnesota law has been given.

3. The Petitioner has declared or affirmed that the representations contained in the Petition are true and
    complete to the best of Petitioner's knowledge or information.

4. The Petitioner is an interested person as defined by Minnesota law.

5. The Personal Representative, has paid or transferred all of the property of the Estate of Decedent to the
    persons entitled to the property, paid all taxes required to be paid by the Personal Representative and
    filed proof of those payments, complied with all the orders and decree of the Court and with the
    provisions of law applicable to this Estate and to the Personal Representative, and has fully discharged
    the Personal Representative's duties.

    IT IS ORDERED:

1. The Petition is granted.

2. The Personal Representative and the surety on the Personal Representative's bond, if any, are now
    discharged.

                                        _____/S/ Richard B. Evans_____

        (COURT SEAL)   Judge   October 20, 2001   Date

MD   MCLE P-642   Order Discharging Personal Representative

Source: This form is property of Miller/Davis Company, St. Paul, MN, Telephone 651–642–1988. Reprinted with permission.

Form 41 Petition for Formal Appointment of Special Administrator

MD Form No. P-405   Minn. Stat. 524.3-614(2); 524.3-617; Minn. Gen. R. Prac. 409(a)   Miller/Davis Co., St. Paul, MN (800) 752-4221
Minnesota Continuing Legal Education © 1994 MCLE

STATE OF MINNESOTA

COUNTY OF _____

DISTRICT COURT
PROBATE DIVISION
_____ **JUDICIAL DISTRICT**

Court File No. _____

Estate of

_____
_____
Decedent

PETITION FOR
FORMAL APPOINTMENT OF
SPECIAL ADMINISTRATOR

I, _____ , state:

1. My address is:

2. I am an interested person as defined by Minnesota law because I am:

3. Decedent was born on _____ , at (city, state) _____ .

4. Decedent died on _____ , at (city, state) _____ .

5. Decedent at the time of death resided in _____ County, at (address):

6. Decedent's Social Security number is _____ .

7. The names and addresses of Decedent's spouse, children, heirs, devisees and other persons interested in this proceeding so far as known or ascertainable with reasonable diligence by the Petitioner are:

Name and Mailing Address	Relationship and Interest (list all)	Birthdate of Minors

VOID

(Attach separate schedule, if necessary)
8. Negative Allegation Statement (see Minn. Gen. R. Prac. 409(a)):

MD   MCLE P-405

Petition for Formal Appointment
of Special Administrator

(continued)

Form 41 Petition for Formal Appointment of Special Administrator *continued*

Court File No. _____

9. The Decedent died:
☐ intestate.
or
☐ testate and _____ is named as Personal Representative in the Will and is ☐ available and qualified ☐ unavailable to serve as special administrator.

10. There ☐ is ☐ is not pending an application or petition for probate of the Will of the Decedent or appointment as a personal representative in this or another court.

11. A Special Administrator is needed because:
☐ No personal representative has been appointed in Minnesota or elsewhere.
or
☐ The Personal Representative ☐ has died ☐ is disabled and therefore cannot act.
or
☐ The Personal Representative should not act because:

12. Venue for this proceeding is in this County of the State of Minnesota because:
☐ The Decedent was domiciled in this County at the time of death and was the owner of property located in the State of Minnesota,
or
☐ Though not domiciled in the State of Minnesota, the Decedent was the owner of property located in this County at the time of death.

13. I estimate the Decedent's assets and indebtedness are as follows:

ASSETS

Probate Assets		Non-Probate Assets	
Homestead	$_____	Joint Tenancy	$_____
Other Real Estate	$_____	Insurance	$_____
Cash	$_____	Other	$_____
Securities	$_____		
Other	$_____		

VOID

Approximate Indebtedness $ _____

14. The appointment of a special administrator is necessary to protect the Estate of the Decedent because:

15. An emergency exists to the extent that the appointment should be made without notice because:

16. _____
is a proper person to be appointed special administrator.

MD   MCLE P-405/Page 2

Petition for Formal Appointment
of Special Administrator

(continued)

Form 41 Petition for Formal Appointment of Special Administrator *continued*

WHEREFORE, I request the Court

Court File No. _____

1. Fix a time and place for a hearing of this Petition.

2. Appoint _____
   as special administrator of the Estate, with _____ bond.

3. Authorize issuance of letters of special administration upon qualification and acceptance; and

4. Grant such other relief as may be proper.

Under penalties for perjury, I declare or affirm that I have read this document and I know or believe its representations are true and complete.

VOID

_____

Petitioner   Date

Attorney For Petitioner

THIS INSTRUMENT WAS DRAFTED BY (NAME AND ADDRESS):

MD   MCLE P-405/Page 3

Petition for Formal Appointment
of Special Administrator

Source: This form is property of Miller/Davis Company, St. Paul, MN, Telephone 651–642–1988. Reprinted with permission.

Form 42   Order of Formal Appointment of Special Administrator

M/D Form No. P-406   Minn. Stat. 524.3-614(2)   Miller/Davis Co., St. Paul, MN (800) 752-4221
Minnesota Continuing Legal Education © 1994 MCLE

STATE OF MINNESOTA   **DISTRICT COURT**
                                                                                 PROBATE DIVISION
COUNTY OF _____   _____ **JUDICIAL DISTRICT**

                                                                    Court File No. _____

Estate of

_____   **ORDER OF**
_____   **FORMAL APPOINTMENT**
                        Decedent   **OF SPECIAL ADMINISTRATOR**

The Petition for Formal Appointment of Special Administrator, signed by _____
_____
came before this Court on _____ . The Court, having heard and considered
the Petition, determines the following:

1. This Court has jurisdiction and venue in this Court is proper.

2. The Petition is complete.

3. The Petitioner has declared or affirmed that the representations contained in the Petition are true and complete to the best of the Petitioner's knowledge or belief.

4. The Petitioner is an interested person as defined by Minnesota law.

5. On the basis of the Petition, it appears that the Decedent died:
   ☐ intestate.
   or
   ☐ testate and _____ is named as Personal
   Representative in the Will and is ☐ available and qualified ☐ unavailable to serve as special
   administrator.

6. There ☐ is ☐ is not pending an application or petition for probate of the Will of the Decedent or appointment of a personal representative in this or another court.

7. No personal representative has been appointed whose appointment has not been terminated.

8. Appointment of a special administrator is necessary to protect the Estate because:

VOID

M/D   MCLE P-406   Order of Formal Appointment
                                                              of Special Administrator

(*continued*)

Form 42 Order of Formal Appointment of Special Administrator *continued*

MD Form No. P-406   Minn. Stat. 524.3-614(2)   Miller/Davis Co., St. Paul, MN (800) 752-4221
                                                                Minnesota Continuing Legal Education © 1994 MCLE

Court File No. _____

9. An emergency exists to the extent that appointment should be made without notice because:

10. _____
    is a proper person to be appointed special administrator of the Estate.

    IT IS ORDERED:

1. The Petition is granted.

2. _____
   is formally appointed as the special administrator of the Estate, with_____ bond,
   to preserve the Estate and to secure its proper administration until a general personal representative is
   appointed by the Registrar or by the Court.

3. Upon filing of any required bond and oath or statement of acceptance, letters of special administration
   shall be issued subject to the following limitations, if any:

(COURT SEAL)

_____

Judge   Date

MCLE P-406/Page 2   Order of Formal Appointment
                                                 of Special Administrator

Source: This form is property of Miller/Davis Company, St. Paul, MN, Telephone 051-642-1988 Reprinted with permission.

Form 43   Letters of Special Administration

MD Form No. P-410   Minn. Stat. 524.3-614   Miller/Davis Co., St. Paul, MN (800) 752-4221
Minnesota Continuing Legal Education © 1994 MCLE

STATE OF MINNESOTA   **DISTRICT COURT**
                                                               PROBATE DIVISION
COUNTY OF _____   _____ **JUDICIAL DISTRICT**

                                                               Court File No. _____
Estate of

_____

_____   **LETTERS OF**
                                               SPECIAL ADMINISTRATION
                    Decedent

1. The Decedent died on _____.

2. _____
    has been appointed Special Administrator of Decedent's Estate and is now qualified to act as Special
    Administrator of the Estate and has authority to administer the Estate according to law with the
    following restrictions (If none, so state):

VOID

(COURT SEAL)   _____

                                 Judge/Registrar   Date

MD   MCLE P-410   Letters of Special Administration

Source: This form is property of Miller/Davis Company, St. Paul, MN, Telephone 651–642–1988. Reprinted with permission.

Form 44 Final Account in Special Administration

MID Form No. P-425   Minn. Stat. 524.3-616; 524.3-617   Miller/Davis Co., St. Paul, MN 800-752-4221
Minnesota Continuing Legal Education © 1994 MCLE

STATE OF MINNESOTA

COUNTY OF _____

Estate of

_____

_____

Decedent

DISTRICT COURT
PROBATE DIVISION
_____ **JUDICIAL DISTRICT**

Court File No. _____
FINAL ACCOUNT
IN SPECIAL ADMINISTRATION
☐ **ORIGINAL**
☐ **AMENDED**
☐ **SUPPLEMENTAL**

READ INSTRUCTIONS AT END OF FORM

	DEBITS	CREDITS

DEBITS

Estate described in Inventory
   Schedule A: Real Estate . . . . $_____
   Schedule B: Securities . . . . $_____
   Schedule C: Bank Accounts/Cash . . . . . . $_____
   Schedule D: Other Personal Property . . . . $_____
     SUBTOTAL . . . . $_____
   Less Schedule E: Mortgages/Liens . . . . . ($_____)
     TOTAL . . . . $_____
Increases:
   Assets Omitted from Inventory . . . . $_____
   Advances to Estate . . . . $_____
   Interest . . . . $_____
   Dividends . . . . $_____
   Dividend Reinvestment . . . . $_____
   Refunds . . . . $_____
   Gain on sale of property . . . . $_____
   Other _____ $_____
   _____ $_____
   _____ $_____
   _____ $_____
   _____ $_____
   _____ $_____
   _____ $_____
   _____ $_____
     TOTAL . . . . $_____

ASSET ADJUSTMENTS (see Instruction A and attach schedule) $_____ $_____

CREDITS-DISBURSEMENTS
Decrease in Estate:
   Loss on sale of property . . . . $_____
   Other _____ $_____
   _____ $_____
   _____ $_____
   _____ $_____
   _____ $_____
     TOTAL Decrease . . . . $_____

VOID

MID   MCLE P-425   Final Account in Special Administration

Source: This form is property of Miller/Davis Company, St. Paul, MN, Telephone 651–642–1988. Reprinted with permission.

Form 45   Order Allowing Account and Discharging Special Administrator

MD Form No. P-428   Minn. Stat. 524.3-616; 524.3-617   Miller/Davis Co., St. Paul, MN (800) 752-4221
Minnesota Continuing Legal Education © 1994 MCLE

STATE OF MINNESOTA

COUNTY OF _____   _____

                                                 Court File No. _____
Estate of

_____   **ORDER ALLOWING ACCOUNT AND**
_____   **DISCHARGING SPECIAL ADMINISTRATOR**
            Decedent
_____

The Petition for Allowance of Account and Discharging Special Administrator signed by _____

_____

came before this Court on _____. The Court, having considered
the Petition, determines the following:

1. The Petition is complete.

2. Any notice required by Minnesota law has been given.

3. The Petitioner has declared or affirmed that the representations contained in the Petition are true and
complete to the best of the Petitioner's knowledge or information.

4. The Petitioner was appointed Special Administrator of the Estate for the purpose of:

VOID

5. (Check appropriate box)

☐   The Special Administrator has paid or transferred all of the property of the Estate which the Special
Administrator had control of to the Personal Representative, filed proof of this transfer, complied
with all the orders of the Court and with the provisions of applicable law and has fully discharged
the duties of the Special Administrator.

or

☐   The provisions of the Order appointing the Special Administrator have been met. There is no general
Personal Representative.

IT IS ORDERED:

1. The Petition is granted.

2. The Special Administrator's Account is allowed.

3. The Special Administrator and the surety on the Special Administrator's bond, if any, are now
discharged.

                                                 _____
                          Judge   Date
                                                 Order Allowing Account and
MD   MCLE P-428   Discharging Special Administrator

Source: This form is property of Miller/Davis Company, St. Paul, MN, Telephone 651–642–1988. Reprinted with permission.

Form 46   Petition for Determination of Descent of Omitted Property

MD Form No. P-660   Minn. Stat. 524.3-413   Miller/Davis Co., St. Paul, MN (800) 752-4221
Minnesota Continuing Legal Education © 1994 MCLE

STATE OF MINNESOTA

COUNTY OF _____   _____

Court File No. _____

Estate of

_____

_____
                    Decedent

**PETITION FOR DETERMINATION
OF DESCENT OF
OMITTED PROPERTY**

I,_____ , state:

1. My address is:

2. I am an interested person as defined by Minnesota law because I am:

3. Decedent was born on _____ , at (city, state) _____ .

4. Decedent died on _____ , at (city, state) _____ .

5. Decedent at time of death resided in _____ County at (address):

VOID

6. Decedent's Social Security Number is _____ .

7. The names and addresses of Decedent's spouse, children, heirs, devisees and other persons interested
    in this proceeding so far as known or ascertainable with reasonable diligence by the Petitioner are:

Name and Mailing Address	Relationship and Interest (list all)	Birthdate of Minors

(Attach separate schedule, if necessary)

MD   MCLE P-660

Petition for Determination of Descent
of Omitted Property

Source: This form is property of Miller/Davis Company, St. Paul, MN, Telephone 651–642–1988. Reprinted with permission.

Form 47   Decree of Descent of Omitted Property

MD Form No. P-661   Minn. Stat. 524.3-413   Miller/Davis Co., St. Paul, MN (800) 752-4221
Minnesota Continuing Legal Education © 1994 MCLE

STATE OF MINNESOTA   **DISTRICT COURT**
PROBATE DIVISION
COUNTY OF _____   _____ **JUDICIAL DISTRICT**

Court File No. _____

Estate of

_____   **DECREE OF DESCENT OF**
_____   **OMITTED PROPERTY**

Decedent

The Petition for Decree of Descent for Omitted Property, signed by _____
_____

came before this Court on _____ . The Court, having heard and considered
the petition, determines the following:

1. The Petition is complete.

2. ☐ Any notice required by Minnesota law has been given.
    or
    ☐ Consents to issuance of a Decree of Descent, and waivers of further notice or hearing have been
       signed by all interested persons and filed with the Court.

3. The Petitioner has declared or affirmed that the representations contained in the Petition are true and
    complete to the best of Petitioner's knowledge or belief.

4. The Petitioner is an interested person as defined by Minnesota law or a person claiming an interest in the
    property described below.

5. The Decedent died on _____ , at (city, state)_____

6. On_____ , this Court entered its

    ☐ Order of Distribution   ☐ Decree of Distribution
    ☐ Final Decree Summary Assignment   ☐ Decree of Descent

    in which the property listed in Paragraph 7 was omitted.

7. At the time of death, Decedent was the owner of the following property which was omitted from the
    Order or Decree:

    (A) Personal Property:

VOID

MD   MCLE P-661   Decree of Descent of Omitted Property

Source: This form is property of Miller/Davis Company, St. Paul, MN, Telephone 651–642–1988. Reprinted with permission.

Form 48   Decree of Descent

MD Form No. P-673   Minn. Stat. 525.312   Miller/Davis Co., St. Paul, MN (800) 752-4221
Minnesota Continuing Legal Education © 1994 MCLE

STATE OF MINNESOTA   **DISTRICT COURT**
      PROBATE DIVISION

COUNTY OF _____ _____ **JUDICIAL DISTRICT**

      Court File No. _____

Estate of

_____   **DECREE OF DESCENT**

_____

      Decedent _____

The Petition for Determination of Descent in the Estate, signed by _____

_____

came before this Court on _____ . The Court, having heard and considered
the petition, determines the following:

1. The Court has jurisdiction and venue in this County is proper.

2. The Petition is complete.

3. Any notice required by Minnesota law has been given.

4. The Petitioner has declared or affirmed that the representations contained in the Petition are true and complete to the best of Petitioner's knowledge or belief.

5. The Petitioner is an interested person as defined by Minnesota law.

6. The Decedent died on _____ , at (city, state) _____ .
More than three years have elapsed since the death of the Decedent and the time limit for appointment proceedings has expired.

7. There has been no probate proceeding or administration proceeding commenced in Minnesota.

8. There is no unrevoked testamentary instrument which relates to property in Minnesota, and which has not been filed for probate in this Court.

VOID

MD   MCLE P-673   Decree of Descent

Source: This form is property of Miller/Davis Company, St. Paul, MN, Telephone 651–642–1988. Reprinted with permission.

Form 49 Application for Informal Probate of Will and for Informal Appointment of Personal Representative

MD Form No. P-100 Minn. Stat. 524.3-301; 524.3-307; Minn. Gen. R. Prac. 408(a)   Miller/Davis Co., St. Paul, MN (800) 752-4221
Minnesota Continuing Legal Education © 1994 MCLE

STATE OF MINNESOTA

COUNTY OF ____Hennepin____   Fourth

Estate of

_____Cheryl Ann Kennedy_____

Decedent

DISTRICT COURT
PROBATE DIVISION
JUDICIAL DISTRICT

Court File No. ___198540___

APPLICATION FOR INFORMAL PROBATE OF
WILL AND FOR INFORMAL APPOINTMENT
OF PERSONAL REPRESENTATIVE

I,_____Charles Kennedy_____, state:

1. My address is:

    1010 Willow Street
    Minneapolis, MN 55409

2. I am an interested person as defined by Minnesota law because I am:

    spouse, heir, devisee, and nominated personal
    representative in the will.

3. Decedent was born on _Jan. 13, 1960_ , at (city, state) ___Minneapolis, Minnesota___ .

4. Decedent died on _Aug. 1, 2000_ , at (city, state) ___Minneapolis, Minnesota___ .

5. Decedent at the time of death resided in ___Hennepin___ County, at (address):

    1010 Willow Street, Minneapolis, MN 55409

6. Decedent's Social Security number is ___217-48-4307___ .

7. The names and addresses of Decedent's spouse, children, heirs, devisees and other persons interested in this proceeding so far as known or ascertainable with reasonable diligence by the Applicant are:

Name and Mailing Address	Relationship and Interest (list all)	Birthdate of Minors
Charles Kennedy 1010 Willow Street, Minneapolis, MN 55409	Spouse/heir/devisee/ nominated personal rep.	
Cherry Kennedy, 1010 Willow St., Mpls, MN	Daughter/heir/devisee	4/24/97
Cindy Kennedy, 1010 Willow St., Mpls, MN	Daughter/heir/devisee	4/24/97
Carl Kennedy, 1010 Willow St., Mpls, MN	Son/heir/devisee	6/15/95
Corey Kennedy, 1010 Willow St., Mpls, MN	Son/heir/devisee	7/05/91
Christopher Kennedy, 1010 Willow St., Mpls	Son/heir/devisee	2/07/90
Catherine Kelly, 1010 Willow St., Mpls, MN	Mother/heir	
Karen Kelly, 1010 Willow St., Mpls, MN	Sister/heir/devisee	

(Attach separate schedule, if necessary)

8. Negative Allegation Statement (see Minn. Gen. R. Prac. 408(a)):

    Decedent left surviving no spouse, children, parents, or brothers or sisters,
    other than herein named, and no issue of deceased children.

9. All persons identified as heirs have survived the Decedent by at least 120 hours.

MD   MCLE P-100

Application for Informal Probate of Will and for
Informal Appointment of Personal Representative

(continued)

Form 49 Application for Informal Probate of Will and for Informal Appointment of Personal Representative *continued*

10. (Check appropriate boxes)   **Court File No.** ___198540___
    ☐ Decedent left no surviving spouse.
    ☐ Decedent left no surviving issue.
    ☒ All issue of Decedent are issue of Decedent's surviving spouse except for:
       No exceptions.

    ☐ There are issue of the surviving spouse who are not issue of the Decedent.

11. Venue for this proceeding is in this County of the State of Minnesota because:
    ☒ The Decedent was domiciled in this County at the time of death and was the owner of property located in the State of Minnesota.
    or
    ☐ Though not domiciled in the State of Minnesota, the Decedent was the owner of property located in this County at the time of death.

12. I estimate the Decedent's assets and indebtedness are as follows:

Probate Assets		Non-Probate Assets	
Homestead	$ 95,000.	Joint Tenancy $	57,000.
Other Real Estate	$ 0	Insurance $	5,000.
Cash	$ 0	Other $	0
Securities	$ 2,000.		
Other	$ 16,610.		

Approximate Indebtedness $ ___110.___

13. There is no personal representative of the Decedent appointed in Minnesota or elsewhere whose appointment has not been terminated.

14. ☒ I have not received a demand for notice and am not aware of any demand for notice of any probate or appointment proceeding concerning the Decedent that may have been filed in Minnesota or elsewhere.
    or ☐ Proper notice has been given to those persons who have filed demand for notice.

15. Decedent's Will is comprised of the following:
    ☒ Last will dated ___November 21, 1998___.
    ☐ Codicil(___) dated ___.
    ☐ Separate writing(___) under Minn. Stat. 524.2-513 dated ___.

    ☐ (check if applicable) The Will refers to a separate writing but none has been found.

16. To the best of my knowledge and belief, the Will has been validly executed.

17. Having conducted a reasonably diligent search, I am unaware of any instrument revoking the Will or of any other unrevoked testamentary instrument.

18. The documents comprising the Will:
    ☒ accompany this Application.
    ☐ are in the Court's possession.
    ☐ have been probated elsewhere and an authenticated copy of the Will and statement or order probating the same accompany this Application.

Application for Informal Probate of Will and for
Informal Appointment of Personal Representative

(continued)

Form 49 Application for Informal Probate of Will and for Informal Appointment of Personal Representative *continued*

Court File No. 198540

19. The Will nominates _____ Charles Kennedy _____
as personal representative.

[x] The nominated personal representative is willing to serve and is not disqualified.

or

[ ] The nominated personal representative is unable or has declined to serve.

_____

has priority to serve as personal representative because:

and is willing to serve and is not disqualified.

20. The Will specifies:

Bond: [x] No Bond
[ ] Minimum Bond
[ ] $ _____ bond
[ ] Unspecified

Administration: [x] Undesignated
[ ] Unsupervised
[ ] Supervised

21. At least 120 hours, but not more than 3 years (except as permitted by Minn. Stat. 524.3-108), have elapsed since Decedent's death.

WHEREFORE, I request the Registrar informally:

1. Enter a statement probating the Will;

2. Enter an order appointing _____ Charles Kennedy _____
as personal representative, with $ _____ no _____ bond, in an unsupervised administration;

3. Issue letters testamentary to _____ Charles Kennedy _____ ; and

4. Grant such other relief as may be proper.

Under penalties for perjury, I declare or affirm that I have read this document and I know or believe its representations are true and complete.

_____ /S/ Charles Kennedy _____

Attorney For Applicant

Applicant   August 30, 2000   **Date**

THIS INSTRUMENT WAS DRAFTED BY (NAME AND ADDRESS):

Susan G. Brown
1400 Main Street
Minneapolis, MN 55455
Telephone: (612) 773-3777
Attorney License No. 9876543

M/D   MCLE P-100/Page3

Application for Informal Probate of Will and for Informal Appointment of Personal Representative

Source: This form is property of Miller/Davis Company, St. Paul, MN, Telephone 651–642–1988. Reprinted with permission.

Form 50 Verification Under Oath

MD Form No. P-034 Minn. Stat. 524.3-601 Miller/Davis Co., St. Paul, MN (800) 752-4221
Minnesota Continuing Legal Education © 1994 MCLE

STATE OF MINNESOTA **DISTRICT COURT**
PROBATE DIVISION
COUNTY OF _____ _____ **JUDICIAL DISTRICT**

Court File No. _____

Estate of

_____ **VERIFICATION UNDER OATH**

_____
Decedent

STATE OF **MINNESOTA** _____
} ss
COUNTY OF _____

I, _____,
being duly sworn state that I am ☐ the party ☐ one of the parties who signed the attached document,
entitled _____
dated _____;
that I have read the document and know its contents; and that the statements contained in the document
are true or I believe them to be true. I understand that penalties for perjury may follow from deliberate
falsification.

VOID

_____
Signature Date

Signed and sworn to (or affirmed) before me on
_____ by
_____ .
Affiant.

NOTARIAL STAMP OR SEAL (OR OTHER TITLE OR RANK)

_____
SIGNATURE OF NOTARY PUBLIC OR OTHER OFFICIAL

Attorney For Personal Representative

THIS INSTRUMENT WAS DRAFTED BY (NAME AND ADDRESS):

MD MCLE P-034 Verification Under Oath

Source: This form is property of Miller/Davis Company, St. Paul, MN, Telephone 651–642–1988. Reprinted with permission.

Form 51   Statement of Informal Probate of Will and Order of Informal Appointment of Personal Representative

M⫶D Form No. P-110   Minn. Stat. 524.3-302; 524.3-303; 524.3-306; 524.3-307   Miller/Davis Co., St. Paul, MN (800) 752-4221
Minnesota Continuing Legal Education © 1994 MCLE

STATE OF MINNESOTA

COUNTY OF ___Hennepin___   Probate Court

                                   Court File No. ___198540___

Estate of

                                   STATEMENT OF INFORMAL PROBATE
___Cheryl Ann Kennedy___   **OF WILL AND ORDER OF**
_____ **INFORMAL APPOINTMENT OF**
          Decedent   **PERSONAL REPRESENTATIVE**

The Application for the Informal Probate of Will and Informal Appointment of Personal Representative, signed by ___Charles Kennedy___,
came before the Registrar on ___August 30, 2000___ . The Registrar, having considered the Application, determines the following:

1. The Application is complete.

2. The Applicant has declared or affirmed that the representations contained in the Application are true to the best of Applicant's knowledge or belief.

3. The Applicant appears from the Application to be an interested person as defined by Minnesota law.

4. On the basis of the statements in the Application, venue in this County is proper.

5. Any notice required by Minnesota law has been given.

6. Decedent's will is comprised of the following:
    - [x] Last will dated ___November 21, 1998___ .
    - [ ] Codicil(__) dated _____ .
    - [ ] Separate writing(__) under Minn. Stat. 524.2-513 dated _____ .

    - [ ] (check if applicable) The Will refers to a separate writing but none has been found.

7. The documents comprising the Will:
    - [x] are in the Registrar's possession.
    - [ ] have been probated elsewhere and an authenticated copy of the Will and statement or order probating the same accompanied the Application.

8. Decedent died on ___August 1, 2000___ and at least 120 hours, but not more than 3 years, (except as permitted by Minn. Stat. 524.3-108) have elapsed since the Decedent's death.

9. (Check appropriate boxes)

    - [ ] Decedent left no surviving spouse.

    - [ ] Decedent left no surviving issue.

    - [x] All issue of Decedent are issue of Decedent's surviving spouse except for:
      No exceptions.

    - [ ] There are issue of the surviving spouse who are not issue of the Decedent.

M⫶D   MCLE P-110

Statement of Informal Probate of Will and Order of
Informal Appointment of Personal Representative

(continued)

Form 51   Statement of Informal Probate of Will and Order of Informal Appointment of Personal Representative   *continued*

Court File No. _____198540_____

10. From the statements in the Application, the person appointed below has priority and is entitled to be appointed personal representative, and is not disqualified to serve as personal representative.

20. The Will specifies:

Bond: [x] No Bond
       [ ] Minimum Bond
       [ ] $ _____ bond
       [ ] Unspecified

Administration: [x] Undesignated
                 [ ] Unsupervised
                 [ ] Supervised

12. The Application indicates that there is no personal representative appointed in this or another county of Minnesota whose appointment has not been terminated.

IT IS ORDERED

1. The Application is granted.

2. The Will is informally probated.

3. _____Charles Kennedy_____
   is informally appointed as the personal representative of the Decedent's Estate, with ____no_____
   bond.

4. Upon filing any required bond and statement of acceptance and oath, letters testamentary will be issued.

____/S/ Lorina B. Arneson_____

Registrar   September 7, 2000   Date

Statement of Informal Probate of Will and Order of
Informal Appointment of Personal Representative

Source: This form is property of Miller/Davis Company, St. Paul, MN, Telephone 651–642–1988. Reprinted with permission.

Form 52   Notice of Informal Probate of Will and Appointment of Personal Representative and Notice to Creditors

M/D Form No. P-120   Minn. Stat. 524.3-306; 524.3-310; 524.3-801   Miller/Davis Co., St. Paul, MN (800) 752-4221
Minnesota Continuing Legal Education © 1994 MCLE

STATE OF MINNESOTA

COUNTY OF ___Hennepin_____   ___Fourth_____

**DISTRICT COURT
PROBATE DIVISION
JUDICIAL DISTRICT**

Court File No. ___198540_____

Estate of

_____Cheryl Ann Kennedy_____
_____
                        Decedent

**NOTICE OF INFORMAL PROBATE OF WILL
AND APPOINTMENT OF PERSONAL
REPRESENTATIVE AND
NOTICE TO CREDITORS**

   Notice is given that an application for informal probate of the Decedent's will dated _Nov. 21, 1998___ , and codicil(__) to the will dated _____ , and separate writing (__) under Minn. Stat. 524.2-513 ("Will"), has been filed with the Registrar. The application has been granted.

   Notice is also given that the Registrar has informally appointed   _____
                 Charles Kennedy_____
lwhose address is:

         1010 Willow Street
         Minneapolis, MN 55409

as personal representative of the Estate of the Decedent. Any heir, devisee or other interested person may be entitled to appointment as personal representative or may object to the appointment of the personal representative. Unless objections are filed with the Court (pursuant to Minn. Stat. 524.3-607) and the Court otherwise orders, the personal representative has full power to administer the Estate including, after 30 days from the date of issuance of letters, the power to sell, encumber, lease or distribute real estate.

   Any objections to the probate of the will or appointment of the Personal Representative must be filed with this Court and will be heard by the Court after the filing of an appropriate petition and proper notice of hearing.

   Notice is also given that (subject to Minn. 524.3-801) all creditors having claims against the Estate are required to present the claims to the personal representative or to the Court Administrator within four months after the date of this Notice or the claims will be barred.

                                        ___/S/ Lorina B. Arneson_____

                                        Registrar   September 7, 2000   Date

                                        ___/S/ Bradford R. Mitlar_____

Attorney For Personal Representative

THIS INSTRUMENT WAS DRAFTED BY (NAME AND ADDRESS):
Susan G. Brown 1400 Main Street Minneapolis, MN 55455 Telephone: (612) 773-3777 Attorney License No. 9876543

                                        Court Administrator   September 7, 2000   Date

NOTE: If notice to creditors has been previously given, delete the notice to creditors.
NOTE TO PUBLISHER: Do not publish the text of Notes.

M/D   MCLE P-120

Notice of Informal Probate of Will and Appointment of
Personal Representative and Notice to Creditors

Source: This form is property of Miller/Davis Company, St. Paul, MN, Telephone 651–642–1988. Reprinted with permission.

Form 53   Proof of Placing Order for Publication

STATE OF MINNESOTA

COUNTY OF HENNEPIN

PROBATE COURT—UNSUPERVISED

COURT FILE NO. <u>198540</u>

In Re: Estate of

<u>   Cheryl Ann Kennedy   </u>

Deceased

PROOF OF PLACING ORDER

<u>FOR PUBLICATION</u>

TO THE CLERK OF PROBATE COURT:

That is to verify that   <u>Susan G. Brown</u>

<u>Attorney for</u>   , applicant(s)

has ~~have~~ made arrangements for the publication of:

☐ NOTICE OF INFORMAL APPOINTMENT OF PERSONAL REPRESENTATIVE(S) AND NOTICE TO CREDITORS

☒ NOTICE OF INFORMAL PROBATE OF WILL AND APPOINTMENT OF PERSONAL REPRESENTATIVE(S) AND NOTICE TO CREDITORS

☐

once a week for two consecutive weeks in the   <u>**FINANCE AND COMMERCE**</u>

Daily Newspaper

and this is to confirm that the same will be published accordingly commencing in the next available issue, and that arrangements for payment of the cost of said publication have been made.

Dated: <u>September 8, 2000</u>

<u>/s/ D. C. Morrison</u>

Publisher

Form 54   Affidavit of Mailing Notice of Informal Probate of Will

---

M/D Form No. P-015   Minn. Stat. 524.1-401; 525.83   Miller/Davis Co., St. Paul, MN (800) 752-4221
Minnesota Continuing Legal Education © 1994 MCLE

STATE OF MINNESOTA

COUNTY OF   Hennepin   Probate Court

                                                        Court File No.   198540

Estate of

_____ Cheryl Ann Kennedy _____   **AFFIDAVIT OF MAILING**
                                                          ORDER OR NOTICE

                Decedent

STATE OF ____ Minnesota ____   }
                                                     } ss.
COUNTY OF ____ Hennepin ____   }

I, _____ Susan G. Brown _____
being first duly sworn, on oath state that on ____ September 8, 2000 ____ ,
____ Minneapolis, MN ____ (city, state), I mailed a copy of the
attached Order or Notice to each person or entity named below by mailing a copy in a sealed envelope,
postage prepaid, with the U.S. Postal Service as follows:

Name and Mailing Address	Relationship and Interest (list all)	Birthdate of Minors
Charles Kennedy 1010 Willow Street, Minneapolis, MN 55409	Spouse/heir/devisee/ personal representative	
Cherry Kennedy, same address	Daughter/heir/devisee	4/24/97
Cindy Kennedy, same address	Daughter/heir/devisee	4/24/97
Carl Kennedy, same address	Son/heir/devisee	6/15/95
Corey Kennedy, same address	Son/heir/devisee	7/05/91
Christopher Kennedy, same address	Son/heir/devisee	2/07/90
Catherine Kelly, same address	Mother/heir	
Karen Kelly, same address	Sister/heir/devisee	

(Attach separate schedule, if necessary)

____ /S/ Susan G. Brown ____

Affiant   September 8, 2000   Date

Signed and sworn to (or affirmed) before me on
____ September 8, 2000 ____ by
____ Susan G. Brown ____.
Affiant.

NOTARIAL STAMP OR SEAL (OR OTHER TITLE OR RANK)

____ /S/ Astrid M. Martensen ____
SIGNATURE OF NOTARY PUBLIC OR OTHER OFFICIAL

INSTRUCTIONS: (1) A copy of the Order or Notice must be mailed to each heir, devisee, personal representative, the foreign consul
pursuant to Minn. Stat. 524.3-306 and 524.3-403, lawyers representing interested parties pursuant to Minn. Stat. 524.1-401(a), and
the Minnesota Attorney General, if a devisee is a charitable organization or if the decedent left no devisee or heirs. In determining the
persons or entities entitled to receive this order or notice, see Minn. Stats. 501B.41(5), 524.1-201(19), 524.1-403 and 524.1-404
and Minn. Gen. Rules of Practice 404(b) and 408(d). If the Decedent is survived by a spouse or minor child, also use Notice to
Spouse and Children. (2) Attach to this affidavit another copy of the Order or Notice which was sent. (3) It may be necessary to give
notice to creditors. See Minn. Stat. 524.3-801(3) and Supplementary Notice to Known and Identified Creditors form.

M/D   MCLE P-015

                                                        Affidavit of Mailing Order or Notice

---

Source: This form is property of Miller/Davis Company, St. Paul, MN, Telephone 651–642–1988. Reprinted with permission.

Form 55 Notice to Spouse and Children and Affidavit of Mailing

MD Form No. P-016 | Minn. Stat. 524.1-401 | Miller/Davis Co., St. Paul, MN (800) 752-4221
Minnesota Continuing Legal Education © 1994 MCLE

STATE OF MINNESOTA

COUNTY OF __Hennepin_____

Estate of

_____Cheryl Ann Kennedy_____

_____

Decedent

DISTRICT COURT
PROBATE DIVISION
Fourth____ JUDICIAL DISTRICT

Court File No. ___198540___

NOTICE TO SPOUSE AND CHILDREN
AND AFFIDAVIT OF MAILING

TO: Surviving spouse and children of the Decedent.

This notice is to advise you of your rights regarding the Estate of ___Cheryl Ann Kennedy_____ .
Under Minnesota law you, as surviving spouse or children or the Decedent, may have some or all of the rights summarized below.

Surviving Spouse:

1.   The right to elect a percentage of the "augmented estate" which is provided under Minnesota Statutes §§ 524.2-201 through 524.2-214. This right to elect is personal to the surviving spouse and must be made within 9 months after the date of the Decedent's death; except that for property subject to probate the election may be made within 6 months after the probate of the Decedent's will, even if the 9 month period has already expired.

2.   If the Decedent's will was made prior to your marriage to the Decedent, the right to choose the intestate share of the Estate under Minnesota Statutes § 524.2-301. This right has some limitations and exceptions.

3.   The right, under Minnesota Statutes § 524.2-402 to the entire homestead if the Decedent did not leave any surviving descendants or the right to a life estate if the Decedent left surviving descendants.

4.   The right to allowances under Minnesota Statutes § 524.2-403, which permits the surviving spouse the right to select:

   a.   Household furniture, furnishings, appliances, and personal effects not exceeding $10,000, net of security interests, but subject to an award of sentimental value property under Minnesota Statutes § 525.152; provided, however, if the encumbered property and the value in excess of security interests, plus that of other exempt property, is less than $10,000, or if there is not $10,000 worth of exempt property in the Estate, the surviving spouse is entitled to other personal property of the Estate, if any, to the extent necessary to make up the $10,000 value; and

   b.   One automobile, if any, without regard to value.

5.   The right to a family allowance from the Estate under Minnesota Statutes § 524.2-404 of up to $1,500 per month (or more if authorized by the court) for one year if the estate is insolvent or for 18 months if the Estate is solvent.

Minor Children of Decedent:

6.   If the Decedent had an obligation to support you, the right to family allowance from the Estate under Minnesota Statutes § 524.2-404 of up to $1,500 per month (or more if authorized by the court) for one year if the Estate is insolvent or for 18 months if the Estate is solvent.

MD   MCLE P-016

Notice to Spouse and Children and Affidavit of Mailing

(continued)

Form 55   Notice to Spouse and Children and Affidavit of Mailing   *continued*

Court File No. _____198540_____

Adult Children of Decedents

7. If you were being supported by Decedent, the right to family allowance from the Estate under Minnesota Statutes § 524.2-404 of up to $1,500 (or more if authorized by the court) per month for one year if the Estate is insolvent or for 18 months if the Estate is solvent.

Minor and Adult Children of Decedent:

8. If there is no surviving spouse, the right to allowances under Minnesota Statutes § 524.2-403:

    a. Household furniture, furnishings, appliances, and personal effects not exceeding $10,000, net of security interests, but subject to an award of sentimental value property under Minnesota Statutes § 525.152; provided, however, if the encumbered property and the value in excess of security interests, plus that of other exempt property, is less than $10,000, or if there is not $10,000 worth of exempt property in the Estate, the children are entitled to other personal property of the Estate, if any, to the extent necessary to make up the $10,000 value; and

    a. One automobile, if any, without regard to value.

If you have any questions regarding interpretation of these statutes or the effect of these or other rights, please consult with an attorney of your own choice or the attorney for the Personal Representative. Copies of the statutes can be obtained at the local county law library or from the Personal Representative.

_____/S/ Charles Kennedy_____

September 8, 2000

Personal Representative   **Date**

Attorney For Personal Representative

THIS INSTRUMENT WAS DRAFTED BY (NAME AND ADDRESS):

Susan G. Brown
1400 Main Street
Minneapolis, MN 55455
Telephone: (612) 773-3777
Attorney License No. 9876543

(continued)

Form 55   Notice to Spouse and Children and Affidavit of Mailing   *continued*

Court File No. ___198540___

STATE OF __MINNESOTA__ _____ } ss.

COUNTY OF __Hennepin__ _____ }

I, _____ Susan G. Brown _____,
being first duly sworn, on oath state that on _____ September 8, 2000 _____, at
_____ Minneapolis, MN ___ (city, state), I mailed a copy of the attached Notice to each person
or entity named below by mailing a copy in a sealed envelope, postage prepaid, with the U.S. Postal Service
as follows:

Name and Mailing Address	Relationship and Interest (list all)	Birthdate of Minors
Charles Kennedy 1010 Willow Street, Minneapolis, MN 55409	Spouse/heir/devisee/ personal representative	
Cherry Kennedy, same address	Daughter/heir/devisee	4/24/97
Cindy Kennedy, same address	Daughter/heir/devisee	4/24/97
Carl Kennedy, same address	Son/heir/devisee	6/15/95
Corey Kennedy, same address	Son/heir/devisee	7/05/91
Christopher Kennedy, same address	Son/heir/devisee	2/07/90

(Attach separate schedule, if necessary)

___/S/ Susan G. Brown_____

Affiant   September 8, 2000   Date

Signed and sworn to (or affirmed) before me on
___September 8, 2000_____ by
___Susan G. Brown_____.
Affiant.

NOTARIAL STAMP OR SEAL (OR OTHER TITLE OR RANK)

___/S/ Astrid M. Martensen_____
SIGNATURE OF NOTARY PUBLIC OR OTHER OFFICIAL

Source: This form is property of Miller/Davis Company, St. Paul, MN, Telephone 651–642–1988. Reprinted with permission.

Form 56   Acceptance of Appointment as Personal Representative and Oath by Individual

---

MD Form No. P-001   Minn. Stat. 524.3-601   Miller/Davis Co., St. Paul, MN (800) 752-4221
                                                                   Minnesota Continuing Legal Education © 1994 MCLE

STATE OF MINNESOTA

COUNTY OF   Hennepin   Probate Court

                                                       Court File No. _____ 198540 _____
Estate of

_____ Cheryl Ann Kennedy _____   **ACCEPTANCE OF APPOINTMENT**
                                                       AS PERSONAL REPRESENTATIVE
_____   **AND OATH BY INDIVIDUAL**
            Decedent

STATE OF   Minnesota
                                                 } ss
COUNTY OF   Hennepin

   I, _____ Charles Kennedy _____ ,
residing at ,   1010 Willow Street
                Minneapolis, MN 55409

as a condition to receiving letters as Personal Representative in this Estate, (1) accept the duties of the
office, (2) agree to be bound by the provisions of the statutes relating to the office, (3) submit to the
jurisdiction of the Court in any proceeding relating to this Estate, and (4) swear that I will faithfully perform
all duties of the office that I now assume to the best of my ability.

                                        _____ /S/ Charles Kennedy _____

                                        Signature   September 7, 2000   **Date**

                                        Signed and sworn to (or affirmed) before me on
                                        _____ September 7, 2000 _____ **by**
+------------------------------------+ Charles Kennedy
| NOTARIAL STAMP OR SEAL (OR OTHER | Personal Representative
| TITLE OR RANK) |
| | _____ /S/ Mariana S. Halsted _____
| | SIGNATURE OF NOTARY PUBLIC OR OTHER OFFICIAL
| |
+------------------------------------+

Attorney For Personal Representative

+--+
| THIS INSTRUMENT WAS DRAFTED BY (NAME AND ADDRESS): |
| |
| Susan G. Brown |
| 1400 Main Street |
| Minneapolis, MN 55455 |
| Telephone: (612) 773-3777 |
| Attorney License No. 9876543 |
+--+

MD   MCLE P-001   Acceptance of Appointment as
                                           Personal Representative and Oath by Individual

---

Source: This form is property of Miller/Davis Company, St. Paul, MN, Telephone 651–642–1988. Reprinted with permission.

Form 57   Letters Testamentary

MD Form No. P-010   Minn. Stat. 524.3-601   Miller/Davis Co., St. Paul, MN (800) 752-4221
                                                         Minnesota Continuing Legal Education © 1994 MCLE

STATE OF MINNESOTA   **DISTRICT COURT**
                                                         PROBATE DIVISION
COUNTY OF   Hennepin   Fourth   **JUDICIAL DISTRICT**

                                            Court File No.   198540

Estate of
                                            LETTERS
          Cheryl Ann Kennedy   [x] **TESTAMENTARY**
                                            [ ] **OF GENERAL ADMINISTRATION**

          Decedent

1. The Decedent died on _Aug. 1, 2000_ .

2. _____ Charles Kennedy _____ has
   been appointed Personal Representative of Decedent's Estate in

   [x] an unsupervised
   [ ] a supervised administration

   and is now qualified to act as Personal Representative of the Estate and has authority to administer the
   Estate according to law.

                              /S/ Lorina B. Arneson

                              ~~Judge~~/Registrar   September 7, 2000   Date

          (COURT SEAL)

MD   MCLE P-010   [ ] Testamentary [ ] of General Administration   Letters

Source: This form is property of Miller/Davis Company, St. Paul, MN, Telephone 651–642–1988. Reprinted with permission.

Form 58 Inventory

MD Form No. P-600   Minn. Stat. 524.3-706   Miller/Davis Co., St. Paul, MN (800) 752-4221
                                                                      Minnesota Continuing Legal Education © 1994 MCLE

STATE OF MINNESOTA

COUNTY OF ____Hennepin____   Probate Court

                                                    Court File No. ____198540____
Estate of

                                                    INVENTORY
                                                    [x] **ORIGINAL**
                                                    [ ] **AMENDED**
                                                    [ ] **SUPPLEMENTAL**

_____Cheryl Ann Kennedy_____

_____   Date of Death ___August 1, 2000___
                Decedent   Social Security Number ___217-48-4307___

_____Charles Kennedy_____ ,
the Personal Representative of the Estate, states:

1. The following is a true and correct inventory at date of death values of all the property of the Estate, both real and personal, which has come into my possession as Personal Representative. If an appraisal of any asset has been made, the name and address of each appraiser used is included. After diligent search and inquiry concerning the assets of the Estate, the following is a list of the Estate assets by category:

SCHEDULE	VALUE
Schedule A: Real Estate	95,000.
Schedule B: Stocks, Bonds, and Other Securities	2,000.
Schedule C: Bank Accounts, Mortgages, Contracts for Deed, Notes and Cash	0
Schedule D: Other Personal Property	16,610.
SUBTOTAL	113,610.
Less Schedule E: Mortgages and Liens	(0)
TOTAL	113,610.

2. A copy of this Inventory, including all schedules, has been mailed to the surviving spouse, if any, and to all residuary distributees of the Decedent and to interested persons and creditors who have requested a copy of the Inventory.

   Under penalties for perjury, I declare or affirm that I have read the Inventory and I know or believe its representations are true and complete.

Attorney For **Personal Representative**

THIS INSTRUMENT WAS DRAFTED BY (NAME AND ADDRESS):
Susan G. Brown
1400 Main Street
Minneapolis, MN 55455
Telephone: (612) 773-3777
Attorney License No. 9876543

____/S/ Charles Kennedy____

Personal Representative Sept. 17, 2000   **Date**

MD   MCLE P-600   Inventory

Form 58 Inventory *continued*

Court File No. ___198540___

SCHEDULE A: REAL ESTATE

INSTRUCTIONS for Schedule A:

1. Include both the legal description and the street address. If rural property also include acreage.
2. For Contracts for Deed: If Decedent owned a Vendor/Seller's interest describe the land on Schedule A, valuing it at zero and show the remaining contract balance on Schedule C. If Decedent owned a Vendee/Buyer's interest, describe the property on Schedule A valuing it at its fair market value.
3. County Assessor's market value can be obtained from the County Assessor or department of taxation.
4. List only Minnesota real estate. DO NOT list real estate located in other states.

Item Number	Description of Property	County Assessor's Market Value	Fair Market Value
1	Homestead in the County of ___Hennepin___ 1010 Willow Street, Minneapolis, MN Legally described as follows, to wit: Lot 3, Block 1, Loring Park Addition to Minneapolis (Plat #17068 Parcel #3196)	$ 91,200.	$ 95,000.
		Sub Total	95,000.
	Other Real Estate in the County of _____ None	$	$
		Sub Total	
	Schedule A: Real Estate	TOTAL	95,000.

(continued)

Form 58 Inventory *continued*

Court File No. ___198540___

SCHEDULE B: STOCKS, BONDS AND OTHER SECURITIES

INSTRUCTIONS for Schedule B:

1. Specify face value of bonds, number of shares of stock, stock certificate number and CUSIP number, if available.
2. List each bond issue, stock, or certificate separately.

Item Number	Description of Property	Unit Value	Fair Market Value
		$	$
1	<u>Stock:</u> 50 Shares Users, Inc., Common Stock, Certificate No. U0556484 dated 01/13/78	40.	2,000.
		Sub Total	2,000.
	Schedule B: Stocks, Bonds and Other Securities	TOTAL	2,000.

MD   MCLE P-600/Page 3   Inventory

(continued)

Form 58 Inventory *continued*

Court File No. _____198540_____

SCHEDULE C: BANK ACCOUNTS, MORTGAGES, CONTRACTS FOR DEED, NOTES AND CASH

INSTRUCTIONS for Schedule C:

1. List Vendor/Seller's interest in Contract for Deed on this Schedule. Also include the date of the contract, name of Vendee/Buyer, interest rate and unpaid balance at date of death, and accrued interest, if any. List Mortgages owned by Decedent as assets, NOT mortgages for which Decedent is liable or mortgages
2. secured by property in the Estate.

Item Number	Description of Property	Fair Market Value
		$
	None	
		Sub Total
	Schedule C: Bank Accounts, Mortgages, Contracts for Deed, Notes and Cash	**TOTAL** _____

(*continued*)

Form 58 Inventory *continued*

Court File No. _____198540_____

SCHEDULE D: OTHER PERSONAL PROPERTY

INSTRUCTIONS for Schedule D:

1. List on this schedule, any personal property owned by Decedent and not reported on other schedules. Examples of property to be listed on this schedule include: refunds, wearing apparel, household goods, automobiles, furniture, business interests, and insurance payable to the Estate.
2. Where appropriate, specify the location of the property.
3. Use actual value or specify if asset has no pecuniary value.
4. DO NOT list non-probate property.

Item Number	Description of Personal Property	Fair Market Value
		$
1	Furniture and household goods.	5,000.
2	Furs – Mink coat.	4,000.
3	Diamond ring.	1,500.
4	Clothing.	200.
5	Wigs (2).	110.
6	1998 Ford, Vehicle Identification No. 5342718653, Title No. 04142313.	5,500.
7	Miscellaneous	300.
	Sub Total	16,610.
	Schedule D: Other Property TOTAL	16,610.

(continued)

Form 58 Inventory *continued*

Court File No. _____198540_____

SCHEDULE E: MORTGAGES AND LIENS

INSTRUCTIONS for Schedule E:

1. Show any mortgages and liens secured by property in the Estate. Detail the date of the installment, names of the parties, interest rate, payment terms, and any other relevant data. Indicate the Schedule and Item Number of the secured property from prior schedule. The remaining balance of Contracts for Deed in which Decedent was the Vendee/Buyer or was the mortgage debtor should be listed on this Schedule. Also include interest and taxes due at date of death.

Item Number	Description of Mortgage or Lien	Asset Secured (Schedule and Item Number)	Balance as of Date of Death $
	None		
		TOTAL	
	Schedule E: Mortgages and Liens	TOTAL	

MCLE P-600/Page 6

Inventory

Source: This form is property of Miller/Davis Company, St. Paul, MN, Telephone 651–642–1988. Reprinted with permission.

Form 59   Written Statement of Claim

MD Form No. P-505   Minn. Stat. 524.3-804   Miller/Davis Co., St. Paul, MN (800) 752-4221
Minnesota Continuing Legal Education © 1994 MCLE

STATE OF MINNESOTA   **DISTRICT COURT**
                                                         PROBATE DIVISION
COUNTY OF ___Hennepin___   ___Fourth___   **JUDICIAL DISTRICT**

                                                 Court File No. ___198540___
Estate of

_____Cheryl Ann Kennedy_____
_____   **WRITTEN STATEMENT OF CLAIM**
              Decedent

I, _____Martin R. Kromstad of Beauty Products, Inc._____ ,
Claimant, state:

1. My address is:

   230 Dunkirk Lane
   Minnetonka, MN 55606

2. The Estate is or will become indebted, to me in the amount of $ ___110.___ .

3. The nature of the claim is: merchandise (wigs) bought by decedent.
   Primavera (#7743) $ 64.
   Carefree (#7739)   46.
   Total $110.

4. The claim arose [x] prior to the death of the Decedent on or about ___July 27, 2000___ .
   or [ ] after the death of Decedent, on or about _____ .

5. The claim is   [x] unsecured, or
                  [ ] secured by:

6. The claim [ ] is [x] is not based on a contract which makes a provision for interest.

7. The claim was or will be due and payable on ___August 27, 2000___ .

8. If the claim is contingent or unliquidated, the nature of the uncertainty is as follows:

Under penalties for perjury, I declare or affirm that I have read this document and I know or believe its representations are true and complete.

                                        BEAUTY PRODUCTS, INC.

Attorney For Claimant   BY: /S/ Martin R. Kromstad

THIS INSTRUMENT WAS DRAFTED BY (NAME AND ADDRESS):

Rafael Y. Santelo   Claimant   September 18, 2000   Date
1341 Stevens Avenue
Minneapolis, MN 55410
Telephone: (612) 841-7662
Attorney License No. 5347194

NOTES: Claim may be presented to Personal Representative or filed with Court Administrator.
Presentation of claim does **not** commence any proceeding. See Minn.Stat.524.3-806

MD   MCLE P-505   Written Statement of Claim

Source: This form is property of Miller/Davis Company, St. Paul, MN, Telephone 651–642–1988. Reprinted with permission.

Form 60 Receipt for Assets by Distributee

MD Form No. P-615   Minn. Stat. 524.3-1001(4);   Miller/Davis Co., St. Paul, MN (800) 752-4221
                                524.3-1003(2)   Minnesota Continuing Legal Education © 1994 MCLE

STATE OF MINNESOTA   **DISTRICT COURT**
                                                                PROBATE DIVISION
COUNTY OF ___Hennepin_____   ___Fourth_____   **JUDICIAL DISTRICT**

                                                                Court File No. ___198540_____

Estate of

_____Cheryl Ann Kennedy_____

_____   **RECEIPT FOR ASSETS**
                                              BY DISTRIBUTEE
          Decedent

I, _____Karen Kelly_____
the undersigned distributee, acknowledge receipt from the Personal Representative of this Estate, of the
following assets in [x] full [ ] partial satisfaction of my distributive share:

One blue–white marquise cut diamond ring, silver setting, valued at $1,500.

_____/S/ Karen Kelly_____

Distributee   January 8, 2001   Date

MD   MCLE P-615   Receipt for Assets by Distributee

Source: This form is property of Miller/Davis Company, St. Paul, MN, Telephone 651–642–1988. Reprinted with permission.

Form 61   Unsupervised Personal Representative's Statement to Close Estate

M Form No. P-682   Minn. Stat. 524.3-1003   Miller/Davis Co., St. Paul, MN (800) 752-4221
                                                                        Minnesota Continuing Legal Education © 1994 MCLE

STATE OF MINNESOTA   **DISTRICT COURT**
                                                                        PROBATE DIVISION
COUNTY OF ___Hennepin_____   ___Fourth___   **JUDICIAL DISTRICT**

                                                                        Court File No. ___198540_____
Estate of

_____Cheryl Ann Kennedy_____   **UNSUPERVISED**
_____   **PERSONAL REPRESENTATIVE'S**
                 Decedent   **STATEMENT TO CLOSE ESTATE**

STATE OF MINNESOTA

COUNTY OF ___Hennepin_____ } ss

I, _____Charles Kennedy_____ ,
the Personal Representative of the Estate, state that I (or a prior Personal Representative whom I have
succeeded) have:

1. Published notice to creditors. The date of the notice was more than four months prior to the date of
    this statement.

2. Fully administered this Estate by making payment, settlement or other disposition of all claims which
    were presented, expenses of administration, estate and other taxes, except as specified in this
    statement.

3. Inventoried the assets of the Estate and distributed them to the persons entitled to them. Listed below
    are all unpaid claims, expenses or taxes which remain undischarged (If none, so state; otherwise state in
    detail other arrangements which have been made to accommodate all outstanding liabilities.):

    None

4. Sent a copy of this statement to all distributees of this Estate and to all creditors or other claimants

M   MCLE P-682   Unsupervised Personal
                                                                        Representative's Statement to Close Estate

(continued)

Form 61   Unsupervised Personal Representative's Statement to Close Estate   *continued*

Court File No. ____198540____

whose claims are neither paid nor barred and have furnished a full account in writing of this administration to the distributees whose interests are affected by the administration of this Estate.

This statement is filed for the purpose of closing this Estate and terminating my appointment as Personal Representative of the Estate.

____/S/ Charles Kennedy_____

Personal Representative   March 1, 2001   Date

Signed and sworn to (or affirmed) before me on
____March 1, 2001_____ by
____Charles Kennedy_____
_____

Personal Representative.

NOTARIAL STAMP OR SEAL (OR OTHER TITLE OR RANK)

____/S/ Georgeann Holtzer_____
SIGNATURE OF NOTARY PUBLIC OR OTHER OFFICIAL

Attorney For Personal Representative

THIS INSTRUMENT WAS DRAFTED BY (NAME AND ADDRESS):

Susan G. Brown
1400 Main Street
Minneapolis, MN 55455
Telephone: (612) 773-3777
Attorney License No. 9876543

NOTE: Appointment of the personal representative terminates one year following the filing of this statement with the court. Letters of appointment remain in full force and effect during that year.

Unsupervised Personal
Representative's Statement to Close Estate

Source: This form is property of Miller/Davis Company, St. Paul, MN, Telephone 651–642–1988. Reprinted with permission.

Form 62   Application for Informal Appointment of Personal Representative (Intestate)

MD Form No. P-103   Minn. Stat. 524.3-301(4); Minn. Gen. R. Prac. 408(a)   Miller/Davis Co., St. Paul, MN (800) 752-4221
Minnesota Continuing Legal Education © 1994 MCLE

STATE OF MINNESOTA

COUNTY OF ___Hennepin___

DISTRICT COURT
PROBATE DIVISION
Fourth   **JUDICIAL DISTRICT**

Court File No. ___198541___

Estate of

___Cheryl Ann Kennedy___

_____
Decedent

**APPLICATION FOR INFORMAL
APPOINTMENT OF PERSONAL
REPRESENTATIVE (INTESTATE)**

I, ___Charles Kennedy_____ , state:

1. My address is:

    1010 Willow Street
    Minneapolis, MN 55409

2. I am an interested person as defined by Minnesota law because I am:

    spouse and heir.

3. Decedent was born on ___Jan. 13, 1960___ , at (city, state) ___Minneapolis, Minnesota___ .

4. Decedent died on ___Aug. 1, 2000___ , at (city, state) ___Minneapolis, Minnesota___ .

5. Decedent at the time of death resided in ___Hennepin___ County, at (address):
    1010 Willow Street, Minneapolis, MN 55409

6. Decedent's Social Security number is ___217-48-4307___ .

7. The names and addresses of Decedent's spouse, children, heirs, devisees and other persons interested in this proceeding so far as known or ascertainable with reasonable diligence by the Applicant are:

Name and Mailing Address	Relationship and Interest (list all)	Birthdate of Minors
Charles Kennedy 1010 Willow Street, Minneapolis, MN 55409	Spouse/heir	
Cherry Kennedy, 1010 Willow St., Mpls, MN	Daughter/heir	4/24/97
Cindy Kennedy, 1010 Willow St., Mpls, MN	Daughter/heir	4/24/97
Carl Kennedy, 1010 Willow St., Mpls, MN	Son/heir	6/15/95
Corey Kennedy, 1010 Willow St., Mpls, MN	Son/heir	7/05/91
Christopher Kennedy, 1010 Willow St., Mpls	Son/heir	2/07/90
Catherine Kelly, 1010 Willow St., Mpls, MN	Mother/heir	
Karen Kelly, 1010 Willow St., Mpls, MN	Sister/heir	

(Attach separate schedule, if necessary)

8. Negative Allegation Statement (see Minn. Gen. R. Prac. 408(a)):
    Decedent left surviving no spouse, children, parents, or brothers or sisters, other than herein named, and no issue of deceased children.

9. All persons identified as heirs have survived the Decedent by at least 120 hours.

MD   MCLE P-103

Application for Informal Appointment
of Personal Representative (Intestate)

(continued)

Form 62 Application for Informal Appointment of Personal Representative (Intestate) *continued*

10. (Check appropriate boxes)

Court File No. 198541

☐ Decedent left no surviving spouse.
☐ Decedent left no surviving issue.
☒ All issue of Decedent are issue of Decedent's surviving spouse except for:

No exceptions.

☐ There are issue of the surviving spouse who are not issue of the Decedent.

11. Venue for this proceeding is in this County of the State of Minnesota because:

☒ The Decedent was domiciled in this County at the time of death and was the owner of property located in the State of Minnesota.

or

☐ Though not domiciled in the State of Minnesota, the Decedent was the owner of property located in this County at the time of death.

12. I estimate the Decedent's assets and indebtedness are as follows:

Probate Assets		Non-Probate Assets	
Homestead	$ 95,000.	Joint Tenancy $	57,000.
Other Real Estate	$ 0	Insurance $	5,000.
Cash	$ 0	Other $	0
Securities	$ 2,000.		
Other	$ 16,610.		

Approximate Indebtedness $ 110.

13. There is no personal representative of the Decedent appointed in Minnesota or elsewhere whose appointment has not been terminated.

14. ☒ I have not received a demand for notice and am not aware of any a demand for notice of any probate or appointment proceeding concerning the Decedent that may have been filed in Minnesota or elsewhere.

or ☐ Proper notice has been given to those persons who have filed demand for notice.

15. The time limit for informal appointment proceedings as provided by Minnesota law has not expired because three years or less have passed since the Decedent's death.

16. Having conducted a reasonably diligent search, I am unaware of any testamentary instrument under Minnesota law and believe that the Decedent died leaving no will.

17. Charles Kennedy

is entitled to priority and appointment as personal representative because:

he is the spouse of the decedent

and is willing to serve and is not disqualified. There are no persons having a prior or equal right to the appointment under Minnesota law except:

who have either renounced their right for appointment or have joined in nominating _____

Application for Informal Appointment
of Personal Representative (Intestate)

(continued)

Form 62 Application for Informal Appointment of Personal Representative (Intestate) *continued*

Court File No. 198541

18. At least 120 hours have elapsed and not more than 3 years (except as permitted by Minn. Stat. 524.3-108), since Decedent's death.

WHEREFORE, I request the Registrar informally:

1. Enter an order appointing _____Charles Kennedy_____
as personal representative of the Estate, with $___10,000.___ bond, in an unsupervised administration;

2. Issue letters of general administration to _____Charles Kennedy_____ ; and

3. Grant such other relief as may be proper.

Under penalties for perjury, I declare or affirm that I have read this document and I know or believe its representations are true and complete.

Attorney For   Applicant

THIS INSTRUMENT WAS DRAFTED BY (NAME AND ADDRESS):

Susan G. Brown
1400 Main Street
Minneapolis, MN 55455
Telephone: (612) 773-3777
Attorney License No. 9876543

___/S/ Charles Kennedy___

Applicant   August 30, 2000 Date

MD   MCLE P-103/Page 3

Application for Informal Appointment
of Personal Representative (Intestate)

Source: This form is property of Miller/Davis Company, St. Paul, MN, Telephone 651–642–1988. Reprinted with permission.

Form 63   Notice of Informal Appointment of Personal Representative and Notice to Creditors (Intestate)

MD Form No. P-123   Minn. Stat. 524.3-310; 524.3-801   Miller/Davis Co., St. Paul, MN (800) 752-4221
Minnesota Continuing Legal Education © 1994 MCLE

STATE OF MINNESOTA

COUNTY OF ____Hennepin_____

Estate of

_____Cheryl Ann Kennedy_____

_____

Decedent

**DISTRICT COURT
PROBATE DIVISION**
____Fourth____   **JUDICIAL DISTRICT**

Court File No. ____198541_____

**NOTICE OF INFORMAL APPOINTMENT OF
PERSONAL REPRESENTATIVE
AND NOTICE TO CREDITORS
(INTESTATE)**

Notice is given that an application for informal appointment of personal representative has been filed with the Registrar. No will has been presented for probate. The application has been granted.

Notice is also given that the Registrar has informally appointed _____
_____Charles Kennedy_____
whose address is

      1010 Willow Street
      Minneapolis, MN 55409

as personal representative of the Estate of the Decedent. Any heir, or other interested person may be entitled to appointment as personal representative or may object to the appointment of the personal representative. Unless objections are filed with the Court (pursuant to Minn. Stat. 524.3-607) and the Court otherwise orders, the personal representative has full power to administer the Estate including, after 30 days from the date of issuance of letters, the power to sell, encumber, lease or distribute real estate.

Any objections to the probate of the will or appointment of the Personal Representative must be filed with this Court and will be heard by the Court after the filing of an appropriate petition and proper notice of hearing.

Notice is also given that (subject to Minn. 524.3-801) all creditors having claims against the Estate are required to present the claims to the personal representative or to the Court Administrator within four months after the date of this Notice or the claims will be barred.

    /S/ Lorina B. Arneson_____

Registrar   September 8, 2000   Date

    /S/ Bradford R. Mitlar_____

Attorney For Personal Representative

Court Administrator   September 8, 2000   Date

THIS INSTRUMENT WAS DRAFTED BY (NAME AND ADDRESS):

Susan G. Brown
1400 Main Street
Minneapolis, MN 55455
Telephone: (612) 773-3777
Attorney License No. 9876543

NOTE: If notice to creditors has been previously given, delete the notice to creditors.
NOTE TO PUBLISHER: Do not publish text of notes.

MD   MCLE P-123

Notice of Informal Appointment of Personal
Representative and Notice to Creditors (Intestate)

Source: This form is property of Miller/Davis Company, St. Paul, MN, Telephone 651-642-1988. Reprinted with permission.

Form 64   Proof of Placing Order for Publication

STATE OF MINNESOTA

COUNTY OF HENNEPIN

PROBATE COURT—UNSUPERVISED

COURT FILE NO. <u>198540</u>

In Re: Estate of

<u>   Cheryl Ann Kennedy   </u>
<u>Deceased</u>

PROOF OF PLACING ORDER

FOR PUBLICATION

TO THE CLERK OF PROBATE COURT:

That is to verify that   <u>Susan G. Brown</u>

<u>   </u> <u>Attorney for</u> , applicant(s)

has ~~have~~ made arrangements for the publication of:

[X]   NOTICE OF INFORMAL APPOINTMENT OF PERSONAL
REPRESENTATIVE(S) AND NOTICE TO CREDITORS

[ ]   NOTICE OF INFORMAL PROBATE OF WILL AND APPOINTMENT OF
PERSONAL REPRESENTATIVE(S) AND NOTICE TO CREDITORS

[ ]

once a week for two consecutive weeks in the   <u>**FINANCE AND COMMERCE**</u>

Daily Newspaper

and this is to confirm that the same will be published accordingly commencing in the next available issue, and that arrangements for payment of the cost of said publication have been made.

Dated: <u>September 8, 2000</u>

<u>/s/ D. C. Morrison</u>

Publisher

Form 65 Affidavit of Mailing Notice of Informal Appointment of Personal Representative

MD Form No. P-015	Minn. Stat. 524.1-401; 525.83	Miller/Davis Co., St. Paul, MN (800) 752-4221 Minnesota Continuing Legal Education © 1994 MCLE

STATE OF MINNESOTA

COUNTY OF _____Hennepin_____

Estate of

_____Cheryl Ann Kennedy_____

Decedent

Probate Court

Court File No. _____198541_____

**AFFIDAVIT OF MAILING
ORDER OR NOTICE**

STATE OF _____Minnesota_____

COUNTY OF _____Hennepin_____ } ss.

I, _____Susan G. Brown_____ ,
being first duly sworn, on oath state that on _____September 8, 2000_____ , at
_____Minneapolis, MN_____ (city, state), I mailed a copy of the
attached Order or Notice to each person or entity named below by mailing a copy in a sealed envelope,
postage prepaid, with the U.S. Postal Service as follows:

Name and Mailing Address	Relationship and Interest (list all)	Birthdate of Minors
Charles Kennedy 1010 Willow Street, Minneapolis, MN 55409	Spouse/heir	
Cherry Kennedy, same address	Daughter/heir	4/24/97
Cindy Kennedy, same address	Daughter/heir	4/24/97
Carl Kennedy, same address	Son/heir	6/15/95
Corey Kennedy, same address	Son/heir	7/05/91
Christopher Kennedy, same address	Son/heir	2/07/90
Catherine Kelly, same address	Mother/heir	
Karen Kelly, same address	Sister/heir	

(Attach separate schedule, if necessary)

/S/ Susan G. Brown

NOTARIAL STAMP OR SEAL (OR OTHER TITLE OR RANK)

Affiant   September 8, 2000   Date

Signed and sworn to (or affirmed) before me on
_____September 8, 2000_____ by
_____Susan G. Brown_____ .

Affiant.

/S/ Astrid M. Martensen

SIGNATURE OF NOTARY PUBLIC OR OTHER OFFICIAL

INSTRUCTIONS: (1) A copy of the Order or Notice must be mailed to each heir, devisee, personal representative, the foreign consul pursuant to Minn. Stat. 524.3-306 and 524.3-403, lawyers representing interested parties pursuant to Minn. Stat. 524.1-401(a), and the Minnesota Attorney General, if a devisee is a charitable organization or if the decedent left no devisee or heirs. In determining the persons or entities entitled to receive this order or notice, see Minn. Stats. 501B.41(5), 524.1-201(19), 524.1-403 and 524.1-404 and Minn. Gen. Rules of Practice 404(b) and 408(d). If the Decedent is survived by a spouse or minor child, also use Notice to Spouse and Children. (2) Attach to this affidavit another copy of the Order or Notice which was sent. (3) It may be necessary to give notice to creditors. See Minn. Stat. 524.3-801(3) and Supplementary Notice to Known and Identified Creditors form.

MD   MCLE P-015

Affidavit of Mailing Order or Notice

Source: This form is property of Miller/Davis Company, St. Paul, MN, Telephone 651–642–1988. Reprinted with permission.

Form 66   Notice to Spouse and Children and Affidavit of Mailing

MD Form No. P-016   Minn. Stat. 524.1-401   Miller/Davis Co., St. Paul, MN (800) 752-4221
Minnesota Continuing Legal Education © 1994 MCLE

STATE OF MINNESOTA

COUNTY OF   Hennepin

Estate of

     Cheryl Ann Kennedy

Decedent

DISTRICT COURT
PROBATE DIVISION
Fourth   **JUDICIAL DISTRICT**

Court File No.   198541

**NOTICE TO SPOUSE AND CHILDREN
AND AFFIDAVIT OF MAILING**

TO: Surviving spouse and children of the Decedent.

This notice is to advise you of your rights regarding the Estate of _____ Cheryl Ann Kennedy _____.
Under Minnesota law you, as surviving spouse or children or the Decedent, may have some or all of the
rights summarized below.

Surviving Spouse:

1. The right to elect a percentage of the "augmented estate" which is provided under Minnesota Statutes §§ 524.2-201 through 524.2-214. This right to elect is personal to the surviving spouse and must be made within 9 months after the date of the Decedent's death; except that for property subject to probate the election may be made within 6 months after the probate of the Decedent's will, even if the 9 month period has already expired.

2. If the Decedent's will was made prior to your marriage to the Decedent, the right to choose the intestate share of the Estate under Minnesota Statutes § 524.2-301. This right has some limitations and exceptions.

3. The right, under Minnesota Statutes § 524.2-402 to the entire homestead if the Decedent did not leave any surviving descendants or the right to a life estate if the Decedent left surviving descendants.

4. The right to allowances under Minnesota Statutes § 524.2-403, which permits the surviving spouse the right to select:

   a. Household furniture, furnishings, appliances, and personal effects not exceeding $10,000, net of security interests, but subject to an award of sentimental value property under Minnesota Statutes § 525.152; provided, however, if the encumbered property and the value in excess of security interests, plus that of other exempt property, is less than $10,000, or if there is not $10,000 worth of exempt property in the Estate, the surviving spouse is entitled to other personal property of the Estate, if any, to the extent necessary to make up the $10,000 value; and

   b. One automobile, if any, without regard to value.

5. The right to a family allowance from the Estate under Minnesota Statutes § 524.2-404 of up to $1,500 per month (or more if authorized by the court) for one year if the estate is insolvent or for 18 months if the Estate is solvent.

Minor Children of Decedent:

6. If the Decedent had an obligation to support you, the right to family allowance from the Estate under Minnesota Statutes § 524.2-404 of up to $1,500 per month (or more if authorized by the court) for one year if the Estate is insolvent or for 18 months if the Estate is solvent.

MD   MCLE P-016   Notice to Spouse and Children and Affidavit of Mailing

(continued)

Form 66   Notice to Spouse and Children and Affidavit of Mailing   *continued*

Court File No.   198541

Adult Children of Decedents

7.   If you were being supported by Decedent, the right to family allowance from the Estate under Minnesota Statutes § 524.2-404 of up to $1,500 (or more if authorized by the court) per month for one year if the Estate is insolvent or for 18 months if the Estate is solvent.

Minor and Adult Children of Decedent:

8.   If there is no surviving spouse, the right to allowances under Minnesota Statutes § 524.2-403:

a.   Household furniture, furnishings, appliances, and personal effects not exceeding $10,000, net of security interests, but subject to an award of sentimental value property under Minnesota Statutes § 525.152; provided, however, if the encumbered property and the value in excess of security interests, plus that of other exempt property, is less than $10,000, or if there is not $10,000 worth of exempt property in the Estate, the children are entitled to other personal property of the Estate, if any, to the extent necessary to make up the $10,000 value; and

a.   One automobile, if any, without regard to value.

If you have any questions regarding interpretation of these statutes or the effect of these or other rights, please consult with an attorney of your own choice or the attorney for the Personal Representative. Copies of the statutes can be obtained at the local county law library or from the Personal Representative.

/S/ Charles Kennedy

September 8, 2000

Personal Representative   **Date**

Attorney For Personal Representative

THIS INSTRUMENT WAS DRAFTED BY (NAME AND ADDRESS):

Susan G. Brown
1400 Main Street
Minneapolis, MN 55455
Telephone: (612) 773-3777
Attorney License No. 9876543

MD   MCLE P-016/Page 2   Notice to Spouse and Children and Affidavit of Mailing

(*continued*)

Form 66   Notice to Spouse and Children and Affidavit of Mailing   *continued*

Court File No. ___198541___

STATE OF <u>MINNESOTA</u> _____ } ss.

COUNTY OF ___Hennepin___

I, _____ Susan G. Brown _____,

being first duly sworn, on oath state that on ____ September 8, 2000 ____, at

_____ Minneapolis, MN _____ (city, state), I mailed a copy of the attached Notice to each person or entity named below by mailing a copy in a sealed envelope, postage prepaid, with the U.S. Postal Service as follows:

Name and Mailing Address	Relationship and Interest (list all)	Birthdate of Minors
Charles Kennedy 1010 Willow Street, Minneapolis, MN 55409	Spouse/heir	
Cherry Kennedy, same address	Daughter/heir	4/24/97
Cindy Kennedy, same address	Daughter/heir	4/24/97
Carl Kennedy, same address	Son/heir	6/15/95
Corey Kennedy, same address	Son/heir	7/05/91
Christopher Kennedy, same address	Son/heir	2/07/90

(Attach separate schedule, if necessary)

___/S/ Susan G. Brown_____

Affiant   September 8, 2000   Date

NOTARIAL STAMP OR SEAL (OR OTHER TITLE OR RANK)

Signed and sworn to (or affirmed) before me on
___September 8, 2000___ by
___Susan G. Brown___.
Affiant.

___/S/ Astrid M. Martensen___
SIGNATURE OF NOTARY PUBLIC OR OTHER OFFICIAL

Source: This form is property of Miller/Davis Company, St. Paul, MN, Telephone 651–642–1988. Reprinted with permission.

Form 67 Acceptance of Appointment as Personal Representative and Oath by Individual

MD Form No. P-001   Minn. Stat. 524.3-601   Miller/Davis Co., St. Paul, MN (800) 752-4221
Minnesota Continuing Legal Education © 1994 MCLE

STATE OF MINNESOTA

COUNTY OF   Hennepin

DISTRICT COURT
PROBATE DIVISION
Fourth JUDICIAL DISTRICT

Court File No.   198541

Estate of

_____ Cheryl Ann Kennedy _____

Decedent

**ACCEPTANCE OF APPOINTMENT
AS PERSONAL REPRESENTATIVE
AND OATH BY INDIVIDUAL**

STATE OF MINNESOTA

COUNTY OF   Hennepin   } ss

I,   Charles Kennedy ,
residing at,   1010 Willow Street
Minneapolis, MN 55409

as a condition to receiving letters as Personal Representative in this Estate, (1) accept the duties of the office, (2) agree to be bound by the provisions of the statutes relating to the office, (3) submit to the jurisdiction of the Court in any proceeding relating to this Estate, and (4) swear that I will faithfully perform all duties of the office that I now assume to the best of my ability.

_____ /S/ Charles Kennedy _____

Signature   September 8, 2000   Date

Signed and sworn to (or affirmed) before me on
September 8, 2000   by
Charles Kennedy .
Personal Representative

NOTARIAL STAMP OR SEAL (OR OTHER TITLE OR RANK)

/S/ Mariana S. Halsted
SIGNATURE OF NOTARY PUBLIC OR OTHER OFFICIAL

Attorney For Personal Representative

THIS INSTRUMENT WAS DRAFTED BY (NAME AND ADDRESS):

Susan G. Brown
1400 Main Street
Minneapolis, MN 55455
Telephone: (612) 773-3777
Attorney License No. 9876543

MD   MCLE P-001

Acceptance of Appointment as
Personal Representative and Oath by Individual

Source: This form is property of Miller/Davis Company, St. Paul, MN, Telephone 651–642–1988. Reprinted with permission.

Form 68 Bond

MD Form No. P-072   Minn. Stat. 524.3-604; 524.3-606   Miller/Davis Co., St. Paul, MN (800) 752-4221
Minnesota Continuing Legal Education © 1994 MCLE

STATE OF MINNESOTA

COUNTY OF ___Hennepin_____   ___Fourth___

DISTRICT COURT
PROBATE DIVISION
JUDICIAL DISTRICT

Court File No. ___198541_____

Estate of

_____Cheryl Ann Kennedy_____

BOND OF PERSONAL REPRESENTATIVE
CORPORATE SURETY

_____
Decedent

We,_____Charles Kennedy_____ ,
residing at_____1010 Willow Street, Minneapolis, MN 55409_____
_____, Principal,
and _____Midwest Surety Company_____, Surety,
a corporation of the State of _____Minnesota_____ whose address is _____
_____735 Marquette Avenue, Minneapolis, MN 55402_____ ,
and is duly authorized to act as Surety in the State of Minnesota, are bound to the State of Minnesota as obligee for the benefit of the interested persons in this Estate as the Court determines in the sum of ___Ten Thousand and 00/100--------------------------Dollars ($ ___10,000._____),
for which payment we now bind ourselves, and each of our heirs, personal representatives, successors and assigns, jointly and severally, by this bond.

If the Principal faithfully discharges all the duties of personal representative of the Estate according to law, then this bond shall be void; otherwise it shall remain in full force and effect.

_____/S/ Charles Kennedy_____

Principal   September 8, 2000   Date

_____Midwest Surety Company_____

(CORPORATE SEAL)

Surety   September 8, 2000   Date

_____/S/ Ira G. Benson_____

                 September 8, 2000
Attorney-in-Fact for Surety,   Date
(Power of Attorney attached)

MD   MCLE P-072

Bond of Personal Representative
Corporate Surety

(continued)

Form 68 Bond *continued*

Court File No. ____198541____

STATE OF __MINNESOTA__

COUNTY OF ____Hennepin____ } ss **ACKNOWLEDGMENT OF PRINCIPAL**

This instrument was acknowledged before me on ____September 8, 2000____ , by
____Charles Kennedy, Personal Representative____ ,
the Principal.

NOTARIAL STAMP OR SEAL (OR OTHER TITLE OR RANK)	/S/ Mariana S. Halsted
	SIGNATURE OF NOTARY PUBLIC OR OTHER OFFICIAL

STATE OF __MINNESOTA__

COUNTY OF ____Hennepin____ } ss **ACKNOWLEDGMENT OF SURETY**

This instrument was acknowledged before me on ____September 8, 2000____ , by
____Ira G. Benson____ as ____Attorney-in-Fact____
of ____Midwest Surety Company____ ,
the Surety.

NOTARIAL STAMP OR SEAL (OR OTHER TITLE OR RANK)	/S/ Mariana S. Halsted
	SIGNATURE OF NOTARY PUBLIC OR OTHER OFFICIAL

APPROVAL OF BOND

I approve the Bond.

/S/ Lorina B. Arneson

~~Judge~~/Registrar September 8, 2000 Date

Bond of Personal Representative
Corporate Surety

MD MCLE P-072/Page 2

Source: This form is property of Miller/Davis Company, St. Paul, MN, Telephone 651–642–1988. Reprinted with permission.

Form 69 Letters of General Administration

MD Form No. P-010   Minn. Stat. 524.3-601   Miller/Davis Co., St. Paul, MN (800) 752-4221
                                                              Minnesota Continuing Legal Education © 1994 MCLE

STATE OF MINNESOTA   **DISTRICT COURT**
                                                              PROBATE DIVISION
COUNTY OF   Hennepin   _Fourth_   **JUDICIAL DISTRICT**

                                         Court File No.   198541

Estate of
                                         LETTERS
_____Cheryl Ann Kennedy_____   ☐ **TESTAMENTARY**
                                         ☒ **OF GENERAL ADMINISTRATION**
            Decedent

1. The Decedent died on _Aug. 1, 2000_ .

2. _____Charles Kennedy_____ has
   been appointed Personal Representative of Decedent's Estate in

   ☒ an unsupervised
   ☐ a supervised administration

   and is now qualified to act as Personal Representative of the Estate and has authority to administer the
   Estate according to law.

                                    ___/S/ Lorina B. Arneson_____

                                    ~~Judge~~Registrar   September 8, 2000   Date

        (COURT SEAL)

MD   MCLE P-010   Letters
                                                     ☐ Testamentary ☐ of General Administration

Source: This form is property of Miller/Davis Company, St. Paul, MN, Telephone 651–642–1988. Reprinted with permission.

Form 70   Deed of Distribution by Personal Representative

MD 107-M Deed of Distribution: Personal Representative(s)   Minnesota Uniform Conveyancing Blanks (8/24/95)   Miller-Davis Co., St. Paul, MN

Individual Personal Representative(s)

Note: This deed should be used only for distribution

No delinquent taxes and transfer entered; Certificate
of Real Estate Value (   ) filed (   ) not required
Certificate of Real Estate Value No. _____

_____ , _____
                                    (Year)

_____
                    County Auditor

by _____
                                    Deputy

(reserved for recording data)

Date: ___January 8, 2001_____

NO DEED TAX DUE

___Charles Kennedy_____ ,
as Personal Representative(s) of the Estate of ___Cheryl Ann Kennedy_____ , Decedent,
Grantor, conveys to
___Charles Kennedy for Christopher Kennedy, a minor_____ , Grantee,
real property in ____Hennepin_____ County, Minnesota, described as follows:

Lot 3, Block 1, Loring Park Addition to Minneapolis (Plat #17068 Parcel #3196):
   To Charles Kennedy for Christopher Kennedy, a minor, son of the decedent,
   an undivided one-fifth (1/5) of said homestead real estate, subject to the
   life estate of Charles Kennedy.

together with all hereditaments and appurtenances belonging thereto.

PERSONAL REPRESENTATIVE(S)

/S/ Charles Kennedy
_____

_____

STATE OF MINNESOTA

COUNTY OF Hennepin   } *ss.* Check here if part or all of the land is Registered (Torrens) ☐

This instrument was acknowledged before me on ___January 8, 2001_____
                                                                              (Date)
by _____Charles Kennedy_____
_____ , as Personal Representative(s)
of the Estate of ___Cheryl Ann Kennedy_____ , Decedent.

NOTARIAL STAMP OR SEAL (OR OTHER TITLE OR RANK):

/S/ Mariana S. Halsted
_____
SIGNATURE OF NOTARY PUBLIC OR OTHER OFFICIAL

Tax Statements for the real property described in this instrument should
be sent to (include name and address of Grantee):

Charles Kennedy
1010 Willow Street
Minneapolis, MN 55409

THIS INSTRUMENT WAS DRAFTED BY (NAME AND ADDRESS):

Susan G. Brown
1400 Main Street
Minneapolis, MN 55455
Telephone: (612) 773-3777
Attorney License No. 9876543

Source: This form is property of Miller/Davis Company, St. Paul, MN, Telephone 651–642–1988. Reprinted with permission.

Form 71   Receipt for Assets by Distributee

MD Form No. P-615 | Minn. Stat. 524.3-1001(4); 524.3-1003(2) | Miller/Davis Co., St. Paul, MN (800) 752-4221
Minnesota Continuing Legal Education © 1994 MCLE

STATE OF MINNESOTA

COUNTY OF ___Hennepin___

Estate of

___Cheryl Ann Kennedy___

_____
Decedent

DISTRICT COURT
PROBATE DIVISION
___Fourth___   **JUDICIAL DISTRICT**

Court File No. ___198541___

RECEIPT FOR ASSETS BY DISTRIBUTEE

I, _____ Charles Kennedy, for Christopher Kennedy, a minor _____
the undersigned distributee, acknowledge receipt from the Personal Representative of this Estate, of the following assets in [x] full [ ] partial satisfaction of my distributive share:

Lot 3, Block 1, Loring Park Addition to Minneapolis (Plat #17068 Parcel #3196): an undivided one-fifth (1/5) of said homestead real estate, subject to the life estate of Charles Kennedy.

___/S/ Charles Kennedy for Christopher___
Kennedy (a minor)

Distributee   January 8, 2001   Date

MD   MCLE P-615   Receipt for Assets by Distributee

Source: This form is property of Miller/Davis Company, St. Paul, MN, Telephone 651–642–1988. Reprinted with permission.

Form 72   Application for Certificate from Registrar—Release of Bond

MD Form No. P-684 | Minn. Stat. 524.3-1007 | Miller/Davis Co., St. Paul, MN (800) 752-4221
Minnesota Continuing Legal Education © 1994 MCLE

STATE OF MINNESOTA

COUNTY OF   Hennepin

Estate of

_____ Cheryl Ann Kennedy _____

Decedent

DISTRICT COURT
PROBATE DIVISION
Fourth   **JUDICIAL DISTRICT**

Court File No. ___198541___

**APPLICATION FOR CERTIFICATE
FROM REGISTRAR**

I, _____ Charles Kennedy _____ , state:

1. My address is:

   1010 Willow Street
   Minneapolis, MN 55409

2. I am [x] the Personal Representative of this Estate.
   [ ] a surety of the Personal Representative.
   [ ] a successor Personal Representative.
   [ ] a successor to the surety.

3. _____ Charles Kennedy _____
   was the duly appointed Personal Representative of the Estate of Decedent.

4. The appointment of the Personal Representative has terminated.

5. I do not know of any action concerning the Estate of Decedent which may be pending in any court.

   WHEREFORE, I request a certificate from the Registrar stating that the Personal Representative appears to have fully administered the Estate of Decedent as evidence to discharge any lien on any property given to secure the obligation of the Personal Representative in lieu of bond or any surety.

   Under penalties for perjury, I declare or affirm that I have read this document and I know or believe its representations are true and complete.

_____ /S/ Charles Kennedy _____

Applicant   March 8, 2001   Date

Attorney For Applicant

THIS INSTRUMENT WAS DRAFTED BY (NAME AND ADDRESS):

Susan G. Brown
1400 Main Street
Minneapolis, MN 55455
Telephone: (612) 773-3777
Attorney License No. 9876543

MD   MCLE P-684

Application for Certificate from Registrar

Source: This form is property of Miller/Davis Company, St. Paul, MN, Telephone 651–642–1988. Reprinted with permission.

Form 73 Certificate of Registrar—Release of Bond

MD Form No. P-686   Minn. Stat. 524.3-1007   Miller/Davis Co., St. Paul, MN (800) 752-4221
Minnesota Continuing Legal Education © 1994 MCLE

STATE OF MINNESOTA   **DISTRICT COURT**
                                                          PROBATE DIVISION
COUNTY OF ___Hennepin___   ___Fourth___   **JUDICIAL DISTRICT**

                                                          Court File No. ___198541___

Estate of

_____Cheryl Ann Kennedy_____   **CERTIFICATE OF REGISTRAR**
_____
                    Decedent

The Application for the Certificate from the Registrar, signed by _____
_____Charles Kennedy_____

came before the Registrar on ___March 8, 2001___ . The Registrar, having considered
the Application, determines the following:

1. The Application is complete.

2. On the basis of the statements in the Application and from the records on file in the Estate, the
    Application is proper.

    The Registrar now certifies that _____
    _____Charles Kennedy_____
Personal Representative of the Estate of Decedent, appears to have fully administered this Estate.

                              ___/S/ Lorina B. Arneson_____

                    Registrar   March 10, 2001   Date

NOTE: This Certificate evidences discharge of any lien on any property given to secure the obligation of the
       Personal Representative in lieu of bond or any surety, but does not preclude action against the
       Personal Representative or the surety.

MD   MCLE P-686   Certificate of Registrar

Source: This form is property of Miller/Davis Company, St. Paul, MN, Telephone 651–642–1988. Reprinted with permission.

Form 74   U.S. Individual Income Tax Return (Form 1040)

Form 1040

Department of the Treasury—Internal Revenue Service
U.S. Individual Income Tax Return **2000** (99) IRS Use Only—Do not write or staple in this space.

For the year Jan. 1–Dec. 31, 2000, or other tax year beginning , 2000, ending , 20 | OMB No. 1545-0074

Label (See instructions on page 19.)

Use the IRS label. Otherwise, please print or type.

Your first name and initial | Last name | Your social security number

If a joint return, spouse's first name and initial | Last name | Spouse's social security number

Home address (number and street). If you have a P.O. box, see page 19. | Apt. no.

City, town or post office, state, and ZIP code. If you have a foreign address, see page 19.

▲ **Important!** ▲
You **must** enter your SSN(s) above.

Presidential Election Campaign (See page 19.)

Note. Checking "Yes" will not change your tax or reduce your refund.
Do you, or your spouse if filing a joint return, want $3 to go to this fund? . . . ▶

You   Spouse
☐ Yes ☐ No ☐ Yes ☐ No

Filing Status

Check only one box.

1 ☐ Single
2 ☐ Married filing joint return (even if only one had income)
3 ☐ Married filing separate return. Enter spouse's social security no. above and full name here. ▶
4 ☐ Head of household (with qualifying person). (See page 19.) If the qualifying person is a child but not your dependent, enter this child's name here. ▶
5 ☐ Qualifying widow(er) with dependent child (year spouse died ▶). (See page 19.)

Exemptions

6a ☐ **Yourself.** If your parent (or someone else) can claim you as a dependent on his or her tax return, **do not** check box 6a . . . .
b ☐ **Spouse** . . . .

No. of boxes checked on 6a and 6b

c **Dependents:**

(1) First name Last name	(2) Dependent's social security number	(3) Dependent's relationship to you	(4) ✔ if qualifying child for child tax credit (see page 20)
			☐
			☐
			☐
			☐
			☐
			☐

If more than six dependents, see page 20.

No. of your children on 6c who:
• lived with you
• did not live with you due to divorce or separation (see page 20)
Dependents on 6c not entered above
Add numbers entered on lines above ▶

d Total number of exemptions claimed . . . .

Income

Attach Forms W-2 and W-2G here. Also attach Form(s) 1099-R if tax was withheld.

If you did not get a W-2, see page 21.

Enclose, but do not attach, any payment. Also, please use Form 1040-V.

7 Wages, salaries, tips, etc. Attach Form(s) W-2 . . . . | 7
8a **Taxable** interest. Attach Schedule B if required . . . . | 8a
b **Tax-exempt** interest. **Do not** include on line 8a . . . | 8b |
9 Ordinary dividends. Attach Schedule B if required . . . . | 9
10 Taxable refunds, credits, or offsets of state and local income taxes (see page 22) . . | 10
11 Alimony received . . . . | 11
12 Business income or (loss). Attach Schedule C or C-EZ . . . . | 12
13 Capital gain or (loss). Attach Schedule D if required. If not required, check here ▶ ☐ | 13
14 Other gains or (losses). Attach Form 4797 . . . . | 14
15a Total IRA distributions . | 15a | b Taxable amount (see page 23) | 15b
16a Total pensions and annuities | 16a | b Taxable amount (see page 23) | 16b
17 Rental real estate, royalties, partnerships, S corporations, trusts, etc. Attach Schedule E | 17
18 Farm income or (loss). Attach Schedule F . . . . | 18
19 Unemployment compensation . . . . | 19
20a Social security benefits . | 20a | b Taxable amount (see page 25) | 20b
21 Other income. List type and amount (see page 25) | 21
22 Add the amounts in the far right column for lines 7 through 21. This is your **total income** ▶ | 22

Adjusted Gross Income

23 IRA deduction (see page 27) . . . . | 23
24 Student loan interest deduction (see page 27) . . . . | 24
25 Medical savings account deduction. Attach Form 8853 . | 25
26 Moving expenses. Attach Form 3903 . . . . . . | 26
27 One-half of self-employment tax. Attach Schedule SE . | 27
28 Self-employed health insurance deduction (see page 29) | 28
29 Self-employed SEP, SIMPLE, and qualified plans . . | 29
30 Penalty on early withdrawal of savings . . . . . | 30
31a Alimony paid   b Recipient's SSN ▶ | 31a |
32 Add lines 23 through 31a . . . . | 32
33 Subtract line 32 from line 22. This is your **adjusted gross income** . . . . . . ▶ | 33

For Disclosure, Privacy Act, and Paperwork Reduction Act Notice, see page 56.   Cat. No. 11320B   Form **1040** (2000)

(continued)

Form 74 U.S. Individual Income Tax Return (Form 1040) *continued*

Form 1040 (2000)   Page **2**

Tax and Credits	34	Amount from line 33 (adjusted gross income)	34	
	35a	Check if: ☐ **You** were 65 or older, ☐ Blind; ☐ **Spouse** was 65 or older, ☐ Blind. Add the number of boxes checked above and enter the total here . . . . ▶ **35a**		
	b	If you are married filing separately and your spouse itemizes deductions, or you were a dual-status alien, see page 31 and check here . . . . . . ▶ **35b** ☐		
Standard Deduction for Most People	36	Enter your **itemized deductions** from Schedule A, line 28, **or standard deduction** shown on the left. **But** see page 31 to find your standard deduction if you checked any box on line 35a or 35b **or** if someone can claim you as a dependent	36	
Single: $4,400	37	Subtract line 36 from line 34	37	
Head of household: $6,450	38	If line 34 is $96,700 or less, multiply $2,800 by the total number of exemptions claimed on line 6d. If line 34 is over $96,700, see the worksheet on page 32 for the amount to enter .	38	
Married filing jointly or Qualifying widow(er): $7,350	39	**Taxable income.** Subtract line 38 from line 37. If line 38 is more than line 37, enter -0-	39	
	40	**Tax** (see page 32). Check if any tax is from **a** ☐ Form(s) 8814 **b** ☐ Form 4972 . . .	40	
	41	Alternative minimum tax. Attach Form 6251	41	
Married filing separately: $3,675	42	Add lines 40 and 41 . . . . ▶	42	
	43	Foreign tax credit. Attach Form 1116 if required	43	
	44	Credit for child and dependent care expenses. Attach Form 2441	44	
	45	Credit for the elderly or the disabled. Attach Schedule R . .	45	
	46	Education credits. Attach Form 8863	46	
	47	Child tax credit (see page 36)	47	
	48	Adoption credit. Attach Form 8839	48	
	49	Other. Check if from **a** ☐ Form 3800 **b** ☐ Form 8396 **c** ☐ Form 8801 **d** ☐ Form (specify)	49	
	50	Add lines 43 through 49. These are your **total credits**	50	
	51	Subtract line 50 from line 42. If line 50 is more than line 42, enter -0- . . . . . ▶	51	
Other Taxes	52	Self-employment tax. Attach Schedule SE	52	
	53	Social security and Medicare tax on tip income not reported to employer. Attach Form 4137	53	
	54	Tax on IRAs, other retirement plans, and MSAs. Attach Form 5329 if required	54	
	55	Advance earned income credit payments from Form(s) W-2	55	
	56	Household employment taxes. Attach Schedule H	56	
	57	Add lines 51 through 56. This is your **total tax** . . . . ▶	57	
Payments	58	Federal income tax withheld from Forms W-2 and 1099 . .	58	
	59	2000 estimated tax payments and amount applied from 1999 return	59	
If you have a qualifying child, attach Schedule EIC.	60a	**Earned income credit (EIC)**	60a	
	b	Nontaxable earned income: amount . . ▶ and type ▶		
	61	Excess social security and RRTA tax withheld (see page 50)	61	
	62	Additional child tax credit. Attach Form 8812	62	
	63	Amount paid with request for extension to file (see page 50)	63	
	64	Other payments. Check if from **a** ☐ Form 2439 **b** ☐ Form 4136	64	
	65	Add lines 58, 59, 60a, and 61 through 64. These are your **total payments** . . . . ▶	65	
Refund Have it directly deposited! See page 50 and fill in 67b, 67c, and 67d.	66	If line 65 is more than line 57, subtract line 57 from line 65. This is the amount you **overpaid**	66	
	67a	Amount of line 66 you want **refunded to you** . . . . ▶	67a	
	▶ b	Routing number		
		▶ c Type: ☐ Checking ☐ Savings		
	▶ d	Account number		
	68	Amount of line 66 you want **applied to your 2001 estimated tax** . ▶	68	
Amount You Owe	69	If line 57 is more than line 65, subtract line 65 from line 57. This is the **amount you owe.** For details on how to pay, see page 51 . . . . ▶	69	
	70	Estimated tax penalty. Also include on line 69	70	

Sign Here
Joint return? See page 19.
Keep a copy for your records.

Under penalties of perjury, I declare that I have examined this return and accompanying schedules and statements, and to the best of my knowledge and belief, they are true, correct, and complete. Declaration of preparer (other than taxpayer) is based on all information of which preparer has any knowledge.

Your signature	Date	Your occupation	Daytime phone number ( )
Spouse's signature. If a joint return, **both** must sign.	Date	Spouse's occupation	May the IRS discuss this return with the preparer shown below (see page 52)? ☐ **Yes** ☐ **No**

Paid Preparer's Use Only

Preparer's signature		Date	Check if self-employed ☐	Preparer's SSN or PTIN
Firm's name (or yours if self-employed), address, and ZIP code			EIN	
			Phone no. ( )	

Form **1040** (2000)

Form 75 Statement of Person Claiming Refund Due a Deceased Taxpayer (Form 1310)

Form **1310**

(Rev. March 1995)
Department of the Treasury
Internal Revenue Service

Statement of Person Claiming
Refund Due a Deceased Taxpayer

▶ See instructions below and on back.

OMB No. 1545-0073

Attachment
Sequence No. **87**

Tax year decedent was due a refund:

Calendar year _____ , or other tax year beginning _____ , 19 ___ , and ending _____ , 19 ___

Please type or print

Name of decedent	Date of death	Decedent's social security number

Name of person claiming refund

Home address (number and street). If you have a P.O. box, see instructions.	Apt. no.

City, town or post office, state, and ZIP code. If you have a foreign address, see instructions.

Part I Check the box that applies to you. Check only one box. **Be sure to complete Part III below.**

A ☐ Surviving spouse requesting reissuance of a refund check. See instructions.

B ☐ Court-appointed or certified personal representative. You may have to attach a court certificate showing your appointment. See instructions.

C ☐ Person, **other** than A or B, claiming refund for the decedent's estate. Also, complete Part II. You may have to attach a copy of the proof of death. See instructions.

Part II Complete this part only if you checked the box on line C above.

		Yes	No
1	Did the decedent leave a will?		
2a	Has a court appointed a personal representative for the estate of the decedent?		
b	If you answered **"No"** to 2a, will one be appointed?		
	If you answered **"Yes"** to 2a or 2b, the personal representative must file for the refund.		
3	As the person claiming the refund for the decedent's estate, will you pay out the refund according to the laws of the state where the decedent was a legal resident?		
	If you answered **"No"** to 3, a refund cannot be made until you submit a court certificate showing your appointment as personal representative or other evidence that you are entitled under state law to receive the refund.		

Part III Signature and verification. All filers must complete this part.

I request a refund of taxes overpaid by or on behalf of the decedent. Under penalties of perjury, I declare that I have examined this claim, and to the best of my knowledge and belief, it is true, correct, and complete.

Signature of person claiming refund ▶ _____ Date ▶ _____

Paperwork Reduction Act Notice

We ask for the information on this form to carry out the Internal Revenue laws of the United States. You are required to give us the information. We need it to ensure that you are complying with these laws and to allow us to figure and collect the right amount of tax.

The time needed to complete and file this form will vary depending on individual circumstances. The estimated average time is:

Recordkeeping . . . . 7 min.

**Learning about the
law or the form** . . . . 3 min.

Preparing the form . . . . 16 min.

**Copying, assembling,
and sending the
form to the IRS** . . . . 17 min.

If you have comments concerning the accuracy of these time estimates or suggestions for making this form simpler, we would be happy to hear from you. You can write to the **Internal Revenue Service,** Attention: Tax Forms Committee, PC:FP, Washington, DC 20224. **DO NOT** send the form to this address.

General Instructions

Purpose of Form

Use Form 1310 to claim a refund on behalf of a deceased taxpayer.

Who Must File

If you are claiming a refund on behalf of a deceased taxpayer, you must file Form 1310 unless **either** of the following applies:

● You are a surviving spouse filing an original or amended joint return with the decedent, OR

● You are a personal representative (see back of form) filing an original Form 1040, Form 1040A, Form 1040EZ, or Form 1040NR for the decedent and a court certificate showing your appointment is attached to the return.

Example. Assume Mr. Green died on January 4 before filing his tax return. On April 3 of the same year, you were appointed by the court as the personal representative for Mr. Green's estate and you file Form 1040 for Mr. Green. You do not need to file Form 1310 to claim the refund on Mr. Green's tax return. However, you must attach to his return a copy of the court certificate showing your appointment.

Cat. No. 11566B

Form **1310** (Rev. 3-95)

Form 76   Schedule A—Itemized Deductions (Form 1040)

SCHEDULES A&B
(Form 1040)

Department of the Treasury
Internal Revenue Service   (99)

Name(s) shown on Form 1040

Schedule A—Itemized Deductions

(Schedule B is on back)

▶ **Attach to Form 1040.** ▶ **See Instructions for Schedules A and B (Form 1040).**

OMB No. 1545-0074

2000

Attachment
Sequence No. **07**

Your social security number

Medical and Dental Expenses	**Caution.** Do not include expenses reimbursed or paid by others.	
	1 Medical and dental expenses (see page A-2)	1
	2 Enter amount from Form 1040, line 34. **2**	
	3 Multiply line 2 above by 7.5% (.075)	3
	4 Subtract line 3 from line 1. If line 3 is more than line 1, enter -0-	4
Taxes You Paid (See page A-2.)	5 State and local income taxes	5
	6 Real estate taxes (see page A-2)	6
	7 Personal property taxes	7
	8 Other taxes. List type and amount ▶ _____	8
	9 Add lines 5 through 8	9
Interest You Paid (See page A-3.)	10 Home mortgage interest and points reported to you on Form 1098	10
	11 Home mortgage interest not reported to you on Form 1098. If paid to the person from whom you bought the home, see page A-3 and show that person's name, identifying no., and address ▶	
Note. Personal interest is not deductible.		11
	12 Points not reported to you on Form 1098. See page A-3 for special rules	12
	13 Investment interest. Attach Form 4952 if required. (See page A-3.)	13
	14 Add lines 10 through 13	14
Gifts to Charity If you made a gift and got a benefit for it, see page A-4.	15 Gifts by cash or check. If you made any gift of $250 or more, see page A-4	15
	16 Other than by cash or check. If any gift of $250 or more, see page A-4. You **must** attach Form 8283 if over $500	16
	17 Carryover from prior year	17
	18 Add lines 15 through 17	18
Casualty and Theft Losses	19 Casualty or theft loss(es). Attach Form 4684. (See page A-5.)	19
Job Expenses and Most Other Miscellaneous Deductions (See page A-5 for expenses to deduct here.)	20 Unreimbursed employee expenses—job travel, union dues, job education, etc. You **must** attach Form 2106 or 2106-EZ if required. (See page A-5.) ▶ _____	20
	21 Tax preparation fees	21
	22 Other expenses—investment, safe deposit box, etc. List type and amount ▶ _____	22
	23 Add lines 20 through 22	23
	24 Enter amount from Form 1040, line 34. **24**	
	25 Multiply line 24 above by 2% (.02)	25
	26 Subtract line 25 from line 23. If line 25 is more than line 23, enter -0-	26
Other Miscellaneous Deductions	27 Other—from list on page A-6. List type and amount ▶ _____	27
Total Itemized Deductions	28 Is Form 1040, line 34, over $128,950 (over $64,475 if married filing separately)?	
	☐ **No.** Your deduction is not limited. Add the amounts in the far right column for lines 4 through 27. Also, enter this amount on Form 1040, line 36. ▶	28
	☐ **Yes.** Your deduction may be limited. See page A-6 for the amount to enter.	

For Paperwork Reduction Act Notice, see Form 1040 instructions.   Cat. No. 11330X   **Schedule A (Form 1040) 2000**

Form 77 Application for Automatic Extension of Time to File U.S. Individual Income Tax Return (Form 4868)

Form **4868**
Department of the Treasury
Internal Revenue Service (99)

Application for Automatic Extension of Time To File U.S. Individual Income Tax Return

OMB No. 1545-0188

2000

 It's Convenient, Safe, and Secure

IRS e-file is the IRS's electronic filing program. Now you can get an automatic extension of time to file your tax return by filing Form 4868 electronically by April 16, 2001. You will receive an electronic acknowledgment or confirmation number once you complete the transaction. Keep it with your records. **Do not** send in Form 4868 if you file electronically.

If you think you may owe tax and wish to make a payment, you may pay by direct debit using option 1 or 2 below or you may pay by credit card using option 3.

First, complete Form 4868 to use as a worksheet; then, take advantage of one of the three IRS e-file options listed below.

1 **E-file by Phone—April 1–16**

Call **1-888-796-1074** toll free. Be sure to have a copy of last year's tax return — you will be asked to provide two pieces of information from the return for taxpayer verification. If you wish to make a payment, you can pay by direct debit (see page 4) or send your check to the address shown on page 4.

2 **E-file Using Your Personal Computer or Through a Tax Professional**

Refer to your tax software package or tax preparer for ways to file electronically. Be sure to have a copy of last year's tax return — you will be asked to provide two pieces of information from the return for taxpayer verification. If you wish to make a payment, you can pay by direct debit (see page 4) or send your check to the address shown on page 4.

3 **E-file and Pay by Credit Card**

You can get an extension if you pay part or all of your estimate of income tax due by using a credit card (American Express® Card, Discover® Card or MasterCard® card). Your payment must be at least $1. You may pay by phone or over the Internet through one of the service providers listed below.

Each service provider will charge a convenience fee based on the amount of the tax payment you are making. Fees may vary between service providers. You will be told what the fee is during the transaction and will have the option to continue or cancel the transaction. You may also obtain the convenience fee by calling the service providers' automated customer service numbers or visiting their Web Sites. All calls are toll free. Do not add the convenience fee to your tax payment.

Official Payments Corporation

1-800-2PAY-TAX
(1-800-272-9829)
1-877-754-4413 (Customer Service)
www.officialpayments.com

PhoneCharge, Inc.

1-888-ALLTAXX
(1-888-255-8299)
1-877-851-9964 (Customer Service)
www.About1888ALLTAXX.com

Form 709 or 709-A. Although an extension of time to file your income tax return also extends the time to file Form 709 or 709-A, you cannot make payments of the gift or GST tax with a credit card. To make a payment of the gift or GST tax, send a check or money order to the service center where the donor's income tax return will be filed. Enter "2000 Form 709" and the donor's name and social security number on the payment.

 File a Paper Form 4868

If you wish to file on paper instead of electronically, fill in the Form 4868 below and mail it to the address shown on page 4.

▼ DETACH HERE ▼

Form **4868**
Department of the Treasury
Internal Revenue Service (99)

Application for Automatic Extension of Time To File U.S. Individual Income Tax Return

For calendar year 2000, or other tax year beginning , 2000, ending ,

OMB No. 1545-0188

2000

Part I Identification		**Part III** Individual Income Tax	
1 Your name(s) (see instructions)		**4** Total tax liability on your income tax return for 2000 $	
Address (see instructions)		**5** Total 2000 payments	
		6 **Balance.** Subtract 5 from 4	

City, town or post office, state, and ZIP code

Part IV **Gift/GST Tax**—If you are **not filing** a gift or GST tax return, go to Part V now. See the instructions.

2 Your social security number	**3** Spouse's social security number

7 Your gift or GST tax payment . $

8 **Your spouse's** gift/GST tax payment

Part II **Complete ONLY If Filing Gift/GST Tax Return**

Caution: Only for gift/GST extension! Checking box(es) may result in correspondence if Form 709 or 709-A is not filed.

This form also extends the time for filing a gift or generation-skipping transfer (GST) tax return if you file a calendar (not fiscal) year income tax return. Enter your gift or GST tax payment(s) in Part IV and:

Check this box ► ☐ if **you** are requesting a **Gift or GST tax** return extension.

Check this box ► ☐ if **your spouse** is requesting a **Gift or GST tax** return extension.

Part V **Total**

9 **Total liability.** Add lines 6, 7, and 8 $

10 Amount you are paying. . . . . ►

Confirmation Number

If you file electronically, you will receive a confirmation number telling you that your Form 4868 has been accepted. Enter the confirmation number here and keep it for your records . . . . . ►

For Privacy Act and Paperwork Reduction Act Notice, see page 4.

Cat. No. 13141W

Form **4868** (2000)

Form 78 State (Minnesota as Example) Individual Income Tax Return

MINNESOTA Department of Revenue   Dept

Individual Income Tax 2000   M-1

Use label or print

Your first name and initial | Last name | Social Security number | Your date of birth *(mm/dd/yyyy)*

If a joint return, spouse's first name and initial | Last name | Social Security number | Spouse's date of birth *(mm/dd/yyyy)*

Present home address (street, apartment number, route)

City or town | State | Zip code

State Elections Campaign Fund
If you want $5 to go to help candidates for state offices pay campaign expenses, see the instructions on back of this form. Fill in the code number for the party of your choice:

Code number
You:
Spouse:

Check your 2000 federal filing status *(check only one box)*:

☐ Single ☐ Married filing joint ☐ Married filing separate ☐ Head of household ☐ Qualifying widow(er)

If filing separately, enter your spouse's Social Security number _____ and name _____

Minnesota income

1 **Federal taxable income** *(from line 39 of your federal Form 1040, line 25 of Form 1040A, line 6 of Form 1040EZ, or line K of telefile tax record)* 1

2 **State income tax addition.** If you itemized deductions on federal Form 1040, fill out the worksheet on page 8 of the M-1 instructions to determine the amount to fill in here 2

3 Other additions, including non-Minnesota bond interest *(see instructions, page 8)* 3

4 Add lines 1, 2 and 3. If the result is a negative number, put parentheses around the number . . 4

5 Total subtractions from Section A, line 35 on back of this form *(see instructions, page 9)* 5

6 Subtract line 5 from line 4. This is your Minnesota taxable income 6

Determining tax

7 **Tax** from table on pages 22–27, or from Schedule *(check box and attach)*: M-1MT☐ M-1LS☐ M-1NR☐ | M-1NR, line 18: _____ M-1NR, line 23: _____ . . 7

8 Marriage credit (for joint return when both spouses have earned income or taxable retirement income) from Section B, line 40 or line 41 on back of form *(see instructions, page 11)* 8

9 Subtract line 8 from line 7. If line 8 is more than line 7, fill in "0" 9

10 Total credits against tax from Section C, line 47 on back of form. Check box *(and attach schedule)* if claiming: M-1LTI☐ M-KS☐ Employer Transit Pass☐ M-1CR☐ M-1MTC☐ 10

11 Subtract line 10 from line 9. If line 10 is more than line 9, fill in "0" 11

12 Nongame Wildlife Fund contribution. This will reduce your refund or increase amount owed . . 12

13 Add lines 11 and 12 13

Payments

14 **Minnesota withholding** *(from your 2000 W-2 and 1099 forms)* . . 14

15 Minnesota estimated tax and Form M-13 payments made for 2000 . . 15

16 Child and dependent care credit *(attach Schedule M-1CD)* 16

17 Minnesota working family credit *(attach Schedule M-1WFC)* 17

18 $ Minnesota K–12 education credit *(attach Schedule M-1ED)* 18

19 Add lines 14 through 18 19

Refund or amount due

20 If line 19 is more than line 13, subtract line 13 from line 19 *(see instructions, page 14)*. This is **YOUR REFUND** 20

21 For direct deposit of the full refund amount on line 20, fill in all of the following.
Routing number ☐☐☐☐☐☐☐☐☐ Type of account: Checking ☐ Savings ☐
Account number ☐☐☐☐☐☐☐☐☐☐☐☐☐

22 If line 13 is more than line 19, subtract line 19 from line 13. This is the **AMOUNT YOU OWE** . . . . Make check payable to: MN Department of Revenue 22

23 Penalty amount from Schedule M-15 *(see instructions, page 14)* . . 23

Fill out lines 24 and 25 only if you want part of your refund credited to your estimated tax

24 Amount from line 20, if any, you want refunded to you 24

25 Amount from line 20 you want applied to your 2001 estimated tax . . 25

I declare that this form is correct and complete to the best of my knowledge and belief.

Your signature | Spouse's signature | Date | Daytime phone | ☐ I do not want my preparer to file my return electronically.

Paid preparer's signature **ONLY** | MN tax ID, SSN or PTIN | Date | Daytime phone | ☐ I authorize the MN Department of Revenue to discuss my tax return with the preparer.

Stock No. 1000010

Attach a copy of your 2000 federal income tax return and schedules or your federal telefile tax record.

Please staple one copy of each W-2 form here. Also attach any 1099 forms showing Minnesota withholding. Place check or money order here but do not staple.

Form 79 Claim for a Refund Due a Deceased Taxpayer (Minnesota)

MINNESOTA Department of Revenue

Claim for a Refund Due a Deceased Taxpayer   M-23

You must attach a copy of the decedent's death certificate to this form.

Print or type

Name of decedent	Social Security number
Name of person claiming refund	Social Security number

Claimant's address (street, apartment, route)	City or town	State	Zip code

Month, day, and year of decedent's death	Year for which refund is due

Property tax refund

If you are claiming the decedent's Minnesota property tax refund:

Check the one box that applies to you, skip the rest of this form, and sign at the bottom:

☐ I am the decedent's surviving spouse

☐ I am the decedent's dependent *(Read "Who is eligible to claim the property tax refund?" in the instructions on the back to determine if you are a dependent.)*

☐ The refund is part of the estate.

Income tax refund

If you are claiming the decedent's Minnesota income tax refund:

If a personal representative has been appointed by the court to represent the decedent's estate, only the personal representative is entitled to claim the decedent's refund. If you have been appointed as personal representative, you do NOT have to file this form. Instead, when you file the decedent's final income tax form, attach a copy of the court document showing your appointment as personal representative.

If no personal representative has been appointed, you can obtain the decedent's refund if you are the decedent's surviving spouse. You can obtain the decedent's refund without filing this form if you file a joint income tax form for the decedent. If you file a separate final income tax form for the decedent, you must file this form to obtain the decedent's refund.

If no personal representative has been appointed, there is no surviving spouse, and the value of the estate is less than $20,000, you are entitled to claim the decedent's refund only if you are the first living person on the list below. If there is more than one person in your category below, you must have all the other persons in your category sign the waiver on the back of this form to obtain the refund.

Check the one box that applies to you:

☐ I am the decedent's surviving spouse and I am filing a separate final income tax return for the decedent

☐ I am the decedent's child

☐ I am a grandchild of the decedent

☐ I am the decedent's mother or father

☐ I am the decedent's brother or sister

☐ I am the child of the decedent's brother or sister

Sign here

I request that the refund of the decedent named above be made to me.

I declare the information I have filled in on this form is correct and complete to the best of my knowledge and belief.

Signature of person claiming refund	Date	Daytime phone number
		( )

Mail this form to: Minnesota Decedent Refund, Minnesota Department of Revenue, St. Paul MN 55146-4210

Be sure to attach a copy of the decedent's death certificate

Stock No. 1000230
(Rev. 10/97)   Printed on recycled paper with 10% post-consumer waste using soy-based ink.

Form 80   Extension Payment of Income Tax (Minnesota)

MINNESOTA Department of Revenue

Form M-13 instructions

Use this form to pay your tax **only** *if you are filing your Form M-1* **after** *April 16, 2001. Do not use this form if you are filing Form M-1 on or before April 16, 2001.*

If you will be filing your individual income tax return after the due date, use Form M-13 to pay your tax by April 16, 2001. Do not use this form to pay your tax after April 16, 2001. **Payments received later than April 16** will not be credited to your estimated tax account.

There are no extensions to pay your individual income tax. All tax must be paid by April 16 even if you have an extension to file your federal return.

(NEW) If you do not pay at least 90 percent of your total tax by the regular due date, or if you pay at least 90 percent but do not pay the balance due when you file your Form M-1, you will be charged a late payment penalty on the unpaid balance.

The late payment penalty is 3 percent of the unpaid amount for the first 30 days it is late and the penalty increases by 3 percent for every 30-day period (or any part thereof), to a maximum late payment penalty of 24 percent. You will also have to pay interest of 9 percent per year on the unpaid tax and penalties from April 16, 2001.

When you are filling out this form:

- **Make sure your Social Security number** is written correctly. If it is not, we cannot properly credit your account.
- **If you are married and will be filing a joint return,** also fill in your spouse's Social Security number.
- **If you are married and will be filing a separate return,** do not fill in your spouse's Social Security number.
- **Estimate how much tax you owe** and fill in the amount. Round to the nearest whole dollar.

Detach the form, and mail it with your check or money order to: Minnesota Individual Income Tax, Mail Station 0025, St. Paul, MN 55145-0025.

This payment will be credited to your 2000 estimated tax account. When you file your Minnesota return, include this amount on line 15 of your Form M-1.

Stock No. 1000130

Detach here before mailing. **DO NOT PHOTOCOPY.**

- -

MINNESOTA Department of Revenue

Income Tax Extension Payment

Use this form to pay your 2000 individual income tax if you are filing Form M-1 after April 16, 2001.

First name and initial	Last name	Social Security number
Spouse's first name and initial	Last name	Social Security number
Present home address (street, apartment, route)		
City or town	State	Zip code

Mail with payment to: Minnesota Individual Income Tax, St. Paul, MN 55145-0025
Make check payable to: MN Dept. of Revenue

2000   **M-13**

Due April 16, 2001

AMOUNT OF PAYMENT

☐☐ , ☐☐☐ , ☐☐☐ . 00

Form 81 Application for Employer Identification Number (Form SS-4)

Form **SS-4**
(Rev. April 2000)
Department of the Treasury
Internal Revenue Service

Application for Employer Identification Number

(For use by employers, corporations, partnerships, trusts, estates, churches, government agencies, certain individuals, and others. See instructions.)

▶ Keep a copy for your records.

EIN

OMB No. 1545-0003

Please type or print clearly.

1 Name of applicant (legal name) (see instructions)
Estate of Jane M. Doe

2 Trade name of business (if different from name on line 1)
N/A

3 Executor, trustee, "care of" name
John C. Doe, Personal Representative

4a Mailing address (street address) (room, apt., or suite no.)
1005 Elm Street

5a Business address (if different from address on lines 4a and 4b)

4b City, state, and ZIP code
St. Paul, MN 55102

5b City, state, and ZIP code

6 County and state where principal business is located
Ramsey County, Minnesota

7 Name of principal officer, general partner, grantor, owner, or trustor—SSN or ITIN may be required (see instructions) ▶
N/A

8a Type of entity (Check only one box.) (see instructions)

Caution: *If applicant is a limited liability company, see the instructions for line 8a.*

☐ Sole proprietor (SSN) _____
☐ Partnership
☐ REMIC
☐ State/local government
☐ Church or church-controlled organization
☐ Other nonprofit organization (specify) ▶ _____
☐ Other (specify) ▶

☐ Personal service corp.
☐ National Guard
Farmers' cooperative

☒ Estate (SSN of decedent) 321 54 9876
☐ Plan administrator (SSN)
☐ Other corporation (specify) ▶ _____
☐ Trust
☐ Federal government/military
(enter GEN if applicable) _____

8b If a corporation, name the state or foreign country (if applicable) where incorporated

State	Foreign country
N/A	N/A

9 Reason for applying (Check only one box.) (see instructions)
☐ Started new business (specify type) ▶ _____
☐ Hired employees (Check the box and see line 12.)
☐ Created a pension plan (specify type) ▶

☐ Banking purpose (specify purpose) ▶ _____
☐ Changed type of organization (specify new type) ▶ _____
☐ Purchased going business
☐ Created a trust (specify type) ▶ _____
☒ Other (specify) ▶ Fiduciary-Death

10 Date business started or acquired (month, day, year) (see instructions)
September 20, 2000

11 Closing month of accounting year (see instructions)
September

12 First date wages or annuities were paid or will be paid (month, day, year). Note: *If applicant is a withholding agent, enter date income will first be paid to nonresident alien. (month, day, year)* . . . . ▶ N/A

13 Highest number of employees expected in the next 12 months. Note: *If the applicant does not expect to have any employees during the period, enter -0-. (see instructions)* . . . . ▶

Nonagricultural	Agricultural	Household
N/A	N/A	N/A

14 Principal activity (see instructions) ▶ N/A

15 Is the principal business activity manufacturing? . . . . ☐ Yes ☒ No
If "Yes," principal product and raw material used ▶

16 To whom are most of the products or services sold? Please check one box.
☐ Public (retail)   ☐ Other (specify) ▶
☐ Business (wholesale)
☒ N/A

17a Has the applicant ever applied for an employer identification number for this or any other business? . . . . . ☐ Yes ☒ No
Note: *If "Yes," please complete lines 17b and 17c.*

17b If you checked "Yes" on line 17a, give applicant's legal name and trade name shown on prior application, if different from line 1 or 2 above.
Legal name ▶ N/A   Trade name ▶ N/A

17c Approximate date when and city and state where the application was filed. Enter previous employer identification number if known.

Approximate date when filed (mo., day, year)	City and state where filed	Previous EIN
N/A	N/A	N/A

Under penalties of perjury, I declare that I have examined this application, and to the best of my knowledge and belief, it is true, correct, and complete.

Business telephone number (include area code)
(612) 345-5000

Fax telephone number (include area code)
(612) 345-4712

Name and title (Please type or print clearly.) ▶ John C. Doe, Personal Representative

Signature ▶ /S/ John C. Doe

Date ▶ 10/31/00

Note: *Do not write below this line. For official use only.*

Please leave blank ▶	Geo.	Ind.	Class	Size	Reason for applying

For Privacy Act and Paperwork Reduction Act Notice, see page 4.

Cat. No. 16055N

Form **SS-4** (Rev. 4-2000)

Form 82 Notice Concerning Fiduciary Relationship (Form 56)

Form **56**
(Rev. August 1997)
Department of the Treasury
Internal Revenue Service

Notice Concerning Fiduciary Relationship

(Internal Revenue Code sections 6036 and 6903)

OMB No. 1545-0013

Part I Identification		
Name of person for whom you are acting (as shown on the tax return)	Identifying number	Decedent's social security no.
Estate of Jane M. Doe	41-6246975	321 : 54 : 9876

Address of person for whom you are acting (number, street, and room or suite no.)
1005 Elm Street

City or town, state, and ZIP code (If a foreign address, see instructions.)
St. Paul, MN 55102

Fiduciary's name
John C. Doe

Address of fiduciary (number, street, and room or suite no.)
1005 Elm Street

City or town, state, and ZIP code
St. Paul, MN 55102

Telephone number (optional)
(612) 345-5000

Part II Authority

1 Authority for fiduciary relationship. Check applicable box:

a(1) ☒ Will and codicils or court order appointing fiduciary. Attach certified copy . . **(2)** Date of death ... 9/20/00
b(1) ☐ Court order appointing fiduciary. Attach certified copy . . . . **(2)** Date (see instructions) ....
c ☐ Valid trust instrument and amendments. Attach copy
d ☐ Other. Describe ▶ ....

Part III Tax Notices

Send to the fiduciary listed in Part I all notices and other written communications involving the following tax matters:

2 Type of tax (estate, gift, generation-skipping transfer, income, excise, etc.) ▶ Estate, gift, income
3 Federal tax form number (706, 1040, 1041, 1120, etc.) ▶ 706, 709, 1041
4 Year(s) or period(s) (if estate tax, date of death) ▶ September 20, 2000

Part IV Revocation or Termination of Notice

Section A—Total Revocation or Termination

5 Check this box if you are revoking or terminating all prior notices concerning fiduciary relationships on file with the Internal Revenue Service for the same tax matters and years or periods covered by this notice concerning fiduciary relationship . ▶ ☐
Reason for termination of fiduciary relationship. Check applicable box:

a ☐ Court order revoking fiduciary authority. Attach certified copy.
b ☐ Certificate of dissolution or termination of a business entity. Attach copy.
c ☐ Other. Describe ▶

Section B—Partial Revocation

6a Check this box if you are revoking earlier notices concerning fiduciary relationships on file with the Internal Revenue Service for the same tax matters and years or periods covered by this notice concerning fiduciary relationship . . . . ▶ ☐
b Specify to whom granted, date, and address, including ZIP code, or refer to attached copies of earlier notices and authorizations
▶ ....

Section C—Substitute Fiduciary

7 Check this box if a new fiduciary or fiduciaries have been or will be substituted for the revoking or terminating fiduciary(ies) and specify the name(s) and address(es), including ZIP code(s), of the new fiduciary(ies) . . . . ▶ ☐

Part V Court and Administrative Proceedings	
Name of court (if other than a court proceeding, identify the type of proceeding and name of agency)	Date proceeding initiated
Ramsey County District Court, Probate Division	September 26, 2000
Address of court	Docket number of proceeding
65 West Kellogg Blvd.	12

City or town, state, and ZIP code	Date	Time	a.m.	Place of other proceedings
St. Paul, MN 55102	10/31/00	10:00	p.m.	

I certify that I have the authority to execute this notice concerning fiduciary relationship on behalf of the taxpayer.

Please Sign Here

▶ /S/ John C. Doe
Fiduciary's signature | Personal Representative Title, if applicable | 11/30/00 Date

▶
Fiduciary's signature | Title, if applicable | Date

For Paperwork Reduction Act and Privacy Act Notice, see back page.   Cat. No. 16375I   Form **56** (Rev. 8-97)

Form 83 U.S. (Fiduciary) Income Tax Return for Estates and Trusts (Form 1041)

Form **1041**

Department of the Treasury—Internal Revenue Service

U.S. Income Tax Return for Estates and Trusts **2000**

For calendar year 2000 or fiscal year beginning Oct. 1 , 2000, and ending Sept. 30 , 2001

OMB No. 1545-0092

A Type of entity:	Name of estate or trust (If a grantor type trust, see page 10 of the instructions.)	C Employer identification number
☒ Decedent's estate	Estate of Jane M. Doe	41 : 6246975

A Type of entity:
- ☒ Decedent's estate
- ☐ Simple trust
- ☐ Complex trust
- ☐ Grantor type trust
- ☐ Bankruptcy estate–Ch. 7
- ☐ Bankruptcy estate–Ch. 11
- ☐ Pooled income fund

B Number of Schedules K-1 attached (see instructions) ▶ 0

C Employer identification number 41 : 6246975

D Date entity created 09/20/00

Name and title of fiduciary
John C. Doe, Personal Representative

Number, street, and room or suite no. (If a P.O. box, see page 10 of the instructions.)
1005 Elm Street

City or town, state, and ZIP code
St. Paul, MN 55102

E Nonexempt charitable and split-interest trusts, check applicable boxes (see page 10 of the instructions):
- ☐ Described in section 4947(a)(1)
- ☐ Not a private foundation
- ☐ Described in section 4947(a)(2)

F Check applicable boxes:
- ☐ Initial return ☒ Final return ☐ Amended return
- ☐ Change in fiduciary's name ☐ Change in fiduciary's address

G Pooled mortgage account (see page 11 of the instructions):
- ☐ Bought ☐ Sold Date:

Income

1	Interest income	1	23,230
2	Ordinary dividends	2	2,460
3	Business income or (loss) (attach Schedule C or C-EZ (Form 1040))	3	
4	Capital gain or (loss) (attach Schedule D (Form 1041))	4	
5	Rents, royalties, partnerships, other estates and trusts, etc. (attach Schedule E (Form 1040))	5	1,100
6	Farm income or (loss) (attach Schedule F (Form 1040))	6	
7	Ordinary gain or (loss) (attach Form 4797)	7	
8	Other income. List type and amount	8	
9	**Total income.** Combine lines 1 through 8 ▶	9	26,790

Deductions

10	Interest. Check if Form 4952 is attached ▶ ☐	10	10,250
11	Taxes	11	3,900
12	Fiduciary fees	12	10,000
13	Charitable deduction (from Schedule A, line 7)	13	
14	Attorney, accountant, and return preparer fees	14	2,040
15a	Other deductions **not** subject to the 2% floor (attach schedule)	15a	
b	Allowable miscellaneous itemized deductions subject to the 2% floor	15b	
16	**Total.** Add lines 10 through 15b	16	26,190
17	Adjusted total income or (loss). Subtract line 16 from line 9. Enter here and on Schedule B, line 1 ▶	17	600
18	Income distribution deduction (from Schedule B, line 15) (attach Schedules K-1 (Form 1041))	18	
19	Estate tax deduction (including certain generation-skipping taxes) (attach computation)	19	
20	Exemption	20	600
21	**Total deductions.** Add lines 18 through 20 ▶	21	600

Tax and Payments

22	Taxable income. Subtract line 21 from line 17. If a loss, see page 15 of the instructions	22	0
23	Total tax (from Schedule G, line 7)	23	0
24	Payments: a 2000 estimated tax payments and amount applied from 1999 return	24a	
b	Estimated tax payments allocated to beneficiaries (from Form 1041-T)	24b	
c	Subtract line 24b from line 24a	24c	
d	Tax paid with extension of time to file: ☐ Form 2758 ☐ Form 8736 ☐ Form 8800	24d	
e	Federal income tax withheld. If any is from Form(s) 1099, check ▶ ☐	24e	
	Other payments: f Form 2439 _____ ; g Form 4136 _____ ; Total ▶	24h	
25	**Total payments.** Add lines 24c through 24e, and 24h ▶	25	
26	Estimated tax penalty (see page 16 of the instructions)	26	
27	**Tax due.** If line 25 is smaller than the total of lines 23 and 26, enter amount owed	27	0
28	**Overpayment.** If line 25 is larger than the total of lines 23 and 26, enter amount overpaid	28	
29	Amount of line 28 to be: **a Credited to 2001 estimated tax** ▶ _____ ; **b Refunded** ▶	29	

Sign Here

Under penalties of perjury, I declare that I have examined this return, including accompanying schedules and statements, and to the best of my knowledge and belief, it is true, correct, and complete. Declaration of preparer (other than fiduciary) is based on all information of which preparer has any knowledge.

▶ /S/ John C. Doe   10/02/01 ▶

Signature of fiduciary or officer representing fiduciary   Date

EIN of fiduciary if a financial institution (see page 6 of the instructions)

Paid Preparer's Use Only

Preparer's signature ▶		Date	Check if self-employed ▶ ☐	Preparer's SSN or PTIN
Firm's name (or yours if self-employed), address, and ZIP code ▶				EIN ▶
				Phone no. ( )

For Paperwork Reduction Act Notice, see the separate instructions.   Cat. No. 11370H   Form **1041** (2000)

Form 84   Application for Extension of Time to File Fiduciary and Certain Other Returns (Form 2758)

Form **2758** (Rev. June 1998) Department of the Treasury Internal Revenue Service	**Application for Extension of Time To File Certain Excise, Income, Information, and Other Returns** ▶ File a separate application for each return.	OMB No. 1545-0148

Please type or print. File the **original and one copy** by the due date for filing your return. See instructions on back.	Name	Employer identification number
	Number, street, and room or suite no. (or P.O. box no. if mail is not delivered to street address)	
	City, town or post office, state, and ZIP code. For a foreign address, see instructions.	

Note: *Corporate income tax return filers must use* **Form 7004** *to request an extension of time to file. Partnerships, REMICs, and trusts must use* **Form 8736** *to request an extension of time to file Form 1065, 1066, or 1041.*

1   I request an extension of time until .... , ... , to file (check only one):

☐ Form 706-GS(D)	☐ Form 990-T (sec. 401(a) or 408(a) trust)	☐ Form 1120-ND (sec. 4951 taxes)	☐ Form 8612
☐ Form 706-GS(T)	☐ Form 990-T (trust other than above)	☐ Form 3520-A	☐ Form 8613
☐ Form 990 or 990-EZ	☐ Form 1041 (estate) (see instructions)	☐ Form 4720	☐ Form 8725
☐ Form 990-BL	☐ Form 1041-A	☐ Form 5227	☐ Form 8804
☐ Form 990-PF	☐ Form 1042	☐ Form 6069	☐ Form 8831

If the organization does not have an office or place of business in the United States, check this box . . . . . . ▶ ☐

2a   For calendar year .... , or other tax year beginning .... , ... and ending .... , ...

  b   If this tax year is for less than 12 months, check reason: ☐ Initial return ☐ Final return ☐ Change in accounting period

3   Has an extension of time to file been previously granted for this tax year? . . . . ☐ Yes ☐ No

4   State in detail why you need the extension ....
....
....

5a   If this form is for Form 706-GS(D), 706-GS(T), 990-BL, 990-PF, 990-T, 1041 (estate), 1042, 1120-ND, 4720, 6069, 8612, 8613, 8725, 8804, or 8831, enter the tentative tax, less any nonrefundable credits. See instructions. $ _____

  b   If this form is for Form 990-PF, 990-T, 1041 (estate), 1042, or 8804, enter any refundable credits and estimated tax payments made. Include any prior year overpayment allowed as a credit . . . . . $ _____

  c   **Balance due.** Subtract line 5b from line 5a. Include your payment with this form, or deposit with FTD coupon if required. See instructions . . . . $ _____

Signature and Verification

Under penalties of perjury, I declare that I have examined this form, including accompanying schedules and statements, and to the best of my knowledge and belief, it is true, correct, and complete; and that I am authorized to prepare this form.

Signature ▶   Title ▶   Date ▶

FILE ORIGINAL AND ONE COPY. The IRS will show below whether or not your application is approved and will return the copy.

Notice to Applicant—To Be Completed by the IRS

☐ We **HAVE** approved your application. Please attach this form to your return.

☐ We **HAVE NOT** approved your application. However, we have granted a 10-day grace period from the later of the date shown below or the due date of your return (including any prior extensions). This grace period is considered to be a valid extension of time for elections otherwise required to be made on a timely return. Please attach this form to your return.

☐ We **HAVE NOT** approved your application. After considering the reasons stated in item 4, we cannot grant your request for an extension of time to file. We are not granting the 10-day grace period.

☐ We cannot consider your application because it was filed after the due date of the return for which an extension was requested.

☐ Other: ....

_____   By: _____   _____
Director   Date

If you want a copy of this form to be returned to an address other than that shown above, please enter the address to which the copy should be sent.

Please Type or Print	Name
	Number, street, and room or suite no. (or P.O. box no. if mail is not delivered to street address)
	City, town or post office, state, and ZIP code. For a foreign address, see instructions.

For Paperwork Reduction Act Notice, see back of form.   Cat. No. 11976B   Form **2758** (Rev. 6-98)

Form 85 State (Minnesota as Example) Fiduciary Income Tax Return

MINNESOTA Department of Revenue

Fiduciary Income Tax Return 2000 M-2

Income tax return for estates and trusts

For calendar year 2000 or fiscal year beginning 10/01 , 2000, ending *(mm/dd/yyyy)* 09/30/2001

Name of estate or trust	Federal ID number	Minnesota ID number
Estate of Jane M. Doe	Check if name has changed:	41-6246975	41-6246975
Name and title of fiduciary	Decedent's Social Security number	Date of death
John C. Doe, Personal Representative	321-54-9876	09/20/00
Address of fiduciary	Fill in decedent's or trust's last address	
1005 Elm Street	1005 Elm Street	
City or town	State	Zip code	City or town	State	Zip code
St. Paul, MN 55102			St. Paul, MN 55102		

Check all that apply: ☐ Amended return or claim for refund ☒ Estate ☐ Trust. Date trust became irrevocable: _____ ☒ Final return ☐ Mail forms to me next year. | **Number of beneficiaries:**

Print or type

Income

1 Federal taxable income *(from line 22 of federal Form 1041)* .... 1 _____ 0 .
2 Fiduciary's deductions not allowed by Minnesota *(see instructions)* .... 2 _____ 0 .
3 Fiduciary's losses not allowed by Minnesota *(see instructions)* .... 3 _____ .
4 Capital gain amount of lump-sum distribution *(attach federal Form 4972)* .... 4 _____ .
5 Additions *(from line 35, column E, on the back of this form)* .... 5 _____ .
6 Add lines 1 through 5 .... 6 _____ 0 .
7 Subtractions *(from line 35, column E, on the back of this form)* .... 7 _____ .
8 Fiduciary's income from non-Minnesota sources *(see instructions)* ..... 8 _____ .
9 Add lines 7 and 8 .... 9 _____ .
10 Subtract line 9 from line 6. This is your Minnesota taxable net income .... 10 _____ 0 .
11 Tax from table on pages 8 through 10 using the income amount shown on line 10 above .. 11 _____ 0 .
12 Tax on a lump-sum distribution *(attach Schedule M-1LS)* .... 12 _____ .
13 Alternative minimum tax *(attach Schedule M-2MT)* .... 13 _____ .
14 Add lines 11 through 13. This is your total 2000 income tax .... 14 _____ 0 .
15 Total estimated tax payments, extension payment, 2000 Minnesota tax withheld, and credit for shareholders of a financial institution electing to be an S corporation *(see instructions)*. If withholding is included: write in the amount and attach documentation $_____ ..15 _____ .
16 If line 14 is more than line 15, subtract line 15 from line 14 .... 16 _____ .
17 *Trusts only:* Additional charge for underpayment of estimated tax *(attach Schedule M-15)* ..17 _____ .
18 If you listed an amount on line 16, add line 16 and line 17 and fill in **AMOUNT OWED**. Check ☐ if paying by EFT. If not, you must attach **PV43** ...18 _____ .
19 If line 15 is more than the sum of lines 14 and 17, subtract lines 14 and 17 from line 15 and fill in the amount of the overpayment ...19 _____ .
20 For direct deposit of the full refund amount on line 19, fill in all of the following.
   Routing number ☐☐☐☐☐☐☐☐☐ Type of account: Checking ☐ Savings ☐
   Account number ☐☐☐☐☐☐☐☐☐☐☐☐☐☐☐☐☐
21 If you are paying estimated tax for 2001, fill in the amount from line 19 you want applied to it, if any ....21 _____ .
22 Subtract line 21 from line 19 and fill in the amount to be **REFUNDED** .... 22 _____ .

Figuring the tax

Refund or tax owed

Signature of fiduciary or officer representing fiduciary	MN ID or Soc. Sec. number	Date	Daytime phone	☐ I authorize the MN Department of Revenue to discuss this tax return with the person below.
/S/ John C. Doe	374-29-4665	10/2/01	(612) 345-5000	
E-mail address for correspondence, if desired			This e-mail address belongs to (check one box): ☐ Fiduciary ☐ Paid preparer	
Paid preparer's signature	MN ID number, SSN or PTIN	Date	Daytime phone ( )	

Signatures

You must attach a copy of federal Form 1041, Schedules K-1, and other federal schedules
Mail to: Minnesota Fiduciary Income Tax, Mail Station 1310, St. Paul, Minnesota 55145-1310

Stock No. 3000200

Form 86   United States Gift (and Generation-Skipping Transfer) Tax Return (Form 709)

Form **709**	**United States Gift (and Generation-Skipping Transfer) Tax Return**	OMB No. 1545-0020
	(Section 6019 of the Internal Revenue Code) (For gifts made during calendar year 2000)	
Department of the Treasury Internal Revenue Service	▶ **See separate instructions.**	**2000**

Part 1—General Information

1 Donor's first name and middle initial Jane M	**2** Donor's last name Doe		**3** Donor's social security number 321 | 54 | 9876	
4 Address (number, street, and apartment number) 1005 Elm Street			**5** Legal residence (domicile) (county and state) Ramsey County, Minnesota	
6 City, state, and ZIP code St. Paul, MN 55102			**7** Citizenship United States	

		Yes	No
8	If the donor died during the year, check here ▶ ☒ and enter date of death **Sept. 20 2000** .		
9	If you received an extension of time to file this Form 709, check here ▶ ☐ and attach the Form 4868, 2688, 2350, or extension letter .		
10	Enter the total number of separate donees listed on Schedule A—count each person only once. ▶ 1		
11a	Have you (the donor) previously filed a Form 709 (or 709-A) for any other year? If the answer is "No," do not complete line 11b .		X
11b	If the answer to line 11a is "Yes," has your address changed since you last filed Form 709 (or 709-A)?		
12	Gifts by husband or wife to third parties.—Do you consent to have the gifts (including generation-skipping transfers) made by you and by your spouse to third parties during the calendar year considered as made one-half by each of you? (See instructions.) (If the answer is "Yes," the following information must be furnished and your spouse must sign the consent shown below. **If the answer is "No," skip lines 13–18 and go to Schedule A.**)	X	
13	Name of consenting spouse John C. Doe **14** SSN 374-29-4665		
15	Were you married to one another during the entire calendar year? (see instructions)		X
16	If the answer to 15 is "No," check whether ☐ married ☐ divorced or ☒ widowed, and give date (see instructions) ▶ 9/20		
17	Will a gift tax return for this calendar year be filed by your spouse?		X
18	**Consent of Spouse**—I consent to have the gifts (and generation-skipping transfers) made by me and by my spouse to third parties during the calendar year considered as made one-half by each of us. We are both aware of the joint and several liability for tax created by the execution of this consent.		

Consenting spouse's signature ▶   /S/ John C. Doe   Date ▶ 02/15/2001

Part 2—Tax Computation

1	Enter the amount from Schedule A, Part 3, line 15	**1**	0
2	Enter the amount from Schedule B, line 3	**2**	
3	Total taxable gifts (add lines 1 and 2)	**3**	0
4	Tax computed on amount on line 3 (see Table for Computing Tax in separate instructions). . .	**4**	0
5	Tax computed on amount on line 2 (see Table for Computing Tax in separate instructions). . .	**5**	
6	Balance (subtract line 5 from line 4)	**6**	0
7	Maximum unified credit (nonresident aliens, see instructions)	**7**	220,550 | 00
8	Enter the unified credit against tax allowable for all prior periods (from Sch. B, line 1, col. C) . .	**8**	
9	Balance (subtract line 8 from line 7)	**9**	220,550
10	Enter 20% (.20) of the amount allowed as a specific exemption for gifts made after September 8, 1976, and before January 1, 1977 (see instructions)	**10**	
11	Balance (subtract line 10 from line 9)	**11**	220,550
12	Unified credit (enter the smaller of line 6 or line 11)	**12**	0
13	Credit for foreign gift taxes (see instructions)	**13**	
14	Total credits (add lines 12 and 13)	**14**	0
15	Balance (subtract line 14 from line 6) (do not enter less than zero)	**15**	0
16	Generation-skipping transfer taxes (from Schedule C, Part 3, col. H, Total)	**16**	
17	Total tax (add lines 15 and 16).	**17**	0
18	Gift and generation-skipping transfer taxes prepaid with extension of time to file . . .	**18**	
19	If line 18 is less than line 17, enter **balance due** (see instructions)	**19**	0
20	If line 18 is greater than line 17, enter **amount to be refunded**	**20**	

Sign Here

Under penalties of perjury, I declare that I have examined this return, including any accompanying schedules and statements, and to the best of my knowledge and belief, it is true, correct, and complete. Declaration of preparer (other than donor) is based on all information of which preparer has any knowledge.

▶ /S/ John C. Doe, Personal Representative   02/15/2001
Signature of donor   Date

Paid Preparer's Use Only	Preparer's signature ▶	Date	Check if self-employed ▶ ☐
	Firm's name (or yours if self-employed), address, and ZIP code ▶		Phone no. ▶ ( )

Attach check or money order here.

For Disclosure, Privacy Act, and Paperwork Reduction Act Notice, see page 11 of the separate instructions for this form.   Cat. No. 16783M   Form **709** (2000)

(continued)

Form 86 United States Gift (and Generation-Skipping Transfer) Tax Return (Form 709) *continued*

Form 709 (2000) Page **2**

SCHEDULE A	Computation of Taxable Gifts (Including Transfers in Trust)

A Does the value of any item listed on Schedule A reflect any valuation discount? If the answer is "Yes," see instructions . Yes ☐ No ☒

B ☐ ◄ Check here if you elect under section 529(c)(2)(B) to treat any transfers made this year to a qualified state tuition program as made ratably over a 5-year period beginning this year. See instructions. Attach explanation.

Part 1—Gifts Subject Only to Gift Tax. *Gifts less political organization, medical, and educational exclusions—see instructions*

A Item number	B • Donee's name and address • Relationship to donor (if any) • Description of gift • If the gift was made by means of a trust, enter trust's EIN and attach a description or copy of the trust instrument (see instructions) • If the gift was of securities, give CUSIP number	C Donor's adjusted basis of gift	D Date of gift	E Value at date of gift
1	Sandy R. Doe, daughter, cash gift 1005 Elm Street St. Paul, MN 55102 (Gift to be split with spouse) Note: Not required to list gift of $30,000 to spouse, John C. Doe. The only circumstances that require listing gifts to a spouse are: (1) it is a gift of a terminable interest; (2) it is a gift of a future interest; or (3) the spouse was not a citizen of the United States at the time of the gift.	20,000	04/20/00	20,000

Total of Part 1 (add amounts from Part 1, column E) . . . . ►

Part 2—Gifts That are Direct Skips and are Subject to Both Gift Tax and Generation-Skipping Transfer Tax. You must list the gifts in chronological order. *Gifts less political organization, medical, and educational exclusions—see instructions. (Also list here direct skips that are subject only to the GST tax at this time as the result of the termination of an "estate tax inclusion period." See instructions.)*

A Item number	B • Donee's name and address • Relationship to donor (if any) • Description of gift • If the gift was made by means of a trust, enter trust's EIN and attach a description or copy of the trust instrument (see instructions) • If the gift was of securities, give CUSIP number	C Donor's adjusted basis of gift	D Date of gift	E Value at date of gift
1				

Total of Part 2 (add amounts from Part 2, column E) . . . . ►

Part 3—Taxable Gift Reconciliation

1	Total value of gifts of donor (add totals from column E of Parts 1 and 2)	1	20,000
2	One-half of items ___1___ attributable to spouse (see instructions)	2	10,000
3	Balance (subtract line 2 from line 1)	3	10,000
4	Gifts of spouse to be included (from Schedule A, Part 3, line 2 of spouse's return—see instructions) . .	4	0
	If any of the gifts included on this line are also subject to the generation-skipping transfer tax, check here ► ☐ and enter those gifts also on Schedule C, Part 1.		
5	Total gifts (add lines 3 and 4)	5	10,000
6	Total annual exclusions for gifts listed on Schedule A (including line 4, above) (see instructions) . . .	6	10,000
7	Total included amount of gifts (subtract line 6 from line 5)	7	0

Deductions (see instructions)

8	Gifts of interests to spouse for which a marital deduction will be claimed, based on items _____ of Schedule A	8	
9	Exclusions attributable to gifts on line 8	9	
10	Marital deduction—subtract line 9 from line 8	10	
11	Charitable deduction, based on items _____ less exclusions . .	11	
12	Total deductions—add lines 10 and 11	12	
13	Subtract line 12 from line 7	13	0
14	Generation-skipping transfer taxes payable with this Form 709 (from Schedule C, Part 3, col. H, Total) .	14	
15	Taxable gifts (add lines 13 and 14). Enter here and on line 1 of the Tax Computation on page 1 . . .	15	0

(If more space is needed, attach additional sheets of same size.) Form **709** (2000)

(continued)

Form 86   United States Gift (and Generation-Skipping Transfer) Tax Return (Form 709)   *continued*

Form 709 (2000)   Page **3**

SCHEDULE A   Computation of Taxable Gifts *(continued)*

16 Terminable Interest (QTIP) Marital Deduction. (See instructions for line 8 of Schedule A.)

If a trust (or other property) meets the requirements of qualified terminable interest property under section 2523(f), and

   a. The trust (or other property) is listed on Schedule A, and

   b. The value of the trust (or other property) is entered in whole or in part as a deduction on line 8, Part 3 of Schedule A,

then the donor shall be deemed to have made an election to have such trust (or other property) treated as qualified terminable interest property under section 2523(f).

   If less than the entire value of the trust (or other property) that the donor has included in Part 1 of Schedule A is entered as a deduction on line 8, the donor shall be considered to have made an election only as to a fraction of the trust (or other property). The numerator of this fraction is equal to the amount of the trust (or other property) deducted on line 10 of Part 3, Schedule A. The denominator is equal to the total value of the trust (or other property) listed in Part 1 of Schedule A.

   If you make the QTIP election (see instructions for line 8 of Schedule A), the terminable interest property involved will be included in your spouse's gross estate upon his or her death (section 2044). If your spouse disposes (by gift or otherwise) of all or part of the qualifying life income interest, he or she will be considered to have made a transfer of the entire property that is subject to the gift tax (see Transfer of Certain Life Estates on page 4 of the instructions).

17 Election Out of QTIP Treatment of Annuities

☐ ◄ Check here if you elect under section 2523(f)(6) **NOT** to treat as qualified terminable interest property any joint and survivor annuities that are reported on Schedule A and would otherwise be treated as qualified terminable interest property under section 2523(f). (See instructions.) Enter the item numbers (from Schedule A) for the annuities for which you are making this election ►

SCHEDULE B   Gifts From Prior Periods

If you answered "Yes" on line 11a of page 1, Part 1, see the instructions for completing Schedule B. If you answered "No," skip to the Tax Computation on page 1 (or Schedule C, if applicable).

A Calendar year or calendar quarter (see instructions)	**B** Internal Revenue office where prior return was filed	**C** Amount of unified credit against gift tax for periods after December 31, 1976	**D** Amount of specific exemption for prior periods ending before January 1, 1977	**E** Amount of taxable gifts

1 Totals for prior periods (without adjustment for reduced specific exemption)	**1**	
2 Amount, if any, by which total specific exemption, line 1, column D, is more than $30,000	**2**	
3 Total amount of taxable gifts for prior periods (add amount, column E, line 1, and amount, if any, on line 2). (Enter here and on line 2 of the Tax Computation on page 1.)	**3**	

(If more space is needed, attach additional sheets of same size.)   Form **709** (2000)

(continued)

Form 86   United States Gift (and Generation-Skipping Transfer) Tax Return (Form 709)   *continued*

Form 709 (2000)

Page **4**

SCHEDULE C	Computation of Generation-Skipping Transfer Tax

Note: *Inter vivos direct skips that are completely excluded by the GST exemption must still be fully reported (including value and exemptions claimed) on Schedule C.*

Part 1—Generation-Skipping Transfers

A Item No. (from Schedule A, Part 2, col. A)	B Value (from Schedule A, Part 2, col. E)	C Split Gifts (enter ½ of col. B) (see instructions)	D Subtract col. C from col. B	E Nontaxable portion of transfer	F Net Transfer (subtract col. E from col. D)
1					
2					
3					
4					
5					
6					

If you elected gift splitting and your spouse was required to file a separate Form 709 (see the instructions for "Split Gifts"), you must enter all of the gifts shown on Schedule A, Part 2, of your spouse's Form 709 here. In column C, enter the item number of each gift in the order it appears in column A of your spouse's Schedule A, Part 2. We have preprinted the prefix "S-" to distinguish your spouse's item numbers from your own when you complete column A of Schedule C, Part 3. In column D, for each gift, enter the amount reported in column C, Schedule C, Part 1, of your spouse's Form 709.	Split gifts from spouse's Form 709 (enter item number)	Value included from spouse's Form 709	Nontaxable portion of transfer	Net transfer (subtract col. E from col. D)
	S-			
	S-			
	S-			
	S-			
	S-			
	S-			
	S-			
	S-			

Part 2—GST Exemption Reconciliation (Section 2631) and Section 2652(a)(3) Election

Check box ▶ ☐   if you are making a section 2652(a)(3) (special QTIP) election (see instructions)

Enter the item numbers (from Schedule A) of the gifts for which you are making this election ▶ _____

1	Maximum allowable exemption (see instructions)	1
2	Total exemption used for periods before filing this return	2
3	Exemption available for this return (subtract line 2 from line 1)	3
4	Exemption claimed on this return (from Part 3, col. C total, below)	4
5	Exemption allocated to transfers not shown on Part 3, below. **You must attach a Notice of Allocation.** (See instructions.)	5
6	Add lines 4 and 5	6
7	Exemption available for future transfers (subtract line 6 from line 3)	7

Part 3—Tax Computation

A Item No. (from Schedule C, Part 1)	B Net transfer (from Schedule C, Part 1, col. F)	C GST Exemption Allocated	D Divide col. C by col. B	E Inclusion Ratio (subtract col. D from 1.000)	F Maximum Estate Tax Rate	G Applicable Rate (multiply col. E by col. F)	H Generation-Skipping Transfer Tax (multiply col. B by col. G)
1					55% (.55)		
2					55% (.55)		
3					55% (.55)		
4					55% (.55)		
5					55% (.55)		
6					55% (.55)		
					55% (.55)		
					55% (.55)		
					55% (.55)		
					55% (.55)		

Total exemption claimed. Enter here and on line 4, Part 2, above. May not exceed line 3, Part 2, above		**Total generation-skipping transfer tax.** Enter here, on line 14 of Schedule A, Part 3, and on line 16 of the Tax Computation on page 1	

(If more space is needed, attach additional sheets of same size.)   ✪

Form **709** (2000)

Form 87   State (Tennessee as Example) Gift Tax Return

INH 300

TENNESSEE DEPARTMENT OF REVENUE
STATE GIFT TAX RETURN

AMENDED RETURN ☐

CALENDAR YEAR OF GIFT	COUNTY	DONOR'S SOCIAL SECURITY NUMBER

NAME OF DONOR _____

STREET ADDRESS _____

CITY, STATE AND ZIP CODE _____

If Donor is deceased, check here ☐ and enter date of death _____

The Tennessee Gift Tax is due April 15 of the year following the calendar year in which gifts were made.

Make your check payable to the Tennessee Department of Revenue for the amount shown on Line 8 and mail to:
Tennessee Department of Revenue
Andrew Jackson State Office Building
500 Deaderick Street
Nashville, Tennessee 37242

For assistance, you may call in-state toll free 1-800-342-1003 or (615) 741-2594.

TERMINABLE INTEREST MARITAL DEDUCTION

1. Do you elect, under the rules of 2523(f) I.R.C., to claim a marital deduction for gifts of qualified terminable interest property (QTIP)?   YES ☐   NO ☐
2. Is the gift a disposition of qualified terminable interest property (QTIP) under T.C.A. §67-8-101(e)?   YES ☐   NO ☐

CONSENT OF SPOUSE - GIFTS BY HUSBAND OR WIFE TO THIRD PARTIES

Do you consent to have the gifts by you and by your spouse to third parties during the calendar year considered as made one-half by each of you?   YES ☐   NO ☐

If the answer is "yes," complete Lines 1 through 4 and sign the consent line below:

1. Name of spouse _____ Spouse's social security number _____
2. Were you married during the entire calendar year?   YES ☐   NO ☐
3. If the answer to 2 is "NO," check whether ☐ married, ☐ divorced, or ☐ widowed, and give date _____
4. Will a gift tax return for this calendar year be filed by your spouse?   YES ☐   NO ☐

Consent of spouse - I consent to have the gifts made by me and my spouse to third parties during the calendar year considered as made one-half by each of us. We are both aware of the joint and several liability for tax created by the execution of this consent.

Spouse's signature _____   Date _____

COMPUTATION OF TAX

		Dollars	Cents
1.	Total Class A Tax		
2.	Total Class B Tax		
3.	Total Tax (Add Lines 1 and 2)		
4.	Deduct: Extension payment		
5.	Net Tax Due (Line 3 minus Line 4)		
6.	Penalty (5% for each 30-day period of delinquency not to exceed 25% of the tax due)		
7.	Interest (_____ % per annum on any taxes unpaid by the due date)		
8.	Total Amount Due (Add Lines 5, 6, and 7)		

Under the penalties of perjury, I declare that I have examined this report, and to the best of my knowledge and belief, it is true, correct and complete.

Donor's signature _____ Date _____

Preparer's signature _____ Date _____

Address _____ Phone _____

City/State _____ ZIP _____

FOR OFFICE USE ONLY

Acct. # _____

Date Rec'd _____

Amt. Rec'd $ _____

RV-R0001801

(continued)

Form 87 State (Tennessee as Example) Gift Tax Return *continued*

INSTRUCTIONS

WHO MUST FILE A RETURN:

Provided that the total value of all gifts during the calendar year exceeds the applicable exemption levels, the State Gift Tax Return must be filed upon transfer by gift by any person of the following property or any interest therein:

    (a) When the transfer is from a resident of this state:
        (1) Real property situated in Tennessee.
        (2) Tangible personal property, except that which is actually situated outside of Tennessee.
        (3) All intangible personal property.
    (b) When the transfer is from a nonresident of this state:
        (1) Real property situated in Tennessee.
        (2) Tangible personal property which is actually situated in Tennessee.
    (c) Property in which a person holds a qualifying income interest for life, which is included for taxation pursuant to §67-8-101(e) Tennessee Code Annotated.

CLASSIFICATION OF DONEES:

    CLASS A - Husband, wife, son, daughter, lineal ancestor, lineal descendant, brother, sister, son-in-law, daughter-in-law, or step-child. For purposes of the Gift Tax, a person who is related to the donor as a result of legal adoption shall be considered to have the same relationship as a natural lineal ancestor, lineal descendant, brother, sister, or step-child. If a person has no child or grandchild, a niece or nephew of such person and the issue of such niece or nephew shall be a class A donee, for transfers made on or after January 1, 1996.

    CLASS B - Any other relative, person, association, or corporation not specifically designated in Class A.

EXEMPTIONS:

    (a) There shall be allowed against the net gifts made during any calendar year a maximum single exemption of ten thousand dollars ($10,000) against that portion of the net gifts going to donees of class A, and maximum single exemption of five thousand dollars ($5,000) against that portion of the net gifts going to the donees of Class B.

    (b) In the event the aggregate net gifts for any calendar year exceed the allowable maximum single exemptions, the tax shall be applicable only to the extent that the gifts, (other than gifts of future interest in property) to each donee exceed the following amounts:
    CLASS A - Gifts made after 1985 -- the sum of $10,000
    CLASS B - The sum of $3,000
    "Net gifts" mean that total amount of gifts made during any calendar year less allowable deductions.
    IF THE TOTAL VALUE OF ALL GIFTS MADE BY A PERSON DURING ANY CALENDAR YEAR DOES NOT EXCEED THE EXEMPTION LEVELS, NO GIFT TAX RETURN IS REQUIRED OF SUCH PERSON.

SCHEDULE A

Item	Date of Gift	Description of Gift - See Instructions (Include Name of Each Donee)	Value of Gift	Commissioner Appraisal
		TOTAL		

NOTE: To facilitate the Class A and B computations, the items listed above should be segregated into the following categories: (1) gifts to spouse, (2) gifts to Class A donees other than the spouse, (3) gifts to Class B donees, and (4) gifts to charity, public, and similar uses.

DONEES

Name	Address	Age	Relationship

(continued)

Form 87 State (Tennessee as Example) Gift Tax Return *continued*

SCHEDULE B

COMPUTATION OF TAXABLE GIFTS

(1) Total gifts of donor (from Schedule A) ....

(2) One-half of items _____ to _____ attributable to spouse ....

(3) Balance (Line 1 minus Line 2) ....

(4) Gifts of spouse to be included (from Line 2, Schedule B of spouse's return).....................

(5) Total gifts (Line 3 plus Line 4) ....

(6) Deductions

    (a) Total of items_____ to _____ given to spouse .... _____

    (b) Charitable, public and similar gifts .... _____

(7) Total deductions [Line 6(a) plus Line 6(b)]...

(8) Total gifts after deductions (Line 5 minus Line 7) ....

(9) Total gifts to Class A donees .... _____

(10) Total exclusions for the calendar year for each

    Class A donee (except gifts of future interest) .... _____

(11) Exemption: $10,000 less amount on Line 10 (if Line

    10 is $10,000 or greater, enter zero) .... _____

(12) Total Class A exemptions (Line 10 plus Line 11) .... _____

(13) Total taxable Class A gifts (Line 9 minus Line 12)..

(14) Total gifts to Class B donees (Line 8 minus Line 9) .... _____

(15) Total exclusions not exceeding $3,000 for the calendar year

    for each Class B donee (except gifts of future interest) ..... _____

(16) Exemption: $5,000 less amount on Line 15 (if Line 15

    is $5,000 or greater, enter zero) .... _____

(17) Total Class B exemptions (Line 15 plus Line 16)... _____

(18) Total taxable Class B gifts (Line 14 minus Line 17) ....

(19) Total taxable gifts (Line 13 plus Line 18) ....

SCHEDULE C

COMPUTATION OF TAX (For Gifts made after 1983)

(1) Class A taxable gifts from Schedule B, Line 13

	AMOUNT	RATE	TAX
(a) First $40,000, or part thereof =	_____	X 5.5% =	_____
(b) Next $200,000, or part thereof =	_____	X 6.5% =	_____
(c) Next $200,000, or part thereof =	_____	X 7.5% =	_____
(d) Amount over $440,000 ..	_____	X 9.5% =	_____
(e) Total Class A tax (Add lines a through d and transfer to Page 1, Line 1)		=	_____

(2) Class B taxable gifts from Schedule B, Line 18

	AMOUNT	RATE	TAX
(a) First $50,000, or part thereof =	_____	X 6.5% =	_____
(b) Next $50,000, or part thereof =	_____	X 9.5% =	_____
(c) Next $50,000, or part thereof =	_____	X 12.0% =	_____
(d) Next $50,000, or part thereof =	_____	X 13.5% =	_____
(e) Amount over $200,000 ..	_____	X 16.0% =	_____
(f) Total Class B tax (Add lines a through e and transfer to Page 1, Line 2) .... =			_____

must be filed w/in 9 months of dod and taxes paid

Form 88 United States Estate (and Generation-Skipping Transfer) Tax Return (Form 706)

Form **706**
(Rev. July 1999)

Department of the Treasury
Internal Revenue Service

United States Estate (and Generation-Skipping Transfer) Tax Return

Estate of a citizen or resident of the United States (see separate instructions).
To be filed for decedents dying after December 31, 1998.
For Paperwork Reduction Act Notice, see page 1 of the separate instructions.

OMB No. 1545-0015

Part 1.—Decedent and Executor

1a Decedent's first name and middle initial (and maiden name, if any)	1b Decedent's last name		2 Decedent's Social Security No.
Jane M.	Doe		321 54 9876

3a Legal residence (domicile) at time of death (county, state, and ZIP code, or foreign country)	3b Year domicile established	4 Date of birth	5 Date of death
Ramsey County, Minnesota 55102	1960	11/06/12	09/20/00

6a Name of executor (see page 4 of the instructions)	6b Executor's address (number and street including apartment or suite no. or rural route; city, town, or post office; state; and ZIP code)
John C. Doe	1005 Elm Street
6c Executor's social security number (see page 4 of the instructions)	St. Paul, MN 55102
374 29 4665	

7a Name and location of court where will was probated or estate administered	7b Case number
Ramsey County District Court, Probate Division	999999

8 If decedent died testate, check here ▶ ☒ and attach a certified copy of the will. **9** If Form 4768 is attached, check here ▶ ☐

10 If Schedule R-1 is attached, check here ▶ ☐

Part 2.—Tax Computation

1	Total gross estate less exclusion (from Part 5, Recapitulation, page 3, item 12)	1	797,148
2	Total allowable deductions (from Part 5, Recapitulation, page 3, item 23)	2	737,348
3	Taxable estate (subtract line 2 from line 1)	3	59,800
4	Adjusted taxable gifts (total taxable gifts (within the meaning of section 2503) made by the decedent after December 31, 1976, other than gifts that are includible in decedent's gross estate (section 2001(b)))	4	0
5	Add lines 3 and 4	5	59,800
6	Tentative tax on the amount on line 5 from Table A on page 12 of the instructions	6	12,952
7a	If line 5 exceeds $10,000,000, enter the lesser of line 5 or $17,184,000. If line 5 is $10,000,000 or less, skip lines 7a and 7b and enter -0- on line 7c. **7a**		
b	Subtract $10,000,000 from line 7a **7b**		
c	Enter 5% (.05) of line 7b	7c	0
8	Total tentative tax (add lines 6 and 7c)	8	12,952
9	Total gift tax payable with respect to gifts made by the decedent after December 31, 1976. Include gift taxes by the decedent's spouse for such spouse's share of split gifts (section 2513) only if the decedent was the donor of these gifts and they are includible in the decedent's gross estate (see instructions)	9	0
10	Gross estate tax (subtract line 9 from line 8)	10	12,952
11	Maximum unified credit (applicable credit amount) against estate tax . **11** 220,550		
12	Adjustment to unified credit (applicable credit amount). (This adjustment may not exceed $6,000. See page 4 of the instructions.) **12**		
13	Allowable unified credit (applicable credit amount) (subtract line 12 from line 11)	13	220,550
14	Subtract line 13 from line 10 (but do not enter less than zero)	14	0
15	Credit for state death taxes. Do not enter more than line 14. Figure the credit by using the amount on line 3 less $60,000. See Table B in the instructions and **attach credit evidence** (see instructions)	15	0
16	Subtract line 15 from line 14	16	0
17	Credit for Federal gift taxes on pre-1977 gifts (section 2012) (attach computation) **17**		
18	Credit for foreign death taxes (from Schedule(s) P). (Attach Form(s) 706-CE.) **18**		
19	Credit for tax on prior transfers (from Schedule Q) **19**		
20	Total (add lines 17, 18, and 19)	20	0
21	Net estate tax (subtract line 20 from line 16)	21	0
22	Generation-skipping transfer taxes (from Schedule R, Part 2, line 10)	22	0
23	Total transfer taxes (add lines 21 and 22)	23	0
24	Prior payments. Explain in an attached statement **24**		
25	United States Treasury bonds redeemed in payment of estate tax **25**		
26	Total (add lines 24 and 25)	26	0
27	Balance due (or overpayment) (subtract line 26 from line 23)	27	0

Under penalties of perjury, I declare that I have examined this return, including accompanying schedules and statements, and to the best of my knowledge and belief, it is true, correct, and complete. Declaration of preparer other than the executor is based on all information of which preparer has any knowledge.

/S/ John C. Doe	08/03/01
Signature(s) of executor(s)	Date

/S/ John W. Cranwall	First Trust Co. Bldg. St. Paul, MN 55101	08/03/01
Signature of preparer other than executor	Address (and ZIP code)	Date

Cat. No. 20548R

(continued)

Form 88   United States Estate (and Generation-Skipping Transfer) Tax Return (Form 706)   *continued*

Form 706 (Rev. 7-99)

Estate of: Jane M. Doe

Part 3—Elections by the Executor

Please check the "Yes" or "No" box for each question. (See instructions beginning on page 5.)		Yes	No
1 Do you elect alternate valuation?	**1**		x
2 Do you elect special use valuation? If "Yes," you must complete and attach Schedule A–1.	**2**		x
3 Do you elect to pay the taxes in installments as described in section 6166? If "Yes," you must attach the additional information described on page 8 of the instructions.	**3**		x
4 Do you elect to postpone the part of the taxes attributable to a reversionary or remainder interest as described in section 6163?	**4**		x

Part 4—General Information   (Note: *Please attach the necessary supplemental documents.* **You must attach the death certificate.**)
(See instructions on page 9.)

Authorization to receive confidential tax information under Regs. sec. 601.504(b)(2)(i); to act as the estate's representative before the IRS; and to make written or oral presentations on behalf of the estate if return prepared by an attorney, accountant, or enrolled agent for the executor:

Name of representative (print or type)	State	Address (number, street, and room or suite no., city, state, and ZIP code)
John W. Cranwall	MN	First Trust Co. Bldg., St. Paul, MN 55101

I declare that I am the ☒ attorney/ ☐ certified public accountant/ ☐ enrolled agent (you must check the applicable box) for the executor and prepared this return for the executor. I am not under suspension or disbarment from practice before the Internal Revenue Service and am qualified to practice in the state shown above.

Signature	CAF number	Date	Telephone number
/S/ John W. Cranwall	111111119	08/03/01	(651) 555-5555

1   Death certificate number and issuing authority (attach a copy of the death certificate to this return).
   #876543, Minnesota Department of Health

2   Decedent's business or occupation. If retired, check here ▶ ☒ and state decedent's former business or occupation.
   Real Estate Broker

3   Marital status of the decedent at time of death:
   ☒ Married
   ☐ Widow or widower—Name, SSN, and date of death of deceased spouse ▶ ....
   ....
   ☐ Single
   ☐ Legally separated
   ☐ Divorced—Date divorce decree became final ▶

4a Surviving spouse's name	**4b** Social security number	**4c** Amount received (see page 9 of the instructions)
John C. Doe	374 29 4665	$554,078

5   Individuals (other than the surviving spouse), trusts, or other estates who receive benefits from the estate (do not include charitable beneficiaries shown in Schedule O) (see instructions). For Privacy Act Notice (applicable to individual beneficiaries only), see the Instructions for Form 1040.

Name of individual, trust, or estate receiving $5,000 or more	Identifying number	Relationship to decedent	Amount (see instructions)
Jay A. Daw	321-29-8106	Brother	50,000.
Sandy R. Doe	373-16-2693	Daughter	5,000.

All unascertainable beneficiaries and those who receive less than $5,000 . . . . ▶

| **Total** . . . . | | | 55,000. |

Please check the "Yes" or "No" box for each question.		Yes	No
6 Does the gross estate contain any section 2044 property (qualified terminable interest property (QTIP) from a prior gift or estate) (see page 9 of the instructions)?			x

(continued on next page)   **Page 2**

Form 88 United States Estate (and Generation-Skipping Transfer) Tax Return (Form 706) *continued*

Form 706 (Rev. 7-99)

Part 4—General Information *(continued)*

		Yes	No
Please check the "Yes" or "No" box for each question.			
7a Have Federal gift tax returns ever been filed?		x	
If "Yes," please attach copies of the returns, if available, and furnish the following information:			

7b Period(s) covered	**7c** Internal Revenue office(s) where filed
2000	Kansas City, MO 64999-0002

If you answer "Yes" to any of questions 8–16, you must attach additional information as described in the instructions.

		Yes	No
8a Was there any insurance on the decedent's life that is not included on the return as part of the gross estate?			x
b Did the decedent own any insurance on the life of another that is not included in the gross estate?			x
9 Did the decedent at the time of death own any property as a joint tenant with right of survivorship in which **(a)** one or more of the other joint tenants was someone other than the decedent's spouse, and **(b)** less than the full value of the property is included on the return as part of the gross estate? If "Yes," you must complete and attach Schedule E			x
10 Did the decedent, at the time of death, own any interest in a partnership or unincorporated business or any stock in an inactive or closely held corporation?			x
11 Did the decedent make any transfer described in section 2035, 2036, 2037, or 2038 (see the instructions for Schedule G beginning on page 11 of the separate instructions)? If "Yes," you must complete and attach Schedule G		x	
12 Were there in existence at the time of the decedent's death:			
a Any trusts created by the decedent during his or her lifetime?			x
b Any trusts not created by the decedent under which the decedent possessed any power, beneficial interest, or trusteeship?		x	
13 Did the decedent ever possess, exercise, or release any general power of appointment? If "Yes," you must complete and attach Schedule H		x	
14 Was the marital deduction computed under the transitional rule of Public Law 97-34, section 403(e)(3) (Economic Recovery Tax Act of 1981)?			x
If "Yes," attach a separate computation of the marital deduction, enter the amount on item 20 of the Recapitulation, and note on item 20 "computation attached."			
15 Was the decedent, immediately before death, receiving an annuity described in the "General" paragraph of the instructions for Schedule I? If "Yes," you must complete and attach Schedule I		x	
16 Was the decedent ever the beneficiary of a trust for which a deduction was claimed by the estate of a pre-deceased spouse under section 2056(b)(7) and which is not reported on this return? If "Yes," attach an explanation			x

Part 5—Recapitulation

Item number	Gross estate		Alternate value	Value at date of death
1	Schedule A—Real Estate	1		372,750
2	Schedule B—Stocks and Bonds	2		10,648
3	Schedule C—Mortgages, Notes, and Cash	3		76,350
4	Schedule D—Insurance on the Decedent's Life (attach Form(s) 712) . . .	4		170,100
5	Schedule E—Jointly Owned Property (attach Form(s) 712 for life insurance) .	5		42,500
6	Schedule F—Other Miscellaneous Property (attach Form(s) 712 for life insurance)	6		70,000
7	Schedule G—Transfers During Decedent's Life (att. Form(s) 712 for life insurance)	7		0
8	Schedule H—Powers of Appointment	8		50,000
9	Schedule I—Annuities	9		4,800
10	Total gross estate (add items 1 through 9).	10		797,148
11	Schedule U—Qualified Conservation Easement Exclusion	11		0
12	Total gross estate less exclusion (subtract item 11 from item 10). Enter here and on line 1 of Part 2—Tax Computation	12		797,148

Item number	Deductions		Amount
13	Schedule J—Funeral Expenses and Expenses Incurred in Administering Property Subject to Claims . . .	13	25,340
14	Schedule K—Debts of the Decedent	14	1,930
15	Schedule K—Mortgages and Liens	15	140,000
16	Total of items 13 through 15	16	167,270
17	Allowable amount of deductions from item 16 (see the instructions for item 17 of the Recapitulation) .	17	167,270
18	Schedule L—Net Losses During Administration	18	0
19	Schedule L—Expenses Incurred in Administering Property Not Subject to Claims	19	0
20	Schedule M—Bequests, etc., to Surviving Spouse	20	554,078
21	Schedule O—Charitable, Public, and Similar Gifts and Bequests	21	16,000
22	Schedule T—Qualified Family-Owned Business Interest Deduction	22	
23	Total allowable deductions (add items 17 through 22). Enter here and on line 2 of the Tax Computation	23	737,348

Page 3

(continued)

Form 88 United States Estate (and Generation-Skipping Transfer) Tax Return (Form 706)   *continued*

Form 706 (Rev. 7-99)

Estate of: Jane M. Doe

SCHEDULE A—Real Estate

- *For jointly owned property that must be disclosed on Schedule E, see the instructions on the reverse side of Schedule E.*
- *Real estate that is part of a sole proprietorship should be shown on Schedule F.*
- *Real estate that is included in the gross estate under section 2035, 2036, 2037, or 2038 should be shown on Schedule G.*
- *Real estate that is included in the gross estate under section 2041 should be shown on Schedule H.*
- *If you elect section 2032A valuation, you must complete Schedule A and Schedule A-1.*

Item number	Description	Alternate valuation date	Alternate value	Value at date of death
1	House and lot, 1005 Elm St., St. Paul, MN, Lot 615, Block 42, Reiser's Addition to St. Paul, Ramsey County (Plat #22760 Parcel #7600), in name of decedent. Copy of Appraisal attached as Exhibit_____. Mortgage balance at St. Paul Bank and Trust Company – $130,000.			350,000.
2	An undivided one-fourth (1/4) interest in duplex and lots, 776 Cliff Rd., St. Paul, MN, Lots 16 & 17, Block 20, Lovey's Addition to St. Paul, Ramsey County (Plat #32689 Parcel #5562), in name of decedent. (1/4 x $91,000) Copy of Appraisal attached as Exhibit_____. (Assume all rent due and collected prior to death.) Mortgage balance at St. Paul Bank and Trust Company – $10,000 (1/4 x $40,000)			22,750.
	Total from continuation schedules or additional sheets attached to this schedule . . .			
	TOTAL. (Also enter on Part 5, Recapitulation, page 3, at item 1.)			372,750.

(If more space is needed, attach the continuation schedule from the end of this package or additional sheets of the same size.)
(See the instructions on the reverse side.)

Schedule A—Page 4

(continued)

Form 88 United States Estate (and Generation-Skipping Transfer) Tax Return (Form 706) *continued*

Form 706 (Rev. 7-99)

Estate of: Jane M. Doe	Decedent's Social Security Number

SCHEDULE A-1—Section 2032A Valuation

Part 1. Type of Election (Before making an election, see the checklist on page 7.):

☐ **Protective election (Regulations section 20.2032A-8(b)).** Complete Part 2, line 1, and column A of lines 3 and 4. (See instructions.)
☐ **Regular election.** Complete all of Part 2 (including line 11, if applicable) and Part 3. (See instructions.)

Before completing Schedule A-1, see the checklist on page 7 for the information and documents that must be included to make a valid election.

The election is not valid unless the agreement (i.e., Part 3—Agreement to Special Valuation Under Section 2032A)—
• Is signed by each and every qualified heir with an interest in the specially valued property, and
• Is attached to this return when it is filed.

Part 2. Notice of Election (Regulations section 20.2032A-8(a)(3))

Note: *All real property entered on lines 2 and 3 must also be entered on Schedules A, E, F, G, or H, as applicable.*

1 Qualified use—check one ▶ ☐ Farm used for farming, or
                ▶ ☐ Trade or business other than farming

2 Real property used in a qualified use, passing to qualified heirs, and to be specially valued on this Form 706.

A Schedule and item number from Form 706	B Full value (without section 2032A(b)(3)(B) adjustment)	C Adjusted value (with section 2032A(b)(3)(B) adjustment)	D Value based on qualified use (without section 2032A(b)(3)(B) adjustment)
Totals			

Attach a legal description of all property listed on line 2.
Attach copies of appraisals showing the column B values for all property listed on line 2.

3 Real property used in a qualified use, passing to qualified heirs, but not specially valued on this Form 706.

A Schedule and item number from Form 706	B Full value (without section 2032A(b)(3)(B) adjustment)	C Adjusted value (with section 2032A(b)(3)(B) adjustment)	D Value based on qualified use (without section 2032A(b)(3)(B) adjustment)
Totals			

If you checked "Regular election," you must attach copies of appraisals showing the column B values for all property listed on line 3.

(continued on next page)

Schedule A-1—Page 8

(continued)

Form 88   United States Estate (and Generation-Skipping Transfer) Tax Return (Form 706)   *continued*

Form 706 (Rev. 7-99)

4 Personal property used in a qualified use and passing to qualified heirs.

A Schedule and item number from Form 706	B Adjusted value (with section 2032A(b)(3)(B) adjustment)	A (continued) Schedule and item number from Form 706	B (continued) Adjusted value (with section 2032A(b)(3)(B) adjustment)
		"Subtotal" from Col. B, below left	....

Subtotal . . . .   **Total adjusted value** . . .

5 Enter the value of the total gross estate as adjusted under section 2032A(b)(3)(A). ▶

6 Attach a description of the method used to determine the special value based on qualified use.

7 Did the decedent and/or a member of his or her family own all property listed on line 2 for at least 5 of the 8 years immediately preceding the date of the decedent's death? . . . .   ☐ **Yes** ☐ **No**

8 Were there any periods during the 8-year period preceding the date of the decedent's death during which the decedent or a member of his or her family:

	Yes	No
a Did not own the property listed on line 2 above?		
b Did not use the property listed on line 2 above in a qualified use?		
c Did not materially participate in the operation of the farm or other business within the meaning of section 2032A(e)(6)?		

If "Yes" to any of the above, you must attach a statement listing the periods. If applicable, describe whether the exceptions of sections 2032A(b)(4) or (5) are met.

9 Attach affidavits describing the activities constituting material participation and the identity and relationship to the decedent of the material participants.

10 Persons holding interests. Enter the requested information for each party who received any interest in the specially valued property. **(Each of the qualified heirs receiving an interest in the property must sign the agreement, and the agreement must be filed with this return.)**

	Name	Address
A		
B		
C		
D		
E		
F		
G		
H		

	Identifying number	Relationship to decedent	Fair market value	Special use value
A				
B				
C				
D				
E				
F				
G				
H				

You must attach a computation of the GST tax savings attributable to direct skips for each person listed above who is a skip person. (See instructions.)

11 Woodlands election. Check here ▶ ☐ if you wish to make a woodlands election as described in section 2032A(e)(13). Enter the Schedule and item numbers from Form 706 of the property for which you are making this election ▶ ....
You must attach a statement explaining why you are entitled to make this election. The IRS may issue regulations that require more information to substantiate this election. You will be notified by the IRS if you must supply further information.

Schedule A-1—Page 9

(continued)

Form 88 United States Estate (and Generation-Skipping Transfer) Tax Return (Form 706) *continued*

Form 706 (Rev. 7-99)

Part 3. Agreement to Special Valuation Under Section 2032A

Estate of:	Date of Death	Decedent's Social Security Number

There cannot be a valid election unless:

- The agreement is executed by each and every one of the qualified heirs, and
- The agreement is included with the estate tax return when the estate tax return is filed.

We (list all qualified heirs and other persons having an interest in the property required to sign this agreement)

_____

_____ ,

being all the qualified heirs and _____

_____ ,

being all other parties having interests in the property which is qualified real property and which is valued under section 2032A of the Internal Revenue Code, do hereby approve of the election made by _____ ,
Executor/Administrator of the estate of _____ ,
pursuant to section 2032A to value said property on the basis of the qualified use to which the property is devoted and do hereby enter into this agreement pursuant to section 2032A(d).

The undersigned agree and consent to the application of subsection (c) of section 2032A of the Code with respect to all the property described on line 2 of Part 2 of Schedule A-1 of Form 706, attached to this agreement. More specifically, the undersigned heirs expressly agree and consent to personal liability under subsection (c) of 2032A for the additional estate and GST taxes imposed by that subsection with respect to their respective interests in the above-described property in the event of certain early dispositions of the property or early cessation of the qualified use of the property. It is understood that if a qualified heir disposes of any interest in qualified real property to any member of his or her family, such member may thereafter be treated as the qualified heir with respect to such interest upon filing a Form 706-A and a new agreement.

The undersigned interested parties who are not qualified heirs consent to the collection of any additional estate and GST taxes imposed under section 2032A(c) of the Code from the specially valued property.

If there is a disposition of any interest which passes, or has passed to him or her, or if there is a cessation of the qualified use of any specially valued property which passes or passed to him or her, each of the undersigned heirs agrees to file a **Form 706-A,** United States Additional Estate Tax Return, and pay any additional estate and GST taxes due within 6 months of the disposition or cessation.

It is understood by all interested parties that this agreement is a condition precedent to the election of special use valuation under section 2032A of the Code and must be executed by every interested party even though that person may not have received the estate (or GST) tax benefits or be in possession of such property.

Each of the undersigned understands that by making this election, a lien will be created and recorded pursuant to section 6324B of the Code on the property referred to in this agreement for the adjusted tax differences with respect to the estate as defined in section 2032A(c)(2)(C).

As the interested parties, the undersigned designate the following individual as their agent for all dealings with the Internal Revenue Service concerning the continued qualification of the specially valued property under section 2032A of the Code and on all issues regarding the special lien under section 6324B. The agent is authorized to act for the parties with respect to all dealings with the Service on matters affecting the qualified real property described earlier. This authority includes the following:

- To receive confidential information on all matters relating to continued qualification under section 2032A of the specially valued real property and on all matters relating to the special lien arising under section 6324B.
- To furnish the Internal Revenue Service with any requested information concerning the property.
- To notify the Internal Revenue Service of any disposition or cessation of qualified use of any part of the property.
- To receive, but not to endorse and collect, checks in payment of any refund of Internal Revenue taxes, penalties, or interest.
- To execute waivers (including offers of waivers) of restrictions on assessment or collection of deficiencies in tax and waivers of notice of disallowance of a claim for credit or refund.
- To execute closing agreements under section 7121.

(continued on next page)

Schedule A-1— Page 10

(continued)

Form 88 United States Estate (and Generation-Skipping Transfer) Tax Return (Form 706) *continued*

Form 706 (Rev. 7-99)

Part 3. Agreement to Special Valuation Under Section 2032A *(Continued)*

Estate of:	Date of Death	Decedent's Social Security Number

- Other acts (specify) ▶ _____

By signing this agreement, the agent agrees to provide the Internal Revenue Service with any requested information concerning this property and to notify the Internal Revenue Service of any disposition or cessation of the qualified use of any part of this property.

Name of Agent	Signature	Address

The property to which this agreement relates is listed in Form 706, United States Estate (and Generation-Skipping Transfer) Tax Return, and in the Notice of Election, along with its fair market value according to section 2031 of the Code and its special use value according to section 2032A. The name, address, social security number, and interest (including the value) of each of the undersigned in this property are as set forth in the attached Notice of Election.

IN WITNESS WHEREOF, the undersigned have hereunto set their hands at _____,

this _____ day of _____ .

SIGNATURES OF EACH OF THE QUALIFIED HEIRS:

Signature of qualified heir	Signature of qualified heir
Signature of qualified heir	Signature of qualified heir
Signature of qualified heir	Signature of qualified heir
Signature of qualified heir	Signature of qualified heir
Signature of qualified heir	Signature of qualified heir
Signature of qualified heir	Signature of qualified heir

Signatures of other interested parties

Signatures of other interested parties

Schedule A-1—Page 11

(continued)

Form 88 United States Estate (and Generation-Skipping Transfer) Tax Return (Form 706) *continued*

Form 706 (Rev. 7-99)

Estate of: Jane M. Doe

SCHEDULE B—Stocks and Bonds

(For jointly owned property that must be disclosed on Schedule E, see the instructions for Schedule E.)

Item number	Description including face amount of bonds or number of shares and par value where needed for identification. Give 9-digit CUSIP number.	Unit value	Alternate valuation date	Alternate value	Value at date of death
		CUSIP number			
1	100 shares Tenneco, Inc., Common, NYSE.	674322189	50.00		5,000.
2	1000 shares Minnesota Co-op, Common, OTC.	911388135	4.50		4,500.
3	$500 U.S. Savings Bond, Series E, #R4502363E, dated April 1990.				574.
4	$500 U.S. Savings Bond, Series E, #R4502364E, dated April 1990. (Assume no accrued dividends on Items 1 and 2.)				574.

Total from continuation schedules (or additional sheets) attached to this schedule . . .	
TOTAL. (Also enter on Part 5, Recapitulation, page 3, at item 2.)	10,648.

(If more space is needed, attach the continuation schedule from the end of this package or additional sheets of the same size.)
(The instructions to Schedule B are in the separate instructions.) **Schedule B—Page 12**

(continued)

Form 88 United States Estate (and Generation-Skipping Transfer) Tax Return (Form 706) *continued*

Form 706 (Rev. 7-99)

Estate of: Jane M. Doe

SCHEDULE C—Mortgages, Notes, and Cash

(For jointly owned property that must be disclosed on Schedule E, see the instructions for Schedule E.)

Item number	Description	Alternate valuation date	Alternate value	Value at date of death
1	Promissory Note of $10,000 from Johnson Furriers dated 03/20/94 payable 03/20/01 (extended to 09/20/01) with interest at 7% per annum payable 09/20.			10,000.
	Interest accrued on Item 1 from 03/20/00 to 09/20/00.			350.
2	Traveler's checks, American Express Nos. 10008–10017, in the amount of $100 each in name of decedent, uncashed at date of death.			1,000.
3	Checking Account No. 55-5555, First National City Bank of St. Paul, in name of decedent, reconciled balance as of date of death.			50,000.
4	Savings Certificate No. 44-4444, American National Bank of St. Paul, in name of decedent, dated 01/20/00 with interest at 5.5% per annum payable monthly. (Assume interest check in the amount of $68.75 payable 09/20/00 was received and deposited in checking account on 09/20/00.)			15,000.
	Total from continuation schedules (or additional sheets) attached to this schedule . .			
	TOTAL. (Also enter on Part 5, Recapitulation, page 3, at item 3.).			76,350.

(If more space is needed, attach the continuation schedule from the end of this package or additional sheets of the same size.)
(See the instructions on the reverse side.)

Schedule C—Page 13

(continued)

Form 88   United States Estate (and Generation-Skipping Transfer) Tax Return (Form 706)   *continued*

Form 706 (Rev. 7-99)

Estate of: Jane M. Doe

SCHEDULE D—Insurance on the Decedent's Life
You must list **all** policies on the life of the decedent and attach a Form 712 for each policy.

Item number	Description		Alternate valuation date	Alternate value	Value at date of death
1	Minnesota Life Insurance Company Policy J 666221 Estate of Jane M. Doe, Beneficiary Face Amount Accumulated Dividends	$120,000 100 $120,100			120,100.
2	Prudential Life Insurance Company Policy 11-1111-123 Jay A. Daw, Beneficiary Face Amount Forms 712 attached	$ 50,000			50,000.
	Total from continuation schedules (or additional sheets) attached to this schedule . .				
	TOTAL. (Also enter on Part 5, Recapitulation, page 3, at item 4.)				170,100.

(If more space is needed, attach the continuation schedule from the end of this package or additional sheets of the same size.)

(See the instructions on the reverse side.)

Schedule D—Page 15

(continued)

Form 88 United States Estate (and Generation-Skipping Transfer) Tax Return (Form 706)   *continued*

Form 706 (Rev. 7-99)

Estate of: Jane M. Doe

SCHEDULE E—Jointly Owned Property
(If you elect section 2032A valuation, you must complete Schedule E and Schedule A-1.)

PART 1.—Qualified Joint Interests—Interests Held by the Decedent and His or Her Spouse as the Only Joint Tenants (Section 2040(b)(2))

Item number	Description For securities, give CUSIP number.	Alternate valuation date	Alternate value	Value at date of death
1	1000 shares American National Slide Rule Company, Common, NYSE, CUSIP 911384275, at $75.00 per share. (Assume no accrued dividends.)			75,000.
	Total from continuation schedules (or additional sheets) attached to this schedule			

1a Totals	**1a**		75,000.
1b Amounts included in gross estate (one-half of line **1a**)	**1b**		37,500.

PART 2.—All Other Joint Interests

2a State the name and address of each surviving co-tenant. If there are more than three surviving co-tenants, list the additional co-tenants on an attached sheet.

	Name	Address (number and street, city, state, and ZIP code)
A.	Sandy R. Doe	1005 Elm Street, St. Paul, MN 55102
B.		
C.		

Item number	Enter letter for co-tenant	Description (including alternate valuation date if any) For securities, give CUSIP number.	Percentage includible	Includible alternate value	Includible value at date of death
1	A	100 shares Minnesota Company, Common, NYSE, CUSIP 812456213, at $50.00 per share. (Assume no accrued dividends.) (Assume surviving joint tenant provided no consideration.)	100%		5,000.
		Total from continuation schedules (or additional sheets) attached to this schedule			

2b Total other joint interests		5,000.
3 **Total includible joint interests** (add lines 1b and 2b). Also enter on Part 5, Recapitulation, page 3, at item 5		42,500.

(If more space is needed, attach the continuation schedule from the end of this package or additional sheets of the same size.)
(See the instructions on the reverse side.)   **Schedule E—Page 17**

(continued)

Form 88   United States Estate (and Generation-Skipping Transfer) Tax Return (Form 706)   *continued*

Form 706 (Rev. 7-99)

Estate of: Jane M. Doe

SCHEDULE F—Other Miscellaneous Property Not Reportable Under Any Other Schedule
(For jointly owned property that must be disclosed on Schedule E, see the instructions for Schedule E.)
(If you elect section 2032A valuation, you must complete Schedule F and Schedule A-1.)

		Yes	No
1	Did the decedent at the time of death own any articles of artistic or collectible value in excess of $3,000 or any collections whose artistic or collectible value combined at date of death exceeded $10,000? . . . . If "Yes," submit full details on this schedule and attach appraisals.	x	
2	Has the decedent's estate, spouse, or any other person, received (or will receive) any bonus or award as a result of the decedent's employment or death? . . . . If "Yes," submit full details on this schedule.		x
3	Did the decedent at the time of death have, or have access to, a safe deposit box? . . . . If "Yes," state location, and if held in joint names of decedent and another, state name and relationship of joint depositor.		x

If any of the contents of the safe deposit box are omitted from the schedules in this return, explain fully why omitted.

Item number	Description For securities, give CUSIP number.	Alternate valuation date	Alternate value	Value at date of death
1	Furniture and household goods located at homestead.			22,000.
2	Fur – Mink coat. Copy of Appraisal attached as Exhibit_____.			11,500.
3	Clothing and personal effects.			4,500.
4	1998 Mazda, Vehicle Identification Number 6778899926, Title Number 03618957, Bluebook market value.			12,000.
5	Judgment dated February 19, 1997 against Forrest R. Redding, collected in full on December 20, 2000.			20,000.
6	Trust created by decedent's uncle with income distributable to decedent for her lifetime and thereafter to her daughter; St. Paul Trust Co., Trustee; decedent had no power of appointment nor other incidents of ownership, therefore, trust assets are not taxable to decedent's estate. (Assume all income distributable to decedent's date of death had been received by 09/20/00.)			0
	Total from continuation schedules (or additional sheets) attached to this schedule . .			
	TOTAL. (Also enter on Part 5, Recapitulation, page 3, at item 6.)			70,000.

(If more space is needed, attach the continuation schedule from the end of this package or additional sheets of the same size.)
(See the instructions on the reverse side.)

Schedule F—Page 19

(continued)

Form 88   United States Estate (and Generation-Skipping Transfer) Tax Return (Form 706)   *continued*

Form 706 (Rev. 7-99)

Estate of: Jane M. Doe

SCHEDULE G—Transfers During Decedent's Life
(If you elect section 2032A valuation, you must complete Schedule G and Schedule A-1.)

Item number	Description For securities, give CUSIP number.	Alternate valuation date	Alternate value	Value at date of death
A.	Gift tax paid by the decedent or the estate for all gifts made by the decedent or his or her spouse within 3 years before the decedent's death (section 2035(b))	X X X X X		0
B.	Transfers includible under section 2035(a), 2036, 2037, or 2038:			
1				
	(Refer to gift tax return filed 02/15/01)			
	Total from continuation schedules (or additional sheets) attached to this schedule . .			
	TOTAL. (Also enter on Part 5, Recapitulation, page 3, at item 7.)			0

SCHEDULE H—Powers of Appointment
(Include "5 and 5 lapsing" powers (section 2041(b)(2)) held by the decedent.)
(If you elect section 2032A valuation, you must complete Schedule H and Schedule A-1.)

Item number	Description	Alternate valuation date	Alternate value	Value at date of death
1	Trust created under agreement dated 12/02/65 by father of decedent for decedent's benefit under which decedent had a general power of appointment (to distribute income and/or principal) which power had not been exercised during decedent's lifetime, but which decedent exercised under her will. The assets remaining in this trust and subject to this power are 500 shares of Green Giant common stock and undistributed earnings (dividends) thereon. Unit value $100.00 per share.			50,000.
	Total from continuation schedules (or additional sheets) attached to this schedule . .			
	TOTAL. (Also enter on Part 5, Recapitulation, page 3, at item 8.)			50,000.

(If more space is needed, attach the continuation schedule from the end of this package or additional sheets of the same size.)
(The instructions to Schedules G and H are in the separate instructions.)

Schedules G and H—Page 21

(continued)

Form 88 United States Estate (and Generation-Skipping Transfer) Tax Return (Form 706) *continued*

Form 706 (Rev. 7-99)

Estate of: Jane M. Doe

SCHEDULE I—Annuities

Note: *Generally, no exclusion is allowed for the estates of decedents dying after December 31, 1984 (see page 15 of the instructions).*

	Yes	No
A Are you excluding from the decedent's gross estate the value of a lump-sum distribution described in section 2039(f)(2)? . . . . If "Yes," you must attach the information required by the instructions.		x

Item number	Description Show the entire value of the annuity before any exclusions.	Alternate valuation date	Includible alternate value	Includible value at date of death
1	Ecko Life Insurance Company Policy 99-9999. Annuity of $100.00 per month payable to decedent for life, thereafter to John C. Doe, husband of decedent (value of annuity based upon life expectancy of male, age 83, is approximately 4.000 x $1,200.00)			4,800.
	Total from continuation schedules (or additional sheets) attached to this schedule . .			
	TOTAL. (Also enter on Part 5, Recapitulation, page 3, at item 9.).			4,800.

(If more space is needed, attach the continuation schedule from the end of this package or additional sheets of the same size.)

(The instructions to Schedule I are in the separate instructions.)

Schedule I—Page 22

(continued)

Form 88   United States Estate (and Generation-Skipping Transfer) Tax Return (Form 706)   *continued*

Form 706 (Rev. 7-99)

Estate of: Jane M. Doe

SCHEDULE J—Funeral Expenses and Expenses Incurred in Administering Property Subject to Claims

Note: *Do not list on this schedule expenses of administering property not subject to claims. For those expenses, see the instructions for Schedule L.*

If executors' commissions, attorney fees, etc., are claimed and allowed as a deduction for estate tax purposes, they are not allowable as a deduction in computing the taxable income of the estate for Federal income tax purposes. They are allowable as an income tax deduction on Form 1041 if a waiver is filed to waive the deduction on Form 706 (see the Form 1041 instructions).

Item number	Description	Expense amount	Total amount
	A. Funeral expenses:		
1	Newark & Newark Funeral Home – funeral.	9,500.	
2	Morningside Florists – funeral flowers.	100.	
3	Riverside Cemetery – burial.	1,000.	
4	Brown Monument Company – gravestone.	500.	
5	Rev. B. Stone – funeral services.	25.	
	Total funeral expenses. . . . . ▶		11,125.
	B. Administration expenses:		
1	Executors' commissions—amount estimated/agreed upon/paid. (Strike out the words that do not apply.) (Claimed on estate's fiduciary income tax return).		0
2	Attorney fees—~~amount estimated~~/agreed upon/~~paid~~. (Strike out the words that do not apply.). . (Claimed $2,040 on estate's fiduciary income tax return)		12,960.
3	Accountant fees—~~amount estimated/agreed upon~~/paid. (Strike out the words that do not apply.).		250.

		Expense amount
4	Miscellaneous expenses:	
	Fees Probate Court	2.
	Printing fees	5.
	Certified copies	50.
	Miscellaneous expenses	448.
	Philip Masterson Co., Inc., appraisals	500.

Total miscellaneous expenses from continuation schedules (or additional sheets) attached to this schedule		
Total miscellaneous expenses . . . . ▶		1,005.
TOTAL. (Also enter on Part 5, Recapitulation, page 3, at item 13.) . . . . ▶		25,340.

(If more space is needed, attach the continuation schedule from the end of this package or additional sheets of the same size.)
(See the instructions on the reverse side.)   **Schedule J—Page 23**

(continued)

Form 88 United States Estate (and Generation-Skipping Transfer) Tax Return (Form 706) *continued*

Form 706 (Rev. 7-99)

Estate of: Jane M. Doe

SCHEDULE K—Debts of the Decedent, and Mortgages and Liens

Item number	Debts of the Decedent—Creditor and nature of claim, and allowable death taxes	Amount unpaid to date	Amount in contest	Amount claimed as a deduction
1	Porta Veta Hospital – last illness expense.			850.
2	Ace's Plumbing Co. – plumbing debt contracted by decedent, company claims $480 is owed, personal representative claims $230 is owed.		250.	230.
3	St. Paul Telephone Co. – telephone.			50.
4	St. Paul Electric Co. – electricity.			100.
5	Harvey's Garbage Pickup – rubbish removal.			50.
6	Dr. Norma J. Dennison – medical.			600.
7	St. Paul Rents – medical (wheelchair).			50.

Total from continuation schedules (or additional sheets) attached to this schedule . . . .

TOTAL. (Also enter on Part 5, Recapitulation, page 3, at item 14.) . . . .   **1,930.**

Item number	Mortgages and Liens—Description	Amount
1	Mortgage on house and lot at St. Paul Bank and Trust Company, including accrued interest to date of death. (Schedule A, Item 1)	130,000.
2	Mortgage on duplex and lots at St. Paul Bank and Trust Company, including accrued interest to date of death (1/4 x $40,000). (Schedule A, Item 2)	10,000.

Total from continuation schedules (or additional sheets) attached to this schedule . . . .

TOTAL. (Also enter on Part 5, Recapitulation, page 3, at item 15.) . . . .   **140,000.**

(If more space is needed, attach the continuation schedule from the end of this package or additional sheets of the same size.)
(The instructions to Schedule K are in the separate instructions.)   **Schedule K—Page 25**

(continued)

Form 88 United States Estate (and Generation-Skipping Transfer) Tax Return (Form 706) *continued*

Form 706 (Rev. 7-99)

Estate of: Jane M. Doe

SCHEDULE L—Net Losses During Administration and
Expenses Incurred in Administering Property Not Subject to Claims

Item number	Net losses during administration (**Note:** *Do not deduct losses claimed on a Federal income tax return.*)	Amount
1		
	Total from continuation schedules (or additional sheets) attached to this schedule	
	TOTAL. (Also enter on Part 5, Recapitulation, page 3, at item 18.)	0

Item number	Expenses incurred in administering property not subject to claims (Indicate whether estimated, agreed upon, or paid.)	Amount
1		
	Total from continuation schedules (or additional sheets) attached to this schedule	
	TOTAL. (Also enter on Part 5, Recapitulation, page 3, at item 19.)	0

(If more space is needed, attach the continuation schedule from the end of this package or additional sheets of the same size.)

Schedule L—Page 26   (The instructions to Schedule L are in the separate instructions.)

(continued)

Form 88 United States Estate (and Generation-Skipping Transfer) Tax Return (Form 706) *continued*

Form 706 (Rev. 7-99)

Estate of: Jane M. Doe

SCHEDULE M—Bequests, etc., to Surviving Spouse

Election To Deduct Qualified Terminable Interest Property Under Section 2056(b)(7). If a trust (or other property) meets the requirements of qualified terminable interest property under section 2056(b)(7), and

    a. The trust or other property is listed on Schedule M, and

    b. The value of the trust (or other property) is entered in whole or in part as a deduction on Schedule M,

then unless the executor specifically identifies the trust (all or a fractional portion or percentage) or other property to be excluded from the election, the executor shall be deemed to have made an election to have such trust (or other property) treated as qualified terminable interest property under section 2056(b)(7).

    If less than the entire value of the trust (or other property) that the executor has included in the gross estate is entered as a deduction on Schedule M, the executor shall be considered to have made an election only as to a fraction of the trust (or other property). The numerator of this fraction is equal to the amount of the trust (or other property) deducted on Schedule M. The denominator is equal to the total value of the trust (or other property).

Election To Deduct Qualified Domestic Trust Property Under Section 2056A. If a trust meets the requirements of a qualified domestic trust under section 2056A(a) and this return is filed no later than 1 year after the time prescribed by law (including extensions) for filing the return, and

    a. The entire value of a trust or trust property is listed on Schedule M, and

    b. The entire value of the trust or trust property is entered as a deduction on Schedule M,

then unless the executor specifically identifies the trust to be excluded from the election, the executor shall be deemed to have made an election to have the entire trust treated as qualified domestic trust property.

		Yes	No
1 Did any property pass to the surviving spouse as a result of a qualified disclaimer?	**1**		x
If "Yes," attach a copy of the written disclaimer required by section 2518(b).			
2a In what country was the surviving spouse born? United States			
b What is the surviving spouse's date of birth? 06/14/17			
c Is the surviving spouse a U.S. citizen?	**2c**	x	
d If the surviving spouse is a naturalized citizen, when did the surviving spouse acquire citizenship?			
e If the surviving spouse is not a U.S. citizen, of what country is the surviving spouse a citizen?			
3 **Election Out of QTIP Treatment of Annuities**—Do you elect under section 2056(b)(7)(C)(ii) **not** to treat as qualified terminable interest property any joint and survivor annuities that are included in the gross estate and would otherwise be treated as qualified terminable interest property under section 2056(b)(7)(C)? (see instructions)	**3**	x	

Item number	Description of property interests passing to surviving spouse		Amount
1	Jointly owned property, Schedule E, Item 1		37,500.
2	Property passing under will to spouse:		
	Real Estate, Schedule A, Items 1-2	372,750.	
	Stocks & Bonds, Schedule B, Items 1-4	10,648.	
	Mortgages, Notes & Cash, Schedule C, Items 1-4	76,350.	
	Insurance payable to estate, Schedule D, Item 1	120,100.	
	Miscellaneous property, Schedule F, Items 1-5	70,000.	
	Powers of Appointment, Schedule H, Item 1	50,000.	
		699,848.	
	Less:		
	Deductions, Schedules J & K	167,270.	
	Charitable devises, Schedule O	16,000. 183,270.	516,578.
	Total from continuation schedules (or additional sheets) attached to this schedule		

4	**Total** amount of property interests listed on Schedule M	**4**	554,078.
5a	Federal estate taxes payable out of property interests listed on Schedule M	**5a**	
b	Other death taxes payable out of property interests listed on Schedule M	**5b**	
c	Federal and state GST taxes payable out of property interests listed on Schedule M	**5c**	
d	Add items 5a, b, and c	**5d**	0
6	Net amount of property interests listed on Schedule M (subtract 5d from 4). Also enter on Part 5, Recapitulation, page 3, at item 20	**6**	554,078.

(If more space is needed, attach the continuation schedule from the end of this package or additional sheets of the same size.) (See the instructions on the reverse side.)

Schedule M—Page 27

Note: Annuity payable to spouse does not qualify for marital deduction (terminable interest).

(continued)

Form 88 United States Estate (and Generation-Skipping Transfer) Tax Return (Form 706) *continued*

Form 706 (Rev. 7-99)

Estate of: Jane M. Doe

SCHEDULE O—Charitable, Public, and Similar Gifts and Bequests

	Yes	No
1a If the transfer was made by will, has any action been instituted to have interpreted or to contest the will or any of its provisions affecting the charitable deductions claimed in this schedule? . . . . If "Yes," full details must be submitted with this schedule.		x
b According to the information and belief of the person or persons filing this return, is any such action planned? If "Yes," full details must be submitted with this schedule.		x
2 Did any property pass to charity as the result of a qualified disclaimer? . . . . If "Yes," attach a copy of the written disclaimer required by section 2518(b).		x

Item number	Name and address of beneficiary	Character of institution	Amount
1	American Cancer Society 222 Glen Acre Dr., St. Paul, MN 55102	Medical Research	10,000.
2	Girls' Clubs of America 111 Aspen Lane, St. Paul, MN 55102	Charitable	5,000.
3	Newark Institute of Higher Learning 444 Wirth Drive, St. Paul, MN 55102	Educational Research	1,000.

Total from continuation schedules (or additional sheets) attached to this schedule . . . .

3 Total	**3**		16,000.
4a Federal estate tax payable out of property interests listed above	**4a**		
b Other death taxes payable out of property interests listed above	**4b**		
c Federal and state GST taxes payable out of property interests listed above	**4c**		
d Add items 4a, b, and c	**4d**		0
5 Net value of property interests listed above (subtract 4d from 3). Also enter on Part 5, Recapitulation, page 3, at item 21	**5**		16,000.

(If more space is needed, attach the continuation schedule from the end of this package or additional sheets of the same size.)
(The instructions to Schedule O are in the separate instructions.)

Schedule O—Page 31

(continued)

Form 88   United States Estate (and Generation-Skipping Transfer) Tax Return (Form 706)   *continued*

Form 706 (Rev. 7-99)

Estate of: Jane M. Doe

SCHEDULE P—Credit for Foreign Death Taxes

List all foreign countries to which death taxes have been paid and for which a credit is claimed on this return.

If a credit is claimed for death taxes paid to more than one foreign country, compute the credit for taxes paid to one country on this sheet and attach a separate copy of Schedule P for each of the other countries.

The credit computed on this sheet is for the ....
(Name of death tax or taxes)

.... imposed in ....
(Name of country)

Credit is computed under the ....
(Insert title of treaty or "statute")

Citizenship (nationality) of decedent at time of death

(All amounts and values must be entered in United States money.)

1 Total of estate, inheritance, legacy, and succession taxes imposed in the country named above attributable to property situated in that country, subjected to these taxes, and included in the gross estate (as defined by statute)	**1**	
2 Value of the gross estate (adjusted, if necessary, according to the instructions for item 2)	**2**	
3 Value of property situated in that country, subjected to death taxes imposed in that country, and included in the gross estate (adjusted, if necessary, according to the instructions for item 3)	**3**	
4 Tax imposed by section 2001 reduced by the total credits claimed under sections 2010, 2011, and 2012 (see instructions).	**4**	
5 Amount of Federal estate tax attributable to property specified at item 3. (Divide item 3 by item 2 and multiply the result by item 4.)	**5**	
6 Credit for death taxes imposed in the country named above (the smaller of item 1 or item 5). Also enter on line 18 of Part 2, Tax Computation	**6**	

SCHEDULE Q—Credit for Tax on Prior Transfers

Part 1—Transferor Information

	Name of transferor	Social security number	IRS office where estate tax return was filed	Date of death
A				
B				
C				

Check here ▶ ☐ if section 2013(f) (special valuation of farm, etc., real property) adjustments to the computation of the credit were made (see page 18 of the instructions).

Part 2—Computation of Credit (see instructions beginning on page 18)

Item	Transferor			Total A, B, & C
	A	B	C	
1 Transferee's tax as apportioned (from worksheet, (line 7 ÷ line 8) × line 35 for each column) . .				
2 Transferor's tax (from each column of worksheet, line 20)				
3 Maximum amount before percentage requirement (for each column, enter amount from line 1 or 2, whichever is smaller)				
4 Percentage allowed (each column) (see instructions)	%	%	%	
5 Credit allowable (line 3 × line 4 for each column)				
6 TOTAL credit allowable (add columns A, B, and C of line 5). Enter here and on line 19 of Part 2, Tax Computation				

Schedules P and Q—Page 32   (The instructions to Schedules P and Q are in the separate instructions.)

(continued)

Form 88   United States Estate (and Generation-Skipping Transfer) Tax Return (Form 706)   *continued*

Form 706 (Rev. 7-99)

SCHEDULE R—Generation-Skipping Transfer Tax

Note: *To avoid application of the deemed allocation rules, Form 706 and Schedule R should be filed to allocate the GST exemption to trusts that may later have taxable terminations or distributions under section 2612 even if the form is not required to be filed to report estate or GST tax.*

*The GST tax is imposed on taxable transfers of interests in property located **outside the United States** as well as property located inside the United States.*

See instructions beginning on page 19.

Part 1—GST Exemption Reconciliation (Section 2631) and Section 2652(a)(3) (Special QTIP) Election

You no longer need to check a box to make a section 2652(a)(3) (special QTIP) election. If you list qualifying property in Part 1, line 9, below, you will be considered to have made this election. See page 21 of the separate instructions for details.

1 Maximum allowable GST exemption	1
2 Total GST exemption allocated by the decedent against decedent's lifetime transfers	2
3 Total GST exemption allocated by the executor, using Form 709, against decedent's lifetime transfers	3
4 GST exemption allocated on line 6 of Schedule R, Part 2	4
5 GST exemption allocated on line 6 of Schedule R, Part 3	5
6 Total GST exemption allocated on line 4 of Schedule(s) R-1	6
7 Total GST exemption allocated to intervivos transfers and direct skips (add lines 2–6)	7
8 GST exemption available to allocate to trusts and section 2032A interests (subtract line 7 from line 1)	8

9 Allocation of GST exemption to trusts (as defined for GST tax purposes):

A Name of trust	B Trust's EIN (if any)	C GST exemption allocated on lines 2–6, above (see instructions)	D Additional GST exemption allocated (see instructions)	E Trust's inclusion ratio (optional—see instructions)

9D Total. May not exceed line 8, above   **9D**

10 GST exemption available to allocate to section 2032A interests received by individual beneficiaries (subtract line 9D from line 8). You must attach special use allocation schedule (see instructions)   **10**

(The instructions to Schedule R are in the separate instructions.)   **Schedule R—Page 33**

(continued)

Form 88 United States Estate (and Generation-Skipping Transfer) Tax Return (Form 706) *continued*

Form 706 (Rev. 7-99)

Estate of: Jane M. Doe

Part 2—Direct Skips Where the Property Interests Transferred Bear the GST Tax on the Direct Skips

Name of skip person	Description of property interest transferred	Estate tax value

1 Total estate tax values of all property interests listed above	**1**	
2 Estate taxes, state death taxes, and other charges borne by the property interests listed above .	**2**	
3 GST taxes borne by the property interests listed above but imposed on direct skips other than those shown on this Part 2 (see instructions)	**3**	
4 Total fixed taxes and other charges (add lines 2 and 3).	**4**	
5 Total tentative maximum direct skips (subtract line 4 from line 1)	**5**	
6 GST exemption allocated	**6**	
7 Subtract line 6 from line 5	**7**	
8 GST tax due (divide line 7 by 2.818182).	**8**	
9 Enter the amount from line 8 of Schedule R, Part 3	**9**	
10 **Total GST taxes payable by the estate** (add lines 8 and 9). Enter here and on line 22 of Part 2—Tax Computation, on page 1	**10**	

Schedule R—Page 34

(continued)

Form 88   United States Estate (and Generation-Skipping Transfer) Tax Return (Form 706)   *continued*

Form 706 (Rev. 7-99)

Estate of: Jane M. Doe

Part 3—Direct Skips Where the Property Interests Transferred Do Not Bear the GST Tax on the Direct Skips

Name of skip person	Description of property interest transferred	Estate tax value

1 Total estate tax values of all property interests listed above	1	
2 Estate taxes, state death taxes, and other charges borne by the property interests listed above .	2	
3 GST taxes borne by the property interests listed above but imposed on direct skips other than those shown on this Part 3 (see instructions)	3	
4 Total fixed taxes and other charges (add lines 2 and 3).	4	
5 Total tentative maximum direct skips (subtract line 4 from line 1)	5	
6 GST exemption allocated	6	
7 Subtract line 6 from line 5	7	
8 GST tax due (multiply line 7 by .55). Enter here and on Schedule R, Part 2, line 9	8	

Schedule R—Page 35

(continued)

Form 88 United States Estate (and Generation-Skipping Transfer) Tax Return (Form 706) *continued*

SCHEDULE R-1
(Form 706)
(Rev. July 1999)
Department of the Treasury
Internal Revenue Service

Generation-Skipping Transfer Tax
Direct Skips From a Trust
Payment Voucher

OMB No. 1545-0015

Executor: File one copy with Form 706 and send two copies to the fiduciary. Do not pay the tax shown. See the separate instructions.
Fiduciary: See instructions on the following page. Pay the tax shown on line 6.

Name of trust	Trust's EIN
Name and title of fiduciary	Name of decedent
Address of fiduciary (number and street)	Decedent's SSN / Service Center where Form 706 was filed
City, state, and ZIP code	Name of executor
Address of executor (number and street)	City, state, and ZIP code
Date of decedent's death	Filing due date of Schedule R, Form 706 (with extensions)

Part 1—Computation of the GST Tax on the Direct Skip

Description of property interests subject to the direct skip	Estate tax value

1	Total estate tax value of all property interests listed above	**1**
2	Estate taxes, state death taxes, and other charges borne by the property interests listed above.	**2**
3	Tentative maximum direct skip from trust (subtract line 2 from line 1)	**3**
4	GST exemption allocated	**4**
5	Subtract line 4 from line 3	**5**
6	**GST tax due from fiduciary** (divide line 5 by 2.818182) **(See instructions if property will not bear the GST tax.)**	**6**

Under penalties of perjury, I declare that I have examined this return, including accompanying schedules and statements, and to the best of my knowledge and belief, it is true, correct, and complete.

Signature(s) of executor(s) _____ Date _____

_____ Date _____

Signature of fiduciary or officer representing fiduciary _____ Date _____

Schedule R-1 (Form 706)—Page 36

(*continued*)

Form 88   United States Estate (and Generation-Skipping Transfer) Tax Return (Form 706)   *continued*

Form 706 (Rev. 7-99)

Estate of: Jane M. Doe

SCHEDULE T—Qualified Family-Owned Business Interest Deduction

For details on the deduction, including trades and businesses that do not qualify, see page 22 of the separate Instructions for Form 706.

Part 1—Election

Note: *The executor is deemed to have made the election under section 2057 if he or she files Schedule T and deducts any qualifying business interests from the gross estate.*

Part 2—General Qualifications

1   Did the decedent and/or a member of the decedent's family own the business interests listed on line 5 of this schedule for at least 5 of the 8 years immediately preceding the date of the decedent's death? ☐ **Yes** ☐ **No**

	Yes	No
2 Were there any periods during the 8-year period preceding the date of the decedent's death during which the decedent or a member of his or her family:		
a Did not own the business interests listed on this schedule?		
b Did not materially participate, within the meaning of section 2032A(e)(6), in the operation of the business to which such interests relate?.		

If "Yes" to either of the above, you must attach a statement listing the periods. If applicable, describe whether the exceptions of sections 2032A(b)(4) or (5) are met.

Attach affidavits describing the activities constituting material participation and the identity and relationship to the decedent of the material participants.

3   Check the applicable box(es). The qualified family-owned business interest(s) is:
  ☐ An interest as a proprietor in a trade or business carried on as a proprietorship.
  ☐ An interest in an entity, at least 50% of which is owned (directly or indirectly) by the decedent and members of the decedent's family.
  ☐ An interest in an entity, at least 70% of which is owned (directly or indirectly) by members of 2 families and at least 30% of which is owned (directly or indirectly) by the decedent and members of the decedent's family.
  ☐ An interest in an entity, at least 90% of which is owned (directly or indirectly) by members of 3 families and at least 30% of which is owned (directly or indirectly) by the decedent and members of the decedent's family.

4   Persons holding interests. Enter the requested information for each party who received any interest in the family-owned business. If any qualified heir is not a U.S. citizen, see the line 4 instructions beginning on page 23 of the separate instructions.

  (Each of the qualified heirs receiving an interest in the business must sign the agreement that begins on the following page 40, and the agreement must be filed with this return.)

	Name	Address
A		
B		
C		
D		
E		
F		
G		
H		

	Identifying number	Relationship to decedent	Value of interest
A			
B			
C			
D			
E			
F			
G			
H			

Schedule T (Form 706)—Page 38

(continued)

Form 88 United States Estate (and Generation-Skipping Transfer) Tax Return (Form 706) *continued*

Form 706 (Rev. 7-99)

Part 3—Adjusted Value of Qualified Family-Owned Business Interests

5   Qualified family-owned business interests reported on this return.
Note: *All property listed on line 5 must also be entered on Schedules A, B, C, E, F, G, or H, as applicable.*

A Schedule and item number from Form 706	B Description of business interest and principal place of business	C Reported value

6   **Total** reported value **6**

7   Amount of claims or mortgages deductible under section 2053(a)(3) or (4) (see separate instructions). **7**

8a   Enter the amount of any indebtedness on qualified residence of the decedent (see separate instructions) **8a**

   b   Enter the amount of any indebtedness used for educational or medical expenses (see separate instructions)   **8b**

   c   Enter the amount of any indebtedness other than that listed on line 8a or 8b, but do not enter more than $10,000 (see separate instructions) **8c**

   d   Total (add lines 8a through 8c). **8d**

9   Subtract line 8d from line 7 . . . .   **9**

10   Adjusted value of qualified family-owned business interests (subtract line 9 from line 6) .   **10**

Part 4—Qualifying Estate

11   Includible gifts of qualified family-owned business interests (see separate instructions):

   a   Amount of gifts taken into account under section 2001(b)(1)(B) .   **11a**

   b   Amount of such gifts excluded under section 2503(b) **11b**

   c   Add lines 11a and 11b **11c**

12   Add lines 10 and 11c. **12**

13   Adjusted gross estate (see separate instructions):

   a   Amount of gross estate **13a**

   b   Enter the amount from line 7 . . .   **13b**

   c   Subtract line 13b from line 13a . .   **13c**

   d   Enter the amount from line 11c . .   **13d**

   e   Enter the amount of transfers, if any, to the decedent's spouse (see inst.)   **13e**

   f   Enter the amount of other gifts (see inst.)   **13f**

   g   Add the amounts on lines 13d, 13e, and 13f **13g**

   h   Enter any amounts from line 13g that are otherwise includible in the gross estate **13h**

   i   Subtract line 13h from line 13g   **13i**

   j   Adjusted gross estate (add lines 13c and 13i). **13j**

14   Enter one-half of the amount on line 13j **14**

     Note: *If line 12 does not exceed line 14, stop here; the estate does not qualify for the deduction. Otherwise, complete line 15.*

15   Net value of qualified family-owned business interests you elect to deduct (line 10 reduced by any marital or other deductions)—**DO NOT** enter more than $675,000—(see instructions) (attach schedule)—enter here and on Part 5, Recapitulation, page 3, at item 22 . . . . . .   **15**

Schedule T—Page 39

(continued)

Form 88 United States Estate (and Generation-Skipping Transfer) Tax Return (Form 706) *continued*

Form 706 (Rev. 7-99)

Part 5—Agreement to Family-Owned Business Interest Deduction Under Section 2057

Estate of:	Date of Death	Decedent's Social Security Number

There cannot be a valid election unless:
- The agreement is executed by each and every one of the qualified heirs, and
- The agreement is included with the estate tax return when the estate tax return is filed.

We (list all qualified heirs and other persons having an interest in the business required to sign this agreement)

_____

_____ ,

being all the qualified heirs and   _____

_____ ,

being all other parties having interests in the business(es) which are deducted under section 2057 of the Internal Revenue Code, do hereby approve of the election made by _____ ,

Executor/Administrator of the estate of _____ ,

pursuant to section 2057 to deduct said interests from the gross estate and do hereby enter into this agreement pursuant to section 2057(h).

The undersigned agree and consent to the application of subsection (f) of section 2057 of the Code with respect to all the qualified family-owned business interests deducted on Schedule T of Form 706, attached to this agreement. More specifically, the undersigned heirs expressly agree and consent to personal liability under subsection (c) of 2032A (as made applicable by section 2057(i)(3)(F) of the Code) for the additional estate tax imposed by that subsection with respect to their respective interests in the above-described business interests in the event of certain early dispositions of the interests or the occurrence of any of the disqualifying acts described in section 2057(f)(1) of the Code. It is understood that if a qualified heir disposes of any deducted interest to any member of his or her family, such member may thereafter be treated as the qualified heir with respect to such interest upon filing a new agreement and any other form required by the Internal Revenue Service.

The undersigned interested parties who are not qualified heirs consent to the collection of any additional estate tax imposed under section 2057(f) of the Code from the deducted interests.

If there is a disposition of any interest which passes or has passed to him or her, each of the undersigned heirs agrees to file the appropriate form and pay any additional estate tax due within 6 months of the disposition or other disqualifying act.

It is understood by all interested parties that this agreement is a condition precedent to the election of the qualified family-owned business deduction under section 2057 of the Code and must be executed by every interested party even though that person may not have received the estate tax benefits or be in possession of such property.

Each of the undersigned understands that by making this election, a lien will be created and recorded pursuant to section 6324B of the Code on the interests referred to in this agreement for the applicable percentage of the adjusted tax differences with respect to the estate as defined in section 2057(f)(2)(C).

As the interested parties, the undersigned designate the following individual as their agent for all dealings with the Internal Revenue Service concerning the continued qualification of the deducted property under section 2057 of the Code and on all issues regarding the special lien under section 6324B. The agent is authorized to act for all the parties with respect to all dealings with the Service on matters affecting the qualified interests described earlier. This authority includes the following:

- To receive confidential information on all matters relating to continued qualification under section 2057 of the deducted interests and on all matters relating to the special lien arising under section 6324B.

- To furnish the Service with any requested information concerning the interests.

- To notify the Service of any disposition or other disqualifying events specified in section 2057(f)(1) of the Code.

- To receive, but not to endorse and collect, checks in payment of any refund of Internal Revenue taxes, penalties, or interest.

- To execute waivers (including offers of waivers) of restrictions on assessment or collection of deficiencies in tax and waivers of notice of disallowance of a claim for credit or refund.

- To execute closing agreements under section 7121.

(continued on next page)

Schedule T, Part 5—Page 40

(continued)

Form 88 United States Estate (and Generation-Skipping Transfer) Tax Return (Form 706) *continued*

Form 706 (Rev. 7-99)

Part 5. Agreement to Family-Owned Business Interest Deduction Under Section 2057 (continued)

Estate of:	Date of Death	Decedent's Social Security Number

● Other acts (specify) ▶ _____

By signing this agreement, the agent agrees to provide the Internal Revenue Service with any requested information concerning the qualified business interests and to notify the Internal Revenue Service of any disposition or other disqualifying events with regard to said interests.

_____	_____	_____
Name of Agent	Signature	Address

The interests to which this agreement relates are listed in Form 706, United States Estate (and Generation-Skipping Transfer) Tax Return, along with their fair market value according to section 2031 (or, if applicable, section 2032A) of the Code. The name, address, social security number, and interest (including the value) of each of the undersigned in this business(es) are as set forth in the attached Schedule T.

IN WITNESS WHEREOF, the undersigned have hereunto set their hands at _____ ,

this _____ day of _____ .

SIGNATURES OF EACH OF THE QUALIFIED HEIRS:

_____	_____
Signature of qualified heir	Signature of qualified heir
_____	_____
Signature of qualified heir	Signature of qualified heir
_____	_____
Signature of qualified heir	Signature of qualified heir
_____	_____
Signature of qualified heir	Signature of qualified heir
_____	_____
Signature of qualified heir	Signature of qualified heir
_____	_____
Signature of qualified heir	Signature of qualified heir

_____

Signature(s) of other interested parties

_____

Signature(s) of other interested parties

Schedule T, Part 5—Page 41

(continued)

Form 706 (Rev. 7-99)

Estate of: Jane M. Doe

SCHEDULE U. Qualified Conservation Easement Exclusion

Part 1—Election

Note: *The executor is deemed to have made the election under section 2031(c)(6) if he or she files Schedule U and excludes any qualifying conservation easements from the gross estate.*

Part 2—General Qualifications

1   Describe the land subject to the qualified conservation easement (see separate instructions) _____

2   Did the decedent or a member of the decedent's family own the land described above during the 3-year period ending on the date of the decedent's death? . . . . ☐ **Yes** ☐ **No**

3   The land described above is located (check whichever applies) (see separate instructions):
   ☐ In or within 25 miles of an area which, on the date of the decedent's death, is a metropolitan area.
   ☐ In or within 25 miles of an area which, on the date of the decedent's death, is a national park or wilderness area.
   ☐ In or within 10 miles of an area which, on the date of the decedent's death, is an Urban National Forest.

4   Describe the conservation easement with regard to which the exclusion is being claimed (see separate instructions).

Part 3—Computation of Exclusion

5	Estate tax value of the land subject to the qualified conservation easement (see separate instructions)		**5**	
6	Date of death value of any easements granted prior to decedent's death and included on line 11 below (see instructions)	**6**		
7	Add lines 5 and 6	**7**		
8	Value of retained development rights on the land (see instructions)	**8**		
9	Subtract line 8 from line 7	**9**		
10	Multiply line 9 by 30% (.30)	**10**		
11	Value of qualified conservation easement for which the exclusion is being claimed (see instructions)	**11**		
	Note: *If line 11 is less than line 10, continue with line 12. If line 11 is equal to or more than line 10, skip lines 12 through 14, enter ".40" on line 15, and complete the schedule.*			
12	Divide line 11 by line 9. Figure to 3 decimal places (e.g., .123) . .	**12**		
	If line 12 is equal to or less than .100, stop here; the estate does not qualify for the conservation easement exclusion.			
13	Subtract line 12 from .300. Enter the answer in hundredths by rounding any thousandths up to the next higher hundredth (i.e., .030 = .03; but .031 = .04).	**13**		
14	Multiply line 13 by 2	**14**		
15	Subtract line 14 from .40	**15**		
16	Deduction under section 2055(f) for the conservation easement (see separate instructions)	**16**		
17	Amount of indebtedness on the land (see separate instructions)	**17**		
18	Total reductions in value (add lines 8, 16, and 17)		**18**	
19	Net value of land (subtract line 18 from line 5)		**19**	
20	Multiply line 19 by line 15		**20**	
21	Enter the smaller of line 20 or the exclusion limitation (see instructions). Also enter this amount on item 11, Part 5, Recapitulation, Page 3		**21**	

Schedule U—Page 42

Form 89 Life Insurance Statement (Form 712)

Form **712** (Rev. May 2000) Department of the Treasury Internal Revenue Service	**Life Insurance Statement**	OMB No. 1545-0022

Part I **Decedent—Insured** (To be filed by the executor with **Form 706**, United States Estate (and Generation-Skipping Transfer) Tax Return, or **Form 706-NA**, United States Estate (and Generation-Skipping Transfer) Tax Return, Estate of nonresident not a citizen of the United States.)

1 Decedent's first name and middle initial	2 Decedent's last name	3 Decedent's social security number (if known)	4 Date of death
Jane M.	Doe	321–54–9876	9/20/00

5 Name and address of insurance company

Minnesota Life Insurance Company, 15121 Oak Street, Minneapolis, MN 55101

6 Type of policy	7 Policy number
Ordinary Life	J 666221

8 Owner's name. If decedent is not owner, attach copy of application.	9 Date issued	10 Assignor's name. Attach copy of assignment.	11 Date assigned
Jane M. Doe	11/06/68		

12 Value of the policy at the time of assignment	13 Amount of premium (see instructions)	14 Name of beneficiaries
	$738.	Estate of Jane M. Doe

15	Face amount of policy	15 $ 120,000.
16	Indemnity benefits	16 $
17	Additional insurance	17 $
18	Other benefits	18 $
19	Principal of any indebtedness to the company that is deductible in determining net proceeds	19 $
20	Interest on indebtedness (line 19) accrued to date of death	20 $
21	Amount of accumulated dividends	21 $ 100.
22	Amount of post-mortem dividends	22 $
23	Amount of returned premium	23 $
24	Amount of proceeds if payable in one sum	24 $ 120,100.
25	Value of proceeds as of date of death (if not payable in one sum)	25 $

26 Policy provisions concerning deferred payments or installments.
Note: If other than lump-sum settlement is authorized for a surviving spouse, attach a copy of the insurance policy.

....

....

27	Amount of installments	27 $

28 Date of birth, sex, and name of any person the duration of whose life may measure the number of payments.

....

....

29	Amount applied by the insurance company as a single premium representing the purchase of installment benefits	29 $

30 Basis (mortality table and rate of interest) used by insurer in valuing installment benefits.

....

31	Were there any transfers of the policy within the three years prior to the death of the decedent?	☐ Yes ☒ No
32	Date of assignment or transfer: ____ / ____ / ____ Month Day Year	
33	Was the insured the annuitant or beneficiary of any annuity contract issued by the company?	☐ Yes ☒ No
34	Did the decedent have any incidents of ownership on any policies on his/her life, but not owned by him/her at the date of death?	☐ Yes ☒ No

35 Names of companies with which decedent carried other policies and amount of such policies if this information is disclosed by your records.

....

....

The undersigned officer of the above-named insurance company (or appropriate Federal agency or retirement system official) hereby certifies that this statement sets forth true and correct information.

Signature ▶ /S/ Charles S. McDonald	Title ▶ Vice President	Date of Certification ▶ 1/05/01

Cat. No. 10170V

Form **712** (Rev. 5-2000)

Form 90 Power of Attorney and Declaration of Representative (Form 2848)

Form **2848** (Rev. December 1997) Department of the Treasury Internal Revenue Service	**Power of Attorney** **and Declaration of Representative** ▶ See the separate instructions.	OMB No. 1545-0150

For IRS Use Only
Received by:
Name
Telephone _____
Function
Date ___ / ___ / ___

Part I **Power of Attorney** (Please type or print.)

1 Taxpayer information (Taxpayer(s) must sign and date this form on page 2, line 9.)

Taxpayer name(s) and address John C. Doe, Personal Representative 1005 Elm Street St. Paul, MN 55102 Estate of Jane M. Doe	Social security number(s) 374 : 29 : 4665 321 : 54 : 9876 Daytime telephone number (612) 345-5000	Employer identification number 41 : 6246975 Plan number (if applicable)

hereby appoint(s) the following representative(s) as attorney(s)-in-fact:

2 Representative(s) (Representative(s) must sign and date this form on page 2, Part II.)

Name and address John W. Cranwall First Trust Co. Bldg. St. Paul, MN 55101	CAF No. .... 111111119 .... Telephone No. .(651) 555-5555......... Fax No. .... (651) 555-7777......... Check if new: Address ☐ Telephone No. ☐
Name and address	CAF No. .... Telephone No. .... Fax No. .... Check if new: Address ☐ Telephone No. ☐
Name and address	CAF No. .... Telephone No. .... Fax No. .... Check if new: Address ☐ Telephone No. ☐

to represent the taxpayer(s) before the Internal Revenue Service for the following tax matters:

3 Tax matters

Type of Tax (Income, Employment, Excise, etc.)	Tax Form Number (1040, 941, 720, etc.)	Year(s) or Period(s)
Estate Tax	706	Death 09/20/00
Gift Tax	709	2000
Fiduciary Income Tax	1041	10/1/00 – 9/30/01

4 Specific use not recorded on Centralized Authorization File (CAF). If the power of attorney is for a specific use not recorded on CAF, check this box. (See instruction for **Line 4—Specific uses not recorded on CAF.**) . . . . ▶ ☐

5 Acts authorized. The representatives are authorized to receive and inspect confidential tax information and to perform any and all acts that I (we) can perform with respect to the tax matters described on line 3, for example, the authority to sign any agreements, consents, or other documents. The authority does not include the power to receive refund checks (see line 6 below), the power to substitute another representative unless specifically added below, or the power to sign certain returns (see instruction for **Line 5—Acts authorized**).

List any specific additions or deletions to the acts otherwise authorized in this power of attorney: ....
....
....

Note: *In general, an unenrolled preparer of tax returns cannot sign any document for a taxpayer. See Revenue Procedure 81-38, printed as Pub. 470, for more information.*

Note: *The tax matters partner of a partnership is not permitted to authorize representatives to perform certain acts. See the instructions for more information.*

6 Receipt of refund checks. If you want to authorize a representative named on line 2 to receive, **BUT NOT TO ENDORSE OR CASH**, refund checks, initial here _____ and list the name of that representative below.

Name of representative to receive refund check(s) ▶

For Paperwork Reduction and Privacy Act Notice, see the separate instructions.   Cat. No. 11980J   Form **2848** (Rev. 12-97)

(continued)

Form 90 Power of Attorney and Declaration of Representative (Form 2848) *continued*

Form 2848 (Rev. 12-97)   Page **2**

7 Notices and communications. Original notices and other written communications will be sent to you and a copy to the first representative listed on line 2 unless you check one or more of the boxes below.

a If you want the first representative listed on line 2 to receive the original, and yourself a copy, of such notices or communications, check this box . . . . ▶ ☐

b If you also want the second representative listed to receive a copy of such notices and communications, check this box . . . . ▶ ☐

c If you do not want any notices or communications sent to your representative(s), check this box . . . . ▶ ☐

8 Retention/revocation of prior power(s) of attorney. The filing of this power of attorney automatically revokes all earlier power(s) of attorney on file with the Internal Revenue Service for the same tax matters and years or periods covered by this document. If you **do not** want to revoke a prior power of attorney, check here . . . . ▶ ☐
YOU MUST ATTACH A COPY OF ANY POWER OF ATTORNEY YOU WANT TO REMAIN IN EFFECT.

9 Signature of taxpayer(s). If a tax matter concerns a joint return, **both** husband and wife must sign if joint representation is requested, otherwise, see the instructions. If signed by a corporate officer, partner, guardian, tax matters partner, executor, receiver, administrator, or trustee on behalf of the taxpayer, I certify that I have the authority to execute this form on behalf of the taxpayer.

▶ **IF NOT SIGNED AND DATED, THIS POWER OF ATTORNEY WILL BE RETURNED.**

/S/ John C. Doe	8/3/01	Personal Representative
Signature	Date	Title (if applicable)

John C. Doe		
Print Name		

Signature	Date	Title (if applicable)

Print Name		

Part II **Declaration of Representative**

Under penalties of perjury, I declare that:

- I am not currently under suspension or disbarment from practice before the Internal Revenue Service;
- I am aware of regulations contained in Treasury Department Circular No. 230 (31 CFR, Part 10), as amended, concerning the practice of attorneys, certified public accountants, enrolled agents, enrolled actuaries, and others;
- I am authorized to represent the taxpayer(s) identified in Part I for the tax matter(s) specified there; and
- I am one of the following:

    a Attorney—a member in good standing of the bar of the highest court of the jurisdiction shown below.

    b Certified Public Accountant—duly qualified to practice as a certified public accountant in the jurisdiction shown below.

    c Enrolled Agent—enrolled as an agent under the requirements of Treasury Department Circular No. 230.

    d Officer—a bona fide officer of the taxpayer's organization.

    e Full-Time Employee—a full-time employee of the taxpayer.

    f Family Member—a member of the taxpayer's immediate family (i.e., spouse, parent, child, brother, or sister).

    g Enrolled Actuary—enrolled as an actuary by the Joint Board for the Enrollment of Actuaries under 29 U.S.C. 1242 (the authority to practice before the Service is limited by section 10.3(d)(1) of Treasury Department Circular No. 230).

    h Unenrolled Return Preparer—an unenrolled return preparer under section 10.7(c)(viii) of Treasury Department Circular No. 230.

▶ **IF THIS DECLARATION OF REPRESENTATIVE IS NOT SIGNED AND DATED, THE POWER OF ATTORNEY WILL BE RETURNED.**

Designation—Insert above letter **(a–h)**	Jurisdiction (state) or Enrollment Card No.	Signature	Date
a	MN	/S/ John W. Cranwall	8/3/01

*U.S. Government Printing Office: 1999 — 455-238/10054

Form 91   Application for Extension of Time to File a Return and/or Pay U.S. Estate Taxes (Form 4768)

Form **4768**	**Application for Extension of Time To File a Return and/or Pay U.S. Estate (and Generation-Skipping Transfer) Taxes**	
(Rev. January 2000)		OMB No. 1545-0181
Department of the Treasury Internal Revenue Service	For filers of Form 706, 706-A, 706-D, or 706-NA (circle only one)	

Note: *Use Form 2758 to request an extension for Forms 706-GS(D) and 706-GS(T).*

Part I   Identification

Decedent's first name and middle initial	Decedent's last name	Date of death
Name of executor	Name of application filer (if other than the executor)	**Decedent's social security number**
Address of executor (Number, street, and room or suite no.)		Estate tax return due date

City, state, and ZIP code

Part II   Extension of Time To File (Sec. 6081)

You must attach your written statement to explain in detail why it is impossible or impractical to file a reasonably complete return within 9 months after the date of the decedent's death.	Extension date requested

Part III   Extension of Time To Pay (Sec. 6161)

You must attach your written statement to explain in detail why it is impossible or impractical to pay the full amount of the estate (or GST) tax by the return due date. If the taxes cannot be determined because the size of the gross estate is unascertainable, check here ▶ ☐ and enter "-0-" or other appropriate amount on Part IV, line 3. You must attach an explanation.	Extension date requested

Part IV   Payment To Accompany Extension Request

1	Amount of estate and GST taxes estimated to be due	1	
2	Amount of cash shortage (complete Part III)	2	
3	**Balance due (subtract line 2 from line 1) (Pay with this application.)**	3	

Signature and Verification

If filed by executor—Under penalties of perjury, I declare that I am an executor of the estate of the above-named decedent and that to the best of my knowledge and belief, the statements made herein and attached are true and correct.

Executor's signature	Title	Date

If filed by someone other than the executor—Under penalties of perjury, I declare that to the best of my knowledge and belief, the statements made herein and attached are true and correct, that I am authorized by the executor to file this application, and that I am (check box(es) that applies):

☐ A member in good standing of the bar of the highest court of (specify jurisdiction) ▶ ....

☐ A certified public accountant duly qualified to practice in (specify jurisdiction) ▶ ....

☐ A person enrolled to practice before the Internal Revenue Service.

☐ A duly authorized agent holding a power of attorney. (The power of attorney need not be submitted unless requested.)

Filer's signature (other than the executor)	Date

Part V   Notice to Applicant—To be completed by the Internal Revenue Service

1 The application for extension of time to file (Part II) is:	2 The application for extension of time to pay (Part III) is:
☐ Approved	☐ Approved
☐ Not approved because	☐ Not approved because ....
☐ Other	☐ Other ....

Internal Revenue Service official	Date	Internal Revenue Service official	Date

For Paperwork Reduction Act Notice, see instructions on the back of this form.   Cat. No. 41984P   Form **4768** (Rev. 1-2000)

Form 92 State (Minnesota as Example) Estate Tax Return

MINNESOTA Department of Revenue

Estate Tax Return

MN-706

Check box if this is an amended return ☐

Decedent's first name, middle initial		Last name	Decedent's Social Security number
Jane M		Doe	321–54–9876

Last home address (street, apartment, route)				Date of death
1005 Elm Street				09/20/2000

City or town	State	Zip	Minnesota probate county and file number
St. Paul	MN	55102	Ramsey County 999999

Executor's first name, middle initial	Last name	Executor's Social Security number
John C	Doe	374–29–4665

Name of firm (if applicable)	Attach approved federal extension *(if applicable)* and fill in the filing extension date *(mm/dd/yyyy)*: ___/___/___

Address (street, apartment, route)	City or town	State	Zip code
1005 Elm Street	St. Paul	MN	55102

Estates of residents of Minnesota

1 Credit for state death taxes from line 15 of federal Form 706 . . . . **1** _____ 0

2 Estate or inheritance tax actually paid to other states *(attach other states' returns and receipts)* . . **2** _____

3 Gross value of all tangible personal and real property in other states *(attach itemized list)* . . **3** _____

4 Fill in the total gross estate from line 1 of federal Form 706. . . . . **4** _____

5 Divide line 3 by line 4. The result is a percentage. . . . . **5** _____ %

6 Multiply line 1 by line 5 . . . . **6** _____

7 Fill in the amount from line 2 or line 6, whichever is smaller . . . . **7** _____

8 Subtract line 7 from line 1. The result is the Minnesota estate tax . . . . **8** _____ 0

Estates of nonresidents of Minnesota

9 Fill in the credit for state death taxes from line 15 of federal Form 706 . . . . **9** _____

10 Gross value of all tangible personal and real property in Minnesota *(attach itemized list)* . **10** _____

11 Fill in the total gross estate from line 1 of federal Form 706 . . . . **11** _____

12 Divide line 10 by line 11. The result is a percentage . . . . **12** _____ %

13 Multiply line 9 by line 12. The result is the Minnesota estate tax . . . . **13** _____

All estates

14 Total payments, including any Form PV86 extension payments, made prior to filing this return . **14** _____

15 If line 8 or line 13 is more than line 14, subtract line 14 from line 8 or line 13 . . . . **15** _____

16 Penalty *(determine from instructions on page 6)* . . . . **16** _____

17 Interest, if any, from: _____ to: _____ *(complete worksheet on back)* . **17** _____

18 Add lines 15, 16 and 17, and fill in the **TOTAL DUE**. You must attach **PV47** . . . . **18** _____ 0

19 If your total payments are more than the sum of Minnesota estate tax, penalty, and interest, subtract the amounts on lines 8, 13, 16 and 17 from line 14 and fill in your **REFUND** . . . . . . **19** _____

20 If paying federal estate tax in installments, attach copy of IRS approval and check box ☐

I declare that I have examined this return and all accompanying schedules and statements, and that they are true and complete to the best of my knowledge and belief.

Signature(s) of executor(s)	Date	I have appointed the person named on back as power of attorney or to hold the powers indicated.
/S/ John C. Doe	08/03/2001	☒
Signature(s) of executor(s)	Date	

Signature of preparer, other than executor	MN tax ID or PTIN	Date	Daytime phone number ( )

You must attach a copy of the estate's federal Form 706, required schedules and death certificate.
Mail to: Minnesota Estate Tax, Mail Station 1315, St. Paul, Minnesota 55146-1315

Stock No. 6000706
I (Rev. 10/00)

(continued)

Form 92   State (Minnesota as Example) Estate Tax Return   *continued*

Worksheet for determining the amount of interest to fill in on line 17
Interest accrues on any unpaid tax and penalty beginning nine months from the decedent's date of death.

1 Fill in the amount of tax not paid within nine months after the decedent's date of death . . . . **1** _____

2 Fill in penalty, if any, from line 16 on the front of this form . . . . **2** _____

3 Add step 1 and step 2. The result is the unpaid tax and penalty on which interest will accrue . . . . **3** _____

4 Determine the number of days that your payment of tax and/or penalty is late.   **Year:** _____   **Year:** _____
If the days fall in more than one calendar year, you must determine the number
of days separately for each year . . . . **4** _____   _____

5 Divide step 4 for each year by 365. Round off the result to four places
after the decimal point . . . . **5** _____   _____

6 Multiply step 3 by the result in step 5 for each year . . . . **6** _____   _____

7 From the list below, fill in the interest rate in effect for the calendar year . . . . **7** _____ %   _____ %

8 Multiply step 6 by the interest rate in step 7 for each year . . . . **8** _____   _____

9 Add the amounts in step 8. Fill in the result here and on line 17 of your Form MN-706 . . . . **9** _____

Interest rates for step 7 above:

2001 .... 9%	1999 ... 8%	1997 ...8%	1995... 7%
2000 .... 8%	1998 ... 9%	1996 ...9%	1994 ... 6%

*If you need the interest rate for a year after 2001, call the department at 651-296-3475 or 1-800-657-3871.
The rates are also available at the department website at **www.taxes.state.mn.us***

Powers of Attorney

I, the executor (personal representative) of the decedent's estate, appoint the person named below as Attorney-in-Fact for the decedent's estate to hold the powers listed below. This power of attorney will remain in effect until the date on which the Minnesota Department of Revenue receives a written notice of revocation signed by me. I hereby revoke all powers of attorney previously filed by me in connection with the estate of this decedent.

Name of person (appointee) given power of attorney	Daytime phone number
John W. Cranwall	(651) 555-5555

Name of firm *(if applicable)*

Address (street, apartment, route)
First Trust Co. Bldg.

City or town	State	Zip code
St. Paul	MN	55101

Powers granted

I grant the Attorney-in-Fact the power to (check the appropriate boxes):

[x] receive written and oral communications from the Minnesota Department of Revenue concerning the involvement of the decedent's estate with any Minnesota and federal tax matters, and to discuss these matters with employees of the Department of Revenue;

[x] examine the contents of all types of Minnesota and federal tax returns of the decedent concerning matters of Minnesota and federal tax liability;

[x] conclude agreements to extend the period of time in which redeterminations can be made of information used in determining the amount of the estate's Minnesota estate tax;

[ ] notify the Department of Revenue of the estate's intention to make installment payments of estate tax, and to provide the schedule of payments;

[x] request a reduction in the amount of any penalty;

[ ] receive Minnesota estate tax refunds; and

[ ] hold the following additional powers:

Form 93   State (Tennessee as Example) Inheritance Tax Return

INH 301   TENNESSEE DEPARTMENT OF REVENUE
INHERITANCE TAX RETURN

AMENDED RETURN ☐

DATE OF DEATH	COUNTY	DECEDENT'S SOCIAL SECURITY NUMBER

NAME OF DECEDENT _____

ADDRESS (AT TIME OF DEATH) _____

_____

CITY, STATE AND ZIP CODE _____

This return should be used for estates of decedents whose date of death is on or after January 1, 1990. This return is due nine (9) months after the date of the decedent's death, unless an extension of time is granted by the Department.

Make your check payable to the Tennessee Department of Revenue for the amount shown on Line 10 and mail to:
Tennessee Department of Revenue
Andrew Jackson State Office Building
500 Deaderick Street
Nashville, Tennessee 37242

For assistance, you may call in-state toll free 1-800-342-1003 or (615) 741-2594.

	Yes	No
Election of Alternate Valuation	_____	_____
Election of Special Use Valuation	_____	_____
Gross Estate contains T.C.A. §67-8-304 (10) property	_____	_____

Age of Decedent _____ Did decedent have a will? ☐ Yes ☐ No (If Yes, attach a copy to the return).

Personal Representative's Name (executor, etc.) _____

Address (street, city, state, zip code) _____

Personal Representative's Name (executor, etc.) _____

Address (street, city, state, zip code) _____

Preparer of Return _____ Phone _____

Address (street, city, state, zip code) _____

Attorney Representing Estate _____ Phone _____

Address (street, city, state, zip code) _____

COMPUTATION OF TAX

		Dollars	Cents
1.	Inheritance Tax	_____	_____
2.	Deduct: Applicable Credits	_____	_____
3.	Inheritance Tax Payable (Line 1 minus Line 2)	_____	_____
4.	Tennessee Estate Tax	_____	_____
5.	Total taxes Due (Add Lines 3 and 4)	_____	_____
6.	Deduct: Extension Payments	_____	_____
7.	Balance of Tax Due (Line 5 minus Line 6)	_____	_____
8.	Penalty (5% for each 30-day period of delinquency not to exceed 25% of the tax due)	_____	_____
9.	Interest (_____% per annum on any taxes unpaid by the due date)	_____	_____
10.	Total Amount Due (Add Lines 7, 8, and 9)	_____	_____

Under the penalties of perjury, I declare that I have examined this report, and to the best of my knowledge and belief, it is true, correct and complete.

Personal Representative's signature _____ Date _____

Preparer's signature _____ Date _____

FOR OFFICE USE ONLY

Acct. # _____

Date Rec'd _____

Amt. Rec'd $ _____

RV-R0001602

(continued)

Form 93   State (Tennessee as Example) Inheritance Tax Return   *continued*

GENERAL INFORMATION
(A copy of the decedent's death certificate may be submitted in lieu of completing Lines 1 through 6.)

1. Decedent's date of birth _____ Place of birth _____

2. Place of death if different than decedent's address (e.g. name of hospital) _____
   _____

3. Cause of death _____ Length of last illness _____

4. Decedent's physician(s):   Name _____   Name _____
                                    Address _____   Address _____
                                    _____   _____

5. Decedent's business or occupation: _____

   If decedent was retired, check here ☐

6. Decedent's marital status at time of death:

   ☐ Married -- date of marriage to surviving spouse _____

   ☐ Widow or widower-- Name of Deceased spouse _____

                  -- Date of spouse's death _____

   ☐ Single

   ☐ Legally separated -- Name of spouse _____

   ☐ Divorced -- Date divorce decree became final _____

7. Names, ages, addresses, and the value of all interests of the heirs, next of kin or devisees of the decedent are as follows:

NAME	AGE	ADDRESS	RELATIONSHIP	AMOUNT

(continued)

Form 93   State (Tennessee as Example) Inheritance Tax Return   *continued*

RECAPITULATION - GROSS ESTATE

IMPORTANT: Please attach a copy of Schedules A through K, M and O of the federal estate tax return (FORM 706). Schedule L of the federal return is not to be included with this return. If you did not file a federal return, the state forms for filing these schedules may be obtained by contacting the Department of Revenue toll free 1-800-342-1003 in state or (615) 741-2594.

	Schedule	Classification of Property	Alternate Value DOLLARS	CENTS	Value at Date of Death DOLLARS	CENTS
1.	A	Real Estate				
2.	B	Stocks and Bonds				
3.	C	Cash, Notes, Mortgages				
4.	D	Insurance on Decendent's Life				
5.	E	Jointly Owned Property				
6.	F	Miscellaneous Property				
7.	G	Transfers During Decedent's Life ...				
8.	H	Powers of Appointment				
9.	I	Annuities				
10.		Total Gross Estate (Add Lines 1 through 9)				

	Schedule	Deductions	Amount DOLLARS	CENTS
11.	J	Funeral Expenses and Administration Expenses		
12.	K	Debts and Mortgages		
13.	M	Bequests to Surviving Spouse (Marital Deduction)		
14.	O	Bequests: Public, Charitable, Religious, and Educational		
15.		Amount deductible from gross estate (Add Lines 11 through 14)		
16.		Taxable Estate (Line 10 minus Line 15)		

INFORMATION CONCERNING FEDERAL ESTATE TAX RETURN (FORM 706)

			DOLLARS	CENTS
1.	Was a federal estate tax return filed? Yes ☐ No ☐			
	If yes, answer the following questions concerning entries on the federal return.			
2.	Total gross estate			
3.	Total allowable deductions			
4.	Taxable estate			
5.	Adjusted taxable gifts			
6.	Credit for state death taxes available			

(continued)

Form 93   State (Tennessee as Example) Inheritance Tax Return   *continued*

INHERITANCE TAX COMPUTATION

The state inheritance tax is imposed upon the net taxable estate of a decedent. In the case of resident decedent's dying between January 1, 1990 and June 30, 1998 the allowable exemption is $600,000; from July 1, 1998 to December 31, 1998 the allowable exemption is $625,000; in 1999 the allowable exemption is $650,000; in 2000 and 2001 the allowable exemption is $675,000; in 2002 and 2003 the allowable exemption is $700,000; in 2004 the allowable exemption is $850,000; in 2005 the allowable exemption is $950,000; in 2006 and thereafter the allowable exemption is $1,000,000.

		DOLLARS	CENTS
1.	Taxable estate (From Line 16, Page 3)		
2.	Deduct: Statutory exemption		
3.	Net taxable estate (Line 1 minus 2)		
4.	Inheritance tax (Compute the tax by using the applicable tax rate shown below and transfer to Line 1, Page 1)		

If Line 3 is:	The tax is:
Not over $40,000	5.5% of the net taxable estate
Over $40,000 but not over $240,000	$2,200, plus 6.5% of the excess over $40,000
Over $240,000 but not over $440,000	$15,200, plus 7.5% of the excess over $240,000
Over $440,000	$30,200, plus 9.5% of the excess over $440,000

SUPPLEMENTAL INFORMATION:

If entries on the federal return regarding the value of the gross estate or the reported total allowable deductions differ from the corresponding entries on the Tennessee return, please explain the difference below. If no federal estate tax return was filed, enter below: assets not taxable in Tennessee or deductions not allowable in Tennessee.

ITEM NO.	EXPLANATION

(If more space is required, attach additional sheets of same size.)

SAMPLE MARITAL DEDUCTION TESTAMENTARY TRUST

LAST WILL AND TESTAMENT OF JOHN P. DOE

I, John P. Doe, a/k/a _____, of _____, City of _____, County of _____, State of _____, being of sound and disposing mind and memory, and not acting under undue influence of any person, do make, publish, and declare this document to be my last will and testament, and do hereby expressly revoke all wills and codicils previously made by me.

Article I

I hereby direct my personal representative, hereinafter named, to pay all my just debts, administrative expenses, and expenses for my last illness, funeral, and burial out of my estate.

Article II

I give my homestead legally described as _____, which I own in _____ County, State of _____, to my wife _____, in fee simple, if she survives me.

Article III

I give my diamond ring to my son, _____, (name and address) and my collection of guns and rifles to my son, _____. (name and address)

Article IV

I give all my other personal property including my automobiles, household furnishings, clothing, jewelry, ornaments, books, and personal effects of every kind used about my home or person to my wife, _____, to do with as she sees fit, if she survives me.

Article V

If my wife, _____, survives me, I give to the _____ of (name of individual of corporate trustee, e.g., a bank) _____ as trustee of a trust to be known as (address), (city), and (state) "TRUST A," assets of my estate to be selected by my personal representative and having a value which, when added to the value of all interests in property that pass or have passed to my wife, either by this will or by other means, in a manner which qualifies for and will be equal to the maximum marital deduction allowable in my estate under the provisions of the United States Internal Revenue Code in effect at the time of my death. Only assets qualifying for the marital deduction shall be allocated to Trust A. My personal representative shall satisfy the foregoing transfer (devise) with such assets as will qualify for said marital deduction and shall compute all values of assets for these purposes in accordance with the Federal Estate Tax values finally computed in my estate except the assets allocated to "TRUST A" shall have an aggregate market value which fairly represents the net appreciation or depreciation of the available property on the date or dates of distribution.

TRUST A shall be administered and distributed by my trustee as follows:

1. Beginning on the date of my death, the net income from TRUST A shall be paid to my wife, _____, in convenient installments to be determined by my trustee, but at least annually, during her life.

2. My trustee shall pay to my wife or apply for her benefit such amounts from the principal of TRUST A as she shall request at any time in writing. In addition, my trustee may pay to my wife or apply for her benefit amounts of the principal of TRUST A as it determines is necessary or advisable for her care, comfort, support, maintenance and welfare, including reasonable luxuries.

3. Upon the death of my wife, my trustee shall distribute the entire assets in TRUST A, including income, to appointee or appointees in the manner and proportions as my wife may designate by her last will which shall expressly refer to this general power of appointment; included in the power shall be her right to appoint free of any other trust provisions hereunder. This general power of

appointment conferred upon my wife shall exist immediately upon my death and shall be exercisable by my wife exclusively and in all events.

4. If, under the above provisions, any portion of TRUST A is not disposed of, it shall be added to TRUST B of ARTICLE VII and administered and distributed as a part of TRUST B.

5. It is my intention that TRUST A shall qualify for the marital deduction which is allowed under the Federal Estate Tax provisions of the Internal Revenue Code in effect at the time of my death. Any provisions of this will which relate to TRUST A shall be so construed and questions pertaining to TRUST A shall be resolved accordingly.

6. If my wife predeceases me or the creation of TRUST A does not effectively reduce the Federal Estate Tax payable by reason of my death, the devise and bequest of this ARTICLE V shall lapse and no TRUST A shall be established.

Article VI

I hereby direct my personal representative to pay out of my residuary estate (and not from TRUST A) all estate, income, and inheritance taxes assessed against my taxable estate or the recipients thereof, whether passing by this will or by other means, without contribution or reimbursement from any person.

Article VII

I give the residue of my estate to _____ of _____, as trustee
(name of individual or corporate trustee)   (address, city, state)
of a separate trust which shall be known as "TRUST B", the bypass trust, and which shall be administered and distributed by my trustee as follows:

1. During the life of my wife, _____.
   (a). Beginning on the date of my death, the net income form TRUST B shall be paid to my wife, _____, in convenient installments to be determined by my trustee, but at least annually, during her life.

   (b). If there are not sufficient principal funds readily available in TRUST A, then in addition to the net income from TRUST B, my trustee may pay to my wife or apply for her benefit sums from the principal of TRUST B as my trustee determines to be necessary or advisable to provide for her proper care, support, and maintenance.

(c). My trustee may also pay to or apply for the benefit of any child or other issue of mine sums from the principal of TRUST B as my trustee determines to be necessary in order to provide for their proper care, support, maintenance and education. It is not required that such payments be for the equal benefit of my children and other issue.

2. After the death of my wife, _____, or in the event she does not survive me, then upon my death, my trustee shall administer and distribute TRUST B as follows:
   (a). Until my youngest living child reaches the age of twenty-five (25) years, my trustee may pay to or apply directly for the benefit of my children and other issue sums from the net income and principal of TRUST B as my trustee determines necessary to provide for their proper care, support, maintenance and education. It is not required that such payments be for the equal benefit of my children and other issue.

   (b). When my youngest living child has reached the age of twenty-five (25) years, my trustee shall divide TRUST B into equal shares and shall provide one share for each of my then living children, and one share to be divided equally among the living issue, collectively, of each deceased child of mine. In making such division, my trustee shall take into account all advances of principal to a child made after such child reached the age of twenty-five (25) years. It shall be within the discretion of my trustee to take into account some, none or all advances of principal to a child made before such child had reached the age of twenty-five (25) years. After such division has been made, said shares shall be distributed outright to such children and to the issue of deceased children by right of representation.

Article VIII

If at any time before final distribution of my estate or trust estate, it happens that there not be in existence anyone who is or might become entitled to receive benefits therefrom as hereinabove provided, then upon the occurrence of such event, all of my estate and trust estate then remaining shall be paid over and distributed outright to my heirs at law, in such proportions as though I had at that time died without a will, a resident of the State of _____, in accordance with the intestate succession laws of personal property of the State of _____ now/then in effect.

Article IX

It is an express condition of this will, which shall control over all other provisions, that in no event shall the duration of any trust created herein continue for a period longer than the lives of all of my wife, _____, and of any of my issue who may be living at the time of my death, and the survivor of all of them and twenty-one (21) years thereafter, and at the end of such time the trustee shall distribute the entire trust estate, principal and any undistributed income outright to the persons then entitled to receive the income therefrom or to have it accumulated for their benefit, in shares which shall be the same as those in which such income is then being distributed to, or accumulated for, them.

Article X

My trustee shall have all powers and authority necessary or advisable to ensure the proper administration and distribution of each trust created by my will. Except as I may otherwise expressly direct or require in my will and in extension but not in limitation of the powers provided by applicable _____ law, I hereby grant to my (state)

trustee as to any properties, real, personal, or mixed, at any time constituting a part of any trust hereunder and without the necessity of notice to or license or approval of any court or person, full power and authority during the term of such and in the continuing sole discretion of my trustee:

1. To retain any assets, including cash, for so long as it deems advisable, whether or not such assets are hereinafter authorized for investment; to sell, exchange, mortgage, lease, or otherwise dispose of any assets of my trust estate for terms within and extending beyond the term of such trust; and to receive any additional properties acceptable to the trustee, from whatever source.

2. Within the trustee's discretion, to invest, reinvest, or exchange assets for, any securities and properties, including but not limited to common and preferred stocks, and no statutes, rules of law, custom or usage shall limit the selection of investments; and to commingle for the purpose of investment all or any part of the funds of said trust in any common trust fund or funds now or hereafter maintained by the trustee.

3. To collect, receive, and obtain receipts for any principal or income; to enforce, defend against, compromise or settle any claim by or against the trust; and to vote or issue proxies to vote, oppose or join in any plans for reorganization, and to exercise any other rights incident to the ownership of any stocks, bonds or other properties which constitute all or a part of the trust estate.

4. To hold assets in bearer form, in the name of the trustee, or in the name of the trustee's nominee or nominees without being required to disclose any fiduciary relationship; and to deposit cash assets as a general deposit in a special bank account without liability for interest thereon; provided that, at all times, such cash and assets shall be shown to be a part of the trust on the books of the trustee.

5. To charge premiums on bonds and other similar investments against principal. The trustee shall not be required to charge any depreciation or depletion against income from any real estate or personal property.

6. To make, without the necessity of intervention or consent of any legal guardian, any payments by the terms of this will payable to or for the benefit of any minor person in any or all of the following ways: (1) Directly for the maintenance, education and welfare of any such minor beneficiary; (2) To the parent or natural guardian of such minor beneficiary; or (3) To any person at that time having custody and care of the person of said minor beneficiary. The receipt of such person shall be full acquittance of the trustee and the trustee shall have no responsibility to oversee the application of the funds so paid.

7. To hold or make division or distribution whenever herein required in whole or in part in money, securities or other property, and in undivided interests therein, and to continue to hold any such undivided interest in any trust hereunder, and in such division or distribution the judgment of the trustee concerning the propriety thereof and the valuation of the properties and securities concerned shall be binding and conclusive on all persons in interest.

8. To charge against the trust principal and to receive on behalf of the trustee reasonable compensation for services hereunder and payment for all reasonable expenses and charges of the trust.

Article XI

In the event that my said wife, _____, predeceases me or should we both die in some common accident, even though she should survive me by an appreciable length of time, such as one-hundred twenty (120) days, then my wife shall be deemed to have survived me with regard to all dispositive provisions for her benefit in this, my last will and testament. In the event that one or more of my children does not survive me, then I hereby give, devise, and bequeath the share of my property which that child would normally have taken under this will, to the living issue, collectively, of each deceased child of mine.

Article XII

If assets of my estate are to become a part of any trust by the terms of this will, and if such assets will immediately distribute upon receipt thereof by the trustee, the trustee may distribute such assets in exactly the same manner as provided in such trust without requiring such trust to be established.

Article XIII

Except for the income and general testamentary power of appointment reserved to my wife in TRUST A or ARTICLE V, no title in the trusts created by this will, or in the income from said trusts shall vest in any beneficiary and neither the principal nor the income of said trusts shall be liable for the debts of any beneficiary, and none of the beneficiaries herein shall have any power to sell, assign, transfer, encumber, or in any other manner to dispose of his or her interest in any such trust, or the income produced by such trust, prior to the actual distribution in fact, by the trustee to said beneficiary.

Article XIV

As used in this will, the singular includes the plural and the masculine includes the feminine, and the terms "issue" and "child" are defined as follows:

> **"issue"** means all persons who are descended from the persons referred to, either by legitimate birth to or legally adopted by him or any of his legitimately born or legally adopted descendants.
> **"child"** means an issue of the first generation.

Article XV

I hereby waive any and all requirements that any trust herein created be submitted to the jurisdiction of any court, that the trustee be appointed or confirmed by any court, that evidence of such appointment or confirmation be filed in any court, and that the trustee's accounts be examined, heard, filed with or allowed by any court. This provision shall be overridden by a request by any trust beneficiaries, trustees or executors to require the procedures waived in this article.

Article XVI

Any trusts herein created shall terminate if the trustee shall determine that the continued administration of such trusts could be unduly expensive or burdensome

to the beneficiaries, and if such event should occur the assets of any such trusts shall be distributed to the beneficiaries then entitled to receive the net income of said trusts in such proportions as they are entitled to receive said net income.

Article XVII

If my estate includes any business, I hereby expressly authorize my personal representative and trustee to retain and carry on any such business regardless of the fact that such business may constitute a large or major portion of my estate or trust estate. My personal representative and trustee shall have all necessary powers to enable them to do any and all things deemed appropriate by them for the carrying on of such business, including the power to incorporate and reorganize the business, to put in additional capital, and to hire a business manager or other such employees as they shall deem necessary. My estate and trust estate shall bear the sole risk of any business interest so retained, and my personal representative and trustee shall not be liable for any loss incurred thereby except when such loss is caused by their own negligence. Since the desirability of retaining any such business interests may be affected by many factors, any powers given in this Article to my personal representative and trustee shall not be mandatory. My personal representative and trustee shall have the power to close out and liquidate or sell such business interests upon such terms as they in their sole discretion shall deem best.

Article XVIII

In the event that my trustee under this will is the beneficiary of proceeds of any pension, profit-sharing or stock bonus plans which qualify under applicable provisions of the Internal Revenue Code, said trustee shall not use any of such proceeds to pay any taxes, debts or other obligations enforceable against my estate, including both probate and nonprobate assets. All such funds shall be allocated to "TRUST B".

Article XIX

The payment by an insurance company of the proceeds of any policy of insurance to my trustee under this will as beneficiary, shall fully discharge all obligation of such insurance company on account of such policy and such insurance company shall bear no responsibility for the proper discharge of my trust or any part thereof. I direct my trustee to administer and distribute such insurance proceeds as follows:

1. If my wife survives me, my trustee shall allocate said insurance proceeds between "TRUST A", and

"TRUST B", according to provisions in this will and as directed by my personal representative.

2. When acting under this will with respect to insurance proceeds as insurance beneficiary, rather than as distributee of my probate estate, my trustee shall have all duties, powers, rights, privileges and discretions given to my personal representative, and I direct that my trustee shall cooperate with my personal representative to ensure the most efficient and economical administration of my total gross estate.

Article XX

In the event my wife, _____, does not survive me, I hereby nominate and appoint _____ as

<small>(name and address)</small>

guardian of the person for my minor child or children. The guardian may use the income from "TRUST B" for the support, education and well being of said child or children. In the event _____ is unable or unwilling to act as personal guardian, I hereby appoint _____ to serve in his place as personal guardian.

<small>(name and address)</small>

Article XXI

I hereby nominate _____ of _____ as the per-

<small>(address)</small>

sonal representative of this my last will and testament, and I give and grant unto my personal representative with respect to my estate and to each and every portion thereof, real, personal, or mixed, all such duties, powers, and discretions herein given and granted to my trustee hereof with respect to my trust estate, all of which duties, powers, and discretions shall be in addition to and not in limitation of those which normally my personal representative would possess.

If at any time after my death, my wife shall file a request in writing with the herein named personal representative and trustee that she wishes to become a co-personal representative and/or co-trustee hereunder, I hereby nominate her as co-personal representative and/or co-trustee. Until such request is filed, the personal representative herein named shall be the sole personal representative and trustee.

Any trustee herein named may at any time after my death, resign by giving notice in writing to the then income beneficiary. The date of delivery shall be specified in such instrument of resignation, and such resignation shall take effect no earlier than thirty (30) days after delivery of such written resignation. Upon such effective resignation the resigning trustee shall be relieved of all further duties and responsibilities and shall bear no liability or responsibility for the acts of any successor trustee.

I hereby direct that my personal representative or trustee shall have custody and possession of all assets, shall bear the responsibility for all receipts and disbursements, and all accounting. I direct that bond shall not be required of my personal representative and trustee.

In witness whereof, I have hereunto set my hand to this my last will and testament, consisting of _____ typewritten pages, including this page and each bearing my signature, on this _____ day of _____, _____ at _____, _____, in the presence of each and all the

<small>(city)   (state)</small>

subscribing witnesses, each of whom I have requested in the presence of the others to subscribe his/her name, with his/her address written opposite thereto, as an attesting witness, in my presence and in the presence of all the others.

_____

The above and foregoing instrument was on the date thereof, signed, published, sealed, and declared by the testator, _____, to be his last will and testament in our presence, and we at his request and in his presence and in the presence of each other, have hereunto subscribed our names as witnesses thereto.

_____ Residing at _____
_____ Residing at _____

[Notary]

UNIFORM PROBATE CODE

PART 1
SHORT TITLE, CONSTRUCTION, GENERAL PROVISIONS

§1–101. [Short Title.]
This Act shall be known and may be cited as the Uniform Probate Code.

§1–102. [Purposes; Rule of Construction.]
(a) This Code shall be liberally construed and applied to promote its underlying purposes and policies.

(b) The underlying purposes and policies of this Code are:

(1) to simplify and clarify the law concerning the affairs of decedents, missing persons, protected persons, minors and incapacitated persons;

(2) to discover and make effective the intent of a decedent in distribution of his property;

(3) to promote a speedy and efficient system for liquidating the estate of the decedent and making distribution to his successors;

(4) to facilitate use and enforcement of certain trusts;

(5) to make uniform the law among the various jurisdictions.

§1–103. [Supplementary General Principles of Law Applicable.]
Unless displaced by the particular provisions of this Code, the principles of law and equity supplement its provisions.

§1–104. [Severability.]
If any provision of this Code or the application thereof to any person or circumstances is held invalid, the invalidity shall not affect other provisions or applications of the Code which can be given effect without the invalid provision or application, and to this end the provisions of this Code are declared to be severable.

§1–105. [Construction Against Implied Repeal.]

This Code is a general act intended as a unified coverage of its subject matter and no part of it shall be deemed impliedly repealed by subsequent legislation if it can reasonably be avoided.

§1–106. [Effect of Fraud and Evasion.]

Whenever fraud has been perpetrated in connection with any proceeding or in any statement filed under this Code or if fraud is used to avoid or circumvent the provisions or purposes of this Code, any person injured thereby may obtain appropriate relief against the perpetrator of the fraud or restitution from any person (other than a bona fide purchaser) benefitting from the fraud, whether innocent or not. Any proceeding must be commenced within 2 years after the discovery of the fraud, but no proceeding may be brought against one not a perpetrator of the fraud later than 5 years after the time of commission of the fraud. This section has no bearing on remedies relating to fraud practiced on a decedent during his lifetime which affects the succession of his estate.

§1–107. [Evidence of Death or Status.]

In addition to the rules of evidence in courts of general jurisdiction, the following rules relating to a determination of death and status apply:

(1) Death occurs when an individual [is determined to be dead under the Uniform Determination of Death Act] [has sustained either (i) irreversible cessation of circulatory and respiratory functions or (ii) irreversible cessation of all functions of the entire brain, including the brain stem. A determination of death must be made in accordance with accepted medical standards].

(2) A certified or authenticated copy of a death certificate purporting to be issued by an official or agency of the place where the death purportedly occurred is prima facie evidence of the fact, place, date, and time of death and the identity of the decedent.

(3) A certified or authenticated copy of any record or report of a governmental agency, domestic or foreign, that an individual is missing, detained, dead, or alive is prima facie evidence of the status and of the dates, circumstances, and places disclosed by the record or report.

(4) In the absence of prima facie evidence of death under paragraph (2) or (3), the fact of death may be established by clear and convincing evidence, including circumstantial evidence.

(5) An individual whose death is not established under the preceding paragraphs who is absent for a continuous period of 5 years, during which he [or she] has not been heard from, and whose absence is not satisfactorily explained after diligent search or inquiry, is presumed to be dead. His [or her] death is presumed to have occurred at the end of the period unless there is sufficient evidence for determining that death occurred earlier.

(6) In the absence of evidence disputing the time of death stated on a document described in paragraph (2) or (3), a document described in paragraph (2) or (3) that states a time of death 120 hours or more after the time of death of another individual, however the time of death of the other individual is determined, establishes by clear and convincing evidence that the individual survived the other individual by 120 hours.

As amended in 1987 and 1991.

§1–108. [Acts by Holder of General Power.]

For the purpose of granting consent or approval with regard to the acts or accounts of a personal representative or trustee, including relief from liability or penalty for failure to post bond, to register a trust, or to perform other duties, and for purposes of consenting to modification or termination of a trust or to deviation from its terms, the sole holder or all co-holders of a presently exercisable general power of appointment, including one in the form of a power of amendment or revocation, are deemed to act for beneficiaries to the extent their interests (as objects, takers in default, or otherwise) are subject to the power.

PART 2
DEFINITIONS

§1–201. General Definitions.

Subject to additional definitions contained in the subsequent Articles that are applicable to specific Articles, parts, or sections, and unless the context otherwise requires, in this Code:

(1) "Agent" includes an attorney-in-fact under a durable or nondurable power of attorney, an individual authorized to make decisions concerning another's health care, and an individual authorized to make decisions for another under a natural death act.

(2) "Application" means a written request to the Registrar for an order of informal probate or appointment under Part 3 of Article III.

(3) "Beneficiary," as it relates to a trust beneficiary, includes a person who has any present or future interest, vested or contingent, and also includes the owner of an interest by assignment or other transfer; as it relates to a charitable trust, includes any person entitled to enforce the trust; as it relates to a "beneficiary of a beneficiary designation," refers to a beneficiary of an insurance or annuity policy, of an account with POD designation, of a security registered in beneficiary form (TOD), or of a pension, profit-sharing, retirement, or similar benefit plan, or other nonprobate transfer at death; and, as it relates to a "beneficiary designated in a governing

instrument," includes a grantee of a deed, a devisee, a trust beneficiary, a beneficiary of a beneficiary designation, a donee, appointee, or taker in default of a power of appointment, or a person in whose favor a power of attorney or a power held in any individual, fiduciary, or representative capacity is exercised.

(4) "Beneficiary designation" refers to a governing instrument naming a beneficiary of an insurance or annuity policy, of an account with POD designation, of a security registered in beneficiary form (TOD), or of a pension, profit-sharing, retirement, or similar benefit plan, or other nonprobate transfer at death.

(5) "Child" includes an individual entitled to take as a child under this Code by intestate succession from the parent whose relationship is involved and excludes a person who is only a stepchild, a foster child, a grandchild, or any more remote descendant.

(6) "Claims," in respect to estates of decedents and protected persons, includes liabilities of the decedent or protected person, whether arising in contract, in tort, or otherwise, and liabilities of the estate which arise at or after the death of the decedent or after the appointment of a conservator, including funeral expenses and expenses of administration. The term does not include estate or inheritance taxes, or demands or disputes regarding title of a decedent or protected person to specific assets alleged to be included in the estate.

(7) "Court" means the [......... Court] or branch in this State having jurisdiction in matters relating to the affairs of decedents.

(8) "Conservator" means a person who is appointed by a Court to manage the estate of a protected person.

(9) "Descendant" of an individual means all of his [or her] descendants of all generations, with the relationship of parent and child at each generation being determined by the definition of child and parent contained in this Code.

(10) "Devise," when used as a noun, means a testamentary disposition of real or personal property and, when used as a verb, means to dispose of real or personal property by will.

(11) "Devisee" means a person designated in a will to receive a devise. For the purposes of Article II, in the case of a devise to an existing trust or trustee, or to a trustee on trust described by will, the trust or trustee is the devisee and the beneficiaries are not devisees.

(12) "Disability" means cause for a protective order as described in Section 5–401.

(13) "Distributee" means any person who has received property of a decedent from his [or her] personal representative other than as a creditor or purchaser. A testamentary trustee is a distributee only to the extent of distributed assets or increment thereto remaining in his [or her] hands. A beneficiary of a testamentary trust to whom the trustee has distributed property received from a personal representative is a distributee of the personal representative. For the purposes of this provision, "testamentary trustee" includes a trustee to whom assets are transferred by will, to the extent of the devised assets.

(14) "Estate" includes the property of the decedent, trust, or other person whose affairs are subject to this Code as originally constituted and as it exists from time to time during administration.

(15) "Exempt property" means that property of a decedent's estate which is described in Section 2–403.

(16) "Fiduciary" includes a personal representative, guardian, conservator, and trustee.

(17) "Foreign personal representative" means a personal representative appointed by another jurisdiction.

(18) "Formal proceedings" means proceedings conducted before a judge with notice to interested persons.

(19) "Governing instrument" means a deed, will, trust, insurance or annuity policy, account with POD designation, security registered in beneficiary form (TOD), pension, profit-sharing, retirement, or similar benefit plan, instrument creating or exercising a power of appointment or a power of attorney, or a dispositive, appointive, or nominative instrument of any similar type.

(20) "Guardian" means a person who has qualified as a guardian of a minor or incapacitated person pursuant to testamentary or court appointment, but excludes one who is merely a guardian ad litem.

(21) "Heirs," except as controlled by Section 2–711, means persons, including the surviving spouse and the state, who are entitled under the statutes of intestate succession to the property of a decedent.

(22) "Incapacitated person" means an individual described in Section 5–103.

(23) "Informal proceedings" means those conducted without notice to interested persons by an officer of the Court acting as a registrar for probate of a will or appointment of a personal representative.

(24) "Interested person" includes heirs, devisees, children, spouses, creditors, beneficiaries, and any others having a property right in or claim against a trust estate or the estate of a decedent, ward, or protected person. It also includes persons having priority for appointment as personal representative, and other fiduciaries representing interested persons. The meaning as it relates to particular persons may vary from time to time and must be determined according to the particular purposes of, and matter involved in, any proceeding.

(25) "Issue" of a person means descendant as defined in subsection (9).

(26) "Joint tenants with the right of survivorship" and "community property with the right of survivorship" includes co-owners of property held under circumstances

that entitle one or more to the whole of the property on the death of the other or others, but excludes forms of co-ownership registration in which the underlying ownership of each party is in proportion to that party's contribution.

(27) "Lease" includes an oil, gas, or other mineral lease.

(28) "Letters" includes letters testamentary, letters of guardianship, letters of administration, and letters of conservatorship.

(29) "Minor" means a person who is under [21] years of age.

(30) "Mortgage" means any conveyance, agreement, or arrangement in which property is encumbered or used as security.

(31) "Nonresident decedent" means a decedent who was domiciled in another jurisdiction at the time of his [or her] death.

(32) "Organization" means a corporation, business trust, estate, trust, partnership, joint venture, association, government or governmental subdivision or agency, or any other legal or commercial entity.

(33) "Parent" includes any person entitled to take, or who would be entitled to take if the child died without a will, as a parent under this Code by intestate succession from the child whose relationship is in question and excludes any person who is only a stepparent, foster parent, or grandparent.

(34) "Payor" means a trustee, insurer, business entity, employer, government, governmental agency or subdivision, or any other person authorized or obligated by law or a governing instrument to make payments.

(35) "Person" means an individual or an organization.

(36) "Personal representative" includes executor, administrator, successor personal representative, special administrator, and persons who perform substantially the same function under the law governing their status. "General personal representative" excludes special administrator.

(37) "Petition" means a written request to the Court for an order after notice.

(38) "Proceeding" includes action at law and suit in equity.

(39) "Property" includes both real and personal property or any interest therein and means anything that may be the subject of ownership.

(40) "Protected person" is as defined in Section 5–103.

(41) "Protective proceeding" means a proceeding described in Section 5–103.

(42) "Registrar" refers to the official of the Court designated to perform the functions of Registrar as provided in Section 1–307.

(43) "Security" includes any note, stock, treasury stock, bond, debenture, evidence of indebtedness, certificate of interest or participation in an oil, gas, or mining title or lease or in payments out of production under such a title or lease, collateral trust certificate, transferable share, voting trust certificate or, in general, any interest or instrument commonly known as a security, or any certificate of interest or participation, any temporary or interim certificate, receipt, or certificate of deposit for, or any warrant or right to subscribe to or purchase, any of the foregoing.

(44) "Settlement," in reference to a decedent's estate, includes the full process of administration, distribution, and closing.

(45) "Special administrator" means a personal representative as described by Sections 3–614 through 3–618.

(46) "State" means a state of the United States, the District of Columbia, the Commonwealth of Puerto Rico, or any territory or insular possession subject to the jurisdiction of the United States.

(47) "Successor personal representative" means a personal representative, other than a special administrator, who is appointed to succeed a previously appointed personal representative.

(48) "Successors" means persons, other than creditors, who are entitled to property of a decedent under his [or her] will or this Code.

(49) "Supervised administration" refers to the proceedings described in Article III, Part 5.

(50) "Survive" means that an individual has neither predeceased an event, including the death of another individual, nor is deemed to have predeceased an event under Section 2–104 or 2–702. The term includes its derivatives, such as "survives," "survived," "survivor," "surviving."

(51) "Testacy proceeding" means a proceeding to establish a will or determine intestacy.

(52) "Testator" includes an individual of either sex.

(53) "Trust" includes an express trust, private or charitable, with additions thereto, wherever and however created. The term also includes a trust created or determined by judgment or decree under which the trust is to be administered in the manner of an express trust. The term excludes other constructive trusts and excludes resulting trusts, conservatorships, personal representatives, trust accounts as defined in Article VI, custodial arrangements pursuant to [each state should list its legislation, including that relating to [gifts] [transfers] to minors, dealing with special custodial situations], business trusts providing for certificates to be issued to beneficiaries, common trust funds, voting trusts, security arrangements, liquidation trusts, and trusts for the primary purpose of paying debts, dividends, interest, salaries, wages, profits, pensions, or employee benefits of any kind, and any arrangement under which a person is nominee or escrowee for another.

(54) "Trustee" includes an original, additional, or successor trustee, whether or not appointed or confirmed by court.

(55) "Ward" means an individual described in Section 5-103.

(56) "Will" includes codicil and any testamentary instrument that merely appoints an executor, revokes or revises another will, nominates a guardian, or expressly excludes or limits the right of an individual or class to succeed to property of the decedent passing by intestate succession.

[FOR ADOPTION IN COMMUNITY PROPERTY STATES]

[(57) "Separate property" (if necessary, to be defined locally in accordance with existing concept in adopting state).

(58) "Community property" (if necessary, to be defined locally in accordance with existing concept in adopting state).]

As revised in 1990 and amended in 1991 and 1993.

PART 3
SCOPE, JURISDICTION AND COURTS

§1–301.   [Territorial Application.]
Except as otherwise provided in this Code, this Code applies to (1) the affairs and estates of decedents, missing persons, and persons to be protected, domiciled in this state, (2) the property of nonresidents located in this state or property coming into the control of a fiduciary who is subject to the laws of this state, (3) incapacitated persons and minors in this state, (4) survivorship and related accounts in this state, and (5) trusts subject to administration in this state.

§1–302.   [Subject Matter Jurisdiction.]
(a) To the full extent permitted by the constitution, the Court has jurisdiction over all subject matter relating to (1) estates of decedents, including construction of wills and determination of heirs and successors of decedents, and estates of protected persons; (2) protection of minors and incapacitated persons; and (3) trusts.

(b) The Court has full power to make orders, judgments and decrees and take all other action necessary and proper to administer justice in the matters which come before it.

(c) The Court has jurisdiction over protective proceedings and guardianship proceedings.

(d) If both guardianship and protective proceedings as to the same person are commenced or pending in the same court, the proceedings may be consolidated.

§1–303.   [Venue; Multiple Proceedings; Transfer.]
(a) Where a proceeding under this Code could be maintained in more than one place in this state, the Court in which the proceeding is first commenced has the exclusive right to proceed.

(b) If proceedings concerning the same estate, protected person, ward, or trust are commenced in more than one Court of this state, the Court in which the proceeding was first commenced shall continue to hear the matter, and the other courts shall hold the matter in abeyance until the question of venue is decided, and if the ruling Court determines that venue is properly in another Court, it shall transfer the proceeding to the other Court.

(c) If a Court finds that in the interest of justice a proceeding or a file should be located in another Court of this state, the Court making the finding may transfer the proceeding or file to the other Court.

§1–304.   [Practice in Court.]
Unless specifically provided to the contrary in this Code or unless inconsistent with its provisions, the rules of civil procedure including the rules concerning vacation of orders and appellate review govern formal proceedings under this Code.

§1–305.   [Records and Certified Copies.]
The [Clerk of Court] shall keep a record for each decedent, ward, protected person or trust involved in any document which may be filed with the Court under this Code, including petitions and applications, demands for notices or bonds, trust registrations, and of any orders or responses relating thereto by the Registrar or Court, and establish and maintain a system for indexing, filing or recording which is sufficient to enable users of the records to obtain adequate information. Upon payment of the fees required by law the clerk must issue certified copies of any probated wills, letters issued to personal representatives, or any other record or paper filed or recorded. Certificates relating to probated wills must indicate whether the decedent was domiciled in this state and whether the probate was formal or informal. Certificates relating to letters must show the date of appointment.

§1–306.   [Jury Trial.]
(a) If duly demanded, a party is entitled to trial by jury in [a formal testacy proceeding and] any proceeding in which any controverted question of fact arises as to which any party has a constitutional right to trial by jury.

(b) If there is no right to trial by jury under subsection (a) or the right is waived, the Court in its discretion may call a jury to decide any issue of fact, in which case the verdict is advisory only.

§1–307.   [Registrar; Powers.]
The acts and orders which this Code specifies as performable by the Registrar may be performed either by a judge of the Court or by a person, including the clerk,

designated by the Court by a written order filed and recorded in the office of the Court.

§1–308. [Appeals.]

Appellate review, including the right to appellate review, interlocutory appeal, provisions as to time, manner, notice, appeal bond, stays, scope of review, record on appeal, briefs, arguments and power of the appellate court, is governed by the rules applicable to the appeals to the [Supreme Court] in equity cases from the [court of general jurisdiction], except that in proceedings where jury trial has been had as a matter of right, the rules applicable to the scope of review in jury cases apply.

§1–309. [Qualifications of Judge.]

A judge of the Court must have the same qualifications as a judge of the [court of general jurisdiction.]

§1–310. [Oath or Affirmation on Filed Documents.]

Except as otherwise specifically provided in this Code or by rule, every document filed with the Court under this Code including applications, petitions, and demands for notice, shall be deemed to include an oath, affirmation, or statement to the effect that its representations are true as far as the person executing or filing it knows or is informed, and penalties for perjury may follow deliberate falsification therein.

PART 4
NOTICE, PARTIES AND REPRESENTATION IN ESTATE LITIGATION AND OTHER MATTERS

§1–401. [Notice; Method and Time of Giving.]

(a) If notice of a hearing on any petition is required and except for specific notice requirements as otherwise provided, the petitioner shall cause notice of the time and place of hearing of any petition to be given to any interested person or his attorney if he has appeared by attorney or requested that notice be sent to his attorney. Notice shall be given:

(1) by mailing a copy thereof at least 14 days before the time set for the hearing by certified, registered or ordinary first class mail addressed to the person being notified at the post office address given in his demand for notice, if any, or at his office or place of residence, if known;

(2) by delivering a copy thereof to the person being notified personally at least 14 days before the time set for the hearing; or

(3) if the address, or identity of any person is not known and cannot be ascertained with reasonable diligence, by publishing at least once a week for 3 consecutive weeks, a copy thereof in a newspaper having general circulation in the county where the hearing is to be held, the last publication of which is to be at least 10 days before the time set for the hearing.

(b) The Court for good cause shown may provide for a different method or time of giving notice for any hearing.

(c) Proof of the giving of notice shall be made on or before the hearing and filed in the proceeding.

§1–402. [Notice; Waiver.]

A person, including a guardian ad litem, conservator, or other fiduciary, may waive notice by a writing signed by him or his attorney and filed in the proceeding. A person for whom a guardianship or other protective order is sought, a ward, or a protected person may not waive notice.

§1–403. [Pleadings; When Parties Bound by Others; Notice.]

In formal proceedings involving trusts or estates of decedents, minors, protected persons, or incapacitated persons, and in judicially supervised settlements, the following apply:

(1) Interests to be affected shall be described in pleadings which give reasonable information to owners by name or class, by reference to the instrument creating the interests, or in other appropriate manner.

(2) Persons are bound by orders binding others in the following cases:

(i) Orders binding the sole holder or all co-holders of a power of revocation or a presently exercisable general power of appointment, including one in the form of a power of amendment, bind other persons to the extent their interests (as objects, takers in default, or otherwise) are subject to the power.

(ii) To the extent there is no conflict of interest between them or among persons represented, orders binding a conservator bind the person whose estate he controls; orders binding a guardian bind the ward if no conservator of his estate has been appointed; orders binding a trustee bind beneficiaries of the trust in proceedings to probate a will establishing or adding to a trust, to review the acts or accounts of a prior fiduciary and in proceedings involving creditors or other third parties; and orders binding a personal representative bind persons interested in the undistributed assets of a decedent's estate in actions or proceedings by or against the estate. If there is no conflict of interest and no conservator or guardian has been appointed, a parent may represent his minor child.

(iii) An unborn or unascertained person who is not otherwise represented is bound by an order to the extent his interest is adequately represented by another party having a substantially identical interest in the proceeding.

(3) Notice is required as follows:

(i) Notice as prescribed by Section 1–401 shall be given to every interested person or to one who can bind an interested person as described in (2)(i) or (2)(ii) above. Notice may be given both to a person and to another who may bind him.

(ii) Notice is given to unborn or unascertained persons, who are not represented under (2)(i) or (2)(ii) above, by giving notice to all known persons whose interests in the proceedings are substantially identical to those of the unborn or unascertained persons.

(4) At any point in a proceeding, a court may appoint a guardian ad litem to represent the interest of a minor, an incapacitated, unborn, or unascertained person, or a person whose identity or address is unknown, if the Court determines that representation of the interest otherwise would be inadequate. If not precluded by conflict of interests, a guardian ad litem may be appointed to represent several persons or interests. The Court shall set out its reasons for appointing a guardian ad litem as a part of the record of the proceeding.

ARTICLE II
INTESTACY, WILLS, AND DONATIVE TRANSFERS (1990)

PART 1
INTESTATE SUCCESSION

PART 1
INTESTATE SUCCESSION

§2–101. Intestate Estate.

(a) Any part of a decedent's estate not effectively disposed of by will passes by intestate succession to the decedent's heirs as prescribed in this Code, except as modified by the decedent's will.

(b) A decedent by will may expressly exclude or limit the right of an individual or class to succeed to property of the decedent passing by intestate succession. If that individual or a member of that class survives the decedent, the share of the decedent's intestate estate to which that individual or class would have succeeded passes as if that individual or each member of that class had disclaimed his [or her] intestate share.

§2–102. Share of Spouse.

The intestate share of a decedent's surviving spouse is:

(1) the entire intestate estate if:

  (i) no descendant or parent of the decedent survives the decedent; or

  (ii) all of the decedent's surviving descendants are also descendants of the surviving spouse and there is no other descendant of the surviving spouse who survives the decedent;

(2) the first [$200,000], plus three-fourths of any balance of the intestate estate, if no descendant of the decedent survives the decedent, but a parent of the decedent survives the decedent;

(3) the first [$150,000], plus one-half of any balance of the intestate estate, if all of the decedent's surviving descendants are also descendants of the surviving spouse and the surviving spouse has one or more surviving descendants who are not descendants of the decedent;

(4) the first [$100,000], plus one-half of any balance of the intestate estate, if one or more of the decedent's surviving descendants are not descendants of the surviving spouse.

[ALTERNATIVE PROVISION FOR COMMUNITY PROPERTY STATES]

[§2–102A. Share of Spouse.

2–102A. Share of Spouse.

(a) The intestate share of a surviving spouse in separate property is:

(1) the entire intestate estate if:

  (i) no descendant or parent of the decedent survives the decedent; or

  (ii) all of the decedent's surviving descendants are also descendants of the surviving spouse and there is no other descendant of the surviving spouse who survives the decedent;

(2) the first [$200,000], plus three-fourths of any balance of the intestate estate, if no descendant of the decedent survives the decedent, but a parent of the decedent survives the decedent;

(3) the first [$150,000], plus one-half of any balance of the intestate estate, if all of the decedent's surviving descendants are also descendants of the surviving spouse and the surviving spouse has one or more surviving descendants who are not descendants of the decedent;

(4) the first [$100,000], plus one-half of any balance of the intestate estate, if one or more of the decedent's surviving descendants are not descendants of the surviving spouse.

(b) The one-half of community property belonging to the decedent passes to the [surviving spouse] as the intestate share.]

§2–103. Share of Heirs other than Surviving Spouse.

Any part of the intestate estate not passing to the decedent's surviving spouse under Section 2–102, or the entire intestate estate if there is no surviving spouse, passes in the following order to the individuals designated below who survive the decedent:

(1) to the decedent's descendants by representation;

(2) if there is no surviving descendant, to the decedent's parents equally if both survive, or to the surviving parent;

(3) if there is no surviving descendant or parent, to the descendants of the decedent's parents or either of them by representation;

(4) if there is no surviving descendant, parent, or descendant of a parent, but the decedent is survived by one or more grandparents or descendants of grandparents, half of the estate passes to the decedent's paternal grandparents equally if both survive, or to the surviving paternal grandparent, or to the descendants of the decedent's paternal grandparents or either of them if both are deceased, the descendants taking by representation; and the other half passes to the decedent's maternal relatives in the same manner; but if there is no surviving grandparent or descendant of a grandparent on either the paternal or the maternal side, the entire estate passes to the decedent's relatives on the other side in the same manner as the half.

§2–104. Requirement that Heir Survive Decedent for 120 Hours.

An individual who fails to survive the decedent by 120 hours is deemed to have predeceased the decedent for purposes of homestead allowance, exempt property, and intestate succession, and the decedent's heirs are determined accordingly. If it is not established by clear and convincing evidence that an individual who would otherwise be an heir survived the decedent by 120 hours, it is deemed that the individual failed to survive for the required period. This section is not to be applied if its application would result in a taking of intestate estate by the state under Section 2–105.

§2–105. No Taker.

If there is no taker under the provisions of this Article, the intestate estate passes to the [state].

§2–106. Representation.

(a) [Definitions.] In this section:

(1) "Deceased descendant," "deceased parent," or "deceased grandparent" means a descendant, parent, or grandparent who either predeceased the decedent or is deemed to have predeceased the decedent under Section 2-104.

(2) "Surviving descendant" means a descendant who neither predeceased the decedent nor is deemed to have predeceased the decedent under Section 2–104.

(b) [Decedent's Descendants.] If, under Section 2–103(1), a decedent's intestate estate or a part thereof passes "by representation" to the decedent's descendants, the estate or part thereof is divided into as many equal shares as there are (i) surviving descendants in the generation nearest to the decedent which contains one or more surviving descendants and (ii) deceased descendants in the same generation who left surviving descendants, if any. Each surviving descendant in the nearest generation is allocated one share. The remaining shares, if any, are combined and then divided in the same manner among the surviving descendants of the deceased descendants as if the surviving descendants who were allocated a share and their surviving descendants had predeceased the decedent.

(c) [Descendants of Parents or Grandparents.] If, under Section 2–103(3) or (4), a decedent's intestate estate or a part thereof passes "by representation" to the descendants of the decedent's deceased parents or either of them or to the descendants of the decedent's deceased paternal or maternal grandparents or either of them, the estate or part thereof is divided into as many equal shares as there are (i) surviving descendants in the generation nearest the deceased parents or either of them, or the deceased grandparents or either of them, that contains one or more surviving descendants and (ii) deceased descendants in the same generation who left surviving descendants, if any. Each surviving descendant in the nearest generation is allocated one share. The remaining shares, if any, are combined and then divided in the same manner among the surviving descendants of the deceased descendants as if the surviving descendants who were allocated a share and their surviving descendants had predeceased the decedent.

§2–107.   Kindred of Half Blood.
Relatives of the half blood inherit the same share they would inherit if they were of the whole blood.

§2–108.   Afterborn Heirs.
An individual in gestation at a particular time is treated as living at that time if the individual lives 120 hours or more after birth.

§2–109.   Advancements.
(a) If an individual dies intestate as to all or a portion of his [or her] estate, property the decedent gave during the decedent's lifetime to an individual who, at the decedent's death, is an heir is treated as an advancement against the heir's intestate share only if (i) the decedent declared in a contemporaneous writing or the heir ac-knowledged in writing that the gift is an advancement or (ii) the decedent's contemporaneous writing or the heir's written acknowledgment otherwise indicates that the gift is to be taken into account in computing the division and distribution of the decedent's intestate estate.

(b) For purposes of subsection (a), property advanced is valued as of the time the heir came into possession or enjoyment of the property or as of the time of the decedent's death, whichever first occurs.

(c) If the recipient of the property fails to survive the decedent, the property is not taken into account in computing the division and distribution of the decedent's intestate estate, unless the decedent's contemporaneous writing provides otherwise.

§2–110.   Debts to Decedent.
A debt owed to a decedent is not charged against the intestate share of any individual except the debtor. If the debtor fails to survive the decedent, the debt is not taken into account in computing the intestate share of the debtor's descendants.

§2–111.   Alienage.
No individual is disqualified to take as an heir because the individual or an individual through whom he [or she] claims is or has been an alien.

[§2–112.   Dower and Curtesy Abolished.
The estates of dower and curtesy are abolished.]

§2–113.   Individuals Related to Decedent Through Two Lines.
An individual who is related to the decedent through two lines of relationship is entitled to only a single share based on the relationship that would entitle the individual to the larger share.

§2–114.   Parent and Child Relationship.
(a) Except as provided in subsections (b) and (c), for purposes of intestate succession by, through, or from a person, an individual is the child of his [or her] natural parents, regardless of their marital status. The parent and child relationship may be established under [the Uniform Parentage Act] [applicable state law] [insert appropriate statutory reference].

(b) An adopted individual is the child of his [or her] adopting parent or parents and not of his [or her] natural parents, but adoption of a child by the spouse of either natural parent has no effect on (i) the relationship between the child and that natural parent or (ii) the right of the child or a descendant of the child to inherit from or through the other natural parent.

(c) Inheritance from or through a child by either natural parent or his [or her] kindred is precluded unless that natural parent has openly treated the child as his [or hers], and has not refused to support the child.

PART 2
ELECTIVE SHARE OF SURVIVING SPOUSE

§2–201. Definitions.

In this Part:

(1) As used in sections other than Section 2–205, "decedent's nonprobate transfers to others" means the amounts that are included in the augmented estate under Section 2–205.

(2) "Fractional interest in property held in joint tenancy with the right of survivorship," whether the fractional interest is unilaterally severable or not, means the fraction, the numerator of which is one and the denominator of which, if the decedent was a joint tenant, is one plus the number of joint tenants who survive the decedent and which, if the decedent was not a joint tenant, is the number of joint tenants.

(3) "Marriage," as it relates to a transfer by the decedent during marriage, means any marriage of the decedent to the decedent's surviving spouse.

(4) "Nonadverse party" means a person who does not have a substantial beneficial interest in the trust or other property arrangement that would be adversely affected by the exercise or nonexercise of the power that he [or she] possesses respecting the trust or other property arrangement. A person having a general power of appointment over property is deemed to have a beneficial interest in the property.

(5) "Power" or "power of appointment" includes a power to designate the beneficiary of a beneficiary designation.

(6) "Presently exercisable general power of appointment" means a power of appointment under which, at the time in question, the decedent, whether or not he [or she] then had the capacity to exercise the power, held a power to create a present or future interest in himself [or herself], his [or her] creditors, his [or her] estate, or creditors of his [or her] estate, and includes a power to revoke or invade the principal of a trust or other property arrangement.

(7) "Probate estate" means property that would pass by intestate succession if the decedent died without a valid will.

(8) "Property" includes values subject to a beneficiary designation.

(9) "Right to income" includes a right to payments under a commercial or private annuity, an annuity trust, a unitrust, or a similar arrangement.

(10) "Transfer," as it relates to a transfer by or of the decedent, includes (A) an exercise or release of a presently exercisable general power of appointment held by the decedent, (B) a lapse at death of a presently exercisable general power of appointment held by the decedent, and (C) an exercise, release, or lapse of a general power of appointment that the decedent created in himself [or herself] and of a power described in Section 2–205(2)(ii) that the decedent conferred on a nonadverse party.

§2–202. Elective Share.

(a) [Elective-Share Amount.] The surviving spouse of a decedent who dies domiciled in this State has a right of election, under the limitations and conditions stated in this Part, to take an elective-share amount equal to the value of the elective-share percentage of the augmented estate, determined by the length of time the spouse and the decedent were married to each other, in accordance with the following schedule:

If the decedent and the spouse were married to each other:	The elective-share percentage is:
Less than 1 year	Supplemental Amount Only.
1 year but less than 2 years	3% of the augmented estate.
2 years but less than 3 years	6% of the augmented estate.
3 years but less than 4 years	9% of the augmented estate.
4 years but less than 5 years	12% of the augmented estate.
5 years but less than 6 years	15% of the augmented estate.
6 years but less than 7 years	18% of the augmented estate.
7 years but less than 8 years	21% of the augmented estate.
8 years but less than 9 years	24% of the augmented estate.
9 years but less than 10 years	27% of the augmented estate.
10 years but less than 11 years	30% of the augmented estate.
11 years but less than 12 years	34% of the augmented estate.
12 years but less than 13 years	38% of the augmented estate.
13 years but less than 14 years	42% of the augmented estate.
14 years but less than 15 years	46% of the augmented estate.
15 years or more	50% of the augmented estate.

(b) [Supplemental Elective-Share Amount.] If the sum of the amounts described in Sections 2–207, 2–209(a)(1), and that part of the elective-share amount payable from the decedent's probate estate and nonprobate transfers to others under Section 2–209(b) and (c) is less than [$50,000], the surviving spouse is entitled to a supplemental elective-share amount equal to [$50,000], minus the sum of the amounts described in those sections. The supplemental elective-share amount is payable from the decedent's probate estate and from recipients of the decedent's nonprobate transfers to others in the order of priority set forth in Section 2–209(b) and (c).

(c) [Effect of Election on Statutory Benefits.] If the right of election is exercised by or on behalf of the surviving spouse, the surviving spouse's homestead allowance, exempt property, and family allowance, if any, are not charged against but are in addition to the elective-share and supplemental elective-share amounts.

(d) [Non-Domiciliary.] The right, if any, of the surviving spouse of a decedent who dies domiciled outside this State to take an elective share in property in this State is governed by the law of the decedent's domicile at death.

§2–203. Composition of the Augmented Estate.

Subject to Section 2–208, the value of the augmented estate, to the extent provided in Sections 2–204, 2–205, 2–206, and 2–207, consists of the sum of the values of all property, whether real or personal; movable or immovable, tangible or intangible, wherever situated, that constitute the decedent's net probate estate, the decedent's nonprobate transfers to others, the decedent's nonprobate transfers to the surviving spouse, and the surviving spouse's property and nonprobate transfers to others.

§2–204. Decedent's Net Probate Estate.

The value of the augmented estate includes the value of the decedent's probate estate, reduced by funeral and administration expenses, homestead allowance, family allowances, exempt property, and enforceable claims.

§2–205. Decedent's Nonprobate Transfers to Others.

The value of the augmented estate includes the value of the decedent's nonprobate transfers to others, not included under Section 2–204, of any of the following types, in the amount provided respectively for each type of transfer:

(1) Property owned or owned in substance by the decedent immediately before death that passed outside probate at the decedent's death. Property included under this category consists of:

(i) Property over which the decedent alone, immediately before death, held a presently exercisable general power of appointment. The amount included is the value of the property subject to the power, to the extent the property passed at the decedent's death, by exercise, release, lapse, in default, or otherwise, to or for the benefit of any person other than the decedent's estate or surviving spouse.

(ii) The decedent's fractional interest in property held by the decedent in joint tenancy with the right of survivorship. The amount included is the value of the decedent's fractional interest, to the extent the fractional interest passed by right of survivorship at the decedent's death to a surviving joint tenant other than the decedent's surviving spouse.

(iii) The decedent's ownership interest in property or accounts held in POD, TOD, or co-ownership registration with the right of survivorship. The amount included is the value of the decedent's ownership interest, to the extent the decedent's ownership interest passed at the decedent's death to or for the benefit of any person other than the decedent's estate or surviving spouse.

(iv) Proceeds of insurance, including accidental death benefits, on the life of the decedent, if the decedent owned the insurance policy immediately before death or if and to the extent the decedent alone and immediately before death held a presently exercisable general power of appointment over the policy or its proceeds. The amount included is the value of the proceeds, to the extent they were payable at the decedent's death to or for the benefit of any person other than the decedent's estate or surviving spouse.

(2) Property transferred in any of the following forms by the decedent during marriage:

(i) Any irrevocable transfer in which the decedent retained the right to the possession or enjoyment of, or to the income from, the property if and to the extent the decedent's right terminated at or continued beyond the decedent's death. The amount included is the value of the fraction of the property to which the decedent's right related, to the extent the fraction of the property passed outside probate to or for the benefit of any person other than the decedent's estate or surviving spouse.

(ii) Any transfer in which the decedent created a power over income or property, exercisable by the decedent alone or in conjunction with any other person, or exercisable by a nonadverse party, to or for the benefit of the decedent, creditors of the decedent, the decedent's estate, or creditors of the decedent's estate. The amount included with respect to a power over property is the value of the property subject to the power, and the amount included with respect to a power over income is the value of the property that produces or produced the income, to the extent the power in either case was exercisable at the decedent's death to or for the benefit of any person other than the decedent's surviving spouse or to the extent the property passed at the decedent's death, by exercise, release, lapse, in default, or otherwise, to or for the benefit of any person other than the decedent's estate or surviving spouse. If the power is a power over both income and property and the preceding sentence produces different amounts, the amount included is the greater amount.

(3) Property that passed during marriage and during the two-year period next preceding the decedent's death as a result of a transfer by the decedent if the transfer was of any of the following types:

(i) Any property that passed as a result of the termination of a right or interest in, or power over, property that would have been included in the augmented estate under paragraph (1)(i), (ii), or (iii), or under paragraph (2), if the right, interest, or power had not terminated until the decedent's death. The amount included is the value of the property that would have been included under those paragraphs if the property

were valued at the time the right, interest, or power terminated, and is included only to the extent the property passed upon termination to or for the benefit of any person other than the decedent or the decedent's estate, spouse, or surviving spouse. As used in this subparagraph, "termination," with respect to a right or interest in property, occurs when the right or interest terminated by the terms of the governing instrument or the decedent transferred or relinquished the right or interest, and, with respect to a power over property, occurs when the power terminated by exercise, release, lapse, default, or otherwise, but, with respect to a power described in paragraph (1)(i), "termination" occurs when the power terminated by exercise or release, but not otherwise.
(ii) Any transfer of or relating to an insurance policy on the life of the decedent if the proceeds would have been included in the augmented estate under paragraph (1)(iv) had the transfer not occurred. The amount included is the value of the insurance proceeds to the extent the proceeds were payable at the decedent's death to or for the benefit of any person other than the decedent's estate or surviving spouse.
(iii) Any transfer of property, to the extent not otherwise included in the augmented estate, made to or for the benefit of a person other than the decedent's surviving spouse. The amount included is the value of the transferred property to the extent the aggregate transfers to any one donee in either of the two years exceeded $10,000.

§2–206. Decedent's Nonprobate Transfers to the Surviving Spouse.

Excluding property passing to the surviving spouse under the federal Social Security system, the value of the augmented estate includes the value of the decedent's nonprobate transfers to the decedent's surviving spouse, which consist of all property that passed outside probate at the decedent's death from the decedent to the surviving spouse by reason of the decedent's death, including:
(1) the decedent's fractional interest in property held as a joint tenant with the right of survivorship, to the extent that the decedent's fractional interest passed to the surviving spouse as surviving joint tenant,
(2) the decedent's ownership interest in property or accounts held in co-ownership registration with the right of survivorship, to the extent the decedent's ownership interest passed to the surviving spouse as surviving co-owner, and
(3) all other property that would have been included in the augmented estate under Section 2–205(1) or (2) had it passed to or for the benefit of a person other than the decedent's spouse, surviving spouse, the decedent, or the decedent's creditors, estate, or estate creditors.

§2–207. Surviving Spouse's Property and Nonprobate Transfers to Others.

(a) [Included Property.] Except to the extent included in the augmented estate under Section 2–204 or 2–206, the value of the augmented estate includes the value of:
(1) property that was owned by the decedent's surviving spouse at the decedent's death, including:
(i) the surviving spouse's fractional interest in property held in joint tenancy with the right of survivorship,
(ii) the surviving spouse's ownership interest in property or accounts held in co-ownership registration with the right of survivorship, and
(iii) property that passed to the surviving spouse by reason of the decedent's death, but not including the spouse's right to homestead allowance, family allowance, exempt property, or payments under the federal Social Security system; and
(2) property that would have been included in the surviving spouse's nonprobate transfers to others, other than the spouse's fractional and ownership interests included under subsection (a)(1)(i) or (ii), had the spouse been the decedent.
(b) [Time of Valuation.] Property included under this section is valued at the decedent's death, taking the fact that the decedent predeceased the spouse into account, but, for purposes of subsection (a)(1)(i) and (ii), the values of the spouse's fractional and ownership interests are determined immediately before the decedent's death if the decedent was then a joint tenant or a co-owner of the property or accounts. For purposes of subsection (a)(2), proceeds of insurance that would have been included in the spouse's nonprobate transfers to others under Section 2–205(1)(iv) are not valued as if he [or she] were deceased.
(c) [Reduction for Enforceable Claims.] The value of property included under this section is reduced by enforceable claims against the surviving spouse.

§2–208. Exclusions, Valuation, and Overlapping Application.

(a) [Exclusions.] The value of any property is excluded from the decedent's nonprobate transfers to others (i) to the extent the decedent received adequate and full consideration in money or money's worth for a transfer of the property or (ii) if the property was transferred with the written joinder of, or if the transfer was consented to in writing by, the surviving spouse.
(b) [Valuation.] The value of property:
(1) included in the augmented estate under Section 2–205, 2–206, or 2–207 is reduced in each category by enforceable claims against the included property; and
(2) includes the commuted value of any present or future interest and the commuted value of amounts

payable under any trust, life insurance settlement option, annuity contract, public or private pension, disability compensation, death benefit or retirement plan, or any similar arrangement, exclusive of the federal Social Security system.

(c) [Overlapping Application; No Double Inclusion.] In case of overlapping application to the same property of the paragraphs or subparagraphs of Section 2–205, 2–206, or 2–207, the property is included in the augmented estate under the provision yielding the greatest value, and under only one overlapping provision if they all yield the same value.

§2–209.   **Sources from Which Elective-Share Payable.**
(a) [Elective-Share Amount Only.] In a proceeding for an elective share, the following are applied first to satisfy the elective-share amount and to reduce or eliminate any contributions due from the decedent's probate estate and recipients of the decedent's nonprobate transfers to others:

(1) amounts included in the augmented estate under Section 2–204 which pass or have passed to the surviving spouse by testate or intestate succession and amounts included in the augmented estate under Section 2–206; and

(2) amounts included in the augmented estate under Section 2–207 up to the applicable percentage thereof. For the purposes of this subsection, the "applicable percentage" is twice the elective-share percentage set forth in the schedule in Section 2–202(a) appropriate to the length of time the spouse and the decedent were married to each other.

(b) [Unsatisfied Balance of Elective-Share Amount; Supplemental Elective-Share Amount.] If, after the application of subsection (a), the elective-share amount is not fully satisfied or the surviving spouse is entitled to a supplemental elective-share amount, amounts included in the decedent's probate estate and in the decedent's nonprobate transfers to others, other than amounts included under Section 2–205(3)(i) or (iii), are applied first to satisfy the unsatisfied balance of the elective-share amount or the supplemental elective-share amount. The decedent's probate estate and that portion of the decedent's nonprobate transfers to others are so applied that liability for the unsatisfied balance of the elective-share amount or for the supplemental elective-share amount is equitably apportioned among the recipients of the decedent's probate estate and of that portion of the decedent's nonprobate transfers to others in proportion to the value of their interests therein.

(c) [Unsatisfied Balance of Elective-Share and Supplemental Elective-Share Amounts.] If, after the application of subsections (a) and (b), the elective-share or supplemental elective-share amount is not fully satisfied, the remaining portion of the decedent's nonprobate transfers to others is so applied that liability for the unsatisfied balance of the elective-share or supplemental elective-share amount is equitably apportioned among the recipients of the remaining portion of the decedent's nonprobate transfers to others in proportion to the value of their interests therein.

§2–210.   **Personal Liability of Recipients.**
(a) Only original recipients of the decedent's nonprobate transfers to others, and the donees of the recipients of the decedent's nonprobate transfers to others, to the extent the donees have the property or its proceeds, are liable to make a proportional contribution toward satisfaction of the surviving spouse's elective-share or supplemental elective-share amount. A person liable to make contribution may choose to give up the proportional part of the decedent's nonprobate transfers to him [or her] or to pay the value of the amount for which he [or she] is liable.

(b) If any section or part of any section of this Part is preempted by federal law with respect to a payment, an item of property, or any other benefit included in the decedent's nonprobate transfers to others, a person who, not for value, receives the payment, item of property, or any other benefit is obligated to return the payment, item of property, or benefit, or is personally liable for the amount of the payment or the value of that item of property or benefit, as provided in Section 2–209, to the person who would have been entitled to it were that section or part of that section not preempted.

§2–211.   **Proceeding for Elective-Share; Time Limit.**
(a) Except as provided in subsection (b), the election must be made by filing in the court and mailing or delivering to the personal representative, if any, a petition for the elective-share within nine months after the date of the decedent's death, or within six months after the probate of the decedent's will, whichever limitation later expires. The surviving spouse must give notice of the time and place set for hearing to persons interested in the estate and to the distributees and recipients of portions of the augmented estate whose interests will be adversely affected by the taking of the elective-share. Except as provided in subsection (b), the decedent's nonprobate transfers to others are not included within the augmented estate for the purpose of computing the elective-share, if the petition is filed more than nine months after the decedent's death.

(b) Within nine months after the decedent's death, the surviving spouse may petition the court for an extension of time for making an election. If, within nine months after the decedent's death, the spouse gives notice of the petition to all persons interested in the decedent's nonprobate transfers to others, the court for cause shown by the surviving spouse may extend the time for election. If the court grants the spouse's petition for an extension, the decedent's nonprobate transfers to others are not excluded from the augmented estate for the purpose of computing the elective-share and supplemental elective-share amounts, if the spouse makes an election by filing in the court and mailing or delivering to the personal representative, if any, a petition for the elective share within the time allowed by the extension.

(c) The surviving spouse may withdraw his [or her] demand for an elective share at any time before entry of a final determination by the court.

(d) After notice and hearing, the court shall determine the elective-share and supplemental elective-share amounts, and shall order its payment from the assets of the augmented estate or by contribution as appears appropriate under Sections 2–209 and 2–210. If it appears that a fund or property included in the augmented estate has not come into the possession of the personal representative, or has been distributed by the personal representative, the court nevertheless shall fix the liability of any person who has any interest in the fund or property or who has possession thereof, whether as trustee or otherwise. The proceeding may be maintained against fewer than all persons against whom relief could be sought, but no person is subject to contribution in any greater amount than he [or she] would have been under Sections 2–209 and 2–210 had relief been secured against all persons subject to contribution.

(e) An order or judgment of the court may be enforced as necessary in suit for contribution or payment in other courts of this State or other jurisdictions.

§2–212. Right of Election Personal to Surviving Spouse; Incapacitated Surviving Spouse.

(a) [Surviving Spouse Must Be Living at Time of Election.] The right of election may be exercised only by a surviving spouse who is living when the petition for the elective-share is filed in the court under Section 2–211(a). If the election is not exercised by the surviving spouse personally, it may be exercised on the surviving spouse's behalf by his [or her] conservator, guardian, or agent under the authority of a power of attorney.

(b) [Incapacitated Surviving Spouse.] If the election is exercised on behalf of a surviving spouse who is an incapacitated person, that portion of the elective-share and supplemental elective-share amounts due from the decedent's probate estate and recipients of the decedent's nonprobate transfers to others under Section 2–209(b) and (c) must be placed in a custodial trust for the benefit of the surviving spouse under the provisions of the [Enacting state] Uniform Custodial Trust Act, except as modified below. For the purposes of this sub-

section, an election on behalf of a surviving spouse by an agent under a durable power of attorney is presumed to be on behalf of a surviving spouse who is an incapacitated person. For purposes of the custodial trust established by this subsection, (i) the electing guardian, conservator, or agent is the custodial trustee, (ii) the surviving spouse is the beneficiary, and (iii) the custodial trust is deemed to have been created by the decedent spouse by written transfer that takes effect at the decedent spouse's death and that directs the custodial trustee to administer the custodial trust as for an incapacitated beneficiary.

(c) [Custodial Trust.] For the purposes of subsection (b), the [Enacting state] Uniform Custodial Trust Act must be applied as if Section 6(b) thereof were repealed and Sections 2(e), 9(b), and 17(a) were amended to read as follows:

(1) Neither an incapacitated beneficiary nor anyone acting on behalf of an incapacitated beneficiary has a power to terminate the custodial trust; but if the beneficiary regains capacity, the beneficiary then acquires the power to terminate the custodial trust by delivering to the custodial trustee a writing signed by the beneficiary declaring the termination. If not previously terminated, the custodial trust terminates on the death of the beneficiary.

(2) If the beneficiary is incapacitated, the custodial trustee shall expend so much or all of the custodial trust property as the custodial trustee considers advisable for the use and benefit of the beneficiary and individuals who were supported by the beneficiary when the beneficiary became incapacitated, or who are legally entitled to support by the beneficiary. Expenditures may be made in the manner, when, and to the extent that the custodial trustee determines suitable and proper, without court order but with regard to other support, income, and property of the beneficiary [exclusive of] [and] benefits of medical or other forms of assistance from any state or federal government or governmental agency for which the beneficiary must qualify on the basis of need.

(3) Upon the beneficiary's death, the custodial trustee shall transfer the unexpended custodial trust property in the following order: (i) under the residuary clause, if any, of the will of the beneficiary's predeceased spouse against whom the elective share was taken, as if that predeceased spouse died immediately after the beneficiary; or (ii) to that predeceased spouse's heirs under Section 2–711 of [this State's] Uniform Probate Code.

[STATES THAT HAVE NOT ADOPTED THE UNIFORM CUSTODIAL TRUST ACT SHOULD ADOPT THE

FOLLOWING ALTERNATIVE SUBSECTION (b) AND NOT ADOPT SUBSECTION (b) OR (c) ABOVE]

[(b) [Incapacitated Surviving Spouse.] If the election is exercised on behalf of a surviving spouse who is an incapacitated person, the court must set aside that portion of the elective-share and supplemental elective-share amounts due from the decedent's probate estate and recipients of the decedent's nonprobate transfers to others under Section 2–209(b) and (c) and must appoint a trustee to administer that property for the support of the surviving spouse. For the purposes of this subsection, an election on behalf of a surviving spouse by an agent under a durable power of attorney is presumed to be on behalf of a surviving spouse who is an incapacitated person. The trustee must administer the trust in accordance with the following terms and such additional terms as the court determines appropriate:

(1) Expenditures of income and principal may be made in the manner, when, and to the extent that the trustee determines suitable and proper for the surviving spouse's support, without court order but with regard to other support, income, and property of the surviving spouse [exclusive of] [and] benefits of medical or other forms of assistance from any state or federal government or governmental agency for which the surviving spouse must qualify on the basis of need.

(2) During the surviving spouse's incapacity, neither the surviving spouse nor anyone acting on behalf of the surviving spouse has a power to terminate the trust; but if the surviving spouse regains capacity, the surviving spouse then acquires the power to terminate the trust and acquire full ownership of the trust property free of trust, by delivering to the trustee a writing signed by the surviving spouse declaring the termination.

(3) Upon the surviving spouse's death, the trustee shall transfer the unexpended trust property in the following order: (i) under the residuary clause, if any, of the will of the predeceased spouse against whom the elective share was taken, as if that predeceased spouse died immediately after the surviving spouse; or (ii) to the predeceased spouse's heirs under Section 2–711.]

§2–213. Waiver of Right to Elect and of Other Rights.

(a) The right of election of a surviving spouse and the rights of the surviving spouse to homestead allowance, exempt property, and family allowance, or any of them, may be waived, wholly or partially, before or after marriage, by a written contract, agreement, or waiver signed by the surviving spouse.

(b) A surviving spouse's waiver is not enforceable if the surviving spouse proves that:

(1) he [or she] did not execute the waiver voluntarily; or

(2) the waiver was unconscionable when it was executed and, before execution of the waiver, he [or she]:

(i) was not provided a fair and reasonable disclosure of the property or financial obligations of the decedent;

(ii) did not voluntarily and expressly waive, in writing, any right to disclosure of the property or financial obligations of the decedent beyond the disclosure provided; and

(iii) did not have, or reasonably could not have had, an adequate knowledge of the property or financial obligations of the decedent.

(c) An issue of unconscionability of a waiver is for decision by the court as a matter of law.

(d) Unless it provides to the contrary, a waiver of "all rights," or equivalent language, in the property or estate of a present or prospective spouse or a complete property settlement entered into after or in anticipation of separation or divorce is a waiver of all rights of elective-share, homestead allowance, exempt property, and family allowance by each spouse in the property of the other and a renunciation by each of all benefits that would otherwise pass to him [or her] from the other by intestate succession or by virtue of any will executed before the waiver or property settlement.

§2–214. Protection of Payors and Other Third Parties.

(a) Although under Section 2–205 a payment, item of property, or other benefit is included in the decedent's nonprobate transfers to others, a payor or other third party is not liable for having made a payment or transferred an item of property or other benefit to a beneficiary designated in a governing instrument, or for having taken any other action in good faith reliance on the validity of a governing instrument, upon request and satisfactory proof of the decedent's death, before the payor or other third party received written notice from the surviving spouse or spouse's representative of an intention to file a petition for the elective share or that a petition for the elective-share has been filed. A payor or other third party is liable for payments made or other actions taken after the payor or other third party received written notice of an intention to file a petition for the elective-share or that a petition for the elective share has been filed.

(b) A written notice of intention to file a petition for the elective-share or that a petition for the elective-share has been filed must be mailed to the payor's or other third party's main office or home by registered or certified mail, return receipt requested, or served upon the payor or other third party in the same manner as a summons in a civil action. Upon receipt of written notice of intention to file a petition for the elective-share or that a petition for the elective-share has been filed, a payor or other third party may pay any amount owed or transfer or deposit any item of property held by it to or with the court having jurisdiction of the probate proceedings relating to the decedent's estate, or if no proceedings have been commenced, to or with the court having jurisdiction of probate proceedings relating to decedents' estates located in the county of the decedent's residence. The court shall hold the funds or item of property, and, upon its determination under Section 2–211(d), shall order disbursement in accordance with the determination. If no petition is filed in the court within the specified time under Section 2–211(a) or, if filed, the demand for an elective share is withdrawn under Section 2–211(c), the court shall order disbursement to the designated beneficiary. Payments or transfers to the court or deposits made into court discharge the payor or other third party from all claims for amounts so paid or the value of property so transferred or deposited.

(c) Upon petition to the probate court by the beneficiary designated in a governing instrument, the court may order that all or part of the property be paid to the beneficiary in an amount and subject to conditions consistent with this Part.

PART 3

SPOUSE AND CHILDREN UNPROVIDED FOR IN WILLS

§2–301.   Entitlement of Spouse; Premarital Will.

(a) If a testator's surviving spouse married the testator after the testator executed his [or her] will, the surviving spouse is entitled to receive, as an intestate share, no less than the value of the share of the estate he [or she] would have received if the testator had died intestate as to that portion of the testator's estate, if any, that neither is devised to a child of the testator who was born before the testator married the surviving spouse and who is not a child of the surviving spouse nor is devised to a descendant of such a child or passes under Sections 2–603 or 2–604 to such a child or to a descendant of such a child, unless:

(1) it appears from the will or other evidence that the will was made in contemplation of the testator's marriage to the surviving spouse;

(2) the will expresses the intention that it is to be effective notwithstanding any subsequent marriage; or

(3) the testator provided for the spouse by transfer outside the will and the intent that the transfer be in lieu of a testamentary provision is shown by the testator's statements or is reasonably inferred from the amount of the transfer or other evidence.

(b) In satisfying the share provided by this section, devises made by the will to the testator's surviving spouse, if any, are applied first, and other devises, other than a devise to a child of the testator who was born before the testator married the surviving spouse and who is not a child of the surviving spouse or a devise or substitute gift under Section 2–603 or 2–604 to a descendant of such a child, abate as provided in Section 3–902. As amended in 1993.

§2–302.   Omitted Children.

(a) Except as provided in subsection (b), if a testator fails to provide in his [or her] will for any of his [or her] children born or adopted after the execution of the will, the omitted after-born or after-adopted child receives a share in the estate as follows:

(1) If the testator had no child living when he [or she] executed the will, an omitted after-born or after-adopted child receives a share in the estate equal in value to that which the child would have received had the testator died intestate, unless the will devised all or substantially all of the estate to the other parent of the omitted child and that other parent survives the testator and is entitled to take under the will.

(2) If the testator had one or more children living when he [or she] executed the will, and the will devised property or an interest in property to one or more of the then-living children, an omitted after-born or after-adopted child is entitled to share in the testator's estate as follows:

(i) The portion of the testator's estate in which the omitted after-born or after-adopted child is entitled to share is limited to devises made to the testator's then-living children under the will.

(ii) The omitted after-born or after-adopted child is entitled to receive the share of the testator's estate, as limited in subparagraph (i), that the child would have received had the testator included all omitted after-born and after-adopted children with the children to whom devises were made under the will and had given an equal share of the estate to each child.

(iii) To the extent feasible, the interest granted an omitted after-born or after-adopted child under this section must be of the same character, whether equitable or legal, present or future, as that devised to the testator's then-living children under the will.

(iv) In satisfying a share provided by this paragraph, devises to the testator's children who were living when the will was executed abate ratably. In abating the devises of the then-living children, the court shall preserve to the maximum extent possible the character of the testamentary plan adopted by the testator.

(b) Neither subsection (a)(1) nor subsection (a)(2) applies if:

(1) it appears from the will that the omission was intentional; or

(2) the testator provided for the omitted after-born or after-adopted child by transfer outside the will and the intent that the transfer be in lieu of a testamentary provision is shown by the testator's statements or is reasonably inferred from the amount of the transfer or other evidence.

(c) If at the time of execution of the will the testator fails to provide in his [or her] will for a living child solely because he [or she] believes the child to be dead, the child is entitled to share in the estate as if the child were an omitted after-born or after-adopted child.

(d) In satisfying a share provided by subsection (a)(1), devises made by the will abate under Section 3–902. As amended in 1991 and 1993.

PART 4
EXEMPT PROPERTY AND ALLOWANCES

§2–401.   Applicable Law.

This Part applies to the estate of a decedent who dies domiciled in this State. Rights to homestead allowance, exempt property, and family allowance for a decedent who dies not domiciled in this State are governed by the law of the decedent's domicile at death.

§2–402.   Homestead Allowance.

A decedent's surviving spouse is entitled to a homestead allowance of [$15,000]. If there is no surviving spouse, each minor child and each dependent child of the decedent is entitled to a homestead allowance amounting to [$15,000] divided by the number of minor and dependent children of the decedent. The homestead allowance is exempt from and has priority over all claims against the estate. Homestead allowance is in addition to any share passing to the surviving spouse or minor or dependent child by the will of the decedent, unless otherwise provided, by intestate succession, or by way of elective share.

[§2–402A.   Constitutional Homestead.

The value of any constitutional right of homestead in the family home received by a surviving spouse or child must be charged against the spouse or child's homestead allowance to the extent the family home is part of the decedent's estate or would have been but for the homestead provision of the constitution.]

§2–403.   Exempt Property.

In addition to the homestead allowance, the decedent's surviving spouse is entitled from the estate to a value, not exceeding $10,000 in excess of any security interests therein, in household furniture, automobiles, furnishings, appliances, and personal effects. If there is no surviving spouse, the decedent's children are entitled jointly to the same value. If encumbered chattels are selected and the value in excess of security interests, plus that of other exempt property, is less than $10,000, or if there is not $10,000 worth of exempt property in the estate, the spouse or children are entitled to other assets of the estate, if any, to the extent necessary to make up the $10,000 value. Rights to exempt property and assets needed to make up a deficiency of exempt property have priority over all claims against the estate, but the right to any assets to make up a deficiency of exempt property abates as necessary to permit earlier payment of homestead allowance and family allowance. These rights are in addition to any benefit or share passing to the surviving spouse or children by the decedent's will, unless otherwise provided, by intestate succession, or by way of elective share.

§2–404.   Family Allowance.

(a) In addition to the right to homestead allowance and exempt property, the decedent's surviving spouse and minor children whom the decedent was obligated to support and children who were in fact being supported by the decedent are entitled to a reasonable allowance in money out of the estate for their maintenance during the period of administration, which allowance may not continue for longer than one year if the estate is inadequate to discharge allowed claims. The allowance may be paid as a lump sum or in periodic installments. It is payable to the surviving spouse, if living, for the use of the surviving spouse and minor and dependent children; otherwise to the children, or persons having their care and custody. If a minor child or dependent child is not living with the surviving spouse, the allowance may be made partially to the child or his [or her] guardian or other person having the child's care and custody, and partially to the spouse, as their needs may appear. The family allowance is exempt from and has priority over all claims except the homestead allowance.

(b) The family allowance is not chargeable against any benefit or share passing to the surviving spouse or children by the will of the decedent, unless otherwise provided, by intestate succession or by way of elective share. The death of any person entitled to family allowance terminates the right to allowances not yet paid.

§2–405.   Source, Determination, and Documentation.

(a) If the estate is otherwise sufficient, property specifically devised may not be used to satisfy rights to homestead allowance or exempt property. Subject to this restriction, the surviving spouse, guardians of minor children, or children who are adults may select property of the estate as homestead allowance and exempt property. The personal representative may make those selections if the surviving spouse, the children, or the guardians of the minor children are unable or fail to do so within a reasonable time or there is no guardian of a minor child. The personal representative may execute an instrument or deed of distribution to establish the ownership of property taken as homestead allowance or exempt property. The personal representative may determine the family allowance in a lump sum not exceeding $18,000 or periodic installments not exceeding $1,500 per month for one year, and may disburse funds of the estate in payment of the family allowance and any part of the homestead allowance payable in cash. The personal representative or an interested person aggrieved by any selection, determination, payment, proposed payment, or failure to act under this section may petition the court for appropriate relief, which may include a family allowance other than that which the personal representative determined or could have determined.

(b) If the right to an elective share is exercised on behalf of a surviving spouse who is an incapacitated person, the personal representative may add any unexpended portions payable under the homestead allowance, exempt property, and family allowance to the trust established under Section 2–212(b).

As amended in 1993.

PART 5
WILLS, WILL CONTRACTS, AND CUSTODY AND DEPOSIT OF WILLS

§2–501.   Who May Make Will.

An individual 18 or more years of age who is of sound mind may make a will.

§2–502.   Execution; Witnessed Wills; Holographic Wills.

(a) Except as provided in subsection (b) and in Sections 2–503, 2–506, and 2–513, a will must be:

(1) in writing;

(2) signed by the testator or in the testator's name by some other individual in the testator's conscious presence and by the testator's direction; and

(3) signed by at least two individuals, each of whom signed within a reasonable time after he [or she] witnessed either the signing of the will as described in paragraph (2) or the testator's acknowledgment of that signature or acknowledgment of the will.

(b) A will that does not comply with subsection (a) is valid as a holographic will, whether or not witnessed, if the signature and material portions of the document are in the testator's handwriting.

(c) Intent that the document constitute the testator's will can be established by extrinsic evidence, including, for holographic wills, portions of the document that are not, in the testator's handwriting.

§2–503.   Writings Intended as Wills, etc.

Although a document or writing added upon a document was not executed in compliance with Section 2–502, the document or writing is treated as if it had been executed in compliance with that section if the proponent of the document or writing establishes by clear and convincing evidence that the decedent intended the document or writing to constitute (i) the decedent's will, (ii) a partial or complete revocation of the will, (iii) an addition to or an alteration of the will, or (iv) a partial or complete revival of his [or her] formerly revoked will or of a formerly revoked portion of the will.

§2–504.   Self-Proved Will.

(a) A will may be simultaneously executed, attested, and made self-proved, by acknowledgment thereof by the testator and affidavits of the witnesses, each made before an officer authorized to administer oaths under the laws of the state in which execution occurs and evidenced by the officer's certificate, under official seal, in substantially the following form:

I, _____ , the testator, sign my name to this instrument this _____ day of _____ , and being first duly sworn, do hereby declare to the undersigned authority that I sign and execute this instrument as my will and that I sign it willingly (or willingly direct another to sign for me), that I execute it as my free and voluntary act for the purposes therein expressed, and that I am eighteen years of age or older, of sound mind, and under no constraint or undue influence.

_____
Testator

We, _____ , _____ , the witnesses, sign our names to this instrument, being first duly sworn, and do hereby declare to the undersigned authority that the testator signs and executes this instrument as [his] [her] will and that [he] [she] signs it willingly (or willingly directs another to sign for [him] [her]), and that each of us, in the presence and hearing of the testator, hereby signs this will as witness to the testator's signing, and that to the best of our knowledge the testator is eighteen years of age or older, of sound mind, and under no constraint or undue influence.

_____
Witness

_____
Witness

The State of _____
County of _____
Subscribed, sworn to and acknowledged before me by _____ , the testator, and subscribed and sworn to before me by _____ , and _____ , witness, this _____ day of _____ .
(Seal)

(Signed) _____

_____
(Official capacity of officer)

(b) An attested will may be made self-proved at any time after its execution by the acknowledgment thereof by the testator and the affidavits of the witnesses, each made before an officer authorized to administer oaths under the laws of the state in which the acknowledgment occurs and evidenced by the officer's certificate, under the official seal, attached or annexed to the will in substantially the following form:

The State of _____
County of _____
We, _____ , _____ , and _____ , the testator and the witnesses, respectively, whose names are signed to the attached or foregoing instrument, being first duly sworn, do hereby declare to the undersigned authority that the testator signed and executed the instrument as the testator's will and that [he] [she] had signed willingly (or willingly directed another to sign for [him] [her]), and that [he] [she] executed it as [his] [her] free and voluntary act for the purposes therein expressed, and that each of the witnesses, in the presence and hearing of the testator, signed the will as witness and that to the best of [his] [her] knowledge the testator was at that time eighteen years or age or older, of sound mind, and under no constraint or undue influence.

_____
Testator

_____
Witness

_____
Witness

Subscribed, sworn to and acknowledged before me by _____ , the testator, and subscribed and sworn to before me by _____ , and _____ , witnesses, this _____ of _____ .
(Seal)

(Signed) _____

_____
(Official capacity of officer)

(c) A signature affixed to a self-proving affidavit attached to a will is considered a signature affixed to the will, if necessary to prove the will's due execution.

§2–505. Who May Witness.
(a) An individual generally competent to be a witness may act as a witness to a will.
(b) The signing of a will by an interested witness does not invalidate the will or any provision of it.

§2–506. Choice of Law as to Execution.
A written will is valid if executed in compliance with Section 2-502 or 2-503 or if its execution complies with the law at the time of execution of the place where the will is executed, or of the law of the place where at the time of execution or at the time of death the testator is domiciled, has a place of abode, or is a national.

§2–507. Revocation by Writing or by Act.
(a) A will or any part thereof is revoked:
(1) by executing a subsequent will that revokes the previous will or part expressly or by inconsistency; or
(2) by performing a revocatory act on the will, if the testator performed the act with the intent and for the purpose of revoking the will or part or if another individual performed the act in the testator's conscious presence and by the testator's direction. For purposes of this paragraph, "revocatory act on the will" includes burning, tearing, canceling, obliterating, or destroying the will or any part of it. A burning, tearing, or canceling is a "revocatory act on the will," whether or not the burn, tear, or cancellation touched any of the words on the will.
(b) If a subsequent will does not expressly revoke a previous will, the execution of the subsequent will wholly revokes the previous will by inconsistency if the testator intended the subsequent will to replace rather than supplement the previous will.
(c) The testator is presumed to have intended a subsequent will to replace rather than supplement a previous will if the subsequent will makes a complete disposition of the testator's estate. If this presumption arises and is not rebutted by clear and convincing evidence, the previous will is revoked; only the subsequent will is operative on the testator's death.
(d) The testator is presumed to have intended a subsequent will to supplement rather than replace a previous will if the subsequent will does not make a complete disposition of the testator's estate. If this presumption arises and is not rebutted by clear and convincing evidence, the subsequent will revokes the previous will only to the extent the subsequent will is inconsistent with the previous will; each will is fully operative on the testator's death to the extent they are not inconsistent.

§2–508.   Revocation by Change of Circumstances.
Except as provided in Sections 2–803 and 2–804, a change of circumstances does not revoke a will or any part of it.

§2–509.   Revival of Revoked Will.
(a) If a subsequent will that wholly revoked a previous will is thereafter revoked by a revocatory act under Section 2–507(a)(2), the previous will remains revoked unless it is revived. The previous will is revived if it is evident from the circumstances of the revocation of the subsequent will or from the testator's contemporary or subsequent declarations that the testator intended the previous will to take effect as executed.
(b) If a subsequent will that partly revoked a previous will is thereafter revoked by a revocatory act under Section 2–507(a)(2), a revoked part of the previous will is revived unless it is evident from the circumstances of the revocation of the subsequent will or from the testator's contemporary or subsequent declarations that the testator did not intend the revoked part to take effect as executed.
(c) If a subsequent will that revoked a previous will in whole or in part is thereafter revoked by another, later, will, the previous will remains revoked in whole or in part, unless it or its revoked part is revived. The previous will or its revoked part is revived to the extent it appears from the terms of the later will that the testator intended the previous will to take effect.

§2–510.   Incorporation by Reference.
A writing in existence when a will is executed may be incorporated by reference if the language of the will manifests this intent and describes the writing sufficiently to permit its identification.

§2–511.   Testamentary Additions to Trusts.
(a) A will may validly devise property to the trustee of a trust established or to be established (i) during the testator's lifetime by the testator, by the testator and some other person, or by some other person, including a funded or unfunded life insurance trust, although the settlor has reserved any or all rights of ownership of the insurance contracts, or (ii) at the testator's death by the testator's devise to the trustee, if the trust is identified in the testator's will and its terms are set forth in a written instrument, other than a will, executed before, concurrently with, or after the execution of the testator's will or in another individual's will if that other individual has predeceased the testator, regardless of the existence, size, or character of the corpus of the trust. The devise is not invalid because the trust is amendable or revocable, or because the trust was amended after the execution of the will or the testator's death.

(b) Unless the testator's will provides otherwise, property devised to a trust described in subsection (a) is not held under a testamentary trust of the testator, but it becomes a part of the trust to which it is devised, and must be administered and disposed of in accordance with the provisions of the governing instrument setting forth the terms of the trust, including any amendments thereto made before or after the testator's death.
(c) Unless the testator's will provides otherwise, a revocation or termination of the trust before the testator's death causes the devise to lapse.

§2–512.   Events of Independent Significance.
A will may dispose of property by reference to acts and events that have significance apart from their effect upon the dispositions made by the will, whether they occur before or after the execution of the will or before or after the testator's death. The execution or revocation of another individual's will is such an event.

§2–513.   Separate Writing Identifying Devise of Certain Types of Tangible Personal Property.
Whether or not the provisions relating to holographic wills apply, a will may refer to a written statement or list to dispose of items of tangible personal property not otherwise specifically disposed of by the will, other than money. To be admissible under this section as evidence of the intended disposition, the writing must be signed by the testator and must describe the items and the devisees with reasonable certainty. The writing may be referred to as one to be in existence at the time of the testator's death; it may be prepared before or after the execution of the will; it may be altered by the testator after its preparation; and it may be a writing that has no significance apart from its effect on the dispositions made by the will.

§2–514.   Contracts Concerning Succession.
A contract to make a will or devise, or not to revoke a will or devise, or to die intestate, if executed after the effective date of this Article, may be established only by (i) provisions of a will stating material provisions of the contract, (ii) an express reference in a will to a contract and extrinsic evidence proving the terms of the contract, or (iii) a writing signed by the decedent evidencing the contract. The execution of a joint will or mutual wills does not create a presumption of a contract not to revoke the will or wills.

§2–515.   Deposit of Will with Court in Testator's Lifetime.
A will may be deposited by the testator or the testator's agent with any court for safekeeping, under rules of the court. The will must be sealed and kept confidential.

During the testator's lifetime, a deposited will must be delivered only to the testator or to a person authorized in writing signed by the testator to receive the will. A conservator may be allowed to examine a deposited will of a protected testator under procedures designed to maintain the confidential character of the document to the extent possible, and to ensure that it will be resealed and kept on deposit after the examination. Upon being informed of the testator's death, the court shall notify any person designated to receive the will and deliver it to that person on request; or the court may deliver the will to the appropriate court.

§2–516.   Duty of Custodian of Will; Liability.

After the death of a testator and on request of an interested person, a person having custody of a will of the testator shall deliver it with reasonable promptness to a person able to secure its probate and if none is known, to an appropriate court. A person who wilfully fails to deliver a will is liable to any person aggrieved for any damages that may be sustained by the failure. A person who wilfully refuses or fails to deliver a will after being ordered by the court in a proceeding brought for the purpose of compelling delivery is subject to penalty for contempt of court.

§2–517.   Penalty Clause for Contest.

A provision in a will purporting to penalize an interested person for contesting the will or instituting other, proceedings relating to the estate is unenforceable if probable cause exists for instituting proceedings.

PART 6
RULES OF CONSTRUCTION APPLICABLE ONLY TO WILLS

§2–601.   Scope.

In the absence of a finding of a contrary intention, the rules of construction in this Part control the construction of a will.

§2–602.   Will May Pass All Property and After-Acquired Property.

A will may provide for the passage of all property the testator owns at death and all property acquired by the estate after the testator's death.

§2–603.   Antilapse; Deceased Devisee; Class Gifts.

(a) [Definitions.] In this section:

(1) "Alternative devise" means a devise that is expressly created by the will and, under the terms of the will, can take effect instead of another devise on the happening of one or more events, including survival of the testator or failure to survive the testator, whether an event is expressed in condition-precedent, condition-subsequent, or any other form. A residuary clause constitutes an alternative devise with respect to a nonresiduary devise only if the will specifically provides that, upon lapse or failure, the nonresiduary devise, or nonresiduary devises in general, pass under the residuary clause.

(2) "Class member" includes an individual who fails to survive the testator but who would have taken under a devise in the form of a class gift had he [or she] survived the testator.

(3) "Devise" includes an alternative devise, a devise in the form of a class gift, and an exercise of a power of appointment.

(4) "Devisee" includes (i) a class member if the devise is in the form of a class gift, (ii) an individual or class member who was deceased at the time the testator executed his [or her] will as well as an individual or class member who was then living but who failed to survive the testator, and (iii) an appointee under a power of appointment exercised by the testator's will.

(5) "Stepchild" means a child of the surviving, deceased, or former spouse of the testator or of the donor of a power of appointment, and not of the testator or donor.

(6) "Surviving devisee" or "surviving descendant" means a devisee or a descendant who neither predeceased the testator nor is deemed to have predeceased the testator under Section 2–702.

(7) "Testator" includes the donee of a power of appointment if the power is exercised in the testator's will.

(b) [Substitute Gift.] If a devisee fails to survive the testator and is a grandparent, a descendant of a grandparent, or a stepchild of either the testator or the donor of a power of appointment exercised by the testator's will, the following apply:

(1) Except as provided in paragraph (4), if the devise is not in the form of a class gift and the deceased devisee leaves surviving descendants, a substitute gift is created in the devisee's surviving descendants. They take by representation the property to which the devisee would have been entitled had the devisee survived the testator.

(2) Except as provided in paragraph (4), if the devise is in the form of a class gift, other than a devise to "issue," "descendants," "heirs of the body," "heirs," "next of kin," "relatives," or "family," or a class described by language of similar import, a substitute gift is created in the surviving descendant's of any deceased devisee. The property to which the devisees would have been entitled had all of them survived the testator passes to the surviving devisees

and the surviving descendants of the deceased devisees. Each surviving devisee takes the share to which he [or she] would have been entitled had the deceased devisees survived the testator. Each deceased devisee's surviving descendants who are substituted for the deceased devisee take by representation the share to which the deceased devisee would have been entitled had the deceased devisee survived the testator. For the purposes of this paragraph, "deceased devisee" means a class member who failed to survive the testator and left one or more surviving descendants.

(3) For the purposes of Section 2–601, words of survivorship, such as in a devise to an individual "if he survives me," or in a devise to "my surviving children," are not, in the absence of additional evidence, a sufficient indication of an intent contrary to the application of this section.

(4) If the will creates an alternative devise with respect to a devise for which a substitute gift is created by paragraph (1) or (2), the substitute gift is superseded by the alternative devise only if an expressly designated devisee of the alternative devise is entitled to take under the will.

(5) Unless the language creating a power of appointment expressly excludes the substitution of the descendants of an appointee for the appointee, a surviving descendant of a deceased appointee of a power of appointment can be substituted for the appointee under this section, whether or not the descendant is an object of the power.

(c) [More Than One Substitute Gift; Which One Takes.] If, under subsection (b), substitute gifts are created and not superseded with respect to more than one devise and the devises are alternative devises, one to the other, the determination of which of the substitute gifts takes effect is resolved as follows:

(1) Except as provided in paragraph (2), the devised property passes under the primary substitute gift.

(2) If there is a younger generation devise, the devised property passes under the younger–generation substitute gift and not under the primary substitute gift.

(3) In this subsection:

(i) "Primary devise" means the devise that would have taken effect had all the deceased devisees of the alternative devises who left surviving descendants survived the testator.

(ii) "Primary substitute gift" means the substitute gift created with respect to the primary devise.

(iii) "Younger-generation devise" means a devise that (A) is to a descendant of a devisee of the primary devise, (B) is an alternative devise with respect to the primary devise, (C) is a devise for which a substitute gift is created, and (D) would have taken effect had all the deceased devisees who left surviving descendants survived the testator except the deceased devisee or devisees of the primary devise.

(iv) "Younger-generation substitute gift" means the substitute gift created with respect to the younger-generation devise.

As amended in 1991 and 1993.

§2–604. Failure of Testamentary Provision.

(a) Except as provided in Section 2-603, a devise, other than a residuary devise, that fails for any reason becomes a part of the residue.

(b) Except as provided in Section 2-603, if the residue is devised to two or more persons, the share of a residuary devisee that fails for any reason passes to the other residuary devisee, or to other residuary devisees in proportion to the interest of each in the remaining part of the residue.

§2–605. Increase in Securities; Accessions.

(a) If a testator executes a will that devises securities and the testator then owned securities that meet the description in the will, the devise includes additional securities owned by the testator at death to the extent the additional securities were acquired by the testator after the will was executed as a result of the testator's ownership of the described securities and are securities of any of the following types:

(1) securities of the same organization acquired by reason of action initiated by the organization or any successor, related, or acquiring organization, excluding any acquired by exercise of purchase options;

(2) securities of another organization acquired as a result of a merger, consolidation, reorganization, or other distribution by the organization or any successor, related, or acquiring organization; or

(3) securities of the same organization acquired as a result of a plan of reinvestment.

(b) Distributions in cash before death with respect to a described security are not part of the devise.

§2–606. Nonademption of Specific Devises; Unpaid Proceeds of Sale, Condemnation, or Insurance; Sale by Conservator or Agent.

(a) A specific devisee has a right to the specifically devised property in the testator's estate at death and:

(1) any balance of the purchase price, together with any security agreement, owing from a purchaser to the testator at death by reason of sale of the property;

(2) any amount of a condemnation award for the taking of the property unpaid at death;

(3) any proceeds unpaid at death on fire or casualty insurance on or other recovery for injury to the property;

(4) property owned by the testator at death and acquired as a result of foreclosure, or obtained in lieu of foreclosure, of the security interest for a specifically devised obligation;

(5) real or tangible personal property owned by the testator at death which the testator acquired as a replacement for specifically devised real or tangible personal property; and

(6) unless the facts and circumstances indicate that ademption of the devise was intended by the testator or ademption of the devise is consistent with the testator's manifested plan of distribution, the value of the specifically devised property to the extent the specifically devised property is not in the testator's estate at death and its value or its replacement is not covered by paragraphs (1) through (5).

(b) If specifically devised property is sold or mortgaged by a conservator or by an agent acting within the authority of a durable power of attorney for an incapacitated principal, or if a condemnation award, insurance proceeds, or recovery for injury to the property are paid to a conservator or to an agent acting within the authority of a durable power of attorney for an incapacitated principal, the specific devisee has the right to a general pecuniary devise equal to the net sale price, the amount of the unpaid loan, the condemnation award, the insurance proceeds, or the recovery.

(c) The right of a specific devisee under subsection (b) is reduced by any right the devisee has under subsection (a).

(d) For the purposes of the references in subsection (b) to a conservator, subsection (b) does not apply if after the sale, mortgage, condemnation, casualty, or recovery, it was adjudicated that the testator's incapacity ceased and the testator survived the adjudication by one year.

(e) For the purposes of the references in subsection (b) to an agent acting within the authority of a durable power of attorney for an incapacitated principal, (i) "incapacitated principal" means a principal who is an incapacitated person, (ii) no adjudication of incapacity before death is necessary, and (iii) the acts of an agent within the authority of a durable power of attorney are presumed to be for an incapacitated principal.

§2–607. Nonexoneration.

A specific devise passes subject to any mortgage interest existing at the date of death, without right of exoneration, regardless of a general directive in the will to pay debts.

§2–608. Exercise of Power of Appointment.

In the absence of a requirement that a power of appointment be exercised by a reference, or by an express or specific reference, to the power, a general residuary clause in a will, or a will making general disposition of all of the testator's property, expresses an intention to exercise a power of appointment held by the testator only if (i) the power is a general power and the creating instrument does not contain a gift if the power is not exercised or (ii) the testator's will manifests an intention to include the property subject to the power.

§2–609. Ademption by Satisfaction.

(a) Property a testator gave in his [or her] lifetime to a person is treated as a satisfaction of a devise in whole or in part, only if (i) the will provides for deduction of the gift, (ii) the testator declared in a contemporaneous writing that the gift is in satisfaction of the devise or that its value is to be deducted from the value of the devise, or (iii) the devisee acknowledged in writing that, the gift is in satisfaction of the devise or that its value is to be deducted from the value of the devise.

(b) For purposes of partial satisfaction, property given during lifetime is valued as of the time the devisee came into possession or enjoyment of the property or at the testator's death, whichever occurs first.

(c) If the devisee fails to survive the testator, the gift is treated as a full or partial satisfaction of the devise, as appropriate, in applying Sections 2-603 and 2-604, unless the testator's contemporaneous writing provides otherwise.

PART 7
RULES OF CONSTRUCTION APPLICABLE TO WILLS AND OTHER GOVERNING INSTRUMENTS

§2–701. Scope.

In the absence of a finding of a contrary intention, the rules of construction in this Part control the construction of a governing instrument. The rules of construction in this Part apply to a governing instrument of any type, except as the application of a particular section is limited by its terms to a specific type or types of provision or governing instrument.

As amended in 1991.

§2–702. Requirement of Survival by 120 Hours.

(a) [Requirement of Survival by 120 Hours Under Probate Code.] For the purposes of this Code, except as provided in subsection (d), an individual who is not established by clear and convincing evidence to have survived an event, including the death of another individual, by 120 hours is deemed to have predeceased the event.

(b) [Requirement of Survival by 120 Hours under Governing Instrument.] Except as provided in subsection (d), for purposes of a provision of a governing instrument that relates to an individual surviving an event, including the death of another individual, an individual who is not established by clear and convincing evidence to have survived the event by 120 hours is deemed to have predeceased the event.

(c) [Co-owners With Right of Survivorship; Requirement of Survival by 120 Hours.] Except as provided in subsection (d), if (i) it is not established by clear and convincing evidence that one of two co-owners with right of survivorship survived the other co-owner by 120 hours, one-half of the property passes as if one had survived by 120 hours and one-half as if the other had survived by 120 hours and (ii) there are more than two co-owners and it is not established by clear and convincing evidence that at least one of them survived the others by 120 hours, the property passes in the proportion that one bears to the whole number of co-owners. For the purposes of this subsection, "co-owners with right of survivorship" includes joint tenants, tenants by the entireties, and other co-owners of property or accounts held under circumstances that entitles one or more to the whole of the property or account on the death of the other or others.

(d) [Exceptions.] Survival by 120 hours is not required if:

(1) the governing instrument contains language dealing explicitly with simultaneous deaths or deaths in a common disaster and that language is operable under the facts of the case;

(2) the governing instrument expressly indicates that an individual is not required to survive an event, including the death of another individual, by any specified period or expressly requires the individual to survive the event by a specified period; but survival of the event or the specified period must be established by clear and convincing evidence;

(3) the imposition of a 120-hour requirement of survival would cause a nonvested property interest or a power of appointment to fail to qualify for validity under Section 2–901(a)(1), (b)(1), or (c)(1) or to become invalid under Section 2–901(a)(2), (b)(2), or (c)(2); but survival must be established by clear and convincing evidence; or

(4) the application of a 120-hour requirement of survival to multiple governing instruments would result in an unintended failure or duplication of a disposition; but survival must be established by clear and convincing evidence.

(e) [Protection of Payors and Other Third Parties.]

(1) A payor or other third party is not liable for having made a payment or transferred an item of property or any other benefit to a beneficiary designated in a governing instrument who, under this section, is not entitled to the payment or item of property, or for having taken any other action in good faith reliance on the beneficiary's apparent entitlement under the terms of the governing instrument, before the payor or other third party received written notice of a claimed lack of entitlement under this section. A payor or other third party is liable for a payment made or other action taken after the payor or other third party received written notice of a claimed lack of entitlement under this section.

(2) Written notice of a claimed lack of entitlement under paragraph (1) must be mailed to the payor's or other third party's main office or home by registered or certified mail, return receipt requested, or served upon the payor or other third party in the same manner as a summons in a civil action. Upon receipt of written notice of a claimed lack of entitlement under this section, a payor or other third party may pay any amount owed or transfer or deposit any item of property held by it to or with the court having jurisdiction of the probate proceedings relating to the decedent's estate, or if no proceedings have been commenced, to or with the court having jurisdiction of probate proceedings relating to decedents' estates located in the county of the decedent's residence. The court shall hold the funds or item of property and, upon its determination under this section, shall order disbursement in accordance with the determination. Payments, transfers, or deposits made to or with the court discharge the payor or other third party from all claims for the value of amounts paid to or items of property transferred to or deposited with the court.

(f) [Protection of Bona Fide Purchasers; Personal Liability of Recipient.]

(1) A person who purchases property for value and without notice, or who receives a payment or other item of property in partial or full satisfaction of a legally enforceable obligation, is neither obligated under this section to return the payment, item of property, or benefit nor is liable under this section for the amount of the payment or the value of the item of property or benefit. But a person who, not for value, receives a payment, item of property, or any other benefit to which the person is not entitled under this section is obligated to return the payment, item of property, or benefit, or is personally liable for the amount of the payment or the value of the item of property or benefit, to the person who is entitled to it under this section.

(2) If this section or any part of this section is preempted by federal law with respect to a payment, an item of property, or any other benefit covered by this section, a person who, not for value, receives the payment, item of property, or any other benefit to which the person is not entitled under this section is obligated to return the payment, item of property, or benefit, or

is personally liable for the amount of the payment or the value of the item of property or benefit, to the person who would have been entitled to it were this section or part of this section not preempted.

As amended in 1991 and 1993.

§2–703. Choice of Law as to Meaning and Effect of Governing Instrument.

The meaning and legal effect of a governing instrument is determined by the local law of the state selected in the governing instrument, unless the application of that law is contrary to the provisions relating to the elective share described in Part 2, the provisions relating to exempt property and allowances described in Part 4, or any other public policy of this State otherwise applicable to the disposition.

As amended in 1991 and 1993.

§2–704. Power of Appointment; Meaning of Specific Reference Requirement.

If a governing instrument creating a power of appointment expressly requires that the power be exercised by a reference, an express reference, or a specific reference, to the power or its source, it is presumed that the donor's intention, in requiring that the donee exercise the power by making reference to the particular power or to the creating instrument, was to prevent an inadvertent exercise of the power.

§2–705. Class Gifts Construed to Accord With Intestate Succession.

(a) Adopted individuals and individuals born out of wedlock, and their respective descendants if appropriate to the class, are included in class gifts and other terms of relationship in accordance with the rules for intestate succession. Terms of relationship that do not differentiate relationships by blood from those by affinity, such as "uncles," "aunts," "nieces," or "nephews", are construed to exclude relatives by affinity. Terms of relationship that do not differentiate relationships by the half blood from those by the whole blood, such as "brothers," "sisters," "nieces," or "nephews", are construed to include both types of relationships.

(b) In addition to the requirements of subsection (a), in construing a dispositive provision of a transferor who is not the natural parent, an individual born to the natural parent is not considered the child of that parent unless the individual lived while a minor as a regular member of the household of that natural parent or of that parent's parent, brother, sister, spouse, or surviving spouse.

(c) In addition to the requirements of subsection (a), in construing a dispositive provision of a transferor who is not the adopting parent, an adopted individual is not considered the child of the adopting parent unless the adopted individual lived while a minor, either before or after the adoption, as a regular member of the household of the adopting parent.

As amended in 1991.

§2–706. Life Insurance; Retirement Plan; Account With POD Designation; Transfer-on-Death Registration; Deceased Beneficiary.

(a) [Definitions.] In this section:

(1) "Alternative beneficiary designation" means a beneficiary designation that is expressly created by the governing instrument and, under the terms of the governing instrument, can take effect instead of another beneficiary designation on the happening of one or more events, including survival of the decedent or failure to survive the decedent, whether an event is expressed in condition-precedent, condition-subsequent, or any other form.

(2) "Beneficiary" means the beneficiary of a beneficiary designation under which the beneficiary must survive the decedent and includes (i) a class member if the beneficiary designation is in the form of a class gift and (ii) an individual or class member who was deceased at the time the beneficiary designation was executed as well as an individual or class member who was then living but who failed to survive the decedent, but excludes a joint tenant of a joint tenancy with the right of survivorship and a party to a joint and survivorship account.

(3) "Beneficiary designation" includes an alternative beneficiary designation and a beneficiary designation in the form of a class gift.

(4) "Class member" includes an individual who fails to survive the decedent but who would have taken under a beneficiary designation in the form of a class gift had he [or she] survived the decedent.

(5) "Stepchild" means a child of the decedent's surviving, deceased, or former spouse, and not of the decedent.

(6) "Surviving beneficiary" or "surviving descendant" means a beneficiary or a descendant who neither predeceased the decedent nor is deemed to have predeceased the decedent under Section 2–702.

(b) [Substitute Gift.] If a beneficiary fails to survive the decedent and is a grandparent, a descendant of a grandparent, or a stepchild of the decedent, the following apply:

(1) Except as provided in paragraph (4), if the beneficiary designation is not in the form of a class gift and the deceased beneficiary leaves surviving descendants, a substitute gift is created in the beneficiary's surviving descendants. They take by representation the property to which the beneficiary would have been entitled had the beneficiary survived the decedent.

(2) Except as provided in paragraph (4), if the beneficiary designation is in the form of a class gift, other than a beneficiary designation to "issue," "descendants," "heirs of the body," "heirs," "next of kin," "relatives," or "family," or a class described by language of similar import, a substitute gift is created in the surviving descendants of any deceased beneficiary. The property to which the beneficiaries would have been entitled had all of them survived the decedent passes to the surviving beneficiaries and the surviving descendants of the deceased beneficiaries. Each surviving beneficiary takes the share to which he [or she] would have been entitled had the deceased beneficiaries survived the decedent. Each deceased beneficiary's surviving descendants who are substituted for the deceased beneficiary take by representation the share to which the deceased beneficiary would have been entitled had the deceased beneficiary survived the decedent. For the purposes of this paragraph, "deceased beneficiary" means a class member who failed to survive the decedent and left one or more surviving descendants.

(3) For the purposes of Section 2–701, words of survivorship, such as in a beneficiary designation to an individual "if he survives me," or in a beneficiary designation to "my surviving children," are not, in the absence of additional evidence, a sufficient indication of an intent contrary to the application of this section.

(4) If a governing instrument creates an alternative beneficiary designation with respect to a beneficiary designation for which a substitute gift is created by paragraph (1) or (2), the substitute gift is superseded by the alternative beneficiary designation only if an expressly designated beneficiary of the alternative beneficiary designation is entitled to take.

(c) [More Than One Substitute Gift; Which One Takes.] If, under subsection (b), substitute gifts are created and not superseded with respect to more than one beneficiary designation and the beneficiary designations are alternative beneficiary designations, one to the other, the determination of which of the substitute gifts takes effect is resolved as follows:

(1) Except as provided in paragraph (2), the property passes under the primary substitute gift.

(2) If there is a younger-generation beneficiary designation, the property passes under the younger-generation substitute gift and not under the primary substitute gift.

(3) In this subsection:

(i) "Primary beneficiary designation" means the beneficiary designation that would have taken effect had all the deceased beneficiaries of the alternative beneficiary designations who left surviving descendants survived the decedent.

(ii) "Primary substitute gift" means the substitute gift created with respect to the primary beneficiary designation.

(iii) "Younger-generation beneficiary designation" means a beneficiary designation that (A) is to a descendant of a beneficiary of the primary beneficiary designation, (B) is an alternative beneficiary designation with respect to the primary beneficiary designation, (C) is a beneficiary designation for which a substitute gift is created, and (D) would have taken effect had all the deceased beneficiaries who left surviving descendants survived the decedent except the deceased beneficiary or beneficiaries of the primary beneficiary designation.

(iv) "Younger-generation substitute gift" means the substitute gift created with respect to the younger-generation beneficiary designation.

(d) [Protection of Payors.]

(1) A payor is protected from liability in making payments under the terms of the beneficiary designation until the payor has received written notice of a claim to a substitute gift under this section. Payment made before the receipt of written notice of a claim to a substitute gift under this section discharges the payor, but not the recipient, from all claims for the amounts paid. A payor is liable for a payment made after the payor has received written notice of the claim. A recipient is liable for a payment received, whether or not written notice of the claim is given.

(2) The written notice of the claim must be mailed to the payor's main office or home by registered or certified mail, return receipt requested, or served upon the payor in the same manner as a summons in a civil action. Upon receipt of written notice of the claim, a payor may pay any amount owed by it to the court having jurisdiction of the probate proceedings relating to the decedent's estate or, if no proceedings have been commenced, to the court having jurisdiction of probate proceedings relating to decedents' estates located in the county of the decedent's residence. The court shall hold the funds and, upon its determination under this section, shall order disbursement in accordance with the determination. Payment made to the court discharges the payor from all claims for the amounts paid.

(e) [Protection of Bona Fide Purchasers; Personal Liability of Recipient.]

(1) A person who purchases property for value and without notice, or who receives a payment or other item of property in partial or full satisfaction of a legally enforceable obligation, is neither obligated under this section to return the payment, item of property, or benefit nor is liable under this section for the amount of the payment or the value of the item of property or benefit. But a person who, not for

value, receives a payment, item of property, or any other benefit to which the person is not entitled under this section is obligated to return the payment, item of property, or benefit, or is personally liable for the amount of the payment or the value of the item of property or benefit, to the person who is entitled to it under this section.

(2) If this section or any part of this section is preempted by federal law with respect to a payment, an item of property, or any other benefit covered by this section, a person who, not for value, receives the payment, item of property, or any other benefit to which the person is not entitled under this section is obligated to return the payment, item of property, or benefit, or is personally liable for the amount of the payment or the value of the item of property or benefit, to the person who would have been entitled to it were this section or part of this section not preempted.

As amended in 1993.

§2–707. Survivorship with Respect to Future Interests under Terms of Trust; Substitute Takers.

(a) [Definitions.] In this section:

(1) "Alternative future interest" means an expressly created future interest that can take effect in possession or enjoyment instead of another future interest on the happening of one or more events, including survival of an event or failure to survive an event, whether an event is expressed in condition-precedent, condition-subsequent, or any other form. A residuary clause in a will does not create an alternative future interest with respect to a future interest created in a nonresiduary devise in the will, whether or not the will specifically provides that lapsed or failed devises are to pass under the residuary clause.

(2) "Beneficiary" means the beneficiary of a future interest and includes a class member if the future interest is in the form of a class gift.

(3) "Class member" includes an individual who fails to survive the distribution date but who would have taken under a future interest in the form of a class gift had he [or she] survived the distribution date.

(4) "Distribution date," with respect to a future interest, means the time when the future interest is to take effect in possession or enjoyment. The distribution date need not occur at the beginning or end of a calendar day, but can occur at a time during the course of a day.

(5) "Future interest" includes an alternative future interest and a future interest in the form of a class gift.

(6) "Future interest under the terms of a trust" means a future interest that was created by a transfer creating a trust or to an existing trust or by an exercise of a power of appointment to an existing trust, directing the continuance of an existing trust, designating a beneficiary of an existing trust, or creating a trust.

(7) "Surviving beneficiary" or "surviving descendant" means a beneficiary or a descendant who neither predeceased the distribution date nor is deemed to have predeceased the distribution date under Section 2–702.

(b) [Survivorship Required; Substitute Gift.] A future interest under the terms of a trust is contingent on the beneficiary's surviving the distribution date. If a beneficiary of a future interest under the terms of a trust fails to survive the distribution date, the following apply:

(1) Except as provided in paragraph (4), if the future interest is not in the form of a class gift and the deceased beneficiary leaves surviving descendants, a substitute gift is created in the beneficiary's surviving descendants. They take by representation the property to which the beneficiary would have been entitled had the beneficiary survived the distribution date.

(2) Except as provided in paragraph (4), if the future interest is in the form of a class gift, other than a future interest to "issue," "descendants," "heirs of the body," "heirs," "next of kin," "relatives," or "family," or a class described by language of similar import, a substitute gift is created in the surviving descendants of any deceased beneficiary. The property to which the beneficiaries would have been entitled had all of them survived the distribution date passes to the surviving beneficiaries and the surviving descendants of the deceased beneficiaries. Each surviving beneficiary takes the share to which he [or she] would have been entitled had the deceased beneficiaries survived the distribution date. Each deceased beneficiary's surviving descendants who are substituted for the deceased beneficiary take by representation the share to which the deceased beneficiary would have been entitled had the deceased beneficiary survived the distribution date. For the purposes of this paragraph, "deceased beneficiary" means a class member who failed to survive the distribution date and left one or more surviving descendants.

(3) For the purposes of Section 2–701, words of survivorship attached to a future interest are not, in the absence of additional evidence, a sufficient indication of an intent contrary to the application of this section. Words of survivorship include words of survivorship that relate to the distribution date or to an earlier or an unspecified time, whether those words of survivorship are expressed in condition-precedent, condition-subsequent, or any other form.

(4) If a governing instrument creates an alternative future interest with respect to a future interest for which a substitute gift is created by paragraph (1) or (2), the substitute gift is superseded by the alternative future interest only if an expressly designated beneficiary of the alternative future interest is entitled to take in possession or enjoyment.

(c) [More Than One Substitute Gift; Which One Takes.] If, under subsection (b), substitute gifts are created and not superseded with respect to more than one future interest and the future interests are alternative future interests, one to the other, the determination of which of the substitute gifts takes effect is resolved as follows:

(1) Except as provided in paragraph (2), the property passes under the primary substitute gift.

(2) If there is a younger-generation future interest, the property passes under the younger-generation substitute gift and not under the primary substitute gift.

(3) In this subsection:

(i) "Primary future interest" means the future interest that would have taken effect had all the deceased beneficiaries of the alternative future interests who left surviving descendants survived the distribution date.

(ii) "Primary substitute gift" means the substitute gift created with respect to the primary future interest.

(iii) "Younger-generation future interest" means a future interest that (A) is to a descendant of a beneficiary of the primary future interest, (B) is an alternative future interest with respect to the primary future interest, (C) is a future interest for which a substitute gift is created, and (D) would have taken effect had all the deceased beneficiaries who left surviving descendants survived the distribution date except the deceased beneficiary or beneficiaries of the primary future interest.

(iv) "Younger-generation substitute gift" means the substitute gift created with respect to the younger-generation future interest.

(d) [If No Other Takers, Property Passes Under Residuary Clause or to Transferor's Heirs.] Except as provided in subsection (e), if, after the application of subsections (b) and (c), there is no surviving taker, the property passes in the following order:

(1) if the trust was created in a nonresiduary devise in the transferor's will or in a codicil to the transferor's will, the property passes under the residuary clause in the transferor's will; for purposes of this section, the residuary clause is treated as creating a future interest under the terms of a trust.

(2) if no taker is produced by the application of paragraph (1), the property passes to the transferor's heirs under Section 2–711.

(e) [If No Other Takers and If Future Interest Created by Exercise of Power of Appointment.] If, after the application of subsections (b) and (c), there is no surviving taker and if the future interest was created by the exercise of a power of appointment:

(1) the property passes under the donor's gift-in-default clause, if any, which clause is treated as creating a future interest under the terms of a trust; and

(2) if no taker is produced by the application of paragraph (1), the property passes as provided in subsection (d). For purposes of subsection (d), "transferor" means the donor if the power was a nongeneral power and means the donee if the power was a general power.

As amended in 1993.

§2–708. Class Gifts to "Descendants," "Issue," or "Heirs of the Body"; Form of Distribution if None Specified.

If a class gift in favor of "descendants," "issue," or "heirs of the body" does not specify the manner in which the property is to be distributed among the class members, the property is distributed among the class members who are living when the interest is to take effect in possession or enjoyment, in such shares as they would receive, under the applicable law of intestate succession, if the designated ancestor had then died intestate owning the subject matter of the class gift.

§2–709. Representation; Per Capita at Each Generation; Per Stirpes.

(a) [Definitions.] In this section:

(1) "Deceased child" or "deceased descendant" means a child or a descendant who either predeceased the distribution date or is deemed to have predeceased the distribution date under Section 2–702.

(2) "Distribution date," with respect to an interest, means the time when the interest is to take effect in possession or enjoyment. The distribution date need not occur at the beginning or end of a calendar day, but can occur at a time during the course of a day.

(3) "Surviving ancestor," "surviving child," or "surviving descendant" means an ancestor, a child, or a descendant who neither predeceased the distribution date nor is deemed to have predeceased the distribution date under Section 2–702.

(b) [Representation; Per Capita at Each Generation.] If an applicable statute or a governing instrument calls for property to be distributed "by representation" or "per capita at each generation," the property is divided into as many equal shares as there are (i) surviving descendants in the generation nearest to the designated ancestor which contains one or more surviving descendants (ii) and deceased descendants in the same generation who left surviving descendants, if any. Each surviving descendant in the nearest generation is allocated one share. The remaining shares, if any, are combined and then divided in the same manner among the surviving descendants of the deceased descendants as if the surviving descendants who were allocated a share and their surviving descendants had predeceased the distribution date.

(c) [Per Stirpes.] If a governing instrument calls for property to be distributed "per stripes," the property is divided into as many equal shares as there are (i) surviving children of the designated ancestor and (ii) deceased children who left surviving descendants. Each surviving child, if any, is allocated one share. The share of each deceased child with surviving descendants is divided in the same manner, with subdivision repeating at each succeeding generation until the property is fully allocated among surviving descendants.

(d) [Deceased Descendant With No Surviving Descendant Disregarded.] For the purposes of subsections (b) and (c), an individual who is deceased and left no surviving descendant is disregarded, and an individual who leaves a surviving ancestor who is a descendant of the designated ancestor is not entitled to a share.

As amended in 1993.

§2–710.   Worthier-Title Doctrine Abolished.

The doctrine of worthier-title is abolished as a rule of law and as a rule of construction. Language in a governing instrument describing the beneficiaries of a disposition as the transferor's "heirs," "heirs at law," "next of kin," "distributees," "relatives," or "family," or language of similar import, does not create or presumptively create a reversionary interest in the transferor.

As amended in 1991.

§2–711.   Interests in "Heirs" and Like.

If an applicable statute or a governing instrument calls for a present or future distribution to or creates a present or future interest in a designated individual's "heirs," "heirs at law," "next of kin," "relatives," or "family," or language of similar import, the property passes to those persons, including the state, and in such shares as would succeed to the designated individual's intestate estate under the intestate succession law of the designated individual's domicile if the designated individual died when the disposition is to take effect in possession or enjoyment. If the designated individual's surviving spouse is living but is remarried at the time the disposition is to take effect in possession or enjoyment, the surviving spouse is not an heir of the designated individual.

As amended in 1991 and 1993.

PART 8
GENERAL PROVISIONS CONCERNING PROBATE AND NONPROBATE TRANSFERS

§2–801.   Disclaimer of Property Interests.

(a) [Right to Disclaim Interest in Property.] A person, or the representative of a person, to whom an interest in or with respect to property or an interest therein devolves by whatever means may disclaim it in whole or in part by delivering or filing a written disclaimer under this section. The right to disclaim exists notwithstanding (i) any limitation on the interest of the disclaimant in the nature of a spendthrift provision or similar restriction or (ii) any restriction or limitation on the right to disclaim contained in the governing instrument. For purposes of this subsection, the "representative of a person" includes a personal representative of a decedent, a conservator of a disabled person, a guardian of a minor or incapacitated person, and an agent acting on behalf of the person within the authority of a power of attorney.

(b) [Time of Disclaimer.] The following rules govern the time when a disclaimer must be filed or delivered:

(1) If the property or interest has devolved to the disclaimant under a testamentary instrument or by the laws of intestacy, the disclaimer must be filed, if of a present interest, not later than [nine] months after the death of the deceased owner or deceased donee of a power of appointment and, if of a future interest, not later than [nine] months after the event determining that the taker of the property or interest is finally ascertained and his [or her] interest is indefeasibly vested. The disclaimer must be filed in the [probate] court of the county in which proceedings for the administration of the estate of the deceased owner or deceased donee of the power have been commenced. A copy of the disclaimer must be delivered in person or mailed by registered or certified mail, return receipt requested, to any personal representative or other fiduciary of the decedent or donee of the power.

(2) If a property or interest has devolved to the disclaimant under a nontestamentary instrument or contract, the disclaimer must be delivered or filed, if of a present interest, not later than [nine] months after the effective date of the nontestamentary instrument or contract and, if of a future interest, not later than [nine] months after the event determining that the taker of the property or interest is finally ascertained and his [or her] interest is indefeasibly vested. If the person entitled to disclaim does not know of the existence of the interest, the disclaimer must be delivered or filed not later than [nine] months after the

person learns of the existence of the interest. The effective date of a revocable instrument or contract is the date on which the maker no longer has power to revoke it or to transfer to himself [or herself] or another the entire legal and equitable ownership of the interest. The disclaimer or a copy thereof must be delivered in person or mailed by registered or certified mail, return receipt requested, to the person who has legal title to or possession of the interest disclaimed.

(3) A surviving joint tenant [or tenant by the entireties] may disclaim as a separate interest any property or interest therein devolving to him [or her] by right of survivorship. A surviving joint tenant [or tenant by the entireties] may disclaim the entire interest in any property or interest therein that is the subject of a joint tenancy [or tenancy by the entireties] devolving to him [or her], if the joint tenancy [or tenancy by the entireties] was created by act of a deceased joint tenant [or tenant by the entireties], the survivor did not join in creating the joint tenancy [or tenancy by the entireties], and has not accepted a benefit under it.

(4) If real property or an interest therein is disclaimed, a copy of the disclaimer may be recorded in the office of the [Recorder of Deeds] of the county in which the property or interest disclaimed is located.*

*If Torrens system is in effect, add provisions to comply with local law.

(c) [Form of Disclaimer.] The disclaimer must (i) describe the property or interest disclaimed, (ii) declare the disclaimer and extent thereof, and (iii) be signed by the disclaimant.

(d) [Effect of Disclaimer.] The effects of a disclaimer are:

(1) If property or an interest therein devolves to a disclaimant under a testamentary instrument, under a power of appointment exercised by a testamentary instrument, or under the laws of intestacy, and the decedent has not provided for another disposition of that interest, should it be disclaimed, or of disclaimed, or failed interests in general, the disclaimed interest devolves as if the disclaimant had predeceased the decedent, but if by law or under the testamentary instrument the descendants of the disclaimant would share in the disclaimed interest by representation or otherwise were the disclaimant to predecease the decedent, then the disclaimed interest passes by representation, or passes as directed by the governing instrument, to the descendants of the disclaimant who survive the decedent. A future interest that takes effect in possession or enjoyment after the termination of the estate or interest disclaimed takes effect as if the disclaimant had predeceased the decedent. A disclaimer relates back for all purposes to the date of death of the decedent.

(2) If property or an interest therein devolves to a disclaimant under a nontestamentary instrument or contract and the instrument or contract does not provide for another disposition of that interest, should it be disclaimed, or of disclaimed or failed interests in general, the disclaimed interest devolves as if the disclaimant has predeceased the effective date of the instrument or contract, but if by law or under the nontestamentary instrument or contract the descendants of the disclaimant would share in the disclaimed interest by representation or otherwise were the disclaimant to predecease the effective date of the instrument, then the disclaimed interest passes by representation, or passes as directed by the governing instrument, to the descendants of the disclaimant who survive the effective date of the instrument. A disclaimer relates back for all purposes to that date. A future interest that takes effect in possession or enjoyment at or after the termination of the disclaimed interest takes effect as if the disclaimant had died before the effective date of the instrument or contract that transferred the disclaimed interest.

(3) The disclaimer or the written waiver of the right to disclaim is binding upon the disclaimant or person waiving and all persons claiming through or under either of them.

(e) [Waiver and Bar.] The right to disclaim property or an interest therein is barred by (i) an assignment, conveyance, encumbrance, pledge, or transfer of the property or interest, or a contract therefor, (ii) a written waiver of the right to disclaim, (iii) an acceptance of the property or interest or a benefit under it or (iv) a sale of the property or interest under judicial sale made before the disclaimer is made.

(f) [Remedy Not Exclusive.] This section does not abridge the right of a person to waive, release, disclaim, or renounce property or an interest therein under any other statute.

(g) [Application.] An interest in property that exists on the effective date of this section as to which, if a present interest, the time for filing a disclaimer under this section has not expired or, if a future interest, the interest has not become indefeasibly vested or the taker finally ascertained, may be disclaimed within [nine] months after the effective date of this section.

As amended in 1993.

§2–802. Effect of Divorce, Annulment, and Decree of Separation.

(a) An individual who is divorced from the decedent or whose marriage to the decedent has been annulled is not a surviving spouse unless, by virtue of a subsequent marriage, he [or she] is married to the decedent at the time of death. A decree of separation that does not terminate the status of husband and wife is not a divorce for purposes of this section.

(b) For purposes of Parts 1, 2, 3, and 4 of this Article, and of Section 3–203, a surviving spouse does not include:

(1) an individual who obtains or consents to a final decree or judgment of divorce from the decedent or an annulment of their marriage, which decree or judgment is not recognized as valid in this State, unless subsequently they participate in a marriage ceremony purporting to marry each to the other or live together as husband and wife;

(2) an individual who, following an invalid decree or judgment of divorce or annulment obtained by the decedent, participates in a marriage ceremony with a third individual; or

(3) an individual who was a party to a valid proceeding concluded by an order purporting to terminate all marital property rights.

§2–803. Effect of Homicide on Intestate Succession, Wills, Trusts, Joint Assets, Life Insurance, and Beneficiary Designations.

(a) [Definitions.] In this section:

(1) "Disposition or appointment of property" includes a transfer of an item of property or any other benefit to a beneficiary designated in a governing instrument.

(2) "Governing instrument" means a governing instrument executed by the decedent.

(3) "Revocable," with respect to a disposition, appointment, provision, or nomination, means one under which the decedent, at the time of or immediately before death, was alone empowered, by law or under the governing instrument, to cancel the designation, in favor of the killer, whether or not the decedent was then empowered to designate himself [or herself] in place of his [or her] killer and whether or not the decedent then had capacity to exercise the power.

(b) [Forfeiture of Statutory Benefits.] An individual who feloniously and intentionally kills the decedent forfeits all benefits under this Article with respect to the decedent's estate, including an intestate share, an elective share, an omitted spouse's or child's share, a homestead allowance, exempt property, and a family allowance. If the decedent died intestate, the decedent's intestate estate passes as if the killer disclaimed his [or her] intestate share.

(c) [Revocation of Benefits Under Governing Instruments.] The felonious and intentional killing of the decedent:

(1) revokes any revocable (i) disposition or appointment of property made by the decedent to the killer in a governing instrument, (ii) provision in a governing instrument conferring a general or nongeneral power of appointment on the killer, and (iii) nomination of the killer in a governing instrument, nominating or appointing the killer to serve in any fiduciary or representative capacity, including a personal representative, executor, trustee, or agent; and (2) severs the interests of the decedent and killer in property held by them at the time of the killing as joint tenants with the right of survivorship [or as community property with the right of survivorship], transforming the interests of the decedent and killer into tenancies in common.

(d) [Effect of Severance.] A severance under subsection (c)(2) does not affect any third-party interest in property acquired for value and in good faith reliance on an apparent title by survivorship in the killer unless a writing declaring the severance has been noted, registered, filed, or recorded in records appropriate to the kind and location of the property which are relied upon, in the ordinary course of transactions involving such property, as evidence of ownership.

(e) [Effect of Revocation.] Provisions of a governing instrument are given effect as if the killer disclaimed all provisions revoked by this section or, in the case of a revoked nomination in a fiduciary or representative capacity, as if the killer predeceased the decedent.

(f) [Wrongful Acquisition of Property.] A wrongful acquisition of property or interest by a killer not covered by this section must be treated in accordance with the principle that a killer cannot profit from his [or her] wrong.

(g) [Felonious and Intentional Killing; How Determined.] After all right to appeal has been exhausted, a judgment of conviction establishing criminal accountability for the felonious and intentional killing of the decedent conclusively establishes the convicted individual as the decedent's killer for purposes of this section. In the absence of a conviction, the court, upon the petition of an interested person, must determine whether, under the preponderance of evidence standard, the individual would be found criminally accountable for the felonious and intentional killing of the decedent. If the court determines that, under that standard, the individual would be found criminally accountable for the felonious and intentional killing of the decedent, the determination conclusively establishes that individual as the decedent's killer for purposes of this section.

(h) [Protection of Payors and Other Third Parties.]

(1) A payor or other third party is not liable for having made a payment or transferred an item of property or any other benefit to a beneficiary designated in a governing instrument affected by an intentional and felonious killing, or for having taken any other action in good faith reliance on the validity of the governing instrument, upon request and satisfactory proof of the decedent's death, before the payor or other third party received written notice of a claimed forfeiture or revocation under this section. A payor or other third party is liable for a payment made or other action taken after the payor or other third party received

written notice of a claimed forfeiture or revocation under this section.

(2) Written notice of a claimed forfeiture or revocation under paragraph (1) must be mailed to the payor's or other third party's main office or home by registered or certified mail, return receipt requested, or served upon the payor or other third party in the same manner as a summons in a civil action. Upon receipt of written notice of a claimed forfeiture or revocation under this section, a payor or other third party may pay any amount owed or transfer or deposit any item of property held by it to or with the court having jurisdiction of the probate proceedings relating to the decedent's estate, or if no proceedings have been commenced, to or with the court having jurisdiction of probate proceedings relating to decedent's estates located in the county of the decedent's residence. The court shall hold the funds or item of property and, upon its determination under this section, shall order disbursement in accordance with the determination. Payments, transfers, or deposits made to or with the court discharge the payor or other third party from all claims for the value of amounts paid to or items of property transferred to or deposited with the court.

(i) [Protection of Bona Fide Purchasers; Personal Liability of Recipient.]

(1) A person who purchases property for value and without notice, or who receives a payment or other item of property in partial or full satisfaction of a legally enforceable obligation, is neither obligated under this section to return the payment, item of property, or benefit nor is liable under this section for the amount of the payment or the value of the item of property or benefit. But a person who, not for value, receives a payment, item of property, or any other benefit to which the person is not entitled under this section is obligated to return the payment, item of property, or benefit, or is personally liable for the amount of the payment or the value of the item of property or benefit, to the person who is entitled to it under this section.

(2) If this section or any part of this section is preempted by federal law with respect to a payment, an item of property, or any other benefit covered by this section, a person who, not for value, receives the payment, item of property, or any other benefit to which the person is not entitled under this section is obligated to return the payment, item of property, or benefit, or is personally liable for the amount of the payment or the value of the item of property or benefit, to the person who would have been entitled to it were this section or part of this section not preempted.

As amended in 1993.

§2–804. Revocation of Probate and Nonprobate Transfers by Divorce; No Revocation by other Changes of Circumstances.

(a) [Definitions.] In this section:

(1) "Disposition or appointment of property" includes a transfer of an item of property or any other benefit to a beneficiary designated in a governing instrument.

(2) "Divorce or annulment" means any divorce or annulment, or any dissolution or declaration of invalidity of a marriage, that would exclude the spouse as a surviving spouse within the meaning of Section 2–802. A decree of separation that does not terminate the status of husband and wife is not a divorce for purposes of this section.

(3) "Divorced individual" includes an individual whose marriage has been annulled.

(4) "Governing instrument" means a governing instrument executed by the divorced individual before the divorce or annulment of his [or her] marriage to his [or her] former spouse.

(5) "Relative of the divorced individual's former spouse" means an individual who is related to the divorced individual's former spouse by blood, adoption, or affinity and who, after the divorce or annulment, is not related to the divorced individual by blood, adoption, or affinity.

(6) "Revocable," with respect to a disposition, appointment, provision, or nomination, means one under which the divorced individual, at the time of the divorce or annulment, was alone empowered, by law or under the governing instrument, to cancel the designation in favor of his [or her] former spouse or former spouse's relative, whether or not the divorced individual was then empowered to designate himself [or herself] in place of his [or her] former spouse or in place of his [or her] former spouse's relative and whether or not the divorced individual then had the capacity to exercise the power.

(b) [Revocation Upon Divorce.] Except as provided by the express terms of a governing instrument, a court order, or a contract relating to the division of the marital estate made between the divorced individuals before or after the marriage, divorce, or annulment, the divorce or annulment of a marriage:

(1) revokes any revocable (i) disposition or appointment of property made by a divorced individual to his [or her] former spouse in a governing instrument and any disposition or appointment created by law or in a governing instrument to a relative of the divorced individual's former spouse, (ii) provision in a governing instrument conferring a general or non-

general power of appointment on the divorced individual's former spouse or on a relative of the divorced individual's former spouse, and (iii) nomination in a governing instrument, nominating a divorced individual's former spouse or a relative of the divorced individual's former spouse to serve in any fiduciary or representative capacity, including a personal representative, executor, trustee, conservator, agent, or guardian; and

(2) severs the interests of the former spouses in property held by them at the time of the divorce or annulment as joint tenants with the right of survivorship [or as community property with the right of survivorship], transforming the interests of the former spouses into tenancies in common.

(c) [Effect of Severance.] A severance under subsection (b)(2) does not affect any third-party interest in property acquired for value and in good faith reliance on an apparent title by survivorship in the survivor of the former spouses unless a writing declaring the severance has been noted, registered, filed, or recorded in records appropriate to the kind and location of the property which are relied upon, in the ordinary course of transactions involving such property, as evidence of ownership.

(d) [Effect of Revocation.] Provisions of a governing instrument are given effect as if the former spouse and relatives of the former spouse disclaimed all provisions revoked by this section or, in the case of a revoked nomination in a fiduciary or representative capacity, as if the former spouse and relatives of the former spouse died immediately before the divorce or annulment.

(e) [Revival if Divorce Nullified.] Provisions revoked solely by this section are revived by the divorced individual's remarriage to the former spouse or by a nullification of the divorce or annulment.

(f) [No Revocation for Other Change of Circumstances.] No change of circumstances other than as described in this section and in Section 2–803 effects a revocation.

(g) [Protection of Payors and Other Third Parties.]

(1) A payor or other third party is not liable for having made a payment or transferred an item of property or any other benefit to a beneficiary designated in a governing instrument affected by a divorce, annulment, or remarriage, or for having taken any other action in good faith reliance on the validity of the governing instrument, before the payor or other third party received written notice of the divorce, annulment, or remarriage. A payor or other third party is liable for a payment made or other action taken after the payor or other third party received written notice of a claimed forfeiture or revocation under this section.

(2) Written notice of the divorce, annulment, or remarriage under subsection (g)(2) must be mailed to the payor's or other third party's main office or home by registered or certified mail, return receipt requested, or served upon the payor or other third party in the same manner as a summons in a civil action. Upon receipt of written notice of the divorce, annulment, or remarriage, a payor or other third party may pay any amount owed or transfer or deposit any item of property held by it to or with the court having jurisdiction of the probate proceedings relating to the decedent's estate or, if no proceedings have been commenced, to or with the court having jurisdiction of probate proceedings relating to decedents' estates located in the county of the decedent's residence. The court shall hold the funds or item of property and, upon its determination under this section, shall order disbursement or transfer in accordance with the determination. Payments, transfers, or deposits made to or with the court discharge the payor or other third party from all claims for the value of amounts paid to or items of property transferred to or deposited with the court.

(h) [Protection of Bona Fide Purchasers; Personal Liability of Recipient.]

(1) A person who purchases property from a former spouse, relative of a former spouse, or any other person for value and without notice, or who receives from a former spouse, relative of a former spouse, or any other person a payment or other item of property in partial or full satisfaction of a legally enforceable obligation, is neither obligated under this section to return the payment, item of property, or benefit nor is liable under this section for the amount of the payment or the value of the item of property or benefit, But a former spouse, relative of a former spouse, or other person who, not for value, received a payment, item of property, or any other benefit to which that person is not entitled under this section is obligated to return the payment, item of property, or benefit, or is personally liable for the amount of the payment or the value of the item of property or benefit, to the person who is entitled to it under this section.

(2) If this section or any part of this section is preempted by federal law with respect to a payment, an item of property, or any other benefit covered by this section, a former spouse, relative of the former spouse, or any other person who, not for value, received a payment, item of property, or any other benefit to which that person is not entitled under this section is obligated to return that payment, item of property, or benefit, or is personally liable for the amount of the payment or the value of the item of property or benefit, to the person who would have been entitled to it were this section or part of this section not preempted.

As amended in 1993.

PART 9
STATUTORY RULE AGAINST PERPETUITIES; HONORARY TRUSTS

SUBPART 1.
[STATUTORY RULE AGAINST PERPETUITIES]

§2–901.   Statutory Rule Against Perpetuities.

(a) [Validity of Nonvested Property Interest.] A nonvested property interest is invalid unless:

(1) when the interest is created, it is certain to vest or terminate no later than 21 years after the death of an individual then alive; or

(2) the interest either vests or terminates within 90 years after its creation.

(b) [Validity of General Power of Appointment Subject to a Condition Precedent.] A general power of appointment not presently exercisable because of a condition precedent is invalid unless:

(1) when the power is created, the condition precedent is certain to be satisfied or becomes impossible to satisfy no later than 21 years after the death of an individual then alive; or

(2) the condition precedent either is satisfied or becomes impossible to satisfy within 90 years after its creation.

(c) [Validity of Nongeneral or Testamentary Power of Appointment.] A nongeneral power of appointment or a general testamentary power of appointment is invalid unless:

(1) when the power is created, it is certain to be irrevocably exercised or otherwise to terminate no later than 21 years after the death of an individual then alive; or

(2) the power is irrevocably exercised or otherwise terminates within 90 years after its creation.

(d) [Possibility of Post-death Child Disregarded.] In determining whether a nonvested property interest or a power of appointment is valid under subsection (a)(1), (b)(1), or (c)(1), the possibility that a child will be born to an individual after the individual's death is disregarded.

(e) [Effect of Certain "Later-of" Type Language.] If, in measuring a period from the creation of a trust or other property arrangement, language in a governing instrument (i) seeks to disallow the vesting or termination of any interest or trust beyond, (ii) seeks to postpone the vesting or termination of any interest or trust until, or (iii) seeks to operate in effect in any similar fashion upon, the later of (A) the expiration of a period of time not exceeding 21 years after the death of the survivor of specified lives in being at the creation of the trust or other property arrangement or (B) the expiration of a period of time that exceeds or might exceed 21 years after the death of the survivor of lives in being at the cre-ation of the trust or other property arrangement, that language is inoperative to the extent it produces a period of time that exceeds 21 years after the death of the survivor of the specified lives.

§2–902.   When Nonvested Property Interest or Power of Appointment Created.

(a) Except as provided in subsections (b) and (c) and in Section 2–905(a), the time of creation of a nonvested property interest or a power of appointment is determined under general principles of property law.

(b) For purposes of Subpart 1 of this Part, if there is a person who alone can exercise a power created by a governing instrument to become the unqualified beneficial owner of (i) a nonvested property interest or (ii) a property interest subject to a power of appointment described in Section 2–901(b) or (c), the nonvested property interest or power of appointment is created when the power to become the unqualified beneficial owner terminates. [For purposes of Subpart 1 of this Part, a joint power with respect to community property or to marital property under the Uniform Marital Property Act held by individuals married to each other is a power exercisable by one person alone.]

(c) For purposes of Subpart 1 of this Part, a nonvested property interest or a power of appointment arising from a transfer of property to a previously funded trust or other existing property arrangement is created when the nonvested property interest or power of appointment in the original contribution was created.

§2–903.   Reformation.

Upon the petition of an interested person, a court shall reform a disposition in the manner that most closely approximates the transferor's manifested plan of distribution and is within the 90 years allowed by Section 2–901(a)(2), 2–901(b)(2), or 2–901(c)(2) if:

(1) a nonvested property interest or a power of appointment becomes invalid under Section 2–901 (statutory rule against perpetuities);

(2) a class gift is not but might become invalid under Section 2–901 (statutory rule against perpetuities) and the time has arrived when the share of any class member is to take effect in possession or enjoyment; or

(3) a nonvested property interest that is not validated by Section 2–901(a)(1) can vest but not within 90 years after its creation.

§2–904.   Exclusions from Statutory Rule Against Perpetuities.

Section 2–901 (statutory rule against perpetuities) does not apply to:

(1) a nonvested property interest or a power of appointment arising out of a nondonative transfer, except a nonvested property interest or a power of appoint-

ment arising out of (i) a premarital or postmarital agreement, (ii) a separation or divorce settlement, (iii) a spouse's election, (iv) a similar arrangement arising out of a prospective, existing, or previous marital relationship between the parties, (v) a contract to make or not to revoke a will or trust, (vi) a contract to exercise or not to exercise a power of appointment, (vii) a transfer in satisfaction of a duty of support, or (viii) a reciprocal transfer;

(2) a fiduciary's power relating to the administration or management of assets, including the power of a fiduciary to sell, lease, or mortgage property, and the power of a fiduciary to determine principal and income;

(3) a power to appoint a fiduciary;

(4) a discretionary power of a trustee to distribute principal before termination of a trust to a beneficiary having an indefeasibly vested interest in the income and principal;

(5) a nonvested property interest held by a charity, government, or governmental agency or subdivision, if the nonvested property interest is preceded by an interest held by another charity, government, or governmental agency or subdivision;

(6) a nonvested property interest in or a power of appointment with respect to a trust or other property arrangement forming part of a pension, profit-sharing, stock bonus, health, disability, death benefit, income deferral, or other current or deferred benefit plan for one or more employees, independent contractors, or their beneficiaries or spouses, to which contributions are made for the purpose of distributing to or for the benefit of the participants or their beneficiaries or spouses the property, income, or principal in the trust or other property arrangement, except a nonvested property interest or a power of appointment that is created by an election of a participant or a beneficiary or spouse; or

(7) a property interest, power of appointment, or arrangement that was not subject to the common-law rule against perpetuities or is excluded by another statute of this State.

§2–905. Prospective Application.

(a) Except as extended by subsection (b), Subpart 1 of this Part applies to a nonvested property interest or a power of appointment that is created on or after the effective date of Subpart 1 of this Part. For purposes of this section, a nonvested property interest or a power of appointment created by the exercise of a power of appointment is created when the power is irrevocably exercised or when a revocable exercise becomes irrevocable.

(b) If a nonvested property interest or a power of appointment was created before the effective date of Subpart 1 of this Part and is determined in a judicial proceeding, commenced on or after the effective date of Subpart 1 of this Part, to violate this State's rule against

perpetuities as that rule existed before the effective date of Subpart 1 of this Part, a court upon the petition of an interested person may reform the disposition in the manner that most closely approximates the transferor's manifested plan of distribution and is within the limits of the rule against perpetuities applicable when the nonvested property interest or power of appointment was created.

§2–906. [Supersession][Repeal].

Subpart 1 of this Part [supersedes the rule of the common law known as the rule against perpetuities][repeals (list statutes to be repealed)].

SUBPART 2.
[HONORARY TRUSTS]

§2–907. Honorary Trusts; Trusts for Pets.

(a) [Honorary Trust.] Subject to subsection (c), if (i) a trust is for a specific lawful noncharitable purpose or for lawful noncharitable purposes to be selected by the trustee and (ii) there is no definite or definitely ascertainable beneficiary designated, the trust may be performed by the trustee for [21] years but no longer, whether or not the terms of the trust contemplate a longer duration.

(b) [Trust for Pets.] Subject to this subsection and subsection (c), a trust for the care of a designated domestic or pet animal is valid. The trust terminates when no living animal is covered by the trust. A governing instrument must be liberally construed to bring the transfer within this subsection, to presume against the merely precatory or honorary nature of the disposition, and to carry out the general intent of the transferor. Extrinsic evidence is admissible in determining the transferor's intent.

(c) [Additional Provisions Applicable to Honorary Trusts and Trusts for Pets.] In addition to the provisions of subsection (a) or (b), a trust covered by either of those subsections is subject to the following provisions:

(1) Except as expressly provided otherwise in the trust instrument, no portion of the principal or income may be converted to the use of the trustee or to any use other than for the trust's purposes or for the benefit of a covered animal.

(2) Upon termination, the trustee shall transfer the unexpended trust property in the following order:

(i) as directed in the trust instrument;

(ii) if the trust was created in a nonresiduary clause in the transferor's will or in a codicil to the transferor's will, under the residuary clause in the transferor's will; and

(iii) if no taker is produced by the application of subparagraph (i) or (ii), to the transferor's heirs under Section 2–711.

(3) For the purposes of Section 2–707, the residuary clause is treated as creating a future interest under the terms of a trust.

(4) The intended use of the principal or income can be enforced by an individual designated for that purpose in the trust instrument or, if none, by an individual appointed by a court upon application to it by an individual.

(5) Except as ordered by the court or required by the trust instrument, no filing, report, registration, periodic accounting, separate maintenance of funds, appointment, or fee is required by reason of the existence of the fiduciary relationship of the trustee.

(6) A court may reduce the amount of the property transferred, if it determines that that amount substantially exceeds the amount required for the intended use. The amount of the reduction, if any, passes as unexpended trust property under subsection (c)(2).

(7) If no trustee is designated or no designated trustee is willing or able to serve, a court shall name a trustee. A court may order the transfer of the property to another trustee, if required to assure that the intended use is carried out and if no successor trustee is designated in the trust instrument or if no designated successor trustee agrees to serve or is able to serve. A court may also make such other orders and determinations as shall be advisable to carry out the intent of the transferor and the purpose of this section.]

As amended in 1993.

PART 10
UNIFORM INTERNATIONAL WILLS ACT
[INTERNATIONAL WILL; INFORMATION REGISTRATION]
NUMBERING SECTIONS OF ACT

§1. [2–1001.]   [Definitions.]

In this Act: [Part:]

(1) "International will" means a will executed in conformity with sections 2 [2–1002] through 5 [2–1005].

(2) "Authorized person" and "person authorized to act in connection with international wills" mean a person who by section 9 [2–1009], or by the laws of the United States including members of the diplomatic and consular service of the United States designated by Foreign Service Regulations, is empowered to supervise the execution of international wills.

§2. [2–1002.]   [International Will; Validity.]

(a) A will shall be valid as regards form, irrespective particularly of the place where it is made, of the location of the assets and of the nationality, domicile, or residence of the testator, if it is made in the form of an international will complying with the requirements of this Act. [Part.]

(b) The invalidity of the will as an international will shall not affect its formal validity as a will of another kind.

(c) This Act [Part] shall not apply to the form of testamentary dispositions made by two or more persons in one instrument.

§3. [2–1003.]   [International Will; Requirements.]

(a) The will shall be made in writing. It need not be written by the testator himself. It may be written in any language, by hand or by any other means.

(b) The testator shall declare in the presence of two witnesses and of a person authorized to act in connection with international wills that the document is his will and that he knows the contents thereof. The testator need not inform the witnesses, or the authorized person, of the contents of the will.

(c) In the presence of the witnesses, and of the authorized person, the testator shall sign the will or, if he has previously signed it, shall acknowledge his signature.

(d) When the testator is unable to sign, the absence of his signature does not affect the validity of the international will if the testator indicates the reason for his inability to sign and the authorized person makes note thereof on the will. In these cases, it is permissible for any other person present, including the authorized person or one of the witnesses, at the direction of the testator to sign the testator's name for him, if the authorized person makes note of this also on the will, but it is not required that any person sign the testator's name for him.

(e) The witnesses and the authorized person shall there and then attest the will by signing in the presence of the testator.

§4. [2–1004.]   [International Will; Other Points of Form.]

(a) The signatures shall be placed at the end of the will. If the will consists of several sheets, each sheet will be signed by the testator or, if he is unable to sign, by the person signing on his behalf or, if there is no such person, by the authorized person. In addition, each sheet shall be numbered.

(b) The date of the will shall be the date of its signature by the authorized person. That date shall be noted at the end of the will by the authorized person.

(c) The authorized person shall ask the testator whether he wishes to make a declaration concerning the safekeeping of his will. If so and at the express request of the testator the place where he intends to have his will kept shall be mentioned in the certificate provided for in Section 5.

(d) A will executed in compliance with Section 3 shall not be invalid merely because it does not comply with this section.

§5. [2–1005.]   [International Will; Certificate.]

The authorized person shall attach to the will a certificate to be signed by him establishing that the requirements of this Act [Part] for valid execution of an international will have been complied with. The authorized person shall keep a copy of the certificate and deliver another to the testator. The certificate shall be substantially in the following form:

CERTIFICATE

(Convention of October 26, 1973)

1. I, _____ (name, address and capacity), a person authorized to act in connection with international wills

2. Certify that on _____ (date) at _____ (place)

3. (testator) _____ (name, address, date and place of birth) in my presence and that of the witnesses

4. (a) _____ (name, address, date and place of birth)

   (b) _____ (name, address, date and place of birth) has declared that the attached document is his will and that he knows the contents thereof.

5. I furthermore certify that:

6. (a) in my presence and in that of the witnesses

   (1) the testator has signed the will or has acknowledged his signature previously affixed.

   *(2) following a declaration of the testator stating that he was unable to sign his will for the following reason _____ , I have mentioned this declaration on the will * and the signature has been affixed by _____ (name and address)

7. (b) the witnesses and I have signed the will;

8. *(c) each page of the will has been signed by _____ and numbered;

9. (d) I have satisfied myself as to the identity of the testator and of the witnesses as designated above;

10. (e) the witnesses met the conditions requisite to act as such according to the law under which I am acting;

11. * (f) the testator has requested me to include the following statement concerning the safekeeping of his will:

12. PLACE OF EXECUTION

13. DATE

14. SIGNATURE and, if necessary, SEAL

* to be completed if appropriate

§6. [2–1006.]   [International Will; Effect of Certificate.]

In the absence of evidence to the contrary, the certificate of the authorized person shall be conclusive of the formal validity of the instrument as a will under this Act. [Part.] The absence or irregularity of a certificate shall not affect the formal validity of a will under this Act. [Part.]

§7. [2–1007.]   [International Will; Revocation.]

The international will shall be subject to the ordinary rules of revocation of wills.

§8. [2–1008.]   [Source and Construction.]

Sections 1 [2–1001] through 7 [2–1007] derive from Annex to Convention of October 26, 1973, Providing a Uniform Law on the Form of an International Will. In interpreting and applying this Act [Part], regard shall be had to its international origin and to the need for uniformity in its interpretation.

§9. [2–1009.]   [Persons Authorized to Act in Relation to International Will; Eligibility; Recognition by Authorizing Agency.]

Individuals who have been admitted to practice law before the courts of this state and who are in good standing as active law practitioners in this state, are hereby declared to be authorized persons in relation to international wills.

§10. [2–1010.]   [International Will Information Registration.]

The [Secretary of State] shall establish a registry system by which authorized persons may register in a central information center, information regarding the execution of international wills, keeping that information in strictest confidence until the death of the maker and then making it available to any person desiring information about any will who presents a death certificate or other satisfactory evidence of the testator's death to the center. Information that may be received, preserved in confidence until death, and reported as indicated is limited to the name, social-security or any other individual-identifying number established by law, address, and date and place of birth of the testator, and the intended place of deposit or safekeeping of the instrument pending the death of the maker. The [Secretary of State], at the request of the authorized person, may cause the information it receives about execution of any international will to be transmitted to the registry system of another jurisdiction as identified by the testator, if that other system adheres to rules protecting the confidentiality of the information similar to those established in this state.]

ARTICLE III
PROBATE OF WILLS AND ADMINISTRATION

PART 1
GENERAL PROVISIONS

PART 1
GENERAL PROVISIONS

§3–101.   [Devolution of Estate at Death; Restrictions.]

The power of a person to leave property by will, and the rights of creditors, devisees, and heirs to his property are subject to the restrictions and limitations contained in this Code to facilitate the prompt settlement of estates. Upon the death of a person, his real and personal property devolves to the persons to whom it is devised by his last will or to those indicated as substitutes for them in cases involving lapse, renunciation, or other circumstances affecting the devolution of testate estate, or in the absence of testamentary disposition, to his heirs, or to those indicated as substitutes for them in cases involving renunciation or other circumstances affecting devolution of intestate estates, subject to homestead allowance, exempt property and family allowance, to rights of creditors, elective share of the surviving spouse, and to administration.

ALTERNATIVE SECTION FOR COMMUNITY PROPERTY STATES
[§3–101A.   [Devolution of Estate at Death; Restrictions.]

The power of a person to leave property by will, and the rights of creditors, devisees, and heirs to his property are subject to the restrictions and limitations contained in this Code to facilitate the prompt settlement of estates. Upon the death of a person, his separate property devolves to the persons to whom it is devised by his last will, or to those indicated as substitutes for them in cases involving lapse, renunciation or other circumstances affecting the devolution of testate estates, or in the absence of testamentary disposition to his heirs, or to those indicated as substitutes for them in cases involving renunciation or other circumstances affecting the devolution of intestate estates, and upon the death of a husband or wife, the decedent's share of their community property devolves to the persons to whom it is devised by his last will, or in the absence of testamentary disposition, to his heirs, but all of their community property which is under the management and control of the decedent is subject to his debts and administration, and that portion of their community property which is not under the management and control of the decedent but which is necessary to carry out the provisions of his will is subject to administration; but the devolution of all the above described property is subject to rights to homestead allowance, exempt property and family allowances, to renunciation, to rights of creditors, [elective share of the surviving spouse] and to administration.]

§3–102. [Necessity of Order of Probate For Will.]

Except as provided in Section 3-1201, to be effective to prove the transfer of any property or to nominate an executor, a will must be declared to be valid by an order of informal probate by the Registrar, or an adjudication of probate by the Court:

As amended in 1993.

§3–103. [Necessity of Appointment For Administration.]

Except as otherwise provided in Article IV, to acquire the powers and undertake the duties and liabilities of a personal representative of a decedent, a person must be appointed by order of the Court or Registrar, qualify and be issued letters. Administration of an estate is commenced by the issuance of letters.

§3–104. [Claims Against Decedent; Necessity of Administration.]

No proceeding to enforce a claim against the estate of a decedent or his successors may be revived or commenced before the appointment of a personal representative. After the appointment and until distribution, all proceedings and actions to enforce a claim against the estate are governed by the procedure prescribed by this Article. After distribution a creditor whose claim has not been barred may recover from the distributees as provided in Section 3–1004 or from a former personal representative individually liable as provided in Section 3–1005. This section has no application to a proceeding by a secured creditor of the decedent to enforce his right to his security except as to any deficiency judgment which might be sought therein.

§3–105. [Proceedings Affecting Devolution and Administration; Jurisdiction of Subject Matter.]

Persons interested in decedents' estates may apply to the Registrar for determination in the informal proceedings provided in this Article, and may petition the Court for orders in formal proceedings within the Court's jurisdiction including but not limited to those described in this Article. The Court has exclusive jurisdiction of formal proceedings to determine how decedents' estates subject to the laws of this state are to be administered, expended and distributed. The Court has concurrent jurisdiction of any other action or proceeding concerning a succession or to which an estate, through a personal representative, may be a party, including actions to determine title to property alleged to belong to the estate, and of any action or proceeding in which property distributed by a personal representative or its value is sought to be subjected to rights of creditors or successors of the decedent.

§3–106. [Proceedings Within the Exclusive Jurisdiction of Court; Service; Jurisdiction Over Persons.]

In proceedings within the exclusive jurisdiction of the Court where notice is required by this Code or by rule, and in proceedings to construe probated wills or determine heirs which concern estates that have not been and cannot now be open for administration, interested persons may be bound by the orders of the Court in respect to property in or subject to the laws of this state by notice in conformity with Section 1–401. An order is binding as to all who are given notice of the proceeding though less than all interested persons are notified.

§3–107. [Scope of Proceedings; Proceedings Independent; Exception.]

Unless supervised administration as described in Part 5 is involved, (1) each proceeding before the Court or Registrar is independent of any other proceeding involving the same estate; (2) petitions for formal orders of the Court may combine various requests for relief in a single proceeding if the orders sought may be finally granted without delay. Except as required for proceedings which are particularly described by other sections of this Article, no petition is defective because it fails to embrace all matters which might then be the subject of a final order; (3) proceedings for probate of wills or adjudications of no will may be combined with proceedings for appointment of personal representatives; and (4) a proceeding for appointment of a personal representative is concluded by an order making or declining the appointment.

§3–108. [Probate, Testacy and Appointment Proceedings; Ultimate Time Limit.]

(a) No informal probate or appointment proceeding or formal testacy or appointment proceeding, other than a proceeding to probate a will previously probated at the testator's domicile and appointment proceedings relating to an estate in which there has been a prior appointment, may be commenced more than three years after the decedent's death, except:

(1) if a previous proceeding was dismissed because of doubt about the fact of the decedent's death, appropriate probate, appointment, or testacy proceedings may be maintained at any time thereafter upon a finding that the decedent's death occurred before the initiation of the previous proceeding and the applicant or petitioner has not delayed unduly in initiating the subsequent proceeding;

(2) appropriate probate, appointment, or testacy proceedings may be maintained in relation to the estate of an absent, disappeared or missing person for whose estate a conservator has been appointed, at

any time within three years after the conservator becomes able to establish the death of the protected person;

(3) a proceeding to contest an informally probated will and to secure appointment of the person with legal priority for appointment in the event the contest is successful, may be commenced within the later of twelve months from the informal probate or three years from the decedent's death;

(4) an informal appointment or a formal testacy or appointment proceeding may be commenced thereafter if no proceedings concerning the succession or estate administration has occurred within the three year period after the decedent's death, but the personal representative has no right to possess estate assets as provided in Section 3–709 beyond that necessary to confirm title thereto in the successors to the estate and claims other than expenses of administration may not be presented against the estate; and

(5) a formal testacy proceeding may be commenced at any time after three years from the decedent's death for the purpose of establishing an instrument to direct or control the ownership of property passing or distributable after the decedent's death from one other than the decedent when the property is to be appointed by the terms of the decedent's will or is to pass or be distributed as a part of the decedent's estate or its transfer is otherwise to be controlled by the terms of the decedent's will.

(b) These limitations do not apply to proceedings to construe probated wills or determine heirs of an intestate.

(c) In cases under subsection (a)(1) or (2), the date on which a testacy or appointment proceeding is properly commenced shall be deemed to be the date of the decedent's death for purposes of other limitations provisions of this Code which relate to the date of death. As amended in 1987 and 1993.

§3–109. [Statutes of Limitation on Decedent's Cause of Action.]

No statute of limitation running on a cause of action belonging to a decedent which had not been barred as of the date of his death, shall apply to bar a cause of action surviving the decedent's death sooner than four months after death. A cause of action which, but for this section, would have been barred less than four months after death, is barred after four months unless tolled.

PART 2
VENUE FOR PROBATE AND ADMINISTRATION; PRIORITY TO ADMINISTER; DEMAND FOR NOTICE

§3–201. [Venue for First and Subsequent Estate Proceedings; Location of Property.]

(a) Venue for the first informal or formal testacy or appointment proceedings after a decedent's death is:

(1) in the [county] where the decedent had his domicile at the time of his death; or

(2) if the decedent was not domiciled in this state, in any [county] where property of the decedent was located at the time of his death.

(b) Venue for all subsequent proceedings within the exclusive jurisdiction of the Court is in the place where the initial proceeding occurred, unless the initial proceeding has been transferred as provided in Section 1–303 or (c) of this section.

(c) If the first proceeding was informal, on application of an interested person and after notice to the proponent in the first proceeding, the Court, upon finding that venue is elsewhere, may transfer the proceeding and the file to the other court.

(d) For the purpose of aiding determinations concerning location of assets which may be relevant in cases involving non-domiciliaries, a debt, other than one evidenced by investment or commercial paper or other instrument in favor of a non-domiciliary is located where the debtor resides or, if the debtor is a person other than an individual, at the place where it has its principal office. Commercial paper, investment paper and other instruments are located where the instrument is. An interest in property held in trust is located where the trustee may be sued.

§3–202. [Appointment or Testacy Proceedings; Conflicting Claim of Domicile in Another State.]

In conflicting claims as to the domicile of a decedent are made in a formal testacy or appointment proceeding commenced in this state, and in a testacy or appointment proceeding after notice pending at the same time in another state, the Court of this state must stay, dismiss, or permit suitable amendment in, the proceeding here unless it is determined that the local proceeding was commenced before the proceeding elsewhere. The determination of domicile in the proceeding first commenced must be accepted as determinative in the proceeding in this state.

§3–203. [Priority Among Persons Seeking Appointment as Personal Representative.]

(a) Whether the proceedings are formal or informal, persons who are not disqualified have priority for appointment in the following order:

(1) the person with priority as determined by a probated will including a person nominated by a power conferred in a will;

(2) the surviving spouse of the decedent who is a devisee of the decedent;

(3) other devisees of the decedent;

(4) the surviving spouse of the decedent;

(5) other heirs of the decedent;

(6) 45 days after the death of the decedent, any creditor.

(b) An objection to an appointment can be made only in formal proceedings. In case of objection the priorities stated in (a) apply except that

(1) if the estate appears to be more than adequate to meet exemptions and costs of administration but inadequate to discharge anticipated unsecured claims, the Court, on petition of creditors, may appoint any qualified person;

(2) in case of objection to appointment of a person other than one whose priority is determined by will by an heir or devisee appearing to have a substantial interest in the estate, the Court may appoint a person who is acceptable to heirs and devisees whose interests in the estate appear to be worth in total more than half of the probable distributable value, or, in default of this accord any suitable person.

(c) A person entitled to letters under (2) through (5) of (a) above, and a person aged [18] and over who would be entitled to letters but for his age, may nominate a qualified person to act as personal representative. Any person aged [18] and over may renounce his right to nominate or to an appointment by appropriate writing filed with the Court. When two or more persons share a priority, those of them who do not renounce must concur in nominating another to act for them, or in applying for appointment.

(d) Conservators of the estates of protected persons, or if there is no conservator, any guardian except a guardian ad litem of a minor or incapacitated person, may exercise the same right to nominate, to object to another's appointment, or to participate in determining the preference of a majority in interest of the heirs and devisees that the protected person or ward would have if qualified for appointment.

(e) Appointment of one who does not have priority, including priority resulting from renunciation or nomination determined pursuant to this section, may be made only in formal proceedings. Before appointing one without priority, the Court must determine that those having priority, although given notice of the proceedings, have failed to request appointment or to nominate another for appointment, and that administration is necessary.

(f) No person is qualified to serve as a personal representative who is:

(1) under the age of [21];

(2) a person whom the Court finds unsuitable in formal proceedings.

(g) A personal representative appointed by a court of the decedent's domicile has priority over all other persons except where the decedent's will nominates different persons to be personal representative in this state and in the state of domicile. The domiciliary personal representative may nominate another, who shall have the same priority as the domiciliary personal representative.

(h) This section governs priority for appointment of a nuccessor personal representative but does not apply to the selection of a special administrator.

§3–204. [Demand for Notice of Order or Filing Concerning Decedent's Estate.]

Any person desiring notice of any order or filing pertaining to a decedent's estate in which he has a financial or property interest, may file a demand for notice with the Court at any time after the death of the decedent stating the name of the decedent, the nature of his interest in the estate, and the demandant's address or that of his attorney. The clerk shall mail a copy of the demand to the personal representative if one has been appointed. After filing of a demand, no order or filing to which the demand relates shall be made or accepted without notice as prescribed in Section 1–401 to the demandant or his attorney. The validity of an order which is issued or filing which is accepted without compliance with this requirement shall not be affected by the error, but the petitioner receiving the order or the person making the filing may be liable for any damage caused by the absence of notice. The requirement of notice arising from a demand under this provision may be waived in writing by the demandant and shall cease upon the termination of his interest in the estate.

PART 3

INFORMAL PROBATE AND APPOINTMENT PROCEEDINGS; SUCCESSION WITHOUT ADMINISTRATION

§3-301. [Informal Probate or Appointment Proceedings; Application; Contents.]

(a) Applications for informal probate or informal appointment shall be directed to the Registrar, and verified by the applicant to be accurate and complete to the best of his knowledge and belief as to the following information:

(1) Every application for informal probate of a will or for informal appointment of a personal representative, other than a special or successor representative, shall contain the following:

(i) a statement of the interest of the applicant;

(ii) the name, and date of death of the decedent, his age, and the county and state of his domicile at the time of death, and the names and addresses of the spouse, children, heirs and devisees and the ages of any who are minors so far as known or ascertainable with reasonable diligence by the applicant;

(iii) if the decedent was not domiciled in the state at the time of his death, a statement showing venue;

(iv) a statement identifying and indicating the address of any personal representative of the decedent appointed in this state or elsewhere whose appointment has not been terminated;

(v) a statement indicating whether the applicant has received a demand for notice, or is aware of any demand for notice of any probate or appointment proceeding concerning the decedent that may have been filed in this state or elsewhere; and

(vi) that the time limit for informal probate or appointment as provided in this Article has not expired either because 3 years or less have passed since the decedent's death, or, if more than 3 years from death have passed, circumstances as described by Section 3–108 authorizing tardy probate or appointment have occurred.

(2) An application for informal probate of a will shall state the following in addition to the statements required by (1):

(i) that the original of the decedent's last will is in the possession of the court, or accompanies the application, or that an authenticated copy of a will probated in another jurisdiction accompanies the application;

(ii) that the applicant, to the best of his knowledge, believes the will to have been validly executed;

(iii) that after the exercise of reasonable diligence, the applicant is unaware of any instrument revoking the will, and that the applicant believes that the instrument which is the subject of the application is the decedent's last will.

(3) An application for informal appointment of a personal representative to administer an estate under a will shall describe the will by date of execution and state the time and place of probate or the pending application or petition for probate. The application for appointment shall adopt the statements in the application or petition for probate and state the name, address and priority for appointment of the person whose appointment is sought.

(4) An application for informal appointment of an administrator in intestacy shall state in addition to the statements required by (1):

(i) that after the exercise of reasonable diligence, the applicant is unaware of any unrevoked testamentary instrument relating to property having a situs in this state under Section 1–301, or, a statement why any such instrument of which he may be aware is not being probated;

(ii) the priority of the person whose appointment is sought and the names of any other persons hav-

ing a prior or equal right to the appointment under Section 3–203.

(5) An application for appointment of a personal representative to succeed a personal representative appointed under a different testacy status shall refer to the order in the most recent testacy proceeding, state the name and address of the person whose appointment is sought and of the person whose appointment will be terminated if the application is granted, and describe the priority of the applicant.

(6) An application for appointment of a personal representative to succeed a personal representative who has tendered a resignation as provided in 3–610(c), or whose appointment has been terminated by death or removal, shall adopt the statements in the application or petition which led to the appointment of the person being succeeded except as specifically changed or corrected, state the name and address of the person who seeks appointment as successor, and describe the priority of the applicant.

(b) By verifying an application for informal probate, or informal appointment, the applicant submits personally to the jurisdiction of the court in any proceeding for relief from fraud relating to the application, or for perjury, that may be instituted against him.

§3–302. [Informal Probate; Duty of Registrar; Effect of Informal Probate.]

Upon receipt of an application requesting informal probate of a will, the Registrar, upon making the findings required by Section 3–303 shall issue a written statement of informal probate if at least 120 hours have elapsed since the decedent's death. Informal probate is conclusive as to all persons until superseded by an order in a formal testacy proceeding. No defect in the application or procedure relating thereto which leads to informal probate of a will renders the probate void.

§3–303. [Informal Probate; Proof and Findings Required.]

(a) In an informal proceeding for original probate of a will, the Registrar shall determine whether:

(1) the application is complete;

(2) the applicant has made oath or affirmation that the statements contained in the application are true to the best of his knowledge and belief;

(3) the applicant appears from the application to be an interested person as defined in Section 1–201(24);

(4) on the basis of the statements in the application, venue is proper;

(5) an original, duly executed and apparently unrevoked will is in the Registrar's possession;

(6) any notice required by Section 3–204 has been given and that the application is not within Section 3–304; and

(7) it appears from the application that the time limit for original probate has not expired.

(b) The application shall be denied if it indicates that a personal representative has been appointed in another [county] of this state or except as provided in subsection (d) below, if it appears that this or another will of the decedent has been the subject of a previous probate order.

(c) A will which appears to have the required signatures and which contains an attestation clause showing that requirements of execution under Section 2–502, 2–503 or 2–506 have been met shall be probated without further proof. In other cases, the Registrar may assume execution if the will appears to have been properly executed, or he may accept a sworn statement or affidavit of any person having knowledge of the circumstances of execution, whether or not the person was a witness to the will.

(d) Informal probate of a will which has been previously probated elsewhere may be granted at any time upon written application by any interested person, together with deposit of an authenticated copy of the will and of the statement probating it from the office or court where it was first probated.

(e) A will from a place which does not provide for probate of a will after death and which is not eligible for probate under subsection (a) above, may be probated in this state upon receipt by the Registrar of a duly authenticated copy of the will and a duly authenticated certificate of its legal custodian that the copy filed is a true copy and that the will has become operative under the law of the other place.

§3–304. [Informal Probate; Unavailable in Certain Cases.]

Applications for informal probate which relate to one or more of a known series of testamentary instruments (other than a will and one or more codicils thereto), the latest of which does not expressly revoke the earlier, shall be declined.

As amended in 1987.

§3–305. [Informal Probate; Registrar Not Satisfied.]

If the Registrar is not satisfied that a will is entitled to be probated in informal proceedings because of failure to meet the requirements of Sections 3–303 and 3–304 or any other reason, he may decline the application. A declination of informal probate is not an adjudication and does not preclude formal probate proceedings.

§3–306. [Informal Probate; Notice Requirements.]

[*] The moving party must give notice as described by Section 1–401 of his application for informal probate to any person demanding it pursuant to Section 3–204, and to any personal representative of the decedent whose appointment has not been terminated. No other notice of informal probate is required.

[(b) If an informal probate is granted, within 30 days thereafter the applicant shall give written information of the probate to the heirs and devisees. The information shall include the name and address of the applicant, the name and location of the court granting the informal probate, and the date of the probate. The information shall be delivered or sent by ordinary mail to each of the heirs and devisees whose address is reasonably available to the applicant. No duty to give information is incurred if a personal representative is appointed who is required to give the written information required by Section 3–705. An applicant's failure to give information as required by this section is a breach of his duty to the heirs and devisees but does not affect the validity of the probate.]

*This paragraph becomes (a) if optional subsection (b) is accepted.

§3–307. [Informal Appointment Proceedings; Delay in Order; Duty of Registrar; Effect of Appointment.]

(a) Upon receipt of an application for informal appointment of a personal representative other than a special administrator as provided in Section 3-614, if at least 120 hours have elapsed since the decedent's death, the Registrar, after making the findings required by Section 3–308, shall appoint the applicant subject to qualification and acceptance; provided, that if the decedent was a non-resident, the Registrar shall delay the order of appointment until 30 days have elapsed since death unless the personal representative appointed at the decedent's domicile is the applicant, or unless the decedent's will directs that his estate be subject to the laws of this state.

(b) The status of personal representative and the powers and duties pertaining to the office are fully established by informal appointment. An appointment, and the office of personal representative created thereby, is subject to termination as provided in Sections 3–608 through 3–612, but is not subject to retroactive vacation.

§3–308. [Informal Appointment Proceedings; Proof and Findings Required.]

(a) In informal appointment proceedings, the Registrar must determine whether:

(1) the application for informal appointment of a personal representative is complete;

(2) the applicant has made oath or affirmation that the statements contained in the application are true to the best of his knowledge and belief;

(3) the applicant appears from the application to be an interested person as defined in Section 1–201(24);

(4) on the basis of the statements in the application, venue is proper;

(5) any will to which the requested appointment relates has been formally or informally probated; but

this requirement does not apply to the appointment of a special administrator;

(6) any notice required by Section 3–204 has been given;

(7) from the statements in the application, the person whose appointment is sought has priority entitling him to the appointment.

(b) Unless Section 3–612 controls, the application must be denied if it indicates that a personal representative who has not filed a written statement of resignation as provided in Section 3–610(c) has been appointed in this or another [county] of this state, that (unless the applicant is the domiciliary personal representative or his nominee) the decedent was not domiciled in this state and that a personal representative whose appointment has not been terminated has been appointed by a Court in the state of domicile, or that other requirements of this section have not been met.

§3–309. [Informal Appointment Proceedings; Registrar Not Satisfied.]

If the Registrar is not satisfied that a requested informal appointment of a personal representative should be made because of failure to meet the requirements of Sections 3–307 and 3–308, or for any other reason, he may decline the application. A declination of informal appointment is not an adjudication and does not preclude appointment in formal proceedings.

§3–310. [Informal Appointment Proceedings; Notice Requirements.]

The moving party must give notice as described by Section 1–401 of his intention to seek an appointment informally: (1) to any person demanding it pursuant to Section 3–204; and (2) to any person having a prior or equal right to appointment not waived in writing and filed with the Court. No other notice of an informal appointment proceeding is required.

§3–311. [Informal Appointment Unavailable in Certain Cases.]

If an application for informal appointment indicates the existence of a possible unrevoked testamentary instrument which may relate to property subject to the laws of this state, and which is not filed for probate in this court, the Registrar shall decline the application.

§3–312. [Universal Succession; In General.]

The heirs of an intestate or the residuary devisees under a will, excluding minors and incapacitated, protected, or unascertained persons, may become universal successors to the decedent's estate by assuming personal liability for (1) taxes, (2) debts of the decedent, (3) claims against the decedent or the estate, and (4) distributions due other heirs, devisees, and persons entitled to prop-

erty of the decedent as provided in Sections 3–313 through 3–322.

§3-313. [Universal Succession; Application; Contents.]

(a) An application to become universal successors by the heirs of an intestate or the residuary devisees under a will must be directed to the [Registrar], signed by each applicant, and verified to be accurate and complete to the best of the applicant's knowledge and belief as follows:

(1) An application by heirs of an intestate must contain the statements required by Section 3–301(a)(1) and (4)(i) and state that the applicants constitute all the heirs other than minors and incapacitated, protected, or unascertained persons.

(2) An application by residuary devisees under a will must be combined with a petition for informal probate if the will has not been admitted to probate in this State and must contain the statements required by Section 3–301(a)(1) and (2). If the will has been probated in this State, an application by residuary devisees must contain the statements required by Section 3–301(a)(2)(iii). An application by residuary devisees must state that the applicants constitute the residuary devisees of the decedent other than any minors and incapacitated, protected, or unascertained persons. If the estate is partially intestate, all of the heirs other than minors and incapacitated, protected, or unascertained persons must join as applicants.

(b) The application must state whether letters of administration are outstanding, whether a petition for appointment of a personal representative of the decedent is pending in any court of this State, and that the applicants waive their right to seek appointment of a personal representative.

(c) The application may describe in general terms the assets of the estate and must state that the applicants accept responsibility for the estate and assume personal liability for (1) taxes, (2) debts of the decedent, (3) claims against the decedent or the estate and (4) distributions due other heirs, devisees, and persons entitled to property of the decedent as provided in Sections 3–316 through 3–322.

§3–314. [Universal Succession; Proof and Findings Required.]

(a) The [Registrar] shall grant the application if:

(1) the application is complete in accordance with Section 3–313;

(2) all necessary persons have joined and have verified that the statements contained therein are true, to the best knowledge and belief of each;

(3) venue is proper;

(4) any notice required by Section 3–204 has been given or waived;

(5) the time limit for original probate or appointment proceedings has not expired and the applicants claim under a will;

(6) the application requests informal probate of a will, the application and findings conform with Sections 3–301(a)(2) and 3–303(a)(c)(d) and (e) so the will is admitted to probate; and

(7) none of the applicants is a minor or an incapacitated or protected person.

(b) The [Registrar] shall deny the application if letters of administration are outstanding.

(c) Except as provided in Section 3–322, the [Registrar] shall deny the application if any creditor, heir, or devisee who is qualified by Section 3–605 to demand bond files an objection.

§3–315. [Universal Succession; Duty of Registrar; Effect of Statement of Universal Succession.]

Upon receipt of an application under Section 3–313, if at least 120 hours have elapsed since the decedent's death, the [Registrar], upon granting the application, shall issue a written statement of universal succession describing the estate as set forth in the application and stating that the applicants (i) are the universal successors to the assets of the estate as provided in Section 3–312, (ii) have assumed liability for the obligations of the decedent, and (iii) have acquired the powers and liabilities of universal successors. The statement of universal succession is evidence of the universal successors' title to the assets of the estate. Upon its issuance, the powers and liabilities of universal successors provided in Sections 3–316 through 3–322 attach and are assumed by the applicants.

§3–316. [Universal Succession; Universal Successors' Powers.]

Upon the [Registrar's] issuance of a statement of universal succession:

(1) Universal successors have full power of ownership to deal with the assets of the estate subject to the limitations and liabilities in this [Act]. The universal successors shall proceed expeditiously to settle and distribute the estate without adjudication but if necessary may invoke the jurisdiction of the court to resolve questions concerning the estate.

(2) Universal successors have the same powers as distributees from a personal representative under Sections 3–908 and 3–909 and third persons with whom they deal are protected as provided in Section 3–910.

(3) For purposes of collecting assets in another state whose law does not provide for universal succession, universal successors have the same standing and power as personal representatives or distributees in this State.

§3–317. [Universal Succession; Universal Successors' Liability to Creditors, Other Heirs, Devisees and Persons Entitled to Decedent's Property; Liability of Other Persons Entitled to Property.]

(a) In the proportions and subject to limits expressed in Section 3–321, universal successors assume all liabilities of the decedent that were not discharged by reason of death and liability for all taxes, claims against the decedent or the estate, and charges properly incurred after death for the preservation of the estate, to the extent those items, if duly presented, would be valid claims against the decedent's estate.

(b) In the proportions and subject to the limits expressed in Section 3–321, universal successors are personally liable to other heirs, devisees, and persons entitled to property of the decedent for the assets or amounts that would be due those heirs, were the estate administered, but no allowance having priority over devisees may be claimed for attorney's fees or charges for preservation of the estate in excess of reasonable amounts properly incurred.

(c) Universal successors are entitled to their interests in the estate as heirs or devisees subject to priority and abatement pursuant to Section 3–902 and to agreement pursuant to Section 3–912.

(d) Other heirs, devisees, and persons to whom assets have been distributed have the same powers and liabilities as distributees under Sections 3–908, 3–909, and 3–910.

(e) Absent breach of fiduciary obligations or express undertaking, a fiduciary's liability is limited to the assets received by the fiduciary.

§3–318. [Universal Succession; Universal Successors' Submission to Jurisdiction; When Heirs or Devisees May Not Seek Administration.]

(a) Upon issuance of the statement of universal succession, the universal successors become subject to the personal jurisdiction of the courts of this state in any proceeding that may be instituted relating to the estate or to any liability assumed by them.

(b) Any heir or devisee who voluntarily joins in an application under Section 3–313 may not subsequently seek appointment of a personal representative.

§3–319. [Universal Succession; Duty of Universal Successors; Information to Heirs and Devisees.]

Not later than thirty days after issuance of the statement of universal succession, each universal successor shall inform the heirs and devisees who did not join in the application of the succession without administration. The information must be delivered or be sent by ordinary mail to each of the heirs and devisees whose address is reasonably available to the universal successors. The information must include the names and addresses of the universal successors, indicate that it is being sent to persons who have or may have some interest in the estate, and describe the court where the application and statement of universal succession has been filed. The failure of a universal successor to give this information is a breach of duty to the persons concerned but does not affect the validity of the approval of succession without administration or the powers or liabilities of the universal successors. A universal successor may inform other persons of the succession without administration by delivery or by ordinary first class mail.

§3–320. [Universal Succession; Universal Successors' Liability For Restitution to Estate.]

If a personal representative is subsequently appointed, universal successors are personally liable for restitution of any property of the estate to which they are not entitled as heirs or devisees of the decedent and their liability is the same as a distributee under Section 3–909, subject to the provisions of Sections 3–317 and 3–321 and the limitations of Section 3–1006.

§3–321. [Universal Succession; Liability of Universal Successors for Claims, Expenses, Intestate Shares and Devises.]

The liability of universal successors is subject to any defenses that would have been available to the decedent. Other than liability arising from fraud, conversion, or other wrongful conduct of a universal successor, the personal liability of each universal successor to any creditor, claimant, other heir, devisee, or person entitled to decedent's property may not exceed the proportion of the claim that the universal successor's share bears to the share of all heirs and residuary devisees.

§3–322. [Universal Succession; Remedies of Creditors, Other Heirs, Devisees or Persons Entitled to Decedent's Property.]

In addition to remedies otherwise provided by law, any creditor, heir, devisee, or person entitled to decedent's property qualified under Section 3–605, may demand bond of universal successors. If the demand for bond precedes the granting of an application for universal succession, it must be treated as an objection under Section 3–314(c) unless it is withdrawn, the claim satisfied, or the applicants post bond in an amount sufficient to protect the demandant. If the demand for bond follows the granting of an application for universal succession, the universal successors, within 10 days after notice

of the demand, upon satisfying the claim or posting bond sufficient to protect the demandant, may disqualify the demandant from seeking administration of the estate.

PART 4
FORMAL TESTACY AND APPOINTMENT PROCEEDINGS

§3–401. [Formal Testacy Proceedings; Nature; When Commenced.]

A formal testacy proceeding is litigation to determine whether a decedent left a valid will. A formal testacy proceeding may be commenced by an interested person filing a petition as described in Section 3–402(a) in which he requests that the Court, after notice and hearing, enter an order probating a will, or a petition to set aside an informal probate of a will or to prevent informal probate of a will which is the subject of a pending application, or a petition in accordance with Section 3–402(b) for an order that the decedent died intestate.

A petition may seek formal probate of a will without regard to whether the same or a conflicting will has been informally probated. A formal testacy proceeding may, but need not, involve a request for appointment of a personal representative.

During the pendency of a formal testacy proceeding, the Registrar shall not act upon any application for informal probate of any will of the decedent or any application for informal appointment of a personal representative of the decedent.

Unless a petition in a formal testacy proceeding also requests confirmation of the previous informal appointment, a previously appointed personal representative, after receipt of notice of the commencement of a formal probate proceeding, must refrain from exercising his power to make any further distribution of the estate during the pendency of the formal proceeding. A petitioner who seeks the appointment of a different personal representative in a formal proceeding also may request an order restraining the acting personal representative from exercising any of the powers of his office and requesting the appointment of a special administrator. In the absence of a request, or if the request is denied, the commencement of a formal proceeding has no effect on the powers and duties of a previously appointed personal representative other than those relating to distribution.

§3–402. [Formal Testacy or Appointment Proceedings; Petition; Contents.]

(a) Petitions for formal probate of a will, or for adjudication of intestacy with or without request for appointment of a personal representative, must be directed to the Court, request a judicial order after notice and hearing and contain further statements as indicated in this section. A petition for formal probate of a will

(1) requests an order as to the testacy of the decedent in relation to a particular instrument which may or may not have been informally probated and determining the heirs,

(2) contains the statements required for informal applications as stated in the six subparagraphs under Section 3–301(a)(1), the statements required by subparagraphs (ii) and (iii) of Section 3–301(a)(2), and

(3) states whether the original of the last will of the decedent is in the possession of the Court or accompanies the petition.

If the original will is neither in the possession of the Court nor accompanies the petition and no authenticated copy of a will probated in another jurisdiction accompanies the petition, the petition also must state the contents of the will, and indicate that it is lost, destroyed, or otherwise unavailable.

(b) A petition for adjudication of intestacy and appointment of an administrator in intestacy must request a judicial finding and order that the decedent left no will and determining the heirs, contain the statements required by (1) and (4) of Section 3–301(a) and indicate whether supervised administration is sought. A petition may request an order determining intestacy and heirs without requesting the appointment of an administrator, in which case, the statements required by subparagraph (ii) of Section 3–301(a)(4) above may be omitted.

§3–403. [Formal Testacy Proceedings; Notice of Hearing on Petition.]

(a) Upon commencement of a formal testacy proceeding, the Court shall fix a time and place of hearing. Notice shall be given in the manner prescribed by Section 1–401 by the petitioner to the persons herein enumerated and to any additional person who has filed a demand for notice under Section 3–204 of this Code.

Notice shall be given to the following persons: the surviving spouse, children, and other heirs of the decedent, the devisees and executors named in any will that is being, or has been, probated, or offered for informal or formal probate in the [county,] or that is known by the petitioner to have been probated, or offered for informal or formal probate elsewhere, and any personal representative of the decedent whose appointment has not been terminated. Notice may be given to other persons. In addition, the petitioner shall give notice by publication to all unknown persons and to all known persons whose addresses are unknown who have any interest in the matters being litigated.

(b) If it appears by the petition or otherwise that the fact of the death of the alleged decedent may be in doubt, or on the written demand of any interested person, a copy of the notice of the hearing on said petition shall be sent by registered mail to the alleged decedent at his last known address. The Court shall direct the petitioner to report the results of, or make and report back concerning, a reasonably diligent search for the alleged decedent in any manner that may seem advisable, including any or all of the following methods:

(1) by inserting in one or more suitable periodicals a notice requesting information from any person having knowledge of the whereabouts of the alleged decedent;

(2) by notifying law enforcement officials and public welfare agencies in appropriate locations of the disappearance of the alleged decedent;

(3) by engaging the services of an investigator.

The costs of any search so directed shall be paid by the petitioner if there is no administration or by the estate of the decedent in case there is administration.

§3–404. [Formal Testacy Proceedings; Written Objections to Probate.]

Any party to a formal proceeding who opposes the probate of a will for any reason shall state in his pleadings his objections to probate of the will.

§3–405. [Formal Testacy Proceedings; Uncontested Cases; Hearings and Proof.]

If a petition in a testacy proceeding is unopposed, the Court may order probate or intestacy on the strength of the pleadings if satisfied that the conditions of Section 3–409 have been met, or conduct a hearing in open court and require proof of the matters necessary to support the order sought. If evidence concerning execution of the will is necessary, the affidavit or testimony of one of any attesting witnesses to the instrument is sufficient. If the affidavit or testimony of an attesting witness is not available, execution of the will may be proved by other evidence or affidavit.

§3–406. [Formal Testacy Proceedings; Contested Cases; Testimony of Attesting Witnesses.]

(a) If evidence concerning execution of an attested will which is not self-proved is necessary in contested cases, the testimony of at least one of the attesting witnesses, if within the state, competent and able to testify, is required. Due execution of an attested or unattested will may be proved by other evidence.

(b) If the will is self-proved, compliance with signature requirements for execution is conclusively presumed and other requirements of execution are presumed subject to rebuttal without the testimony of any witness upon filing the will and the acknowledgment and affidavits annexed or attached thereto, unless there is proof of fraud or forgery affecting the acknowledgment or affidavit.

§3–407. [Formal Testacy Proceedings; Burdens in Contested Cases.]

In contested cases, petitioners who seek to establish intestacy have the burden of establishing prima facie proof of death, venue, and heirship. Proponents of a will have the burden of establishing prima facie proof of due execution in all cases, and, if they are also petitioners, prima facie proof of death and venue. Contestants of a will have the burden of establishing lack of testamentary intent or capacity, undue influence, fraud, duress, mistake or revocation. Parties have the ultimate burden of persuasion as to matters with respect to which they have the initial burden of proof. If a will is opposed by the petition for probate of a later will revoking the former, it shall be determined first whether the later will is entitled to probate, and if a will is opposed by a petition for a declaration of intestacy, it shall be determined first whether the will is entitled to probate.

§3–408. [Formal Testacy Proceedings; Will Construction; Effect of Final Order in Another Jurisdiction.]

A final order of a court of another state determining testacy, the validity or construction of a will, made in a proceeding involving notice to and an opportunity for contest by all interested persons must be accepted as determinative by the courts of this state if it includes, or is based upon, a finding that the decedent was domiciled at his death in the state where the order was made.

§3–409. [Formal Testacy Proceedings; Order; Foreign Will.]

After the time required for any notice has expired, upon proof of notice, and after any hearing that may be necessary, if the Court finds that the testator is dead, venue is proper and that the proceeding was commenced within the limitation prescribed by Section 3–108, it shall determine the decedent's domicile at death, his heirs and his state of testacy. Any will found to be valid and unrevoked shall be formally probated. Termination of any previous informal appointment of a personal representative, which may be appropriate in view of the relief requested and findings, is governed by Section 3–612. The petition shall be dismissed or appropriate amendment allowed if the court is not satisfied that the alleged decedent is dead. A will from a place which does not provide for probate of a will after death, may be proved for probate in this state by a duly authenticated certificate of its legal custodian that the copy introduced is a true copy and that the will has become effective under the law of the other place.

§3–410. [Formal Testacy Proceedings; Probate of More Than One Instrument.]

If two or more instruments are offered for probate before a final order is entered in a formal testacy proceeding, more than one instrument may be probated if neither expressly revokes the other or contains provisions which work a total revocation by implication. If more than one instrument is probated, the order shall indicate what provisions control in respect to the nomination of an executor, if any. The order may, but need not, indicate how any provisions of a particular instrument are affected by the other instrument. After a final order in a testacy proceeding has been entered, no petition for probate of any other instrument of the decedent may be entertained, except incident to a petition to vacate or modify a previous probate order and subject to the time limits of Section 3–412.

§3–411. [Formal Testacy Proceedings; Partial Intestacy.]

If it becomes evident in the course of a formal testacy proceeding that, though one or more instruments are entitled to be probated, the decedent's estate is or may be partially intestate, the Court shall enter an order to that effect.

§3–412. [Formal Testacy Proceedings; Effect of Order; Vacation.]

Subject to appeal and subject to vacation as provided in this section and in Section 3–413, a formal testacy order under Sections 3–409 to 3–411, including an order that the decedent left no valid will and determining heirs, is final as to all persons with respect to all issues concerning the decedent's estate that the court considered or might have considered incident to its rendition relevant to the question of whether the decedent left a valid will, and to the determination of heirs, except that:

(1) The court shall entertain a petition for modification or vacation of its order and probate of another will of the decedent if it is shown that the proponents of the later-offered will: (i) were unaware of its existence at the time of the earlier proceeding: or (ii) were unaware of the earlier proceeding and were given no notice thereof, except by publication.

(2) If intestacy of all or part of the estate has been ordered, the determination of heirs of the decedent may be reconsidered if it is shown that one or more persons were omitted from the determination and it is also shown that the persons were unaware of their relationship to the decedent, were unaware of his death or were given no notice of any proceeding concerning his estate, except by publication.

(3) A petition for vacation under paragraph (1) or (2) must be filed prior to the earlier of the following time limits:

(i) if a personal representative has been appointed for the estate, the time of entry of any order approving final distribution of the estate, or, if the estate is closed by statement, six months after the filing of the closing statement;

(ii) whether or not a personal representative has been appointed for the estate of the decedent, the time prescribed by Section 3–108 when it is no longer possible to initiate an original proceeding to probate a will of the decedent; or

(iii) twelve months after the entry of the order sought to be vacated.

(4) The order originally rendered in the testacy proceeding may be modified or vacated, if appropriate under the circumstances, by the order of probate of the later-offered will or the order redetermining heirs.

(5) The finding of the fact of death is conclusive as to the alleged decedent only if notice of the hearing on the petition in the formal testacy proceeding was sent by registered or certified mail addressed to the alleged decedent at his last known address and the court finds that a search under Section 3–403(b) was made.

If the alleged decedent is not dead, even if notice was sent and search was made, he may recover estate assets in the hands of the personal representative. In addition to any remedies available to the alleged decedent by reason of any fraud or intentional wrongdoing, the alleged decedent may recover any estate or its proceeds from distributees that is in their hands, or the value of distributions received by them, to the extent that any recovery from distributees is equitable in view of all of the circumstances.

As amended in 1993.

§3–413. [Formal Testacy Proceedings; Vacation of Order For Other Cause.]

For good cause shown, an order in a formal testacy proceeding may be modified or vacated within the time allowed for appeal.

§3–414. [Formal Proceedings Concerning Appointment of Personal Representative.]

(a) A formal proceeding for adjudication regarding the priority or qualification of one who is an applicant for appointment as personal representative, or of one who previously has been appointed personal representative in informal proceedings, if an issue concerning the testacy of the decedent is or may be involved, is governed by Section 3–402, as well as by this section. In other cases, the petition shall contain or adopt the statements required by Section 3–301(1) and describe the question relating to priority or qualification of the personal representative which is to be resolved. If the proceeding precedes any appointment of a personal representative, it shall stay any pending informal appointment proceedings as well as any commenced thereafter. If the proceeding is commenced after appointment, the previously appointed personal representative, after receipt of notice thereof, shall refrain from exercising any power

of administration except as necessary to preserve the estate or unless the Court orders otherwise.

(b) After notice to interested persons, including all persons interested in the administration of the estate as successors under the applicable assumption concerning testacy, any previously appointed personal representative and any person having or claiming priority for appointment as personal representative, the Court shall determine who is entitled to appointment under Section 3–203, make a proper appointment and, if appropriate, terminate any prior appointment found to have been improper as provided in cases of removal under Section 3–611.

PART 5

SUPERVISED ADMINISTRATION

§3–501. [Supervised Administration; Nature of Proceeding.]

Supervised administration is a single in rem proceeding to secure complete administration and settlement of a decedent's estate under the continuing authority of the Court which extends until entry of an order approving distribution of the estate and discharging the personal representative or other order terminating the proceeding. A supervised personal representative is responsible to the Court, as well as to the interested parties, and is subject to directions concerning the estate made by the Court on its own motion or on the motion of any interested party. Except as otherwise provided in this Part, or as otherwise ordered by the Court, a supervised personal representative has the same duties and powers as a personal representative who is not supervised.

§3–502. [Supervised Administration; Petition; Order.]

A petition for supervised administration may be filed by any interested person or by a personal representative at any time or the prayer for supervised administration may be joined with a petition in a testacy or appointment proceeding. If the testacy of the decedent and the priority and qualification of any personal representative have not been adjudicated previously, the petition for supervised administration shall include the matters required of a petition in a formal testacy proceeding and the notice requirements and procedures applicable to a formal testacy proceeding apply. If not previously adjudicated, the Court shall adjudicate the testacy of the decedent and questions relating to the priority and qualifications of the personal representative in any case involving a request for supervised administration, even though the request for supervised administration may be denied. After notice to interested persons, the Court shall order supervised administration of a decedent's estate: (1) if the decedent's will directs supervised administration, it shall be ordered unless the Court finds that circumstances bearing on the need for supervised administration have changed since the execution of the will and that there is no necessity for supervised administration; (2) if the decedent's will directs unsupervised administration, supervised administration shall be ordered only upon a finding that it is necessary for protection of persons interested in the estate; or (3) in other cases if the Court finds that supervised administration is necessary under the circumstances.

§3–503. [Supervised Administration; Effect on Other Proceedings.]

(a) The pendency of a proceeding for supervised administration of a decedent's estate stays action on any informal application then pending or thereafter filed.

(b) If a will has been previously probated in informal proceedings, the effect of the filing of a petition for supervised administration is as provided for formal testacy proceedings by Section 3–401.

(c) After he has received notice of the filing of a petition for supervised administration, a personal representative who has been appointed previously shall not exercise his power to distribute any estate. The filing of the petition does not affect his other powers and duties unless the Court restricts the exercise of any of them pending full hearing on the petition.

§3–504. [Supervised Administration; Powers of Personal Representative.]

Unless restricted by the Court, a supervised personal representative has, without interim orders approving exercise of a power, all powers of personal representatives under this Code, but he shall not exercise his power to make any distribution of the estate without prior order of the Court. Any other restriction on the power of a personal representative which may be ordered by the Court must be endorsed on his letters of appointment and, unless so endorsed, is ineffective as to persons dealing in good faith with the personal representative.

§3–505. [Supervised Administration; Interim Orders; Distribution and Closing Orders.]

Unless otherwise ordered by the Court, supervised administration is terminated by order in accordance with time restrictions, notices and contents of orders prescribed for proceedings under Section 3–1001. Interim orders approving or directing partial distributions or granting other relief may be issued by the Court at any time during the pendency of a supervised administration on the application of the personal representative or any interested person.

PART 6
PERSONAL REPRESENTATIVE; APPOINTMENT, CONTROL AND TERMINATION OF AUTHORITY

§3–601. [Qualification.]

Prior to receiving letters, a personal representative shall qualify by filing with the appointing Court any required bond and a statement of acceptance of the duties of the office.

§3–602. [Acceptance of Appointment; Consent to Jurisdiction.]

By accepting appointment, a personal representative submits personally to the jurisdiction of the Court in any proceeding relating to the estate that may be instituted by any interested person. Notice of any proceeding shall be delivered to the personal representative, or mailed to him by ordinary first class mail at his address as listed in the application or petition for appointment or as thereafter reported to the Court and to his address as then known to the petitioner.

§3–603. [Bond Not Required Without Court Order, Exceptions.]

No bond is required of a personal representative appointed in informal proceedings, except (1) upon the appointment of a special administrator; (2) when an executor or other personal representative is appointed to administer an estate under a will containing an express requirement of bond or (3) when bond is required under Section 3–605. Bond may be required by court order at the time of appointment of a personal representative appointed in any formal proceeding except that bond is not required of a personal representative appointed in formal proceedings if the will relieves the personal representative of bond, unless bond has been requested by an interested party and the Court is satisfied that it is desirable. Bond required by any will may be dispensed with in formal proceedings upon determination by the Court that it is not necessary. No bond is required of any personal representative who, pursuant to statute, has deposited cash or collateral with an agency of this state to secure performance of his duties.

§3–604. [Bond Amount; Security; Procedure; Reduction.]

If bond is required and the provisions of the will or order do not specify the amount, unless stated in his application or petition, the person qualifying shall file a statement under oath with the Registrar indicating his best estimate of the value of the personal estate of the decedent and of the income expected from the personal and real estate during the next year, and he shall execute and file a bond with the Registrar, or give other suitable security, in an amount not less than the estimate.

The Registrar shall determine that the bond is duly executed by a corporate surety, or one or more individual sureties whose performance is secured by pledge of personal property, mortgage on real property or other adequate security. The Registrar may permit the amount of the bond to be reduced by the value of assets of the estate deposited with a domestic financial institution (as defined in Section 6–101) in a manner that prevents their unauthorized disposition. On petition of the personal representative or another interested person the Court may excuse a requirement of bond, increase or reduce the amount of the bond, release sureties, or permit the substitution of another bond with the same or different sureties.

§3–605. [Demand For Bond by Interested Person.]

Any person apparently having an interest in the estate worth in excess of [$1000], or any creditor having a claim in excess of [$1000], may make a written demand that a personal representative give bond. The demand must be filed with the Registrar and a copy mailed to the personal representative, if appointment and qualification have occurred. Thereupon, bond is required, but the requirement ceases if the person demanding bond ceases to be interested in the estate, or if bond is excused as provided in Section 3–603 or 3–604. After he has received notice and until the filing of the bond or cessation of the requirement of bond, the personal representative shall refrain from exercising any powers of his office except as necessary to preserve the estate. Failure of the personal representative to meet a requirement of bond by giving suitable bond within 30 days after receipt of notice is cause for his removal and appointment of a successor personal representative.

§3–606. [Terms and Conditions of Bonds.]

(a) The following requirements and provisions apply to any bond required by this Part:

(1) Bonds shall name the [state] as obligee for the benefit of the persons interested in the estate and shall be conditioned upon the faithful discharge by the fiduciary of all duties according to law.

(2) Unless otherwise provided by the terms of the approved bond, sureties are jointly and severally liable with the personal representative and with each other. The address of sureties shall be stated in the bond.

(3) By executing an approved bond of a personal representative, the surety consents to the jurisdiction of the probate court which issued letters to the primary obligor in any proceedings pertaining to the fiduciary duties of the personal representative and naming the surety as a party. Notice of any proceeding shall be delivered to the surety or mailed to him by registered or certified mail at his address as listed with the court where the bond is filed and to his address as then known to the petitioner.

(4) On petition of a successor personal representative, any other personal representative of the same decedent, or any interested person, a proceeding in the Court may be initiated against a surety for breach of the obligation of the bond of the personal representative.

(5) The bond of the personal representative is not void after the first recovery but may be proceeded against from time to time until the whole penalty is exhausted.

(b) No action or proceeding may be commenced against the surety on any matter as to which an action or proceeding against the primary obligor is barred by adjudication or limitation.

§3–607. [Order Restraining Personal Representative.]

(a) On petition of any person who appears to have an interest in the estate, the Court by temporary order may restrain a personal representative from performing specified acts of administration, disbursement, or distribution, or exercise of any powers or discharge of any duties of his office, or make any other order to secure proper performance of his duty, if it appears to the Court that the personal representative otherwise may take some action which would jeopardize unreasonably the interest of the applicant or of some other interested person. Persons with whom the personal representative may transact business may be made parties.

(b) The matter shall be set for hearing within 10 days unless the parties otherwise agree. Notice as the Court directs shall be given to the personal representative and his attorney of record, if any, and to any other parties named defendant in the petition.

§3–608. [Termination of Appointment; General.]

Termination of appointment of a personal representative occurs as indicated in Sections 3–609 to 3–612, inclusive. Termination ends the right and power pertaining to the office of personal representative as conferred by this Code or any will, except that a personal representative, at any time prior to distribution or until restrained or enjoined by court order, may perform acts necessary to protect the estate and may deliver the assets to a successor representative. Termination does not discharge a personal representative from liability for transactions or omissions occurring before termination, or relieve him of the duty to preserve assets subject to his control, to account therefor and to deliver the assets. Termination does not affect the jurisdiction of the Court over the personal representative, but terminates his authority to represent the estate in any pending or future proceeding.

§3–609. [Termination of Appointment; Death or Disability.]

The death of a personal representative or the appointment of a conservator for the estate of a personal representative, terminates his appointment. Until appointment and qualification of a successor or special representative to replace the deceased or protected representative, the representative of the estate of the deceased or protected personal representative, if any, has the duty to protect the estate possessed and being administered by his decedent or ward at the time his appointment terminates, has the power to perform acts necessary for protection and shall account for and deliver the estate assets to a successor or special personal representative upon his appointment and qualification.

§3–610. [Termination of Appointment; Voluntary.]

(a) An appointment of a personal representative terminates as provided in Section 3–1003, one year after the filing of a closing statement.

(b) An order closing an estate as provided in Section 3–1001 or 3–1002 terminates an appointment of a personal representative.

(c) A personal representative may resign his position by filing a written statement of resignation with the Registrar after he has given at least 15 days written notice to the persons known to be interested in the estate. If no one applies or petitions for appointment of a successor representative within the time indicated in the notice, the filed statement of resignation is ineffective as a termination of appointment and in any event is effective only upon the appointment and qualification of a successor representative and delivery of the assets to him.

§3–611. [Termination of Appointment by Removal; Cause; Procedure.]

(a) A person interested in the estate may petition for removal of a personal representative for cause at any time. Upon filing of the petition, the Court shall fix a time and place for hearing. Notice shall be given by the petitioner to the personal representative, and to other persons as the Court may order. Except as otherwise ordered as provided in Section 3–607, after receipt of notice of removal proceedings, the personal representative shall not act except to account, to correct maladministration or preserve the estate. If removal is ordered, the Court also shall direct by order the disposition of the assets remaining in the name of, or under the control of, the personal representative being removed.

(b) Cause for removal exists when removal would be in the best interests of the estate, or if it is shown that a personal representative or the person seeking his appointment intentionally misrepresented material facts in the proceedings leading to his appointment, or that the personal representative has disregarded an order of the Court, has become incapable of discharging the duties of his office, or has mismanaged the estate or failed to perform any duty pertaining to the office. Unless the decedent's will directs otherwise, a personal representative appointed at the decedent's domicile, incident to securing appointment of himself or his nominee as ancillary personal representative, may obtain removal of another who was appointed personal representative in this state to administer local assets.

§3–612. [Termination of Appointment; Change of Testacy Status.]

Except as otherwise ordered in formal proceedings, the probate of a will subsequent to the appointment of a personal representative in intestacy or under a will which is superseded by formal probate of another will, or the vacation of an informal probate of a will subsequent to the appointment of the personal representative thereunder, does not terminate the appointment of the personal representative although his powers may be reduced as provided in Section 3–401. Termination occurs upon appointment in informal or formal appointment proceedings of a person entitled to appointment under the later assumption concerning testacy. If no request for new appointment is made within 30 days after expiration of time for appeal from the order in formal testacy proceedings, or from the informal probate, changing the assumption concerning testacy, the previously appointed personal representative upon request may be appointed personal representative under the subsequently probated will, or as in intestacy as the case may be.

§3–613. [Successor Personal Representative.]

Parts 3 and 4 of this Article govern proceedings for appointment of a personal representative to succeed one whose appointment has been terminated. After appointment and qualification, a successor personal representative may be substituted in all actions and proceedings to which the former personal representative was a party, and no notice, process or claim which was given or served upon the former personal representative need be given to or served upon the successor in order to preserve any position or right the person giving the notice or filing the claim may thereby have obtained or preserved with reference to the former personal representative. Except as otherwise ordered by the Court, the successor personal representative has the powers and duties in respect to the continued administration which the former personal representative would have had if his appointment had not been terminated.

§3–614. [Special Administrator; Appointment.]

A special administrator may be appointed:

(1) informally by the Registrar on the application of any interested person when necessary to protect the estate

of a decedent prior to the appointment of a general personal representative or if a prior appointment has been terminated as provided in Section 3–609;

(2) in a formal proceeding by order of the Court on the petition of any interested person and finding, after notice and hearing, that appointment is necessary to preserve the estate or to secure its proper administration including its administration in circumstances where a general personal representative cannot or should not act. If it appears to the Court that an emergency exists, appointment may be ordered without notice.

§3–615. [Special Administrator; Who May Be Appointed.]

(a) If a special administrator is to be appointed pending the probate of a will which is the subject of a pending application or petition for probate, the person named executor in the will shall be appointed if available, and qualified.

(b) In other cases, any proper person may be appointed special administrator.

§3–616. [Special Administrator; Appointed Informally; Powers and Duties.]

A special administrator appointed by the Registrar in informal proceedings pursuant to Section 3–614(1) has the duty to collect and manage the assets of the estate, to preserve them, to account therefor and to deliver them to the general personal representative upon his qualification. The special administrator has the power of a personal representative under the Code necessary to perform his duties.

§3–617. [Special Administrator; Formal Proceedings; Power and Duties.]

A special administrator appointed by order of the Court in any formal proceeding has the power of a general personal representative except as limited in the appointment and duties as prescribed in the order. The appointment may be for a specified time, to perform particular acts or on other terms as the Court may direct.

§3–618. [Termination of Appointment; Special Administrator.]

The appointment of a special administrator terminates in accordance with the provisions of the order of appointment or on the appointment of a general personal representative. In other cases, the appointment of a special administrator is subject to termination as provided in Sections 3–608 through 3–611.

PART 7
DUTIES AND POWERS OF PERSONAL REPRESENTATIVES

§3-701. [Time of Accrual of Duties and Powers.]

The duties and powers of a personal representative commence upon his appointment. The powers of a personal representative relate back in time to give acts by the person appointed which are beneficial to the estate occurring prior to appointment the same effect as those occurring thereafter. Prior to appointment, a person named executor in a will may carry out written instructions of the decedent relating to his body, funeral and burial arrangements. A personal representative may ratify and accept acts on behalf of the estate done by others where the acts would have been proper for a personal representative.

§3–702. [Priority Among Different Letters.]

A person to whom general letters are issued first has exclusive authority under the letters until his appointment is terminated or modified. If, through error, general letters are afterwards issued to another, the first appointed representative may recover any property of the estate in the hands of the representative subsequently appointed, but the acts of the latter done in good faith before notice of the first letters are not void for want of validity of appointment.

§3–703. [General Duties; Relation and Liability to Persons Interested in Estate; Standing to Sue.]

(a) A personal representative is a fiduciary who shall observe the standards of care applicable to trustees as described by Section 7–302. A personal representative is under a duty to settle and distribute the estate of the decedent in accordance with the terms of any probated and effective will and this Code, and as expeditiously and efficiently as is consistent with the best interests of the estate. He shall use the authority conferred upon him by this Code, the terms of the will, if any, and any order in proceedings to which he is party for the best interests of successors to the estate.

(b) A personal representative shall not be surcharged for acts of administration or distribution if the conduct in question was authorized at the time. Subject to other obligations of administration, an informally probated will is authority to administer and distribute the estate according to its terms. An order of appointment of a personal representative, whether issued in informal or formal proceedings, is authority to distribute apparently intestate assets to the heirs of the decedent if, at the time of distribution, the personal representative is not aware of a pending testacy proceeding, a proceeding to vacate an order entered in an earlier testacy proceeding, a formal proceeding questioning his appointment or fitness to continue, or a supervised administration proceeding. Nothing in this section affects the duty of the personal representative to administer and distribute the estate in accordance with the rights of claimants, the surviving spouse, any minor and dependent children and any pretermitted child of the decedent as described elsewhere in this Code.

(c) Except as to proceedings which do not survive the death of the decedent, a personal representative of a decedent domiciled in this state at his death has the same standing to sue and be sued in the courts of this state and the courts of any other jurisdiction as his decedent had immediately prior to death.

§3–704.   [Personal Representative to Proceed Without Court Order; Exception.]

A personal representative shall proceed expeditiously with the settlement and distribution of a decedent's estate and, except as otherwise specified or ordered in regard to a supervised personal representative, do so without adjudication, order, or direction of the Court, but he may invoke the jurisdiction of the Court, in proceedings authorized by this Code, to resolve questions concerning the estate or its administration.

§3–705.   [Duty of Personal Representative; Information to Heirs and Devisees.]

Not later than 30 days after his appointment every personal representative, except any special administrator, shall give information of his appointment to the heirs and devisees, including, if there has been no formal testacy proceeding and if the personal representative was appointed on the assumption that the decedent died intestate, the devisees in any will mentioned in the application for appointment of a personal representative. The information shall be delivered or sent by ordinary mail to each of the heirs and devisees whose address is reasonably available to the personal representative. The duty does not extend to require information to persons who have been adjudicated in a prior formal testacy proceeding to have no interest in the estate. The information shall include the name and address of the personal representative, indicate that it is being sent to persons who have or may have some interest in the estate being administered, indicate whether bond has been filed, and describe the court where papers relating to the estate are on file. The information shall state that the estate is being administered by the personal representative under the [State] Probate Code without supervision by the Court but that recipients are entitled to information regarding the administration from the personal representative and can petition the Court in any matter relating to the estate, including distribution of assets and expenses of administration. The personal representative's failure to give this information is a breach of his duty to the persons concerned but does not affect the validity of his appointment, his powers or other duties. A personal representative may inform other persons of his appointment by delivery or ordinary first class mail.
As amended in 1987.

§3–706.   [Duty of Personal Representative; Inventory and Appraisement.]

Within 3 months after his appointment, a personal representative, who is not a special administrator or a successor to another representative who has previously discharged this duty, shall prepare and file or mail an inventory of property owned by the decedent at the time of his death, listing it with reasonable detail, and indicating as to each listed item, its fair market value as of the date of the decedent's death, and the type and amount of any encumbrance that may exist with reference to any item.
The personal representative shall send a copy of the inventory to interested persons who request it. He may also file the original of the inventory with the court.

§3–707.   [Employment of Appraisers.]

The personal representative may employ a qualified and disinterested appraiser to assist him in ascertaining the fair market value as of the date of the decedent's death of any asset the value of which may be subject to reasonable doubt. Different persons may be employed to appraise different kinds of assets included in the estate. The names and addresses of any appraiser shall be indicated on the inventory with the item or items he appraised.

§3–708.   [Duty of Personal Representative; Supplementary Inventory.]

If any property not included in the original inventory comes to the knowledge of a personal representative or if the personal representative learns that the value or description indicated in the original inventory for any item is erroneous or misleading, he shall make a supplementary inventory or appraisement showing the market value as of the date of the decedent's death of the new item or the revised market value or descriptions, and the appraisers or other data relied upon, if any, and file it with the Court if the original inventory was filed, or furnish copies thereof or information thereof to persons interested in the new information.

§3–709.   [Duty of Personal Representative; Possession of Estate.]

Except as otherwise provided by a decedent's will, every personal representative has a right to, and shall take possession or control of, the decedent's property, except that any real property or tangible personal property may be left with or surrendered to the person presumptively entitled thereto unless or until, in the judgment of the personal representative, possession of the property by him will be necessary for purposes of administration. The request by a personal representative for delivery of any property possessed by an heir or devisee is conclusive evidence, in any action against the heir or devisee for possession thereof, that the possession of the property by the personal representative is necessary for purposes of administration. The personal representative shall pay taxes on, and take all steps reasonably necessary for the management, protection and preservation of, the estate in his possession. He may maintain an action to recover possession of property or to determine the title thereto.

§3–710. [Power to Avoid Transfers.]

The property liable for the payment of unsecured debts of a decedent includes all property transferred by him by any means which is in law void or voidable as against his creditors, and subject to prior liens, the right to recover this property, so far as necessary for the payment of unsecured debts of the decedent, is exclusively in the personal representative.

§3–711. [Powers of Personal Representatives; In General.]

Until termination of his appointment a personal representative has the same power over the title to property of the estate that an absolute owner would have, in trust however, for the benefit of the creditors and others interested in the estate. This power may be exercised without notice, hearing, or order of court.

§3–712. [Improper Exercise of Power; Breach of Fiduciary Duty.]

If the exercise of power concerning the estate is improper, the personal representative is liable to interested persons for damage or loss resulting from breach of his fiduciary duty to the same extent as a trustee of an express trust. The rights of purchasers and others dealing with a personal representative shall be determined as provided in Sections 3-713 and 3-714.

§3–713. [Sale, Encumbrance or Transaction Involving Conflict of Interest; Voidable; Exceptions.]

Any sale or encumbrance to the personal representative, his spouse, agent or attorney, or any corporation or trust in which he has a substantial beneficial interest, or any transaction which is affected by a substantial conflict of interest on the part of the personal representative, is voidable by any person interested in the estate except one who has consented after fair disclosure, unless
(1) the will or a contract entered into by the decedent expressly authorized the transaction; or
(2) the transaction is approved by the Court after notice to interested persons.

§3–714. [Persons Dealing with Personal Representative; Protection.]

A person who in good faith either assists a personal representative or deals with him for value is protected as if the personal representative properly exercised his power. The fact that a person knowingly deals with a personal representative does not alone require the person to inquire into the existence of a power or the propriety of its exercise. Except for restrictions on powers of supervised personal representatives which are endorsed on letters as provided in Section 3–504, no provision in any will or order of court purporting to limit the power of a personal representative is effective except as to persons with actual knowledge thereof. A person is not bound to see to the proper application of estate assets paid or delivered to a personal representative. The protection here expressed extends to instances in which some procedural irregularity or jurisdictional defect occurred in proceedings leading to the issuance of letters, including a case in which the alleged decedent is found to be alive. The protection here expressed is not by substitution for that provided by comparable provisions of the laws relating to commercial transactions and laws simplifying transfers of securities by fiduciaries.

§3–715. [Transactions Authorized for Personal Representatives; Exceptions.]

Except as restricted or otherwise provided by the will or by an order in a formal proceeding and subject to the priorities stated in Section 3–902, a personal representative, acting reasonably for the benefit of the interested persons, may properly:
(1) retain assets owned by the decedent pending distribution or liquidation including those in which the representative is personally interested or which are otherwise improper for trust investment;
(2) receive assets from fiduciaries, or other sources;
(3) perform, compromise or refuse performance of the decedent's contracts that continue as obligations of the estate, as he may determine under the circumstances. In performing enforceable contracts by the decedent to convey or lease land, the personal representative, among other possible courses of action, may:
(i) execute and deliver a deed of conveyance for cash payment of all sums remaining due or the purchaser's note for the sum remaining due secured by a mortgage or deed of trust on the land; or
(ii) deliver a deed in escrow with directions that the proceeds, when paid in accordance with the escrow agreement, be paid to the successors of the decedent, as designated in the escrow agreement;
(4) satisfy written charitable pledges of the decedent irrespective of whether the pledges constituted binding obligations of the decedent or were properly presented as claims, if in the judgment of the personal representative the decedent would have wanted the pledges completed under the circumstances;

(5) if funds are not needed to meet debts and expenses currently payable and are not immediately distributable, deposit or invest liquid assets of the estate, including moneys received from the sale of other assets, in federally insured interest-bearing accounts, readily marketable secured loan arrangements or other prudent investments which would be reasonable for use by trustees generally;

(6) acquire or dispose of an asset, including land in this or another state, for cash or on credit, at public or private sale; and manage, develop, improve, exchange, partition, change the character of, or abandon an estate asset;

(7) make ordinary or extraordinary repairs or alterations in buildings or other structures, demolish any improvements, raze existing or erect new party walls or buildings;

(8) subdivide, develop or dedicate land to public use; make or obtain the vacation of plats and adjust boundaries; or adjust differences in valuation on exchange or partition by giving or receiving considerations; or dedicate easements to public use without consideration;

(9) enter for any purpose into a lease as lessor or lessee, with or without option to purchase or renew, for a term within or extending beyond the period of administration;

(10) enter into a lease or arrangement for exploration and removal of minerals or other natural resources or enter into a pooling or unitization agreement;

(11) abandon property when, in the opinion of the personal representative, it is valueless, or is so encumbered, or is in condition that it is of no benefit to the state;

(12) vote stocks or other securities in person or by general or limited proxy;

(13) pay calls, assessments, and other sums chargeable or accruing against or on account of securities, unless barred by the provisions relating to claims;

(14) hold a security in the name of a nominee or in other form without disclosure of the interest of the estate but the personal representative is liable for any act of the nominee in connection with the security so held;

(15) insure the assets of the estate against damage, loss and liability and himself against liability as to third persons;

(16) borrow money with or without security to be repaid from the estate assets or otherwise; and advance money for the protection of the estate;

(17) effect a fair and reasonable compromise with any debtor or obligor, or extend, renew or in any manner modify the terms of any obligation owing to the estate. If the personal representative holds a mortgage, pledge or other lien upon property of another person, he may, in lieu of foreclosure, accept a conveyance or transfer of encumbered assets from the owner thereof in satisfaction of the indebtedness secured by lien;

(18) pay taxes, assessments, compensation of the personal representative, and other expenses incident to the administration of the estate;

(19) sell or exercise stock subscription or conversion rights; consent, directly or through a committee or other agent, to the reorganization, consolidation, merger, dissolution, or liquidation of a corporation or other business enterprise;

(20) allocate items of income or expense to either estate income or principal, as permitted or provided by law;

(21) employ persons, including attorneys, auditors, investment advisors, or agents, even if they are associated with the personal representative, to advise or assist the personal representative in the performance of his administrative duties; act without independent investigation upon their recommendations; and instead of acting personally, employ one or more agents to perform any act of administration, whether or not discretionary;

(22) prosecute or defend claims, or proceedings in any jurisdiction for the protection of the estate and of the personal representative in the performance of his duties;

(23) sell, mortgage, or lease any real or personal property of the estate or any interest therein for cash, credit, or for part cash and part credit, and with or without security for unpaid balances;

(24) continue any unincorporated business or venture in which the decedent was engaged at the time of his death (i) in the same business form for a period of not more than 4 months from the date of appointment of a general personal representative if continuation is a reasonable means of preserving the value of the business including good will, (ii) in the same business form for any additional period of time that may be approved by order of the Court in a formal proceeding to which the persons interested in the estate are parties; or (iii) throughout the period of administration if the business is incorporated by the personal representative and if none of the probable distributees of the business who are competent adults object to its incorporation and retention in the estate;

(25) incorporate any business or venture in which the decedent was engaged at the time of his death;

(26) provide for exoneration of the personal representative from personal liability in any contract entered into on behalf of the estate;

(27) satisfy and settle claims and distribute the estate as provided in this Code.

§3–716. [Powers and Duties of Successor Personal Representative.]

A successor personal representative has the same power and duty as the original personal representative to complete the administration and distribution of the estate, as expeditiously as possible, but he shall not exercise any power expressly made personal to the executor named in the will.

§3–717. [Co-representatives; When Joint Action Required.]

If two or more persons are appointed co-representatives and unless the will provides otherwise, the concurrence of all is required on all acts connected with the administration and distribution of the estate. This restriction does not apply when any co-representative receives and receipts for property due the estate, when the concurrence of all cannot readily be obtained in the time reasonably available for emergency action necessary to preserve the estate, or when a co-representative has been delegated to act for the others. Persons dealing with a co-representative if actually unaware that another has been appointed to serve with him or if advised by the personal representative with whom they deal that he has authority to act alone for any of the reasons mentioned herein, are as fully protected as if the person with whom they dealt had been the sole personal representative.

§3–718. [Powers of Surviving Personal Representative.]

Unless the terms of the will otherwise provide, every power exercisable by personal co-representatives may be exercised by the one or more remaining after the appointment of one or more is terminated, and if one of 2 or more nominated as co-executors is not appointed, those appointed may exercise all the powers incident to the office.

§3–719. [Compensation of Personal Representative.]

A personal representative is entitled to reasonable compensation for his services. If a will provides for compensation of the personal representative and there is no contract with the decedent regarding compensation, he may renounce the provision before qualifying and be entitled to reasonable compensation. A personal representative also may renounce his right to all or any part of the compensation. A written renunciation of fee may be filed with the Court.

§3–720. [Expenses in Estate Litigation.]

If any personal representative or person nominated as personal representative defends or prosecutes any proceeding in good faith, whether successful or not he is entitled to receive from the estate his necessary expenses and disbursements including reasonable attorneys' fees incurred.

§3–721. [Proceedings for Review of Employment of Agents and Compensation of Personal Representatives and Employees of Estate.]

After notice to all interested persons or on petition of an interested person or on appropriate motion if administration is supervised, the propriety of employment of any person by a personal representative including any attorney, auditor, investment advisor or other specialized agent or assistant, the reasonableness of the compensation of any person so employed, or the reasonableness of the compensation determined by the personal representative for his own services, may be reviewed by the Court. Any person who has received excessive compensation from an estate for services rendered may be ordered to make appropriate refunds.

PART 8
CREDITORS' CLAIMS

§3–801. [Notice to Creditors.]

(a) Unless notice has already been given under this section, a personal representative upon appointment [may] [shall] publish a notice to creditors once a week for three successive weeks in a newspaper of general circulation in the [county] announcing the appointment and the personal representative's address and notifying creditors of the estate to present their claims within four months after the date of the first publication of the notice or be forever barred.

(b) A personal representative may give written notice by mail or other delivery to a creditor, notifying the creditor to present his [or her] claim within four months after the published notice, if given as provided in subsection (a), or within 60 days after the mailing or other delivery of the notice, whichever is later, or be forever barred. Written notice must be the notice described in subsection (a) above or a similar notice.

(c) The personal representative is not liable to a creditor or to a successor of the decedent for giving or failing to give notice under this section.

As amended in 1989.

§3–802. [Statutes of Limitations.]

(a) Unless an estate is insolvent, the personal representative, with the consent of all successors whose interests would be affected, may waive any defense of limitations available to the estate. If the defense is not waived, no claim barred by a statute of limitations at the time of the decedent's death may be allowed or paid.

(b) The running of a statute of limitations measured from an event other than death or the giving of notice to creditors is suspended for four months after the decedent's death, but resumes thereafter as to claims not barred by other sections.

(c) For purposes of a statute of limitations, the presentation of a claim pursuant to Section 3–804 is equivalent to commencement of a proceeding on the claim.
As amended in 1989.

§3–803. [Limitations on Presentation of Claims.]

(a) All claims against a decedent's estate which arose before the death of the decedent, including claims of the state and any subdivision thereof, whether due or to become due, absolute or contingent, liquidated or unliquidated, founded on contract, tort, or other legal basis, if not barred earlier by another statute of limitations or non-claim statute, are barred against the estate, the personal representative, and the heirs and devisees of the decedent, unless presented within the earlier of the following:

(1) one year after the decedent's death; or

(2) the time provided by Section 3–801(b) for creditors who are given actual notice, and within the time provided in 3–801(a) for all creditors barred by publication.

(b) A claim described in subsection (a) which is barred by the non-claim statute of the decedent's domicile before the giving of notice to creditors in this State is barred in this State.

(c) All claims against a decedent's estate which arise at or after the death of the decedent, including claims of the state and any subdivision thereof, whether due or to become due, absolute or contingent, liquidated or unliquidated, founded on contract, tort, or other legal basis, are barred against the estate, the personal representative, and the heirs and devisees of the decedent, unless presented as follows:

(1) a claim based on a contract with the personal representative, within four months after performance by the personal representative is due; or

(2) any other claim, within the later of four months after it arises, or the time specified in subsection (a)(1).

(d) Nothing in this section affects or prevents:

(1) any proceeding to enforce any mortgage, pledge, or other lien upon property of the estate;

(2) to the limits of the insurance protection only, any proceeding to establish liability of the decedent or the personal representative for which he is protected by liability insurance; or

(3) collection of compensation for services rendered and reimbursement for expenses advanced by the personal representative or by the attorney or accountant for the personal representative of the estate.
As amended in 1989.

§3–804. [Manner of Presentation of Claims.]

Claims against a decedent's estate may be presented as follows:

(1) The claimant may deliver or mail to the personal representative a written statement of the claim indicating its basis, the name and address of the claimant, and the amount claimed, or may file a written statement of the claim, in the form prescribed by rule, with the clerk of the Court. The claim is deemed presented on the first to occur of receipt of the written statement of claim by the personal representative, or the filing of the claim with the Court. If a claim is not yet due, the date when it will become due shall be stated. If the claim is contingent or unliquidated, the nature of the uncertainty shall be stated. If the claim is secured, the security shall be described. Failure to describe correctly the security, the nature of any uncertainty, and the due date of a claim not yet due does not invalidate the presentation made.

(2) The claimant may commence a proceeding against the personal representative in any Court where the personal representative may be subjected to jurisdiction, to obtain payment of his claim against the estate, but the commencement of the proceeding must occur within the time limited for presenting the claim. No presentation of claim is required in regard to matters claimed in proceedings against the decedent which were pending at the time of his death.

(3) If a claim is presented under subsection (1), no proceeding thereon may be commenced more than 60 days after the personal representative has failed a notice of disallowance; but, in the case of a claim which is not presently due or which is contingent or unliquidated, the personal representative may consent to an extension of the 60-day period, or to avoid injustice the Court, on petition, may order an extension of the 60-day period, but in no event shall the extension run beyond the applicable statute of limitations.

§3–805. [Classification of Claims.]

(a) If the applicable assets of the estate are insufficient to pay all claims in full, the personal representative shall make payment in the following order:

(1) costs and expenses of administration;

(2) reasonable funeral expenses;

(3) debts and taxes with preference under federal law;

(4) reasonable and necessary medical and hospital expenses of the last illness of the decedent, including compensation of persons attending him;

(5) debts and taxes with preference under other laws of this state;

(6) all other claims.

(b) No preference shall be given in the payment of any claim over any other claim of the same class, and a claim due and payable shall not be entitled to a preference over claims not due.

§3–806. [Allowance of Claims.]

(a) As to claims presented in the manner described in Section 3–804 within the time limit prescribed in 3–803, the personal representative may mail a notice to any claimant stating that the claim has been disallowed. If, after allowing or disallowing a claim, the personal representative changes his decision concerning the claim, he shall notify the claimant. The personal representative may not change a disallowance of a claim after the time for the claimant to file a petition for allowance or to commence a proceeding on the claim has run and the claim has been barred. Every claim which is disallowed in whole or in part by the personal representative is barred so far as not allowed unless the claimant files a petition for allowance in the Court or commences a proceeding against the personal representative not later than 60 days after the mailing of the notice of disallowance or partial allowance if the notice warns the claimant of the impending bar. Failure of the personal representative to mail notice to a claimant of action on his claim for 60 days after the time for original presentation of the claim has expired has the effect of a notice of allowance.

(b) After allowing or disallowing a claim the personal representative may change the allowance or disallowance as hereafter provided. The personal representative may prior to payment change the allowance to a disallowance in whole or in part, but not after allowance by a court order or judgment or an order directing payment of the claim. He shall notify the claimant of the change to disallowance, and the disallowed claim is then subject to bar as provided in subsection (a). The personal representative may change a disallowance to an allowance, in whole or in part, until it is barred under subsection (a); after it is barred, it may be allowed and paid only if the estate is solvent and all successors whose interests would be affected consent.

(c) Upon the petition of the personal representative or of a claimant in a proceeding for the purpose, the Court may allow in whole or in part any claim or claims presented to the personal representative or filed with the clerk of the Court in due time and not barred by subsection (a) of this section. Notice in this proceeding shall be given to the claimant, the personal representative and those other persons interested in the estate as the Court may direct by order entered at the time the proceeding is commenced.

(d) A judgment in a proceeding in another court against a personal representative to enforce a claim against a decedent's estate is an allowance of the claim.

(e) Unless otherwise provided in any judgment in another court entered against the personal representative, allowed claims bear interest at the legal rate for the pe-

riod commencing 60 days after the time for original presentation of the claim has expired unless based on a contract making a provision for interest, in which case they bear interest in accordance with that provision.
As amended in 1987.

§3–807. [Payment of Claims.]

(a) Upon the expiration of the earlier of the time limitations provided in Section 3–803 for the presentation of claims, the personal representative shall proceed to pay the claims allowed against the estate in the order of priority prescribed, after making provision for homestead, family and support allowances, for claims already presented that have not yet been allowed or whose allowance has been appealed, and for unbarred claims that may yet be presented, including costs and expenses of administration. By petition to the Court in a proceeding for the purpose, or by appropriate motion if the administration is supervised, a claimant whose claim has been allowed but not paid may secure an order directing the personal representative to pay the claim to the extent funds of the estate are available to pay it.

(b) The personal representative at any time may pay any just claim that has not been barred, with or without formal presentation, but is personally liable to any other claimant whose claim is allowed and who is injured by its payment if:

(1) payment was made before the expiration of the time limit stated in subsection (a) and the personal representative failed to require the payee to give adequate security for the refund of any of the payment necessary to pay other claimants; or

(2) payment was made, due to negligence or willful fault of the personal representative, in such manner as to deprive the injured claimant of priority.
As amended in 1989.

§3–808. [Individual Liability of Personal Representative.]

(a) Unless otherwise provided in the contract, a personal representative is not individually liable on a contract properly entered into in his fiduciary capacity in the course of administration of the estate unless he fails to reveal his representative capacity and identify the estate in the contract.

(b) A personal representative is individually liable for obligations arising from ownership or control of the estate or for torts committed in the course of administration of the estate only if he is personally at fault.

(c) Claims based on contracts entered into by a personal representative in his fiduciary capacity, on obligations arising from ownership or control of the estate or on torts committed in the course of estate administration may be asserted against the estate by proceeding against the personal representative in his fiduciary capacity, whether or not the personal representative is individually liable therefor.

(d) Issues of liability as between the estate and the personal representative individually may be determined in a proceeding for accounting, surcharge or indemnification or other appropriate proceeding.

§3–809. [Secured Claims.]

Payment of a secured claim is upon the basis of the amount allowed if the creditor surrenders his security; otherwise payment is upon the basis of one of the following:

(1) if the creditor exhausts his security before receiving payment, [unless precluded by other law] upon the amount of the claim allowed less the fair value of the security; or

(2) if the creditor does not have the right to exhaust his security or has not done so, upon the amount of the claim allowed less the value of the security determined by converting it into money according to the terms of the agreement pursuant to which the security was delivered to the creditor, or by the creditor and personal representative by agreement, arbitration, compromise or litigation.

§3–810. [Claims Not Due and Contingent or Unliquidated Claims.]

(a) If a claim which will become due at a future time or a contingent or unliquidated claim becomes due or certain before the distribution of the estate, and if the claim has been allowed or established by a proceeding, it is paid in the same manner as presently due and absolute claims of the same class.

(b) In other cases the personal representative or, on petition of the personal representative or the claimant in a special proceeding for the purpose, the Court may provide for payment as follows:

(1) if the claimant consents, he may be paid the present or agreed value of the claim, taking any uncertainty into account;

(2) arrangement for future payment, or possible payment, on the happening of the contingency or on liquidation may be made by creating a trust, giving a mortgage, obtaining a bond or security from a distributee, or otherwise.

§3–811. [Counterclaims.]

In allowing a claim the personal representative may deduct any counterclaim which the estate has against the claimant. In determining a claim against an estate a Court shall reduce the amount allowed by the amount of any counterclaims and, if the counterclaims exceed the claim, render a judgment against the claimant in the amount of the excess. A counterclaim, liquidated or unliquidated, may arise from a transaction other than that upon which the claim is based. A counterclaim may give rise to relief exceeding in amount or different in kind from that sought in the claim.

§3–812. [Execution and Levies Prohibited.]

No execution may issue upon nor may any levy be made against any property of the estate under any judgment against a decedent or a personal representative, but this section shall not be construed to prevent the enforcement of mortgages, pledges or liens upon real or personal property in an appropriate proceeding.

§3–813. [Compromise of Claims.]

When a claim against the estate has been presented in any manner, the personal representative may, if it appears for the best interest of the estate, compromise the claim, whether due or not due, absolute or contingent, liquidated or unliquidated.

§3–814. [Encumbered Assets.]

If any assets of the estate are encumbered by mortgage, pledge, lien, or other security interest, the personal representative may pay the encumbrance or any part thereof, renew or extend any obligation secured by the encumbrance or convey or transfer the assets to the creditor in satisfaction of his lien, in whole or in part, whether or not the holder of the encumbrance has presented a claim, if it appears to be for the best interest of the estate. Payment of an encumbrance does not increase the share of the distributee entitled to the encumbered assets unless the distributee is entitled to exoneration.

§3–815. [Administration in More Than One State; Duty of Personal Representative.]

(a) All assets of estates being administered in this state are subject to all claims, allowances and charges existing or established against the personal representative wherever appointed.

(b) If the estate either in this state or as a whole is insufficient to cover all family exemptions and allowances determined by the law of the decedent's domicile, prior charges and claims, after satisfaction of the exemptions, allowances and charges, each claimant whose claim has been allowed either in this state or elsewhere in administrations of which the personal representative is aware, is entitled to receive payment of an equal proportion of his claim. If a preference or security in regard to a claim is allowed in another jurisdiction but not in this state, the creditor so benefited is to receive dividends from local assets only upon the balance of his claim after deducting the amount of the benefit.

(c) In case the family exemptions and allowances, prior charges and claims of the entire estate exceed the total value of the portions of the estate being administered separately and this state is not the state of the decedent's last domicile, the claims allowed in this state shall be paid their proportion if local assets are adequate for the purpose, and the balance of local assets shall be transferred to the domiciliary personal representative. If local assets are not sufficient to pay all claims allowed in this state the amount to which they are entitled, local assets shall be marshalled so that each claim allowed in this state is paid its proportion as far as possible, after taking into account all dividends on claims allowed in this state from assets in other jurisdictions.

§3–816. [Final Distribution to Domiciliary Representative.]

The estate of a non-resident decedent being administered by a personal representative appointed in this state shall, if there is a personal representative of the decedent's domicile willing to receive it, be distributed to the domiciliary personal representative for the benefit of the successors of the decedent unless (1) by virtue of the decedent's will, if any, and applicable choice of law rules, the successors are identified pursuant to the local law of this state without reference to the local law of the decedent's domicile; (2) the personal representative of this state, after reasonable inquiry, is unaware of the existence or identity of a domiciliary personal representative; or (3) the Court orders otherwise in a proceeding for a closing order under Section 3–1001 or incident to the closing of a supervised administration. In other cases, distribution of the estate of a decedent shall be made in accordance with the other Parts of this Article.

PART 9
SPECIAL PROVISIONS RELATING TO DISTRIBUTION

§3–901. [Successors' Rights if No Administration.]

In the absence of administration, the heirs and devisees are entitled to the estate in accordance with the terms of a probated will or the laws of intestate succession. Devisees may establish title by the probated will to devised property. Persons entitled to property by homestead allowance, exemption or intestacy may establish title thereto by proof of the decedent's ownership, his death, and their relationship to the decedent. Successors take subject to all charges incident to administration, including the claims of creditors and allowances of surviving spouse and dependent children, and subject to the rights of others resulting from abatement, retainer, advancement, and ademption.

§3–902. [Distribution; Order in Which Assets Appropriated; Abatement.]

(a) Except as provided in subsection (b) and except as provided in connection with the share of the surviving spouse who elects to take an elective share, shares of distributees abate, without any preference or priority as between real and personal property, in the following order: (1) property not disposed of by the will; (2) residuary devises; (3) general devises; (4) specific devises. For purposes of abatement, a general devise charged on any specific property or fund is a specific devise to the extent of the value of the property on which it is charged, and upon the failure or insufficiency of the property on which it is charged, a general devise to the extent of the failure or insufficiency. Abatement within each classification is in proportion to the amounts of property each of the beneficiaries would have received if full distribution of the property had been made in accordance with the terms of the will.

(b) If the will expresses an order of abatement, or if the testamentary plan or the express or implied purpose of the devise would be defeated by the order of abatement stated in subsection (a), the shares of the distributees abate as may be found necessary to give effect to the intention of the testator.

(c) If the subject of a preferred devise is sold or used incident to administration, abatement shall be achieved by appropriate adjustments in, or contribution from, other interests in the remaining assets.

[§3–902A. [Distribution; Order in Which Assets Appropriated; Abatement.]

(addendum for adoption in community property states)

[(a) and (b) as above.]

(c) If an estate of a decedent consists partly of separate property and partly of community property, the debts and expenses of administration shall be apportioned and charged against the different kinds of property in proportion to the relative value thereof.

[(d) same as (c) in common law state.]]

§3–903. [Right of Retainer.]

The amount of a non-contingent indebtedness of a successor to the estate if due, or its present value if not due, shall be offset against the successor's interest; but the successor has the benefit of any defense which would be available to him in a direct proceeding for recovery of the debt.

§3–904. [Interest on General Pecuniary Devise.]

General pecuniary devises bear interest at the legal rate beginning one year after the first appointment of a personal representative until payment, unless a contrary intent is indicated by the will.

§3–905. [Penalty Clause for Contest.]

A provision in a will purporting to penalize any interested person for contesting the will or instituting other proceedings relating to the estate is unenforceable if probable cause exists for instituting proceedings.

§3–906. [Distribution in Kind; Valuation; Method.]
(a) Unless a contrary intention is indicated by the will, the distributable assets of a decedent's estate shall be distributed in kind to the extent possible through application of the following provisions:

(1) A specific devisee is entitled to distribution of the thing devised to him, and a spouse or child who has selected particular assets of an estate as provided in Section 2–403 shall receive the items selected.

(2) Any homestead or family allowance or devise of a stated sum of money may be satisfied in kind provided

(i) the person entitled to the payment has not demanded payment in cash;

(ii) the property distributed in kind is valued at fair market value as of the date of its distribution, and

(iii) no residuary devisee has requested that the asset in question remain a part of the residue of the estate.

(3) For the purpose of valuation under paragraph (2) securities regularly traded on recognized exchanges, if distributed in kind, are valued at the price for the last sale of like securities traded on the business day prior to distribution, or if there was no sale on that day, at the median between amounts bid and offered at the close of that day. Assets consisting of sums owed the decedent or the estate by solvent debtors as to which there is no known dispute or defense are valued at the sum due with accrued interest or discounted to the date of distribution. For assets which do not have readily ascertainable values, a valuation as of a date not more than 30 days prior to the date of distribution, if otherwise reasonable, controls. For purposes of facilitating distribution, the personal representative may ascertain the value of the assets as of the time of the proposed distribution in any reasonable way, including the employment of qualified appraisers, even if the assets may have been previously appraised.

(4) The residuary estate shall be distributed in any equitable manner.

(b) After the probable charges against the estate are known, the personal representative may mail or deliver a proposal for distribution to all persons who have a right to object to the proposed distribution. The right of any distributee to object to the proposed distribution on the basis of the kind or value of asset he is to receive, if not waived earlier in writing, terminates if he fails to object in writing received by the personal representative within 30 days after mailing or delivery of the proposal. As amended in 1987.

§3–907. [Distribution in Kind; Evidence.]
If distribution in kind is made, the personal representative shall execute an instrument or deed of distribution assigning, transferring or releasing the assets to the distributee as evidence of the distributee's title to the property.

§3–908. [Distribution; Right or Title of Distributee.]
Proof that a distributee has received an instrument or deed of distribution of assets in kind, or payment in distribution, from a personal representative, is conclusive evidence that the distributee has succeeded to the interest of the estate in the distributed assets, as against all persons interested in the estate, except that the personal representative may recover the assets or their value if the distribution was improper.

§3–909. [Improper Distribution; Liability of Distributee.]
Unless the distribution or payment no longer can be questioned because of adjudication, estoppel, or limitation, a distributee of property improperly distributed or paid, or a claimant who was improperly paid, is liable to return the property improperly received and its income since distribution if he has the property. If he does not have the property, then he is liable to return the value as of the date of disposition of the property improperly received and its income and gain received by him.

§3–910. [Purchasers from Distributees Protected.]
If property distributed in kind or a security interest therein is acquired for value by a purchaser from or lender to a distributee who has received an instrument or deed of distribution from the personal representative, or is so acquired by a purchaser from or lender to a transferee from such distributee, the purchaser or lender takes title free of rights of any interested person in the estate and incurs no personal liability to the estate, or to any interested person, whether or not the distribution was proper or supported by court order or the authority of the personal representative was terminated before execution of the instrument or deed. This section protects a purchaser from or lender to a distributee who, as personal representative, has executed a deed of distribution to himself, as well as a purchaser from or lender to any other distributee or his transferee. To be protected under this provision, a purchaser or lender need not inquire whether a personal representative acted properly in making the distribution in kind, even if the personal representative and the distributee are the same person, or whether the authority of the personal representative had terminated before the distribution. Any recorded instrument described in this section on which a state documentary fee is noted pursuant to [insert appropriate reference] shall be prima facie evidence that such transfer was made for value.

§3–911. [Partition for Purpose of Distribution.]
When two or more heirs or devisees are entitled to distribution of undivided interests in any real or personal

property of the estate, the personal representative or one or more of the heirs or devisees may petition the Court prior to the formal or informal closing of the estate, to make partition. After notice to the interested heirs or devisees, the Court shall partition the property in the same manner as provided by the law for civil actions of partition. The Court may direct the personal representative to sell any property which cannot be partitioned without prejudice to the owners and which cannot conveniently be allotted to any one party.

§3–912. [Private Agreements Among Successors to Decedent Binding on Personal Representative.]

Subject to the rights of creditors and taxing authorities, competent successors may agree among themselves to alter the interests, shares, or amounts to which they are entitled under the will of the decedent, or under the laws of intestacy, in any way that they provide in a written contract executed by all who are affected by its provisions. The personal representative shall abide by the terms of the agreement subject to his obligation to administer the estate for the benefit of creditors, to pay all taxes and costs of administration, and to carry out the responsibilities of his office for the benefit of any successors of the decedent who are not parties. Personal representatives of decedents' estates are not required to see to the performance of trusts if the trustee thereof is another person who is willing to accept the trust. Accordingly, trustees of a testamentary trust are successors for the purposes of this section. Nothing herein relieves trustees of any duties owed to beneficiaries of trusts.

§3–913. [Distributions to Trustee.]

(a) Before distributing to a trustee, the personal representative may require that the trust be registered if the state in which it is to be administered provides for registration and that the trustee inform the beneficiaries as provided in Section 7–303.

(b) If the trust instrument does not excuse the trustee from giving bond, the personal representative may petition the appropriate Court to require that the trustee post bond if he apprehends that distribution might jeopardize the interests of persons who are not able to protect themselves, and he may withhold distribution until the Court has acted.

(c) No inference of negligence on the part of the personal representative shall be drawn from his failure to exercise the authority conferred by subsections (a) and (b).

§[§3–914. [Disposition of Unclaimed Assets.]

(a) If an heir, devisee or claimant cannot be found, the personal representative shall distribute the share of the missing person to his conservator, if any, otherwise to the [state treasurer] to become a part of the [state escheat fund].

(b) The money received by [state treasurer] shall be paid to the person entitled on proof of his right thereto or, if the [state treasurer] refuses or fails to pay, the person may petition the Court which appointed the personal representative, whereupon the Court upon notice to the [state treasurer] may determine the person entitled to the money and order the [treasurer] to pay it to him. No interest is allowed thereon and the heir, devisee or claimant shall pay all costs and expenses incident to the proceeding. If no petition is made to the [court] within 8 years after payment to the [state treasurer], the right of recovery is barred.]

§3–915. [Distribution to Person Under Disability.]

(a) A personal representative may discharge his obligation to distribute to any person under legal disability by distributing in a manner expressly provided in the will.

(b) Unless contrary to an express provision in the will, the personal representative may discharge his obligation to distribute to a minor or person under other disability as authorized by Section 5–101 or any other statute. If the personal representative knows that a conservator has been appointed or that a proceeding for appointment of a conservator is pending, the personal representative is authorized to distribute only to the conservator.

(c) If the heir or devisee is under disability other than minority, the personal representative is authorized to distribute to:

(1) an attorney in fact who has authority under a power of attorney to receive property for that person; or

(2) the spouse, parent or other close relative with whom the person under disability resides if the distribution is of amounts not exceeding [$10,000] a year, or property not exceeding [$10,000] in value, unless the court authorizes a larger amount or greater value.

Persons receiving money or property for the disabled person are obligated to apply the money or property to the support of that person, but may not pay themselves except by way of reimbursement for out-of-pocket expenses for goods and services necessary for the support of the disabled person. Excess sums must be preserved for future support of the disabled person. The personal representative is not responsible for the proper application of money or property distributed pursuant to this subsection.

As amended in 1987.

§3–916. [Apportionment of Estate Taxes.]

(a) For purposes of this section:

(1) "estate" means the gross estate of a decedent as determined for the purpose of federal estate tax and the estate tax payable to this state;

(2) "person" means any individual, partnership, association, joint stock company, corporation,

government, political subdivision, governmental agency, or local governmental agency;

(3) "person interested in the estate" means any person entitled to receive, or who has received, from a decedent or by reason of the death of a decedent any property or interest therein included in the decedent's estate. It includes a personal representative, conservator, and trustee;

(4) "state" means any state, territory, or possession of the United States, the District of Columbia, and the Commonwealth of Puerto Rico;

(5) "tax" means the federal estate tax and the additional inheritance tax imposed by _____ and interest and penalties imposed in addition to the tax;

(6) "fiduciary" means personal representative or trustee.

(b) Except as provided in subsection (i) and, unless the will otherwise provides, the tax shall be apportioned among all persons interested in the estate. The apportionment is to be made in the proportion that the value of the interest of each person interested in the estate bears to the total value of the interests of all persons interested in the estate. The values used in determining the tax are to be used for that purpose. If the decedent's will directs a method of apportionment of tax different from the method described in this Code, the method described in the will controls.

(c)(1) The Court in which venue lies for the administration of the estate of a decedent, on petition for the purpose may determine the apportionment of the tax.

(2) If the Court finds that it is inequitable to apportion interest and penalties in the manner provided in subsection (b), because of special circumstances, it may direct apportionment thereof in the manner it finds equitable.

(3) If the Court finds that the assessment of penalties and interest assessed in relation to the tax is due to delay caused by the negligence of the fiduciary, the Court may charge him with the amount of the assessed penalties and interest.

(4) In any action to recover from any person interested in the estate the amount of the tax apportioned to the person in accordance with this Code the determination of the Court in respect thereto shall be prima facie correct.

(d)(1) The personal representative or other person in possession of the property of the decedent required to pay the tax may withhold from any property distributable to any person interested in the estate, upon its distribution to him, the amount of tax attributable to his interest. If the property in possession of the personal representative or other person required to pay the tax and distributable to any person interested in the estate is insufficient to satisfy the proportionate amount of the

tax determined to be due from the person, the personal representative or other person required to pay the tax may recover the deficiency from the person interested in the estate. If the property is not in the possession of the personal representative or the other person required to pay the tax, the personal representative or the other person required to pay the tax may recover from any person interested in the estate the amount of the tax apportioned to the person in accordance with this Act.

(2) If property held by the personal representative is distributed prior to final apportionment of the tax, the distributee shall provide a bond or other security for the apportionment liability in the form and amount prescribed by the personal representative.

(e)(1) In making an apportionment, allowances shall be made for any exemptions granted, any classification made of persons interested in the estate and for any deductions and credits allowed by the law imposing the tax.

(2) Any exemption or deduction allowed by reason of the relationship of any person to the decedent or by reason of the purposes of the gift inures to the benefit of the person bearing such relationship or receiving the gift; but if an interest is subject to a prior present interest which is not allowable as a deduction, the tax apportionable against the present interest shall be paid from principal.

(3) Any deduction for property previously taxed and any credit for gift taxes or death taxes of a foreign country paid by the decedent or his estate inures to the proportionate benefit of all persons liable to apportionment.

(4) Any credit for inheritance, succession or estate taxes or taxes in the nature thereof applicable to property or interests includable in the estate, inures to the benefit of the persons or interests chargeable with the payment thereof to the extent proportionately that the credit reduces the tax.

(5) To the extent that property passing to or in trust for a surviving spouse or any charitable, public or similar purpose is not an allowable deduction for purposes of the tax solely by reason of an inheritance tax or other death tax imposed upon and deductible from the property, the property is not included in the computation provided for in subsection (b) hereof, and to that extent no apportionment is made against the property. The sentence immediately preceding does not apply to any case if the result would be to deprive the estate of a deduction otherwise allowable under Section 2053(d) of the Internal Revenue Code of 1954, as amended, of the United States, relating to deduction for state death taxes on transfers for public, charitable, or religious uses.

(f) No interest in income and no estate for years or for life or other temporary interest in any property or fund is subject to apportionment as between the temporary interest and the remainder. The tax on the temporary interest and the tax, if any, on the remainder is chargeable against the corpus of the property or funds subject to the temporary interest and remainder.

(g) Neither the personal representative nor other person required to pay the tax is under any duty to institute any action to recover from any person interested in the estate the amount of the tax apportioned to the person until the expiration of the 3 months next following final determination of the tax. A personal representative or other person required to pay the tax who institutes the action within a reasonable time after the 3 months' period is not subject to any liability or surcharge because any portion of the tax apportioned to any person interested in the estate was collectible at a time following the death of the decedent but thereafter became uncollectible. If the personal representative or other person required to pay the tax cannot collect from any person interested in the estate the amount of the tax apportioned to the person, the amount not recoverable shall be equitably apportioned among the other persons interested in the estate who are subject to apportionment.

(h) A personal representative acting in another state or a person required to pay the tax domiciled in another state may institute an action in the courts of this state and may recover a proportionate amount of the federal estate tax, of an estate tax payable to another state or of a death duty due by a decedent's estate to another state, from a person interested in the estate who is either domiciled in this state or who owns property in this state subject to attachment or execution. For the purposes of the action the determination of apportionment by the Court having jurisdiction of the administration of the decedent's estate in the other state is prima facie correct.

(i) If the liabilities of persons interested in the estate as prescribed by this act differ from those which result under the Federal Estate tax law, the liabilities imposed by the federal law will control and the balance of this Section shall apply as if the resulting liabilities had been prescribed herein.

As amended in 1982.

PART 10
CLOSING ESTATES

§3–1001. [Formal Proceedings Terminating Administration; Testate or Intestate; Order of General Protection.]

(a) A personal representative or any interested person may petition for an order of complete settlement of the estate. The personal representative may petition at any time, and any other interested person may petition after one year from the appointment of the original personal representative except that no petition under this section may be entertained until the time for presenting claims which arose prior to the death of the decedent has expired. The petition may request the Court to determine testacy, if not previously determined, to consider the final account or compel or approve an accounting and distribution, to construe any will or determine heirs and adjudicate the final settlement and distribution of the estate. After notice to all interested persons and hearing the Court may enter an order or orders, on appropriate conditions, determining the persons entitled to distribution of the estate, and, as circumstances require, approving settlement and directing or approving distribution of the estate and discharging the personal representative from further claim or demand of any interested person.

(b) If one or more heirs or devisees were omitted as parties in, or were not given notice of, a previous formal testacy proceeding, the Court, on proper petition for an order of complete settlement of the estate under this section, and after notice to the omitted or unnotified persons and other interested parties determined to be interested on the assumption that the previous order concerning testacy is conclusive as to those given notice of the earlier proceeding, may determine testacy as it affects the omitted persons and confirm or alter the previous order of testacy as it affects all interested persons as appropriate in the light of the new proofs. In the absence of objection by an omitted or unnotified person, evidence received in the original testacy proceeding shall constitute prima facie proof of due execution of any will previously admitted to probate, or of the fact that the decedent left no valid will if the prior proceedings determined this fact.

§3–1002. [Formal Proceedings Terminating Testate Administration; Order Construing Will Without Adjudicating Testacy.]

A personal representative administering an estate under an informally probated will or any devisee under an informally probated will may petition for an order of settlement of the estate which will not adjudicate the testacy status of the decedent. The personal representative may petition at any time, and a devisee may petition after one year, from the appointment of the original personal representative, except that no petition under this section may be entertained until the time for presenting claims which arose prior to the death of the decedent has expired. The petition may request the Court to consider the final account or compel or approve an accounting and distribution, to construe the will and adjudicate final settlement and distribution of the estate. After notice to all devisees and the personal representative and hearing, the Court may enter an order or orders, on appropriate conditions, determining the persons entitled to distribution of the estate under the will, and, as circumstances require, approving settlement and directing or approving distribution of the estate and discharging the personal representative from further claim or demand of any devisee who is a party to the proceeding and those he represents. If it appears that a part of the estate is intestate, the proceedings shall be dismissed or amendments made to meet the provisions of Section 3–1001.

§3–1003. [Closing Estates; By Sworn Statement of Personal Representative.]

(a) Unless prohibited by order of the Court and except for estates being administered in supervised administration proceedings, a personal representative may close an estate by filing with the court no earlier than six months after the date of original appointment of a general personal representative for the estate, a verified statement stating that the personal representatives or a previous personal representative, has:

(1) determined that the time limited for presentation of creditors' claims has expired.

(2) fully administered the estate of the decedent by making payment, settlement, or other disposition of all claims that were presented, expenses of administration and estate, inheritance and other death taxes, except as specified in the statement, and that the assets of the estate have been distributed to the persons entitled. If any claims remain undischarged, the statement must state whether the personal representative has distributed the estate subject to possible liability with the agreement of the distributees or state in detail other arrangements that have been made to accommodate outstanding liabilities; and

(3) sent a copy of the statement to all distributees of the estate and to all creditors or other claimants of whom the personal representative is aware whose claims are neither paid nor barred and has furnished a full account in writing of the personal representative's administration to the distributees whose interests are affected thereby.

(b) If no proceedings involving the personal representative are pending in the Court one year after the closing statement is filed, the appointment of the personal representative terminates.

As amended in 1989.

§3–1004. [Liability of Distributees to Claimants.]

After assets of an estate have been distributed and subject to Section 3–1006, an undischarged claim not barred may be prosecuted in a proceeding against one or more distributees. No distributee shall be liable to claimants for amounts received as exempt property, homestead or family allowances, or for amounts in excess of the value of his distribution as of the time of distribution. As between distributees, each shall bear the cost of satisfaction of unbarred claims as if the claim had been satisfied in the course of administration. Any distributee who shall have failed to notify other distributees of the demand made upon him by the claimant in sufficient time to permit them to join in any proceeding in which the claim was asserted against him loses his right of contribution against other distributees.

§3–1005. [Limitations on Proceedings Against Personal Representative.]

Unless previously barred by adjudication and except as provided in the closing statement, the rights of successors and of creditors whose claims have not otherwise been barred against the personal representative for breach of fiduciary duty are barred unless a proceeding to assert the same is commenced within 6 months after the filing of the closing statement. The rights thus barred do not include rights to recover from a personal representative for fraud, misrepresentation, or inadequate disclosure related to the settlement of the decedent's estate.

§3–1006. [Limitations on Actions and Proceedings Against Distributees.]

Unless previously adjudicated in a formal testacy proceeding or in a proceeding settling the accounts of a personal representative or otherwise barred, the claim of a claimant to recover from a distributee who is liable to pay the claim, and the right of an heir or devisee, or of a successor personal representative acting in their behalf, to recover property improperly distributed or its value from any distributee is forever barred at the later of three years after the decedent's death or one year after the time of its distribution thereof, but all claims of creditors of the decedent, are barred one year after the decedent's death. This section does not bar an action to recover property or value received as a result of fraud. Amended in 1989.

§3–1007. [Certificate Discharging Liens Securing Fiduciary Performance.]

After his appointment has terminated, the personal representative, his sureties, or any successor of either, upon the filing of a verified application showing, so far as is known by the applicant, that no action concerning the estate is pending in any court, is entitled to receive a certificate from the Registrar that the personal representative appears to have fully administered the estate in question. The certificate evidences discharge of any lien on any property given to secure the obligation of the personal representative in lieu of bond or any surety, but does not preclude action against the personal representative or the surety.

§3–1008. [Subsequent Administration.]

If other property of the estate is discovered after an estate has been settled and the personal representative discharged or after one year after a closing statement has been filed, the Court upon petition of any interested person and upon notice as it directs may appoint the same or a successor personal representative to administer the subsequently discovered estate. If a new appointment is made, unless the Court orders otherwise, the provisions of this Code apply as appropriate; but no claim previously barred may be asserted in the subsequent administration.

PART 11
COMPROMISE OF CONTROVERSIES

§3–1101. [Effect of Approval of Agreements Involving Trusts, Inalienable Interests, or Interests of Third Persons.]

A compromise of any controversy as to admission to probate of any instrument offered for formal probate as the will of a decedent, the construction, validity, or effect of any governing instrument, the rights or interests in the estate of the decedent, of any successor, or the administration of the estate, if approved in a formal proceeding in the Court for that purpose, is binding on all the parties thereto including those unborn, unascertained or who could not be located. An approved compromise is binding even though it may affect a trust or an inalienable interest. A compromise does not impair the rights of creditors or of taxing authorities who are not parties to it.
As amended in 1993.

§3–1102. [Procedure for Securing Court Approval of Compromise.]

The procedure for securing court approval of a compromise is as follows:

(1) The terms of the compromise shall be set forth in an agreement in writing which shall be executed by all competent persons and parents acting for any minor child having beneficial interests or having claims which will or may be affected by the compromise. Execution is not required by any person whose identity cannot be ascertained or whose whereabouts is unknown and cannot reasonably be ascertained.

(2) Any interested person, including the personal representative, if any, or a trustee, then may submit the agreement to the Court for its approval and for execution by the personal representative, the trustee of every affected testamentary trust, and other fiduciaries and representatives.

(3) After notice to all interested persons or their representatives, including the personal representative of any estate and all affected trustees of trusts, the Court, if it finds that the contest or controversy is in good faith and that the effect of the agreement upon the interests of persons represented by fiduciaries or other representatives is just and reasonable, shall make an order approving the agreement and directing all fiduciaries subject to its jurisdiction to execute the agreement. Minor children represented only by their parents may be bound only if their parents join with other competent persons in execution of the compromise. Upon the making of the order and the execution of the agreement, all further disposition of the estate is in accordance with the terms of the agreement.
As amended in 1993.

PART 12
COLLECTION OF PERSONAL PROPERTY BY AFFIDAVIT AND SUMMARY ADMINISTRATION PROCEDURE FOR SMALL ESTATES

§3–1201. [Collection of Personal Property by Affidavit.]

(a) Thirty days after the death of a decedent, any person indebted to the decedent or having possession of tangible personal property or an instrument evidencing a debt, obligation, stock or chose in action belonging to the decedent shall make payment of the indebtedness or deliver the tangible personal property or an instrument evidencing a debt, obligation, stock or chose in action to a person claiming to be the successor of the decedent upon being presented an affidavit made by or on behalf of the successor stating that:

(1) the value of the entire estate, wherever located, less liens and encumbrances, does not exceed $5,000;

(2) 30 days have elapsed since the death of the decedent;

(3) no application or petition for the appointment of a personal representative is pending or has been granted in any jurisdiction; and

(4) the claiming successor is entitled to payment or delivery of the property.

(b) A transfer agent of any security shall change the registered ownership on the books of a corporation from the decedent to the successor or successors upon the presentation of an affidavit as provided in subsection (a).

§3–1202. [Effect of Affidavit.]

The person paying, delivering, transferring, or issuing personal property or the evidence thereof pursuant to affidavit is discharged and released to the same extent as if he dealt with a personal representative of the decedent. He is not required to see to the application of the personal property or evidence thereof or to inquire into the truth of any statement in the affidavit. If any person to whom an affidavit is delivered refuses to pay, deliver, transfer, or issue any personal property or evidence thereof, it may be recovered or its payment, delivery, transfer, or issuance compelled upon proof of their right in a proceeding brought for the purpose by or on behalf of the persons entitled thereto. Any person to whom payment, delivery, transfer or issuance is made is answerable and accountable therefor to any personal representative of the estate or to any other person having a superior right.

§3–1203. [Small Estates; Summary Administration Procedure.]

If it appears from the inventory and appraisal that the value of the entire estate, less liens and encumbrances, does not exceed homestead allowance, exempt property, family allowance, costs and expenses of administration, reasonable funeral expenses, and reasonable and necessary medical and hospital expenses of the last illness of the decedent, the personal representative, without giving notice to creditors, may immediately disburse and distribute the estate to the persons entitled thereto and file a closing statement as provided in Section 3–1204.

§3–1204. [Small Estates; Closing by Sworn Statement of Personal Representative.]

(a) Unless prohibited by order of the Court and except for estates being administered by supervised personal representatives, a personal representative may close an estate administered under the summary procedures of Section 3–1203 by filing with the Court, at any time after disbursement and distribution of the estate, a verified statement stating that:

(1) to the best knowledge of the personal representative, the value of the entire estate, less liens and encumbrances, did not exceed homestead allowance, exempt property, family allowance, costs and expenses of administration, reasonable funeral expenses, and reasonable, necessary medical and hospital expenses of the last illness of the decedent;

(2) the personal representative has fully administered the estate by disbursing and distributing it to the persons entitled thereto; and

(3) the personal representative has sent a copy of the closing statement to all distributees of the estate and to all creditors or other claimants of whom he is aware whose claims are neither paid nor barred and has furnished a full account in writing of his administration to the distributees whose interests are affected.

(b) If no actions or proceedings involving the personal representative are pending in the Court one year after the closing statement is filed, the appointment of the personal representative terminates.

(c) A closing statement filed under this section has the same effect as one filed under Section 3–1003.

ARTICLE IV
FOREIGN PERSONAL REPRESENTATIVES; ANCILLARY ADMINISTRATION

PART 1
DEFINITIONS

Section
4–101. [Definitions.]

PART 2
POWERS OF FOREIGN PERSONAL REPRESENTATIVES

4–201. [Payment of Debt and Delivery of Property to Domiciliary Foreign Personal Representative Without Local Administration.]
4–202. [Payment or Delivery Discharges.]
4–203. [Resident Creditor Notice.]
4–204. [Proof of Authority-Bond.]
4–205. [Powers.]
4–206. [Powers of Representatives in Transition.]
4–207. [Ancillary and Other Local Administrations; Provisions Governing.]

PART 3
JURISDICTION OVER FOREIGN REPRESENTATIVES

4–301. [Jurisdiction by Act of Foreign Personal Representative.]
4–302. [Jurisdiction by Act of Decedent.]
4–303. [Service on Foreign Personal Representative.]

PART 4
JUDGMENTS AND PERSONAL REPRESENTATIVE

4–401. [Effect of Adjudication For or Against Personal Representative.]

PART 1
DEFINITIONS

§4–101. [Definitions.]

In this Article

(1) "local administration" means administration by a personal representative appointed in this state pursuant to appointment proceedings described in Article III.

(2) "local personal representative" includes any personal representative appointed in this state pursuant to appointment proceedings described in Article III and excludes foreign personal representatives who acquire the power of a local personal representative pursuant to Section 4–205.

(3) "resident creditor" means a person domiciled in, or doing business in this state, who is, or could be, a claimant against an estate of a non-resident decedent.

PART 2
POWERS OF FOREIGN PERSONAL REPRESENTATIVES

§4–201. [Payment of Debt and Delivery of Property to Domiciliary Foreign Personal Representative Without Local Administration.]

At any time after the expiration of sixty days from the death of a nonresident decedent, any person indebted to the estate of the nonresident decedent or having possession or control of personal property, or of an instrument evidencing a debt, obligation, stock or chose in action belonging to the estate of the nonresident decedent may pay the debt, deliver the personal property, or the instrument evidencing the debt, obligation, stock or chose in action, to the domiciliary foreign personal representative of the nonresident decedent upon being presented with proof of his appointment and an affidavit made by or on behalf of the representative stating:

(1) the date of the death of the nonresident decedent,

(2) that no local administration, or application or petition therefor, is pending in this state,

(3) that the domiciliary foreign personal representative is entitled to payment or delivery.

§4–202. [Payment or Delivery Discharges.]

Payment or delivery made in good faith on the basis of the proof of authority and affidavit releases the debtor or person having possession of the personal property to the same extent as if payment or delivery had been made to a local personal representative.

§4–203. [Resident Creditor Notice.]

Payment or delivery under Section 4–201 may not be made if a resident creditor of the nonresident decedent has notified the debtor of the nonresident decedent or the person having possession of the personal property belonging to the nonresident decedent that the debt should not be paid nor the property delivered to the domiciliary foreign personal representative.

§4–204. [Proof of Authority—Bond.]

If no local administration or application or petition therefor is pending in this state, a domiciliary foreign personal representative may file with a Court in this State in a [county] in which property belonging to the decedent is located, authenticated copies of his appointment and of any official bond he has given.

§4–205. [Powers.]

A domiciliary foreign personal representative who has complied with Section 4–204 may exercise as to assets in this state all powers of a local personal representative and may maintain actions and proceedings in this state subject to any conditions imposed upon nonresident parties generally.

§4–206. [Power of Representatives in Transition.]

The power of a domiciliary foreign personal representative under Section 4–201 or 4–205 shall be exercised only if there is no administration or application therefor pending in this state. An application or petition for local administration of the estate terminates the power of the foreign personal representative to act under Section 4–205, but the local Court may allow the foreign personal representative to exercise limited powers to preserve the estate. No person who, before receiving actual notice of a pending local administration, has changed his position in reliance upon the powers of a foreign personal representative shall be prejudiced by reason of the application or petition for, or grant of, local administration. The local personal representative is subject to all duties and obligations which have accrued by virtue of the exercise of the powers by the foreign personal representative and may be substituted for him in any action or proceedings in this state.

§4–207. [Ancillary and Other Local Administrations; Provisions Governing.]

In respect to a nonresident decedent, the provisions of Article III of this Code govern (1) proceedings, if any, in a Court of this state for probate of the will, appointment, removal, supervision, and discharge of the local personal representative, and any other order concerning the estate; and (2) the status, powers, duties and liabilities of any local personal representative and the rights of claimants, purchasers, distributees and others in regard to a local administration.

PART 3
JURISDICTION OVER FOREIGN REPRESENTATIVES

§4–301. [Jurisdiction by Act of Foreign Personal Representative.]

A foreign personal representative submits personally to the jurisdiction of the Courts of this state in any proceeding relating to the estate by (1) filing authenticated copies of his appointment as provided in Section 4–204, (2) receiving payment of money or taking delivery of personal property under Section 4–201, or (3) doing any act as a personal representative in this state which would have given the state jurisdiction over him as an individual. Jurisdiction under (2) is limited to the money or value of personal property collected.

§4–302. [Jurisdiction by Act of Decedent.]

In addition to jurisdiction conferred by Section 4–301, a foreign personal representative is subject to the jurisdiction of the courts of this state to the same extent that his decedent was subject to jurisdiction immediately prior to death.

§4–303. [Service on Foreign Personal Representative.]

(a) Service of process may be made upon the foreign personal representative by registered or certified mail, addressed to his last reasonably ascertainable address, requesting a return receipt signed by addressee only. Notice by ordinary first class mail is sufficient if registered or certified mail service to the addressee is unavailable. Service may be made upon a foreign personal representative in the manner in which service could have been made under other laws of this state on either the foreign personal representative or his decedent immediately prior to death.

(b) If service is made upon a foreign personal representative as provided in subsection (a), he shall be allowed at least [30] days within which to appear or respond.

PART 4
JUDGMENTS AND PERSONAL REPRESENTATIVE

§4–401. [Effect of Adjudication For or Against Personal Representative.]

An adjudication rendered in any jurisdiction in favor of or against any personal representative of the estate is as binding on the local personal representative as if he were a party to the adjudication.

ARTICLE V
PROTECTION OF PERSONS UNDER DISABILITY AND THEIR PROPERTY

PART 1
GENERAL PROVISIONS AND DEFINITIONS

PART 2
GUARDIANS OF MINORS

PART 3
GUARDIANS OF INCAPACITATED PERSONS

PART 4
PROTECTION OF PROPERTY OF PERSONS UNDER DISABILITY AND MINORS

PART 5
DURABLE POWER OF ATTORNEY

Section

PART 1
GENERAL PROVISIONS AND DEFINITIONS
§5–101. [Facility of Payment or Delivery.]

(a) Any person under a duty to pay or deliver money or personal property to a minor may perform the duty, in amounts not exceeding $5,000 a year, by paying or delivering the money or property to:

(1) the minor if 18 or more years of age or married;

(2) any person having the care and custody of the minor with whom the minor resides;

(3) a guardian of the minor; or

(4) a financial institution incident to a deposit in a state or federally insured savings account or certifi-cate in the sole name of the minor with notice of the deposit to the minor.

(b) This section does not apply if the person making payment or delivery knows that a conservator has been appointed or proceedings for appointment of a conservator of the estate of the minor are pending.

(c) Persons, other than the minor or any financial institution, receiving money or property for a minor, are obligated to apply the money to the support and education of the minor, but may not pay themselves except by way of reimbursement for out-of-pocket expenses for goods and services necessary for the minor's support. Any excess sums must be preserved for future support and education of the minor and any balance not so used and any property received for the minor must be turned over to the minor when majority is attained. A person who pays or delivers money or property in accordance with provisions of this section is not responsible for the proper application thereof.

§5–102. [Delegation of Powers by Parent or Guardian.]

A parent or guardian of a minor or incapacitated person, by a properly executed power of attorney, may delegate to another person, for a period not exceeding 6 months, any power regarding care, custody or property of the minor child or ward, except the power to consent to marriage or adoption of a minor ward.

§5–103. [General Definitions.]

As used in Parts 1, 2, 3 and 4 of this Article:

(1) "Claims," in respect to a protected person, includes liabilities of the protected person, whether arising in contract, tort, or otherwise, and liabilities of the estate which arise at or after the appointment of a conservator, including expenses of administration.

(2) "Court" means the [_____] court.

(3) "Conservator" means a person who is appointed by a Court to manage the estate of a protected person and includes a limited conservator described in Section 5–419(a).

(4) "Disability" means cause for a protective order as described in Section 5–401.

(5) "Estate" includes the property of the person whose affairs are subject to this Article.

(6) "Guardian" means a person who has qualified as a guardian of a minor or incapacitated person pursuant to parental or spousal nomination or court appointment and includes a limited guardian as described in Sections 5–209(e) and 5–306(c), but excludes one who is merely, a guardian and litem.

(7) "Incapacitated person" means any person who is impaired by reason of mental illness, mental deficiency, physical illness or disability, chronic use of drugs,

chronic intoxication, or other cause (except minority) to the extent of lacking sufficient understanding or capacity to make or communicate responsible decisions.

(8) "Lease" includes an oil, gas, or other mineral lease.

(9) "Letters" includes letters of guardianship and letters of conservatorship.

(10) "Minor" means a person who is under [21] years of age.

(11) "Mortgage" means any conveyance, agreement, or arrangement in which property is used as collateral.

(12) "Organization" includes a corporation, business trust, estate, trust, partnership, association, 2 or more persons having a joint or common interest, government, governmental subdivision or agency, or any other legal entity.

(13) "Parent" includes any person entitled to take, or who would be entitled to take if the child died without a will, as a parent by intestate succession from the child whose relationship is in question and excludes any person who is only a stepparent, foster parent, or grandparent.

(14) "Person" means an individual or an organization.

(15) "Petition" means a written request to the Court for an order after notice.

(16) "Proceeding" includes action at law and suit in equity.

(17) "Property" includes both real and personal property or any interest therein and means anything that may be the subject of ownership.

(18) "Protected person" means a minor or other person for whom a conservator has been appointed or other protective order has been made as provided in Sections 5–407 and 5–408.

(19) "Protective proceeding" means a proceeding under the provisions of Part 4 of this Article.

(20) "Security" includes any note, stock, treasury stock, bond, debenture, evidence of indebtedness, certificate of interest or participation in an oil, gas, or mining title or lease or in payments out of production under such a title or lease, collateral trust certificate, transferable share, voting trust certificate or, in general, any interest or instrument commonly known as a security, or any certificate of interest or participation, any temporary or interim certificate, receipt or certificate of deposit for, or any warrant or right to subscribe to or purchase any of the foregoing.

(21) "Visitor" means a person appointed in a guardianship or protective proceeding who is trained in law, nursing, or social work, is an officer, employee, or special appointee of the Court, and has no personal interest in the proceeding.

(22) "Ward" means a person for whom a guardian has been appointed. A "minor ward" is a minor for whom a guardian has been appointed solely because of minority.

As amended in 1989.

§5–104. [Request for Notice; Interested Person.]

Upon payment of any required fee, an interested person who desires to be notified before any order is made in a guardianship proceeding, including any proceeding subsequent to the appointment of a guardian under Section 5–312, or in a protective proceeding under Section 5–401, may file a request for notice with the clerk of the court in which the proceeding is pending. The clerk shall mail a copy of the request to the guardian and to the conservator if one has been appointed. A request is not effective unless it contains a statement showing the interest of the person making it and the address of that person or an attorney to whom notice is to be given. The request is effective only as to proceedings occurring after the filing. Any governmental agency paying or planning to pay benefits to the person to be protected is an interested person in protective proceedings.

PART 2
GUARDIANS OF MINORS

§5–201. [Appointment and Status of Guardian of Minor.]

A person may become a guardian of a minor by parental appointment or upon appointment by the Court. The guardianship status continues until terminated, without regard to the location from time to time of the guardian or minor ward.

§5–202. [Parental Appointment of Guardian for Minor.]

(a) The parent of an unmarried minor may appoint a guardian for the minor by will, or other writing signed by the parent and attested by at least 2 witnesses.

(b) Subject to the right of the minor under Section 5–203, if both parents are dead or incapacitated or the surviving parent has no parental rights or has been adjudged to be incapacitated, a parental appointment becomes effective when the guardian's acceptance is filed in the Court in which a nominating instrument is probated, or, in the case of a non-testamentary nominating instrument, in the Court at the place where the minor resides or is present. If both parents are dead, an effective appointment by the parent who died later has priority.

(c) A parental appointment effected by filing the guardian's acceptance under a will probated in the state of the testator's domicile is effective in this State.

(d) Upon acceptance of appointment, the guardian shall give written notice of acceptance to the minor and to the person having the minor's care or the minor's nearest adult relative.

§5–203. [Objection by Minor of Fourteen or Older to Parental Appointment.]

A minor 14 or more years of age who is the subject of a parental appointment may prevent the appointment or cause it to terminate by filing in the Court in which the nominating instrument is filed a written objection to the appointment before it is accepted or within 30 days after receiving notice of its acceptance. An objection may be withdrawn. An objection does not preclude appointment by the Court in a proper proceeding of the parental nominee or any other suitable person.

§5–204. [Court Appointment of Guardian of Minor; Conditions for Appointment.]

(a) The Court may appoint a guardian for an unmarried minor if all parental rights have been terminated or suspended by circumstances or prior Court order. A guardian appointed pursuant to Section 5–202 whose appointment has not been prevented or nullified under Section 5–203 has priority over any guardian who may be appointed by the Court, but the Court may proceed with another appointment upon a finding that the parental nominee has failed to accept the appointment within 30 days after notice of the guardianship proceeding.

(b) If necessary, and on appropriate petition or application, the Court may appoint a temporary guardian who shall have the full authority of a general guardian of a minor, but the authority of a temporary guardian may not last longer than 6 months. The appointment of a temporary guardian for a minor may occur even though the conditions described in subsection (a) have not been established.

§5–205. [Venue.]

The venue for guardianship proceedings for a minor is in the court at the place where the minor resides or is present at the time the proceedings are commenced.

§5–206. [Procedure for Court Appointment of Guardian of Minor.]

(a) A minor or any person interested in the welfare of the minor may petition for appointment of a guardian.

(b) After the filing of a petition, the Court shall set a date for hearing, and the petitioner shall give notice of the time and place of hearing the petition in the manner prescribed by Section 1–401 to:

 (1) the minor, if 14 or more years of age and not the petitioner;

 (2) any person alleged to have had the principal care and custody of the minor during the 60 days preceding the filing of the petition; and

 (3) any living parent of the minor.

(c) Upon hearing, if the Court finds that a qualified person seeks appointment, venue is proper, the required notices have been given, the conditions of Section 5–204(a) have been met, and the welfare and best interest of the minor will be served by the requested appointment, it shall make the appointment and issue letters. In other cases, the Court may dismiss the proceedings or make any other disposition of the matter that will serve the best interest of the minor.

(d) If the Court determines at any time in the proceeding that the interests of the minor are or may be inadequately represented, it may appoint an attorney to represent the minor, giving consideration to the preference of the minor if the minor is 14 or more years of age.

§5–207. [Court Appointment of Guardian of Minor; Qualifications; Priority of Minor's Nominee.]

The Court may appoint as guardian any person whose appointment would be in the best interest of the minor. The Court shall appoint a person nominated by the minor, if the minor is 14 or more years of age, unless the Court finds the appointment contrary to the best interest of the minor.

§5–208. [Consent to Service by Acceptance of Appointment; Notice.]

By accepting a parental or court appointment as guardian, a guardian submits personally to the jurisdiction of the Court in any proceeding relating to the guardianship that may be instituted by any interested person. The petitioner shall cause notice of any proceeding to be delivered or mailed to the guardian at the guardian's address listed in the Court records and to the address then known to the petitioner. Letters of guardianship must indicate whether the guardian was appointed by court order or parental nomination.

§5–209. [Powers and Duties of Guardian of Minor.]

(a) A guardian of a minor ward has the powers and responsibilities of a parent regarding the ward's support, care, and education, but a guardian is not personally liable for the ward's expenses and is not liable to third persons by reason of the relationship for acts of the ward.

(b) In particular and without qualifying the foregoing, a guardian shall:

 (1) become or remain personally acquainted with the ward and maintain sufficient contact with the ward to know of the ward's capacities, limitations, needs, opportunities, and physical and mental health;

 (2) take reasonable care of the ward's personal effects and commence protective proceedings if necessary to protect other property of the ward;

 (3) apply any available money of the ward to the ward's current needs for support, care, and education;

(4) conserve any excess money of the ward for the ward's future needs, but if a conservator has been appointed for the estate of the ward, the guardian, at least quarterly, shall pay to the conservator money of the ward to be conserved for the ward's future needs; and

(5) report the condition of the ward and of the ward's estate that has been subject to the guardian's possession or control, as ordered by the Court on petition of any person interested in the ward's welfare or as required by Court rule.

(c) A guardian may:

(1) receive money payable for the support of the ward to the ward's parent, guardian, or custodian under the terms of any statutory benefit or insurance system or any private contract, devise, trust, conservatorship, or custodianship, and money or property of the ward paid or delivered pursuant to Section 5–101;

(2) if consistent with the terms of any order by a court of competent jurisdiction relating to detention or commitment of the ward, take custody of the person of the ward and establish the ward's place of abode within or without this State;

(3) if no conservator for the estate of the ward has been appointed, institute proceedings, including administrative proceedings, or take other appropriate action to compel the performance by any person of a duty to support the ward or to pay sums for the welfare of the ward;

(4) consent to medical or other professional care, treatment, or advice for the ward without liability by reason of the consent for injury to the ward resulting from the negligence or acts of third persons unless a parent would have been liable in the circumstances;

(5) consent to the marriage or adoption of the ward; and

(6) if reasonable under all of the circumstances, delegate to the ward certain responsibilities for decisions affecting the ward's well-being.

(d) A guardian is entitled to reasonable compensation for services as guardian and to reimbursement for room, board and clothing personally provided to the ward, but only as approved by order of the Court. If a conservator, other than the guardian or one who is affiliated with the guardian, has been appointed for the estate of the ward, reasonable compensation and reimbursement to the guardian may be approved and paid by the conservator without order of the Court controlling the guardian.

(e) In the interest of developing self-reliance on the part of a ward or for other good cause, the Court, at the time of appointment or later, on its own motion or on appropriate petition or motion of the minor or other interested person, may limit the powers of a guardian other-

wise conferred by this section and thereby create a limited guardianship. Any limitation on the statutory power of a guardian of a minor must be endorsed on the guardian's letters or, in the case of a guardian by parental appointment, must be reflected in letters that are issued at the time any limitation is imposed. Following the same procedure, a limitation may be removed and appropriate letters issued.

§5–210. [Termination of Appointment of Guardian; General.]

A guardian's authority and responsibility terminates upon the death, resignation, or removal of the guardian or upon the minor's death, adoption, marriage, or attainment of majority, but termination does not affect the guardian's liability for prior acts or the obligation to account for funds and assets of the ward. Resignation of a guardian does not terminate the guardianship until it has been approved by the Court. A parental appointment under an informally probated will terminates if the will is later denied probate in a formal proceeding.

§5–211. [Proceedings Subsequent to Appointment; Venue.]

(a) The Court at the place where the ward resides has concurrent jurisdiction with the Court that appointed the guardian or in which acceptance of a parental appointment was filed over resignation, removal, accounting, and other proceedings relating to the guardianship.

(b) If the Court at the place where the ward resides is neither the appointing court nor the court in which acceptance of appointment is filed, the court in which proceedings subsequent to appointment are commenced in all appropriate cases shall notify the other court, in this or another state, and after consultation with that court determine whether to retain jurisdiction or transfer the proceedings to the other court, whichever is in the best interest of the ward. A copy of any order accepting a resignation or removing a guardian must be sent to the appointing court or the court in which acceptance of appointment is filed.

§5–212. [Resignation, Removal, and Other Post-appointment Proceedings.]

(a) Any person interested in the welfare of a ward or the ward, if 14 or more years of age, may petition for removal of a guardian on the ground that removal would be in the best interest of the ward or for any other order that is in the best interest of the ward. A guardian may petition for permission to resign. A petition for removal or for permission to resign may, but need not, include a request for appointment of a successor guardian.

(b) Notice of hearing on a petition for an order subsequent to appointment of a guardian must be given to the ward, the guardian, and any other person as ordered by the court.

(c) After notice and hearing on a petition for removal or for permission to resign, the Court may terminate the guardianship and make any further order that may be appropriate.

(d) If the Court determines at any time in the proceeding that the interest of the ward is or may be inadequately represented, it may appoint an attorney to represent the minor, giving consideration to the preference of the minor if the minor is 14 or more years of age.

PART 3
GUARDIANS OF INCAPACITATED PERSONS

§5–301. [Appointment of Guardian for Incapacitated Person by Will or Other Writing.]

(a) The parent of an unmarried incapacitated person may appoint by will, or other writing signed by the parent and attested by at least 2 witnesses, a guardian of the incapacitated person. If both parents are dead or the surviving parent is adjudged incapacitated, a parental appointment becomes effective when, after having given 7 days prior written notice of intention to do so to the incapacitated person and to the person having the care of the person or to the nearest adult relative, the guardian files acceptance of appointment in the court in which the will is [informally or formally] probated, or in the case of a non-testamentary nominating instrument, in the Court at the place where the incapacitated person resides or is present. The notice shall state that the appointment may be terminated by filing a written objection in the Court, as provided by subsection (d). If both parents are dead, an effective appointment by the parent who died later has priority.

(b) The spouse of a married incapacitated person may appoint by will, or other writing signed by the spouse and attested by at least 2 witnesses, a guardian of the incapacitated person. The appointment becomes effective when, after having given 7 days prior written notice of intention to do so to the incapacitated person and to the person having care of the incapacitated person or to the nearest adult relative, the guardian files acceptance of appointment in the Court in which the will is informally or formally probated or, in the case of nontestamentary nominating instrument, in the Court at the place where the incapacitated person resides or is present. The notice shall state that the appointment may be terminated by filing a written objection in the Court, as provided by subsection (d). An effective appointment by a spouse has priority over an appointment by a parent.

(c) An appointment effected by filing the guardian's acceptance under a will probated in the state of the decedent's domicile is effective in this State.

(d) Upon the filing in the Court in which the will was probated or, in the case of a non-testamentary nominating instrument, in the Court at the place where the incapacitated person resides or is present, of written objection to the appointment by the incapacitated person for whom a parental or spousal appointment of guardian has been made, the appointment is terminated. An objection does not prevent appointment by the Court in a proper proceeding of the parental or spousal nominee or any other suitable person upon an adjudication of incapacity in proceedings under the succeeding sections of this Part.

As amended in 1987.

§5–302. [Venue.]

The venue for guardianship proceedings for an incapacitated person is in the place where the incapacitated person resides or is present at the time the proceedings are commenced. If the incapacitated person is admitted to an institution pursuant to order of a court of competent jurisdiction, venue is also in the [county] in which that court is located.

§5–303. [Procedure for Court Appointment of a Guardian of an Incapacitated Person.]

(a) An incapacitated person or any person interested in the welfare of the incapacitated person may petition for appointment of a guardian, limited or general.

(b) After the filing of a petition, the Court shall set a date for hearing on the issue of incapacity so that notices may be given as required by Section 5–304, and, unless the allegedly incapacitated person is represented by counsel, appoint an attorney to represent the person in the proceeding. The person so appointed may be granted the powers and duties of a guardian ad litem. The person alleged to be incapacitated must be examined by a physician or other qualified person appointed by the Court who shall submit a report in writing to the Court. The person alleged to be incapacitated also must be interviewed by a visitor sent by the Court. The visitor also shall interview the person who appears to have caused the petition to be filed and any person who is nominated to serve as guardian and visit the present place of abode of the person alleged to be incapacitated and the place it is proposed that the person will be detained or reside if the appointment is made and submit a report in writing to the Court. The Court may utilize the service of any public or charitable agency as an additional visitor to evaluate the condition of the allegedly incapacitated person and to make appropriate recommendations to the Court.

(c) A person alleged to be incapacitated is entitled to be present at the hearing in person. The person is entitled to be represented by counsel, to present evidence, to cross-examine witnesses, including the Court-appointed physician or other qualified person and any visitor [, and to trail by jury]. The issue may be determined at a closed hearing [or without a jury] if the person alleged to be incapacitated or counsel for the person so requests.

(d) Any person may apply for permission to participate in the proceeding, and the Court may grant the request, with or without hearing, upon determining that the best interest of the alleged incapacitated person will be served thereby. The Court may attach appropriate conditions to the permission.

§5–304. [Notice in Guardianship Proceeding.]

(a) In a proceeding for the appointment of a guardian of an incapacitated person, and, if notice is required in a proceeding for appointment of a temporary guardian, notice of hearing must be given to each of the following:

(1) the person alleged to be incapacitated and spouse, or, if none, adult children, or if none, parents;

(2) any person who is serving as guardian, conservator, or who has the care and custody of the person alleged to be incapacitated;

(3) in case no other person is notified under paragraph (1), at least one of the nearest adult relatives, if any can be found; and

(4) any other person as directed by the Court.

(b) Notice of hearing on a petition for an order subsequent to appointment of a guardian must be given to the ward, the guardian and any other person as ordered by the Court.

(c) Notice must be served personally on the alleged incapacitated person. Notices to other persons as required by subsection (a)(1) must be served personally if the person to be notified can be found within the state. In all other cases, required notices must be given as provided in Section 1–401.

(d) The person alleged to be incapacitated may not waive notice.

§5–305. [Who May Be Guardian; Priorities.]

(a) Any qualified person may be appointed guardian of an incapacitated person.

(b) Unless lack of qualification or other good cause dictates the contrary, the Court shall appoint a guardian in accordance with the incapacitated person's most recent nomination in a durable power of attorney.

(c) Except as provided in subsection (b), the following are entitled to consideration for appointment in the order listed:

(1) the spouse of the incapacitated person or a person nominated by will of a deceased spouse or by other writing signed by the spouse and attested by at least 2 witnesses;

(2) an adult child of the incapacitated person;

(3) a parent of the incapacitated person, or a person nominated by will of a deceased parent or by other writing signed by a parent and attested by at least two witnesses;

(4) any relative of the incapacitated person with whom the person has resided for more than 6 months prior to the filing of the petition; and

(5) a person nominated by the person who is caring for or paying for the care of the incapacitated person.

(d) With respect to persons having equal priority, the Court shall select the one it deems best qualified to serve. The Court, acting in the best interest of the incapacitated person, may pass over a person having priority and appoint a person having a lower priority or no priority.

§5–306. [Findings; Order of Appointment.]

(a) The Court shall exercise the authority conferred in this Part so as to encourage the development of maximum self-reliance and independence of the incapacitated person and make appointive and other orders only to the extent necessitated by the incapacitated person's mental and adaptive limitations or other conditions warranting the procedure.

(b) The Court may appoint a guardian as requested if it is satisfied that the person for whom a guardian is sought is incapacitated and that the appointment is necessary or desirable as a means of providing continuing care and supervision of the person of the incapacitated person. The Court, on appropriate findings, may (i) treat the petition as one for a protective order under Section 5–401 and proceed accordingly, (ii) enter any other appropriate order, or (iii) dismiss the proceedings.

(c) The Court, at the time of appointment or later, on its own motion or on appropriate petition or motion of the incapacitated person or other interested person, may limit the powers of a guardian otherwise conferred by Parts 1, 2, 3 and 4 of this Article and thereby create a limited guardianship. Any limitation on the statutory power of a guardian of an incapacitated person must be endorsed on the guardian's letters or, in the case of a guardian by parental or spousal appointment, must be reflected in letters issued at the time any limitation is imposed. Following the same procedure, a limitation may be removed or modified and appropriate letters issued.

§5–307. [Acceptance of Appointment; Consent to Jurisdiction.]

By accepting appointment, a guardian submits personally to the jurisdiction of the Court in any proceeding relating to the guardianship that may be instituted by any interested person. Notice of any proceeding must be delivered or mailed to the guardian at the address listed in the Court records and at the address as then known to the petitioner.

§5–308. [Emergency Orders; Temporary Guardians.]

(a) If an incapacitated person has no guardian, an emergency exists, and no other person appears to have authority to act in the circumstances, on appropriate petition the Court may appoint a temporary guardian whose authority may not extend beyond [15 days] [the period of effectiveness of ex parte restraining orders], and who may exercise those powers granted in the order.

(b) If an appointed guardian is not effectively performing duties and the Court further finds that the welfare of the incapacitated person requires immediate action, it may appoint, with or without notice, a temporary guardian for the incapacitated person having the powers of a general guardian for a specified period not to exceed 6 months. The authority of any permanent guardian previously appointed by the Court is suspended as long as a temporary guardian has authority.

(c) The Court may remove a temporary guardian at any time. A temporary guardian shall make any report the Court requires. In other respects the provisions of Parts 1, 2, 3 and 4 of this Article concerning guardians apply to temporary guardians.

§5–309. [General Powers and Duties of Guardian.]

Except as limited pursuant to Section 5–306(c), a guardian of an incapacitated person is responsible for care, custody, and control of the ward, but is not liable to third persons by reason of that responsibility for acts of the ward. In particular and without qualifying the foregoing, a guardian has the same duties, powers and responsibilities as a guardian for a minor as described in Section 5–209(b), (c) and (d).

§5–310. [Termination of Guardianship for Incapacitated Person.]

The authority and responsibility of a guardian of an incapacitated person terminates upon the death of the guardian or ward, the determination of incapacity of the guardian, or upon removal or resignation as provided in Section 5–311. Testamentary appointment under an informally probated will terminates if the will is later denied probate in a formal proceeding. Termination does not affect a guardian's liability for prior acts or the obligation to account for funds and assets of the ward.

§5–311. [Removal or Resignation of Guardian; Termination of Incapacity.]

(a) On petition of the ward or any person interested in the ward's welfare, the Court, after hearing, may remove a guardian if in the best interest of the ward. On petition of the guardian, the Court, after hearing, may accept a resignation.

(b) An order adjudicating incapacity may specify a minimum period, not exceeding six months, during which a petition for an adjudication that the ward is no longer incapacitated may not be filed without special leave. Subject to that restriction, the ward or any person interested in the welfare of the ward may petition for an order that the ward is no longer incapacitated and for termination of the guardianship. A request for an order may also be made informally to the Court and any person who knowingly interferes with transmission of the request may be adjudged guilty of contempt of court.

(c) Upon removal, resignation, or death of the guardian, or if the guardian is determined to be incapacitated, the Court may appoint a successor guardian and make any other appropriate order. Before appointing a successor guardian, or ordering that a ward's incapacity has terminated, the Court shall follow the same procedures to safeguard the rights of the ward that apply to a petition for appointment of a guardian.

As amended in 1987.

§5–312. [Proceedings Subsequent to Appointment; Venue.]

(a) The Court at the place where the ward resides has concurrent jurisdiction with the Court that appointed the guardian or in which acceptance of a parental or spousal appointment was filed over resignation, removal, accounting, and other proceedings relating to the guardianship, including proceedings to limit the authority previously conferred on a guardian or to remove limitations previously imposed.

(b) If the Court at the place where the ward resides is not the Court in which acceptance of appointment is filed, the Court in which proceedings subsequent to appointment are commenced, in all appropriate cases, shall notify the other Court, in this or another state, and after consultation with that Court determine whether to retain jurisdiction or transfer the proceedings to the other Court, whichever may be in the best interest of the ward. A copy of any order accepting a resignation, removing a guardian, or altering authority must be sent to the Court in which acceptance of appointment is filed.

PART 4

PROTECTION OF PROPERTY OF PERSONS UNDER DISABILITY AND MINORS

§5–401. [Protective Proceedings.]

(a) Upon petition and after notice and hearing in accordance with the provisions of this Part, the Court may appoint a conservator or make any other protective order for cause as provided in this section.

(b) Appointment of a conservator or other protective order may be made in relation to the estate and affairs of a minor if the Court determines that a minor owns money or property requiring management or protection that cannot otherwise be provided or has or may have business affairs that may be jeopardized or prevented by minority, or that funds are needed for support and education and that protection is necessary or desirable to obtain or provide funds.

(c) Appointment of a conservator or other protective order may be made in relation to the estate and affairs of a person if the Court determines that (i) the person is unable to manage property and business affairs effectively for such reasons as mental illness, mental deficiency, physical illness or disability, chronic use of drugs, chronic intoxication, confinement, detention by a foreign power, or disappearance; and (ii) the person has property that will be wasted or dissipated unless property management is provided or money is needed for the support, care, and welfare of the person or those entitled to the person's support and that protection is necessary or desirable to obtain or provide money.

As amended in 1989.

§5–402. [Protective Proceedings; Jurisdiction of Business Affairs of Protected Persons.]

After the service of notice in a proceeding seeking the appointment of a conservator or other protective order and until termination of the proceeding, the Court in which the petition is filed has:

(1) exclusive jurisdiction to determine the need for a conservator or other protective order until the proceedings are terminated;

(2) exclusive jurisdiction to determine how the estate of the protected person which is subject to the laws of this State must be managed, expended, or distributed to or for the use of the protected person, the protected person's dependents, or other claimants; and

(3) concurrent jurisdiction to determine the validity of claims against the person or estate of the protected person and questions of title concerning any estate asset.

§5–403. [Venue.]

Venue for proceedings under this Part is:

(1) in the Court at the place in this State where the person to be protected resides whether or not a guardian has been appointed in another place; or

(2) if the person to be protected does not reside in this State, in the Court at any place where property of the person is located.

§5–404. [Original Petition for Appointment or Protective Order.]

(a) The person to be protected or any person who is interested in the estate, affairs, or welfare of the person, including a parent, guardian, custodian, or any person who would be adversely affected by lack of effective management of the person's property and business affairs may petition for the appointment of a conservator or for other appropriate protective order.

(b) The petition must set forth to the extent known the interest of the petitioner; the name, age, residence, and address of the person to be protected; the name and address of the guardian, if any; the name and address of the nearest relative known to the petitioner; a general statement of the person's property with an estimate of the value thereof, including any compensation, insurance, pension, or allowance to which the person is entitled; and the reason why appointment of a conservator or other protective order is necessary. If the appointment of a conservator is requested, the petition must also set forth the name and address of the person whose appointment is sought and the basis of the claim to priority for appointment.

§5–405. [Notice.]

(a) On a petition for appointment of a conservator or other protective order, the requirements for notice described in Section 5–304 apply, but (i) if the person to be protected has disappeared or is otherwise situated so as to make personal service of notice impracticable, notice to the person must be given by publication as provided in Section 1–401, and (ii) if the person to be protected is a minor, the provisions of Section 5–206 also apply.

(b) Notice of hearing on a petition for an order subsequent to appointment of a conservator or other protective order must be given to the protected person, any conservator of the protected person's estate, and any other person as ordered by the Court.

§5–406. [Procedure Concerning Hearing and Order on Original Petition.]

(a) Upon receipt of a petition for appointment of a conservator or other protective order because of minority, the Court shall set a date for hearing. If the Court determines at any time in the proceeding that the interests of the minor are or may be inadequately represented, it may appoint an attorney to represent the minor, giving consideration to the choice of the minor if 14 or more years of age. An attorney appointed by the Court to represent a minor may be granted the powers and duties of a guardian ad litem.

(b) Upon receipt of a petition for appointment of a conservator or other protective order for reasons other than minority, the Court shall set a date for hearing. Unless the person to be protected has chosen counsel, the Court shall appoint an attorney to represent the person who may be granted the powers and duties of a guardian ad litem. If the alleged disability is mental illness, mental deficiency, physical illness or disability, chronic use of drugs, or chronic intoxication, the Court may direct that the person to be protected be examined by a physician designated by the Court, preferably a physician who is not connected with any institution in which the person is a patient or is detained. The Court may send a visitor to interview the person to be protected. The visitor may be a guardian ad litem or an officer or employee of the Court.

(c) The Court may utilize, as an additional visitor, the service of any public or charitable agency to evaluate the condition of the person to be protected and make appropriate recommendations to the Court.

(d) The person to be protected is entitled to be present at the hearing in person. The person is entitled to be represented by counsel, to present evidence, to cross-examine witnesses, including any Court-appointed physician or other qualified person and any visitor [,and to trial by jury]. The issue may be determined at a closed hearing [or without a jury] if the person to be protected or counsel for the person so requests.

(e) Any person may apply for permission to participate in the proceeding and the Court may grant the request, with or without hearing, upon determining that the best interest of the person to be protected will be served thereby. The Court may attach appropriate conditions to the permission.

(f) After hearing, upon finding that a basis for the appointment of a conservator or other protective order has been established, the Court shall make an appointment or other appropriate protective order.

As amended in 1989.

§5–407. [Permissible Court Orders.]

(a) The Court shall exercise the authority conferred in this Part to encourage the development of maximum self-reliance and independence of a protected person and make protective orders only to the extent necessitated by the protected person's mental and adaptive limitations and other conditions warranting the procedure.

(b) The Court has the following powers that may be exercised directly or through a conservator in respect to the estate and business affairs of a protected person:

(1) While a petition for appointment of a conservator or other protective order is pending and after preliminary hearing and without notice to others, the Court may preserve and apply the property of the person to be protected as may be required for the support of the person or dependents of the person.

(2) After hearing and upon determining that a basis for an appointment or other protective order exists with respect to a minor without other disability, the Court has all those powers over the estate and business affairs of the minor which are or may be necessary for the best interest of the minor and members of the minor's immediate family.

(3) After hearing and upon determining that a basis for an appointment or other protective order exists with respect to a person for reasons other than minority, the Court, for the benefit of the person and members of the person's immediate family, has all the powers over the estate and business affairs which the person could exercise if present and not under disability, except the power to make a will. Those powers include, but are not limited to, power to make gifts; to convey or release contingent and expectant interests in property, including marital property rights and any right of survivorship incident to joint tenancy or tenancy by the entirety; to exercise or release powers held by the protected person as trustee, personal representative, custodian for minors, conservator, or donee of a power of appointment; to enter into contracts; to create revocable or irrevocable trusts of property of the estate which may extend beyond the disability or life of the protected person; to exercise options of the protected person to purchase securities or other property; to exercise rights to elect options and change beneficiaries under insurance and annuity policies and to surrender the policies for their cash value; to exercise any right to an elective share in the estate of the person's deceased spouse and to renounce or disclaim any interest by testate or intestate succession or by inter vivos transfer.

(c) The Court may exercise or direct the exercise of the following powers only if satisfied, after notice and hearing, that it is in the best interest of the protected person, and that the person either is incapable of consenting or has consented to the proposed exercise of power:

(1) to exercise or release powers of appointment of which the protected person is donee;

(2) to renounce or disclaim interests;

(3) to make gifts in trust or otherwise exceeding 20 percent of any year's income of the estate; and

(4) to change beneficiaries under insurance and annuity policies.

(d) A determination that a basis for appointment of a conservator or other protective order exists has no effect on the capacity of the protected person.

§5–408. [Protective Arrangements and Single Transactions Authorized.]

(a) If it is established in a proper proceeding that a basis exists as described in Section 5–401 for affecting the property and business affairs of a person, the Court, without appointing a conservator, may authorize, direct or ratify any transaction necessary or desirable to achieve any security, service, or care arrangement meeting the foreseeable needs of the protected person. Protective arrangements include payment, delivery, deposit, or retention of funds or property; sale, mortgage, lease, or other transfer of property; entry into an annuity contract, a contract for life care, a deposit contract, or a contract for training and education; or addition to or establishment of a suitable trust.

(b) If it is established in a proper proceeding that a basis exists as described in Section 5–401 for affecting the property and business affairs of a person, the Court, without appointing a conservator, may authorize, direct, or ratify any contract, trust, or other transaction relating to the protected person's property and business affairs if the Court determines that the transaction is in the best interest of the protected person.

(c) Before approving a protective arrangement or other transaction under this section, the Court shall consider the interests of creditors and dependents of the protected person and, in view of the disability, whether the protected person needs the continuing protection of a conservator. The Court may appoint a special conservator to assist in the accomplishment of any protective arrangement or other transaction authorized under this section who shall have the authority conferred by the order and serve until discharged by order after report to the Court of all matters done pursuant to the order of appointment.

§5–409. [Who May Be Appointed Conservator; Priorities.]

(a) The Court may appoint an individual or a corporation with general power to serve as trustee or conservator of the estate of a protected person. The following are entitled to consideration for appointment in the order listed:

(1) a conservator, guardian of property, or other like fiduciary appointed or recognized by an appropriate court of any other jurisdiction in which the protected person resides;

(2) an individual or corporation nominated by the protected person 14 or more years of age and of sufficient mental capacity to make an intelligent choice;

(3) the spouse of the protected person;

(4) an adult child of the protected person;

(5) a parent of the protected person, or a person nominated by the will of a deceased parent;

(6) any relative of the protected person who has resided with the protected person for more than 6 months before the filing of the petition; and

(7) a person nominated by one who is caring for or paying benefits to the protected person.

(b) A person in priorities (1), (3), (4), (5), or (6) may designate in writing a substitute to serve instead and thereby transfer the priority to the substitute. With respect to persons having equal priority, the Court shall select the one it deems best qualified to serve. The Court, acting in the best interest of the protected person, may pass over a person having priority and appoint a person having a lower priority or no priority.

§5–410. [Bond.]

The Court may require a conservator to furnish a bond conditioned upon faithful discharge of all duties of the trust according to law, with sureties as it shall specify. Unless otherwise directed, the bond must be in the amount of the aggregate capital value of the property of the estate in the conservator's control, plus one year's estimated income, and minus the value of securities deposited under arrangements requiring an order of the Court for their removal and the value of any land which the fiduciary, by express limitation of power, lacks power to sell or convey without Court authorization. The Court, in lieu of sureties on a bond, may accept other collateral for the performance of the bond, including a pledge of securities or a mortgage of land.

§5–411. [Terms and Requirements of Bonds.]

(a) The following requirements and provisions apply to any bond required under Section 5–410.

(1) Unless otherwise provided by the terms of the approved bond, sureties are jointly and severally liable with the conservator and with each other.

(2) By executing an approved bond of a conservator, the surety consents to the jurisdiction of the Court that issued letters to the primary obligor in any proceeding pertaining to the fiduciary duties of the conservator and naming the surety as a party respondent. Notice of any proceeding must be delivered to the surety or mailed by registered or certified mail to the address listed with the Court at the place where the bond is filed and to the address as then known to the petitioner.

(3) On petition of a successor conservator or any interested person, a proceeding may be initiated against a surety for breach of the obligation of the bond of the conservator.

(4) The bond of the conservator is not void after the first recovery but may be proceeded against from time to time until the whole penalty is exhausted.

(b) No proceeding may be commenced against the surety on any matter as to which an action or proceeding against the primary obligor is barred by adjudication or limitation.

§5–412. [Effect of Acceptance of Appointment.]

By accepting appointment, a conservator submits personally to the jurisdiction of the Court in any proceeding relating to the estate which may be instituted by any interested person. Notice of any proceeding must be delivered to the conservator or mailed by registered or certified mail to the address as listed in the petition for appointment or as thereafter reported to the Court and to the address as then known to the petitioner.

§5–413. [Compensation and Expenses.]

If not otherwise compensated for services rendered, any visitor, attorney, physician, conservator, or special conservator appointed in a protective proceeding and any attorney whose services resulted in a protective order or in an order that was beneficial to a protected person's estate is entitled to reasonable compensation from the estate.

§5–414. [Death, Resignation, or Removal of Conservator.]

The Court may remove a conservator for good cause, upon notice and hearing, or accept the resignation of a conservator. Upon the conservator's death, resignation, or removal, the Court may appoint another conservator. A conservator so appointed succeeds to the title and powers of the predecessor.

§5–415. [Petitions for Orders Subsequent to Appointment.]

(a) Any person interested in the welfare of a person for whom a conservator has been appointed may file a petition in the appointing court for an order:

(1) requiring bond or collateral or additional bond or collateral, or reducing bond;

(2) requiring an accounting for the administration of the trust;

(3) directing distribution;

(4) removing the conservator and appointing a temporary or successor conservator; or

(5) granting other appropriate relief.

(b) A conservator may petition the appointing court for instructions concerning fiduciary responsibility.

(c) Upon notice and hearing, the Court may give appropriate instructions or make any appropriate order.

§5–416. [General Duty of Conservator.]

A conservator, in relation to powers conferred by this Part, or implicit in the title acquired by virtue of the proceeding, shall act as a fiduciary and observe the standards of care applicable to trustees.

§5–417. [Inventory and Records.]

(a) Within 90 days after appointment, each conservator shall prepare and file with the appointing Court a complete inventory of the estate subject to the conservatorship together with an oath or affirmation that the inventory is believed to be complete and accurate as far as information permits. The conservator shall provide a copy thereof to the protected person if practicable and the person has attained the age of 14 years and has sufficient mental capacity to understand the arrangement. A copy also shall be provided to any guardian or parent with whom the protected person resides.

(b) The conservator shall keep suitable records of the administration and exhibit the same on request of any interested person.

§5–418. [Accounts.]

Each conservator shall account to the Court for administration of the trust not less than annually unless the Court directs otherwise, upon resignation or removal and at other times as the Court may direct. On termination of the protected person's minority or disability, a conservator shall account to the Court or to the formerly protected person or the successors of that person. Subject to appeal or vacation within the time permitted, an order after notice and hearing allowing an intermediate account of a conservator adjudicates as to liabilities concerning the matters considered in connection therewith; and an order, following notice and hearing, allowing a final account adjudicates as to all previously unsettled liabilities of the conservator to the protected person or the protected person's successors relating to the conservatorship. In connection with any account, the Court may require a conservator to submit to a physical check of the estate, to be made in any manner the Court specifies.
As amended in 1987.

§5–419. [Conservators; Title By Appointment.]

(a) The appointment of a conservator vests in the conservator title as trustee to all property, or to the part thereof specified in the order, of the protected person, presently held or thereafter acquired, including title to any property theretofore held for the protected person by custodians or attorneys-in-fact. An order specifying that only a part of the property of the protected person vests in the conservator creates a limited conservatorship.

(b) Except as otherwise provided herein, the interest of the protected person in property vested in a conservator by this section is not transferrable or assignable by the protected person. An attempted transfer or assignment by the protected person, though ineffective to affect property rights, may generate a claim for restitution or damages which, subject to presentation and allowance, may be satisfied as provided in Section 5–427.

(c) Neither property vested in a conservator by this section nor the interest of the protected person in that property is subject to levy, garnishment, or similar process other than an order issued in the protective proceeding made as provided in Section 5–427.

§5–420. [Recording of Conservator's Letters.]

(a) Letters of conservatorship are evidence of transfer of all assets, or the part thereof specified in the letters, of a protected person to the conservator. An order terminating a conservatorship is evidence of transfer of all assets subjected to the conservatorship from the conservator to the protected person, or to successors of the person.

(b) Subject to the requirements of general statutes governing the filing or recordation of documents of title to land or other property, letters of conservatorship and orders terminating conservatorships, may be filed or recorded to give record notice of title as between the conservator and the protected person.

§5–421. [Sale, Encumbrance, or Transaction Involving Conflict of Interest; Voidable; Exceptions.]

Any sale or encumbrance to a conservator, the spouse, agent, attorney of a conservator, or any corporation, trust, or other organization in which the conservator has a substantial beneficial interest, or any other transaction involving the estate being administered by the conservator which is affected by a substantial conflict between fiduciary and personal interests is voidable unless the transaction is approved by the Court after notice as directed by the Court.

§5–422. [Persons Dealing With Conservators; Protection.]

(a) A person who in good faith either assists or deals with a conservator for value in any transaction other than those requiring a Court order as provided in Section 5–407 is protected as if the conservator properly exercised the power. The fact that a person knowingly deals with a conservator does not alone require the person to inquire into the existence of a power or the propriety of its exercise, but restrictions on powers of conservators which are endorsed on letters as provided in Section 5–425 are effective as to third persons. A person is not bound to see to the proper application of estate assets paid or delivered to a conservator.

(b) The protection expressed in this section extends to any procedural irregularity or jurisdictional defect occurred in proceedings leading to the issuance of letters and is not a substitution for protection provided by comparable provisions of the law relating to commercial transactions or to simplifying transfers of securities by fiduciaries.

§5–423. [Powers of Conservator in Administration.]

(a) Subject to limitation provided in Section 5–425, a conservator has all of the powers conferred in this section and any additional powers conferred by law on trustees in this State. In addition, a conservator of the estate of an unmarried minor [under the age of 18 years], as to whom no one has parental rights, has the duties and powers of a guardian of a minor described in Section 5–209 until the minor attains [the age of 18 years] or marries, but the parental rights so conferred on a conservator do not preclude appointment of a guardian as provided in Part 2.

(b) A conservator without Court authorization or confirmation, may invest and reinvest funds of the estate as would a trustee.

(c) A conservator, acting reasonably in efforts to accomplish the purpose of the appointment, may act without Court authorization or confirmation, to

(1) collect, hold, and retain assets of the estate including land in another state, until judging that disposition of the assets should be made, and the assets may be retained even though they include an asset in which the conservator is personally interested;

(2) receive additions to the estate;

(3) continue or participate in the operation of any business or other enterprise;

(4) acquire an undivided interest in an estate asset in which the conservator, in any fiduciary capacity, holds an undivided interest;

(5) invest and reinvest estate assets in accordance with subsection (b);

(6) deposit estate funds in a state or federally insured financial institution, including one operated by the conservator;

(7) acquire or dispose of an estate asset, including land in another state, for cash or on credit, at public or private sale, and manage, develop, improve, exchange, partition, change the character of, or abandon an estate asset;

(8) make ordinary or extraordinary repairs or alterations in buildings or other structures; demolish any improvements; and raze existing or erect new party walls or buildings;

(9) subdivide, develop, or dedicate land to public use; make or obtain the vacation of plats and adjust boundaries; adjust differences in valuation or exchange or partition by giving or receiving considerations; and dedicate easements to public use without consideration;

(10) enter for any purpose into a lease as lessor or lessee with or without option to purchase or renew for a term within or extending beyond the term of the conservatorship;

(11) enter into a lease or arrangement for exploration and removal of minerals or other natural resources or enter into a pooling or unitization agreement;

(12) grant an option involving disposition of an estate asset and take an option for the acquisition of any asset;

(13) vote a security, in person or by general or limited proxy;

(14) pay calls, assessments, and any other sums chargeable or accruing against or on account of securities;

(15) sell or exercise stock-subscription or conversion rights;

(16) consent, directly or through a committee or other agent, to the reorganization, consolidation, merger, dissolution, or liquidation of a corporation or other business enterprise;

(17) hold a security in the name of a nominee or in other form without disclosure of the conservatorship so that title to the security may pass by delivery, but the conservator is liable for any act of the nominee in connection with the stock so held;

(18) insure the assets of the estate against damage or loss and the conservator against liability with respect to third persons;

(19) borrow money to be repaid from estate assets or otherwise; advance money for the protection of the estate or the protected person and for all expenses, losses, and liability sustained in the administration of the estate or because of the holding or ownership of any estate assets, for which the conservator has a lien on the estate as against the protected person for advances so made;

(20) pay or contest any claim; settle a claim by or against the estate or the protected person by compromise, arbitration, or otherwise; and release, in whole or in part, any claim belonging to the estate to the extent the claim is uncollectible;

(21) pay taxes, assessments, compensation of the conservator, and other expenses incurred in the collection, care, administration, and protection of the estate;

(22) allocate items of income or expense to either estate income or principal, as provided by law, including creation of reserves out of income for depreciation, obsolescence, or amortization, or for depletion in mineral or timber properties;

(23) pay any sum distributable to a protected person or dependent of the protected person by paying the sum to the distributee or by paying the sum for the use of the distributee to the guardian of the distributee, or, if none, to a relative or other person having custody of the distributee;

(24) employ persons, including attorneys, auditors, investment advisors, or agents, even though they are associated with the conservator, to advise or assist in the performance of administrative duties; act upon their recommendation without independent investigation; and instead of acting personally, employ one or more agents to perform any act of administration, whether or not discretionary;

(25) prosecute or defend actions, claims, or proceedings in any jurisdiction for the protection of estate assets and of the conservator in the performance of fiduciary duties; and

(26) execute and deliver all instruments that will accomplish or facilitate the exercise of the powers vested in the conservator.

§5–424. [Distributive Duties and Powers of Conservator.]

(a) A conservator may expend or distribute income or principal of the estate without Court authorization or confirmation for the support, education, care, or benefit of the protected person and dependents in accordance with the following principles:

(1) The conservator shall consider recommendations relating to the appropriate standard of support, education, and benefit for the protected person or dependent made by a parent or guardian, if any. The conservator may not be surcharged for sums paid to persons or organizations furnishing support, education, or care to the protected person or a dependent pursuant to the recommendations of a parent or guardian of the protected person unless the conservator knows that the parent or guardian derives personal financial benefit therefrom, including relief from any personal duty of support or the recommendations are clearly not in the best interest of the protected person.

(2) The conservator shall expend or distribute sums reasonably necessary for the support, education, care, or benefit of the protected person and dependents with due regard to (i) the size of the estate, the probable duration of the conservatorship, and the likelihood that the protected person, at some future time, may be fully able to be wholly self-sufficient and able to manage business affairs and the estate; (ii) the accustomed standard of living of the protected person and dependents; and (iii) other funds or sources used for the support of the protected person.

(3) The conservator may expend funds of the estate for the support of persons legally dependent on the protected person and others who are members of the protected person's household who are unable to support themselves, and who are in need of support.

(4) Funds expended under this subsection may be paid by the conservator to any person, including the protected person, to reimburse for expenditures that the conservator might have made, or in advance for services to be rendered to the protected person if it is reasonable to expect the services will be performed and advance payments are customary or reasonably necessary under the circumstances.

(5) A conservator, in discharging the responsibilities conferred by Court order and this Part, shall implement the principles described in Section 5–407(a), to the extent possible.

(b) If the estate is ample to provide for the purposes implicit in the distributions authorized by the preceding subsections, a conservator for a protected person other than a minor has power to make gifts to charity and other objects as the protected person might have been expected to make, in amounts that do not exceed in total for any year 20 percent of the income from the estate.

(c) When a minor who has not been adjudged disabled under Section 5–401(c) attains majority, the conservator, after meeting all claims and expenses of administration, shall pay over and distribute all funds and properties to the formerly protected person as soon as possible.

(d) If satisfied that a protected person's disability, other than minority, has ceased, the conservator, after meeting all claims and expenses of administration, shall pay over and distribute all funds and properties to the formerly protected person as soon as possible.

(e) If a protected person dies, the conservator shall deliver to the Court for safekeeping any will of the deceased protected person which may have come into the conservator's possession, inform the executor or beneficiary named therein of the delivery, and retain the estate for delivery to a duly appointed personal representative of the decedent or other persons entitled thereto. If, 40 days after the death of the protected person, no other person has been appointed personal representative and no application or petition for appointment is before the Court, the conservator may apply to exercise the powers and duties of a personal representative in order to be able to proceed to administer and distribute the decedent's estate. Upon application for an order granting the powers of a personal representative to a conservator, after notice to any person nominated personal representative by any will of which the applicant is aware, the Court may grant the application upon determining that there is no objection and endorse the letters of the conservator to note that the formerly protected person is deceased and that the conservator has acquired all of the powers and duties of a personal representative. The making and entry of an order under this section has the effect of an order of appointment of a personal representative [as provided in Section 3–308 and Parts 6 through 10 of Article III], but the estate in the name of the conservator, after administration, may be distributed to the decedent's successors without prior re-transfer to the conservator as personal representative.

§5–425. [Enlargement or Limitation of Powers of Conservator.]

Subject to the restrictions in Section 5–407(c), the Court may confer on a conservator at the time of appointment or later, in addition to the powers conferred by Sections 5–423 and 5–424, any power that the Court itself could exercise under Sections 5–407(b)(2) and 5–407(b)(3). The Court, at the time of appointment or later, may limit the powers of a conservator otherwise conferred by Sections 5–423 and 5–424 or previously conferred by the Court and may at any time remove or modify any limitation. If the Court limits any power conferred on the conservator by Section 5–423 or Section 5–424, or specifies, as provided in Section 5–419(a), that title to some but not all assets of the protected person vest in the conservator, the limitation or specification of assets subject to the conservatorship must be endorsed upon the letters of appointment.

§5–426. [Preservation of Estate Plan; Right to Examine.]

In (i) investing the estate, (ii) selecting assets of the estate for distribution under subsections (a) and (b) of Section 5–424, and (iii) utilizing powers of revocation or withdrawal available for the support of the protected person and exercisable by the conservator or the Court, the conservator and the Court shall take into account any estate plan of the protected person known to them, including a will, any revocable trust of which the person is settlor, and any contract, transfer, or joint ownership arrangement originated by the protected person with provisions for payment or transfer of benefits or interests at the person's death to another or others. The conservator may examine the will of the protected person.

§5–427. [Claims Against Protected Person; Enforcement.]

(a) A conservator may pay or secure from the estate claims against the estate or against the protected person arising before or after the conservatorship upon their presentation and allowance in accordance with the priorities stated in subsection (c). A claim may be presented by either of the following methods:

(1) The claimant may deliver or mail to the conservator a written statement of the claim indicating its basis, the name and mailing address of the claimant, and the amount claimed; or

(2) The claimant may file a written statement of the claim, in the form prescribed by rule, with the clerk of Court and deliver or mail a copy of the statement to the conservator.

(b) A claim is deemed presented on the first to occur of receipt of the written statement of claim by the conservator or the filing of the claim with the Court. A presented claim is allowed if it is not disallowed by written statement mailed by the conservator to the claimant within 60 days after its presentation. The presentation of a claim tolls any statute of limitation relating to the claim until 30 days after its disallowance.

(c) A claimant whose claim has not been paid may petition the [appropriate] Court for determination of the claim at any time before it is barred by the applicable statute of limitation and, upon due proof, procure an order for its allowance, payment, or security from the estate. If a proceeding is pending against a protected person at the time of appointment of a conservator or is initiated against the protected person thereafter, the moving party shall give notice of the proceeding to the conservator if the proceeding could result in creating a claim against the estate.

(d) If it appears that the estate in conservatorship is likely to be exhausted before all existing claims are paid, the conservator shall distribute the estate in money or in kind in payment of claims in the following order:

(1) costs and expenses of administration;

(2) claims of the federal or state government having priority under other laws;

(3) claims incurred by the conservator for care, maintenance, and education, previously provided to the protected person or the protected person's dependents;

(4) claims arising prior to the conservatorship;

(5) all other claims.

(e) No preference may be given in the payment of any claim over any other claim of the same class, and a claim due and payable is not entitled to a preference over claims not due; but if it appears that the assets of the conservatorship are adequate to meet all existing claims, the Court, acting in the best interest of the protected person, may order the conservator to give a mortgage or other security on the conservatorship estate to secure payment at some future date of any or all claims in class 5.

§5–428. [Personal Liability of Conservator.]

(a) Unless otherwise provided in the contract, a conservator is not personally liable on a contract properly entered into in fiduciary capacity in the course of administration of the estate unless the conservator fails to reveal the representative capacity and identify the estate in the contract.

(b) The conservator is personally liable for obligations arising from ownership or control of property of the estate or for torts committed in the course of administration of the estate only if personally at fault.

(c) Claims based on (i) contracts entered into by a conservator in fiduciary capacity, (ii) obligations arising from ownership or control of the estate, or (iii) torts committed in the course of administration of the estate, may be asserted against the estate by proceeding against the conservator in fiduciary capacity, whether or not the conservator is personally liable therefor.

(d) Any question of liability between the estate and the conservator personally may be determined in a proceeding for accounting, surcharge, or indemnification, or other appropriate proceeding or action.

§5–429. [Termination of Proceedings.]

The protected person, conservator, or any other interested person, may petition the Court to terminate the conservatorship. A protected person seeking termination is entitled to the same rights and procedures as in an original proceeding for a protective order. The Court, upon determining after notice and hearing that the minority or disability of the protected person has ceased, shall terminate the conservatorship. Upon termination, title to assets of the estate passes to the formerly pro-

tected person or to successors. The order of termination must provide for expenses of administration and direct the conservator to execute appropriate instruments to evidence the transfer.

§5–430. [Payment of Debt and Delivery of Property to Foreign Conservator without Local Proceedings.]

(a) Any person indebted to a protected person or having possession of property or of an instrument evidencing a debt, stock, or chose in action belonging to a protected person may pay or deliver it to a conservator, guardian of the estate, or other like fiduciary appointed by a court of the state of residence of the protected person upon being presented with proof of appointment and an affidavit made by or on behalf of the fiduciary stating:

(1) that no protective proceeding relating to the protected person is pending in this State; and

(2) that the foreign fiduciary is entitled to payment or to receive delivery.

(b) If the person to whom the affidavit is presented is not aware of any protective proceeding pending in this State, payment or delivery in response to the demand and affidavit discharges the debtor or possessor.

§5–431. [Foreign Conservator; Proof of Authority; Bond; Powers.]

If a conservator has not been appointed in this State and no petition in a protective proceeding is pending in this State, a conservator appointed in the state in which the protected person resides may file in a Court of this State in a [county] in which property belonging to the protected person is located, authenticated copies of letters of appointment and of any bond. Thereafter, the domiciliary foreign conservator may exercise as to assets in this State all powers of a conservator appointed in this State and may maintain actions and proceedings in this State subject to any conditions imposed upon nonresident parties generally.

PART 5

DURABLE POWER OF ATTORNEY

ADOPTION OF UNIFORM DURABLE POWER OF ATTORNEY ACT

§5–501. [Definition.]

A durable power of attorney is a power of attorney by which a principal designates another his attorney in fact in writing and the writing contains the words "This power of attorney shall not be affected by subsequent disability or incapacity of the principal, or lapse of time," or "This power of attorney shall become effective upon the disability or incapacity of the principal," or similar words showing the intent of the principal that the authority conferred shall be exercisable notwithstanding the principal's subsequent disability or incapacity, and, unless it states a time of termination, notwithstanding the lapse of time since the execution of the instrument. As amended in 1984.

§5–502. [Durable Power of Attorney Not Affected By Lapse of Time, Disability or Incapacity.]

All acts done by an attorney in fact pursuant to a durable power of attorney during any period of disability or incapacity of the principal have the same effect and inure to the benefit of and bind the principal and his successors in interest as if the principal were competent and not disabled. Unless the instrument states a time of termination, the power is exercisable notwithstanding the lapse of time since the execution of the instrument. As amended in 1987.

§5–503. [Relation of Attorney in Fact to Court Appointed Fiduciary.]

(a) If, following execution of a durable power of attorney, a court of the principal's domicile appoints a conservator, guardian of the estate, or other fiduciary charged with the management of all of the principal's property or all of his property except specified exclusions, the attorney in fact is accountable to the fiduciary as well as to the principal. The fiduciary has the same power to revoke or amend the power of attorney that the principal would have had if he were not disabled or incapacitated.

(b) A principal may nominate, by a durable power of attorney, the conservator, guardian of his estate, or guardian of his person for consideration by the court if protective proceedings for the principal's person or estate are thereafter commenced. The court shall make its appointment in accordance with the principal's most recent nomination in a durable power of attorney except for good cause or disqualification.

§5–504. [Power of Attorney Not Revoked Until Notice.]

(a) The death of a principal who has executed a written power of attorney, durable or otherwise, does not revoke or terminate the agency as to the attorney in fact or other person, who, without actual knowledge of the death of the principal, acts in good faith under the power. Any action so taken, unless otherwise invalid or unenforceable, binds successors in interest of the principal.

(b) The disability or incapacity of a principal who has previously executed a written power of attorney that is not a durable power does not revoke or terminate the agency as to the attorney in fact or other person, who, without actual knowledge of the disability or incapacity of the principal, acts in good faith under the power. Any action so taken, unless otherwise invalid or unenforceable, binds the principal and his successors in interest.

§5–505. [Proof of Continuance of Durable and Other Powers of Attorney by Affidavit.]

As to acts undertaken in good faith reliance thereon, an affidavit executed by the attorney in fact under a power of attorney, durable or otherwise, stating that he did not have at the time of exercise of the power actual knowledge of the termination of the power by revocation or of the principal's death, disability, or incapacity is conclusive proof of the nonrevocation or nontermination of the power at that time. If the exercise of the power of attorney requires execution and delivery of any instrument that is recordable, the affidavit when authenticated for record is likewise recordable. This section does not affect any provision in a power of attorney for its termination by expiration of time or occurrence of an event other than express revocation or a change in the principal's capacity.

ARTICLE VI
NONPROBATE TRANSFERS ON DEATH (1989)

PART 1
PROVISIONS RELATING TO EFFECT OF DEATH

Section

PART 2
MULTIPLE-PERSON ACCOUNTS

SUBPART 1
DEFINITIONS AND GENERAL PROVISIONS

Section

SUBPART 2
OWNERSHIP AS BETWEEN PARTIES AND OTHERS

PART 1
PROVISIONS RELATING TO EFFECT OF DEATH

§6–101. Nonprobate Transfers on Death.

(a) A provision for a nonprobate transfer on death in an insurance policy, contract of employment, bond, mortgage, promissory note, certificated or uncertificated security, account agreement, custodial agreement, deposit agreement, compensation plan, pension plan, individual retirement plan, employee benefit plan, trust, conveyance, deed of gift, marital property agreement, or other written instrument of a similar nature is nontestamentary. This subsection includes a written provision that:

(1) money or other benefits due to, controlled by, or owned by a decedent before death must be paid after the decedent's death to a person whom the decedent designates either in the instrument or in a separate writing, including a will, executed either before or at the same time as the instrument, or later;

(2) money due or to become due under the instrument ceases to be payable in the event of death of the promisee or the promisor before payment or demand; or

(3) any property controlled by or owned by the decedent before death which is the subject of the instrument passes to a person the decedent designates either in the instrument or in a separate writing, including a will, executed either before or at the same time as the instrument, or later.

(b) This section does not limit rights of creditors under other laws of this State.

PART 2
MULTIPLE-PERSON ACCOUNTS

SUBPART 1
DEFINITIONS AND GENERAL PROVISIONS

§6–201. Definitions.

In this part:

(1) "Account" means a contract of deposit between a depositor and a financial institution, and includes a checking account, savings account, certificate of deposit, and share account.

(2) "Agent" means a person authorized to make account transactions for a party.

(3) "Beneficiary" means a person named as one to whom sums on deposit in an account are payable on request after death of all parties or for whom a party is named as trustee.

(4) "Financial institution" means an organization authorized to do business under state or federal laws relating to financial institutions, and includes a bank, trust company, savings bank, building and loan association, savings and loan company or association, and credit union.

(5) "Multiple-party account" means an account payable on request to one or more of two or more parties, whether or not a right of survivorship is mentioned.

(6) "Party" means a person who, by the terms of an account, has a present right, subject to request, to payment from the account other than as a beneficiary or agent.

(7) "Payment" of sums on deposit includes withdrawal, payment to a party or third person pursuant to check or other request, and a pledge of sums on deposit by a party, or a set-off, reduction, or other disposition of all or part of an account pursuant to a pledge.

(8) "POD designation" means the designation of (i) a beneficiary in an account payable on request to one party during the party's lifetime and on the party's death to one or more beneficiaries, or to one or more parties during their lifetimes and on death of all of them to one or more beneficiaries, or (ii) a beneficiary in an account in the name of one or more parties as trustee for one or more beneficiaries if the relationship is established by the terms of the account and there is no subject of the trust other than the sums on deposit in the account, whether or not payment to the beneficiary is mentioned.

(9) "Receive," as it relates to notice to a financial institution, means receipt in the office or branch office of the

financial institution in which the account is established, but if the terms of the account require notice at a particular place, in the place required.

(10) "Request" means a request for payment complying with all terms of the account, including special requirements concerning necessary signatures and regulations of the financial institution; but, for purposes of this part, if terms of the account condition payment on advance notice, a request for payment is treated as immediately effective and a notice of intent to withdraw is treated as a request for payment.

(11) "Sums on deposit" means the balance payable on an account, including interest and dividends earned, whether or not included in the current balance, and any deposit life insurance proceeds added to the account by reason of death of a party.

(12) "Terms of the account" includes the deposit agreement and other terms and conditions, including the form, of the contract of deposit.

§6–202. Limitation on Scope of Part.
This part does not apply to (i) an account established for a partnership, joint venture, or other organization for a business purpose, (ii) an account controlled by one or more persons as an agent or trustee for a corporation, unincorporated association, or charitable or civic organization, or (iii) a fiduciary or trust account in which the relationship is established other than by the terms of the account.

§6–203. Types of Account; Existing Accounts.
(a) An account may be for a single party or multiple parties. A multiple-party account may be with or without a right of survivorship between the parties. Subject to Section 6–212(c), either a single-party account or a multiple-party account may have a POD designation, an agency designation, or both.

(b) An account established before, on, or after the effective date of this part, whether in the form prescribed in Section 6–204 or in any other form, is either a single-party account or a multiple-party account, with or without right of survivorship, and with or without a POD designation or an agency designation, within the meaning of this part, and is governed by this part.

§6–204. Forms.
(a) A contract of deposit that contains provisions in substantially the following form establishes the type of account provided, and the account is governed by the provisions of this part applicable to an account of that type:

UNIFORM SINGLE-OR MULTIPLE-PARTY
ACCOUNT FORM
PARTIES [Name One or More Parties]:

_____ _____

OWNERSHIP [Select One And Initial]:

_____ SINGLE-PARTY ACCOUNT
_____ MULTIPLE-PARTY ACCOUNT
Parties own account in proportion to net contributions unless there is clear and convincing evidence of a different intent.
RIGHTS AT DEATH [Select One And Initial]:
_____ SINGLE-PARTY ACCOUNT
At death of party, ownership passes as part of party's estate.
_____ SINGLE PARTY ACCOUNT WITH POD (PAY ON DEATH) DESIGNATION
[Name One Or More Beneficiaries]:

_____ _____

At death of party, ownership passes to POD beneficiaries and is not part of party's estate.
_____ MULTIPLE-PARTY ACCOUNT WITH RIGHT OF SURVIVORSHIP
At death of party, ownership passes to surviving parties.
_____ MULTIPLE-PARTY ACCOUNT WITH RIGHT OF SURVIVORSHIP AND POD (PAY ON DEATH) DESIGNATION
[Name One Or More Beneficiaries]:

_____ _____

At death of last surviving party, ownership passes to POD beneficiaries and is not part of last surviving party's estate.
_____ MULTIPLE-PARTY ACCOUNT WITHOUT RIGHT OF SURVIVORSHIP
At death of party, deceased party's ownership passes as part of deceased party's estate.
AGENCY (POWER OF ATTORNEY) DESIGNATION [Optional] Agents may make account transactions for parties but have no ownership or rights at death unless named as POD beneficiaries.
[To Add Agency Designation To Account, Name One Or More Agents]:

_____ _____

[Select One And Initial]:
_____ AGENCY DESIGNATION SURVIVES DISABILITY OR INCAPACITY OF PARTIES
_____ AGENCY DESIGNATION TERMINATES ON DISABILITY OR INCAPACITY OF PARTIES
(b) A contract of deposit that does not contain provisions in substantially the form provided in subsection (a) is governed by the provisions of this part applicable to the type of account that most nearly conforms to the depositor's intent.

§6–205. Designation of Agent.
(a) By a writing signed by all parties, the parties may designate as agent of all parties on an account a person other than a party.
(b) Unless the terms of an agency designation provide that the authority of the agent terminates on disability or incapacity of a party, the agent's authority survives disability and incapacity. The agent may act for a disabled

or incapacitated party until the authority of the agent is terminated.

(c) Death of the sole party or last surviving party terminates the authority of an agent.

§6–206. Applicability of Part.

The provisions of Subpart 2 concerning beneficial ownership as between parties or as between parties and beneficiaries apply only to controversies between those persons and their creditors and other successors, and do not apply to the right of those persons to payment as determined by the terms of the account. Subpart 3 governs the liability and set-off rights of financial institutions that make payments pursuant to it.

SUBPART 2
OWNERSHIP AS BETWEEN PARTIES AND OTHERS

§6–211. Ownership During Lifetime.

(a) In this section, "net contribution" of a party means the sum of all deposits to an account made by or for the party, less all payments from the account made to or for the party which have not been paid to or applied to the use of another party and a proportionate share of any charges deducted from the account, plus a proportionate share of any interest or dividends earned, whether or not included in the current balance. The term includes deposit life insurance proceeds added to the account by reason of death of the party whose net contribution is in question.

(b) During the lifetime of all parties, an account belongs to the parties in proportion to the net contribution of each to the sums on deposit, unless there is clear and convincing evidence of a different intent. As between parties married to each other, in the absence of proof otherwise, the net contribution of each is presumed to be an equal amount.

(c) A beneficiary in an account having a POD designation has no right to sums on deposit during the lifetime of any party.

(d) An agent in an account with an agency designation has no beneficial right to sums on deposit.

§6–212. Rights at Death.

(a) Except as otherwise provided in this part, on death of a party sums on deposit in a multiple-party account belong to the surviving party or parties. If two or more parties survive and one is the surviving spouse of the decedent, the amount to which the decedent, immediately before death, was beneficially entitled under Section 6–211 belongs to the surviving spouse. If two or more parties survive and none is the surviving spouse of the decedent, the amount to which the decedent, immediately before death, was beneficially entitled under Section 6–211 belongs to the surviving parties in equal shares, and augments the proportion to which each sur-

vivor, immediately before the decedent's death, was beneficially entitled under Section 6–211, and the right of survivorship continues between the surviving parties.

(b) In an account with a POD designation:

(1) On death of one of two or more parties, the rights in sums on deposit are governed by subsection (a).

(2) On death of the sole party or the last survivor of two or more parties, sums on deposit belong to the surviving beneficiary or beneficiaries. If two or more beneficiaries survive, sums on deposit belong to them in equal and undivided shares, and there is no right of survivorship in the event of death of a beneficiary thereafter. If no beneficiary survives, sums on deposit belong to the estate of the last surviving party.

(c) Sums on deposit in a single-party account without a POD designation, or in a multiple party account that, by the terms of the account, is without right of survivorship, are not affected by death of a party, but the amount to which the decedent, immediately before death, was beneficially entitled under Section 6–211 is transferred as part of the decedent's estate. A POD designation in a multiple-party account without right of survivorship is ineffective. For purposes of this section, designation of an account as a tenancy in common establishes that the account is without right of survivorship.

(d) The ownership right of a surviving party or beneficiary, or of the decedent's estate, in sums on deposit is subject to requests for payment made by a party before the party's death, whether paid by the financial institution before or after death, or unpaid. The surviving party or beneficiary, or the decedent's estate, is liable to the payee of an unpaid request for payment. The liability is limited to a proportionate share of the amount transferred under this section, to the extent necessary to discharge the request for payment.

As amended in 1991.

§6–213. Alteration of Rights.

(a) Rights at death under Section 6–212 are determined by the type of account at the death of a party. The type of account may be altered by written notice given by a party to the financial institution to change the type of account or to stop or vary payment under the terms of the account. The notice must be signed by a party and received by the financial institution during the party's lifetime.

(b) A right of survivorship arising from the express terms of the account, Section 6–212, or a POD designation, may not be altered by will.

§6-214. Accounts and Transfers Nontestamentary.

Except as provided in Part 2 of Article II (elective share of surviving spouse) or as a consequence of, and to the extent directed by, Section 6–215, a transfer resulting from the application of Section 6–212 is effective by reason of the terms of the account involved and this part and is not testamentary or subject to Articles I through IV (estate administration).

§6–215.   Rights of Creditors and Others.

(a) If other assets of the estate are insufficient, a transfer resulting from a right of survivorship or POD designation under this part is not effective against the estate of a deceased party to the extent needed to pay claims against the estate and statutory allowances to the surviving spouse and children.

(b) A surviving party or beneficiary who receives payment from an account after death of a party is liable to account to the personal representative of the decedent for a proportionate share of the amount received to which the decedent, immediately before death, was beneficially entitled under Section 6–211, to the extent necessary to discharge the claims and allowances described in subsection (a) remaining unpaid after application of the decedent's estate. A proceeding to assert the liability may not be commenced unless the personal representative has received a written demand by the surviving spouse, a creditor, a child, or a person acting for a child of the decedent. The proceeding must be commenced within one year after death of the decedent.

(c) A surviving party or beneficiary against whom a proceeding to account is brought may join as a party to the proceeding a surviving party or beneficiary of any other account of the decedent.

(d) Sums recovered by the personal representative must be administered as part of the decedent's estate. This section does not affect the protection from claims of the personal representative or estate of a deceased party provided in Section 6–226 for a financial institution that makes payment in accordance with the terms of the account.
As amended in 1991.

§6–216.   Community Property and Tenancy by the Entireties.

(a) A deposit of community property in an account does not alter the community character of the property or community rights in the property, but a right of survivorship between parties married to each other arising from the express terms of the account or Section 6–212 may not be altered by will.

(b) This part does not affect the law governing tenancy by the entireties.

SUBPART 3
PROTECTION OF FINANCIAL INSTITUTIONS

§6–221.   Authority of Financial Institution.

A financial institution may enter into a contract of deposit for a multiple-party account to the same extent it may enter into a contract of deposit for a single-party account, and may provide for a POD designation and an agency designation in either a single-party account or a multiple-party account. A financial institution need not inquire as to the source of a deposit to an account or as to the proposed application of a payment from an account.

§6–222.   Payment on Multiple-Party Account.

A financial institution, on request, may pay sums on deposit in a multiple-party account to:

(1) one or more of the parties, whether or not another party is disabled, incapacitated, or deceased when payment is requested and whether or not the party making the request survives another party; or

(2) the personal representative, if any, or, if there is none, the heirs or devisees of a deceased party if proof of death is presented to the financial institution showing that the deceased party was the survivor of all other persons named on the account either as a party or beneficiary, unless the account is without right of survivorship under Section 6–212.

§6–223.   Payment on POD Designation.

A financial institution, on request, may pay sums on deposit in an account with a POD designation to:

(1) one or more of the parties, whether or not another party is disabled, incapacitated, or deceased when the payment is requested and whether or not a party survives another party;

(2) the beneficiary or beneficiaries, if proof of death is presented to the financial institution showing that the beneficiary or beneficiaries survived all persons named as parties; or

(3) the personal representative, if any, or, if there is none, the heirs or devisees of a deceased party, if proof of death is presented to the financial institution showing that the deceased party was the survivor of all other persons named on the account either as a party or beneficiary.

§6–224.   Payment to Designated Agent.

A financial institution, on request of an agent under an agency designation for an account, may pay to the agent sums on deposit in the account, whether or not a party is disabled, incapacitated, or deceased when the request is made or received, and whether or not the authority of the agent terminates on the disability or incapacity of a party.

§6–225.   Payment to Minor.

If a financial institution is required or permitted to make payment pursuant to this part to a minor designated as a beneficiary, payment may be made pursuant to the Uniform Transfers to Minors Act.

§6–226.   Discharge.

(a) Payment made pursuant to this part in accordance with the type of account discharges the financial institution from all claims for amounts so paid, whether or not the payment is consistent with the beneficial ownership of the account as between parties, beneficiaries, or their successors. Payment may be made whether or not a party, beneficiary, or agent is disabled, incapacitated, or deceased when payment is requested, received, or made.

(b) Protection under this section does not extend to payments made after a financial institution has received written notice from a party, or from the personal representative, surviving spouse, or heir or devisee of a deceased party, to the effect that payments in accordance with the terms of the account, including one having an agency designation, should not be permitted, and the financial institution has had a reasonable opportunity to act on it when the payment is made. Unless the notice is withdrawn by the person giving it, the successor of any deceased party must concur in a request for payment if the financial institution is to be protected under this section. Unless a financial institution has been served with process in an action or proceeding, no other notice or other information shown to have been available to the financial institution affects its right to protection under this section.

(c) A financial institution that receives written notice pursuant to this section or otherwise has reason to believe that a dispute exists as to the rights of the parties may refuse, without liability, to make payments in accordance with the terms of the account.

(d) Protection of a financial institution under this section does not affect the rights of parties in disputes between themselves or their successors concerning the beneficial ownership of sums on deposit in accounts or payments made from accounts.

§6–227. Set-Off.

Without qualifying any other statutory right to set-off or lien and subject to any contractual provision, if a party is indebted to a financial institution, the financial institution has a right to set-off against the account. The amount of the account subject to set-off is the proportion to which the party is, or immediately before death was, beneficially entitled under Section 6–211 or, in the absence of proof of that proportion, an equal share with all parties.

PART 3
UNIFORM TOD SECURITY REGISTRATION ACT

§6–301. Definitions.

In this part:

(1) "Beneficiary form" means a registration of a security which indicates the present owner of the security and the intention of the owner regarding the person who will become the owner of the security upon the death of the owner.

(2) "Register," including its derivatives, means to issue a certificate showing the ownership of a certificated security or, in the case of an uncertificated security, to initiate or transfer an account showing ownership of securities.

(3) "Registering entity" means a person who originates or transfers a security title by registration, and includes a broker maintaining security accounts for customers and a transfer agent or other person acting for or as an issuer of securities.

(4) "Security" means a share, participation, or other interest in property, in a business, or in an obligation of an enterprise or other issuer, and includes a certificated security, an uncertificated security, and a security account.

(5) "Security account" means (i) a reinvestment account associated with a security, a securities account with a broker, a cash balance in a brokerage account, cash, interest, earnings, or dividends earned or declared on a security in an account, a reinvestment account, or a brokerage account, whether or not credited to the account before the owner's death, or (ii) a cash balance or other property held for or due to the owner of a security as a replacement for or product of an account security, whether or not credited to the account before the owner's death.

§6–302. Registration in Beneficiary Form; Sole or Joint Tenancy Ownership.

Only individuals whose registration of a security shows sole ownership by one individual or multiple ownership by two or more with right of survivorship, rather than as tenants in common, may obtain registration in beneficiary form. Multiple owners of a security registered in beneficiary form hold as joint tenants with right of survivorship, as tenants by the entireties, or as owners of community property held in survivorship form, and not as tenants in common.

§6–303. Registration in Beneficiary Form; Applicable Law.

A security may be registered in beneficiary form if the form is authorized by this or a similar statute of the state of organization of the issuer or registering entity, the location of the registering entity's principal office, the office of its transfer agent or its office making the registration, or by this or a similar statute of the law of the state listed as the owner's address at the time of registration. A registration governed by the law of a jurisdiction in which this or similar legislation is not in force or was not in force when a registration in beneficiary form was made is nevertheless presumed to be valid and authorized as a matter of contract law.

§6–304. Origination of Registration in Beneficiary Form.

A security, whether evidenced by certificate or account, is registered in beneficiary form when the registration includes a designation of a beneficiary to take the ownership at the death of the owner or the deaths of all multiple owners.

§6–305. Form of Registration in Beneficiary Form.

Registration in beneficiary form may be shown by the words "transfer on death" or the abbreviation "TOD," or by the words "pay on death" or the abbreviation "POD," after the name of the registered owner and before the name of a beneficiary.

§6–306. Effect of Registration in Beneficiary Form.

The designation of a TOD beneficiary on a registration in beneficiary form has no effect on ownership until the owner's death. A registration of a security in beneficiary form may be canceled or changed at any time by the sole owner or all then surviving owners without the consent of the beneficiary.

§6–307. Ownership on Death of Owner.

On death of a sole owner or the last to die of all multiple owners, ownership of securities registered in beneficiary form passes to the beneficiary or beneficiaries who survive all owners. On proof of death of all owners and compliance with any applicable requirements of the registering entity, a security registered in beneficiary form may be reregistered in the name of the beneficiary or beneficiaries who survive the death of all owners. Until division of the security after the death of all owners, multiple beneficiaries surviving the death of all owners hold their interests as tenants in common. If no beneficiary survives the death of all owners, the security belongs to the estate of the deceased sole owner or the estate of the last to die of all multiple owners.

§6–308. Protection of Registering Entity.

(a) A registering entity is not required to offer or to accept a request for security registration in beneficiary form. If a registration in beneficiary form is offered by a registering entity, the owner requesting registration in beneficiary form assents to the protections given to the registering entity by this part.

(b) By accepting a request for registration of a security in beneficiary form, the registering entity agrees that the registration will be implemented on death of the deceased owner as provided in this part.

(c) A registering entity is discharged from all claims to a security by the estate, creditors, heirs, or devisees of a deceased owner if it registers a transfer of the security in accordance with Section 6–307 and does so in good faith reliance (i) on the registration, (ii) on this part, and (iii) on information provided to it by affidavit of the personal representative of the deceased owner, or by the surviving beneficiary or by the surviving beneficiary's representatives, or other information available to the registering entity. The protections of this part do not extend to a reregistration or payment made after a registering entity has received written notice from any claimant to any interest in the security objecting to implementation of a registration in beneficiary form. No other notice or other information available to the registering entity affects its right to protection under this part.

(d) The protection provided by this part to the registering entity of a security does not affect the rights of beneficiaries in disputes between themselves and other claimants to ownership of the security transferred or its value or proceeds.

§6–309. Nontestamentary Transfer on Death.

(a) A transfer on death resulting from a registration in beneficiary form is effective by reason of the contract regarding the registration between the owner and the registering entity and this part and is not testamentary.

(b) This part does not limit the rights of creditors of security owners against beneficiaries and other transferees under other laws of this State.

§6–310. Terms, Conditions, and Forms for Registration.

(a) A registering entity offering to accept registrations in beneficiary form may establish the terms and conditions under which it will receive requests (i) for registrations in beneficiary form, and (ii) for implementation of registrations in beneficiary form, including requests for cancellation of previously registered TOD beneficiary designations and requests for reregistration to effect a change of beneficiary. The terms and conditions so established may provide for proving death, avoiding or resolving any problems concerning fractional shares, designating primary and contingent beneficiaries, and substituting a named beneficiary's descendants to take in the place of the named beneficiary in the event of the beneficiary's death. Substitution may be indicated by appending to the name of the primary beneficiary the letters LDPS, standing for "lineal descendants per stirpes." This designation substitutes a deceased beneficiary's descendants who survive the owner for a beneficiary who fails to so survive, the descendants to be identified and to share in accordance with the law of the beneficiary's domicile at the owner's death governing inheritance by descendants of an intestate. Other forms of identifying beneficiaries who are to take on one or more contingencies, and rules for providing proofs and assurances needed to satisfy reasonable concerns by registering entities regarding conditions and identities relevant to accurate implementation of registrations in beneficiary form, may be contained in a registering entity's terms and conditions.

(b) The following are illustrations of registrations in beneficiary form which a registering entity may authorize:

(1) Sole owner-sole beneficiary: John S Brown TOD (or POD) John S Brown Jr.

(2) Multiple owners-sole beneficiary: John S Brown Mary B Brown JT TEN TOD John S Brown Jr.

(3) Multiple owners-primary and secondary (substituted) beneficiaries: John S Brown Mary B Brown JT TEN TOD John S Brown Jr SUB BENE Peter Q Brown or John S Brown Mary B Brown JT TEN TOD John S Brown Jr LDPS.

[§6–311. Application of Part.

This part applies to registrations of securities in beneficiary form made before or after [effective date], by decedents dying on or after [effective date].]

ARTICLE VII
TRUST ADMINISTRATION

PART 1
TRUST REGISTRATION

Section

PART 2
JURISDICTION OF COURT CONCERNING TRUSTS

PART 3
DUTIES AND LIABILITIES OF TRUSTEES

PART 4
POWERS OF TRUSTEES

PART 1
TRUST REGISTRATION

§7–101. [Duty to Register Trusts.]

The trustee of a trust having its principal place of administration in this state shall register the trust in the Court of this state at the principal place of administration. Unless otherwise designated in the trust instrument, the principal place of administration of a trust is the trustee's usual place of business where the records pertaining to the trust are kept, or at the trustee's residence if he has no such place of business. In the case of co-trustees, the principal place of administration, if not otherwise designated in the trust instrument, is (1) the usual place of business of the corporate trustee if there is but one corporate co-trustee, or (2) the usual place of business or residence of the individual trustee who is a professional fiduciary if there is but one such person and no corporate co-trustee, and otherwise (3) the usual place of business or residence of any of the co-trustees as agreed upon by them. The duty to register under this Part does not apply to the trustee of a trust if registration would be inconsistent with the retained jurisdiction of a foreign court from which the trustee cannot obtain release.

§7–102. [Registration Procedures.]

Registration shall be accomplished by filing a statement indicating the name and address of the trustee in which it acknowledges the trusteeship. The statement shall indicate whether the trust has been registered elsewhere. The statement shall identify the trust: (1) in the case of a testamentary trust, by the name of the testator and the date and place of domiciliary probate; (2) in the case of a written inter vivos trust, by the name of each settlor and the original trustee and the date of the trust instrument; or (3) in the case of an oral trust, by information identifying the settlor or other source of funds and describing the time and manner of the trust's creation and the terms of the trust, including the subject matter, beneficiaries and time of performance. If a trust has been registered elsewhere, registration in this state is ineffective until the earlier registration is released by order of the Court where prior registration occurred, or an instrument executed by the trustee and all beneficiaries, filed with the registration in this state.

§7–103. [Effect of Registration.]

(a) By registering a trust, or accepting the trusteeship of a registered trust, the trustee submits personally to the jurisdiction of the Court in any proceeding under Section 7–201 of this Code relating to the trust that may be initiated by any interested person while the trust remains registered. Notice of any proceeding shall be delivered to the trustee, or mailed to him by ordinary first class mail at his address as listed in the registration or as thereafter reported to the Court and to his address as then known to the petitioner.

(b) To the extent of their interests in the trust, all beneficiaries of a trust properly registered in this state are subject to the jurisdiction of the court of registration for the purposes of proceedings under Section 7–201, provided notice is given pursuant to Section 1–401.

§7–104.   [Effect of Failure to Register.]

A trustee who fails to register a trust in a proper place as required by this Part, for purposes of any proceedings initiated by a beneficiary of the trust prior to registration, is subject to the personal jurisdiction of any Court in which the trust could have been registered. In addition, any trustee who, within 30 days after receipt of a written demand by a settlor or beneficiary of the trust, fails to register a trust as required by this Part is subject to removal and denial of compensation or to surcharge as the Court may direct. A provision in the terms of the trust purporting to excuse the trustee from the duty to register, or directing that the trust or trustee shall not be subject to the jurisdiction of the Court, is ineffective.

§7–105.   [Registration, Qualification of Foreign Trustee.]

A foreign corporate trustee is required to qualify as a foreign corporation doing business in this state if it maintains the principal place of administration of any trust within the state. A foreign co-trustee is not required to qualify in this state solely because its co-trustee maintains the principal place of administration in this state. Unless otherwise doing business in this state, local qualification by a foreign trustee, corporate or individual, is not required in order for the trustee to receive distribution from a local estate or to hold, invest in, manage or acquire property located in this state, or maintain litigation. Nothing in this section affects a determination of what other acts require qualification as doing business in this state.

PART 2
JURISDICTION OF COURT CONCERNING TRUSTS

§7–201.   [Court; Exclusive Jurisdiction of Trusts.]

(a) The Court has exclusive jurisdiction of proceedings initiated by interested parties concerning the internal affairs of trusts. Proceedings which may be maintained under this section are those concerning the administration and distribution of trusts, the declaration of rights and the determination of other matters involving trustees and beneficiaries of trusts. These include, but are not limited to, proceedings to:

(1) appoint or remove a trustee;

(2) review trustees' fees and to review and settle interim or final accounts;

(3) ascertain beneficiaries, determine any question arising in the administration or distribution of any trust including questions of construction of trust instruments, to instruct trustees, and determine the existence or nonexistence of any immunity, power, privilege, duty or right; and

(4) release registration of a trust.

(b) Neither registration of a trust nor a proceeding under this section result in continuing supervisory proceedings. The management and distribution of a trust estate, submission of accounts and reports to beneficiaries, payment of trustee's fees and other obligations of a trust, acceptance and change of trusteeship, and other aspects of the administration of a trust shall proceed expeditiously consistent with the terms of the trust, free of judicial intervention and without order, approval or other action of any court, subject to the jurisdiction of the Court as invoked by interested parties or as otherwise exercised as provided by law.

§7-202.   [Trust Proceedings; Venue.]

Venue for proceedings under Section 7–201 involving registered trusts is in the place of registration. Venue for proceedings under Section 7–201 involving trusts not registered in this state is in any place where the trust properly could have been registered, and otherwise by the rules of civil procedure.

§7–203.   [Trust Proceedings; Dismissal of Matters Relating to Foreign Trusts.]

The Court will not, over the objection of a party, entertain proceedings under Section 7–201 involving a trust registered or having its principal place of administration in another state, unless (1) when all appropriate parties could not be bound by litigation in the courts of the state where the trust is registered or has its principal place of administration or (2) when the interests of justice otherwise would seriously be impaired. The Court may condition a stay or dismissal of a proceeding under this section on the consent of any party to jurisdiction of the state in which the trust is registered or has its principal place of business, or the Court may grant a continuance or enter any other appropriate order.

§7–204.   [Court; Concurrent Jurisdiction of Litigation Involving Trusts and Third Parties.]

The Court of the place in which the trust is registered has concurrent jurisdiction with other courts of this state of actions and proceedings to determine the existence or nonexistence of trusts created other than by will, of actions by or against creditors or debtors of trusts, and of other actions and proceedings involving trustees and third parties. Venue is determined by the rules generally applicable to civil actions.

§7–205. [Proceedings for Review of Employment of Agents and Review of Compensation of Trustee and Employees of Trust.]

On petition of an interested person, after notice to all interested persons, the Court may review the propriety of employment of any person by a trustee including any attorney, auditor, investment advisor or other specialized agent or assistant, and the reasonableness of the compensation of any person so employed, and the reasonableness of the compensation determined by the trustee for his own services. Any person who has received excessive compensation from a trust may be ordered to make appropriate refunds.

§7–206. [Trust Proceedings; Initiation by Notice; Necessary Parties.]

Proceedings under Section 7-201 are initiated by filing a petition in the Court and giving notice pursuant to Section 1-401 to interested parties. The Court may order notification of additional persons. A decree is valid as to all who are given notice of the proceeding though fewer than all interested parties are notified.

PART 3

DUTIES AND LIABILITIES OF TRUSTEES

§7–301. [General Duties Not Limited.]

Except as specifically provided, the general duty of the trustee to administer a trust expeditiously for the benefit of the beneficiaries is not altered by this Code.

§7–302. [Trustee's Standard of Care and Performance.]

Except as otherwise provided by the terms of the trust, the trustee shall observe the standards in dealing with the trust assets that would be observed by a prudent man dealing with the property of another, and if the trustee has special skills or is named trustee on the basis of representations of special skills or expertise, he is under a duty to use those skills.

§7–303. [Duty to Inform and Account to Beneficiaries.]

The trustee shall keep the beneficiaries of the trust reasonably informed of the trust and its administration. In addition:

(a) Within 30 days after his acceptance of the trust, the trustee shall inform in writing the current beneficiaries and if possible, one or more persons who under Section 1-403 may represent beneficiaries with future interests, of the Court in which the trust is registered and of his name and address.

(b) Upon reasonable request, the trustee shall provide the beneficiary with a copy of the terms of the trust which describe or affect his interest and with relevant information about the assets of the trust and the particulars relating to the administration.

(c) Upon reasonable request, a beneficiary is entitled to a statement of the accounts of the trust annually and on termination of the trust or change of the trustee.

§7–304. [Duty to Provide Bond.]

A trustee need not provide bond to secure performance of his duties unless required by the terms of the trust, reasonably requested by a beneficiary or found by the Court to be necessary to protect the interests of the beneficiaries who are not able to protect themselves and whose interests otherwise are not adequately represented. On petition of the trustee or other interested person the Court may excuse a requirement of bond, reduce the amount of the bond, release the surety, or permit the substitution of another bond with the same or different sureties. If bond is required, it shall be filed in the Court of registration or other appropriate Court in amounts and with sureties and liabilities as provided in Sections 3–604 and 3–606 relating to bonds of personal representatives.

§7–305. [Trustee's Duties; Appropriate Place of Administration; Deviation.]

A trustee is under a continuing duty to administer the trust at a place appropriate to the purposes of the trust and to its sound, efficient management. If the principal place of administration becomes inappropriate for any reason, the Court may enter any order furthering efficient administration and the interests of beneficiaries, including, if appropriate, release of registration, removal of the trustee and appointment of a trustee in another state. Trust provisions relating to the place of administration and to changes in the place of administration or of trustee control unless compliance would be contrary to efficient administration or the purposes of the trust. Views of adult beneficiaries shall be given weight in determining the suitability of the trustee and the place of administration.

§7–306. [Personal Liability of Trustee to Third Parties.]

(a) Unless otherwise provided in the contract, a trustee is not personally liable on contracts properly entered into in his fiduciary capacity in the course of administration of the trust estate unless he fails to reveal his representative capacity and identify the trust estate in the contract.

(b) A trustee is personally liable for obligations arising from ownership or control of property of the trust estate or for torts committed in the course of administration of the trust estate only if he is personally at fault.

(c) Claims based on contracts entered into by a trustee in his fiduciary capacity, on obligations arising from ownership or control of the trust estate, or on torts committed in the course of trust administration may be asserted against the trust estate by proceeding against the trustee in his fiduciary capacity, whether or not the trustee is personally liable therefor.

(d) The question of liability as between the trust estate and the trustee individually may be determined in a proceeding for accounting, surcharge or indemnification or other appropriate proceeding.

§7–307. [Limitations on Proceedings Against Trustees After Final Account.]

Unless previously barred by adjudication, consent or limitation, any claim against a trustee for breach of trust is barred as to any beneficiary who has received a final account or other statement fully disclosing the matter and showing termination of the trust relationship between the trustee and the beneficiary unless a proceeding to assert the claim is commenced within [6 months] after receipt of the final account or statement. In any event and notwithstanding lack of full disclosure a trustee who has issued a final account or statement received by the beneficiary and has informed the beneficiary of the location and availability of records for his examination is protected after 3 years. A beneficiary is deemed to have received a final account or statement if, being an adult, it is received by him personally or if, being a minor or disabled person, it is received by his representative as described in Section 1–403(1) and (2).

PART 4
POWERS OF TRUSTEES

ARTICLE VIII
EFFECTIVE DATE AND REPEALER

§8–101. [Time of Taking Effect; Provisions for Transition.]

(a) This Code takes effect on January 1, 19_____.

(b) Except as provided elsewhere in this Code, on the effective date of this Code:

(1) the Code applies to governing instruments executed by decedents dying thereafter;

(2) the Code applies to any proceedings in Court then pending or thereafter commenced regardless of the time of the death of decedent except to the extent that in the opinion of the Court the former procedure should be made applicable in a particular case in the interest of justice or because of infeasibility of application of the procedure of this Code;

(3) every personal representative including a person administering an estate of a minor or incompetent holding an appointment on that date, continues to hold the appointment but has only the powers conferred by this Code and is subject to the duties imposed with respect to any act occurring or done thereafter;

(4) an act done before the effective date in any proceeding and any accrued right is not impaired by this Code. If a right is acquired, extinguished or barred upon the expiration of a prescribed period of time which has commenced to run by the provisions of any statute before the effective date, the provisions shall remain in force with respect to that right;

(5) any rule of construction or presumption provided in this Code applies to governing instruments executed before the effective date unless there is a clear indication of a contrary intent;

(6) a person holding office as judge of the Court on the effective date of this Act may continue the office of judge of this Court and may be selected for additional terms after the effective date of this Act even though he does not meet the qualifications of a judge as provided in Article I.

As amended in 1993.

GLOSSARY

abate To diminish, decrease, or reduce.

abatement The process of determining the order in which gifts made by the testator in a will shall be applied to the payment of the decedent-testator's debts, taxes, and expenses, which may cause the reduction or elimination of the gifts.

abode A person's principal place of residence or home.

accounting A formal written report of all items of property, income produced by the property, and expenses, prepared by a personal representative, trustee, or guardian and given to heirs, beneficiaries, and the probate court.

accrue Either a debt that has become due or a right a person becomes entitled to receive, but the debt has not yet been paid or the right received.

accumulated income The part of the income from a trust that is kept in the account.

active trust A trust that imposes on the trustee the duty of being active in the execution of the trust and performing management and administrative duties.

activities of daily living (ADLs) Six everyday functions and activities people do without help including bathing, eating, dressing, toileting, continence, and transferring.

adeem To take away; to revoke a gift made in a will.

ademption The intentional act of the testator to revoke, recall, or cancel a gift made through the will or by the delivery of the gift to the donee.

adjusted gross estate The value of the decedent's estate after administration expenses, funeral expenses, creditors' claims, and casualty losses have been subtracted from the value of the gross estate.

adjusted taxable gifts All taxable lifetime gifts made after December 31, 1976.

administration expenses The costs of managing the decedent's estate, e.g., filing fees, attorney's fees, and the commission of the personal representative.

administration of an estate The management of an estate by a personal representative that includes collecting estate assets, valuing them, paying decedent's taxes and debts, and distributing the remainder to beneficiaries or heirs.

administrator A male personal representative appointed by the probate court to administer the decedent's estate when there is no will. Also, an administrator can be a corporation, e.g., a bank.

administrator(-trix) *cum testamento annexo* Also called administrator C.T.A. (administrator with the will annexed). The personal representative appointed by the court in two situations: where the maker of the will does not name an executor or executrix, or where the maker of the will does name an executor or executrix but the latter cannot serve due to a deficiency in qualification or competency.

administrator(-trix) *de bonis non* Also called administrator D.B.N. (administrator of goods not administered). A court-appointed personal representative who replaces a previous administrator who has begun but failed to complete the administration of a decedent's estate for any reason, including death.

administratrix A female personal representative appointed by the probate court to administer the decedent's estate when there is no will.

adopted child The person (child) adopted.

adoption A formal legal process of establishing a relationship of parent and child between persons who are not so related by nature.

adoptive parent A person who legally adopts another individual, usually a child.

adult daycare center Senior service centers that are community-based group programs which give care during the day for adults with functional or cognitive impairments and provide assistance to caregivers.

advance directives (also called medical directives) Written documents in which individuals specify the kind of medical treatment they desire if they become incapacitated or terminally ill.

advancement Money or property given by a parent while living to a child in anticipation of the share the child will inherit from the parent's estate and in advance of the proper time for receipt of such property. It is intended to be deducted from the share of the parent's estate that the child receives.

affiant The person who makes, subscribes, and files an affidavit.

affidavit   A sworn written statement of facts affirmed before a notary public.

affinity   Relationship by marriage.

after-acquired property   All property obtained by the maker of a will after the date of the formal execution of a will.

after-born child   A child born after the parent's will has been executed.

agency   An account in which the title to the property constituting the agency remains in the owner of the property and does not pass to the trust institution, and in which the agent is charged with certain duties regarding the property.

agent   A person authorized by another person—called the principal—to act in place of the principal.

alienability   Transferability.

alienation   In the law of real property, alienation is the conveyance or transfer of property from one person to another.

allocation   The crediting of a receipt or the charging of a disbursement in its entirety to one account, as to the principal account or the income account.

allowance   See **Commission**.

alternate valuation date   For federal estate tax purposes, the personal representative may elect to value all the assets of a decedent at a date six months after the decedent's death rather than at the date of death.

ambulatory   Revocable or subject to change.

ambulatory will   A will subject to being revoked or changed, the phrase merely denoting the power a testator or testatrix possesses of altering the will during his or her lifetime.

amendment   A change in a legal document by an addition, deletion, or correction.

amortization   The operation of paying off an indebtedness by installments or by a sinking fund.

anatomical gift   A donation of all or a part of a body after death.

ancestor   Also ascendant. The person from whom one is descended. Also, the claimant to an intestate's share related to the decedent in an ascending lineal bloodline.

ancillary administration   Additional administration used to dispose of and distribute that portion of the decedent's estate located in a state other than the decedent's domiciliary state.

ancillary administrator(-trix)   The personal representative appointed by the court to distribute that part of a decedent's estate located in a jurisdiction (state) other than the decedent's domiciliary state.

annual exclusion   The purpose of the annual exclusion is to eliminate the administrative inconvenience of taxing numerous small gifts by excluding the gifts to each donee during the calendar year below a certain amount, e.g., $10,000.

annuitant   One who is entitled to an annuity, a beneficiary.

annuity   A fixed sum to be paid at regular intervals, such as annually, for a certain or indefinite period, as for a stated number of years or for life.

antenuptial (premarital) agreement   A contract made by a man and woman before their marriage or in contemplation of that marriage whereby the property rights of either or both the prospective husband or wife are determined.

antilapse statute   A statute that prevents a lapse (termination) of a clause in a will which would otherwise occur if the beneficiary who was to receive property under the clause dies before the testator.

appointee   The person who is to receive the benefit of a power of appointment.

apportionment   A division, partition, or distribution of property into proportionate parts.

apportionment clause   Clause in a will that allocates the tax burden among the residuary estate and the beneficiaries of the will.

appraisal (appraisement)   A monetary valuation placed on property by a recognized expert.

appreciation   Increase in value of an asset by the mere passing of time (normally due to market conditions).

approved list   A list of authorized investments that a fiduciary may acquire. It may or may not be a statutory list.

ascendant   Also ancestor. Claimant to an intestate's share related to the decedent in an ascending lineal bloodline.

assets   All property of the deceased, real or personal, tangible or intangible, legal or equitable, that can be made available for or appropriated to payment of debts.

assignee   The person to whom an assignment (transfer) is made.

assignment   A transfer from one person to another of the whole of any property, real or personal, or of any estate or right therein.

assignor   The person making a transfer.

assisted living facility   A community residential living arrangement that provides individual personal care and health services for a person who requires help with activities of daily living.

attachment   In property law, the act by a sheriff of seizing property from a judgment debtor by virtue of a judicial order or summons, thereby bringing the property under the jurisdiction of the court as security for payment of the debt.

attest (a will)   To bear witness; to affirm or verify a will as genuine.

attestation clause   Witnesses to a will state that they have attested the maker's signature. Ordinarily, they sign a clause to this effect.

attorney-client privilege A rule that confidential communications in the course of professional employment between attorney and client may not be divulged by the attorney without the client's consent.

attorney in fact An agent, not necessarily an attorney, who is given authority by the principal in a written document called a power of attorney to perform certain specific acts on behalf of the principal.

audit The review of financial records by an outside party, e.g., the Internal Revenue Service.

augmented estate The augmented estate consists of the value of all of the property, whether real or personal, tangible or intangible, wherever situated, that consists of the sum of four components (1) the decedent's net probate estate; (2) the decedent's nonprobate transfers to others; (3) the decedent's nonprobate transfers to the surviving spouse; (4) the surviving spouse's net assets and nonprobate transfers to others, reduced by funeral and administration expenses, homestead allowance, family allowance, exempt property, and enforceable creditors' claims.

bailment The delivery of goods or personal property by one person to another for some specific purpose but without passing title to the property or goods. The person delivering the goods is known as the *bailor*, the person receiving it is the *bailee*.

basis Original basis is usually an asset's cost, which may be adjusted later when improvements are made to the asset, e.g., the addition of a new roof to a home. Basis is important in tax calculations since capital gain or loss is the excess or loss of selling price compared to basis.

beneficial title See **Equitable title.**

beneficiary (of a trust) (also called *cestui que trust***)** During the existence of the trust, the person or institution holding equitable title to whom the trustee distributes the income earned from the trust property. When the trust terminates, the trustee conveys legal title to the property held in trust to the beneficiary or to some other person designated by the settlor (grantor) by a deed (*inter vivos* trust) or by a will *(testamentary trust)*.

beneficiary (of a will) In the terminology of wills, a person to whom the decedent's property is given or distributed; or the orthodox term for a person or institution to whom the maker of a will gives personal property through the will.

bequest A gift of personal property through a will. See also **Legacy.**

boilerplate Standard and identical language used in legal documents of a like nature.

bona fide In good faith.

bond A certificate whereby a surety company promises to pay money if the personal representative of a de-

ceased fails to faithfully perform the duties of administering the decedent's estate.

bonds A debt of a corporation or government that it acknowledges and agrees to pay to the holder of the bond a certain fixed sum of money on a specific date and interest on that sum in the interim.

buy-sell agreement An agreement among co-owners of a business promising to buy out one of their number on death, disability, or retirement.

bypass trust (also called Trust B of an A-B trust, credit shelter trust, exemption equivalent trust, family trust, or residuary trust) An estate planning device whereby a deceased spouse's estate passes to a trust as a life estate for the surviving spouse rather than entirely to the surviving spouse, thereby reducing the likelihood that the surviving spouse's estate will be subject to federal estate tax.

canons of ethics General rules or principles regarding behavior and professional responsibilities that apply to lawyers in their practice of law.

capacity See **Testamentary capacity.**

capital gain The profit realized on the sale or exchange of capital assets, e.g., assets owned for more than one year.

capital gains tax An income tax on profits from the sale or exchange of a capital asset at a lower rate than the rates applied to ordinary income.

case law The law created by judges' decisions. See also **Common law.**

cash surrender value In ordinary (straight) life insurance, the cash reserve that increases (builds) each year the policy remains in force as a minimum savings feature. After the policy has been in force for a period specified by the insurer (company), the policyholder may borrow an amount not to exceed the cash value.

casualty loss The destruction of property caused by a sudden, unexpected destructive force, e.g., flood, fire, vandalism, etc.

causa mortis In contemplation of approaching death.

cause of action The right of a person to commence a lawsuit.

caveat "Let him beware."

certified copy An authoritative endorsement or guarantee that the copy is accurate, i.e., the same as the original.

cestui que trust See **Beneficiary (of a trust).**

charitable deduction Under tax law IRC § 170(c), a charitable deduction is any contribution by a person to a qualified charity or other tax-exempt institution for which the taxpayer can claim a deduction on her income tax return.

charitable remainder   A gift to a qualified charity after an intervening estate which qualifies as a tax deduction under certain circumstances.

charitable remainder annuity trust   Trust in which a fixed amount of income is given to a beneficiary at least annually for life and after death, the remainder is given to charity.

charitable remainder trust   Trust in which the settlor or a beneficiary retains the income from the trust for a time period (usually for life) after which the remainder is given to charity.

charitable remainder unitrust   Trust in which a fixed percentage of not less than 5 percent of the fair market value of the trust property is determined annually and is given to a beneficiary for life, and after death, the remainder is given to charity.

charitable trust   A charitable (public) trust is an express trust established for the purpose of accomplishing social benefit for the public or the community. Also, it is the only type of trust that can last indefinitely.

chattel   Generally, any item of personal property.

chose in action   A right to recover something through a civil lawsuit.

chronically ill   A continuing or recurring illness that prevents the person from performing activities of daily living or requires supervision because of a cognitive impairment.

citation   The reference to legal authorities such as constitutions, statutes, case decisions, etc., in arguments made to a court or in legal textbooks to identify the source of the authority. Also, the legal form, used in some states, that is the court's order fixing a date, time, and place for hearing the petition to prove a will or for administration, and that the petitioner is required to give notice of the hearing to all interested persons including creditors who must now timely file their claims against the decedent's estate.

civil action   A lawsuit brought to remedy a private, individual wrong, such as a breach of contract or tort.

civil court   Civil matters, i.e., breach of contract and personal injury (tort) cases, must be brought before a civil court. A civil court has no power to hear criminal cases.

claimant   A creditor who files a claim against the decedent's estate.

class gift   A gift of an aggregate sum to a body of persons, uncertain in number, as, for example, the class consisting of the children of the same parents.

"clean hands" doctrine   Equitable relief may be denied to a person who has been guilty of unjust or unfair conduct.

clerk   An officer of the court who receives and files documents and keeps records of court proceedings.

closing statement   An affidavit by the personal representative at the end of informal probate proceedings to close the estate and to be discharged.

code   A collection or revision of laws arranged by table of contents, chapters, subheads, and index and passed and published by legislatures.

codicil   A written amendment to a will that may modify or revoke provisions in the will but does not cancel (invalidate) the will. A codicil must be executed with the same formalities as a will.

cognitive disorder (impairment)   A mental incapacity that causes disorientation, loss of memory, and lack of safety awareness, e.g., Alzheimer's disease.

collateral heirs (relatives)   A person not in a direct line of lineal ascent or descent tracing a kinship relationship to a decedent through a common ancestor (e.g., brothers, sisters, aunts, uncles, nieces, nephews, cousins), forming a collateral line of relationship.

collaterals of the half-blood   Persons related to a decedent through only one common ancestor. Example: Having the same father or mother, but not both parents, in common.

commingling   Combining community and separate property, e.g., into the same account or by using both to acquire a different item of property. Also when a fiduciary (trustee) combines the money from the sale of trust property with his own funds instead of placing the money in the trust account.

commission   Compensation a fiduciary receives for his services, based on a percentage of the principal or of the income or both.

common disaster clause   A clause used in a will to avoid an undesirable result where the order of death of two or more persons cannot be established by proof. Simultaneous deaths (e.g., in an automobile accident) are deaths in a common disaster.

common law   Common law is based on the unwritten principles of law that had their origin in England. These principles were developed according to the customs and traditions of the community or on what was "equitable," "fair," or "just."

common law state   The 41 states of the United States that take their marital property law from the English common law; they are not community property states.

common probate   An informal or independent probate. Referring to one of the two probate procedures established by common law and included and modified in the Uniform Probate Code and called informal probate; the other procedure is solemn probate or the UPC procedure called formal probate.

community property   All property, other than property received by gift, will, or inheritance, acquired by either spouse during marriage is considered to belong to both spouses equally in the nine community property states.

competent witness A person who is legally capable and suitable to act as a witness to a will.

complaint In a civil action, the written pleadings or claims the person suing (plaintiff) lists against the defendant and has served on him.

concurrent ownership One of the various forms of property ownership. Concurrent ownership is a situation where two or more persons share rights as co-owners.

condition precedent A condition or specific event that must occur before an agreement or obligation becomes binding.

condition subsequent A condition that will continue or terminate an existing agreement once the condition does or does not occur. See also **Defeasible**.

conditional gift A gift of property that is subject to the performance of a condition specified in a will or trust.

conflict of interest Divided loyalties (it would be a conflict of interest for an attorney to represent both sides in the dispute).

consanguinity Relationship by blood through at least one common ancestor.

conservator A fiduciary; an individual or trust institution appointed by a court to care for and manage property of an incompetent person.

consideration (1) In contract terminology, the benefit requested and received by a person making a promise in return for that promise. The benefit may be an act, forbearance, or return promise given to the original promisor (person making the promise). In sales contracts, the consideration for each party is either the price or the delivery of the goods; however, initially the consideration is the exchange of promises. (2) The cause, motive, impelling influence (i.e., something of value) that induces two or more contracting parties to enter into a contract.

constructive trust A remedial device invoked by courts of equity to obtain legal title from a person who obtained title by fraud, duress, or other wrongdoing and force him to convey that title to the one who should have it.

continence The ability to control bowel and bladder function.

continuing care retirement community A campus-style community that provides a combination of housing, services, and nursing care, at one location, to meet the various needs of residents as they grow older. The community generally charges a standard fee to enter and a flexible fee for a package of contract-specified services that vary as the resident's needs change.

contract for deed An agreement or contract to sell real property on an installment basis. On payment of the last installment, the title to the property is transferred by delivery of the deed to the purchaser.

convey To give or sell property to another.

conveyance Any transfer by deed or will of legal or equitable title to real property from one party to another, e.g., from one person to another person, a corporation, or the government.

copyright A government grant to an author of an exclusive right to publish, reprint, and sell a manuscript for a period of the life of the author plus 50 years after the author's death for works written after January 1, 1976.

corpus See **Trust estate or Trust property**.

court of equity The court that administers justice according to the rules of equity and fairness. Examples of remedies from this court include a court order forbidding the person sued (defendant) from doing some act, i.e., an injunction, or a reforming of a contract by the court to conform the contract to the parties' intentions.

court of law The court that administers justice according to the rules and practices of both statutory law and common law. An example of a remedy that a court of law grants is damages (money) as compensation for personal injury or breach of contract.

covenant A promise of two or more parties, incorporated in a trust indenture or other formal instrument, to perform certain acts or to refrain from the performance of certain acts.

creditor One who is owed money by another.

creditor's claim A document that must be filed by the creditors of a decedent in order to be paid from the assets of the decedent's estate.

creditor's notice In probate proceedings, the notice that is published stating the decedent's death and the name of the executor or the administrator to whom claims should be presented for payment.

credits Subtractions made directly from a tax that is owed; credits are more beneficial than deductions.

Crummey trust An irrevocable life insurance trust that permits premiums to be paid by the settlor with dollars given to the trust free of gift tax.

curtesy In common law, the right of the surviving husband to a life estate in all of the real property left by his deceased wife. A husband was entitled to curtesy only if the married couple had a child born alive.

custodial (personal) care Care that consists of helping the patient with daily living and personal needs provided by people lacking professional skills or training.

custodian A person who has charge or custody of property for the benefit of another, usually a minor.

custodianship An alternative to a trust or guardianship that allows a person to be appointed by the court to manage property for the benefit of a minor.

cy-pres As near as possible.

cy-pres doctrine   *Cy-pres* means "as near as possible." Where a testator or settlor makes a gift to a charity or for a charitable purpose and subsequently it becomes impossible or impractical to apply the gift to that particular charity, the equity court may order it applied to another charity "as near as may be possible" to the one designated by the settlor.

damages   The monetary remedy from a court of law that can be recovered by the person who has suffered loss or injury to her person, property, or rights by the unlawful act, omission, or negligence of another.

death benefits   Monetary payments from agencies such as Social Security and the Veterans' Administration payable to the decedent's estate.

death certificate   A document signed by a physician evidencing the death of a person.

death transfer taxes   A government levy (rate or amount of taxation) on property transferred to others by an individual on his or her death. Such taxes include estate, inheritance, and/or gift taxes.

decedent   The deceased person, referred to as having died testate or intestate.

declaration of trust   The act or document by which the settlor who holds legal title to property or an estate acknowledges and declares that she retains the title to the property as trustee in a trust for the benefit of another person or for certain specified purposes.

decree   The written judgment (decision) of a court of equity.

decree of distribution   A decree whereby the court determines the persons entitled to the estate, names the heirs or devisees, states their relationship to the decedent, describes the property, determines the property to which each person is entitled, and gives other findings of fact.

deductions   Items that may be subtracted from taxable income, the taxable estate, or taxable gifts, thereby lowering the amount on which the tax is due.

deed   A written, signed document that transfers title or ownership of real property, such as land.

deed of trust   An instrument in writing duly executed and delivered by which the legal title to real property is placed in one or more trustees.

defeasible   Capable of being defeated, annulled, revoked, or undone upon the happening of a future event or the performance of a condition subsequent, or by a conditional limitation, as a defeasible title to property.

degree of relationship   A method of determining which collateral relatives or heirs will inherit from an intestate.

degrees of kindred   The relationship of surviving blood relatives to a decedent who dies intestate.

demand   To assert and file a claim for payment based on a legal right.

demandant   Any person who has a financial or property interest in a decedent's estate and who files with the court a demand for notice of any order or filing pertaining to the estate.

demonstrative gift (legacy)   A gift or bequest of a specific monetary amount to be paid from the sale of a particular item of property or from some identifiable fund.

dependent   One who derives support from another; to be distinguished from one who merely derives a benefit from the earnings of the deceased.

deposition   A written declaration of a witness, under oath and before a qualified officer, to be used in place of the oral testimony of the witness at a trial or other hearing, e.g., a hearing to validate a will.

depreciation   A decline in value of an asset due to its increase in age. Also, a deduction allowed against the income produced by property in the amount of the property's original cost divided by its estimated useful life.

descendant   Claimant to an intestate's share related to the decedent in a descending lineal bloodline.

descent   Succession to the ownership of an estate by inheritance.

descent and distribution   See **Laws of descent and distribution.**

devest   See **Divest.**

devise   A gift of real property through a will. In UPC terminology, "devise" refers to gifts of both real and personal property.

devisee   The recipient of a devise.

devolution   The passing of property by inheritance, including both descent of real property and distribution of personal property.

direct heir   In the direct line of ascent or descent of the decedent, such as father, mother, son, or daughter.

direct skip   A generation-skipping transfer of an interest in property that is transferred to a skip person; a direct skip is subject to the federal estate tax.

disciplinary rules   Statements of minimum professional conduct that, if violated, lead to sanctions against the offending attorney.

disclaimer   A document that will allow an heir or beneficiary to give up the right to inherit or receive property without any adverse tax consequences. Also, the right a person has to refuse or reject appointment as trustee of a trust.

discretionary trust   A trust that provides the trustee with direction as to the management of the fund. This entitles the beneficiary to only as much of the income or principal as the trustee in her discretion shall see fit to give the beneficiary or to apply for his use. It is also called a sprinkling trust.

disposition The parting with, transfer of, or conveyance of property.

dissent Refusal to agree with something already stated or to an act previously performed. For example, a widow asserting her rights under the law and refusing to take the share provided for her in her husband's will is known as her "dissent from the will."

distributee A person who is entitled to share in the distribution of an estate of a decedent who dies intestate, or as defined by the UPC, any person who has received property of a decedent from the personal representative other than a creditor or purchaser. See also **Next of kin.**

distribution The apportionment and division, under authority of a court, of the remainder of the estate of an intestate, after payment of the debts and expenses, among those who are legally entitled to share in the same. Also, the transfer of property to the beneficiaries of a trust.

distributive share A recipient's portion of property left by a decedent who died intestate, as determined by state intestate succession laws.

divest or devest "To take away." Usually referring to an authority, power, property, or title, as to take away a vested right.

dividend The share of profits or property to which the owners of a business are entitled, e.g., stockholders are entitled to dividends authorized by a corporation in proportion to the number of shares they own.

domicile The legal home where a person has a true, fixed, and permanent place of dwelling and to which the person intends to return when absent. A temporary residence, such as a summer home, is not a domicile. A person may have only one domicile but could have more than one residence. Domicile and residence are frequently used interchangeably, but they are distinguished in that domicile is the legal home, the fixed permanent place of habitation, while residence is a transient place of dwelling. Domicile, not residence, determines venue.

domiciliary administration Administration of an estate in the state where a person was domiciled at the time of death.

domiciliary state The state in which the decedent's domicile (legal home) is located.

donee One to whom a gift is made or a bequest given.

donee (of a power of appointment) The person to whom a power of appointment is given, also called the holder, who selects the appointee to receive an estate or income therefrom.

donor One who makes a gift or who creates a trust.

donor (of a power of appointment) The testator or settlor who creates a power or authority upon another

(the donee) to appoint, that is, to select the person(s) (the appointee) to receive an estate or an income therefrom after the testator's or donee's death.

double indemnity Payment of double the face amount of a life insurance policy if the death of the insured (policyholder) is caused by an accident.

dower At common law, the surviving wife's right to a life estate in one-third of the real property her husband owned during the marriage. Most states (except community property states) have replaced common law dower with statutes that give one spouse (wife or husband) the right to an "elective" or "forced" share of the other spouse's property. The spouse may renounce the will and "elect" to take the statutory share.

durable power of attorney A written document whereby a principal grants a power of attorney which continues to be or becomes effective in the event the principal later becomes disabled, e.g., mentally incapacitated. If the power does not take effect until the principal becomes disabled (incapacitated), the power is called a springing durable power of attorney. All states have statutes that establish the exact words required for this document.

durable power of attorney for health care A document that gives an agent, as a substitute for the principal (the patient), the power and authority to make all medical and health care decisions when the patient is disabled and unable to make such decisions, including the authority to direct the withholding or withdrawal of life sustaining treatment.

duress Coercion; acting under the pressure of a threat.

ejectment In the law of real property, a civil action (a lawsuit brought in a court) for the recovery of the possession of land and for damages for the unlawful detention of its possession.

elder law Specialized legal services for our aging population.

elective share See **Forced share statute.**

emergency provision The provision of a will or trust agreement that gives the trustee power to pay or apply principal or accumulated income to meet emergencies in the life of the beneficiary due to unforeseeable events.

employee stock ownership plan (ESOP) A special category of a qualified benefit plan that is funded with the employer's own stock.

employer identification number See **Federal employer identification number.**

encumbrance (incumbrance) A claim or lien against real property, e.g., mortgages, easements, or a judgment, tax, or mechanic's lien.

endowment insurance An insurance contract in which the insurance company agrees to pay a stipulated amount when the policyholder reaches a specified age or upon the policyholder's death if that occurs earlier.

equitable title (of a trust) The right of the party who holds the equitable title or beneficial interest to the benefits of the trust. The party has the right to have the legal title transferred to her.

equity A system of laws or judicial remedies granted by certain courts, called courts of equity (chancery), distinct from the common law courts. Examples of such judicial remedies, granted when no adequate remedy from a court of law is available, are injunctions, reformation of contracts, and specific performance.

escheat The passage of property to the state when an intestate decedent leaves no surviving blood relatives or a spouse entitled to inherit the intestate's estate.

estate The whole of the property, real and personal, owned by any person. Also called the *gross estate*.

estate administration See **Administration of an estate.**

estate checking account A checking account established by the personal representative to hold the decedent's monetary assets.

estate equalization Rearranging property ownership of total estate assets owned by the spouses so that each spouse's individual estate has approximately the same value.

estate for years An estate for a fixed and determinate period of time, e.g., a lease for ten years.

estate plan An arrangement of a person's estate using the law of wills, trusts, tax, insurance, and property to gain maximum financial benefits for the disposition of a person's assets during life and at death.

estate tax (or transfer tax) A tax imposed on the privilege of passing an estate at death. The rate of tax is ordinarily based on the size of the estate and does not depend on the shares of the individual beneficiaries or their relationship to the decedent. To be distinguished from an inheritance tax.

estoppel Words or acts that prohibit a person from alleging or denying certain facts.

ethical considerations Ideals of professional conduct that attorneys should strive to achieve.

exculpatory provision A clause in favor of a trustee in a will or trust instrument that implies that the trustee has the power he purports to execute and clears him of all responsibility where this power is exercised in good faith. Sometimes called an immunity provision.

execute To perform or complete, e.g., to write and sign a will.

execution of a valid will The acts of the testator who writes and signs the will and the two or more witnesses who attest and sign it to establish the will's validity.

executor A man named in the will by the maker to be the personal representative of the decedent's estate and to carry out the provisions of the will. Also can be a corporation, e.g., a bank.

executrix A woman named in the will by the maker to be the personal representative of the decedent's estate and to carry out the provisions of the will.

exempt property The decedent's personal property up to a specific dollar amount that is given to the surviving spouse and/or minor children and is exempt from creditors' claims.

exemption equivalent (applicable exclusion amount) The maximum value of property that can be transferred to others without incurring any federal gift or estate tax because of the application of the unified credit (applicable credit amount).

exordium clause The beginning preamble or introductory clause of a will.

express trust A trust established by voluntary action and represented by a written document or an oral declaration.

face value The dollar amount appearing on a document, e.g., a life insurance policy.

fair market value The monetary amount that an item of property, e.g., a house, would bring if sold on the open market. Generally, the price agreed to by a willing seller and willing buyer, neither party being compelled to offer a price above or below the average price for such an item.

family allowance A statute that allows the court to award to the surviving spouse and/or minor children a monthly cash allowance for their maintenance and support before any debts are paid or distribution made under a will or without a will.

family conference A meeting of surviving family members to discuss the decedent's will or the intestate statute and the administration of the estate.

federal employer identification number A number that must be obtained from the I.R.S. for each individual estate or trust.

federal estate tax A tax imposed on the right to transfer property at death.

fee simple estate A freehold estate that is absolute and unqualified; an estate that is the largest, best, and most extensive estate that can be enjoyed in real property. It is not limited in duration or in the owner's method of disposition. Also known as a fee simple absolute, an estate in fee, or simply a fee.

fiduciary A person who is appointed to serve in a position of trust and who controls and manages property exclusively for the benefit of others. An example would be a trustee acting for the benefit of a trust beneficiary. Other examples would be a guardian acting for a minor, a partner acting for fellow partners, and a personal representative acting for beneficiaries of an estate.

fiduciary capacity   The legal capability of a person or institution such as a bank to act as a fiduciary.

fiduciary duty   A duty or responsibility required of a fiduciary that arises out of a position of loyalty and trust. In the law of trusts, it is a duty that a trustee owes to the beneficiary of a trust.

final account   The personal representative's written account that shows all changes in the assets of the estate during his administration and discloses the balance of property available for distribution to the will's beneficiaries or to the decedent's heirs.

fixture   Real property that may have once been personal property but now is permanently attached to land or buildings.

forced share statute   Forced heirship or elective share. The spouse's statutory right to choose a share of the decedent spouse's estate instead of inheriting under the provisions of the decedent's will.

foreclosure   The termination of all rights in property of the person (the mortgagor) who, in writing, pledges the property for the purpose of securing a debt.

foreign state   Any state other than the decedent's domiciliary state.

formal probate   A probate proceeding conducted by the probate court in the administration of a decedent's estate, with or without a will, that requires court supervision and notice to interested persons. See also **Solemn probate.**

freehold estate   A right of title to land; an estate in land or other real property of uncertain duration. There are three freehold estates: fee simple, fee tail, and life estate.

future estate or interest   Any fixed estate or interest, except a reversion, in which the privilege of possession or enjoyment is future and not present.

garnish   Make a claim against.

garnishment   A three-party statutory proceeding in which a judgment creditor may demand that an employer who owes wages to an employee (the judgment debtor) pay these wages to the creditor to satisfy the creditor's claim against the employee (debtor).

general legacy   A gift of a fixed amount of money from the general assets of the estate.

general power of appointment   The right to pass an interest in property to whomever a donee (the one who is given the power) chooses, including herself or her estate, creditors, or creditors of the estate.

generation-skipping transfer   A transfer of assets to a person two or more generations below the transferor, e.g., from the grandparent to a grandchild.

generation-skipping transfer tax   A federal tax on the transfer of property valued over $1,000,000 (indexed for inflation) to a person who is two or more generations below the generation of the grantor-transferor, e.g., a grandparent transferring property to a grandchild thereby skipping a child.

generation-skipping transfer trust   A trust whereby property or benefits transferred by a grantor are split between persons (beneficiaries) from two or more generations that are younger than the generation of the grantor of the trust. Also, a trust that partially avoids federal gift and estate taxes on large sums of money or other valuable assets between generations of family members.

gift   A transfer of property without payment or an expectation of receiving anything in return for it.

gift *causa mortis*   A gift of personalty made in expectation of death, completed by actual delivery of the property, and effective only if the donor dies.

gift *inter vivos*   Gifts between the living. To be effective, there must be actual delivery of the property during the lifetime of the donor and without reference to the donor's death.

gift splitting   For gift tax purposes, an election by spouses to make a gift by one of them to a third party as being made one-half by each spouse.

gift tax   A graduated tax imposed by the federal government on transfers of property by gift during the donor's lifetime.

gift tax exclusion   A donor can give $10,000 (indexed for inflation) annually to a donee or a like amount to each of any number of donees free from federal gift tax.

grantee   The person to whom a conveyance of real or personal property is made.

grantor   The person who makes a conveyance (transfer) of real or personal property to another. Also, the trustor, settlor, or donor who creates a trust.

gross estate   All of a person's property before deductions (debts, taxes, and other expenses or liabilities) that is subject to the federal estate tax. See **Estate.**

guardian   The person or institution named by the maker of a will or appointed by the court when there is no will to care for the person and/or property of a minor or a handicapped or incompetent person.

guardian   *ad litem*   A person appointed by the court to defend or bring a lawsuit on behalf of a minor or an incompetent person.

guardian of the person   A person who is responsible for the care and custody of a child, or incompetent person.

guardian of the property   A person who is responsible for managing the property of a child or incompetent person.

half-blood   A term denoting the degree of relationship that exists between those who have the same mother *or* the same father, but not both parents in common.

health care proxy A document in which a patient designates a proxy or surrogate who has legal authority to make medical and health care decisions if the patient is too incapacitated to do so personally.

heir Traditionally, a person, including a spouse, who is entitled by statute to the real property of an intestate. Today, a person entitled to any gift (real or personal property) of the intestate or in the decedent's will.

holographic will A will drawn and signed entirely in the maker's own handwriting that often requires no witnesses. State laws establish the conditions for a valid holographic will.

home health care Medical and nonmedical (including household) services provided by doctors, nurses, therapists, home health aides, and homemakers for sick, disabled, or infirmed persons in their homes.

homestead The house and the adjoining land (within statutory limits) where the head of the family lives; the family's fixed place of residence.

homestead allowance A statute that provides a modest cash award for the benefit of a surviving spouse or minor children; it is a priority payment to them and is not subject to creditors' claims.

homestead exemption Property tax reductions or exemptions available in some states for homestead property. A formal declaration is recorded annually to establish the homestead or whenever the property changes owners. A statute that protects a family from eviction from their home by creditors.

homicide or slayer statute A person who is convicted of murdering another person cannot inherit from the victim's estate.

hospice care A public agency or private organization that provides supportive care at home or in an institution, e.g., hospital, for the terminally ill, i.e., persons certified by their doctor to have a life expectancy of six months or less.

householder (also called head of household) A person who is entitled to the homestead exemption.

illegitimate child See **Nonmarital child.**

implied trust Implied trusts are trusts imposed on property by the courts when trust intent is lacking. These trusts are subdivided into resulting and constructive trusts. Both types are also passive trusts and are said to be created by "operation of law."

incident of ownership The right of the insured or her estate to the economic benefits of the insurance policy. Also, an element or right of ownership or degree of control over a life insurance contract. This right includes the options to change the beneficiary, to surrender or cancel the policy, to assign the policy, to pledge the policy for a loan, or to obtain a loan from the insurer (in-surance company) against the cash surrender value of the policy. The retention by the insured of an incident of ownership in the life insurance policy will cause the policy proceeds to be included in the decedent's gross estate.

income Interest, dividends, or other return from money that has been invested; salary, wages, etc.

income beneficiary The beneficiary who is entitled to receive the income produced from trust property.

incompetent person A person under legal disability, e.g., a physically or mentally incapacitated person.

incorporation by reference A reference in a will to another existing document that makes the other document a part of the will itself.

increment An increase; that which is gained or added.

indefeasible That which cannot be defeated, revoked, or made void.

indefinite class A group of persons within the public whose number is not specified and are unknown to the settlor of the trust.

indemnify To reimburse someone for property that was lost, damaged, or stolen.

individual retirement accounts (IRAs) Individuals under the age of 70 1/2 with earned income may make annual contributions under certain circumstances to either a traditional or Roth IRA. Contributions to a traditional IRA may be deductible, subject to limitations, and amounts earned are not taxed until distributed. Contributions to a Roth IRA are never deductible and amounts earned are tax-free when distributed if the individual satisfies a five-year holding period and certain other requirements.

inflation protection A policy option that provides for increases in benefit amounts to help pay for expected increases in the costs of long-term care services due to inflation.

informal probate An unsupervised probate proceeding in which notice to interested persons is not required. See **Common probate.**

inherit To receive property from the estate of an ancestor.

inheritance Property that descends to an heir when an ancestor dies intestate.

inheritance tax (or "succession tax") A tax on the right to receive property from a decedent at death. Usually determined by the size of the share of the particular beneficiary and her relationship to the decedent. To be distinguished from an estate tax.

inheritance tax waiver A notice from a state taxing authority indicating that either no inheritance tax is due on certain property (so that ownership to it may be transferred) or that the tax on the property has been paid.

injunction   A remedy from a court of equity that consists of a court order forbidding the performance of some act.

in loco parentis   In the place of a parent; with a parent's rights, duties, and responsibilities.

in personam jurisdiction   The authority of the court over the individual against whom a lawsuit is brought, i.e., the defendant.

in rem jurisdiction   The authority of the court over things ("res"), i.e., the property of the decedent. A probate court is empowered to hear cases concerning decedent's wills, instruments by which decedents direct the transfer of property or "things." Therefore, the jurisdiction of a probate court is basically *in rem*.

insane delusions   A person with a disordered mind imagines facts to exist for which there is no evidence.

insolvent estate   The estate of a decedent that has more debts than assets.

insurable interest   An interest in the life of an individual or in property by which there will be financial loss if the insured dies or, in the case of property, if it is damaged, lost, or destroyed. Such an interest will entitle the person possessing the interest to obtain insurance on it.

intangible personal property   A personal property interest that cannot be touched or moved, such as a right to sue another person, cash, stocks, bonds, and the like. See also **Chose in action.**

interested party (person)   A person including heirs, devisees, personal representatives, creditors, beneficiaries, and any others having a property right in or claim to the estate of the decedent.

interested witness   A person who is a beneficiary and a witness of the same will.

interlineation   The act of writing between the lines of an instrument, e.g., a will. This could void the will.

in terrorem clause   A clause in a will that states that if a beneficiary of the will objects to probate or challenges the will's distributions, the contestant forfeits all benefits of the will.

inter vivos   "Between the living."

inter vivos gift   A voluntary transfer of property by a living person, called the donor, to a recipient, called the donee. Consideration is not required for an) *inter vivos* gift, as it would be in the case of a contract.

inter vivos   or **living trust**   A trust created by a maker (settlor) during the maker's lifetime. It becomes operational immediately after the trust is created.

intestacy   Death without a valid will.

intestate   As an adjective, meaning "without a will"; as a noun, meaning a person who dies without a valid will.

intestate succession   The manner in which a decedent's property will be distributed when death occurs without a valid will, determined by state law.

intestate succession statutes   Laws passed in each state establishing the manner in which a decedent's property will be distributed when death occurs without a valid will.

inventory   A complete physical check of all the assets of the decedent and a listing of said assets and their value at the time of the decedent's death on the forms provided for the inventory.

irrevocable life insurance trust   A living trust that cannot be revoked or amended that is established by a settlor who assigns the ownership of a new or existing life insurance policy on her life to the trust and contributes money annually to the trust to pay the premiums.

irrevocable trust   A trust that may not be revoked by the settlor after its creation.

issue   All persons who have descended from a common ancestor; a broader term than "children." Includes lineal descendants of any degree (children, grandchildren, etc.).

joint tenancy   Ownership of real or personal property by two or more persons with the right of survivorship.

joint tenants   Two or more persons who own or hold equal undivided interests in property with the right of survivorship.

joint will   A will for spouses that consists of a single document signed by them as their will.

judgment   The official decision of a court of justice establishing the rights and claims of parties in a lawsuit submitted to the court for determination.

jurisdiction   The authority by which a particular court is empowered by statute to decide a certain kind of case and to have its decision enforced.

kin   Relationship by blood.

kindred   Family; relatives; individuals related by blood.

lapse   Failure to distribute a gift in a will because the legatee, beneficiary, or devisee dies before the testator.

lapsed devise   A devise that fails, or takes no effect, by reason of the death, unwillingness, or incapacity of the devisee during the testator's lifetime.

lapsed legacy   When the legatee dies before the testator, or before the legacy is payable, the bequest is said to lapse, as it then falls into the residuary fund of the estate.

last will and testament   A legally enforceable declaration of one's intention to dispose of one's property, both real and personal, after death. It is revocable or amendable up to the time a person dies or loses the mental capacity to make a valid will.

laws of descent and distribution   Succession to the ownership of an estate by inheritance.

leasehold estate   One of the categories into which the law of real property divides the rights of ownership, the other being a freehold estate. The categories are distinguished by the extent and duration of the individual's interest or according to how long and how much an interest a person has in realty.

ledger   A book of account in which a record of monetary transactions is made.

legacy   A disposition of personal property through a will.

legal capacity   Age at which a person acquires capacity to make a valid will, usually 18.

legal description of real estate   A description recognized by law that definitely (specifically) locates real property by reference to government surveys or recorded maps.

legal entity   Something having legal existence, e.g., a natural or artificial person (corporation) that can sue or be sued.

legal investments   See **Statutory investment.**

legal life estate   A life estate created by operation of law and not directly by the parties themselves.

legal title (of a trust)   The form of ownership of trust property held by the trustee giving the trustee the right to control and manage the property for another's benefit, i.e., the holder of the equitable title.

legatee   The person who receives a gift of personal property under a will.

letter of instructions   A document that specifies the testator's instructions for organ donation and funeral and burial plans. It can also be an all-inclusive checklist of various personal and estate information to help the family and personal representative locate and identify property and documents necessary to administer the estate.

Letters of Administration   The formal document of authority and appointment given to a personal representative (administrator) by the proper court to carry out the administration of the decedent's estate according to the proper state intestate succession statute.

Letters of Authority   Certificates of appointment called Letters Testamentary, when there is a will, or Letters of Administration, when there is no will.

Letters Testamentary   The formal document of authority and appointment given to a personal representative (executor) by the proper court to carry out the administration of the decedent's estate according to the terms of a will.

lien   A claim or charge on property for payment of some debt. An estate in real property includes the right to possession and enjoyment of it, while a lien on real property is the right to have it sold or otherwise applied in satisfaction of a debt.

life estate   A freehold estate in which a person, called the life tenant, holds an interest in land during her own or someone else's lifetime.

life in being   A phrase used in the common law and statutory rules against perpetuities, meaning the remaining duration of the life of a person who is in existence at the time the deed or will takes effect.

life insurance   A contract, a legally binding agreement, by which one party (the insurance company) promises to pay another (the policyholder or the designated beneficiary) a certain sum of money if the policyholder sustains a specific loss (i.e., death or total disability). For this protection, the policyholder makes a payment, called a premium, to the insurance company on a regular basis, such as annually.

life insurance trust   See **Irrevocable life insurance trust.**

life interest   A claim or interest not amounting to ownership and limited by a term of life, either that of the person in whom the right is vested or that of another.

life tenant   The person holding a life estate in property.

limited or special power of appointment   See **Special power of appointment**.

lineal   A lineal is a person related to an intestate decedent in a direct line of kinship either upward in an ascending bloodline (e.g., parents, grandparents, or great-grandparents) or downward in a descending bloodline (e.g., children, grandchildren, or great-grandchildren).

lineal ascendants or lineal ancestors   Persons with whom one is related in the ascending line—one's parents, grandparents, great-grandparents, etc.

lineal descendants   Persons with whom one is related in the descending line, one's children, grandchildren, great-grandchildren, etc.

liquidate   To turn assets into cash by their sale.

living trust   A trust that is created and becomes operative during the lifetime of the settlor. The same as an *inter vivos* trust.

living will   A document, separate from a will, that expresses a person's wish to be allowed to die a natural death and not be kept alive by artificial means.

long-term care   The support that disabled, frail, or chronically ill people need when they can no longer care for themselves.

long-term care insurance   Insurance that pays a fixed monetary benefit, usually per day, for a designated benefit period during which the insured generally receives care at home or in a nursing home.

lucid interval   A temporary restoration to sanity during which an incompetent person has sufficient intelligence and judgment to make a valid will.

maintenance allowance   An allowance provided by state statutes from the decedent's estate to the surviving spouse and minor children, which gives them reasonable maintenance during the administration of the decedent's estate for a statutory time period, e.g., 12 to 18 months. In some states, maintenance is also called the family allowance.

malfeasance   Doing an act that a personal representative should not do; a wrongful act or mismanagement.

marital deduction   An unlimited amount of the decedent's gross estate, which may be given to the surviving spouse without being subject to federal estate tax levied against the decedent's estate.

marital deduction trust (also called Trust A of an A-B trust or marital trust)   A trust that is designed to make the most financially advantageous use of the marital deduction against the federal estate tax.

marshaling of assets   The arrangement or ranking of testamentary assets in a certain order to be used for the payment of debts, taking into consideration which claims have priority over others.

medical power of attorney   A written document that enables the principal to appoint an agent, proxy, or surrogate to make decisions for medical care when the principal becomes incapacitated and is unable to make such decisions. It may be called a durable power of attorney for health care, health care proxy, or appointment of a health care agent.

memorandum   A written list of the testator's personal property and the name of the beneficiary who receives each item. It is signed by the testator but is not a legally enforceable document.

minor   A person who is under the legal age of majority, usually eighteen.

Model Code of Professional Responsibility   Rules of conduct governing the legal profession written by the ABA and adopted by some states.

Model Rules of Professional Conduct   Standards of conduct written by the ABA to establish ethical guidelines for the practice of law and adopted by most states.

mortgage   A contract by which a person pledges property to another as security in order to obtain a loan.

mortgagee   The person who takes, holds, or receives a mortgage from the borrower; the creditor.

mortgagor   The person who gives a mortgage to the lender; the debtor.

mutual (reciprocal) wills   Separate and identical wills usually made by spouses containing reciprocal provisions and an agreement that neither spouse will change his or her will after the death of the other.

natural guardian   The father of the child, or the mother if the father is dead or vice versa. In most states, mothers and fathers have equal rights of guardianship over their children.

natural objects of the testator's bounty   Family members and other friends and institutions, e.g., charitable or religious organizations, for whom the testator has affection.

necessaries   Necessary items that supply the personal needs of an individual or family, such as food, clothing, or shelter.

negative will   A will that specifically disinherits a named person or class of persons.

net estate   Under estate tax statutes, "net estate" means that which is left of the gross estate after various deductions allowed by statute in the course of settlement.

next of kin   The nearest blood relatives of the decedent; or those who would inherit from a decedent who died intestate, whether or not they are blood relatives, e.g., a spouse.

no contest clause   See *In terrorem* clause.

nomination   The act of suggesting or proposing a person for an office, position, or duty; to be distinguished from appointment. Thus, the testator nominates, but the court appoints, the executor under a will.

nonadverse party   Any person having a substantial beneficial interest in the trust that would be adversely affected by the exercise or nonexercise of the power that he possesses respecting the trust.

nonforfeiture benefit   A policy feature that returns a portion of the premiums if the insured cancels the insurance policy or allows it to lapse.

nonmarital child   A child born to parents who are not married.

nonprobate asset   This type of property will pass by operation of law.

non-skip person   Any transferee of a direct skip who is not a skip person.

notary public   A person authorized by the state whose function is to administer oaths, certify documents and deeds, and attest to the authenticity of signatures.

notice to creditors   A written notice posted in public places or by notice in newspapers to creditors of an estate to present their claims for what the executor or administrator owes them from the estate assets. It is also a notice to debtors to pay what they owe the estate.

notice to surviving spouse   Notification to a surviving spouse or minor children regarding the allowances of personal property from the decedent's estate to which they are entitled. In addition, a renunciation and election rule applying only to the spouse who has not consented to the will, giving him or her the right to file a statement in writing renouncing and refusing to accept the provisions of such a will.

nuncupative will   An oral will spoken in the presence of a witness or witnesses that is valid only under exceptional circumstances, such as the impending death of the person "speaking" the will. Nuncupative wills are prohibited in some jurisdictions.

nursing home care   A residential institution that provides care and services for the elderly or infirmed.

olographic (or holographic) testament   See **Holographic will**.

omitted child   See **Pretermitted child or heir**.

operation of law   Rights pass to a person by the application of the established rules of law, without the act, knowledge, or cooperation of the person.

opinions   Statements issued by the ABA and state bar associations interpreting and applying their codes and rules that establish ethical guidelines for the practice of law.

ordinary (whole or straight) life insurance   Life insurance that combines protection with a minimum savings feature called cash surrender value. Premium payments are required throughout the policyholder's lifetime. The cash value slowly increases until it equals the face amount of the policy. The policyholder may surrender the policy at any time and take out the money (cash value) for his own use or retain the policy until death for the benefit of the named beneficiary.

orphans' court   Another name for the probate court in some states.

orthodox terminology   Traditional definitions of words relating to wills and probate matters, used universally before the adoption into law of the Uniform Probate Code.

parol evidence   Oral testimony or written evidence.

parol evidence rule   A general rule of contract law that oral or written evidence (testimony) is not allowed to vary, change, alter, or modify any terms or provisions of a written contract (agreement).

partition   The division of real property held by joint tenants or tenants in common into distinct portions so that they may hold the property in severalty, i.e., in single ownership. It does not create or convey a new or additional title or interest, but merely severs the unity of possession.

passive trust   An implied, resulting, constructive trust, or a trust that does not give oral or written affirmative powers and duties to a trustee to perform discretionary acts of management or administration for the benefit of named beneficiaries. A passive trust commissions the trustee to perform only minor acts of a mechanical or formal nature and often creates no active administrative duties.

patent   A government grant to an inventor of an exclusive right to make, use, and sell an invention for a nonrenewable period of 17 years.

pecuniary bequest or legacy   A bequest of a sum of money or of an annuity.

per capita (distribution)   "Individually." When all heirs entitled to a portion of an intestate decedent's estate are related to the deceased in the same degree of relationship (same-generation ascendants or descendants), each receives an identical portion, all sharing equally. Also, a distribution of property based on giving equal shares to all those entitled to the intestate's estate.

perpetuity   Any limitation or condition that may take away or suspend the power of alienation for a period beyond a life or lives in being and 21 years thereafter plus the usual period of gestation.

personal guardian   An individual or trust institution appointed by a court to take custody of and care for a minor or an incompetent person.

personal property   Also referred to as "chattels personal" or movable property. Everything subject to ownership that is not real estate; includes such items as clothing, household furnishings, stocks, money, contract rights, life insurance, and similar holdings.

personal representative   A person who administers the decedent's estate and either carries out the terms of the will or follows the appropriate intestate succession statute in distributing the estate. If the personal representative has been named in the will to carry out such liaison duties, he is called an executor (a woman is an executrix); if the court appoints the personal representative because no valid will exists, he is an administrator (administratrix, in the case of a woman).

per stirpes (distribution)   By "representation." When heirs entitled to a portion of an intestate decedent's estate are related to the deceased in different degrees of relationship (intergenerational ascendants or descendants) with some heirs having predeceased the intestate, the descendants of such persons receive their shares through the predeceased heirs. Also, a distribution of property that depends on the relationship to the intestate of those entitled to the estate.

petition for probate or administration   An application to the proper court (probate court) from the person (called the petitioner) seeking to validate a will or to administer an intestate's estate asking the court to grant the request sought in the application.

posthumous child   A child born after the death of its father or, when a caesarean operation is performed, after that of the mother.

postmortem   After death; pertaining to matters occurring after death.

postnuptial agreement A contract made by spouses after marriage whereby the property rights of either or both spouses are determined.

pour-over will A "pour-over" provision refers to the transfer of property from an estate or trust to another estate or trust upon the happening of an event as provided in the instrument. Also, a provision in a will that directs the residue of the estate into a trust.

power in trust A power that the donee (the trustee) must exercise in favor of the beneficiary of the trust.

power of appointment A power or authority conferred by one person (called the donor) by deed or will on another (called the donee) to select and nominate the person or persons (called the appointees) who are to receive and enjoy an estate or an income therefrom or from a fund, after the testator's death or the donee's death, or after the termination of an existing right or interest.

power of attorney A document, witnessed and acknowledged, authorizing another to act as one's agent or attorney.

precatory trust A trust created by certain words, which are more like words of entreaty and permission than words of command or certainty. Examples of such words are "hope, desire, wish, and request," "have fullest confidence," "heartily beseech," and the like.

precatory words Words such as *hope, desire, request, ask, beseech, wish,* or *recommend* which are ineffective to dispose of property.

predecease To die before another.

pre-existing condition limitation An illness or disability for which the insured was diagnosed or treated during a period of time before applying for a long-term care insurance policy.

prenuptial agreement See **Antenuptial agreement**.

present interest An immediate and unrestricted interest in real or personal property including the privilege of possession or the enjoyment of the property.

present value In the law of trusts, the present value is the value of the trust property to the beneficiaries for gift tax purposes. The present value varies with the length of time the trust runs and is a percentage of the full value of the trust property.

pretermitted (omitted) child or heir A child or other descendant omitted in a parent's will.

prima facie At first sight; on the face of it. A fact presumed to be true unless disproved by evidence to the contrary.

primary beneficiary The person selected by the policyholder of a life insurance contract who is given a superior claim to the benefits of the insurance over all others.

principal The capital or property of an estate or trust, as opposed to the income, which is the product of the capital. Also, a person who authorizes another (called the agent) to act on the person's behalf.

private trust A trust established or created for the financial benefit of a certain designated person or class of persons, clearly identified or capable of being identified by the terms of the trust.

probate administration See **Probate proceedings**.

probate assets (or probate property) Property passed by will or descended as intestate property.

probate court The court that has jurisdiction over the probate of wills, the grant of administration, and supervision of the management and settlement of the estates of decedents, including the collection of assets, the allowance of claims, and the distribution of the estate. In some states, probate courts (also called surrogate courts, orphans' courts, or courts of chancery) have jurisdiction over the estates of minors, including the appointment of guardians and the settlement of their accounts, and the estates of incompetents, habitual drunkards, and spendthrifts.

probate in common form An informal proceeding in court without notice to the interested parties. Probate in common form is revocable.

probate in solemn form A formal probate proceeding that requires court supervision and notice to all interested parties.

probate (of a will) The procedure by which a document is presented to the court to confirm it as a valid will. The process by which a proper court declares the will to be a valid testamentary disposition, or the system provided by law for transferring property of a decedent to successors.

probate proceedings The process of distributing the estate of a person who died testate or intestate; includes all other matters over which probate courts have jurisdiction.

probate property (estate) This includes the decedent's assets that are solely owned, that are property held as tenants in common, and that are subject to administration by the personal representative.

promissory note A promise in writing to pay a specified sum of money to the order of a named payee or to the bearer of the note.

property Anything subject to ownership.

property guardian An individual or trust institution appointed by a court to care for and manage the property of a minor or an incompetent person. The same individual can be both personal and property guardian and is then called simply the guardian.

proponent The petitioner who presents a will to the court for approval.

pro rata   According to a certain rate or percentage.

prorate   To divide, share, or distribute proportionally.

prudent-person rule for trust investment   This rule is used in states that have statutes governing investments by trustees. Originally stated in 1830 by the Supreme Judicial Court of Massachusetts, it says that, in investing, all that is required of trustees is that they conduct themselves faithfully and exercise a sound discretion and observe how people of prudence, discretion, and intelligence manage their own affairs not in regard to speculation but in regard to the permanent disposition of their funds, considering the probable income as well as the probable safety of the capital to be invested. This rule is also used in states where there is no statute governing investments.

public administrator   A public official appointed by the court to administer an estate of an intestate when no interested persons, including family members, are available.

publication   In the law of wills, the formal declaration made by a testator at the time of signing a will that it is her last will and testament.

public (charitable) trust   See **Charitable trust.**

pur autre vie   An estate lasting for the life of a person other than the life tenant.

purchase-money resulting trust   A resulting trust in which property is purchased and paid for by one person, and at his direction, the seller transfers possession and title to another person.

qualified small estate   A decedent's estate that consists entirely of statutory exempt property or allowances, funeral and administration expenses, and is within a certain limited monetary value.

QTIP trust (Qualified Terminable Interest Property) A type of trust that will qualify for the marital deduction in which the surviving spouse receives all the income for life but is not given a general power of appointment. Generally, the marital deduction (for gift and estate tax purposes) is not available if the interest transferred will terminate on the death of the transferee spouse and pass to someone else. For example, if a husband places property in trust for his wife for life, and the remainder to their children when his wife dies, this is a terminable interest that does *not* qualify as a marital deduction for the husband or for the husband's estate. If, however, the QTIP election is made so that the property transferred into the trust is treated as qualified terminable interest property, the terminable interest restriction is waived, and the marital deduction is allowed. In exchange for this deduction, the surviving spouse's (wife's) gross estate must include the value of the QTIP election assets, even though she has no control over the ultimate disposition of these assets, i.e., she has no general power

of appointment. Terminable interest property qualifies for this election if the donee or heir (the wife in this example) is the only beneficiary of the asset during her lifetime, and she receives income distributions from the trust property at least annually. If the trust property is transferred as a gift, the donor spouse (the husband) is the one who makes the QTIP election. If the trust property is transferred by death, the personal representative (executor) of the estate of the deceased spouse (the husband) has the right to make the election on schedule M of Form 706, the United States Estate Tax Return (see Form 88 in Appendix A).

quasi-community property   Property that is acquired outside a community property state and then moved into it or that is owned by spouses who have moved into a community property state.

ratification   The confirmation, approval, or sanction of a previous act done either by persons themselves or by another.

real property   Realty or real estate. Land and generally whatever is built or growing on or affixed (permanently attached) to land. It includes land, buildings, and fixtures. A fixture is real property that may once have been personal property but now is permanently attached to land or buildings. An example of a fixture on land is a tree. In a building, a fixture could be the carpeting nailed to a floor, a built-in dishwasher, and the like.

receivables   Debts (promissory notes and the like) established in the course of business, due from others at present or within a certain time period.

receiver   An indifferent person between the parties to a cause, appointed by the court to receive and preserve the property or fund in litigation, receive its rents, issues, and profits, and apply or dispose of them at the direction of the court when it does not seem reasonable that either party should hold them or where a party is incompetent to do so, as in the case of an infant.

reciprocal wills   See **Mutual wills.**

reformation of contracts   Equitable remedy to conform a written agreement to the actual intention of the contracting parties.

registrar (surrogate)   The judge of the court or, most often, the person designated by the judge to perform the functions on behalf of the court in informal proceedings.

relationship by affinity   A connection by ties of marriage.

relationship by consanguinity   Blood relationship; the relationship of persons descended from the same common ancestor.

remainder   In the law of wills, the remainder is the balance of an estate after all the other provisions of the will have been satisfied. Also referred to as "rest" and "residue." Also, a future estate in real property that takes effect on the termination of a prior estate created by the same instrument (document) at the same time.

remainderman   A person entitled to the remainder of an estate, e.g., a future fee simple estate, after a particular smaller estate, e.g., a life estate, has expired.

renounce   To reject, disclaim, abandon. To divest oneself of a right, power, or privilege.

renunciation   The act by which a person abandons a right acquired without transferring it to another, e.g., to refuse to accept a gift in a will.

representation   See **Right of representation.**

republication   The reexecution, revival, or restoration by a testator of a will that had previously been revoked.

republish   Reestablish; as to reestablish a will.

res   A thing; an object. The phrase "trust res" means trust property. Everything that may form an "object" of rights.

residence   The dwelling in which one temporarily lives or resides. "Residence" is not always synonymous with "domicile," although the terms are frequently interchanged. "Residence" may imply a temporary dwelling, whereas "domicile" always denotes a permanent dwelling.

residuary or residue clause   A clause in a will that disposes of the remaining assets (residue) of the decedent after all debts and gifts in the will are satisfied.

residuary estate (also called the residue of the estate)   The remaining assets (residue) of the decedent's estate after all debts have been paid and all other gifts in the will are distributed.

residuary legacy or devise   A gift of all the testator's estate not otherwise effectively disposed of by a will.

respite care   Care offered to relieve family caregivers for a few hours or up to several days.

Restatement of Trusts   In 1935, recognizing the need to simplify and clarify the law of trusts, a group of trust experts working for the American Law Institute set forth the existing rules of law affecting trust creation and administration and included illustrations and comments. The complete work was called the Restatement of the American Law of Trusts. In 1959, the original Restatement was revised and the revisions were incorporated into the Restatement of Trusts, Second. In 1992, another partial revision was completed. Throughout the trust chapters of this book, relevant sections of the Restatement (Second) or (Third) of Trusts will be cited.

resulting trust   A trust created by operation of law from circumstances implied from the intentions of the parties that the person who holds legal title is obligated to hold it "in trust" for another person's benefit, even though there is no stated intention to create a trust and no fraud is involved. Resulting trusts often occur when an attempt to create a valid express trust fails for lack of one or more of the essential elements.

reversion or reversionary interest   The interest in real property that a grantor retains when a conveyance of the property by deed or by will transfers an estate smaller than what the grantor owns. At some future time, the real property reverts back to the grantor.

revocable   Susceptible of being revoked, annulled, or made void by canceling, rescinding, repealing, or reversing.

revocable trust   A trust that the creator (settlor) has a right or power to revoke (cancel). Generally, such a power must be expressly reserved by the settlor in the trust instrument.

revocation clause   A clause or statement in a will that revokes all prior wills and codicils.

revocation of will   Recalling, annulling, or rendering inoperative an existing will by some subsequent act of the testator or testatrix.

revoke   To cancel.

right of election   The right of a surviving husband or wife to choose to take, under the decedent's state law, his or her statutory share in preference to the provision made in the deceased spouse's will.

right of representation   The right of a child to receive the share of an intestate's property that the child's deceased parent would have received if the parent was still living.

right of succession   The right of an heir or successor to share in a decedent's estate, determined by degree of kindred.

right of survivorship   An important characteristic of a joint tenancy that, on the death of one joint tenant, passes the decedent's interest in the property by operation of law to the surviving joint tenants, with the last joint tenant entitled to the whole property.

right to die   The right of a dying person to refuse extraordinary medical treatment to prolong life.

right to die laws   Cases and statutes that allow a dying person to refuse medical treatment to prolong life.

royalty   A payment made to an author, composer, or inventor by a company that has been licensed to either publish or manufacture the manuscript or invention of that author, composer, or inventor.

Rule Against Perpetuities   A rule that fixes the time within which a future interest must vest (pass). The estate must vest (pass) within a time limited by a life or lives then in being and 21 years thereafter, together with the period of gestation. The rule applies only to private trusts, not to public trusts.

safe deposit box   A locked box in a bank vault to which only the renter of the box has access.

savings bank trust   See **Totten trust.**

secondary (contingent) beneficiary   The person selected by the policyholder as a successor to the benefits of a life insurance policy whenever the proceeds of the policy are not paid to the primary beneficiary.

securities   Stocks, bonds, and other documents issued by corporations.

seisin (or seizin)   Actual possession, where the possessor intends to claim the land as a fee simple or life estate. Seisin is not the same as legal title. The difference between legal title and seisin is that the person who holds seisin over the land does not necessarily hold legal title to it.

self-proved will   A statutory procedure that provides for proving of a will without testimony of witnesses by an acknowledgment of the testator and with an affidavit of witnesses made before a notary public and added to the end of the will.

self-proving affidavit (clause)   A clause at the end of a will that contains an acknowledgment or affidavit of the testator and affidavits of witnesses signed by them in the presence of a notary public who also signs and seals it. This clause is used to replace the traditional attestation clause.

separate property   Property one person owns free from any rights or control of others; as the property that the husband or wife owned prior to their marriage or acquired during marriage by inheritance, will, or gift.

settlement   The final distribution of an estate by an executor or an administrator.

settlement option   One of a number of alternatives that parties to an insurance contract agree to follow to discharge their agreement.

settlor   A person who creates a trust; also called donor, grantor, creator, or trustor.

severalty   Property in severalty is that owned and held by one person only, without any other person having an interest or right in the property.

severance   Act of severing, separating, or partitioning; with respect to joint tenancy, severance is the destruction of any one of the four essential unities accomplished by one of the joint tenants transferring *inter vivos* the interest in real property to another person by deed, thereby creating a tenancy in common for the new owner with the other remaining joint tenants.

short-term trust   An irrevocable trust running for at least 10 years or more, or for the life of the beneficiary, in which the income is payable to a person other than the settlor. The income from a trust of this kind is taxable to the income beneficiary and not to the settlor. Also known as a Clifford, come-back, give and keep, and reversionary trust. Such trusts have been severely limited by the 1986 Tax Reform Act.

simultaneous death clause   A clause in a will that determines the distribution of property in the event there is no evidence as to the priority of time of death of the testator and another, usually the testator's spouse.

skilled nursing facility   A Medicare-qualified facility that specializes in skilled nursing or rehabilitation services under the supervision of licensed nursing personnel and based on a doctor's orders.

skip person   An individual (such as a grandchild) who is two or more generations below the generation of the transferor (grantor). A trust can also be a skip person.

small estate   A decedent's estate with few assets and a limited monetary value.

soldiers' and sailors' wills   Several states have statutes relaxing statutory requirements for wills of soldiers and sailors. They usually require that the will be made by soldiers in actual military service or sailors while at sea. These wills are usually limited to disposing of personalty.

solemn probate   Formal probate. Probate proceedings that require court supervision and notice to interested persons.

sound mind   To have the mental capacity (ability) to make a valid will.

sovereign (governmental) immunity   A common law rule that exempts or frees the government from tort liability. Many states have limited or abolished this immunity.

special administrator   An administrator appointed by the court to take over and safeguard an estate pending the appointment of an executor or general administrator.

special power of appointment   A power of appointment that cannot be exercised in favor of the donee or her estate, but only in favor of an identifiable person(s) other than the donee.

specific bequest or legacy   A gift, by will, of a particular item of personal property or a gift of a class of personal property in a will.

specific devise   A gift, by will, of real property.

specific performance   A remedy from a court of equity requiring the parties to a contract to do what they promised, e.g., perform their contract according to its terms.

spend-down   A procedure that requires an individual to spend enough income and resources to qualify for Medicaid eligibility.

spendthrift   One who spends money unwisely and wastefully.

spendthrift clause   A clause in a will that prevents the beneficiary from having the power to transfer his interest in the principal or income of a trust in any manner, preventing such interest from being subject to the claims of his creditors, attachment, execution, or other process of law.

spendthrift trust   A trust created to provide a fund for the maintenance of a beneficiary and at the same time to secure it against his improvidence or incapacity.

spouse's allowance   Allowance made by the court to the surviving husband or wife for the purpose of providing him or her with funds for living expenses during the period of settlement of the estate.

spouse's statutory, forced or elective share   See **Forced share statute**.

sprinkling trust   A trust in which the income or principal is distributed among the members of a designated class in amounts and proportions determined by the discretion of the trustee. Also called spraying trusts.

standing   The requirement that a person stands to lose a pecuniary interest in a decedent's estate if a will is allowed.

stare decisis   The practice of following previous court decisions. A Latin term meaning "to stand by previous decisions."

statute   A law passed by a state or federal legislature. Statutory law is one source of law, i.e., state statutes, federal statutes. State and federal governments publish books of law that are called statutes.

Statute of Frauds   State laws which provide that no suit or civil action shall be maintained on certain classes of oral contracts unless the agreement is put in writing and signed by the party to be charged, i.e., the person being sued, or by an authorized agent of that person.

statute of limitations   Each state has its own statute of limitations that bars lawsuits on valid claims after the expiration of a specific period of time. The period varies for different kinds of claims.

statutes of descent   See **Laws of descent and distribution.**

statutes of distribution   See **Laws of descent and distribution.**

statutory investment   An investment that a trustee is specifically authorized to make under the terms of the statutes governing investments by trustees.

statutory lists   Lists of conservative investments set forth by statute in which a trustee is to invest. These statutes are of two types: (1) "permissive," where the trustee may invest outside the list but has the burden of justifying any investments not on the list; (2) "mandatory," where the trustee is liable for any investment not on the list. These lists are also known as "legal lists."

statutory will   A fill-in-the-blank type of will that is authorized by statute in a few states.

stepped-up basis   A provision whereby the heir's basis in inherited property is equal to its value at the date of the decedent's death.

stock dividend   A dividend of shares of stock distributed to stockholders.

stocks   Fractional shares (certificates) representing an ownership in a corporation.

stock split   One share of stock is split into a larger number of shares resulting in a proportional change in the number of shares owned by each stockholder.

stock transfer   The transfer of stock from one person to another by sale or gift handled by a party designated by the corporation called a transfer agent (often a bank).

straw man   A person used to create a joint tenancy of real property between the existing owner of the property and one or more other persons. The owner transfers a deed to the straw man, and the straw man immediately reconveys, by a second deed, the property back to the original owner and the new co-owner as joint tenants.

subject matter jurisdiction   The power a court must have to render the kind of judgment requested by a party to an action-at-law.

subrogation   The substitution of one person in the place of another with reference to a lawful claim, demand, or right. An equitable remedy borrowed from civil law to compel the ultimate discharge of a debt or obligation by a person who in good conscience should pay it.

subscribe (a will)   To sign a will.

subscribing witness   One who sees a writing executed, or hears it acknowledged, and at the request of the party thereupon signs her name as a witness.

subscription   The act of signing one's name to a written document.

succession   The act of acquiring property of a deceased person, whether by operation of law on the person's dying intestate or by taking under a will.

succession tax   A tax imposed on the privilege of receiving property from a decedent by devise or inheritance. It is imposed on each legacy or distributive share of the estate as it is received; inheritance tax.

successive beneficiary   One who takes the place of another beneficiary by succession. For example, under a will in which property is left to A for life, then to B for life, and then to C outright, B and C are successive beneficiaries.

successor   An all-inclusive UPC term meaning those persons, other than creditors, who are entitled to real or personal property of a decedent either under the will or through intestate succession.

summary proceeding   Any proceeding by which a controversy is settled, a case is disposed of, or a trial is conducted in a prompt and simple manner without the aid of a jury, without presentment or indictment, or in other respects out of the regular course of common law. An example would be a process used to settle an estate without the probate procedure.

summons   In a civil action (lawsuit), the notification to a defendant that he is being sued and that he must answer it at a time or place named in the notice document.

support trust   A trust containing a direction that the trustee shall pay or apply only so much of the income and principal as is necessary for the education and support of the beneficiary and to spend the income only for that purpose. This type of trust can be used where spendthrift trusts are not recognized.

surcharge An overcharge beyond what is just and right, e.g., an amount the fiduciary is required by court decree to make good because of negligence or willful failure of duty.

surety An individual or insurance company that, at the request of a personal representative, agrees to pay money up to the amount of a bond in the event that the personal representative fails to faithfully perform his duties.

surrogate The name given in some of the states to the judge or judicial officer who has the authority to act concerning the administration of probate matters, guardianships, etc.

surrogate court See **Probate court.**

tangible personal property Property that can be touched, e.g., furniture, jewelry, or a car.

taxable distribution Any distribution of income or principal from a trust to a skip person.

taxable estate The balance of an estate after the various expenses, claims, and deductions allowed by statute are subtracted from the gross estate.

taxable gift A transfer of property that is both voluntary and complete by an individual for less than an adequate and full consideration in money or money's worth.

taxable termination Any termination of an interest in property held in trust; however, a termination is not a taxable termination if (1) immediately afterward any non-skip person has an interest in the trust property or (2) distribution can never thereafter be made to a skip person.

tax-qualified long-term care insurance policy A policy that conforms to specific standards under federal law and offers certain federal tax advantages.

tax waiver A written consent from the state tax department allowing the withdrawal of property belonging to the estate of a decedent by the administrator or the executor for the purpose of assembling the assets and to permit distribution.

tenancy An interest in or ownership of property by any kind of legal right or title. Not necessarily limited to the more restricted meaning of one (called a tenant) who has temporary use and possession of real property, e.g., an apartment, owned by another (called the landlord).

tenancy at sufferance A person who has tenancy at sufferance has come into possession of land by lawful title and continues to hold the property even after her title or interest has terminated.

tenancy at will A person who has tenancy at will holds possession of premises by permission of the owner or landlord but without a fixed term. The person has no sure estate because he is at the will or pleasure of the owner.

tenancy by the entirety A form of joint tenancy with the right of survivorship available only to a husband and wife. It is essentially a *joint tenancy* modified by the common law theory that husband and wife are one person, but it is distinguished from the usual joint tenancy in that it cannot be terminated by one joint tenant's *inter vivos* conveyance of his or her interest. Neither one of the tenants by the entirety can convey (transfer) the property or sever the tenancy by the entirety without the consent of the other spouse. The predominant and distinguishing feature of both joint tenancy and tenancy by the entirety is the "right of survivorship."

tenancy (estate) for years The temporary use and possession of lands or tenements not one's own, for a determinate period of time, as for a year or a fixed number of years.

tenancy in common The ownership of an undivided interest of real or personal property by two or more persons without the right of survivorship. Each person has the right to hold or occupy the whole property in common with the other co-tenants, and each is entitled to share in the profits derived from the property. Unlike a joint tenancy, when a tenant in common dies, the decedent's interest goes to an heir or as directed in a will.

tenancy in partnership Co-ownership of real property held by partners in a partnership.

tenants in common Two or more persons who own property in a tenancy in common.

terminable interest An interest in property that terminates on the death of the holder or on the occurrence of some other specified event.

term insurance Life insurance that is pure protection without savings (cash value). It is also the cheapest insurance. It requires the insurance company to pay the face amount of insurance, i.e., the proceeds, to the beneficiary if the policyholder dies within a given time period (term).

territorial jurisdiction A court has authority only over matters affecting persons and property within the geographic limits assigned to the court by statute.

testacy Death with a valid will.

testament A will.

testamentary capacity The sanity (sound mind) requirement for a person to make a valid will. That measure of mental ability that is recognized in law as sufficient for the making of a will.

testamentary devise In orthodox terminology, a transfer of real property through a will.

testamentary disposition   A disposition of property by way of gift that is not to take effect unless or until the grantor dies.

testamentary guardian   A guardian of a minor or an incompetent person appointed in the decedent's last will.

testamentary intent   Requirement for a valid will that the testator must intend the instrument to operate as his/her last will.

testamentary trust   A trust created in a will. It becomes operational only after death.

testate   As an adjective, having made a valid will; as a noun, one, either a man or a woman, who makes and/or dies with a valid will.

testator   A man who makes and/or dies with a valid will.

testatrix   A woman who makes and/or dies with a valid will.

testimonium clause   A clause in a will in which the maker states that she has freely signed and dated the will and requests the proper number of witnesses to do the same.

"tickler" system   A chronological list of all the important steps and dates in the stages of the administration of the decedent's estate.

title   The right to or legal ownership of property.

toileting   Getting to and from, on and off the toilet, and performing personal hygiene.

Torrens title proceeding   A judicial proceeding for the registration of title to real property in which all interests, encumbrances, and estates in the property are determined and entered on the record and on the legal document called the certificate of title, which is used to transfer ownership.

tort   A private or civil wrong or injury independent of contract law.

Totten trust   A trust created by the deposit by one person of his own money in his own name as a trustee for another.

transfer   An act of the parties (e.g., individuals, corporations, or the government) by which the title to property is conveyed from one party to another.

transfer agent   The party designated by a corporation (usually a bank) to be contacted whenever a stock transfer, e.g., a sale or gift of stock, occurs. The bank records changes in the ownership of the stock and keeps the list of stockholders of the corporation.

transferee   The party to whom the title to property is conveyed.

transferor   The party who transfers or conveys the title to property. Also, the decedent or donor who creates a generation-skipping transfer trust.

transferring   Moving in or out of bed, a chair, or wheelchair.

transfer tax   A tax on the passing of the title to property or a valuable interest out of or from the estate of a decedent by inheritance, devise, or bequest; estate tax.

trust   A right of property, real or personal, held by one person (trustee) for the benefit of another (beneficiary). The trustee holds legal title to the property; the beneficiary holds equitable title.

trust account   This general term includes all types of accounts in a trust department, such as agencies, guardianships, and estates.

trust agreement   A written agreement (contract) between the settlor and trustee(s) that creates the trust and is signed by them.

trust corpus   See **Trust property** or **Trust estate.**

trustee   The person or institution named by the maker of a will to administer property for the benefit of another (the beneficiary) according to provisions in a testamentary trust or by the settlor of a trust in an *inter vivos* trust.

trust estate   The property that is the subject matter of the trust.

trust fund   All the property held in trust in a given account. See also **Trust property.**

trust income   All ordinary receipts from use or investment of the trust property, such as interest, rents, and dividends.

trust instrument   Any writing under which a trust is created, such as a will, trust agreement, declaration of trust, or court order.

trust investments   A broad term that includes not just securities but all kinds of property in which trust funds are invested.

trustor   A person who intentionally creates a trust. Also known as a settlor, grantor, or donor.

trust powers   The authority to engage in the trust business.

trust property   Also called the trust corpus, res, fund, estate, or subject matter of the trust. The property interest that the trustee holds subject to the right of someone else.

trust res   See **Trust property.**

unauthorized practice of law   Engaging in any legal work that involves exercising professional judgment or advice usually reserved for a lawyer.

undivided interest   A right to an undivided portion of property that is owned by one of two or more tenants in common or joint tenants before the property is divided (partitioned).

undue influence   The influence one person exerts over another person to the point where the latter is overpowered and induced to do or forbear an act that she would not do or would do if left to act freely.

unified credit (applicable credit amount)　The credit given against the federal estate tax after death, or credit against the gift tax for certain transfers prior to death.

Uniform Anatomical Gift Act　Any individual who is competent and of legal age may give all or a part of her body to any hospital, surgeon, physician, accredited medical or dental school, college or university, or any bank or storage facility for education, research, advancement of medical or dental science, therapy or transplantation, or to any specified individual for therapy or transplantation. The gift of all or part of the body may be made by a document other than a will, e.g., a card designed to be carried on the person that must be signed by the donor in the presence of witnesses, who in turn must sign the card in the presence of the donor.

Uniform Probate Code (UPC)　A uniform law available for adoption by the states to modernize and improve the efficiency of estate administration. To help alleviate the confusion of having 50 states with different procedures for handling decedents' estates, the National Conference of Commissioners on Uniform State Laws and the American Law Institute prepared model uniform statutes and recommended their adoption by the states. The Uniform Probate Code is one such model. These codes are not the law of a particular state until that state adopts them.

Uniform Simultaneous Death Act　An act that provides that where the inheritance of property depends on the priority of death of the decedents and where there is no sufficient evidence that the decedents have died other than simultaneously, the property of each decedent involved shall be distributed as if each had survived the other.

Uniform Transfers to Minors Act　A law that enables a gift of specified types of real or personal property to be given to a custodian and held for a minor until the minor reaches adulthood.

unity of possession　One of the essential elements of concurrent forms of ownership, i.e., ownership involving two or more persons. It requires that concurrent owners must hold the same undivided possession of the whole property and that each owner has the right to share proportionately in profits derived from it, e.g., cultivated crops, livestock, and the like.

unsupervised administration　A method of administering an estate without court action unless requested by an interested person.

venue　The particular place, county or city, where a court having jurisdiction may hear and decide a case.

vested interest　An interest in which there is a present fixed right in real or personal property although the right of possession and enjoyment may be postponed until some future date or until the happening of some event.

vested remainder　An estate by which a present interest passes to the party, with the right of possession and enjoyment postponed until the termination of the prior estate.

voluntary trust　A trust created by the voluntary act of the settlor and not conditioned upon his death. The actual title passes to a *cestui que trust* while the legal title is retained by the settlor, to be held by him for the purposes of the trust.

voucher　A bank voucher that contains a check and a ledger or voucher that allows for a documented record of the use, date, and amount of the business transaction, e.g., a payment of a decedent's debt.

waiting (elimination) period　The amount of time in calendar or benefit days before benefits are paid after qualifying for long-term care services in a nursing home or at home.

waiver of premium payment　A provision in a long-term care insurance policy that allows the insured to stop paying premiums once benefits are received.

ward　A minor or incompetent person placed by the probate court under the care and supervision of a guardian.

waste　Any act or omission that does permanent damage to real property or unreasonably changes its character or value.

whole life insurance　See **Ordinary (straight) life insurance.**

widow's allowance　An allowance consisting of personal property made by the court to a widow to cover her immediate needs after her husband's death.

will　The legally enforceable written declaration of a person's intended distribution of property after death.

will contest　Litigation to overturn a decedent's will.

work product privilege　Work of an attorney for a client that includes private memoranda prepared in anticipation of litigation or for trials that does not have to be disclosed (given to the opposing party).

Selected definitions reprinted from Black's Law Dictionary, coauthors Joseph R. Nolan and Jacqueline M. Nolan-Haley, Sixth Edition, Copyright © 1991, with permission of the West Group.

INDEX